The SAGE
Handbook of

Personality Theory
and Assessment

Vol 2 Personality Measurement and Testing

The SAGE
Handbook of

Personality Theory
and Assessment

Vol 2 Personality Measurement and Testing

Edited by
Gregory J. Boyle
Gerald Matthews
Donald H. Saklofske

Los Angeles • London • New Delhi • Singapore

Chapter 1 Introduction and editorial arrangement © Gregory J. Boyle, Gerald Matthews and Donald H. Saklofske 2008

Chapter 2 © Gerard Saucier 2008

Chapter 3 © Fons J.R. van de Vijver and Dianne A. van Hemert 2008

Chapter 4 © Chris J. Jackson 2008

Chapter 5 © Douglas P. Boer, Nicola J. Starkey and Andrea M. Hodgetts 2008

Chapter 6 © Andrew L. Comrey 2008

Chapter 7 © Heather E.P. Cattell and Alan D. Mead 2008

Chapter 8 © Gregory J. Boyle and Keith Barton 2008

Chapter 9 © In the Public Domain. Paul T. Costa, Jr. and Robert R. McCrae 2008

Chapter 10 © Adrian Furnham, Sybil B.G. Eysenck and Donald H. Saklofske 2008

Chapter 11 © Marvin Zuckerman 2008

Chapter 12 © Michael C. Ashton and Kibeom Lee 2008

Chapter 13 © Auke Tellegen and Niels G. Waller 2008

Chapter 14 © John J. Furedy 2008

Chapter 15 © Eco de Geus and David L. Neumann 2008

Chapter 16 © Eliza Congdon and Turhan Canli 2008

Chapter 17 © Jan Strelau and Bogdan Zawadzki 2008

Chapter 18 © Vivian Zayas, Donna D. Whitsett, Jenna J.Y. Lee, Nicole Wilson and Yuichi Shoda 2008

Chapter 19 © Ephrem Fernandez 2008

Chapter 20 © Leonard M. Horowitz, Bulent Turan, Kelly R. Wilson and Pavel Zolotsev 2008

Chapter 21 © Susan E. Rivers, Marc A. Brackett and Peter Salovey 2008

Chapter 22 © Richard D. Roberts, Ralf Schulze and Carolyn MacCann 2008

Chapter 23 © Ryan Y. Hong and Sampo V. Paunonen 2008

Chapter 24 © Konrad Schnabel, Jens B. Asendorpf and Anthony G. Greenwald 2008

Chapter 25 © James M. Schuerger 2008

Chapter 26 © Ellen W. Rowe, Alyssa M. Perna and Randy W. Kamphaus 2008

Chapter 27 © Mark A. Blais and Matthew R. Baity 2008

Chapter 28 © Edward Helmes 2008

Chapter 29 © W. John Livesley and Roseann M. Larstone 2008

Chapter 30 © Leslie C. Morey and Suman Ambwani 2008

Chapter 31 © Samuel E. Krug 2008

Chapter 32 © Theodore Millon 2008

First published 2008

SAGE Publications Ltd
1 Oliver's Yard
55 City Road
London EC1Y 1SP

SAGE Publications Inc.
2455 Teller Road
Thousand Oaks,
California 91320

SAGE Publications India Pvt Ltd
B 1/I 1 Mohan Cooperative
    Industrial Area
Mathura Road
New Delhi 110 044

SAGE Publications Asia-Pacific Pte Ltd
33 Pekin Street #02-01
Far East Square
Singapore 048763

Library of Congress Control Number: 2007943494

British Library Cataloguing in Publication data
A catalogue record for this book is available from the British Library

ISBN 978-1-4129-4652-0

Typeset by Cepha Imaging Pvt. Ltd., Bangalore, India
Printed in Great Britain by The Cromwell Press Ltd, Trowbridge, Wiltshire
Printed on paper from sustainable resources

Dedications

Two of the greatest and most prolific contributors to the science of human personality during the 20th century were Raymond B. Cattell, PhD, DSc., and Hans J. Eysenck, PhD, DSc. While Professor Cattell pursued his academic career in prestigious USA universities (Harvard, Clark, Illinois), Professor Eysenck undertook his lifelong work at the Institute of Psychiatry, University of London. So prominent were these two men, that their work is now enshrined in the Cattellian and Eysenckian Schools of Psychology, respectively. Cattell concentrated on primary factors, while Eysenck focused on broader secondary dimensions. Indeed, at the second-order 16PF level, the degree of communality between the Eysenckian and Cattellian factors is striking!

'The Cattell and Eysenck constructs and theories should be seen, not as mutually contradictory, but as complementary and mutually supportive.'

Eysenck (1984). Cattell and the theory of Personality.
Multivariate Behavioral Research, 19(2–3): 323–336.

Both Ray Cattell and Hans Eysenck were our mentors and friends. Both men gave freely of their time, and their kindness and generosity was abundant. Our own academic careers were facilitated by the intellectual support and moral encouragement of both these great men who made a profound and lasting contribution to personality research and testing. Each was an exemplary scientist, humanitarian and mentor, qualities that all three editors respect and aspire to. We will remain forever indebted to both Ray Cattell and Hans Eysenck.

This book is also dedicated to:

My parents, my wife and family – GJB

Diana – GM

Frances and Harold, my parents – DHS

Contents

Notes on Contributors

Suman Ambwani is an intern in clinical psychology at the Medical University of South Carolina and a doctoral candidate in clinical psychology at Texas A&M University. Her research interests include eating disorders, personality assessment, and cross-cultural issues in psychopathology, with publications in journals such as *Sex Roles*, *Psychotherapy Research*, and the *European Journal of Psychological Assessment*. She was the 2005 recipient of the Research Excellence Award from the *American Psychological Association – Division 52*, and 2003 recipient of the Donald G. Paterson Award from the Minnesota Psychological Association.

Jens Asendorpf is professor of psychology at Humboldt University, Berlin since 1994. He received his PhD from the University of Giessen, Germany in 1981. He studies transactions between personality and social relationships over the lifespan. Other interests include evolutionary approaches to personality and assessment of self-concept using the implicit association task. He is editor of the *European Journal of Personality*, and is author of more than 100 publications in the areas of personality and developmental psychology.

Michael Ashton is professor of psychology at Brock University. He received his PhD from the University of Western Ontario in 1998. His interests include the structure and measurement of personality characteristics and of related individual differences. He has published many articles and book chapters and is author of the textbook *Individual Differences and Personality*. He is currently on the editorial boards of the *British Journal of Social Psychology*, the *European Journal of Personality*, the *Journal of Personality and Social Psychology*, and the *Journal of Research in Personality*.

Matthew Baity is an instructor in psychology at Harvard Medical School and a staff psychologist at Massachusetts General Hospital. He received his PhD from the University of Arkansas in 2001. His research interests include the cognitive and personality assessment of psychopathology, as well as psychotherapy process and treatment outcomes. He is currently program manager for the MGH Treatment Outcome Measurement Project. He is co-author of chapters in books such as *Rorschach Assessment to the Personality Disorders,* and has articles in the *Journal of Personality Assessment, the American Journal of Psychotherapy, Journal of Nervous and Mental Disease, and the American Journal of Psychiatry.*

Keith Barton is professor emeritus at the University of California, Davis. He obtained his PhD from Peabody College (now Vanderbilt University) in 1969. His interests lie in personality measurement and personality correlates. He worked for four years in Cattell's laboratory at the University of Illinois and has co-authored many publications with Cattell. He is author of the Child Rearing Practices Questionnaire, and of the IPAT Central Trait-State Scales, and co-author of the book *Child Personality Structure and Development.*

Mark Blais is associate professor of psychology at Harvard Medical School and an associate chief of psychology at Massachusetts General Hospital where he has been since receiving his PsyD from Nova Southeastern University in 1990. His major interest is personality assessment and measurement. Other interests include outcomes measurement and quality management. He is the author of over 70 papers and 20 book chapters. His co-authored articles appear in journals such as the *Journal of Personality Disorders, Comprehensive Psychiatry, the Journal of Nervous and Mental Disease, and Psychotherapy and Psychosomatics.* He is associate editor of the *Journal of Personality Assessment.*

Douglas Boer is associate professor of psychology at the University of Waikato, New Zealand. He received his PhD from the University of Alberta in 1989. His major research interest is the study of risk and risk manageability in sexual offenders and intellectually disabled individuals. He has published widely and is co-author of several risk assessment manuals including the *Sexual Violence Risk – 20 (SVR-20).* He is the New Zealand editor for the *Australia-New Zealand Treatment of Sexual Abuse* journal and is associate editor of the online journal *Sexual Offender Treatment.*

Gregory Boyle is professor of psychology at Bond University, Australia. He earned separate PhDs from both the University of Delaware in 1983, and the University of Melbourne in 1985. He also received a DSc from the University of Queensland in 2006, for his research into personality and individual differences. He is a fellow of the Association for Psychological Science, and the Australian Psychological Society, and recipient of the Buros Institute of Mental Measurements Distinguished Reviewer Award in 2005. He is on a number of editorial boards including *Personality and Individual Differences.* He has over 200 publications, is co-author of a book on statistical methods, and co-editor of *Sage Benchmarks in Psychology: The Psychology of Individual Differences (4 Vols.).* He is also co-editor of the current volumes.

Marc Brackett is an associate research scientist in Psychology at Yale University and Deputy Director of the Health, Emotion, and Behavior Laboratory at the same *institution.* He obtained his PhD from the University of New Hampshire in 2003. He focuses on the measurement of emotional intelligence in children and adults, and the links between emotional intelligence and the quality of interpersonal relationships, well-being, academic performance, and workplace success. He has contributed to more than four-dozen scholarly publications, and is the author of multiple curricula that teach emotional literacy to students, teachers, and school administrators.

Turhan Canli is associate professor of psychology at Stony Brook University. He obtained his PhD from Yale University in 1993. He focuses on the neural basis of emotion, emotional memory, and personality, combining neuroimaging with molecular genetics to investigate how individual differences in brain function relate to variation within specific genes, and their interaction with individuals' unique life experience. He has many book chapters and empirical publications in *PNAS, Science, Nature Neuroscience,* and is editor of the book *Biology of Personality and Individual Differences.* He is associate editor of the journal *Social Neuroscience.*

Heather Cattell is research consultant at the Institute for Personality and Ability Testing (IPAT). She received her PhD from Michigan State University in 1982 in clinical and quantitative psychology. She is co-author of the 16PF Fifth Edition Questionnaire, constructed with her parents, Raymond and Karen Cattell, the original developers of the 16PF instrument. She is also co-author of the Psych-Eval Personality Questionnaire, measuring clinical traits, and the Spanish-American 16PF. She is co-author of the book *Essentials of 16PF Assessment,* and of the 16PF Cattell Comprehensive Personality Interpretation Report. She is on the American Board of Assessment Psychology and is a fellow of the Society for Personality Assessment.

Andrew Comrey is emeritus professor of psychology at UCLA. He completed his PhD in 1949 in psychometrics at the University of Southern California under supervision of J.P. Guilford. After a year each at the University of Illinois and the University of Southern California, he joined the department of psychology, UCLA, where he has remained his entire academic career. His major research interests include personality measurement and factor analysis. He elucidated a taxonomy of personality traits measured in the *Comrey Personality Scales*, which he constructed using factor analytic methodology described in his book, *A First Course in Factor Analysis*. He has over 200 publications and is also author of *A Sourcebook for Mental Health Measures*. He has served on the editorial boards of *Multivariate Behavioral Research*, and the *Journal of Personality and Social Psychology*, among others. He has been past president of the *Society for Multivariate Experimental Psychology*, and fellow and charter member of the *Association for Psychological Science*.

Eliza Congdon is a doctoral candidate at Stony Brook University. Her research is focused on the biological bases of impulsivity. Specifically, she is working to integrate neuroimaging and genetics in elucidating the neurogenetics of behavioural inhibition. Her work is currently funded by an NRSA grant. She has co-authored articles that appear in the *Journal of Personality*, *Neuropsychiatric Genetics*, *Journal of Neural Transmission*, *Proceedings of the National Academy of Sciences, USA*, and in *Behavioral and Cognitive Neuroscience Reviews*.

Paul Costa, Jr. is chief of the Laboratory of Personality and Cognition, National Institute on Aging's Intramural Research Program and professor of psychiatry and behavioral sciences at the Johns Hopkins University School of Medicine. He obtained his PhD from the University of Chicago in 1970. His enduring interests are in the structure and measurement of personality and in lifespan development. He co-authored the NEO Personality Inventory-Revised and has actively developed the five-factor model of personality. He has published extensively in the area of personality assessment and he is co-editor of the book *Recent Advances in Psychology and Aging: Advances In Cell Aging and Gerontology* (Vol. 15).

Sybil Eysenck has been a senior lecturer in psychology at the Institute of Psychiatry, University of London (now retired). She obtained her PhD from the University of London in 1955. She was married to the late Professor H.J. Eysenck. She has over 180 publications and is co-author of the books *Personality Structure and Measurement* and *Psychoticism as a Dimension of Personality*, as well as of *Individual Differences in Children and Adolescents*. She is also co-editor-in-chief of the international journal, *Personality and Individual Differences*.

Ephrem Fernandez is professor of clinical psychology at the University of Texas, San Antonio. Previously, he held faculty appointments at Southern Methodist University, and at the University Queensland, Australia. He received his PhD from Ohio State University in1989. His research spans medical psychology and affect science, including the psychometric assessment and cognitive-behavioural management of pain, and assessment and integrative psychotherapy for maladaptive anger. He has numerous publications, and is author of the book *Anxiety, Depression, and Anger in Pain: Research Findings and Clinical Options* and co-editor of the *Handbook of Pain Syndromes: Biopsychosocial Approaches*. He has served on the editorial boards of *Headache* and the *Annals of Behavioral Medicine*. His research is funded by the US National Institutes of Health.

John Furedy is emeritus professor of psychology at the University of Toronto, where he worked for nearly 40 years, before returning to Australia in 2005. He obtained his PhD from the University of Sydney in 1965, in experimental psychophysiology. His research interests include psychophysiology, and the philosophy of science in psychology. He has over 350 publications and is co-author of the book *Theories and Applications in the Detection of Deception: Psychophysiological and Cultural Perspectives*. He has served on 13 editorial boards including *Behavioral and Brain Sciences, Biological Psychology, International Journal of Psychophysiology*, and *New Ideas in Psychology*. He was elected a fellow of the Association for Psychological Science, the Canadian Psychological Association, and the Australian Psychological Society.

Adrian Furnham is professor of psychology at University College London where he has worked for 25 years. He obtained his DPhil from Oxford University in 1981, his DSc from the University of London in 1991, and his DLitt from the University of Natal in 1997. He has research interests in applied, differential and evolutionary psychology. Other interests include economic socialisation, lay theories, and complementary medicine. He has 700 publications, plus 54 books including *Personality and Intelligence at Work*, as well as *The Psychology of Physical Attraction*, and is on the editorial boards of 12 journals. He is a past president of the International Society for the Study of Individual Differences.

Eco de Geus is professor of psychology and co-director of the Netherlands Twin Registry at Vrije Universiteit Amsterdam, where he received his PhD in 1992. His research interests include behavioural and molecular genetic research into psychophysiological endophenotypes of individual differences in affective and cognitive function. Other interests include genetic epidemiological research into lifestyle, stress and cardiovascular risk factors and their co-morbidity with anxiety and depression. He has over 160 publications and developed the *VU Ambulatory Monitoring System* for measuring ANS responses. He has been guest editor of *Behavior Genetics*, and is an associate editor of *Biological Psychology*. He is also on the editorial board of *Psychosomatic Medicine*.

Anthony Greenwald is professor of psychology at the University of Washington. He received his PhD from Harvard in 1963. He has published over 150 scholarly articles, served on editorial boards of 13 psychological journals, and received both the Donald T. Campbell Research Award from the Society of Personality and Social Psychology and Distinguished Scientist Award from the Society of Experimental Social Psychology. He constructed the *Implicit Association Test* for assessing individual differences in implicit social cognition.

Edward Helmes is professor of psychology at James Cook University where he has been on the faculty since 2001. He obtained his PhD from the University of Western Ontario in 1978. His research interests include personality assessment, neuropsychology and cognitive ageing. He has over 120 publications and is co-editor of the book, *Problems and Solutions in Human Assessment: Honoring Douglas N. Jackson at Seventy*. He is associate editor of the *Australian Psychologist*, and is a fellow of the Australian Psychological Society and of the Australian Association for Gerontology.

Dianne van Hemert is a postdoctoral research associate at the University of Amsterdam. She received her PhD in cross-cultural psychology from Tilburg University in 2002. Her research interests include cultural differences in personality and social behavior, multilevel models, and meta-analysis. She is on the editorial board of the *Journal of Cross-Cultural Psychology* and is co-editor of the book, *Individuals and Cultures in Multilevel Analysis*. She has published in journals such as *Personality and Individual Differences, Cognition and Emotion*, and the *Journal of Personality*.

Andrea Hodgetts recently completed her internship in clinical psychology at the University of Waikato, New Zealand, having received her PhD from Massey University in 2000. She worked in the neurorehabilitation unit of St John's Health Care Corporation in Newfoundland, Canada, and has also worked in the organisational development unit of the London Borough of Camden, UK. Her research interests revolve around lower socioeconomic groups' experiences of unemployment and homelessness and she has co-authored a number of peer-reviewed articles in journals such as the *Journal of Community and Applied Social Psychology, Journal of Health Psychology and Journal of Social and Cultural Geography*.

Ryan Hong is assistant professor of psychology at the National University of Singapore. He obtained his PhD in 2008 from the University of Western Ontario, Canada. His research interests include personality and psychopathology, and their interface. His publications have appeared in journals such as *Behaviour Research and Therapy*, and *Personality and Individual Differences*.

Leonard Horowitz is professor of psychology at Stanford University. He received his PhD from Johns Hopkins University in 1960. He was a Fulbright fellow at University College, London, and obtained his clinical training at Mt Zion Psychiatric Clinic, San Francisco. He is co-editor of the book *Measuring Patient Changes in Mood, Anxiety, and Personality Disorders: Toward a Core Battery*, and author of the book, *Interpersonal Foundations of Psychopathology*. He is past president of the Society for Psychotherapy Research and of the Society for Interpersonal Theory and Research. He has served on editorial boards such as the *Journal of Experimental Psychology*, the *Journal of Personality Disorders*, the *Journal of Personal and Social Relationships*, and *Psychotherapy Research*.

Chris Jackson is professor of business psychology at the University of New South Wales. He obtained his PhD from the University of Coventry, UK in 1989. His research interests concern the overlap between learning and personality, including the effect of "left and right" brain and the biological influence of personality processes in the workplace. He has recently published the *Learning Styles Profiler* (LSP) which provides a measure of functional and dysfunctional learning. He is author of the book, *An Applied Neuropsychological Model of Functional and Dysfunctional Learning*, and co-author of the *Eysenck Personality Profiler (EPP-S)*.

Randy Kamphaus is dean of the College of Education and Distinguished Research Professor at the University of Georgia, where he obtained his PhD in educational psychology in 1983. His research interests include applied clinical assessment and diagnosis, mental health screening, and classification methods. He has authored dozens of journal articles and book chapters, four psychological tests, and 12 books including, *Clinical Assessment of Child and Adolescent Intelligence*, and also, *Clinical Assessment of Child and Adolescent Personality and Behavior*. He is a fellow of the American Psychological Association and editor of the *School Psychology Quarterly*.

Samuel Krug is chairman of MetriTech Inc., and of Industrial Psychology International Ltd, Champaign, Illinois. He received his PhD from the University of Illinois at Urbana-Champaign in 1971. His research has primarily focused on issues in applied personality and educational measurement. He is the author of more than 100 articles, books, tests, and computer-based assessment products. He is author of *Psychware Sourcebook: A Reference Guide to Computer-based Products for Assessment in Psychology, Business, and Education*, and co-author of the book, *Responsible Test Use: Case Studies for Assessing Human Behavior*.

Roseann Larstone is a doctoral student in educational psychology at the University of British Columbia. Her research interests include the contribution of emotion regulation to conduct problems, resilience, and developmental trajectories of aggression. She has co-authored articles in *Social Behavior and Personality, Personality and Individual Differences*, plus book chapters in the *Handbook of Research Methods in Abnormal and Clinical Psychology*, and in *Personality and Psychopathology: Building Bridges*. She is the editorial assistant for the *Journal of Personality Disorders*.

Jenna Lee is a doctoral candidate in social/personality psychology at the University of Washington. Her research interests include culture and self-evaluation, acquaintance sexual aggression, and recommendation algorithms.

Kibeom Lee is associate professor of psychology at the University of Calgary. He received his PhD from the University of Western Ontario in 2000. His research interests include the structure and measurement of personality characteristics and workplace attitudes and behaviours. He has several dozen publications and he currently serves on the editorial boards of the *Journal of Occupational and Organizational Psychology and European Journal of Personality*.

John Livesley is emeritus professor of psychiatry at the University of British Columbia. He obtained his PhD from the University of Liverpool in 1969, and a degree in medicine (MB ChB) from the same university in 1974. His research focuses on the classification, assessment, and aetiology of personality disorders. He is author of *Practical Management of Personality Disorder*, editor of the books *DSM-IV Personality Disorders*, the *Handbook of Personality Disorders: Theory, Research and Treatment*, and co-editor of the book, *Severe Personality Disorders*. He is editor of the *Journal of Personality Disorders*, and fellow of the Royal Society of Canada.

Carolyn MacCann is a post-doctoral fellow at the Center for New Constructs, Educational Testing Service, Princeton, New Jersey. She obtained her PhD from the University of Sydney in 2006. Her research interests include personality assessment, faking, situation judgment testing, and emotional intelligence. She has co-authored several articles published in journals such as *Personality and Individual Differences, Emotion, International Journal of Organizational Analysis*, and *Human Development*, and book chapters on assessment issues in emotional intelligence in the books *Measuring Emotional Intelligence* and *Emotional Intelligence and Elites: Sex, Gender and the Brain*.

Robert McCrae is a research psychologist in the Laboratory of Personality and Cognition at the National Institute on Aging. He received his PhD from Boston University in 1976. His research interests include personality structure, development and assessment, as well as cross-cultural studies. He has 300 publications and is co-author of the Revised NEO Personality Inventory, and *Personality in Adulthood: A Five-Factor Theory Perspective*. He is on the editorial boards of the *European Journal of Personality*, and *Psychological Assessment*. He is a fellow of the American Psychological Association, the Association for Psychological Science, the Gerontology Society of America, and the Society for Personality Assessment.

Gerald Matthews is professor of psychology at the University of Cincinnati. He received his PhD from Cambridge University in 1984. His research interests include the effects of personality and stress on performance, information-processing models, applied personality research and emotional intelligence as well as the assessment of transient subjective states. He has over 150 publications and has co-authored the textbooks *Personality Traits* and *Human Performance: Cognition, Stress and Individual Differences*. He is editor of the book *Cognitive Science Perspectives on Personality and Emotion* and co-editor of *The Science of Emotional Intelligence: Knowns and Unknowns*. He is secretary-treasurer of the International Society for the Study of Individual Differences, and also is co-editor of the current volumes.

Alan Mead is assistant professor of psychology at the Illinois Institute of Technology. He received his PhD from the University of Illinois, Urbana in industrial and organisational psychology. His background includes the position of research scientist at the Institute for Personality and Ability Testing (IPAT). His research interests include psychometric applications such as differential item functioning, scoring non-cognitive assessments, and computerised testing. He has published in journals such as *Psychological Bulletin, Applied Psychological Measurement, Educational and Psychological Measurement, Applied Measurement in Education, and Personnel Psychology.*

Theodore Millon is the scientific director at the Institute for Advanced Studies in Personology and Psychopathology. He obtained his PhD from the University of Connecticut in 1954. Professor emeritus of psychology and psychiatry at Harvard Medical School, he was editor-in-chief of the *Journal of Personality Disorders* and inaugural president of the *International Society for the Study of Personality Disorders*. He is author or editor of over 30 books including, *Masters of the Mind,* and *Resolving Difficult Clinical Syndromes: A Personalized Psychotherapeutic Approach.* He is also recipient of the *American Psychological Association Foundation's 2008 Gold Medal Life Achievement Award* in the Application of Psychology.

Leslie Morey is professor and department head of psychology at Texas A&M University. He received his PhD from the University of Florida and has served on the faculty at Harvard Medical School, and the Yale University School of Medicine. He has over 160 publications on the assessment and diagnosis of mental disorders. He is the author of the Personality Assessment Inventory, the Personality Assessment Screener, the *Interpretive Guide to the Personality Assessment Inventory*, and *Essentials of PAI Assessment*. He is past associate editor of the journal *Assessment* and of the *Journal of Personality Assessment*. He is a fellow of both the Society for Personality Assessment, and the American Association of Applied and Preventive Psychology.

David Neumann is a senior lecturer in psychology at Griffith University. He received his PhD from the University of Queensland in 1998. His research into cognitive psychophysiology focuses on attention and learning. His research interests include emotion and learning during Pavlovian conditioning in humans, the role of attention for the enhancement of performance in sport, and the effects of nicotine on cognition and affect. His published articles have appeared in journals such as *Psychophysiology, Biological Psychology*, and *Behaviour Research and Therapy*. He was elected the Australian Research Council Young Researcher of the Year (2000).

Sampo Paunonen is professor of psychology at the University of Western Ontario, where he received his PhD in 1984. His research interests include person perception, personality assessment and personnel selection. He also has interests in multivariate methods, such as factor analys' and in psychometric theory. He has published extensively in leading psychology journals including the *American Psychologist, Psychological Review, Psychological Bulletin,* and the *Journal of Personality and Social Psychology.* Also, he has served on the editorial boards of the *Journal of Personality* and the *Journal of Personality* and *Social Psychology.*

Alyssa Perna is a doctoral candidate in applied developmental psychology at George Mason University. Her research interests include the social and emotional development of preschool children and its relation to school readiness and academic achievement. More specifically, she is interested in the development of self-regulatory mechanisms as a critical component of development during the toddler and preschool years.

Susan Rivers is an associate research scientist in psychology at Yale University, where she earned her PhD in 2005. Her research focuses on emotional development, and the role that emotion knowledge and skills play in effective social and intrapersonal functioning in children and adults. She is co-author of school-based curricula that teach emotion knowledge and skills to children, and conducts research to evaluate their effectiveness. She is co-editor of the book *Emotional Literacy in the Classroom.* Her co-authored articles appear in the *Journal of Personality and Social Psychology,* the *Journal of Health Psychology, and Developmental Review.*

Richard Roberts is principal research scientist at the Educational Testing Service, Princeton, New Jersey. He received his PhD from the University of Sydney in 1996. His research interests focus especially on the assessment of cognitive abilities and personal skills, especially as they apply in educational contexts. He has published over 120 articles and book chapters. He is co-author of *Emotional Intelligence: Science and Myth* and co-editor of the books *Learning and Individual Differences: Content, Trait, and Process Determinants,* and *Extending Intelligence: Enhancement and New Constructs,* as well as *Emotional Intelligence: Knowns and Unknowns.* He was a National Research Council Fellow from 1996–1999.

Ellen Rowe is assistant professor of psychology at George Mason University. She received her PhD from the University of Georgia in 2005. Her research interests include the assessment and remediation of emotional, behavioural, and adjustment problems among children and adolescents. She is also interested in classification methods, and applied measurement. In addition to a number of book chapters, her published articles appear in journals such as the *Journal of Child Psychology and Psychiatry, and Genetic, Social, and General Psychology Monographs.*

Donald Saklofske is professor of applied psychology and associate dean of research at the University of Calgary. He received his PhD from the University of Calgary in 1973. His research interests include individual differences, personality, intelligence and emotional intelligence, cognition, and psychological assessment. He has co-authored and edited books on intelligence, the assessment of intelligence, individual differences and educational psychology. He is on editorial boards for three psychology journals and is a book series co-editor. He is a fellow of ˑth the Canadian Psychological Association and the Association for Psychological Science ˑ also co-editor of the current volumes.

vey is the Chris Argyris professor of psychology at Yale University and the dean ˑge. He completed his undergraduate education at Stanford University and his PhD ˑ6. He has over 300 publications and 13 books including *The Wisdom in Feeling: ˑl Processes in Emotional Intelligence,* and *Key Readings in the Social Psychology of Health*, as well as *The Emotionally Intelligent Manager*. He served on the National Advisory Mental Health Council of the US National Institute of Mental Health. He was associate editor of *Psychological Bulletin* and *Emotion*, editor of *Review General Psychology*, and past president of the Society for General Psychology. He has received research excellence awards from the US Substance Abuse and Mental Health Administration, the US National Cancer Institute's Cancer Information Service, and the National Science Foundation's Presidential Young Investigator program.

Gerard Saucier is professor of psychology at the University of Oregon, where he received his PhD in 1991. His research interests include the generalisable structure and optimal assessment of personality attributes, and the related structure and assessment of dispositional patterns in beliefs and values. He is an associate editor of the *Journal of Personality and Social Psychology*, and past associate editor of the *Journal of Research in Personality*. He received the Cattell Award in 1999 from the Society of Multivariate Experimental Psychology and is a fellow of the Association for Psychological Science.

Konrad Schnabel is assistant professor of psychology at Humboldt-University, Berlin. His research interests focus on differences between implicit and explicit self-representations. He has published extensively in journals such as the *British Journal of Social Psychology*, *Experimental Psychology*, and the *European Journal of Personality*, on the behavioural validation of implicit measures and on the use of multiple implicit measurement procedures. His current projects investigate the validity of non-evaluative implicit self-representations and the malleability of social anxiety reflected by explicit and implicit measures.

James Schuerger has been professor of psychology at Cleveland State University for more than 30 years. He obtained his PhD from Kent State University in 1967. Also, he was research assistant professor in Cattell's laboratory at the University of Illinois. His major research interests include objective personality testing. He has more than a 100 publications on topics in psychological measurement, is author of the Adolescent Personality Questionnaire and co-author (with Raymond B. Cattell) of the Objective Analytic Test Battery. He is currently field-testing a revision of the Children's Personality Questionnaire.

Ralf Schulze is a research scientist at the Westfälische Wilhelms-Universität Münster, Germany. He earned his PhD from the University of Münster in 2001. His research interests span the fields of personality and social psychology as well as psychometrics and research methods. In the area of individual differences research, he focuses on emotional intelligence and self-motivated cognition. He has published dozens of articles and book chapters in his fields of interest. In addition, he is co-author of the book *Meta-analysis: A Comparison of Approaches,* and co-editor of the books *Meta-analysis: New Developments and Applications in Medical and Social Sciences, and Emotional Intelligence: An International Handbook*

Yuichi Shoda is professor of psychology, University of Washington. He received his PhD from Columbia University in 1990. His research is aimed at identifying and understanding stable within-person patterns of variation in the stream, over time and across situations, of an individual's cognition, affect, and behaviour. He is co-author of a personality psychology textbook and co-editor of the books *The Coherence of Personality: Social-Cognitive Bases of Personality Consistency, Variability*, and *Persons in Context: Constructing a Science of the Individual*. He is a fellow of the Association for Psychological Science.

Nicola Starkey Nicola Starkey is senior lecturer in psychology at the University of Waikato, New Zealand. She obtained her PhD from the University of Leeds, UK in 2000. Her major research interests include animal models of psychiatric disorders, psychological assessment, neuropsychology and young driver behaviour. She has co-authored several articles in journals such as *Physiology and Behavior, Neuroscience and Biobehavioral Reviews,* and the *Archives of Clinical Neuropsychology.*

Jan Strelau is professor at the Warsaw School of Social Psychology. He received his PhD in 1963 from the University of Warsaw. He is a member of the Polish Academy of Sciences and Academia Europaea and holds *Doctor honoris causa* degrees from the Universities of Gdańsk and Poznań, Poland, and from the State University of Humanistic Sciences in Moscow, Russia. He was the first president of the European Association of Personality Psychology, past president of the International Society for the Study of Individual Differences, and vice-president of the International Union of Psychological Science. He is author of 220 papers and book chapters, and author or co-editor of 39 books in the field of individual differences.

Auke Tellegen is emeritus professor of psychology at the University of Minnesota, where he received his PhD in 1962. He has published on the theory, dimensional structure, and assessment of personality, affect, and hypnosis, and on the behaviour genetics of personality. He is author of the Multidimensional Personality Inventory and of the MMPI-2 Restructured Clinical (RC) Scales. He received the Bruno Klopfer Award from the Society of Personality Assessment and the Jack Block Award from the Society of Personality and Social Psychology. He has been associate editor of the *Journal of Research in Personality*, and the *American Journal of Clinical Hypnosis*. He is a fellow of both the American Psychological Association, and the Society for Personality Assessment.

Bulent Turan is a doctoral candidate in psychology at Stanford University. His research interests include normative knowledge structures and individual differences in accessing different components of knowledge related to trust and supportiveness in close relationships. He has several published articles in journals including, the *Journal of Personality and Social Psychology*, *Personality and Social Psychology Review*, the *Journal of Social and Clinical Psychology*, and *Communication and Cognition*, as well as book chapters.

Fons van de Vijver is professor of psychology at Tilburg University, where he received his PhD in 1991. He also is professor at North-West University, South Africa. He has 250 publications on methodological issues in cross-cultural comparisons, intelligence, multiculturalism and acculturation. He is co-editor of the book, *Individuals and Cultures in Multilevel Analysis*. He is past editor of the *Journal of Cross-Cultural Psychology* and is on editorial boards including the *European Journal of Psychological Assessment*, the *International Journal of Testing*, and the *Psychology Science Quarterly*. He is a fellow of the International Academy for Intercultural Research.

Niels Waller is professor of psychology at the University of Minnesota, where he received his PhD in 1990. He has published widely on psychometric models of personality and psychopathology. He is co-author of the book *Multivariate Taxometric Procedures* and co-editor of the book *A Paul Meehl Reader: Essays on the Practice of Scientific Psychology*. He is the recipient of numerous awards including the 1999 American Psychological Association Distinguished Scientific Award for Early Career Contribution to Psychology in the area of individual differences and the 1997 Raymond B. Cattell Award, Society for Multivariate Experimental Psychology.

Donna Whitsett is a postdoctoral research associate at the University of Washington, where she received her PhD in social/personality psychology in 2007. Her research interests include emotion regulation, emotional support, and more recently, the promotion of environmentally sustainable behaviours. She has contributed to publications in a variety of journals including the *Journal of Positive Psychology* and the *Journal of Community Psychology*.

Kelly Wilson is a doctoral candidate in psychology at Stanford University. She is also a member of the PTSD Clinical Team at the San Francisco VA Medical Center. Her primary research interests include adult attachment and the recognition of others' mental states, interpersonal perception, and personality disorders. She has several co-authored articles in journals such as *Personality and Social Psychology Review*, the *Journal of Social and Clinical Psychology*, and the *Journal of Personality*. She is also co-author of chapters in books such as the *Handbook of Personology and Psychopathology*.

Nicole Wilson is a doctoral candidate in social/personality psychology at the University of Washington. Her research interests include stress and coping and her publications appear in the *Journal of Aging and Health*, the *Journal of Aging and Physical Activity*, the *Journal of Gerontology: Medical Sciences*, and the *Journal of Gerontology: Psychological Sciences*.

Bogdan Zawadzki is professor of psychology at Warsaw University. He obtained his PhD from the University of Warsaw in 1992. His research interests include individual differences, the psychology of temperament, behaviour genetics, cross-cultural psychology, psychological diagnosis, psychometrics and clinical psychology including the impact of natural disasters on mental health of victims, and posttraumatic stress disorder. He has 100 publications, including handbooks for four personality inventories.

Vivian Zayas is assistant professor of psychology at Cornell University. She completed her PhD in 2003 and postdoctoral training in 2006 at the University of Washington. Her research examines the cognitive-affective processes that regulate behaviour within close relationships and which may affect the quality of individuals' mental health. She adopts a multi-level interdisciplinary perspective that integrates the study of attachment processes, executive control and self-regulation from cognitive psychology and cognitive neuroscience. Her research has been funded by the US National Science Foundation and the US National Institutes of Health and appears in journals such as *Personality and Social Psychology Bulletin, Psychological Science, and the Journal of Personality.*

Pavel Zolotsev is a doctoral candidate in psychology at Stanford University. His primary research interest is how individual differences in personality variables manifest themselves in actual behaviour. He has undertaken research into dating couples' interpersonal behaviours and the effects of verbal and non-verbal communication on couples' wellbeing. Using the circumplex model of interpersonal behaviour and motives, he is currently examining behaviours of dependent and self-critical people. He has published in the *Personality and Social Psychology Review.*

Marvin Zuckerman is professor emeritus at the University of Delaware, where he taught and conducted research for 33 years. He obtained his PhD from New York University in 1954.

His research has focused on sensation seeking, and the psychobiology of personality. He is author or co-author of well over 200 journal articles and book chapters. Recent books include *Sensation Seeking and Risky Behavior* and the *Psychobiology of Personality*. He is a past president of the International Society for the Study of Individual Differences and fellow of both the American Psychological Association and the Association for Psychological Science.

Personality Measurement and Testing: An Overview

Gregory J. Boyle, Gerald Matthews and Donald H. Saklofske

A colleague recently remarked:

> Psychologists who specialize in the study of personality and individual differences spend a lot of time coming up with various descriptions of people, like Machiavellianism, external locus of control, openness to experience, and neuroticism. Even more effort is spent trying to measure these ideas with tests like the MMPI-2, brief anxiety scales, and Rorschach Inkblots. But do they really tell us anything about human behaviour in general or about the individual? Does it make a difference in how we view people, select them for jobs, or guide therapy choices and assist in evaluating outcomes?

This is a very loaded question, and the one that appears to challenge both the technical adequacy of our personality measures, but especially the construct and criterion validity or effectiveness of personality instruments in describing individual differences, clinical diagnosis and guiding and evaluating interventions. Technically, there are very few actual 'tests' of personality – the Objective-Analytic Battery being an exception. Most so-called 'tests' of personality are in fact, self-report scales or rating scales based on reports of others. Such scales quantify subjective introspections, or subjective impressions of others' personality make-up. At the same

time, it is a relevant question and one that we will continue to face in the study of personality and the application of the findings, including assessment of personality, within psychological practice areas such as clinical and school psychology, and within settings such as the military, business and sports psychology, among others. Volume 1 in this two-volume series is devoted to a critical analysis of the theories, models and resulting research that drive the personality descriptions and assessment discussed in Volume 2. Demonstrating both the construct and practical validity of personality descriptions is essential to psychology as a scientific discipline and empirically grounded practice/profession.

THE STATUS OF PSYCHOLOGICAL ASSESSMENT

In a recently published paper focusing on psychological assessment, the following claim was made:

> Data from more than 125 meta-analyses on test validity and 800 samples examining multimethod

assessment suggest four general conclusions: (a) Psychological test validity is strong and compelling, (b) psychological test validity is comparable to medical test validity, (c) distinct assessment methods provide unique sources of information, and (d) clinicians who rely exclusively on interviews are prone to incomplete understandings. (Meyer et al., 2001: 128)

The authors also stated that multiple methods of assessment in the hands of 'skilled clinicians' further enhanced the validity of the assessments so that the focus should now move on to how we use these scales in clinical practice to inform diagnosis and prescription. This is a remarkable accomplishment, if accurate, and even a bold claim that has not gone unchallenged. Claims (a) and (b) have been attacked on various grounds (e.g. see critiques by Fernández-Ballesteros, 2002; Garb et al., 2002; Hunsley, 2002; Smith, 2002). Furthermore, the debate about the clinical or treatment validity of psychological assessment and the added or incremental value of multimethod assessment is argued by some not to rest on solid empirical ground (e.g. Hunsley, 2002; Hunsley and Meyer, 2003), in spite of such carefully argued presentations on the utility of integrative assessment of personality with both adults (e.g. Beutler and Groth-Marnat, 2003) and children (e.g. Riccio and Rodriguez, 2007; Flanagan, 2007). In fact, this is very much the argument put forward by supporters of RTI (response to intervention) in challenge to the view that diagnostic assessment, using multiple assessment methods, should point the way to both diagnosis and intervention planning (see special issue of *Psychology in the Schools*, 43(7), 2006).

While the Meyer et al. review focused on all areas of psychological assessment, it does suggest that the theories and models, as well as research findings describing various latent traits underlying individual differences have produced sufficient information to allow for reliable and valid measurement and in turn, application of these assessment findings to understanding, predicting and even changing human behaviour associated with intelligence, personality and conation

(see Boyle and Saklofske, 2004). While there has been considerable progress, but certainly not a consensus in the models and measures used to describe intelligence and cognitive abilities, the other main individual differences' areas of personality and conation have travelled a somewhat different path to their current position in psychological assessment.

Calling this a remarkable accomplishment also has to be put in the context of time. Psychological science is only slightly more than 125 years old. As a profession that applies the research findings from both experimental and correlational studies in diagnosis, intervention and prevention in healthcare settings, schools, business and so on, psychology is even younger. Specializations that are heavily grounded in psychological assessment such as clinical, school, counselling and industrial-organizational psychology only began to appear more or less in their present form in the mid-twentieth century. While it can be debated, the success of the Binet intelligence scales in both Europe and North America in the early 1900s, followed by the widespread use of ability and personality instruments for military selection during World War I in the US, and the growing interest in psychoanalysis complimented by development and use of projective measures to tap 'hidden' personality structures, provided the strong foundation for the contemporary measurement and assessment of personality.

A BRIEF HISTORICAL NOTE ON PSYCHOLOGICAL ASSESSMENT

However, history shows that the description and assessment of individual differences is not new to psychology. Sattler (2001) and Aiken (2000) have provided brief outlines of key events in cognitive and educational assessment during the several hundred years prior to the founding of psychology, and one can clearly sense that the 'tasks' of psychological measurement were being determined during this time. Prior to the creative scientific studies by Galton in the nineteenth century, the first psychological laboratory established in 1879 by Wundt, and psychology's earliest efforts at measuring the 'faculties of the mind' during the Brass Instruments era (e.g. James McKeen Cattell), there is a long history documenting efforts to describe the basis for human behaviour and what makes us alike all others and yet unique in other ways. As early as 4,000 years ago in China, there is evidence of very basic testing programs for determining the 'fit' for various civil servants followed by the use of written exams some 2,000 years ago that continued in various forms through to the start of the twentieth century. Efforts to understand and assess human personality also have a long history that predates the study of psychology. Centuries before the psychoanalytic descriptions of Freud, who argued for the importance of the unconscious and suggested that the putative tripartite personality structure of the id, ego and superego were shaped by a developmental process reflected in psychosexual stages, the Roman physician Galen contended that human personality was a function of the body secretions (humors). Galen subsequently outlined the first personality typology characterized by the choleric, melancholic, sanguine and phlegmatic types.

Interest in such processes as memory and reaction time, and efforts to assess and distinguish between mental retardation and mental illness were already underway before the establishment of Galton's psychometric laboratory in London and Wundt's and Cattell's psychophysical laboratories in Germany and the US respectively. While much of this work was focused on the study of intelligence and cognitive abilities, it laid the foundation for psychological testing and assessment that has shaped the face of psychology today. Probably the greatest impetus for test development came as a result of the success of the Binet intelligence tests, first in France and then in the US. The use of tests to classify school children according to ability was followed by the development and use of the Army Alpha and Beta tests to aid in the selection of recruits (in terms of their cognitive abilities) for military service in the US Army. However at that same time, it was also recognised that there was a need to identify military recruits who might be prone to, or manifest the symptoms of, psychological disorders. Woodworth (1919) created the Personal Data Sheet that presented examinees with a questionnaire not unlike those found on scales tapping psychiatric disorders to which a 'yes–no' response could be made. While there was not a control or check for 'faking good–faking bad' protocols, the measure was deemed to be a success. Thus, well before the Minnesota Multiphasic Personality Inventory (MMPI), constructed by Hathaway and McKinley (1940, 1943) and its revised version (MMPI-2, 1989), as well as the California Psychological Inventory (CPI; see Gough, 1987), and other more recent personality measures, Woodworth's (1919) Personal Data Sheet, was followed shortly after by other personality scales such as the Thurstone Personality Schedule (Thurstone and Thurstone, 1930) and the Bernreuter Personality Inventory (Bernreuter, 1931), which may be considered the earliest personality measures, atleast employing a contemporary questionnaire format. Of interest is that other measures being constructed around the same time highlighted the divergent views on personality assessment methods at the time including the Rorschach Inkblot Test (Rorschach, 1921) and the Human Figure Drawings (Goodenough, 1926) and the Sentence Completion Tests (Payne, 1928).

PSYCHOLOGICAL SCIENCE VERSUS PSEUDOSCIENCE

The basis by which current psychological assessment methods and practices can be separated from other attempts to describe the latent traits and processes underlying differences in human behaviour is the very fact that they are grounded in scientific research, as outlined in the editors' introduction to Vol. 1. It is science that forces a method of study, including objectivity, experimentation and empirical support of hypotheses, and requires the creation and testing of theories. Psychology requires the operationalizing of variables and factors to be used in a description of human behaviour. In contrast to pseudosciences that operate outside of this framework and rest their case in beliefs, personal viewpoints, and idiosyncratic opinions, psychology also demands replication and, where possible, quantification of measures.

Measurement is the cornerstone of psychology and has spawned a number of methods for gathering the very data that may demonstrate the usefulness or lack of usefulness of a theory or provide the information needed to describe a particular human personality characteristic or even diagnose a personality disorder or clinical condition. Pseudosciences such as astrology, palmistry and phrenology, which compete with psychological views of personality, do not require such objective evidence to support their claims; rather, vague 'theories' are treated as fact and so-called evidence is often tautological. Thus a strength of psychology is that it has as its basis measurement that includes varying methods of gathering data to test theoretical ideas and hypotheses, as well as strict adherence to psychometric measurement principles such as reliability, validity and standardization (cf. Boyle, 1985).

FOUNDATIONS OF PERSONALITY MEASUREMENT AND ASSESSMENT

As mentioned above, it was concurrent with the advent of World War I that a major effort to assess personality characteristics was first witnessed. Prior to that time, the closest measure of personality would likely be considered as the word association techniques

used by Jung. Today almost everyone is familiar with personality measures, self-report questionnaires and rating scales that most often appear in the form of a statement or question (e.g. 'I am a very nervous person'; 'I enjoy activities where there are a lot of people and excitement') that the client answers with a 'yes–no,' 'true–false' or an extended scale such as a 5 or 7 point or greater Likert-type scale with anchors such as 'always true of me–never true of me' or 'definitely like me–not at all like me.' These highly structured measures contrast with the more ambiguous, subjective and open-ended techniques most often found in projective instruments such as the Rorschach Inkblot or Thematic Apperception tests.

Indeed, there is a longstanding tension between objective and subjective strategies for personality assessment (see Cattell and Johnson, 1986; Schuerger, 1986, Vol. 2). Use of questionnaires based on subjective insights and self-reports has dominated the field, but one may wonder how much this dominance reflects the convenience and low cost of questionnaire assessment. Advocates of objective testing may legitimately question the validity of subjective experience and the apparent ease with which desirable responses may be faked. Table 1.1 sets out the key issues dividing the two camps; both have strengths and weaknesses. We do not take a position on which approach is ultimately to be preferred; the chapters in Vol. 2 illustrate the vitality of both subjective and objective measurement approaches. Ideally, multimethod measurement models in which subjective and objective indices converge on common latent traits are to be desired, but current measurement technology remains some way from achieving this goal.

Given the more common use of standardized personality measures such as, for example, the Minnesota Multiphasic Personality Inventory-2 (MMPI-2), the California Psychological Inventory (CPI), the Sixteen Personality Factor Questionnaire (16PF), the Eysenck Personality Questionnaire - Revised (EPQ-R), and the NEO Personality

Table 1.1   Objective vs. subjective assessments of personality – some key issues

	Objective testing perspective	Subjective testing perspective
Meaningfulness of self-reports	People often lack insight into their true personalities. Personality may be shaped by unconscious forces (psychoanalysis) or by situationally specific implicit learning processes.	Self-reports are a class of behaviours that may usefully index latent personality traits. As Cattell (1973) pointed out, self-reports may be treated as behaviours whose meaning can be established through research (Q data) rather than as veridical insights (Q data).
Role of response bias	Self-reports often reflect no more than trivial response styles (e.g. acquiescence), (e.g. or deliberate impression management faking). Techniques for assessment of response bias may themselves be open to manipulation.	Response bias may be assessed independently from latent traits. Furthermore, some 'biases' may be integral to personality and worth investigating as substantive traits (Paulhus, 2002).
Biological basis of personality as the basis for measurement	If personality is biologically based, it is unlikely that self-reports map directly onto the brain systems controlling traits. Research should work towards direct assessment of individual differences in neural functioning and their molecular-genetic sources.	Traits may be higher-level emergent personal qualities that are not isomorphic with any single brain system (Zuckerman, 2005). Thus, it is difficult to capture traits in their entirety using biological indices. Specific biological theories also have only mixed support from empirical tests (Matthews and Gilliland, 1999).
Status of objective, implicit and projective tests	It is questionable whether subjective experience possesses the scaling properties necessary for quantitative measurement models (cf. Barrett, 2005). Tests based on objective behaviours may be intrinsically superior to subjective reports in supporting adequate measurement.	Historically, the reliability and validity of leading projective tests has been controversial. The new generation of implicit measures do not yet have the extensive nomological net of traits assessed by questionnaire. Such traits currently possess superior criterion, construct and consequential validity.

Inventory – Revised (NEO-PI-R), a brief description of the strategies underlying their construction will be presented here. Kaplan and Saccuzzo (2005) provide a useful description of the various strategies employed in constructing personality measures. Deductive strategies employ both face validity (logical–content strategy) and theory-driven views of personality. However, the assumption that an item followed by a 'yes' response, on the basis of content alone ('I am frequently on edge') taps anxiety or the broader neuroticism dimension found on scales assessing the Big Five (NEO-PI-R) or the three Eysenckian dimensions (EPQ-R) may or may not be accurate. And for instruments that employ a face-validity perspective, the rational approach to constructing items to measure particular characteristics may provide the client motivated by other alternative needs with the opportunity to provide

inaccurate and biased responses (e.g. see Boyle et al., 1995; Boyle and Saklofske, 2004). For example, a scale purportedly tapping aggression with items such as 'I often start fights' or 'I have never backed down from a chance to fight' may be so transparent as to increase the likelihood that examinees will also be more able to create a 'false' impression, depending on their motivation (e.g. early parole or lighter court sentence, malingering).

The foundational basis for many contemporary personality scales includes empirical strategies that employ the responses of various criterion groups (e.g. anxious vs. non-anxious adolescents) to determine how they differ on particular items and scales. For example, the very successful psychopathology scales, namely the MMPI (Hathaway and McKinley, 1940, 1943) and the revised MMPI-2 published in 1989, and the Millon

Clinical Multiaxial Inventories I, II and III (Millon, 1977, 1987, 2006) as well as the 'normal' personality trait scale, the California Personality Inventory or CPI (Gough, 1987), are examples of instruments grounded in this approach to test construction and clinical use. Criterion-keyed inventories employ the approach that is less tied to what an item 'says' or any *a priori* views of what it might be assessing, but rather whether the item discriminates or differentiates a known extreme group (e.g. clinical groups such as depressed, schizophrenic, etc.) from other clinical and normal respondents.

In other instances, statistical techniques, particularly factor analysis, are also used to infer or guide psychologists in determining the meaning of items and, thus, to define the major personality trait dimensions. Cattell's Sixteen Personality Factor Questionnaire or 16PF began as a large set of items based on a lengthy trait list that were then reduced to 36 'surface traits' and then further to 16 source traits, said to describe the basic dimensions of personality structure (see Boyle, 2006). In turn, structural equation modelling (see Cuttance and Ecob, 1987) allows personality structure to be examined in the larger context of other psychological variables to portray a more comprehensive and integrated description of human behaviour.

Finally, theory-driven measures draw from descriptions of 'what should be' or 'folk concepts' (e.g. CPI) and use this as the basis for constructing personality instruments, an example being the Edwards Personal Preference Schedule based on Murray's description of human needs. The major personality theories that have influenced the measurement of personality include psychoanalysis (e.g. Rorschach Inkblot Test; Vaillant's (1977) Interview Schedule for assessing defence mechanisms), phenomenology (Rogers and Dymond's Q-sort), behavioural and social learning (Rotter's I-E Scale) and trait conceptions (Cattell's 16 PF; Eysenck's EPQ-R; and Costa and McCrae's NEO-PI-R).

Certainly, the personality scales and assessment techniques most often employed today, in both research and clinical practice, include a combination of all the above approaches. The Eysenckian measures (e.g. MPI, EPI, EPQ/EPQ-R), the Cattellian measures (e.g. 16PF, HSPQ, CPQ; CAQ), as well as Big Five measures such as the NEO-PI-R have relied on empirical and factor analytic input into scale construction. Thus, the argument may be made that the NEO-PI-R, in spite of varying criticisms (see Boyle, Vol. 1), is a popular instrument for assessing putative trait dimensions labelled extraversion, neuroticism, conscientiousness, agreeableness and openness to experience. However, as Boyle et al. (1995: 432) reported, the NEO-PI-R measures less than two-thirds of the known trait variance within the normal personality sphere alone. Indeed, the proponents of any one of the major personality measures we have listed would claim that the measure concerned is based on theory, supported by research findings and is of practical value in clinical psychology and other applied fields.

TYPES OF PERSONALITY ASSESSMENT

When one thinks of personality assessment, what usually comes to mind is the self-report questionnaire. This almost exclusive reliance on questionnaires asking the respondent to answer a series of questions is showing signs of change and will continue to do so as genetic, biological and neurological markers, for particular personality traits come to the fore over time. At this time, the emphasis is on multimethod assessment approaches to ensure a convergence of results related to personality (and other) assessment as well as diagnosis of cognitive and affective disorders, includes case history and other extant data, interview, observation, behavioural and a pot pourri of informal assessment strategies, in combination with standardized tests and questionnaires. However, it would appear from the Meyer et al. (2001) review, that standardized, norm referenced measures (standard set of questions, method of administration, scoring) are the most valid and reliable of the currently available methods for assessing personality constructs.

The use of questionnaires and self-report inventories has dominated the field of personality measurement. In contrast to performance measures used in the assessment of cognitive ability (intelligence tests) and the assessment of skills through the use of, for example, driving tests, musical competitions and electrical apprenticeship practica, personality assessment has largely employed somewhat subjective self-report techniques or reports of others using questionnaires, checklists and rating scales. While questionnaire methods predated projective scales, their development was spurred by the need for standardized scales that would minimize human error in administration, scoring and interpretation. Use of such measures also allowed quantification of the personality dimensions being examined. Accordingly, psychologists could not only determine the direction (e.g. introversion vs. extraversion) but also the magnitude (e.g. very high score on extraversion at say, the 98th percentile) of a particular trait. This in turn, allowed for further refinements in assessment as well as replicability and cross-validation of the instruments themselves. Standardized personality instruments are most often associated with the assessment of personality traits (see Matthews et al., 2003) including those described by H.J. Eysenck, R.B. Cattell, P.T. Costa and R.R. McCrae, D.N. Jackson and others.

Projective measures are grounded in the tenets of dynamic psychology, beginning with the early psychoanalytic work of Freud. These measures were developed as a way of probing into unconscious content and motivations and to give a 'window' into the basic personality of the client. Here it is the subjectivity that is celebrated both in terms of the structure-free format that clients are given to respond to, often ambiguous stimuli, that will presumably allow for the expression of personality but also the openness of interpretation afforded the clinician who is well grounded in the views and 'clinical experiences' of dynamic psychology. While there are a number of projective measures ranging from the Szondi and Blacky Pictures to the Rosenzweig Picture Frustration Test, sentence completion techniques and House-Tree-Person Test that were created during the early and middle part of the last century, the Thematic Apperception Test (Morgan and Murray, 1935) and Rorschach Inkblot Test (Rorschach, 1921) remain the most often used projective measures today. Even with some waning in the interest of subjective/projective measures, in recent years, the well known Draw-A-Person and Bender Gestalt tests, among others, have been further extended to include the assessment of psychopathology and affective indicators (e.g. Draw A Person: Screening Procedure for Emotional Disturbance; Naglieri et al., 1991). Langens and Schmalt (Vol. 1) discuss more recent work that builds on the TAT.

As a reaction to the psychodynamic influence in psychology and further drawing from the earlier success of Pavlov and Watson's work in describing and changing behaviour, Skinner's model of operant conditioning was extensively embraced following World War II and for the following 30 years. Here, there is no interest in inferring latent traits underlying the expressions of human behaviour, or searching for unconscious mechanisms (the so-called 'Black Box') that might help explain individual differences. Rather personality is viewed or operationalized as observable behaviour reflecting the interaction between the person and his/her environment. Thus a behaviour that has been identified as potentially relevant for intervention (e.g. hitting others; talking out of turn) is observed in terms of frequency, duration and so on, in the context of its antecedent and consequent conditions. Thus it can be determined if the behaviour requires change, and if so, the prescriptive approach for doing so is to change those antecedent (environmental factors such as a noisy and distracting classroom) and/or consequent (e.g. reinforcement) conditions that would maintain the behaviour in question. Furthermore, this method has considerable predictive utility regarding the likelihood of the occurrence of particular behaviours. Based on systematic behavioural observation, there is no need to infer personality factors or an underlying personality structure. However, it is the use of observational data, most salient in the behavioural approaches, that is also central to the clinical and research study of personality.

Interviews have been a mainstay of psychological information and continue to form the cornerstone of such specialized areas as counselling psychology. Clinical psychology, industrial/organizational psychology and many other branches of applied psychology employ both structured and more open-ended interviews to gather critical information about a client's personal history, worries and concerns, career aspirations, mental health problems and so on. While self report personality questionnaires are essentially a form of structured interview, the use of interview techniques in general are considered to be less reliable and valid in diagnosis and treatment planning. However, in the service of a multimethod approach to personality assessment, interview data can have both exploratory and confirmatory usefulness. To paraphrase Gordon Allport, if you want to know what people think or feel, ask them!

In more recent years, explorations of the biological and neurological bases of human behaviour, from fields such as behaviour genetics and neuropsychology have contributed significantly to the study of personality. These contributions are extensively described in Vol. 1 in chapters by Stelmack and Rammsayer (psychophysiology) and also by Johnson et al. (behaviour genetics). While many personality theories are firmly grounded in brain-behaviour and genetic explanations (e.g. Eysenck's E and N factors), tests of these hypothetical links are now much more possible with the use of MRI and fMRI, as well as metabolic, neurotransmitter and genetic measures.

In line with the dominant tradition of the field, many of the contributions to Vol. 2 are concerned with questionnaire assessments. The various uni- and multidimensional personality questionnaires may be evaluated against agreed standards for determining the efficacy of a given psychological measurement instrument (AERA/APA/NCME Test Standards, 1999). These standards lay out a framework for interpreting reliability and validity, so that the questionnaire developer has the following obligations:

1 To provide evidence for the reliability of the measure in question and information on the standard error of measurement.
2 To demonstrate that a meaningful relationship exists between the test's content and the construct that it is intended to measure (similar to 'content validity').
3 To provide theoretical and empirical analyses supporting (or disconfirming) relationships between the construct and the responses provided by the test-taker (e.g. checking that responses are not driven by social desirability or other biasing factors).
4 To demonstrate that the internal structure of the construct is as suggested by the underlying theoretical framework (e.g. whether it is uni- or multidimensional, whether it is hierachical in structure, etc.).
5 To localize the construct within a nomological net; that is, other individual differences variables to which the assessment relates, as specified by theory. This criterion relates to 'construct validity', including establishing both convergent and discriminant evidence, test-criterion relationships, and investigating how validity generalizes across samples, situations and cultures.

Readers may determine for themselves how well the leading questionnaires match up to these test standards. We have indicated previously in this introduction the need for alternatives to questionnaires, including objective tests. Volume 2 also addresses these alternatives, in reviewing psychophysiological techniques that may lend themselves to assessment, and also implicit, objective and projective tests. Historically, it has often proved difficult to obtain evidence for reliability and validity that matches corresponding evidence for questionnaire assessments, but the chapters here provide optimism that a new era of computer-interactive objective testing of personality constructs may be at hand.

INTRODUCTION TO VOLUME TWO

This volume contains a series of in-depth and critical chapters on the broad topics of personality measurement and assessment written by leading experts. The chapters are grouped into several themes including general methodological issues, multidimensional personality instruments, assessing biologically based and self-regulative traits, followed then by projective and objective personality measures, and lastly by measures assessing abnormal personality.

GENERAL METHODOLOGICAL ISSUES

It is often said in relation to psychological assessment that the key to moving forward with psychometrically sound measurement rests with the definitions that are determined to best represent a particular domain of behaviour, psychological disturbance (or wellbeing), or underlying traits such as extraversion or neuroticism. From the start, we realize that this is a daunting task for psychologists that will invariably require an interdisciplinary perspective and effort. John et al. (1988) quite rightly asserted that 'personality psychology has not yet established a generally accepted taxonomy of its subject matter which includes all variation in the overt social behaviour and the internal experiences of individuals' (1988: 171). This is based on the view that personality attributes, like so many other psychological constructs, including intelligence, are abstract concepts that are not directly observable, but rather are inferred. The search for a generally supported taxonomy would provide the needed basis for personality research, in spite of differences in theoretical orientation by bringing 'an order' to the huge collection of personality variables

that have been created and studied over the years. In turn, this has direct relevance to what we measure in our personality instruments and how we can use this information in understanding individual differences.

Saucier (Vol. 2) contends that how we define, organize and measure personality can be guided from lexical studies of natural language. In turn, these studies have formed the basis for a personality structure that runs the gamut from a single factor solution somewhat akin to 'g' in intelligence theory and measurement, to seven lexical factors. While language may partly determine the number of factors that emerge in an examination of personality structure based on human lexicons, the issue becomes even more apparent when we attempt to develop measures to assess personality. The question can be asked: are personality characteristics universal? If so, then other than their expression or the actual behaviours observed to infer a personality characteristic, the universality of personality traits for example should allow for the translation and adaptation of an instrument from one language and culture to another. But as we search further into the cultural and linguistic fabric of differing societies, we find unique examples of personality factors that do not seem to have an equivalent elsewhere. Comparing and contrasting cultures that are defined by an independent versus interdependent view of the self, the Japanese concept of 'omoiyari' would seem to exhibit some relationship with prosocial behaviour and empathy as defined in Western psychology. However, it is also unique because of the intuitive aspect ('sasshi') that is valued so highly in societies that are grounded in an interdependent view of the person. The chapter by van de Vijver and van Hemert (Vol. 2) describes the critical aspects of the methodology required in cross-cultural research and instrument construction and then follows this with some of the advances in the cross-cultural measurement of personality. It readily becomes apparent that the search for both universal personality factors and potentially unique clusters of personality variables will not be uncovered by simply comparing the responses to scales administered in two different countries or cultures, even if the measures are translated.

In response to the diversity of views on personality that have resulted from various theoretical, research and measurement perspectives in psychology and allied disciplines, Jackson (Vol. 2) proposes a 'hybrid model' that should serve both heuristic and practical functions. Integrating biological, experiential and social-cognitive theories, Jackson describes how this model departs from earlier views that appears to have fragmented rather than unified the study of personality (e.g. viewing approach-avoidance as orthogonal constructs; separating temperament and character). Of particular interest to practitioners is Jackson's contention that the proposed hybrid model will guide the implementation of various psychological treatment interventions. This has been a major concern of clinical, school/educational, counselling and I/O psychologists, as well as those who practice psychology in health, military, sport, forensic and other venues. As one psychologist known to the authors quipped recently, 'What good does it do for the psychologist and client to know the client's scores on the Big Five or to tell the client that s/he is a stable introvert'! Predicting successful and unsuccessful outcomes with and without interventions will provide personality psychology with the status accorded to intelligence and intelligence tests.

MULTIDIMENSIONAL PERSONALITY INSTRUMENTS

The second group of chapters is focused on an examination of some of best-known and most often used measures of personality. In contrast to scales that are intended to assess psychopathology such as the MMPI-2, these measures reflect an eclectic underpinning of theory, trait descriptions, and factor analysis that rather describe the structure of

personality. As the late Professor Hans Eysenck so often reminded us, the psychoticism or the P factor in his theory of personality, and also assessed on the EPQ and EPQ-R, is not a measure of psychotic behaviour or psychopathology. Rather it reflects a tough minded/tender minded dimension that may predispose a person to psychopathy or schizophrenia.

The well known California Psychological Inventory is now over 50-years-old and is considered to be very much akin to a 'folk description' of personality in contrast to instruments either driven by theory or derived empirically from factor analysis. There is some disagreement about the actual factor structure and whether this measure is best described within the currently popular five-factor model (FFM). Also, some of the scales on the CPI 260 and 434 are less reliable than is minimally ideal. However, exploration of the current 20 CPI scales has resulted in some new scales summarized by Boer et al. (Vol. 2). The CPI is one of the more often used measures in the business sector by I/O psychologists for personnel selection but has also been used extensively in counselling and forensic settings.

Factor analysis has been a driving influence on the development of both intelligence and personality instruments. For example, the widely recognized three strata structure of intelligence described by Carroll was based on an analysis of 456 factor-analytic studies of intelligence. On the other hand, proposed models of intelligence, for example by Spearman and Thurstone many years earlier, have been tested with factor analysis (both exploratory and confirmatory) to determine if the proposed structure can be replicated with large data sets. Certainly, many of the trait descriptions of personality are in part derived from factor analysis (e.g. Cattell's 16 PF), or the theoretical structure is supported with the aid of factor analysis (e.g. Eysenck's PEN model reflected in the EPQ/EPQ-R).

The Comrey Personality Scales (CPS) are a very good example of how factor analysis has been employed over time to create the eight factors found in this measure (Comrey, 1994; Comrey and Lee, 1992). As is now expected with all scales that employ a questionnaire format and self-ratings, a validity and response bias scale are included to assist in determining various biases that would then challenge the accuracy of the report and its clinical usefulness. Comrey (Vol. 2) has provided solid empirical evidence in support of the factor structure as well as the validity and clinical use of these scales. A question sometimes asked about personality scales is: 'What does it mean to be extraverted ... what does this tell the psychologist or even the client?' Comrey has provided clear clinical descriptions of what it means to score high or low on measures such as orderliness vs. lack of compulsion, or trust vs. defensiveness. A.L. Comrey's psychometric work has stood the test of critical scrutiny over many years and remains an exemplary contribution to the scientific (factor analytic) construction of multidimensional personality scales, alongside the parallel outstanding contributions of R.B. Cattell and H.J. Eysenck (see Boyle, Vol. 1).

Probably one of the very best examples of the early use of factor analysis to define and measure personality characteristics as well as to expand and refine the scale is found in the 16PF developed by R.B. Cattell that was first published in 1949 (see Cattell et al., 1970), with the fifth revision being published in 1993. Cattell (1973) described personality as comprised of three levels. Starting with the 16 primary personality traits, factor analysis produced the second-order global factors that very much interface with the current Big Five personality factors (Boyle, 1989b; Krug and Johns, 1986). Such a model does allow for a personality description at several levels (strata) but also contributes to an understanding of individual differences as can be seen, for example, with global extraversion. Such a scale permits both research on large-scale population comparisons (e.g. cross-cultural comparisons) but also at the level of the individual who has requested counselling for interpersonal problems or work-related

stress. The chapter by Heather Cattell and Alan Mead (Vol. 2) also portrays the significant role played by the 16PF in defining variants of the Big Five (see Boyle et al., 1995) but further delves into the debate surrounding the correlated vs. orthogonal relationship of these factors, drawing our attention to the 'power' of factor analysis (oblique solutions) in defining the relational structure of personality. Another interesting issue is the relationship between the psychometric cornerstones of reliability and validity and how they interact to an optimal level on measures such as the 16PF. Of particular interest to the readers of this chapter are the comprehensive references to the clinical use and applications of the past and current versions of the 16PF.

Boyle and Barton (Vol. 2) have extended the chapter by Heather Cattell to first remind us that Raymond B. Cattell (as indexed by journal citations) is one of the most influential psychologists of the twentieth century (Haggbloom et al., 2002: 142). We are also reminded of the huge compendium of research and measurement instruments in the personality field alone that Cattell gave us including the Sixteen Personality Questionnaire, the High School Personality Questionnaire, the Adolescent Personality Questionnaire, the Children's Personality Questionnaire, the Early School Personality Questionnaire, the Preschool Personality Questionnaire, the Central Trait-State Kit, the Objective-Analytic Battery and the Clinical Analysis Questionnaire along with its more recent version, the PsychEval Personality Questionnaire (Cattell et al., 2003). This chapter then turns to an analysis of personality measures using Barton's nine-parameter model that targets key 'who, what, how' questions and echoes Cattell's call for the development of personality measures that go beyond the use not only of subjective L-data and Q-data measures, but also draw from the objective testing of behaviour (T-data). Such an approach will provide psychologists with the multimethod assessment framework needed to converge on the most accurate and meaningful description of an individual's personality. On another note, as one reads through these two volumes and possibly becomes concerned about the diversity of personality models and measurement approaches, we are reminded of a statement by Eysenck (1984), also named as one of the most influential contributors to twentieth century psychology (see Haggbloom et al., 2002). In an analysis of Cattell's personality theory and measures, Eysenck stated that 'the Cattell and Eysenck constructs and theories should be seen not as mutually contradictory, but as complementary and mutually supportive' (1984: 336).

The Big Five personality factors have dominated the personality trait literature over recent years. More references are seen to the putative constructs labelled: extraversion, neuroticism, openness to experience, agreeableness and conscientiousness as measured, for example, by the NEO-PI-R than to any other set of personality traits, in spite of the substantial lack of agreement among psychologists (e.g. Cattell, 1995; Eysenck, 1992; McAdams, 1992; Schneider et al., 1995). However, Costa and McCrae have provided a very detailed 'inside' look at the construction of the NEO-PI-R in relation to the position of trait psychology, and criticisms of earlier personality measurement including other trait measures based on Eysenck's P, E, N model and Cattell's 16PF. Moving beyond N, E and O, and influenced by Norman and Goldberg's factors defining the structure of personality, Costa and McCrae engaged in an extensive research programme that resulted in the NEO-FFI, NEO-PI and the more recent NEO-PI-R and NEO-PI 3 (a detailed critique of the factor analytic methodology employed in construction of the NEO-PI-R is provided by Boyle et al., 1995: 431–433).

While considerable research pertaining to scale reliability and validity has been undertaken and some of the key findings are included in this chapter, the question of accuracy in self-report measures has been addressed quite simply in the NEO-PI and NEO-PI-R questionnaires. A last item asks respondents to say if they have answered items honestly and accurately and if all items

have been responded to and the answer sheet completed correctly. However, this response can easily be manipulated. Even if a person thinks at a conscious level that s/he has answered 'honestly', it does not follow necessarily that the responses are accurate, particularly if the individual has poor self-insight. This simple approach is quite in contrast to many other scales such as the 16PF, MMPI, PAI and BASC that have included a number of 'validity' checks; however the computer scored version of the NEO-PI-R does give further indications of such potentially relevant indicators of response accuracy and bias in reporting such as the number of missing items. Although in recent times the proposed Big Five personality factors have tended to take 'centre stage' in personality research, the use of the NEO-PI-R in applied settings is tempered by Costa and McCrae's view that 'more research is still needed to optimize its application'.

As stated above, the debate over the number of traits that would 'best' define personality, and in turn, that will have the greatest application to 'real world' settings, ranging from personnel selection to therapeutic intervention prescriptions, has been heard for many years. Based on both taxonomic descriptions and factor-analytic investigations, it would appear that the three most often cited positions are those reflected in H. Eysenck's (1991) paper, 'Dimensions of Personality: 16, 5 or 3? Criteria for a taxonomic paradigm'. Eysenck's personality theory, while having undergone various revisions (as outlined by O'Connor, Vol. 2), has stayed true to the position that the three major personality dimensions of extraversion, neuroticism and psychoticism are sufficient to account for individual differences across a wide spectrum of human behaviours. However, the proportion of the personality sphere variance accounted for by Eysenck's three broad factors almost certainly is less than optimal (cf. Mershon and Gorsuch, 1988). Eysenck's model has resulted in the publication of a number of scales beginning with the MPI tapping extraversion and neuroticism followed by the EPI and even-tually the EPQ and EPQ-R that included the P scale (see Furnham et al., Vol. 2). Children's versions of the EPI and EPQ scales have been concurrently constructed by S. Eysenck and are referred to as the 'junior' versions (e.g. JEPQ; Eysenck and Eysenck, 1975). While Eysenck's model clearly described a number of primary traits from which the second-order factors of E, N and P emerged, there was less effort invested in developing scales to measure each of these. However, over time the components of extraversion, initially focusing on impulsivity and sociability, were split off with sociability remaining as part of E along with such other primary traits as sensation seeking and venturesomeness. While the Eysencks developed several scales to assess impulsivity, venturesomeness and empathy, there was also some effort to select those items from the EPQ defining the three-factor space to predict criminal propensity and antisocial behaviour. The EPI and EPQ are still used extensively in research studies and have been translated and adapted for use in many different countries (Boyle and Saklofske, 2004).

Entering the taxonomic debate regarding the number of personality factors that are needed to account for individual differences in behaviour, the Zuckerman–Kuhlman Personality Questionnaire (ZKPQ) has redefined the factor space described by the Big Five. As Zuckerman (Vol. 2) explains in his chapter, the ZKPQ was developed to derive a personality structure appropriate for measuring basic personality traits with their roots in biological traits. Zuckerman provides a detailed discussion of the evolution of the ZKPQ into its current five-factor structure and the labelling of the factors as ImpSS (impulsive sensation seeking), N-Anx (neuroticism–Anxiety), Agg-Hos (aggression-hostility) and Sy (sociability). While the factor structure and psychometric integrity of the ZKPQ and also the short-form (Zuckerman, 2005) has been replicated in cross-cultural studies, some studies have also attested to the potential for use in a variety of settings ranging from risk taking in university students (Zuckerman and Kuhlman, 2000) to the reactions of migrant groups to moving into a new and different culture (Schmitz, 2004). However, because of its underpinnings in the psychobiology of personality, Zuckerman contends that possibly one of the greatest uses of the ZKPQ should be to explore the underlying basis of personality in the brain.

Ashton et al. (Vol. 2) have offered yet another model that comprised of six factors, assessed using the HEXACO-PI (Ashton et al., 2006). They have argued that studies of more than a dozen languages show that six personality factors appear common to all. The name of this model (HEXACO) serves as an acronym for the names of the factors including: honesty–humility (H), emotionality (E), extraversion (X), agreeableness (A), conscientiousness (C) and openness to experience (O). In their chapter, Ashton and Lee write that, 'Despite its lexical origins, the HEXACO model uses the name openness to experience rather than intellect/imagination/unconventionality.' The major addition to this model, in comparison with the proposed Big Five factors, and resulting scale, again in comparison with the NEO-PI, is the H factor. However, Ashton and Lee further suggest that the six personality factors described in their model reflect two dimensions representing altruistic in contrast to antagonistic tendencies, and engagement within different areas of endeavour. It is the contention of the authors that the honesty–humility and emotionality factors are what give the HEXACO model an advantage over the currently popular Big Five. This chapter provides Croatian, Greek, and Filipino data supporting the cross-cultural factor structure.

Tellegen and Waller (Vol. 2) describe the process of constructing a measure of personality from both deductive and external approaches to scale construction. However, they argue that an 'exploratory' approach used during the 10 year construction period of the Multidimensional Personality Questionnaire (MPQ) (Tellegen, 1982, 1995) has the advantage of permitting changes during the research and development phases of test construction. The authors state that, 'The intent in constructing the MPQ was to clarify and demarcate major dimensions in the self-descriptive personality trait domain' and offer strong support for their scale (e.g. heuristic virtues, substantial heritabilities, links with neurobehavioural personality models, shared factor loadings with other major personality scales such as the EPQ, CPI, PRF, NEO, and Cattell's 16 PF, as well as respectable scale reliabilities). An interesting and controversial issue is raised in this chapter regarding the congruence between self-ratings and ratings of others, as well as with external criteria. When comparing subjective self-report personality ratings with ratings by knowledgeable others (e.g. spouse, friends/peers, employer/employees), it is not uncommon to see some, and possibly, considerable divergence. This could be construed as measurement error related to the varying reliabilities of the scales or that the descriptors (e.g. items and scales) are aimed more at assessing latent traits versus overt behavioural manifestations that are less readily observed by significant others. Score discrepancies might also reflect biases in responding (social desirability, or malingering) by the 'client' leading to a difference in self-ratings versus ratings by others. Tellegen and Waller, in fact, argue that the very nature of the MPQ will possibly result in 'reliable discrepancies which are potentially informative and should not be dismissed as simply demonstrating the fallibility of self-report'. One has to appreciate the view taken in this chapter about the use of and feedback from personality measures such as the MPQ in everyday applied settings: 'With use of appropriate norms, feedback contributes to self-clarification by translating discrete self-statements into coherent and telling characterizations.'

ASSESSMENT OF BIOLOGICALLY BASED TRAITS

The third section of this volume is titled 'Assessment of biologically based traits' and includes five chapters focusing on the biological underpinnings of personality structure and measurement. A major criticism of many personality measures is that they are often so phenotypical in content and purpose that they miss describing the causal and underlying correlates of key personality traits and factors. Saklofske and Eysenck (1994) stated that 'trait models of personality are sometimes criticized for apparently pretending to explain differences in behaviour by simply postulating the existence of traits based on that behaviour.... Factor analysis and other correlational methods are not meant to tell us anything about causality but to act as tools for the discovery of a proper personality taxonomy. Having solved the problem, we may then go on to carry out the more difficult task of finding out why some people are more sociable, others shy, why some people are extraverted, others introverted.'

Brain-behaviour studies began with the earlier EEG studies and are now driven by technologically sophisticated techniques such as fMRI used in neuropsychological research. The fields of psychobiology and psychophysiology using early measures such as EMG, GSR and HR, have more recently engaged in direct studies of neurotransmitters such as dopamine and serotonin. The specialty areas such as behaviour genetics, initially studying human behaviour between individuals of varying degrees of genetic relatedness (e.g. kinship studies) now have access to DNA data. All are essential for a full understanding of human personality that links the phenotypic expression of personality with the underlying genotypic foundations.

Furedy's chapter (Vol. 2) provides an historical backdrop for the relevance of psychophysiological measurement in the study of personality. He then describes how the following psychophysiological measures may be considered by personality researchers: 'peripheral vs. central measures, baseline vs. response-to-challenge measures, tonic vs. phasic measures; uniphasic vs. multiphasic measures; lo-tech vs. hi-tech measures; physiological "respectability" vs. psychological validity; temporal vs. localization measures; specific vs. reactive sensitivity; psycho-physiological vs. behavioural measures; reliability vs. validity.' But before psychologists who rely on self-report question-naires, and observation and interview data begin to feel that their measures are less ade-quate and not a 'direct' measure of personality, Furedy provides a very good example of the high reliability but low validity of the poly-graph for classification purposes (e.g. truthful vs. deceptive individuals).

Extending this work, de Geus and Neumann (Vol. 2) provide two very good reasons for the significance of psychophysio-logical measurement in furthering our under-standing of personality. They point to the limitations of an over-reliance on self- and other-report 'paper and pencil' measures that may be prone to various biases, distortions and psychometric shortcomings. In contrast, psychophysiological indices have the advan-tage that 'voluntary control over the recorded biological signals is limited if not absent'. At more of a construct validity level, these authors argue that personality may only be completely understood by also describing the biological processes underlying the major dimensions of personality. Focusing on the two most agreed-upon personality traits, extraversion and neuroticism, compelling evidence is provided to show their psychoph-siological underpinnings, ranging from ERP to fMRI data. In a similar tone to Furedy, however, de Geus and Neumann also agree that the 'reliability of psychophysiological measures is currently less convincing than those for paper-and-pencil measures and validity has been far more rigorously tested for the latter'. They suggest two reasons for the 'shortfall' of psychophysiological data to provide a solid foundation on which to build comprehensive understandings of per-sonality. First, many studies rely only on a single measure (e.g. cerebral blood flow, EEG asymmetry) rather than examining the complex and often interactive nature of mul-tiple causal pathways. Second, 'mainstream neuroscience is still very much focused on universal affective and cognitive brain processes at the expense of individual differ-ences ... by not taking individual differences

into account, or considering them a mere nuisance variable, many neuroscience studies may have failed to detect a link between a brain structure and the putative affective and cognitive processes in which it is involved.'

Congdon and Canli (Vol. 2) focus their analysis of the biological basis of personality on the 'primary' personality factor of impulsivity. While impulsivity is considered a multidimensional construct found in many personality descriptions, included in many personality scales, and identified in various psychopathological (e.g. bipolar disorder, DSM-IV-TR Axis-II disorders) and neurobe-havioural (e.g. AD/HD) conditions, 'the fact that patients are classified based on a taxon-omy that is not biologically based poses a serious challenge to efforts to investigate the biological basis of impulsivity.' Noting the shortcomings of fitting impulsivity into the larger framework of personality, they describe research from non-invasive neu-roimaging and molecular genetic studies that have separately provided support for a bio-logical foundation. However, their reliance of these studies on heterogeneous diagnostic categories and self-report measures, 'obscure any effect that a genotype may have on the phenotype of interest, especially when the size of the effect is small'. Thus the authors argue for an 'endophenotype' approach that would combine neuroimaging and molecular genetic approaches and show its efficacy in an investigation of dopaminergic gene variation on impulsivity.

Strelau and Zawadski (Vol. 2) follow up on a lifetime of work on temperament which Strelau defines as a stable set of personality traits, essentially present from birth or early infancy. Although tempera-ment has a neurobiochemical basis, changes may occur due to external conditions. This chapter briefly outlines the more significant theoretical views of temperament and describes some of the key measures that have evolved within the psychometric tradi-tion. The very fact that there are some 30 temperament instruments and more than 80 temperament scales reported in the literature, suggests that either the construct is so broad as to not be particularly useful in theory, research and practice, or that there is considerable overlap. Strelau and Zawadski state that 'the results of factor analysis confirm the expectation of a broad five-factor domain of personality with temperamental scales located mainly in two "arousability" factors: "emotionality/neuroticism" and "extraversion/activity"'. However, Strelau and Zawadski argue that much work is still required to add specificity to the very broad concept of temperament and to develop reliable and valid measures.

ASSESSMENT OF SELF-REGULATIVE TRAITS

'Styles of self-regulation are integral aspects of personality' (Matthews et al., 2000: 199). They further argue that the integration of personality traits and self-regulation requires a resolution of two divergent viewpoints: 'The trait approach views personality as stable across time and across different situations … much of the literature on self-regulation adopts a social-cognitive perspective that conceptualizes personality as the outcome of idiographic, contextually sensitive cognitive processes' (2000: 171). While most primary (e.g. impulsivity) and higher-order personality traits (e.g. extraversion) relate to styles of self-regulation, the chapters in section 3 highlight this critical feature of human behaviour.

The chapter by Zayas et al. (Vol. 2) complements the two chapters in Vol. 1 that examine social-cognitive views of personality (Cervone, Vol. 1; Matthews, Vol. 1). Zayas and colleagues further provide a detailed analysis of the social-cognitive perspective on key questions that have confronted the study of personality. Earlier views of behaviour in more simple terms were described as a function of persons interacting with their environment (PxE). However, the growing

realization of the complexity of both these variables was most obvious when observing both individual and intraindividual differences. While there is a predictability to human behaviours that is surely grounded in personality, there is also the observation that a person's behaviours will vary across situations. It is not uncommon to hear expressions such as 'he is a situational extravert' suggesting that under particular situations, and the demands arising from particular circumstances, a person may behave or act somewhat differently than under other conditions. Thus a purely trait perspective does not account adequately for such variability across situations, but at the same time, human behaviour is not continuously random. Zayas et al. argue that such variability can best be understood by knowing what features in a given situation are 'psychologically active' for each of us. It is the psychologically important or 'if features' of situations that activate both cognitive and affective processes, which in turn result in thoughts, feeling and actions. This social cognitive perspective outlined by Zayas et al. suggests that 'if … then … profiles provide clues for identifying individuality and personality coherence within individuals' cross-situational variability … This variability need not be considered a source of error to be eliminated'.

As highlighted in the chapter by Fernandez (Vol. 2), anger, hostility and aggression have been studied in psychology since the early formulations of Freud that elevated aggression to one of the major human 'instincts'(cf. Fernandez, 2002). The early work of Rosenzweig using the Picture-Frustration Test, the questionnaire analysis of aggression developed by Buss and Durkee (1957), the theoretical analysis of aggression by Bandura (1983) and the more recent cognitive-behavioural descriptions presented by Dodge (e.g. Crick and Dodge, 1996) are but some examples of the interest in understanding and measuring aggression, anger and hostility. Fernandez distinguishes the qualitative aspects of anger from other emotions such as sadness and also the quantitative aspects of low (annoyance) to high levels (rage) but further contends that 'anger can assume the form of an emotion, a mood, or a temperament, depending on whether it is phasic, tonic, or cyclic'. While questionnaires have served as the major methods of assessing anger and hostility, the major contribution of this chapter by Fernandez is the description of six core dimensions in the expression of anger including direction, locus, reaction, modality, impulsivity and objective of anger. Using this model, Fernandez shows how anger profiles are created using the anchor points of these six dimensions.

In contrast to the strict trait approach for defining and measuring personality, Horowitz et al. (Vol. 2) have drawn from the interpersonal model of personality and have identified four interpersonal measures (behaviours, traits, interpersonal goals, interpersonal problems) that are further organized around the two interpersonal dimensions of communion and agency. This allows for the creation of a profile (or 'nomological net') describing the individual using eight interpersonal variables. The measures derived from this model and their application to personality assessment are illustrated in this chapter but more importantly serve to 'show how the four interpersonal measures (the IMI, IAS, IIP, and CSIV) may be used together to clarify other concepts in clinical psychology' such as personality disorders.

Probably one of the major catalysts for stimulating an examination of the interface between personality and intelligence called for by Saklofske and Zeidner (1995) is the more recent examination of emotional intelligence (EI). The two somewhat divergent views of EI reflected in the trait formulation with its closer links with personality traits, and the ability model proposed by Mayer and Salovey (1997) are described in the chapter by Austin et al. (see Vol. 1). What sets the so-called ability approach apart from the trait EI view is the focus on the interaction between emotion and cognition. As Rivers et al. (Vol. 2) outline in their chapter,

'Emotional intelligence (EI) refers to the capacity to both reason about emotion and use emotion to enhance thinking and problem solving.' It is the skills of perceiving, using, understanding and managing emotions that are the foundation of EI. Furthermore, the method of measuring EI can be contrasted. While trait scales (e.g. Bar-On, 1997; Schutte et al. 1998) mimic traditional self-report personality questionnaires where a person's position on the scale(s) is usually determined using normative comparisons, the ability scales (MSCEIT and MSCEIT-YV) discussed in this chapter employ a problem-solving approach applied to emotional situations, using both consensus and expert scoring (MSCEIT) and veridical scoring (MSCEIT-YV).

The MSCEIT is a departure from standard personality assessment using self-report measures but rather, like intelligence tests, one that employs problem situations to which the respondent's answers are compared with expert opinion. Thus, the low correlations between the two forms of EI assessment may reflect differing conceptual underpinnings of EI or method variance or both. And the far from high correlations with intelligence tests for both trait and ability measures raises the interesting question of whether EI should be considered 'an intelligence' (Austin and Saklofske, 2005). These are key issues raised by Roberts et al. in their chapter (Vol. 2) which continues to look critically at EI models and measures following the first and more recent books by Matthews et al. (2002, 2007). Focusing on the 'intelligence' aspect of EI, Roberts et al. argue that self-report measures do not assess intelligence and thus should not be construed as measures of EI, in contrast to ability-based models that are 'the only appropriate ones to delineate, and hence investigate, emotional *intelligence*'. Arguing for a constrained view of EI, the authors then suggest that the ability (or maximum performance) model reflected in the MSCEIT kind of measures holds the greatest promise for assessing EI. However, they are currently limited by their 'mono-operation and mono-method biases' and will benefit as well from 'using new paradigms from emotions research, and new test construction techniques from I/O psychology'.

IMPLICIT, PROJECTIVE AND OBJECTIVE MEASURES OF PERSONALITY

The next section of this volume turns to an examination of implicit, objective and projective personality measurement. Probably no other topic in the personality assessment literature has generated the same level of debate as that seen between proponents of standardized instruments versus projective tests. On another level, cross-cultural issues have also risen to the fore in relation to both personality as well as intelligence measures. The 'emic–etic' perspectives on cross-cultural comparisons have raised a number of questions about how well both the constructs used in one culture to operationalize and assess, say intelligence or personality, can travel across national, cultural and linguistic borders. The reader may also refer to Saucier's chapter (Vol. 2) on the significance of the lexicon in determining how a culture describes and values various human characteristics.

Hong and Paunonen (Vol. 2) describe two 'non-verbal' personality measures, the NPQ and FF-NPQ. In contrast to the more psycho-dynamic measures such as the TAT, these two measures focus on explicit (rather than unconscious) personality characteristics, are samples of behaviour reflecting personality traits rather than 'signs' of some underlying personality disposition, and use a structured response format to ensure objective scoring and increase scorer reliability. A key advantage argued for this format by Hong and Paunonen is that these measures are likely more portable and flexible when assessing individuals from different cultural and language backgrounds because the problem of translation, and also reading skills level, is reduced. In particular, the FF-NPQ should provide an alternative

measure for determining the robustness of the putative Big Five across cultures.

The basic difference in the assumptions posed by projective versus standardized personality instruments relates to whether personality traits and factors are explicitly known to the person who is self-reporting or instead, that personality is more implicit and may be assessed with techniques referred to as Implicit Association Tests (IATs). Schnabel et al. (Vol. 2) argue that IATs have a number of advantages over traditional questionnaire methods for assessing personality. As described by Schnabel et al., IAT measures are designed to 'assess automatic associations between a contrasted pair of target (such as "me" versus "others") and attribute (such as "anxious" versus "confident") concepts through a series of discrimination tasks that require fast responding'. A basic premise of these measures is that such motivational distortion factors as faking good/bad, and so on, are less likely to confound or yield misleading results. However, while social cognitive research has provided a foundation on which to build IATs, explanations for IAT effects are still less than fully understood, and the psychometric properties, especially reliability, of standard IAT measures is somewhat lower than considered desirable. At the same time, there is growing evidence from validity studies that IATs may provide another 'method' for assessing personality that would allow researchers and clinicians to potentially address the issue of contaminating method variance that likely occurs when exclusively relying on self-report questionnaires. However at this time, there is not sufficient evidence that IAPs should be used in clinical decision making related to diagnosis and treatment planning and/or selection.

Schuerger (Vol. 2) provides yet a further alternative to assessing personality based on the efforts of Cattell and Warburton (1967) to create actual performance tests (T-data) of personality, a careful selection of which have been included in the Objective-Analytic Test Battery or OAB. While Schuerger concedes that that original versions were very cumbersome and not widely adopted, the idea underlying the OAB is quite contemporary and one that clearly supports a multi-trait, multimethod, multimodal approach to assessing human characteristics. A consensus is lacking regarding the factor structure of the OAB with Schuerger stating that only six of the factors originally reported by Cattell have been replicated in research conducted outside Cattell's laboratory. However, Schuerger also contends that the OA tests still hold remarkable promise as demonstrated in both educational and clinical settings, and there may be even greater untapped potential in individual OA variables. In contrast to the time when Cattell was developing the OA tests, the advent of modern computer technology and widespread computer use may yet be the format for reviving interest in such performance tests of personality structure. It would be surprising not to find more performance measures being presented by computer in the very near future. Our clinical laboratories already have this capability but microcomputers will also make this is a reality for the 'travelling clinician' such as the school psychologist.

Standardized personality instruments, such as the Eysenck and Cattell measures and projective techniques including the Rorschach inkblots and TAT, have certainly dominated the field of personality assessment for much of the twentieth century. While personality scales are still a mainstay in contemporary psychology, including those described in the chapters of Vol. 2, both research and practicing psychologists are also interested in assessing the manifestations and related behaviours of underlying personality dimensions such as anxiety, depression and aggression. Thus, while the tendency towards aggressive behaviour can be plotted on a three-dimensional matrix defined by E, N, and P, of greater clinical utility to psychologists is to have more 'direct' measures of the level and type of aggressive behaviour. For example, the early Buss–Durkee scale was more focused on assessing the direct expression of aggression

in its own right just as were the depression and anxiety scales developed by Beck (e.g. Beck and Steer, 1993). Not all scales are focused on the 'negative' or pathological side, and in particular, we now see scales tapping happiness, life satisfaction and subjective wellbeing.

The past several decades have witnessed the development of multiscale measures that tap a wide range of psychologically important behaviours. Scales developed by Achenbach and Connors for multidimensional measures paved the way for many of the new scales that tap a number of behavioural factors of relevance to clinical diagnosis and intervention planning. The first and now recently revised Behaviour Assessment System for Children developed by Reynolds and Kamphaus (1992, 2004) is not a personality measure in the strict sense of tapping those traits thought to underlie behaviour, but rather a more direct assessment of behaviour itself. The advantages they offer to the practicing psychologist are described by Rowe et al. (Vol. 2) who also remind us that this, or any other scale, should never 'stand alone' as the sole basis for diagnosis or prescription. The current BASC-II provides statements that the respondent (child, parent, teacher) answers using a four-point (or true–false) Likert-type format yielding composite, primary and content scores. For example, the mixture of items on the primary self-report scales range from anxiety to attention problems, self-esteem to sense of inadequacy, and locus of control to sensation seeking, thus reflecting a very eclectic mix of scales all focusing on behaviour and the behaviours argued to describe, say, locus of control. Of interest is that the BASC-II has become the most often used behavioural measure by school and child-adolescent clinical psychologists, in part because of its solid psychometric properties and time–cost benefits, but more so because it provides a 'direct' method of assessment of both 'strengths and problem areas'.

There is clearly consensus among psychologists for a multimethod approach to personality assessment based on empirically supported models and methods. Blais and Baity (Vol. 2) have critically assessed the position of the two most well known projective measures, the Rorschach Ink Blot Test and the TAT in the context of clinical diagnosis by examining the DSM-IV Axis-II personality disorders and diagnostic efficacy of current scoring methods for both measures. While there is certainly controversy and disagreement about the use of projective instruments in assessing not just personality, but also psychopathology (e.g. Gacono et al., 2002), psychologists must remember that these are empirical questions that remain to be decided by the evidence. More to the point, Blais and Baity also remind us that there is not a direct correspondence between the various Rorschach or TAT scoring systems and an actual DSM-IV diagnosis. Rather the contribution of these 'performance' measures can best be realized when they are integrated into systems and perspectives describing personality and psychopathology. In a recent paper that the reader may also wish to consult, Hughes et al. (2007) focused attention on the use of the Rorschach by school psychologists and after an extensive review of the Rorschach and Exner's Comprehensive System for administration and interpretation, concluded that they 'meet current ethical and legal standards for tests' (2007: 288).

ABNORMAL PERSONALITY TRAIT INSTRUMENTS

The last section of Vol. 2 examines several very specific measures for assessing abnormal personality traits either through an examination of those personality characteristics known or believed to underlie psychopathological behaviour, or by a more 'behavioural' examination of particular clinical conditions and syndromes that have been described in DSM and ICD classifications. Just as the Wechsler Intelligence Scales were deemed the most often used measures for

assessing cognitive ability in the twentieth century, so too, the MMPI and more recently the MMPI-2 have been among the most popular and often used self-report measures for assessing psychopathology. In fact, the MMPI was so widely used that it found its way from primarily psychiatric and forensic settings, to personnel selection and university counselling settings.

Again, much like intelligence tests of the earlier part of the twentieth century that attempted to assess the full complement of cognitive abilities, the MMPI was intended as a comprehensive measure of the gamut of psychopathological conditions. Thus, in some ways, as the chapter by Helmes (Vol. 2) points out, the MMPI does stand out as compared with the shorter and more specifically focused measures of abnormal personality of more recent years. As both a screening instrument and for distinguishing broad types of psychopathology (e.g. depression vs. psychopathy), both versions of the MMPI have served us well. However, the MMPI is more limited for differential diagnosis (e.g. anxiety vs. depression), but then that is an unrealistic expectation for any measure, even one as lengthy as the MMPI, since the diagnosis of psychological disorders requires the convergence of clinical data from a multi-method approach. A review of the literature (Helmes and Reddon, 1993) does not provide a great deal of evidence to support the use of the clinical scales for differential diagnosis. With any instrument that has survived as long as the MMPI, there is the tendency for some myth or beliefs to 'trump' what the evidence actually tells us about the MMPI's clinical efficacy and empirically validated best practices use. However, Helmes states that 'there is promise that the new RC scales will be better able to make such distinctions than the traditional clinical scales, but the relevant studies have yet to appear in print'.

The debate surrounding the MMPI/ MMPI-2 scales raises an interesting issue about the current role of such measures in clinical assessment and the issue of efficiency. The tendency now seems to be towards use of shorter, more time-efficient and more focused measures, although the more recently published BASC/BASC-II, for example, are not so brief. The advantage of the MMPI/MMPI-2 is that it does serve as a broad screening measure for evaluating various broad types of psychopathology (or the lack thereof). In contrast, the use of say a brief depression inventory, would only be more useful if the psychologist was either attempting to rule out depressive symptomatology or had formed the hypothesis of depression, based on other indicators (e.g. interview and presenting symptoms, family and previous clinical history) and was adding confirmatory evidence.

What is in store for this 'battleship' measure? Helmes summarizes:

> The MMPI-2 does not represent a highly sophisticated approach to assessment that is based upon the state-of-the-art in diagnosis and conceptualizations of psychopathology. Successive introductions of new scales have modernized aspects of the interpretation of the test, at the cost of providing increased opportunities for conflicting scores that need to be reconciled during the overly complex interpretive process. The escalating collection of scales for the MMPI-2, with each successive set providing at best modest increases in incremental validity for some applications, simply multiply the number of potential sources of interpretive conflict. ... the future of the MMPI/MMPI-2 thus remains difficult to predict.

While new measures, including personality, behaviour and psychopathology measures continue to abound in psychology and certainly present a challenge to formerly well-established measures, Krug (Vol. 2) reviews the Cattellian Clinical Analysis Questionnaire (CAQ) and its revised version, the PEPQ, as comprehensive measures of both normal personality and psychopathology. In spite of some support for the psychometric strengths of the separate and composite scales, they do not appear to be often used in either research or in clinical settings, although in military contexts the CAQ has received considerable use (e.g. the Australian Army Psychology Corps has used the CAQ extensively in its psychological research, assessment and selection procedures – see Boyle, 1989).

This chapter raises the interesting issue of whether we have been too quick to abandon the theoretical, research and measurement contributions of such key figures in psychology as Cattell and Eysenck. As noted above, Eysenck's E and N scales included in the EPQ and EPQ-R instruments are psychometrically sound and central to a trait description of personality. Similarly, a thorough study of the Cattellian instruments is needed before we too quickly engage in an 'out with the old and in with the new' attitude and later discover that we may have simply 'reinvented the wheel' (e.g. see the number of different scales that assess risk taking, sensation seeking, thrill seeking, etc.)

In contrast to the MMPI and MMPI-2 that are not grounded in a contemporary model of either personality or psychopathology, the measures described in the remaining chapters provide reassuring alternatives. The Dimensional Assessment of Personality Pathology (DAPP) measures employ a construct validation approach to arrive at a classification of personality disorder. Empirical evaluations leading to revisions in the initial theoretical description of personality disorder are supported by increases in the validity of the classification scheme. The DAPP has also evolved from a somewhat different approach than many of the current personality and clinical scales that start with a description of the personality trait (e.g. extraversion) or disorder (e.g. anxiety). Rather than beginning with this a priori view, Livesley and Larstone (Vol. 2) state that the DAPP 'incorporates a bottom-up approach in which diagnostic constructs evolve based on empirical evidence of the way the features of personality disorder are organized'. The advantage of this approach is that it provides for a dynamic rather than static view of personality criteria and categories that is forced to modify or change with new evidence from both research studies and clinical use (e.g. Cattell et al., 2002; Roberts et al., 2006a, 2006b). Even more compelling is the reconciliation between normal and abnormal personality that were treated quite separately even into the latter part of the twentieth century. This may well be why measures such as the EPQ and NEO-FFI and NEO-PI appeared in stark contrast to the many separate pathology scales (e.g. MMPI), with the latter not grounded in underlying personality factors, but rather collections of psychiatric symptoms based on archaic psychiatric nosology (Cronbach, 1990, p. 539). The DAPP and its counterparts have provided the foundation for the much-needed reconciliation between basic descriptions of personality models and traits on the one hand, and personality disorders and psychopathology on the other.

As noted above, while there has been a tendency towards constructing more specifically focused and brief measures of both normal and abnormal personality traits, in contrast, the Personality Assessment Inventory (PAI) devised by Morey (1991, 2007), has been constructed on the basis of contemporary diagnostic classifications, and as an attempt to overcome the well-documented limitations of the MMPI/MMPI-2 instruments (Helmes and Reddon, 1993). The PAI comprises no fewer than 344 items with a mix of validity, clinical, treatment consideration and interpersonal scales. Morey and Ambwani (Vol. 2) summarize findings showing that this multidimensional inventory has received increasing attention in both research and clinical practice settings. Studies supporting the validity of the PAI subscales in the assessment of a wide range of psychological problem areas, ranging from eating disorders to emotional injury, will ensure its continued use in both applied and research settings.

This section ends with a summary of the Millon inventories and view of personality assessment. All would agree that no single theory or measurement instrument, no matter how robust or broad, can ever give a complete description of an individual's personality structure. As Millon (Vol. 2) argues, our efforts to measure human personality with a predefined set of traits that are reflected in our assessment tools is complicated by the very nature of examining a breakdown of these traits for each individual, and then reconstructing a description of personality;

the 'loop' from idiographic individuality to nomothetic commonality to nomothetic individuality is brought to closure. Millon's chapter provides a detailed overview of the inventories that he has developed over the past several decades, highlighting the links with both the DSM and ICD taxonomies of personality disorders, as well as the theoretical basis for conceptualizing both personality and abnormal behaviour. The critical question that has so often been posed regarding the direct association between assessment, diagnosis and treatment planning or therapy is addressed by Millon who argues that his inventories provide a necessary basis for associating polarity schemes and clinical domains with corresponding therapies: 'Any discussion of *personalized psychotherapy* … must take place at a level of abstraction or integration commensurate with that of personality itself. Personality disorders and clinical syndromes cannot be remedied if the person is thoroughly integrated while the therapy is not. Therapy must be as individualized as the person'.

SUMMARY COMMENTS

The chapters included in this volume are testimony to the incredible progress that has been made in the measurement and assessment of personality, particularly in more recent years. Guided by various theoretical models and research findings as well as extensive interdisciplinary collaboration, the sophistication of psychological measurement will continue to provide the necessary assessment tools to further our basic and applied analysis of human personality. Each chapter in this volume is a celebration of the research contributions and clinical knowledge of leading experts in personality measurement and assessment. We thank all of the authors for sharing with us their critical analyses of the models and methods for measuring personality and especially their insights and creativity that will serve well the measurement and assessment of human personality.

REFERENCES

Aiken, L.R. (2000) *Rating Scales and Checklists: Evaluating Behavior, Personality, and Attitude*. New York: Wiley.

American Educational Research Association, American Psychological Association, National Council on Measurement in Education (1999) *Standards for Educational and Psychological Testing*. Washington, DC: American Educational Research Association.

Ashton, M.C., Lee, K., de Vries, R.E., Perugini, M., Gnisci, A. and Sergi, I. (2006) 'The HEXACO model of personality structure and indigenous lexical personality dimensions in Italian, Dutch, and English', *Journal of Research in Personality*, 40(6): 851–75.

Austin, E.J. and Saklofske, D.H. (2005) 'Far too many intelligences? On the communalities and differences between social, practical, and emotional intelligence', in R. Schulze and R.D. Roberts (eds), *Emotional Intelligence: An International Handbook*. Cambridge, MA: Hogrefe and Huber, pp. 107–128.

Bandura, A. (1983) 'Psychological mechanisms of aggression', in R.G. Geen and E.I. Donnerstein (eds), *Aggression: Theoretical and Empirical Reviews* (Vol. 1). New York: Academic, pp. 1–40.

Bar-On, R. (1997) *BarOn Emotional Quotient Inventory (EQ-i): Technical Manual*. Toronto: Multi-Health Systems.

Barrett, P. (2005) 'What if there were no psychometrics?: Constructs, complexity, and measurement', *Journal of Personality Assessment*, 85(2): 134–40.

Beck, A.T. and Steer, R.A. (1993) '*Manual for the Beck Depression Inventory*', San Antonio, TX: The Psychological Corporation.

Bernreuter R.G. (1931) *The Personality Inventory*. Stanford, CA: Stanford University Press.

Beutler, L.E. and Groth-Marnat, G. (2003) (eds), *Integrative Assessment of Adult Personality* (2nd edn). New York: Guilford.

Block, J. (1995) 'A contrarian view of the five-factor approach to personality description', *Psychological Bulletin*, 117(2): 187–229.

Boyle, G.J. (1985) 'Self-report measures of depression: Some psychometric considerations', *British Journal of Clinical Psychology*, 24(1): 45–59.

Boyle, G.J. (1989a) '*A Guide to Use of the Sixteen Personality Factor Questionnaire and Clinical Analysis Questionnaire in Military Selection*', Canberra: Australian Army Directorate of Psychology, 1st Psychological Research Unit.

Boyle, G.J. (1989b) 'Re-examination of the major personality-type factors in the Cattell, Comrey and Eysenck scales: Were the factor solutions by Noller et al. optimal?', *Personality and Individual Differences*, 10(12): 1289–99.

Boyle, G.J. (2006) 'Scientific analysis of personality and individual differences', DSc thesis, University of Queensland.

Boyle, G.J. and Saklofske, D.H. (2004) (eds), *Sage Benchmarks in Psychology: The Psychology of Individual Differences* (Vols. 1–4). London: Sage.

Boyle, G.J., Stankov, L. and Cattell, R.B. (1995) 'Measurement and statistical models in the study of personality and intelligence', in D.H. Saklofske and M. Zeidner (eds), *International Handbook of Personality and Intelligence*. New York: Plenum.

Buss, A. and Durkee, A. (1957) 'An inventory for assessing different kinds of hostility', *Journal of Consulting Psychology*, 21(4): 343–9.

Cattell, R.B. (1973) *Personality and Mood by Questionnaire*. New York: Jossey Bass.

Cattell, R.B. (1995) 'The fallacy of five factors in the personality sphere', *The Psychologist*, 8(5): 207–8.

Cattell, R.B., Boyle, G.J. and Chant, D. (2002) 'The enriched behavioral prediction equation and its impact on structured learning and the dynamic calculus', *Psychological Review*, 109(1), 202–5.

Cattell, R.B., Cattell, A.K., Cattell, H.E., Russell, M.T. and Bedwell, S. (2003) '*The PsychEval Personality Questionnaire*', Champaign, IL: Institute for Personality & Ability Testing, Inc.

Cattell, R.B., Eber, H.W. and Tatsuoka, M.M. (1970) *Handbook for the Sixteen Personality Factor Questionnaire*. Champaign, IL: Institute for Personality and Ability Testing, Inc.

Cattell, R.B. and Johnson, R.C. (1986) (eds), *Functional Psychological Testing: Principles and Instruments*. New York: Brunner/Mazel.

Cattell, R.B. and Warburton, F.W. (1967) *Objective Personality and Motivation Tests: A Theoretical Introduction and Practical Compendium*. Champaign, IL: University of Illinois Press.

Comrey, A.L. (1994) *Revised Manual and Handbook of Interpretations for the Comrey Personality Scales*. San Diego. CA: Educational and Industrial Testing Service.

Comrey, A.L. and Lee, H.B. (1992) *A First Course in Factor Analysis* (2nd edn). Hillsdale, NJ: Erlbaum.

Costa, P.T. and McCrae, R.R. (1992) *The NEO Personality Inventory (Revised) Manual*. Odessa, FL: Psychological Assessment Resources.

Crick, N.R. and Dodge, K.A. (1996) 'Social information-processing mechanisms in reactive and proactive aggression', *Child Development*, 67(3): 993–1002.

Cronbach, L.J. (1990) *Essentials of Psychological Testing* (5th edn). New York: Harper & Row.

Cuttance, P. and Ecob, R. (1987) (eds), *Structural Modeling by Example: Applications in Educational, Sociological, and Behavioral Research*. Cambridge, UK: Cambridge University Press, pp. 241–79.

Eysenck, H.J. (1984) 'Cattell and the theory of personality', *Multivariate Behavioral Research*, 19(2–3): 323–36.

Eysenck, H.J. (1991) 'Dimensions of personality: 16, 5, or 3? Criteria for a taxonomic paradigm', *Personality and Individual Differences*, 12(8): 773–90.

Eysenck H.J. (1992) 'Four ways five factors are not basic', *Personality and Individual Differences*, 13(6): 667–73.

Eysenck, H.J. and Eysenck, S.B.G. (1975) *Manual of the Eysenck Personality Questionnaire (Adult and Junior)*. London, UK: Hodder & Stoughton.

Fernandez, E. (2002) 'Anxiety, depression, and anger in pain: Research findings and clinical options', Dallas, TX: *Advanced Psychological Resources*.

Fernández-Ballesteros, R. (2002) 'How should psychological assessment be considered', *American Psychologist*, 57(2): 138–9.

Flanagan, R. (2007) 'Comments on the miniseries: Personality assessment in school psychology', *Psychology in the Schools*, 44(3): 311–18.

Gacono, C.B., Evans, F.B. and Viglione, D.J. (2002) 'The Rorschach in forensic practice', *Journal of Forensic Psychology Practice*, 2(3): 33–53.

Garb, H.N., Klein, D.F. and Grove, W.M. (2002) 'Comparison of medical and psychological tests', *American Psychologist*, 57(2): 137–8.

Goodenough, F.L. (1929) *Measurement of Intelligence by Drawings*. New York: Harcourt, Brace & World.

Gough, H.G. (1987) *California Psychological Inventory Manual*. Palo Alto, CA: Consulting Psychological Press.

Haggbloom, S.J., Warnick, R., Warnick, J.E., Jones, V.K., Yarbrough, G.L., Russell, T.M., Borecky, C.M., McGahhey, R., Powell III, J.L., Beavers, J. and Monte, E. (2002) 'The 100 most eminent psychologists of the 20th century', *Review of General Psychology*, 6(2): 139–52.

Hathaway, S.R. and McKinley, J.C. (1940) 'A multiphasic personality schedule (Minnesota): 1. Construction of the schedule', *Journal of Psychology*, 10: 249–54.

Hathaway, S.R. and McKinley, J.C. (1943) '*The Minnesota Multiphasic Personality Inventory* (rev edn)', Minneapolis: University of Minnesota Press.

Helmes, E. and Reddon, J.R. (1993) 'A perspective on developments in assessing psychopathology: A critical review of the MMPI and MMPI-2', *Psychological Bulletin*, 113(3): 453–71.

Hunsley, J. (2002) 'Psychological testing and psychological assessment: A closer examination', *American Psychologist*, 57(2): 139–40.

Hunsley, J. and Meyer, G.J. (2003) 'The incremental validity of psychological testing and assessment: Conceptual, methodological, and statistical issues', *Psychological Assessment*, 15(4): 446–55.

Hughes, T.L., Gacono, C.B. and Owen, P.F. (2007) 'Current status of Rorschach assessment implications for the school psychologist', *Psychology in the Schools*, 44(3): 281–91.

John, O.P., Angleitner, A. and Ostendorf, F. (1988) 'The lexical approach to personality: A historical review of trait taxonomic research', *European Journal of Personality*, 2(3): 171–203.

Kaplan, R.M. and Saccuzzo, D.P. (2005) *Psychological Testing: Principles, Applications, and Issues* (6th edn). Belmont, CA: Thomson Wadsworth.

Krug, S.E. and Johns, E.F. (1986) 'A large scale cross-validation of second-order personality structure defined by the 16PF', *Psychological Reports*, 5(2): 683–93.

Matthews, G. and Gilliland, K. (1999) 'The personality theories of H.J. Eysenck and

J.A. Gray: A comparative review', *Personality and Individual Differences*, 26(4): 583–626.

Matthews, G., Deary, I.J. and Whiteman, M.C. (2003) *Personality Traits* (2nd edn). Cambridge. UK: Cambridge University Press.

Matthews, G., Schwean, V.L., Campbell, S.E., Saklofske, D.H. and Mohamed, A.A.R. (2000) 'Personality, self-regulation, and adaptation: A cognitive-social framework', in M. Borksrtyd, P.R. Pintrich and M. Zeidner (eds), *Handbook of Self-regulation*. San Diego: Academic, pp. 171–207.

Matthews, G., Zeidner, M. and Roberts, R.D. (2002) *Emotional Intelligence: Science and Myth*. Cambridge, MA: MIT Press.

Mayer, J.D. and Salovey, P. (1997) 'What is emotional intelligence?', in P. Salovey and D.J. Sluyter (eds), *Emotional Development and Emotional Intelligence: Educational Implications*. New York: Basic Books, pp. 3–31.

McAdams, D.P. (1992) 'The five-factor model in personality: A critical appraisal', *Journal of Personality*, 60(2): 329–61.

Mershon, B. and Gorsuch, R.L. (1988) 'Number of factors in the personality sphere: Does increase in factors increase predictability of real-life criteria?', *Journal of Personality and Social Psychology*, 55(4): 675–80.

Meyer, G.J., Finn, S.E., Eyde, L.D., Kay, G.G., Moreland, K.L., Dies, R.R., Eisman, E.J., Kubiszyn, T.W. and Reed, G.M. (2001) 'Psychological testing and psychological assessment: A review of evidence and issues', *American Psychologist*, 56(2): 128–65.

Millon, T. (1977) *Manual for the Millon Clinical Multiaxial Inventory (MCMI)*. Minneapolis: National Computer Systems.

Millon, T. (1987) *Manual for the Millon Clinical Multiaxial Inventory-II (MCMI-II)*. Minneapolis: National Computer Systems.

Millon, T. (2006) *Millon Clinical Multiaxial Inventory-III Manual* (3rd edn). Minneapolis: NCS Pearson.

Morey, L.C. (1991) *The Personality Assessment Inventory Professional Manual*. Odessa, FL: Psychological Assessment Resources.

Morey, L.C. (2007) *The Personality Assessment Inventory Professional Manual* (2nd edn). Odessa, FL: Psychological Assessment Resources.

Morgan, C.D. and Murray, H.A. (1935) 'A method for investigating phantasies: The Thematic Apperception Test', *Archives of Neurology and Psychiatry*, 34(2): 289–306.

Naglieri, J., McNeish, T. and Bardos, A. (1991) *Draw-A-Person: Screening Procedure of Emotional Disturbance*. Austin: Proed.

Paulhus, D.L. (2002) 'Socially desirable responding: The evolution of a construct', in H.I. Braun and D.N. Jackson (eds), *The Role of Constructs in Psychological and Educational Measurement*. Mahwah, NJ: Erlbaum, pp. 49–69.

Payne, A.F. (1928) *Sentence Completions*. New York: New York Guidance Clinic.

Reynolds, C.R. and Kamphaus, R. (1992) *Behavior Assessment System for Children*. Circle Pines, MN: American Guidance Service.

Reynolds, C.R. and Kamphaus, R.W. (2004) *Behavior Assessment System for Children* (2nd edn manual). Circles Pines, MN: American Guidance Service.

Riccio, C.A. and Rodriguez, O.L. (2007) 'Integration of psychological assessment approaches in school psychology', *Psychology in the Schools*, 44(3): 243–55.

Roberts, B.W., Walton, K.E. and Viechtbauer, W. (2006a) Patterns of mean-level change in personality traits across the life course: A meta-analysis of longitudinal studies. *Psychological Bulletin*, 132(1): 1–25.

Roberts, B.W., Walton, K.E. and Viechtbauer, W. (2006b) 'Personality traits change in adulthood: Reply to Costa and McCrae (2006)', *Psychological Bulletin*, 132(1): 29–32.

Rogers, C.R. and Dymond, R.F. (1954) (eds), *Psychotherapy and Personality Change*. Chicago, IL: University of Chicago Press.

Rorschach, H. (1921) *Psychodiagnostik*. Berne: Birchen.

Rotter, J.B. (1975) 'Some problems and misconceptions related to the construct of internal versus external control of reinforcement', *Journal of Consulting and Clinical Psychology*, 43(1): 56–67.

Saklofske, D.H. and Eysenck, H.J. (1994) 'Extraversion–introversion', in V.S. Ramachandran (ed.), *Encyclopedia of Human Behavior*. New York: Academic, pp. 321–32.

Saklofske, D.H. and Zeidner, M. (1995) *International Handbook of Personality and Intelligence*. New York: Plenum.

Sattler, J.M. (2001) *Assessment of Children: Cognitive Applications* (4th edn). San Diego: CA: Jerome M. Sattler, Publisher, Inc.

Schuerger, J.M. (1986) 'Personality assessment by objective tests', in R.B. Cattell and R.C. Johnson (eds), *Functional Psychological Testing: Principles and Instruments*. New York: Brunner/Mazel, pp. 260–87.

Schmitz, P.G. (2004) 'On the alternative five-factor model: Structure and correlates', in R.M. Stelmack (ed.), *On the Psychobiology of Personality: Essays in Honor of Marvin Zuckerman*. Amsterdam: Elsevier, pp. 65–87.

Schneider, R.J., Hough, L.M. and Dunnette, M.D. (1995) 'Broadsided by broad traits: How to sink science in five dimensions or less', *Journal of Organizational Behavior*, 17(6): 639–55.

Schutte, N.S., Malouff, J.M., Hall, L.E., Haggerty, D.J., Cooper. J.T., Golden, C.J. and Dornheim, L. (1998) 'Development and validation of a measure of emotional intelligence', *Personality and Individual Differences*, 25(2): 167–77.

Smith, D.A. (2002) 'Validity and values: Monetary and otherwise', *American Psychologist*, 57(2): 136–7.

Tellegen, A. (1982) 'Brief manual of the *Multidimensional Personality Questionnaire*', Unpublished manuscript, University of Minnesota.

Tellegen, A. (1995) '*Multidimensional Personality Questionnaire*', Unpublished document, University of Minnesota.

Thurstone, L.L. and Thurstone, T. (1930) 'A neurotic inventory', *Journal of Social Psychology*, 1(1): 3–30.

Vaillant, G.E. (1977) *Adaptation to Life*. Boston, MA: Little Brown.

Woodworth, R.S. (1919) 'Examination of emotional fitness for warfare', *Psychological Bulletin*, 16(2): 59–60.

Zuckerman, M. and Kuhlman, D.M. (2000) 'Personality and risk-taking: Common biosocial factors', *Journal of Personality*, 68(6): 999–1029.

Zuckerman, M. (2005) *Psychobiology of Personality* (2nd rev edn). New York: Cambridge University Press.

PART I

General Methodological Issues

2

Measures of the Personality Factors Found Recurrently in Human Lexicons

Gerard Saucier

How can attributes of personality best be organized and measured? Answers to this crucial scientific question provide the foundation not only for personality tests, but also for much research on personality and individual differences. Studies of natural languages provide an important source of answers. In this chapter I review the approach used in such lexical studies of personality attributes, as well as basic findings and major measures associated with these studies.

Lexical measures of personality factors are used primarily in research settings. Because the items themselves are terms from the lexicon, they are easily embedded within lexical-study stimuli, where they provide the most direct representation of lexical factors. They have also proven to be extremely useful templates for the development of more sophisticated assessment instruments. Moreover, because lexical factors have a solid content-validity basis, they can be used in the validation of other measures. This chapter presents an array of measures for lexical personality factors, concentrating on those measures based

most directly on lexical structures; that is, those designed to be markers of these structures. Inquiries into the structure of attributes hinge strongly on how personality is defined. Therefore, the definition of personality is a good place to begin a discussion of structure.

DEFINING PERSONALITY

Definitions make one's assumptions explicit. How one defines personality is consequential, affecting how one selects variables when studying personality. There is no single canonical definition in current use. Personality is defined either as (a) a set of attributes characterizing an individual, or as (b) the underlying system that generates the set of attributes. Funder (1997) provided a definition that includes both (a) and (b): Personality is 'an individual's characteristic patterns of thought, emotion, and behavior, together with the psychological mechanisms – hidden or not – behind those patterns' (1997: 1–2). Funder refers to a broad array of attributes that simultaneously are (i) ascribed to individuals, (ii) stable over time, and (iii) psychological in nature.

But there are other ways to define personality. In a classic early textbook, Allport (1937) catalogued 50 distinct meanings found in definitions of personality. These meanings can be arrayed in a continuum ranging from one's externally observable manner to one's internal self. Reacting against broad omnibus definitions of personality (e.g. Prince, 1924), Allport's definition – 'personality is the dynamic organization within the individual of those psychophysical systems that determine his unique adjustments to his environment' (1937: 48) – highlights attributes that are seen as residing 'within' the individual.

However, other ways of defining personality, consistent with a 'biosocial' view that Allport deprecated, emphasize attributes that are more external or that involve the effect the individual tends to have on others. These include (a) attributes of external appearance (including qualities like physical size), (b) attributes associated with the role one assumes or the status one has achieved in society (e.g. professional, motherly, famous), and (c) attributes of an evocative type, that involve the pattern of reactions that the individual generates in others given the kind of stimulus s/he is (e.g. charming, intimidating, boring, believable, lovable, respected, offensive). Such social effects represent a person's social stimulus value (Allport, 1937: 41; based on May, 1932).

Another class with controversial status as personality attributes is that containing highly evaluative terms (e.g. stupid, evil, abnormal, good). Most personality concepts are decidedly evaluative (clearly favorable or unfavorable; Goldberg, 1982), but these are distinct in the high ratio of the evaluative to the descriptive component. Highly evaluative terms are not 'pure evaluation'; one can find descriptive dimensions from selections consisting purely of such terms (Benet-Martinez and Waller, 2002), so they do have *some* descriptive component.

What about patterns of belief and attitudes? Allport (1937) generally regarded attitudes

as behavioral dispositions of a specific and external sort, being 'bound to an object or value' (1937: 294); that is, aroused in the presence of a specifiable class of stimuli. If, however, an attitude is 'chronic and temperamental', expressed in almost any sphere of the person's behavior' (1937: 294), as in for example radicalism or conservatism, then for Allport it differed little from a trait. Thus, generalized attitudes – those for which it is difficult to specify the object – can be considered personality traits. Factors derived from the correlations among large numbers of more specific attitudes and beliefs define traits, in that they represent consistent patterns across many attitude objects.

Values can be seen as beliefs regarding 'how one ought or ought not to behave, or about some end-state of existence worth or not worth attaining' (Rokeach, 1968: 124), and, echoing Allport's distinctions, 'not tied to any specific attitude object or situation' (Rokeach, 1968: 124). Super (1995) characterized interests as related to values, being preferences for classes of activities in which individual expect to attain their values. Interests involve assessing objects according to how liked or disliked they are (rather than their favorability or importance more generally). Career-interest measures show even higher stability than do personality measures (Low et al., 2005). And there are dimensions of variation in career-interest items that are relatively independent of currently popular trait dimensions (Ackerman, 1996; Ackerman and Heggestad, 1997).

Including all such additional variables, one arrives at a broader definition of personality: all of the relatively stable attributes, qualities, or characteristics that distinguish the behavior, thoughts, and feelings of individuals. Such a broad definition is close to that proposed by Roback (1931): 'an integrative combination of all our cognitive (knowledge), affective (feeling), conative (volitional) and even physical qualities' (1931: 31–32).

Such broad definitions are not unusual. However, since Allport and Odbert (1936), personality has often been defined broadly but operationalized narrowly, so that many classes of relevant variables are excluded. These narrow variable selections have been achieved by either (a) starting with a full range of attributes of persons and then purging those judged to fall in categories considered unsuitable using exclusion rules (e.g. Allport and Odbert, 1936; Ashton et al., 2004; Goldberg, 1990; Norman, 1967), or (b) relying on vaguely defined 'personality relevance' ratings of judges. In effect, a narrower definition is being used, that personality is pattern of behavior (including stable affective tendencies but generally not patterns of thinking) that are believed to reside within the individual and that cannot be disqualified as attitudes, temporary states, social effects, or social roles, or because they are overly evaluative. Such definition-by-exclusion makes personality into a remarkably gerrymandered construct.

Previous research indicates that the structure of personality attributes encoded in lexicons depends in major ways upon the upstream selection of variables. This is unsurprising. If astronomers forbade themselves from investigating regions of the sky beyond that narrow band of the firmament where the most obvious objects of interest (the sun, the moon, the planets) move across the sky, astronomy's conclusions about the universe would certainly be altered. To remove the risk that we ignore important phenomena and miss major discoveries, we need a wider view. We should couple our focus on the most prototypical attributes of personality with a simultaneous 'bigger picture' examination of a wider range of psychological attributes.

PARSIMONY IN PERSONALITY MODELS

How many important traits are there? Surveying the scales in current personality inventories, one finds a bewildering variety of constructs. And if one turns to single words in modern world languages, the situation becomes overwhelming: Allport and Odbert (1936), for example, found nearly 18,000 words in *Webster's Second International Dictionary* referring to characteristics that might distinguish one human being from another. One needs a parsimonious summary of this vast domain of concepts.

In the field of personality the search for a scientifically compelling classification of the huge number of personality attributes excites increasing interest. A classification systematically divides phenomena into ordered groups or categories; it 'chunks' things. A scientific classification helps organize and integrate knowledge and research findings, providing a standard scientific nomenclature that facilitates communication and aids in the accumulation of empirical findings. Because personality attributes describe continua and not categories, such a classification will naturally be a 'dimensional classification' – more like those used for classifying colors than like those for classifying species.

In constructing a classification a variety of procedures could be used to group the phenomena under study. The most useful is a class of statistical methods generically referred to as factor analysis. Factor analysis can be considered a variable-reduction procedure, in which many variables are organized by a few factors that summarize the interrelations among the variables (Goldberg and Velicer, 2006).

THE BASIS FOR THE LEXICAL APPROACH

However, prior to conducting factor analysis, one must determine which variables to include in the analysis. Variable selection is vitally dependent on how personality is defined. It is also guided, to some degree, by the investigator's beliefs about the criteria for the goodness of a structural model (see Saucier and Simonds, 2006, for a listing of such criteria).

As has long been recognized (e.g. Allport and Odbert, 1936; Cattell, 1943; Goldberg, 1981; Norman, 1963), basic personality dimensions might be discovered by studying conceptions embedded in the natural language. The key premise of the lexical approach is this: The degree of representation of an attribute in language has some correspondence with the general importance of the attribute in real-world transactions. If terms in a language are used as variables, an attribute that is represented by multiple terms in that language will likely appear as a factor. Moreover, if the factor includes terms that are used with high frequency, the importance of the factor is underscored.

Such factors are but a starting point for several reasons. The lexicon could omit or underemphasize some scientifically important variables. Moreover, the meaning of single natural-language terms can be vague, ambiguous, or context-dependent (John et al., 1988). Folk concepts of personality (Tellegen, 1993) provide basic but not exhaustive (necessary but not sufficient) components for a science of personality attributes (Goldberg and Saucier, 1995). These components operate on the descriptive or phenotypic level, without implication as to what might be the underlying biological or other causal basis. An established causal basis is an important criterion for the goodness of a structural model (Saucier and Simonds, 2006). Ultimately, a structural model of personality ought to align the descriptive level with the causal level, and there may turn out not to be perfect homology between the two levels.

Nonetheless, lexicalized concepts – especially those represented in very frequently used words – tend to have high social importance. So variables and factors based on lexicalized concepts have a virtual guarantee of being important. Lexicalized concepts can be found in standard sources created by disinterested parties (e.g. linguists and lexicographers), and basing variable selection on such a source reduces the likelihood of investigator bias in the selection process. And because lexicalized concepts constitute a finite domain, one can sample them representatively and so establish content-validity benchmarks for personality variables. For drawing

conclusions regarding personality structure, these concepts thereby have a major advantage over statements and sentences: Drawing on the generative capacity of a human language, a nearly infinite number of personality-descriptive sentences might be formed, meaning that establishing any selection of statements and sentences is representative would be quite difficult.

The lexical-study paradigm gives special importance to one other demanding criterion. *Cross-cultural generalizability* can be used to judge among competitor structures. Structural models derived within one limited population, or a limited sample from that population, are prone to reflect the unique patterns found within that population or sample. Although culture-specific patterns are certainly interesting, models that transfer well – across populations, languages, and sociocultural settings – better satisfy scientific standards of replicability and generalizability.

We can apply this criterion in either a lenient or a stringent way. The lenient way is to export a set of variables (e.g. those in a single personality inventory) for use in other populations, and then examine whether these preselected variables (after translation, if necessary) generate the same factor structure in each new language or culture (as in Rolland et al., 1998; Rossier et al., 2005). If the inventory's scales generate similar factors across populations, one might argue (as in McCrae and Costa, 1997) that the structure is widely generalizable. A more stringent test is to identify the most salient and important personality concepts *within* each linguistic/cultural context, derive an indigenous factor structure from those variables, and then examine how much this new structure corresponds to previously proposed structures. A structure that met this demanding test in any language could be considered more truly ubiquitous and universal than a merely 'translatable' structure.

The lexical approach involves such an indigenous research strategy. Analyses are carried out separately within each language, using a representative set of native-language descriptors, rather than merely importing selections of variables from other languages (e.g. English).

The following review will detail the structures that have emerged from lexical studies of some 16 languages, and that appear most replicable. These structures involve alternatively one, two, three, five, six, and seven factors. In all cases, measures of lexically derived factors will be described in conjunction with the structure.

What if we were constrained to only one factor?

Several lexical studies have reported evidence about factor solutions containing only one factor (Boies et al., 2001; di Blas and Forzi, 1999; Goldberg and Somer, 2000; Saucier, 1997, 2003b; Saucier et al., 2006). Findings have been quite consistent. The single factor contrasts a heterogeneous mix of desirable attributes at one pole with a mix of undesirable attributes at the other pole. This unrotated factor can be labelled 'evaluation'. A more specific interpretation, which fits reported findings from lexical studies, would be 'virtues' versus 'bad character'.

Evaluation is the first factor to emerge in the cognitions of young children. Whereas older children employ more differentiated trait concepts, younger children typically rely on global, evaluative inference (Alvarez et al., 2001). One can refer also to a classic finding in cognitive psychology: In judgments about the meanings of diverse objects in a wide array of cultural settings, a global evaluation factor (good vs. bad) was found recurrently to be the first and largest factor (Osgood, 1962; Osgood et al., 1975). Osgood hypothesized that the ubiquity of this evaluative factor was related to basic evolutionary principles: Our forebears would not have survived if they had not become adapted at a very basic level to any signals of good versus bad objects or events – those to approach versus those to avoid, those leading to pleasure versus those leading to pain (e.g. 'Can I eat it or will it eat me?'). This motivational dimension – what is liked and approached, as opposed to what is disliked and avoided – provides one possible theoretical account for the one-factor model. There is no widely used measure of this 'Big One' factor. Indeed, the factor has had relatively little attention in personality studies. This contrasts strikingly with the situation in the field of cognitive abilities where a one-factor taxonomy has long been dominant (Carroll, 1993).

For measuring a general evaluation factor, several research measures are available. Saucier (1994b) developed an adjectival marker scale for the single 'general evaluation' (Ge) factor. This scale was intended to be relatively orthogonal to four non-evaluative dimensions derived in the same study. The content at the favorable pole was characterized as largely a combination of likeability, good judgment, and perceived maturity. Constituent terms and psychometric indices are provided in Table 2.1, both for the longer 24-adjective scale (Ge-24) and a briefer 12-item subset (Ge-12). An alternative measure was developed specifically to minimize correlations with the octant scales for the Non-Evaluative Personality Circumplex (NEPC) (Saucier et al., 2001; described later under three-factor models). Terms and indices for this scale (NEPC-E) are also presented in the table. As part of a study of the structure of English type-nouns, Saucier (2003b) used an economical ten-adjective marker scale for the one broad factor (derived from the Big One factor in the lexical study of Saucier, 1997) labeled 'socially desirable qualities'. As another alternative, one could employ terms from the bipolar scales recommended by Osgood et al., 1975, table 4:18), among which good–bad, pleasant–unpleasant, nice–awful, and beautiful–ugly proved the most ubiquitously useful across a wide range of cultural settings. Table 2.1 presents such a set. A characteristic of Osgood's items is that they can be used to describe inanimate objects as well as animals or people, because they use terms (e.g. pleasant, beautiful) without strong and specific moral/ethical connotations.

Table 2.1 Psychometric Indices for Marker Scales for Lexical One- and Two-Factor Structures

Marker Scale	No. of Items	Sample	Coefficient Alpha	Mean r	SD of r	% of Variance 1st – 2nd Factor	Mean	SD	Skew
General Evaluation (Ge-24) (Saucier, 1994b)	24	ESCS-1993	.87	.23	.09	26 – 8	5.60	.54	-.56
		ICS	.84	.18					
General Evaluation (Ge-12) (Saucier, 1994b)	12	ESCS-1993	.78	.24	.08	31 – 10	5.69	.57	-.65
		ICS	.72	.18					
		OCS-Self	.64	.14					
		OCS-Peer	.77	.23					
NEPC Evaluation Scale (Saucier et al., 2001)	20	ESCS-1998a	.81	.19	.09	24 – 9	5.46	.64	-.68
		OCS-Self/Peer	.70						
SDQ	10	ESCS-1995	.65	.18	.10	27 – 14	5.80	.60	-1.17
Osgood Unipolar-Item Evaluation Scale	10	ESCS-1995	.70	.23	.15	33 – 18	5.67	.60	-.80
Big-Two Social Propriety and Morality (S)	10	ESCS-1995	.73	.24	.10	32 – 13	5.82	.66	-.84
Big-Two Dynamism (D)	10	ESCS-1995	.79	.28	.09	35 – 13	4.97	.83	-.44

Note: ESCS – Eugene-Springfield Community Sample (ESCS-1993, N=1125; ESCS-1995, N=700; ESCS-1998a, N=733; for intercorrelations, N=592). ICS – Illinois College Students (see Saucier, 1994b), N=250. OCS - Oregon College Student Sample, Self-Ratings N=320, Peer-Ratings N=316. NEPC – Non-Evaluative Personality Circumplex. % of variance figures based on a principal-axes analysis of all items in the scale. SDQ – Socially Desirable Qualities, for which items are Responsible, Patient, Warm, Clever, Sociable versus Cruel, Irritable, Disorganized, Corrupt, Dishonest. Osgood Scale items are Good, Nice, Lovely, Beautiful, Pleasant versus Bad, Cruel, Dangerous, Awful, Uncomfortable. Ge-12 items are all part of the Ge-24. S items are Tolerant, Patient, Courteous, Responsible versus Cruel, Harsh, Irritable, Reckless, Corrupt, Egotistical. D items are Expressive, Talkative, Bold, Clever, Sociable, Good-looking, Humorous versus Timid, Dull, Bashful.

Several psychometric indices are included in Table 2.1 and succeeding tables. Two reference internal consistency: coefficient alpha and the mean inter-item correlation. Two are relevant to unidimensionality: (a) the standard deviation of the inter-item correlations, which decreases as unidimensionality increases, and (b) the ratio of variance between the first and second unrotated factors from the scale items, which becomes more lop-sided as unidimensionality increases. Finally, the table includes the scale mean, where scores are the average response on a 1-to-7 multipoint rating scale, as well as the scale standard deviation and the skewness statistic (where values less than −1 or greater than +1 indicate extreme negative or positive skew, respectively). Comparing the five alternative marker scales with respect to these indices, it appears that the Ge-24 and Ge-12 scales are superior, as they combine strong internal consistency and unidimensionality with somewhat less skewness than the other measures.

If dimensions of psychopathology are constrained to be only one, that dimension would represent general maladjustment. General maladjustment is probably strongly related to the evaluation factor in personality. One difference is that studies of psyhopathology, understandably, pay little attention to favorable qualities. Abnormal psychology tends to contrast varieties of dysfunction with the mere absence of dysfunction (i.e. normality).

The big two

Two-factor solutions from lexical studies also suggest a consistent pattern: One factor includes attributes associated with positively valued dynamic qualities and individual ascendancy, whereas the other factor includes attributes associated with socialization, social propriety, solidarity, and community cohesion (Caprara et al., 1997; di Blas and Forzi, 1999; Digman, 1997; Goldberg and Somer, 2000; Hrebíckov· et al., 1999; Paulhus and John, 1998; Saucier, 1997, 2003b; Saucier et al.,

2005, 2006; Shweder, 1972; White, 1980). These two factors may be aligned with some of the other sets of dual personological constructs reviewed by Digman (1997) and by Paulhus and John (1998), including Hogan's (1983) distinction between 'getting ahead' (dynamism) and 'getting along' (social propriety). They seem also to resemble higher-order factors of the Big Five (DeYoung, 2006; Digman, 1997).

To date, this two-factor structure appears to be as ubiquitous across languages and cultures as the one-factor structure. Moreover, like the one-factor structure and unlike structures described later, it appears to be relatively impervious to variable-selection effects. These two factors seem to appear whether there is a relatively restricted or inclusive selection of variables (Saucier, 1997), and whether one studies adjectives or type-nouns (Saucier, 2003b) or even more diverse combinations of variable types (De Raad and Barelds, 2006; Saucier et al., 2006). Not yet known is the extent to which the two-factors will be robust across even broader selections of variables (e.g. those that also include variables representing beliefs, attitudes, values, and interests). If both the one- and two-factor structures eventually turn out to be universal, the latter has a clear advantage, because two factors provide more information than one.

No consensual theory is as yet associated with the Big Two, but Paulhus and John (1998) reviewed a number of theories associated with two-factor structures of personality. De Young has specifically proposed that the two higher-order factors, which he labels 'stability' and 'plasticity', are related respectively to individual differences in serotonin and in dopamine functioning. These two factors might alternatively stem from the operation of basic human motivations that operate in the observer: 'social propriety' might reference the degree to which an observed person is safe versus dangerous or hazardous (i.e. punishing) for others, whereas 'dynamism' might reference the degree to which an observed person is stimulating versus boring (i.e. rewarding) for others. Studies are needed to evaluate these hypotheses.

There are as yet no widely used standard measures of the Big Two. Measures of the interpersonal circumplex (e.g. Wiggins et al., 1988) will not serve, because its two dimensions are too narrow – omitting contributions, for example, of openness/intellect, conscientiousness, and emotional stability. The same is true of Eysenck's older 'Big Two' – extraversion and neuroticism – which obviously leave out contributions of a different combination of three Big Five factors.

As markers of the Big Two in lexical studies in newly studied languages, Saucier has used a relatively brief collection of English adjectives derived from the two-factor structure in an English lexical analysis (Saucier, 1997). Constituent terms and psychometric indices for these 'initial approximation' scales are provided in Table 2.1.

There may be strong homology between structures in the domains of personality and psychopathology at the two-factor level. A favored two-dimensional model for psychopathology separates externalizing and internalizing disorders, conceived as two correlated factors (e.g. Krueger and Markon, 2006). A reasonable hypothesis is that externalizing disorders represent low social propriety (morality) whereas internalizing disorders have a stronger relation to low dynamism. More studies are needed to establish homologies between domains at the two-factor level. Just as the single evaluative factor is a higher-order combination of the favorable poles of the Big Two, the single psychopathology factor (i.e. maladjustment) is a higher-order combination of the externalizing and internalizing dimensions.

Personality descriptors in three-dimensional space

In three-factor solutions, studies of most languages of European origin (plus those in Turkish, Korean, and Chinese) have produced factors corresponding to extraversion,

agreeableness, and conscientiousness. This structure was not observed in Filipino, French, Greek, or Maasai studies. Still, this three-factor structure does appear readily in a large subset of languages, and in more languages than the Big Five (De Raad and Peabody, 2005).

Peabody (1987; Peabody and Goldberg, 1989) demonstrated that the unrotated-factor versions of this Big Three can be labeled as evaluation, assertive versus unassertive (or aggressive vs. accommodating), and tight versus loose (or impulse control vs. impulse expression). The first two of these are the most ubiquitous, as they rotate into the social propriety (morality) and dynamism factors that make up the Big Two. The Big Three does not replicate in all lexical studies simply because a tight–loose factor does not necessarily appear third, but rather sometimes fourth or later, in the sequence of unrotated factors.

For the rotated versions of these three dimensions, scales for the first three of the Big Five – that is, for extraversion, agreeableness, and conscientiousness (see Table 2.3) – will function reasonably well. But the unrotated versions are also of interest, because they concentrate social-desirability responding in only one of the factors (i.e. evaluation), and thus remove it from the other two. This was demonstrated by Saucier et al. (2001), who likewise showed that these unrotated factors are quite similar in English and in German. This set of factors includes one evaluative factor and two non-evaluative factors, and the latter were presented as a non-evaluative circumplex (cf. di Blas et al., 2000). Saucier et al. (2001) provided psychometric indices for the octant scales taken separately. These scales produce unusually symmetric (non-skewed) distributions but tend to be multidimensional and only moderately homogeneous.

An additional three-factor model is the affective-meaning dimensions of Osgood and colleagues, which have a quasi-lexical basis, being drawn from ratings of a wide variety of objects and entities. The most ubiquitous bipolar-scale markers for activity and potency across cultures (Osgood et al., 1975, table 4:18) appear to be strong–weak, big–little/small, and heavy–light (for potency), and fast–slow, young–old, active–passive, and alive–dead (for activity). Although the three Osgood dimensions are known to apply well across a very broad range of target entities, activity and potency have not provided a particularly good account of lexical factors.

Another three-factor alternative is evident in the convergence between models of Eysenck (Eysenck and Eysenck, 1975), of Tellegen and colleagues (Tellegen, in press; Clark and Watson, 1999), and of Rothbart (Rothbart and Bates, 1998), all of which share an emphasis on affect and on biological bases of temperament. One factor is extraversion, approach, or positive emotionality. A second is neuroticism, negative affectivity, or negative emotionality. A third is psychoticism (which might be better labeled as some combination of psychopathy and impulsive sensation seeking), constraint (labeled by the opposite pole), or effortful control (labeled by the opposite pole). Although this model is prominent in contemporary psychology, it is yet to be reported from a lexical study, perhaps because it tends to omit content from agreeableness, a large and prominent constituent of the personality lexicon.

Saucier (1997) found that, for English adjectives, this structure was as robust across variable selections as were the one- and two-factor structures described previously. However, that remains the only demonstration of this sort. Saucier's (2003b) study of the structure of English type-nouns failed to confirm this three-factor structure although it did confirm the Big One and Big Two. And the three factors did not appear in two recent lexical studies with more inclusive selections of variables (Saucier et al., 2005; Saucier et al., 2006). A conclusion is that they are not very robust across variable selections.

The same variable-selection caveat pertains to the next two structural models to be discussed. In the case of the Big Five and the Cross-Language Six, the structure seems to be dependent on a narrow way of operationalizing personality (using exclusion rules). And all of these models may be dependent on the use of adjectives, to the exclusion of other word-forms. In order to increase our understanding of the contingencies between variable selection and obtained structure, all lexical studies should ideally compare results from a conventional, narrow variable selection with that from a more inclusive selection of variables (as in Saucier, 1997; Goldberg and Somer, 2000; Saucier et al., 2006).

At this point, the reader may be interested in how the one-, two-, and three-factor levels are related. Table 2.2 provides the correlations among all of the adjective marker scales described in this chapter; some of the higher correlations are affected by item overlap between marker sets at different levels. The general evaluation factor, regardless of the scale for it, is related to both S (social propriety) and D (dynamism) but more to S than to D.

Regularities at the five-factor level

The Big Five factors are extraversion, agreeableness, conscientiousness, emotional stability, and intellect/imagination. Lexical studies in Germanic and Slavic languages (including English) have been supportive of the Big Five, and so has a study in Turkish (Goldberg and Somer, 2000). But studies in Italian (De Raad et al., 1998) and Hungarian (Szirmàk and De Raad, 1994) found no counterpart to the intellect factor in five-factor solutions. Extraction of additional factors was necessary to find a factor related to intellect. In a study of modern Greek (Saucier et al., 2005), there was no intellect or imagination factor (intellect terms were more associated with a factor emphasizing courage and self-confidence).

Several lexical studies have included a relatively broad selection of variables, each including many terms that could be classified as referring to emotions and moods or as

Table 2.2   Intercorrelations among adjective marker scales for structures of one to seven factors

	1	2	3	4	5	6	7	8	9	10	11	12	13	14	15	16	17	18	19	20	21	22	23	24	25	26	27	28
1. Ge-24																												
2. Ge-12	95																											
3. NEPC-E	62	60																										
4. SDQ	55	54	52																									
5. Osgood E	50	51	45	68																								
6. S	49	49	47	75	58																							
7. D	36	33	40	43	41	58																						
8. TL	05	03	-04	05	-07	00	04																					
9. TALU	-04	-08	-06	-14	-20	-35	00	-22																				
10. AU	-01	-03	-03	-08	-07	-45	-35	10	43																			
11. ALUT	04	04	08	04	04	-21	-45	43	11	58																		
12. B5MM-I	27	25	31	33	30	00	-21	57	-50	03	40																	
13. B5MM-II	52	53	51	71	65	75	27	84	-13	09	44	57																
14. B5MM-III	39	35	31	58	40	36	20	27	-25	-46	-29	04	21															
15. B5MM-IV	46	44	48	50	38	52	19	20	48	11	10	-19	17	31														
16. B5MM-V	25	23	39	27	19	07	41	19	11	06	00	19	37	28	16													
17. CL6-H	57	58	41	59	49	65	10	09	-26	-29	08	61	40	16	61	16												
18. CL6-E	-31	-28	-27	-27	-17	-05	-36	81	02	-09	-26	-32	06	-27	40	37	03											
19. CL6-X	36	34	37	45	41	14	81	02	-09	-36	-51	-15	92	36	-43	24	-27	-25										
20. CL6-A	41	43	44	65	49	81	02	15	50	08	05	-06	14	65	21	25	22	-08	07									
21. CL6-C	45	41	32	55	40	40	15	50	08	05	-26	14	34	23	55	09	46	-20	20	23								
22. CL6-O	29	26	40	27	23	05	51	-16	17	26	32	29	16	20	23	07	02	-31	27	06	04							
23. ML7-gr	17	16	41	18	16	51	68	-33	05	-16	28	79	24	16	34	20	05	-03	81	-04	-05	04						
24. ML7-sa	48	47	44	50	45	18	53	05	38	34	26	24	33	22	16	04	23	-75	46	18	30	17	20					
25. ML7-et	39	38	38	54	37	07	07	02	-20	-36	-05	09	19	12	24	47	37	-21	16	17	35	06	04	41				
26. ML7-cfo	41	40	41	50	39	62	06	06	-16	-47	-42	02	69	75	48	19	66	20	79	51	06	20	-03	09	06	32		
27. ML7-co	24	21	44	37	26	19	11	09	52	10	-27	11	18	10	69	15	30	-09	15	06	35	75	-03	20	03	20	22	
28. ML7-ov	30	28	24	26	21	04	45	-07	18	27	19	22	14	16	10	02	84	02	09	36	49	10	84	04	35	06	-05	05
29. ML7-nv	34	36	24	58	53	56	10	24	-06	-11	-21	13	43	45	35	00	48	-16	22	36	49	10	-03	04	-03	04	34	-04

Note: Eugene-Springfield Community Sample (ESCS), N=533. Decimal points omitted. Between-set correlations above 0.60 in magnitude are printed in boldface type. All correlations within set (the same level, structure, and number of factors) are in italics. For Big Five, correlations are based on ESCS-1995. Some scales from different sets have overlapping items, which may inflate the correlations among the more closely related scales.

being unusually highly evaluative, and two of these studies (Goldberg and Somer, 2000; Saucier, 1997) included terms referring to physical appearance. In these studies, there has been no difficulty in replicating the one- and two-factor structures reviewed earlier. But none of these analyses has found the Big Five in a five-factor solution.

Because of the long history of Big Five models and its long salience in lexical studies, numerous measures of the lexical Big Five have been constructed. Saucier and Goldberg (2002) provide a detailed account of the some major adjectival Big Five marker scales in English. A shorter summary is provided here.

Goldberg (1990) originally experimented with bipolar and cluster scoring methods for measuring the Big Five as found in adjectives. Then he settled on a standard set of 100 'unipolar' adjectives, 20 for each factor (Goldberg, 1992). Although this marker set has been widely used, it is now judged overly long for many purposes. This influential marker set became the starting point for reduced-length marker scale sets. The first was the Mini-Markers (Saucier, 1994a), which included only a 40-item subset of the 100, those most univocally loading on each of the five factors; there are indications that validity is comparable with that for the longer marker set (Dwight et al., 1998). An alternative subset is the Ortho-40 (Saucier, 2002), differing from the Mini-Markers in having lower interscale correlations. Another problem with the 100 unipolar adjectives, and to some degree these reduced-length descendents, was the use of many negations (un- terms) (Graziano et al., 1998). By including some adjectives not contained in the 100 unipolar set, Saucier (2002) devised an alternative 40-adjective set (the 3M40) that had fewer negations while retaining interscale correlations as low as those from the Ortho-40.

Constituent terms and psychometric indices are provided in Table 2.3 for the Mini-Markers for peer-ratings as well as self-ratings. The 569 peer-ratings are averaged

ratings from three well-acquainted peers nominated by each of the 569 persons who provided self-ratings, who were described by the three peers. The scales scored from peer ratings sometimes have higher internal consistency – specifically for agreeableness, conscientiousness, and emotional stability (the Big Five factors most highly associated with the broader social propriety/morality factor). When aggregated, peer ratings have the potential for psychometric properties superior to what self-ratings can provide (Hofstee, 1994). Correlations between self and aggregated peer ratings were 0.66, 0.45, 0.50, 0.41, and 0.49, respectively, for extraversion, agreeableness, conscientiousness, emotional stability, and intellect/imagination.

Big Five scales are also available from the items of the International Personality Item Pool (Goldberg, 1999). Goldberg used the 100 markers as orienting points for selecting items for 20-item scales (in the IPIP-100) and 10-item scales (in the IPIP-50), with an eye to maximizing internal consistency while balancing the number of forward- and reverse-keyed items (Saucier and Goldberg, 2002). Donnellan et al. (2006) recently developed a 'mini-IPIP' questionnaire by shortening the IPIP-50 to only 20 items. These IPIP scales can be expected to measure factors similar to the lexical ones captured by the 100 markers; however, they are one step removed from the lexical studies (Goldberg, 1990, 1992) that led to the 100 markers, and they do not share method variance with adjective scales. Thus, they are not lexical-factor measures by a strict criterion.

The same can be said for the NEO Personality Inventory (Costa and McCrae, 1985, 1992), described in another chapter in this volume, as well as its short form, the NEO Five Factor Inventory (NEO-FFI). It is worth noting, however, that the development of the agreeableness and conscientiousness domain scales for the NEO measures was strongly influenced by earlier lexical measures of the corresponding Big Five factors (McCrae and Costa, 1985).

Table 2.3 Psychometric indices for marker scales for the Big Five

Marker scale	No. of items	Sample	2-year retest r	Coefficient alpha	Mean r	SD of r	% of variance 1st – 2nd Factor	Mean	SD	Skew
Mini-markers (self-ratings)										
I - Extraversion	8	ESCS-1993	0.83	0.83	0.38	0.13	47 – 13	4.10	0.56	–0.02
II - Agreeableness	8	ESCS-1993	0.70	0.79	0.34	0.08	42 – 12	5.74	0.65	–0.91
III - Conscientiousness	8	ESCS-1993	0.78	0.83	0.38	0.11	46 – 12	5.30	0.84	–0.70
IV - Emotional stability	8	ESCS-1993	0.73	0.76	0.28	0.12	39 – 14	4.59	0.88	–0.14
V - Intellect/imagination	8	ESCS-1993	0.77	0.79	0.33	0.13	42 – 17	5.17	0.82	–0.38
Mini-markers (self-ratings)										
I - Extraversion	8	ESCS-1998b		0.86	0.42	0.13	50 – 12	3.47	0.80	–0.36
II - Agreeableness	8	ESCS-1998b		0.81	0.36	0.11	45 – 13	4.30	0.53	–0.76
III - Conscientiousness	8	ESCS-1998b		0.86	0.43	0.14	51 – 11	4.08	0.66	–0.86
IV - Emotional stability	8	ESCS-1998b		0.80	0.33	0.13	42 – 16	3.67	0.70	–0.38
V - Intellect/imagination	8	ESCS-1998b		0.83	0.38	0.14	46 – 18	3.85	0.64	–0.49
Mini-markers (peer-ratings)										
I - Extraversion	8	ESCS-1998b		0.86	0.43	0.13	51 – 12	3.70	0.66	–0.54
II - Agreeableness	8	ESCS-1998b		0.87	0.46	0.08	53 – 12	4.28	0.50	–0.95
III - Conscientiousness	8	ESCS-1998b		0.89	0.49	0.13	57 – 10	4.12	0.61	–0.96
IV - Emotional stability	8	ESCS-1998b		0.84	0.40	0.15	48 – 17	3.57	0.63	–0.26
V - Intellect/imagination	8	ESCS-1998b		0.81	0.36	0.17	44 – 20	3.98	0.49	–0.43

Note: ESCS – Eugene-Springfield Community Sample (1993, N = 1125; 1998b and 1998b samples, N = 569). ESCS-1998b used a 1-5 rating scale rather than 1–7. % of variance figures based on a principal-axes analyses of all items in the scale. See source articles (Saucier (1994a, 2002) or author's web-pages for list of Mini-marker items and for indices based on other samples. Some comparable indices for the 100 markers, Ortho-40, and 3M40 are available in previous publications (Saucier, 2002; Saucier and Goldberg, 2002).

Two other lexically influenced questionnaires deserve mention. One is the Big Five Inventory (BFI) (Benet-Martinez and John, 1998). This measure has 44 short phrase items. The content and positions for the five factors on this instrument were clearly influenced by both the Big Five adjective scales and by the NEO inventory. For example, in Big Five measures one factor is intellect or imagination, whereas the corresponding NEO domain is labeled as openness to experience. In the BFI, the corresponding scale has elements of all three kinds of content, and so overall represents a sort of compromise. Hendriks and her colleagues developed the Five Factor Personality Inventory (FFPI) (Hendriks et al., 1999), a 100-item Big Five inventory using an IPIP-style item format that has been translated and used in numerous languages (Hendriks et al., 2003). The FFPI was constructed based in large part on results of Dutch lexical studies, especially the innovative study of Hofstee and De Raad (1991). The BFI and FFPI are useful Big Five measures, although not lexical-factor measures by a strict criterion.

Even shorter measures of the Big Five have begun to appear. Gosling et al. (2003) developed a ten-item Big Five measure that showed adequate retest reliability and adequate convergence both with other Big Five measures and between self and observer ratings. Major sources for the items were Goldberg's marker sets and the BFI.

As these examples of Big Five measures illustrate, measures of lexical personality factors tend to be provisional and are used primarily in research, but they have also provided a useful template for the development of more sophisticated assessment instruments.

Lexical six-factor models

Ashton et al. (2004) have presented evidence that many of the lexical studies conducted to date yield a consistent pattern in six-factor solutions. Although the structure was first detected in studies of Korean (Hahn et al., 1999) and

French (Boies et al., 2001), it has also appeared to a recognizable degree in Dutch, German, Hungarian, Italian, and Polish. This structure seems less bound to the Germanic and Slavic language families than the Big Five.

Empirically, the extraversion, conscientiousness, and intellect factors in this six-factor model differ relatively little from corresponding factors in the Big Five. Emotionality is more related to (low) emotional stability than to any other Big Five factor. The other two factors emerge largely out of the interstitial areas between Big Five factors: agreeableness from big five agreeableness and emotional stability, and honesty/humility from big five agreeableness and conscientiousness. However, as Table 2.2 indicates, emotionality and honesty in particular tend to have relations to more than two Big Five factors.

Evidence to date indicates that the replicability of the six-factor structure across languages probably exceeds that for the Big Five. Moreover, this 'Cross-Language Six' might be considered superior because it provides more information than the Big Five. In the first reported 'horse races' between the models, replication comparisons in lexical study of modern Greek (Saucier et al., 2005) and of the language of the Maasai (Saucier et al., 2006), the six-factor model seemed about equally as replicable as the Big Five. In neither study, however, were five- or six-factor models nearly as well replicated as were one- and two-factor models.

Other measures focused on in this chapter have included adjectives as items, and one might employ adjective markers to index these six factors. The best approach would be to utilize as many as possible of the adjectives that Ashton et al. present in their 'summary of the six-factor solutions' (2004: 363) in various languages. Table 2.4 presents the constituent terms and psychometric indices for a set of marker scales so constructed; large subsets of these terms (in translation) have been used as marker scales for the Cross-Language Six in two previous lexical studies (Saucier et al., 2005, 2006).

Table 2.4 Psychometric indices for adjective marker scales for the Cross-Language Six

Marker scale	No. of items	sample	Coeff. alpha	Mean r	SD of r	% of variance 1st – 2nd factor	Mean	SD	Skew	r with HEXACO-PI					
										H	E	X	A	C	O
Honesty/Humility (H)	10	ESCS	0.71	0.24	0.12	33 – 13	5.94	0.58	-0.69	0.40	0.10	0.02	0.25	0.22	-0.08
Emotionality (E)	11	ESCS	0.65	0.14	0.15	23 – 18	3.80	0.67	0.17	0.05	0.57	-0.17	-0.02	-0.15	-0.13
Extraversion (X)	8	ESCS	0.75	0.28	0.11	37 – 15	4.89	0.89	-0.21	-0.01	0.08	0.70	0.00	0.12	0.08
Agreeableness (A)	9	ESCS	0.76	0.29	0.11	38 – 12	5.25	0.79	-0.54	0.27	0.02	-0.08	0.59	0.04	0.02
Conscientiousness (C)	9	ESCS	0.76	0.26	0.11	35 – 13	5.70	0.72	-0.96	0.13	0.00	0.06	-0.01	0.69	-0.16
Openness (O)	11	ESCS	0.76	0.23	0.14	31 – 13	5.18	0.70	-0.48	-0.15	-0.16	0.33	-0.02	0.03	0.60

Note: ESCS – Eugene–Springfield community sample, *N* = 533, except *N* = 519 for correlations with HEXACO-PI. % of variance figures based on a principal-axes analysis of all items in the scale. Adjectives selected as markers for Cross-Language Six are drawn from those cited as most recurrent across languages by Ashton et al. (2004), and are as follows: (honesty/humility) honest, sincere, fair, loyal, modest, vs. deceitful, hypocritical, conceited, sly, greedy; (emotionality) anxious, fearful, vulnerable, emotional, sensitive, sentimental vs. strong, courageous, independent, tough, independent, self-assured; (extraversion) talkative, sociable, cheerful, energetic vs. quiet, shy, passive, withdrawn; (agreeableness) gentle, tolerant, peaceful, agreeable, good-natured vs. irritable, argumentative, aggressive, short-tempered; (conscientiousness) orderly, precise, careful, self-disciplined vs. disorganized, lazy, negligent, reckless, irresponsible; (openness) creative, intellectual, philosophical, talented, educated, witty unconventional vs. uncreative, unintellectual, uneducated, conventional. Psychometric indices for the HEXACO Personality Inventory (HEXACO-PI) can be obtained from Lee and Ashton (2004).

However, the standard way to measure these six factors is with a questionnaire called the HEXACO Personality Inventory (HEXACO-PI) (Lee and Ashton, 2004). In this inventory, each of the six factors has four subscales measuring facets of the six factors. Psychometric indices for the six higher-order scales are presented elsewhere (Lee and Ashton, 2004). Correlations between HEXACO scales and adjective markers for the Cross-Language Six are also included in Table 2.4. The correlations indicate good lexically based content validity for the HEXACO scales, with one exception: The convergence of lexical and questionnaire honesty/humility ($r = 0.40$) is rather weak. This is probably due to the H scale's use of fairly specific contextualized items. Generally, the questionnaire scale appears less suffused with evaluation and agreeableness than the lexical version.

This six-factor model may be found only in the adjective domain. Saucier (2003b) found that the structure of type-nouns in English yielded six factors very similar to those found in studies of Dutch (De Raad and Hoskens, 1990) and German (Henss, 1998). However, these six factors – liveliness, antagonism, malignancy/cowardice, masculinity, intellect/openness, and attractiveness – as a set do not correspond closely to the Cross-Language Six described here.

Seven-factor models found with a wider inclusion of lexical variables

Analyses leading to the five- or six-factor structure have involved, in effect, removal of the most extremely evaluative terms at an early stage of the variable-selection process. Indeed, Allport (Allport and Odbert, 1936) and Norman (1963) both favored removal of highly evaluative terms. Also removed have been (a) terms indicating relative eccentricity (e.g. average, strange, unusual); (b) terms that can refer to both stable and temporary attributes (e.g. happy, tired, bored); (c) tendencies to affect others in a consistent way

(e.g. likeable, annoying); (d) social status indicators (e.g. wealthy, famous); and (e) attributes of physique and health (e.g. tall, fat, sickly). When investigators have used wider variable selections (i.e. those including many or all of these excluded types of variables), the Big Five has not appeared readily in five-factor solutions. Studies in English and Turkish, however, did find Big-Five-like factors within a seven-factor solution (Goldberg and Somer, 2000; Saucier, 1997; Tellegen and Waller, 1987).

Of the two additional factors, one was found in all three studies: 'negative valence' is a factor emphasizing attributes with extremely low desirability and endorsement rates and with descriptive content involving morality/depravity, dangerousness, worthlessness, peculiarity, and stupidity (cf. Benet-Martinez and Waller, 2002). Its overall themes – extreme social impropriety, failing a threshold for social acceptability, and not being worthy of trust or credence – involve non-normativeness: Does one stand outside of social norms to a high enough degree that one becomes liable for exclusion from the group? The other factor varied more across the three studies and involved descriptors indicating some kind of power to impress others, either in the form of a 'positive valence' factor emphasizing positive attributes (possibly social effects) like 'impressive' and 'outstanding' (found by Tellegen and Waller, 1987) or, where attractiveness terms were included, an 'attractiveness' factor (found by Goldberg and Somer, 2000; Saucier, 1997; also Saucier, 2003b). Whether attractiveness or negative valence fall within the domain of personality can be debated, but both factors involve phenomena of great interest to social psychologists.

The structure labeled the Big Seven was established in an unpublished lexical study of English descriptors that used the method of sampling one descriptors from one in every four pages of a dictionary (Tellegen and Waller, 1987). The structure includes five Big-Five-like factors, except that 'intellect/ imagination' is reconceived as 'unconventionality'.

The two additional factors are labeled 'positive valence' and 'negative valence'. Scrutiny of empirical indices of replication indicate that two attempts to replicate this structure, in studies of Spanish (Benet-Martinez and Waller, 1997) and Hebrew (Almagor et al., 1995) had only modest success, although each of these studies found structures of interest in their own right. A standard lexical measure of the Big Seven in its original English-study structural form is the Inventory of Personal Characteristics (IPC-7) (Tellegen et al., 1991).

Studies in some other languages with broad variable-selection criteria indicate an alternative seven-factor structure. The convergences between these studies occurred in spite of their many differences in methodology. Lexical studies in Filipino (Church et al., 1997, 1998) and Hebrew (Almagor et al., 1995) – languages from unrelated language-families and cultures – yielded a highly convergent seven-factor structure, even though this similarity was obscured by

discrepant labels. The English translations of marker adjectives for the Filipino and Hebrew factors have been shown to correspond in a one-to-one way (Saucier, 2003a).

One of these new factors resembles the negative valence factor just described. Two of them resemble Big Five factors – conscientiousness and intellect. The other three Big Five factors – extraversion, agreeableness, and emotional stability – correlate substantially with the remaining *four* factors, which map an affective-interpersonal domain (cf. Saucier, 1992). These four can be labeled 'gregariousness' (or 'liveliness'), 'self-assurance' (or 'fortitude'), 'even temper' ('tolerant' versus 'temperamental'), and 'concern for others' (versus 'egotism'). Big Five extraversion is related to gregariousness and self-assurance, emotional stability to self-assurance and even temper, and agreeableness to even temper and concern for others.

The relation of the Multi-Language Seven (ML7) to the Cross-Language Six (CL6) is best explained with the help of Figure 2.1. This

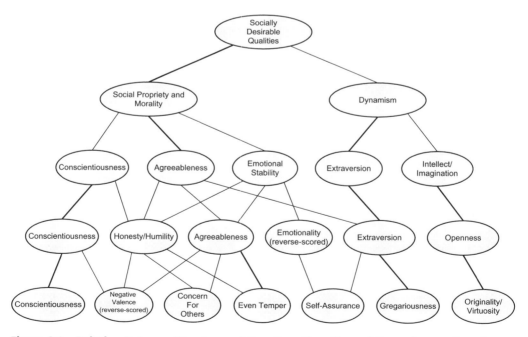

Figure 2.1   Relation Between Structures of One, Two, Five, Six, and Seven Factors Based on Adjective Markers

figure shows the relations between lexical structures of one, two, five, six, and seven factors. It joins any factors at adjacent levels that have a substantial correlation (more than 0.35 in magnitude) in Table 2.2. The SDQ scale was used for the one-factor level. Pairs of factors correlated most highly (above 0.70) are joined by a thick and bold line. The figure depicts very strong relations between CL6 extraversion and ML7 gregariousness, between CL6 agreeableness and ML7 even temper, between the conscientiousness factors, and between CL6 openness and ML7 originality/virtuosity. ML7 self-assurance is related to both CL6 emotionality (reverse-scored) and extraversion, whereas ML7 concern for others and negative valence (reverse-scored) are both related both to CL6 agreeableness and honesty/humility, negative valence being related also to CL6 conscientiousness.

It is noteworthy that negative valence is substantially correlated with CL6 honesty (H), conscientiousness (C), and agreeableness (A) (-0.36 to -0.49 with each), another indicator is that this factor contains descriptive content. Unlike extraversion, emotionality, and openness, these three factors (H, C, and A) concern moral and prosocial behavior, and are clearly related to the broad social propriety and morality factor (and not to dynamism). The aspect of social propriety and morality uniquely captured by so-called negative valence is normality violation; that is, the tendency to behave in ways that are awry, askew, and violative of normal standards for behavior, by way of undependability, recklessness, abusiveness, incompetence, or sheer eccentricity. The favorable pole of this dimension is characterized by 'vanilla' descriptors like normal and trustworthy (Saucier, 2003a). The unfavorable pole is particularly richly represented (in English) by type-nouns, like creep, idiot, fool, twit, crook, and deadbeat, terms whose use implies that the target is being singled out for social exclusion (Saucier, 2003b). The contempt implied in these descriptors may not be unusual when we encounter others who

violate the standards of what we consider normal.

Saucier (2003a) developed a 60-adjective marker set for the seven factors. Constituent terms and psychometric indices are provided in Table 2.5.

An integrative framework for structures of one to seven lexical factors

How are the structures (and measures) of one, two, three, five, six, and seven lexical factors related to one another? Some answers might be found by examining the intercorrelations of the scales measuring their factors (Table 2.2). This table leads to a clear picture of the relation of the one- and two-factor structures with each other and with the five-, six-, and seven-factor structures. The general evaluation factor bifurcates into S and D. Social propriety divides into agreeableness, conscientiousness, and emotional stability (Big Five), or into honesty, agreeableness, and conscientiousness (Cross-Language Six), or into even temper, concern for others, conscientiousness, and (reversed) normality violation (ML7). Dynamism divides into extraversion and intellect/imagination (Big Five), into extraversion, openness, and (low) emotionality (CL6), or into gregariousness, self-assurance, and originality/virtuosity (ML7). Thus, the Big Two is a sensible higher-order organization for each of these three structures. However, it is far more difficult to give a simple description of how the five-, six-, and seven-factor structures relate to each other. Indicating complexity, in Figure 2.1 the lines joining levels of five, six, and seven factors have several crossing lines.

A hierarchical structural representation combining both broader and narrower constructs will provide the best compromise between parsimony and accuracy. The broad levels, with wider bandwidth constructs, offers higher efficiency (i.e. parsimony). The narrower levels offer higher fidelity

Table 2.5   Psychometric indices for adjective marker scales for the Multi-Language Seven

Marker Scale	No. of items	Sample	Coefficient alpha	Mean r	SD of r	% of variance 1st – 2nd factor	Mean	SD	Skew
Gregariousness (GR)	8	ESCS	0.78	0.30	0.13	40 – 14	4.07	0.96	0.06
Self-assurance (SA)	9	ESCS	0.74	0.25	0.11	34 – 13	5.21	0.78	−0.63
Even temper (ET)	8	ESCS	0.81	0.35	0.15	45 – 12	4.60	1.06	−0.29
Concern for others (CFO)	8	ESCS	0.70	0.25	0.12	35 – 17	5.46	0.71	−0.41
Conscientiousness (CO)	9	ESCS	0.72	0.23	0.16	35 – 13	4.84	0.81	−0.44
Originality/virtuosity (OV)	9	ESCS	0.73	0.25	0.12	34 – 14	4.98	0.79	−0.32
Negative valence or Normality violation (NV)	9	ESCS	0.76	0.27	0.10	36 – 15	6.39	0.64	−1.72

Note: N = 592. % of variance figures based on a principal-axes analysis of all items in the scale

(i.e. predictive accuracy). Given the differences in covariation structure between languages, it seems appropriate to defer such studies of lexically derived facets until a consensual hierarchical structure at the broad levels is better defined.

Belief, value, and attitude factors as additions to the dimensional classification

As the above review indicates, the Big Five and Cross-Language Six are structures whose appearance seems contingent on a relatively narrow selection of variables, and thus on an operational definition of personality that has many exclusion clauses. The Multi-Language Seven may be contingent on a more inclusive variable selection and definition of personality. Structures with one or two broad factors seem less dependent on the variable selection on the definition of personality. However, none of the previous lexical studies of personality has included a substantial representation of belief, value, and attitude variables. Would including such variables lead to additional factors?

Unfortunately, the research literature on the structure of beliefs, values, and attitudes has been poorly developed. To rectify this situation, Saucier (2000) used a lexical rationale, extracting from a large dictionary all English nouns ending in '-ism,' such terms postulated to represent many of the most important beliefs and attitudes. From the definitions of these terms, Saucier developed 389 questionnaire items, which he administered to a large sample of college students, who indicated their extent of agreement with each item. Analyses revealed four broad dimensions of beliefs and attitudes, which were replicated in a follow-up sample, and later in Romanian (Krauss, 2006). The study yielded important increments to knowledge about belief/attitude dispositions: Two of the four factors are little represented in previous measures.

Saucier's (2000) four 'isms' factors are labeled as traditional religiousness (α),

subjective spirituality (δ), unmitigated self-interest (β), and protection of civil institutions (γ). These four dimensions showed low correlations with markers for the Big Five (Saucier, 2000), indicating that adding the stable dispositions underlying beliefs and attitudes in a dimensional classification of personality will result in at least four additional factors. Contemporary personality inventories, however, include scales for constructs like self-transcendence, traditionalism, and openness to experience, which are more highly related to belief, value, and attitude dispositions.

Saucier (2006) has developed a brief set of marker items for these four factors, the items being based mostly on dictionary definitions from the earlier study (Saucier, 2000). Table 2.6 provides psychometric indices for these scales. In addition to reasonable internal consistency (a from 0.69 to 0.79), the scales show impressive retest stability (r from 0.64 to 0.85) across nearly four years, and retest stability for tradition-oriented religiousness (0.85) well exceeds that for the typical personality measure. Table 2.7 provides the correlations between the four isms scales and lexical marker scales reviewed earlier in this chapter. The highest r is 0.31 (between subjective spirituality and loose vs. tight) and, consistent with these being factors additional to those in the lexical marker scales, there are few correlations above 0.20 in magnitude.

As for values, Renner (2003a, 2003b) developed a questionnaire from a lexical study of German, and found four factors in common across adjective and noun variable selections. These factors were labeled: salvation, profit, intellectualism, and balance; the first two may correspond to tradition-oriented religiousness and unmitigated self-interest from Saucier (2000). The same author completed a similar project using the Northern Sotho language from South Africa (Renner et al., 2003). Again, factors related to salvation and profit (though differently labeled), plus three additional factors, were found. Renner's program of studies makes

Table 2.6 Psychometric indices for dictionary-based marker scales for the Four Isms Factors

Marker scale	No. of items	Sample	4-year retest r	Coefficient alpha	Mean inter-item r	SD of inter-item r	% of variance 1st – 2nd factor	Mean	SD	Skew
Tradition-oriented religiousness (TR; α)	6	ESCS	0.85	0.79	0.39	0.11	50 – 14	2.94	0.90	−0.10
Unmitigated self-interest (USI; β)	8	ESCS	0.65	0.70	0.23	0.08	33 – 15	1.72	0.50	0.77
Protection of civil institutions (PCI; γ)	8	ESCS	0.64	0.69	0.22	0.10	33 – 16	4.28	0.46	−1.05
Subjective spirituality (SS; δ)	6	ESCS	0.77	0.75	0.33	0.08	45 – 15	2.94	0.81	−0.15

Note: N = 703, except retest r, based on N = 652. % of variance figures based on a principal-axes analysis of all items in the scale.

Table 2.7   Correlations between Isms Factor Scales and adjective marker scales for structures of one to seven factors

Adjective scale	TR (α)	USI (β)	PCI (γ)	SS (δ)
Ge-24	−0.09	−0.11	0.19	0.07
Ge-12	−0.08	−0.10	0.18	0.08
NEPC-E	−0.08	−0.17	0.18	0.10
SDQ	−0.01	−0.07	**0.25***	0.00
Osgood E	0.02	−0.09	0.18	0.09
S	0.05	−0.12	**0.22***	0.03
D	−0.10	−0.02	0.07	0.08
TL	0.00	−0.03	0.15	**−0.31***
TALU	−0.17	0.10	−0.04	−0.18
AU	−0.16	0.10	0.01	−0.07
ALUT	−0.09	0.06	−0.17	0.19
B5MM-I	−0.03	−0.03	0.08	0.04
B5MM-II	0.07	−0.14	**0.22***	0.12
B5MM-III	0.04	−0.02	**0.22***	−0.13
B5MM-IV	−0.07	−0.07	**0.20***	−0.11
B5MM-V	−0.15	−0.11	−0.07	0.07
CL6-H	0.14	−0.16	**0.24***	−0.03
CL6-E	0.18	−0.02	−0.02	0.11
CL6-X	−0.02	−0.02	0.14	0.06
CL6-A	0.02	−0.05	**0.20***	0.06
CL6-C	0.07	−0.08	**0.27***	−0.14
CL6-O	**−0.20***	−0.09	−0.08	0.10
ML7-gr	0.00	−0.02	0.07	0.11
ML7-sa	−0.10	0.02	0.11	−0.03
ML7-et	0.03	−0.06	0.13	−0.04
ML7-cfo	**0.23***	−0.07	0.16	0.16
ML7-co	**0.24***	−0.05	**0.27***	−0.14
ML7-ov	**−0.21***	−0.10	−0.03	0.09
ML7-nv	−0.02	0.08	**−0.29***	**0.22***

Note: Eugene-Springfield Community Sample, *N* = 521. All correlations 0.09 and above are significant, *p* < .05. For Big Five, correlations are based on ESCS-1995, which is closer in time to the administration of the isms measures. *correlations over 0.20 in magnitude. Highest correlation in each column is underlined. TR – tradition-oriented religiousness, USI – unmitigated self-interest, PCI – protection of civil Institutions, SS – subjective spirituality

clear that values can be studied by the lexical approach, and that lexical value factors probably have some relation to lexical isms factors. These studies promise to lead eventually to lexically based measures of values. Analogous lexical studies of interests would be very useful.

CONCLUSIONS

Lexical studies of personality attributes, narrowly defined, have now reached a stage mature enough that key aspects of their structure are becoming evident in the recurrent findings from these studies. However, the 'personality' represented in most of these studies is a considerably narrower phenomenon than personality as it is typically defined, and the structure of personality attributes encoded in lexicons depends in major ways upon the upstream selection of variables. Therefore, personality psychology should couple the focus that it already has, on the most prototypical attributes of personality, with a simultaneous 'bigger picture' examination of all psychological attributes on which there are stable individual differences.

Recurrent aspects of the factors at the top of the personality-attribute hierarchy – the one- and two-factor levels – are already quite clear. Beneath this top level, findings seem more dependent on variable selection. Given relatively narrow variable selection procedures, the Big Five emerges readily from some languages (mainly those having origins in northern Europe) while the Cross-Language Six emerges readily from an apparently even wider range of languages. Given more inclusive procedures, studies to date are too few to permit firm conclusions. More studies are needed, and the direct measures of lexicon-derived personality factors reviewed in this chapter are a vital tool for these studies. These measures help facilitate the search for what is recurrent and ubiquitous (and what is not) in the personality tendencies that differentiate humans, as sedimented in human lexicons.

ACKNOWLEDGMENTS

Work on this article was supported by Grant MH-49227 from the National Institute of Mental Health, US Public Health Service. I am grateful to Lewis R. Goldberg for editing suggestions. Correspondence regarding this article may be addressed to: Gerard Saucier, Department of Psychology, 1227 University of Oregon, Eugene, OR 97403, USA (E-mail: gsaucier@uoregon.edu)

REFERENCES

Ackerman, P.L. (1996) 'A theory of adult intellectual development: Process, personality, interests, and knowledge', *Intelligence*, 22(2): 227–57.

Ackerman, P.L. and Heggestad, E.D. (1997) 'Intelligence, personality, and interests: Evidence for overlapping traits', *Psychological Bulletin*, 121(2): 218–45.

Allport, G.W. (1937) *Personality: A Psychological Interpretation*. New York: Holt.

Allport, G.W. and Odbert, H.S. (1936) 'Trait names: A psycho-lexical study', *Psychological Monographs*, 47(211): 171–220.

Almagor, M., Tellegen, A. and Waller, N. (1995) 'The Big Seven model: A cross-cultural replication and further exploration of the basic dimensions of natural language of trait descriptions', *Journal of Personality and Social Psychology*, 69(2): 300–7.

Alvarez, J.M., Ruble, D.N. and Bolger, N. (2001) 'Trait understanding or evaluative reasoning? An analysis of children's behavioral predictions', *Child Development*, 72(5): 1409–25.

Ashton, M.C., Lee, K., Perugini, M., Szarota, P. De Vries, R.E., di Blas, L., Boies, K. and De Raad, B. (2004) 'A six-factor structure of personality-descriptive adjectives: Solutions from psycholexical studies in seven languages', *Journal of Personality and Social Psychology*, 86(2): 356–66.

Benet-Martínez, V. and John, O.P. (1998) '*Los Cinco Grandes* across cultures and ethnic groups: Multitrait multimethod analyses of the Big Five in Spanish and English', *Journal of Personality and Social Psychology*, 75(3): 729–50.

Benet-Martinez, V. and Waller, N.G. (1997) 'Further evidence for the cross-cultural generality of the Big Seven factor model: Indigenous and imported Spanish personality constructs', *Journal of Personality*, 65(3): 567–98.

Benet-Martinez, V. and Waller, N.G. (2002) 'From adorable to worthless: Implicit and self-report structure of highly evaluative personality descriptors', *European Journal of Personality*, 16(1): 1–41.

Boies, K., Lee, K., Ashton, M.C., Pascal, S. and Nicol, A.A.M. (2001) 'The structure of the French personality lexicon', *European Journal of Personality*, 15(4): 277–95.

Caprara, G.V., Barbanelli, C. and Zimbardo, P.G. (1997) '"Politicians" uniquely simple personalities', *Nature*, 385(6616): 493.

Carroll, J.B. (1993) *Human Cognitive Abilities: A Survey of Factor-analytic Studies*. New York: Cambridge University Press.

Cattell, R.B. (1943) 'The description of personality: Basic traits resolved into clusters', *Journal of Abnormal and Social Psychology*, 38(4): 476–506.

Church, A.T., Katigbak, M.S. and Reyes, J.A.S. (1998) 'Further exploration of Filipino personality structure using the lexical approach: Do the Big Five or Big Seven dimensions emerge?', *European Journal of Personality*, 12(4): 249–69.

Church, A.T., Reyes, J.A.S., Katigbak, M.S. and Grimm, S.D. (1997) 'Filipino personality structure and the Big Five model: A lexical approach', *Journal of Personality*, 65(3): 477–528.

Clark, L.A. and Watson, D. (1999) 'Temperament: A new paradigm for trait psychology', in L.A. Pervin and O.P. John (eds), *Handbook of Personality: Theory and Research* (2nd edn). New York: Guilford, pp. 399–423.

Costa, P.T. and McCrae, R.R. (1985) *The NEO Personality Inventory Manual*. Odessa, FL: Psychological Assessment Resources.

Costa, P.T. and McCrae, R.R. (1992) *Revised NEO Personality Inventory (NEO PI-R) and NEO Five-Factor Inventory (NEO-FFI) Professional Manual*. Odessa, FL: Psychological Assessment Resources.

De Raad, B. and Barelds, D. (2006) 'A new taxonomy of Dutch personality traits based on a comprehensive and unrestricted list of descriptors', Unpublished manuscript, University of Groningen.

De Raad, B., di Blas, L. and Perugini, M. (1998) 'Two independently constructed Italian trait taxonomies: Comparisons within Italian and between Italian and Germanic languages', *European Journal of Personality,* 12(1): 19–41.

De Raad, B. and Hoskens, M. (1990) 'Personality-descriptive nouns', *European Journal of Personality*, 4(2): 131–46.

De Raad, B. and Peabody, D. (2005) 'Cross-culturally recurrent personality factors: Analyses of three factors', *European Journal of Personality*, 19(6): 451–74.

DeYoung, C.G. (2006) 'Higher-order factors of the Big Five in a multi-informant sample', *Journal of Personality and Social Psychology,* 91(6): 1138–51.

di Blas, L. and Forzi, M. (1998) 'An alternative taxonomic study of personality descriptors in the Italian language', *European Journal of Personality*, 12(2): 75–101.

di Blas, L. and Forzi, M. (1999) 'Refining a descriptive structure of personality attributes in the Italian language: The abridged Big Three circumplex structure', *Journal of Personality and Social Psychology*, 76(3): 451–81.

di Blas, L., Forzi, M. and Peabody, D. (2000) 'Evaluative and descriptive dimensions from Italian personality factors', *European Journal of Personality*, 14(4): 279–90.

Digman, J.M. (1997) 'Higher order factors of the Big Five', *Journal of Personality and Social Psychology*, 73(6): 1246–56.

Donnellan, M.B., Oswald, F.L., Baird, B.M. and Lucas, R.E. (2006) 'The Mini-IPIP Scales: Tiny yet effective measures of the Big Five factors of personality', *Psychological Assessment*, 18(2): 192–203.

Dwight, S.A., Cummings, K.M. and Glenar, J.L. (1998) 'Comparison of criterion-related validity coefficients for the Mini-Markers and for Goldberg's markers of the Big Five personality factors', *Journal of Personality Assessment*, 70(3): 541–50.

Eysenck, H.J. and Eysenck, S.B.G. (1975) *Manual of the Eysenck Personality Questionnaire*. London: Hodder & Stoughton.

Funder, D.C. (1997) *The Personality Puzzle*. New York: Norton.

Goldberg, L.R. (1981) 'Language and individual differences: The search for universals in personality lexicons', in L.W. Wheeler (ed.), *Review of Personality and Social Psychology* (Vol. 2). Beverly Hills, CA: Sage, pp. 141–65.

Goldberg, L.R. (1982) 'From Ace to Zombie: Some explorations in the language of personality', in C.D. Spielberger and J.N. Butcher (eds), *Advances in Personality Assessment* (Vol. 1). Hillsdale, NJ: Erlbaum, pp. 203–34.

Goldberg, L.R. (1990) 'An alternative "description of personality": The Big-Five factor structure', *Journal of Personality and Social Psychology*, 59(6): 1216–29.

Goldberg, L.R. (1992) 'The development of markers for the Big-Five factor structure', *Psychological Assessment*, 4(1): 26–42.

Goldberg, L.R. (1999) 'A broad-bandwidth, public-domain, personality inventory measuring the lower-level facets of several five-factor models', in I. Mervielde, I. Deary, F. De Fruyt and F. Ostendorf (eds), *Personality Psychology in Europe* (Vol. 7). Tilburg, The Netherlands: Tilburg University Press, pp. 7–28.

Goldberg, L.R. and Saucier, G. (1995) 'So what do you propose we use instead? A reply to Block', *Psychological Bulletin*, 117(2): 221–5.

Goldberg, L.R. and Somer, O. (2000) 'The hierarchical structure of common Turkish person-descriptive adjectives', *European Journal of Personality*, 14(6): 497–531.

Goldberg, L.R. and Velicer, W.F. (2006) 'Principles of exploratory factor analysis', in S. Strack (ed.), *Differentiating Normal and Abnormal Personality* (2nd edn). New York: Springer, pp. 209–37.

Gosling, S.D., Rentfrow, P.J. and Swann, W.B. (2003) 'A very brief measure of the Big Five personality domains', *Journal of Research in Personality*, 37(6): 504–28.

Graziano, W.G., Jensen-Campbell, L.A., Steele, R.G. and Hair, E.C. (1998) 'Unknown words in self-reported personality: Lethargic and provincial in Texas', *Personality and Social Psychology Bulletin*, 24(8): 893–905.

Hahn, D.W., Lee, K. and Ashton, M.C. (1999) 'A factor analysis of the most frequently used Korean personality trait adjectives', *European Journal of Personality*, 13(4): 261–82.

Hendriks, A.A.J., Hofstee, W.K.B. and De Raad, B. (1999) 'The Five-Factor Personality Inventory (FFPI)', *Personality and Individual Differences*, 27(2): 307–25.

Hendriks, A.A.J., Perugini, M., Angleitner, A., Ostendorf, F., Johnson, J.A., De Fruyt, F., Hřebíčková, M., Kreitler, S., Murakami, T., Bratko, D., Conner, M., Nagy, J., Rodriguez-Fornells, A. and Ruisel, I. (2003) 'The Five-Factor Personality Inventory: Cross-cultural generalizability across 13 countries', *European Journal of Personality*, 17(5): 347–73.

Henss, R. (1998) 'Type nouns and the five factor model of personality description', *European Journal of Personality*, 12(1): 57–71.

Hofstee, W.K.B. (1994) 'Who should own the definition of personality?', *European Journal of Personality*, 8(3): 149–62.

Hofstee, W.K.B. and De Raad, B. (1991) 'Persoonlijkheidsstructuur: de AB-sub-5C-taxonomie van Nederlandse eigenschapstermen [Personality structure: The Abridged Big Five-Dimensional Circumplex (AB5C) structure of Dutch trait adjectives]', *Nederlands Tijdschrift voor de Psychologie en haar Grensgebieden*, 46(6): 262–74.

Hogan, R. (1983) 'A socioanalytic theory of personality', in M.M. Page (ed.), *Nebraska Symposium on Motivation*. Lincoln: University of Nebraska Press, pp. 336–55.

Hřebíčková, M., Ostendorf, F., Osecká, L. and Čermák, I. (1999) 'Taxonomy and structure of Czech personality-relevant verbs', in I. Mervielde, I.J. Deary, F. De Fruyt and F. Ostendorf (eds), *Personality Psychology in Europe* (Vol. 7). Tilburg, The Netherlands: Tilburg University Press, pp. 51–65.

John, O.P., Angleitner, A. and Ostendorf, F. (1988) 'The lexical approach to personality: A historical review of trait taxonomic research', *European Journal of Personality*, 2(3): 171–203.

Krauss, S. (2006) 'Does ideology transcend culture? A preliminary examination in Romania', *Journal of Personality*, 74(4): 1219–56.

Krueger, R.F. and Markon, K.E. (2006) 'Reinterpreting comorbidity: A model-based approach to understanding and classifying psychopathology', *Annual Review of Clinical Psychology*, 2: 111–33.

Lee, K. and Ashton, M.C. (2004) 'Psychometric properties of the HEXACO Personality Inventory', *Multivariate Behavioral Research*, 39(2): 329–58.

Low, K.S.D., Yoon, M., Roberts, B.W., and Rounds, J. (2005) 'Stability of vocational interests from early adolescence to middle adulthood: A quantitative review of longitudinal studies', *Psychological Bulletin*, 131(5): 713–37.

May, M.A. (1932) 'The foundations of personality', in P.S. Achilles (ed.), *Psychology at Work*. New York: McGraw-Hill.

McCrae, R.R. and Costa, P.T. (1985) 'Updating Norman's "adequate taxonomy": Intelligence and personality dimensions in natural language and in questionnaires', *Journal of Personality and Social Psychology*, 49(3): 710–21.

McCrae, R.R. and Costa, P.T. (1997) 'Personality trait structure as a human universal', *American Psychologist*, 52(5): 509–16.

Norman, W.T. (1963) 'Toward an adequate taxonomy of personality attributes: Replicated factor structure in peer nomination personality ratings', *Journal of Abnormal and Social Psychology*, 66(6): 574–83.

Norman, W.T. (1967) *2800 Personality Trait Descriptors: Normative Operating Characteristics for a University Population*. Ann Arbor: Department of Psychology, University of Michigan.

Osgood, C.E. (1962) 'Studies on the generality of affective meaning systems', *American Psychologist*, 17(1): 10–28.

Osgood, C.E., May, W. and Miron, M. (1975) *Cross-cultural Universals of Affective Meaning*. Urbana: University of Illinois Press.

Paulhus, D.L. and John, O.P. (1998) 'Egoistic and moralistic biases in self-perception: The interplay of self-descriptive styles with basic traits and motives', *Journal of Personality*, 66(6): 1025–60.

Peabody, D. (1987) 'Selecting representative trait adjectives', *Journal of Personality and Social Psychology*, 52(1): 59–71.

Peabody, D. and Goldberg, L.R. (1989) 'Some determinants of factor structures from personality-trait descriptors', *Journal of Personality and Social Psychology*, 57(3): 552–67.

Prince, M. (1924) *Psychotherapy and Multiple Personality: Selected Essays*. Cambridge, MA: Harvard University Press.

Renner, W. (2003a) 'A German value questionnaire developed on a lexical basis: Construction and steps toward validation', *Review of Psychology*, 10(2): 107–23.

Renner, W. (2003b) 'Human values: A lexical perspective', *Personality and Individual Differences*, 34(1): 127–41.

Renner, W., Peltzer, K. and Phoswana, M.G. (2003) 'The structure of values among Northern Sotho speaking people in South Africa', *South African Journal of Psychology*, 33(2): 103–8.

Roback, A.A. (1931) *Personality: The Crux of Social Intercourse*. Cambridge, MA: Sci-Art.

Rokeach, M. (1968) *Beliefs, Attitudes, and Values: A Theory of Organization and Change*. San Francisco: Jossey-Bass.

Rolland, J.P., Parker, W.D. and Stumpf, H. (1998) 'A psychometric examination of the French translations of the NEO-PI-R and NEO-FFI', *Journal of Personality Assessment*, 71(2): 269–91.

Rossier, J., Dahouru, D. and McCrae, R.R. (2005) 'Structural and mean-level analyses of the five-factor model and locus of control: Further evidence from Africa', *Journal of Cross-Cultural Psychology*, 36(2): 227–46.

Rothbart, M.K. and Bates, J.E. (1998) 'Temperament', in W. Damon (series ed.) and N. Eisenberg (vol. ed.), *Handbook of Child Psychology: Vol. 3, Social, Emotional and Personality Development* (5th edn). New York: Wiley, pp. 105–76.

Saucier, G. (1992) 'Benchmarks: Integrating affective and interpersonal circles with the Big-Five personality factors', *Journal of Personality and Social Psychology*, 62(6): 1025–35.

Saucier, G. (1994a) 'Mini-markers: A brief version of Goldberg's unipolar Big-Five markers', *Journal of Personality Assessment*, 63(3): 506–16.

Saucier, G. (1994b) 'Separating description and evaluation in the structure of personality attributes', *Journal of Personality and Social Psychology*, 66(1): 141–54.

Saucier, G. (1997) 'Effects of variable selection on the factor structure of person descriptors', *Journal of Personality and Social Psychology*, 73(6): 1296–312.

Saucier, G. (2000) 'Isms and the structure of social attitudes', *Journal of Personality and Social Psychology*, 78(2): 366–85.

Saucier, G. (2002) 'Orthogonal markers for orthogonal factors: The case of the Big Five', *Journal of Research in Personality*, 36(1): 1–31.

Saucier, G. (2003a) 'An alternative multi-language structure of personality attributes', *European Journal of Personality*, 17(3): 179–205.

Saucier, G. (2003b) 'Factor structure of English-language personality type-nouns', *Journal of Personality and Social Psychology*, 85(4): 695–708.

Saucier, G. (2005) 'Framework for integrating lexical structures of five, six, and seven factors', ORI Technical Report, 45(3). Eugene: Oregon Research Institute.

Saucier, G. (2006) 'A brief measure of the four factors in the Survey of Dictionary-based Isms (SDI)', Unpublished manuscript, University of Oregon.

Saucier, G., Georgiades, S., Tsaousis, I. and Goldberg, L.R. (2005) 'The factor structure of Greek personality adjectives', *Journal of Personality and Social Psychology*, 88(5): 856–75.

Saucier, G. and Goldberg, L.R. (2002) 'Assessing the Big Five: Applications of 10 psychometric criteria to the development of marker scales', in B. De Raad and M. Perugini (eds), *Big Five Assessment*. Seattle: Hogrefe & Huber, pp. 29–58.

Saucier, G., Ole-Kotikash, L. and Payne, D.L. (2006) 'The structure of personality and character attributes in the language of the Maasai', Unpublished report, University of Oregon.

Saucier, G., Ostendorf, F. and Peabody, D. (2001) 'The non-evaluative circumplex of personality adjectives', *Journal of Personality*, 69(4): 537–82.

Saucier, G. and Simonds, J. (2006) 'The structure of personality and temperament', in D.K. Mroczek and T.D. Little (eds), *Handbook of Personality Development*. Mahwah, NJ: Erlbaum, pp. 109–28.

Shweder, R.A. (1972) 'Semantic structure and personality assessment', Unpublished doctoral dissertation, Harvard University.

Super, D.E. (1924) 'Values: Their nature, assessment, and practical use', in D.E. Super and B. Sverko (eds), *Life Roles, Values, and Careers: International Findings of the Work Importance Study*. San Francisco: Jossey Bass, pp. 54–61.

Szirmák, Z. and De Raad, B. (1994) 'Taxonomy and structure of Hungarian personality traits', *European Journal of Personality*, 8(2): 95–118.

Tellegen, A. (1993) 'Folk concepts and psychological concepts of personality and personality disorder', *Psychological Inquiry*, 4(2): 122–30.

Tellegen, A. (in press) *Manual for the Multidimensional Personality Questionnaire*. Minneapolis: University of Minnesota Press.

Tellegen, A., Grove, W. and Waller, N.G. (1991) 'Inventory of personal characteristics # 7', Unpublished measure, University of Minnesota.

Tellegen, A. and Waller, N.G. (1987) 'Re-examining basic dimensions of natural language trait descriptors', Paper presented at the 95th Annual Convention of the American Psychological Association.

White, G.M. (1980) 'Conceptual universals in interpersonal language', *American Anthropologist*, 82(4): 759–81.

Wiggins, J.S., Trapnell, P. and Phillips, N. (1988) 'Psychometric and geometric characteristics of the Revised Interpersonal Adjective Scales (IAS-R)', *Multivariate Behavioral Research*, 23(4): 517–30.

3

Cross-Cultural Personality Assessment

Fons J.R. van de Vijver and Dianne A. van Hemert

The chapter describes issues in the assessment of personality in a cross-cultural context. For example, how can we establish whether personality structure is universal? How can we examine universal and culture-specific aspects of personality? How do we know whether observed differences in scores across cultures reflect personality differences or whether these reflect differences in response styles, such as social desirability and acquiescence? Are Western personality questionnaires suitable for identifying the structure of personality in non-Western groups? Do we find the same personality structure in non-Western groups if we administer local and Western instruments? What are adequate translation and adaptation procedures in cross-cultural personality assessment? The common assessment issue behind all these questions is validity (Messick, 1989): How can we ensure that the inferences of cross-cultural studies, in particular when these involve non-Western groups, are adequate? The current chapter provides an overview of ways in which assessment issues of cross-cultural personality psychology have been addressed.

Each part of the chapter deals with a different way in which assessment issues have been dealt with. The first part of the chapter reviews methodological approaches to deal with the problems of cross-cultural personality assessment, focusing on bias and equivalence (Van de Vijver and Leung, 1997). The starting point in this approach is an application of an instrument in two or more cultures. A detailed study of psychometric properties of the instruments is made to determine whether the same psychological constructs are measured in each group and, if needed, whether scores can be compared across cultural groups.

The next three parts of the chapter describe more substantive approaches to cross-cultural personality assessment. The second part deals with response styles. It is argued there that the conventional view of response styles as validity threats (such as the view that social desirability can be interpreted as lying) is counterproductive in cross-cultural personality assessment; response styles can also be construed as consistent communication characteristics of participants that show systematic differences across cultures.

The third part of the chapter gives an overview of studies using indigenous approaches. These studies attend to assessing personality in a specific cultural context; the aim of these studies is not to develop a model of personality that can be employed in different cultures but to provide a comprehensive picture of personality in a specific cultural context. Indigenous studies indirectly address the question of whether the personality structure that is found in Western studies is also found when an assessment instrument is developed 'from scratch' and does not start from an existing Western instrument. The fourth part of the chapter describes studies in which other methods than self-reports have been used to assess personality in different cultures. Finally, conclusions are drawn in the final part.

BIAS AND EQUIVALENCE: AN INTEGRATED APPROACH

A few thorny methodological issues challenge cross-cultural personality assessment. The first one deals with the question of comparability of personality structure. Do the same concepts apply in all cultural groups? Can introversion be used to describe the personality of both Chinese and Americans? A second issue refers to the comparability of scores across cultures. Suppose that we have administered a questionnaire in two cultures that measures conformity and that we are interested in the question of which culture has higher scores. Even if we would find that conformity is a concept that can be measured in the same way in different cultures, the question still has to be addressed as to whether scores are directly comparable across cultures. Response styles are a major threat to the direct comparability of scores across cultures. If conformity is a much more desirable characteristic in one culture than in the other (and as we discuss later, there is strong evidence that cultures differ systematically in social desirability), there is a fair

chance that observed score differences are influenced by differential social desirability. As a consequence, real cross-cultural differences in conformity and differences in social desirability are confounded and scores are not directly comparable.

Threats to the comparability of scores are known as bias (Van de Vijver and Leung, 1997). More precisely, bias refers to all confounding influences on test scores that do not belong to the construct under study. Equivalence is a closely related concept that refers to the comparability of test scores. This comparability can be challenged if bias affects the cross-cultural comparison.

Following Van de Vijver and Leung (1997), three sources of bias in cross-cultural research are distinguished. The first is called *construct bias*, which occurs when the construct measured is not identical across groups or when behaviors that constitute the domain of interest from which items are sampled, are not identical across cultures. Triandis and Vassiliou (1972) have argued that philotimo (being respectful, virtuous, reliable, proud, and self-sacrificing) is a person-describing adjective that is unique to the Greek language and culture. The absence of this factor in existing personality inventories would then point to construct bias when the cross-cultural comparison involves Greeks. Other examples of culture-specific phenomena can be found in clinical psychology, notably the so-called culture-bound syndromes, such as Amok, which occurs in some Asian countries such as Indonesia and Malaysia. It is characterized by a brief period of violent aggressive behavior among men (Azhar and Varma, 2000). The period is often preceded by an insult and the patient shows persecutory ideas and automatic behaviors. After the period the patient is usually exhausted and has no recollection of the event.

A second type of bias, called *method bias*, can result from sample incomparability, instrument characteristics, tester and interviewer effects, and the method (mode) of administration. In general, method bias is a label for all sources of bias emanating from aspects that are described in the method section of empirical papers. Important sources of method bias are sample incomparability (e.g. confounding cross-cultural differences in educational background), differential stimulus familiarity (in mental testing), and differential response styles (in personality and survey research). Method bias constitutes an important source of alternative explanations of observed cross-cultural differences. Method bias usually presents itself in the data analysis as a confounding factor. If the confounding factor has been included in the design of the study, it can be dealt with in the statistical analysis. For example, if social desirability is expected to influence the cross-cultural differences on some personality measure, it is possible to employ covariance analysis to correct for confounding cross-cultural differences in social desirability, assuming that a questionnaire has been administered to measure it. If not included in the design of the study, method bias factors often constitute post hoc alternative interpretations of cross-cultural differences. It is our experience that in most cases confounding variables do not emerge unexpectedly but that it is easy to anticipate on their impact. Cross-cultural studies are more conclusive if confounding variables have been measured and their impact is evaluated in the analyses.

The last type of bias involves anomalies at item level and is called *item bias* or *differential item functioning*. According to a widely adopted definition, an item is biased if persons with the same standing on the underlying construct (e.g. they are equally extraverted), but coming from different cultural groups do not have the same average score on the item. The score on the construct is usually derived from the total test score. If a geography test administered to pupils in Australia and the Netherlands contains the item 'What is the capital of Australia?', Australian pupils can be expected to show higher scores on the item than Dutch students, even when pupils with the same total test score would be compared. The item is

biased because it favors one cultural group across all test score levels. Of all bias types, item bias has been most extensively studied. Various psychometric techniques are available to identify item bias (e.g. Camilli and Shepard, 1994; Van de Vijver and Leung, 1997).

Building on these types of bias, four different types of equivalence can be defined (cf. Van de Vijver and Leung, 1997). The first type is labeled *construct nonequivalence*. It amounts to comparing 'apples and oranges'. Because there is no shared attribute, no cross-cultural comparison can be made. Examples are philotimo (as discussed above) and culture-bound syndromes in clinical psychology. The second is called *structural (or functional) equivalence*. An instrument administered in different cultural groups shows structural equivalence if it measures the same construct in these groups. Structural equivalence has been examined for various cognitive tests (Jensen, 1980; Van de Vijver, 1997). We discuss studies on the structural equivalence of personality instruments below. Functional equivalence, sometimes treated as identical to structural equivalence, is often associated with equal nomological networks in different cultures. Nomological networks (often amounting to a check on the convergent and divergent validity) can be compared even if the target instruments are not identical.

The third type of equivalence is called *measurement unit equivalence*. Instruments show this type of equivalence if their measurement scales have the same units of measurement and a different origin (such as the Celsius and Kelvin scales in temperature measurement). This type of equivalence assumes interval- or ratio-level scores (with the same measurement units in each culture). At first sight it may seem unnecessary or even counterproductive to define a level of equivalence with the same measurement units but different scale origins. Why would scales have different origins across cultural groups? Our example about cross-cultural differences in social desirability that confound differences in conformity illustrates the need for distinguishing this level of equivalence. At least some of the observed cross-cultural score differences in conformity may have to be accounted for by social desirability. The latter will obscure real cross-cultural differences. Measurement unit equivalence is a consequence of confounding cross-cultural differences, often the consequence of method bias, because method bias often leads to a difference in score means on observed variables that cannot be attributed to the target construct of the test (e.g. extraversion) but to confounding factors such as method bias (e.g. social desirability). Within- and between-culture differences in scores do not have the same meaning if there are such confounding differences.

Only in the case of scalar (or full score) equivalence can direct comparisons of scores (at both individual and country level) be made; it is the only type of equivalence that allows for statistical tests that compare means (such as t-tests and analyses of variance). This type of equivalence assumes the same interval or ratio scales across groups and the absence of any type of bias. Conclusions about which of the latter two types of equivalence applies are often difficult to draw and can easily create controversy. For example, racial differences in intelligence test scores have been interpreted as largely due to valid differences (scalar equivalence) and as mainly reflecting measurement artifacts (measurement unit equivalence). Intelligence is also a good example where within-country differences (presumably more biologically rooted) and between-country differences (presumably culture related, such as educational differences) have different meanings.

Structural, measurement unit, and scalar equivalence are hierarchically ordered. The third presupposes the second, which presupposes the first. As a consequence, higher levels of equivalence are more difficult to establish. It is easier to demonstrate that an instrument measures the same construct in different cultural groups (structural equivalence)

than to demonstrate numerical comparability across cultures (scalar equivalence). On the other hand, higher levels of equivalence allow for more precise comparisons of scores across cultures. Whereas in the case of structural equivalence, only factor structures and nomological networks (Cronbach and Meehl, 1955) can be compared, measurement unit and full score scalar equivalence allow for more fine-grained analyses of cross-cultural similarities and differences. It is only in the latter that mean scores can be compared across cultures in t-tests and analyses of (co)variance.

Findings on equivalence of personality measures

The previous section distinguished four types of cross-cultural equivalence in quantitative instruments: construct inequivalence, structural/functional equivalence, measurement unit equivalence, and full score (scalar) equivalence. In this section we review studies in which the equivalence of personality measures has been assessed. Most personality research focusing on equivalence issues deals with structural equivalence in measures based on the Big Five and the Eysenck Personality Questionnaire. As mentioned before, establishing cross-cultural structural equivalence is a prerequisite for comparing scores on questionnaires across cultures. In addition, a more substantial reason for the relative preponderance of research on structural equivalence lies in the assumed biological basis of personality (Allik and McCrae, 2002; McCrae and Costa, 1999; Eysenck and Eysenck, 1975, 1976). If the structure of personality is similar across cultures, suggesting universality in personality, a biological basis is more likely. This section will end with suggestions on how to improve common cross-cultural research designs.

Big Five

Many measures have evolved from the idea of describing individual differences in personality in terms of five factors (Big Five); that is, the Five-Factor Model (FFM) (McCrae and Costa, 1997). The most widely used instrument is the revised NEO Personality Inventory (NEO-PI-R) (Costa and McCrae, 1992). The NEO-PI-R consists of five scales, namely extraversion, agreeableness, conscientiousness, neuroticism (emotional stability), and openness to experience. Many studies have addressed the cross-cultural generalizability of the NEO-PI-R structure. For example, McCrae and Costa (1997) compared first-order (five personality factors) and second-order (30 facets) factor structures from six countries (Germany, Portugal, Israel, China, Korea, and Japan) with the American structure. They found similar second-order structure at face value and acceptable congruence for the first-order factors, except for extraversion and agreeableness in the Japanese sample. Rolland (2002) reviewed the available evidence and concluded that cross-cultural structural equivalence for the neuroticism, openness, and conscientiousness scales is very strong. Comparability of the agreeableness and extraversion scales is sometimes less convincing, but justifies the use of the five factors of personality even in non-Western countries.

In addition to self-reports, McCrae and colleagues studied cross-cultural equivalence of observer ratings, in which respondents had to rate a person they know well using the items of the NEO-PI-R (McCrae et al., 2005a). Compared to the US self-report structure, they found similar factor structures across 50 countries, but congruence coefficients were more often below 0.90 for the openness to experience scale and for African countries. The authors concluded that universality of the five factors in trait psychology was confirmed.

McCrae and Terracciano (2008) reported data on the equivalence of the five-factor structure within and across countries. Individual-level and culture-level factor loadings, based on different datasets of 36–51 countries, proved to be comparable (factorial agreement index > 0.85) for all scales but extraversion. The culture-level meaning of the extraversion scale cannot be assumed identical to the individual-level meaning.

A second FFM-based instrument that has been administered cross-culturally is the Five Factor Personality Inventory (FFPI) (Hendriks et al., 1999). It was developed in the Netherlands and consists of four scales similar to the NEO-PI-R (i.e. extraversion, agreeableness, conscientiousness, and emotional stability) and a fifth factor that is variable across different Big Five measures, called autonomy. In a study comparing factor structures of nine European countries, the US, Israel, and Japan to the Netherlands and to the US as benchmark structures, values of Tucker's phi appeared to be generally above 0.90 (Hendriks et al., 2003). However, congruence coefficients were lower when compared to the US instead of to the Netherlands, for the agreeableness factor. It can be concluded that substantial evidence has been found for the cross-cultural equivalence of the five-factor structure personality. As research on full score equivalence is still limited, comparisons of country mean scores on the Big Five measures should be treated with care (see also Poortinga et al., 2002).

Eysenck Personality Questionnaire

The Eysenck Personality Questionnaire (EPQ) was published in 1975 (Eysenck and Eysenck, 1975) and consists of four scales: the psychoticism scale (EPQ-P), designed to measure tough-mindedness, the extraversion scale (EPQ-E), designed to measure extraversion versus introversion, the neuroticism scale (EPQ-N), designed to measure emotionality or emotional instability, and the lie scale (EPQ-L), initially intended to measure a response tendency but shown to tap a stable personality characteristic as well (Eysenck and Eysenck, 1976; McCrae and Costa, 1983).

Several studies established structural equivalence of the EPQ using a UK sample as reference (e.g. Barrett and Eysenck, 1984;

Eysenck et al., 1986). This comparison method, using a procedure for factor comparison described by Kaiser et al. (1971), could yield misleadingly high coefficients of factorial similarity (Bijnen et al., 1986; Bijnen and Poortinga, 1988) and does not have a high power to detect biased items (Van de Vijver and Poortinga, 1994). However, Barrett et al. (1998) presented substantial evidence using an improved comparison procedure based on target rotation of countries' factor matrices toward the UK factor structure. These analyses showed factorial similarity of all four EPQ scales across 34 countries, indicating that the meaning of the four factors is (nearly) identical in each of these countries.

Van Hemert et al. (2002) compared individual-based structures with country-based structures of the EPQ across 24 countries in an attempt to establish multilevel structural equivalence. EPQ-E and EPQ-N were convincingly equivalent at an individual and country level. For the two other scales (EPQ-P and EPQ-L) aggregating individual scores to country level seems to affect the psychological meaning of the scores. It can be concluded that the structural equivalence of the EPQ scales is well supported across countries, but that the meaning of country-level scores remains unclear for the psychoticism and lie scales.

Other instruments

Cross-cultural equivalence has been studied for some other measures of personality. The *Minnesota Multiphasic Personality Inventory* (MMPI) is a clinical self-report questionnaire on personality and psychopathology consisting of 10 clinical scales (such as depression, paranoia, and schizophrenia), 15 content scales (such as anxiety, anger, and cynicism), additional scales on concepts such as marital distress and addiction, and several validity scales to assess response styles. The instrument has been translated into more than 100 languages and has been used in at least 46 countries (Butcher et al., 2004). Detailed cross-national data on the second edition, the

MMPI-2, from more than 20 cultures were reported in Butcher (1996). Considerable efforts were taken to ensure translation equivalence of the MMPI-2 scales. A general translation strategy was outlined by Butcher, stipulating the use of (at least) two translators, back-translation by an independent translator, comparison of the original and back-translated versions, and examination of the equivalence of the translation in a field study. This strategy has been widely adapted and translations of the MMPI-2 are considered to be largely linguistically equivalent (Nichols et al., 2000). The factor structures of the instrument seemed to be similar across cultures (Handel and Ben-Porath, 2000), but adequate factor congruence indices such as Tucker's phi lack in most studies (Nichols et al., 2000).

The *Sixteen Personality Factor (16PF) Questionnaire* was developed from a list of person descriptors in English language. Peer- and self-ratings and behavioral measures of these descriptors were cluster-analyzed and factor-analyzed, leading to 16 primary traits. Subsequent factor analyses revealed five second-order factors (extraversion, anxiety, tough-mindedness, independence, and self-control) that have been shown to correlate highly with the five NEO-PI factors (Cattell, 2004). Cattell reports high similarity in the primary factor structure of the 16 PF across European countries, Japan, and Latin America (see also Hofer and Eber, 2002). However, no explicit comparisons of factor structures across cultures were made and cross-cultural congruence of the second-order structure has not been clearly established (Rossier, 2005).

Holland (1985) proposed six personality types in his *model of vocational interests*: realistic (R), investigative (I), artistic (A), social (S), enterprising (E), and conventional (C), represented by a hexagonal (circular-order) model referred to as RIASEC. Adjacent personality types are assumed to show higher intercorrelations than personality types which are further apart. Rounds and Tracey (1996) examined the model fit across 19 countries and 5 ethnic groups within the US by analyzing RIASEC correlation matrices. When compared with the benchmark US data, individual countries and ethnic groups showed poor correspondence indices for the circular model and to a lesser extent for alternative models that entailed a partition in three groups of personality types.

Schmitt and Allik (2005) reported findings on equivalence of the *Rosenberg Self-Esteem Scale (RSES)* across 53 countries. A one-factorial structure appeared adequate in most countries and showed acceptable similarity compared to the US solution, thereby providing evidence for the structural equivalence of the scale. Moreover, functional equivalence was found across cultures such that high self-esteem goes together with high extraversion and low neuroticism (as measured by the Big Five Inventory) in almost all countries.

A considerable number of cross-cultural and multi-ethnic studies have studied the *Locus of Control (LOC)* construct. Originally, the LOC scale by Rotter (1966) was designed to measure one dimension, indicating the extent of internal versus external control that persons experience. However, Dyal (1984) provided a detailed review of cross-cultural equivalence studies on the LOC construct showing that many cross-cultural studies found two factors instead of one, reflecting personal control and political control. Across ethnic groups within the US and across nations, no similarity of factor structure can be assumed. A multination study on LOC was performed by Smith et al. (1995). They used multidimensional scaling on standardized country scores ($n = 43$) and found three dimensions: personal-political, which was highly correlated with internality country means, individual-social, and luck. As these dimensions were based on the total dataset, it is unclear whether the solution showed adequate fit for each specific country. It can be concluded that the LOC construct lacks cross-cultural structural equivalence.

RESPONSE STYLES FROM A SUBSTANTIVE PERSPECTIVE

It was mentioned in the previous section that asking respondents to report on their own personality entails a number of methodological problems. One particular source of method bias in cross-cultural personality research deserves further attention. People often show tendencies to respond according to certain systematic patterns (response styles) lowering the validity of instruments. Three main types of response styles are extreme responding (preferring the endpoints of a scale), acquiescent responding (agreeing with items irrespective of item content), and social desirability (portraying oneself in a favorable manner). The latter two response styles are different in that acquiescence pertains to endorsing items independent of their contents, whereas social desirability pertains to endorsing items dependent of their contents. This distinction is only apparent when scales use a combination of positively and negatively worded items; when all items are scaled in the same direction it is impossible to disentangle the two response styles.

In addition to individuals, cultures also differ with respect to the frequency with which they show different types of responding behavior (see Johnson and Van de Vijver, 2003, for an overview of the literature on socially desirable responding; Johnson et al., 2005). Many authors provided evidence for consistent cross-cultural differences in response styles. In a meta-analysis across 41 countries, Fischer et al. (submitted) calculated acquiescence scores for various scales in the personality, social-psychological, and organizational domains. They showed that 3.1% of the overall variance was shared among all scales, pointing to a systematic influence of response styles in cross-cultural comparisons. Similarly, in a large-scale study involving 26 countries, Harzing (2006) found consistent cross-cultural differences in acquiescence and extremity responding. Moreover, she found that cross-cultural differences in response styles are systematically related to various country characteristics.

All studies conducted thus far in which response styles are compared across several countries report the same findings: There are systematic differences across countries and country differences in response styles are related to other country variables. It is counterproductive to dismiss response styles as confounding factors in cross-cultural research that should be eliminated or, at least, statistically controlled. As shown below, cross-cultural research shows that response styles can be viewed as communication styles, as ways in which participants present themselves. Therefore, the relevant question is how to interpret the common response styles in terms of their correlates with other cultural characteristics.

Culture-level correlates of response styles

Not many large-scale cross-cultural studies have been done to shed light on the cross-cultural meaning of response styles; most studies involve two-culture comparisons (e.g. Bachman and O'Malley, 1984; Grimm and Church, 1999; Heine and Renshaw, 2002; Hui and Triandis, 1989) or provide only post-hoc explanations of differences. In a comparison of European countries, Van Herk et al. (2004) found that Mediterranean countries, particularly Greece, showed higher acquiescent and extreme responding than northwestern European countries in surveys on consumer research. They explained these differences in terms of the individualism versus collectivism dimension, at the same time acknowledging that the causal relationship might well be reversed, so that response styles are responsible for country scores on individualism and collectivism (see also Berry et al., 2002).

Two classes of country variables have been shown to be associated with response styles in cross-cultural studies, namely socioeconomic context and cultural values.

Socioeconomic and political indicators such as gross national product (GNP), political rights, and level of democracy seem to be relevant to socially desirable and acquiescent responding. Van Hemert et al. (2002) reported significant correlations between these indicators and social desirability as measured by the Eysenck Personality Questionnaire Lie scale across 31 countries; lower scores were found in wealthier and more democratic countries. Similarly, Fischer et al. (submitted) correlated ARS scores based on 17 different instruments or scales to a number of socioeconomic indicators and found the level of acquiescence to be negatively correlated with survey quality, wealth-related indices, democratic rights, and positive correlations with prevalence rates for psychiatric disorders. They suggest that survey responses are systematic indicators of culturally appropriate expressiveness that are also reflected in the larger sociopolitical climate of the societies. An explanation of these findings might be found in the concept of resources. Ross and Mirowsky (1984) found that external resources influence cross-cultural differences in social desirability; less powerful (i.e. less resourceful) social groups often give more socially desirable responses.

Multicountry research on the importance of cultural values for response styles started with Bond and Smith's (1996) meta-analysis of studies on the Asch conformity paradigm. Conformity can be expected to tap something similar to social desirability. They found several measures of cultural values, such as individualism (several measures), autonomy and conservatism (Schwartz, 1994), to be strong predictors of conformity. The authors argue that these measures reflect the individualism versus collectivism dimension in such a way that more individualistic countries showed less conformity. Another concept close to social desirability was studied by Triandis et al. (2001) in a 12-country study of deception (both self-reported and other-reported) in scenarios of negotiation situations. High vertical (hierarchical) collectivism was positively related to the tendency to deceive.

Yet, the pattern was reversed at the individual level. Van Hemert et al. (2002) also found higher collectivism to be associated with higher social desirability.

Harzing (2006) found in a study involving 26 countries that acquiescence and extreme responding are more prevalent in countries with higher scores on Hofstede's collectivism and power distance, and GLOBE's uncertainty avoidance. She also reported that extraversion (at country level) is a positive predictor of acquiescence and extremity scoring. Finally, she found that English-language questionnaires tend to evoke less extremity scoring and that answering items in one's native language is associated with more extremity scoring.

A convincing case for a substantive cultural interpretation of response styles was made by Smith (2004). He calculated acquiescence scores for variables from five multi-country surveys on values, beliefs, reports of own behavior, and reports of others' behavior (Hofstede, 1980; House et al., 2004; Leung et al., 2002; Schwartz, 1994; Smith et al., 2002), and added social desirability scores based on the EPQ (Van Hemert et al., 2002). The GLOBE study (House et al., 2004) provided indices on society 'as it should be' and society 'as it is'. All six acquiescent response bias indices were positively interrelated, and correlations with GLOBE 'as should be' were much stronger than correlations with GLOBE 'as is'. This can be taken as evidence for a common factor. Congruent with Harzing's (2006) findings, acquiescent bias scores were positively related to Hofstede's collectivism and power distance and GLOBE uncertainty avoidance. In addition, depending on whether 'as is' or 'as should be' scores were used to predict acquiescent bias, 'as is' family collectivism or 'as should be' institutional collectivism and uncertainty avoidance explained cross-cultural variance. Smith concluded that response bias at a country level can be meaningfully interpreted in terms of cultural values and reflects cultural communication styles and patterns of intergroup relations.

This idea features in many recent cross-national studies, but specific correlations sometimes differ. For example, Johnson et al. (2005) studied country-level correlates of individual-level extreme responding across respondents from 19 countries and acquiescent responding across respondents from 10 countries using hierarchical linear modeling. Extreme responding was positively related to power distance and masculinity, and acquiescence was negatively related to power distance, uncertainty avoidance, individualism, masculinity, and GNP. These findings were only partly in agreement with other research. The correlations found for extreme responding fitted the hypotheses and the negative correlations of acquiescence with individualism and GNP replicated previous findings (Smith, 2004; Van Hemert et al., 2002). Diverging results included the role of power distance in predicting acquiescence, which was reversed in Smith's (2004) and Harzing's (2006) studies. This difference might be explained by the limited number of countries for the acquiescence analyses and the multilevel design of the study in which individual-level response styles were used rather than country-level scores, and individual-level control variables such as gender, age, and employment were used.

Another multilevel study on extreme responding was performed by De Jong et al. (2007). They used a method based on item response theory for measuring extreme responding, allowing for differential usefulness of items in the calculation of extreme responding. A multilevel analysis (26 countries, 12,500 individuals) with individual-level demographic variables (i.e. age, gender, and education) and Hofstede's measures revealed significant effects of gender and age and positive correlations with individualism, uncertainty avoidance, and masculinity. These results differ from findings by Johnson et al. (2005), who did report a relationship with power distance and not with individualism and uncertainty avoidance, and findings by Harzing (2006), who also observed a positive correlation with power distance.

New developments

In our view, the study of response styles slowly gets the attention it deserves in cross-cultural research. We see several promising directions in which research on cross-cultural response styles can advance our insight in cross-cultural differences on self-report measures. First, Lalwani et al. (2006) distinguish two distinct ways of socially desirable responding in individualistic and collectivistic cultures rather than focus on the frequency only. Social desirability has been viewed as both other-deception (i.e. conscious lying or impression management) and (unconscious) self-deception, reflecting a personality trait akin to conformity or agreeableness (Paulhus, 1984). Lalwani and colleagues found that persons in more horizontally individualistic societies, which value being independent, self-reliant, self-directed, and unique, show more self-deceptive enhancement, a predisposition supposedly related to narcissism. In contrast, persons in more horizontally collectivist societies, which focus on sociability and maintaining good relationships, show more impression management and put forward a favorable self-image.

Second, work has been done on the effects of questionnaire characteristics in relation to cross-cultural differences. For example, Van Dijk et al. (submitted) tested whether the domain (i.e. subject) of a questionnaire has an impact on the extent of acquiescence or extremity responding in a multicountry International Social Survey Program dataset. They found some evidence for higher acquiescence and extreme responding scores in domains with high personal relevance, such as family, than in domains with low personal relevance, such as government. Furthermore, culture-level correlations with socioeconomic indices and values indicated that wealthier countries have lower acquiescence scores, and individualist, happy countries and countries with low uncertainty avoidance have lower acquiescence scores for personally relevant domains. Extremity responding turned out to be higher in uncertainty avoidant countries (in concordance with De Jong et al., 2007, and Harzing, 2006), and countries with low subjective wellbeing, independent of the domain of the questions.

A third development can be found in multilevel studies focusing on the interaction of individual-level and culture-level variables. Smith and Fischer (2008) performed a multilevel analysis of acquiescence, extreme responding, and culture. They demonstrated interactions in response styles between individuals' predispositions and cultural context in such a way that interdependent persons show more acquiescence in more collectivistic cultures and independent persons respond more extremely in more individualistic cultures. They argue that cultural context acts as a 'press' towards different communication styles, but these effects can be reinforced or mitigated by personal characteristics. Another example of a multilevel approach that includes interaction effects was provided by De Jong (2006). He included individual-level sociodemographic and personality variables as well as country-level value dimensions in a study on social desirable responding across 25 countries and more than 12,000 respondents. Main effects were found for individualism (negatively related to social desirability) and uncertainty avoidance, power distance, and masculinity (positive correlations). In addition, the effect of individual-level conscientiousness was stronger in countries high on uncertainty avoidance, the effect of agreeableness was mitigated by country-level individualism, and the effect of extraversion was stronger in more masculine countries and countries high on power distance.

Conclusions

Most research on response styles, across cultures, finds systematic and not just random variation, indicating a substantive basis of response styles at the country level. Differences can be interpreted in terms of socioeconomic context as well as values and norms. A consistent finding is the lower level of acquiescence and social desirability in wealthy and individualistic countries. This consistency in findings is easy to explain theoretically as individualistic societies value independence and uniqueness more, whereas collectivist societies value group relations more. Therefore, communication patterns in the latter are more likely to focus on avoiding conflict and maintaining harmony, enforcing socially desirable interaction. Findings on extreme responding are a bit more mixed, but individualism seems to be relevant here as well.

In the future, researchers should be more aware of the psychological meaning of response styles in cross-cultural studies. Rather than seeing response styles as sources of bias to be eliminated, more substantive explanations should be considered. Recent research on response styles might help to advance the cross-cultural study of personality in conceptualizing response styles as communication styles that are promoted in specific cultural settings. Viewed in this light, response styles are culture-level reflections of personality and interaction patterns, and as such very relevant for the cross-cultural study of personality.

INDIGENOUS APPROACHES TO ASSESS PERSONALITY

Indigenous approaches to personality attempt to develop models of personality for a specific cultural context (Sinha, 1997). The theoretical discussion on the strengths and weaknesses of these approaches is closely related to the distinction between so-called 'emic' and 'etic' approaches that has played an important role in cross-cultural psychology (Pike, 1967). An etic approach of personality has the aim of developing a single model that captures all features of personality across the cultures of a study. An emic approach works from the premise that psychological phenomena can only be studied in

their cultural context and that applications of Western models in a non-Western context can easily lead to the inadequate imposition of Western models; so, an indigenous approach can be called emic. Traditionally, emic studies are often associated with models that are developed for use in non-Western cultures. The two approaches have often been construed as incompatible and based on different methodologies (the etic approach is more quantitative and the emic approach is more qualitative). It is now increasingly appreciated that the two approaches may be more complementary than previously assumed.

Indigenous studies of personality are particularly relevant for cross-cultural psychology when the models found in these studies are compared, explicitly or implicitly, with those developed and tested in other cultures. If such a comparison shows that some personality traits are found in both Western and non-Western countries, strong evidence is found for their universality. However, indigenous studies may not replicate Western findings. Lack of replicability could point to two kinds of construct bias in Western models of personality. First, Western factors may not show up in a non-Western context; Western factors may themselves be culture-specific. Second, personality features found in a non-Western context may not be present in a Western context. If the studies have been properly conducted, these differences between Western and non-Western personality traits provide important information about which personality traits may not be universal. As a consequence, it would be counterproductive to dismiss these indigenous factors as unimportant for psychology.

We describe the largest indigenous study of personality in more detail as it exemplifies the approach and provides insight in both the methodology of the study and the implications of such a study for Western psychology. The study has been conducted by Fanny Cheung and colleagues from Hong Kong (Cheung, 2006; Cheung et al., 1996). They were interested in the assessment of Chinese personality, starting from a local conceptualization of the concept. Their first research question involved the identification of the Chinese concept of personality. The authors used numerous sources of information to get more insight in the implicit theories of personality in China. They analyzed dictionaries, literature, and various other sources of information; in addition, they held interviews with a large sample of informants who were asked to describe their family members, friends, and other people. The purpose of this qualitative stage of the study was to get a broad picture of Chinese personality and of the way in which personality is described in Chinese. The massive number of descriptions of persons were categorized and reduced to a smaller set of questionnaire items. The final instrument, called the Chinese Personality Assessment Inventory (CPAI), consisted of 22 normal personality scales, which measure four factors: dependability, interpersonal relatedness, social potency, and individualism. Although the labels are different, these factors are quite similar to four factors of the Big Five; the only factor that was not represented was openness.

The original CPAI was revised so as to increase its clinical applicability. In addition, some scales were added, such as esthetics, with the aim of representing openness in the scale. The new scale was administered together with a standard instrument of the Big Five. A factor analysis in which the data of the latter instrument and the CPAI were combined showed that all five factors could be replicated, including openness. In addition, a sixth factor emerged that was also found when the CPAI was factor analyzed on its own. This sixth factor was called interpersonal relatedness; it is measured by various relationship-oriented constructs, such as harmony, face, renqing (relationship orientation), discipline, thrift (vs. extravagance), and traditionalism (vs. modernity).

The interpersonal relatedness factor does not show overlap with the Big Five. It may seem, therefore, that the Chinese researchers identified an indigenous construct. Cheung and colleagues provided evidence that the relatedness factor is not a linear combination of the other five factors and is correlated with real-life criteria, which provides strong support for its relevance. Much cross-cultural literature shows that China is more collectivistic than Western countries. It is probably not surprising that a comprehensive Chinese study identifies a social aspect of personality that is not well represented in Western instruments. However, there is increasing evidence that this factor is not unique for China, but that relatedness may also be a salient personality construct in Western cultures. Lin and Church (2004), investigating the replication of the interpersonal relatedness dimensions of the CPAI in Chinese American and European American samples, found good replication, suggesting that this dimension is not culture specific. Although more studies are needed to address the universality of the sixth factor, it is already clear that the relatedness factor is not indigenous for China or East Asia.

ALTERNATIVE ASSESSMENT METHODS

The field of cognitive psychology is advanced in terms of alternative assessment method. In addition to individual and group administrations of standardized intelligence tests, various alternative measures have been proposed, such as the use of real-life tasks, the assessment of elementary cognitive tasks, and psychophysiological registrations (overviews can be found in Sternberg, 2000). Furthermore, various kinds of stimuli have been employed for assessing the same underlying skill. For example, digits and names of common objects have been used to measure short-term memory span. These variations in stimuli and administration modes are relevant for cross-cultural psychology, because the patterning of cross-cultural differences may not be invariant across modes of stimuli and responses. In general, the use of stimuli with higher ecological validity is associated with a higher cognitive performance (Van de Vijver, 1997). The issue of ecological validity is particularly salient when working with illiterates and with groups that have a widely different cultural background. Historically, the pursuit of culture-free cognitive tests has always been on the agenda of cross-cultural cognitive assessment. The interest in the theme of developing an instrument in which competence and performance are identical or at least as similar as possible has not changed since the publication of the first culture-free cognitive test by Cattell (1940).

Is there a similar problem in cross-cultural personality assessment? To some extent there is. The cross-cultural validity of personality scales may be attenuated by response styles, such as social desirability, acquiescence, and extremity responding (see previous section). In addition, it may well be that the use of shorter or longer descriptions of psychological characteristics in terms of habits, preferences, or behaviors is not equally appropriate in all cultural groups. Some personality questionnaires were not developed for use in other cultures. The use of metaphors and colloquialisms may create translation problems. The clarity and conciseness of the expression in the original language may have to be sacrificed in the translation process in order to preserve the psychological meaning of the expression. In short, there are various reasons for using non-standard methods of personality assessment, that is, methods other than self-reports, in cross-cultural psychology.

There is surprisingly little interest in the use of alternative methods in cross-cultural personality. To our knowledge, there are only two kinds of non-standard assessment of personality in cross-cultural psychology. The first one builds on the culture-and-personality school (Bock, 1988), and mainly involves the use of projective instruments in a non-Western context. There are a few notable exceptions such as the use of an instrument similar to the Thematic Apperception Test to assess implicit power motives in Zambian and German children (Hofer and Chasiotis, 2004), but the general tendency is that issues of bias and equivalence are hardly ever addressed in these studies (Van de Vijver, 2000). It is unlikely that projective instruments will hold a promising future in cross-cultural personality testing as long as their psychometric basis is so shallow.

The second line of non-standard assessment of personality and cross-cultural framework is based on the work with the Nonverbal Personality Questionnaire (NPQ) (Paunonen et al., 1990; see also Paunonen and Ashton, 1998). The NPQ is a measure of the needs model developed by Murray (1938), measuring 16 traits. The stimuli consist of 136 'line drawings of a target person engaging in various trait-related behaviors, and respondents are asked to estimate the likelihood that they would engage in similar behaviors' (Paunonen et al., 2000: 221). The drawings depict situations that are similar to those described in verbal items, but with the advantage of avoiding translation problems. The questionnaire has been administered to students in Canada, England, the Netherlands, Norway, and Israel. The psychometric properties were adequate. Moreover, a concurrently administered personality questionnaire (the Personality Research Form, Jackson, 1984) showed a similar factorial structure to the NPQ. Support for the five-factor model of personality was found, both when the NPQ was analyzed separately and when the instrument was analyzed together with the Personality Research Form. This study provides evidence for the viability of non-verbal personality assessment in cross-cultural psychology. More studies using this instrument and newly developed instruments that are used in cultures that are culturally more dissimilar from one another are needed to appreciate the potential of non-verbal personality assessment in cross-cultural psychology.

CONCLUSION

Cross-cultural personality assessment and personality theory are closely linked. Theoretical developments may lead to new ways of assessing personality and new measurement tools may generate new theoretical insights. Since our chapter deals with developments in assessment, we define here three promising avenues in assessment that, if pursued properly, could lead to a better understanding of cross-cultural similarities and differences in personality. First, the impact of bias and equivalence is still underrated in cross-cultural personality psychology. As described in this chapter, the quality of some instruments has been well-established in various cultures, but it should be appreciated that the set of tested instruments is small and that equivalence cannot be taken for granted. In particular, structural equivalence should have continued attention of personality researchers. Establishing structural equivalence is a prerequisite for the examination of mean score levels across countries. Cross-cultural administration of personality measures should therefore start with comparing factor structures and nomological networks across countries, in order to accumulate information on structural and functional equivalence. Only if both structural and functional equivalence have been identified could the study of cross-cultural score comparability begin.

Second, there is a need to be more sensitive to the influence of method factors on the outcomes of cross-cultural personality assessment. We described various examples of studies in which response styles are shown to be related to country characteristics such as affluence. However, there are more method factors than response styles to take into account. Van Hemert (in press) calculated that, in a subset of 361 cross-cultural comparisons on personality variables taken from the literature, method-related factors such as the type of instrument (self-report or not), the complexity of the instrument, the cultural origin of the task, and the type of sample explained 25.8% of all cross-cultural variance. Taken together with variance accounted for by sample size, the contribution of methodological factors in cross-cultural differences exceeds 30%.

This is much more than culture-level substantial factors such as values and socioeconomic variables could explain (total of 8.7%). More information needs to be collected on comparability of specific methods of personality research.

Third, there is a need to critically examine the adequacy of close translations which ignore the potential need to adapt items (Hambleton et al., 2004). Brislin (1986) described the translation–back-translation procedure, entailing (1) a translation to the target language by an independent translator, (2) back-translation of this translated version into the original language by a second translator, and (3) comparison of the original and back-translated versions of a questionnaire in order to detect problems in the translation. In addition to this procedure, Spielberger (2006) suggests to perform translation–back-translation on a pool of items that is larger than needed, and statistically select the best items for inclusion in the questionnaire. In doing so, obtaining idiomatic comparability across languages (i.e. producing items having the same psychological meaning across languages), is more important than linguistic equivalence.

Much progress has been made in cross-cultural personality research in the last few decades. Large-scale studies have been conducted, which have increased our understanding of similarities and differences of personality structure across cultures. A good appreciation of method issues in cross-cultural personality assessment and a sophisticated use of these methods may further enhance our insights.

REFERENCES

Allik, J. and McCrae, R.R. (2002) 'A five-factor theory perspective', in R.R. McCrae and J. Allik (eds), *The Five-Factor Model of Personality Across Cultures*. New York: Kluwer Academic/Plenum Publishers, pp. 303–22.

Azhar, M.Z. and Varma, S.L. (2000) 'Mental illness and its treatment in Malaysia', in

I. Al-Issa (ed.), *Al-Junun: Mental Illness in the Islamic World*. Madison, CT: International Universities Press, pp. 163–86.

Bachman, J.G. and O'Malley, P.M. (1984) 'Yea-saying, nay-saying, and going to extremes: Black-white differences in response styles', *Public Opinion Quarterly*, 48(2): 491–509.

Barrett, P.T. and Eysenck, S. (1984) 'The assessment of personality factors across 25 countries', *Personality and Individual Differences*, 5(6): 615–32.

Barrett, P.T., Petrides, K.V., Eysenck, S.B.G. and Eysenck, H.J. (1998) 'The Eysenck Personality Questionnaire: An examination of the factorial similarity of P, E, N, and L across 34 countries', *Personality and Individual Differences*, 25(5): 805–19.

Berry, J.W., Poortinga, Y.H., Segall, M.S. and Dasen, P.R. (2002) *Cross-cultural Psychology. Research and Applications* (2nd edn). Cambridge, UK: Cambridge University Press.

Bijnen, E.J. and Poortinga, Y.H. (1988) 'The questionable value of cross-cultural comparisons with the Eysenck Personality Questionnaire', *Journal of Cross-Cultural Psychology*, 19(2): 193–202.

Bijnen, E.J., Van der Net, T.Z.J. and Poortinga, Y.H. (1986) 'On cross-cultural comparative studies with the Eysenck Personality Questionnaire', *Journal of Cross-Cultural Psychology*, 17(1): 3–16.

Bock, P.K. (1988) *Rethinking Psychological Anthropology: Continuity and Change in the Study of Human Action*. New York: Freeman.

Bond, R. and Smith, P.B. (1996) 'Culture and conformity: A meta-analysis of studies using Asch's (1952b, 1956) line judgment task', *Psychological Bulletin*, 119(1): 111–37.

Brislin, R.W. (1986) 'The wording and translation of research instruments', in W.J. Lonner and J.W. Berry (eds), *Field Methods in Cross-cultural Research*. Thousand Oaks, CA: Sage, pp. 137–64.

Butcher, J.N. (1996) (ed.), *International Adaptations of the MMPI-2: Research and Clinical Applications*. Minneapolis, MN: University of Minnesota Press.

Butcher, J.N., Atlis, M.M. and Hahn, J. (2004) 'The Minnesota Multiphasic Personality Inventory-2 (MMPI-2)', in M.J. Hilsenroth and D.L. Segal (eds), *Comprehensive Handbook of Psychological Assessment (Vol. 2): Personality Assessment*. Hoboken, NJ: Wiley, pp. 30–8.

Camilli, G. and Shepard, L.A. (1994) *Methods for Identifying Biased Test Items* (Vol. 4). Thousand Oaks: Sage.

Cattell, H.E.P. (2004) 'The Sixteen Personality Factor (16PF) Questionnaire', in M.J. Hilsenroth and D.L. Segal (eds), *Comprehensive Handbook of Psychological Assessment (Vol. 2): Personality Assessment*. Hoboken, NJ: Wiley, pp. 39–49.

Cattell, R.B. (1940) 'A culture-free intelligence test', *Journal of Educational Psychology*, 31(3): 161–79.

Cheung, F. (2006) 'A combined emic–etic approach to cross-cultural personality test development: The case of the CPAI', in Q. Jing, H. Zhang and K. Zhang (eds), *Psychological Science Around the World* (Vol. 2). London: Psychology Press, pp. 91–103.

Cheung, F.M., Leung, K., Fan, R., Song, W.Z., Zhang, J.X. and Zhang, J.P. (1996) 'Development of the Chinese Personality Assessment Inventory (CPAI)', *Journal of Cross-Cultural Psychology*, 27(2): 181–99.

Costa, P.T. Jr. and McCrae, R.R. (1992) *NEO-PI-R: Professional Manual*. Odessa, FL: Psychological Assessment Resources.

Cronbach, L.J. and Meehl, P.E. (1955) 'Construct validity in psychological tests', *Psychological Bulletin*, 52(4): 281–302.

De Jong, M. (2006) 'Response bias in international marketing research', Unpublished doctoral dissertation, Tilburg University, Tilburg.

De Jong, M.G., Steenkamp, J.B.E.M., Fox, J.P. and Baumgartner, H. (2007) 'Using Item Response Theory to measure extreme response style in marketing research: A global investigation', *Journal of Marketing Research*, 45(1): 104–15.

Dyal, J.A. (1984) 'Cross-cultural research with the Locus of Control construct', in H.M. Lefcourt (ed.), *Research with the Locus of Control Construct (Vol. 3). Extensions and Limitations*. New York: Academic Press, pp. 209–305.

Eysenck, H.J. and Eysenck, S.B.G. (1975) *Manual of the Eysenck Personality Questionnaire*. London: Hodder & Stoughton.

Eysenck, H.J. and Eysenck, S.B.G. (1976) *Psychoticism as a Dimension of Personality*. London: Hodder & Stoughton.

Eysenck, S.B.G., Barrett, P., Spielberger, C., Evans, F.J. and Eysenck, H.J. (1986) 'Cross-cultural comparisons of personality dimensions: England and America', *Personality and Individual Differences*, 7(2): 209–14.

Fischer, R., Fontaine, J.R.J., Van de Vijver, F.J.R. and Van Hemert, D.A. (submitted) 'What is style and what is bias in cross-cultural comparisons? An examination of acquiescent response styles in cross-cultural research'.

Grimm, S.D. and Church, A.T. (1999) 'A cross-cultural study of response biases in personality measures', *Journal of Research in Personality*, 33(4): 415–41.

Hambleton, R.K., Merenda, P. and Spielberger, C. (2004) (eds), *Adapting Educational and Psychological Tests for Cross-cultural Assessment*. Hillsdale, NJ: Lawrence Erlbaum.

Handel, R.W. and Ben-Porath, Y.S. (2000) 'Multicultural assessment with the MMPI-2: Issues for research and practice', in R.H. Dana (ed.), *Handbook of Cross-Cultural and Multicultural Personality Assessment*. Mahwah, NJ: Lawrence Erlbaum, pp. 229–45.

Harzing, A-W. (2006) 'Response styles in cross-national survey research. A 26-country study', *International Journal of Cross-Cultural Management*, 6(2): 243–66.

Heine, S.J. and Renshaw, K. (2002) 'Interjudge agreement, self-enhancement, and liking: Cross-cultural divergences', *Personality and Social Psychology Bulletin*, 28(5): 578–87.

Hendriks, A.A.J., Perugini, M., Angleitner, A., Bratko, D., Conner, M., De Fruyt, E., Hrebickova, M., Johnson, J. A., Murakami, T., Nagy, J., Nussbaum, S., Ostendorf, F., Fornells, A. and Ruisel, I. (2003) 'The Five-Factor Personality Inventory: Cross-cultural generalizability across 13 countries', *European Journal of Personality*, 17(5): 347–73.

Hendriks, A.A.J., Hofstee, W.K.B. and De Raad, B. (1999) 'The Five-Factor Personality Inventory (FFPI)', *Personality and Individual Differences*, 27(2): 307–25.

Hofer, J. and Chasiotis, A. (2004) 'Methodological considerations of applying a tat-type picture-story test in cross-cultural research: A comparison of German and Zambian adolescents', *Journal of Cross-Cultural Psychology*, 35(2): 224–41.

Hofer, S.M. and Eber, H.W. (2002) 'Second-order factor structure of the Cattell Sixteen Personality Factor Questionnaire', in B. De Raad and M. Perugini (eds), *Big Five Assessment*. Göttingen: Hogrefe & Huber, pp. 397–409.

Hofstede, G. (1980) *Culture's Consequences*. Beverly Hills, CA: Sage.

Holland, J.L. (1985) *Making Vocational Choices: A Theory of Vocational Personalities and Work Environments* (2nd edn). Englewood Cliffs, NJ: Prentice Hall.

House, R.J., Hanges, P.J., Javidan, M., Dorfman, P.W. and Gupta, V. (2004) (eds), *Culture, Leadership, and Organizations: The GLOBE Study of 62 Societies*. Thousand Oaks, CA: Sage.

Hui, C.H. and Triandis, H.C. (1989) 'Effects of culture and reponse format on extreme response style', *Journal of Cross-Cultural Psychology*, 20(3): 296–309.

Jackson, D.N. (1984) *Personality Research Form Manual*. Port Huron, MI: Research Psychologists Press.

Jensen, A.R. (1980) *Bias in Mental Testing*. New York: The Free Press.

Johnson, T.P., Kulesa, P., Cho, Y.I. and Shavitt, S. (2005) 'The relation between culture and response styles: Evidence from 19 countries', *Journal of Cross-Cultural Psychology*, 36(2): 264–77.

Johnson, T.P. and Van de Vijver, F.J.R. (2003) 'Social desirability in cross-cultural research', in J.A. Harkness, F.J.R. Van de Vijver and P. Ph. Mohler (eds), *Cross-cultural Survey Methods*. New York: Wiley, pp. 195–204.

Kaiser, H.F., Hunka, S. and Bianchini, J.C. (1971) 'Relating factors between studies based upon different individuals', *Multivariate Behavioral Research*, 6(4): 409–22.

Lalwani, A.K., Shavitt, S. and Johnson, T. (2006) 'What is the relation between cultural orientation and socially desirable responding?', *Journal of Personality and Social Psychology*, 90(1): 165–78.

Leung, K., Bond, M.H., De Carrasquel, S., Munoz, C., Hernandez, M., Murakami, F., Yamaguchi, S., Bierbrauer, G. and Singelis, T. M. (2002) 'Social axioms: The search for universal dimensions of general beliefs about how the world functions', *Journal of Cross-Cultural Psychology*, 33(3): 286–302.

Lin, T.Y. and Church, A.T. (2004) 'Are indigenous Chinese personality dimensions culture-specific? An investigation of the Chinese Personality Assessment Inventory in Chinese American and European

American samples', *Journal of Cross-Cultural Psychology*, 35(5): 586–605.

McCrae, R.R. and Costa, P.T. Jr. (1983) 'Social desirability scales: More substance than style', *Journal of Consulting and Clinical Psychology*, 51(6): 882–88.

McCrae, R.R. and Costa, P.T. Jr. (1996) 'Toward a new generation of personality theories: Theoretical contexts for the Five-Factor Model', in J.S. Wiggins (ed.), *The Five-Factor Model of Personality: Theoretical Perspectives*. New York: Guilford, pp. 51–87.

McCrae, R.R. and Costa, P.T. Jr. (1997) 'Personality structure as a human universal', *American Psychologist*, 52(5): 509–16.

McCrae, R.R. and Costa, P.T. Jr. (1999) 'A Five-Factor Theory of personality', in L.A. Pervin and O.P. John (eds), *Handbook of Personality: Theory and Research* (2nd edn). New York: Guilford, pp. 139–53.

McCrae, R.R. and Terracciano, A. (2008) 'The five-factor model and its correlates in individuals and cultures', in F.J.R. Van de Vijver, D.A. Van Hemert and Y.H. Poortinga (eds), *Individuals and Cultures in Multilevel Analysis*. Mahwah, NJ: Erlbaum, pp. 249–83.

McCrae, R.R., Terracciano, A. and 78 Members of the Personality Profiles of Cultures Project (2005a) 'Universal features of personality traits from the observer's perspective: Data from 50 cultures', *Journal of Personality and Social Psychology*, 88(3): 547–61.

McCrae, R.R., Terracciano, A. and 78 Members of the Personality Profiles of Cultures Project (2005b) 'Personality profiles of cultures: Aggregate personality traits', *Journal of Personality and Social Psychology*, 89(3): 407–25.

Messick, S. (1989) 'Validity', in R.L. Linn (ed.), *Educational Measurement* (3rd edn). London: Collier Macmillan Publishers, pp. 13–104.

Murray, H.A. (1938) *Explorations in Personality*. New York: Oxford Press.

Nichols, D., Padilla, J. and Gomez-Maqueo, E. (2000) 'Issues in the cross-cultural adaptation and use of the MMPI-2', in R.H. Dana (ed.), *Handbook of Cross-Cultural and Multicultural Personality Assessment*. Mahwah, NJ: Lawrence Erlbaum, pp. 247–66.

Paulhus, D.L. (1984) 'Two-component models of socially desirable responding', *Journal of Personality and Social Psychology*, 46(3): 598–609.

Paunonen, S.V. and Ashton, M.C. (1998) 'The structured assessment of personality across cultures', *Journal of Cross-Cultural Psychology*, 29(1): 150–70.

Paunonen, S.V., Jackson, D.N. and Keinonen, M. (1990) 'The structured nonverbal assessment of personality', *Journal of Personality*, 58(3): 481–502.

Paunonen, S.V., Zeidner, M., Engvik, H.A., Oosterveld, P., Maliphant, R. (2000) 'The nonverbal assessment of personality in five cultures', *Journal of Cross-Cultural Psychology*, 31(2): 220–39.

Pike, K. (1967) *Language in Relation to a Unified Theory of the Structure of Human Behavior*. The Hague: Mouton

Poortinga, Y.H., Van de Vijver, F.J.R. and Van Hemert, D.A. (2002) 'Cross-cultural equivalence of the Big Five: A tentative interpretation of the evidence', in R.R. McCrae and J. Allik (eds), *The Five-Factor Model of Personality Across Cultures*. New York: Kluwer Academic/Plenum Publishers, pp. 281–302.

Rolland, J.P. (2002) 'The cross-cultural generalizability of the Five-Factor Model of personality', in R.R. McCrae and J. Allik (eds), *The Five-Factor Model of Personality Across Cultures*. New York: Kluwer Academic/Plenum Publishers, pp. 7–28.

Ross, C.E. and Mirowsky, J. (1984) 'Socially-desirable response and acquiescence in a cross-cultural survey of mental health', *Journal of Health and Social Behavior*, 25(2): 189–97.

Rossier, J. (2005) 'A review of the cross-cultural equivalence of frequently used personality inventories', *International Journal for Educational and Vocational Guidance*, 5(2): 175–88.

Rotter, J.B. (1966) 'Generalized expectancies for internal versus external control of reinforcement', *Psychological Monographs*, 80(1): whole no. 609.

Rounds, J. and Tracey, T.J. (1996) 'Cross-cultural structural equivalence of RIASEC models and measures', *Journal of Counseling Psychology*, 43(3): 310–29.

Schmitt, D. and Allik, J. (2005) 'Simultaneous administration of the Rosenberg Self-Esteem Scale in 53 nations: Exploring the universal and culture-specific features of global self-esteem', *Journal of Personality and Social Psychology*, 89(4): 623–42.

Schwartz, S.H. (1994) 'Beyond individualism/collectivism: New cultural dimensions of values', in U. Kim, H.C. Triandis, C. Kagitcibasi, S.C. Choi and G. Yoon (eds), *Individualism and Collectivism*. Thousand Oaks, CA: Sage, pp. 85–119.

Sinha, D. (1997) 'Indigenizing psychology', in J.W. Berry, Y.H. Poortinga and J. Pandey (eds), *Handbook of Cross-cultural Psychology: Vol. 1. Theory and Method* (2nd edn). Boston: Allyn and Bacon, pp. 129–69.

Smith, P.B. (2004) 'Acquiescent response bias as an aspect of cultural communication style', *Journal of Cross-Cultural Psychology*, 35(1): 50–61.

Smith, P.B. and Fischer, R. (2008) 'Acquiescence, extreme response bias and levels of cross-cultural analysis', in F.J.R. Van de Vijver, D.A. Van Hemert and Y.H. Poortinga (eds), *Individuals and Cultures in Multilevel Analysis*. Mahwah, NJ: Erlbaum, pp. 285–314.

Smith, P.B., Peterson, M.F., Schwartz, S.H., Ahmad, A.H., Akande, D., Andersen, J.A. et al. (2002) 'Culture values, sources of guidance, and their relevance to managerial behavior: A 47-nation study', *Journal of Cross-Cultural Psychology*, 33(2): 188–208.

Smith, P.B., Trompenaars, F. and Dugan, S. (1995) 'The Rotter Locus of Control scale in 43 countries: A test of cultural relativity', *International Journal of Psychology*, 30(3): 377–400.

Spielberger, C.D. (2006) 'Cross-cultural assessment of emotional states and personality traits', *European Psychologist*, 11(4): 297–303.

Sternberg, R.J. (2000) (ed.), *Handbook of Intelligence*. Cambridge, UK: Cambridge University Press.

Triandis, H.C. and Vassiliou, V. (1972) 'A comparative analysis of subjective culture', in H.C. Triandis (ed.), *The Analysis of Subjective Culture*. New York: Wiley, pp. 299–335.

Triandis, H.C., Carnevale, P., Gelfand, M., Robert, C., Wasti, A., Probst, T., Kashima, E.S., Dragonas, T., Chan, D., Chen, X.P., Kim, U., De Dreu, C., Van De Vliert, E., Iwao, S., Ohbuchi, K. and Schmitz, P. (2001) 'Culture and deception in business negotiations: A multilevel analysis', *International Journal of Cross-Cultural Management*, 1(1): 73–90.

Van de Vijver, F.J.R. (1997) 'Meta-analysis of cross-cultural comparisons of cognitive test performance', *Journal of Cross-Cultural Psychology*, 28(6): 678–709.

Van de Vijver, F.J.R. (2000) 'The nature of bias', in R.H. Dana (ed.), *Handbook of Cross-cultural and Multicultural Personality Assessment*. Mahwah, NJ: Erlbaum, pp. 87–106.

Van de Vijver, F.J.R. and Leung, K. (1997) *Methods and Data Analysis for Cross-Cultural Research*. Newbury Park, CA: Sage.

Van de Vijver, F.J.R. and Poortinga, Y.H. (1994) 'Methodological issues in cross-cultural studies on parental rearing behavior and psychopathology', in C. Perris, W.A. Arrindell and M. Eisemann (eds), *Parenting and Psychopathology*. Chichester: Wiley, pp. 173–97.

Van Dijk, T.K., Datema, F., Piggen, A.J.H.F., Welten, S.C.M. and Van de Vijver, F.J.R. (submitted) 'Toward a model of acquiescence and extremity scoring for cross-cultural research'.

Van Hemert, D.A. (in press) 'Cross-cultural meta-analysis', in D. Matsumoto and F.J.R. Van de Vijver (eds), *Cross-Cultural Research Methods*. Oxford University Press.

Van Hemert, D.A., Van de Vijver, F.J.R., Poortinga, Y.H. and Georgas, J. (2002) 'Structural and functional equivalence of the Eysenck Personality Questionnaire within and between countries', *Personality and Individual Differences*, 33(8): 1229–49.

Van Herk, H., Poortinga, Y.H., Verhallen, T.M.M. (2004) 'Response styles in rating scales: Evidence of method bias in data from six EU countries', *Journal of Cross-Cultural Psychology*, 35(3): 346–60.

4

Measurement Issues Concerning a Personality Model Spanning Temperament, Character, and Experience

Chris J. Jackson

INTRODUCTION

Personality research (i.e. the study of individual differences in affect, cognition, behavior, experience, and learning) has had a considerable impact across the whole of psychology and its applications. Nevertheless, the study of personality is split by different research foci (i.e. theories and perspectives) that traditionally appear to be incompatible with each other. This chapter aims to contrast the biological, social-cognitive and experiential foci, and propose a hybrid model of personality and learning that uniquely also places similar emphasis on theory and measurement. The scope of this review is limited to approach and avoidance pathways that span these different research foci. Discussion of the different foci is limited to an integrative and measurement perspective as opposed to providing a complete review of the evidence in favor of one focus or the other. It is

argued that the proposed hybrid methodology outlined in this chapter will lead to a better understanding of personality, motivation, and learning.

Approach and avoidance are motivational tendencies presumed to account for individual differences in behavior, mood, and cognition and learning (Elliot and Thrash, 2002; Gable et al., 2003). Approach and avoidance motivations differ as a function of valence, such that *approach* motivation occurs when behavior is instigated by the possibility of reward and positive outcomes, whereas *avoidance* motivation involves a desire to avoid punishment and negative outcomes (Elliot, 1999). Recently, the significance of approach and avoidance pathways in personality theory has increased because they have been considered as unifying constructs in personality (e.g. Carver et al., 2000; Elliot and Thrash, 2002). It has been argued that the idea of approach and avoidance is 'so conceptually central that it may be used to organize and integrate seemingly diverse approaches to personality' (Elliot and Thrash 2002: 804), and that the dual processes of approach and avoidance collectively provide a conceptual lens through which diverse approaches to personality may be understood. Additionally, the idea that approach and avoidance pathways are associated with learnt responses to environmental stimuli associated with reward and punishment leads to the perspective that approach and avoidance pathways are associated with learning and motivation (e.g. Gray and McNaughton, 2000). This perspective argues that approach and avoidance pathways might provide an explanation of the dynamics of personality as opposed to a simple description of personality.

The fundamental importance of approach and avoidance is clarified by its prominence in almost all major foci of personality research. Biological and Big Five theorists explain approach and avoidance in terms of extraversion and neuroticism (Eysenck, 1967; Costa and McCrae, 1992); Gray (1970) explains approach and avoidance in terms of the behavioral activation system (BAS) and the behavioral inhibition system (BIS); and Zuckerman (1994) makes reference to sensation seeking which he argues is a combination of the two (i.e. high approach and low avoidance). Socio-cognitive theorists, on the other hand, understand approach and avoidance in terms of learning and avoidance goals (Vandewalle, 1997) and the approach engendered by self-efficacy in achieving goals (Bandura, 1997).

Overlaps between the different models associated with the different research foci are illustrated in Figure 4.1 It is emphasized that this represents a simplification since different authors have often taken a variety of perspectives. Eysenck, for example, primarily claims a biological basis for his personality model (e.g. Eysenck, 1967), while also later making reference to socio-cognitive influences from learning. While acknowledging that most of the models listed in Figure 4.1 can be construed to cover multiple foci,

the figure still remains useful in listing the primary focus of each model.

Despite the clear centrality of approach and avoidance pathways across these different research foci, the emphasis on their importance differs. On the one hand, Gray's constructs of approach and avoidance are theory driven and well developed a priori explanations of approach and avoidance (e.g. Corr, 2004; Gray, 1970, 1982; Gray and McNaughton, 2000), whereas others are statistically derived, in that approach and avoidance theory was added post hoc to explain dimensions underlying surface level behavior (e.g. Eysenck, 1967; Zuckerman, 1994). There are also personality models with no major theoretical basis (such as the Big Five) and some models of experiential learning with no discernible basis in personality (e.g. Kolb, 1984). All this is pertinent because *theory driven* models of approach and avoidance learning tend to have weak measurement systems. For instance, considerable research documents the constant problems in measuring Gray's model (e.g. Jackson, 2003; Smillie et al., 2006; Quilty and Oakman, 2004) whereas measurement-first models such as the Big Five (e.g. Costa and McCrae, 1992) tend to have a weaker theoretical basis (see Block, 1995).

As far as is known, there are just two broad personality models that explicitly aim to develop a hybrid model of personality and learning. For the purpose of this discussion, the word 'hybrid' is used to describe a model that is designed *from the outset* to span more than one of the multiple research foci described in Figure 4.1. The first is Cloninger's personality-based model (Cloninger et al., 1993) and the second is Jackson's learning in personality model (Jackson, 2005). Jackson's proposed hybrid model corresponds more closely to the middle path between learning and personality, resides at the juxtaposition between biological, cognitive, and experiential research foci, and was developed with a focus on theory and measurement. The result is a model of learning in personality which has a basis in approach and avoidance and

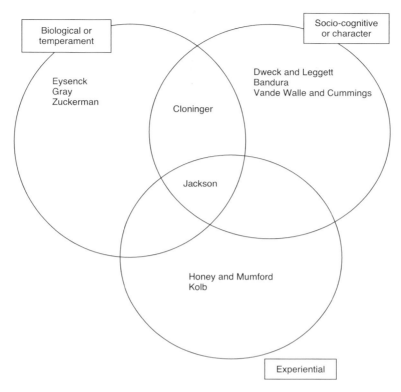

Figure 4.1   A simplified figurative representation of the major models of approach and avoidance

which has the additional aim of differentiating between functional and dysfunctional learning.

IMPULSIVITY-SENSATION SEEKING (IMP-SS) CLUSTER AS THE BIOLOGICAL BASIS OF APPROACH AND AVOIDANCE WITHIN THE PROPOSED HYBRID MODEL

The central relevance of impulsivity-sensation seeking (Imp-SS) as a trait cluster is highlighted by its centrality in many personality taxonomies (e.g. Cloninger et al., 1993; Gray, 1981; Zuckerman, 1979). Even Hans J. Eysenck, who strongly advocated super-factors of personality (e.g. Eysenck, 1967) developed a specific taxonomy of impulsivity

(Eysenck and Eysenck, 1978), and accepted the importance of this dimension (Eysenck, 1993). Considerable evidence suggests that Imp-SS has a particularly strong heritability (Eysenck, 1993; Pickering, 2004) even against a background that there is now reasonable evidence in favor of at least a partial physiological or genetically driven basis to much of personality (Eaves et al., 1989; Fulker et al., 1980; Revelle, 1995).

Researchers however tend to differ in how they view the details of the biological basis of Imp-SS since there is some dispute over its basis in dopamine or serotonin pathways (e.g. Cloninger, 1987; Coscina, 1997; Gray, 1970; Zuckerman, 1979). Dopamine has been argued to be a biological basis for Imp-SS behaviors such as disinhibition, substance abuse, and antisocial behavior (e.g. Davids et al., 2003; Di Chiara, 1995; Goldman and

Fishbein, 2000) and serotonin has also been argued to be related to Imp-SS behaviors such as substance abuse, antisocial behavior and aggression (e.g. Dolan and Anderson, 2003; Moeller et al., 1994). Some research, however, advocate a cognitive basis (e.g. Dickman, 1990).

From this viewpoint, it is not surprising that Imp-SS is seen as predicting dysfunctional approach oriented behaviors such as criminality, gambling, alcohol use, and adultery (Eysenck and Gudjonsson, 1989; Kambouropoulos and Staiger, 2001; McAlister et al., 2005; Parker and Bagby, 1997; Zuckerman, 1994). In organizational settings, Imp-SS has been associated with a variety of negative outcomes, such as propensity to quit, job strain, and low job performance in service workers (Reio and Sanders-Reio, 2006).

There is, however a smaller literature concerning potential positive outcomes of Imp-SS. First, impulsivity may be both functional as well as dysfunctional. Functional impulsivity involves seizing the moment and making appropriate but quick decisions. Dickman demonstrates that functional impulsivity is related to functional outcomes (Dickman, 1990). Brunas-Wagstaff et al. (1994) argue dysfunctional impulsives have difficulty inhibiting inappropriate responses and functional impulsives have a rapid information-processing style, which is advantageous when positive outcomes are dependent on quick decision-making. Jackson (2001) reports that this trait cluster positively predicts work performance.

Second, Imp-SS is associated with successful learning. Ball and Zuckerman (1990, 1992) found people high in Imp-SS learnt faster regardless of the availability of reinforcement, and Pickering (2004) argued high Imp-SS is associated with successful learning and problem solving. Raine et al. (2002) took behavioral measures of Imp-SS in children who were 3 years old. They found support for their prediction that, by 11 years of age, high Imp-SS scorers would have higher IQs. They conclude that young children's stimulus seeking creates an enriched environment that stimulates cognitive development and learning.

In summary, research indicates substantial evidence in favor of the biological basis of Imp-SS that would reflect an appetitive drive (an approach system presumably related to dopamine) while also reflecting a low inhibition drive (presumably based on an avoidance system linked to serotonin). While Zuckerman (1994) mainly focuses on dysfunctional components of sensation seeking, Dickman (1990) and Arnett (1994) expressly argue that Imp-SS can be related to functional outcomes, especially if a cognitive perspective to Imp-SS is introduced. However, none of these perspectives capitalize on another positive attribute related to Imp-SS which is its potential basis for learning as proposed by Ball and Zuckerman (1992) and Raine et al. (2002). One controversial conclusion from these findings is that Imp-SS is related to 'real-world' learning in which stimuli possess a confusing mix of approach and avoidance reinforcement such that Imp-SS is generally related to high approach and low avoidance learning. Potentially the separate measures of approach and avoidance advocated in Gray's RST may be better suited to the laboratory in which reward and punishment stimuli can be independently provided.

Based on these arguments the proposed hybrid model (Jackson, 2005) incorporates Imp-SS as a psychobiological construct in a model of 'learning in personality'. Sensation seeking (i.e. the Imp-SS cluster) represents the measurable biological basis of exploratory learning and is related to high approach and low avoidance. Jackson places an emphasis on the capacity of sensation seekers to be exploratory and curious as opposed to the emphasis of Zuckerman's (1978) model of risk taking and danger seeking. Moreover the design of the scale overcomes many of the criticisms that have been made of Zuckerman's sensation seeking scales by Arnett (1994) and J. Jackson and Maraun (1996). According to the proposed hybrid model, sensation seeking is the biological basis of functional and dysfunctional learning.

In line with the argument that socio-cognitive and environmental influences might lead to functional learning (see Arnett, 1994; Dickman, 1990), Jackson is also influenced by Cloninger et al.'s (1993) notion of temperament and character, with temperament representing the stable, biological basis of personality and character representing the more socio-cognitive components of learning. Elliot and Thrash (2002) advocate a similar kind of split to Cloninger without using this terminology.

For sensation seeking to be beneficial it may need to be focused, controlled, delayed or redirected, thus accounting for its positive and negative consequences. According to Jackson's model, socio-cognitive processes modify sensation seeking to produce functionally learnt outcomes. It is argued that the socio-cognitive processes have developed at a later evolutionary point in time to modify the instinctive urge to explore so that it becomes a functional pro-social activity. Without the positive influence of advanced socio-cognitive processes, the instinctive urge to explore is much more dysfunctional (a classic example being failure to delay gratification resulting in smash-and-grab behavior typical of delinquency).

The socio-cognitive processes developed by Jackson (2005) are very different to Cloninger et al.'s (1993) character components of personality, yet both models claim to have a basis in the socio-cognitive research focus shown in Figure 4.1. To understand Jackson's model of functional and dysfunctional learning it is crucial to examine the strengths and weaknesses of Cloninger's model which might already be thought of as achieving most of these aims already.

APPROACH AND AVOIDANCE ACROSS TEMPERAMENT AND CHARACTER – A MOVE FROM CLONINGER'S MODEL TO THE PROPOSED HYBRID MODEL

From a general approach and avoidance perspective, Cloninger et al. (1993) differentiates between biological and social-cognitive constructs based on their respective differences in terms of procedural learning (data-driven habit and skill learning) and propositional learning (concept-driven learning). According to Cloninger's model, perceptual memory processes relating to temperament operate independently of conceptual processes related to character. Research supports this disassociation in the central nervous system (Roediger et al., 1990).

Temperament is argued to be found in the subcortical, primeval part of the brain. Another way of thinking of temperament is that it is thought to be a distal, biologically based cause of personality, grounded in phylogenetically old learning systems (Cloninger, 1987). It may also be defined as the automatic associative responses to basic emotional stimuli that determine habits and skills (Cloninger, 1987). Finally, temperament components are argued to be stable and uninfluenced by socio-cultural learning. Alternative and similar words for 'temperament' used by other researchers include 'biological', 'non-conscious', 'procedurally learnt', 'non-controlled', and 'instinctive'.

Cloninger et al. (1993) contended that neocortical or conscious processes of the brain relate to character and as a consequence associated behaviors are weakly heritable, subject to learning by insight. Character refers to concepts about self and relations to others that develop over time as a function of social learning and maturation of interpersonal behavior. Character influences behavior through conscious decision-making, self-regulation, insight learning and self-awareness (Cloninger et al., 1993). Alternative words for 'character' include 'conscious', 'social', 'learnt', 'controlled', 'agentic doing', 'self-regulated', 'self-aware', 'voluntary', and 'cognitive'.

In terms of measurement, Cloninger developed the Temperament and Character Inventory (TCI) to measure temperament and character dimensions. Cloninger's model divides temperament into four scales. Harm avoidance (HA) represents the avoidance system in that it refers to a tendency to avoid punishment, novelty, and omission of rewards. Novelty seeking (NS) concerns a tendency to frequently engage in exploratory activity and to experience intense exhilaration in response to novel stimuli. Novelty seeking represents the approach system, is associated with response to reward and is based on the meso-limbic dopaminergic pathways (Cloninger, 1987; Gray, 1987; Pickering and Gray, 1999). Two other scales are also concerned with temperament, but are much less clearly related to approach and avoidance. These are reward dependence (RD) – which is not as similar to BAS as novelty seeking – and persistence (Cloninger et al., 1993). Character is divided into three scales termed self-directedness (SD) – which measures something akin to conscientiousness; cooperativeness (C) – which refers to something akin to sociability and agreeableness; and self-transcendence (ST) – which refers to feelings about nature and the universe (Cloninger et al., 1993).

Cloninger's structural model of personality provides a well-defined framework within which to describe potential biological and socio-cognitive influences on personality. Cloninger's theoretical contribution should not be underestimated. The model, however, has the following limitations:

1   There has not been a great deal of research into the temperament/character split, and whether it can simply be represented by the dichotomy envisaged by Cloninger.
2   Cloninger et al.'s (1993) proposed measurement model argues for a hierarchical structure to personality which is in fact also associated with Eysenck and Eysenck's (1991) Giant Three model and Costa and McCrae's (1992) Big Five model. The hierarchical model of personality provides structure by arguing that superfactors of personality are aggregates of primary scales. The hierarchical model is a consequence of these researchers' model development based on exploratory factor analysis and suggests that there is little real interaction between the temperament and character constructs in Cloninger's model.
3   While temperament primary scales have a general basis in approach and avoidance and a clear

link to Gray's model, Cloninger's choice of character variables is based largely on observation and factor analysis (Cloninger et al., 1993). Cloninger's model fails to build upon well-known cognitive and social models of personality (such as goal orientation as shown in Figure 4.1) and in fact remains firmly within the trait theory perspective of personality.
4   While the temperament dimensions seem heritable, at least one study has found that character is as heritable as temperament (Gillespie et al., 2003). Cloninger's own theory would suggest that character should be less heritable than temperament.
5   The model has a very clinical orientation and has achieved little impact outside of this field.
6   The model does not attempt to include the research focus of experiential learning.
7   The model does not attempt to measure functional and dysfunctional learning.

Developing Cloninger's general concepts of temperament and character, the proposed hybrid model argues that sensation seeking is a distal predictor of behavior, and character or conscious scales are proximal mediators of the distal scale. Proximal character components are seen as re-expressions of distal temperament such that functional or dysfunctional outcomes might result. Use of structural equation modeling (SEM) terms is deliberate since SEM provides a theoretical perspective as well as an applied measurement methodology, in which the prediction of actual behavior is expressly built into a theory-based model of learning in personality. Such a perspective extends and develops initial exploratory work by Cloninger et al., (1993), Elliot and Thrash (2002), Humphreys and Revelle (1984), Jackson and Francis (2004), and Ortony et al. (2005). While Cloninger's theory hints at a possible mediating relationship of character on temperament (e.g. Cloninger et al., 1993), a review of the literature shows such a possibility has yet to be instigated.

The proposed hybrid model deviates from Cloninger in arguing that prior theoretical work from the socio-cognitive and experiential research foci should be incorporated into character and to understand why, it is essential to review the main socio-cognitive and experiential models of learning in personality.

THE THEORETICAL STRUCTURE OF THE PROPOSED HYBRID MODEL

Chen et al. (2000) propose and validate a socio-cognitive applied model including goals (Locke and Latham, 1990), general self-efficacy, specific self-efficacy for a given situation (Bandura, 1999), goal orientation (VanderWalle and Cummings, 1997) and state anxiety. Their model was not tested outside of the educational domain, and did not include the biological basis of personality. It does, however, provide a very different perspective to Cloninger's character variables. Influenced by Chen et al.'s (2000) choice of socio-cognitive variables, Jackson (2005) argues character can be conceptualized in terms of goal-oriented achievers, conscientious achievers, and emotionally intelligent achievers as well as an experiential learning pathway that includes deep learning achievers. It is argued that sensation seeking is mediated by a series of pathways comprising these scales such that high sensation seeking can be re-expressed as functional or dysfunctional behavior according to the effects of the socio-cognitive and experiential components of the model.

GOAL-ORIENTED ACHIEVER

Goal orientation suggests that people vary in the extent to which they have a learning orientation toward tasks (e.g. Dweck, 1986, 1989). The most useful and adaptive goal orientation is learning goal orientation which refers to a tendency to develop competence by acquiring new skills and mastering new situations (Dweck and Leggett, 1988; VandeWalle and Cummings, 1997). A learning orientation reflects a desire to develop competence by mastering new skills and developing oneself to deal with new situations. People with a learning orientation tend to pursue an adaptive or learning response pattern which is associated with persistence in the face of failure. They use more complex learning strategies and pursue specific, difficult and challenging goals and tasks. In line with the views of Elliot and Thrash (2002) and Locke and Latham (1990) a learning goal orientation is seen as a socio-cognitive approach mechanism (see Figure 4.1). In the learning goal orientation, effort is instrumental for developing the ability needed for future task mastery.

High goal orientation on its own is unlikely to be enough to redirect sensation seeking toward functional and adaptive learning. Take dysfunctional outcomes, such as substance abuse and binge eating, which involve a process consisting of planning and goal-focused behavior. In concrete terms this consists of a purchase, preparation, and consummation (Dawe and Loxton, 2004). The same can be said for organized crime and white-collar crimes, such as identity theft or fraud, which involve a great deal of carefully considered business-like activity, but is nonetheless dysfunctional and antisocial. Goal orientation provides the motivation to effectively achieve either functional or dysfunctional success but has little to say about what goals are initially set. It is therefore argued that other cognitions are required that guide the goal focus towards functional or dysfunctional outcomes. Therefore, the learning pathway between sensation seeking and goal-oriented achiever is mediated by pro-social cognitions which orient goals towards directing behavior towards functional outcomes.

The cognitions that seem likely to influence goal orientation were chosen to represent three different components of learning in personality. Each can be thought of as mediating the relationship between sensation seeking and goal-oriented achieving such that high scorers will have a tendency towards functional behaviors and low scorers will have a tendency towards dysfunctional behaviors.

CONSCIENTIOUS ACHIEVER – A PROPENSITY TO BE RESPONSIBLE AND TO WORK HARD

Conscientiousness is the second socio-cognitive scale included in the proposed hybrid model and is derived from the Big Five which has a basis in exploratory factor analysis. Conscientiousness refers to behavior that is 'responsible, dependable, persistent, and achievement-oriented' (Barrick and Mount, 1993: 111) and describes a desire for self-regulation and consequently to follow one's conscience (Costa and McCrae, 1992). Moreover, conscientious individuals are represented as being organized, reliable, hard-working, determined, self-disciplined, and achievement oriented (Costa and McCrae, 1992). Several authors maintain that conscientiousness is important to functional learning outcomes, especially in organizational settings (Barrick and Mount, 1991; Hogan and Holland, 2003; Martocchio and Judge, 1997). The idea of the conscientious achiever being dependable, responsible, orderly and cautious fits in well with a model in which conscientiousness is a learned, cognitive based skill.

A great deal of empirical evidence argues that conscientiousness is probably the most predictive of the Big Five personality traits (Byrne et al, 2005; Hogan and Holland, 2003; Liao and Chuang, 2004). Several meta-analyses have also concluded that conscientiousness is related to functional learning outcomes such as job performance and beneficial health (Barrick and Mount, 1991; Bogg and Roberts, 2004; Dudley et al., 2006; Hogan and Holland, 2003; Ones and Viswesvaran, 1996; Tett et al., 1991).

However conscientiousness can be seen as simply part of a more complex cognitive process. Barrick et al. (1993) report that goals mediate the relationship between conscientiousness and two measures of job proficiency supervisory ratings for sales representatives. Gellatly (1996) finds that goals and expectancy mediate relationships between conscientiousness and performance on arithmetic tasks, and Barrick et al. (2002) report that conscientiousness was mediated by motivational constructs in the prediction of job performance in a sales job. As a result, conscientiousness is seen as a potential pathway, but not the sole pathway, between sensation seeking and goal orientation.

EMOTIONALLY INTELLIGENT ACHIEVER – A RATIONAL AND EMOTIONALLY INDEPENDENT THINKER

Trait emotional intelligence refers to the ability to direct and regulate emotions in a constructive and independent way such that positive outcomes are achieved. It is argued that emotional intelligence refers to an emotional state that leaves constructive behaviors open to oneself (Petrides and Furnham, 2000). According to the hybrid model, a calm, rational, and independent person is better able to choose appropriate behaviors (i.e. emotionally intelligent person), whereas a person dependent upon chance, luck, and others has a limited repertoire of behaviors available (i.e. non-emotionally intelligent person). An emotionally intelligent achiever is a functional learner who has the capacity to be objective in understanding problems, and has emotional independence from others and from chance. In being emotionally intelligent, intuition and chance are rejected and logical and rational ways of understanding are developed. This is a somewhat different definition of emotional intelligence to the more mainstream ones.

While the relationship between emotional intelligence and functional learning outcomes is likely to be positive, its relationship to dysfunctional learning outcomes is likely to be either positive or negative. High-scoring emotional intelligent achievers will tend to be functional learners due to their rationality and independence and low scorers will tend to be dysfunctional due to their dependence on chance and others. However, the relationship between emotional intelligent achievers with other scales in the proposed hybrid will be more complex with some positive and some negative relationships. It is argued that conscientious achievers tend to be emotionally dependent upon others (thus the relationship between conscientious achievers and emotional intelligent achievers will be negative), because the learning involved in becoming conscientious, hardworking, and striving will be related to emotional neediness. The relationship between emotionally intelligent achievers and goal-oriented achievers is likely to be negative because emotionally independent people will tend to be emotionally independent and therefore reject the self-imposed constraints of goals.

The negative pathways between conscientious achievers and emotionally intelligent achievers and between emotionally intelligent achievers and goal orientation achievers add complexity and depth to the proposed model of learning in personality. These negative pathways provide constraints on the way that both deep learning achievers and conscientious achievers become goal-oriented achievers. The final scale in the proposed hybrid model of learning in personality is experientially based which therefore includes the third research focus as shown in Figure 4.1.

EXPERIENTIALLY BASED LEARNING

Similar to the socio-cognitive perspective, another research focus which rejects the biological basis of personality and learning is that of experiential learning (see Figure 4.1). Here, the argument is that 'we are what we learn from our experiences.' The concept of experiential learning explores the cyclical pattern of all learning from experience through reflection and conceptualizing to action and on to further experience (Kolb, 1984).

Experiential learning is often measured by Honey and Mumford's Learning Styles Questionnaire (LSQ), which is designed specifically to measure the way people learn and is often used to provide information about preferred learning styles. Each of the four elements of Kolb's (1984) learning cycle is measured in a simple way that has led to the questionnaire gaining a wide following. The LSQ has, however, been subject to repeated criticisms based on its poor representation of theory and inadequate psychometric properties (Duff and Duffy, 2002; Swailes and Senior, 1999). According to the model of learning upon which the LSQ is predicated, people learn by experience from within four phases of a learning cycle (i.e. activist, reflector, theorist, and pragmatist). These phases reflect activities that people are thought to do when they learn and are associated with their preferences for these activities, as opposed to their achievement orientations.

Within the proposed hybrid model, experiential learning is included as a deep learning achiever scale which reflects the cognitions associated with resources allocated to the study of experiences. Research demonstrates that deep processing (that involves elaboration, critical thinking, and the integration of new information with prior knowledge) tends to produce high performance on cognitively demanding tasks. High ability individuals typically use more complex learning methods. Low ability individuals, however, have fewer cognitive resources and tend to use less complex learning strategies (Kanfer, 1991; Kanfer and Ackerman, 1989; Kanfer et al., 1994).

The proposed hybrid model argues that high sensation seeking is related to high deep learning achieving because the search and curiosity associated with sensation seeking tends to correspond with high experiential learning. Deep learners tend to reflect and think about their learning experiences and will tend to draw pro-social conclusions. Deep learners are likely to seek out useful stimuli and therefore enter a cycle of functional learning that also leads to emotional intelligence (i.e. a rational and logical way of learning). On the other hand people who tend to allocate fewer resources to the study of new sensations will tend to be dysfunctional learners because they will not be able to draw complex pro-social conclusions (such as how delay of gratification will tend to be a useful pro-social strategy).

PROPOSING THE HYBRID MODEL OF FUNCTIONAL AND DYSFUNCTIONAL LEARNING-SPANNING TEMPERAMENT AND CHARACTER

The proposed hybrid model measures approach and avoidance learning in personality and is designed to span biological, cognitive, and experiential foci (see Figure 4.1). The proposed model argues in favor of a non-directional (i.e. both functional and dysfunctional) biologically based scale of sensation seeking being a distal component of the learning basis to personality. Sensation seeking is a high approach and low avoidance instinctive urge to learn which is the basis of both functional and dysfunctional learning in personality. While Zuckerman (1994) advocates the role of sensation seeking in dysfunctional and risk-taking tendencies, Jackson emphasizes the role of sensation seeking in providing a basic drive to explore and be curious about the environment.

The view that non-directional sensation seeking or impulsivity is a basis for both functional and dysfunctional behavior was perhaps first argued by Arnett (1994) and Dickman (1990). Arnett proposed (but did not test) that the failure to socialize a high sensation seeker could lead to psychopathy, whereas correct socialization leads to leadership, career enhancement, and creativity. The proposed hybrid model of learning in personality adds the flesh to Arnett's proposal by detailing the socio-cognitive and experiential pathways that lead to functional and dysfunctional learning.

The basis for the proposed biosocial model of personality is mainly derived from the biological theories of Eysenck (1967), Gray (1990), Gray and McNaughton (2000) and Zuckerman (1994); the cognitive theories of

Bandura (1999), Dweck (1986, 1989), and Vandewalle and Cummings (1997); conscientiousness from the Big Five (Costa and McCrae, 1992); cognitions of negative emotionality and emotional intelligence (Petrides and Furnham, 2000); and the experiential model of Kolb (1984). It is also based on the integrationist ideas of Chen et al. (2000), Cloninger et al. (1993), Elliot and Thrash (2002), Humphreys and Revelle (1984), and Ortony et al. (2005). In particular, the model suggests that socio-cognitive and experiential factors mediate the biological drive of sensation seeking. Such a perspective is based on a theoretical perspective implicit in the writings of Cloninger et al. (1993), and utilizes a measurement model based on SEM

Table 4.1 shows the means, standard deviations, and alphas of the five learning-in-personality scales. Each scale has 15 items and can be scored as 'true', 'false', and 'can't decide'.

The proposed measurement model of 'learning in personality' shown in Figure 4.2 is based on a sample of 3,124 people who have completed the Learning Styles Profiler (LSP) (Jackson, 2005). The two-step approach to structural equation modeling (SEM) was used to validate the theoretical structure as recommended by Anderson and Gerbing (1988). One-factor congeneric measurement models were specified and tested prior to the testing of the full structural model. The aim in developing the measurement models prior to the full structural model is to assess the validity and reliability of the constructs prior to their use in the full model (Anderson and

Table 4.1   Means, standard deviations and Cronbach's alphas of the proposed hybrid model of learning in personality (n = 3124)

	Mean	SD	alpha
Sensation seeking	22.15	5.44	0.75
Goal-oriented achiever	22.29	5.55	0.80
Deep learning achiever	16.56	6.20	0.74
Conscientious achiever	21.50	5.60	0.75
Emotionally intelligent achiever	20.34	6.69	0.81

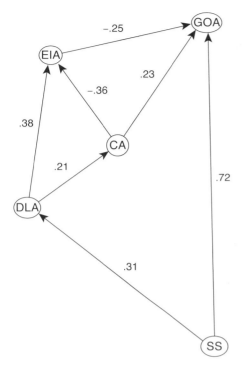

Figure 4.2 The proposed hybrid model of learning in personality – testing the theory using SEM

the subsequent structural model analysis. This procedure followed Holmes-Smith's (2001) recommendations.

Consistent with the hypothesized the nature of sensation seeking (strongly biological, genetic, developed early in evolution), based on the literature review, this scale is considered the most distal. This distal 'instinctive or temperament' scale is mediated across a series of pathways in the prediction of behaviors by means of 'conscious or character' based socio-cognitive or experiential scales which possess a complex structure with some similarity to that proposed by Chen et al. (2000) and according to the arguments developed in this literature review. In the previous section, it has been argued that the desire to approach sensations and a low tendency to avoid punishment will be cognitively re-expressed both through goal orientation and knowledge accrued from learning experience. Having a tendency to be a deep learner is itself re-expressed in terms of conscientiousness and emotional intelligence. Conscientiousness is re-expressed in terms of goals and the rationality of emotional intelligence is expressed in terms of low goal orientation.

Given that Chi-squared is sensitive to a large sample size, it is not surprising that it is significant. However, excellent 'goodness of fit' is achieved on all other widely used measures (RMR = 0.046; GFI = 0.997; AGFI = 0.984; CFI = 0.989, RMSEA = 0.049, RHO = 0.959). All paths shown in Figure 4.2 are significant ($p < 0.001$) and all indirect paths are significant ($p < 0.001$). No error covariances were fitted to improve model fit.

Table 4.2 presents correlations between the scales of the proposed measurement model as well as correlations with other measures. Jackson's sensation seeking is significantly positively correlated with all representative biologically based measures of approach (EPQ-extraversion, Carver and White's (1994) three scales of BAS, Dickman's functional and dysfunctional impulsivity, and Zuckerman's four scales of sensation

Gerbing, 1988). The one-factor model was initially calculated using four parcels of items from the relevant scales. Standardized lambda coefficients and standardized error terms were inspected to identify those items considered most important in the one-factor model and those variables considered least important as a measure of the latent construct (i.e. with small lambda coefficients and large error variance according to the specifications provided by Holmes-Smith, 2001). All one-factor congeneric models achieved an excellent 'goodness of fit'. Factor scores from these one-factor models were used to create composite variables with maximized reliabilities. With the standard deviation and variance of the composite variable, and the maximized reliability value, parameter coefficients and error coefficients for the composite variable were calculated. These values were then used in

Table 4.2 Correlations of Jackson's Learning Styles Profiler with other scales

	SS	GOA	DLA	CA	EIA	n
a) Scale intercorrelations						
GOA	0.55**					3124
DLA	0.26**	0.14**				3124
CA	-0.00	0.25**	0.17**			3124
EIA	-0.09**	0.18**	-0.19**	0.20**		3124
b) Correlations with representative biological approach and avoidance models						
EPQ-E	0.52**	0.40**	0.06	-0.05	-0.15**	3124
SSS-TAS	0.32**	0.13*	0.07	-0.08	0.09	386
SSS-ES	0.27**	0.10*	0.10*	-0.30**	0.05	386
SSS-DIS	0.12*	-0.02	-0.08	-0.35**	-0.03	386
SSS-BS	0.23**	0.09	-0.01	-0.31**	-0.22**	386
C&W BAS DR	0.41**	0.40**	0.11**	0.11**	-0.22**	927
C&W BAS FU	0.49**	0.19**	0.15**	-0.09**	-0.22**	927
C&W BAS RR	0.20**	0.11**	0.08*	0.07*	-0.05	927
Dickman FI	0.49**	0.44**	0.06	-0.09**	0.02	913
Dickman DFI	0.21**	0.01	0.04	-0.28**	-0.45**	913
EPQ-N	-0.12**	-0.21**	0.12**	0.08*	-0.29**	3124
C&W BIS	-0.16**	-0.18**	0.06	0.09**	-0.04	927
c) Correlations with representative cognitive approach and avoidance models						
Chen GSE	0.48**	0.67**	0.16**	0.17**	0.03	802
Learning goal	0.49**	0.47**	0.26**	0.19**	-0.02	923
Proving goal	0.22**	0.18**	0.17**	0.10**	-0.23**	923
Avoidant goal	-0.08*	-0.10**	0.03	0.04	-0.22**	923
d) Correlations with experiential learning						
LSQ Activist	0.56**	0.18**	0.11	-0.27**	-0.46**	249
LSQ Reflector	-0.04	0.18**	0.17**	0.60**	0.10	249
LSQ Pragmatist	0.13*	0.24**	0.09	0.35**	-0.13*	249
LSQ Theorist	0.04	0.27**	0.21**	0.51**	-0.05	249
e) Correlations with functional self-reported behavior						
Job perform.	0.24**	0.35**	0.12**	0.21**	0.12**	851
Org. commit	0.12**	0.12**	0.04	0.10**	0.06	698
Job satis.	0.14**	0.15**	0.06	0.05	0.10**	729

f) Correlations with self-reported leadership behavior

MLQ Char.	0.38**	0.31**	0.21**	0.22**	0.14**	334
MLQ Inte.	0.35**	0.33**	0.33**	0.18***	0.04	334
MLQ Indi.	0.30**	0.22**	0.19**	0.13*	0.13*	334
MLQ Con.	0.23**	0.19**	0.20**	0.19**	0.09	334

g) Correlations with self-reported dysfunctional behavior

PPI-total	0.24**	0.41**	0.11*	-0.22**	-0.42**	354
Gambling SOGS	0.05	0.05	0.16**	0.03	-0.30**	354
Workplace deviance	-0.03	0.02	-0.04	0.14**	-0.21**	717
Prolific Sex	-0.00	0.15**	0.07	-0.14**	-0.13**	415
Drug use DAST20	0.05	0.09	0.10	0.01	-0.15**	343

Jackson's (2005) LSP: SS = sensation seeking; GOA = goal-oriented achiever; DLA = deep learning achiever; CA = conscientious achiever; EIA = emotionally intelligent achiever

Eysenck and Eysenck's (1991) EPQ-R: E PQ-E = extraversion; EPQ-N = neuroticism

Zuckerman's (1978) Sensation Seeking Scale: SSS-TAS = thrill and adventure seeking; SSS-ES = experience seeking;

SSS-DIS = disinhibition; SSS − BS = boredom susceptibility

Carver and White's (1994) BIS-BAS scales: C & W BAS DR = BAS drive; C & W BAS FU = BAS fun seeking; C & W BAS RR = BAS reward responsiveness; C & W BIS = BIS

Dickman's (1990) Functional (Dickman FI) and Dysfunctional Impulsivity scales (Dickman DFI)

Chen et al.'s (2000) General Self-Efficacy Scale (GSE)

VanderWalle and Cummings (1997): Learning goal, Proving goal, Avoidant goal

Learning Styles Questionnaire: LSQ activist; LSQ reflector, LSQ pragmatist; LSQ theorist

Johnson's (1998) Job performance (Job perform.) and Organizational commitment (org. commit.)

Warr and Payne's (1993) Job Satisfaction Questionnaire (Job Satis.)

Multifactor Leadership Questionnaire (Modified MLQ; Bass and Avolio, 1995). Transformational leadership measured in terms of charisma (MLQ Char), intellectual stimulation (MLQ Inte.); individual consideration (MLQ Indi.), and contingent reward (MLQ Con.)

Lilienfeld and Andrews' (1996) Psychopathic Personality Index (PPI)

Lesieur and Blume's (1987) South Oaks Gambling Scale (Gambling SOGS)

Bennett and Robinson's (2000) Workplace Deviance

Bailey et al.'s (2000) Prolific Sexual Activity

Skinner's (1982) Drug-use Scale (DAST-20)

seeking). Jackson's sensation seeking and Zuckerman's sensation seeking measures differ because Jackson's is designed to be neither functional nor dysfunctional, whereas Zuckerman's is purposefully more dysfunctional. It is noted that biologically based models of approach are generally positively correlated with goal-oriented achiever and negatively correlated with conscientiousness. These correlational trends explain why approach measures are generally unpredictive of behavior such as work place performance since the positive component of goals is cancelled-out by the negative relationship with conscientiousness. The proposed hybrid model uniquely measures all these components.

Like Zuckerman's sensation seeking, Jackson's sensation seeking represents low avoidance as well as approach. This is shown by the negative correlations between Jackson's sensation seeking with EPQ neuroticism. Jackson argues that sensation seeking represents both high approach and low avoidance and this is shown by the pattern of positive and negative correlations with measures that aim to capture approach and avoidance separately.

It is also noted that Dickman's (2000) functional impulsivity is much more strongly related to sensation seeking and goal-oriented achiever, whereas Dickman's dysfunctional impulsivity is more related to sensation seeking, low conscientiousness, and low emotional autonomy. The relationship between the scales of the Learning Styles Profiler and Dickman's impulsivity measures show that the proposed model performed extremely well since both functional and dysfunctional impulsivity relate to high sensation seeking, whereas functional impulsive behavior is positively associated with goal-oriented achiever. Dysfunctional impulsive behavior is negatively associated with conscientious achiever and emotional intelligent achiever.

Also shown in Table 4.2 are the correlations with widely accepted measures of cognitive approach and avoidance (Chen et al.'s, 2001, self-efficacy and VanderWalle

and Cummings, 1997, measures of goal orientation). As expected, these two measures correlate most highly with sensation seeking and goal-oriented achiever. In contrast, VanderWalle's avoidance goal orientation correlates negatively with sensation seeking, and so is consistent with Jackson's theory. Its dysfunctional nature is also highlighted by negative correlations with emotional intelligent achiever and goal-oriented achiever. VanderWalle's proving goal orientation shows a combination of both functional and dysfunctional components noted by its positive relationships with sensation seeking, goal-oriented achiever, deep learning achiever, and conscientious achiever, and its negative relationship with emotionally intelligent achiever.

A further section of Table 4.2 provides evidence in favor of the overlap between the proposed hybrid model and experiential learning. The pattern of results between Jackson's model and Honey and Mumford's Learning Styles Questionnaire suggests that sensation seeking overlaps with the activist scale and conscientious achiever overlaps with Honey and Mumford's reflector, pragmatist, and theorist scales. Results further suggest that the activist scale of Honey and Mumford's Learning Styles Questionnaire may generally possess low validity as activist learning is also associated with low conscientious achievement and low emotional intelligent achievement. Interestingly, Honey and Mumford's scales do not seem highly related to the deep learning achiever scale which further demonstrates the well known psychometric problems with the Learning Styles Questionnaire (Duff and Duffy, 2002; Swailes and Senior, 1999).

The validity of the proposed hybrid model is also shown in Table 4.2 in terms of the positive correlations between most of the LSP scales and self-reported functional workplace behavior (job performance, organizational commitment, and job satisfaction). This viewpoint is confirmed by noting that the proposed model is also strongly predictive of transformational leadership.

Finally, the validity of the proposed model can be shown in its ability to predict dysfunctional behavior. It is suggested that dysfunctional behavior should have the following:

1 A positive but not necessarily significant relationship with sensation seeking. The positive relationship indicates that sensation seeking is positively related to dysfunctional learning. However the correlation between sensation seeking and dysfunctional behavior does not need to be significant because, in line with many others, it is argued that step 1 of Baron and Kenny's (1986) test of mediation (which tests for a link between the IV and the DV) does not have to be significant to demonstrate mediation.
2 A pattern of generally negative correlations between Jackson's cognitive scales and dysfunctionally learnt behavior, with the possible exception of goal orientation which may be positive when dysfunctional behaviors involve a great deal of planning. In general these patterns are shown in Figure 4.2. Psychopathy (measured by means of the PPI; Lilienfeld and Andrews, 1996) is positively related to sensation seeking and goal-oriented achievement and negatively related to conscientious achievement and emotionally intelligent achievement. Gambling (measured by SOGS; Lesieur and Blume, 1987), workplace deviance (Bennett and Robinson, 2000), prolific sexual activity (Bailey et al., 2000) and drug use (DAST-20; Skinner, 1982) are significantly negatively related to emotionally intelligent achiever and generally negatively related to conscientious achiever.

Collectively, therefore, these results provide reasonably strong evidence in favor of Jackson's (2005) proposed hybrid model. The five scales of the Learning in Personality model have good alpha reliability (Table 4.1). A structural model of learning is developed in which all proposed direct and indirect pathways are statistically significant (Figure 4.2) and the hypothesized model is consistent with the empirical data, as indicated by the model fit indices. Moreover, the proposed theoretical model is also consistent with other approach and avoidance models of personality as shown by the correlations in

Table 4.2. The model also predicts both functional and dysfunctional behavior as also shown in Table 4.2.

OUTCOMES – FUNCTIONAL/ DYSFUNCTIONAL/NON-LEARNER/STEADY

Jackson's (2005) argues a functional learner is someone who has the instinctive drive to learn (i.e. is a high sensation seeker) and who can harness, redirect, delay, or re-express this drive by means of cognitions to achieve a functional understanding of today's complex world. This is a self-developed competent learner perhaps best symbolized by an entrepreneur.

A dysfunctional learner is someone who has the instinctive drive to learn, but who is generally a low scorer on the socio-cognitive and experiential learning scales. Such a perspective argues that dysfunctional appetitive behaviors such as delinquency, alcohol consumption, workplace crime, and so on, are the result of cognitive deficits in the regulation of high sensation seeking. To some extent such a view is broadly supported by research in similar areas such as McFall's (1976) social deficit model, which follows this perspective since problematic behavior is seen as a consequence of an underdeveloped repertoire of socially acceptable skills.

Jackson's model also identifies a competent non-learner. This is someone who is a low scorer on sensation seeking and is therefore not very curious about the world but who is a high scorer on the socio-cognitive scales. Such a person is likely to be functionally competent and a good worker but not very adventurous. In many jobs, in which mistakes are inappropriate and adventurousness is not valued, the competent non-learner will be an excellent employee. However this person will to some extent get 'stuck in a rut'. It needs to be emphasized that the low sensation seeking reflects a low desire to engage in new self-development learning as opposed to a low desire to learn knowledge.

A low scorer on sensation seeking on the socio-cognitive, and on experiential scales is likely to be a non-competent non-learner. This person lacks the cognitive skills to be effective and lacks the drive to explore and self-develop. Such a person may be knowledgeable (since learning in personality is not concerned with the accrual of facts, except perhaps the deep learning achiever scale) but is generally neither curious nor pro-social.

The structure of the model is accepting of psychological interventions, unlike many of the present trait models of personality, such as the Big Five, Giant Three or Reinforcement Sensitivity Theory. The latter models argue in favor of behavioral consistency whereas the proposed hybrid model is dynamic and developmental. It is argued that the socio-cognitive and experiential scales should be more open to training, CBT, coaching, and self-development than the biological (a view also shared by Cloninger et al., 1993). This is a fundamentally important difference since identifying whether or not traits are primarily biological or socio-cognitive provides the theoretical framework for behavioral interventions as desired by Blackburn (2000; see Levine and Jackson, 2004). This allows us to apply personality assessment to not only describe behavior, but to really use it to drive issues such as the management of dangerous offenders, clinical intervention, educational intervention, as well as in the targeting of interventions in training, coaching, and organizational psychology.

A further use could be in personnel selection. At present, personality questionnaires are generally used as a basis for selection or rejection. The proposed hybrid model identifies possible areas for development and training as well as selection. This could be useful for example military officer selection in which there is a shortage of applicants such that there is an increasing desire to pass applicants. Using the Learning Styles Profiler would enable applicants to be split into 'recoverable rejects' and 'rejects'. Recoverable rejects are those people who could meet the person specification if they benefit from training.

CONCLUSIONS

The proposed hybrid model of learning in personality provides a significant and innovative opportunity to integrate biological, socio-cognitive, and experiential models of personality (see Figure 4.1). The proposed hybrid model is theoretical and has wide applicability and appeal to personality researchers and practitioners. While innovative in scope, the basis of the proposed hybrid model logically extends and integrates many prior theories (e.g. Chen et al., 2000; Cloninger et al., 1993; Elliot and Thrash, 2002; Gray and McNaughton, 2000; Humphreys and Revelle, 1984; Revelle, 1993, 1995). A considerable influence on the model is derived from biological, socio-cognitive theorists and experiential theorists. It is argued that near-simultaneous development of a measurement model that corresponds to the theoretical structure provides the appropriate balance between previous work that emphasizes measurement at the expense of theory (such as the Big Five model), post-hoc theory to match measurement (e.g. Eysenck's model), and post-hoc measurement to match theory (e.g. Gray's RST). It is argued that the focus on approach and avoidance in personality psychology is useful but that a combined pathway has considerable merit compared to the dual pathways as argued, for example, by Elliot and Thrash (2002), Eysenck (1967), and Gray and McNaughton (2000).

The proposed model of learning in personality achieves the following theoretical outcomes:

1   Development of a hybrid model of biological, experiential, and social-cognitive theories of personality, such that social and experiential cognitions are seen as proximal mediators of a distal biological construct.

2 Relegation of sensation seeking to temperament thereby permitting the social-cognitive perspective; and relegation of social-cognitive theory to character to allow sensation seeking room to flourish.
3 Development of the idea that sensation seeking relates to both functional and dysfunctional learning and the opportunity to understand personality antecedents of functional and dysfunctional learning in personality by common biological basis and divergent cognitions.
4 The opportunity to integrate a variety of social and cognitive models along the lines suggested by Chen et al. (2000).
5 A departure from Eysenck's hierarchical model of personality influenced by exploratory factor analysis towards a theory-driven structural model influenced by SEM.
6 A departure from a strict dichotomy of temperament and character envisaged by Cloninger et al. (1993) into more of a continuum flowing from distal biological constructs to proximal socio-cognitive constructs.
7 A departure from the separate measurement of approach and avoidance as extraversion and neuroticism or BAS and BIS by advocating a single biological scale of high approach and low avoidance. Such a perspective does not dispute the biological evidence of separate approach and avoidance pathways (e.g. Depue and Collins, 1999; Gray and McNaughton, 2000). It does acknowledge that it is hard to measure these pathways as orthogonal constructs (as noted by Jackson and Smillie, 2004; Smillie and Jackson, 2005) and acknowledges that complex and relevant stimuli in the real-world often contain a mix of rewarding and punishing stimuli which lead to both BAS and BIS activation.
8 The development of a model of personality which provides direct advice on how to implement interventions such as by training, CBT, coaching, and self-development as required by Blackburn (2000).
9 Prediction of functional and dysfunctional learning outcomes. The proposed hybrid model focuses on developmental learning outcomes instead of simply describing personality (as the Big Five model, for example, sets out to do).
10 The opportunity to understand personality antecedents of functional and dysfunctional learning in personality in terms of common biological basis and divergent cognitive basis.
11 There are numerous applications of the model in organizational, educational, forensic and clinical psychology as well as in the community.

ACKNOWLEDGEMENTS

The Manual, Paper versions and a Software expert system of the hybrid model of learning ('The Learning Styles Profiler') are available from Cymeon at (http://www.cymeon.com). Thanks to the excellent endeavors of my notable graduate students including Stephen Levine, Luke Smillie, and Peter O'Connor for their help and assistance with my learning.

REFERENCES

Anderson, J.C. and Gerbing, D.W. (1988) 'Structural equation modeling in practice: A review and recommended two-step approach', *Psychological Bulletin*, 103(2): 411–23.
Arnett, J. (1994) 'Sensation seeking: A new conceptualization and a new scale', *Personality and Individual Differences*, 16(2): 289–96.
Bailey, J.M., Kirk, K.M., Zhu, G., Dunne, M.P. and Martin, N.G. (2000) 'Do individual differences in sociosexuality represent genetic or environmentally contingent strategies? Evidence from the Australian twin registry', *Journal of Personality and Social Psychology*, 78(3): 537–45.
Ball, S.A. and Zuckerman, M. (1990) 'Sensation seeking, Eysenck's personality dimensions and reinforcement sensitivity in concept formation', *Personality and Individual Differences*, 11(4): 343–53.
Ball, S.A. and Zuckerman, M. (1992) 'Sensation seeking and selective attention: Focused and divided attention on a dichotic listening task', *Journal of Personality and Social Psychology*, 63(5): 825–31.
Bandura, A. (1997) *Self-efficacy: The Exercise of Control*. New York: Freeman, pp. 154–96.
Bandura, A. (1999) 'Social cognitive theory of personality', in A. Pervin and O.P. John (eds), *Handbook of Personality: Theory and Research* (2nd edn) New York: Guilford, pp. 154–96.
Baron, R.M. and Kenny, D.A. (1986) 'The moderator–mediator variable distinction in social psychological research: Conceptual, strategic, an statistical considerations', *Journal of Personality and Social Psychology*, 51(6): 1173–82.

Barrick, M.R. and Mount, M.K. (1991) 'The big five personality dimensions and job performance: A meta-analysis', *Personnel Psychology*, 44(1): 1–26.

Barrick, M.R., Mount, M.K. and Strauss, J.P. (1993) 'Conscientiousness and performance of sales representatives: Test of the mediating effects of goal setting', *Journal of Applied Psychology*, 78(5): 715–22.

Barrick, M.R., Stewart, G.L. and Piotrowski, M. (2002) 'Personality and job performance: Test of the mediating effects of motivation among sales representatives', *Journal of Applied Psychology*, 87(1): 43–51.

Bennett, R.J. and Robinson, S.L. (2000) 'The development of a measure of workplace deviance', *Journal of Applied Psychology*, 85(3): 349–60.

Blackburn, R. (2000) 'Treatment or incapacitation? Implications of research on personality disorders for the management of dangerous offenders', *Legal and Criminological Psychology*, 5(1): 1–23.

Block, J. (1995) 'A contrarian view of the five-factor approach to personality description', *Psychological Bulletin*, 117(2): 187–215.

Bogg, T. and Roberts, B.W. (2004) 'Conscientiousness and health related behaviors: A meta-analysis or the leading behavioral contributors to mortality', *Psychological Bulletin*, 130(6): 887–919.

Brunas-Wagstaff, J., Berquist, A. and Wagstaff, G.F. (1994) 'Cognitive correlates of functional and dysfunctional impulsivity', *Personality and Individual Differences*, 17(2): 289–92.

Byrne, Z.J. Stoner, K. Thompson, W. and Hochwarter. W. Carver, C.S., Sutton, S.K. and Scheier, M.F. (2005) 'The interactive effects of conscientiousness, work effort, and psychological climate on job performance', *Journal of Vocational Behavior*, 66: 326–38.

Carver, C.S., Sutton, S.K. and Scheier, M.F. (2000) 'Action, emotion, and personality: Emerging conceptual integration', *Personality and Social Psychology Bulletin*, 26(6): 741–51.

Carver, C.S. and White, T. (1994) 'Behavioral inhibition, behavioral activation, and affective responses to impending reward and punishment: The BIS/BAS scales', *Journal of Personality and Social Psychology*, 67(2): 319–33.

Chen, G., Gully, S. and Eden, D. (2001) 'Validation of a new general self-efficacy scale', *Organizational Research Methods*, 4(1): 62–83.

Chen, G., Gully, S.M., Whiteman, J.A. and Kilcullen, R.N. (2000) 'Examination of relationships among trait-like individual differences, state-like individual differences and learning performance', *Journal of Applied Psychology*, 85(6): 835–47.

Cloninger, C.R. (1987) 'A systematic method for clinical description and classification of personality variants', *Archives of General Psychiatry*, 44(6): 573–88.

Cloninger, C.R., Svrakic, D.M. and Przybeck, T.R. (1993) 'A psychobiological model of temperament and character', *Archives of General Psychiatry*, 50(12): 975–90.

Corr, P.J. (2004) 'Reinforcement sensitivity theory and personality', *Neuroscience and Biobehavioral Reviews*, 28(3): 317–32.

Coscina, D.V. (1997) 'The biopsychology of impulsivity: Focus on brain serotonin', in C.D. Webster and M.A. Jackson (eds), *Impulsivity: Theory, Assessment and Treatment*. London: Guilford, pp. 95–115.

Costa, P.T. Jr. and McCrae, R.R. (1992) *Revised NEO Personality R and NEO Five-Factor Inventory (NEO FFI) Professional Manual*. Odessa, FL: Psychological Assessment Resources.

Davids, E., Zhang, K., Tarazi, F.I. and Baldessarini, R.J. (2003) 'Animal models of attention-deficit hyperactivity disorder', *Brain Research Reviews*, 42(1): 1–21.

Dawe, S. and Loxton, N.J. (2004) 'The role of impulsivity in the development of substance use and eating disorders', *Neuroscience and Biobehavioural Reviews*, 28(3): 343–51.

Depue, R.A. and Collins, P.F. (1999) 'Neurobiology of the structure of personality: Dopamine, facilitation of incentive motivation, and extraversion', *Behavioural and Brain Sciences*, 22: 491–569.

Dickman, S.J. (1990) 'Functional and dysfunctional impulsivity: Personality and cognitive correlates', *Journal of Personality and Social Psychology*, 58(1): 95–102.

Dickman, S.J. (2000) 'Impulsivity, arousal and attention', *Personality and Individual Differences*, 28(3): 563–81.

Di Chiara G. (1995) 'The role of dopamine in drug abuse viewed from the perspective of its role in motivation', *Drug and Alcohol Dependence*, 38(2): 95–137.

Dolan, M. and Anderson, I.M. (2003) 'The relationship between serotonergic function and the Psychopathy Checklist: Screening Version', *Journal of Psychopharmacology*, 17(2): 211–17.

Dudley, N., Orvis, K., Lebiecki, J. and Cortina J. (2006) 'A meta-analytic investigation of conscientiousness in the prediction of job performance: Examining the intercorrelations and the incremental validity of narrow traits', *Journal of Applied Psychology*, 91(1): 40–57.

Duff, A. and Duffy, T. (2002) 'Psychometric qualities of Honey and Mumford's Learning Styles Questionnaire', *Personality and Individual Differences*, 33(1): 147–64.

Dweck, C.S. (1986) 'Motivational processes affecting learning', *American Psychologist*, 41(10): 1040–8.

Dweck, C.S. (1989) 'Motivation', in A. Lesgold and R. Glaser (eds), *Foundations for a Psychology of Education*. Hillsdale, NJ: Erlbaum, pp. 87–136.

Dweck, C.S. and Leggett, E.L. (1988) 'A social-cognitive approach to motivation and personality', *Psychological Review*, 95(2): 256–73.

Eaves, L., Eysenck, H.J. and Martin, N. (1989) *Genes, Culture, and Personality: An Empirical Approach*. New York: Academic Press.

Elliot, A.J. (1999) 'Approach and avoidance motivation and achievement goals', *Educational Psychologist*, 34: 169–89.

Elliot, A.J. and Thrash, T.M. (2002) 'Approach-avoidance motivation in personality: Approach and avoidance temperaments and goals', *Journal of Personality and Social Psychology*, 82(5): 804–18.

Eysenck, H. (1967) *The Biological Basis of Personality*. Springfield, IL: Charles C. Thomas.

Eysenck, H.J. (1993) 'The nature of impulsivity', in W.G. McCown, J.L. Johnson and M.B. Shure (eds), *The Impulsive Client: Theory, Research and Treatment* Washington, DC: American Psychological Association, pp. 57–69.

Eysenck, H.J. and Eysenck, S.B.G. (1991) *Manual of the Eysenck Personality Scales*. London: Hodder & Stoughton.

Eysenck, H.J. and Gudjonsson, G.H. (1989) *The Causes and Cures of Criminality*. London: Plenum Press.

Eysenck, S.B.G. and Eysenck, H.J. (1978) 'Impulsiveness and venturesomeness: Their position in a dimensional system', *Psychological Reports*, 43: 1247–55.

Fulker, D.W., Eysenck, S.B. and Zuckerman, M. (1980) 'A genetic and environmental analysis of sensation seeking', *Journal of Research in Personality*, 14: 261–81.

Gable, S.L., Reis, H.T. and Elliot, A.J. (2003) 'Evidence of bivariate systems: An empirical test of appetition and aversion across domains', *Journal of Research in Personality*, 37(5): 349–72.

Gellatly, I. (1996) 'Conscientiousness and task performance: Test of a cognitive process model', *Journal of Applied Psychology*, 81(5): 474–82.

Gillespie, N., Cloninger, C.R., Heath, A.C. and Martin, N.G. (2003) 'The genetic and environmental relationship between Cloninger's dimensions of temperament and character', *Personality and Individual Differences*, 35(8): 1931–46.

Goldman, D. and Fishbein, D.H. (2000) 'Genetic basis for impulsive and antisocial behaviours: Can their course be altered?', in D.H. Fishbein (ed.), *The Science, Treatment, and Prevention of Antisocial Behaviours: Application to the Criminal Justice System*. Kingston, NJ: Civic Research Institute.

Gray J.A. (1970) 'The psychophysiological basis of introversion-extraversion', *Behaviour Research and Therapy*, 8(3): 249–66.

Gray, J.A. (1981) 'A critique of Eysenck's theory of personality', in H.J. Eysenck (ed.), *A Model for Personality*. Berlin: Springer, pp. 246–76.

Gray, J.A. (1982) *The Neuropsychology of Anxiety: An Enquiry into the Function of the Septo-hippocampal System*. New York: Oxford University Press.

Gray, J.A. (1987) 'The neuropsychology of emotion and personality', in S.M. Stahl, S.D. Iverson and E.C. Goodman (eds), *Cognitive Neurochemistry*. Oxford: Oxford University Press.

Gray, J.A. and McNaughton, N. (2000) *The Neuropsychology of Anxiety*. Oxford: Oxford University Press.

Hogan, J. and Holland, B. (2003) 'Using theory to evaluate personality and job performance relations: A socioanalytic perspective', *Journal of Applied Psychology*, 88(1): 100–112.

Holmes-Smith, P. (2001) *Applied Structural Equation Modeling*. Canberra: School Research, Evaluation and Measurement Services.

Humphreys, M.S. and Revelle, W. (1984) 'Personality, motivation and performance: A theory of the relationship between individual differences and information processing', *Psychological Review*, 91(2): 153–84.

Jackson, C.J. (2001) 'Comparison between Eysenck and Gray's models of personality in the prediction of motivational work criteria', *Personality and Individual Differences*, 31(2): 129–44.

Jackson, C.J. (2002) 'Mapping Gray's model of personality onto the Eysenck Personality Profiler (EPP)', *Personality and Individual Differences*, 32(3): 495–507.

Jackson, C.J. (2003) 'Gray's RST: A psychometric critique', *Personality and Individual Differences*, 34: 533–44.

Jackson, C.J. (2005) *An Applied Neuropsychological Model of Functional and Dysfunctional Learning: Applications for Business, Education, Training and Clinical Psychology*. Cymeon: Australia.

Jackson, C.J. and Francis, L.J. (2004) 'Are interactions in Gray's Reinforcement Sensitivity Theory proximal or distal in the prediction of religiosity: A test of the joint subsystems hypothesis', *Personality and Individual Differences*, 36(5): 1197–209.

Jackson, C.J. and Smillie, L.D. (2004) 'Appetitive motivation predicts the majority of personality and an ability measure: A comparison of BAS measures and a re-evaluation of the importance of RST', *Personality and Individual Differences*, 36(7): 1627–36.

Jackson, J.S.H. and Maraun, M. (1996) 'The conceptual validity of empirical scale construction: The case of the Sensation Seeking Scale', *Personality and Individual Differences*, 21(1): 103–10.

Johnson, D.E. (1998) *Applied Multivariate Methods for Data Analysts*. Pacific Grove, CA: Duxbury Press.

Kambouropoulos N. and Staiger P.K. (2004) 'Reactivity to alcohol-related cues: Relationship among cue type, motivational processes, and personality', *Psychology of Addictive Behaviors*, 18(3): 275–83.

Kanfer, R. (1991) 'Motivation theory and organizational psychology', in M.D. Dunnette and L. Hough (eds), *Handbook of Industrial and Organizational Psychology* (2nd edn, Vol. 1). Palo Alto: Consulting Psychologists Press, pp. 75–170.

Kanfer, R. and Ackerman, P.L. (1989) 'Motivation and cognitive abilities: An integrative/aptitude-treatment interaction approach to skill acquisition', *Journal of Applied Psychology*, 74(4): 657–90.

Kanfer, R., Ackerman, P.L., Murtha, T.C., Dugdale, B. and Nelson, L. (1994) 'Goal setting, conditions of practice, and task performance: A resource allocation perspective', *Journal of Applied Psychology*, 79(6): 826–35.

Kolb, D. (1984) *Experiential Learning*. Englewood Cliffs, NJ: Prentice Hall.

Lesieur H.R. and Blume S.B. (1987) 'The South Oaks Gambling Screen (SOGS): A new instrument for the identification of pathological gamblers', *American Journal of Psychiatry*, 144(9): 1184–8.

Levine, S.Z. and Jackson, C.J. (2004) 'Eysenck's theory of crime revisited: Factors or primary scales?', *Legal and Criminological Psychology*, 9(1): 1–18.

Liao, H. and Chuang, A. (2004) 'A multilevel investigation of factors influencing employee service performance and customer outcomes', *Academy of Management Journal*, 47(1): 41–58.

Lilienfeld, S.O. and Andrews, B.P. (1996) 'Development and preliminary validation of a self-report measure of psychopathic personality traits in noncriminal populations', *Journal of Personality Assessment*, 66(3): 488–524.

Locke, E.A. and Latham, G.P. (1990) *A Theory of Goal Setting and Task Performance*. Englewood Cliffs, NJ: Prentice Hall.

Martocchio, J.J. and Judge, T.A. (1997) 'Relationship between conscientiousness and learning in employee training: Mediating influences of self-deception and self-efficacy', *Journal of Applied Psychology*, 82(5): 764–73.

McAlister, A.R., Pachana, N. and Jackson, C.J. (2005) 'Predictors of young dating adults' inclination to engage in extradyadic sexual activities: A multi-perspective study', *British Journal of Psychology*, 96(3): 331–50.

McFall, R.M. (1976) *Behavioral Training: Acquisition Approach to Clinical Problems*. Morristown, NJ: General Learning Press.

Moeller, F.G., Steinberg, J.L., Petty, F., Fulton, M., Cherek, D.R., Kramer, C and Garver, D.L. (1994) 'Low CSF 5-HIAA concentrations and severe aggression and impaired impulse control in nonhuman primates', *American Journal of Psychiatry*, 151: 1485–91.

Ortony, A., Norman, D.A. and Revelle, W. (2005) 'Effective functioning: A three level model of affect, motivation, cognition, and behavior', in J.M. Fellous and M.A. Arbib (eds), *Who Needs Emotions? The Brain*

Meets the Machine. New York: Oxford University Press.

Parker, J.D. and Bagby, R.M. (1997) 'Impulsivity in adults: A critical review of measurement approaches', in C.D. Webster and M.A. Jackson (eds), *Impulsivity: Theory, Assessment and Treatment*. New York, Guilford, pp. 142–57.

Petrides, K.V. and Furnham, A. (2000) 'On the dimensional structure of emotional intelligence', *Personality and Individual Differences*, 29(2): 313–20.

Pickering, A.D. (2004) 'The neuropsychology of impulsive antisocial sensation seeking personality traits: From dopamine to hippocampal function?', in R.M Stelmack (ed.), *On the Psychobiology of Personality: Essays in Honour of Marvin Zuckerman*. London: Elsevier, pp. 455–78.

Pickering, A.D. and Gray, J.A. (1999) 'The neuroscience of personality', in O.P. John (ed.), *Handbook of Personality: Theory and Research* (2nd edn). New York: Guilford, pp. 277–99.

Quilty, L.C. and Oakman, J.M. (2004) 'The assessment of behavioural activation – the relationship between impulsivity and behavioural activation', *Personality and Individual Differences*, 37(2): 429–42.

Raine, A., Reynolds, C., Venables, P.H. and Mednick, S.A. (2002) 'Stimulation seeking and intelligence: A prospective longitudinal study', *Journal of Personality and Social Psychology*, 82: 663–74.

Reio, T. and Sanders-Reio, J. (2006) 'Sensation seeking as an inhibitor of job performance', *Personality and Individual Differences*, 40(4): 631–42.

Revelle, W. (1993) 'Individual differences in personality and motivation: Non-cognitive determinants of cognitive performance', in A. Baddeley and L. Weiskrantz (eds), *Attention: Selection, Awareness and Control: A Tribute to Donald Broadbent*. Oxford: Oxford University Press, pp. 346–73.

Revelle, W. (1995) 'Personality processes', *Annual Review of Psychology*, 46: 295–328.

Roediger, H.L., Rajaram, S. and Srinivas, K. (1990) 'Specifying criteria for postulating memory systems', *Annals of the New York Academy of Sciences*, 608(1): 572–89.

Skinner, H.A. (1982) *Drug Use Questionnaire, DAST-20*. Toronto: Addiction Research Foundation.

Smillie, L.D. and Jackson, C.J. (2005) 'The appetitive motivation scale and other BAS measures in the prediction of approach and active-avoidance', *Personality and Individual Differences*, 38(4): 981–94.

Smillie, L.D., Jackson, C.J. and Dalgleish, L.I. (2006) 'Conceptual differences among Carver and White's (1994) BAS scales: A reward-reactivity versus trait impulsivity perspective', *Personality and Individual Differences*, 40(5): 1039–50.

Swailes, S. and Senior, B. (1999) 'The dimensionality of Honey and Mumford's Learning Styles Questionnaire', *International Journal of Selection and Assessment*, 7(1): 1–11.

Tett, R., Jackson, D. and Rothstein, M. (1991) 'Personality measures as predictors of job performance: A meta-analytic review', Personnel Psychology, 44(4): 703–42.

VandeWalle, D. and Cummings, L.L. (1997) 'A test of the influence of goal orientation on the feedback-seeking process', *Journal of Applied Psychology*, 82(3): 390–400.

Warr, P. and Payne, R. (1983) 'Social class and reported changes in behaviour after job loss', *Journal of Applied Social Psychology*, 13(3): 206–22.

Zuckerman, M. (1978) 'Dimensions of sensation seeking', in H. London and J. Exner (eds), *Dimensions of Personality*. New York: Wiley, pp. 487–549.

Zuckerman, M. (1979) *Sensation Seeking: Beyond the Optimal Level of Arousal*. Hillsdale, NJ: Lawrence Erlbaum

Zuckerman, M. (1994) *Behavioral Expressions and Biosocial Bases of Sensation Seeking*. New York: Cambridge University Press.

Zuckerman, M., Ball, S. and Black, J., (1990) 'Influences of sensation, gender, risk appraisal, and situational motivation on smoking', *Addictive Behavior*, 15: 209–20.

PART II

Multidimensional Personality Instruments

5

The California Psychological Inventory – 434- and 260-item Editions

Douglas P. Boer, Nicola J. Starkey and Andrea M. Hodgetts

INTRODUCTION

The California Psychological Inventory (CPI)[1] was first copyrighted in 1951 and subsequently published by Consulting Psychologists Press (CPP) with the aim of producing a measure that assessed enduring personality traits across many different cultural groups, and which accurately predicted behaviour of generally well-functioning people in interpersonal contexts. To this end, the CPI uses common descriptors of personality which are frequently used and understood by lay people across different cultures. The present versions of the test continue to espouse lay terminologies such as 'self-control', 'dominance', and 'tolerance', terms referred to as 'folk concepts' which are seen as having widespread 'functional validity' or cross-cultural applicability by Gough (2000).

Unlike most objective personality tests in current use, the CPI was not been developed from any particular personality theory, nor was it developed on the basis of sound psychometric properties. Rather the focus of the test's development has been on its practical usefulness. Most of the scales were developed using a combination of the rational approach and empirical criterion keying. The resulting easy to understand nature of the test has encouraged the widespread translation and use of the instrument and as noted by Groth-Marnat, the test has 'become one of the more frequently used tests by professional psychologists' (2003: 355). To this end, the CPI has long been known as 'the sane man's MMPI' (Thorndike, 1959) as it is generally intended to be used with individuals who are not mentally ill. In fact, the test uses a minimum of symptom-eliciting questions, focusing instead on skills-oriented questions of an interpersonal nature.

The overall aim of the CPI has remained unchanged since its original publication with the most recent versions of the instrument. The CPI has gone through a number of revisions: the 1957 and 1975 versions had 480 items and 18 scales, the 1986 version added two more folk scales (independence and empathy) but reduced the total number of items to 462, and in the 1996 third edition, the item count was further reduced to 434 items (Manoogian, 2005). According to Groth-Marnat, the 1996 revision deleted 28 items as a result of a 'combination of continuing research and a wish to conform to the 1990 Americans with Disabilities Act' (2003: 356). The most recent development in the CPI legacy has been the development of the CPI 260 form (Gough and Bradley, 2002), using the same scales as the CPI 434, but reducing the item count via the use of an expert panel aware of the statistical importance of the items. No new items were added, but the CPI 260 is certainly a test that is geared to the new millennium – computer administrable, computer scored, and an easily interpreted computer report generated for feedback purposes.

At the present time, the test is most frequently used in areas of personnel selection, interpersonal adjustment, and antisocial behaviour (Gough, 2000). A survey published by Camara et al. (2000) revealed that the CPI is among the most commonly used personality tests. With the release of the newest 260-item version (Gough and Bradley, 2002), a test aimed directly at the industrial-organizational (I/O) psychology assessment market, the popularity of the CPI test family can only increase.

The present chapter is not a scale by scale examination of the CPI 434 or CPI 260. The test manuals (Gough and Bradley, 1996; Gough and Bradley, 2002) provide excellent scale descriptions and Groth-Marnat (2003) provides an in-depth, independent review of the scales beyond the purview of this chapter. It is our considered and unsolicited opinion that the Groth-Marnat (2003) text is arguably the best text in terms of the CPI for practitioners and researchers alike, if not for the other tests covered in that same book.

THE CPI 434-ITEM VERSION (GOUGH AND BRADLEY, 1996)

The most current full version of the CPI is the third edition (CPI 434; Gough and Bradley, 1996). The CPI 434 consists of 434 items providing scores for 20 standard (folk) scales, 3 vectors and 13 special purpose or research scales (Gough and Bradley, 1996).

For the norm sample, internal reliabilities ranged between 0.62 and 0.84 for the standard scales, 0.77 and 0.88 for the vector scales, and 0.45 and 0.88 for the special purpose scales. Of the standard scales, four failed to reach the traditionally acceptable minimum internal consistency of 0.7 (self acceptance, empathy, psychological mindedness, flexibility), as did four of the special purpose scales (anxiety, Dickens scale for social desirability, Dickens scale for acquiescence, law-enforcement orientation). These are listed in Tables 5.1 and 5.2, along with a brief summary of the purpose of each scale. Test–retest reliabilities (over a year) range between 0.51 for flexibility to 0.84 to femininity/masculinity (Gough and Bradley, 1996).

FACTOR STRUCTURE OF THE CPI

The CPI was not developed on the basis of its factor structure, and therefore there is an unsurprising degree of item overlap between scales. Nevertheless, factor analyses have been conducted which have resulted in a two-, four-, or five-factor solution (Groth-Marnat, 2003). Gough and Bradley (1996) reported a five-factor solution for the CPI 434 comprising of ascendence, dependability, conventionality, originality, and femininity/masculinity. Other researchers have attempted to link the CPI to the five-factor model (FFM) of personality (i.e. neuroticism, extraversion, openness to experience, agreeableness, and conscientiousness) and initial reports suggested that all 20 CPI scales, apart from communality, were meaningfully

Table 5.1 CPI 434 standard scales, their purpose, clusters, and internal reliabilities (adapted from Groth-Marnat, 2004; Gough and Bradley, 1996; McAllister, 1996)

Scale		Purpose	Internal reliability
Standard Scales			
Cluster I: Interpersonal style and orientation			
Do	Dominance	Leadership, confidence assertiveness, persuasiveness	0.83
Cs	Capability for status	Current status and predictors of future status, e.g. ambition, self confidence, drive to succeed	0.72
Sy	Sociability	Enjoyment of interacting with people, range of interests, introversion/extraversion	0.77
Sp	Social presence	Self-assurance, assertiveness, poise and spontaneity in social situations	0.71
Sa	Self-acceptance	Personal worth, independent thinking and action, confidence	0.67
In	Independence	Self-assurance, self sufficiency, reliance on own initiative, evaluation and direction	0.74
Em	Empathy	Understanding of others feelings and attitudes, insight	0.63
Cluster II: Normative orientation and values			
Re	Responsibility	Dependability, conscientiousness, reliability	0.77
So	Socialization	Delinquency, acceptance and following of rules and social norms	0.78
Sc	Self control	Self-directed behaviour, impulsivity, self discipline, self-control	0.83
Gi	Good impression	Creating a favourable impression, helpfulness; a validity scale for 'faking good'	0.81
Cm	Communality	Fitting in, similarity to average; a validity scale to detect random responding	0.71
Wb	Wellbeing	Perception of current health and psychological adjustment; a validity scale to detect those 'faking bad' in terms of their wellbeing	0.84
To	Tolerance	Acceptance of others beliefs or values, social tolerance, rigidity and openness	0.79
Cluster III: Cognitive and intellectual functioning			
Ac	Achievement via conformance	Orientation to achievement, need for explicit goals and criteria, conformity	0.78
Ai	Achievement via independence	Orientation to achievement, creativity, independence of thought, work from own initiative	0.80
Ie	Intellectual efficiency	Intellectual ability, making use of own ability, organization	0.79
Cluster IV: Role and personal style			
Py	Psychological mindedness	Perception and insight with regard to others, concentration, enjoyment of occupation	0.62
Fx	Flexibility	Adaptability and flexibility in behaviour, temperament and thinking	0.64
F/M	Femininity/masculinity	Assess beliefs which are traditionally masculine or feminine e.g. sensitivity, reaction to criticism	0.73

related to one of the five factors (McCrea et al., 1993). However, McCrea and colleagues also found that agreeableness was under represented by CPI scales. In contrast, a more recent study by Fleenor and Eastman (1997) suggested that all five factors of the FFM are represented in the CPI scales. However, further study is needed to confirm the fourth and fifth factors relating to neuroticism and agreeableness as both were made up of only one scale (Fleenor and Eastman, 1997).

In general, the effectiveness of the CPI in assessing the FFM is still in doubt and several researchers suggest that if one wanted to measure these factors, then using a measure designed on that theoretical perspective ought to provide the most accurate data. In particular this applies to greatly improved criterion validity for conscientiousness and emotional stability in personnel selection (Salgado, 2003). Inconsistencies with the factor loadings of the CPI may occur for several reasons.

Table 5.2   CPI vector and special purpose scales, their purpose, and internal reliabilities (adapted from Groth-Marnat, 2004; Gough and Bradley, 1996; McAllister, 1996)

Scale		Purpose	Internal reliability
Vectors			
V1.	Externality/internality	Continuum from involvement, participation and extraversion to detachment, privacy and introversion	0.82
V2.	Norm doubting/norm favouring	Continuum from conscientiousness, rule respecting to unconventional and changeable	0.77
V3.	Ego integration/self-realization	How positively people evaluate themselves as having achieved their potential	0.88
Special purpose scales (from Form 462)			
Mp	Managerial potential	Identifies those with flair for supervisory roles	0.81
Wo	Work orientation	Identifies a strong work ethic, dedication to work	0.78
CT	Creative temperament	Identifies those who are unconventional, with creative and artistic potential	0.73
B-MS	Baucom's unipolar scale for masculinity	Identifies those with typically masculine attributes, e.g. self confidence and aggression	0.88
B-FM	Baucom's unipolar scale for femininity	Identifies those with typically feminine attributes e.g. gentleness, patience, sincerity	0.75
Anx	Anxiety	Nervousness, tension and evasion	0.49
D-SD	Dickens scale for social desirability	For research to study socially desirable responding, not recommended for interpretation of individual profiles	0.69
D-AC	Dickens scale for acquiescence	For research to study acquiescent responding, not recommended for interpretation of individual profiles	0.47
Special purpose scales (from Form 434)			
Lp	Leadership	Identifies those who have good leadership skills, e.g. enterprising, energetic, resourceful	0.88
Ami	Amicability	Identifies those who are friendly and considerate, e.g. dependable, warm, compassionate	0.79
Leo	Law enforcement orientation	Identifies those who are favourable about societal rules and laws and would be successful in the law enforcement field, e.g. stable, optimistic, ambitious, direct, honest	0.45
Tm	Toughmindedness	Assesses emotionality, objectivity, rationality and confidence	0.79
Nar	Narcissism	Exaggerated self-esteem, inflated sense of worth, self-centred	0.76

First, definitions of the five factors comprising the FFM used by CPI researchers often differ. Second, factor analysis on the CPI is invariably undertaken at the level of the subscales, rather than at the level of the items. Thus, results from factor analysis indicate which CPI scales load together on a factor rather than which individual items load on particular factors. This is potentially problematic to a meaningful factor analytic solution as some items contribute to more than one subscale score. To further complicate this sort of analysis, it is common practice to eliminate items that do not load significantly on a factor in tests which are constructed using factor analysis. This was certainly not the case in the derivation of items in the CPI, so it not surprising that the scales both overlap and are

not independent. In summary, these issues make factor-analytic research, particularly that aimed at validating the FFM using the CPI, of dubious value. Furthermore, since FFM-based tests have better criterion validity than tests like the CPI for certain personality characteristics, such as conscientiousness and emotional stability (Salgado, 2003), psychologists using tests for purposes where these values are paramount need to be aware of the relative strengths and weaknesses of their testing options.

On a positive note, some studies on the CPI have found that the factor structure of the test is similar in many cultures, including Japan (Gough and Bradley, 1996). In addition, achievement through conformance and achievement through independence predict

GPA in North America and in other countries such as Italy and Greece (Paunonen and Ashton, 1998). Even though the factor structure is similar in a variety of countries, the items may not be equally relevant. For example, the items fail to discriminate between issues that are particularly important in one culture compared to another (Paunonen and Ashton, 1998).

NEWER SCALES BASED ON THE CPI 434

In keeping with the 'open system' approach of the CPI 434, several additional subscales have been developed, which are summarized in Table 5.3 and briefly described below. These are separated into general scales and those used within I/O areas. Anyone interested in using any of these scales are urged to consult the original references for further detailed information.

General scales

With regard to general scales, Klohnen (1996) developed a scale to measure ego resiliency (ER) from the CPI. Klohnen defined ER as the 'general capacity for flexible and resourceful adaptation to internal and external stressors' (1996: 1067). This scale consists of consists of 29 items from the CPI 434, which show good internal reliability (0.81–0.88) and good convergent validity with an observer-based measure of ER (Klohnen, 1996).

The next scale to be developed, hostility (H), was proposed as a result of the documented links between high levels of this characteristic and poor health outcomes and unhealthy behaviour. The H scale consists of 33 items reportedly having good internal reliability (alpha 0.74–0.77) and high correlations with other measures of hostility (Adams and John, 1997).

Subsequently, Johnson (1997) published an article describing the construction of

seven scales from the CPI to assess social performance. These scales were originally developed in the late 1970s but were not published until relatively recently. The scales were based on Hogan's (1983) socioanalytic theory-based interpretation of the FFM: sociability, ambition, likeability, prudence, adjustment, intellectance, and ego control. The internal reliabilities of the scales are good (> 0.7) for sociability, ambition, adjustment and intellectance, but less than 0.7 for likeability, prudence, and ego control. However, even these values are in keeping with those reported for the standard CPI scales.

The most recent of the general scales to be developed is the Depression scale (Jay and John, 2004), consisting of 33 items, which provide a broad coverage of DSM-IV symptoms of depression (American Psychiatric Association, 1994). The Depression scale possesses similar content to the Beck Depression Inventory II (BDI) (Beck et al., 1996) and the Centre for Epidemiological Studies Depression Scale (CES-D) (Radloff, 1977). Administration of the Depression scale embedded in the entire CPI or administered separately resulted in internal reliability of 0.88–0.90, which is comparable to that of the BDI and CES-D. The scale shows good convergent, discriminant, and external validity. These scales are summarized in Table 5.3.

I/O-related scales

As the CPI is widely used within I/O settings, other researchers have been concentrating on developing scales which may prove useful in this area. For example, Hakstian and Farrell (2001) developed a measure of openness (Op) which has been shown to be predictive of training proficiency and creative management behaviours, and thus this scale has relevance for personnel selection. The Op scale is related to the CPI special purpose scale, creative temperament, but measures a wider range of

Table 5.3   Recently developed scales for the CPI 434: scale type, reliability, developer and items

Scale name	Internal reliability	Developer (author and year)	CPI items contributing to the scale
General-use scales			
Ego resiliency	0.81–0.88	Klohnen, 1996	From CPI Form 472 (research version) (Gough, 1986) True keyed: 331(61*), 363 (21), 366 (245) and 448 (226) False keyed: 12, 15, 16 (411), 31, 38, 46 (NI), 59 (362), 74, 111, 147, 177, 188(422), 205(390), 238, 243, 248, 258, 328(186), 365, 374(270), 385(76), 416, 418, 428 (145) and 454 (94)
Hostility	0.74–0.77	Adams and John, 1997	From CPI Form 480 (Gough 1957) True keyed: 10, 11, 27, 32, 49, 56, 57, 60, 117, 124, 128, 136, 142, 173, 176, 188, 194, 206, 209, 219, 225, 247 (NI), 266, 282(NI), 294, 349, 351, 375, 405, 426 (NI), 446 (175), 457 (381). False keyed: 107
Sociability	0.70–0.74	Johnson, 1997	From CPI Form 462 (Gough, 1986) True keyed: 1, 4, 52, 102, 163, 167, 168, 208, 218, 231, 239, 242, 251, 296, 319, 395 False keyed: 83, 87, 188, 215, 249, 318, 340
Ambition	0.81–0.82	"	From CPI Form 462 (Gough, 1986) True keyed: 6, 53, 112, 171, 179, 202, 216, 224, 256, 260, 264, 320, 346, 359, 376, 380, 403, 412, 448 (226) False keyed: 7, 31, 145, 379, 385, 422, 426, 443 (151)
Likeability	0.67–0.69	"	From CPI Form 462 (Gough, 1986) True keyed: 45, 127, 198 False keyed: 29, 44, 56, 57, 71, 81, 94, 137, 153, 161, 233, 270, 290, 293, 342, 364, 374, 428
Prudence	0.59–0.69	"	From CPI Form 462 (Gough, 1986) True keyed: 125, 149, 165, 174, 181, 212, 223, 314, 367 False keyed: 77, 93, 101, 185, 214, 250, 275, 288, 302, 336, 396, 420, 431
Adjustment	0.83–0.88	"	From CPI Form 462 (Gough, 1986) True keyed: 21, 108, 200, 245, 259 False keyed: 12, 38, 40, 54, 76, 111, 124, 150, 159, 176, 177, 186, 225, 227, 232, 257, 258, 284, 416, 418, 419 (NI), 429, 452 (313)
Intellectance	0.62–0.89	"	From CPI Form 462 (Gough, 1986) True keyed: 8, 17, 50, 61, 84, 97, 140, 152, 160, 166, 228, 269, 280, 283, 292, 391 False keyed: 121, 199, 281, 311, 352, 382, 401, 436 (67)
Ego control	0.65–0.66	"	From CPI Form 462 (Gough, 1986) True keyed: 14, 24, 35, 85, 88, 229, 230, 246, 328, 361, 363, 387, 408 False keyed: 99, 119, 132, 143, 157, 170, 331, 456 (362)
Depression	0.88–0.90	Jay and John, 2004	From CPI Form 462 (Gough, 1987). True keyed: 13, 15, 54, 70, 99, 124, 147, 156, 161, 238, 257, 279, 299, 311, 339, 353, 365, 369, 390, 398, 416, 419 (NI), 426, 456 (362), 459 (402). False keyed: 21, 50, 133, 135 (NI), 245, 259, 280, 400.

Table 5.3   Recently developed scales for the CPI 434: scale type, reliability, developer and items—cont'd

Scale name	Internal reliability	Developer (author and year)	CPI items contributing to the scale
General-use scales			
Personnel selection/managerial scales			
Openness	0.75	Hakstian and Farrell, 2001	Items available in the print version of the original article
Counterproductivity	0.8–0.90	Hakstian, Farrell and Tweed, 2002	From CPI Form 434 (Gough, 1996) True keyed: 20, 26, 36, 39, 42, 44, 52, 54, 66, 67, 77, 81, 93, 99, 101, 102, 114, 120, 132, 139, 145, 156, 161, 163, 164, 170, 185, 189, 191, 194, 203, 208, 214, 218, 248, 250, 251, 267, 268, 270, 275, 297, 302, 307, 331, 336, 349, 388, 396, 399, 405, 420, 425, 431. False keyed: 14, 35, 61, 68, 69, 96, 123, 134, 181, 195, 204, 212, 223, 230, 235, 254, 260, 276, 278, 286, 328, 343, 380, 394, 408, 409
Employment-related motivational distortion	0.72–0.86	Hakstian and Ng, 2005	From CPI Form 434 (Gough, 1996) True keyed: 5, 14, 52, 65, 69, 167, 179, 195, 202, 218, 222, 223, 226, 239, 254, 255, 278, 292, 305, 319, 345, 354, 355, 359, 361, 370, 371, 376, 382, 392, 403, 408, 424 False keyed: 30, 38, 55, 66, 91, 124, 139, 151, 156, 191, 203, 238, 258, 262, 268, 275, 313, 334, 379, 414, 416, 418, 426

*Where items in the original article are derived from an older version of the CPI, numbers in brackets refer to item on Form 434. Where no number is indicated in brackets the item number is unchanged. NI = not included in Form 434

characteristics. Items were chosen to reflect tolerance, liberalism, adaptability, flexibility, and a searching, inquiring intellect. The final Op scale is comprised of 36 items, which is best administered as part of the CPI. Initial studies suggest it shows good internal reliability (0.75), and test–retest reliability (0.84 at two weeks) and it has been shown to correlate highly with the facets of actions, ideas, and values from the NEO-PI (Costa and McCrae, 1992).

A year later, Hakstain et al. (2002) developed a scale to assess counterproductive tendencies, which cover areas such as theft, dishonesty, absenteeism, tardiness, substance abuse, laziness, and disruptiveness, rather than just delinquency. This scale consists of 80 items which overall has good internal reliability (0.8–0.9) and test–retest reliability (0.88–0.89) which are best administered as part of the whole CPI, in order to make their purpose less obvious. The most recent scale to be developed by this group assesses employment related motivational

distortion, which is defined as 'the intentional altering of personality test responses from what examinees believe is true for themselves to increase the likelihood of getting a job for which they have applied' (Hakstian and Ng, 2005: 406). The scale consists of 56 items (reported in the original article) with good internal reliability (0.72–0.86) and test–retest reliability (0.80–0.86). A summary of the newly developed scales and their items is presented in Table 5.3.

INTERPRETATION

The following section presents a brief overview of the interpretation of the CPI. Further detailed interpretive guidelines can be found in the CPI manual (Gough and Bradley, 1996) or the text by McAllister (1996).

First, during administration, it is important to note the time taken to complete the CPI (usually 40 and 60 minutes). A shorter completion time suggests the profile may be invalid, or the respondent was answering impulsively. If the completion time is much longer, this could indicate the presence of depression, a high degree of indecisiveness, too great a focus on detail, or possibly poor reading ability (Groth-Marnat, 2003). Second, the validity of the profile should be checked for: (1) completeness (more than 25 blank items suggest the test results may not be valid); (2) double answering (true and false to the same question); and (3) random answering (suggested by low score (< 30 T) on Cm). Other validity issues, such as faking good, can usually be determined by examining the Gi score (> 70 T suggests faking good), alternatively a low Gi score (< 35 T) suggests faking bad. In addition, a low Wb score (< 30 T) suggests a fake bad profile or very poor self-concept. Gough has also presented equations designed to more accurately detect fake good, fake bad, and random answering profiles (Gough and Bradley, 1996; Groth-Marnat, 2003; McAllister, 1996). Once the validity of the profile is confirmed, the next step is to interpret the vector or structural scales.

The CPI boasts three structural scales or vectors. Combining the first two vectors (externality/internality and norm doubting/norm favouring) allows the user to place a person into one of four personality types (alpha, beta, gamma and delta). The third vector provides information regarding self-realization, rated on a scale of 1–7. The low end of the scale represents poor or little self-realization/integration, 4 is average and a score of 7 suggests a very high level of self-realization and psychological integration (Gough and Bradley, 1996; Groth-Marnat, 2003; McAllister, 1996).

With regard to the four personality types, alphas are extraverted, outgoing, active, and respect societal norms. They tend to be task-focused, ambitious, and often fulfil managerial or leadership roles. Those who are well developed (high score on vector 3) can be charismatic, while those who score much lower can be quite selfish and manipulative.

Similarly, betas also show respect for societal norms but tend to be more private individuals. They are happy as followers, show a high degree of self-control, and are dependable. They frequently consider others' needs before their own. Those who are highly self-actualized are viewed as inspiring and perceptive, while those who are less so may appear inflexible, overly conforming, and rigid. In contrast, gamma types enjoy social participation and are extraverted, like alphas. But they question, rather than accept traditional norms. They are creative and function in the most innovative areas of their field. If they score low on vector 3, they may come across as self-indulgent, intolerant, and disruptive. Finally, deltas tend to be introverted and choose personal value systems rather than those of the community. They are detached and often reflective, sometimes becoming overly absorbed in their own daydreams. Deltas who have reached optimal realization can often be creative and imaginative, but this often goes unnoticed. Those who are poorly developed may appear withdrawn, self-defeating and poorly organized (Groth-Marnat, 2003; McAllister, 1996). This model of personality has been used to examine the relationship between personality type and vocational choice/success and educational choice/success. Studies show that alphas most frequently major in the applied sciences, pre-professional programs, business administration, and engineering. Deltas tend to choose arts, music and humanities. Gammas are most often found in social sciences such as psychology, while teaching and nursing attracts Beta types (Gough and Bradley, 1996). As yet, the utility of this system is unknown but it is certainly an area worthy of further study.

The next step in interpretation is to examine the overall level of the profiles. Scores of greater than T = 50 generally suggest positive adjustment, while scores far below this suggest problem areas. However, these scores have to be interpreted in the context of the test-taker's age, education level, situation, and occupation as high scores for one person may be an expected score for another

(Groth-Marnat, 2003; McAllister, 1996). Following this, the scores on different groups (clusters) of scales are compared. These clusters are based on conceptual similarity rather than statistical relatedness, and are clearly delineated on the CPI profile. Cluster 1 (or class 1) measures interpersonal style and orientation (consisting of Do, Cs, Sy, Sp, Sa, In, and Em); cluster 2 assesses normative orientation and values (Re, So, Sc, Gi, Cm, Wb, and To); cluster 3 measures cognitive and intellectual functioning (Ac, Ai, and Ie); and cluster 4 is associated with role and personal style (Py, Fx, and F/M). The scales contributing to each of these clusters are summarized in Table 5.1 (Gough and Bradley, 1996).

An alternative approach to examining groups of scores is to examine them on the basis of the statistically derived five factors. Factor 1 comprises Do, Cs, Sy, Sp, Sa, In, and Em (as does cluster 1) and measures social poise and interpersonal effectiveness; factor 2 assesses overall wellbeing and personal adjustment (Re, So, Sc, Gi, Wb, To, and Ac); factor 3 is related to independent behaviour and action (Ai, Fx, To, Ie, and Py); factor 4 measures adherence to social norms (Cm, Re, So, and Wb) and the fifth factor (F/M) assesses sensitivity, aesthetic interests and dependency (Groth-Marnat, 2003; McAllister, 1996)

Once these steps are completed, the individual scales can be interpreted, which are described and summarized in Tables 5.1 and 5.2. The CPI manual provides detailed descriptions of each of these scales and also details the adjectives most commonly associated with them. This greatly assists in constructing an accurate description of the respondent (Gough and Bradley, 1996). Following this, further analyses can be conducted based on interpreting combinations of scores (see McAllister, 1996) and/or by using CPI equations which have been developed for making predictions regarding a variety of issues such as high-school achievement, college attendance, grade point averages, teaching effectiveness, medical promise, dental performance, leadership, parole success, and social maturity (Groth-Marnat, 2003). Thus,

the information that can be derived from the CPI is extensive and detailed. Clearly it needs to be interpreted in light of the respondent's life circumstances and other measures. However, to use the CPI to its full potential and provide accurate interpretations, users are encouraged to read as many case studies as possible, paying close attention to the interpretation.

THE CPI 260 (GOUGH AND BRADLEY, 2002)

More recently, a shorter version of the CPI has been developed, namely the 260-item version (CPI 260) which is specifically for use within work and I/O settings (Manoogian, 2002, 2005). There are 29 scales, arranged as 20 folk scales, 3 structural scales and 6 special purpose scales, which are administered online. The scales are largely similar to the CPI 434, although 4 of the folk scales, 3 vector scales and 1 of the special purpose scales have been respectively renamed as follows:

* Socialization (So) is social conformity (So);
* Intellectual efficiency (Ie) is conceptual fluency (Cf);
* Psychological mindedness (Py) is insightfulness (Is);
* Femininity/masculinity (F/M) is sensitivity (Sn);
* Externality/internality (v.1) is participating/private (v.1);
* Norm-favouring/norm-doubting is approving/questioning (v.2);
* Ego integration (v.3) is fulfilment (v.3); and
* Leadership potential (Lp) is leadership (Lp).

Interestingly, the toughmindedness scale has been dropped completely in the CPI 260 for reasons not made clear in the manual. The alpha reliabilities for this shortened version are similar to the full length CPI. The lowest alpha was 0.54 for sensitivity and the highest alpha was 0.86 for dominance. There are high interscale correlations between the short and long forms of the CPI, suggesting that the shortened version possesses similar properties (Pinfold, 2004). As yet, little published research has been undertaken with the CPI

260 to determine its utility in personnel management and leadership. However, the feedback forms are clearly orientated more to leadership and management qualities compared to those from the CPI 434. For example, the feedback forms provide information related to issues such as dealing with others, self-management, motivation and thinking styles (Gough and Bradley, 2003). As with CPI Form 434, the three vector scales of the CPI 260 allow a person to be described as a particular personality type. For the CPI 260 these are: (1) implementer, (2) supporter, (3) innovator, and (4) visualizer. Sample reports for both versions of the CPI are available for illustrative purposes at no charge on the test publisher's website (<http://www.cpp-db.com>).

NEW AREAS OF RESEARCH

In this section we attempted to focus on studies which have used the CPI as a research tool (not including scale development based on the CPI 434 which was discussed earlier in this chapter) published since and including the year 2000. While we refer to studies prior to 2000 (depending on the subject area) for background information, we have focused our attention on innovative applications of the CPI in research efforts either as an adjunct to the study (e.g. to help discern which subjects to exclude from a study) or as a focal point for a study that is innovative. We admit that our selection does not cover all subject areas in the literature; however, we were somewhat surprised by the limited nature and scope of the current CPI research literature. This may be because neither the CPI 434 nor the CPI 260 provide materials or answer keys for hand scoring by researchers, thus diminishing interest by potential researchers. Also, as can be seen by the literature we examined, some studies are still using the older versions of the CPI, which allow for hand scoring by researchers. Despite the ease of utility of the older CPI versions for research purposes, the findings of these studies may be viewed as of limited value in the application to the current CPI forms.

Personality dimensions

Studies suggest that the 'egosytonicity' of items may affect the validity of some of the scales. 'Egosytonic' items are hypothesized to be those 'which a respondent finds congenial . . . on which giving an opinion is a rewarding act . . . (and from which respondents) experience a certain sense of satisfaction . . . a small surge of positive affect . . . answering "true"' (Gough and Bradley, 1996: 10). Participants are reported to enjoy responding to communality scale items (to which most people agree), items relating to positive emotions and attitudes related to higher extraversion, conscientiousness, emotional stability, and openness to experience. Thus people may be more likely to respond truthfully to these types of items. This may be worth taking into account if using subscales with a high number of negatively worded items or those addressing negative feelings or situations as this may bias a respondent's answers (Johnson, 2006).

Schweizer (2002) used the impulsivity scale (Gough, 1957) along with other instruments to study the interaction of impulsivity and reasoning performance. His findings showed that impulsivity and reasoning performance were negatively correlated, and that high levels of impulsivity clearly impaired a subject's ability to complete reasoning tasks.

Another area of interest is that of giftedness and parental personality dimensions. As part of their longitudinal study of giftedness and achievement, Runco and Albert (2005) examined exceptionally gifted adolescents and their parents on the CPI 480 (Gough, 1975) and found that parental personality profiles were similar between boys with high IQs and boys with exceptional math/science abilities. Of a particular interest, the mothers and fathers of both groups of subjects had elevated achievement via independence scores, but low achievement via conformance scores. Runco and Albert indicated that such this difference between the achievement scales was evidence of 'critical tendencies and persistence' (2005: 365). The boys also showed similarities in terms of showing low scores on the wellbeing and good impression scales of the CPI 480.

Substance abuse and forensic applications

Not all articles reviewed in this section involve both substance abuse issues and forensic issues. However, many recent articles do examine crossover topics in these areas and hence we have combined these two areas in this section.

Of the subscales derived prior to the development of the CPI 434, one of the most frequently used for research purposes in the forensic and substance abuse areas is the CPI-So (socialization) developed by Gough (1957) and subsequently validated by Rosen and Schalling (1974). Research conducted on this subscale indicates that CPI-So may be used to predict antisocial and prosocial behaviour. For example, Gough and Bradley (1992) found that CPI-So differentiated between men and women with and without criminal backgrounds. In another study, baseline antisociality as measured by the CPI-So scale was found to be significantly correlated with treatment non-completion (Alterman et al., 1998).

Gomà-i-Freixanet (2001) found that the CPI-So differentiated between female subjects divided into groups by level and type of risk-taking behaviours (including female armed robbers and three other non-criminal groups of women who engaged in varying levels of risk-taking). Gomà-i-Freixanet's (2001) data analysis indicates that the antisocial group obtained significantly lower CPI-So scores than the other three groups and the latter three groups (including the group which did not participate in any risk-taking behaviour) did not show any significant difference in terms of their CPI-So scores. While Gomà-i-Freixanet (2001) interpreted these data as supported of a particular model of risk-taking behaviour, we would suggest caution when antisocial behaviour is equated with risk-taking behaviour, as the differences found in his study

(in terms of the CPI-So) may be due to antisociality as opposed to risk-taking behaviour.

Studies suggest that the CPI-So scale is made up of four factors: positive affect; self-discipline; cathexis of social norms; interpersonal awareness (Gough, 1994). This factor structure has been found to be consistent in criminal and non-criminal populations, suggesting that scores along the prosocial to antisocial continuum can be interpreted (Collins and Bagozzi, 1999). This scale is being increasingly used within addiction and treatment areas. For example, the CPI-So scale has been used to match alcoholics with the most appropriate treatment modality. That is, it accurately identified poorly socialized alcoholics who responded better to Cognitive Behaviour Therapy than Interactional Group Therapy (Kadden et al., 1996).

In related research, CPI-So scores (from the CPI 480 by Gough, 1975) were reported as being lower in polysubstance users than single substance users (Conway et al., 2003). In another study using a small sample of rural college students divided into groups by level and type of substance, Wolff and Wolff (2002) opined that occasional drug or alcohol users had somewhat 'healthier' personality features than abstainers or more regular users. However, the data indicate that individuals who do not use drugs (abstainers) had significantly higher scores on the CPI-So and achievement through conformance scales than occasional drug users and the latter scored significantly higher on these scales than regular drugs users. While the occasional users of drugs or alcohol had higher scores on scales such as good impression, psychological mindedness and achievement through independence, the author's overall conclusion is questionable. This study also used the 462-item version of the CPI (Gough, 1986).

In a somewhat related area, the CPI-So has been used to differentiate between pathological gamblers with and without antisocial personality disorder (Pietrzak and Petry, 2005). Unsurprisingly, pathological gamblers with antisocial personality disorder had significantly lower scores on the CPI-So than those without this personality disorder.

Similarly, Fein et al. (2004) found that male and female abstinent alcoholics had significantly lower scores on the CPI-So scale than did the non-alcoholic (but alcohol using) control group.

I/O and cross-cultural applications

A great deal of research has been conducted on the CPI in terms of I/O and cross-cultural applications of the test, including some research where these two applications cross over to examine I/O applications in non-North American cultures to show the widespread utility of the test.

In an innovative prospective study with a small sample of new telemarketing employees, Hakstian et al. (1997) showed that a composite index utilizing three CPI scales from the CPI 480 (achievement through conformance, socialization, and self-acceptance) had predictive validity for job performance. In another study that examined work performance, Cook et al. (2000) reported on correlations between scales of the CPI 462 and self-ratings of various aspects of work behaviour such as technical proficiency, effort, personal discipline, general proficiency, and leadership by 899 city employees in the UK who volunteered to participate in the study. Essentially, Cook and his colleagues (2000) found very little by way of overall correlations to the work indicators, but concluded that their data indicated some support for the differential validity of the CPI and the importance of examining a wide range of criteria when studying work performance.

Young et al. (2000) utilized the 34-item Managerial Potential Scale (MPS) devised by Gough (1984). Young and his colleagues (2000) found that MPS was one of only two significant factors in terms of correlation to overall performance in a sample of 566 managerial employees from a variety of Fortune 500 companies.

There is good evidence regarding the cross-cultural reliability of the CPI scales, particularly with regards to its use in selecting job applicants. The good impression scale of CPI is often used to detect 'faking good' in job applicants. A recent study showed that a Norwegian student sample scored significantly lower on this scale compared to a US student sample, which has implications with regard to personnel selection among different cultures (Sandal and Endresen, 2002). However, other studies suggest good cross-cultural reliability as the CPI exists in 29 languages designed to represent 'dispositions having universal status' (Gough, 1965). One recent study that examined job satisfaction in Romanian engineers (Van den Berg and Pitariu, 2005), used the CPI 462 (Gough, 1986), but collapsed the scales of the CPI 462 and the Sixteen Personality Factor Questionnaire (Cattell et al, 1970) via factor analysis. Some of the findings by Van den Berg and Pitariu (2005) were discrepant with other studies and these authors noted that from a theoretical point of view 'the external validity of the Big Five personality model (FFM) is partly dependent on socio-cultural factors' (2005: 233).

Adjunct applications

A number of recent studies were reviewed for this chapter which used the CPI or more frequently the socialization subscale (CPI-So) to control for antisocial traits between subject groups (e.g., Martin et al., 2004; Gonzalez et al., 2005). An interesting study by Sorocco et al. (2006) also utilized the CPI-So scores as a measure of antisocial tendencies. Sorocco and her colleagues (2006) did not find any difference in emotional or physiological response, namely diurnal cortisol release, to the stressors employed in their study.

In summary, the current research that employs the CPI, plus the crossover literature between these various areas have been particularly fertile and shows promise for continued work. In addition, the CPI-So subscale is considered by many researchers as an important adjunct method to ascertain the antisociality of test subjects and either to measure or to control for such tendencies across sample groups.

CRITICISMS

There are several issues that could complicate research efforts or limit the ability to draw conclusions from one's CPI data. First, we noted that much of the current research literature utilizes older versions of the test which may limit the validity of findings in terms of their extrapolation to test results using newer versions of the CPI. Second, much of the recent research has employed the CPI-So, which is again, almost always based on the 1975 CPI 480 or the 1986 CPI 462, both of which allow for researcher hand scoring unlike the current versions of the CPI. Third, there are many studies which utilizes the CPI, but few of these studies publish internal reliability data. For research conducted with the most recent edition of the CPI, this may be because the scoring keys are kept confidential and all scoring is done at CPP. Thus, the researcher receives individual reports which detail the scale scores for each participant, but these reports do not provide item level responses, which are necessary to calculate reliability statistics. However, the publisher suggested to the present authors that the research team at CPP may be able to help with this but 'item level scoring is not widely available' (R.J. Devine, pers. comm., February 14, 2007). The need to return forms to CPP for scoring appears to be at odds to the concept of the 'open system' of questionnaire development (Goldberg et al., 2006) and certainly adds an important restriction on reliability estimation. As many researchers have already done (as indicated above), any new researchers wishing to use the CPI and conduct item level analysis, an alternative approach would be to use the older version of the CPI, such as the CPI 480 or CPI 462, both of which provide hand-scoring instructions. Alternatively, the International Personality Item Pool (IPIP) (Goldberg, 1999; <http://ipip.ori.org>) is a set of over 2,000 items which are freely available. Psychometric properties of the current IPIP scales are updated frequently and there are keys for scoring the current scales. The constructs in the most frequently used personality inventories, including those in the newest versions of the CPI (CPI 260 and CPI 434), can be measured by the IPIP. However, this latter approach needs to be undertaken with caution as there may be construct definition differences. In particular, this has been shown for the Dominance scale (Goldberg et al, 2006).

The fourth issue is in relation to how the subscales are administered. The CPI is designed to be administered as a whole but numerous studies use subscales in isolation and until recently the consequences of this departure from the recommended administration of the test have not been addressed. Surprisingly, a study using the CPI-So scale suggests that isolated administration may lead to more reliable results than when this scale is embedded within the entire CPI, possibly because CPI-So is not a unique construct, but instead forms part of a larger factor which represents general prosocial disposition (Alterman et al., 2003). However, using other scales in a similar isolated fashion should be carried out with caution until studies have demonstrated the equivalence of the two forms of subscale administration.

There are other grounds for criticism, but most of these have already been discussed by Groth-Marnat (2003). For example, the absence of factor-analytic work during scale development has been noted. Also, perhaps more importantly from a clinical point of view, test users are faced with the problem of interpreting multiple scale elevations as there are no reference books for this purpose and a paucity of research on this topic. The MMPI, by contrast, has both reference books for two and three factor elevations, along with a great deal of supporting research.

CONCLUSION

The CPI continues to provide fertile ground for research. The CPI 434 has generated a great deal of interest in a wide variety of research areas and has shown promise, particularly in relation to I/O psychological assessment areas.

If one wanted to measure the so-called 'folk scales' described by the CPI, using a personality assessment instrument for the reasons outlined in the manual, the CPI is probably a good choice. However, if one was interested in FFM-related research, other tests based on the FFM offer a greater degree of flexibility and a more sound psychometric basis on which to base your research. Indeed, the large number of recent publications based on the FFM and its assessment suggests that this is increasing in popularity both in the research and I/O areas. However, the CPI 260 provides very stiff competition for the I/O test user and is arguably the most user-friendly I/O-related instrument for personality assessment currently on the market. Nonetheless, if used for the reasons just cited in this paragraph, Bolton's (1992) widely cited conclusion about the CPI remains relevant, if perhaps somewhat less true in a relative sense than when it was written: '[The] CPI is an excellent normal personality assessment device, more reliable than the manual adverts, with good normative data and outstanding interpretive information' (1992: 139).

NOTES

Please note that we have used the abbreviation 'CPI' to refer to the California Psychological Inventory *in general* (regardless of version), and when we are referring to a particular version of the test we indicate the version under discussion.

REFERENCES

Adams, S.H. and John, O.P. (1997) 'A hostility scale for the California Psychological Inventory: MMPI, Observer Q Sort, and Big Five correlates', *Journal of Personality Assessment*, 69(2): 408–24.

Alterman, A.I., McDermott, P.A., Mulvaney, F.D., Cacciola, J.S., Rutherford, M.J., Searles, J.S., Lynch, K. and Cnaan, A. (2003) 'Comparison of embedded and isolated administrations of the California Psychological Inventory's socialization subscale', *Psychological Assessment*, 15(1): 64–70.

Alterman, A.I., Rutherford, M.J., Cacciola, J.S., McKay, J.R. and Boardman, C.R. (1998) 'Prediction of 7 month methadone maintenance treatment response by four measures of antisociality', *Drug and Alcohol Dependence*, 49(3): 217–23.

American Psychiatric Association (1994) *Diagnostic and Statistical Manual of Mental Disorders* (4th edn). Washington, DC: American Psychiatric Association.

Beck, A.T., Steer, R.A. and Brown, G.K. (1996) *Beck Depression Inventory Manual* (2nd edn). San Antonio, TX: Psychological Corporation.

Bolton, B. (1992) 'Review of the California Psychological Inventory, revised edition', in J.J. Framer and J.C. Conely (eds), *Eleventh Mental Measurements Yearbook*. Lincoln, NE: Buros Institute of Mental Measurement, pp. 558–62.

Cattell, R.B., Eber, H.W. and Tatsuoka, M.M. (1970) *Handbook for the Sixteen Personality Factor Questionnaire (16PF)*. Champaign: Institute for Personality and Ability Testing (IPAT).

Camara, W.J., Nathan, J.S. and Puente, A.E. (2000) 'Psychological test usage: Implications in professional psychology', *Professional Psychology: Research and Practice*, 31(2): 141–54.

Collins, J.M. and Bagozzi, R.P. (1999) 'Testing the equivalence of the socialization factor structure for criminals and noncriminals', *Journal of Personality Assessment*, 72(1): 68–73.

Conway, K.P., Kane, R.J., Ball, S.A., Poling, J.C. and Rounsaville, B.J. (2003) 'Personality, substance of choice and polysubstance involvement among substance dependent patients', *Drug and Alcohol Dependence*, 71(1): 65–75.

Cook, M., Young, A., Taylor, D. and Bedford, A.P. (2000) 'Personality and self rated work performance', *European Journal of Psychological Assessment*, 16(3): 202–8.

Costa, P.T. Jr. and McCrae, R.R. (1992) *Revised NEO Personality Inventory (NEO PI-R) and NEO Five-Factor Inventory (NEO-FFI): Professional Manual*. Odessa, FL: Psychological Assessment Resources.

Fein, G., Klein, L. and Finn, P. (2004) 'Impairment on a simulated gambling task in long-term abstinent alcoholics',

Alcoholism: Clinical and Experimental Research, 28(10): 1487–91.

Fleenor, J.W. and Eastman, L. (1997) 'The relationship between the five-factor model of personality and the California Psychological Inventory', *Educational and Psychological Measurement*, 57(4): 698–704.

Goldberg, L.R., Johnson, J.A., Eber, H.W., Hogan, R., Ashton, M.C., Cloninger, C.R. and Gough, H.G. (2006) 'The international personality item pool and the future of public-domain personality measures', *Journal of Research in Personality*, 40(1): 84–96.

Goldberg, L.R. and Saucier, G. (1999) 'International personality item pool. A scientific collaboratory for the development of advanced measures of personality and other individual differences', Retrieved February 16, 2007 from http://ipip.ori.org.

Gomà-i-Freixanet, M. (2001) 'Prosocial and antisocial aspects of personality in women: A replication study', *Personality and Individual Differences*, 30(8): 1401–11.

Gonzalez, R., Vassileva, J., Bechara, A., Grbesic, S., Sworowski, L., Novak, R.M., Nunnally, G. and Martin, E.M. (2005) 'The influence of executive functions, sensation seeking, and HIV serostatus on the risky sexual practices of substance-dependent individuals', *Journal of the International Neuropsychological Society*, 11(2): 121–31.

Gough, H.G. (1957) *Manual for the California Psychological Inventory*. Palo Alto, CA: Consulting Psychologists Press.

Gough, H.G. (1975) *The California Psychological Inventory*. Palo Alto, CA: Consulting Psychologists Press.

Gough, H.G. (1984) 'A managerial potential scale for the California Psychological Inventory', *Journal of Applied Psychology*, 69(2): 233–40.

Gough, H.G. (1986) *The California Psychological Inventory*. Palo Alto, CA: Consulting Psychologists Press.

Gough, H.G. (1987) *The California Psychological Inventory: Administrator's Guide*. Palo Alto, CA: Consulting Psychologists Press.

Gough, H.G. (1994) 'Theory, development and interpretation of the CPI socialization scale', *Psychological Reports*, 75(suppl.1): 651–700.

Gough, H.G. and Bradley, P. (1992) 'Delinquent and criminal behavior as assessed by the revised California Psychological Inventory', *Journal of Clinical Psychology*, 48(3): 298–308.

Gough, H.G. (2000) 'The California Psychological Inventory', in C.E. Watkins and V.L. Campbell (eds), *Testing and Assessment in Counseling Practice* (2nd edn). Mahwah, NJ: Lawrence Erlbaum Associates, pp. 45–71.

Gough, H.G. (1965) 'Cross-cultural validation of a measure of asocial behavior', *Psychological Reports*, 17(2): 379–87.

Gough, H.G. and Bradley, P. (1996) *California Psychological Inventory manual* (3rd edn). Palo Alto, CA: Consulting Psychologists Press.

Gough, H.G. and Bradley, P. (2002) *California Psychological Inventory 260 (CPI 260)*. Palo Alto, CA: Consulting Psychologists Press.

Gough, H.G. and Bradley, P. (2003) *CPI 260 Client Feedback Report*. Palo Alto, CA: Consulting Psychologists Press.

Groth-Marnat, G. (2003) *Handbook of Psychological Assessment* (4th edn). Hoboken, NJ: John Wiley & Sons.

Hakstian, A.R. and Farrell, S. (2001) 'An openness scale for the California Psychological Inventory', *Journal of Personality Assessment*, 76(1): 107–34.

Hakstain, A.R., Farrell, S. and Tweed, R.T. (2002) 'The assessment of counterproductive tendencies by means of the California Psychological Inventory', *International Journal of Selection and Assessment*, 10(1/2): 58–86.

Hakstian, A.R. and Ng, E.L. (2005) 'Employment related motivational distortion: Its nature, measurement and reduction', *Educational and Psychological Measurement*, 65(3): 405–41.

Hakstian, A.R., Scratchley, L.S., MacLeod, A.A., Tweed R.G. and Siddarth S, (1997) 'Selection of telemarketing employees by standardised assessment procedures', *Psychology and Marketing*, 14(7): 703–26.

Hogan, R. (1983) 'A socioanalytic theory of personality', in M.M. Page (ed.), *Nebraska Symposium on Motivation 1982: Personality – Current Theory and Research*. Lincoln: University of Nebraska Press, pp. 55–89.

Jay, M. and John, O.P. (2004) 'A depressive symptom scale for the California Psychological Inventory: Construct validation of CPI-D', *Psychological Assessment*, 16(3): 299–309.

Johnson, J.A. (1997) 'Seven social performance scales for the California Psychological

Inventory', *Human Performance*, 10(1): 1–30.

Johnson, J.A. (2006) 'Ego-syntonicity in response to items in the California Psychological Inventory', *Journal of Research in Personality*, 40(1): 73–83.

Kadden, R.M., Litt, M.D., Donovan, D. and Cooney, N.L. (1996) 'Psychometric properties of the California Psychological Inventory socialisation scale in treatment seeking alcoholics', *Psychology of Addictive Behaviours*, 10(3): 131–46.

Klohnen, E.C. (1996) 'Conceptual analysis and measurement of the construct of ego resiliency', *Journal of Personality and Social Psychology*, 70(5): 1067–79.

Manoogian, S. (2002) *CPI 260 Coaching Report for Leaders User's Guide (A)*. Palo Alto, CA: Consulting Psychologists Press.

Manoogian, S. (2005) *CPI 260 Coaching Report for Leaders User's Guide*. Palo Alto, CA: Consulting Psychologists Press.

Martin, E.M., Pitrak, D.L., Weddington, W., Rains, N.A., Nunnally, G., Nixon, H., Grbesic, S., Vassileva, J. and Bechara, A. (2004) 'Cognitive impulsivity and HIV serostatus in substance dependent males', *Journal of the International Neuropsychological Society*, 10(7): 931–8.

McAllister, L. (1996) *A Practical Guide to CPI Interpretation*. Palo Alto, CA: Consulting Psychologists Press.

McCrae, R.R., Costa, P.T. and Piedmont, R.L. (1993) 'Folk concepts, natural language, and psychological constructs: The California Psychological Inventory and the five-factor model', *Journal of Personality*, 61(1): 1–26.

Paunonen, S.V. and Ashton, M.C. (1998) 'The structured assessment of personality across cultures', *Journal of Cross Cultural Psychology*, 29(1): 150–70.

Pietrzak, R.H. and Petry, N.M. (2005) 'Antisocial personality disorder is associated with increased severity of gambling, medical, drug and psychiatric problems among treatment-seeking pathological gamblers', *Addiction*, 100(8): 1183–93.

Pinfold, A. (2004) *Comparison of the CPI 260 and 434*. Retrieved February 16, 2007 from <http://www.nzcer.org.nz/pdfs/comparisonofCPI434andCPI260.pdf>

Radloff, L.S. (1977) 'The CES-D scale: A self report depression scale for research in the general population', *Applied Psychological Measurement*, 1(3): 385–401.

Rosen, A. and Schalling, D. (1974) 'On the validity of the California Psychological Inventory socialization scale: A multivariate approach', *Journal of Consulting and Clinical Psychology*, 42(6): 757–65.

Runco, M.A. and Albert, R.S. (2005) 'Parents' personality and the creative potential of exceptionally gifted boys', *Creativity Research Journal*, 17(4): 355–67.

Salgado J.F. (2003) 'Predicting job performance using FFM and non-FFM personality measures', *Journal of Occupational and Organizational Psychology*, 76(3): 323–46.

Sandal, G.M. and Endresen, I.M. (2002) 'The sensitivity of the CPI good impression scale for detecting "faking good" among Norwegian students and job applicants', *International Journal of Selection and Assessment*, 10(4): 304–11.

Schweizer, K. (2002) 'Does impulsivity influence performance in reasoning?', *Personality and Individual Differences*, 33(7): 1031–43.

Sorocco, K.H., Lovallo, W.R., Vincent, A.S. and Collins, F.L. (2006) 'Blunted hypothalamic-pituitary-adrenocortical axis responsivity to stress in persons with a family history of alcoholism', *International Journal of Psychophysiology*, 59(3): 210–7.

Thorndike, R.L. (1959) 'The California Psychological Inventory: A review', in O.K. Buros (ed.), *Fifth Mental Measurements Yearbook*. Highland Park, NJ: Gryphon Press.

Van den Berg, P.T. and Pitariu, H. (2005) 'The relationship between perosnality and well-being during societal change', *Personality and Individual Differences*, 39(3): 229–34.

Wolff, M.W. and Wolff, K.A. (2002) 'Personality characteristics as a function of frequency and type of substance use', *Adolescence*, 37(148): 705–16.

Young, B.S., Arthur, W. Jr. and Finch, J. (2000) 'Predictors of managerial performance: More than cognitive ability', *Journal of Business and Psychology*, 15(1): 53–72.

6

The Comrey Personality Scales

Andrew L. Comrey[1]

This chapter summarizes the development, validation, and interpretation of the Comrey Personality Scales (Comrey, 1970a, 1970b, 1980, 1993, 1994), an inventory of factored personality traits. The Comrey Personality Scales, hereafter abbreviated as the CPS, were designed to measure the variables that make up a taxonomy of personality traits developed over a period of years by the author with the aid of many of his students. The factored traits included in this taxonomy are the following: T – trust versus defensiveness; O – orderliness versus lack of compulsion; C – Social Conformity versus Rebelliousness; A – activity versus lack of energy; S – emotional stability versus neuroticism; E – extraversion versus introversion; M – masculinity versus femininity[2]; and P – empathy versus egocentrism.

The factored personality scales for measuring these traits evolved in a series of steps as the taxonomy itself developed, with improvements in both occurring at each step. The attempt to develop this taxonomy was inspired originally by discrepancies in the personality taxonomies proposed by Guilford, Cattell, and Eysenck, three of the most important writers on personality measurement. The taxonomic research undertaken by the author had, as its initial objective,

a resolution of the differences among these well-known writers. The intention was to independently seek out and identify the major factors of personality with the idea of comparing the resulting taxonomy of traits with those of the three authors mentioned.

As the research progressed, it became clear that the author's own taxonomy would not closely match that of any one of these previous writers. Instead, a taxonomic system began to emerge that, while sharing much with these previous systems, was nevertheless distinct from any of them. As the form of this taxonomy took shape, methods of identifying the major factors were developed and refined, along with methods of measuring the factors, ultimately leading to the published version of the CPS (Comrey, 1970a, 1970b).

STUDIES OF MMPI ITEMS

Since the objective of the planned research program called for the identification of the main factors needed to describe human personality, the decision was made to study the items of several well-known personality test instruments under the assumption that they would define at least some of the needed personality factors well enough to permit their identification.

The MMPI was selected as the first instrument to be studied because it was the most widely used personality inventory and also because the usual scores derived from the MMPI appeared to be factorially complex and overlapping. Factor analyses of the items scored on these scales would serve the double function of (a) yielding clues to the important personality dimensions and (b) clarifying the factor composition of these widely used scales. It was decided, therefore, to factor analyze the items on each of the main scales of the original MMPI. These ten published studies are described more fully in the original CPS manual (Comrey, 1970b). Because computers were new in psychology when this work was begun, it took three years to develop a completely computerized procedure for factor analyzing large matrices of correlations among the items on the MMPI scales. This work involved a considerable amount of experimentation with different kinds of correlation coefficients, methods of factor extraction, and methods of factor rotation.

These studies demonstrated that the scales of the MMPI are indeed factorially complex, with many of the same factors appearing on more than one scale. Moreover, the connections between the scale names and the apparent content of the factors found in the scale items are rather tenuous for most of the scales. Beyond this, however, these factor studies of MMPI items provided the initial identification of three of the final CPS personality taxonomy factors. The cynicism factor in the MMPI analyses ultimately led to the trust versus defensiveness factor. Agitation, sex concern, and neuroticism item factors from the MMPI analyses led eventually to the present emotional stability versus neuroticism factor, and finally, the MMPI shyness factor is now represented in the CPS by the extraversion versus introversion factor. The initial identification of these factors was poor, as were the methods of

measuring them. The present-day factor measures and the factors themselves were developed through a long series of refinements over the subsequent 12 years. As newer factors were being sought and developed, work continued on the refinement of factors already identified.

THE FHID APPROACH

These initial studies with MMPI items were followed by several investigations designed to locate important constructs in the personality domain through a consideration of other personality tests (Levonian et al., 1959; Comrey and Soufi, 1960, 1961). Ideas derived from these studies and from the published works of other investigators provided the basis for the first empirical investigation by the author aimed directly at developing a factor analytic taxonomy of personality traits (Comrey, 1961). This article also outlined a first approximation to the strategy that was to guide subsequent research efforts culminating in the publication of the CPS.

A very important feature of this research strategy is the use of the Factored Homogeneous Item Dimension (FHID) as the basic unit of analysis in factor analytic studies designed to locate the main factors for a taxonomy of personality. A study of past factor analytic investigations, the author's as well as those of others, revealed that many obtained factors are virtual artifacts produced by the analysis of variable collections that include subsets of variables that are too similar in character. If a random selection of personality-test items from a specified pool is factor analyzed, for example, it is probable that some of the items will be very similar to other items in the pool, creating subsets of items that are essentially alternate ways of asking the same question. Because of the great similarity of the items in such a homogeneous subset, they will correlate considerably higher among themselves than they will with items outside the subset.

Because of this, these highly related items will be very apt to define their own separate factor in the solution.

A factor produced by the unwitting or even intentional insertion of highly similar items into an analysis is not the kind of broad factor construct that is needed for a taxonomy to describe the whole of human personality. In factor analytic studies designed to locate broader and more meaningful constructs, it is necessary to take steps to avoid the production of factors that are not at an appropriate level in the hierarchy of factors.

The development and use of the FHID as the basic unit in the factor analysis has helped to accomplish this objective in the studies leading to the production of the CPS. The FHID is a total score variable calculated by summing scores over several items that are required to satisfy the following two criteria: (a) the items must be originally developed and logically conceived as measures of the variable under consideration, or chosen with this in mind; (b) the items must be found to define the same factor in a factor analysis of items. By meeting both these requirements, the items forming a FHID are shown to have both conceptual and demonstrated empirical statistical homogeneity. To control for acquiescence response bias (tendency to agree or to disagree), half the items are phrased positively with respect to the FHID name and half of the items are phrased negatively. Item scores for the negatively worded items are reversed before adding them with the positively worded item scores to obtain the total FHID score. This score reversal is accomplished by subtracting the number of the selected response from an appropriate value at or higher than the highest numbered response. With the CPS, which uses response scales numbered from 1 to 7, the negatively worded response values are subtracted from 8.

The early studies carried out in this programmatic research revealed that many factors emerging from the studies were essentially nothing more than FHIDs. The experience gained from these and subsequent studies showed that it was relatively easy to develop a pool of conceptually homogeneous items that would define a single factor when included in a factor analysis of items. Not all items, of course, would emerge with loadings of sufficient magnitude to be acceptable. Items that failed to yield an adequately high loading were modified or replaced. Through a succession of analyses, a set of items could usually be developed that would meet the criteria for a FHID. Although it proved to be relatively easy to develop these item factors, or FHIDs, to represent numerous defined personality concepts, success was not always attained, by any means. A poorly defined concept usually leads to failure of developing a FHID. The items may split up into more than one item factor when included in a factor analysis of items or they may fail to define any factor at all. In such cases, the concept must be redefined and new items written for another attempt or the concept must be dropped.

The relative ease with which such item factors were produced led the author to reject the notion that FHID factors represent those major constructs that are needed to provide the basis for scientific development in the field of personality. In areas of measurement that do not depend on items, factors of a similarly arbitrary sort can be produced by using highly overlapping measures in the same analysis; for example, diastolic and systolic blood pressure included together in the same analysis of physiological variables. Such factors are considered to be at a very low level in the hierarchy of factors.

Factor analysis of properly selected FHIDs, however, can force the production of factors at a higher level in the factor hierarchy. The FHIDs analyzed must be selected in such a fashion as to avoid inclusion of two or more FHIDs that overlap each other too much conceptually in what they measure; that is, alternate forms of each other. If two or more alternate-form types of FHIDs are included, it is like including two very similar items in an analysis of items in which the effect is to drive out a factor that is very low in the hierarchy of factors. In analyses of FHIDs, this problem is avoided by making certain that each FHID included as a variable is conceptually distinct from every other FHID in the analysis. When this is done, the factors that emerge fall at a higher level than the FHID level in the hierarchy of factors, and hence, are much more likely to represent the broad constructs needed for a taxonomy to provide the basis for development of a science. Thus, factors produced by the common variance found among conceptually distinct FHIDS represent constructs at a level of generality above the FHID level.

The advantages of factor analyzing FHIDs instead of items to locate the major constructs in a given field such as personality, are not limited to being able to control the level in the factor hierarchy where the factors will emerge (Comrey, 1984). When items are combined to form a FHID, such as in the CPS, each FHID score is based on four items and has a range of possible scores from 4 to 28. Not only is the unreliable two-choice item replaced by a much more reliable seven-choice item, but the total FHID score itself is further enhanced in reliability through the use of several items instead of just one. Thus, the basic building blocks of the analysis are much better variables with much higher reliabilities than two-choice items. It inevitably follows that factor analytic results using FHIDs will be much more stable than those based on items, especially two-choice items (Comrey and Montag, 1982).

The second level in the factor hierarchy, where factors that come from analyses of conceptually distinct FHIDs lie, might be called the 'primary' level, following Thurstone's use of the term in his famous studies of the primary mental abilities. The factors at this primary level are conceived as providing the kind of constructs most likely to be useful for developing a science of personality, for example. It is extremely important to note that the number of factors that have emerged at this level is very limited. Only eight have been verified so far in the CPS system, although others may well be

added in the future. The number of factors that can be produced at the FHID level, however, is almost without limit. As long as new groups of similar items can be found, new FHID factors can be identified. The principle of scientific parsimony demands that we limit the number of main constructs that we use to form our scientific taxonomies. Primary level factors are sufficiently numerous and broad enough to cover the domain but they are limited in number. FHID factors are not.

Although these primary-level factors are considerably broader in character than FHIDs, they are not so broad as to represent 'type' factors. Type factors are found at a higher level in the factor hierarchy, being based on the correlations that occur naturally among the primary-level factors. Type factors are too few, too broad, and too complex to be most useful for the task of building a general taxonomy for scientific purposes, although they may be very useful for certain applications. General intelligence would be an example of a well-established type-level factor in the domain of human abilities. It is a high-level factor in the hierarchy of factors that exists because the basic primary-level human ability factors are substantially correlated in the general population.

Application of the FHID approach to the task of building a taxonomy of factored personality traits gradually led to the emergence of the following general strategy (Comrey, 1984):

1   Formulate verbal definitions of many personality concepts that might lead to the development of FHIDs;
2   Develop a pool of items for each of these defined concepts, half stated positively and half stated negatively with respect to the concept name;
3   Carry out factor analyses of items in which all the items for a given concept are included in the same analysis together with items designed to measure other concepts. Avoid including items in the same analysis for concepts that are expected to measure the same primary-level factor construct. If two item pools from the same primary-level factor are included in the same analysis,

the factor analytic results may not produce only FHIDs but may produce the primary-level factor or some hybrid factor that represents a mixture of the two levels.

4   Revise the items and item pools and reanalyze until an acceptable FHID is available for each concept retained. Concepts that fail to produce acceptable FHIDs in the refinement process are dropped out.

5   Factor analyze the FHIDs to develop a first approximation impression of the number and nature of the primary-level factor constructs. On the basis of these results, formulate a verbal conception of each factor construct identified at the primary-factor level.

6   Develop new FHIDs and revise or drop old ones with the objective of providing several variables with high loadings on each factor. Diversity of content is desirable among the variables defining a factor so that all important aspects of the factor construct will be represented. FHIDs that prove to be factorially complex, that is, with major loadings on more than one primary-level factor, are eliminated.

7   Carry out new analyses in which the primary-level factors expected are specified along with the FHIDs that are supposed to define them. Drop, modify or redefine factors and FHIDs that fail to replicate in successive studies with different subjects. Retain the factors, and the FHIDs defining them, that replicate successfully in a series of studies. Continue, however, to search for FHIDs that might do an even better job of defining these replicated factors.

8   Formulate hypotheses about new factor constructs that might constitute useful additions to the taxonomy of replicated factors. Try to expand the taxonomy, in other words, into as yet unrepresented but important areas of the domain. Develop FHIDs that should define such hypothesized factors, and carry out new analyses to determine if such factors do emerge and whether or not they can be replicated. Continue the attempt to expand the taxonomy until no new primary-level factors can be found.

PRELIMINARY FACTOR ANALYTIC STUDIES

The research strategy using the FHID, as described in the previous section, was applied in a series of investigations undertaken during the 1960s to develop the personality taxonomy upon which the CPS is based. All of these studies, both published and unpublished, are described more fully and referenced in the original CPS manual (Comrey, 1970b). To save space, the references will not be given here. The earliest of these studies concentrated on methodology, developing FHIDs, and some preliminary identification of primary factors. Factors T, O, S, and E were already identified by this time, although under different names.

These factors continued to emerge in subsequent studies, undergoing successive refinements and improvements in the FHIDs designed to measure them. Empathy versus egocentrism (P) was the next factor to be strongly identified, followed by social conformity versus rebelliousness (C). In each study, the previously identified factors emerged along with the newly identified ones. Factors that failed to replicate were dropped from consideration. The remaining two factors in the taxonomy, activity versus lack of energy (A) and masculinity versus femininity (M), were added as a result of a study in which FHIDs from the previous studies were analyzed together with quasi-FHIDs derived from an analysis of the Guilford–Zimmerman Temperament Survey (GZTS). These 'quasi-FHIDs' were groups of items found in the GZTS that appeared upon inspection to meet the criteria for FHIDs reasonably well. In this analysis, all the previously established CPS factors were replicated but, in addition, the GZTS general activity and masculinity factors emerged as distinct from the CPS factors. In subsequent studies, these two factors were replicated using new items and FHIDs to define them, so they were added to the taxonomy as activity versus lack of energy (A) and masculinity versus femininity (M). This study also established the strong similarity between the GZTS emotional stability and the CPS factor that had been called 'neuroticism' up to this point.

Additional studies of the CPS FHIDs and factors with factor scores from the Eysenck

Personality Inventory and the Cattell 16 PF revealed the essential similarity between the CPS neuroticism, the GZTS emotional stability, the Eysenck neuroticism, and Cattell's second-order neuroticism factor. For these reasons, the CPS factor name was changed to 'emotional stability versus neuroticism' (S). Eysenck's extraversion–introversion factor was also found to be very similar to Cattell's second-order extraversion–introversion factor, and to the CPS factor that up to this point had been called 'shyness', so shyness was renamed 'extraversion versus introversion' (E). Other name changes in the CPS factors were initiated to provide a bipolar name for each factor with the more culturally approved pole mentioned first.

At the conclusion of these studies, eight repeatedly replicated factors had been identified along with several FHIDs to measure each of them. Although not all the FHIDs had loadings on their respective factors as high as one might like, the decision was made to go ahead with the publication of the CPS even though later studies might identify some better FHIDs and one or more additional valid factors not included in the original eight. Development of the CPS taxonomy was viewed, at this point, as a work in progress rather than as a completed endeavor. The results of the final pre-publication empirical replication study, described more fully in the original CPS Manual (Comrey, 1970b), are summarized in the next section.

FACTOR ANALYSIS OF THE FHIDS IN THE CPS

After the final decision had been made about what primary-level factors had demonstrated sufficient independence and replicability to be included in the CPS personality taxonomy, a new sample of subjects was drawn to serve as the basis for deriving the final normative data and for obtaining a final factor solution. The final published version of the CPS was administered to 746 volunteer

subjects, 362 males, and 384 females. About one-third of these subjects were visitors to a university Open House day at UCLA, comprising friends, acquaintances, and families of students for the most part. The remaining two-thirds of the cases consisted of university students, their friends, and UCLA employees. The sample, therefore, represented predominantly the educated upper-middle class with a heavy concentration of subjects in the college-age group but with some representation for all adult age groups.

The variables

Forty-four variables were included in the analysis: 40 FHIDs defining the 8 CPS factors; 2 validation scales, validity (V) and response bias (R); plus the variables of age and sex. Each of the personality factors was represented by 5 FHIDs. Each FHID in turn contained 4 items, 2 positively stated with respect to the FHID name and 2 negatively stated. Each item was answered by using one of the following two response scales:

- Scale X: 7 = always, 6 = very frequently, 5 = frequently, 4 = occasionally, 3 = rarely, 2 = very rarely, 1 = never.
- Scale Y: 7 = definitely, 6 = very probably, 5 = probably, 4 = possibly, 3 = probably not, 2 = very probably not, 1 = definitely not.

The validation scales, V and R, were designed to provide information about the genuineness of the test protocol. The V scale presents items to which the respondent should give a particular extreme response, either a '1' for a positively stated item or a '7' for a negatively stated item. Since there are eight items on this scale, the expected total score is 8 due to the fact that an item score of 7 becomes 1 when the score is reversed for a negatively stated item. If the respondent has a score that departs too far from 8 on the V scale, for example if values approach 25 or more, the test protocol becomes suspect. Random marking should produce on the average a score of 32 on the V scale.

The R scale, on the other hand, is designed as a 'response bias' scale, to indicate whether the subjects are responding in a 'socially desirable' way (i.e. making themselves look good). Very low scores on the R scale would suggest that the subjects might be deliberately giving a socially undesirable impression of themselves for some reason. The 44 variables included in the analysis are listed below. Following each FHID name (variables 1 to 40) a letter is given in parentheses to show what factor this FHID is supposed to measure. A sample item is also given with its item number in the CPS test booklet. The X or Y after the item number indicates the preferred scale to be used by the respondent in choosing a test statement answer. If the item number is underlined, the item is negatively stated with respect to the FHID name (Table 6.1).

The analysis

The 44 variables described in the previous section were intercorrelated using the Pearson product-moment correlation coefficient. This 44 × 44 matrix of correlation coefficients was factor analyzed by the minimum residual method (Comrey, 1962; Comrey and Ahumada, 1965; Comrey, 1973; Comrey and Lee, 1992), with 15 factors extracted to be certain that more than enough factors would be taken out. By the fifteenth factor, the loadings were of negligible importance and the residuals contained no appreciable true variance remaining to be extracted. No iteration of the minimum residual solution was carried out, hence the obtained communalities and factor loadings are underestimated to some extent.

The 15 minimum residual factors were rotated by criterion I of the tandem criteria for orthogonal analytic rotation (Comrey, 1967; Comrey, 1973; Comrey and Lee, 1992). This procedure spreads the variance from the

minimum residual solution out, but only as far as the intercorrelations among the variables permit since the method seeks to place as much variance on one factor as possible given that the variables placed on the same factor must be correlated with each other. Most extraction methods can squeeze the variance down even more than criterion I rotations do because they can place variables on the same factor that are not correlated with each other and typically do.

Only eight of the criterion I factors were of appreciable importance; the remaining criterion I factors were too small in the proportion of variance accounted for to be considered further. Since only the first eight of the criterion I factors had enough high loadings to be considered as possible major factors, only these factors were re-rotated by criterion II of the tandem criteria in the attempt to produce a solution in which the variance is distributed more evenly among the retained factors, such as is customarily obtained in a simple structure solution.

The eight rotated criterion II factors are shown in Table 6.2. Only loadings of 0.30 or more are shown to make the table easier to read. These results represent the final orthogonal rotated loadings for the 44 variables defining the eight CPS taxonomy factors. The sharp break in the number of important criterion I factors at exactly eight when there were eight factors expected would not normally occur. These results were achieved after a long series of studies in which the factors and the variables defining them had been carefully refined to produce a very sharp factor structure.

Although the orthogonal solution in Table 6.2 presents a sharp factor structure, plots of the factors with each other suggested the need for oblique rotations if simple structure criteria were to be maximally satisfied. Details of the extensive steps involved in the oblique rotations are given elsewhere (Comrey, 1973; Comrey and Lee, 1992) so, to save space, they will not be repeated here. An additional reason is that the variables that had major loadings in the orthogonal solution also

Table 6.1 Factored Homogeneous Item Dimensions (FHIDs), V, R, Age, and Sex

1.	Lack of cynicism (T)	1X.	The average person is honest.
2.	Lack of defensiveness (T)	19X.	You can get what is coming to you without having to be aggressive or competitive.
3.	Belief in human worth (T)	37Y.	Most people are valuable human beings.
4.	Trust in human nature (T)	10X.	Other people are selfishly concerned about themselves in what they do.
5.	Lack of paranoia (T)	20X.	Some people will deliberately say things to hurt you.
6.	Neatness (O)	2Y.	I could live in a pig pen without letting it bother me.
7.	Routine (O)	20Y.	Living according to a schedule is something I like to avoid.
8.	Order (O)	38X.	My room is in a mess.
9.	Cautiousness (O)	11X.	I am a cautious person.
10.	Meticulousness (O)	29X.	I will go to great lengths to correct mistakes in my work which other people wouldn't even notice.
11.	Law enforcement (C)	3Y.	This society provides too much protection for criminals.
12.	Acceptance of social order (C)	21Y.	The laws governing the people of this country are sound and need only minor changes, if any.
13.	Intolerance of nonconformity (C)	39Y.	Young people should be more willing than they are to do what their elders tell them to do.
14.	Respect for law (C)	12X.	If the laws of society are unjust, they should be disobeyed.
15.	Need for approval (C)	30X.	I ignore what my neighbors might think of me.
16.	Exercise (A)	4X.	If I think about exercising, I lie down until the idea goes away.
17.	Energy (A)	22X.	I seem to lack the drive necessary to get things done.
18.	Need to excel (A)	40Y.	Being a big success in life requires more effort than I am willing to make.
19.	Liking for work (A)	13X.	I love to work long hours.
20.	Stamina (A)	31X.	I can work a long time without feeling tired.
21.	Lack of inferiority feelings (S)	6X.	I feel inferior to the people I know.
22.	Lack of depression (S)	24X.	I feel so down-in-the-dumps that nothing can cheer me up.
23.	Lack of agitation (S)	42X.	My nerves seem to be on edge.
24.	Lack of pessimism (S)	15X.	I expect things to turn out for the best.
25.	Mood stability (S)	33X.	My mood remains rather constant, neither going up nor down.
26.	Lack of reserve (E)	7X.	I am a very talkative person.
27.	Lack of seclusiveness (E)	25X.	At a party I like to meet as many people as I can.
28.	No loss for words (E)	43X.	It is easy for me to talk with people.
29.	Lack of shyness (E)	16X.	I find it difficult to talk with a person I have just met.
30.	No stage fright (E)	34Y.	It would be hard for me to do anything in front of an audience.
31.	No fear of bugs (M)	8X.	Big bugs and other crawling creatures upset me.
32.	No crying (M)	26X.	A sad movie makes me feel like crying.
33.	No romantic love (M)	44X.	I like movies which tell the story of two people in love.
34.	Tolerance of blood (M)	17Y.	I could assist in a surgical operation without fainting if I had to.
35.	Tolerance of vulgarity (M)	35X.	I can tolerate vulgarity.
36.	Sympathy (P)	144X.	I am rather insensitive to the difficulties that other people are having.
37.	Helpfulness (P)	27Y.	I enjoy helping people even if I don't know them very well.
38.	Service (P)	45Y.	I would like to devote my life to the service of others.
39.	Generosity (P)	18Y.	I would hate to make a loan to a poor family I didn't know very well.
40.	Unselfishness (P)	36X.	I take care of myself before I think about other people's needs.
41.	Validity scale (V)	5Y.	If I were asked to lift a ten-ton weight, I could do it.
42.	Response bias scale (R)	41X.	My morals are above reproach.
43.	Age (recorded as a two-digit number)		
44.	Sex (scored 1 = male, 0 = female)		

Table 6.2   Orthogonal Rotated Matrix for 40 CPS FHIDs, V, R, Age, and Sex

FHID	Factor	T	O	C	A	S	E	M	P	h^2
Trust vs.Defensiveness (T)										
1	T	0.68								0.54
2	T	0.59								0.43
3	T	0.57								0.45
4	T	0.66								0.49
5	T	0.63								0.48
Orderliness vs. Lack of Compulsion (O)										
6	O		0.57							0.43
7	O		0.59							0.44
8	O		0.69							0.52
9	O		0.35							0.29
10	O		0.54							0.39
Social Conformity vs. Rebelliousness (C)										
11	C			0.76						0.64
12	C			0.67						0.51
13	C		0.31	0.72						0.61
14	C			0.67						0.57
15	C			0.44						0.31
Activity vs. Lack of Energy (A)										
16	A				0.51					0.33
17	A				0.67	0.30	0.31			0.68
18	A		0.34		0.38					0.38
19	A		0.34		0.51					0.49
20	A				0.70					0.62
Emotional Stability vs. Neuroticism (S)										
21	S					0.59	0.32			0.50
22	S					0.69				0.62
23	S					0.66				0.51
24	S					0.61				0.54
25	S					0.57				0.44
Extraversion vs. Introversion (E)										
26	E						0.68			0.50
27	E						0.60			0.50
28	E						0.84			0.82
29	E						0.79			0.69
30	E						0.49			0.36
Mental Toughness vs. Sensitivity (M)										
31	M							0.61		0.45
32	M							0.60		0.46
33	M							0.43		0.23
34	M							0.43		0.27
35	M			−0.44				0.34		0.44
Empathy vs. Egocentrism (P)										
36	P								0.66	0.55
37	P								0.77	0.71
38	P								0.66	0.48
39	P								0.67	0.51
40	P								0.57	0.43

Continued

Table 6.2   Orthogonal Rotated Matrix for 40 CPS FHIDs, V, R, Age, and Sex—cont'd

FHID	Factor	T	O	C	A	S	E	M	P	h^2
Validity Scale										
41								0.23		0.07
Response Bias										
42				0.31					0.40	0.41
Age (Years)										
43		0.20								0.10
Sex (Male vs. Female)										
44								0.54		0.37

Notes: Loadings < 0.30 have been omitted (except for variables 41 and 43, which have no loadings ≥ 0.30).
All FHIDs are scored in the direction of the factor (thereby minimizing negative loadings).
Names for the FHIDS (Variables 1–40) are shown in Table 6.1
(N = 746; 362 males and 384 females).

had major loadings in the oblique solution. Oblique factor pattern coefficients, however, will be reported along with the orthogonal loadings when the factors are described below.

Description of the CPS factors

For each CPS factor, a brief description will be given below along with the FHIDs that have loadings of 0.30 or more in either the orthogonal or the oblique solution.

I. Trust versus Defensiveness (T)

Individuals who are high on this personality factor indicate that they believe more than the average person in the basic honesty, trustworthiness, and good intentions of other people. They believe that others wish them well and they have faith in human nature. Individuals who are low on T are cynical, defensive, suspicious, and have a low opinion of the value of the average person. FHIDs 1 through 5 were expected to define this factor. FHIDs and/or variables with loadings of 0.30 or more on this factor are as shown in Table 6.3.

II. Orderliness versus Lack of Compulsion (O)

Individuals who are high on this factor tend to be very concerned with neatness and orderliness. They report being cautious,

meticulous, and say they like to live in a routine way. Individuals who are low on this factor are inclined to be careless, sloppy, unsystematic in their style of life, reckless, and untidy. FHIDs 6 through 10 were expected to define this factor. FHIDs and/or variables with loadings of 0.30 or more on this factor are shown in Table 6.4.

III. Social Conformity versus Rebelliousness (C)

Individuals who are high on this factor depict themselves as accepting the society as it is, respecting the law, believing in law enforcement, seeking the approval of society, and resenting nonconformity in others. Individuals who are low on this factor are inclined to challenge the laws and institutions of the society, resent control, accept nonconformity in others, and are nonconforming themselves. FHIDs 11 through 15 were expected to define this factor. FHIDs

Table 6.3   Trust versus Defensiveness (T)

Variable	Orthogonal	Oblique
1. Lack of cynicism	0.68	0.71
2. Lack of defensiveness	0.59	0.60
3. Belief in human worth	0.57	0.53
4. Trust in human nature	0.66	0.68
5. Lack of paranoia	0.63	0.63

Table 6.4 Orderliness versus Lack of Compulsion (O)

Variable	Orthogonal	Oblique
6. Neatness	0.57	0.47
7. Routine	0.59	0.50
8. Order	0.69	0.67
9. Cautiousness	0.35	0.25
10. Meticulousness	0.54	0.53
18. Need to Excel	0.34	0.31
19. Liking for Work	0.34	0.35

and/or variables with loadings of 0.30 or more on this factor are shown in Table 6.5.

IV. Activity versus Lack of Energy (A)

Individuals who are high on this factor report liking physical activity, hard work, and exercise, having great energy and stamina, and striving to excel. Individuals who are low on A are inclined to be physically inactive, lack drive and energy, tire quickly, and have little motivation to excel. FHIDs 16 through 20 were expected to define this factor. FHIDs and/or variables with loadings of 0.30 or more on this factor are shown in Table 6.6.

V. Emotional Stability versus Neuroticism (S)

Individuals who are high on this factor report being happy, calm, optimistic, stable in mood, and having confidence in themselves. Individuals who are low on the factor have inferiority feelings, are agitated, depressed, pessimistic, and have frequent mood swings. FHIDs 21 through 25 were expected to define this factor. FHIDs and/or variables

Table 6.5 Social Conformity versus Rebelliousness (C)

Variable	Orthogonal	Oblique
2. Lack of defensiveness	-0.21	-0.30
7. Routine	0.28	0.30
11. Law Enforcement	0.76	0.80
12. Acceptance of the social order	0.67	0.66
13. Intolerance of nonconformity	0.72	0.77
14. Respect for law	0.67	0.70
15. Need for approval	0.44	0.46
35. Tolerance of vulgarity	-0.44	-0.46
40. Unselfishness	0.23	0.32
42. Response bias scale (R)	0.31	0.36

Table 6.6 Activity versus Lack of Energy (A)

Variable	Orthogonal	Oblique
9. Cautiousness	0.28	-0.31
16. Exercise	0.51	0.55
17. Energy	0.67	0.71
18. Need to excel	0.38	0.38
19. Liking for work	0.51	0.55
20. Stamina	0.70	0.74

with loadings of 0.30 or more on this factor are shown in Table 6.7.

VI. Extraversion versus Introversion (E)

Individuals who are high on this factor depict themselves as outgoing, easy to meet, seeking the company of others, meeting strangers easily, and speaking before groups with little fear. Individuals low on the factor are reserved, reclusive, shy, cannot easily find things to talk about with others, and suffer from stage fright. FHIDs 26 through 30 were expected to define this factor. FHIDs and/or variables with loadings of 0.30 on this factor are shown in Table 6.8.

VII. Masculinity versus Femininity (M)

Individuals who are high on this factor report being rather tough-minded individuals who are not bothered by crawling creatures, the sight of blood, vulgarity, who do not cry easily, and who have little interest in love stories. Individuals who are low on this factor are inclined to cry easily, are bothered by blood and crawling things such as snakes and insects, are disturbed by vulgarity, and have a high interest in romantic love. FHIDs 31 through 35 and the sex variable were expected

Table 6.7 Emotional Stability versus Neuroticism (S)

Variable	Orthogonal	Oblique
17. Energy	0.30	0.11
21. Lack of inferiority feelings	0.59	0.54
22. Lack of depression	0.69	0.65
23. Lack of agitation	0.66	0.66
24. Lack of pessimism	0.61	0.56
25. Mood stability	0.57	0.60

Table 6.8 Extraversion versus Introversion (E)

Variable	Orthogonal	Oblique
17. Energy	0.31	0.10
21. Lack of inferiority feelings	0.32	0.25
26. Lack of reserve	0.68	0.72
27. Lack of seclusiveness	0.60	0.58
28. No loss for words	0.84	0.86
29. Lack of shyness	0.79	0.82
30. No stage fright	0.49	0.52

Table 6.10 Empathy versus Egocentrism (P)

Variable	Orthogonal	Oblique
36. Sympathy	0.66	0.65
37. Helpfulness	0.77	0.79
38. Service	0.66	0.67
39. Generosity	0.67	0.68
40. Unselfishness	0.57	0.60
42. Response bias scale (R)	0.40	0.39

to have major loadings on this factor. FHIDs and/or variables with loadings of 0.30 or more on this factor are shown in Table 6.9.

Masculinity versus femininity (M) has several FHIDs with rather small loadings so it is the least homogeneous of the CPS factors and the one that needs the most work to find additional FHIDs with high loadings.

VIII. Empathy versus Egocentrism (P)

Individuals who are high on this factor describe themselves as sympathetic, helpful, generous, unselfish, and interested in devoting their lives to the service of other people. Individuals who are low on this factor are not particularly sympathetic or helpful to others, tend to be concerned about themselves and their own goals, and are relatively uninterested in dedicating their lives to serving other people. FHIDs 36 through 40 were expected to define this factor. FHIDs and/or variables with loadings of 0.30 or more on this factor are shown in Table 6.10.

DISCUSSION OF RESULTS

The orthogonal criterion II solution (Table 6.2) and the oblique factor pattern solution

agree rather well in showing that in most cases the variables had major loadings on the factors they were expected to define and not elsewhere. The two variables that were most disappointing in this respect were FHIDs 9 and 35. FHID variable 9, cautiousness, was expected to have a major loading on factor O, orderliness versus lack of compulsion. It had loadings of 0.35 in the orthogonal solution and 0.25 in the oblique solution while exhibiting loadings almost as high in other factors. This FHID, therefore, would be regarded as a prime candidate for revision or replacement in carrying out another study designed to improve the factor taxonomy and the test instrument.

In this study, variable 35, tolerance for vulgarity, appears to be too complex factorially, measuring factor C as much as it measures factor M since its loadings are of comparable magnitude in both factors. If such results continue to be replicated, in a revision of the test instrument, this particular FHID would also be marked for revision or replacement. Variable 18, need to excel, has its highest loading on the factor it is supposed to define, factor A, but the loading was only 0.38. This FHID had higher loadings on factor A, however, in later replications of this study (see Table 6.11).

The loadings for variables 33 and 34 are not very high on factor M, about 0.43, in both solutions, but they have no appreciable loadings on any other factors. This tends to make factor M somewhat broader and less homogeneous in composition compared to other factors but this is not necessarily unacceptable. It would be desirable, however, to increase these loadings in a revised version of the taxonomy and test if at all possible.

Table 6.9 Masculinity versus Femininity (M)

Variable	Orthogonal	Oblique
25. Mood stability	0.27	0.30
30. No stage fright	0.28	0.38
31. No fear of bugs	0.61	0.64
32. No crying	0.60	0.63
33. No romantic love	0.43	0.43
34. Tolerance of blood	0.43	0.44
35. Tolerance of vulgarity	0.34	0.34
44. Sex (male versus female)	0.54	0.56

Table 6.11 Loadings of CPS FHIDs for Six Different Samples

Factor	FHID	NO	BZ	NZ	MA	DV	AU
T1.	Lack of cynicism	68	56	63	71	78	66
T2.	Lack of defensiveness	59	51	43	48	54	49
T3.	Belief in human worth	57	52	58	52	59	61
T4.	Trust in human nature	66	54	61	63	69	57
T5.	Lack of paranoia	63	43	49	46	67	62
O6.	Neatness	57	57	48	58	65	60
O7.	Routine	59	59	70	42	56	59
O8.	Order	69	59	73	62	79	75
O9.	Cautiousness	35	51	45	21	35	45
O10.	Meticulousness	54	29	54	09	38	40
C11.	Law enforcement	76	56	64	55	67	66
C12.	Acceptance of social order	67	66	57	39	03	48
C13.	Intolerance of nonconformity	72	69	63	46	68	75
C14.	Respect for law	67	51	57	65	49	66
C15.	Need for approval	44	26	49	06	36	30
A16.	Exercise	51	61	64	35	56	56
A17.	Energy	67	35	73	66	65	66
A18.	Need to excel	38	26	58	36	53	56
A19.	Liking for work	51	69	50	48	66	56
A20.	Stamina	70	59	61	58	66	64
S21.	Lack of inferiority feelings	59	38	44	49	49	54
S22.	Lack of depression	69	64	68	68	58	61
S23.	Lack of agitation	66	47	64	54	69	61
S24.	Lack of pessimism	61	60	60	52	55	60
S25.	Mood stability	57	41	63	65	71	64
E26.	Lack of reserve	68	71	67	71	73	71
E27.	Lack of seclusiveness	60	57	54	70	71	73
E28.	No loss for words	84	77	82	77	92	88
E29.	Lack of shyness	79	77	78	72	85	84
E30.	No stage fright	49	52	55	38	58	52
M31.	No fear of bugs	61	40	59	70	64	65
M32.	No crying	60	57	67	53	59	62
M33.	No interest in love stories	43	43	38	32	52	43
M34.	Tolerance of blood	43	39	46	37	38	42
M35.	Tolerance of vulgarity	34	35	50	34	28	32
P36.	Sympathy	66	53	52	53	64	54
P37.	Helpfulness	77	72	73	70	74	68
P38.	Service	66	60	64	59	57	62
P39.	Generosity	67	63	56	70	71	70
P40.	Unselfishness	57	60	55	52	63	58

Note: Decimal points have been omitted. The samples referred to in the columns of this table are: NO = normative group, BZ = Brazil college students, NZ = New Zealand college students, MA = Mexican-American students, DV = Denver residents, AU = Australian residents. Factor names are T = trust vs. defensiveness, O = orderliness vs. lack of compulsion, C = social conformity vs. lack of rebelliousness, A = activity vs. lack of energy, E = extraversion vs. introversion, M = masculinity vs. femininity, and P = empathy vs. egocentrism

STUDIES DESIGNED TO VALIDATE THE CPS FACTORS

Validity information concerning the CPS has been derived from many different sources, empirical, theoretical, and clinical. For example, many studies have been carried out for the purpose of determining the robustness of the CPS factor structure under different motivational conditions and in different cultural settings. Other studies have been concerned with the utility of the factor scales themselves in research, in selection, and in the clinic. Still other studies have represented concurrent validation efforts in which the CPS factors have been related to scales from other well-known personality tests. The author has had extensive personal experience in examining CPS test results in relation to other characteristics of individuals in clinical and other settings. Information from these various sources as it applies to interpreting the meaning of CPS factor scores will be summarized in the remainder of this chapter.

A construct validation study

An example of a simple construct validation investigation of the CPS is contained in the factor analytic study reported above through the inclusion of 'sex' as a variable. It was predicted that variable 44, sex, should have a substantial positive loading on factor M, masculinity versus femininity. Both loadings for the gender-identity variable 44, sex, were above 0.50 on M. There are easier ways of determining sex than by giving the CPS, of course, but the verification of this deduction is a point in favor of the interpretation advanced for factor M. That is, if CPS masculinity versus femininity (M) factor is measuring something that is associated with differences in men and women, gender identity should be substantially loaded on this factor and indeed it is.

Replication of the CPS taxonomy

Many studies have been undertaken since the CPS was published to determine how well the CPS taxonomy would replicate in other settings and under varying motivational conditions. Noller et al. (1988), for example, report a replication of the norm group study, described earlier in this chapter, using a stratified sample of 669 Australian volunteer subjects balanced for age, sex, and social class. They summarize (see Table 6.11) their results (AU) and compare them with those from the norm group (NO) and several other previously published studies using roughly comparable kinds of samples; for example,

Forbes et al. (NZ) (1974), Rodrigues and Comrey (BZ) (1974), Vandenberg and Price (DE) (1978), and Zamudio et al. (MA) (1983). (The letter pair in parentheses with each reference identifies the group involved in the results summarized in Table 6.11 (see Note).)

Table 6.11 shows that there was a remarkable degree of stability in the major factor loadings from these various studies despite vast differences in the populations from which these samples were drawn. Comparable findings were obtained in another study using a sample of 394 psychiatric outpatients (Comrey and Schiebel, 1985b). The subjects in all these studies, however, were volunteers. In a similar study of Israeli applicants for drivers' licenses (Montag and Comrey, 1982b), all the CPS factors were replicated reasonably well except social conformity versus rebelliousness (C). This was attributed to the reluctance of applicants to admit to anti-establishment attitudes and values. In a similar study with 226 Hare Krishna subjects, Weiss and Comrey (1987c) also verified all the CPS factors except social conformity versus rebelliousness (C). Although these were volunteer subjects, they were very homogeneous with respect to their scores on the FHIDs defining Factor C, preventing its emergence in the analysis.

More recently, good confirmation of the CPS factor structure has been obtained in Italy, Russia, and South Africa. Using an Italian edition of the CPS (Comrey, 1991; Caprara et al., 1991), CPS FHID scores were intercorrelated and factor analyzed for 268 Italian subjects. All eight CPS personality factors appeared as expected (Caprara et al., 1992). Using a Russian translation of the CPS, Brief and Comrey (1993) factor analyzed the FHID scores for 457 Russian subjects and found strong support for the eight CPS factor structure (see also Brief et al., 1994). Using an Afrikaans translation of the CPS, de Bruin et al. (1997) intercorrelated and factor analyzed the FHID scores for a sample of 804 South African university students, finding nine factors, eight of which were clearly recognizable as the eight factors comprising the CPS taxonomy. Other recent studies have explored the relationship between the CPS factors and the five factors of the NEO-PI personality inventory (Hahn, 1994; Caprara et al., 1995; Caprara et al., 2001). In general, three of the Big Five factors are very similar to CPS factors orderliness versus lack of compulsion, emotional stability versus neuroticism, and extraversion versus introversion. One Big Five factor is related to two CPS factors, trust versus defensiveness and empathy versus egocentrism. The fifth Big Five factor bears some resemblance to the CPS social conformity versus rebelliousness factor.

The CPS taxonomy and Erikson's ages of man

As the CPS taxonomy took shape through a series of factor analytic investigations, the author was struck by the fact that there appeared to be a close correspondence between the emerging factor constructs and the eight ages of man proposed by Erik Erikson (1963), a neo-Freudian psychoanalyst. Elaborating on Freud's psychosexual theory, Erikson proposed a social theory of development, describing eight stages through which an individual should progress in passing from infancy to maturity. Each of these stages has a characteristic developmental task and characteristic modes of behavior designed to achieve the goals of that period. Erikson elaborated eight ages of man, but the eighth one, ego integrity versus despair, represents the end result of the accumulated effects of adjustments made in the first seven stages. The CPS

taxonomic traits and their hypothesized corresponding ages of man are shown in Table 6.12.

> Two CPS factors are paired with intimacy versus isolation, one related to social adjustment in a non-sexual role (E) and the other in a sex-specific role (M). Erikson's theory merges these kinds of adjustments but empirical findings establish that these are distinct types of adjustment that require separate constructs. At the time of publication, the order of the CPS factors was chosen to be identical to that for the Erikson ages of man due to the apparent correspondence of these constructs.

At this point in time, the putative correspondence between the CPS factor traits and Erikson's ages of man enjoys the status of a plausible hypothesis that needs more substantial confirmation through further empirical research. To the extent that such a correspondence can be verified, a wealth of additional interpretive possibilities for CPS factor scores becomes available through the use of psychoanalytic theory. These possible interpretations are elaborated at greater length in Comrey (1980). The foregoing represents an example of enhancing and validating factor interpretation by relating factor analytic results to outside theory and knowledge.

Concurrent validation studies

In a concurrent validation study carried out prior to the publication of the CPS (Comrey and Duffy, 1969), an earlier version of the CPS was administered along with the Eysenck Personality Inventory and the Cattell 16 PF to the same subjects. It was established

Table 6.12   CPS Traits versus Erikson's 'Ages of Man'

T Trust vs. defensiveness	Basic trust vs. mistrust
O Orderliness vs. lack of compulsion	Autonomy vs. shame and doubt
C Social conformity vs. rebelliousness	Initiative vs. guilt
A Activity vs. lack of energy	Industry vs. inferiority
S Emotional stability vs. neuroticism	Identity vs. role confusion
E Extraversion vs. introversion	Intimacy vs. isolation
M Masculinity vs. femininity	Intimacy vs. isolation
P Empathy vs. egocentrism	Generativity vs. stagnation, ego integrity vs. despair

that the Eysenck items factor analyzed into two factors, as expected, neuroticism and extraversion-versus-introversion. It was further shown that these two factors are highly related to the CPS neuroticism and shyness factors, now renamed 'emotional stability versus neuroticism' and 'extraversion versus introversion', respectively. These findings were confirmed in a similar study several years later with a large, representative sample of Australian subjects (Noller et al., 1987). A follow-up study by Boyle (1989) also supported these findings. Cattell 16 PF scales were also shown to be related to these factors although these major factor constructs emerge at the second-order level in the 16 PF rather than at the primary level as in the CPS.

Knapp and Comrey (1973) administered the Shostrum Personal Orientation Inventory (POI) and the CPS to the same subjects predicting that self-actualization as measured by major POI scales time competence (Tc) and inner directed (I) would be significantly related to emotional stability versus neuroticism (S), a prediction that was confirmed. Also predicted and confirmed was a positive relationship between the POI nature of man-constructive (Nc) and the CPS trust versus defensiveness (T) scale, both of which measure a basic belief in the goodness of human nature. Finally, a negative relationship was predicted and confirmed between the POI existentiality (Ex) scale and the CPS social conformity versus rebelliousness (C). The Ex scale measures the ability situationally to react without rigid adherence to principles.

In an entirely different kind of study, translated versions of the Minnesota Multiphasic Personality Inventory, the Eysenck Personality Inventory, and the CPS were administered to 179 applicants for driving licenses in Israel (Montag and Comrey, 1982a). Intercorrelations were obtained for three lie detection scales, three emotional stability scales, three extraversion–introversion scales, and two masculinity–femininity scales. Using a modified multitrait–multimethod procedure, these correlations were evaluated

to show good convergent and discriminant validity for most of these measures.

Construct validation studies

A doctoral dissertation study by Fabian, also reported in Fabian and Comrey (1971), has provided evidence for the construct validity of the emotional stability versus neuroticism factor. As part of the study, she administered an early version of the factor scale designed to measure factor S to 69 normal, non-neurotic general medical and surgical hospital patients, 31 neuropsychiatric outpatients, and 68 neuropsychiatric inpatients. All of the neuropsychiatric patients had been diagnosed as neurotics. The prediction was that the lowest mean neuroticism score (or highest emotional stability score) would be shown by the general medical and surgical patients with the highest neuroticism mean score occurring for the inpatient neurotics. Outpatient neurotics were expected to have an intermediate mean neuroticism score. The mean neuroticism scores for the normals, outpatients, and inpatients, respectively, were 85.1, 110.1, and 119.1, giving a highly significant F-ratio of 32.6 in a one-way analysis of variance test of the differences between means.

Comrey and Backer (1970) administered the CPS and a biographical inventory to 209 male and female volunteer students at UCLA. The questions on the biographical inventory were hypothesized to show a relationship in a predicted direction with one or more of the CPS. The most striking degree of confirmation occurred for the social conformity versus rebelliousness (C) scale. Variables correlated significantly at the 1% level with social conformity versus rebelliousness in this study were the following: amount of marijuana consumed, -0.54; having some religious preference versus having none, 0.39; degree of participation in campus demonstrations, -0.39; amount of addictive drugs used, -0.36; extent of premarital sexual activity, -0.27; amount of interest in joining the Peace Corps, -0.26; number of mental problems listed, −0.26; degree of unconventionality of dress, −0.25; and several other variables with lower but still significant values. All the significant relationships except one had been predicted in advance on the basis of what the factor should represent. The association of substance abuse with low scores on social conformity versus rebelliousness (C) has also been confirmed by Knecht et al. (1972). Comrey et al. (1978) showed that Asian students scored higher than non-Asians on the CPS C scale and that it is also positively correlated with political conservatism, both outcomes as predicted.

Weiss and Comrey (1987a, 1987b) compared the personality characteristics of 132 males and 94 females of the Hare Krishna movement with those of normal and psychiatric patients using the CPS. They found that the main way in which Hare Krishnas differed from normal patients was that they exhibited a very high average score on the orderliness versus lack of compulsion (O) scale, indicating a strong tendency to compulsivity. This finding is consistent with an analysis of the daily living habits of cult members. In other respects, they were more similar to normal than to psychiatric patients.

The value of the CPS for detecting emotional disturbance has been demonstrated rather conclusively in studies of psychiatric patients compared with normals (Comrey et al., 1978; Comrey and Schiebel, 1983, 1985a). Results from a study with normal subjects are in substantial agreement (Comrey, 1981). A review of additional studies providing evidence for the validity of the Comrey Personality Scales is to be found in the most recent *Manual and Handbook of Interpretations for the CPS* (Comrey, 1994).

INTERPRETATION OF CPS FACTOR SCORES

A wealth of material on how to interpret CPS factor scores is contained in the original CPS manual (Comrey, 1970b) and in the *Handbook of Interpretations for the CPS* (Comrey, 1980, 1994). Studies cited above that were not described in these references offer additional validity information that is useful in test score interpretation. A major premise elaborated in the CPS handbook is that an extreme score on any of the CPS personality scales, high or low, is indicative of a personality aberration that may represent a serious threat to good adjustment. The presence of two extreme scores is an even more serious sign of emotional disturbance. The author has never seen a valid protocol containing three or more extreme scores for any individual who was not a psychiatric inpatient or outpatient. The validity scales have also been found to be useful adjuncts to the personality scales for interpretive purposes. Many considerations must be taken into account, of course, in trying to determine the true meaning of a CPS protocol. However, some of the better supported and more likely possible interpretations of high and low scores on CPS scales will be summarized briefly below.

Validity (V) scale

High scores
The record may be invalid; the respondent may be choosing answers randomly, have a low IQ, not understand English well, or may suffer from a thought disorder or other psychiatric disability.

Low scores
A low score is expected on this scale so it is not an indication of any problem.

Response bias (R) scale

High scores
Faking good (social desirability responding), deliberate or unconscious favorable self-presentation, naivety, lack of worldly experience, tradition bound, low IQ, somatic complaints, and diminished physical capacity. High scores have been found to be strongly associated with psychiatric disturbance.

Low scores

Faking bad; delinquent behavior; self blame and feelings of worthlessness (especially in females); anger, hostility, and projection of blame onto others (especially in males); callousness; withdrawal; reclusiveness; history of antisocial acting out. Low scores have been found to be strongly associated with psychiatric disturbance.

Trust versus Defensiveness (T)

High scores

Naive belief in the good intentions of others, gullibility, denial of negative feelings toward others, statistically significant evidence of inhibition of anger toward others, and obsessive-compulsive neurosis found in females.

Low scores

Paranoid suspiciousness; distrust of others' motives; anger and hostility toward others; resentment; violent ideation; projection of blame onto others. Low scores have been found to be strongly associated with psychiatric disturbance in females and to a lesser extent in males. Males low on T may be less willing to seek psychiatric assistance than females.

Orderliness versus Lack of Compulsion (O)

High scores

Individuals with above average scores on this scale have good work habits, are dependable, conscientious, neat, and orderly. As the scores move up to very high levels, however, the indicated behavior takes on a rigid, obsessive-compulsive character which may interfere with effective functioning in many areas of life. Such individuals are unable to adapt well to changing circumstances. High scores have been shown to be associated with obsessive-compulsive behavior and psychiatric diagnosis. A disproportionately high number of individuals with high scores on O have been found in psychiatrically disturbed groups and in Hare Krishnas.

Low scores

Individuals low on O may be disorganized, undisciplined, sloppy, disorderly, indolent, irresponsible, and/or incompetent. They tend to have poor work habits. Statistical comparisons show low O scores to be associated with tardiness, fatigue, some suicide risk, memory and/or attention deficit, depression, withdrawal, reclusiveness, a lack of concern for others, and simple schizophrenia. Low scores on O have been found to be moderately associated with a variety of antisocial behaviors and with membership in emotionally disturbed groups.

Social Conformity versus Rebelliousness (C)

High scores

Individuals with above average scores on C tend to be older, more conforming, conservative, resistant to change, and pro-establishment. As the scores move up to the very high level, the indicated behavior merges over toward fanatic intolerance of non-conformity and differing views by others along with extreme resistance to change. Very high scores may be associated with right-wing extremist political views. High scores on C are strongly associated with psychiatric disturbance. Some evidence suggests that high scores on C are more characteristic of alcohol abusers than low scores.

Low scores

Nonconforming, rebellious, rejecting of society and its values, anti-establishment, truculent, and resistant to any form of authority. Found to be associated with use of marijuana, addictive drugs, tobacco addiction, trouble with the police, mental problems, and sexual promiscuity. Associated with participation in demonstrations, unconventional dress and radical revolutionary political attitudes. Such individuals can be expected to be trouble makers wherever they are found. Low scores are strongly associated with psychiatric disturbance.

Activity versus Lack of Energy (A)

High scores

Energetic, physically active, ambitious, hard working, and tireless. At higher levels may indicate hyperactivity, a tendency to be a workaholic, overcompensation for unconscious feelings of inferiority. Found to be associated statistically with obsessive-compulsive behavior and trouble with the law. Criminals tend to have higher than normal A scores. High A scores are not strongly associated with membership in institutionalized psychiatrically disturbed groups. High A subjects tend to deny any psychiatric disability.

Low scores

Chronic malaise, inertia, neurasthenia, lethargy, lack of energy or ambition, sedentary, somatic complaints, and inability to cope. Found statistically to be associated with these characteristics and also with fear, anxiety, dread, depression, withdrawal, and feelings of inadequacy and worthlessness. Low A scores are very strongly associated with psychiatric disturbance.

Emotional Stability versus Neuroticism

High scores

Individuals with above average scores on S are emotionally stable, controlled, reserved, and inclined to suppress feelings. As the scores move up into the very high range, the indicated behavior merges into strong denial of depression, anxiety, and feelings of inadequacy. There tends to be a rigid control of affect and an insensitivity to the emotional side of life. High scores have been shown to be associated statistically with denial of problems, evasiveness, and hysterical neurosis in males. High scores have not been found to be strongly associated with membership in institutionalized psychiatric groups.

Low scores

Depressed, anxious, insecure, feelings of inferiority, worthlessness and inadequacy,

emotionally disturbed. Low scores are very highly associated with membership in institutionalized psychiatrically disturbed groups. Statistically associated with fear, dread, agitation, withdrawal, reclusiveness, dependence, self-blaming, blaming others, and violent ideation.

Extraversion versus Introversion (E)

High scores

Individuals with above average scores on E are outgoing, gregarious, sociable, have good social skills, and are dependent on social contact. As the scores move into the very high range, the indicated behavior merges over into excessive gregariousness characterized by extreme superficiality of interpersonal relations. High scores on E have been found to be statistically associated with cyclothymic personality, hysterical personality disorder, denial of problems, and evasiveness.

Low scores

Shy, lacking in social poise, poor social skills, withdrawn, reclusive, and schizoid. Statistically shown to be associated with these characteristics and also with lack of energy, depression, feelings of inadequacy, anger, hostility, and schizoid personality disorder diagnosis. Low scores on E have been found to be very strongly associated with membership in institutionalized psychiatrically disturbed groups.

Masculinity versus Femininity (M)

High scores

Individuals with above average scores on M are aggressive and dominant, competitive, realistic, forceful, and somewhat insensitive. As the scores move into the very high level, the indicated behavior merges over into the domineering, combative, unfeeling, crudely insensitive, and 'ultramacho'. High M scores have been found to be associated statistically in females with homosexuality and in males with schizoid personality diagnosis and trouble with the law. High M scores are not usually found in institutionalized psychiatric male groups.

Low scores

Non-aggressive, submissive, non-competitive, artistic; domestic interests, sensitive, tender-minded, romantic, unrealistic thinking patterns, and squeamish. Low scores on M have been very strongly associated with psychiatric group membership in males and to some extent in females. Very low scores in males are suggestive of a failure to develop a normal masculine identity. In females, it is suggestive of insufficient assertiveness for effective adjustment.

Empathy versus Egocentrism (P)

High scores

Individuals with above average scores on P are inclined to be service oriented, helpful to others, self-effacing, and to subordinate their own personal goals for the benefit of others. As the scores move to higher levels, the indicated behavior merges over into self-sacrificing martyrdom, total subordination of personal aggrandizement to the needs of others as a socially acceptable means of escaping from the necessity of developing personal expertise to achieve success in the real world. High scores have been found to be related statistically to self-sacrificing martyrdom, interest in joining the Peace Corps, emotionalism and sentimentality in females, and a poor employment record in males. High scores have not been found to be strongly associated with membership in psychiatrically disturbed groups.

Low scores

Self-centered, egocentric, selfish, preoccupied with personal concerns, indifferent to the needs of others, and unhelpful. Low scores have been found to be statistically associated with a callous lack of concern for others, fatigue, lack of energy, withdrawal, trouble with the law, and passive-aggressive personality disorder diagnosis. Psychiatrically disturbed groups have not been found to have

substantially lower mean scores on this factor than normals. On the other hand, the author has observed, however, that an extremely low score on P occurs fairly often in psychiatrically disturbed individuals.

Interpretation of scores must always take into account the context in which the testing was done. Interpreting records for individuals applying for assistance at a psychological clinic is very different from interpreting records obtained from individuals applying for a job where the success of their application is thought to depend on their test results. Detection of faking on the CPS is highly sophisticated, depending upon the interplay of validity scale scores, the pattern of response-alternative utilization, and the pattern of high, low, and moderate scores (Comrey, 1970b, 1980; Comrey and Backer, 1975). Where there is evidence of serious response distortion in the record, the kinds of interpretations offered above may not be appropriate (Comrey, 1994).

NOTES

1 The author is Professor Emeritus in the Department of Psychology, UCLA, Los Angeles, California 90095.

2 With the publication of the *Revised Manual and Handbook of Interpretations for the Comrey Personality Scales* (Comrey, 1994), the name of factor M was changed from 'Masculinity vs. Femininity' to 'Mental Toughness vs. Sensitivity'. The reason for this change was the emotionally charged meanings associated with these words in everyday language. This often led to unwarranted interpretations of extreme M scores by some testees. The new name for the factor is designed to reduce this kind of interpretive distortion of the factor scores. Since most of the publications cited in this chapter use the old name, however, the new name will not be used here. Currently available profile sheets, however, do employ the new terminology for this factor.

REFERENCES

Boyle, G.J. (1989) 'Re-examination of the major personality-type factors in the Cattell,

Comrey, and Eysenck scales: Were the factor solutions by Noller et al. optimal?', *Personality and Individual Differences*, 10(12): 1289–99.

Brief, D.E. and Comrey, A.L. (1993) 'A profile of personality for a Russian sample: As indicated by the Comrey Personality Scales', *Journal of Personality Assessment*, 60(2): 267–84.

Brief, D.E., Comrey, A.L. and Collins, B.E. (1994) 'The Comrey Personality Scales in Russian: A study of concurrent, predictive, and external validity', *Personality and Individual Differences*, 16(1): 113–22.

Caprara, G.V., Barbaranelli, C., Perugini, M. and Comrey, A.L. (1991) *Scale di Personalita di Comrey: Manuale*. Firenze, Italy: Organizzazioni Speciali.

Caprara, G.V., Barbaranelli, C. and Comrey, A.L. (1992) 'Validation of the Comrey Personality Scales on an Italian sample', *Journal of Research in Personality*, 26(1): 21–31.

Caprara, G.V., Barbaranelli, C. and Comrey, A.L. (1992b) 'A personological approach to the study of aggression', *Personality and Individual Differences*, 13(1): 77–84.

Caprara, G.V., Barbaranelli, C. and Comrey, A.L. (1995) 'Factor analysis of the NEO-PI Inventory and the Comrey Personality Scales in an Italian sample', *Personality and Individual Differences*, 18(2): 193–200.

Caprara, G.V., Barbaranelli, C., Hahn, R. and Comrey, A.L. (2001) 'Factor analyses of the NEO-PI-R Inventory and the Comrey Personality Scales in Italy and the United States', *Personality and Individual Differences*, 30(2): 217–28.

Caprara, G.V., Barbaranelli, C., Perugini, M. and Comrey, A.L. (1991) *Scale di Personalita di Comrey: Manuale*. Firenze: Organizzazioni Speciali.

Comrey, A.L. (1962) 'The minimum residual method of factor analysis', *Psychological Reports*, 11(1): 15–18.

Comrey, A.L. (1967) 'Tandem criteria for analytic rotation in factor analysis', *Psychometrika*, 32(1): 143–54.

Comrey, A.L. (1970a) *The Comrey Personality Scales*. San Diego: Educational and Industrial Testing Service.

Comrey, A.L. (1970b) *Manual for the Comrey Personality Scales*. San Diego: Educational and Industrial Testing Service.

Comrey, A.L. (1973) *A First Course in Factor Analysis*. New York: Academic.

Comrey, A.L. (1980) *Handbook of Interpretations for the Comrey Personality Scales*. San Diego: Educational and Industrial Testing Service.

Comrey, A.L. (1981) 'Detecting emotional disturbance with the Comrey Personality Scales', *Psychological Reports*, 48(4): 703–71.

Comrey, A.L. (1984) 'Comparison of two methods to identify major personality factors', *Applied Psychological Measurement*, 4(3): 397–408.

Comrey, A.L. (1991) *CPS Scale di Personalita*. Firenze: O.S. Organizzazioni Speciali.

Comrey, A.L. (1993) *Manual Supplement for the Short Form of the Comrey Personality Scales*. San Diego: Educational and Industrial Testing Service.

Comrey, A.L. (1994) *Revised Manual and Handbook of Interpretations for the Comrey Personality Scales*. San Diego: Educational and Industrial Testing Service.

Comrey, A.L. and Ahumada, A. (1965) 'Note and Fortran IV program for minimum residual factor analysis', *Psychological Reports*, 17(3): 446.

Comrey, A.L. and Backer, T.E. (1970) 'Construct validation of the Comrey Personality Scales', *Multivariate Behavioral Research*, 5(3): 469–77.

Comrey, A.L. and Backer, T.E. (1975) 'Detection of faking on the Comrey Personality Scales', *Multivariate Behavioral Research*, 10(2): 311–20.

Comrey, A.L. and Lee, H.B. (1992) *A First Course in Factor Analysis* (2nd edn). Hillsdale, NJ: Erlbaum.

Comrey, A.L. and Montag, I. (1982) 'Comparison of factor analytic results with two-choice and seven-choice personality item formats', *Applied Psychological Measurement*, 6(2): 285–9.

Comrey, A.L. and Schiebel, D. (1983) 'Personality test correlates of psychiatric outpatient status', *Journal of Consulting and Clinical Psychology*, 51(4): 757–62.

Comrey, A.L. and Schiebel, D. (1985a) 'Personality test correlates of psychiatric case history data', *Journal of Consulting and Clinical Psychology*, 53(3): 470–9.

Comrey, A.L. and Schiebel, D. (1985b) 'Personality factor structure in psychiatric outpatients and normals', *Multivariate Behavioral Research*, 20(3): 419–26.

Comrey, A.L., Soufi, A. and Backer, T.E. (1978) 'Psychiatric screening with the Comrey Personality Scales', *Psychological Reports*, 42(6): 1127–30.

Comrey, A.L., Wong, C. and Backer, T.E. (1978) 'Further validation of the Social Conformity scale of the Comrey Personality Scales', *Psychological Reports*, 43(1): 165–6.

de Bruin, G.P., Zak, J.N. and Comrey, A.L. (1997) 'Factor analysis of an Afrikaans translation of the Comrey Personality Scales', *Psychological Reports*, 81(5): 867–76.

Erikson, E.H. (1963) *Childhood and Society* (2nd edn). New York: Norton.

Fabian, J.J. and Comrey, A.L. (1971) 'Construct validation of factored neuroticism scales', *Multivariate Behavioral Research*, 6(2): 287–99.

Forbes, A.R., Dexter, W.R. and Comrey, A.L. (1974) 'A cross-cultural comparison of certain personality factors', *Multivariate Behavioral Research*, 9(2): 383–93.

Hahn, R. and Comrey, A.L. (1994) 'Factor analysis of the NEO-PI and the Comrey Personality Scales', *Psychological Reports*, 75(2): 355–65.

Knapp, R.R. and Comrey, A.L. (1973) 'Further construct validation of a measure of self actualization', *Educational and Psychological Measurement*, 33(3): 419–25.

Knecht, S.D., Cundick, B.P., Edwards, D. and Gunderson, E.K.E. (1972) 'The prediction of marijuana use from personality scales', *Educational and Psychological Measurement*, 32(6): 1111–7.

Levonian, E., Comrey, A.L., Levy, W. and Procter, D. (1959) 'A statistical evaluation of the Edwards Personal Preference Schedule', *Journal of Applied Psychology*, 43(2): 355–9.

Montag, I. and Comrey, A.L. (1982a) 'Comparison of certain MMPI, Eysenck, and Comrey personality constructs', *Multivariate Behavioral Research*, 17(1): 93–7.

Montag, I. and Comrey, A.L. (1982b) 'Personality construct similarity in Israel and the United States', *Applied Psychological Measurement*, 6(1): 61–7.

Noller, P., Law, H. and Comrey, A.L. (1987) 'Cattell, Comrey, and Eysenck personality factors compared: More evidence for the five robust factors?', *Journal of Personality and Social Psychology*, 53(4): 775–82.

Noller, P., Law, H. and Comrey, A.L. (1988) 'Factor structure of the Comrey Personality Scales in an Australian sample', *Multivariate Behavioral Research*, 23(3): 397–411.

Rodrigues, A. and Comrey, A.L. (1974) 'Personality structure in Brazil and the United States', *Journal of Social Psychology*, 92(1): 19–26.

Vandenberg, S.G. and Price, R.A. (1978) 'Replication of the factor structure of the Comrey Personality Scales', *Psychological Reports*, 42(2): 343–52.

Weiss, A.S. and Comrey, A.L. (1987a) 'Personality characteristics of Hare Krishnas', *Journal of Personality Assessment*, 51(3): 399–413.

Weiss, A.S. and Comrey, A.L. (1987b) 'Personality and mental health of Hare Krishnas compared with psychiatric outpatients and "normals"', *Personality and Individual Differences*, 8(4): 721–30.

Weiss, A.S. and Comrey, A.L. (1987c) 'Personality factor structure among Hare Krishnas', *Educational and Psychological Measurement*, 47(2): 317–28.

Zamudio, A., Padilla, A.M. and Comrey, A.L. (1983) 'Personality structure of Mexican-Americans using the Comrey Personality Scales', *Journal of Personality Assessment*, 47(1): 100–6.

The Sixteen Personality Factor Questionnaire (16PF)

Heather E.P. Cattell and Alan D. Mead

INTRODUCTION

The Sixteen Personality Factor Questionnaire (16PF) is a comprehensive measure of normal-range personality found to be effective in a variety of settings where an in-depth assessment of the whole person is needed. The 16PF traits, presented in Table 7.1, are the result of years of factor-analytic research focused on discovering the basic structural elements of personality (Cattell, R.B., 1957, 1973).

In addition to discovering the sixteen normal-range personality traits for which the instrument is named, these researchers identified the five broad dimensions – a variant of the 'Big Five' factors (Cattell, R.B., 1957, 1970). From the beginning, Cattell proposed a multi-level, hierarchical structure of personality: the second-order global measures describe personality at a broader, conceptual level, while the more precise primary factors reveal the fine details and nuances that make each person unique, and are more powerful in predicting actual behavior. In addition, this factor-analytic structure includes a set of third-order factors, also discussed in this chapter.

Due to its scientific origins, the 16PF Questionnaire has a long history of empirical research and is embedded in a well-established theory of individual differences. This questionnaire's extensive body of research stretches back over half a century, providing evidence of its utility in clinical, counseling, industrial-organizational, educational, and research settings (Cattell, R.B. et al., 1970; H.E.P. Cattell and Schuerger, 2003; Conn and Rieke, 1994; Krug and Johns, 1990; Russell and Karol, 2002). A conservative estimate of 16PF research since 1974 includes more than 2,000 publications (Hofer and Eber, 2002). Most studies have found the 16PF to be among the top five most commonly used normal-range instruments in both research and practice (Butcher and Rouse, 1996; Piotrowski and Zalewski, 1993; Watkins et al., 1995). The measure is also widely used internationally, and since its inception has been adapted into over 35 languages worldwide.

HISTORY AND DEVELOPMENT OF THE 16PF QUESTIONNAIRE

The history of the 16PF Questionnaire spans almost the entire history of standardized

Table 7.1   16PF Scale Names and Descriptors

Descriptors of Low Range	Primary Scales	Descriptors of High Range
Reserved, Impersonal, Distant	Warmth (A)	Warm-hearted, Caring, Attentive To Others
Concrete, Lower Mental Capacity	Reasoning (B)	Abstract, Bright, Fast-Learner
Reactive, Affected By Feelings	Emotional Stability (C)	Emotionally Stable, Adaptive, Mature
Deferential, Cooperative, Avoids Conflict	Dominance (E)	Dominant, Forceful, Assertive
Serious, Restrained, Careful	Liveliness (F)	Enthusiastic, Animated, Spontaneous
Expedient, Nonconforming	Rule-Consciousness (G)	Rule-Conscious, Dutiful
Shy, Timid, Threat-Sensitive	Social Boldness (H)	Socially Bold, Venturesome, Thick-Skinned
Tough, Objective, Unsentimental	Sensitivity (I)	Sensitive, Aesthetic, Tender-Minded
Trusting, Unsuspecting, Accepting	Vigilance (L)	Vigilant, Suspicious, Skeptical, Wary
Practical, Grounded, Down-To-Earth	Abstractedness (M)	Abstracted, Imaginative, Idea-Oriented
Forthright, Genuine, Artless	Privateness (N)	Private, Discreet, Non-Disclosing
Self-Assured, Unworried, Complacent	Apprehension (O)	Apprehensive, Self-Doubting, Worried
Traditional, Attached To Familiar	Openness to Change (Q1)	Open To Change, Experimenting
Group-Orientated, Affiliative	Self-Reliance (Q2)	Self-Reliant, Solitary, Individualistic
Tolerates Disorder, Unexacting, Flexible	Perfectionism (Q3)	Perfectionistic, Organized, Self-Disciplined
Relaxed, Placid, Patient	Tension (Q4)	Tense, High Energy, Driven
	Global Scales	
Introverted, Socially Inhibited	Extraversion	Extraverted, Socially Participating
Low Anxiety, Unperturbable	Anxiety Neuroticism	High Anxiety, Perturbable
Receptive, Open-Minded, Intuitive	Tough-Mindedness	Tough-Minded, Resolute, Unempathic
Accommodating, Agreeable, Selfless	Independence	Independent, Persuasive, Willful
Unrestrained, Follows Urges	Self-Control	Self-Controlled, Inhibits Urges

Adapted with permission from S.R. Conn and M.L. Rieke (1994). 16PF Fifth Edition Technical Manual. Champaign, IL: Institute for Personality and Ability Testing, Inc.

personality measurement. Instead of being developed to measure preconceived dimensions of interest to a particular author, the instrument was developed from the unique perspective of a scientific quest to try to discover the basic structural elements of personality.

Raymond Cattell's personality research was based on his strong background in the physical sciences; born in 1905, he witnessed first-hand the awe-inspiring results of science, from electricity and telephones to automobiles, airplanes, and medicine. He wanted to apply these scientific methods to the uncharted domain of human personality with the goal of discovering the basic elements of personality (much as the basic elements of the physical world were discovered and organized into the periodic table). He believed that human characteristics such as creativity, authoritarianism, altruism, or leadership skills could be predicted from these fundamental personality traits (much as water was a weighted combination of the elements of

hydrogen and oxygen). For psychology to advance as a science, he felt it also needed basic measurement techniques for personality. Thus, through factor analysis – the powerful new tool for identifying underlying dimensions behind complex phenomena – Cattell believed the basic dimensions of personality could be discovered and then measured.

Over several decades, Cattell and his colleagues carried out a program of comprehensive, international research seeking a thorough, research-based map of normal personality. They systematically measured the widest possible range of personality dimensions, believing that 'all aspects of human personality which are or have been of importance, interest, or utility have already become recorded in the substance of language' (Cattell, R.B., 1943: 483). They studied these traits in diverse populations, using three different methodologies (Cattell, R.B., 1973): observation of natural, in-situ life behavior or L-data (e.g. academic grades, number of traffic accidents, or social contacts); questionnaire or Q-data from the self-report domain; and objective behavior measured in standardized, experimental settings or T-data (e.g. number of original solutions to problem presented, responses to frustrations). Eventually, this research resulted in the 16 unitary traits of the 16PF Questionnaire shown in Table 7.1.

From the beginning, Cattell's goal was to investigate universal aspects of personality. Thus, his University of Illinois laboratory included researchers from many different countries who later continued their research abroad. Ongoing collaborative research was carried out with colleagues around the world, for example, in Japan (Akira Ishikawa and Bien Tsujioka), Germany (Kurt Pawlik and Klaus Schneewind), India (S. Kapoor), South Africa (Malcolm Coulter), England (Frank Warburton, Dennis Child), and Switzerland (Karl Delhees).

Since its first publication in 1949, there have been four major revisions – the most recent release being the 16PF Fifth Edition (Cattell, R.B. et al., 1993). The main goals of the latest revision were to develop updated, refined item content and collect a large, new norm sample. The item pool included the best items from all five previous forms of the 16PF plus new items written by the test authors and 16PF experts. Items were refined in a four-stage, iterative process using large samples. The resulting instrument has shorter, simpler items with updated language, a more standardized answer format, and has been reviewed for gender, cultural, and ethnic bias and ADA (Americans With Disabilities Act) compliance. Psychometric characteristics are improved, hand scoring is easier, and the standardization contains over 10,000 people.

Because of its international origins, the 16PF Questionnaire was quickly translated and adapted into many other languages. Since its first publication in 1949, the instrument has been adapted into more than 35 languages worldwide. These are not simply translations, as many questionnaires provide, but careful cultural adaptations, involving new norms and reliability and validity research in each new country. Introduction of Web-based administration in 1999 allowed international test-users easy access to administration, scoring, and reports in many different languages, using local norms

CATTELL'S THEORY OF PERSONALITY

Primary and secondary-level traits

From its inception, the 16PF Questionnaire was a multi-level measure of personality based on Cattell's factor-analytic theory (Cattell, R.B., 1933, 1946). Cattell and his colleagues first discovered the primary traits, which provide the most basic definition of individual personality differences. These more specific primary traits are more powerful in understanding and predicting the complexity of actual behavior (Ashton, 1998; Judge et al., 2002; Mershon and Gorsuch, 1988; Paunonen and Ashton, 2001; Roberts et al., 2005).

Next, these researchers factor-analyzed the primary traits themselves in order to investigate personality structure at a higher level. From this, the broader 'second-order' or global factors emerged – the original Big Five. These researchers found that the numerous primary traits consistently coalesced into these broad dimensions, each with its own independent focus and function within personality, as described in Table 7.2. More recently, a similar set of Big Five factors has been rediscovered by other researchers (Costa and McCrae, 1992a; Goldberg, 1990), but using forced, orthogonal factor definitions. The five global factors also have been found in factor analyses of a wide range of current personality instruments (as Dr. Herb Eber, one of the original 16PF authors, used to say, 'These broad factors validate across very different populations and methods because they are as big as elephants and can be found in any large data set!').

Thus, these five 'second-order' or global factors were found to define personality at a

Table 7.2 16PF global factors and the primary trait` make-up

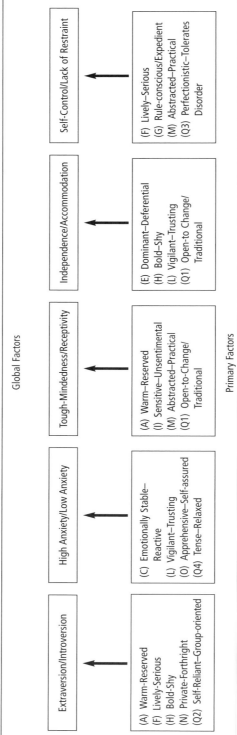

Global Factors

Extraversion/Introversion	High Anxiety/Low Anxiety	Tough-Mindedness/Receptivity	Independence/Accommodation	Self-Control/Lack of Restraint

(A) Warm–Reserved
(F) Lively–Serious
(H) Bold–Shy
(N) Private–Forthright
(Q2) Self-Reliant–Group-oriented

(C) Emotionally Stable–Reactive
(L) Vigilant–Trusting
(O) Apprehensive–Self-assured
(Q4) Tense–Relaxed

(A) Warm–Reserved
(I) Sensitive–Unsentimental
(M) Abstracted–Practical
(Q1) Open-to-Change/Traditional

(E) Dominant–Deferential
(H) Bold–Shy
(L) Vigilant–Trusting
(Q1) Open-to Change/Traditional

(F) Lively–Serious
(G) Rule-conscious/Expedient
(M) Abstracted–Practical
(Q3) Perfectionistic–Tolerates Disorder

Primary Factors

higher, more theoretical level of personality. However, because of their factor-analytic origins, the two levels of personality are essentially inter-related. The global factors provide the larger conceptual, organizing framework for understanding the meaning and function of the primary traits. However, the meanings of the globals themselves were determined by the primary traits which converged to make them up (see Table 7.2).

For example, the Extraversion/Introversion global factor was defined by the convergence of the five primary scales that represent basic human motivations for moving toward versus away from social interaction. Similarly, the four primary traits that merged to define Tough-Mindedness versus Receptivity describe four different aspects of openness to the world: openness to feelings and emotions (Sensitivity – I), openness to abstract ideas and imagination (Abstractedness – M), openness to new approaches and ideas (Openness-to-Change – Q1), and openness to people (Warmth – A).

Cattell's hierarchical structure is based on the idea that all traits are inter-correlated in the real world (for example, intelligence and anxiety, although conceptually quite distinct, are usually strongly inter-correlated). Because the basic 16PF primary traits were naturally inter-correlated, they could be factor-analyzed to find the secondary-level global traits. Thus, the data itself determined the definitions of the primary and global factors (in contrast to the forced orthogonal definitions of factors in the currently popular Big Five models).

Thus, the global traits provide a broad overview of personality, while the primary traits provide the more detailed information about the richness and uniqueness of the individual. For example, two people may have the same score on global Extraversion but may have quite different social styles. Someone who is warm and supportive (A+) but shy and modest (H−) may have the exact same Extraversion score as someone who is socially bold and gregarious (H+) but emotionally aloof and detached (A−). However, the first person is likely to come across as warm, modest, and concerned about others, while the second is likely to seem bold, talkative, and attention seeking (less concerned about others). Thus, although both may seek social interaction to an equal degree, they do so for very different reasons and are likely to have a very different impact on their social environment.

The primary and global levels of 16PF traits combine to provide a comprehensive, in-depth understanding of an individual's personality. For example, although knowing someone's overall level of Self-Control/conscientiousness is important, successfully motivating that person to accomplish a particular goal depends on also knowing whether their self-control is motivated more by strong obedience to societal standards (Rule-Consciousness – G+), by a temperamental tendency to be self-disciplined and organized (Perfectionism – Q3+), or by a practical, focused perceptual style (low Abstractedness – M−). Thus, the 16PF Questionnaire can provide an in-depth, integrated understanding of an individual's whole personality.

The super factors of personality: third-order factors

From the beginning, Cattell's comprehensive trait hierarchy was three-tiered: A wide sampling of everyday behaviors were factor-analyzed to find the primary factors; these primary traits were factor-analyzed, resulting in the five second-order, global traits; and then the global factors were factor-analyzed into third-order traits at the highest, most abstract level of personality organization (Cattell, R.B., 1946, 1957, 1973). Factor analysis of secondary factors to find third-order factors was practiced first in the ability domain (e.g. Spearman, 1932), but a few personality theorists have also looked at this highest level of personality structure (e.g. Eysenck, 1978; Hampson, 1988; Digman, 1997; Peabody and Goldberg, 1989).

Because factor-analytic results at each level depend on the clarity of the traits being factor-analyzed, early attempts to find third-order traits were less reliable. However, several independent studies have recently used large-scale samples to investigate the third-order factor structure of the 16PF (H.E.P. Cattell, 1996; Dancer and Woods, 2007; Gorsuch, 2007; Lounsbury et al., 2004). H.E.P. Cattell (1996) applied a common factor analysis to the global traits of the 16PF Fifth Edition norm sample ($n = 2,500$), and found two well-defined third-order factors. Richard Gorsuch (pers. comm., 12 February 2007) applied a common factor analysis to the 16PF global scores of 11,000 subjects, and found two very similar third-order factors. Most recently, Dancer and Woods (2007) found very similar results working with a sample of 4,405 working adults, and this factor pattern is presented in Table 7.3.

Each of these independent studies found the same two-factor solution. The first factor, factor I, involves human activities that are directed outward toward the world. This includes both Extraversion (movement toward social engagement, 'communion' or 'attachment'), as well as Independence (mastery/dominance of the social and non-social environment). Thus, third-order factor I encompasses tendencies to move assertively outward into the world toward both social connection and toward exploration/mastery of the environment, and might be called active outward engagement.

Third-order factor II involves internal types of processes and events. It includes first the age-old dimension of instinctual impulsivity versus self-restraint (global

Self-Control or conscientiousness); but also the dimensions of internal perceptual sensitivity, reactivity, and creativity – openness to feelings, imagination, esthetics, and new ideas (global Receptivity/openness versus Tough-Mindedness). Note that higher levels of Self-Control/conscientiousness are related to *lower* levels of openness/Receptivity: Thus, highly conscientiousness, self-controlled people also tend to be tough-minded and less open to emotions and new ideas. Conversely, those who are more impulsive and undisciplined also tend to be more creative and open to feelings and ideas (and to experience life more vividly). This third-order factor is well illustrated in the contrasting styles of having a conscientious focus on concrete, objective, practical tasks, versus occupations that focus on abstract, imaginative, and innovative ideas. Thus, superfactor II might be called self-disciplined practicality versus unrestrained creativity.

The fifth global factor, Anxiety/neuroticism, then loads on both of these third-order factors. This suggests that the distress described by Anxiety could arise either in the inward/outward engagement domain or in the more internalized unrestrained creativity/ self-disciplined practicality domain. Additionally, high levels of distress may affect either of these areas. This is consistent with the wide range of outward and inward human capacities that can potentially become unbalanced, or can be affected by stress.

These results are consistent with Cattell's original belief that these third-order factors may not represent personality traits in the usual sense, but might reflect some broad, abstract level of sociological or biological influences on human temperament (Cattell, R.B., 1957; 1973). For example, there may be some biological/neurological structure that affects outward engagement versus inhibition (superfactor I), or affects impulse control/restraint and perceptual sensitivity/reactivity (superfactor II). Definition and understanding of these third-order factors await further investigation.

Table 7.3 Varimax rotated factor loadings of the second-order factors of the 16PF5 questionnaire ($n = 4,405$)

	Rotated factor I	Rotated factor II
Extraversion	0.821	
Independence	0.669	
Anxiety	−0.638	−0.522
Self-control		0.816
Tough-mindedness		0.737

Comparison of the 16PF global scales with other five-factor models

For over 50 years, the 16PF has included the broad, second-order dimensions currently called 'the Big Five' (Cattell, R.B., 1946; Krug and Johns, 1986). In fact, Cattell located three of these five factors in his earliest studies of temperament (1933) – which Digman (1996) called 'the first glimpse of the Big Five'. Four of the five current traits were already described in Cattell's 1957 book. All five traits have been clearly identified and scorable from the questionnaire since the release of the fourth edition around 1970. Although Cattell continued to believe that there were more than five factors, so have many other prominent psychologists (Block, 1995; Fiske, 1994; Hogan et al., 1996; Jackson et al., 2000; Lee et al., 2005; Ostendorf, 1990; Saucier 2001).

The 16PF scales and items also played an important role in the development of the other Big Five factor models (e.g. Costa and McCrae, 1976, 1985; Norman, 1963; McKenzie et al., 1997; Tupes and Christal, 1961). For example, the first NEO manual (Costa and McCrae, 1985: 26) describes the development of the questionnaire as beginning with cluster analyses of 16PF scales, which these researchers had been using for over 20 years in their own research. However, this origin, or even acknowledgement of the existence of the five 16PF global factors, does not appear in any current accounts of the development of the Big Five (Costa and McCrae, 1992a; Digman, 1990; Goldberg, 1990).

Furthermore, when the 16PF correlation matrix, which was used in the original development of the Big Five, is re-analyzed using more modern, rigorous factor-analytic methods, Costa and McCrae's results do not replicate (McKenzie, 1998). Instead, appropriate factoring (see R.B. Cattell, 1978; Gorsuch, 1983) of the original matrix produces the five 16PF global factors, rather than the three orthogonal NEO factors that Costa and McCrae chose to use.

A range of studies comparing the five 16PF global factors and the set of NEO Big Five factors show a striking resemblance between the two (Carnivez and Allen, 2005; H.E.P. Cattell, 1996; Conn and Rieke, 1994; Gerbing and Tuley, 1991; Schneewind and Graf, 1998). These studies show strong correlational and factor-analytic alignment between the two models: Between the two extraversion factors, between anxiety and neuroticism, between self-control and conscientiousness, between tough-mindedness/receptivity and openness-to-experience, and between independence and dis-agreeableness. In fact, the average correlation between the 16PF global factors and their respective NEO five factors are just as high as those between the NEO five factors and the Big Five markers which the NEO was developed to measure (H.E.P. Cattell, 1996; Goldberg, 1992). The alignments among the Big Five models are summarized in Table 7.4.

However, there are important differences between the two models. Although proponents of the other five-factor models have done much in the last decade to try to bring about a consensus in psychology about the existence of five global factors, their particular set of traits have been found to be problematic. In the development process, the NEO Big Five factors were forced to be statistically uncorrelated or orthogonal for reasons of theoretical and statistical simplicity. However, few have found this as a satisfactory approach for defining the basic dimensions

Table 7.4   Alignments among the three main five-factor models

16PF (Cattell)	NEO-PI-R (Costa and McCrae)	Big Five (Goldberg)
Extraversion/Introversion	Extraversion	Surgency
Low Anxiety/High Anxiety	Neuroticism	Emotional stability
Tough-Mindedness/Receptivity	Openness	Intellect or culture
Independence/Accommodation	Agreeableness	Agreeableness
Self-Control/Lack of Restraint	Conscientiousness	Conscientiousness or dependability

of human personality. For example, Big Five supporter Jack Digman (1997) stated: 'The apparent orthogonality of the Big Five is a direct result of the general employment of varimax rotation, a procedure that imposes rather than finds independent factors.' Additionally, Loevinger writes:

> There is no reason to believe that the bedrock of personality is a set of orthogonal ... factors, unless you think that nature is constrained to present us a world in rows and columns. That would be convenient for many purposes, particularly given the statistical programs already installed on our computers. But is this realistic? (1994: 6)

The decision to impose orthogonal locations had fundamental effects on the resulting factors and their meanings. In his analysis of this basic issue of factor analysis, Child states:

> Oblique solutions can spread the common variance between and within factors; orthogonal rotation can only spread variance between factors. That is why it is so important to carry out an oblique solution, to allow no escape of important variance ... Unfortunately, the orthogonal compromise disguises both the relationship between domains and the number of factors which could possibly be present in hyperspace. (1998: 353–354)

In contrast to the orthogonal definitions that were fundamental to the development of the NEO factors, recent studies have found that the NEO five factors are actually substantially inter-correlated (Carnivez and Allen, 2005; Goldberg, 1992; Smith et al., 2001). Even the latest NEO-PI-R manual (Costa and McCrae, 1992: 100) shows neuroticism and conscientiousness to inter-correlate − 0.53, and extraversion and openness to inter-correlate 0.40. Goldberg's Big Five markers also show substantial inter-correlations. These inter-correlations contradict the original premise on which the NEO Big Five factors were defined.

The forced orthogonal factor locations of the five-factor model have had substantial effects on the meanings of the traits. For example, although the basic traits of dominance (or agency) and warmth (or communion) have long been seen as two of the most fundamental dimensions of human personality (Wiggins, 2003), the five-factor model has no factor that centrally includes either dominance or warmth. Rather factor analyses of the NEO-PI-R show that the central traits of dominance and warmth are widely dispersed and spread thinly among several of the five factors, particularly extraversion and agreeableness (H.E.P. Cattell, 1996; Child, 1998; Conn and Rieke, 1994; Costa and McCrae, 1992).

However, in the 16PF Questionnaire, the Independence global factor is organized around traits of assertiveness and influence in the world (high scorers are dominant, independent-minded and innovative, low scorers are deferential, cooperative, and agreeable). Thus, the 16PF global Independence factor is defined around traits of dominance or 'agency', while in the NEO model, the basic trait of dominance is split and relegated to small roles in several factors including extraversion and dis-agreeableness (where dominance is centered in a negative, hostile context).

In a similar way, factor-analyses of the NEO-PI-R have found that the basic trait of warmth (or communion) is also divided, with low loadings on several factors including extraversion and agreeableness (H.E.P. Cattell, 1996; Child, 1998; Conn and Rieke, 1994; Smith et al., 2001). However, in the 16PF, Warmth plays a central role in Extraversion, the factor that focuses on the basic dimensions of interpersonal relating. Additionally, these factor analyses of the NEO-PI-R indicate that the openness trait (called 'intellect' in Goldberg's model) tends to focus more on cognitive or intellectual curiosity, rather than equally measuring the whole domain, which includes openness to feelings, emotions, and esthetics. Also, the Big Five factor 'conscientiousness' appears to be narrower in content than 16PF Self-Control and doesn't include the whole domain of human methods for self-control and self-restraint versus impulsivity (Roberts et al., 2005).

Thus, the imposed orthogonality of the NEO has had multiple impacts on its factor definitions. Furthermore, researchers have found that when oblique methods are used on the NEO-PI-R items, allowing the data itself to determine factor definitions, the resulting factor definitions are different, and show more clarity and simple structure than do the current NEO-PI-R factors (Child, 1998).

However, the biggest difference between the two approaches is the method of development of the primary level traits. In the 16PF Questionnaire, the first-order primary trait definitions are based on decades of scientific research, and have been confirmed in a wide range of independent studies (see the section on Validity). In contrast, the NEO-PI primary-level personality facets were decided by consensus among a small group of psychologists (who selected what they felt should appear in each NEO domain). Child (1998) comments:

> It does seem miraculous that the personality domains divided exactly into six facets. Of course, as the NEO PI-R is a "top-down" theory, the researchers can choose whatever number they wish before tying up the parcel. The snag with this procedure is its arbitrary nature and proneness to creating factors or traits to fit a theory. (1998: 352)

This method of selecting the fundamental facets of personality raises some basic questions about the NEO model. First of all, this arbitrary approach to choosing the facets leaves them open to debate by every other psychologist who happens to conceptualize personality differently (e.g. Gough, 1987; Hogan et al., 1996; Wiggins, 2003). More importantly, these facets are now used to define and calculate scores on the basic Big Five factors, which have resulted in changed definitions of the Big Five domains themselves.

Additionally, many correlational and factor-analytic studies have found the underlying factor structure of the NEO facets inconsistent and confusing, and that the domains do not actually hold together (Child, 1998; Church and Burke, 1994; Conn and Rieke, 1994; Loevinger, 1994; Parker et al., 1993; Roberts et al., 2005; Smith et al., 2001). These researchers have found that a large proportion of the NEO facets actually correlate

just as well with other Big Five domains than their own (even the test authors stated that the 1992 revision of the NEO was prompted by the fact that the facets for neuroticism and extraversion did not cohere psychometrically (McCrae and Costa, 1992)). For example, Roberts et al. (2005) found that three of the six conscientiousness facets do not adhere to that domain, but are as strongly related to other Big Five domains as they are to conscientiousness.

Overall, the strong correlations of many facets with theoretically unrelated domains and facets bring into question the definition of the Big Five factors. This lack of adherence of the NEO facets to their assigned domains is inconsistent with the basic model of the questionnaire (and probably a result of the non-empirical origins of the facets). Thus, a number of important issues have been raised about the integrity of the NEO model, as a result of both the arbitrary choice of facet trait meanings and orthogonal global factor definitions.

Another important distinction between the 16PF and other questionnaires is the contextualized nature of its items. For example, items on the NEO-PI-R involve a high degree of transparent self-rating or self-assessment of traits (e.g. 'I'm an even-tempered person'; 'I am dominant, forceful, and assertive'; 'I am known as a warm and friendly person'). Although this type of transparent item may do well in research settings, in most assessment situations where there are strong motivational components, these items tend to be vulnerable to distortion. For example, various studies have found that the basic factor structure of the NEO-PI-R is different in job applicant samples, thus bringing into question the validity of the questionnaire in settings where motivation and social desirability are issues (Schmit and Ryan, 1993; Smith et al., 2001). In contrast, 16PF items tend to be more indirect and involve more contextualized questions about actual behavior or experience (e.g. 'When I find myself in a boring situation, I usually "tune out" and daydream about other things'; 'I hardly ever feel hurried or rushed as I go about my daily tasks'; 'I some-times feel that I need my friends more than they need me').

Furthermore, there is substantial research indicating that self-ratings are different from observer ratings in their factor structure, and that they are only moderately correlated with actual behavior (e.g. Paunonen, 1993; Peabody and Goldberg, 1989). This suggests that much of the variance or meaning in self-ratings is not explained by the actual trait value, but rather is substantially affected by self-perception or self-image. For example, self-ratings do not capture the important dimensions of personality that are outside of a person's awareness or inconsistent with their self-image. Therefore, indirect questions that ask about actual everyday behavior (as 16PF items do) tend to measure personality more accurately, than asking a person to rate themselves on the trait – particularly where social desirability is involved or when no validity scales are available on the instrument.

BASIC FEATURES OF THE 16PF QUESTIONNAIRE

First published in 1949, the 16PF Questionnaire has had four major revisions, in 1956, 1962, 1968, and the fifth edition in 1993 (Cattell, R.B. et al.). The latest edition contains 185 multiple-choice items, with a three-point answer format. Item content is non-threatening, asking about daily behavior, interests, and opinions. The short ability scale items (Factor B) are grouped together at the end of the questionnaire with separate instructions. The questionnaire is written at a fifth grade reading level, and meant for use with people 16 years and older.

The instrument provides scores on the 16 primary scales, 5 global scales, and 3 response bias scales. All personality scales are bipolar (have clear, meaningful definitions at both ends), and are given in 'stens'

(standardized-ten scores) ranging from 1 to 10, with a mean of 5.5 and a standard deviation of 2.0. The latest standardization includes over 10,000 people and was published in 2001.

Because the questionnaire is un-timed and has simple, straightforward instructions, administration requires minimal supervision in either individual or group settings. Administration time is about 35–50 minutes for paper-and-pencil format, and about 25–40 minutes for computer administration. Easy scoring procedures are provided for paper-and-pencil, computer, or Internet formats. The publisher provides various scoring services (mail-in, fax, software, and Internet) and a range of interpretive reports for different applications. Detailed instructions for administration and scoring can be found in numerous places (H.E.P. Cattell and Schuerger, 2003; Russell and Karol, 2002).

The questionnaire is available in many different languages (international translations exceed 35 languages worldwide). Unlike many commercially available personality measures, recent 16PF translations are culturally adapted, with local norms and reliability and validity information available in individual manuals. Internet administration also allows use of international norms for scoring, plus reports in over a dozen different language groups.

The 16PF traits are also measured in parallel versions for younger age ranges. For example, the 16PF Adolescent Personality Questionnaire measures the 16PF traits in 12–18 year olds (Schuerger, 2001). A shorter (20-minute) version of the questionnaire, consisting of a subset of somewhat-shortened scales, was developed for use in employee selection settings – the 16PF Select (Cattell, R.B. et al., 1999). The 16PF Express (Gorsuch, 2006) provides a very short, 15-minute measure of all the traits (with four or five items per factor). The 16PF traits also appear in the PsychEval Personality Questionnaire (PEPQ; Cattell, R.B. et al., 2003), a comprehensive instrument which includes both normal and abnormal personality dimensions.

USES AND APPLICATIONS

Because of its strong scientific background, the 16PF Questionnaire is used in a wide range of settings, including industrial/organizational, counseling and clinical, basic research, educational, and medical settings. The instrument's ability to provide comprehensive, objective information in an efficient manner makes it a particularly powerful tool for industrial/organization applications, such as employee selection, promotion, development, coaching, or outplacement counseling. The questionnaire is also widely used in career counseling settings.

Although the 16PF Questionnaire is a measure of normal-range personality, it can be used in counseling/clinical settings to provide an in-depth, integrated picture of the whole person. Many experts have promoted the use of normal-range measures in clinical settings (e.g. Butcher and Rouse, 1996; Costa and McCrae, 1992b). For example, 16PF dimensions have proven useful in efficiently developing a comprehensive picture of the whole person (including strengths and weaknesses), facilitating rapport and empathy, helping clients develop greater self-awareness, identifying relevant adjustment issues, choosing appropriate therapeutic strategies, and planning developmental goals (H.B. and H.E.P. Cattell, 1997; Karson et al., 1997).

Information about questionnaire interpretation can be found in numerous 16PF resource books. These include the test manuals, clinically oriented interpretive books (e.g. H.B. Cattell, 1989; Karson et al., 1997; Meyer, 1996), resource books for I/O settings (e.g. Schuerger and Watterson, 1998; Lord, 1999; Watterson, 2002); and comprehensive interpretive guidebooks (e.g. H.E.P. Cattell and Schuerger, 2003; H.E.P. Cattell, 2007), plus computer-generated interpretive reports.

RELIABILITY AND HOMOGENEITY

Test–retest reliability

Test–retest reliabilities (measuring temporal consistency or stability) are documented in the *16PF Fifth Edition Technical Manual* (Conn and Rieke, 1994). For the 16PF primary scales, test–retest reliabilities average 0.80 over a two-week interval (ranging from 0.69 to 0.87), and 0.70 over a two-month interval (ranging from 0.56 to 0.79). The five global scales of the 16PF Questionnaire show even higher test–retest reliabilities (they have more items); they average 0.87 for a two-week interval (ranging from 0.84 to 0.91), and 0.78 for a two-month interval (ranging from 0.70 to 0.82).

International 16PF editions also show strong test–retest reliabilities. For example, two-week test–retest reliabilities for the Norwegian edition average 0.80 for primary scales and 0.87 for global scales (IPAT, 2004b); for the German edition, primary scale reliabilities average 0.83 over a one-month interval (Schneewind and Graf, 1998); for the Danish edition, primary scale reliabilities average 0.86 over a two-week interval (IPAT, 2004c); and for the French edition, one-month reliabilities average 0.73 (IPAT, 1995).

Internal consistency

Internal consistency indicates the degree of inter-relatedness or homogeneity of the items in a scale, and is thus a good estimate of reliability for narrowly defined scales. Internal consistency estimates for the 16PF primary scales on a diverse sample of 4,660, range from 0.66 to 0.86, with a mean of 0.75 (Conn and Rieke, 1994). Normal internal consistency estimates are not appropriate for the global scales, because of their heterogeneous nature as weighted composites of primary scales. However, recently developed equations (F. Drasgow, pers. comm., January 2005) for estimating internal consistency in heterogeneous composites were applied, and average 0.87 over the five global scales (S. Bedwell, pers. comm., February 2007).

Internal consistency for international versions of the instrument also meets professionally accepted standards. For example, Cronbach alphas averaged 0.74 in the German edition (Schneewind and Graf, 1998), 0.72 in the French edition (Rolland and Mogenet, 1996), 0.75 in the Japanese edition (IPAT, 2007), 0.69 in the Chinese edition (Jia-xi and Guo-peng, 2006), and 0.73 in the Spanish-American or Pan-Spanish edition (H.E.P. Cattell, 2005).

Too much homogeneity?

Test developers often select items to maximize the internal consistency of a scale by deleting heterogeneous items. Cattell and others (Cattell, R.B. and Tsujioka, 1964; Rosnowski, 1987) have questioned this practice because it can lead to seemingly highly reliable scales which actually measure only a very narrow, homogeneous segment of the target construct, or measure it only in a narrow group of people.

In fact, personality scales can be too homogeneous. Lord (1980: 9) shows how, for dichotomous items, a single scale cannot maximize both internal consistency reliability and validity. Reliability may be defined as:

$$\rho_{xx'} = \frac{n}{n-1}\left(1 - \frac{\sum \sigma_i^2}{\sum\sum \sigma_i \sigma_j \rho_{ij}}\right) \quad (7.1)$$

where n is the number of items on the scale, $\rho_{xx'}$ is the internal consistency reliability, ρ_{ij} is the correlation of items i and j, and σ_i and σ_j are the standard deviations of items i and j. Validity may be defined as:

$$\rho_{xc} = \frac{\sum \sigma_i \rho_{iC}}{\sqrt{\sum\sum \sigma_i \sigma_j \rho_{ij}}} \quad (7.2)$$

where ρ_{XC} is the criterion-related validity of the scale, ρ_{iC} is the criterion correlation of item i, and other terms are as defined in Equation 7.1. The term involving a ratio of numbers of items in Equation 7.1 approaches one quickly and can be ignored. The remainder of Equation 7.1 looks quite like Equation 7.2; both equations contain ratios of sums with similar denominators. The denominator is maximized when the items are highly correlated (and a large denominator leads to a small ratio). The key difference between the two equations is that the ratio is subtracted from 1 in Equation 7.1.

Thus, opposite conditions lead to maximization of Equations 7.1 and 7.2. Equation 7.1 shows that internal consistency is maximized when items are highly correlated, and Equation 7.2 shows that criterion-related validity is maximized when items are uncorrelated. In practical terms, this means it is mathematically impossible to simultaneously maximize reliability and validity of a scale. Therefore, test developers must choose between making very homogeneous scales that reliably predict only a narrow set of behaviors versus creating more heterogeneous scales that measure more comprehensive scale content. Because the predictive validity of a scale is the ultimate measure of its worth, internal consistency reliability should not be the main criterion used in scale development.

FACTORIAL VALIDITY

One important source of validity for the 16PF Questionnaire has been factor-analytic studies of the structure of the primary and global traits across diverse samples of people (e.g. Boyle, 1989; Carnivez and Allen, 2005; H.E. Cattell, 1996; Cattell, R.B. et al., 1970; Cattell, R.B. and Krug, 1986; Chernyshenko et al., 2001; Conn and Rieke, 1994; Dancer and Woods, 2007; Gerbing and Tuley, 1991; R. Gorsuch, pers. comm., February 2007; Hofer et al., 1997; Krug and Johns, 1986;

McKenzie et al., 1997; Ormerod et al., 1995). These studies have used exploratory and confirmatory factor analysis to confirm the number, identity, and independence of the primary factors; and to confirm the number, identity, and primary factor make-up of the global factors.

For example, Dancer and Woods (2007) factor-analyzed the primary traits in a sample of 4,414 business employees and found strong support for the 16PF global factor structure. R. Gorsuch (pers. comm., February 2007) factor-analyzed the primary traits to find the global traits on a sample of 11,000 test-takers, and then applied a common factor analysis to the globals to confirm the third-order factors. Hofer et al. (1997) used confirmatory factor analysis and structural equation modeling tests of factorial invariance to study the measurement properties of the questionnaire across six large, diverse, samples ($n = 30,732$), and concluded that 'the factor structure of the 16PF holds remarkably well across radically different samples of people, across gender, and across different forms of the 16PF' (266).

Factor analyses of international editions have also confirmed the structure of the 16PF primary and global traits. For example, factor analyses have confirmed the factor structure in the German edition (Schneewind and Graf, 1998), the French edition (Rolland and Mogenet, 1996), the Japanese edition (IPAT, 2007), the Chinese edition (Jia-xi and Guo-peng, 2006), the Castilian Spanish edition (Prieto et al., 1996), the Italian edition (Argentero, 1989), the South African edition (Van Eeden and Prinsloo, 1997; Schepers and Hassett, 2006); the Norwegian edition (IPAT, 2004b); and the Dutch edition (IPAT, 2004a).

CONSTRUCT VALIDITY

Construct validity of the 16PF scales has been demonstrated by their correlations with scales on other instruments. *The 16PF Fifth Edition Administrator's Manual* (Russell and Karol, 2002) and the *16PF Fifth Edition Technical Manual* (Conn and Rieke, 1994) present correlations between the 16PF primary and global scales and a range of other measures of normal, adult personality. These include the California Psychological Inventory (Gough, 1987), the Myers-Briggs Type Indicator (Myers and McCaulley, 1985), the NEO-PI-R (Costa and McCrae, 1992a), the Personality Research Form (Jackson, 1989), the Coopersmith Self-Esteem Inventory (Coopersmith, 1981), the Holland occupational themes, as well as other measures of creativity, leadership, and social skills. These results consistently validate the meanings of the 16PF scales.

There are numerous independent studies showing strong relationships between the 16PF scales and other questionnaire scales; for example, Boyle (1989) studied relationships with the Eysenck and Comrey scales; Dancer and Woods (2007) investigated relationships with the FIRO-B; and many studies have investigated the relationships between the 16PF scales and the NEO-PI scales (Carnivez and Allen, 2005; H.E.P. Cattell, 1996; Conn and Rieke, 1994; Gerbing and Tuley, 1991).

International 16PF editions have also shown strong relationships with other instruments. For example, the Japanese 16PF manual (IPAT, 2007) provides inter-correlations with the OPQ and the SPI (a Myers-Briggs type measure); the German edition provides inter-correlations and multi-level factor analyses with the NEO-PI-R, the PRF, and the Locus of Control Inventory (Schneewind and Graf, 1998); the Dutch Manual provides inter-correlations with the MBTI as well as with peer-ratings of personality (IPAT, 2004a); the French edition (IPAT, 1995) provides inter-correlations with the CPI, the Gordon Personality Inventory, and the MBTI; and Schepers and Hassett (2006) provide correlational, factor-analytic, and canonical correlations between the South African 16PF and the Locus of Control Inventory.

PREDICTIVE VALIDITY

For over half a century, the 16PF Questionnaire has proven useful in understanding and predicting a wide range of important behaviors, thus providing a rich source of information for test users. For example, the instrument has been effective in predicting such diverse areas as creativity (Guastello and Rieke, 1993b), social skills and empathy (Conn and Rieke, 1994), marital compatibility (Russell, 1995), and leadership potential (Conn and Rieke, 1994), as well as over a hundred occupational profiles (Cattell, R.B. et al., 1970; Conn and Rieke, 1994; Schuerger and Watterson, 1998; Walter, 2000).

The 16PF Questionnaire has been particularly productive in the domain of basic personality measurement research. For example, in studies of underlying personality structure (Roberts et al., 2005), research into measurement equivalence across cultures (Ellis and Mead, 2000); studies into differences between peer-ratings and self-reports (IPAT, 2004a), and studies of response bias (Christiansen et al., 1994) and social desirability (Seisdedos, 1996). The instrument has also been useful in social and cognitive psychology, for example, in studies of social perception and judgments (Rohmer and Louvet, 2004), attributional style (Wang and Zhang, 2005), cognitive style and decision-making (Bisset, 2000), and cult membership (Kintlerova, 2000).

The measure has also been productive in educational settings, for example, in predicting academic achievement (Schuerger, 2001), characteristics of college drop-outs (Sanchez et al., 2001), choice of college major or spe-cialization (Hartung et al., 2005), and university sports participation (Arora, 2005). The instrument has also been useful in medical studies, for example, of treatment issues in end-stage liver disease (Bonaguidi, 1996) and illnesses such as coronary artery disease (Miller et al., 1996) or cancer (Nair et al., 1993). Because of space limitations, this review will focus on two broad areas of use: organizational applications, such as employee selection and career development, and counseling and clinical uses.

Employee selection, promotion, and development

The 16PF Questionnaire has proven itself invaluable in making a range of organizational decisions, such as employee hiring, promotion, development, coaching, outplacement, and retirement counseling. There is an extensive body of research demonstrating the 16PF Questionnaire's ability to predict a wide variety of occupational profiles (Cattell, R.B. et al., 1970; Conn and Rieke, 1994; Guastello and Rieke, 1993a, 1993b; Russell and Karol, 2002; Schuerger and Watterson, 1998; Walter, 2000). Additionally, the 16PF has been useful in predicting many important job-related dimensions, for example, creativity (Guastello and Rieke, 1993b), leadership styles (Watterson, 2002), team roles and team climate (Burch and Anderson, 2004; Fisher et al., 1998), social skills (Conn and Rieke, 1994), job training success (Tango and Kolodinsky, 2004), and job satisfaction (Lounsbury et al., 2004). International versions have also been effective in predicting important work dimensions, for example, punctuality, job preparedness, and ability to work alone in the Netherlands (IPAT, 2004a); call-center customer service performance in Britain (Williams, 1999); and leadership effectiveness ratings in Norwegian managers (Hetland and Sandal, 2003).

Note that almost all research results are linear and assume that 'more is better' on personality dimensions, which may not be the case. For example, although police officers as a group generally score above average on Rule-Consciousness (G+); higher on-the-job performance is often predicted by *lower* scores on Rule-Consciousness within this above average group – probably because extremely G+ people may be rigidly rule-bound (Adcox et al., 1999). Therefore, job performance results need to be taken in the context of the group's general score range, and curvilinear relationships should be considered.

Meta-analytic job performance evidence

Over two decades, a large body of evidence has shown that various Big Five measures of personality are valid predictors of job performance (Hough and Ones, 2001; Hurtz and Donovan, 2000; Salgado, 1997; Tett et al., 1991). Indeed, the 16PF Questionnaire shows even greater ability to predict occupational outcomes through its more fine-grained primary traits, which are more powerful in capturing important variance about specific behaviors (Ashton, 1998; Judge et al., 2002; Mershon and Gorsuch, 1988; Paunonen and Ashton, 2001; Gorsuch, 2006).

Managers, executives, and leaders

The 16PF Questionnaire has a long history of identifying the personality traits of successful supervisors, managers, executives, and other leaders (Cattell, R.B. et al., 1970; Cattell, R.B. et al., 1999; Cattell, R.B. and Stice, 1954; Christiansen et al., 1994; Conn and Rieke, 1994; Guastello and Rieke, 1993a; Johns et al., 1980; Roy, 1995; Schuerger and Watterson, 1998; Walter, 2000; Watterson, 2002). These studies consistently indicate that three clusters of traits are important for managerial success. First, effective managers tend to be higher on Global Independence and its primary traits of Dominance (E+), Social Boldness (H+), and Openness-to-Change (Q1+). Second, leaders tend to be below average on Anxiety and its traits of Apprehension (O−) and Emotional Stability (C+). Third, leaders tend to be above average on Extraversion and its traits of Warmth (A+), Social Boldness (H+), Liveliness (F+), and Group-Orientation (Q2−). Leaders also tend to be above average on Reasoning Ability (B+), and somewhat above average on self-control traits.

Many of these studies also predicted important differences in management style and behaviors. For example, top-level executives whose roles involve developing long-term, innovative goals, tend to score higher on Openness-to-Change (Q1+), Abstractedness (M+), Reasoning Ability (B+); average (below other managers) on Extraversion traits such as Warmth (A), Forthrightness (N), and Group-Orientation (Q2); and average to below on Rule-Consciousness (G−) (H.B. Cattell, 1989; Walter, 2000; Watterson, 2002). On the other hand, managers who are in applied manufacturing and operations roles tend to score below average on Abstractedness (M−) and Sensitivity (I−), and above average on Rule-Consciousness (G+) and Perfectionism (Q3+). Many studies have predicted other aspects of managerial style such as achievement motivation or supervision style, such as task-oriented versus relationship-oriented focus (Clark and Clark, 1990; Dutta, 1995; Guastello and Rieke, 1993a; Hinton and Barrow 1976; Johns et al., 1980; Roy, 1995; Walter, 2000).

Similar results have also been found in international samples, such as German managers, executives, and consultants (Schneewind and Graf, 1998); Norwegian managers and executives (IPAT, 2004b); middle- and senior-level British managers (Bartram, 1992; Singh, 1989; Williams, 1999); high-performing Japanese managers (IPAT, 2006); autocratic versus democratic styles of managers in India (Singh and Kaur, 2001); and predictions of management level and income in Dutch samples (IPAT, 2004a).

Entrepreneurship

Aldridge (1997) studied the personalities of entrepreneurs and found them to be significantly below average on anxiety traits – low on Apprehensiveness (Self-Assured (O−)) and above average on Emotional Stability (C+). They were also above average on Independence and its traits of Dominance (E+), Social Boldness (H+), and Openness-to-Change (Q1+). They were also higher on Self-Reliance (Q2+), Rule-Consciousness (G+), and Reasoning Ability (B+), and low on Sensitivity (Utilitarian (I−)).

H.B. Cattell confirmed many of these results in her applied research (H.B. Cattell, 1989; H.B. Cattell and H.E.P. Cattell, 1997), identifying traits that distinguished entrepreneurs from other executives: innovative thinking (Openness-to-Change (Q+)); ability to step back and focus on the 'big picture' (Abstractedness (M+)); and a preference for working independently (Self-Reliance (Q2+)). Aldridge (1997) and Fraboni and Saltstone (1990) also found that entrepreneurs tended to be less sociable than regular managers (low Warmth (A−), and low Trust (L+)), and prefer to work independently (Self-Reliance (Q2+)). Many of these results have also been confirmed in international samples, for example, Norwegian entrepreneurs (IPAT, 2004b). Thus, the traits that particularly distinguish entrepreneurs from other business managers include traits that cluster around qualities of innovation and self-reliance.

Sales

Many studies have identified a similar 16PF profile for effective salespeople (e.g. Cattell, R.B. et al., 1970; Guastello and Rieke, 1993b; Rieke and Russell, 1987; Schuerger and Watterson, 1991; Tucker, 1991; Walter, 2000). Salespeople tend to be high on Extraversion and its traits of Warmth (A+), Social Boldness (H+), Liveliness (F+), and Group-Orientation (Q2−). They also tend to be low on Anxiety and its sub-traits of Apprehensiveness (Self-Assured (O−)), Vigilance (Trusting (L−)), and high on Emotional Stability (C+). They also tend to be somewhat above average on Independence and its traits of Social Boldness (H+) and Dominance (E+); and somewhat above average on Rule-Consciousness (G+) and Reasoning Ability (B+). Thus, salespeople tend to be generally similar to managers; however, salespeople tend to be even higher on the traits of Extraversion (especially F+, H+, and A+) and lower on Anxiety traits (more Self-Assured (O−), and are Stable (C+)). This profile has also been validated in numerous international

samples, for example in several groups of British salespeople (Williams, 1999), German salespeople (Schneewind, 1998), and Norwegian salespeople (IPAT, 2004b).

Social/helping occupations

16PF profiles have also been identified for social or helping occupations such as teaching, counseling, customer service, human resource personnel, ministers/priests, nurses, and physical therapists (e.g. Cattell, R.B. et al., 1970; H.B. Cattell and H.E.P. Cattell, 1997; Phillips et al., 1985; Roy, 1995; Schuerger and Watterson, 1998; Walter, 2000). People in social/helping occupations tend to be above average on Extraversion, and particularly on Warmth (A+); they also tend to be below average on Tough-Mindedness (in the Receptive/open direction) – above average on Sensitivity (I+) and Open-to-Change (Q1+). They also tend to be below average on Anxiety: Relaxed (Q4−), Self-Assured (O−), Trusting (L−), and Emotionally Stable (C+); and above average on Self-Control traits of Perfectionism (Q3) and Rule-Consciousness (G+). These results have been validated in various international samples, such as British counselors of adolescents (Lee, 1994) and customer service personnel (Williams, 1999).

Police, security, and protective service personnel

The 16PF Questionnaire has a long history of predicting the personality profiles of effective police officers, prison guards, firefighters, and other protective service and security personnel (e.g. Adcox et al., 1999; Cattell, R.B. et al., 1970; Cattell, R.B. et al., 1999; H. Eber, pers. comm., 10 February 2007; Hofer et al., 1997; IPAT, 2003; Jones et al., 2006; Schuerger and Watterson, 1998; Walter, 2000). These studies indicate that protective service officers tend to be calm and resilient under stress (low Anxiety, Emotionally Stable (C+); Self-Assured (O−); and Trusting (L−)).

They also tend to be responsible, self-disciplined, and task-focused (high self-control; Rule-Conscious, G+; Perfectionistic, Q3+; Practical, M−; and Serious, F−). They also tend to be tough and pragmatic (high on Tough-Mindedness; Unsentimental (I−); Practical (M−); and Traditional (Q1−)). Additionally, protective service personnel are consistently bold and fearless (high on Social Boldness (H+), but not on other Extraversion traits), and somewhat above average on Dominance (E+).

These results have been confirmed across very large samples. For example, Herb Eber's sample of 30,700 police officers confirms all 12 of the trait findings noted above (H. Eber, pers. comm., 10 February, 2007). Additional trait patterns have been found to be associated with particular job roles and functions, for example, officers who work alone versus in community-patrol situations, those who perform investigative roles, or those who work on high-stress assignments tend to show particular trait profiles.

Scientific, technology, and research personnel

Distinct 16PF profiles have also been found for scientific or technological professions such as computer scientists, physicists, engineers, and research and development personnel (Cattell, R.B. et al., 1970; Schuerger and Watterson, 1998; Walter, 2000). In addition to being high on Abstract Reasoning (B+), they tend be high on Independence and its traits of Dominance (E+) and Openness-to-Change (Q1+); low on Extraversion Traits of Reserved (A−), Serious (F−), and Self-Reliant (Q2+); and below average on Anxiety traits of Self-Assured (O-), Relaxed (Q4−), and Emotionally Stable (C+). These results have been confirmed in international samples, for example, groups of Norwegian researchers, engineers, and computer programmers (IPAT, 2004b), British engineers (Williams, 1999), and German technical professionals (Schneewind and Graf, 1998).

Creativity

Many studies have examined the relationship between 16PF scores and creativity. Conn and Rieke (1994) summarized much of this research, and these results have been confirmed in recent American and international samples (e.g. Joy and Hicks, 2004; Jurcova, 2000; Roy, 1995, 1996). Consistent predictors of creativity include high scores on Independence and its primary scales Dominance (E+), Social Boldness (H+), and Openness-to-Change (Q1+); low scores on Tough-Mindedness (in the Receptive or open direction) and its traits of Openness-to-Change (Q1+), Sensitivity (I+), and Abstractedness (M+); and somewhat below average scores on Self-Control (unrestrained). These results have been confirmed in international samples, for example in Norwegian artists (IPAT, 2004b) and in Korean, American, Finnish, and Slovak students (Shaughnessy et al., 2004).

Career development counseling and coaching

The 16PF Questionnaire is widely used in career development planning, counseling, and coaching, both inside and outside organizations, to help clients understand their strengths and limitations, and plan self-development goals and effective career paths (Carson, 1998; Cattell, R.B. et al., 1970; H.E.P. Cattell and Schuerger, 2003; Conn and Rieke, 1994; Krug and Johns, 1990; Lowman, 1991; Schuerger, 1995; Schuerger and Watterson, 1998; Watterson, 2002). In addition to using the numerous 16PF occupational profiles to determine person–job fit, the questionnaire has been useful because of its long history of predicting the six Holland RIASEC occupational dimensions (Schuerger and Watterson, 1998; Schuerger and Sfiligoj, 1998). There is also empirical evidence of the relationship between 16PF scores and important career outcomes such as career satisfaction (Lounsbury et al., 2004) and job-training success (Tango and Kolodinsky, 2004).

Counseling and clinical uses

The 16PF Questionnaire was developed as a measure of *normal* adult personality, and cannot be used to diagnosis psychiatric disorders (e.g. Lally, 2003). However, 16PF dimensions have proven quite useful in counseling and clinical settings; for example, in quickly developing a picture of the individual's overall personality functioning (including strengths and weaknesses), in facilitating the development of empathy and rapport, helping the client gain greater self-awareness, planning developmental goals, anticipating the course of therapy, selecting optimal therapeutic interventions, and identifying relevant adjustment issues (H.B. Cattell, 1989; Karson et al., 1997; Meyer, 1996; Russell, 1995; Schuerger, 2001).

16PF scores have also been successful in predicting a diverse range of behaviors of interest to clinicians; for example, effects of group therapy (Wang and Li, 2003), war-related stress (Poikolainen, 1993), alienation (Yi-Hui et al., 2004), types of substance abuse (Carey et al., 1995), suicidal tendencies (Ferrero et al., 1997), delinquency (Junmai, 2005), law-breaking tendencies (Low et al., 2004), and excessive Internet use (Xiaoming, 2005).

One source of useful clinical information has been the qualitative research carried out in clinical settings (H.B. Cattell, 1989; H.B. Cattell and H.E.P. Cattell, 1997; Karson et al., 1997). For example, H.B. Cattell studied over 1,100 clients who were assessed or treated over a 20-year period, and found that specific 16PF score combinations were related to distinct patterns of thinking, feeling, and behavior. She found that score combinations predicted individuals' capacity for insight and introspection, difficulties in establishing trust and rapport, sensitivity to power dynamics in relationships, effective treatment modalities, and capacity for successful termination.

The 16PF Questionnaire has proven particularly useful in marital or couples counseling, where it provides information about how the two partners' unique traits combine and interact (Russell, 1995). In particular, 16PF research has predicted various aspects of marital satisfaction as a function of absolute or relative levels of personality traits. For example, Krug (1976) found that different types of marital dissatisfaction were related to large score differences between partners on certain traits. He also found that dissatisfaction in wives was related to particular personality traits in husbands, while husbands' dissatisfaction was related to largely different traits in wives.

Russell (1995) studied 321 couples and found that several aspects of marital satisfaction were related to higher levels of particular 16PF traits. She also found that several 16PF traits predicted greater consensus between the partners on important topics, and that better problem-solving communication was related to another set of traits. She also found that 16PF traits predicted more traditional gender roles in relationships. Craig and Olson (1995) also studied 145 marital therapy clients, and found that five different 16PF trait clusters represented different marital types that required different types of therapeutic goals.

SUMMARY

The 16PF Questionnaire is a comprehensive and widely used measure of normal, adult personality which was developed from factor-analytic research into the basic structural elements of personality. First published in 1949, and now in its fifth edition, the questionnaire is based on Cattell's multi-level personality theory, and measures 16 primary factors, 5 global or second-stratum factors (the original Big Five), and 2 third-stratum factors. Although this chapter could not review the decades of research on the 16PF Questionnaire, a summary of reliability studies indicates that the questionnaire provides reliable information, and a selection of validity studies illustrates how the instrument is used effectively in a variety of contexts.

REFERENCES

Adcox, K., Taylor, W. and Mead, A.D. (1999) 'Leveraging personality assessment to reduce law enforcement officers' accidents', Paper presented at the Annual Meeting of the Society for Industrial and Organizational Psychology, Atlanta, GA.

Aldridge, J.H. (1997) 'An occupational personality profile of the male entrepreneur as assessed by the 16PF Fifth Edition', Unpublished doctoral dissertation, Cleveland State University.

Argentero, P. (1989) 'Second-order factor structure of Cattell's 16 Personality Factor Questionnaire', *Perceptual and Motor Skills*, 68(3): 1043–47.

Arora, S. (2005) 'Personality profiles of university sports players', *Social Science International*, 21(2): 115–20.

Ashton, M.C. (1998) 'Personality and job performance: The importance of narrow traits', *Journal of Organizational Behavior*, 19(3): 289–303.

Bartram, E. (1992) 'The personality of UK managers: 16PF norms for short-listed applicants', *Journal of Occupational and Organizational Psychology*, 65(2): 159–72.

Birkett-Cattell, H. (1989) *The 16PF: Personality in Depth*. Champaign, IL: Institute for Personality and Ability Testing.

Birkett-Cattell, H. and Cattell, H.E.P. (1997) *16PF Cattell Comprehensive Personality Interpretation Manual*. Champaign, IL: Institute for Personality and Ability Testing.

Bisset, I.A. (2000) 'Comment on Gadzella and Penland (1995) Creativity and critical thinking', *Psychological Reports*, 86(3): 848–50.

Block, J. (1995) 'A contrarian view of the five-factor approach to personality description', *Psychological Bulletin*, 117(2): 187–215.

Bonaguidi, F., Michelassi, C., Trivella, M.G., Carpeggiani, C., Pruneti, C.A., Cesana, G. and L'Abbate, A. (1996) 'Cattell's 16 PF and PSY Inventory: Relationship between personality traits and behavioral responses in patients with acute myocardial infarction', *Psychological Reports*, 78(2): 691–702.

Boyle, G.J. (1989) 'Re-examination of the major personality factors in the Cattell, Comrey and Eysenck scales: Were the factor solutions of Noller et al. optimal?', *Personality and Individual Differences*, 10(12): 1289–99.

Burch, G.S.J. and Anderson, N. (2004) 'Measuring person-team fit: Development and validation of the team selection inventory', *Journal of Managerial Psychology*, 19(4): 406–26.

Butcher, J.N. and Rouse, S.V. (1996) 'Personality: Individual differences and clinical assessment', *Annual Review of Psychology*, 47: 87–111.

Carnivez, G.L. and Allen, T.J. (2005) 'Convergent and factorial validity of the 16PF and the NEO-PI-R', Paper presented at the Annual Convention of the American Psychological Association, Washington, DC.

Carey, G., Stallings, M.C., Hewitt, J.K. and Fulker, D.W. (1995) 'The familial relationships among personality, substance abuse, and other problem behavior in adolescents', *Behavior Genetics*, 25(3): 258.

Carson, A.D. (1998) 'The integration of interests, aptitudes and personality traits: A test of Lowman's Matrix', *Journal of Career Assessment*, 6(1): 83–105.

Cattell, H.E.P. (1996) 'The original big five: A historical perspective', *European Review of Applied Psychology*, 46(1): 5–14.

Cattell, H.E.P. (2005) *Spanish-American 16PF Questionnaire Technical Manual: A Pan-Spanish Psychological Assessment*. Champaign, IL: Institute for Personality and Ability Testing.

Cattell, H.E.P. (2007) *Exploring your 16PF Profile*. Oxford: Oxford Psychologist Press.

Cattell, H.E.P. and Schuerger, J.M. (2003) *Essentials of the 16PF Assessment*. New York: Wiley.

Cattell, R.B. (1933) 'Temperament tests: II. Tests', *British Journal of Psychology*, 24: 20–49.

Cattell, R.B. (1943) 'The description of personality: Basic traits resolved into clusters', *Journal of Abnormal and Social Psychology*, 38(4): 476–506.

Cattell, R.B. (1946) *The Description and Measurement of Personality*. New York: Harcourt, Brace & World.

Cattell, R.B. (1957) *Personality and Motivation Structure and Measurement*. New York: World Book.

Cattell, R.B. (1973) *Personality and Mood by Questionnaire*. San Francisco: Jossey-Bass.

Cattell, R.B. (1978) *The Scientific Use of Factor Analysis in Behavioral and Life Sciences*. New York: Plenum.

Cattell, R.B., Cattell, A.K. and Cattell, H.E.P. (1993) *16PF Fifth Edition Questionnaire*. Champaign, IL: Institute for Personality and Ability Testing.

Cattell, R.B., Cattell, A.K., Cattell, H.E.P. and Kelly, M.L. (1999) *The 16PF Select Manual*. Champaign, IL: Institute for Personality and Ability Testing.

Cattell, R.B., Cattell, A.K., Cattell, H.E.P., Russell, M.T. and Bedwell, S. (2003) *The PsychEval Personality Questionnaire*. Champaign, IL: Institute for Personality and Ability Testing.

Cattell, R.B., Eber, H.W. and Tatsuoka, M.M. (1970) *Handbook for the Sixteen Personality Factor Questionnaire*. Champaign, IL: Institute for Personality and Ability Testing.

Cattell, R.B. and Krug, S.E. (1986) 'The number of factors in the 16PF: A review of the evidence with special emphasis on methodological problems', *Educational and Psychological Measurement*, 46(3): 509–22.

Cattell, R.B. and Stice, G.F. (1954) 'Four formulae for selecting leaders on the basis of personality', *Human Relations*, 7(4): 493–507.

Cattell, R.B. and Tsujioka, B. (1964) 'The importance of factor-trueness and validity versus homogeneity and orthogonality in test scales', *Educational and Psychological Measurement*, 24(1): 3–30.

Chernyshenko, O.S., Stark, S. and Chan, K.Y. (2001) 'Investigating the hierarchical factor structure of the fifth edition of the 16PF: An application of the Schmid-Leiman orthogonalisation procedure', *Educational and Psychological Measurement*, 61(2): 290–302.

Child, D. (1998) 'Some technical problems in the use of personality measures in occupational settings illustrated using the "Big-Five"', in S. Shorrocks-Taylor (ed.), *Directions in Educational Psychology*. London: Whurr Publishing, pp. 346–64.

Christiansen, N.D., Goffin, R.D., Johnston, N.G. and Rothstein, M.G. (1994) 'Correcting for faking: Effects on criterion-related validity and individual hiring decisions', *Personnel Psychology*, 47(4): 847–60.

Church, A.T. and Burke, P.J. (1994) 'Exploratory and confirmatory tests of the Big-Five and Tellegen's three- and four-dimensional models', *Journal of Personality and Social Psychology*, 66(1): 93–114.

Clark, K.E. and Clark, M.B. (1990) *Measures of Leadership*. West Orange, NJ: Leadership Library of America.

Conn, S.R. and Rieke, M.L. (1994) *The 16PF Fifth Edition Technical Manual*. Champaign, IL: Institute for Personality and Ability Testing.

Coopersmith, S. (1981) *Self-esteem Inventories*. Palo Alto, CA: Consulting Psychologists Press.

Costa, P.T., Jr. and McCrae, R.R. (1976) 'Age differences in personality structure: A cluster analytic approach', *Journal of Gerontology*, 31(5): 564–70.

Costa, P.T., Jr. and McCrae, R.R. (1985) *The NEO-PI-R Personality Inventory Manual*. Odessa, FL: Psychological Assessment Resources.

Costa, P.T., Jr. and McCrae, R.R. (1992a) *Revised NEO-PI-R Personality Inventory (NEO-PI-R) and NEO-PI-R Five-Factor Inventory (NEO-PI-R-FFI) Professional Manual*. Odessa, FL: Psychological Assessment Resources.

Costa, P.T., Jr. and McCrae, R.R. (1992b) 'Normal personality assessment in clinical practice: The NEO Personality Inventory', *Psychological Assessment*, 4(1): 5–13.

Craig, R.J. and Olson, R.E. (1995) '16 PF profiles and typologies for patients seen in marital therapy', *Psychological Reports*, 77(2): 187–94.

Dancer, L.J. and Woods, S.A. (2007) 'Higher-order factor structures and intercorrelations of the 16PF5 and FIRO-B', *International Journal of Selection and Assessment*, 14(4): 385–91.

Digman, J.M. (1990) 'Personality structure: Emergence of the five-factor model', *Annual Review of Psychology*, 41: 417–40.

Digman, J.M. (1996) 'A curious history of the five-factor model', in J.S. Wiggins (ed.), *The Five-factor Model of Personality: Theoretical Perspectives*. New York: Guilford.

Digman, J.M. (1997) 'Higher order factors of the big five', *Journal of Personality and Social Psychology*, 73(6): 1246–56.

Dutta, R.D. (1995) 'Differences in personality factors of experienced teachers, physicians, bank managers, and fine artists', *Psychological Studies*, 40(1): 51–6.

Ellis, B.B. and Mead, A.D. (2000) 'Assessment of the measurement equivalence of a Spanish translation of the 16PF Questionnaire', *Educational and Psychological Measurement*, 60(5): 787–807.

Eysenck, H. (1978) 'Superfactors P, E, and N in a comprehensive factors space', *Multivariate Behavioral Research*, 13(2): 475–82.

Fisher, S.G., Macrosson, W.D.K. and Wong, J. (1998) 'Cognitive style and team role preference', *Journal of Managerial Psychology*, 13(8): 544–57.

Fiske, D.W. (1994) 'Two cheers for the Big Five!', *Psychological Inquiry*, 5(1): 123–4.

Fraboni, M. and Saltstone, R. (1990) 'First and second generation entrepreneur typologies: Dimensions of personality', *Journal of Social Behavior and Personality*, 5(3): 105–13.

Gerbing, D.W. and Tuley, M.R. (1991) 'The 16PF related to the five-factor model of personality: Multiple-indicator measurement versus the *a priori* scales', *Multivariate Behavioral Research*, 26(2): 271–89.

Goldberg, L.R. (1990) 'An alternative "description of personality": The big-five factor structure', *Journal of Personality and Social Psychology*, 59(6): 1216–29.

Goldberg, L.R. (1992) 'The development of markers for the big-five factor structure', *Psychological Assessment*, 4(1): 26–42.

Gorsuch, R.L. (1983) *Factor Analysis* (2nd rev edn). Hillsdale, NJ: Erlbaum.

Gorsuch, R.L. (2006) *The 16PF Express Edition: A Supplemental Chapter to the 16PF Fifth Edition Administrator's Manual*. Champaign, IL: Institute for Personality and Ability Testing.

Gough, H.G. (1987) *California Psychological Inventory Administrator's Guide*. Mountain View, CA: Consulting Psychologists Press.

Guastello, S.J. and Rieke, M.L. (1993a) *The 16PF and Leadership: Summary of Research Findings 1954–1992*. Champaign, IL: Institute for Personality and Ability Testing.

Guastello, S.J. and Rieke, M.L. (1993b) *Selecting Successful Salespersons with the 16PF. Form A Validity Studies*. Champaign, IL: Institute for Personality and Ability Testing.

Hampson, S.E. (1988) *The Construction of Personality* (2nd edn). London: Routledge.

Hartung, P.J., Borges, N.J. and Jones, B.J. (2005) 'Using person matching to predict career specialty choice', *Journal of Vocational Behavior*, 67(1): 102–17.

Hetland, H. and Sandal, G.M. (2003) 'Transformational leadership in Norway: Outcomes and personality correlates', *European Journal of Work and Organizational Psychology*, 12(2): 147–70.

Hinton, B.L. and Barrow, J.C. (1976) 'Personality correlates of the reinforcement propensities of leaders', *Personnel Psychology*, 29(1): 61–6.

Hofer, S.M. and Eber, H.W. (2002) 'Second-order factor structure of the Cattell Sixteen Personality Factor Inventory (16PF)', in B. De Raad and M. Perugini (eds), *Big-Five Assessment*. Ashland, OH: Hogrefe & Huber, pp. 397–404.

Hofer, S.M., Horn, J.L. and Eber, H.W. (1997) 'A robust five-factor structure of the 16PF: Strong evidence from independent rotation and confirmatory factorial invariance procedures', *Personality and Individual Differences*, 23(2): 247–69.

Hogan, J., Brinkmeyer, K. and Hogan, R. (1996) *Hogan Personality Inventory Form Manual*. Tulsa, OK: Hogan Assessment Systems.

Hough, L.M. and Ones, D.S. (2001) 'The structure, measurement, validity, and use of personality variables in industrial, work, and organisational psychology', in N. Anderson, D.S. Ones, H. Sinangil and C. Viswesvaran (eds), *Handbook of Industrial, Work, and Organizational Psychology* (Vol. 1). London: Sage, pp. 233–77.

Hurtz, G.M. and Donovan, J.J. (2000) 'Personality and job performance', *Journal of Applied Psychology*, 85(6): 869–79.

IPAT (1995) *16PF5 Manuel: French Version*. Champaign, IL: Institute for Personality and Ability Testing.

IPAT (2003) *The Protective Service Report Manual*. Champaign, IL: Institute for Personality and Ability Testing.

IPAT (2004a) *Dutch 16PF5 User's Manual*. Champaign, IL: Institute for Personality and Ability Testing.

IPAT (2004b) *16PF5 Manual: Norwegian Version*. Champaign, IL: Institute for Personality and Ability Testing.

IPAT (2004c) *16PF5 Manual: Danish Version*. Champaign, IL: Institute for Personality and Ability Testing.

IPAT (2005) *16PF5 Manual: Swedish Version*. Champaign, IL: Institute for Personality and Ability Testing.

IPAT (2006) *The 16PF5 User's Manual: South African Version*. Champaign, IL: Institute for Personality and Ability Testing.

IPAT (2007) *Japanese 16PF5 Technical Manual*. Champaign, IL: Institute for Personality and Ability Testing.

Jackson, D.N. (1989) *Personality Research Form Manual*. Port Huron, MI: Sigma Assessment Systems.

Jackson, D.N., Paunonen, S.V. and Tremblay, P.F. (2000) *Six Factor Personality Questionnaire*. Port Huron, MI: Sigma Assessment Systems.

Jia-xi, C. and Guo-peng, C. (2006) '[The validity and reliability research of 16PF 5th in China]', *Chinese Journal of Clinical Psychology*, 14(1): 13–46.

Jones, J.W., Newhouse, N.K. and Stowers, M.R. (2006) *Civilian Police Officer Profiles: An IPAT Technical Report*. Champaign, IL: Institute for Personality and Ability Testing.

Johns, E.F., Schuerger, J.M. and Watterson, D.G. (1980) '*Personality measures as predictors of managerial performance and salaries*', Paper presented at the meeting of the Midwest Society for Multivariate Experimental Psychology, May, St. Louis, MO.

Joy, S. and Hicks, S. (2004) 'The need to be different: Primary trait structure and impact on projective drawing', *Creativity Research Journal*, 16(2–3): 331–9.

Judge, T.A., Bono, J.E., Erez, A., Locke, E.A. and Thoresen, C.J. (2002) 'The scientific merit of valid measures of general concepts: Personality research and core self-evaluations', in J.M. Brett and F. Drasgow (eds), *The Psychology of Work: Theoretically Based Empirical Research*. Mahwah, NJ: Erlbaum, pp. 55–77.

Junmei, J. (2005) '[A Research on the Personality Traits of Young Criminals]', *Psychological Science (China)*, 28(1): 217–9.

Jurcova, M. (2000) 'Socialna kompetentnost tvorivych adolescentov – jej kognitivne a osobnostni zdroje [Social competence of creative adolescents – its cognitive and personality sources]', *Ceskoslovenske Psychologie*, 44(6): 481–92.

Karson, M., Karson, S. and O'Dell, J. (1997) *16PF Interpretation in Clinical Practice: A Guide to the Fifth Edition*. Champaign, IL: Institute for Personality and Ability Testing.

Kintlerova, T. (2000) 'Osobnostni charakteristiky clenov siekt a kultov [Personality characteristics of members of sects and cults]', *Ceskoslovenske Psychologie*, 44(2): 180–9.

Krug, S.E. (1976) 'Personality correlates of marital satisfaction and conflict', Unpublished manuscript, Institute for Personality and Ability Testing.

Krug, S.E. and Johns, E.F. (1986) 'A large-scale cross-validation of second-order personality structure defined by the 16PF', *Psychological Reports*, 59(2): 683–93.

Krug, S.E. and Johns, E.F. (1990) 'The 16 Personality Factor Questionnaire', in E.E. Watkins and V.L. Campbell (eds), *Testing in Counseling Practice*. Hillsdale, NJ: Lawrence Erlbaum.

Lally, S.J. (2003) 'What tests are acceptable for use in forensic evaluations? A survey of experts', *Professional Psychology: Research and Practice*, 34(5): 491–8.

Lee, K., Ogunfowora, B. and Ashton, M.C. (2005) 'Personality traits beyond the Big Five: Are they within the HEXACO space?', *Journal of Personality*, 73(5): 1437–63.

Lee, R.E. (1994) 'Personality characteristics of very desirable and undesirable childcare workers in a residential setting', *Psychological Reports*, 74(2): 579–84.

Loevinger, J. (1994) 'Has psychology lost its conscience?', *Journal of Personality Assessment*, 62(1): 2–8.

Lord, F.M. (1980) *Applications of Item Response Theory to Practical Testing Problems*. Hillsdale, NJ: Lawrence Erlbaum.

Lord, W. (1999) *16PF5: Overcoming Obstacles to Interpretation*. Windsor: NFER-Nelson Publishing Company (available from IPAT).

Lounsbury, J., Park, S.H., Sundstrom, E., Williamson, J.M. and Pemberton, A.E. (2004) 'Personality, career satisfaction, and life satisfaction: Test of a directional model', *Journal of Career Assessment*, 12(4): 395–406.

Low, J.M., Williamson, D. and Cottingham, J. (2004) 'Predictors of university student lawbreaking behaviors', *Journal of College Student Development*, 45(5): 535–48.

Lowman, R.L. (1991) *The Clinical Practice of Career Assessment*. Washington, DC: American Psychological Association.

McKenzie, J. (1998) 'Fundamental flaws in the Five Factor Model: A re-analysis of the seminal correlation matrix from which the "Openness-to-Experience" factor was extracted', *Personality and Individual Differences*, 24(4): 475–80.

McKenzie, J., Tindell, G. and French, J. (1997) 'The great triumvirate: Agreement between lexically and psycho-physiologically based models of personality', *Personality and Individual Differences*, 22(2): 269–77.

Mershon, B. and Gorsuch, R.L. (1988) 'Number of factors in the personality sphere: Does increase in factors increase predictability of real-life criteria?', *Journal of Personality and Social Psychology*, 55(4): 675–80.

Meyer, R.G. (1996) *The Clinician's Handbook* (5th edn). Boston: Allyn and Bacon/ Longman.

Miller, T.Q., Smith, T.W., Turner, C.W., Guijarro, M.L. and Hallet, A.J. (1996) 'Una rassegna meta-analitica della ricerca su ostilita e salute fisica [A meta-analytic review of research on hostility and physical health]', *Bollettino di Psicologia Applicata*, 220(1): 3–40.

Myers, I.B. and McCaulley, M.G. (1985) *Manual: A Guide to the Development and Use of the Myers-Briggs Type Indicator*. Mountain View, CA: Consulting Psychologist Press.

Norman, W.T. (1967) *2800 Personality Trait Descriptors: Normative Operating Charac- teristics for a University Population*. Ann Arbor: University of Michigan, Department of Psychology.

Ormerod, M.B., McKenzie, J. and Woods, A. (1995) 'Final report on research relating to the concept of five separate dimensions of personality – or six including intelligence', *Personality and Individual Differences*, 18(4): 451–61.

Ostendorf, F. (1990) *Language and Personality Structure: On the Validity of the Five-factor Model of Personality*. Regensburg, Germany: S. Roderer Verlag.

Parker, J.D.A., Bagby, R.M. and Summerfeldt, L.J. (1993) 'Confirmatory factor analysis of the NEO PI-R', *Personality and Individual Differences'*, 15(4): 463–6.

Paunonen, S.V. (1993) 'Sense, nonsense, and the Big-Five factors of personality', Paper pre- sented at the Annual Meeting of the American Psychological Association, August, Toronto.

Paunonen, S.V. and Ashton, M.S. (2001) 'Big Five factors and facets and the prediction of behavior', *Journal of Personality and Social Psychology*, 81(3): 524–39.

Peabody, D. and Goldberg, L.R. (1989) 'Some determinants of factor structures from personality-trait descriptors', *Journal of Personality and Social Psychology*, 57(3): 552–67.

Phillips, D.A., Carlisle, C.S., Hautala, R. and Larson, R. (1985) 'Personality traits and teacher- student behaviors in physical education', *Journal of Educational Psychology*, 77(4): 408–16.

Piotrowski, C. and Zalewski, C. (1993) 'Training in psychodiagnostic testing in APA-approved PsyD and PhD clinical psychology programs', *Journal of Personality Assessment*, 61(2): 394–405.

Prieto, J.M., Gouveia, V.V. and Ferandez, M.A. (1996) 'Evidence on the primary source trait structure in the Spanish 16PF Fifth Edition', *European Review of Applied Psychology*, 46(1): 33–43.

Rieke, M.L. and Russell, M.T. (1987) *Narrative Score Report User's Guide*. Champaign, IL: Institute for Personality and Ability Testing.

Roberts, B.W., Chernyshenko, O.S., Stark, S. and Goldberg, L.R. (2005) 'The structure of conscientiousness: an empirical investigation based on seven major personality question- naires', *Personnel Psychology*, 58(1): 103–39.

Rohmer, O. and Louvet, E. (2004) 'Familiarite et reactions affectives de l'egard des personnes handicapes physiques [Familiarity and affec- tive reactions regarding physically handi- capped persons]', *Bulletin de Psychologie*, 57(2): 165–70.

Rolland, J.P. and Mogenet, J.L. (1996) 'Evidence on the primary dimensions of the 16PF5 French Form', *European Review of Applied Psychology*, 46(1): 25–31.

Rosnowski, M. (1987) 'Use of tests manifesting sex differences as measures of intelligence: Implications for measurement bias', *Journal of Applied Psychology*, 72(3): 480–3.

Roy, D.D. (1995) 'Differences in personality fac- tors of experienced teachers, physicians, bank managers, and fine artists', *Psychological Studies*, 40(1): 51–6.

Roy, D.D. (1996) 'Personality model of fine artists', *Creativity Research Journal*, 9(4): 391–4.

Russell, M.T. (1995) *The 16PF Couple's Counseling Report User's Guide*. Champaign, IL: Institute for Personality and Ability Testing.

Russell, M.T. and Karol, D. (1994) *16PF Fifth Edition Administrator's Manual with Updated Norms*. Champaign, IL: Institute for Personality and Ability Testing.

Salgado, J. (1997) 'The five factor model of personality and job performance in the European Community', *Journal of Applied Psychology*, 82(1): 30–43.

Sanchez, M.M., Rejano, E.I. and Rodriguez, Y.T. (2001) 'Personality and academic productivity in the university student', *Social Behavior and Personality*, 29(3): 299–305.

Saucier, G. (2001) 'Going beyond the Big-Five', Paper presented at the Annual Conference of the American Psychological Association, August, San Francisco.

Schepers, J.M. and Hassett, C.F. (2006) 'The relationship between the Fourth Edition (2003) of the Locus of Control Inventory and the Sixteen Personality Factor Questionnaire Fifth Edition', *South African Journal of Industrial Psychology*, 32(2): 9–18.

Schmit, M.K. and Ryan, A.M. (1993) 'The Big-Five in personnel selection: Factor structure in applicant and non-applicant populations', *Journal of Applied Psychology*, 78(6): 966–74.

Schneewind, K.A. and Graf, J. (1998) *16-Personlichkeits-Factoren-Test Revidierte Fassung Test-Manual [The 16 Personality Factor Test – Revised Version Test Manual]*. Bern, Switzerland: Verlag Hans Huber.

Schuerger, J.M. (1995) 'Career assessment and the Sixteen Personality Factor Questionnaire', *Journal of Career Assessment*, 3(2): 157–75.

Schuerger, J.M. and Sfiligoj, T. (1998) 'Holland codes and the 16PF global factors: Sixty-nine samples', *Psychological Reports*, 82(3): 1299–306.

Schuerger, J.M. and Watterson, D.G. (1998) *Occupational Interpretation of the 16PF Questionnaire*. Cleveland, OH: Watterson and Associates.

Seisdedos, N. (1996) 'The "IM" (Impression Management) Scale', *European Review of Applied Psychology*, 46(1): 45–54.

Shaughnessy, M.F., Kang, M.H., Greene, M., Misutova, M., Suomala, J. and Siltala, R. (2004) '16 PF personality profile of gifted children: Preliminary report of an international study', *North American Journal of Psychology*, 6(1): 51–4.

Singh, S. (1989) 'Projective and psychometric correlates of managerial success', *British Journal of Projective Psychology*, 34(1): 28–36.

Singh, S. and Kaur, R. (2001) 'A comparative study of the personality characteristics, motives, and work values of the autocratic and democratic executives', *Journal of the Indian Academy of Applied Psychology*, 27(1–2): 143–9.

Smith, M.A., Moriarty, K.O. and Lutrick, E.C. (2001) 'Exploratory factor analysis of the NEO-PI-R for job applicants: Evidence against the Big Five', Paper presented at the Annual Meeting of the Society for Industrial and Organizational Psychology, April, San Diego.

Spearman, C. (1932) *The Abilities of Man*. London: Macmillan.

Tango, R.A. and Kolodinsky, P. (2004) 'Investigation of placement outcomes 3 years after a job skills training program for chronically unemployed adults', *Journal of Employment Counseling*, 41(2): 80–92.

Tett, R.P., Jackson, D.N. and Rothstein, M. (1991) 'Personality measures as predictors of job performance: A meta-analytic review', *Personnel Psychology*, 44(4): 703–42.

Tucker, T.L. (1991) 'Investigating sales effectiveness in the automobile industry in relation to personality variables as measured by the 16PF Questionnaire', Unpublished dissertation, Fuller Theological Seminary.

Tupes, E.C. and Christal, R.E. (1961) *Recurrent Personality Factors Based on Trait Ratings*. Tech. Rep. Nos 61–67. Lackland, TX: US Air Force Aeronautical Systems Division.

Van Eeden, R. and Prinsloo, C.H. (1997) 'Using the South African version of the 16PF in a multicultural context', *South African Journal of Psychology*, 27(3): 151–9.

Walter, V. (2000) *16PF Personal Career Development Profile Technical and Interpretive Manual*. Champaign, IL: Institute for Personality and Ability Testing.

Wang, Y. and Li, Y. (2003) '[The effect of group counseling on improvement of self-confidence of college students]', *Chinese Mental Health Journal*, 17(4): 235–9.

Wang, C. and Zhang, N. (2005) '[Personality Correlates of Attributional Style in Undergraduates]', *Chinese Journal of Clinical Psychology*, 13(1): 53–4.

Watkins, C.E., Campbell, V.L., Nieberding, R. and Hallmark, R. (1995) 'Contemporary practice of psychological assessment of clinical psychologist', *Professional Psychology: Research and Practice*, 26(1): 54–60.

Watterson, D.G. (2002) *The 16PF Leadership Coaching Report Manual*. Champaign,

IL: Institute for Personality and Ability Testing.

Wiggins, J.S. (2003) *Paradigms of Personality Assessment*. Guilford.

Williams, R. (1999) *16PF5: Profiling Personality for Potential – A Data Supplement to the UK Edition*. Champaign, IL: Institute for Personality and Ability Testing.

Xiaoming, Y. (2005) '[The mental health problems of internet-addicted college students]', *Psychological Science (China)*, 28(6): 1476–8.

Yi-Hui, T., Hai, H. and Liang-Xin, L. (2004) '[Relationship among the family functioning, personality, and alienation of adolescents]', *Chinese Journal of Clinical Psychology*, 12(2): 158–60.

8

Contribution of Cattellian Personality Instruments

Gregory J. Boyle and Keith Barton

Raymond B. Cattell, PhD, DSc (London) was ranked among the top ten most highly cited psychologists of the twentieth century (along with Freud, Piaget, Eysenck, and Skinner), as indexed in the peer-reviewed psychological journal literature (Haggbloom et al., 2002: 142). Over the span of more than half a century, Cattell undertook an extensive programmatic series of empirical research studies into the taxonomy of psychological structure (across the domains of intellectual abilities, normal and abnormal personality traits, dynamic (motivation) traits, and transitory mood states). Subsequently, a wide range of functional multidimensional psychological testing instruments were constructed (see Cattell, 1986d; Cattell and Johnson, 1986; Smith, 1988) to measure the factor-analytically derived constructs. The major personality instruments constructed within the Cattellian School included the Sixteen Personality Questionnaire or 16PF (Birkett-Cattell, 1989; Cattell, 1986g, 1994; Cattell and Krug, 1986; Cattell and H.E.P. Cattell, 1995; H.E.P. Cattell, 2001, 2004; H.E.P. Cattell and Schuerger, 2003; Conn and Rieke, 1994); the High School Personality

Questionnaire or HSPQ (Cattell and M.D. Cattell, 1975) as well as its more recent version, the Adolescent Personality Questionnaire or APQ; the Children's Personality Questionnaire or CPQ (Porter and Cattell, 1985); the Early School Personality Questionnaire or ESPQ (Coan and Cattell, 1959); the Preschool Personality Questionnaire or PSPQ (Lichtenstein et al., 1986; Dreger et al., 1995), the Central Trait-State Kit or CTS (Barton and Cattell, 1981; Barton, 1985b), the Objective-Analytic Battery or OAB (Cattell and Schuerger, 1978; Schuerger, 1986), and the Clinical Analysis Questionnaire or CAQ (Krug, 1980), along with its more recent version, the PsychEval Personality Questionnaire or PEPQ (see instruments on the Institute for Personality and Ability Testing website at <http://www.ipat.com>).

The highly cited fourth edition of the 16PF (16PF4) consists of 187 items (Forms A and B) measuring 16 primary factors (e.g. see Krug, 1981). When these 16 source traits were intercorrelated and subjected to factor analysis, several broad second-stratum dimensions were derived (see Boyle, 2006, for a summary). Scale reliabilities (including dependability coefficients, stability coefficients, and equivalence coefficients), as well as direct and indirect validities of the full 16PF and some combined forms may all be obtained from the relevant technical manual (e.g. for the more recent 16PF fifth edition or 16PF5, see Conn and Rieke, 1994). There is also available from the same sources much data on regression coefficients to predict a wide variety of criteria such as achievement, accident proneness, leadership, and so on. The 16PF (and CAQ/ PEPQ) instruments are often used in a 'negative selection' mode, whereby instead of attempting to make positive predictions about future performance in specific situations, the instruments are used to exclude from the selection process 'at risk' individuals who have obtained extreme scores (i.e. a sten of 10) on specific trait scales (especially the psychopathological trait dimensions measured in Part 2 of the CAQ/PEPQ).

The Cattellian personality questionnaires measure primary source traits at different age levels (16PF for adults, the HSPQ/APQ for adolescents, as well as the CPQ, ESPQ, and PSPQ for children of various age groups). Each of these Q-data instruments takes roughly up to one hour to administer, and except for the PSPQ, there is a standard questionnaire form together with an answer sheet that can be computer scored. These instruments can be administered either in an individual or a group setting. A complete listing of the factors measured in the 16PF using popular, professional labels is shown in Johnson (1986: 221). The personality scales for the primary factors in younger children, such as the ESPQ and PSPQ, do not cover quite as many factors as at the adult level. For example, the HSPQ drops down from 16 to 14 factors. This reflects the developmental differentiation that occurs in personality structure, and it also recognizes that some factors may be larger and more formed in childhood and others in adult life (Barton, 1986c). Cross-validation of the factor structures from numerous cross-cultural studies of the 16PF and HSPQ (e.g. Cattell and Johnson, 1986; Cattell et al., 1983) has contributed

greatly to our knowledge about the universality of human personality structure.

More specifically, the 16PF has the advantages of (1) having been factored to meaningful simple structure source traits; (2) permitting scoring of second-stratum factors; (3) having been cross-validated in its standardization and foreign-language translations; (4) having corresponding downward extensions for use with teenagers and children (HSPQ/APQ, CPQ, ESPQ, and PSPQ, respectively); (5) showing strong alignment of its second-stratum Q-data factors with the first-stratum objective test (T-data) factors measured in the OAB; and (6) having empirically derived criterion relations for major clinical syndrome categories, and for more than 40 occupational categories. Moreover, the 16PF4 has stood the test of critical scrutiny over many years and several editions of the *Test Critiques* series and the *Buros Mental Measurements Yearbooks* (MMY). The 16PF4, with the option of combined administration of its multiple parallel forms, has the potential to exhibit very high levels of test–retest reliability (both dependability and stability).

More recently, Cattell and Cattell (1995) described the development of the new fifth edition of the 16PF, undertaken with the goal of updating and improving item content, standardizing on the current population sample, and refining the instrument psychometrically. Item selection involved an iterative process, commencing with selected items from all earlier versions of the 16PF (presumably excluding items which showed significant sex differences). Factor analyses (H.E.P. Cattell, 2001, 2004; Hofer et al., 1997) supported the factor structure of the 16PF5 and demonstrated its continuity with earlier versions, but for this version provided only five second-stratum factors in line with the currently popular Big Five personality dimensions and the corresponding static five-factor model (FFM). However, it is important to note that both Gorsuch and Cattell (1967) as well as Cattell and Nichols (1972) had previously undertaken extensive investigations into the delineation of higher-stratum Q-data personality factors. For example, from an examination of ten separate studies, Cattell and Nichols had identified no fewer than eight second-stratum 16PF factors. Therefore, the Big Five (FFM) was seen by Cattell as being overly restrictive (Cattell, 1995). This issue has been examined independently (Boyle et al., 1995; Boyle and Saklofske, 2004), showing the inadequacy of the FFM which accounts for less than 60% of the known trait variance within the normal personality sphere alone, not including the abnormal trait domain (Boyle et al., 1995: 432; Boyle and Smári, 1997, 1998, 2002).

In regard to the abnormal personality trait domain, the CAQ (Krug, 1980) was developed by factoring the entire MMPI item pool, together with hundreds of additional items pertaining to various aspects of depression and psychopathology (Boyle, 1990; Boyle and Comer, 1990). Altogether, the CAQ measures $(16 + 12 = 28)$ primary source trait dimensions. The CAQ comprises two parts. Part 1 measures the 16PF normal personality factors, while Part 2 measures 12 additional (abnormal) trait factors elucidated factor-analytically. In practice, and for greater reliability, the 16PF itself is often administered instead of Part 1 of the CAQ (which has reduced reliability with only eight items per subscale included). The difference between the two frequently used questionnaire instruments for clinical diagnosis – the MMPI and the CAQ – is that the former was constructed to separate superficial syndrome types (such as the DSM-IV recognizes), whereas the CAQ measures underlying source traits. The CAQ can and does permit type classifications, but it does so through first getting profiles on the functionally unitary traits and then classifying by similarities of profiles.

Instead of operating with both primary and secondary traits, as in the 16PF, HSPQ, CAQ, and so on, permitting *depth psychometry* (Cattell, 1987), many psychologists tend to use *either* primary *or* secondary trait scores. At the first-stratum (primary) factor level, several normal personality trait factors (the first 16 of which were included in the 16PF), along with 12 abnormal (psychopathological) trait

dimensions have been elucidated, which together account for most of the known normal and abnormal personality trait variance. The largest and most useful second-stratum factors are also measured via the Central Trait-State Kit or CTS (Barton, 1985b). There are advantages in having a *family* of instruments aimed at measuring the same personality trait structures across developmental ages, and also cross-validated and standardized cross-culturally.

NINE-PARAMETER MODEL OF PSYCHOLOGICAL ASSESSMENT

Providing a detailed description of the various personality assessment instruments from the Cattellian laboratory, we also discuss these measures within the framework of a nine-parameter model of psychological assessment shown in Figure 8.1 (Barton, 1985a). Providing a multidimensional definition of psychological assessment in line with Boyle (1991a), Eysenck (1997), as well as Eysenck and Eysenck (1985), the nine-parameter model can also be used for taxonomic classification of psychological instruments themselves (Barton, 1986c). By identifying the Cattellian instruments within the framework of this model one can see the breadth of coverage of each personality instrument, as well as highlighting those areas that are not presently covered.

Barton's (1985a) nine-parameter model does not attempt to address the 'process' aspects of assessment (i.e. the steps which must be followed) but views assessment in terms of nine questions that must be answered to define fully the domain of psychological assessment. The nine parameters may be grouped roughly into sets of three. The first set concerns questions about *who* is being assessed (e.g. How old are they? Are they from a 'normal' population or from a clinical group?). The second set is related to *what* is being assessed (e.g. personality, cognition or motivation, Questionnaire, projective, or objective test?). The third set has to do with the *how* of assessment (e.g. Do we need

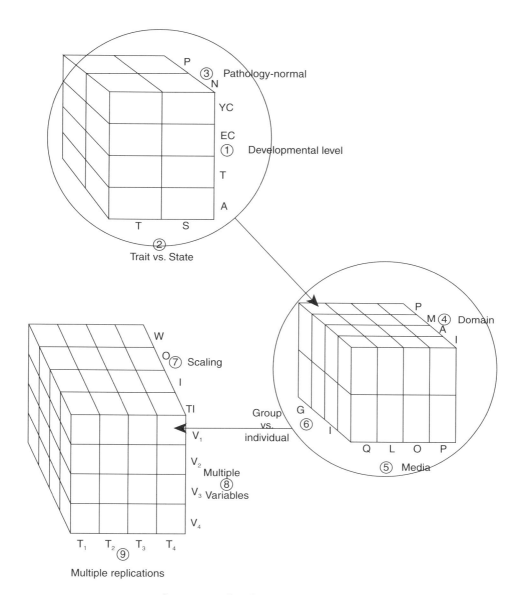

Figure 8.1   The nine-parameter model

multiple measures? Multiple variables? On what scale will we assess: nominal, ordinal, or interval?).

Parameter 1: developmental level

What is the appropriate developmental level at which to measure a given individual? What aspects of the developmental level should influence the choice of measures used

in the assessment (e.g. language or reading level)? It is this dimension that the Cattellian Institute for Personality and Ability Testing (IPAT) had in mind when it designed and constructed a wide array of psychometric instruments to measure factor-analytically elucidated personality traits. While the 16PF is the instrument of choice when measuring adult personality traits (Birkett-Cattell, 1989; Boyle, 1990), the HSPQ was specifically designed for adolescents; the items on this instrument were all focused on the lifestyle and interests of the typical North American teenager. While the CPQ was intended for use with 8–12 year olds, the ESPQ was constructed for use with 6–8 year olds, and the PSPQ for use with children younger than 6 years. In the construction of these instruments it was shown empirically that different numbers of factors needed to be extracted at different age levels (Boyle et al., 2001; Cattell, 1973; Cattell and Kline, 1977). The reduced number of factors measured in the various downward extensions of the 16PF instrument (HSPQ, CPQ, ESPQ, and PSPQ) is consistent with the increasing complexity of personality structure over the early lifespan as a function of maturation, socialization and experiential learning (Cattell, 1983, 1996). Indeed, in recent years, it has become increasingly evident that personality traits are subject to change throughout the lifespan (Cattell et al., 2002; Eysenck, 1994c; Roberts et al., 2006a, 2006b).

When items are rewritten for different age levels, can the factors they represent be considered the 'same'? The construction of related instruments for various age levels has a definite advantage over a single measure since the different versions can be tailored to fit developmental levels by using items that tap personality through the differing interests and behaviours from childhood to adulthood (Cattell and Dreger, 1978; Eysenck, 1984). However, some distinct disadvantages come to mind. The first is that developmental cutoff points for the instruments may be arbitrary. Some 16–17 year olds can readily cope with responding to the 'adult' 16PF, whereas for others at 18 or 19 years of age, the HSPQ might be more suitable. Another issue that is relevant when we choose to use different questions for different age levels is that of changing mores and fads of society. The HSPQ was constructed more than 30 years ago (see R.B. Cattell and M.D. Cattell, 1975) and the teenagers of the twenty-first century have a vastly different set of potential behaviours through which they can express their personalities. If the HSPQ were to be updated

today, the range of potential items would be greatly increased due to the expansion of the high technology world.

Parameter 2: trait versus state

The major Cattellian personality instruments (OAB, 16PF, CAQ, CTS, HSPQ, CPQ, ESPQ and PSPQ) were all designed to measure relatively enduring trait dimensions. However, the state–trait distinction is an important one that must be considered in personality assessment. Cattell was perhaps the first to highlight this distinction in relation to state–trait anxiety (see Cattell, 1986e; Cattell and Scheier, 1961). Historically, a personality trait has been defined as a set of related behaviours that remain relatively consistent over a long time period (e.g. Comrey, 1980; Eysenck, 1988, 1994a, 1994c; Fisher and Boyle, 1997). A situationally sensitive state on the other hand is again a set of behaviours which fluctuate from moment to moment and from day to day (i.e. over time and circumstances). Any given individual has a characteristic trait level of anxiety (A-trait) or curiosity (C-trait), but depending on the situation, may vary in the level of A-state or C-state, respectively (Boyle, 1983, 1989a). The relationship between personality traits and related emotional states has been highlighted in several empirical studies. Thus, personality questionnaire data have been subjected to P-technique and/or differential dR-technique factor analyses revealing transitory state dimensions (e.g. Barton and Flocchini, 1985; Boyle, 1987a, 1988, 1989d; Boyle and Cattell, 1984; Cattell, 1978, 1982a; also see Boyle, 1987b, as well as Cattell and Kameoka, 1985, for a list of abnormal state dimensions derived from dR-factoring of Part 2 of the Clinical Analysis Questionnaire or CAQ).

The Cattellian motivation measures (cf. Cattell, 1985, 1992a), including the Motivation Analysis Test (MAT) at the adult level (Boyle, 1986, 1988; Boyle and Cattell, 1984, 1987; Boyle et al., 1985; Cattell, 1982b, 1985) and its downward extensions, the School Motivation Analysis Test (SMAT) used with adolescents (Boyle, 1989b; Boyle et al., 1988), and the experimental version of the Children's Motivation Analysis Test (CMAT) – (Barton et al., 1986; Boyle, 1989c; Boyle and Start, 1988) all provide objective test measures of dynamic traits that are somewhat less stable than personality traits, but relatively more stable than transitory mood-state dimensions. In addition, the Eight State Questionnaire or 8SQ (Curran and Cattell, 1976) measures personality variables in a state form (Barton, 1986b; Boyle, 1986, 1989d, 1991b). The 8SQ subscales are labelled: anxiety, stress, depression, regression, fatigue, guilt, extraversion, and arousal. Variables such as anxiety or stress have been singled out for special treatment in test development by IPAT presumably because of their high usage in clinical psychological practice (Cattell, 1987).

Parameter 3: normal (non-psychopathology) – extreme (psychopathology)

Is the individual being assessed expected to be similar to most others (i.e. within plus or minus one standard deviation or so from the mean) on the dimensions measured? If the answer to this question is in the negative, then often it may be preferable to select other measures designed specifically for extreme scorers and which do not exhibit such high unreliability of measurement at the bottom and top ends of their scales (cf. Barton and Dreger, 1986; Cattell, 1986a). In some cases, for example in personality assessment, individuals with 'extreme' scores might be administered qualitatively different scales to describe their personality structure (Barton, 1986a, 1986c; Barton and Cattell, 1975). Parenthetically, the Culture Fair Intelligence Tests or CFIT (Cattell and Cattell, 1977) illustrate this parameter. Here a separate scale is available if one is measuring around the average intelligence level, another scale is designed for below average intelligence, and a third

scale concentrates on providing a score for individuals with higher than average intelligence. In the personality arena, this parameter is illustrated by the fact that the 16PF series for example measures variables within the 'normal personality sphere' (Boyle, 1989e, 1989f, 2006). Part 2 of the CAQ (Krug, 1980), however, measures the abnormal or psychopathological personality trait domain. In the case of motivation measurement, only the 'normal' sphere has instruments that represent it (i.e. the MAT/SMAT/CMAT) – (see Barton et al., 1986; Boyle, 1986; Cattell, 1992a; Schuerger, 1986). Here Barton's (1985a) nine-parameter model has heuristic value in suggesting that measures of 'abnormal motivation' might also be constructed. Aside from their use in research studies, such measures of abnormal motivation might be useful in several applied areas of psychological practice, including, for example, clinical and forensic psychology (Barton and Wood, 1993).

Parameter 4: domain (field of measurement)

What general area of mental life are we dealing with and what dimensions are needed to fully define this domain? A dictionary definition of domain is a 'field of thought or action'. Here, the question has to do with what kind of measures are we dealing with: personality, motivation, cognition, and so on? It is no coincidence that the Cattellian measures illustrate this parameter since we find multiple instruments published for all of the major domains. The 16PF series of instruments with its downward extensions (HSPQ, CPQ, ESPQ, and PSPQ) covers the domain of normal personality (Barton, 1986c; Barton and Dreger, 1986). Indeed, the 16PF is the most highly cited measure of normal personality and there are now five editions of this highly regarded psychometric instrument attesting to its acceptance among the mainstream psychological community (see H.E.P. Cattell, 2001, 2004; for discussion of the 16PF fifth edition). Abnormal/psychopathological personality is assessed using Part 2 of the CAQ, while the MAT/SMAT/CMAT series of objective-test instruments covers the normal motivation domain (Cattell, 1985; Sweney et al., 1986), and the 8SQ provides a quantitative assessment of several clinically important mood states derived from dR-factoring of the personality instruments. Separately, the CFIT series of objective tests (Cattell and Cattell, 1977) as well as the Comprehensive Ability Battery or CAB (Hakstian and Cattell, 1982) enable quantitative measurement of the domain of cognitive abilities (cf. Cattell and Horn, 1982).

Parameter 5: media of measurement (method)

What are the different methods that, at least theoretically, could be used to tap and measure the dimensions of interest? By measurement media is meant the means, agencies or instruments through which data is collected for assessment purposes (Cattell, 1973, 1986b; Cattell and Nesselroade, 1988). Methods of personality measurement currently employed, including self-report questionnaires, rating scales (reports of others – see Johnson, 1986), interviews (formal/informal; structured/unstructured), naturalistic observation, experimental observation, projective techniques, objective tests, essays, standardized self-report instruments, diaries, demographic and biographic data, and so on. Cattell (1973), as well as Cattell and Kline (1977) argued that it should be possible to identify personality traits through multiple-measurement media including ratings or life-record data (L-data), questionnaire data (Q-data), or objective test data (T-data). Choice of specific media to be used in any assessment procedure will depend on many factors such as the relative importance attached to fakeability or motivational response distortion (Cattell, 1992b), the degree to which validities and reliabilities must be demonstrably high, the diversity and scope of the assessors' practical skills, the

emphasis on actual behaviours versus attitudes, and so on. In an ideal assessment situation the same (or similar) variables would be targeted using several different measurement media. A consistent pattern of results across different media would suggest high convergent validity, a fact that Campbell and Fiske (1959) have highlighted in their multitrait, multi-method theory. The term multimethod that Campbell and Fiske used is equivalent here to the idea of multiple media (Barton, 1986a).

This assessment parameter involving choice of measurement media is a complex one that not only subsumes the issue of convergent validity but also such topics as face validity, concept validity, discriminative validity, construct validity, social desirability of items, the construction of correction scales to minimize faking (good or bad), lie scales, instruments for random marking, as well as the more sophisticated trait view theory approach (Cattell, 1979: 370–372; Cattell and Krug, 1971). It is essential, therefore, that in constructing any assessment procedure the literature on the advantages and disadvantages of a variety of measurement media be taken into account (Cattell, 1986c, 1986f; Johnson et al., 1986).

Although the majority of Cattellian instruments involve Q-data media, much of the research that was undertaken within Cattell's laboratory at the University of Illinois also involved other kinds of measurement media. The Objective Analytic Battery or OAB (Cattell and Schuerger, 1978; Cattell et al., 1980; Schuerger, 1986) is the compilation of several objective tests and has been used extensively to confirm the basic personality structure in a different media from questionnaires – especially the 16PF second-stratum factors which align with first-stratum OAB trait dimensions (Boyle, 2006; Boyle and Robertson, 1989; Cattell and Birkett, 1980; Cattell and Nichols, 1972; Cattell and Schuerger, 1978; Krug and Johns, 1986). As compared with the Q-data media, it is almost impossible to fake one's responses to objective (T-data) test measures.

Parameter 6: nomothetic (group) – idiographic (individual)

Is our intention here to understand relationships within an individual (idiographic) or to be able to generalize to large groups of individuals (nomothetic)? This question helps to pinpoint more precisely exactly which measures will be used in any given assessment and has to do with the decision to utilize either group testing or individual assessment. If the major objective of an assessment procedure is to generate or investigate nomothetic laws (relationships that hold over large groups of individuals), group instruments may be desired, since they are efficient in terms of cost, time and amount of data generated. However, if idiographic knowledge (investigation of consistent relationships within a single individual) is the aim, then individual testing often will be required. The Cattellian Q-data personality instruments (16PF, CAQ, HSPQ, CPQ, ESPQ, PSPQ) have been designed to be administered either individually or in groups. The norms provided in the test manuals themselves encourage a nomothetic approach since one can compare each individual's score with the mean scores obtained on large, representative standardization samples (Cattell, 1986c). In addition, P-technique factor analyses have often been used to identify idiographic (idiosyncratic) factors that may be unique to the individual (Cattell, 1983; Cattell and Kline, 1977; Kline, 1986).

Parameter 7: scaling (nominal, ordinal, interval)

To what extent do our measures reflect qualitative (e.g. categorical or nominal) versus quantitative (e.g. interval) measurement of the dimensions in question? Several taxonomies of scaling have been suggested by psychometrists whose major goal is the quantification of psychological measures. For example, anxiety might be assessed dichotomously through 'yes or no' responses to a simple question (nominal scaling since the individual may merely be classed say as 'anxious' or 'not anxious'). Alternatively, anxiety might be ranked as to its degree of intensity in say, three different situations (or it might be measured on a five-point Likert-type ordinal scale, with item responses varying from, 'very anxious' to 'not very anxious' (interval). Depending on the type of scale used, the assessment will have different statistical options available (see Boyle and Langley, 1989). Data collected at the nominal level, for example, lends itself to non-parametric statistical methods but not to the more powerful parametric statistical methods. Data collected at an interval level of scaling can usually be converted to an ordinal or nominal level, making available a much wider choice of statistical techniques (see Boyle and Langley, 1989). Clearly though, scaling decisions should be made in a deliberate fashion *before* any data collection is accomplished (Barton, 1986c; Cattell, 1986c).

Except for ability instruments such as the CFIT or CAB, the items on the Cattellian personality, Q-data questionnaires often measure at the categorical level and it is only when we sum across several items that we obtain a final scale score that is at the interval level. Thus, at the item level the question is often of the form 'Do you prefer (a) or (b)?' This is clearly at the nominal/categorical level since (a) is in no way greater or smaller than (b). If choice (a) is, for example, 'going to a party' and (b) is 'staying home with a book,' and the choice is made for (a), this may count as a unit on an 'extraversion' scale and be summed over a number of such choices. Eventually, the respondent is assigned a place on an interval scale but all the individual questions required nominal choices! Parenthetically, with items on measures of abilities, the scaling situation is somewhat different. IQ test items typically have definite right and wrong answers (i.e. convergent reasoning rather than the divergent reasoning involved in tests of creativity). Nonetheless, because IQ scale units are not completely equivalent at different levels of intelligence, the IQ scale technically provides a quasi-interval level of measurement (Glass and

Stanley, 1970: 13). This applies also to all the items measuring factor B (intelligence) on the 16PF series of personality instruments (see Cattell and Brennan, 1994, for a discussion of methods of deriving equal interval unit scores).

Parameter 8: multiple variables (multivariate measurement)

Can we use or devise multiple measures of the same variables *within* any given medium? Campbell and Fiske (1959) emphasized the usefulness of multi-trait multi-method (media) matrix in psychological measurement (cf. Barton, 1986c). Here we extrapolate their model to include multiple variables. For example, if we are assessing 'anxiety', often it would be preferable to do so employing several measurement media, including questionnaires, interviews and objective instruments, and also to undertake multidimensional assessment in the context of other traits such as depression, or stress (Cattell, 1986b). It would also help to have multiple measures of a psychological construct within any medium (e.g. 16PF second-stratum anxiety/neuroticism factor and the score on say Eysenck's neuroticism dimension – Eysenck, 1988, 1994a, 1994b; Eysenck and Eysenck, 1975). This arrangement would permit the estimation of convergent validity not only across media or methods but within measurement media as well. Use of multiple variables within the same measurement media will provide greater confidence in any inferential statements made about the data, since in effect, any relationships will have been multiply verified and not rest on single measures alone (Barton and Wood, 1993; Boyle, 1991a).

Parameter 9: multiple replications (test–retest reliability)

Is the nature of personality measures selected such as to allow multiple retesting (repeated-measures design) at both short and long intervals? This parameter is important in the design of longitudinal assessments and in the demonstration of the consistency reliability properties of personality instruments. As discussed in Cattell (1973), often the same psychometric measures may be used for both short-term or immediate retesting (dependability) as well as longer-term retesting (stability). In other cases, especially when memory of items may influence subsequent responses, separate parallel forms of an instrument have to be constructed for retesting purposes (see Cattell, 1986f). Since the *process* of assessment ideally involves future retesting or assessments, then it is easy to see how selection of measures must incorporate criteria that ensure that retesting is possible in the absence of methodological problems (Barton, 1986b, 1986c).

Uses of the nine-parameter model

As a classification system or taxonomy

It is hoped that the model described above (Barton, 1985a) will be found useful as a means of both classifying existing personality instruments and assessment methods and also as a stimulant to the creation of new measures that as yet only exist in theory. For example, the model suggests the new concepts of state motivation and state cognition. Few, if any, existing instruments exist that represent these ideas and the usefulness of such concepts can hardly be estimated until such measurement instruments are constructed and empirical studies undertaken (Barton, 1986a, 1986c). In using the nine-parameter model to classify existing psychometric instruments, it is anticipated that the parameters suggested in the model will provide a context or perspective which will help to emphasize the strengths and weaknesses of specific instruments, and thus encourage modifications and further changes in the design of personality instruments (as well as other categories of psychometric instruments).

As part of the definition of psychological assessment

Earlier, psychological assessment was defined in terms that included decisions, data collection, and procedures. This model is intended, in part, to further clarify how the data is to be collected, what data is to be collected and what attributes of the testee must be considered. The other components of the definition involving decision-making criteria and procedures are discussed in Barton (1985a).

As an aid in the critical analysis of instruments

The series of parameters in the model may be used as a checklist of questions to be asked of any instrument to be scrutinized. For example, it may be useful to identify the three-dimensional 'position' of a specific instrument, say Cattell's 16PF, within the model and then use the parameter questions to determine its strengths and weaknesses (Barton, 1986c). It is remarkable how much focused criticism, positive and negative, can be generated by using the model as a framework for critical analysis of a single instrument.

OTHER ASPECTS OF PERSONALITY ASSESSMENT BY QUESTIONNAIRE

Omnibus instruments such as the Cattellian personality questionnaires, which within an hour or less, cover 12 to 16 personality dimensions, cannot have the validity and reliability levels of, say, an intelligence test that devotes to the measurement of one factor as much time as these do to a dozen or more factors. However, to meet the needs of the researcher or practitioner who requires high reliabilities, these instruments are constructed with several parallel forms. For example, the 16PF (fourth edition) has no fewer than six parallel forms, namely A, B, C, D, E, and F. To ensure adequate reliability, Cattell has always recommended that at least two forms of the 16PF (forms A + B or forms C + D) should be administered conjointly.

The 16PF parallel forms are deliberately adapted to meet the needs of different populations. Forms A and B are equivalent and are suitable for individuals with a high-school level of education. Forms C and D place a somewhat reduced demand on vocabulary and are also shorter, so that each can be administered in about half an hour. Forms E and F are designed for individuals with low literacy levels. All forms include an intelligence test (factor B), which provides a brief measure of fluid intelligence, achieving a reduction of the impact of crystallized intelligence, by taking complex relationships among very simple words.

The 16PF handbook gives weights for scoring the various second-stratum factors (cf. Boyle and Robertson, 1989; Cattell and Nichols, 1972; Gorsuch and Cattell, 1967; Krug and Johns, 1986). The alignment with the OAB objective test factors is discussed in Cattell and Birkett (1980). The scoring service that IPAT provides automatically calculates the second-stratum scores from the primary scores derived from the answer sheet. Presumably, a principal reason for using second-stratum scores has been the desire of psychologists to score fewer dimensions and to have a simpler, more manageable picture than is given by all 16 primary factors. Psychometrically, the prediction of any kind of behaviour, clinical or normal, from say five second-stratum scores is decidedly poorer (accounting for significantly less variance) than prediction from the full set of primary scores (Mershon and Gorsuch, 1988). The most effective approach is to use primary and secondary scores together in what Cattell has called 'depth psychometry' (Cattell, 1987). Since age curves and heritability estimates are now known for these personality factors, just as for intellectual abilities (Cattell et al., 1980), it is now possible to project predictions to some extent into the future.

The Cattellian instruments are widely applied today in clinical diagnosis, forensic psychology, school achievement, vocational counselling and in occupational selection (e.g. see Fisher and Boyle, 1997; Piotrowski and Zalewski, 1993; Watkins et al., 1995). However, due to problems with item transparency and resultant motivational/response distortion (Boyle, 1985), it is more desirable to use objective personality tests rather than subjective questionnaires (Boyle et al., 1995; Boyle and Saklofske, 2004). The arguments for objective test instruments are that they are not readily fakeable, whereas questionnaires can be faked all too easily. However, while we argue for greater use of objective instruments, we also recognize that there have been significant developments in the construction of motivational distortion scales and in trait view theory corrections, which help to minimize the effects of response distortion in questionnaires (see Cattell, 1986a; Cattell and Krug, 1971).

APPROPRIATENESS OF ASSESSING PERSONALITY VIA QUESTIONNAIRES

Wording of items

It is often falsely assumed that to get a valid picture of a person's personality via a questionnaire, the person being measured must 'know' his or her own personality to start with. If the items on the questionnaire refer only to specific and well-defined behaviours (e.g. 'how many books have you read during the last year?' then the respondent need make no inferences at all about the responses. The wording of items is thus very important and calls for the elimination of vague and ambiguous terms. Items presented in operational terms are to be preferred for personality assessment. As soon as one allows judgments of doubtful validity (such as a question like 'Do others consider you very outgoing?'), then the criticism of subjectivity is to a large extent a valid one.

Composition of item pool

At least in the area of normal personality assessment, the current consensus among test designers seems to be to include only items of a general, non-controversial nature, avoiding, for example, controversial items pertaining to religion, sex, and politics, and also minimizing their 'social desirability' and susceptibility to other response sets. This recent tendency towards the production of neutral ('unisex') personality inventories (by removing items that differ across sex) makes it well nigh impossible to obtain complete and accurate personality profiles. There are important sex differences in psychological functioning resulting from differences in genes (XX vs. XY chromosomes), brain anatomy (e.g. greater development of the corpus callosum in females leading to more integrated functioning of left and right cerebral hemispheres in contrast to greater specialization of abilities in males), sex hormone levels (testosterone vs. oestrogen), as well as marked differences in acculturation and social conditioning. Clearly, for comprehensive assessment of individual differences in personality, it is important to measure what Cattell has defined as the total 'personality sphere' (see Boyle and Saklofske, 2004).

Potential consequences of test-taking

If the consequences of taking a personality questionnaire are potentially neutral, then the appropriateness of the Q-data method of assessment is probably much higher than when such consequences are significant. Thus, when the consequences could be negative (e.g. admission to a mental institution, or incarceration in prison), or positive (e.g. selection for a job, approval from the therapist, or release from prison or mental institution) then there may be a strong motive (conscious or unconscious) on the part of the respondent to distort his/her responses. To identify and control for these distortions, many instruments incorporate lie scales (e.g. the Eysenck Personality Questionnaire – see Eysenck and Eysenck, 1975), social desirability estimates, 'faking good' and 'faking bad' scales (e.g. 16PF), scales for detecting random responses and scales that identify response sets, and on a deeper theoretical basis, correction by *trait view theory* (Cattell, 1986a; Cattell and Krug, 1971). Trait view corrections show that there is not a *single* 'social desirability', but rather *several* distinct 'desirability response tendencies', which impact differentially depending on the particular testing situation.

Other considerations that may influence the degree to which a personality questionnaire is an appropriate instrument in any given situation include (a) the *length* of the instrument (i.e. number of items); (b) the face validity of items (often some items are so annoying; for example, 'This morning my heart was beating', that the whole questionnaire suffers a loss of credibility and subsequent loss in validity); (c) the format of responses (i.e. forced choice yes/no items; or a Likert-type *scale* of possible responses ranging from, say, 'strongly agree' to 'strongly disagree').

STANDARDS FOR USE OF QUESTIONNAIRES IN PERSONALITY ASSESSMENT

Factor-analytic methodology

Exploratory factor analytic (EFA) methodology has progressed considerably since the publication of Cattell's (1978) treatise (for a detailed discussion of EFA methodological requirements, see Boyle, 1993; Boyle et al., 1995; Boyle and Saklofske, 2004; Child, 1990; Gorsuch, 1983). Over the past three decades, not only has EFA methodology advanced considerably (e.g. inclusion of (1) Cattell's Scree Test; and (2) Promax oblique rotation options within the SPSS statistical package), but also confirmatory factor analysis (CFA), and the more sophisticated structural equation modelling (SEM) that combines factor analysis, multiple regression analysis, and path analysis (implemented via LISREL and EQS statistical packages) have become commonplace. Perhaps the most fundamental drawback in implementing EFA procedures, however, has

been (and often remains) undue reliance on inadequate sample sizes, with many EFA studies reported in the social sciences literature being based on 100 or even fewer observations. More than 30 years ago, Cattell (1973: 284) had recommended that at least 250 participants are needed to enable accurate factor solutions to be derived. Since then, this prescription itself has been shown to be insufficient. Thus, according to Cuttance:

> MacCallum (1985) investigated the process of the exploratory fitting of models in simulated data ... for which the true model was known. He found that only about half of the exploratory searches located the true model. ... He obtained this limited rate of success ... in samples of 300 observations ... and his success rate in smaller samples ($n = 100$) was zero. ... An exploratory analysis of data thus entails the risk of inducing an interpretation founded on the idiosyncracies of individual samples. (1987: 243)

Evidently, much caution must be exercised when undertaking EFA analyses, which tend to promote theory conflation, as opposed to the more scientifically defensible hypothetico-deductive CFA and SEM approaches which enable testing of competing hypotheses and theories.

Standards for reliability and validity

When a proper distinction is drawn between dependability, stability, and homogeneity forms of consistency, we nevertheless find some controversy regarding the desirability of the latter. The 'older' tradition advocates the highest possible degree of correlation among all items within any one scale as indexed via the Cronbach alpha coefficient on the assumption that this leads to 'internal consistency'. In contrast, the 'newer' functional testing position (Cattell and Johnson, 1986) argues that optimum (rather than maximum) homogeneity is desirable if breadth of measurement of a construct (factor) is to be obtained (for a detailed discussion, see Boyle, 1991a; Cattell, 1982b; Kline, 1986). Indeed, high item homogeneity could be achieved merely by rewording the same items in many different ways leading to significant 'item redundancy'. This point is not a minor issue, since reviewers of psychometric instruments often erroneously point to low homogeneity coefficients as evidence of low overall reliability. A concise summary of consistency coefficients was provided by Cattell (1973: 354), along with a detailed discussion of validity issues (1973: 349–379). These principles are just as important in contemporary psychometric test construction, as they were when formulated by Cattell more than 30 years ago.

SUMMARY AND CONCLUSIONS

The utility of the 16PF itself is enhanced by virtue of the fact that it is a *family* of instruments: the 16PF for adults, the HSPQ for teenagers, the CPQ for children aged 8–12 years, the ESPQ for ages 6–8 years, and the PSPQ for children below 6 years of age (Butcher and Rouse, 1996; Hofer and Eber, 2002). The objective has been to deal (through the whole age range) with the same factor-analytically derived personality structures (Cattell and Krug, 1986). In most cases, these personality factors have been shown to persist across the family of related instruments, though with some changing expressions and changes of variance. The 16PF family of personality questionnaires has its value in terms of (1) developmental research into personality origins (Barton, 1986c); (2) conceptual insights into the source traits (Boyle, 1990; Cattell and Krug, 1986); (3) prediction of criteria over different timespans; and (4) utility of second-stratum Q-data factors (Boyle, 2006; Cattell and Nichols, 1972; Krug and Johns, 1986).

Obtaining both primary and secondary trait scores is the basis of *depth psychometry* (Cattell, 1987), and the simultaneous measurement of both normal and abnormal personality trait dimensions is indispensable in clinical psychological practice, as well as other applications such as occupational selection. As stated above, the CAQ is particularly valuable

in clinical practice as it combines a measure of the 16 normal personality trait factors, followed by measures of 12 abnormal personality (psychopathological) trait dimensions. The CAQ has also been used extensively in organizational psychology settings involving selection of personnel. For example, the Australian Army Psychology Corps has a long history of administering the 16PF and CAQ instruments as part of its routine psychological assessment procedures.

Questionnaires can only be properly appraised within the perspective of the three media of measurement (L-data, Q-data, and T-data). Subjective measures are subject to perceptual distortion (L-data and Q-data), whereas objective measures involve actual tests (T-data). The empirical evidence suggests that L-data and Q-data factors deal with the same personality source traits, whereas second-stratum personality factors in Q-data align with first-stratum T-data factors as measured via the Objective Analytic Battery (OAB – Cattell and Birkett, 1980; Cattell and Schuerger, 1978; Schuerger, 1986). In light of the serious validity problems associated with item transparency and motivational/ response distortion of L-data and Q-data instruments (Boyle, 1985), and despite the current popularity of personality questionnaires (as perusal of the *Buros Mental Measurements Yearbooks* indicates), it is to be hoped that in the future, use of objective personality (T-data) instruments will become the 'gold standard'. The plethora of 'personality tests' has literally exploded in recent years. Virtually all of these are simple rating scales (subjective ratings of others or subjective self ratings). Aside from response sets and superficial reporting, a major problem with rating scales of personality/motivation is that they depend upon transparent, face valid items. Item transparency is associated with problematic response or motivational distortion so that most current personality assessment is based on flawed methodology. Correction scales can go only so far, and in some cases (e.g. K-scale in MMPI) application of the correction may just as often produce less accurate results.

In summary, what is needed are truly *objective interactive personality tests* (implemented via computer with stimulus items individualized for each respondent). While Cattell and Warburton produced a compendium of over 2,000 objective personality tests as long ago as 1967, aside from the innovative Objective-Analytic Test Battery which includes such T-data tests (see Cattell and Schuerger, 1978; Schuerger, 1986), little effort has been devoted subsequently to the construction of truly objective personality tests. Regrettably, virtually all new personality instruments constructed have been based on subjective L-data or Q-data measurement approaches. Merely eliciting subjective responses to questions in rating scales and questionnaires, rather than observing actual behaviours in actual (T-data) test situations, remains a major ongoing difficulty for the scientific advancement of personality assessment (cf. Cattell, 1979: 123). Clearly, the field of personality assessment needs to be transformed out of its present subjective measurement quandary and lifted onto an altogether more technologically sophisticated level of objective-interactive testing as advocated by Boyle (2006).

REFERENCES

Barton, K. (1985a) 'A nine parameter model for psychological assessment', *Journal of Personality Assessment*, 49(4): 399–405.

Barton, K. (1985b) *The Central Trait–State Scales. A Kit of 20 Subtests Measuring Five Central Personality Dimensions as Traits and States, with Equivalent Forms*. Champaign, IL: Institute for Personality and Ability Testing.

Barton, K. (1986a) 'Assessment viewed from an experimental perspective: A marriage of practitioner and researcher', *Journal of Social Behavior and Personality*, 1(1): 61–75.

Barton, K. (1986b) 'Measuring emotional states and temporary role adoptions', in R.B. Cattell and R.C. Johnson (eds), *Functional Psychological Testing: Principles and Instruments*. New York: Brunner/Mazel, pp. 334–47.

Barton, K. (1986c) 'Personality assessment by questionnaire', in R.B. Cattell and R.C. Johnson (eds), *Functional Psychological Testing: Principles and Instruments*. New York: Brunner/Mazel, pp. 237–59.

Barton, K. and Cattell, R.B. (1975) 'An investigation of the common factor space of some well-known questionnaire scales: The Eysenck EPI, the Comrey Scales and the IPAT Central Trait-State Kit (CST)', *Journal of Multivariate Experimental Personality and Clinical Psychology*, 1(4): 268–77.

Barton, K. and Cattell, R.B. (1981) *The Central Trait–State Kit (CTS): Experimental Version*. Champaign, IL: Institute for Personality and Ability Testing.

Barton, K., Dielman T.E. and Cattell, R.B. (1986) 'Prediction of objective child motivation test scores from parents' reports of child-rearing practices', *Psychological Reports*, 59(2): 343–52.

Barton, K. and Dreger, R.M. (1986) 'Prediction of marital roles from normal and pathological dimensions of personality: 16PF and MMPI', *Psychological Reports*, 59(2): 459–68.

Barton, K. and Flocchini, S. (1985) 'P-Technique factor analysis and the construct validity of emotional state scales', *Multivariate Experimental Clinical Research*, 7(2): 61–7.

Barton, K. and Wood, S. (1993) 'Psychological assessment from clinical research perspectives: Some empirical evidence for stereotypes', *Journal of Social Behavior and Personality*, 8(1): 27–42.

Birkett-Cattell, H. (1989) *The 16PF: Personality in Depth*. Champaign, IL: Institute for Personality and Ability Testing.

Boyle, G.J. (1983) 'Critical review of state–trait curiosity test development', *Motivation and Emotion*, 7(4): 377–97.

Boyle, G.J. (1985) 'Self-report measures of depression: Some psychometric considerations', *British Journal of Clinical Psychology*, 24(1): 45–59.

Boyle, G.J. (1986) 'Intermodality superfactors in the Sixteen Personality Factor Questionnaire, Eight State Battery and Objective Motivation Analysis Test', *Personality and Individual Differences*, 7(4): 583–6.

Boyle, G.J. (1987a) 'Evidence of typological mood states from change-score (dR)-factoring of the Clinical Analysis Questionnaire', *Psychologische Beiträge*, 29(2–3): 290–99.

Boyle, G.J. (1987b) 'Psychopathological depression superfactors in the Clinical Analysis Questionnaire', *Personality and Individual Differences*, 8(5): 609–14.

Boyle, G.J. (1988) 'Elucidation of motivation structure by dynamic calculus', in J.R. Nesselroade and R.B. Cattell (eds), *Handbook of Multivariate Experimental Psychology* (2nd edn). New York: Plenum, pp. 737–87.

Boyle, G.J. (1989a) 'Breadth-depth or state-trait curiosity? A factor analysis of state-trait curiosity and state anxiety scales', *Personality and Individual Differences*, 10(2): 175–83.

Boyle, G.J. (1989b) 'Central dynamic traits measured in the School Motivation Analysis Test', *Multivariate Experimental Clinical Research*, 9(1): 11–26.

Boyle, G.J. (1989c) 'Children's Motivation Analysis Test (CMAT): Normative data', *Psychological Reports*, 65(3): 920–22.

Boyle, G.J. (1989d) 'Factor structure of the Differential Emotions Scale and the Eight State Questionnaire revisited', *Irish Journal of Psychology*, 10(1): 56–66.

Boyle, G.J. (1989e) 'Re-examination of the major personality-type factors in the Cattell, Comrey and Eysenck scales: Were the factor solutions by Noller et al. optimal?', *Personality and Individual Differences*, 10(12): 1289–99.

Boyle, G.J. (1989f) 'Review of R.B. Cattell and R.C. Johnson's (1986) "Functional psychological testing: Principles and instruments"', *Multivariate Experimental Clinical Research*, 9(1): 41–3.

Boyle, G.J. (1990) 'A review of the factor structure of the Sixteen Personality Factor Questionnaire and the Clinical Analysis Questionnaire', *Psychological Test Bulletin*, 3(1): 40–45.

Boyle, G.J. (1991a) 'Experimental psychology does require a multivariate perspective', *Contemporary Psychology*, 36(4): 350–1.

Boyle, G.J. (1991b) 'Item analysis of the subscales in the Eight State Questionnaire (8SQ): Exploratory and confirmatory factor analyses', *Multivariate Experimental Clinical Research*, 10(1): 37–65.

Boyle, G.J. (1993) 'Special Review: Evaluation of the exploratory factor analysis programs provided in SPSSX and SPSS/PC+', *Multivariate Experimental Clinical Research*, 10(2): 129–35.

Boyle, G.J. (2006) 'Scientific analysis of personality and individual differences', DSc thesis, University of Queensland, St. Lucia, Queensland.

Boyle, G.J. and Cattell, R.B. (1984) 'Proof of situational sensitivity of mood states and dynamic traits to disturbing stimuli', *Personality and Individual Differences*, 5(5): 541–8.

Boyle, G.J. and Cattell, R.B. (1987) 'A first survey of the similarity of personality and motivation prediction of "in situ" and experimentally controlled learning, by structured learning theory', *Australian Psychologist*, 22(2): 189–96.

Boyle, G.J. and Comer, P.G. (1990) 'Personality characteristics of direct-service personnel in community residential units', *Australia and New Zealand Journal of Developmental Disabilities*, 16(2): 125–31.

Boyle, G.J. and Langley, P.D. (1989) *Elementary Statistical Methods: For Students of Psychology, Education and the Social Sciences*. Sydney: Pergamon.

Boyle, G.J., Ortet, G. and Ibáñez, M.I. (2001) 'Evaluación de la personalidad y la inteligencia: Una perspectiva cattelliana [Evaluation of personality and intelligence: A Cattellian perspective]', *Universitas Tarraconensis Revista de Psicologìa*, 23(1–2): 73–92.

Boyle, G.J. and Robertson, J. M. (1989) 'Anomaly in equation for calculating 16PF second-order factor QIII', *Personality and Individual Differences*, 10(9): 1007–8.

Boyle, G.J. and Saklofske, D.H. (2004) (eds), 'Editors' Introduction', in G.J. Boyle, and D.H. Saklofske (eds), *Sage Benchmarks in Psychology: The Psychology of Individual Differences, Vol. 1: Intelligence, Vol. 2: Personality, Vol. 3: Cognition, Emotion and Conation, Vol. 4: Clinical and Applied Research*. London: Sage.

Boyle, G.J. and Smári, J. (1997) 'De fem stora och personlighetspsykologins matningsproblem [The big five and measurement problems in personality psychology]. *Nordisk Psykologi [Nordic Psychology]*, 49(1): 12–21.

Boyle, G.J. and Smári, J. (1998) 'Statiska femfaktorpersonlighets-modeller-Svar till Engvik [Static five-factor models of personality: A reply to Engvik]', *Nordisk Psykologi [Nordic Psychology]*, 50(3): 216–22.

Boyle, G.J. and Smári, J. (2002) 'Vers une simplification du modèle Cattellien de la personnalité [Towards a simplification of the Cattellian model of personality]', *Bulletin de Psychologie*, 55(6): 635–43.

Boyle, G.J., Stankov, L. and Cattell, R.B. (1995) 'Measurement and statistical models in the study of personality and intelligence', in D.H. Saklofske and M. Zeidner (eds), *International Handbook of Personality and Intelligence*. New York: Plenum, pp. 417–46.

Boyle, G.J., Stanley, G.V. and Start, K.B. (1985) 'Canonical/redundancy analyses of the Sixteen Personality Factor Questionnaire, the Motivation Analysis Test, and the Eight State Questionnaire', *Multivariate Experimental Clinical Research*, 7(3): 113–22.

Boyle, G.J. and Start, K.B. (1988) 'A first delineation of higher-order factors in the Children's Motivation Analysis Test (CMAT)', *Psychologische Beiträge*, 30(4): 556–67.

Boyle, G.J., Start, K.B. and Hall, E.J. (1988) 'Comparison of Australian and American normative data for the School Motivation Analysis Test', *Psychological Test Bulletin*, 1(1): 24–7.

Butcher, J.N. and Rouse, S.V. (1996) 'Personality: Individual differences and clinical assessment', *Annual Review of Psychology*, 47: 87–111.

Campbell, D.P. and Fiske, D.W. (1959) 'Convergent and discriminant validation by the multitrait-multimethod matrix', *Psychological Bulletin*, 56(2): 91–105.

Cattell, H.E.P. (2001) 'The Sixteen Personality Factor (16PF) Questionnaire', in W.I. Dorfman and M. Hersen (eds), *Understanding Psychological Assessment*. Dordrecht: Kluwer, pp. 187–215.

Cattell, H.E.P. (2004) 'The Sixteen Personality Factor (16PF) questionnaire', in M.J. Hilsenroth and D.L. Segal (eds), *Comprehensive Handbook of Psychological Assessment, Vol. 2: Personality Assessment*. Hoboken, NJ: Wiley, pp. 39–49.

Cattell, H.E.P and Schuerger, J.M. (2003) *Essentials of 16PF Assessment*. Hoboken, NJ: Wiley.

Cattell, R.B. (1973) *Personality and Mood by Questionnaire*. San Francisco: Jossey-Bass.

Cattell, R.B. (1978) *The Scientific Use of Factor Analysis in Behavioral and Life Sciences*. New York: Plenum.

Cattell, R.B. (1979) *Personality and Learning Theory, Vol. 1: The Structure of Personality in its Environment*. New York: Springer.

Cattell, R.B. (1982a) 'The clinical use of difference scores: Some psychometric problems', *Multivariate Experimental Clinical Research*, 6(2): 87–98.

Cattell, R.B. (1982b) 'The psychometry of objective motivation measurement: A response to the critique of Cooper and Kline', *British Journal of Educational Psychology*, 52(2): 234–41.

Cattell, R.B. (1983) *Structured Personality-Learning Theory: A Wholistic Multivariate Research Approach*. New York: Praeger.

Cattell, R.B. (1985) *Human Motivation and the Dynamic Calculus*. New York: Praeger.

Cattell, R.B. (1986a) 'Dodging the third error source: Psychological interpretation and use of given scores', in R.B. Cattell and R.C. Johnson (eds), *Functional Psychological Testing: Principles and Instruments*. New York: Brunner/Mazel, pp. 496–543.

Cattell, R.B. (1986b) 'General principles across the media of assessment', in R.B. Cattell and R.C. Johnson (eds), *Functional Psychological Testing: Principles and Instruments*. New York: Brunner/Mazel, pp. 15–32.

Cattell, R.B. (1986c) 'Selecting, administering, scoring, recording, and using tests in assessment', in R.B. Cattell and R.C. Johnson (eds), *Functional Psychological Testing: Principles and Instruments*. New York: Brunner/Mazel, pp. 105–126.

Cattell, R.B. (1986d) 'Structured tests and functional diagnoses', in R.B. Cattell and R.C. Johnson (eds), *Functional Psychological Testing: Principles and Instruments*. New York: Brunner/Mazel, pp. 3–14.

Cattell, R.B. (1986e) 'The actual trait, state, and situation structures important in functional testing', in R.B. Cattell and R.C. Johnson (eds), *Functional Psychological Testing: Principles and Instruments*. New York: Brunner/Mazel, pp. 33–53.

Cattell, R.B. (1986f). The psychometric properties of tests: Consistency, validity, and efficiency', in R.B. Cattell and R.C. Johnson (eds), *Functional Psychological Testing: Principles and Instruments*. New York: Brunner/Mazel, pp. 54–78.

Cattell, R.B. (1986g) 'The 16PF personality structure and Dr. Eysenck', *Journal of Social Behavior and Personality*, 1(2): 153–60.

Cattell, R.B. (1987) *Psychotherapy by Structured Learning Theory*. New York: Springer.

Cattell, R.B. (1992a) 'Human motivation objectively, experimentally analysed', *British Journal of Medical Psychology*, 65(3): 237–43.

Cattell, R.B. (1992b) 'Superseding the motivational distortion scale', *Psychological Reports*, 70(2): 499–502.

Cattell, R.B. (1994) 'A cross-validation of primary personality structure in the 16PF. by two parcelled factor analyses', *Multivariate Experimental Clinical Research*, 10(3): 181–90.

Cattell, R.B. (1995) 'The fallacy of five factors in the personality sphere', *The Psychologist*, 8(5): 207–8.

Cattell, R.B. (1996) 'Personality and structured learning', *European Review of Applied Psychology*, 46(1): 73–5.

Cattell, R.B. and Birkett, H. (1980) 'The known personality factors aligned between first-order T-data and second-order Q-data factors, with new evidence on the inhibitory control, independence and regression traits', *Personality and Individual Differences*, 1(3): 229–38.

Cattell, R.B. and Brennan, J. (1994) 'Finding personality structure when ipsative measurements are the unavoidable basis of the variables', *American Journal of Psychology*, 107(2): 261–74.

Cattell, R.B., Boyle, G.J. and Chant, D. (2002) 'The enriched behavioral prediction equation and its impact on structured learning and the dynamic calculus', *Psychological Review*, 109(1): 202–5.

Cattell, R.B. and Cattell, M.D. (1975) *Handbook for the Junior and Senior High School Personality Questionnaire*. Champaign, IL: Institute for Personality and Ability Testing.

Cattell, R.B. and Cattell, A.K.S. (1977) *Measuring Intelligence with the Culture Fair Tests*. Champaign, IL: Institute for Personality and Ability Testing.

Cattell, R.B. and Cattell, H.E.P. (1995) 'Personality structure and the new fifth edition of the 16PF', *Educational and Psychological Measurement*, 55(6): 926–37.

Cattell, R.B., Danko, G., Cattell, H.B. and Raymond, J. (1983) 'A cross-cultural study of primary personality factor structure in the preparation of the Hawaiian HSPQ', *Multivariate Experimental Clinical Research*, 7(1): 1–23.

Cattell, R.B. and Dreger, R.M. (1978) (eds), *Handbook of Modern Personality Theory*. New York: Wiley.

Cattell, R.B. and Horn, J.L. (1982) 'Whimsy and misunderstanding of Gf-Gc theory: A comment on Guilford', *Psychological Bulletin*, 91(3): 621–33.

Cattell, R.B. and Johnson, R.C. (1986) (eds), *Functional Psychological Testing: Principles and Instruments*. New York: Brunner/Mazel.

Cattell, R.B. and Kameoka, V.A. (1985) 'Psychological states measured in the Clinical Analysis Questionnaire (CAQ)', *Multivariate Experimental Clinical Research*, 7(2): 69–87.

Cattell, R.B. and Kline, P. (1977) *The Scientific Analysis of Personality and Motivation*. New York: Academic.

Cattell, R.B. and Krug, S.E. (1971) 'A test of the trait-view theory of distortion in measurement of personality questionnaire', *Educational and Psychological Measurement*, 31(3): 721–34.

Cattell, R.B. and Krug, S.E. (1986) 'The number of factors in the 16PF: A review of the evidence with special emphasis on methodological problems', *Educational and Psychological Measurement*, 46(3): 509–22.

Cattell, R.B. and Nesselroade, J.R. (1988) (eds), *Handbook of Multivariate Experimental Psychology* (2nd edn). New York: Plenum.

Cattell, R.B. and Nichols, K.E. (1972) 'An improved definition, from 10 researches, of second-order personality factors in Q-Data (with cross-cultural checks)', *Journal of Social Psychology*, 86(2): 187–203.

Cattell, R.B., Rao, D.C., Schuerger, J.M. and Vaughan, D.S. (1980) 'Unitary personality traits analyzed for heritability', *Human Heredity*, 31(5): 261–75.

Cattell, R.B. and Scheier, I. (1961) *The Meaning and Measurement of Neuroticism and Anxiety*. New York: Ronald.

Cattell, R.B. and Schuerger, J.M. (1978) *Personality Theory in Action: Handbook for the Objective-Analytic (O-A) Test Kit*. Champaign, IL: Institute for Personality and Ability Testing.

Cattell, R.B. and Warburton, F.W. (1967) *Objective Personality and Motivation Tests: A Theoretical Introduction and Practical Compendium*. Champaign, IL: University of Illinois Press.

Child, D. (1990) *The Essentials of Factor Analysis* (2nd edn). London: Cassell.

Coan, R.W. and Cattell, R.B. (1959) 'The development of the Early School Personality Questionnaire', *Journal of Experimental Education*, 28(3): 143–52.

Comrey, A.L. (1980) *Handbook of Interpretations for the Comrey Personality Scales*. San Diego: Educational and Industrial Testing Service.

Conn, S.R. and Rieke, M.L. (1994) *Technical Manual for the 16PF* (5th edn). Champaign, IL: Institute for Personality and Ability Testing.

Curran, J.P. and Cattell, R.B. (1976) *Manual for the Eight State Questionnaire*. Champaign, IL: Institute for Personality and Ability Testing.

Cuttance, P. (1987) 'Issues and problems in the application of structural equation models', in P. Cuttance and R. Ecob (eds), *Structural Modeling by Example: Applications in Educational, Sociological, and Behavioral Research*. Cambridge, UK: Cambridge University Press, pp. 241–79.

Dreger, R.M., Lichtenstein, D. and Cattell, R.B. (1995) 'Manual for the Experimental edition of the Personality Questionnaire for Preschool Children Form A', *Journal of Social Behavior and Personality,* 10 (suppl.): 1–50.

Eysenck, H.J. (1984) 'Cattell and the theory of personality', *Multivariate Behavioral Research*, 19(2–3): 323–36.

Eysenck, H.J. (1988) *Dimensions of Personality*. New Brunswick, NJ: Transaction Publishers.

Eysenck, H.J. (1994a) 'Normality–abnormality and the three-factor model of personality',in S. Strack and M. Lorr (1994) (eds), *Differentiating Normal and Abnormal Personality*. New York: Springer, pp. 3–25.

Eysenck, H.J. (1994b) 'Personality and intelligence: Psychometric and experimental approaches', in R.J. Sternberg and P. Ruzgis (eds), *Personality and Intelligence*. New York: Cambridge University Press, pp. 3–31.

Eysenck, H.J. (1994c) 'Personality: Biological foundations', in P.A. Vernon (ed.), *The Neuropsychology of Individual Differences*. San Diego: Academic, pp. 151–207.

Eysenck, H.J. (1997) 'Personality and experimental psychology: The unification of psychology and the possibility of a paradigm', *Journal of Personality and Social Psychology*, 73(6): 1224–37.

Eysenck, H.J. and Eysenck, S.B.G. (1975) *Manual of the Eysenck Personality Questionnaire (Junior and Adult)*. London: Hodder and Stoughton.

Eysenck, H.J. and Eysenck, M.W. (1985) *Personality and Individual Differences: A Natural Science Approach*. New York: Plenum.

Fisher, C.D. and Boyle, G.J. (1997) 'Personality and employee selection: Credibility regained', *Asia Pacific Journal of Human Resources*, 35(2): 26–40.

Glass, G.V. and Stanley, J.C. (1970) *Statistical Methods in Education and Psychology*. Englewood Cliffs, NJ: Prentice-Hall.

Gorsuch, R.L. and Cattell, R.B. (1967) 'Second stratum personality factors defined in the questionnaire realm by the 16PF', *Multivariate Behavioral Research*, 2(2): 211–24.

Gorsuch, R.L. (1983) *Factor Analysis* (2nd rev edn). Hillsdale, NJ: Erlbaum.

Haggbloom, S.J., Warnick, R., Warnick, J.E., Jones, V.K., Yarbrough, G.L., Russell, T.M., Borecky, C.M., McGahhey, R., Powell III, J.L., Beavers, J. and Monte, E. (2002) 'The 100 most eminent psychologists of the 20th century', *Review of General Psychology*, 6(2): 139–52.

Hakstian, A.R. and Cattell, R.B. (1982) *Manual for the Comprehensive Ability Battery*. Champaign, IL: Institute for Personality and Ability Testing.

Hofer, S.M., Horn, J.L. and Eber, H.W. (1997) 'A robust five-factor structure of the 16PF: Strong evidence from independent rotation and confirmatory factorial invariance procedures', *Personality and Individual Differences*, 23(2): 247–69.

Hofer, S.M. and Eber, H.W. (2002) 'Second-Order Factor Structure of the Cattell Sixteen Personality Factor Questionnaire', in B. de Raad, and M. Perugini (eds), *Big Five Assessment*. Göttingen, Germany: Hogrefe & Huber, pp. 397–409.

Johnson, R.C. (1986) 'Personality assessment by observers in normal and psychiatric data', in R.B. Cattell and R.C. Johnson (eds), *Functional Psychological Testing: Principles and Instruments*. New York: Brunner/Mazel, pp. 208–36.

Johnson, R.C., Porteus, B.D. and Cattell, R.B. (1986) 'The wider scientific and social aspects of psychological testing', in R.B. Cattell and R.C. Johnson (eds), *Functional Psychological Testing: Principles and Instruments*. New York: Brunner/Mazel, pp. 142–65.

Kline, P. (1986) *A Handbook of Test Construction: Introduction to Psychometric Design*. New York: Methuen.

Krug, S.E. (1980) *Clinical Analysis Questionnaire Manual*. Champaign, IL: Institute for Personality and Ability Testing.

Krug, S.E. (1981) *Interpreting 16PF Profile Patterns*. Champaign, IL, Institute for Personality and Ability Testing.

Krug, S.E. and Johns, E.F. (1986) 'A large scale cross-validation of second-order personality structure defined by the 16PF', *Psychological Reports*, 59(2): 683–93.

Lichtenstein, D., Dreger, R.M. and Cattell, R.B. (1986) 'Factor structure and standardization of the Preschool Personality Questionnaire', *Journal of Social Behavior and Personality*, 1(2): 165–82.

MacCallum, R. (1985) 'Some problems in the process of model modification in covariance structure modeling', Paper presented to the European Meeting of the Psychonomic Society, Cambridge, UK.

Mershon, B. and Gorsuch, R.L. (1988) 'Number of factors in the personality sphere: Does increase in factors increase predictability of real-life criteria?', *Journal of Personality and Social Psychology*, 55(4): 675–80.

Piotrowski, C and Zalewski, C. (1993) 'Training in psychodiagnostic testing in APA-approved PsyD. and PhD. clinical psychology programs', *Journal of Personality Assessment*, 61(2): 394–405.

Porter, R.B. and Cattell, R.B. (1985) *Handbook for the Children's Personality Questionnaire (CPQ)*. Champaign, IL: Institute for Personality and Ability Testing.

Roberts, B.W., Walton, K.E. and Viechtbauer, W. (2006a) 'Patterns of mean-level change in personality traits across the life course: A meta-analysis of longitudinal studies', *Psychological Bulletin*, 132(1): 1–25.

Roberts, B.W., Walton, K.E. and Viechtbauer, W. (2006b) 'Personality traits change in adulthood: Reply to Costa and McCrae (2006)', *Psychological Bulletin*, 132(1): 29–32.

Schuerger, J.M. (1986) 'Personality assessment by objective tests', in R.B. Cattell and R.C. Johnson (eds), *Functional Psychological Testing: Principles and Instruments*. New York: Brunner/Mazel, pp. 260–87.

Smith, B.D. (1988) 'Personality: Multivariate systems theory and research', in J.R. Nesselroade and R.B. Cattell (eds), *Handbook of Multivariate Experimental Psychology* (2nd edn). New York: Plenum.

Sweney, A.R., Anton and Cattell, R.B. (1986) 'Evaluating motivation structure, conflict, and adjustment', in R.B. Cattell and R.C. Johnson (eds), *Functional Psychological Testing: Principles and Instruments*. New York: Brunner/Mazel, pp. 288–315.

Watkins, C.E., Campbell, V.L., Nieberding, PR. and Hallmark, R. (1995) 'Contemporary practice of psychological assessment by clinical psychologists', *Professional Psychology: Research and Practice*, 26(1): 54–60.

9

The Revised NEO Personality Inventory (NEO-PI-R)

Paul T. Costa, Jr. and Robert R. McCrae

In some respects, the Revised NEO Personality Inventory (NEO-PI-R) (Costa and McCrae, 1985b, 1989a, 1992b) is a cutting-edge instrument. Our research on neuroticism, extraversion, and openness to experience began in the mid-1970s, but already by 1983 we had begun to add measures of agreeableness and conscientiousness. Research has continued since publication of the NEO-PI in 1985, resulting in a manual supplement issued in 1989 and a major revision introducing facet scales for agreeableness and conscientiousness in 1992. Item changes to improve internal consistency and readability recently led to the NEO-PI-3 (McCrae et al., 2005c). We hope and believe the NEO-PI-R incorporates the latest advances in personality structure and assessment; the 'neo' in the title is an intended pun.

In other respects, the NEO-PI-R is profoundly conservative, deeply rooted in the research of generations of personality psychologists. Most of the traits it measures have long been familiar, and scale labels have been chosen to emphasize continuity with past conceptualizations. The psychometric strategies for item selection and scale validation benefited from the insight and experience of many previous researchers and theorists. Even the data we used to formulate our model and validate our instrument were, in many cases, collected years ago by colleagues in longitudinal studies. We hope to carry on the proud traditions of personality assessment.

THE EVOLUTION OF THE NEO-PI-R

The 1970s were not the most auspicious time to undertake the development of a new personality inventory. Personality psychology was in crisis, rocked by critiques from Mischel (1968), Fiske (1974), and Shweder (1975). If the field had a future, it seemed to be in interactionism (Magnusson and Endler, 1977) rather than in trait psychology. And if one insisted on using conventional personality measures, why add another instrument to an already crowded field? What did we hope to accomplish by introducing the NEO-PI?

Our decision was based on two beliefs. First, we were committed to the basic correctness of trait psychology: We believed that there were consistent and enduring individual differences in ways of thinking, feeling, and acting; that individuals were capable of describing themselves with reasonable accuracy if asked appropriate questions; and that psychometric tools (such as factor analysis) and principles (such as construct validation) could be used to develop useful measures of traits. These tenets would not have been controversial in the 1930s or the 1950s, and can hardly be considered inflammatory today, but they were not widely shared at that time.

Second, we felt that existing instruments were less than optimal. Quite aside from the many scales of dubious validity that contributed so much to what Block (1977) called the 'litter-ature' of personality, we found that even the best instruments were lacking in some respect. Eysenck and Eysenck's (1975) extraversion and neuroticism scales, for example, were reliable and valid measures of two fundamental dimensions of personality, but they could hardly encompass the full range of individual differences, and they did not allow any differentiation among the more specific traits that each dimension subsumed. Cattell et al.'s (1970) Sixteen Personality Factor Questionnaire (16PF) offered more scope and specificity, but its scales had been widely criticized for a lack of replicable factor structure (see Howarth, 1976).

A three-factor model

Our research began with analyses of the 16PF in the Veterans Administration's Normative Aging Study (Costa and McCrae, 1976). At first, we were interested in the question of structural changes with age: Were the relations among traits, summarized as higher-order factors or clusters, different for old than for young or middle-aged men? It is impossible to answer this question until one knows what the structure is at each age, and thus we were faced with the perennial problem of determining the 'correct' number of factors and their appropriate rotation. Our later

research (Costa and McCrae, 1980b) showed that there are no age differences in structure, but by that time we had become interested in the problem of structure for its own sake. We ultimately decided on a fairly parsimonious solution: a three-factor model that included neuroticism (N), extraversion (E), and openness (O). The first two factors were common in analyses of the 16PF (as anxiety and 'exvia'); and, in addition, clearly corresponded to the major dimensions of Eysenck's system. The third dimension allowed us to go a step beyond Eysenck's work, identifying a new fundamental dimension (Costa and McCrae, 1986).

We quickly became convinced of the importance of this new dimension of openness to experience (McCrae and Costa, 1985b, 1997a), seen first in the 16PF bright, tender-minded, imaginative, and liberal-thinking scales. Although it had rarely been viewed as a basic trait dimension, related concepts had often been proposed: Rogers' (1961) openness to feelings and the low pole of Rokeach's (1960) dogmatism were clearly related, and Fitzgerald (1966) and Coan (1974) had not only developed the idea, but had also created scales and showed that such facets as openness to esthetics and ideas co-varied in a single dimension. It was from them that we took the term *openness*. We were subsequently delighted to find that Tellegen and Atkinson (1974) had also identified this as a third major dimension, which they called *absorption*.

Richard Coan's Experience Inventory became the basis for our own scales to measure openness (Costa and McCrae, 1978), and our success in measuring facets of this dimension led us to create scales to measure aspects of N and E. The EASI-III scales of Buss and Plomin (1975) were an important influence, both in form and content. We admired the simple, straightforward wording Buss and Plomin used, as well as some of the distinctions they drew. For example, we included anxiety and angry hostility as facets of N, just as they had included fear and anger in their 'general emotionality' domain.

Rather than adopt the factor-analytic language of first-order and second-order factors, we began to speak of N, E, and O as broad *domains* of traits, and more specific traits as their *facets* (Costa and McCrae, 1995). Our approach was to measure each domain by summing scores on a half-dozen facet scales. The user would thus have highly reliable measures of three global domains, as well as more specific information on traits within each domain. (Mershon and Gorsuch, 1988, gave an empirical demonstration of the predictive value of measuring specific traits as well as broad factors, confirming the utility of the domain-and-facet approach.)

We called the resulting questionnaire the NEO Inventory and brought it to Baltimore when we joined the National Institute on Aging (Costa and McCrae, 1980b). Research with that instrument showed the utility of the three-dimensional model in understanding such phenomena as somatic complaints (Costa and McCrae, 1980a), psychological wellbeing (Costa and McCrae, 1984), ego development (McCrae and Costa, 1980), and vocational interests (Costa et al., 1984). The validity of the scales themselves was demonstrated by convergence with other instruments and with spouse ratings on a third-person form of the NEO Inventory (McCrae, 1982). The three domains of N, E, and O were clearly central variables in personality psychology, but they were just as clearly incapable of addressing the full range of individual differences. What about trust and altruism? What about self-control and need for achievement?

Rediscovery of the five-factor model

Although we were aware of its limitations, we – like most personality psychologists – had come to accept them as inevitable. Surely every personality test would have omissions; how could we hope to measure all traits? How many traits *should* an inventory measure? At about this time, Goldberg (1981, 1983) revived a line of research that claimed a solution to this problem (John et al., 1988). His analyses were based on the assumption that individual differences in personality are so important for social interaction that every culture must have evolved words to express them. Over the centuries, all important traits would have been encoded in the natural language. The scope of personality traits is thus given by the scope of trait names; if we can determine the structure of the traits listed in the dictionary, we can determine the structure of personality (Norman, 1963). Although this rationale was not accepted by many psychologists (e.g. Block, 1995), who doubted the ability of laypersons to perceive the full range of psychological characteristics, the approach was strengthened by the fact that different researchers in this field consistently identified similar dimensions, which Norman called extraversion or surgency, agreeableness, conscientiousness, emotional stability, and culture. This five-factor model appeared to provide a robust and comprehensive description of the natural language of traits, if not traits themselves.

It was clear to us that Norman's extraversion strongly resembled ours, and that his emotional stability was the polar opposite of our N. There was some suggestion that culture was a variant of O. An empirical test (McCrae and Costa, 1985c) confirmed these hypotheses and also pointed to the importance of agreeableness (A) and conscientiousness (C), domains unrepresented in the NEO Inventory. We therefore constructed brief scales to measure these two domains (McCrae and Costa, 1987) and published the final instrument as the NEO Personality Inventory (Costa and McCrae, 1985b). A series of subsequent analyses showed that the five-factor model operationalized by the NEO-PI was in fact extraordinarily comprehensive: It encompassed dimensions in Murray's needs (Costa and McCrae, 1988a); the interpersonal circumplex (McCrae and Costa, 1989e); Jungian typologies (McCrae and Costa, 1989c); and the items of Block's (1961) California Adult Q-Set (McCrae et al., 1986).

The major limitation of the NEO-PI was the lack of facet scales for A and C. We were confident that important facets of these domains could be identified and measured, but we did not want to delay publication of the instrument while we conducted the necessary research. Item selection and facet validation studies were conducted in several samples (Costa et al., 1991), and the Revised NEO Personality Inventory (NEO-PI-R) was published in 1992. In addition to adding facet scales for A and C, the revision replaced 10 of the original 144 N, E, and O items. The NEO-PI-R version has 240 items, new and more representative norms, a hand-scoring answer sheet that incorporates the scoring template, and enhanced computer scoring and interpretation (see tables in McCrae and Costa, Vol. 1, for facet labels).

The most recent revision arose from the observation that adolescents aged 12–18 could use the NEO-PI-R, but that some individuals in that age range did not understand a few of the items (De Fruyt et al., 2000; McCrae et al., 2002). We wrote new items with a simpler vocabulary, and also took the opportunity to replace readable items that showed relatively poor item-total correlations. Using data from a new sample of adolescents, we replaced 37 NEO-PI-R items, leading to a test, the NEO-PI-3, with higher readability and slightly better psychometrics than the NEO-PI-R, but essentially equivalent to it (McCrae et al., 2005a).

ITEM SELECTION AND SCALE DEVELOPMENT

Rational, theoretical, and factor-analytic approaches

Our early work with other personality instruments involved a number of item analyses, and we spent many hours interpreting the resulting factors. We were struck by the ease of interpretation. Items that formed factors generally asked the same question in somewhat different form; rational interpretation was therefore straightforward. We eventually came to believe that most respondents understood questions in much the same way that we did, so there was no particular mystery about writing items: Define the construct and ask about it in simple terms, and you can probably create a decent scale. This conclusion has been supported by research by Jackson (1975) and Burisch (1984), but it contrasts sharply with the premises that lead to such instruments as the Minnesota Multiphasic Personality Inventory (Hathaway and McKinley, 1943). We do not believe that individuals have perfect knowledge of themselves or that they are unfailingly candid in their responses to inventory items, but for most respondents in most situations there appears to be no better way to learn about people than to ask them directly. Where problems with self-reports are anticipated, the observer-rating version of the NEO-PI-R can be used.

The fact that most factors can be interpreted rationally does not mean that reason can replace data in the construction of scales. Items that seem appropriate a priori may turn out to be poor measures of the intended construct: perhaps they have a low endorsement frequency, or the words are interpreted differently by many respondents, or perhaps one's original understanding of the construct was simply wrong. Item analyses are always necessary, and we have relied heavily on factor analyses for this purpose (cf. Briggs and Cheek, 1986).

Factor analysis has been central to personality assessment because it allows the researcher to discover independent and internally consistent clusters of items simultaneously. That is to say, factored scales tend to have both convergent and discriminant validity. Factor analysts differ tremendously, however, in how they view and employ the technique. Our approach has been to emphasize the theoretical and conceptual aspects of the solution rather than statistical or mathematical criteria. We have allowed our model, rather than eigenvalues or scree tests, to determine the number of factors, and prefer orthogonally rotated principle components to more elaborate, and sometimes more difficult-to-understand oblique and common factor solutions.

The respect in which we have departed most from conventional factor analytic usage is in factor rotation. All rotations are mathematically equivalent in terms of their ability to represent the correlations among variables. A geography based on northeast–southwest and northwest–southeast axes would be equally effective in pinpointing locations, although there are good and practical reasons to adopt the north–south, east–west conventions. Similarly, we have occasionally used theoretical considerations to rotate factors when there are reasons to think that varimax rotations are not optimal.

Conventional varimax rotation was inappropriate for analyses of the structure of the original NEO-PI scales, because three of the domains – N, E, and O – were represented by six scales each, whereas A and C had only a single marker apiece. Varimax rotation tends to distribute variance equally across factors and so was unlikely to yield the intended structure. When five factors were extracted from a joint analysis of the 18 N, E, and O facet scales and the A and C domain scales, varimax rotation gave clear N and O factors, but tended to split the E facets among E, A, and C factors. We therefore proposed an alternative to varimax rotation that we called *validimax rotation* (McCrae and Costa, 1989d). Instead of guiding the position of the factors by internal criteria of simple structure, the technique used external criteria of convergent and discriminant validity. We had six alternative measures of the five factors on our subjects from different instruments and observers, and rotated the NEO-PI factors to the position that maximized the 30 convergent correlations while simultaneously minimizing the 120 divergent correlations with these measures. The resulting factors closely approximated our theoretical model, were replicable across samples and observers, and appeared to offer an optimal scoring of the NEO-PI for the five factors. With the introduction of facet

scales for A and C, traditional (and more familiar) varimax rotation sufficed to show the intended structure (Costa et al., 1991), and varimax factor scores based on the normative sample are now used in computer interpretation of the NEO-PI-R.

Theoretical and structural considerations in selecting facets

Although agreement among supporters of the five-factor model (Digman and Inouye, 1986; Hogan, 1986) is not perfect, it far exceeds agreement on specific facets within each domain; attention to this level of analysis may be the next important step in personality measurement (Briggs, 1989). We originally construed the relation between domains and facets as one of sets and subsets in a mathematical sense. Subsets draw all their elements from the set, but may themselves be large or small, overlapping or mutually exclusive. This kind of metaphor is useful for describing existing personality scales, which differ in breadth and focus, and do not form neat vertical or horizontal structures. Eysenck's N scale, Spielberger's (1972) trait anxiety scale, the resentment subscale of the Buss–Durkee (1957) Hostility Inventory, and the item 'I often feel lonely and blue' all fall within the domain of neuroticism.

In constructing a new instrument, however, the most useful approach might be to divide the full domain into mutually exclusive categories of approximately equal breadth. Our strategy was to review the literature to identify as many traits as possible relevant to each domain; to draw distinctions among them when we felt it would be useful (e.g. dividing sociability into warmth and gregariousness), and to combine traits that seemed closely related (e.g. including guilt-proneness and hopelessness in the depression scale).

If the five domains are considered to be independent, non-intersecting sets, then our sets-and-subsets analogy would suggest that facets belong in only one domain. In the language of factor analysis, we should find simple structure in analyses, and in fact, three-factor solutions of our N, E, and O scales did yield relatively clear simple structures (McCrae and Costa, 1983a). When we added scales measuring A and C, however, we found that several of the N, E, and O facet scales also had loadings on these two dimensions. This was particularly true of extraversion facets: warmth was positively related to agreeableness, whereas assertiveness was negatively related; activity was positively related; and excitement seeking negatively related to conscientiousness. We thus faced a dilemma: If we wished to preserve simple structure in a five-dimensional instrument, we would need to abandon some of our facet scales; if we wished to retain the facets, we would need to abandon simple structure.

We opted for the second solution. Simple structure provides guidance in exploratory analyses because it offers the most parsimonious explanation; other things being equal, simple structure should be preferred. But other things are not equal: There are excellent reasons to adopt a five-factor model, and also excellent reasons to measure traits that are related to more than one of the factors. Warmth and assertiveness are important interpersonal characteristics for laypersons and psychologists alike; to omit them from our inventory merely because they showed joint loadings would be arbitrary and counterproductive. (Geography, too, would be more elegant if the equator neatly divided North America from South America, but map-makers must place the continents where they fall.)

This position may seem unorthodox, but it has solid precedent in personality research. In particular, many writers have argued that a circular arrangement is necessary to describe the structure of interpersonal traits (Leary, 1957; Wiggins, 1979). We have shown that the interpersonal circumplex is defined by the two dimensions of E and A (McCrae and Costa, 1989e), so it is not surprising that NEO-PI-R E facets also have loadings on the A factor. Circumplexes defined by other combinations of the five factors have also been proposed (e.g. Conley, 1985), and the computer interpretive report for the NEO-PI-R generates ten 'style graphs' that describe combinations of pairs of factors (see Costa and Piedmont, 2003).

Specific variance in facet scales

Many inventories based on the five-factor model offer only five global scales (De Raad and Perugini, 2002), and one group of researchers (Hendriks et al., 1999; Hofstee et al., 1992), noting that some facets overlap two or more domains, have proposed that facets can be obtained simply by linear combinations of factors. In that view, facets add nothing to the information in the factors; they merely package it in convenient form. Angry hostility, for example, might be construed as nothing but a combination of high N and low A.

The facets of the NEO-PI-R are intended to be more than that. Each is supposed to measure a discrete trait and thus to contribute something above and beyond the five factors, and there is now ample evidence that they do so. Paunonen and Ashton (2001) showed that the facets add incrementally to the prediction of behaviors, and Reynolds and Clark (2001) found that facets were superior to factors in explaining personality disorders.

Technically, NEO-PI-R facets can explain more than factors because they contain valid specific variance; that is, meaningful individual differences are unrelated to the common factors. There is now a substantial body of data demonstrating this, found by analyzing residual scores from which the variance attributable to the factors has been partialled. Jang et al. (1998) showed that specific variance was reliable over time and that for 26 of the 30 facets, it was significantly heritable. Small but consistent age trends have been reported for residual facet scores (McCrae et al., 1999). In the first study of specific variance (McCrae and Costa, 1992), we reported that partial correlations between self-reported and peer- or spouse-rated facets, controlling for the five factors in each data source, showed significant associations for the majority of facets.

New evidence of cross-observer agreement on specific variance comes from data on the NEO-PI-3 (McCrae et al., 2005c). Both self-reports and observer ratings were obtained from 266 pairs of individuals, mostly spouses. In both data sets, the five factors were extracted, and each of the 30 NEO-PI-3 facet scales was predicted from all five factors. The residual scores were saved, and correlations between Form S (self-report) residuals and Form R (observer rating) residuals ranged from 0.18 to 0.58, $n = 532$, all p's < 0.001, with a median value of 0.33. Thus, each of the facets assesses observable characteristics of the individual that go beyond the five factors.

The NEO Five-Factor Inventory

Despite our interest in pursuing both the domain and facet levels of personality assessment, many investigators (particularly survey researchers) face serious limitations of time that make in-depth assessment difficult. Short scales to measure the five factors provide

a comprehensive portrait of the individual at a global level, and would be of value in many applications. To meet this need we developed the NEO Five-Factor Inventory (NEO-FFI), a shortened version of the self-report form of the original NEO-PI, with 12-item scales to measure each of the facets.

Our validimax factor rotation procedure was used in initial item selection. The 180 NEO-PI items were factored in a sample of 983 men and women (Costa and McCrae, 1988b); five principal components were extracted. These item factors were next rotated to maximize convergent and discriminant validity with the NEO-PI validimax factors. For each domain, the 12 highest loading items were selected as preliminary NEO-FFI items. About 10 substitutions were then made to diversify item content, eliminate items with joint loadings, and balance keying of the scales.

The resulting scales retained much, although not all, of the validity of the full NEO-PI domain scales. Table 9.1 shows correlations of the NEO-FFI scales with self-report adjective factors and with NEO-PI factors in spouse and peer ratings. Convergent correlations range

Table 9.1   Validity coefficients for the NEO Five-Factor Inventory

	NEO-FFI scale				
	N	E	O	A	C
Adjective factors ($n = 375$)					
N	62***	00	03	−11*	16**
E	−20***	60***	02	01	20***
O	−16**	18***	56***	−08	−05
A	02	11*	04	57***	−03
C	−19***	11*	−08	07	61***
NEO–PI factors in spouse ratings ($n = 144$)					
N	48***	−10	−02	−24**	−11
E	−02	51***	22**	13	01
O	−08	−01	53***	01	−13
A	−07	16	20*	44***	00
C	−09	−17*	−11	30***	39***
NEO–PI factors in mean peer ratings ($n = 213$)					
N	35***	−05	05	−02	−07
E	02	38***	06	−12	−09
O	−01	−01	59***	00	−06
A	10	−10	00	37***	−19**
C	−15*	−12	−07	11	34***

Note: Decimal points are omitted. Convergent correlations are given in boldface. *$p < 0.05$; **$p < 0.01$; ***$p < 0.001$

from 0.34 to 0.62; divergent correlations are typically much smaller. In these data, the NEO-FFI scales account for about 75% as much variance in convergent criteria as do the full NEO-PI factors; subsequent estimates put that figure as high as 85% (Costa and McCrae, 1992b). As is usually the case with abbreviated scales, some precision is traded for speed and convenience.

Internal consistencies of the NEO-FFI N, E, O, A, and C scales were 0.89, 0.79, 0.76, 0.74, and 0.84, respectively. In a college sample, the two-week retest reliabilities of NEO-FFI scales were 0.89, 0.86, 0.88, 0.86, and 0.90 for N, E, O, A, and C, respectively (Robins et al., 2001). A comparison of NEO-FFI scores from men and women shows that women are higher in both N and A, a finding that mirrors results from the full scales.

It appears that the NEO-FFI offers acceptable measures of the five factors in a convenient form. We would encourage both researchers and clinicians to use the full NEO-PI-R whenever practicable, because it gives more precise measures of the five factors and, as importantly, additional information on facets. We recognize, however, that this will not always be possible, and that other users may not share our views on the need for detailed information. Perhaps experience with the NEO-FFI will be a stepping stone for some users to a more complete approach to personality assessment.

The success of the NEO-FFI in research contexts is shown in the fact that there are over 680 citations to it in the psychological literature. A few of the articles were critical, however (e.g. Egan et al., 2000), so new analyses were undertaken using the full item pool of the NEO-PI-R (McCrae and Costa, 2004). These analyses form the basis of a projected NEO-FFI-3.

The road not taken: validity scales

A great deal of psychometric ingenuity and research has gone into the creation of validity scales to detect gross and subtle falsification,

random responding, acquiescence, and other response tendencies, and clinicians are often trained that 'the validity of a psychological test, when used in clinical assessment, must be evaluated and established for each individual to whom the test is administered' (Ben-Porath and Waller, 1992: 16). The argument here is that a personality scale may show construct validity at the group level, but be invalid in some individual cases – a claim we would not dispute. Validity scales are supposed to identify these occasional invalid protocols, yet there is a hopeless circularity here: Even if we have a well-validated validity scale, how would we know that it was valid for this particular protocol? Clearly, we must establish its validity, perhaps by using meta-validity scales. Logically, Ben-Porath and Waller's argument implies an infinite regress, and if we adopted their standard, clinical assessment would be impossible. We take a more pragmatic view.

The original NEO-PI had only one standard validity check: The final item asked subjects if they 'have tried to answer all these questions honestly and accurately'. This item was originally included to verify that subjects had used the response format correctly (i.e. used the rightmost response category to mean *strongly agree*), because our early experience had pointed to a few individuals who reversed the scale and thus obtained an inverted personality profile. As a screen, this item also has the merit of detecting a few subjects who are willing to admit that they have not been candid, and may also detect random responding if the respondent happens to mark *strongly disagree or disagree* on this item. In volunteer samples, less than 1% of subjects are rejected because of this validity check.

It may seem to bespeak considerable naivety on our part to include as the only validity scale in an otherwise transparent instrument an honesty item that is itself transparent. In fact, however, it is a studied decision. We have adopted the self-disclosure model of item responding (Johnson, 1981) because there is considerable evidence that it works; and we have rejected the creation of social desirability (SD) and inconsistency scales (Costa and McCrae, 1997) because there is considerable evidence that they do not work (Piedmont et al., 2000). We acknowledge the fact that individuals differ in acquiescent responding, but feel that balanced keying of items (a criterion for item selection in all NEO-PI-R scales) is sufficient to control for the effects of this tendency (McCrae et al., 2001). Finally, we have chosen not to include infrequency scales, not because they do not work, but because they are intrusive and of limited application.

In a series of articles (Costa and McCrae, 1988a; McCrae, 1986; McCrae and Costa, 1983b; McCrae et al., 1989), we have argued that most SD scales ask substantive questions and, as a result, measure socially desirable characteristics rather than response artifacts. The test of SD scales is their ability to increase the validity of substantive scales, and this can best be assessed by using non-self-report criteria. Previous research has shown that neither the Crowne–Marlowe SD scale, nor the EPI Lie scale, nor the Edwards SD scale, nor the MMPI *K* scale is successful in increasing correlations with such criteria – in fact, 'correcting' scores often reduces valid variance in the self-reports. Data in these studies came from volunteers with no particular motivation to distort their responses, but some studies have reached similar conclusions under evaluative conditions (Barrick and Mount, 1996; Michaelis and Eysenck, 1971). In any case, it seems clear to us that the value of SD scales has been exaggerated, and their omission from the NEO-PI-R is both efficient and justified by the data.

We have also deliberately omitted infrequency scales from the NEO-PI-R. These scales combine items of very low (or very high) endorsement frequency; high scores are statistically implausible, and suggest that subjects were responding randomly or perversely. Such scales probably work, but they do so at considerable cost. Not only do they add a significant number of items; they also tend to stand out as 'trick' questions, and test-wise respondents may consider them annoying or insulting. In an instrument that relies on candor and cooperation between administrator and respondent, such items are simply out of place.

Random responding is most likely to occur when respondents are not motivated to complete the questionnaire accurately, and in our experience is most often not random at all, but highly systematic. In their hurry to finish the task, some respondents will simply fill out a single column (often the neutral, center response) for all items. Answer sheets like this are obvious to visual inspection, and should of course be discarded. But isn't it possible that some subjects give legitimate responses that happen to be the same for a long string of items? We considered this possibility by examining the responses of 983 normal volunteers. In this cooperative sample, no subject answered *strongly disagree* to more than 6 consecutive items, *disagree* to more than 9 consecutive items, *neutral* to more than 10, *agree* to more than 14, or *strongly agree* to more than 9 consecutive items. Scanning for patterns of responses that exceed these numbers can be used to identify random responders.

The NEO-PI-R retains the original validity check item at the end of the answer sheet, and also asks respondents if they have responded to all the items, and marked their responses in the correctly numbered spaces on the answer sheet. The Interpretive Report generated by computer administration and mail-in scoring includes a section on test validity based on these questions, the number of missing items, a count of *agree* and *strongly agree* responses (which yield warnings for acquiescence and nay-saying), and a scan of repetitive, presumably random responses. These checks provide unobtrusive measures of the validity of individual test results. In cases of questionable validity, an *interpretive report* is still generated, and the administrator is urged to explore with the respondent the meaning of test responses before deciding whether the interpretation is valid or not.

Carter and colleagues (2001) reported an informative study of test validity in a population of opioid-dependent outpatients, where cooperation with test administrators is problematic. They found that nearly one-quarter of their respondents had potentially invalid protocols identified through computer administration and scoring. The four-month retest stability of NEO-PI-R scales was significantly lower in the potentially invalid group for all 5 factors and 16 facets, suggesting that the NEO-PI-R validity checks are effective. However, even within the potentially invalid group, the median retest correlation was 0.35 (compared to 0.58 in the valid subsample), suggesting that protocols were not wholly invalid. Researches are advised to analyze data with and without questionable protocols, and clinicians should not hastily discard data from which some information, however imperfect, may be obtained.

APPROACHES TO VALIDATION

Most contemporary personologists subscribe to the tenets of construct validation (Hogan and Nicholson, 1988). Like them, we believe that the validity of a measure is established by a nomological network of supporting data; that one must be concerned about the content validity of measures (e.g. the representativeness of facets in each domain); that both convergent and discriminant validity are required; and that trait measures must point beyond test scores to meaningful social criteria. Because of our interest in psychology and aging, we would also ask that traits, which are enduring dispositions, show longitudinal evidence of stability over at least part of the adult lifespan.

We have, therefore, conducted a variety of validity studies on NEO-PI-R scales. We have correlated them with other self-report scales such as the Eysenck Personality Questionnaire (McCrae and Costa, 1985a) and the Guilford–Zimmerman Temperament Survey (Costa and McCrae, 1985a); with sentence completions (McCrae and Costa, 1980), divergent thinking tests (McCrae, 1987), and measures of the spontaneous self-concept

(McCrae and Costa, 1988); and with peer, spouse, and clinician ratings (McCrae and Costa, 1989d). We have demonstrated impressive levels of stability intervals up to 15 years (Costa and McCrae, 1988b; Terracciano et al., 2006), and shown that our scales predict such real-life outcomes as occupational change (McCrae and Costa, 1985b), life satisfaction (Costa and McCrae, 1984), and coping with a nuclear accident (Costa and McCrae, 1989b).

Like Block (1981), we tend to believe that simple behavior counts may not be appropriate criteria for personality measures, and prefer the judgments of knowledgeable informants, who can take situational factors into account in assessing the meaning of behavior. Consequently, a major portion of our research has been concerned with agreement between self-reports and peer or spouse ratings. We first developed the third-person form of the NEO-PI-R (Form R) as a means of validating self-reports (McCrae, 1982). Subsequent research (McCrae and Costa, 1989a; McCrae et al., 2004) has consistently shown correlations between self-reports and spouse or mean peer ratings ranging from 0.40 to 0.60, suggesting that about half the variance in NEO-PI-R scales is attributable to the underlying traits themselves (Ozer, 1985).

It is important to note that these data provide validity evidence for both Form S (self-reports) and Form R (observer ratings) of the NEO-PI-R. Additional evidence for the validity of Form R scales comes from correlations among peer ratings and between peer ratings and spouse ratings (McCrae and Costa, 1989a), and from correlations with external criteria such as well-being (Costa and McCrae, 1984), coping behaviors (McCrae and Costa, 1986), and divergent thinking tests (McCrae, 1987). Spouse ratings of N, E, and O have also shown high levels of stability over a six-year interval (Costa and McCrae, 1988b), and peer ratings on all five factors show stability over seven years (Costa and McCrae, 1992c). McCrae et al. (2005d) showed that Form R worked well in translation in 50 cultures.

Observer ratings provides a valuable complement to self-reports in many studies, particularly when there is reason to suspect bias in self-reports. For other studies (e.g. of individuals with cognitive or psychiatric impairment), ratings by informants may be the only feasible way to assess personality (Siegler et al., 1991). One of the unique strengths of the NEO-PI-R is the provision of reliable and well-validated observer rating scales.

APPLICATIONS OF THE NEO-PI-R

The NEO-PI-R is intended to provide a comprehensive description of personality traits: the individual's characteristic and enduring emotional, interpersonal, experiential, attitudinal, and motivational styles. As such, it is potentially useful whenever individual differences in personality are relevant. We have used it primarily as a tool for research, examining such questions as the structure and stability of personality and its influence on the life course. Questions about the origins of personality, its psychophysiological basis and expression, its relation to cognitive performance, and its impact on mental and physical health can also be addressed. Because all five major domains of personality – and many impor-tant facets – are measured by the NEO-PI-R, investigations using this instrument may discover relations that would be missed with a more narrowly focused set of scales.

The NEO-PI-R was developed and validated on adult samples ranging in age from 20 to 90, and is clearly appropriate for this age group. There are appreciable age differences between college students and adults over the age of 30 (Costa and McCrae, 1994b), and separate norms have been published. The basic validity of the instrument in college settings, however, appears to be unaltered (Costa et al., 1989; Piedmont, 1994). More recently, the NEO-PI-3 has been slightly modified for use by children age 12 and over (McCrae et al., 2004). The five-factor model may make possible a fuller integration of developmental psychology and personality (Kohnstamm et al., 1998; McCrae et al., 2000).

Evaluating other scales: Cloninger's TPQ

New theories often call for new measures, but the resulting proliferation of scales has made communication between researchers difficult. Correlating scales with measures of the five-factor model allows us to place them in a known context and can facilitate an understanding and evaluation of them.

During the 1980s, a new theory was proposed by psychiatrist Robert Cloninger (1988), whose three-dimensional model of personality attempted to synthesize experimental neurobehavioral studies, and had particular relevance to the understanding of personality disorders. Cloninger asserted that there are three independent dimensions of personality corresponding to three chemically coded neural networks or brain systems: dopaminergic neurons regulate the dimension of novelty seeking; serotonergic neurons regulate harm avoidance; and norepinephrinergic neurons regulate reward dependence. While other neurotransmitters, peptides, and hormones have an acknowledged influence, these three specific neurotransmitters are hypothesized to have a 'principal neuromodulatory role in only one system . . . this may explain the consistent observation that there are at least three uncorrelated dimensions of adaptive personality traits' (Cloninger, 1988: 85).

Although consistent with much of the animal literature, Cloninger's adoption of a three-factor model appears to have been based on the faulty assumption that there was widespread agreement on the three personality dimensions in humans. Tellegen (1985), Eysenck and Eysenck (1975), and even McCrae and Costa (1983a) had all proposed three-factor models which shared the common dimensions of N and E. But whereas we originally suggested adding O as the third dimension, Tellegen's constraint factor appears to resemble C, and the Eysencks' psychoticism blends low A and low C (McCrae and Costa, 1985a). Clearly, the full five-factor model is needed to accommodate even these three systems, and any three-factor system is likely either to be incomplete or to conflate distinct dimensions.

Evidence of this can be seen in the adjectives that Cloninger (1988; table 1) used to describe his dimensions. Novelty Seeking, for example, contrasts *curious* (a part of O), and *enthusiastic* (E) with *methodical* and *orderly* (C). His Harm Avoidance dimension contrasts N-related traits such as *worrying* and *fearful* with E-related traits such as *outgoing* and *energetic*. Finally, his Reward Dependence dimension includes elements of several factors: *sentimental* (A) and *persistent* (C) are contrasted with *practical* (low O) and *detached* (low E).

Cloninger's conceptualizations were reflected in an instrument he developed to measure his model, a 100-item true/false questionnaire called the Tridimensional Personality Questionnaire (TPQ). Version 4 of the TPQ measures four subscales for each of the three major dimensions, and correlation of these scales with the NEO-PI can be used to examine the dimensions Cloninger proposed. Data from a sample of 78 college students are presented in Table 9.2, which gives correlations for the full scales and subscales with the five NEO-PI validimax factors. By and large, the rational interpretations suggested above are supported by these data; Novelty Seeking is positively related to E and negatively related to C; Harm Avoidance is chiefly related to N, but secondarily to low E and low O; and Reward Dependence is related to four of the five dimensions. The TPQ and the theory on which it is based do not appear to describe the organization of personality traits very well.

Based in part on such findings, Cloninger subsequently expanded his model and developed a new measure, the Temperament and Character Inventory (TCI; Cloninger and Svrakic, 1994). The persistence subscale became a separate factor, and three character-related scales (Self-Directedness, Cooperativeness, and Self-Transcendence) were added. Joint factor analyses with NEO-PI-R factors show that Self-Directedness is related chiefly to low N, Cooperativeness to A, and Self-Transcendence to O (McCrae et al., 2001).

The correlations in Table 9.2 have some historic significance. In an article in *Nature Genetics* that effectively launched the study of the molecular genetics of personality, Benjamin and colleagues (1996) used them to estimate Novelty Seeking from NEO-PI-R scores, which was then related to the D4 dopamine receptor gene. A large part of the subsequent literature on the genetics of personality has used measures from Cloninger or the NEO-PI-R (e.g. Schinka et al., 2004).

Assessment of the individual

However, the NEO-PI-R is not merely a research instrument. It is intended to be used by the clinician, counselor, or personnel psychologist who wishes to understand a particular individual and to use the conclusions of research in making specific decisions (Costa and McCrae, 1992a; McCrae, 1991; McCrae and Costa, 1991). Profile sheets and computer interpretations are among the tools designed to facilitate this use by giving a clear description of the individual.

In clinical psychology, it seemed to us that knowing what sort of person the client was would be of considerable value, and we were gratified to find that a number of clinicians concurred in this judgment (see McCrae and Costa, 1989b). Clinical use of the NEO-PI-R has continued (Costa and McCrae, in press; Singer, 2005), although more research is still needed to optimize its application.

Several distinct uses can be mentioned. Understanding the client's personality can lead to (a) rapid rapport and more accurate empathy; (b) a better understanding of the problem and its situational and characterological bases; (c) a more realistic assessment of likely outcomes and a better basis for treatment

Table 9.2   Correlations of Cloninger's TPQ scales with NEO-PI validimax factors

TPQ scale		Validimax factor				
		N	*E*	*O*	*A*	*C*
Novelty Seeking		−09	32**	17	−10	−60***
	Exploratory-Excitability	−12	40***	40***	−01	−21
	Impulsiveness	09	07	01	−15	−42***
	Extravagance	−19	16	05	08	−46***
	Disorderliness	−04	24*	04	−16	−50***
Harm Avoidance		74***	−32***	−27*	05	11
	Worry and Pessimism	74***	−21	−28*	−03	07
	Fear of Uncertainty	56***	−21	−31**	11	19
	Shyness	45***	−45***	−10	08	11
	Fatigability	59***	−17	−18	−04	00
Reward Dependence		33**	43***	26*	27*	24
	Sentimentality	17	26*	42***	42***	29*
	Persistence at Work	21	31**	09	07	41***
	Attachment	28*	39***	09	11	−07
	Dependence	15	07	23*	30**	08

Note: n = 78. Decimal points are omitted. $*p < 0.05$; $**p < 0.01$; $***p < 0.001$

goals; (d) anticipation of the client's cooperativeness (agreeableness) and motivation (conscientiousness) in therapy; (e) identification of the client's strengths, which might not be immediately apparent from a discussion focused on problems; and (f) the choice of a mode of therapy that will be both effective and acceptable to the client. The choice of therapy in particular is a clear area in which research is needed, and the five-factor model provides a framework for the systematic search for Trait × Treatment interaction effects.

There is one further clinical application of NEO-PI-R scales that has proven increasingly important. Wiggins and Pincus (1989) originally showed that NEO-PI domain scales provided a useful framework for understanding measures of personality disorders. As the links between DSM-IV Axis II disorders and fundamental dimensions of personality become clearer, personality measures became increasingly important in psychiatric diagnosis. Consideration of the five-factor model may even lead to better conceptualization of personality disorders themselves (Costa and Widiger, 2002) and to new approaches to the assessment and diagnosis of personality pathology (McCrae et al., 2005b).

Self-understanding

Personality inventories are sophisticated devices that may tap sensitive issues for some respondents, and we have insisted that the NEO-PI-R be used only by those qualified by appropriate professional training in personality theory and psychometrics (Costa and McCrae, 1992b). Early in the development of the inventory, however, we became convinced that under certain conditions, the results of personality tests can be shared with respondents. Students in personality theory, or testing courses, are often given the results of their own tests, and the Myers-Briggs Type Indicator (Myers and McCaulley, 1985) has extensive provisions for explaining the respondent's type to him or her. Feedback from personality inventories can be useful as a way of engaging the respondent in the research enterprise and can be a tool for self-understanding as well. McReynolds (1985) viewed the therapeutic use of shared test results – what he called 'client-centered assessment' – as an important trend in psychotherapy, and Tellegen (1985) suggested that providing feedback might help establish the trust and cooperation needed to obtain valid personality assessments. Two decades of experience with personality feedback suggests that problems are minimal and rewards substantial.

Computer interpretations and profile sheets are too technical for many respondents and might be confusing and misleading. We therefore designed a simplified feedback sheet, *Your NEO Summary*, which gives non-threatening descriptions of high, average, and low scorers for each of the five factors. The administrator who wishes to provide feedback scores the NEO-PI-R or NEO-FFI, consults appropriate norms, and checks off the applicable description for each respondent (Costa and McCrae, 1989a).

Your NEO Summary was evaluated by 44 college students who had taken the NEO-PI-R as part of a course on personality theory. All of the students felt the sheet was easy to understand. They believed the descriptions were 'very accurate' (48%) or 'fairly accurate' (52%); none thought the descriptions were 'not very accurate' or 'inaccurate.' For most students (61%), the feedback confirmed their self-image; the rest (39%) believed they had learned something new about themselves. All the students enjoyed receiving feedback; none felt it was disturbing. Two of the students indicated that they would like to discuss the feedback with a professional.

It is well known that almost any general statement about personality will be accepted as accurate by many respondents (Forer, 1949). However, Furnham and Varian (1988) have shown that individuals can generally distinguish accurate feedback, and the presence on the feedback sheet of descriptions for different ranges of scores for each factor, that are *not* checked, helps respondents understand the distinctive nature of their personality profile. We tested the meaningfulness of respondents' acceptance of feedback in a second study of 77 college students. These individuals were given a blank *Your NEO Summary* sheet and asked to check off the descriptions they expected to receive; they then completed the NEO-PI, and their prior expectations were compared with the actual summary sheet. Correlations between expected and actual summary scores showed

agreement ranging from 0.24 for agreeableness to 0.60 for conscientiousness (all $p < 0.05$). These values are high enough to suggest validity for the feedback information, but low enough to demonstrate the need for standardized assessment: global self-ratings could not be used as a substitute for the NEO-PI-R.

Some clinicians believe that more extensive feedback than that offered by *Your NEO Summary* is valuable for some clients, and discuss their profile sheets with them (Mutén, 1991; Singer, 2005). In response to clinician demand, an optional section of the computer-generated interpretive report (Costa et al., 1994) provides more extensive client feedback, including interpretations of the facet scores.

CONCLUSION

Much has changed in the field of personality since the NEO-PI-R was first conceived. Traits were out of fashion then; today, even classic demonstrations of the power of the situation are being reinterpreted to acknowledge the role of the person (Carnahan and McFarland, 2007). In part, this change came about because the five-factor model effectively solved the long-standing problem of personality structure; in part, because good operationalizations of the five-factor model, including the NEO-PI-R, were made available to researchers. As a result, a solid body of knowledge has been accumulated on the stability, heritability, universality, and utility of personality traits, and this has prompted a new generation of personality theories (e.g. McAdams and Pals, 2006; McCrae and Costa, in press). Epstein (1977) was right: Traits are alive and well, and tools for their assessment are flourishing (Costa and McCrae, in press).

ACKNOWLEDGMENTS

Paul T. Costa Jr., and Robert R. McCrae receive royalties from the Revised NEO

Personality Inventory. This research was supported by the Intramural Research Program of the NIH, National Institute on Aging. Early unpublished versions of this chapter were referenced as:

Costa, P.T. Jr. and McCrae, R.R. (in preparation) 'The NEO Personality Inventory', in S.R. Briggs and J. Cheek (eds), *Personality Measures* (Vol. 1). Greenwich, CT: JAI Press.

Costa, P.T. Jr. and McCrae, R.R. (in press) 'The Revised NEO Personality Inventory (NEO-PI-R)', in S.R. Briggs, J.M. Cheek and E.M. Donahue (eds), *Handbook of Adult Personality Inventories*. New York: Plenum.

Excerpts from an earlier version were printed in:

Cohen, R.J. and Swerdlik, M.E. (1999) *Psychological Testing and Assessment: An Introduction to Tests and Measurement* (4th edn). Mountain View, CA: Mayfield Publishing, pp. 410–13.

Cohen, R.J. (ed.) (2002, 2005) *Exercises in psychological testing and assessment* (5th edn, 6th edn). San Francisco, CA: McGraw-Hill, pp. 182–5.

REFERENCES

Barrick, M.R. and Mount, M.K. (1996) 'Effects of impression management and self-deception on the predictive validity of personality constructs', *Journal of Applied Psychology*, 81(3): 261–72.

Benjamin, J., Li, L., Patterson, C., Greenberg, B.D., Murphy, D.L. and Hamer, D.H. (1996) 'Population and familial association between the D4 dopamine receptor gene and measures of novelty seeking', *Nature Genetics*, 12(1): 81–4.

Ben-Porath, Y.S. and Waller, N.G. (1992) '"Normal" personality inventories in clinical assessment: General requirements and the potential for using the NEO Personality Inventory', *Psychological Assessment*, 4(1): 14–19.

Block, J. (1961) *The Q-sort Method in Personality Assessment and Psychiatric Research*. Springfield, IL: Charles C Thomas.

Block, J. (1977) 'Advancing the psychology of personality: Paradigmatic shift or improving the quality of research?', in D. Magnusson and N.S. Endler (eds), *Personality at the Cross-roads: Current Issues in Interactional Psychology*. Hillsdale, NJ: Lawrence Erlbaum Associates, pp. 37–64.

Block, J. (1981) 'Some enduring and consequential structures of personality', in A.I. Rabin, J. Aronoff, A.M. Barclay and R.A. Zucker (eds), *Further Explorations in Personality*. New York: Wiley-Interscience, pp. 27–43.

Block, J. (1995) 'A contrarian view of the five-factor approach to personality description', *Psychological Bulletin*, 117(2): 187–215.

Briggs, S.R. (1989) 'The optimal level of measurement for personality constructs', in D.M. Buss and N. Cantor (eds), *Personality Psychology: Recent Trends and Emerging Directions*. New York: Springer-Verlag, pp. 246–60.

Briggs, S.R. and Cheek, J.N. (1986) 'The role of factor analysis in the development and evaluation of personality scales', *Journal of Personality*, 54(1): 106–48.

Burisch, M. (1984) 'Approaches to personality inventory construction: A comparison of merits', *American Psychologist*, 39(3): 214–27.

Buss, A.H. and Durkee, A. (1957) 'An inventory for assessing different kinds of hostility', *Journal of Consulting Psychology*, 21(4): 343–8.

Buss, A.H. and Plomin, R. (1975) *A Temperament Theory of Personality Development*. New York: Wiley.

Carnahan, T. and McFarland, S. (2007) 'Revisiting the Stanford Prison Experiment: Could participant self-selection have led to the cruelty?', *Personality and Social Psychology Bulletin*, 33(5): 603–14.

Carter, J.A., Herbst, J.H., Stoller, K.B., King, V.L., Kidorf, M.S., Costa, P.T. Jr. and Brooner, R.K. (2001) 'Short-term stability of NEO-PI-R personality trait scores in opioid-dependent outpatients', *Psychology of Addictive Behaviors*, 15(3): 255–60.

Cattell, R.B., Eber, H.W. and Tatsuoka, M.M. (1970) *The Handbook for the Sixteen Personality Factor Questionnaire*. Champaign, IL: Institute for Personality and Ability Testing.

Cloninger, C.R. (1988) 'A unified biosocial theory of personality and its role in the development of anxiety states: A reply to commentaries', *Psychiatric Development*, 6(2): 83–120.

Cloninger, C.R. and Svrakic, D.M. (1994) 'Differentiating normal and deviant personality by the seven-factor personality model', in S. Strack and M. Lorr (eds), *Differentiating Normal and Abnormal Personality*. New York: Springer, pp. 40–64.

Coan, R.W. (1974) *The Optimal Personality*. New York: Columbia University Press.

Conley, J.J. (1985) 'A personality theory of adulthood and aging', in R. Hogan and W.H. Jones (eds), *Perspectives in Personality* (Vol. 1). Greenwich, CT: JAI Press, pp. 81–115.

Costa, P.T. Jr. and McCrae, R.R. (1976) 'Age differences in personality structure: A cluster analytic approach', *Journal of Gerontology*, 31(5): 564–70.

Costa, P.T. Jr. and McCrae, R.R. (1978) 'Objective personality assessment', in M. Storandt, I.C. Siegler and M.F. Elias (eds), *The Clinical Psychology of Aging*. New York: Plenum Press, pp. 119–43.

Costa, P.T. Jr. and McCrae, R.R. (1980a) 'Somatic complaints in males as a function of age and neuroticism: A longitudinal analysis', *Journal of Behavioral Medicine*, 3(3): 245–57.

Costa, P.T. Jr. and McCrae, R.R. (1980b) 'Still stable after all these years: Personality as a key to some issues in adulthood and old age', in P.B. Baltes and O.G. Brim Jr. (eds), *Life Span Development and Behavior* (Vol. 3). New York: Academic Press, pp. 65–102.

Costa, P.T. Jr. and McCrae, R.R. (1984) 'Personality as a lifelong determinant of well-being', in C. Malatesta and C. Izard (eds), *Affective Processes in Adult Development and Aging*. Beverly Hills, CA: Sage, pp. 141–57.

Costa, P.T. Jr. and McCrae, R.R. (1985a) 'Concurrent validation after 20 years: Implications of personality stability for its assessment', in J.N. Butcher and C.D. Spielberger (eds), *Advances in Personality Assessment* (Vol. 4). Hillsdale, NJ: Lawrence Erlbaum Associates, pp. 31–54.

Costa, P.T. Jr. and McCrae, R.R. (1985b) *The NEO Personality Inventory Manual*. Odessa, FL: Psychological Assessment Resources.

Costa, P.T. Jr. and McCrae, R.R. (1986) 'Major contributions to personality psychology', in S. Modgil and C. Modgil (eds), *Hans Eysenck: Consensus and Controversy*. Barcombe Lewes: Falmer, pp. 63–72, 86, 87.

Costa, P.T. Jr. and McCrae, R.R. (1988a) 'From catalog to classification: Murray's needs and the Five-Factor Model', *Journal of Personality and Social Psychology*, 55(2): 258–65.

Costa, P.T. Jr. and McCrae, R.R. (1988b) 'Personality in adulthood: A six-year longitudinal study of self-reports and spouse ratings on the NEO Personality Inventory', *Journal of Personality and Social Psychology*, 54(5): 853–63.

Costa, P.T. Jr. and McCrae, R.R. (1989a) *The NEO-PI/NEO-FFI Manual Supplement*. Odessa, FL: Psychological Assessment Resources.

Costa, P.T. Jr. and McCrae, R.R. (1989b) 'Personality, stress, and coping: Some lessons from a decade of research', in K.S. Markides and C.L. Cooper (eds), *Aging, Stress, Social Support and Health*. New York: Wiley, pp. 267–83.

Costa, P.T. Jr. and McCrae, R.R. (1992a) 'Normal personality assessment in clinical practice: The NEO Personality Inventory', *Psychological Assessment*, 4(1): 5–13.

Costa, P.T. Jr. and McCrae, R.R. (1992b) *Revised NEO Personality Inventory (NEO-PI-R) and NEO Five-Factor Inventory (NEO-FFI) Professional Manual*. Odessa, FL: Psychological Assessment Resources.

Costa, P.T. Jr. and McCrae, R.R. (1992c) 'Trait psychology comes of age', in T.B. Sonderegger (ed.), *Nebraska Symposium on Motivation: Psychology and Aging*. Lincoln, NE: University of Nebraska Press, pp. 169–204.

Costa, P.T. Jr. and McCrae, R.R. (1994) 'Stability and change in personality from adolescence through adulthood', in C.F. Halverson, G.A. Kohnstamm and R.P. Martin (eds), *The Developing Structure of Temperament and Personality from Infancy to Adulthood*. Hillsdale, NJ: Lawrence Erlbaum Associates, pp. 139–50.

Costa, P.T. Jr. and McCrae, R.R. (1995) 'Domains and facets: Hierarchical personality assessment using the Revised NEO Personality Inventory', *Journal of Personality Assessment*, 64(1): 21–50.

Costa, P.T. Jr. and McCrae, R.R. (1997) 'Stability and change in personality assessment: The Revised NEO Personality Inventory in the Year 2000', *Journal of Personality Assessment*, 68(1): 86–94.

Costa P.T. Jr. and McCrae, R.R. (in press) 'The NEO Inventories', in R.P. Archer and S.R. Smith (eds), *A Guide to Personality Assessment: Evaluation, Application, and Integration*. Mahwah, NJ: Erlbaum.

Costa, P.T. Jr., McCrae, R.R. and Dembroski, T.M. (1989) 'Agreeableness vs. antagonism: Explication of a potential risk factor for CHD', in A. Siegman and T.M. Dembroski (eds), *In Search of Coronary-prone Behavior: Beyond Type A*. Hillsdale, NJ: Lawrence Erlbaum Associates, pp. 41–63.

Costa, P.T. Jr., McCrae, R.R. and Dye, D.A. (1991) 'Facet scales for Agreeableness and Conscientiousness: A revision of the NEO Personality Inventory', *Personality and Individual Differences*, 12(9): 887–98.

Costa, P.T. Jr., McCrae, R.R. and Holland, J.L. (1984) 'Personality and vocational interests in an adult sample', *Journal of Applied Psychology*, 69(3): 390–400.

Costa, P.T. Jr., McCrae, R.R. and PAR Staff (1994) *NEO Software System* [Computer software]. Odessa, FL: Psychological Assessment Resources.

Costa, P.T. Jr. and Piedmont, R.L. (2003) 'Multivariate assessment: NEO-PI-R profiles of Madeline G', in J.S. Wiggins (ed.), *Paradigms of Personality Assessment*. New York: Guilford, pp. 262–80.

Costa, P.T. Jr. and Widiger, T.A. (2002) (eds), *Personality Disorders and the Five-Factor Model of Personality* (2nd edn). Washington, DC: American Psychological Association.

De Fruyt, F., Mervielde, I., Hoekstra, H.A. and Rolland, J.-P. (2000) 'Assessing adolescents' personality with the NEO-PI-R,' *Assessment*, 7(4): 329–45.

De Raad, B. and Perugini, M. (2002) (eds), *Big Five Assessment*. Gottingen: Hogrefe & Huber.

Digman, J.M. and Inouye, J. (1986) 'Further specification of the five robust factors of personality', *Journal of Personality and Social Psychology*, 50(1): 116–23.

Egan, V., Deary, I. and Austin, E. (2000) 'The NEO-FFI: Emerging British norms and an item-level analysis suggest N, A, and C are more reliable than O and E', *Personality and Individual Differences*, 29(5): 907–20.

Epstein, S. (1977) 'Traits are alive and well', in D. Magnusson and N.S. Endler (eds), *Personality at the Crossroads: Current Issues in Interactional Psychology*. Hillsdale, NJ: Lawrence Erlbaum Associates, pp. 83–98.

Eysenck, H.J. and Eysenck, S.B.G. (1975) *Manual of the Eysenck Personality Questionnaire*. San Diego: EDITS.

Fiske, D.W. (1974) 'The limits for the conventional science of personality', *Journal of Personality*, 42(1): 1–11.

Fitzgerald, E.T. (1966) 'Measurement of openness to experience: A study of regression in the service of the ego', *Journal of Personality and Social Psychology*, 4(6): 655–63.

Forer, B.R. (1949) 'The fallacy of personal validation: A classroom demonstration of gullibility', *Journal of Abnormal and Social Psychology*, 44(1): 118–23.

Furnham, A. and Varian, C. (1988) 'Predicting and accepting personality test scores', *Personality and Individual Differences*, 9(4): 735–48.

Goldberg, L.R. (1981) 'Language and individual differences: The search for universals in personality lexicons', in L. Wheeler (ed.), *Review of Personality and Social Psychology* (Vol. 2). Beverly Hills, CA: Sage, pp. 141–65.

Goldberg, L.R. (1983) 'The magical number five, plus or minus two: Some considerations on the dimensionality of personality descriptors', Paper presented at a Research Seminar, June, Gerontology Research Center, Baltimore.

Hathaway, S.R. and McKinley, J.C. (1943) *The Minnesota Multiphasic Personality Inventory* (revised edn). Minneapolis: University of Minnesota Press.

Hendriks, A.A.J., Hofstee, W.K.B. and De Raad, B. (1999) 'The Five-Factor Personality Inventory (FFPI)', *Personality and Individual Differences*, 27(2): 307–25.

Hofstee, W.K.B., De Raad, B. and Goldberg, L.R. (1992) 'Integration of the Big Five and circumplex approaches to trait structure', *Journal of Personality and Social Psychology*, 63(1): 146–63.

Hogan, R. (1986) *Hogan Personality Inventory Manual*. Minneapolis, MN: National Computer Systems.

Hogan, R. and Nicholson, R.A. (1988) 'The meaning of personality test scores', *American Psychologist*, 43(8): 621–6.

Howarth, E. (1976) 'Were Cattell's "personality sphere" factors correctly identified in the first instance?', *British Journal of Psychology*, 67(2): 213–36.

Jackson, D.N. (1975) 'The relative validity of scales prepared by naive item writers and those based on empirical methods of personality scale construction', *Educational and Psychological Measurement*, 35(2): 361–70.

Jang, K.L., McCrae, R.R., Angleitner, A., Riemann, R. and Livesley, W.J. (1998) 'Heritability of facet-level traits in a cross-cultural twin sample: Support for a hierarchical model of personality', *Journal of Personality and Social Psychology*, 74(6): 1556–65.

John, O.P., Angleitner, A. and Ostendorf, F. (1988) 'The lexical approach to personality: A historical review of trait taxonomic research', *European Journal of Personality*, 2(3): 171–203.

Johnson, J.A. (1981) 'The "self-disclosure" and "self-presentation" views of item response dynamics and personality scale validity', *Journal of Personality and Social Psychology*, 40(4): 761–9.

Kohnstamm, G.A., Havlerson, C.F. Jr., Mervielde, I. and Havill, V.L. (1998) (eds), *Parental Descriptions of Child Personality: Developmental Antecedents of the Big Five?* Hillsdale, NJ: Lawrence Erlbaum Associates.

Leary, P. (1957) *Interpersonal Diagnosis of Personality*. New York: Ronald Press.

Magnusson, D. and Endler, N.S. (1977) *Personality at the Crossroads: Current Issues in Interactional Psychology*. Hillsdale, NJ: Lawrence Erlbaum Associates.

McAdams, D.P. and Pals, J.L. (2006) 'A new Big Five: Fundamental principles for an integrative science of personality', *American Psychologist*, 61(3): 204–17.

McCrae, R.R. (1982) 'Consensual validation of personality traits: Evidence from self-reports and ratings', *Journal of Personality and Social Psychology*, 43(2): 293–303.

McCrae, R.R. (1986) 'Well-being scales do not measure social desirability', *Journal of Gerontology*, 41(3): 390–2.

McCrae, R.R. (1987) 'Creativity, divergent thinking, and Openness to Experience', *Journal of Personality and Social Psychology*, 52(6): 1258–65.

McCrae, R.R. (1991) 'The Five-Factor Model and its assessment in clinical settings', *Journal of Personality Assessment*, 57(3): 399–414.

McCrae, R.R. and Costa, P.T. Jr. (1980) 'Openness to experience and ego level in Loevinger's sentence completion test: Dispositional contributions to developmental models of personality', *Journal of Personality and Social Psychology*, 39(6): 1179–90.

McCrae, R.R. and Costa, P.T. Jr. (1983a) 'Joint factors in self-reports and ratings: Neuroticism, Extraversion, and openness to experience', *Personality and Individual Differences*, 4(3): 245–55.

McCrae, R.R. and Costa, P.T. Jr. (1983b) 'Social desirability scales: More substance than style', *Journal of Consulting and Clinical Psychology*, 51(6): 882–88.

McCrae, R.R. and Costa, P.T. Jr. (1985a) 'Comparison of EPI and Psychoticism scales with measures of the Five-Factor Model of personality', *Personality and Individual Differences*, 6(5): 587–97.

McCrae, R.R. and Costa, P.T. Jr. (1985b) 'Openness to experience', in R. Hogan and W.H. Jones (eds), *Perspectives in Personality* (Vol. 1). Greenwich, CT: JAI Press, pp. 145–72.

McCrae, R.R. and Costa, P.T. Jr. (1985c) 'Updating Norman's "adequate taxonomy": Intelligence and personality dimensions in natural language and in questionnaires', *Journal of Personality and Social Psychology*, 49(3): 710–21.

McCrae, R.R. and Costa, P.T. Jr. (1986) 'Personality, coping, and coping effectiveness in an adult sample', *Journal of Personality*, 54(2): 385–405.

McCrae, R.R. and Costa, P.T. Jr. (1987) 'Validation of the Five-Factor Model of personality across instruments and observers', *Journal of Personality and Social Psychology*, 52(1): 81–90.

McCrae, R.R. and Costa, P.T. Jr. (1988) 'Age, personality, and the spontaneous self-concept', *Journal of Gerontology: Social Sciences*, 43(6): S177–S185.

McCrae, R.R. and Costa, P.T. Jr. (1989a) 'Different points of view: Self-reports and ratings in the assessment of personality', in J.P. Forgas and M.J Innes (eds), *Recent Advances in Social Psychology: An International Perspective*. Amsterdam: Elsevier, pp. 429–39.

McCrae, R.R. and Costa, P.T. Jr. (1989b) 'More reasons to adopt the Five-Factor Model', *American Psychologist*, 44(2): 451–2.

McCrae, R.R. and Costa, P.T. Jr. (1989c) 'Reinterpreting the Myers-Briggs Type Indicator from the perspective of the Five-Factor Model of personality', *Journal of Personality*, 57(1): 17–40.

McCrae, R.R. and Costa, P.T. Jr. (1989d) 'Rotation to maximize the construct validity of factors in the NEO Personality Inventory', *Multivariate Behavioral Research*, 24(1): 107–24.

McCrae, R.R. and Costa, P.T. Jr. (1989e) 'The structure of interpersonal traits: Wiggins's circumplex and the Five-Factor Model', *Journal of Personality and Social Psychology*, 56(4): 586–95.

McCrae, R.R. and Costa, P.T. Jr. (1991) 'The NEO Personality Inventory: Using the Five-Factor Model in counseling', *Journal of Counseling and Development*, 69(4): 367–72, 375–6.

McCrae, R.R. and Costa, P.T. Jr. (1992) 'Discriminant validity of NEO-PI-R facets', *Educational and Psychological Measurement*, 52(1): 229–37.

McCrae, R.R. and Costa, P.T. Jr. (1997) 'Conceptions and correlates of Openness to Experience', in R. Hogan, J.A. Johnson and S.R. Briggs (eds), *Handbook of Personality Psychology*. Orlando, FL: Academic Press, pp. 269–90.

McCrae, R.R. and Costa, P.T. Jr. (2004) 'A contemplated revision of the NEO Five-Factor Inventory', *Personality and Individual Differences*, 36(3): 587–96.

McCrae, R.R. and Costa, P.T. Jr. (in press) 'The Five-Factor Theory of personality', in O.P. John, R.W. Robins and L.A. Pervin (eds), *Handbook of Personality: Theory and Research* (3rd edn). New York: Guilford.

McCrae, R.R., Costa, P.T. Jr. and Busch, C.M. (1986) 'Evaluating comprehensiveness in personality systems: The California Q-Set and the Five-Factor Model', *Journal of Personality*, 54(2): 430–46.

McCrae, R.R., Costa, P.T. Jr., Dahlstrom, W.G., Barefoot, J.C., Siegler, I.C. and Williams, R.B. Jr. (1989) 'A caution on the use of the MMPI K-correction in research on psychosomatic medicine', *Psychosomatic Medicine*, 51(1): 58–65.

McCrae, R.R., Costa, P.T. Jr., Lima, M. P., Simões, A., Ostendorf, F., Angleitner, A., Marušić, I., Bratko, D., Caprara, G.V., Barbaranelli, C., Chae, J-H. and Piedmont, R.L. (1999) 'Age differences in personality across the adult life span: Parallels in five cultures', *Developmental Psychology*, 35(2): 466–77.

McCrae, R.R., Costa, P.T. Jr. and Martin, T.A. (2005a) 'The NEO-PI-3: A more readable Revised NEO Personality Inventory', *Journal of Personality Assessment*, 84(3): 261–70.

McCrae, R.R., Costa, P.T. Jr., Martin, T.A., Oryol, V.E., Rukavishnikov, A.A., Senin, I. G., Hřebíčková, M. and Urbánek, T. (2004) 'Consensual validation of personality traits across cultures', *Journal of Research in Personality*, 38(2): 179–201.

McCrae, R.R., Costa, P.T. Jr., Ostendorf, F., Angleitner, A., Hřebíčková, M., Avia, M. D., Sanz, J., Sánchez-Bernardos, M.L., Kusdil, M.E., Woodfield, R., Saunders, P.R. and Smith, P.B. (2000) 'Nature over nurture: Temperament, personality, and lifespan development', *Journal of Personality and Social Psychology*, 78(1): 173–86.

McCrae, R.R., Costa, P.T. Jr., Terracciano, A., Parker, W.D., Mills, C.J., De Fruyt, F. and Mervielde, I. (2002) 'Personality trait development from 12 to 18: Longitudinal, cross-sectional, and cross-cultural analyses', *Journal of Personality and Social Psychology*, 83(6): 1456–68.

McCrae, R.R., Herbst, J.H. and Costa, P.T. Jr. (2001) 'Effects of acquiescence on personality factor structures', in R. Riemann, F. Ostendorf and F. Spinath (eds), *Personality and Temperament: Genetics, Evolution, and Structure*. Berlin: Pabst Science, pp. 217–31.

McCrae, R.R., Löckenhoff, C.E. and Costa, P.T. Jr. (2005b) 'A step towards DSM-V: Cataloging personality-related problems in living', *European Journal of Personality*, 19(4): 269–86.

McCrae, R.R., Martin, T.A. and Costa, P.T. Jr. (2005c) 'Age trends and age norms for the NEO Personality Inventory-3 in adolescents and adults', *Assessment*, 12(4): 363–73.

McCrae, R.R., Terracciano, A. and 78 Members of the Personality Profiles of Cultures Project. (2005d) 'Universal features of personality traits from the observer's perspective: Data from 50 cultures', *Journal of Personality and Social Psychology*, 88(3): 547–61.

McReynolds, P. (1985) 'Psychological assessment and clinical practice: Problems and prospects', in J.N. Butcher and C.D. Spielberger (eds), *Advances in Personality Assessment* (Vol. 4). Hillsdale, NJ: Lawrence Erlbaum Associates, pp. 1–30.

Mershon, B. and Gorsuch, R.L. (1988) 'Number of factors in the personality sphere: Does increase in factors increase predictability of real-life criteria?', *Journal of Personality and Social Psychology*, 55(4): 675–80.

Michaelis, W. and Eysenck, H.J. (1971) 'The determination of personality inventory factor patterns and intercorrelations by changes in real-life motivation', *Journal of Genetic Psychology*, 118(2): 223–4.

Mischel, W. (1968) *Personality and Assessment*. New York: Wiley.

Mutén, E. (1991) 'Self-reports, spouse ratings, and psychophysiological assessment in a behavioral medicine program: An application of the Five-Factor Model', *Journal of Personality Assessment*, 57(3): 449–64.

Myers, I.B. and McCaulley, M.H. (1985) *Manual: A Guide to the Development and Use of the Myers-Briggs Type Indicator*. Palo Alto: Consulting Psychologists Press.

Norman, W.T. (1963) 'Toward an adequate taxonomy of personality attributes: Replicated factor structure in peer nomination personality ratings', *Journal of Abnormal and Social Psychology*, 66(6): 574–83.

Ozer, D.J. (1985) 'Correlation and the coefficient of determination', *Psychological Bulletin*, 97(2): 307–15.

Paunonen, S.V. and Ashton, M.C. (2001) 'Big Five factors and facets and the prediction of behavior', *Journal of Personality and Social Psychology*, 81(3): 524–39.

Piedmont, R.L. (1994) 'Validation of the NEO-PI-R observer form for college students: Toward a paradigm for studying personality development', *Assessment*, 1(3): 259–68.

Piedmont, R.L., McCrae, R.R., Riemann, R. and Angleitner, A. (2000) 'On the invalidity of validity scales: Evidence from self-reports and observer ratings in volunteer samples', *Journal of Personality and Social Psychology*, 78(3): 582–93.

Reynolds, S.K. and Clark, L.A. (2001) 'Predicting dimensions of personality disorder from domains and facets of the Five-Factor Model', *Journal of Personality*, 69(2): 199–222.

Robins, R.W., Fraley, R.C., Roberts, B.W. and Trzesniewski, K.H. (2001) 'A longitudinal study of personality change in young adulthood', *Journal of Personality*, 69(4): 617–40.

Rogers, C.R. (1961) *On Becoming a Person: A Therapist's View of Psychotherapy*. Boston: Houghton Mifflin.

Rokeach, M. (1960) *The Open and Closed Mind*. New York: Basic Books.

Schinka, J.A., Busch, R.M. and Robichaux-Keene, N. (2004) 'A meta-analysis of the association between the serotonin transporter gene polymorphism (5HTTLPR) and anxiety-related personality traits', *Molecular Psychiatry*, 9(2): 197–202.

Shweder, R.A. (1975) 'How relevant is an individual difference theory of personality?', *Journal of Personality*, 43(3): 455–84.

Siegler, I.C., Welsh, K.A., Davison, D.V., Fillenbaum, G.G., Earl, N.L., Kaplan, E.B. and Clark, C.M. (1991) 'Ratings of personality change in patients being evaluated for memory disorders', *Alzheimer Disease and Associated Disorders*, 5(4): 240–50.

Singer, J.A. (2005) *Personality and Psychotherapy: Treating the Whole Person*. New York: Guilford Press.

Spielberger, C.D. (1972) 'Anxiety as an emotional state', in C.D. Spielberger (ed.), *Anxiety: Current Trends in Theory and Research* (Vol. 1). New York: Academic Press, pp. 23–49.

Tellegen, A. (1985) 'Structures of mood and personality and their relevance to assessing anxiety, with an emphasis on self-report', in A.H. Tuma and J.D. Maser (eds), *Anxiety and the Anxiety Disorders*. Hillsdale, NJ: Lawrence Erlbaum Associates, pp. 681–706.

Tellegen, A. and Atkinson, G. (1974) 'Openness to absorbing and self-altering experiences ("absorption"), a trait related to hypnotic susceptibility', *Journal of Abnormal Psychology*, 83(3): 268–77.

Terracciano, A., Costa, P.T. Jr. and McCrae, R.R. (2006) 'Personality plasticity after age 30', *Personality and Social Psychology Bulletin*, 32(8): 999–1009.

Wiggins, J.S. (1979) 'A psychological taxonomy of trait-descriptive terms: The interpersonal domain', *Journal of Personality and Social Psychology*, 37(3): 395–412.

Wiggins, J.S. and Pincus, A.L. (1989) 'Conceptions of personality disorders and dimensions of personality', *Psychological Assessment: A Journal of Consulting and Clinical Psychology*, 1(4): 305–16.

10

The Eysenck Personality Measures: Fifty Years of Scale Development

Adrian Furnham, Sybil B.G. Eysenck and Donald H. Saklofske

INTRODUCTION

It is difficult to imagine the problems faced by psychologists wanting to measure personality 100 or even 60 years ago. A visit to PAN, PsycINFO on the web, or to the Buros Mental Measurement Yearbooks and the many psychology journals that focus on assessment (e.g. *Psychological Assessment*, *Assessment*), and one is offered a plethora of psychological tests including many measuring personality. These personality measures range from psychometrically and empirically sophisticated and lengthy questionnaires and inventories to simple checklists of a few items. Some measures date back to the early and middle part of the last century, but most that are still in common use by psychologists are post-1980s tests. It is probably not an exaggeration to suggest that there are hundreds if not thousands of tests available to measure normal personality functioning, let alone the personality descriptions found in scales tapping psychopathology (e.g. MMPI-2). What is most

apparent is that these scales differ enormously in their theoretical and psychometric rigour including the published research that supports their clinical use.

Prior to the end of the Second World War there were very few personality measures. Of course there were some projective techniques (e.g. Szondi test, the well-known Rorschach Inkblot test first introduced in the early 1920s) that were used by psychoanalytically oriented practitioners. However, personality assessment based on objective measures including the use of questionnaires and inventories was not so much a part of the psychological practices and theories of the day during the first half of the twentieth century. The measurement of intelligence was progressing from early Galton tests (that showed little correlation with any behaviour of interest to psychologists) to the first Binet tests in 1905 and then the Wechsler tests beginning with the Wechlser–Bellevue in 1939. However, only a few isolated papers and journals that have been rediscovered (Deary, 1996) suggest that personality assessment might be approached in a similar way. Although it may be claimed that Woodsworth's Personal Data Sheet, published in 1917, was the first published personality measure, the idea and impetus for the psychometrically valid measurement of theoretically based and empirically supported personality descriptions was to come sometime later. There is likely to be agreement from the majority of psychologists that much of the credit for the development of modern personality tests focuses on two London Schools. University College London trained personality theorists who were not only to 'spar' on issues of personality theory for well over 30 years, but were to develop tests that are still in use today. Professor Raymond B. Cattell and Professor Hans J. Eysenck very much shaped psychology in general, and more specifically personality measurement and the applications of their tests in both clinical and educational contexts. A recent four-volume series entitled *The Psychology of Individual Differences* began with this dedication.

This compendium is dedicated to the memory of two of the most highly respected and cited psychologists of the twentieth century – Professor Hans J. Eysenck and Professor Raymond B. Cattell. Both prodigious men made a profound and lasting contribution to the psychology of individual differences. Each was an exemplary scientist, humanitarian and mentor. (Boyle and Saklofske, 2004)

This chapter will describe the history, theoretical underpinnings and psychometric properties of the various Eysenckian tests developed, modified and extended by Professor Hans Eysenck and Dr Sybil B.G. Eysenck. A number of these, particularly the Eysenck Personality Questionnaire (EPQ, EPQ-R) (Eysenck and Eysenck, 1975) are still used in both research and clinical settings. One testament to the popularity and use of this test are the citation counts and references in journal articles. There are five major Eysenckian measures. At the beginning of 2006 their citation count stands at:

1 Maudsley Personality Inventory (MPQ) (Eysenck, 1959): 750

2 Eysenck Personality Inventory (EPI) (Eysenck and Eysenck, 1964a): 950
3 Eysenck Personality Questionnaire (EPQ) (Eysenck and Eysenck, 1975): 2,600
4 Eysenck Personality Questionnaire-Revised (EPQ-R) (Eysenck and Eysenck, 1991): 800
5 Eysenck Personality Profiler (EPPI) (Eysenck and Wilson, 1991): 55

TEST LONGEVITY, POPULARITY AND USAGE

Before beginning a discussion of the various personality questionnaires created by Professor Eysenck, and especially those developed in collaboration with Dr Sybil Eysenck, it would seem relevant to address the question of why a particular model of personality and the measures that are derived from it would achieve a certain status and longevity. In spite of what we may wish to think as research and applied psychological scientists, it is somewhat naive to believe that test usage is only a function of sound theoretical and research underpinnings and psychometric qualities of the test. There are many measures that appear under the personality assessment rubric that have little empirical support, but still are often included in research and client reports. In fact, a search on what now appears to be the most common forum for obtaining information, 'the Web', yields lengthy lists of personality measures including some that 'mimic' Eysenck's 'Super Three' factors (extraversion, neuroticism, psychoticism) or the 'Big Five' trait description (extraversion, neuroticism, conscientiousness, agreeableness, openness to experience) so often linked with the work of Digman (1997), Goldberg (1993) and Costa and McCrae (1992b).

There are various factors which lead to test popularity and usage and include the marketing power of test publishers and current fashion. Another factor related to testing is quite simply cost effectiveness. While research psychologists are certainly aware of the impact of method variance, and well-trained practicing psychologists (e.g. clinical and school psychologists) endorse a multiple method approach to collecting information about clients (e.g. tests, history, interview, observation), it should also be noted that Meyer et al. (2001) concluded that the best tests in psychology are as good as the best tests in medicine. Finally, high-profile cases of success or failure of organisations (e.g. industry, education) using tests can have a significant effect on the use of tests. Certainly the use of intelligence tests has shown a vulnerability to this kind of situation (e.g. court cases, government legislation) in the US. As a consequence, newspapers and magazines frequently cover stories about psychological testing thereby increasing debate about both the psychometric properties and usefulness of tests. Indeed, there are now well-known and well-rehearsed arguments for and against the use of tests in many different applied settings. Unfortunately, many of these are more based on beliefs and myth than 'the facts'. The use of psychological tests, outside the narrow world of the research laboratory, is dependent on a number of common beliefs. Furnham (2005) has listed common objections against as well as arguments for, the use of psychometric tests in applied settings (clinical, educational and organisational). Some objections to the use of personality tests include:

- Many of these tests can be faked.
- Some people do not have sufficient self-insight to report on their own feelings and behaviour.
- Tests are unreliable; temporary factors such as anxiety, boredom, weariness or ill-health can lead people to give different answers on different occasions.
- Tests may lack validity as they do not measure what they purport to measure and, equally, the scores do not predict performance.
- Tests measure all sorts of dimensions of behaviour, but not necessarily those crucial to the information needed.
- Respondents have to be sufficiently literate or articulate to accurately complete; familiarity with tests and with test jargon can impact results.
- Test norms may be very extensive in some cases but limited in others, at least for the populations that schools or companies want to test.
- A frequent claim is that tests are unfair and biased in favour of particular groups. It is up to the user to know whom the test has been standardised on and if this is an appropriate comparison group.
- Interpretation of the tests takes skill, insight and experience. Without appropriately trained personnel, test misuse is certainly a high possibility.
- Freedom of information legislation may mean that candidates can see and perhaps challenge the scores themselves, the way scores are interpreted or the decisions made on them. But if a test has been inappropriately or unfairly used with a client, then the situation must be corrected and prevented from happening in future instances.
- As tests of both ability and personality become well known, potential clients may be able to obtain copies resulting in test performances that have more to do with preparation and practice than actual ability.

These criticisms in some instances, and considering some tests, are more than justified. In the process of addressing the criticisms, the responses may also in fact present a strong case for personality and other testing. Examples are:

- Tests such as the EPQ and EPQ-R provide quantitative information, which means individuals can more easily be compared on the same criteria.
- With data-based records, a person's development can be tracked over time. Test results in an individual's file can actually demonstrate if, and by how much, the tests were predictive of later work-related or achievement behaviour. Further, such tests allow researchers to assess the stability of major personality traits over shorter and longer time periods.
- Tests give explicit and specific results on temperament and ability rather than the vague, ambiguous, coded platitudes so often found in references.
- Tests introduce an element of fairness because they eliminate bias, false evidence and limit favouritism in decision making where specific and measurable criteria are established.
- Tests that are derived from a particular theory and are comprehensive may cover all the basic dimensions of personality and ability from which other behaviour patterns derive. The EPQ and EPQ-R tap the three crucial facets of human personality described by Eysenck, namely extraversion–introversion, neuroticism–stability, and tender vs. tough-mindedness. E and N are found in other major trait models including the Big Five and Cattell's 16PF.

- Tests are scientific in that they are soundly empirically based on theoretical foundations. Besides strong theoretical grounding and psychometric properties, many of the current personality measures are supported by a wealth of studies. E and N are especially powerful predictors of a wide range of human behaviours and this is likely why they hold such a key position in trait personality theory and measurement.

The Eysenckian measures have been used in a wide range of applied settings from education to industry. Initially, Professor Eysenck's research and earlier questionnaires such as the MPI seemed most clearly linked with clinical psychology, but later the sphere of interest and application expanded to educational psychology and more recently with organisational psychology.

WHAT CHARACTERISES EYSENCKIAN MEASURES?

The key debate is not whether E and N are major personality traits, although there is still somewhat less consensus regarding P. Nor is there debate regarding the need to carefully and accurately measure personality traits. Rather the issue that should be addressed revolves around two interconnected points; namely, are the Eysenck personality questionnaires psychometrically as good if not better than other measures assessing E, N and P (or proxies for these trait names), and is a questionnaire that does assess only these three traits versus these three plus C, O and A, or the larger spectrum of primary personality traits found in, say, the 16PF of relevance in both research and applied settings? Examining the main Eysenckian measures, still in wide use today in this context, it is possible to identify at least five salient points supporting their continued use.

Parsimony

The well-known PEN model initially described by Eysenck (1952, 1960b, 1970)

provides the theoretical underpinnings of the EPQ which was, and possibly is, the most parsimonious personality model and resulting measure. It compares nicely with the 16 dimensions of Cattell's 16PF or the Big Five, Six or Seven. In some ways, focusing on second-order factors is akin to the role of 'g' in the measurement of intelligence. Whilst some psychologists have argued through the bandwidth-fidelity debate for finer grain analysis at the facet (primary and lower-order) factor level, to some extent the Eysencks resisted this trend although the creation of measures such as the I_6 and I_7 did provide an assessment of several key variables including venturesomeness, impulsivity and empathy. More recently, there has been a focus on primary factors and their acolytes have started working with the EPP (Jackson et al., 2000). There has also been considerable interest in the EPP and the facet/primary factor level of analysis (Jackson et al., 2000) recently. While the Eysencks always measured super-factors or traits (i.e. the Gigantic Three), some researchers have argued that a finer grained level of analysis (i.e. facet level) enables one to understand the nature of processes better (Petrides et al., 2003).

Of course, the position espoused by both Professor Eysenck and Dr Sybil Eysenck is that the PEN dimensional system is necessary, but also sufficient, to describe human personality functioning and individual differences. It is also fair to say that while Eysenck has been the major architect of the PEN model, other prominent psychologists such as Cloninger, Gray, Revelle, Tellegen and Zuckerman have recognised in their own way, the significance of these three super-factors (Eysenck, 1990b; Revelle, 1997).

Explanation of process

More than any other test developers in the twentieth century, the Eysencks were not contented to describe and categorise traits: they sought to escape tautology by explanation. Thus we have the first counter-intuitive theory of arousal to explain extraversion.

Hans Eysenck showed nearly a decade before the publication of the EPQ (Eysenck, 1947 (1998), 1952, 1953) that his work and interests were solidly grounded in the biological basis of personality and he set about exploring that for the next 30 years (Eysenck, 1960a, 1960b, 1967 (2006), 1982b; Eysenck et al., 1989). More than any other personality theorist, he was concerned with describing and explaining the mechanisms and processes which account for systematic individual differences. Eysenck's theory and model of individual differences is fully described in an earlier chapter by O'Connor and will not be repeated here; only a thumbnail sketch will be provided to provide the context for the development of the various personality measures developed by both Hans and Sybil Eysenck and colleagues.

Extraversion is perhaps the best known of the three major personality dimensions that defined Eysenck's model and in some ways is at the 'heart' of the theory. Eysenck's cortical arousal theory of extraversion has been extensively described in numerous books (e.g. Eysenck, 1973), book chapters and articles (e.g. Saklofske and Eysenck, 1994). Revelle (1997) succinctly and clearly summarised the classic Eysenckian arousal theory that underpins the theory of extraversion. The basic assumptions were: (1) introverts are more aroused than extraverts; (2) stimulation increases arousal; (3) arousal related to performance is curvilinear; (4) the optimal level of arousal for a task is negatively related to task difficulty; and (5) arousal related to hedonic tone is curvilinear. Assumption (1) was based upon many studies associating EPI-E with (low) physiological arousal (Eysenck, 1967 (2006)). Assumptions (3) and (4) were based upon the Yerkes–Dodson law (Yerkes and Dodson, 1908) and the subsequent support for it by Broadhurst (1959). Assumption (5) was founded on Berlyne's discussion of curiosity and arousal (1960). Based upon assumptions (1)–(4), it can be predicted that introverts should perform better than extraverts under low levels of stimulation but should perform less well at high levels of stimulation. Similarly, assumptions (1), (2), and (5) lead to the prediction that

extraverts should seek out more stimulation than introverts.' (Revelle, 1997: 199)

Neuroticism is based on activation thresholds in the sympathetic nervous system or visceral brain. This is the part of the brain that is responsible for the fight-or-flight response in the face of danger. High N persons have a low activation threshold and when confronted with even mild stressors or anxiety producing situations, will experience negative affect and become easily upset. These manifestations can range from physiological changes in heart rate, blood pressure, cold hands, sweating and muscular tension to feelings of apprehension and nervousness to the full effects of fear and anxiety. In contrast to high N or emotionally unstable and labile persons, emotionally stable people have a much higher activation threshold, and thus will experience negative affect only when confronted by very major stressors. They appear much calmer relative to the high N person in situations that could be described as anxiety inducing or pressure laden. A full description of neurosis is provided by Eysenck in the 1977 book *You and Neurosis*.

Psychoticism, the most controversial and debated of Eysenck's three super-factors, was most fully described by Eysenck and Eysenck (1976) in the book *Psychoticism as a Dimension of Personality*. High P scorers are more predisposed to psychotic episodes, but also tend to manifest a higher probability of engaging in aggression and demonstrating the kind of cold, tough-mindedness that characterises psychopathy and persons more likely to engage in crime (Eysenck, 1977). While somewhat less fully described and with less empirical support than either E or N, the research that has been done has indicated that P also has a biological basis (e.g. increased testosterone levels).

Experimentation

Hans Eysenck was rigorously schooled in the experimental tradition at a time when behaviourism triumphed. He believed, like Cronbach (1957), that it was essential that the correlational (individual difference) and experimental branches of psychology unite, so that personality effects were not treated as error variance (Howarth and Eysenck, 1968). This basic premise was the foundational underpinning for the creation of both the International Society for the Study of Individual Differences and also the official journal, *Personality and Individual Differences*. The Eysencks had little time for the approach found in the DSM manual revision where politics rather than empirical findings determined categorisation.

Wide application

The Eysencks were both psychological pioneers and risk takers; they were eager to extend their research programme to look at the significance of personality functioning in areas as disparate as sex (Eysenck and Wilson, 1979), crime (Eysenck and Nias, 1978; Eysenck and Gudjonsson, 1989), the paranormal and astrology (Eysenck and Sargent, 1982; Eysenck and Nias, 1982), health (Eysenck, 1980), intelligence (Eysenck, 1982a), therapy (Eysenck and Martin, 1988), business, education, art and music, and to further examine the role of genetics and culture (Eysenck, 1982b; Eysenck et al., 1989; Saklofske and S.B.G. Eysenck, 1988 (1998)), as they impact and shape personality. They believed that individual differences were systematically and predictably present in all aspects of human functioning. To many, particularly favouring a sociological and more environmental only perspective, this was radical indeed.

Continuous improvement and development

For nearly 40 years the Eysencks have engaged in a systematic research programme to improve, update and validate their personality measures. Because the scales have been so widely used in research worldwide they

have been subject to detailed, but at times dismissive, scrutiny by many people. Their observations and research studies, particularly those emphasising a cross-cultural perspective, have suggested various improvements. Thus, over time, questionnaire items have been removed, changed, and added and new scales have been developed. It has not been commercial or forces of fashion that have led this to occur but rather empirical studies.

THE TAXONOMY OF PERSONALITY

At present the Eysenckian model still has three – and only three – super-factors in the PEN model (psychoticism, extraversion, neuroticism). Eysenck was quite convinced that these three conceptual and descriptive categories are necessary and sufficient to describe an individual's personality. Of course, he was the first to be heard to say that his investment in this theory was more to stimulate research that would lead to a comprehensive and replicable description of personality than to simply commit to an a priori view that his theory was in fact correct.

These three super-factors of E, N and P are made up of primary factors that could be thought of as habits. Thus anxiety-proneness, obsessiveness and hypochondriasis are components of neuroticism and reflect stable habitual patterns of thinking, seeing and feeling. These primary factors are made up of very specific definable behaviours which make up individual questionnaire items. While various situational influences and states may cause variability in the behaviours when these are aggregated, it is noticeable that traits are stable over time and consistent across situations. In this sense, the Eysencks would support the fundamental tenets of trait theory as clearly described by Deary and Matthews (1993). First, *the primary causality of traits* argues that it is the traits that cause behaviour, and although feedback mechanisms occur, they are less important. Second, *the inner locus of traits* reflects the idea that traits sufficiently describe the central, core qualities of individuals.

The past decade or more has witnessed a serious dispute between the pro-Eysenckians who support the Gigantic Three Eysenckian system and those who support the Big Five. The two positions were clearly debated between proponents in conferences and journal articles. For those who were so fortunate to witness the debates between Hans Eysenck and Paul Costa, and others such as Lou Goldberg (e.g. ISSID conference, Oxford University, 1991), these were truly akin to the 'clash of the titans'. While the debate was always intense, each 'proponent' bringing out more data to support their position, it was always so respectful of each person's work and commitment as a scientist.

Costa and McCrae (1992a) summarised the evidence for the validity of the five-factor model by stating the 'four ways the five factors are basic'. First, that longitudinal and cross-sectional studies have shown five robust factors to be enduring behavioural dispositions; second, traits associated with the five factors emerge from different personality systems and from studies of natural language (i.e. lexicon); third, the five factors are found in different age, sex, race and language groups, and fourth, heritability studies demonstrate some biological basis for each of the five factors. They have subsequently added evidence of cross-cultural similarities in the ageing trajectories of the five factors and asserted that the five factors are a human universal, with the traits being primarily genetically influenced.

H.J. Eysenck (1991, 1992) rigorously criticised the five-factor models of personality. He suggested that the criteria set out by Costa and McCrae for accepting the five-factor model are necessary but not sufficient for determining the important dimensions of personality. He argued that agreeableness and conscientiousness are primary-level traits which are both facets of his higher-order factor psychoticism. Additionally, he contended that openness forms a part of extraversion and (low) conscientiousness a part of neuroticism. Thus O, A and C were primary, not super-factors. He also pointed to the meta-analysis of factor analytic studies carried out by Royce and Powell (1983) which indicated a three-factor model similar to his own. Eysenck suggested that the five-factor model lacks a nomological or theoretical network and is, therefore, arbitrary; he contrasted this with the theoretical basis of his psychoticism dimension which has roots in mental illness phenomena. As ever, data were carefully marshalled to support a clear theory.

Eysenck (1992) always believed that it is the nomological network in which a dimension is embedded that provides its psychometric validity. This network must specify its biological and psychophysiological bases, its cultural invariance, its relationship to social behaviour and psychological illness. Without doubt Eysenck's main substantial contribution to personality research was the formulation of a robust theory of the biological bases of the E, N and P personality dimensions (Eysenck, 1967).

Matthews et al. have attempted an evaluation of this debate:

> We may conclude that trait psychology is in a healthy state, with signs of growing agreement on the structure of human personality. However, although some old combatants may have signed an armistice, there remain significant conflicts between partisans of the various perspectives described in this chapter. With this proviso, a cautious view of the current consensus is as follows. Extraversion and Neuroticism stimulate no detectable controversy; they are almost universally represented in psychometric personality systems. Conscientiousness and Agreeableness are the objects of a little more doubt, and a higher-order factor such as Psychoticism might challenge their status. Additionally, different systems have rotated these dimensions slightly differently to give them altered emphases. It might be argued that the Gigantic Three and Big Five simply reflect different levels of description, and so are not fundamentally incompatible. The most problematic issue is the status of Openness. There is some dispute over whether there is a distinction between dimensions of Intellect/Culture and Openness, and whether Openness should be ranked as a 'Big Five' factor at all. It is unlikely that such issues will be resolved entirely from psychometric studies. (2003: 37)

THE FOUR EYSENCK QUESTIONNAIRES

The history of the development of the four main Eysenckian personality measures is clearly told in the introduction of the EPQ Manual (Eysenck and Eysenck, 1975):

The Eysenck Personality Questionnaire (EPQ) is a development of various earlier personality questionnaires; it differs from the latest of these (the EPI or Eysenck Personality Inventory) by including an additional scale, and hopefully by having made certain improvements in the other scales. The first questionnaire in this series was the Maudsley Medical Questionnaire; this was a forty-item measure of N (neuroticism or emotionality). This was followed by the MPI (Maudsley Personality Inventory), which contained scales for the measurement of N and E (extraversion–introversion). The MPI (Eysenck, 1959) was in turn followed by the EPI (Eysenck and Eysenck, 1964a); this added a 'Lie' (L) scale to measure dissimulation, and provided two alternative forms (A and B) for repeated testing of the same population. In addition, the EPI was written in somewhat simplified English, in order to make it easier for less highly educated subjects to understand the questions without having to have their meaning explained to them. The EPI was also designed in order to provide certain psychometrically desirable improvements over the MPI; e.g. the dimensions of E and N were completely independent in the EPI, whereas they had been slightly correlated in the MPI. Also, the reliability of the EPI was somewhat higher. Corresponding scales on the two inventories do of course correlate so highly that they must be assumed to measure identical dimensions of personality, and for most practical purposes they are interchangeable; similarly the E and N scales of the present questionnaire are so similar to the corresponding scales of the other questionnaires that whatever has been discovered about correlates of E and N with the use of the older scales must be assumed to apply with equal force to the new scales. The main advantage of the new scale is the introduction of a new variable, which we have labelled P for psychoticism, although this psychiatric term should not be taken to imply that the scales are not useful for the measurement of personality traits in normal persons. The word 'psychoticism', as we shall explain presently in some detail, simply refers to an underlying personality trait present in varying degrees in all persons; if present in marked degree, it predisposes a person to the development of psychiatric abnormalities. However, the possession of such a predisposition is a far cry from actual psychosis, and only a very small proportion of people with high P scores are likely to develop a psychosis in the course of their lives. For many practical purposes and certainly for discussing the results of the inventory with lay persons, it may be useful to omit psychiatric terms like 'neuroticism' and 'psychoticism' altogether, and refer instead to 'emotionality' and 'tough-mindedness'. In this Manual, these more acceptable terms will be used as synonymous with N and P. (1975: 5)

MAUDSLEY PERSONALITY INVENTORIES

Over the years, Eysenck published various (very) short measures of the E and N constructs. Eysenck (1956) published a paper describing two 24-item questionnaires measuring neuroticism and extraversion and followed this with another 12-item scale (Eysenck, 1958) that presented psychometric data on 1,600 individuals. This work culminated in the Maudsley Personality Inventory (MPI) that was intended to measure the two orthogonal dimensions of introversion–extraversion and neuroticism–stability. Despite it being developed almost 50 years ago, researchers still use the MPI and papers continue to appear using it as the central, usually only measure of personality (Akiyoshi et al, 1998). Indeed recent studies still report findings related to the discriminate and predictive validity of the MPI (Kasai et al., 2004).

One question remains: Why, after all this time, do researchers use the MPI and not any of the Eysenckian instruments that effectively replaced it? There are probably three (related) answers to this question. The first likely reflects a lesser emphasis placed by some on the psychometric qualities of an older instrument such as the MPI. For example, areas such as psychiatry tend to be less aware of the critical aspects of test construction (reliability, standardisation and norm tables) and its use, and may not have been updated on more recent developments because this is far removed from their area of expertise. Second, the MPI seems to be still used in non-English speaking countries (like Japan) although the EPQ has been translated into Japanese (Iwawaki et al., 1980). Third, the MPI still does a very good job at measuring E and N, the two core dimensions of personality, although what is lacking are contemporary norms and more detailed and reported analysis of the psychometric integrity of this measure

EYSENCK PERSONALITY INVENTORY (EPI)

In the EPI Manual, Eysenck and Eysenck (1964a, 1964b) explained the rationale and advantages of the EPI over the MPI:

'The Eysenck Personality Inventory (EPI) is a development of the Maudsley Personality Inventory (MPI – Eysenck, 1959; Knapp, 1962). Like the parent instrument, it sets out to measure two major dimensions of personality, extraversion and neuroticism. It is sufficiently similar to the MPI and correlates sufficiently highly with it, to make it almost certain that the experimental findings reported for the older instrument will also apply to the newer; nevertheless, the improvements incorporated in the EPI make it more useful from many practical points of view. These advantages are as follows:

1   The EPI consists of two parallel forms, thus making possible retesting after experimental treatment without interference from memory factors.
2   The EPI items have been carefully reworded so as to make them understandable even by subjects of low intelligence and/or education; the MPI items were found to be rather too difficult with subjects of this type.
3   The correlation between Extraversion and Neuroticism on the MPI was small but nevertheless marginally significant; suitable item selection has caused it to disappear in the EPI.
4   The EPI contains a Lie Scale which may be used to eliminate subjects showing 'desirability response set'; no such scale was contained in the published form of the MPI.
5   The retest reliability of the EPI is somewhat higher than that of the MPI even after periods of several months it is still in excess of 0.85.
6   Direct evidence is available of the validity of the EPI as a descriptive instrument of the behaviour manifestations of personality.' (1964a, 1964b: 3)

Both form A and B of the EPI had 57 questions that were responded to by 'yes' or 'no'. The manual reports excellent test–retest reliability of between 0.81 and 0.97 for 9 months to a year. The split half reliability of the scales ranged from 0.74 to 0.91. Correlations between the dimensions in normal, neurotic and psychotic populations was reassuringly low at less than $r = 0.10$ except for form B which rose to $r = -0.22$ for psychotics. There was a discussion of the 18-item Lie Scale which evidenced low scores (< 3) but impressive test–retest reliability of around $r = 0.70$. Impressive norms are provided on 'normal' groups as diverse as teachers, postmen and telephone operators. There were also norms for female prisoners, a hospitalised alcoholic group, two psychotic groups (depressive, schizophrenic) and four neurotic groups (anxiety, obsessional, hysteric and mixed). There was no systematic evidence of age, sex or social class correlates of the EPI. Interestingly well before its time, the manual ends with what now looks like an enormously complex computer programme for scoring the EPI.

As often noted with the ever-practical Eysencks, they developed a short version of the EPI. It was comprised of 12-items drawn from the 57-item Eysenck Personality Inventory, (Eysenck and Eysenck, 1964a, 1964b) recalling that the EPI was, in turn, created through a series of factor analyses of various sets of items of the former Maudsley Personality Inventory (Eysenck, 1959). Items were selected on the basis of extensive factor analyses of the 108 items considered for inclusion in the 57-item EPI. The 12-item EPI also yielded measures of the two major dimensions of personality, extraversion and neuroticism (6 items on each).

Correlations of the short scales with the long are as follows: 0.82 for extraversion and 0.79 for neuroticism. The correlation between the short extraversion and neuroticism scales is –0.05.

Advantages of the EPI over the MPI include the careful rewording of the questions so as to make them understandable for subjects of low intelligence and/or education, and the retest reliability of the EPI is somewhat higher than that of the MPI. Even after periods of several months it is in excess of 0.85. In all, the short form of the EPI permitted psychologists to quickly and accurately assess two of the most recognisable and studied personality factors described in trait theory. In many ways, it was these efforts that has resulted in the trend for many measures of both personality, intelligence and also various conative factors such as motivation to appear in both longer and shorter forms; the former being more relevant to differential diagnosis and a fuller and in-depth coverage of both the 'general factor' (e.g. extraversion) and possibly first-order factors or subscales (e.g. sociability, venturesomeness) while the short versions lend themselves to serving as brief indicators of personality and as screeners when a quick estimate is required.

EYSENCK–WITHERS QUESTIONNAIRE, 1965

A personality questionnaire for subjects between IQ 50 and 80 was standardised and published in 1965. However the MPI and EPI scales were, by then, well established and this measure was less often and less widely used in both research and clinical practice.

EYSENCK PERSONALITY QUESTIONNAIRE – (EPQ) (EYSENCK AND EYSENCK, 1975)

Without doubt the most important and most often used of the Eysenckian measures was and still is the EPQ. There are two somewhat similar manuals for the EPQ. The 1975, 47-page manual describes both the 'Junior' and 'Adult' versions of the EPQ (Eysenck and Eysenck 1975) and the 1991 manual further includes the EPQ-R, EPQ-R-short scale, addiction and criminality scales as well as details

of the Impulsiveness Venturesomeness and Empathy Scales (Eysenck and Eysenck, 1991).

Naturally because the major change between the EPI and the EPQ was the addition of the P (psychoticism) Scale, much of the manual is dedicated to its description and validation. The latter is described primarily in terms of criterion groups and construct validity. In fact, the results of at least 16 empirical studies demonstrate that P is significantly associated with other human factors as varied as drug addiction and venereal disease to reaction-time speed and vulnerability and impulsiveness. The 1991 manual quotes many studies published subsequent to 1975 that provide evidence for the validity and reliability of the P factor such as its factorial stability and its biological basis. Thus studies were quoted which showed a statistically significant and theoretically predictable series of correlations between P and aggression, delusions and hallucinations, latent inhibition, reaction time, arousal, conditioning, visual perception, stimulus and response, uncertainty, sexual behaviour, extra punitiveness, drug dependence, health as well as social interests and occupational choices.

The manual also describes the Lie Scale that is considered to be more than merely a measure of dissimulation but rather reflects some stable personality factor in its own right. Whatever else, it can be effectively used to raise concerns about the accuracy of the self-report descriptions of E, N and P. Test–retest reliabilities were reported for all four scales and eight populations. Most were between 0.80 and 0.90. Similarly, internal consistency (alpha) coefficients were impressive again and mainly in the 0.80s although the P scale did not quite achieve the more acceptable reliabilities observed for E and N. Norms are provided (with an $n > 3000$) by age group and sex because of slight but noticeable trends. Norms are also provided for over 50 occupational groups from accountants to architects and unskilled labourers to lecturers. As these personality dimensions are considered to be the very traits that underlie both normal and abnormal human behaviour, norms are also published on eight 'abnormal groups' including alcohol and drug addicts, prisoners and personality disordered people as well as psychotics and neurotics. Intercorrelations between the four scales did however indicate that the dimensions may not be truly orthogonal.

Data are also provided for the Junior EPQ, designed for children and adolescents. Most studies suggest that the scale works quite well for children in the 7–8 year age range and above (e.g. S.B.G. Eysenck and Saklofske, 1983). Reliabilities tend to be lower and inter-correlations between scales higher than in the adult version. Further, there is some, albeit modest validity evidence. Like the EPQ, the junior version was quickly adapted for use in other countries (see Saklofske and Eysenck, 1988 (1998)).

In 1990, *Current Contents* (May 28th) featured the EPQ as a citation classic. Fifteen years after it was published it was cited 770 times. Hans Eysenck was invited to write a short reflective piece on the origin of the EPQ. He noted:

I started work on personality during the war, working at the Mill Hill Emergency Hospital for psychiatric war casualties. As an experimental psychologist, I was very suspicious of personality inventories, because of their apparent subjectivity, the contradictory results that had been reported, and the poor methodology that characterised their use. However, when I constructed the Maudsley Medical Questionnaire after my transfer to the Maudsley, as a measure of neuroticism (N), I found it so useful, practically and theoretically, that I became convinced of the usefulness of such instruments as long as they were developed by the experimental testing of deductions from a theoretical framework and were constructed in line with the best traditions of psychometrics. The original inventory was never published independently, but later on I published the Maudsley Personality Inventory, which added an extraversion scale to the N scale. This inventory was successful, but it needed improvement and together with my wife, Sybil, I set about to produce the Eysenck Personality Inventory (EPI), which added a lie (dissimulation) scale and appeared in two forms, A and B, to allow easier comparisons and retests. There was a third major dimension of personality that I had originally postulated, but I did not think that this would be accessible through questionnaires. Sybil disagreed and was proved right;

together we produced the Eysenck Personality Questionnaire (EPQ), which added a psychoticism (P) scale and completed my original plan. This scale had some psychometric weaknesses and has since been improved to produce the EPQ-R, which will presently be commercially available.

The EPQ has been used in translation in 35 countries all over the world, from Uganda to the USSR, from mainland China to the US, and has been found to give practically identical factor solutions when analysed. Its use has grown with the increasing support given to the underlying theory by many experimental studies; also useful were demonstrations of its predictive power in relation to education, criminality, accident proneness, mental disease and many other applied fields. Its development owes much to Sybil Eysenck, who has been mainly responsible for the successful transition from EPI to EPQ. It is unique in being part of a hard nosed, testable theory; as Kurt Lewin said: 'There is nothing as practical as a good theory!' Maybe that is why these inventories have been cited and used so frequently.

One of the big changes between the EPI and the EPQ, in addition to the new third factor of psychoticism, was the 'migration' of many items measuring impulsivity from extraversion to psychoticism. In a celebrated study, Rocklin and Revelle (1981) examined the change in extraversion measurement as the EPI was developed into the EPQ. The EPI 59 extraversion items were a mix (a shotgun wedding) of roughly half and half items measuring sociability and those measuring impulsivity. The EPQ was thus seen as an attempt to 'purify' extraversion as a measure primarily of sociability. While impulsivity and sociability are closely empirically related they can be seen as distant constructs.

More importantly Rocklin and Revelle (1981) pointed out that these two constructs are differentially related to specific behaviours. Thus impulsivity, but not sociability, is related to vigilance decrements, caffeine-induced stress, driver safety and conditionability. More importantly, they argue that extraversion as measured by the EPQ is no longer an adequate measure of the arousal theory of extraversion. Thus studies using the EPQ and EPI measure of extraversion may indeed yield different results.

Revelle (1997) noted that many researchers found a different pattern of correlations for the extraversion scale using the EPI and EPQ versions. He noted also that the Eysencks, rather than giving up on the concept of impulsivity, actually developed multi-dimensional but narrower more specific measures of impulsivity (Eysenck et al., 1985c; Saklofske and Eysenck, 1983).

THE REVISED AND SHORTENED EPQ

Despite extensive research into and a robust defence of the Eysenckian third dimension of psychoticism, it continued to receive criticism (Eysenck and Eysenck, 1976; Claridge, 1981). Eysenck et al. (1985b) described three 'major faults' with the P scale: the (comparative) low internal reliabilities of the P scale (suggesting the lack of theoretical coherence) in the items; the low range of scoring, indicating means of around 3 despite there being 21 items; and related to this, a grossly skewed positive distribution. Hence, they set about revising and validating the EPQ.

The new EPQ (R) has 100 items, 32 measuring P, 23 E, 24 N and 21 L. Interestingly, all N items were scored 'yes' (i.e. had no reverse items) while 20 of the 23 items for E were also scored 'yes' (in the direction of E). Around half of the P items, and one third of the L items were scored 'yes'.

Because the N and E scales had demonstrated theoretical and psychometric integrity, the focus was less on them but rather on the P scale. In all 19 of the original EPQ items were retained, 6 dropped and 13 new items written. The old E scale (from the EPQ) received only two new items and the N scale one new item. The Lie Scale remained unchanged. There is also a short EPQ(R) version with 12 items, from each scale, including the Lie Scale, for a total of 48 items.

The distribution of the new P scale reflecting skew and kurtosis still shows a serious (albeit reduced) skew, which may be due to the observation that high P scorers, being uncooperative, do not complete or discard rather than complete questionnaires, thus leaving more low than high scores available on P.

EYSENCK PERSONALITY PROFILER (EYSENCK AND WILSON, 1991)

The EPP was devised to measure traits at both the domain or *super-factor* level (the Big Three P, E and N) but also at the *primary* factor or facet level. It is not clear what motivated the authors to construct this measure, which neither author seemed particularly eager to publicise in the academic literature. It has been suggested that a software publisher, on reading the earlier book entitled *Know Your Own Personality* (Eysenck and Wilson, 1975), was eager to develop an early online measure and used the questionnaire in the book.

The EPP was constructed for use in work-related settings and most of its applications focus on organisational psychology issues such as job satisfaction (Furnham et al., 2002) or are based on employee samples (e.g. Jackson et al., 2000). However, the inventory can also be used in non-occupational settings (e.g. Francis et al., 2001; Wilson and Jackson, 1994). The EPP is a measure of normal adult personality, but, like other similar inventories, it may prove useful in the investigation of psychological disorders (e.g. Bienvenu et al., 2001).

The Eysencks always favoured the parsimony of the three-factor level as noted in the EPI and EPQ. However, some psychologists in both the research and practices areas prefer to describe traits at the primary or facet level much as some psychologists argue about the meaningfulness of cognitive ability measures at the level of full scale IQ, factor scores and subtest scores. Further, various researchers like Dr. C Jackson who holds copyright and sales rights has worked consistently on improving the measure (Jackson et al., 2000). This has included developing a short version (Petrides et al., 2003). The measure has also attracted serious psychometric investigation (Costa and McCrae, 1995; Petrides et al., 2003).

The long version of the EPP consists of 440 items (questions) yielding 21 scores (7 for each of the 3 major factors) plus, if administered by questionnaire 3 other measures: dissimulation (i.e. lie), time taken (to complete the whole test) and the number of 'can't decide' responses.

The 21 traits are:

- Extraversion: activity, sociability, expressiveness, assertiveness, ambition, dogmatism and aggressiveness.
- Neuroticism: inferiority, unhappiness, anxiety, dependence, hypochondria, guilt and obsessiveness.
- Psychoticism: risk-taking, impulsivity, irresponsibility, manipulativeness, sensation seeking, tough-mindedness and practicality.
- A Lie Scale is also included.

Costa and McCrae (1995), in one of the few validity studies on the EPP, are highly critical of it. Commenting on the results reported by Eysenck et al. (1992), they state:

> Factor analyses of EPP scales in large sample of men and women (n = 982, 542, respectively) provided mixed support for the original model. A three-factor solution yielded an N factor defined by six of the seven intended scales. The P factor was defined by five of the a priori psychoticism scales, along with Expressive and Aggressive traits intended to measure E. The third factor, however, bore little resemblance to E. It was defined chiefly by Obsessive, Ambitious and Responsible, a combination that five-factor researchers would recognise as Conscientiousness. The most familiar markers of E – Active, Sociable and Assertive – defined the opposite pole of the N factor. However, a targeted rotation showed that a better fit to the theory was also consistent with the structure of the data: 17 of the 21 variables could be forced on to the intended factor, although most of the E and P variables had sustainable secondary loadings. A final point of note is that the Practical versus Reflective scale had no loading over 0.30 in either analysis. (1995: 309)

Jackson et al. (2000) responded to this critique with a similar analysis but on a much bigger and diverse sample. Little evidence was found to support Costa and McCrae's (1995) unequivocal comment that a five-factor solution fitted the data well. Confirmatory factor analysis was also used, by means of structural equation modelling, to estimate the goodness of fit of three- and five-factor models and little evidence was found to favour one solution over the other. A shorter version of the EPP, which consists of just nine scales, seemed to favour a three-factor solution. However, the authors do add two additional criticisms of the EPP:

> First, the primary scales of Neuroticism (except for N7 (Obsessiveness)) are highly correlated, suggesting that it is not necessary to measure seven scales of Neuroticism when possibly just two or three will provide the same amount of information. Secondly each item of the EPP is scored 'Yes', 'No', or 'Can't Decide'. Jackson et al. (2000) provided evidence that the 'Can't Decide' option may be chosen to relieve conflict experienced when faced with 'Yes' or 'No' choices that seem to be equally attractive or unattractive, depending on the amount of item neutrality, uncertainty, ambiguity and the situation (see Goldberg, 1993). It seems likely that this response scale is less straightforward than the test's authors probably intended. (1995: 234)

Furnham et al. (2001) explored various test correlates (e.g. concurrent validity) of the EPP. The factor structure of the EPP has been the object of several psychometric investigations, most of which involved various forms of exploratory factor analyses (EFA) (Costa and McCrae, 1995; Eysenck et al., 1992; Jackson et al., 2000). These studies have suggested that some EPP scales either measure more than one super-factor (i.e. they are 'factorially complex') or do not fit well into the Eysenckian personality hierarchy (but may fit into other hierarchies such as the Big Five; see Costa and McCrae, 1995).

Petrides et al. (2003) using structure equation modelling explored the structure of the short form of the EPP. They show the nine-factor short form to be superior to the long version. They note:

> The revised short form of the EPP constitutes an efficient instrument to measure normal adult personality on nine primary facets marking the three Eysenckian dimensions of Psychoticism, Extraversion

and Neuroticism. The structure and factor pattern of the questionnaire are largely invariant across men and women. The former tend to score higher on Psychoticism, but there seem to be no gender differences in either Extraversion or Neuroticism. There are correlations of considerable magnitude between Extraversion and the other two super-factors. (2003: 278)

Reliability data on the short form of the EPP have also been presented in several studies and are summarised in Table 10.1.

PERSONALITY STRUCTURE CROSS-CULTURALLY

Most personality theorists hypothesise that major individual difference variables such as intelligence and personality are in fact universal constructs. While they may vary in their expression (phenotype) as a function of culture and other psychosocial factors, basic traits are common across human kind. Some psychologists would also argue that the measurement of their specifically described

traits or constructs would prove universal across all countries and cultures (at all time periods) because of the universally based biological structure of personality across racial, gender and educational groups. Considerable research has been published over the years examining the genetic, biological, neurological and environmental basis (e.g. culture, ethnicity, family) of personality and has demonstrated the significant contribution of both biology and socio-cultural factors in determining and shaping the expression of intelligence and personality.

For over 20 years Sybil Eysenck published studies comparing the results of studies on adults and children using the Adult and Junior version of the EPQ. Furthermore, over years with this impressive data they set about doing multi-cultural comparative research. Thus in 1981 they summarised the results of 14 studies using just under 15,000 subjects (Eysenck and Eysenck, 1981). In 1985, they extended their analysis to 24 countries (Eysenck et al., 1985a) and in 1998 this was further extended to 34 countries (Barrett

Table 10.1   Internal consistencies for the Revised EPP-SF scales based on four previous studies

Factor and scale	Descriptive adjectives	Costa and McCrae, (1995)[b]	Eysenck et al. (1992)[a] M	Eysenck et al. (1992)[a] F	Jackson et al. (2000)[c]	Muris et al. (2000)[d]
Psychoticism						
RIS	Adventurous, daring hesitant (R)	0.71	0.69	0.68	0.66	0.69
IMP	Hurried, impetuous, careful (R)	0.79	0.75	0.75	0.75	0.76
SEN	Excitement-seeking, disinhibited, subdued (R)	0.81	0.75	0.76	0.74	0.74
Extraversion						
ACT	Energetic, fast-paced, sluggish (R)	0.83	0.75	0.77	0.71	0.74
SOC	Talkative, outgoing, reserved (R)	0.84	0.82	0.81	0.78	0.75
AMB	Competitive, hard-working, apathetic (R)	0.82	0.80	0.80	0.77	0.72
Neuroticism						
UNH	Gloomy, miserable, cheerful (R)	0.87	0.85	0.89	0.83	0.88
ANX	Nervous, worried, relaxed (R)	0.83	0.83	0.85	0.80	0.80
DEP	Helpless, vulnerable, autonomous (R)	0.63	0.75	0.77	0.73	0.71

Note: These alphas are based on studies that administered the long form of the Eysenck Personality Profiler (EPP). EPP-SF = short form of the EPP; Eysenck et al. = H.J. Eysenck, Barrett, Wilson and Jackson; Jackson et al., = Jackson, Furnham, Forde and Cotter; Muris et al. = Muris, Schmidt, Merckelbach and Rassin; RIS = risk taking; IMP = impulsivity; SEN = sensation seeking; ACT = activity; SOC = sociability; AMB = ambitiousness; UNH = unhappiness; ANX = anxiety; DEP = dependence. [a]*n* = 1,559; gender-specific data (M = males; F = females). [b]*n* = 229. [c]*n* = 655. [d]*n* = 215; Dutch data.

et al., 1998). As each national group was added so inevitably the population sample increased but more impressively so did the nature of the analysis. As mentioned before, Sybil Eysenck also published a book detailing specific studies of the Eysenck scales used in different countries with children and adolescents (Saklofske and Eysenck, 1988, 1998).

Barrett et al. (1998) argued that part of the analytic procedure used by Eysenck et al. (1985a) was inappropriate and suggested a modified version. Their analysis provides data from the countries set out below. Table 10.2 also shows the different languages that the EPQ has been successfully translated into. Furthermore, it indicates that reasonable population norms exist for these countries and thus, it became possible to do many within and between continent, race, linguistic, area comparisons many, by no means all, of which have been published.

Their conclusion was that the EPQ factors are strongly replicable across all 34 countries; that is, the original UK data can be replicated using data from any countries. It should be mentioned that cross-cultural studies and standardisations were also undertaken with the Junior EPQ in over 20 countries.

CONCLUSION

Jeffrey Gray once famously described Hans Eysenck's personality theory as akin to somebody finding St Pancras Railway Station in the jungle. The station is an extremely impressive piece of highly elaborate, complex and beautiful Victorian architecture situated in central London. What he meant was that the theory stands out dramatically from all around it. Compared to all other theories of personality from 1950 to the current day, the PEN model is peerless.

The Eysencks have always acknowledged the necessity of empirical verification of theory and of the importance of measurement. Professor Eysenck was often heard to remark that he was less concerned that his

Table 10.2 The sample sizes of the datasets used, comparing each of the countries with the respective male and female UK datasets

Country	Males	Females
Australia	336	318
Brazil	636	579
Bulgaria	506	516
Canada	432	780
Catalan	412	393
Czechoslovakia	416	1,496
Egypt	596	1,196
Finland	501	448
France	983	466
Germany	747	374
Hong Kong	268	461
India	972	959
Israel	688	362
Italy	403	378
Japan	717	808
Korea	661	539
Lebanon	634	605
Lithuania	555	849
Mexico	474	514
Netherlands	401	475
Nigeria	825	455
Norway	377	425
Poland	532	661
Portugal	1,109	1,269
Puerto Rico	535	558
Romania	465	549
Sicily	374	401
Singapore	493	501
Spain	434	595
Sri Lanka	507	523
USA	508	873
USSR	538	529
Uganda	918	555
Zimbabwe	473	365

theory be proven correct as he was for his theory to stimulate the kind and quantity of research needed to fully describe human personality. Of course, the need to measure the varied constructs they created to describe individual differences resulted in the development of the various self-report measures reviewed in this chapter. However, three important points need to be made.

First, the Eysencks understood both the limitations of all self-report methodology (questionnaire, interview) and believed that personality questions could and should be supplemented by other behavioural and biological measures. Hence, Eysenck showed early interest in such things as the lemon drop test (Eysenck and Eysenck, 1967) and other indices reflecting personality, or more specifically, the hypothesised response (e.g. galvanic skin response) of persons varying in their personality. In fact, the Eysencks were enthusiastic sceptics of questionnaire methodology.

Second, they always displayed the KAISEN philosophy of continuous improvement. The Eysencks accepted the necessity to improve on their questionnaires. Throughout the 50-year span from the MPI to the EPQ(R), there was a constant analysis and re-analysis of items and psychometric validity. The popularity of the scales was a great advantage because studies in clinical, educational, experimental, occupational and organisational psychology showed evidence of test reliability and validity.

Third, the Eysencks steadfastly resisted to 'giving in' to popular trends. While they were happy to popularise the understanding of personality in popular paperbacks, they were never at all interested in compromising their scientific credibility.

So have the Gigantic Three been swept away by the Big Five? Has the PEN model been drowned by the OCEAN tide? Are the Eysenckian measures on the decline with respect to usage? There is no doubt that if one examines the many journals in the area of personality, it will be observed that the five-factor model is particularly popular. There has never been a European versus American 'standoff' over this issue, but as there are so many more personality psychologists in America, compared to Europe, it is almost inevitable that home-grown instruments take precedence. Hans Eysenck died in 1997 and Sybil Eysenck has retired. But this has not stopped an army of admirers and acolytes from continuing the psychological study of the PEN model and the instruments designed to assess it.

REFERENCES

Akiyoshi, J., Yamandu, A., Katsuragi, F., Kohno, Y., Yamamoto, Y., Miyamoto, M., Tsutsumi, T.,

Isogawa, K. and Fuju, I. (1998) 'Relationship between SCL-90, Maudsley Personality Inventory and CCK4-induced intracellular calcium response in T cells', *Psychiatry Research*, 81(3): 381–6.

Barrett, P. (1999) 'Rejoinder to: The Eysenckian personality structure: A "Giant Three" or "Big Five" model in Hong Kong?', *Personality and Individual Differences*, 26(1): 175–86.

Barrett, P.T., Petrides, K.V., Eysenck, S.B.G. and Eysenck, H.J. (1998) 'The Eysenck Personality Questionnaire: An examination of the factorial similarity of P, E, N, and L across 34 countries', *Personality and Individual Differences*, 25(5): 805–19.

Berlyne, D.E. (1960) *Conflict, Arousal and Curiosity*. New York: McGraw Hill.

Bienvenu, O.J., Nestadt, G., Samuels, J.F., Costa, P.T., Jr., Howard, W.T. and Eaton, W.W. (2001) 'Phobic, panic and major depressive disorders and the five-factor model of personality', *Journal of Nervous and Mental Disease*, 189(3): 154–61.

Block, J. (2001) 'Millennial contrarianism: The five-factor approach to personality description 5 years later', *Journal of Research in Personality*, 35(1): 98–107.

Borkenau, P. and Ostendorf, F. (1990) 'Comparing exploratory and confirmatory factor analysis: A study on the 5-factor model of personality', *Personality and Individual Differences*, 11(5): 515–24.

Boyle, G.J. and Saklofske, D.H (2004) (eds), *The Psychology of Individual Differences*. London: Sage Publications.

Broadhurst, P. (1959) 'The interaction of task difficulty and motivation: The Yerkes-Dodson law revived', *Acta Psychologica*, 16(1): 321–8.

Byrne, B. M., Shavelson, R. J. and Muthen, B. (1989) 'Testing for the equivalence of factor covariance and mean structures: The issue of partial measurement invariance', *Psychological Bulletin*, 105(3): 456–466.

Cattell, R.B. (1973) *Personality and Mood by Questionnaire*. San Francisco: Jossey-Bass.

Cattell, R.B., Eber, H. W. and Tatsuoka, M.M. (1970) *Handbook for the 16 Personality Factor Questionnaire*. Champaign, IL: Institute for Personality and Ability Testing.

Church, A.T. and Burke, P.J. (1994) 'Exploratory and confirmatory tests of the Big Five and Tellegen's three- and four-dimensional models',

Journal of Personality and Social Psychology, 66(1): 93–114.

Claridge, G. (1981) 'Psychoticism', in R. Lynn (ed.), *Dimensions of Personality*. New York: Pergamon Press, pp. 79–110.

Costa, P.T. Jr. and McCrae, R.R. (1992a) 'Four ways five factors are basic', *Personality and Individual Differences*, 13(6): 653–65.

Costa, P.T. Jr. and McCrae, R.R. (1992b) *The Revised NEO Personality Inventory (NEO-PI-R) and NEO Five Factor Inventory (NEO-FFI) Professional Manual*. Odessa, FL: Psychological Assessment Resources.

Costa, P.T. Jr. and McCrae, R.R. (1995) 'Primary traits of the Eysenck P-E-N system: Three and five-factor solutions', *Journal of Personality and Social Psychology*, 69(2): 308–17.

Costa, P.T. Jr., Terracciano, A. and McCrae, R. R. (2001) 'Gender differences in personality traits across cultures: Robust and surprising findings', *Journal of Personality and Social Psychology*, 81(2): 322–31.

Cronbach, L.J. (1957) 'The two disciplines of scientific psychology', *American Psychologist*, 12(11), 671–84.

Deary, I. (1996) 'A (latent) big five personality model in 1915? A reanalysis of Webb's data', *Journal of Personality and Social Psychology*, 71(5): 992–5.

Deary, I. and Matthews, G. (1993) 'Personality traits are alive and well', *Psychologist*, 6(7): 299–311.

Dickman, S.J. (1990) 'Functional and dysfunctional impulsivity: Personality and cognitive correlates', *Journal of Personality and Social Psychology*, 58(1): 95–102.

Digman, J.M. (1997) 'Higher-order factors of the Big Five', *Journal of Personality and Social Psychology*, 73(6): 1246–56.

Eagly, A.H. (1995) 'The science and politics of comparing women and men', *American Psychologist*, 50(3): 145–58.

Eysenck, H.J. (1947) *Dimensions of Personality*. New York: Praeger. Reissued in 1998 by Transaction Publishers, New York.

Eysenck, H.J. (1952) *The Scientific Study of Personality*. London: Routledge and Kegan Paul.

Eysenck, H.J. (1953) *The Structure of Human Personality*. London: Methuen.

Eysenck, H.J. (1956) 'The questionnaire measurement of neuroticism and extraversion', *Revista de Psicologia*, 50(1): 113–40.

Eysenck, H.J. (1958) 'A short questionnaire for the measurement of two dimensions of personality', *Journal of Applied Psychology*, 42(1): 14–17.

Eysenck, H.J. (1959) *The Maudsley Personality Inventory*. London: University of London Press.

Eysenck, H.J. (1960a) *Experiments in Personality* (2 Vol.). London: Routledge and Kegan Paul.

Eysenck, H.J. (1960b) *The Structure of Human Personality* (2nd edn). London: Methuen.

Eysenck, H.J. (1967) *The Biological Basis of Personality*. Springfield: CC Thomas. Reissued in 2006 by Transaction Publishers, New York.

Eysenck, H.J. (1970) 'A dimensional system of psychodiagnostics', in R.R. Mahrer (ed.), *New Approaches to Personality Classification*. New York: Columbia University Press, pp. 169–208.

Eysenck, H.J. (1973) 'Historical introduction', in H.J. Eysenck (ed.), *Eysenck on Extraversion*. London: John Wiley, pp. 3–16.

Eysenck, H.J. (1977) *You and Neurosis*. London: Maurice Temple Smith.

Eysenck, H.J. (1980) *The Causes and Effects of Smoking*. London: Maurice Temple Smith.

Eysenck, H.J. (1981) 'General features of the model', in H.J. Eysenck (ed.), *A Model for Personality*. Berlin: Springer-Verlag, pp. 1–37.

Eysenck, H.J. (1982a) *A Model for Intelligence*. New York: Springer-Verlag.

Eysenck, H.J. (1982b) *Personality, Genetics and Behaviour*. New York: Praeger.

Eysenck, H.J. (1990a) 'An improvement on the personality inventory. Current Contents: Social and behavioral sciences', *Citation Classic*, 18: 22.

Eysenck, H.J. (1990b) 'Genetic and environmental contributions to individual differences: The three major dimensions of personality', *Journal of Personality*, 58(1): 245–61.

Eysenck, H.J. (1991) 'Dimensions of Personality: 16, 5 or 3? Criteria for a taxonomic paradigm', *Personality and Individual Differences*, 12(8): 773–90.

Eysenck, H.J. (1992) 'Four ways five factors are not basic', *Personality and Individual Differences*, 13(6): 667–73.

Eysenck, H.J. (1997) 'Personality and experimental psychology: The unification of psychology and the possibility of a paradigm', *Journal of Personality and Social Psychology*, 73(6): 1224–37.

Eysenck, H.J., Barrett, P.T. and Eysenck, S.B.G. (1985a) 'Indices of factor comparison for homologous and non-homologous personality scales in 24 different countries', *Personality and Individual Differences*, 6(4): 503–4.

Eysenck, H.J., Barrett, P.T., Wilson, G.D. and Jackson, C.J. (1992) 'Primary trait measurement of the 21 components of the P-E-N system', *European Journal of Psychological Assessment*, 8(2): 109–17.

Eysenck, H.J., Eaves, L. and Martin, N. (1989) *Genes, Culture and Personality. An Empirical Approach*. New York: Academic Press.

Eysenck, H.J. and Eysenck, M.W. (1985) *Personality and Individual Differences: A Natural Science Approach*. New York: Plenum.

Eysenck, H.J. and Eysenck, S.B.G. (1964a) *The Eysenck Personality Inventory*. London: Hodder & Stoughton.

Eysenck, H.J. and Eysenck, S.B.G. (1975) *Manual of the Eysenck Personality Questionnaire (Junior and Adult)*. London: Hodder & Stoughton.

Eysenck, H.J. and Eysenck, S.B.G. (1976) *Psychoticism as a Dimension of Personality*. London: Hodder & Stoughton.

Eysenck, H.J. and Eysenck, S.B.G. (1981) 'Culture and personality abnormalities', in I. Al-Issa (ed.), *Culture and Psychopathology*. Maryland: University Park Press, pp. 277–301.

Eysenck, H.J. and Eysenck, S.B.G. (1991) *Manual of the Eysenck Personality Scales*. London: Hodder & Stoughton.

Eysenck, H.J. and Gudjonsson, G.H. (1989) *The Causes and Cures of Criminality*. New York: Plenum Press.

Eysenck, H.J. and Martin, I. (1988) (eds), *Theoretical Foundations of Behaviour Therapy*. New York: Plenum Press.

Eysenck, H.J. and Nias, D. (1978) *Sex, Violence and the Media*. London: Maurice Temple Smith.

Eysenck, H.J. and Nias, D. (1982) *Astrology – Science or Superstition?* London: Maurice Temple Smith.

Eysenck, H.J. and Sargent, C. (1982) *Explaining the Unexplained. Mysteries of the Paranormal*. London: Weidenfeld & Nicholson.

Eysenck, H.J. and Wilson, G.D. (1975) *Know Your Own Personality*. London: Maurice Temple Smith. Reissued in 1976 by Penguin, Harmondsworth.

Eysenck, H.J. and Wilson, G.D. (1979) *The Psychology of Sex*. London: Dent.

Eysenck, H.J. and Wilson, G.D. (1991) *The Eysenck Personality Profiler*. London: Corporate Assessment Network.

Eysenck, H.J., Wilson, G.D. and Jackson, C.J. (1996) *The Eysenck Personality Profiler (short)*. Guildford: Psi-Press.

Eysenck, S.B.G. and Eysenck, H.J. (1964b) 'An improved short questionnaire for the measurement of extraversion and neuroticism', *Life Sciences*, 3(10): 1103–9.

Eysenck, S.B.G. and Eysenck, H.J. (1967) 'Salivary response to lemon juice as a measure of introversion', *Perceptual and Motor Skills*, 24(3): 1047–53.

Eysenck, S.B.G. and Eysenck, H.J. (1977) 'The place of impulsiveness in a dimensional system of personality description', *British Journal of Social and Clinical Psychology*, 16(1): 57–68.

Eysenck, S.B.G., Eysenck, H.J. and Barrett, P.T. (1985b) 'A revised version of the Psychoticism scale', *Personality and Individual Differences*, 6(1): 21–9.

Eysenck, S.B.G., Pearson, P., Easting, G. and Allsopp, J. (1985c) 'Age norms for impulsiveness, venturesomeness, and empathy in adults', *Personality and Individual Differences*, 6(5): 613–19.

Eysenck, S.B.G. and Saklofske, D.H. (1983) 'A comparison of responses of Canadian and English children on the Junior Eysenck Personality Questionnaire', *Canadian Journal of Behavioural Science*, 15(2): 121–30.

Eysenck, S.B.G. and Withers, M. (1965) *Manual of the Eysenck–Withers Personality Inventory for Subnormal Subjects (50–80 IQ)*. London: University of London Press.

Francis, L., Jones, S.H., Jackson, C.J. and Robbins, M. (2001) 'The feminine personality profile of male Anglican clergy in Britain and Ireland: A study employing the Eysenck Personality Profiler', *Review of Religious Research*, 43(1): 14–23.

Furnham, A. (2005) *The Psychology of Behaviour at Work*. Hove: Psychologist Press.

Furnham, A., Jackson, C., Forde, L. and Cotter, T. (2001) 'Correlates of the Eysenck Personality

Profiler', *Personality and Individual Differences*, 30(4): 587–94.

Furnham, A., Petrides, K.V., Jackson, C.J. and Cotter, T. (2002) 'Do personality factors predict job satisfaction?', *Personality and Individual Differences*, 33(8): 1325–42.

Goldberg, L.R. (1993) 'The structure of phenotypic personality traits', *American Psychologist*, 48(1): 26–34.

Howarth, E. and Eysenck, H.J. (1968) 'Extraversion, arousal, and paired associate recall', *Journal of Experimental Research in Personality*, 3(2): 114–16.

Iwawaki, S., Eysenck, S.B.G. and Eysenck, H.J. (1980) 'Japanese and English personality structure: A cross-cultural study', *Psychologia*, 23(4): 195–205.

Jackson, C.J., Furnham, A., Forde, L. and Cotter, T. (2000) 'The structure of the Eysenck Personality Profiler', *British Journal of Psychology*, 91(2): 223–39.

Kaiser, H.F. (1970) 'A second generation Little Jiffy', *Psychometrika*, 35(4): 401–15.

Kasai, Y., Takegami, K. and Ududa, A. (2004) 'A study of patients with spinal disease using the Maudsley Personality Inventory', *International Orthopaedics*, 28(1): 56–9.

Knapp, R.R. (1962) *Manual of the Maudsley Personality Inventory*. San Diego: Educational and Industrial Testing Services.

Lynn, R. and Martin, T. (1997) 'Gender differences in extraversion, neuroticism and psychoticism in 37 nations', *Journal of Social Psychology*, 137(3): 369–73.

Matthews, G., Deary, I. and Whiteman, M. (2003) *Personality Traits*. Cambridge: Cambridge University Press.

Meyer, G.J., Finn, S.E., Eyde, L.D., Kay, G.G., Moreland, K.L., Dies, R.R., Eisman, E.J., Kubiszyn, T.W. and Reed, G.M. (2001) 'Psychological testing and psychological assessment: A review of evidence and issues', *American Psychologist*, 56(2): 128–65.

Muris, P., Schmidt, M., Merckelbach, H. and Rassin, E. (2000) 'Reliability, factor structure and validity of the Dutch Eysenck Personality Profiler', *Personality and Individual Differences*, 29(5): 857–68.

Petrides, K.V., Jackson, C., Furnham, A. and Levine, S. (2003) 'Exploring issues of personality measurement and structure through the development of a short form of the Eysenck Profiler', *Journal of Personality Assessment*, 81(3): 271–80.

Revelle, W. (1997) 'Extraversion and impulsivity: The lost dimension?', in H. Nyborg (ed.), *The Scientific Study of Human Nature: Tribute to Hans J. Eysenck at Eighty*. New York: Pergamon, pp. 189–212.

Rocklin, T. and Revelle, W. (1981) 'The measurement of extraversion: A comparison of the Eysenck Personality Inventory and the Eysenck Personality Questionnaire', *British Journal of Social Psychology*, 20(4): 279–84.

Royce, J.R. and Powell, A. (1983) *Theory of Personality and Individual Differences: Factors, Systems and Processes*. Englewood Cliffs: Prentice Hall.

Saklofske, D.H. and Eysenck, H.J. (1994) 'Extraversion-introversion in V.S Ramachandran', (ed.), *Encyclopedica of Human Behavior*. San Diego: Academic Press, pp. 321–32.

Saklofske, D.H. and Eysenck, S.B.G. (1983) 'Impulsiveness and Venturesomeness in Canadian Children. *Psychological Reports*, 52(1): 147–152.

Saklofske, D.H. and Eysenck, S.B.G. (1988) *Individual Differences in Children and Adolescents*. London: Hodder & Stoughton.

Saklofske, D.H. and Eysenck, S.B.G. (1998) (eds), *Individual Differences in Children and Adolescents* (republished in North America with new preface). New Jersey: Transaction Publishers Rutgers.

Saucier, G. (2002) 'Orthogonal markers for orthogonal factors: The case of the big five', *Journal of Research in Personality*, 36(1): 1–31.

Thompson, B. (1994) 'Guidelines for authors', *Educational and Psychological Measurement*, 54(4): 837–47.

Vassend, O. and Skrondal, A. (1997) 'Validation of the NEO Personality Inventory and the Five-Factor model. Can findings from exploratory and confirmatory factor analysis be reconciled?', *European Journal of Personality*, 11(2): 147–66.

Wainer, H. (1976) 'Estimating coefficients in linear models: It don't make no nevermind', *Psychological Bulletin*, 83(2): 213–17.

Wiggins, J.S. and Trobst, K.K. (1999) 'The fields of interpersonal behaviour', in L.A. Pervin and O.P. John (eds), *Handbook of Personality:*

Theory and Research (2nd edn). New York: Guilford, pp. 653–70.

Wilson, G.D. and Jackson, C. (1994) 'The personality of physicists', *Personality and Individual Differences*, 16(1): 187–89.

Yerkes, R.M. and Dodson, J.R. (1908) 'The relative strength of stimuli to rapidity of habit information', *Journal of Comparative Neurology and Psychology*, 18: 459–82.

11

Zuckerman–Kuhlman Personality Questionnaire (ZKPQ): An Operational Definition of the Alternative Five Factorial Model of Personality

Marvin Zuckerman

The development of the ZKPQ has been described in chapters in other books (Joireman and Kuhlman, 2004; Zuckerman, 2002a) and an initial article (Zuckerman et al., 1993). This chapter will bring the description of the test and its reliability and validity up to date. Personality scientists in different countries have been important in the test development and establishment of its reliability and validity as will be described here.

Test validity is an ongoing effort. The point at which a test becomes the definition of a construct depends on the outcome of many studies of the test and the theory linking it to observable phenomena (Cronbach and Meehl, 1955). Verbal self-descriptions, as in personality questionnaires, cannot be assumed to have 'face validity' any more than responses to ink blots can be accepted as

surrogates for responses to the real world. For now we define the five factors of the ZKPQ as 'operational definitions' of the traits described.

TEST DEVELOPMENT

Work on the search for basic factors of personality began when Costa and McCrae's 'Big Five' was still only three and the 'Big Five' was based on lexical analyses of self and other ratings using adjectives rather than a questionnaire. The dominant model was Eysenck's 'Big Three': extraversion (E), neuroticism (N), and psychoticism (P). Only E and N in Eysenck's model were congruent with Costa and McCrae's 'Big Three'.

Their third factor 'openness to experience' (O) did not resemble Eysenck's third dimension of P. Neither this model seemed to have sufficient specificity, for instance, not differentiating between anxiety and aggression as traits. Furthermore, I felt that Eysenck's P factor was inaccurately characterized as 'psychoticism' when antisocial tendencies or 'psychopathy' would have been a more accurate clinical term.

My approach to personality has been a psychobiological one in which basic personality traits are adaptive behavioral solutions which can be seen in other species of animals and are predisposed by inherited biological differences within species (Zuckerman, 1984, 1991, 2005). Translations across species can be helped when the constructs are in comparative language; for instance, 'aggression' rather than 'agreeableness', and 'impulsivity' rather than 'conscientiousness.' Of course 'a rose by any other name' may still be a rose but if we call it something else and it describes something other than the prototype it may actually be a tulip. Questionnaire items describe behaviors, intentions and attitudes, but the Big Five was based on analyses of general trait words by which humans describe one another. It is true that some of the Big Five traits can be reliably identified in other species, particularly primates, but this requires leaps of translation (Gosling, 2001). Conscientiousness, for instance, cannot be directly identified in non-human primates and certainly not in rats.

Some traits which are important across species, like explorativeness, or a positive rather than a fearful response to novel stimuli, are not adequately represented in the lexicon to become primary factors. The trait of sensation seeking, which I have studied for many years, has proven to have a high heritability and a strong biological basis in physiological and biochemical studies (Zuckerman, 1979, 1994, 2006). But there are few words like 'adventurousness' or 'daring' in the lexicon to power a factor in a factor analysis. It is a truism that you only get out of a factor analysis what you put into it.

We began our factor analytic studies of traits using questionnaire scales that had been involved in studies of temperament, genetics, and biological correlates of personality (Zuckerman et al., 1988). We tried to use at least several markers for each postulated latent factor, including sensation seeking and impulsivity, as well as the standard factors of extraversion, emotionality, and socialization (E, N, and P). No measures of cultural interests or intellectual styles were included because of our comparative conception of basic personality traits. In all, there were 46 scales or subscales selected from 8 different personality or temperament questionnaires. Of course, this precluded finding a factor like O in the Big Five. Although a scree test suggested that four or five factors would be sufficient, we conducted factor analyses rotating three, five, and seven factors to see what happened to factors going from the broader analyses to the more specific ones.

The three factors at the broader level closely resembled Eysenck's primary three, and in fact, his E and N scales had the highest loading on the first two, and the P scale had the second highest loading on the third factor. The factors were therefore named E-sociability (E-Sy), N-emotionality (N-Emot), and P-impulsive unsocialized sensation seeking (P-ImpUSS) in terms of the primary scales defining them. At the five-factor level, 'activity' separated itself as a separate factor from E-Sy and N-Emot), and P-ImpUSS separated from 'aggression' in the P-ImpUSS factor. At the seven-factor level, N-Emot separated into 'anger' and N-Anx, and P-ImpUSS separated into 'autonomy versus conformity' and P-Imp. However, the seven-factor solution did not yield factors that were reliable in structure across gender.

A second study (Zuckerman et al., 1991) was done with a larger sample of subjects and a reduction in the number of scales to 33 representing the best markers for the factors discovered in the earlier study. Rotations were done for three, four, five, and six factors. The E-Sy factor remained unchanged from the six to the three factor solutions.

Activity (Act) which started as an independent factor in the six-factor analysis became a part of the E-Sy factor in the three-factor analysis. N-Anx and aggression-hostility (Agg-Host), which were separate factors at the six-factor level blended into the broader N-Emot factor in the three-factor analysis. Impulsivity and P-unsocialized sensation seeking were separate factors at the six-factor level but blended into the P-ImpUSS factor in the five-factor analysis and this remained the same through the four- and three-factor analyses. The six-factor solution was less reliable than the others and the impulsivity factor could not be identified in women. This is what led to our combining Imp and SS in the more stable factor of P-ImpUSS. The combination of sensation seeking with a non-planning, quick decision type of impulsivity was not new in the literature and past research had led to the conceptualization of 'a marriage of traits made in biology' (Zuckerman, 1993).

Derivation of the ZKPQ full scale was first described in the article by Zuckerman et al. (1993). The items came from the test scales used in the Zuckerman et al. (1991) study with the exception of those from the Eysenck Personality Questionnaire (EPQ). The separate items were correlated first with the factors derived from the total scale scores: N-Anx, Agg-Host, ImpSS, Sy, and Act. Twenty items for each factor scale were selected on the basis of high correlations with the designated factor, lower correlations with the other factors, and low correlations with a scale for social desirability. These 100 items were factor analyzed. A scree test indicated five major factors. Eighty-nine of the 100 items loaded highly and selectively on the factors to which they had been assigned on the basis of item-total correlations. Ten new items were added to comprise a validity scale on the basis of infrequency and social desirability. This is not a reliable scale and is used to eliminate individual test records of dubious validity. The final form of the ZKPQ consists of the 99 true–false items. A short form of half the length of the full form will be described in a later section.

Factor analyses of the items within the major five scales were done in order to identify possible subfactors. Scree plots indicated that one factor was sufficient to describe both the N-Anx and Agg-Host scales. Two factor solutions were found for the remaining three scales. The Sy scale contained one subfactor for liking lively parties and relationships (PR) and another for an intolerance of social isolation (IS). The ImpSS divided into one subfactor for impulsivity (Imp) and another for sensation seeking (SS). The two subfactors within the Activity scale were a need for general activity (GA) and a specific need for work activity (WA).

Schmitz (2004) factor analyzed the ZKPQ scale scores starting with the subfactors and moving from five to four to three factor solutions. Figure 11.1 shows the relationships between the subscales and the scales derived from the five-factor solution and the relationships between the major factors going from five to four and from four to three factors. At the five-factor level the factors were identical with the major factors in the alternative five, but at the four-factor level, N-Anx merged with Agg-Host to form an emotionality factor. The three-factor solution is essentially Eysenck's Big Three: E, N, and P.

RELIABILITY

Factor replicability

Schmitz (2004) translated the ZKPQ into German and factor analyzed the items. He found that all 19 items of the N-Anx scale, 18 of the 19 items on the ImpSS scale, 16 of the 17 items on the Act scale, and 12 of the 17 items on the Agg-Host scale loaded primarily on the scale to which they have been assigned in the American study. Two studies conducted in Spain, one on the test translated into Catalan (Goma-i-Freixanet et al., 2004) and the other into Spanish (Aluja et al., 2004), measured the coefficients of factor congruence

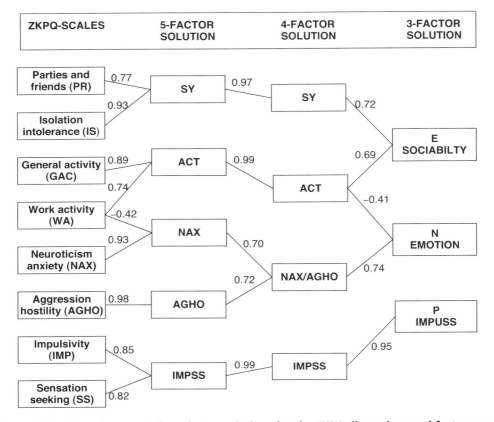

Figure 11.1 Five-, four-, and three-factor solutions for the ZKPQ dimensions and factor score correlations across levels when Eysenck Personality Questionnaire Scales are included in the analysis. E = extraversion; N = neuroticism; P-ImpUSS = psychoticism-impulsive unsocialized sensation seeking. This figure was published in 'On the alternative five-factor model: Structure and correlates' by P.G. Schmitz in R.M. Stelmack (ed.) *On the Psychobiology of Personality: Essays in Honor of Marvin Zuckerman.* **Oxford, UK: Elsevier. pp. 65–88. © 2004 by Elsevier. Reprinted with permission**

between their samples and the American ZKPQ sample. The results are shown in Table 11.1.

Coefficients of over 0.85 are considered evidence for near identity of factors. All coefficients but one exceed this criterion and all but 3 of the 15 exceed 0.90. One can conclude that the same factors are found in Spanish as in American subjects.

Internal reliabilities

Internal reliabilities (Table 11.2) are shown for the American samples and for translated

scales in other countries including: Spain (Aluja et al., 2004) and Catalonia (Goma-i-Freixanet et al., 2004); Germany 1 (Angleitner et al., 2004) and Germany 2 (Schmitz, 2004);

Table 11.1 Factor congruence coefficients between Spanish and American samples

ZKPQ scales	Males (n = 330)	Females (n = 603)	M and F (n = 1006)
N-anxiety	0.90	0.96	0.99
Impulsive-SS	0.84	0.94	0.97
Sociability	0.92	0.93	0.96
Aggression-host	0.85	0.93	0.96
Activity	0.91	0.88	0.95

Table 11.2   Internal reliabilities (Alphas) of ZKPQ scales

Language	Gender	n's'	ImpSS	N-Anx	Agg-Hos	Activity	Sy
English-US	Males	1,144	0.77	0.0.82	0.76	0.74	0.77
	Females	1,825	0.81	0.84	0.76	0.77	0.79
Spanish	Both	1,006	0.83	0.85	0.74	0.78	0.77
Catalan	Both	933	0.79	0.84	0.67	0.75	0.75
German 1	Both	730	0.83	0.86	0.71	0.73	0.75
German 2	Males	480	0.84	0.91	0.73	0.87	0.87
	Females	710	0.83	0.96	0.71	0.80	0.86
Hebrew	Females	372	0.74	0.81	0.67	0.77	0.75
Romanian	Both	100	0.79	0.84	0.57-	0.67	0.71-
Chinese	Both	333	0.68-	0.81-	0.62	0.61-	0.76
Japanese	Males	206	0.77	0.82	0.74	0.69	0.81
	Females	230	0.79	0.85	0.74	0.73	0.73
Median			0.80	0.85	0.725	0.745	0.765
Range			0.68–	0.81–	0.57–	0.61–	0.71–
			0.84	0.91	0.76	0.87	0.87

Note: ImpSS = impulsive sensation seeking; N-Anx = neuroticism-anxiety; Agg-Hos = aggression-hostility; Sy = sociability

Israel (I. Montag, pers. comm., 2001); Roumania (C. Bondci, personal communication, 2003); China, (Wu et al., 2000); and Japan (Shiomi et al., 1996). Italian (De Pascalis and Russo, 2003) and French (Rossier et al., 2008) translations are also available, but no reliabilities were available at the time of writing.

Overall, the internal reliabilities are all satisfactory but highest for N-Anx and ImpSS, and lowest for Agg-Host and Act. With few exceptions most alphas exceed 0.7 and for N-Anx they all exceed 0.8. This shows remarkably stable results given that they are based on translated scales in different cultures.

Retest reliabilities

Table 11.3 shows retest reliabilities from the American and German (Schmitz, 2004) samples. The retest reliabilities are high for

periods ranging from one to seven month interval & between tests.

Short form

Zuckerman–Kuhlman (report in Zuckerman, 2002a, and unpublished manual) described the development of a short form of the ZKPQ with seven items selected for each of the five factors selected on the basis of their correlations with the total scores on the respective factors. As would be expected, internal reliabilities were lower for all but the Sy subscales compared to the long form.

More recently, Aluja et al. (2006) developed a short form which is cross-cultural since it was developed using American, Swiss (French language), German, and Spanish ZKPQ data. Despite the fact that the data came from 4 different languages, subsets of 10 items for each factor (a total

Table 11.3   Retest reliabilities

Country	n's	Intervals	ImpSS	N-Anx	Agg-Hos	Activity	Sy
USA	153	3–4 weeks	0.80	0.84	0.78	0.76	0.83
Germany	150	6 weeks	0.80	0.84	0.72	0.79	0.84
Germany	75	7 months	0.78	0.80	0.79	0.78	0.82

Note: ImpSS = impulsive sensation seeking; N-Anx = neuroticism-anxiety; Agg-Hos = aggression-hostility; Sy = sociability

of 50 items) were found that loaded significantly on that particular factor in all 4 countries. Congruence coefficients between the five factors across all countries were nearly always above 0.90 indicating high similarity of the factors across countries and languages. Alpha measures of reliability were about as high as those obtained for the full scales: 0.8 or higher for N-Anx, and 0.7 or higher for the other scales except for Agg-Host.

The advantage of a cross-cultural scale for research is that scores can be compared from country to country. Without this kind of development one cannot be sure that scores from different countries are not based on language differences even though the factors may be reliable within each country. The scale length and testing time are much reduced without much sacrifice of reliability. Therefore, those who want short scales in any of these four languages should consider using the 50-item cross-cultural form (ZKPQ-50-CC) scale for that language.

VALIDITY

Comparisons with other personality scales

A preliminary phase of validity is comparing the test to other self-report questionnaires measuring what purport to be the same or similar constructs. This is more of a semantic test for personality questionnaires because scales tend to correlate to the degree that their item content is similar. The correlations between similar constructs are related to convergent validity. They assess the degree to which the other measures are measuring similar constructs, something which cannot always be inferred from the label assigned to the scales. However, unless one scale is so established that it constitutes a 'gold standard' or criterion for the other scales, one can only assess construct the validity in terms of relationships to criterion outside of the tests themselves. Arguably no personality questionnaire has reached this stage of unquestionable validity.

A second type of validity is called discriminant validity. Scales that are assumed to measure different constructs should not correlate or should correlate very low relative to the convergent validity correlations. With multi-scale questionnaires the scales can be compared for both convergent and discriminant validity within a multitrait–multimethod matrix (Campbell and Fiske, 1959). Table 11.4 shows this kind of matrix assessing the ZKPQ scales against two established personality questionnaires, the Eysenck Personality Questionnaire (EPQ) (Eysenck and Eysenck, 1975), and the Neuroticism, Extraversion, Openness (NEO) (Costa and McCrae, 1985). Table 11.4 shows the correlations between the ZKPQ and the EPQ and NEO from the study by Zuckerman et al. (1993).

Table 11.4   Correlations of ZKPQ scales with EPQ and NEO scales

| | | ZKPQ scales | | | | |
		Imp-SS	Sociability	N-anxiety	Agg-host	Act
EPQ						
	Psychoticism	**0.55****	−0.05	−0.05	0.32**	−0.05
	Extraversion	0.28**	**0.70****	−0.24**	0.13	0.36**
	Neuroticism	0.01	−0.21*	**0.79****	0.35**	−0.13
NEO						
	Conscientiousness	**−0.51**	−0.04	−0.09	−0.13	0.31**
	Extraversion	0.28**	**0.70****	−0.24**	0.13	0.36**
	Neuroticism	0.01	−0.21	**0.79****	0.35**	−0.13
	Agreeableness	0.23	−0.05	0.04	**−0.63****	0.09
	Openness	0.00	0.06	0.00	−0.15	0.11

Four of the ZKPQ scales show good convergent reliability with the NEO: ImpSS with conscientiousness, sociability with extraversion, N-Anx with neuroticism, and Agg-Host with agreeableness (negative r). All of the remaining correlations between scales based on different constructs are much lower, showing good discriminant validity. The convergence with the EPQ is limited by the fact that this test contains only three factors compared to five in the ZKPQ. However, three of the factors show good convergent validity: ImpSS with psychoticism, sociability with extraversion, and N-Anx with neuroticism. Agg-Host correlates low but significantly with EPQ psychoticism and neuroticism showing poor convergent and no discriminant validity. Activity also shows little convergent validity, probably because it is not represented in any direct way in the EPQ and NEO broad scales.

Factor analysis is another way of testing convergent and discriminant validity since scales measuring the same construct should load on the same factor and not markedly on other factors. Factor analyses were performed for three, four, and five rotated factors in this study using the subscales from the three major tests. Activity in the ZKPQ and openness in the NEO could not form any fifth or sixth factor because there were no other markers for them so the four-factor analysis is presented for clarity (Table 11.5).

The first factor is clearly extraversion including the NEO and EPQ E scales and the ZKPQ sociability scale. The ZKPQ activity scale also loads on this factor although at a somewhat lower level than the E and Sy scales. The second factor is neuroticism with loadings of over 0.9 from the ZKPQ N-Anx and the NEO and EPQ N scales. The third factor has EPQ P and ZKPQ Imp at one pole and NEO conscientiousness at the other. This is clearly the P-ImpUSS factor found in earlier analyses of scales prior to the development of the ZKPQ (Zuckerman et al., 1988, 1991). The fourth factor is agreeableness (NEO) versus Agg-Host (ZKPQ) with a secondary loading from NEO openness.

Discriminant validity is also good since the convergent scales loadings on the four factors are much higher than secondary loadings on other scales.

Some other correlations of interest in this study included those with the Buss-Plomin EASI scale, the Sensation Seeking Scale-form V (SSS-V), and Block's Ego Undercontrol and Ego Resiliency scales. The ZKPQ ImpSS, Sociability, and N-Anx scales correlated respectively with the EASI scales with the same names (r's 0.59–.70). The ImpSS correlated 0.66 with the total score on the SSS-V and somewhat lower but nearly equally with all of the subscales. Apparently, ImpSS represents the general SS factor and not any one particular subtype. ImpSS correlates 0.63 with Block's Ego Undercontrol scale. Although ego resiliency correlates negatively with N-Anx, the correlation is low: −0.30.

Cloninger (1987) developed a model for personality that is of interest to those involved in studying the psychobiology of personality because he and his colleagues have done many studies on this topic. Zuckerman and Cloninger (1996) correlated the ZKPQ scales with those of the Temperament and Character Inventory (TCI). Good convergent and divergent validities were obtained for four of the five scales in each inventory. Convergent correlations were: ImpSS versus novelty seeking, 0.68; N-Anx versus harm avoidance, 0.66; Agg-Host versus cooperativeness, −0.60, activity versus persistence, 0.46. All of these were much higher than with other scales of the two tests. What is missing is a TCI match for ZKPQ sociability. However, there is no extraversion scale in the TCI.

Comparisons with motivational and emotional trait scales

Gray's (1982) motivational theory of personality identifies two major dimensions of personality as anxiety and impulsivity. The former is based on sensitivity to signals of punishment and the latter to sensitivity to signals of reward. Others have suggested that

Table 11.5   Four-factor analysis of NEO, EPQ, and ZKPQ scales

Scales	Factor 1	Factor 2	Factor 3	Factor 4
NEO extraversion	**0.88**	−0.14	−0.05	0.17
EPQ extraversion	**0.79**	−0.32	0.17	−0.08
ZKPQ sociability	**0.76**	−0.16	0.10	−0.07
ZKPQ activity	**0.60**	0.01	−0.18	0.02
ZKPQ N-anxiety	−0.13	**0.92**	−0.01	0.08
NEO neuroticism	−0.16	**0.90**	−0.04	−0.08
EPQ neuroticism	−0.16	**0.91**	−0.04	−0.08
NEO conscientiousness	0.15	−0.07	**−0.86**	−0.02
EPQ psychoticism	−0.09	−0.08	**0.80**	−0.28
ZKPQ ImpSS	0.48	0.08	**0.74**	−0.02
NEO agreeableness	−0.04	−0.07	−0.31	**0.81**
ZKPQ aggression-hostility	0.35	0.34	0.24	**−0.72**
NEO openness	0.27	0.14	0.18	**0.67**

Note: From M. Zuckerman et al. (1993) 'A comparison of three structural models for personality: The Big Three, the Big Five, and the Alternative Five', Journal of Personality and Social Psychology, 65: 762. © 1993 by the American Psychological Association
ImpSS = impulsive sensation seeking
Aggression-Hos = aggression-hostility

neuroticism is associated with negative emotionality and extraversion with positive emotionality. Costa and McCrae (1992) include subscales for positive emotions and warmth in their extraversion factor and subscales for anxiety, hostility, and depression in their neuroticism factor. Zuckerman et al. (1999) included the EPQ and ZKPQ and scales developed by Torrubia et al. (2001) based on Gray's model for sensitivities to signals of reward and punishment, and scales for generalized reward and punishment expectancies developed by Ball and Zuckerman (1990). Also included were trait scales for positive and negative affect (anxiety, depression, and hostility) that are part of the Multiple Affect Adjective Check List-Revised (MAACL-R; Zuckerman and Lubin, 1985; Lubin and Zuckerman, 1999).

A factor analysis found that the extraversion factor (EPQ E, ZKPQ Sy) was associated with sensitivity to signals of reward, generalized reward expectancy and positive affect, particularly of a surgent type. The neuroticism factor (EPQ N, ZKPQ N-Anx) was associated with sensitivity to signals of punishment and generalized punishment expectancy, and negative affects (particularly anxiety). The third factor (EPQ P, ZKPQ ImpSS and Agg-Host) was associated with

sensitivity to signals of reward, but not with generalized reward expectancy. It was negatively related to positive affect and positively related to negative affects, particularly hostility. Depression loaded equally on N and P.

Self-observer correlation

One way to establish some external validity for a self-descriptive questionnaire is to have others describe them. Angleitner et al. (2004) had good friends or relatives of the test takers describe them by filling out the ZKPQ German version as a description of the subject. Goma-i-Freixanet et al. (2005) had spouses fill out the ZKPQ once for their own self-description and again to describe their spouses as they see them. The peer and spouse correlations are shown in Table 11.6.

With only two exceptions the correlations indicate high agreement between self and observer reports with correlations ranging from 0.50 to 0.63. Spouses show higher agreement than friends on the N-anxiety. This is understandable because spouses are usually more aware of the negative moods and attitudes toward self than are friends and relatives.

Table 11.6   Self-observer agreement

ZKPQ Scales	Correlations*	
	Angleitner et al. (2004) friends and relatives	Goma-i-Freixanet (2005) spouse pairs
Neuroticism-anxiety	0.44	0.63
Imp-SS	0.50	0.63
Aggression-hostility	0.57	0.53
Sociability	0.62	0.54
Activity	0.56	0.47

* All correlations significant, $p < 0.0001$
n Angleitner et al. = 141; n Goma-i-Freixanet et al. = 88 pairs

Risky behaviors in community and college populations

The ZKPQ was related to risk taking by college students in six areas: smoking, drinking, drug use, risky sex, reckless driving, and gambling (Zuckerman and Kuhlman, 2000). The risk taking tendencies, particularly smoking drinking, drugs, and sex, tend to be interrelated so we calculated a composite risk taking score based on all 6 and compared high, medium, and low risk takers on the ZKPQ.

High general risk takers of both genders were higher than medium and low risk takers on ImpSS, Agg-Host, and Sy. Gender differences on risk-taking were mediated by the gender differences on ImpSS. Looking at specific forms of risk taking, ImpSS was related to all three kinds of substance use and sexual risk taking in men and women, whereas Agg-Host was only related to drinking and reckless driving in men and to drinking, smoking, and sex in women. Sociability was related to drinking, drugs, sex, and gambling in men, and to drinking and smoking in women.

A large community study of women 18 to 30 years of age, using only the ImpSS and the N-Anx scales from the ZKPQ, found that sensation seeking, but not impulsivity or anxiety, had large indirect effects on risky sexual behavior, drinking, and drug use (Van Zile-Tamsen et al., 2006). A three-year longitudinal study of college students using only the sensation seeking (SS) subscale of the ImpSS found that heavy-stable drinkers were higher on SS than light-stable drinkers whereas those fluctuating in level of drinking or only doing heavy drinking during holiday seasons scored at intermediate levels of sensation seeking (Greenbaum et al., 2005). Drug abusers in clinical samples will be discussed in a later section on psychopathology.

Other studies using the ImpSS scale alone have shown relationships between this scale and drinking in elementary school students (Anderson et al., 2005), and adolescent substance use (Ames et al., 2005). In the latter study the influence of sensation seeking on drinking and marijuana use was mediated by implicit cognition or the strength of substance-related cognitions in associations.

McDaniel and Zuckerman (2003) used only the ImpSS scale from the ZKPQ in a study of 790 randomly selected adults from two eastern metropolitan areas. Respondents were also interviewed regarding their gambling interests and habits. Interest in gambling and the number of different types of gambling correlated significantly with the total ImpSS and each of its two subscales in both men and women. The pattern of correlations with specific types of gambling varied by gender. ImpSS correlated with frequency of sports betting for both men and women, but ImpSS correlated with frequency of lottery and slot machine gambling only for women, and with video poker only for men.

Breen and Zuckerman (1999) studied gambling behavior in the laboratory using an analog that allowed 'chasing behavior'. Chasing is a pattern seen in pathological gambling when the gambler persists in betting and even increases bet sizes after a series of losses. The outcomes of betting over a series of trials were controlled with an increasing proportion of losing over blocks of trials. Those who persisted until they had lost all of their winnings from earlier trials were called 'chasers'. Only the ImpSS scale, scored for Imp and SS components separately, was used. Scores on the Imp subscale were significantly higher in chasers than non-chasers but the SS subscale did not differentiate the two groups.

Sports

A great deal of research has been done relating sensation seeking as measured by the SSS to risky or exceptional sports (Zuckerman, 1994, and Zuckerman, 2007). Although sensation seekers tends to engage in these kind of sports, like mountain climbing, skydiving, scuba diving, downhill skiing, and so on, ordinary competitive sports have not been studied much in relation to sensation seeking. O'Sullivan et al. (1998) studied male teams for baseball and football, and female teams for equestrianism, field hockey, and lacrosse and compared them with scores from the general university population at the same university.

All four team participants showed the same ZKPQ profile relative to the general college norms. All four team participants had higher scores on activity and lower scores on N-Anx than general university students. Male team players actually had lower scores than the general students on ImpSS, but female team participants did not differ from the population on this scale.

Prostitution

Prostitutes, or 'sex workers' to use the current euphemism, have been mythologized by poets and writers in positive and negative ways since the earliest times. However, little personality research has been done studying them. Two previous studies, one using interviews (Greenwald, 1970) and the other the

MMPI (Exner et al., 1977) suggested that the best diagnostic description for sex practitioners was psychopathic or antisocial personality disorder. Other MMPI studies support the conclusion.

A study using the ZKPQ was done on prostitutes working on a highway leading out of a city, soliciting motorists and truck drivers at bars and restaurants (O'Sullivan et al., 1996). Risk was particularly high in this setting. During the previous year a serial killer had been murdering prostitutes along the highway. Prostitutes were interviewed and tested during breaks they took at a restaurant. A group of matched service workers at a university were used for controls. Despite attempts to match the groups on race, age, education, and marital status, the control group was somewhat older and better educated.

The prostitutes scored significantly higher than controls on the ImpSS, N-Anx, and Agg-Host scales, but after controlling for group differences on age and education only the difference on ImpSS remained significant ($p < 0.001$), and the difference on Agg-Host approached significance ($p = 0.08$). Cocaine and polydrug users among the prostitutes scored even higher than non-drug or other drug users on ImpSS.

Acculturation of immigrant groups

Schmitz (2004) studied the reactions of migrant groups in reactions to moving into a new and different culture. He used a model distinguishing four types of adaptation. *Integration* is a reaction in which one's cultural identity is maintained but some aspects of the host society are taken over and integrated in the migrants own behavior and value system. In *assimilation, the* approved behaviors and values of the place of origin are abandoned in favor of total adoption of those of the host country. *Separation* means maintaining one's own cultural identity with no interest in making friendships outside of one's own migrant group or in taking over any of the customs or values of the host society.

In *marginalization* there is abandonment of previous cultural values and identity, but no close contact with the host society or other groups in the country. Correlations of ZKPQ scales with measures of each of the four patterns of acculturation were done in 26 samples. Only the ImpSS was subdivided into its component subscales. The results are the average correlations across samples.

The Imp component of ImpSS correlated negatively with integration and low positively with marginalization. In contrast, SS correlated positively with integration and negatively with separation. Both components correlated positively with marginalization. The net result combining the two components was a nullification for the correlations with integration and separation with the total ImpSS correlation but retention of the correlation with marginalization. These results show the importance of scoring the subscales to reveal cases in which they work in opposite directions.

Sociability correlated positively with integration and negatively with separation as might be expected. Neuroticism-anxiety correlated positively with assimilation, separation, and marginalization but not at all with integration. Aggression-hostility did correlate with integration but in a negative direction. It correlated positively with marginalization. Activity correlated positively with integration and assimilation and negatively with marginalization. I would guess that these correlations are due to the work-activity rather than to the general-activity component of the activity scale. The broadest patterns of personality correlation are with integration and marginalization. The group in marginalization is one with the most psychopathology in the form of substance abuse and antisocial behavioral expressions. On the ZKPQ they are characterized by high scores on ImpSS, N-Anx, and Agg-Host. These are the same scales that relate to severity of drug abuse and antisocial behavior in a clinical sample as will be discussed subsequently. In contrast, the most adaptive pattern, integration, is related to sensation seeking, but to a non-impulsive type characterized by sociability and

a need for high activity (probably work-related) and low aggression-hostility. Separation is negatively related to sensation seeking and sociability and positively related to anxiety. Those in this group are anxious because of novelty in the new culture and defend by rigidly adhering to the old ways.

Love styles

There are many types of love in relationships between unrelated adults. Hendrick and Hendrick (1986) developed scales to measures six types of love:

1 Eros is passionate, focused, and committed love or romantic love.
2 Ludus is playful, sexual, but less committed type of love.
3 Storge represents friendship and closeness more than passion.
4 Agape is selfless devotion to the other with strong commitment.
5 Manic is anxious, obsessive, dependent, possessive, and jealous love.
6 Pragama is mate selection based upon appraisal of mate's potentials for a stable long-term relationship.

The six types of love styles were related to the SSS by Richardson et al. (1988). Ludus was positively correlated with the total SSS and all of the subscales. Pragma was negatively correlated with the Total SSS and TAS and Dis subscales. Agape correlated negatively with ES and Dis subscales.

Schmitz (2004) repeated this study substituting the ZKPQ for the SSS. The ImpSS scale was analyzed for its Imp and SS components separately as well as their total. Total ImpSS correlated positively with ludus and negatively with pragma replicating the results with the SSS. But whereas both components correlated negatively with pragma, only the SS subscale correlated with ludus. Sociability correlated positively and N-Anx correlated negatively with eros. Activity correlated positively with ludus, pragma, and mania. N-Anx and Agg-Host corre-lated low but positively and significantly with mania.

Psychopathology

The personality disorders are a special category of disorders in the DSM of the American Psychiatric Association (Form IV, 1994). They represent more pervasive, persistent, inflexible types of psychopathology on dimensions which often represent abnormal extremes of normal traits (Costello, 1996). It is generally thought that personality disorders represent maladaptive extremes of normal dimensions of personality (Livesley et al., 1994). They can be expected to occur in large general populations with some frequency.

Aluja et al. (2007) used the Millon Clinical Multiaxial Inventory III (MCMI-III) (Millon, et al., 1994) which contains scales for each of the personality disorders (PDs) in the DSM including some provisional unofficial ones. The disorders are grouped into three categories: A – odd and eccentric; B – dramatic, emotional, and erratic; and C – anxious or fearful. Table 11.7 shows the disorders classified in each major category and a score representing the sum of those. Table 11.7 shows the correlations of the disorder scales with the ZKPQ in a student population from three Spanish universities and their friends and relatives from the general population. The average age was 33 years.

ImpSS and Agg-Host correlated most highly with the cluster B which includes antisocial, narcissistic, histrionic, and borderline PDs. N-Anx correlated most prominently with both cluster C (avoidant, and dependent, but not obsessive-compulsive disorders), and cluster A (schizotypal, schizoid and paranoid disorders). Sociability had a very high positive correlation with the histrionic PD and a strong negative correlation with the schizoid PD. Activity showed little strong correlation with the PDs. All of the unclassified PDs (sadistic, masochistic, depressive, and passive-aggressive) correlated with N-Anx, but the sadistic also had a strong correlation with Agg-Host. A factor analysis sharpened these contrasts between the ZKPQ and the three categories of PDs.

A similar kind of study was conducted in a Chinese student population (Wang et al., 2004) using the Dimensional Assessment of Personality Pathology (DAPP-BQ) (Livesley et al., 1998). Unlike the MCMI, the DAPP contains scales of abnormal

Table 11.7   Correlations between MCMI-III personality disorder scales and ZKPQ

	ImpSS	N-Anxiety	Agg-Host	Activity	Sociability
Schizoid (A)	−0.14*	0.27*	−0.03	−0.09	−0.54*
Schizotypal (A)	0.20*	0.46*	0.22*	0.02	−0.14*
Paranoid (A)	0.11	0.34*	0.30*	0.07	−0.11
Cluster A	0.08	0.41*	0.22*	0.01	−0.29*
Histrionic (B)	0.38*	−0.20*	0.13*	0.21*	0.65*
Narcissistic (B)	0.40*	−0.30*	0.35*	0.21*	0.29*
Antisocial (B)	0.58*	0.10	0.44*	0.03	0.17*
Borderline (B)	0.35*	0.52*	0.33*	0.03	0.03
Cluster B	0.62*	0.05	0.45*	0.18*	0.45*
Avoidant (C)	−0.11	0.50*	0.04	−0.09	−0.32*
Dependent (C)	0.05	0.53*	0.00	−0.03	0.01
Ob-Comp (C)	−0.49*	−0.04	−0.26*	0.12	−0.21*
Cluster C	−0.27*	0.44*	−0.12	0.01	−0.24*
Sadistic (U)	0.35*	0.30*	0.54*	0.11	0.04
Masochistic (U)	0.09	0.52*	0.15*	−0.06	−0.15*
Depressive (U)	0.02	0.64*	0.16*	−0.01	−0.16*
Passive-Agg (U)	0.21*	0.56*	0.37*	0.01	−0.04

Based on data from Aluja, A. et al. (2007) not published in the article
Cluster A = odd or eccentric; Cluster B = dramatic, erratic, emotional; Cluster C = anxious or fearful; U = unclassified, not part of DSM-IV
*$p < 0.001$

personality traits rather than diagnoses. ImpSS correlated significantly with scales for: Affective lability, callousness, conduct problems, narcissism, oppositionality, rejection, and stimulus seeking. N-Anx correlated primarily with scales for anxiousness, affective lability, cognitive distortion, identity problems, insecure attachment, oppositionality, social avoidance, submissiveness, and suspiciousness. Agg-Host was related to scales for affective lability, callousness, conduct problems, and rejection. Activity was unrelated to nearly all of the scales except compulsivity. Sociability was negatively related to restricted expression, intimacy problems and social avoidance.

Drug abuse

In contrast to a previous section on drug use, drug abuse is defined by those who have had legal and social problems with drugs and as a consequence entered into treatment. Black (1993) studied drug abusers in an outpatient clinic using the ZKPQ. Contrasts of patients based on their primary drug of use showed that primary alcohol users were higher on sociability than cocaine users, whereas the cocaine users were higher on N-Anx and Agg-Host. Primary marijuana users did not differ from either alcohol or cocaine users. The scale was predictive of outcome of treatment. Those who completed the program successfully were higher on sociability, whereas those who violated the prohibition on drug use during the program were higher than others on N-Anx and Agg-Host.

Ball (1995) gave the ZKPQ to 450 cocaine abusers seeking outpatient treatment. Although the ZKPQ scales are relatively uncorrelated in normal populations, the ImpSS, N-Anx, and Agg-Host were substantially intercorrelated in this population and therefore showed similar results. For instance, severity of drug abuse and addiction and other psychiatric problems were related to all three of these scales. All three also predicted treatment outcome. Cocaine abusers

who continued to use cocaine during treatment scored higher on ImpSS and N-Anx on admission with a marginal effect for Agg-Host. There were some correlations with treatment response that were specific to ImpSS. ImpSS correlated with number of treatment appointments kept and those who scored high on ImpSS and Agg-Host were less successful in remaining at least one month in treatment and were more likely to be judged in need of inpatient treatment.

Cluster analyses of the ZKPQ yielded two subtypes. Subtype 2 had higher scores on ImpSS, Agg-Host, and N-Anx but lower scores on sociability. Type 1 comprized mainly men stipulated by the courts, not abused as children, and free of psychiatric symptoms. Type 2 consisted mainly of women who were abused as children and who reported other psychiatric symptoms. They were more recent users of cocaine. Type 1 seemed to be drug abusers who used drugs primarily for the pleasure and type 2s were more likely to use it to self-medicate in dealing with lifelong problems.

Ball and Schottenfeld (1997) studied 92 pregnant and post-partum drug-abusing women in a day-treatment program. In this study N-Anx was prominently related to drug, legal, and psychiatric severity, and a history of depression, anxiety, and attention-difficulties. A history of violence and criminal arrests was primarily associated with Agg-Host, but both N-Anx and Agg-Host were associated with a history of attention difficulties and suicidal tendencies. ImpSS, N-Anx, and Agg-Host were all correlated with scores on the Beck (1993) Depression Inventory.

In a previous section I described the characteristics of prostitutes, many of whom also had drug problems. Many women who use drugs use prostitution as a source of income to finance their habit. In that study the prostitutes scored higher than controls mainly on ImpSS with a borderline result for Agg-Host. In the Ball and Schottenfeld (1997) study, women who had sex with multiple partners and women who exchanged sex for money and drugs scored higher on ImpSS, N-Anx, and Agg-Host, than those reporting few partners. Having many strangers as sex partners without the protection of condoms is a high-risk activity for anyone. In this group the women who reported being tested many times for HIV virus scored higher on the N-Anx and Agg-Host scales.

Psychopathy

Psychopathic or antisocial personality is frequent in groups of substance abusers; in fact it may be the modal diagnosis. The studies of personality in drug abusers are usually based on admission testing, but the profiles on entry are influenced by the current stress affecting the drug clients. The twin peaks on the psychopathic deviate and hypomania scores on the MMPI are most characteristic of the uncomplicated psychopathic personality. In a study of drug abusers entering a inpatient drug program only 21% showed this kind of profile, but on retesting six months into the program, 63% of residents and 93% of the female residents showed this profile (Zuckerman et al., 1975). Scores on scales indicating anxiety, mood, and psychosis had dropped-off leaving the Pd and Ma scales still elevated. The results were similar in an outpatient program where 61% of a group of cocaine users had the psychopathic MMPI profile after starting treatment (Ball et al., 1997).

It is possible that the elevation of N-Anx in the more severe cocaine addicts in the studies by Ball was a function of the more severe stress they were under at the time of admission into the program. ImpSS and Agg-Host may represent the more permanent and characteristic traits related to psychopathy in these populations. It is important to have more direct measures of psychopathy beyond self-report test scores.

Psychopathic personalities are even more common in prison than in drug populations. Thornquist and Zuckerman (1995) used the Hare (1991) Psychopathy Check List (PCL), based on interview and review of case histories, to assess psychopathy in prison inmates enrolled in a drug program. The ZKPQ was also given and a laboratory task associated with impulsivity was used. Ratings of psychopathy from the PCL correlated significantly with ImpSS and Agg-Host but only in White prisoners and not in Black or Hispanic prisoners. On the laboratory task, errors of commission were correlated only with ImpSS. Errors of commission, or passive avoidance, are errors in learning not to respond when signals of punishment are present.

BIOLOGICAL STUDIES

The author has been interested in the psychobiology of personality and the development of the alternative five-factor model grew out of the need to organize my first book on this topic by defining the basic traits of study (Zuckerman, 1991). Since then, a second volume has been organized around four of the five traits identifiable both in the Big Five and the Alternative Five systems (Zuckerman, 2005).

Genetics

Genetic studies of sensation seeking using twins prior to the development of the ZKPQ ImpSS scale showed a high genetic contribution to the variance of sensation seeking with little effect for shared environment but the remainder effects due to non-shared environment (Zuckerman, 2002b). Until recently, it was not known if these results could be extended to the ImpSS measure of sensation seeking.

Angleitner et al. (2004) conducted the first twin study using their German translation of the ZKPQ. The twin sample included 223–225 monozygotic (identical) twins and 113 dizygotic (fraternal) twins. Table 11.8 shows the correlations of identical and fraternal twins on the main and subtrait or

Table 11.8   Twin Correlations, Heritabilities and Environment Parameters (Reduced Models) for ZKPQ Major and Facet Scales

ZKPQ Scales/Facets	MZr	DZr	h	SE	NSE
Sociability/	.51	.27	.51	___	.49
Parties and Friends	.47	.23	.47	___	.53
Isolation Intolerance	.50	.27	.49	___	.51
Imp-Sensation Seeking/	.42	.30	.43	___	.57
Sensation Seeking	.46	.20	.45	___	.55
Impulsivity	.23	.34	___	.27	.73
Neuroticism-Anxiety	.42	.09	.43*	___	.57
Aggression-Hostility	.46	.22	.45	___	.55
Activity/	.48	.29	.49	___	.53
General Activity	.45	.24	.47	___	.53
Work Effort	.36	.26	.38	___	.62

Note: h = additive genetic variance except for neuroticism* where it equals non-additive genetic variance; SE = Shared environment; NSE = non-shared environment

MZr = monozygotic twin correlation (*n* = 223-225); DZr = dizygotic twin correlation (*n* = 113)

From "Investigating the ZKPQ-III-R" by A. Angleitner, R. Rieman, & F. M. Spinath. In R. M Stelmack (Ed.),2004, *On the psychobiology of personality: Essays in honor of Marvin Zuckerman,* tables 7 & 8, pps 100-101. Oxford, UK: Elsevier. Copyright 2004 by Elsevier Ltd. Reprinted by permission.

facet scores of the ZKPQ and the proportions of variance due to genetics, shared environment, and non-shared environment in the reduced or best-fitting models.

The heritability estimates for the major five scales range from 0.43 to 0.51. Only the impulsivity facet of the ImpSS scale showed no heritability and a significant shared environment effect. In contrast the SS component showed a heritability of 0.45 and no effect of shared environment, consistent with previous research on the sensation-seeking trait, but somewhat lower than the 0.6 heritability usually found for the SSS and its subscales (Zuckerman, 2002b). If we accept these data, ImpSS is a reliable combination of a trait with moderate heritability (SS) and one with primarily environmental determination (Imp). Buss and Plomin (1975) decided to exclude impulsivity as a temperament partly because of the mixed results on evidence for heritability in twin studies. They concluded, 'Of all the temperaments, impulsivity is the most affected by environment' (1975: 146). Jang et al. (1998) found that the impulsiveness component of the NEO, a facet of neuroticism in that test, had only a relatively low heritability (0.37), but there was no evidence of shared environment influence. Impulsivity, however, is defined in different ways and subscales are

only weakly correlated. The type in the ImpSS can be described as non-planning and acting on impulse. Other types may be more heritable and less influenced by environment. It should be noted that the German sample scored much lower than American, Spanish, and Swiss samples on ImpSS (Aluja et al., 2006). This could have had some effect on the results in contrast to the other traits.

Another anomaly in the results is that although the other traits can be explained by a model that postulates additive genetic mechanisms, N-Anx data suggest a non-additive type of genetic mechanism. This is reflected in the lack of correlation in the fraternal twin sample, in contrast to the other traits where the correlations are roughly half of those for identical twins as postulated by an additive genetic model. Neuroticism usually shows the signs of an additive genetic basis of its heritability in other studies.

Perceived parental behavior and attitudes

The relationships between personality and behavior of parents toward children, as reported by children are of interest in terms of social theories of personality formation.

However, such correlations are ambiguous in the sense that one cannot tell if causal direction, if any, between parental treatment are produced by genetic or environmental sources or their interaction. Parents and children share genes that could affect similar behavior, such as aggression or anxiety, in both. The child's behavior may evoke reactions in the parent as well as vice versa. On the basis of the results of most twin studies showing no effect of shared environment on sensation seeking we might expect little correlation between parental behavior and children's personalities.

Kraft and Zuckerman (1999) used the EMBU, a scale based on retrospective recall of how one was treated by one's parents. The same three factor scales are used for mothers' and fathers' behaviors: punishment/rejection, love/warmth, and overprotection/control. The subjects were college students about 19 years of age. Subjects were drawn from those with intact families and those who came from divorced families with a stepfather or stepmother. There were too few in the stepmother group for correlational analyses so these were done only on intact family and families with a stepfather.

There were no significant differences between children from intact and stepparent families on any of the ZKPQ scales, even though there were differences on the EMBU suggesting that differences in the emotional climates of the two types of families made no difference in the personalities of the children emerging from them. In the intact families there were no significant correlations between EMBU father or mother behaviors and ImpSS, Agg-Host, and activity ZKPQ scales. N-Anx had a number of significant correlations with EMBU scores. Father punishment-rejection correlated positively and father love correlated negatively with N-Anx in both males and females. In males only mothers' and fathers' control correlated positively with N-Anx. In families with a stepfather, father punishment correlated positively with N-Anx and Agg-Host for both males and females. Father love correlated positively with sociability in females in both intact and stepfather families.

Augmenting-reducing of the cortical evoked potential

The relationship of the amplitude of the cortical evoked potential (EP) in response to increasing intensities of stimulation has provided an interesting source of individual differences. On a simple psychophysiological basis one would expect the cortical response to increase in a linear fashion with increases in stimulus intensity. This does occur in some individuals to one degree or another and these are called 'augmenters'. However, other individuals show little increase of EP amplitude as a function of stimulus intensity or even a reduction of the EP at the highest intensity, and therefore are called 'reducers'. Actually augmenting-reducing (A-R) is not a typology but a normally distributed function as indexed by the slope of the regression between stimulus intensity and EP amplitude.

The relationship between the A-R of the visually evoked EP and disinhibitory sensation seeking was first demonstrated by Zuckerman et al. (1974). High sensation seekers tended to be augmenters and low sensation seekers were usually reducers. The relationship has been replicated most of the time and extended to A-R of the auditory EP (Zuckerman, 1990, 1994). Various behavioral and psychopathological correlates of the A-R function have been reported in humans and it has been a useful model in animals, differentiating types in cats and subspecies of rats with analogous behaviors to those seen in human high and low sensation seekers (Siegel and Driscoll, 1996).

Brocke et al. (1999) (also see Brocke, 2004) used the auditory EP and related its A-R in relation to both the SSS and the ZKPQ. They found that both the SSS-total and the ZKPQ ImpSS correlated positively with the slope of the P2 (a peak function about 170 ms after the stimulus).

The A-R function is influenced by or related to differences in neurotransmitters, as shown by human and animal studies, and is therefore important in providing hypotheses for biochemical bases of personality at a more basic level of brain function (Zuckerman, 1995).

SUMMARY

The ZKPQ was developed to derive a personality system appropriate for measuring basic traits of personality with their roots in biological traits. This is why we used questionnaires that had already established some connections with psychophysiological and biochemical markers. Five reliable factors were found, first in factor analyses of scales and then in analyses of items from these scales. Four of the five of these factor-derived scales have some relationship to factors in the Big Five of Costa and McCrae, but their fifth factor, openness, is not related to the fifth factor of the ZKPQ, activity. Relationships with Eysenck's Big Three are also strong: E with Sy, N with N-Anx, and P with both ImpSS and Agg-Host.

We have argued that sensation seeking is a basic trait of personality as shown by high heritability, many biological correlates, and a wide range of behavioral expressions. We did find that it was one of our central factors but it was also linked with a type of impulsivity reflecting spontaneity and lack of planning in behavioral expressions, even risky ones. We called the blend 'impulsive sensation seeking' but allowed separate scoring for the two facets in the long form of the ZKPQ.

All five scales have shown good internal reliabilities even in translated scales in seven other countries. On the basis of good factor reliability a short form has been developed which is equivalent in four languages: English, German, French, and Spanish. Retest reliabilities are good for intervals ranging from three weeks to seven months.

Validity as established by correlations with peer or spouse evaluations are excellent. Risky behavior as in substance use and sex are predictable from one or more of the scales in combination, usually ImpSS, N-Anx, and Agg-Host. Other areas of study have included gambling, team sports,

prostitution, migrant acculturation, and love styles. Antisocial expressions and impulsive, egocentric types of personality disorders are related primarily to ImpSS and Agg-Host. ZKPQ scales are useful in assessing drug abusers and predicting reactions to treatment and outcomes. Internalizing, neurotic type personality disorders, like avoidant, dependent, and depressive, are related to N-Anx.

Studies of the psychobiology of personality using the ZKPQ are just beginning. The first biometric twin study shows moderate heritabilities typical of other personality traits. A measure of individual differences based on the dependence of the cortical evoked potential on stimulus intensity which has been useful in comparative studies of sensation seeking has been found to be related to the newer ImpSS scale. The ZKPQ should be explored as an instrument for revealing the underlying basis of personality in the brain.

REFERENCES

Aluja, A., Cuevas, L., Garcia, L.F. and Garcia, O. (2007) 'Zuckerman's personality model predicts MCMI-III personality disorders', *Personality and Individual Differences*, 42(7): 1311–21.

Aluja, A., Garcia, O. and Garcia, L.F. (2004) 'Replicability of the three, four, and five Zuckerman's personality super-factors: Exploratory and confirmatory factor analysis of the EPQ-RS, ZKPQ, and NEO-PI-R', *Personality and Individual Diffferences*, 36(5): 1093–108.

Aluja, A., Rossier, J., Garcia, L.F., Angleitner, A., Kuhlman, M. and Zuckerman, M. (2006) 'A cross-cultural shortened form of the ZKPQ (ZKPQ-50-cc) adapted to English, French, German, and Spanish languages', *Personality and Individual Differences*, 41(4): 619–28.

American Psychiatric Association (1994) *Diagnostic and Statistical Manual of the Mental Disorders* (4th edn). Washington, DC: APA.

Angleitner, A., Riemann, R. and Spinath, F.M. (2004) 'Investigating the ZKPQ-III-R: Psychometric properties, relations to the five-factor model, and genetic and environmental influences on its scales and facets', in R. M. Stelmack (ed.), *On the Psychobiology of Personality: Essays in Honor of Marvin Zuckerman*. Oxford: Elsevier, pp. 89–105.

Ball, S.A. (1995) 'The validity of an alternative five-factor measure of personality in cocaine abusers', *Psychological Assessment*, 7(2): 148–54.

Ball, S.A., Carroll, K.M., Robinson, J.E. and O'Malley, S.S. (1997) 'Addiction severity and MMPI-derived typologies in cocaine abusers', *American Journal on Addictions*, 6(1): 83–6.

Ball, S.A. and Schottenfeld, R.S. (1997) 'A five-factor model of personality and addiction, psychiatric, and AIDS risk severity in pregnant and post-partum cocaine misusers', *Substance Use and Misuse*, 32(1): 25–41.

Ball, S.A. and Zuckerman, M. (1990) 'Sensation seeking, Eysenck's personality dimensions and reinforcement sensitivity in concept formation', *Personality and Individual Differences*, 11(4): 343–53.

Beck, A. (1993) *Beck Depression Inventory/Aaron T. Beck Robert A. Starr*. San Antonio, TX.

Black, J.J. (1993) 'Predictors of outcome at an outpatient substance abuse center', Unpublished doctoral dissertation, University of Delaware, Newark.

Breen, B.B. and Zuckerman, M. (1999) '"Chasing" in gambling behavior: Personality and cognitive determinants', *Personality and Individual Differences*, 27(6): 1097–111.

Brocke, B. (2004) 'The multilevel approach in sensation seeking: Potentials and findings of a four-level research program', in R.M. Stelmack (ed.), *On the Psychobiology of Personality*. Amsterdam: Elsevier, pp. 267–93.

Brocke, B., Beauducel, A. and Tashe, K.G. (1999) 'Biopsychological bases and behavioral correlates of sensation seeking: Contributions to a multilevel validation', *Personality and Individual Differences*, 26(6): 1103–123.

Buss, A.H. and Plomin, R. (1975) *A Temperamental Theory of Personality Development*. New York: Wiley.

Campbell, D.T. and Fiske, D.W. (1959) 'Convergent and discriminant validation by the multitrait-multimethods matrix', *Psychological Bulletin*, 56(2): 81–105.

Cloninger, C.R. (1987) 'A systematic method for clinical description and classification of personality variants', *Archives of General Psychiatry*, 44(6): 573–88.

Costa, P.T. Jr. and McCrae, R.R. (1985) *The NEO Personality Inventory Manual*. Odessa, FL: Psychological Assessment Resources.

Costa, P.T. Jr. and McCrae, R.R. (1992) *NEO-PI-R: Revised NEO Personality Inventory (NEO-PI-R)*. Odessa, FL: Psychological Assessment Resources.

Costello, C.G. (1996) 'The advantages of focusing on the personality characteristics of the personality disordered', in C.G. Costello (ed.), *Personality Characteristics of the Personality Disordered*. New York: Wiley, pp. 1–23.

Cronbach, L.J. and Meehl, P.E. (1955) 'Construct validity in psychological tests', *Psychological Bulletin*, 52(4): 281–302.

De Pascalis, V. and Russo, P.M. (2003) 'Zuckerman–Kuhlman Personality Questionnaire: Preliminary results of the Italian version', *Psychological Reports*, 92(3): 965–74.

Eysenck, H.J. and Eysenck, S.B.G. (1975) *Manual of the Eysenck Personality Questionnaire (Junior and Adult)*. London: Hodder & Stoughton.

Goma-i-Freixanet, M., Valero, S., Punti, J. and Zuckerman, M. (2004) 'Psychometric properties of the Zuckerman–Kuhlman Personality Questionnaire in a Spanish sample', *European Journal of Psychological Assessment*, 20(20): 134–46.

Goma-i-Freixanet, M., Wismeijer, A.J. and Valero, S. (2005) 'Consensual validity parameters of the Zuckerman–Kuhlman Personality Questionnaire: Evidence from self-reports and spouse reports', *Journal of Personality Assessment*, 84(3): 279–86.

Gosling, S.D. (2001) 'From mice to men: What can we learn about personality from animal research?', *Psychological Bulletin*, 127(1): 45–86.

Gray, J.A. (1982) *The Neuropsychology of Anxiety: An Enquiry into the Function of the Septohippocampal System*. New York: Oxford University Press.

Greenbaum, P.E., Del Boca, F.K., Darkes, J., Wang, C-P. and Goldman, M.C. (2005) 'Variation in the drinking trajectories of freshman college students', *Journal of*

Consulting and Clinical Psychology, 73(2): 229–38.

Greenwald, H. (1970) *The Elegant Prostitute.* New York: Walker & Co.

Hare, R.D. (1991) *The Hare Psychopathy Checklist-Revised.* Toronto: Multi-Health Systems.

Hendrick, C. and Hendrick, S.S. (1986) 'A theory and method of love', *Journal of Personality and Social Psychology*, 50(2): 392–402.

Jang, K.L., McCrae, R.R., Angleitner, A., Rieman, R. and Livesley, W.J. (1998) 'Heritability of facet-level traits in a cross-cultural twin sample: Support for a hierarchal model of personality', *Journal of Personality and Social Psychology*, 74(6): 1556–65.

Joireman, J. and Kuhlman, D.M. (2004) 'The Zuckerman–Kuhlman Personality Questionnaire: Origin, development, and validity of a measure to assess an alternative five-factor model of personality', in R.M. Stelmack (ed.), *On the Psychobiology of Personality: Essays in Honor of Marvin Zuckerman.* Amsterdam: Elsevier, pp. 49–64.

Kraft, M.R. Jr. and Zuckerman, M. (1999) 'Parental behavior and attitudes of parents reported by young adults from intact and stepparent families and relationships between perceived parenting and personality', *Personality and Individual Differences*, 27(3): 453–76.

Livesley, W.J., Jang, K.L. and Vernon, P.A. (1998) 'The phenotypic and genetic structure of traits delineating personality disorder', *Archives of General Psychiatry*, 55(10): 941–8.

Livesley, W.J., Schroeder, M.L., Jackson, D.N. and Jang, K.L. (1994) 'Categorical distinctions in the the study of personality disorder: Implications for classification', *Journal of Abnormal Psychology*, 103(1): 6–17.

Lubin, B. and Zuckerman, M. (1999) *MAACL-R: Manual for the Multiple Affect Adjective Check List- Revised.* San Diego, CA: Educational and Industrial Testing Service.

McDaniel, S.R. and Zuckerman, M. (2003) 'The relationship of impulsive sensation seeking and gender to interest and participation in gambling activities', *Personality and Individual Differences*, 35(6): 1385–400.

O'Sullivan, D.M., Zuckerman, M. and Kraft, M. (1996) 'The personality of prostitutes', *Personality and Individual Differences*, 21(1): 445–8.

O'Sullivan, D.M., Zuckerman, M. and Kraft, M. (1998) 'Personality characteristics of male and female participants in team sports', *Personality and Individual Differences*, 25: 119–28.

Richardson, D.R., Medvin, N. and Hammock, G. (1988) 'Love styles, relationship experience, and sensation seeking: A test of validity', *Personality and Individual Differences*, 9(3): 645–51.

Schmitz, P.G. (2004) 'On the alternative five-factor model: Structure and correlates', in R.M. Stelmack (ed.), *On the Psychobiology of Personality: Essays in Honor of Marvin Zuckerman.* Amsterdam: Elsevier, pp. 65–87.

Shiomi, K, Kuhlman, D.M., Zuckerman, M., Joireman, J.A., Sato, M. and Yata, S. (1996) 'Examining the validity and reliability of a Japanese version of the Zuckerman–Kuhlman Personality Questionnaire (ZKPQ)', *Hyago University of Teacher Education Journal*, 2: 1–13.

Thornquist, M.H. and Zuckerman, M. (1995) 'Psychopathy, passive-avoidance learning and basic dimensions of personality', *Personality and Individual Differences*, 19(4): 525–34.

Torrubia, R., Avila, C., Moltó, J. and Caserás, X. (2001) 'The sensitivity to punishment and sensitivity to reward questionnaire (SPSRQ) as a measure of Gray's anxiety and impulsivity dimensions', *Personality and Individual Differences*, 15(6): 837–62.

Van Zile-Tamsen, C., Harlow, L.L. and Livingston, J.A. (2006) 'A measurement model of women's behavioral risk-taking', *Health Psychology*, 25: 249–54.

Wang, W., Du, W., Wang, Y., Livesley, J. and Jang, K.L. (2004) 'The relationship between the Zuckerman–Kuhlman Personality Questionnaire and traits delineating personality pathology', *Personality and Individual Differences*, 36(1): 155–62.

Wu, Y-X, Wang, W., Du, W-Y, Li, J., Jiang, X-F and Wang, Y-H (2000) 'Development of a Chinese version of the Zuckerman–Kuhlman Personality Questionnaire: Reliabilities and gender/age effects', *Social Behavior and Personality*, 28(3): 241–50.

Zuckerman, M. (1979) *Sensation Seeking: Beyond the Optimal Level of Arousal.* Hillsdale, NJ: Erlbaum.

Zuckerman, M. (1984) 'Sensation seeking: A comparative approach to a human trait', *Behavioral and Brain Sciences*, 7(3): 413–34.

Zuckerman, M. (1991) *Psychobiology of Personality*. Cambridge, UK: Cambridge University Press.

Zuckerman, M. (1993) 'Sensation seeking and impulsivity: A marriage of traits made in biology?', in W.G. McCown, J.L. Johnson and M.B. Shure (eds), *The Impulsive Client: Theory, Research, and Treatment*. Washington, DC: American Psychological Association, pp. 71–91.

Zuckerman, M. (1994) *Behavioral Expressions and Biosocial Bases of Sensation Seeking*. New York: Cambridge University Press.

Zuckerman, M. (1995) 'Good and bad humors: Biochemical bases of personality and its disorders', *Psychological Science*, 6(6): 325–32.

Zuckerman, M. (2002a) 'Zuckerman–Kuhlman Personality Questionnaire (ZKPQ): An alternative five-factorial model', in B. De Raad and M. Perugini (eds), *Big Five Assessment*. Seattle, WA: Hogrefe & Huber, pp. 377–96.

Zuckerman, M. (2002b) 'Genetics of sensation seeking', in J. Benjamin, R.P. Ebstein and R.H. Belmaker (eds), *Molecular Genetics and the Human Personality*. Washington, DC: American Psychiatric Publishing, pp. 193–210.

Zuckerman, M. (2005) *Psychobiology of Personality* (2nd edn, revised and updated). New York: Cambridge University Press.

Zuckerman, M. (2006) 'Biosocial bases of sensation seeking', in T. Canli (ed.), *Biology of Personality and Individual Differences*. New York: Guilford, pp. 37–59.

Zuckerman, M. (2007) *Sensation Seeking and Risky Behavior*. Washington, DC: American Psychological Association.

Zuckerman, M. and Cloninger, C.R. (1996) 'Relationships between Cloninger's, Zuckerman's, and Eysenck's dimensions of personality', *Personality and Individual Differences*, 21(2): 283–5.

Zuckerman, M., Joireman, J., Kraft, M. and Kuhlman, D.M. (1999) 'Where do motivational and emotional traits fit within three factor models of personality?', *Personality and Individual Differences*, 26(3): 487–504.

Zuckerman, M. and Kuhlman, D.M. (2000) 'Personality and risk-taking: Common biosocial factors', *Journal of Personality*, 68(6): 999–1029.

Zuckerman, M., Kuhlman, D.M. and Camac, C. (1988) 'What lies beyond E and N? Factor analysis of scales believed to measure basic dimensions of personality', *Journal of Personality and Social Psychology*, 54(3): 96–107.

Zuckerman, M., Kuhlman, D.M., Joireman, J., Teta, P. and Kraft, M. (1993) 'A comparison of three structural models for personality: The big three, the big five, and the alternative five', *Journal of Personality and Social Psychology*, 65(4): 757–68.

Zuckerman, M., Kuhlman, D., Thornquist, M. and Kiers, H. (1991) 'Five (or three) robust questionnaire scale factors of personality without culture', *Personality and Individual Differences*, 12(9): 929–41.

Zuckerman, M. and Lubin, B. (1985) *Manual of the Multiple Affect Adjective Check List-Revised (MAACL-R)*. San Diego: CA: Educational and Industrial Testing Service.

Zuckerman, M., Murtaugh, T.T. and Siegel, J. (1974) 'Sensation seeking and cortical augmenting-reducing', *Psychophysiology*, 11(5): 535–42.

Zuckerman, M., Sola, S., Masterson, J. and Angelone, J.V., (1975) 'MMPI patterns in drug abusers before and after treatment in therapeutic communities', *Journal of Consulting and Clinical Psychology*, 43(3): 286–96.

12

The HEXACO Model of Personality Structure

Michael C. Ashton and Kibeom Lee

By the 1990s, many personality researchers had reached a consensus that the domain of personality variation was best summarized in terms of five broad and roughly independent dimensions known as the Big Five factors. These dimensions were discovered in investigations of English-language personality-descriptive adjectives, and were later popularized via the Five-Factor Model of personality structure and its associated questionnaire instruments.

In recent years, however, there has emerged much new evidence suggesting an alternative representation of personality structure. This newer framework, which we have called the HEXACO model, consists of six rather than five dimensions. Three of the six HEXACO factors have close counterparts in the Big Five or Five-Factor Model (B5/FFM), whereas the other three HEXACO factors have more complex relations with the remaining two dimensions of the B5/FFM.

In this chapter, we will begin by describing the origins and content of the HEXACO dimensions, which were discovered in analyses of the personality lexicons of various languages. After summarizing the results of those studies and the content of the six HEXACO dimensions, we then discuss the theoretical bases of these factors, exploring the likely adaptive trade-offs between high and low levels of each dimension. We then turn to the predictive validity of the HEXACO constructs in accommodating a variety of personality characteristics, particularly those that may be only modestly associated with the B5/FFM dimensions.[1] Next, we discuss the differences between the HEXACO model and some other recently proposed frameworks, as judged both by interpretability of factors as personality constructs and also by the replicability of the structures. Finally, we discuss the results of some recent lexical studies of personality structure conducted in the Croatian, Greek, and Filipino languages.

EMPIRICAL BASIS: RESULTS OF LEXICAL STUDIES OF PERSONALITY STRUCTURE IN MANY LANGUAGES

The statistical technique of factor analysis is useful for identifying the major dimensions that underlie the domain of personality characteristics. But if factor analysis is to generate an accurate model of personality structure, it is necessary to analyze variable sets that are representative of that domain. Such variable sets can be obtained through the lexical strategy, whereby the familiar personality-descriptive words (usually adjectives) of a language are selected as the variables on which participants' self- or peer ratings can be obtained and then factor-analyzed. The important strength of the lexical approach is that the selected variables constitute the full array of subjectively important personality characteristics that have been observed and described by generations of speakers of a language. Thus, this approach greatly reduces the problem of researcher biases in the selection of personality variables (see Ashton and Lee, 2008a, for responses to various criticisms of the lexical approach).

EARLY ENGLISH-LANGUAGE LEXICAL STUDIES: ORIGINS OF THE BIG FIVE AND FIVE-FACTOR MODEL

The first lexically based investigations of personality structure were conducted in the English language. In those early studies (e.g. Cattell, 1947), limited computing power forced researchers to use rather small variable sets (typically less than 50 variables) that represented only a small fraction of the English personality lexicon. Those investigations consistently produced a common set of five factors (see Tupes and Christal, 1961,1992) now called the 'Big Five' (e.g. Goldberg, 1990). The names of these Big Five factors are extraversion (e.g. *talkative, outgoing* versus *quiet, shy*), agreeableness (e.g. *gentle, sympathetic* versus *harsh, cold-hearted*), conscientiousness (e.g. *organized, disciplined* versus *sloppy, lazy*), emotional stability (e.g. *relaxed* versus *moody, anxious*), and intellect/imagination (e.g. *intellectual, imaginative* versus *shallow*).

The Big Five factors have been popularized through the closely related Five-Factor Model,

whose dimensions are operationalized by the the NEO Personality Inventory – Revised and the NEO Five-Factor Inventory (NEO-PI-R and NEO-FFI; Costa and McCrae, 1992). In these instruments, the five factors are conceptualized in ways that depart slightly from the original Big Five identities, but remain very similar overall to the Big Five structure. (One noteworthy difference is that the five-factor model openness to experience factor excludes the intellectual *ability* aspects of the corresponding Big Five factor of intellect/imagination.) Note that the Five-Factor Model does owe its ultimate origins to lexical studies of personality structure (see McCrae, 1989). Three of its dimensions – neuroticism (i.e. low emotional stability), extraversion, and openness to experience – were identified in analyses of Cattell's personality scales, which had been derived from his earlier lexical research (Cattell, 1947). Its other two dimensions – agreeableness and conscientiousness – were later added in response to findings from lexical studies of personality structure in the English language.

During the past decade, the factor structure of the NEO-PI-R has been examined in countries around the world. The results show that the five-factor space consistently corresponds closely to that obtained in samples from the US. But although this result supports the validity of the NEO-PI-R as an operationalization of the B5/FFM, it does not provide independent evidence that the B5/FFM is the optimal cross-culturally replicated representation of personality structure (cf. McCrae and Costa, 1997, 2003). Such evidence can only be forthcoming from analyses of variable sets that are *indigenous* to the cultures in question (not imported from the culture of the model's developers) and *representative* of the personality domain (not selected as markers of a specified set of factor axes).

If the B5/FFM did, in fact, represent the optimal structural model of personality variation, then one would not expect to observe any widespread recovery of a larger set of factors from analyses of personality variable sets that are culturally indigenous and representative of the personality domain. Some proponents of the Five-Factor Model have suggested that there exist five *and only five* factors of personality, a point that is viewed as 'an empirical fact, like the fact that there are seven continents or eight American presidents from Virginia' (McCrae and John, 1992: 194). From the perspective of the B5/FFM, the predicted result of investigations of personality structure is that the familiar five factors – but no more than five factors – should be replicated when the personality lexicons of various languages are analyzed.

LEXICAL STUDIES IN MANY LANGUAGES: EMERGENCE OF THE SIX-DIMENSIONAL (HEXACO) FRAMEWORK

Since the 1980s, lexical studies of personality structure have been conducted in various languages other than English, using adjective selection criteria that have generally followed the logic of the lexical approach by excluding terms that are not plausible descriptors of personality (e.g. terms that are chiefly evaluative or that describe physical characteristics and abilities; see Ashton and Lee, 2001, 2002). In most languages, the five-factor solutions have recovered the space of the Big Five factors as found in English, although often with some differences in the rotational positions of the factor axes. In a few languages, however, five-factor solutions have not recovered the Big Five factor space. Most notably, an intellect/imagination dimension has failed to emerge among the first five factors in lexical studies conducted in Italian (Di Blas and Forzi, 1998), in Hungarian (Szirmak and De Raad, 1994), and in Greek (Saucier et al., 2005; see also reanalysis by Lee and Ashton, 2006a). The most striking findings from these investigations, however, have been the results obtained in six-factor solutions. Contrary to the suggestion that there are five and only five replicable dimensions of personality,

a common set of six factors has emerged across at least 12 languages (see list in Table 12.1). As reported by Ashton et al. (2004), the personality lexicons of the Dutch, French, German, Hungarian, Italian, Korean, and Polish languages produced very similar six-factor solutions. A similar six-dimensional structure has also been recovered more recently in reanalyses of archival data based on the English personality lexicon (Ashton et al., 2004a), and also in reanalyses of investigations of the personality lexicons of the Croatian (Lee et al., 2005a), Greek (Lee and Ashton, 2008), Filipino (Ashton et al., 2006a), and Turkish (Wasti et al., in press) languages. (Later in this chapter, we provide a detailed description of the Croatian, Greek, and Filipino results.)

Listed in Table 12.2 (in English translation) are the adjectives that typically define these six factors as observed in the lexical studies conducted in various languages. Two of the factors in that table are very similar in content to the extraversion and conscientiousness dimensions obtained in five-factor solutions of previous English-language investigations. A third dimension of that table is similar to the English intellect/imagination dimension, with an additional prominent element of unconventionality.

Table 12.1   Languages having known six-factor solutions from lexical studies of personality structure (personality-descriptive adjectives only), classified by language family and (for Indo-European family) by branch of language family

Language Family (Branch)	Languages
Indo-European (Italic/Romance)	French, Italian
Indo-European (Germanic)	Dutch, English, German
Indo-European (Hellenic)	Greek
Indo-European (Slavic)	Croatian, Polish
Korean	Korean*
Malayo-Polynesian	Filipino
Turkic	Turkish*
Uralic	Hungarian

Note: See reviews of lexical study results in Ashton, Lee, Perugini, et al. (2004), Ashton and Lee (in press).
* Some linguists (e.g. Ruhlen, 1991) classify Korean and Turkish within a broad Altaic language family

Table 12.2 Summary of defining content and theoretical interpretations of HEXACO factors

Factor	Common defining adjectives in lexical studies	HEXACO-PI-R facet scales	Theoretical interpretation	Benefits of high level?	Costs of high level?
Honesty-humility	Sincere, honest, faithful/loyal, modest/unassuming, fair-minded versus sly, greedy, pretentious, hypocritical, boastful, pompous	Sincerity, fairness, greed-avoidance, modesty	Reciprocal altruism (fairness)	Gains from cooperation (mutual help and non-aggression)	Loss of potential gains that would result from exploitation of others
Agreeableness (versers anger)	Patient, tolerant, peaceful, mild, agreeable, lenient, gentle versus ill-tempered, quarrelsome, stubborn, choleric	Forgiveness, gentleness, flexibility, patience	Reciprocal altruism (tolerance)	Gains from cooperation (mutual help and non-aggression)	Losses due to being exploited by others
Emotionality	Emotional, oversensitive, sentimental, fearful, anxious, vulnerable versus brave, tough, independent, self-assured, stable	Fearfulness, anxiety, dependence, sentimentality	Kin altruism	Survival of kin (especially offspring); personal survival (especially as favors kin survival)	Loss of potential gains associated with risks to self and kin
Extraversion	Outgoing, lively, extraverted, sociable, talkative, cheerful, active versus shy, passive, withdrawn, introverted, quiet, reserved	Social self-esteem, social boldness, sociability, liveliness	Engagement in social endeavors	Social gains (i.e. friends, mates, allies)	Energy and time; risks from social environment
Conscientiousness	Organized, disciplined, diligent, careful, thorough, precise versus sloppy, negligent, reckless, lazy, irresponsible, absent-minded	Organization, diligence, perfectionism, prudence	Engagement in task-related endeavors	Material gains (i.e., improved use of resources), reduced risks	Energy and time
Openness to Experience	Intellectual, creative, unconventional, innovative, ironic versus shallow, unimaginative, conventional	Aesthetic appreciation, inquisitiveness, creativity, unconventionality	Engagement in idea-related endeavors	Materials and social gains (i.e. resulting from discovery)	Energy and time; risks from social and natural environment

Two other factors of Table 12.2 have more complex relations with the classic English lexical Big Five factors. One factor has elements in common with (low) Big Five emotional stability; however, this factor excludes the anger that mainly defines (low) emotional stability, and includes the sentimentality that mainly defines Big Five agreeableness (cf. Saucier and Goldberg, 1996, table 2). We have called this Table 12.2 factor 'emotionality', a less pejorative term than 'emotional instability' or 'neuroticism' (Ashton et al., 2004b). Conversely, another factor of Table 12.2 resembles Big Five agreeableness to some extent, but excludes sentimentality and includes (lack of) anger. This factor of Table 12.2, being defined by patience, gentleness, and flexibility, is perhaps better summarized by the name 'agreeableness' than is the B5/FFM version, which is defined by sympathy, gentleness, and sentimentality; to differentiate the two versions of the factor, we sometimes refer to the six-dimensional variant as 'agreeableness (versus anger)'. Given these shifts of factor content, emotionality, and agreeableness (versus anger) can be seen roughly as rotational variants of B5/FFM (low) emotional stability and B5/FFM agreeableness.

We have labeled the remaining factor in Table 12.2 as 'honesty-humility' (e.g. Ashton et al., 2004b). As seen in the table, the terms that frequently define this factor suggest honesty (e.g. *sincere, fair*) and humility (e.g. at the low pole, *pretentious, greedy*). Thus, the emergence of these three dimensions – emotionality, agreeableness (versus anger), and honesty-humility – is the feature that distinguishes the cross-language six-factor structure from the B5/FFM.

The content of the six lexical personality factors, as shown in Table 12.2, tends to be very similar across studies and across languages. Nevertheless, there is some variation across investigations in the rotational positions of the factor axes that emerge from the use of simple-structure-seeking algorithms (e.g. varimax). As a result, the core content of the six factors does tend to show some shifts between investigations. An example of this

involves the positions of some emotionality-related terms, such as those describing fearfulness and sentimentality, within the plane of emotionality and extraversion. From one study to the next, there may be small variations in the positions of those two vectors, with the result that fearfulness terms may show substantial negative loadings on extraversion, or that sentimentality terms may show substantial positive loadings on extraversion. Despite variations such as these, however, the factor spaces observed in the various studies remain very similar. Moreover, the factors that typically emerge in simple-structure solutions from lexical studies conducted in various languages are those that are summarized in Table 12.2.

The six-factor structure is also characterized by an interesting variability of the locations of a group of related terms describing sympathy, soft-heartedness, generosity, and associated characteristics. These terms represent *blends* of factors rather than manifestations of any one factor alone, as shown by their tendency, both to have substantial secondary loadings and also to 'migrate' between factors across studies (see discussions in Ashton et al. 2006, 2007). In several investigations, most of these sympathy- related terms have shown their strongest loadings on the agreeableness (versus anger) factor. However, in several other investigations, most of those terms have instead shown their strongest loadings on the honesty-humility factor. Also, in a few other studies, several sympathy-related terms have shown substantial loadings on an emotionality factor; for example, the low pole of the English lexical emotionality factor was defined by terms such as *pitiless*, *unsympathetic*, and *cold-hearted* (Ashton et al., 2004a).

To conclude this section, we should briefly mention the nature of solutions involving more than six factors, as obtained from standard lexical studies of personality structure (i.e. those based on personality-descriptive terms only). There is evidence from a few studies that seven-factor solutions produces a separate factor for intellectual ability

(Ashton et al., 2004b), which defines a factor different from that defined by intellectual openness (i.e. creativity, unconventionality, etc.). Also, there is evidence from a few studies for a separation of two aspects of emotionality – specifically, fearfulness and sentimenta-lity – onto two separate dimensions within seven-factor solutions (Ashton et al., 2004b). In addition, some investigations that have included descriptors of religiosity and spirituality have produced a factor defined by those terms. This suggests that religiosity or spirituality represents an additional dimension beyond the B5/FFM (e.g. Piedmont, 1999), but as we have discussed elsewhere (e.g. Ashton et al., 2004a; Lee et al., 2005c), we believe that religiosity or spirituality falls outside the domain of personality proper.

Summary

Lexical studies of personality structure have produced a common set of six dimensions across at least a dozen languages. Three of these factors are interpreted as extraversion, conscientiousness, and intellect/imagination/unconventionality, and closely resemble three of the English lexical Big Five factors. Of the remaining factors, one is interpreted as honesty-humility, and the other two are interpreted as emotionality and agreeableness (versus anger); these last two factors differ in important respects from B5/FFM (low) emotional stability and B5/FFM agreeableness. One noteworthy result of these studies has been the position of terms describing sympathy and soft-heartedness, which represent blends of honesty-humility, agreeableness (versus anger), and (to a lesser extent) emotionality.

The finding of this six-dimensional structure across diverse cultures has some important implications, as it contradicts the expectation that *only* five factors of personality description would be replicated. In fact, the six-factor solution is actually somewhat *more* widely replicated than is the B5/FFM, which has failed to emerge in some languages that recovered the six-factor structure.

Conversely, there are apparently no languages in which standard lexical studies (i.e. those based solely on personality-descriptive terms) have failed to recover the above six dimensions in the six-factor solution. The emergence of the six-dimensional structure across diverse cultures and languages, from variable sets that are both *indigenous* and *representative* of the personality domain, gives this model a wider basis of independent empirical support than is possessed by the B5/FFM.

Recently, we have referred to the six-factor framework as the HEXACO model of personality structure, and we have operationalized that framework in the HEXACO Personality Inventory (HEXACO-PI) (Lee and Ashton, 2004, 2006b). The name of this model reflects the names of the factors – honesty-humility (H), emotionality (E), extraversion (X), agreeableness (A), conscientiousness (C), and openness to experience (O) – and also their number (i.e. the Greek *hexa*, six). (Note that, despite its lexical origins, the HEXACO model uses the name openness to experience rather than intellect/ imagination/ unconventionality.) Names of the revised HEXACO Personality Inventory (HEXACO-PI-R) facet scales are listed in Table 12.2.

THEORETICAL INTERPRETATION: LINKS WITH CONSTRUCTS FROM EVOLUTIONARY BIOLOGY

As shown in the above summary, lexical studies of personality structure in diverse languages have generated a six-dimensional space that we call the HEXACO structure. But this raises the question of *why* human personality variation would be characterized by *this* particular set of dimensions. We believe that the emergence of the HEXACO factors follows from the importance of the adaptive trade-offs that are associated with behaviors corresponding to several important constructs from theoretical biology. Also, we suggest that these interpretations can explain and predict several important personality phenomena that would not otherwise be understood.

As we describe below, the theoretical framework associated with the HEXACO model is based on two broad concepts. First, the honesty-humility, agreeableness (versus anger), and emotionality factors correspond to biologists' constructs of reciprocal and kin altruism. Second, the extraversion, conscientiousness, and openness to experience factors represent three parallel dimensions each describing engagement or investment within its own respective area or variety of endeavor. Our interpretations of the six factors are summarized below and in Table 12.2, with a focus on the probable adaptive trade-offs associated with high and low levels of each dimension (see also Ashton and Lee, 2001; Lee and Ashton, 2004).

First, we have suggested that the honesty-humility and agreeableness (versus anger) correspond to two complementary aspects of the construct of reciprocal altruism (Trivers, 1971). Honesty-humility represents the tendency to be fair and genuine in dealing with others, in the sense of *cooperating with others even when one might exploit them without suffering retaliation*. Agreeableness (versus anger) represents the tendency to be forgiving and tolerant of others, in the sense of *cooperating with others even when one might have suffered some exploitation by them*. According to this interpretation, high levels of honesty-humility are associated with decreased opportunities for personal gains from the exploitation of others, but also with decreased risks of losses from withdrawal of cooperation (or further retaliation) by others. By the same logic, high levels of agreeableness (versus anger) are associated with increased opportunities for personal gains from long-run reciprocal cooperation with others but also with increased risks of losses from exploitation by others. (Here we use the term altruism in terms of a dimension of altruism versus antagonism, to include both a willingness to help or provide benefits to others but also an *unwillingness to harm or impose costs* on others.)

We have also suggested that emotionality corresponds to tendencies that are associated with the construct of kin altruism (Hamilton, 1964). These tendencies include empathic concern and emotional attachment toward close others (who tend to be one's kin), but also the harm-avoidant and help-seeking behaviors that are associated with investment in kin (see also Lee and Ashton, 2004). Interpreted in this way, high levels of emotionality are associated with increased likelihood of personal and kin survival, but also with decreased opportunities for gains that are often associated with risks to personal and kin survival.

The remaining three personality factors – extraversion, conscientiousness, and openness to experience – are interpreted in our theoretical framework as tendencies to become engaged in three different areas or varieties of endeavor. Specifically, extraversion represents engagement in social endeavors (such as socializing, leading, or entertaining), conscientiousness represents engagement in task-related endeavors (such as working, planning, and organizing), and openness to experience represents engagement in idea-related endeavors (such as learning, imagining, and thinking). According to these interpretations, high levels of any of these three dimensions are associated with increased opportunities for gains resulting from the investment of one's energy and time in those areas. For example, depending on the social and ecological circumstances in a given environment, high extraversion may promote gains of a social nature (i.e. access to friends, allies, and mates), high conscientiousness may promote gains of a material or economic nature (as well as improved health and safety), and high openness to experience may promote social and material gains that result from new discoveries. On the other hand, however, high levels of any of these dimensions would also be associated with increased costs in terms of expended energy and time and, in some cases, of risks from the natural and social environment.

The interpretations of extraversion, conscientiousness, and openness to experience as dimensions of engagement or endeavor suggest links with some constructs from theoretical biology (see details in Ashton and Lee, 2007). As noted elsewhere (Ashton et al., 2002), the interpretation of extraversion as social endeavor suggests similarities to the concept of social-attention holding power, a variant of resource-holding potential. Similarly, the interpretation of conscientiousness as task-related endeavor suggests similarities to some of the (non-altruistic) aspects of the r versus K continuum, particularly, the consistent exploitation of resources. Finally, the interpretation of openness to experience as idea-related endeavor suggests similarities to the contrast between individual learning and imitation.

A noteworthy advantage of the theoretical framework described above is that it parsimoniously explains the existence of *three* separate factors relevant to altruism. That is, the recurrent emergence of the honesty-humility, agreeableness (versus anger), and emotionality factors is immediately understood when these are interpreted with reference to reciprocal altruism and with kin altruism. In contrast, the emergence of these three factors is not explained by any interpretation of the B5/FFM framework, which includes only two dimensions within this three-dimensional segment of the HEXACO space, and provides no hint as to the nature of any more differentiated structure. Moreover, the interpretation of these dimensions in terms of altruism-related constructs allows an understanding of several phenomena that would otherwise be unexplained. For example, the large sex differences on and the diverse content of the emotionality factor are readily grasped when this factor is explained in terms of kin-altruistic tendencies (see Ashton and Lee, 2007, for a detailed discussion).

PRACTICAL SIGNIFICANCE: ACCOMMODATION OF IMPORTANT PERSONALITY VARIABLES

Earlier in this chapter we described the empirical basis of the HEXACO framework in the results of lexical studies of personality structure, and we also discussed the theoretical interpretations of the six dimensions. But there remains the question of practical implications: In particular, does the larger space of the HEXACO structure provide any advantages beyond the B5/FFM space in accommodating personality traits and personality-relevant criteria? Such advantages could be expected, given that some variables associated with the three-dimensional space of the HEXACO honesty-humility, agreeableness (versus anger), and emotionality factors might have weaker projections within the two-dimensional space of B5/FFM agreeableness and emotional stability (versus neuroticism). Below, we briefly summarize some previous studies that have investigated the ability of the HEXACO model and the B5/FFM to capture a variety of personality traits and related criteria.

The HEXACO honesty-humility factor is defined by characteristics that tend either to be weakly represented within measures of the B5/FFM or to be subsumed within a very broad version of B5/FFM agreeableness (see Ashton and Lee, 2005b). As a consequence of this heavier representation of honesty-humility-related traits within the HEXACO model, that framework has outperformed the B5/FFM in predicting several variables of practical importance. These variables – which have shown strong negative associations with honesty-humility – include workplace delinquency (see Lee et al., 2005b), sexual harassment proclivities (see Lee et al., 2003), and the traits of primary psychopathy, Machiavellianism, and narcissism (see Lee and Ashton, 2005).

The practical usefulness of the honesty-humility factor can also be seen by examining the correlates of the NEO-PI-R (Costa and McCrae, 1992), which assesses several narrow traits or facets within each B5/FFM domain. In one study (Ashton and Lee, 2005b), we found that the straightforwardness and modesty facets of NEO-PI-R agreeableness were associated with HEXACO honesty-humility rather than with the English lexical Big Five version of agreeableness. Moreover, these same two facets were also strong predictors of two personality variables involving insincerity – namely (low) self-monitoring and (low) social adroitness. (Note, however, that these two NEO-PI-R facets do not represent the full range of honesty-humility content, and would be unlikely to provide optimal prediction of some other honesty-humility-related variables, including (at the negative pole) materialism or corruption-proneness.)

The HEXACO framework also had some success in accommodating a range of variables that have been suggested to fall 'beyond the Big Five'. A diverse set of such variables has been operationalized in the scales of the Supernumerary Personality Inventory (SPI) (Paunonen et al., 2003), which we examined in a recent study (Lee et al., 2005c). The results of that investigation showed that the HEXACO-PI scales outperformed measures of the B5/FFM dimensions in predicting several variables that are conceptually similar to honesty-humility, including integrity, (low) manipulativeness, (low) egotism, and (low) seductiveness. There was also a substantial predictive advantage of the HEXACO variables over those of the B5/FFM in predicting two SPI scales – femininity and (low) risk taking – that are conceptually related to emotionality. This latter result suggests that the predictive advantages associated with the HEXACO model are not limited to honesty-humility, but also extend to the emotionality domain. Some traits within that domain, including femininity, harm-avoidance, and dependence, are typically not included within measures of any B5/FFM dimension.

Note that although most of the studies summarized above were based exclusively on self-reported personality, similar results have been obtained from peer reports (e.g. in prediction of likelihood to sexually harass; see Lee et al., 2003). In a recent study by Lee et al. (in press), self- and peer reports of honesty-humility, each outperformed self-reports of all B5/FFM variables in predicting scores on an overt integrity test and a business ethical dilemmas task. That is, the cross-source correlations between these outcome variables and honesty-humility exceeded any of the within-source correlations between the outcome variables and the B5/FFM. This result suggests that the strong correlations, previously observed, between honesty-humility and outcome variables are due to actual behavioral co-occurrence, and not merely to artifactual covariation resulting from the use of self-report assessment.

Future validity studies of the kind described above are still warranted, but the results of comparisons conducted thus far do suggest some advantage of the HEXACO model over the B5/FFM in accommodating several important personality variables. As summarized above, the HEXACO honesty-humility and emotionality factors appear to accommodate several personality traits and personality-related constructs that are less well assimilated within the space of the B5/FFM.

CONTRASTS WITH OTHER LEXICALLY DERIVED MODELS: FACTOR INTERPRETATION AND REPLICABILITY

As summarized above, the results of lexical studies of personality structure have shown a rather high degree of consistency, producing a similar six-dimensional structure even across very different languages. In fact, this six-factor solution has actually been replicated somewhat *more* widely across languages than the Big Five structure, which was not recovered in the lexical studies conducted in Hungarian and in Italian (Trieste). Thus, the six-dimensional framework not only provides a more differentiated representation of the personality domain than the five-dimensional framework does, but also does so without incurring any cost in terms of cross-cultural replicability.

Recently, Saucier (2003) has proposed an alternative lexically derived structural model of personality that also involves a space larger than that of the Big Five. This alternative structure, which has been called the 'Multi-Language Seven' (ML7; Saucier, 2003), was derived from results of investigations of the personality lexicons of two languages – Hebrew and Filipino – as supplemented by some analyses of English-language personality-descriptive adjectives. We will discuss the content of the proposed ML7 dimensions below, but we first note that six of the ML7 factors share elements of content with the six factors that have been replicated across languages. The remaining ML7 factor ('negative valence') is defined by terms that have been excluded from most lexical studies of personality structure on the grounds that they provide extreme negative evaluations, rather than descriptions corresponding to normal personality dispositions.

Given the proposal of this alternative lexically based model of personality structure, it would be useful to review some features of that model. Below, we discuss two features of the ML7 structure, specifically (a) the interpretation of the negative valence factor, and (b) the extent to which the remaining six substantive factors of the ML7 are consistent with the six dimensions that have been recovered across many languages.

Interpretation of negative valence

Recall that the purpose of lexical studies of personality structure is to find the major dimensions that underlie the domain of personality characteristics. Therefore, the variable sets of these investigations have generally been restricted to words that serve chiefly as personality descriptors (e.g. *outgoing, stubborn, organized, unemotional, pretentious, inquisitive*); in contrast, adjectives that serve chiefly to evaluate an individual (e.g. *terrible, good-for-nothing, wonderful, excellent*) have been excluded.

In some lexically based investigations, however, researchers have included primarily evaluative terms, on the grounds that such

terms might define factors that would indicate an individual's level of self-esteem (Tellegen, 1993). For example, an individual who describes himself or herself as *terrible* or *good-for-nothing* is likely to have very low self-esteem; therefore, a factor defined by these terms would represent a dimension of low self-esteem.

This inference about the self-esteem of respondents who endorse extremely undesirable terms is probably accurate. However, this does not justify the inclusion of primarily evaluative terms in lexical studies of personality structure. According to the logic of the lexical approach, any hypothesized personality dimension of low self-esteem would have to be defined by terms that *describe* persons having low self-esteem – terms such as *self-critical, self-disparaging*, and so on (see Ashton and Lee, 2001, 2002). To include other terms as potential *signs* (rather than *descriptors*) of low self-esteem is inconsistent with the purpose and rationale of the lexical approach. (Note, of course, that the above argument does not deny the importance of low self-esteem as a personality characteristic.)

Note that when primarily evaluative terms are included in the variable sets of lexical investigations, a 'negative valence' factor often does emerge, being defined by extremely undesirable adjectives that are infrequently endorsed in self-ratings (e.g. Saucier, 1997).[2] Recently, it has been suggested that this factor is indeed a meaningful descriptive dimension of personality variation, on the grounds that some of the defining adjectives of this factor do, in fact, have descriptive aspects (Saucier, 2002, 2003). For example, *stupid* suggests low intellect, *evil* suggests low kindness, and *crazy* suggests low conventionality.

These terms likely do have descriptive aspects, and would be expected to correlate somewhat with various personality scales that share similar descriptive content. However, this does not mean that the negative valence *factor* is a meaningful descriptive dimension. To the extent that terms such as *stupid* and *evil* and *crazy* together define a negative valence factor – instead of separately defining the factors that describe high versus low levels of intellect, of kindness, and of conventionality – this suggests that those terms covary because of a strong *common element* of extreme undesirability and/or infrequent endorsement. This interpretation is supported by the prevalence on negative valence of the more purely evaluative terms (see Saucier, 1997, for example), which further suggests that terms such as *stupid, evil,* and *crazy* (despite their descriptive aspects) serve mainly as terms of negative evaluation rather than as descriptors of personality dispositions.

Related to the above point, it is likely that persons who endorse negative valence adjectives will be rather poorly socialized, and will tend to have markedly low scores on self-report measures of socialization-related traits. This might suggest an interpretation of negative valence as a descriptive dimension of 'social deviance' (e.g. Saucier, 2002) or 'social impropriety' (Saucier, 2003). However, we believe that interpretation is inconsistent with the fact that the negative valence factor is *not* defined by most of the terms that actually *describe* persons' levels of socialization or social conformity (e.g. *conventional, self-controlled, polite, tame, proper* versus *rebellious, impulsive, rude, wild, nonconforming*). Those terms instead load on other dimensions, leaving a negative valence factor that is defined by various extremely undesirable terms that have very low mean self-ratings.[3]

The findings discussed above indicate that the negative valence factor cannot be interpreted substantively. Although some terms that define negative valence do have some descriptive aspects, the crucial fact remains that those terms do not load on the same factors as do the terms that share those descriptive aspects *without* being characterized by extreme negative evaluation. Instead, the *distinguishing common element* of the terms that define negative valence is their extreme social undesirability and/or their low endorsement rates.

Relations of other ML7 factors with cross-language (HEXACO) dimensions

As we have noted elsewhere (see Ashton and Lee, 2002), the remaining six substantive factors of the ML7 correspond fairly closely to the factors that we have proposed as the major dimensions of personality (e.g. Ashton and Lee, 2001). Four ML7 factors – gregariousness, conscientiousness, intellect, and even temper – correspond fairly closely overall to the extraversion, conscientiousness, intellect/imagination/unconventionality (openness to experience), and agreeableness (versus anger) dimensions as observed in lexical studies of personality structure, apart from the somewhat narrower content of the ML7 factors. In addition, ML7 self-assurance resembles to some extent the low pole of cross-language emotionality, but lacks the sentimentality, hypersensitivity, and emotionality that typically define the latter dimension. Finally, ML7 concern for others has some elements in common with cross-language honesty-humility, particularly (at the low pole) conceit. However, ML7 concern for others excludes much prototypical honesty-humility content (e.g. *sincere* and *unassuming* versus *deceitful, hypocritical, materialistic,* and *pretentious*).

RECENT FINDINGS: THE STRUCTURE OF THE CROATIAN, GREEK, AND FILIPINO PERSONALITY LEXICONS

In our 2004 review of lexical studies of personality structure, we drew attention to the similar six-factor solutions obtained from investigations conducted in various languages (Ashton et al., 2004b). Since that time, studies of the personality lexicons of two other languages – Croatian (Mlacic and Ostendorf, 2005) and Greek (Saucier et al., 2005)–have also been published. Although the results of those investigations show six-factor solutions very similar to those that have been replicated across languages, the original articles did not draw attention to these similarities. In the Croatian study, no systematic comparison with previous six-factor solutions was undertaken, and in the Greek study, the analyses do not allow clear comparisons with the results of previous investigations. Therefore, we describe below the six-factor solutions obtained from the Croatian and Greek lexicons (see Lee et al., 2005a; Lee and Ashton, 2008). In addition to the recent Croatian and Greek studies, lexically based investigations of personality structure were conducted in the Filipino language during the 1990s (Church et al., 1997, 1998). However, those investigations were based on variable sets that included 'negative valence' terms, and therefore, we describe here the solutions derived from Filipino variable sets that exclude such terms, and hence are more directly comparable to solutions from other languages (see Ashton et al., 2006a).

Croatian lexical personality factors

In their report describing the structure of the Croatian personality lexicon, Mlacic and Ostendorf (2005) focused on the five-factor solutions obtained from 453 adjectives (self-ratings) and 455 adjectives (peer ratings), but also indicated some features of the six-factor solutions. Here, we will focus mainly on the Croatian self-rating results, but we also mention briefly the similar results obtained from Croatian peerrating data. Using the information reported by Mlacic and Ostendorf in combination with that reported for the same data set by Ostendorf et al. (2004), we have listed in Table 12.3 the Croatian adjectives that best represent each of the varimax-rotated factors in the self-rating six-factor solution. Below, we reinterpret the Croatian six-factor solution on the basis of that factor content.

The adjectives representing the Croatian factors that we interpret as extraversion, conscientiousness, and intellect were taken from the corresponding factors in the five-factor solution reported by Mlacic and Ostendorf

(2005), who arrived at the same interpretations. (Correlations between the corresponding five-factor and six-factor versions of these three factors were 0.98 or above.) Note that the Croatian intellect factor is, indeed, heavily defined by intellect-related terms, with many of those terms describing cognitive *ability* (e.g. *intelligent, smart, bright*), rather than a disposition toward intellectual *endeavor*; in addition, there are several terms suggesting imagination, but no terms suggesting unconventionality (such terms appear to have been largely absent from the Croatian variable set).

For two of the remaining three dimensions of the Croatian six-factor solution, the highest-loading terms were listed explicitly by Ostendorf et al. (2004). One of these factors was very similar in content to the cross-language agreeableness (i.e. agreeableness versus anger) factor (cf. Ashton et al., 2004b, table 2), being defined by adjectives translated as *unirritable* and *gentle* versus *explosive, quick-tempered, stubborn*, and *quarrelsome*. (Recall that this content corresponds to the *cross-language* agreeableness factor, but not to Big Five agreeableness.)

The other factor whose defining terms were listed by Ostendorf et al. (2004) corresponded closely to the cross-language honesty-humility factor (cf. Ashton et al., 2004b, table 5), being defined by adjectives translated as *honest, fair,* and *just* versus *greedy, perfidious, rapacious, covetous, overbearing, conceited, fame-thirsty, self-important, self-interested,* and *hypocritical.* Interestingly, the Croatian honesty-humility factor also shows strong loadings for terms such as *generous* and *good-hearted*; as noted above, these traits largely represent blends of the cross-language, honesty-humility, and agreeableness (versus anger) factors, sometimes showing their strongest loadings on one factor, and sometimes on the other (see discussion above).

For the last of the Croatian self-rating factors, we have listed the strongest defining terms from this dimension in the five-factor solution, which correlated 0.92 with its counterpart in the six-factor solution (cf. Mlacic and Ostendorf, 2005, figure 2, table 3); however, we have removed those terms that shifted to the cross-language agreeableness (versus anger) factor of the six-factor solution. As seen in Table 12.3, the self-rating version of the factor is character-ized by adjectives suggesting unemotionality versus oversensitivity. Thus, the adjectives defining the low pole of this dimension are among those that have consistently defined the emotionality factor in previous lexical studies (cf. Ashton et al., 2004b, table 4). Inspection of the content of this factor, how-ever, suggests that this Croatian dimension is somewhat more narrowly defined than are its counterparts in most other languages, being defined most strongly only by terms related to emotionality and sensitivity, and not by terms suggesting fearfulness and vulnerability.

Turning briefly to the peer rating six-factor solution, the six factors were generally very similar to those of the self-rating solution: three factors were interpreted by Mlacic and Ostendorf (2005) as extraversion, conscien-tiousness, and intellect, and two others were nearly identical in content to the self-rating dimensions that we interpreted as cross-lan-guage agreeableness and honesty-humility. The remaining peer rating factor was small, being defined by only 11 terms, but these were similar to those of the self-rating solution; the six terms listed by Mlacic and Ostendorf were *romantic, emotional, sentimental*, and *naïve* versus *unemotional* and *insensitive*.

To summarize, the Croatian personality lexicon has produced six factors whose defining content corresponds closely to that of the six factors observed in many other lan-guages. The Croatian six-factor solution con-tains dimensions clearly interpretable as extraversion, conscientiousness, agreeable-ness (versus anger), and honesty-humility, and two other dimensions that – although rather narrow in content, probably because of the specific rules used in variable selection – are defined exclusively by terms associated with the intellect and emotionality factors of other languages.

Greek lexical personality factors

The main analyses of Saucier et al. (2005) involved self-ratings of 991 respondents on the 400 most frequently used Greek person-ality terms. The authors reported summaries of analyses on both ipsatized and original (i.e., non-ipsatized) data, but focused mainly on the non-ipsatized responses. However, because almost all other lexical studies of personality structure have been based on ipsatized data, we will focus exclusively on the results obtained from the ipsatized responses. (See Lee and Ashton, 2007, for a discussion of the use of ipsatized and non-ipsatized data.)

As noted in the previous section, another feature of the investigation by Saucier et al. (2005) was its use of a variable set that included primarily evaluative terms (*abject, unpleasant, loser, barbarian, inhuman, dis-gusting*, and *useless*). As would be expected, these terms defined a negative valence factor, which emerged in solutions containing three or more factors. This dimension was defined exclusively by terms with low mean responses: Of the 20 highest-loading terms on negative valence, all had response means below 1.35 on the 1-to-5 response scale; conversely, of the 20 terms with the lowest response means, all loaded at least 0.30 on negative valence and less than 0.30 on all other factors.

We have reanalyzed the Greek adjective data set of Saucier et al. (2005) after exclud-ing the negative valence terms. (As noted above, we ipsatized participants' responses by standardizing across variables within respondents prior to performing factor analy-ses; in this way, our procedures would be consistent with those of all previous lexical studies, and would allow meaningful com-parisons with results of those studies.) Also for the sake of consistency with previous lex-ical studies, we excluded the Greek adjec-tives that represented 'negative valence', by removing the 40 adjectives that loaded 0.30 or above on the negative valence factor in Saucier et al.'s ipsatized seven-factor solu-tion. We factor analyzed the self-ratings of

Table 12.3 Adjectives having highest loadings on the dimensions of the Croatian self- and peer rating six-factor solutions

Factor	Self-rating adjectives	Peer rating adjectives
Conscientiousness	Organiziran (organized), marljiv (industrious), temeljit (thorough), radišan (hard-working), odgovoran (responsible), uredan (orderly), vrijedan (sedulous), sistematičan (systematic), radin (diligent), precizan (precise) versus neorganiziran (disorganized), nemaran (negligent), neodgovoran (irresponsible), lijen (lazy), neoprezan (incautious), nesistematičan (unsystematic), nesustavan (unsystematic), neuredan (disorderly), netočan (inaccurate), nesavjestan (unconscientious)	Organiziran (organized), odgovoran (responsible), temeljit (thorough), radin (diligent), radišan (hard-working), vrijedan (sedulous), marljiv (industrious), sistematičan an (systematic), sustavan (systematic), metodičan (methodical) versus neorganiziran (disorganized), neodgovoran (irresponsible), nemaran (negligent), nesistematičan (unsystematic), lijen (lazy), površan (superficial), nesustavan (unsystematic), zaboravljiv (forgetful), neozbiljan (frivolous), nestalan (unsteady)
Honesty-humility	Sućutan (sympathetic), dobrodušan (good-hearted), obaziv (regardful), human (humane), dobronamjeran (well-intentioned), pošten (honest), velikodušan (generous), pravičan (fair), milosrdan (charitable), sirokogrudan (broad-minded) versus licemjeran (hypocritical), pohlepan (greedy), grabežljiv (rapacious), sebičan (selfish), koristoljubiv (self-interested), gramziv (covetous), uobražen (conceited), egocentričan (self-centered), podmukao (perfidious), umišljen (self-important), podao (mean), slavohlepan (fame-thirsty)	Pošten (honest), sirokogrudan (broad-minded), velikodušan (generous), dobrodušan (good-hearted), human (humane), milosrdan (charitable), pravedan (just), osjećajan (compassionate), topao (warm), sućutan (sympathetic), dobronamjeran (well-intentioned) versus pohlepan (greedy), podmukao (perfidious), grabežljiv (rapacious), sebičan (selfish), podao (mean), gramziv (covetous), prepotentan (overbearing), uobražen (conceited), slavohlepan (fame-thirsty)
Extraversion	Komunikativan (communicative), ekstravertiran (extraverted), razgovorljiv (loquacious), otvoren (open), društven (sociable), energican (energetic), govorljiv (talkative), dinamičan (dynamic), druželjubiv (companionable), aktivan (active) versus zatvoren (reserved) povučen (withdrawn), nedruštven (unsociable), stidljiv (bashful), negovorljiv (untalkative), introvertan (introverted), introvertiran (introverted), šutljiv (taciturn), sramežljiv (shy), neenergičan (unenergetic)	Otvoren (open), razgovorljiv (loquacious), komunikativan (communicative), pokretljiv (brisk), dinamičan (dynamic), poduzetan (enterprising), okretan (nimble), energičan (energetic), pokretan (agile), ekstravertiran (extraverted) versus zatvoren (reserved), šutljiv (taciturn), stidljiv (bashful), negovorljiv (untalkative), povučen (withdrawn), sramežljiv (shy), introvertiran (introverted), introvertan (introverted), pasivan (passive), stidan (demure)
Agreeableness (versus Anger)	Nerazdražljiv (unirritable), smiren (tranquil), blag (gentle), miroljubiv (peaceful) versus ratoboran (belligerent), eksplozivan (explosive), raspaljiv (quick-tempered), žestok (fierce), tvrdoglav (stubborn), razdražljiv (irritable), prkosan (defiant), inatljiv (spiteful), oštar (harsh), nagao (rash), agresivan (aggressive), impulzivan (impulsive), svojeglav (self-willed), buntovan (rebellious), svadljiv (quarrelsome), nepopustljiv (unyielding)	Nerazdražljiv (unirritable), smiren (tranquil), popustljiv (complying), poslušan (obedient), tolerantan (tolerant), strpljiv (patient), blag (gentle) versus eksplozivan (explosive), svadljiv (quarrelsome), raspaljiv (quick-tempered), svojeglav (self-willed), tvrdoglav (stubborn), inatljiv (spiteful), razdražljiv (irritable), oštar (harsh), žestok (fierce), nagao (rash), ratoboran (belligerent), prkosan (defiant), otresit (surly)

Intellect	Darovit (gifted), talentiran (talented), uman (sagacious), stvaralački (originative), bistar (bright), pametan (smart), intelektualan (intellectual), nadaren (endowed), oštrouman (sharp-witted), bistrouman (quick-witted) versus nekreativan (uncreative), nedarovit (ungifted), neinteligentan (unintelligent), neintelektualan (unintellectual), nemaštovit (unimaginative), nevješt (unskillful), neprofinjen (unsophisticated)	Bistar (bright), bistrouman (quick-witted), uman (sagacious), oštrouman (sharp-witted), domišljat (ingenious), intelektualan (intellectual), talentiran (talented), misaon (reflective), maštovit (imaginative), pametan (smart) versus neinteligentan (unintelligent), nedarovit (ungifted), povodljiv (suggestible), nekreativan (uncreative), neintelektualan (unintellectual)
(low) Emotionality*	Neemocionalan (unemotional), neosjetljiv (insensitive), neosjećajan (bezosjećajan (without compassion), hladnokrvan (cool-blooded), flegmatičan (phlegmatic) versus preosjetljiv (oversensitive), osjetljiv (sensitive), romantičan (romantic), strastan (passionate), strastven (impassioned), povodljiv (suggestible), emocionalan? (emotional), sentimentalan? (sentimental)	Neemocionalan? (unemotional), neosjetljiv? (insensitive) versus romantičan? (romantic), emocionalan? (emotional), sentimentalan? (sentimental), naivan? (naïve)

Note: Adjectives for the self- and peer rating factors interpreted as conscientiousness, extraversion, and intellect and for the peer rating factor interpreted as agreeableness (versus anger) were taken from the five-factor solutions reported by Mlacic and Ostendorf (2005, tables 4 and 6). Adjectives for the self- and peer rating factors interpreted as honesty-humility and for the self-rating factor interpreted as agreeableness (versus anger) were taken from Ostendorf et al. (2004). Adjectives for the self-rating factor interpreted as low Emotionality were selected from Mlacic and Ostendorf's (2005) table 4, according to the method described in the text of this article. English translations of adjectives for peer rating factor interpreted as Intellect were those listed by Mlacic and Ostendorf (2005). See text for cautions regarding content of the peer rating factor interpreted as intellect

*The peer-rating version of this factor was defined by 11 terms, 6 of which were listed, in English translation only, by Mlacic and Ostendorf (2005)

all 991 respondents on the remaining set of 360 adjectives by the method of principal components (see Lee and Ashton, 2008).

We applied a varimax rotation to the six Greek lexical factors, and obtained dimensions that corresponded closely to those observed in other languages. However, we noticed that the extraversion and emotionality factors were rotated slightly away from their usual axis locations, so we rotated these two varimax axes by 15 degrees within that plane. Table 12.4 shows the loadings of the highest-loading adjectives on each of the six factors, as obtained from varimax followed by this additional re-rotation.

With regard to interpretation of these dimensions, the first factor corresponded fairly closely to extraversion, being defined by such characteristics as sociability and cheerfulness versus their opposites. The second factor represented conscientiousness, being defined by terms describing organization and industriousness versus their opposites. The third factor resembled the *cross-language* agreeableness dimension, being defined by content suggesting patience and politeness versus irritability and stubbornness.

The fourth factor resembled the cross-language emotionality factor, being defined by content suggesting vulnerability, (hyper) sensitivity, fearfulness, and emotionality versus their opposites. The fifth factor resembled honesty-humility, being defined by adjectives relevant to the various aspects of that factor, including fairness (e.g. *ethical* versus *unscrupulous*) and modesty (e.g. *modest* versus *grandiose* and *exhibitionist*) versus insincerity (e.g. *sly*) and greed (e.g. *profiteer*).

Finally, the sixth factor can be interpreted as an intellect/imagination dimension, being defined by such terms as *talented, inventive*, and *ingenious*. This factor is relatively small compared to the other five factors, but its defining content is broadly similar to that of the intellect/imagination/unconventionality factor observed across languages, except for the absence of content related to unconventionality or philosophicalness in the Greek

version of the factor. Overall, the content of the six factors suggests that this solution is very similar to the common six-factor structure observed across other languages.[4]

Filipino lexical personality factors

The Filipino personality lexicon has been examined in a series of studies (Church et al., 1997, 1998) in which 'negative valence' terms were included along with adjectives that serve primarily as personality descriptors. To facilitate comparisons with results of previous studies, the authors of those studies did comment on the five-factor solutions obtained when negative valence terms were excluded from analyses, noting that the Big Five structure was not recovered. Given the widespread cross-language replication of a six-dimensional solution, the six-factor space derived from the personality-descriptive adjectives of the Filipino language is of some interest, and we summarize those results here.

Table 12.5 shows the highest-loading terms on the varimax-rotated factors of the six-factor solution derived from the set of 232 adjectives obtained by Church et al. (1997) after removal of negative valence terms, and based on self-ratings from 1,529 persons. As seen in that table, the first factor was defined by a variety of terms related to overall altruism and to the core aspects of honesty-humility, and thus represents a broad variant of that factor. The second factor contained terms typical of conscientiousness (e.g. *disciplined, orderly* versus *lazy*), but also has strong elements of religiosity and thriftiness, which obscure somewhat the interpretation of this factor. The content of the third factor involved irritability and ill-temper versus patience, and thus corresponds to cross-language agreeableness versus anger (but not to classic Big Five agreeableness); interestingly, terms describing overall altruism (e.g. *kind, understanding*) tended to divide their loadings between this factor and the first factor (i.e. honesty-humility). The fourth factor corresponded

Table 12.4 Adjectives having highest-loadings on the dimensions of the Greek six-factor solution

Factor	Adjectives
Extraversion	Διασκεδαστικός (amusing), κοινωνικός (sociable), χαρούμενος (cheerful), ανοιχτόκαρδος (openhearted), ευχάριστος (pleasant), άνετος (comfortable), εύθυμος (cheerful), εξωστρεφής (extroverted), ζωηρός (lively, vivid), αξιαγάπητος (lovable)
	versus
	απόμακρος (withdrawn), λιγομίλητος (taciturn), σιωπηλός (silent), μοναχικός (loner), κακοδιάθετος (moody), μονότονος (monotonous), θλιμμένος (sad), αμίλητος (silent), εσωστρεφής (introvert)
Conscientiousness	Εργατικός (hard working), οργανωτικός (organized), επιμελής (industrious), εργασιομανής (workaholic), υπεύθυνος (responsible), συνεπής (consistent), σταθερός (stable), τελειομανής (perfectionist), μεθοδικός (methodical)
	versus
	ανοργάνωτος (disorganised), αμελής (neglectful), ακατάστατος (untidy), απρογραμμάτιστος (unscheduled), τεμπέλης (lazy), ασυνεπής (inconsistent), ανεύθυνος (irresponsible), άστατος (unstable), αφηρημένος (absentminded), ασταθής (unstable), ανυπάκουος (disobedient), αδιόρθωτος (incorrigible), επιπόλαιος (superficial), απρόσεκτος (careless)
Agreeableness (versus anger)	Ήρεμος (calm), ήπιος (mild), υπομονητικός (patient), ήσυχος (quiet), υποχωρητικός (compliant), ευγενής (polite), επιεικής (clement)
	versus
	οξύθυμος (touchy), επιθετικός (aggressive), ευέξαπτος (touchy), απότομος (abrupt), νευρικός (nervous), αντιδραστικός (reactive), γκρινιάρης (fretful), νευρωτικός (neurotic), απαιτητικός (demanding), καυγατζής (brawler), πιεστικός (pushy), ισχυρογνώμων (strong-minded), καταπιεστικός (oppressive), ιδιότροπος (capricious), ανυπόμονος (impatient), πεισματάρης (stubborn)
Emotionality	Υπερευαίσθητος (hypersensitive), ανασφαλής (insecure), φοβητσιάρης (fearful), ευάλωτος (vulnerable), διστακτικός (hesitant), παραπονιάρης (complainer), δειλός (coward), ευαίσθητος (sensitive), ευκολόπιστος (easy to convince), συναισθηματικός (emotional), απαισιόδοξος (pessimistic), αγχωτικός (neurotic), αγχώδης (anxious), μελαγχολικός (melancholic), αμήχανος (self-conscious)
	versus
	θαρραλέος (courageous), αποφασιστικός (determinative), ανεξάρτητος (independent), αισιόδοξος (optimistic), αυτόνομος (autonomous), δυναμικός (dynamic), τολμηρός (bold, daring), γενναίος (brave)
Honesty-humility	Ευσυνείδητος (conscientious), έντιμος (honourable), ευπρεπής (decent), μετριόφρων (modest), εχέμυθος (reticent), ηθικός (ethical), αξιόπιστος (reliable), αμερόληπτος (unbiased), διακριτικός (considerate), συνετός (prudent), έμπιστος (trustworthy), αντικειμενικός (objective), πιστός (faithful)
	versus
	αδίστακτος (unscrupulous), κερδοσκόπος (profiteer), μεγαλομανής (grandiose), επιδειξιομανής (exhibitionist), ύπουλος (sly), προκλητικός (provocative), εκδικητικός (vengeful), πανούργος (cunning, foxy), επικίνδυνος (dangerous), αλαζόνας (arrogant), φιλοχρήματος (avaricious)
Intellect	Ταλαντούχος (talented), πολυτάλαντος (multitalented), μεγαλοφυής (genius), εφευρετικός (inventive), ευφυής (ingenious), ιδιοφυής (genius), δημοφιλής (popular), πρωτοπόρος (pioneer), εξαίρετος (remarkable), ευρηματικός (inventive), εκλεκτικός (eclectic), πανέξυπνος (sharp), αξιοζήλευτος (enviable), επιτυχημένος (successful), έξοχος (excellent), χαρισματικός (charismatic), αξιέπαινος (laudable, praise-worthy), επιλεκτικός (selective)

Note: Factor loadings based on reanalysis of Greek lexical study data from Saucier et al. (2005); see text for details. All results are based on self-ratings, which were the sole rating source of the original study.

rather closely to extraversion, being defined by terms related to talkativeness and cheerfulness; this Filipino variant of extraversion also had a strong element of humorousness. The fifth factor corresponded roughly to emotionality, being defined by terms such as *fearful* and *sensitive* versus their opposites, but appeared to be tilted somewhat toward the low pole of extraversion, as suggested by the loadings of terms such as *shy* versus *lively*. Finally, the content of the sixth factor involved intellectual ability, and thus represented an intellect factor.

We should note that a similar six-factor space is observed when the 405-adjective set described by Church et al. (1998) is analyzed, using self-rating data from their sample of 740 persons. This larger variable set was limited to terms that are chiefly personality-descriptive, with negative valence and positive valence being removed. The varimax-rotated factor axis locations from this solution differed somewhat from those of the dimensions of Table 12.5, but orthogonal re-rotations produce almost identical factors. Interestingly, the larger variable set clarified the interpretation of some factors; for example, the emotionality dimension showed high loadings for additional terms such as *iyadin (cries easily)* and *madamdamin (emotional)*. Thus, the Filipino personality lexicon – like the Croatian and Greek lexicons discussed above – appears to produce a six-factor structure very similar to that observed in the standard lexical studies of personality structure that have been conducted in diverse other languages.

SUMMARY AND CONCLUSIONS

The major points of this chapter can be summarized as follows:

1   The study of personality structure requires the use of variable sets that are representative of the domain of personality characteristics. Such variable sets can be obtained by identifying the familiar personality-descriptive adjectives that are indigenous to a given language.

2   Early lexical studies of personality structure, as conducted in the English language, suggested that the personality domain could be summarized in terms of five dimensions. Subsequent lexical investigations, as conducted in many diverse languages, have recovered a common set of six factors.

3   This six-dimensional structure, called the HEXACO model, is defined by the factors called honesty-humility (H), emotionality (E), extraversion (X), agreeableness (A), conscientiousnes (C), and openness to experience (O). The extraversion, conscientiousness, and openness to experience factors correspond closely to those of the Big Five or Five-Factor Model, whereas the honesty-humility, emotionality, and agreeableness factors have more complex relations with the Big Five or Five-Factor Model dimensions of agreeableness and neuroticism.

4   The HEXACO model is associated with a theoretical framework in which three factors are interpreted as dimensions of altruistic versus antagonistic tendency, and three others are interpreted as dimensions of engagement within different areas of endeavor.

5   Recent studies of the predictive validity of the HEXACO model support the suggestion that this framework provides some important advantages over the Big Five or Five-Factor Model, largely as a function of the honesty-humility and emotionality factors.

6   Some alternative models of personality structure posit a negative valence dimension, but this is not a meaningful descriptive dimension of personality. Although some terms that define this factor have some descriptive aspects, the *distinguishing common element* of negative valence terms is their extreme undesirability and/or low endorsement means.

7   Re-examinations of the personality lexicons of the Croatian, Greek, and Filipino languages show that these languages do recover six-factor solutions that are very similar to those observed in various other languages.

ACKNOWLEDGEMENTS

Correspondence concerning this chapter should be addressed to Michael C. Ashton, Department of Psychology, Brock University, St. Catharines, ON L2S 3A1 Canada (e-mail: mashton@brocku.ca) or to Kibeom Lee,

Table 12.5 Adjectives having highest loadings on the dimensions of the Filipino six-factor solution

Facto	Adjectives
Honesty-humility	Mapagbigay-loob (obliging), mapagbigay (generous), maasikaso (attentive), mapaglingkod (serving others), maalalahanin (thoughtful), magandang-kalooban (kind-hearted), matulungin (helpful), maunawain (understanding), mapang-unawa (understanding), maalaga (cares for others), mapagpakumbaba (humble), maaruga (nurturant)
	versus
	pasikat (boastful), mapagmataas (arrogant), mapagmagaling (show-off), mapagmalaki (haughty), mayabang (boastful), mapagpanggap (pretentious), mapagkunwari (pretentious), mapanlamang (opportunistic), mapaghari-harian (domineering), mahangin (boastful), naninira (slanderous), mapagmarunong (know-it-all)
Conscientiousness (with religiosity and thriftiness)	Matipid (thrifty), espirituwal (spiritual), madasalin (pious, frequently prays), relihiyoso (religious), nananampalataya (believes in god), palasimba (pious, frequently goes to church), palaaral (studious), maka-diyos (godly), mapag-impok (thrifty), banal (holy), disiplinado (disciplined), masinop (orderly)
	versus
	maaksaya (wasteful), mapagwaldas (profligate), gastador (spendthrift), luku-luko (crazy), tamad (lazy), kapritsoso (capricious), gala (wandering), burara (sloppy), malayaw (pampered), ningas-kugon (non-persistent)
Agreeableness (versus anger)	Pasensiyoso (forgiving, patient), mahinahon (calm), mapang-unawa* (understanding), mabait (kind)
	versus
	mainisin (irritable), mainitin ang ulo (hot-headed), tampuhin (sulky), masungit (ill-tempered), magagalitin (irritable), bugnutin (irascible), mayamutin (petulant), sumpungin (moody), maiinipin (impatient), peevish (pikon), suplado (snobbish), seloso (jealous)
Extraversion	Palatawa (giggly), mapagpatawa (humorous), palabiro (always joking), palangiti (smiles a lot), maingay (noisy), madaldal (talkative), cheerful (masayahin), ngitiin (smiles a lot), bungisngis (giggly), galawgaw (naughty), kalog (gregarious), magulo (mischievous)
	versus
	tahimik (quiet), seryoso (serious), pino (refined)
Emotionality	Duwag (cowardly), nerbiyoso (nervous), matatakutin (fearful), mahiyain (shy), mabagal (sluggish), mahina (weak), lambutin (weak), magulatin (skittish), lampa (unsteady), maramdamin (sensitive)
	versus
	alerto (alert), malakas ang loob (strong-willed), matapang (brave), may-tapang (brave), may-tapang (brave), masigla (lively), alisto (alert)
Intellect	Matalas ang tsip (mentally keen), may-talino (talented), matalas ang ulo (sharp, talented), marunong (learned), madunong (intelligent), may-katwiran (rational), magaling (able), mahusay (competent), may-isip (sensible), may-utak (brainy), mautak (brainy), may-ulo (intelligent)

Note: Results are from a varimax-rotated six-factor solution based on the 232-adjective set described by Church et al. (1997). Interpretations of factors are those of Ashton et al. (2006a). All results are based on self-ratings

* had higher loading on honesty-humility factor

Department of Psychology, University of Calgary, Calgary, AB T2N 1N4 Canada (e-mail: kibeom@ucalgary.ca).

This work was supported by grants 410-2007-0700 and 410-2007-2159 from the Social Sciences and Humanities Research Council of Canada.

We thank Timothy Church and Marcia Katigbak for providing the results of the Filipino lexical analyses reported here, and we thank Gerard Saucier, Stelios Georgiades, Ioannis Tsaousis, and Lewis R. Goldberg for providing the Greek lexical data whose analyses are reported here.

NOTES

1 For a somewhat more detailed treatment of the issues regarding the lexical origins, theoretical bases, and predictive validity of the HEXACO model, see Ashton and Lee (2007).

2 Note also that, because the ML7 model is based on variable selections that differ from those on which the B5/FFM and HEXACO models are based, any quantitative comparisons of the extent to which these models are recovered from the same variable set are meaningless. For example, when the variable set includes many negative valence terms, a five- or six-factor solution may well contain a negative valence factor, thereby precluding the emergence of the B5/FFM or HEXACO structures, respectively.

3 The factor interpreted as negative valence in a Hebrew lexical investigation (Almagor et al., 1995) was in fact a *bipolar* dimension that was chiefly defined by terms describing low versus high levels of honesty-humility, and hence differs from the typical negative valence factor.

4 In the five-factor solution, four of the five dimensions were nearly identical to the extraversion, conscientiousness, agreeableness, and honesty-humility factors of the six-factor solution. The remaining dimension of the five-factor solution was mainly defined by Emotionality-related terms (particularly those involving fearfulness and insecurity), but also contained some intellect/imagination-related terms at its opposite pole. The Greek five-factor solution is therefore reminiscent of the five-factor solutions observed in Hungarian and Italian (Trieste), in which there was no factor corresponding directly to intellect/imagination, but in which the other five of the six cross-language factors did emerge.

REFERENCES

Almagor, M., Tellegen, A. and Waller, N.G. (1995) 'The Big Seven Model: A cross-cultural replication and further exploration of the basic dimensions of natural language trait descriptors', *Journal of Personality and Social Psychology*, 69(2): 300–7.

Ashton, M.C. and Lee, K. (2001) 'A theoretical basis for the major dimensions of personality', *European Journal of Personality*, 15: 327–53.

Ashton, M.C. and Lee, K. (2002) 'Six independent factors of personality variation: A response to Saucier', *European Journal of Personality*, 16(1): 63–75.

Ashton, M.C. and Lee, K. (2005a) 'A defence of the lexical approach to the study of personality structure', *European Journal of Personality*, 19(1): 5–24.

Ashton, M.C. and Lee, K. (2005b) 'Honesty-humility, the Big Five, and the Five-Factor Model', *Journal of Personality*, 73(5): 1321–53.

Ashton, M.C. and Lee, K. (2007) 'Empirical, theoretical, and practical advantages of the HEXACO model of personality structure', *Personality and Social Psychology Review*, 11(2): 150–66.

Ashton, M.C., Lee, K., de Vries, R.E., Szarota, P., Marcus, B., Wasti, S.A., Church, A.T. and Katigbak, M.S. (2006a) 'Lexical studies of personality structure: An examination of six-factor solutions', Paper presented at the 13th European Conference on Personality, July 2006, Athens, Greece.

Ashton, M.C., Lee, K., de Vries, R.E., Perugini, M., Gnisci, A. and Sergi, I. (2006b) 'The HEXACO Model of personality structure and indigenous lexical personality dimensions in Italian, Dutch, and English', *Journal of Research in Personality*, 40(6): 851–75.

Ashton, M.C., Lee, K. and Goldberg, L.R. (2004a) 'A hierarchical analysis of 1,710 English personality-descriptive adjectives', *Journal of Personality and Social Psychology*, 87(5): 707–21.

Ashton, M.C., Lee, K., Marcus, B. and de Vries, R.E. (2007) 'German lexical personality factors: Relations with the HEXACO model', *European Journal of Personality,* 21(1): 23–43.

Ashton, M.C., Lee, K. and Paunonen, S.V. (2002) 'What is the central feature of

Extraversion? Social attention versus reward sensitivity', *Journal of Personality and Social Psychology*, 83(1): 245–52.

Ashton, M.C., Lee, K., Perugini, M., Szarota, P., de Vries, R.E., Di Blas, L., Boies, K. and De Raad, B. (2004b) 'A six-factor structure of personality-descriptive adjectives: Solutions from psycholexical studies in seven languages', *Journal of Personality and Social Psychology*, 86(2): 356–66.

Cattell, R.B. (1947) 'Confirmation and clarification of primary personality factors', *Psychometrika*, 12: 197–220.

Church, A.T., Katigbak, M.S. and Reyes, J.A.S. (1998) 'Further exploration of Filipino personality structure using the lexical approach: Do the big-five or big-seven dimensions emerge?', *European Journal of Personality*, 12(4): 249–69.

Church, A.T., Reyes, J.A.S., Katigbak, M.S. and Grimm, S.D. (1997) 'Filipino personality structure and the Big Five model: A lexical approach', *Journal of Personality*, 65(3): 477–528.

Costa, P.T. Jr. and McCrae, R.R. (1992) *NEO Personality Inventory–Revised (NEO-PI-R) and NEO Five-Factor Inventory (NEO-FFI) Professional Manual*. Odessa, FL: Psychological Assessment Resources.

Di Blas, L. and Forzi, M. (1998) 'An alternative taxonomic study of personality-descriptive adjectives in the Italian language', *European Journal of Personality*, 12(2): 75–101.

Goldberg, L.R. (1990) 'An alternative "Description of personality": The Big-Five factor structure', *Journal of Personality and Social Psychology*, 59(6): 1216–29.

Hamilton, W.D. (1964) 'The genetical evolution of social behavior. I, II', *Journal of Theoretical Biology*, 7(1): 1–52.

Lee, K. and Ashton, M.C. (2004) 'Psychometric properties of the HEXACO Personality Inventory', *Multivariate Behavioral Research*, 39(2): 329–58.

Lee, K. and Ashton, M.C. (2005) 'Psychopathy, Machiavellianism, and Narcissism in the Five-Factor Model and the HEXACO Model of Personality Structure', *Personality and Individual Differences*, 38(7): 1571–82.

Lee, K. and Ashton, M.C. (2008) 'Re-analysis of the structure of the Greek personality lexicon', Submitted for publication.

Lee, K. and Ashton, M.C. (2006) 'Further assessment of the HEXACO Personality Inventory: Two new facet scales and an observer report form', *Psychological Assessment*, 18(2): 182–91.

Lee, K., Ashton, M.C. and de Vries, R.E. (2005a) 'Six factors in the Croatian personality lexicon', Unpublished manuscript.

Lee, K., Ashton, M.C. and de Vries, R.E. (2005b) 'Predicting workplace delinquency and integrity with the HEXACO and Five-Factor Models of personality structure', *Human Performance*, 18(2): 179–97.

Lee, K., Ashton, M.C., Morrison, D.L., Cordery, J. and Dunlop, P.D. (2008) 'Predicting integrity with the HEXACO personality model: Use of self- and observer reports', *Journal of Occupational and Organizational Psychology*, 81:147–67.

Lee, K. and Ashton, M.C. (2007) 'Factor analysis in personality research', in R.W. Robins, R.C. Fraley and R. Krueger (eds), *Handbook of Research Methods in Personality Psychology*. New York: Guilford, pp. 424–43.

Lee, K., Gizzarone, M. and Ashton, M.C. (2003) 'Personality and the likelihood to sexually harass', *Sex Roles*, 49(1–2): 59–69.

Lee, K., Ogunfowora, B. and Ashton, M.C. (2005c) 'Personality traits beyond the Big Five: Are they within the HEXACO space?', *Journal of Personality*, 73(5): 1437–63.

McCrae, R.R. (1989) 'Why I advocate the five-factor model: Joint analyses of the NEO-PI with other instruments', in D.M. Buss and N. Cantor (eds), *Personality Psychology: Recent Trends and Emerging Directions*. New York: Springer-Verlag, pp. 237–45.

McCrae, R.R. and Costa, P.T. Jr. (1997) 'Personality trait structure as a human universal', *American Psychologist*, 52(5): 509–16.

McCrae, R.R. and Costa, P.T. Jr. (2003) *Personality in Adulthood*. New York: Guilford.

McCrae, R.R. and John, O.P. (1992) 'An introduction to the five-factor model and its applications', *Journal of Personality*, 60(2): 175–215.

Mlacic, B. and Ostendorf, F. (2005) 'Taxonomy and structure of Croatian personality-descriptive adjectives', *European Journal of Personality*, 19(2): 117–52.

Ostendorf, F., Mlacic, B., Hrebickova, M. and Szarota, P. (2004), 'In search of the sixth big factor of personality in four European languages', Paper presented at the 12th European Conference on Personality, July, 2004, Groningen, The Netherlands.

Paunonen, S.V., Haddock, G., Forsterling, F. and Keinonen, M. (2003) 'Broad versus narrow personality measures and the prediction of behaviour across cultures', *European Journal of Personality*, 17(6): 413–33.

Piedmont, R. (1999) 'Does spirituality represent the sixth factor of personality? Spiritual transcendence and the five-factor model', *Journal of Personality*, 67(6): 985–1013.

Ruhlen, M. (1991) *A Guide to the World's Languages: Volume 1, Classification.* Stanford, CA: Stanford University Press.

Saucier, G. (1997) 'Effects of variable selection on the factor structure of person descriptors', *Journal of Personality and Social Psychology*, 73(6): 1296–312.

Saucier, G. (2002) 'Gone too far – or not far enough? Comments on the article by Ashton and Lee (2001)', *European Journal of Personality*, 16(1): 55–62.

Saucier, G. (2003) 'An alternative multi-language structure for personality attributes', *European Journal of Personality*, 17(3): 179–205.

Saucier, G., Georgiades, S., Tsaousis, I. and Goldberg, L.R. (2005) 'The factor structure of Greek personality adjectives', *Journal of Personality and Social Psychology*, 88(5): 856–75.

Saucier, G. and Goldberg, L.R. (1996) 'Evidence for the Big Five in analyses of familiar English personality adjectives', *European Journal of Personality*, 10(1): 61–77.

Szirmak, Z. and De Raad, B. (1994) 'Taxonomy and structure of Hungarian personality traits', *European Journal of Personality*, 8(2): 95–117.

Tellegen, A. (1993) 'Folk concepts and psychological concepts of personality and personality disorder', *Psychological Inquiry*, 4(2): 122–30.

Trivers, R.L. (1971) 'The evolution of reciprocal altruism', *Quarterly Review of Biology*, 46(1): 35–57.

Tupes, E.C. and Christal, R.E. (1961) *Recurrent Personality Factors Based on Trait Ratings.* USAF Tech. Rep. No. 61-97. US Air Force: Lackland Air Force Base, TX.

Tupes, E.C. and Christal, R.E. (1992) 'Recurrent personality factors based on trait ratings', *Journal of Personality*, 60(2): 225–51.

Wasti, S.A., Lee, K., Ashton, M.C. and Somer, O. (in press) 'The Turkish personality lexicon and the HEXACO model of personality'. *Journal of Cross-Cultural Psychology*.

13

Exploring Personality Through Test Construction: Development of the Multidimensional Personality Questionnaire

Auke Tellegen and Niels G. Waller

INTRODUCTION: APPROACHES TO SCALE CONSTRUCTION

Construction of a self-report personality inventory can be a straightforward undertaking. We may take a 'rational' or 'deductive' approach (Burisch, 1984) and begin by formulating a construct from which to 'deduce' basic descriptors – in our case a set of construct-based self-report items. We might even draw on already developed constructs and start writing items immediately; Murray's (1938) carefully elaborated motivational trait constructs have served that function several times. Once enough items have been generated, scale construction, if purely deductive, is complete.

A deductive orientation does not rule out the use of data to improve one's initial scales. Data-based deletion or addition of items can increase the internal consistency of a deductive scale. If our objective is to create a multi-scale inventory, we can also empirically enhance scale distinctiveness and independence. But even if deductive scale construction includes extensive and sophisticated data-based streamlining (see Jackson, 1970, 1971), its unchanging purpose is to accommodate the initial constructs, not to examine them.

A very different method is the 'external' approach (Burisch, 1984). We select a non-test variable to serve as a criterion (e.g. peer-ratings of friendliness, clinical diagnoses of antisocial personality vs. its absence, records of community leadership), and assemble a test-item pool. Next we collect data to identify pool items that correlate substantially with our criterion. These items are combined to form an external scale. External scale construction is often considered non-theoretical or 'blindly' empirical. In contrast to rational scale constructors, strict practitioners of the external method pay no attention to the substantive or statistical coherence of their scales.

Yet, external scale construction does not take place in a conceptual vacuum. It requires choosing reputational, diagnostic, or life-record criteria, and assembling an item pool. Presumably, these choices are guided by some conception of the criterion variable: why it is important and how it relates to self-reports. Conversely, the deductive approach is not without non-theoretical empiricism. Its streamlining phase (using internal rather than external correlational evidence) often results in discarding items that do not 'work' statistically, and selecting those that do. Deductive and external approaches are both therefore to some extent responsive to blind fact and mere reason. But a more telling common feature is their one-way straightforwardness: both are highly structured methods for specifying and pursuing fixed psychometric goals. Neither approach encourages data collection for the purpose of examining and possibly changing the very trait concepts that guide the test construction effort.

A markedly different methodology is to let constructs evolve as a planned part of the test construction process itself. Our approach is then no longer 'structured' in the deductive or external sense, but 'exploratory' (Tellegen, 1985). This approach does not lack direction. It is bidirectional, moving from ideas to data and vice versa. One's initial constructs guide the assembling of a construct-appropriate item pool. Analysis of data collected with this pool guides construct revision and is followed by a new round of data collection. Exploratory scale construction is not a quasi-formulaic translation of constructs into measures. It is a slower journey of trial and error, a psychometric exploration of personality. With some luck it leads to better constructs, and to scales that match these constructs.

To conduct such an exploration, it helps to believe that traits are real and make an important difference in life. Adopting this 'realistic' view, we define 'trait' as an inferred psychobiological structure underlying an extended family of behavioral dispositions. These dispositions are emphatically not construed as generalized 'situation-free' action

tendencies, but as tendencies to behave in certain ways in certain situations (Tellegen, 1991). A dimensional trait recurs in essentially the same qualitative form in different people, but with quantitative variations; that is, individual differences in amount or level. Response measures that closely reflect individual differences on the same trait dimension are expected to covary. This covariation of trait indicators is crucial to the viability of a trait construct (Meehl, 1986).

Covariation of very similar responses permits only narrow inferences. For example, covariation between self-report statements, each indicating a tendency to worry, is 'meaningful', but from a personality trait perspective the meaning is narrow. If statements of tension, apprehension, and jumpiness are also in the cluster, a broader construct like 'anxiety' needs to be considered. And if correlational evidence tells us to include additional emotional descriptors – for example irritability and unstable mood – even 'anxiety' is underinclusive. A still broader dispositional construct is needed; for example, proneness to react as if under stress, or 'stress reactivity'.

Diverse content sampling of a hypothesized trait domain makes it not only more likely that we recognize underinclusive constructs for that domain, it may also facilitate our recognition of overinclusive constructs. A familiar alternative construct proposed for stress reactivity is social desirability. It is clearly overinclusive since several desirable and undesirable characteristics (e.g., leadership qualities, vindictiveness, punctuality) are primarily associated with traits other than stress reactivity, such as social potency, aggression, and control versus impulsiveness. However, as an overinclusive construct, social desirability has been a useful source of discriminant correlations. We rely on convergent correlations between diverse candidate indicators to infer a trait and recognize the breadth of its manifestations, but to draw its boundaries we need discriminant correlations.

To achieve adequate convergent and discriminant validation, Loevinger (1957) has recommended an overinclusive item pool:

'Items in the pool should be drawn from an area of content defined more broadly than the trait expected to be measured. When possible, the items of the pool should be chosen so as to sample all possible contents which might comprise the putative trait according to all known alternative theories of the trait' (1957: 659). As these words imply, each psychometric trait construct is at minimum a rudimentary theory entailing empirically testable item choices. A comprehensive evaluation of such a theory is not possible with a theoretically underinclusive item pool, and will require an overinclusive pool if the evaluation is to include discriminant validation.

Our stress reactivity/social desirability example shows that highly informative discriminant correlations can be discovered by exploring several distinctive traits rather than a single trait. It opens the possibility of understanding non-correlates of a given trait, T, as manifestations of other traits, U, V, ..., Z, and thus deepening understanding of T itself (and of U, V,..., Z). We better understand a trait by better understanding things it is not. As more traits are considered, discriminant correlations play an increasingly important role in defining each trait. For example, if the number of factors increases from two to ten, and the number of factor markers is the same for all factors, then the ratio of discriminant to convergent correlations increases ninefold.[1]

Even if our initial item pool of candidate trait indicators is descriptively diverse, reflecting a variety of alternative conceptions for each of several hypothesized traits, it is still not likely to yield definitive results. An infusion of new facts will not merely eliminate invalid views, it will suggest new ones, leading to the inclusion of new descriptors. Only through successive cycles of item generation, data collection, and analysis, can our initial and subsequent guesses be brought in line with the actual facts of covariation and become increasingly informative and informed.

The exploratory process outlined here differs in two main respects from the one Loevinger has recommended. Though stressing the need for an overinclusive item pool, she proposed 'that this requirement be met not in a lengthy series of investigations ... but primarily in the very constitution of the pool of items from which the test is chosen' (1957: 659). As we just noted, this recommendation discounts the possibility of the test construction process itself producing findings that suggest new conjectures leading to new descriptors. The exploratory approach makes the ascent of the 'inductive-hypothetico-deductive spiral' (Cattell, 1966, 1978) an explicit part of test construction. Loevinger's later psychometric work (Loevinger and Wessler, 1970) exemplifies such an extended iterative effort. It sustained the elucidation of the Ego Development trait through the progressive evolution of its measure.

We also emphasize more strongly than Loevinger did in 1957 the heuristic value, from a discriminant or construct demarcation point of view, of exploring simultaneously several target traits. Again the Ego Development scale construction project provides an example: although the developmental milestone variables (impulsiveness, conformity, conscientiousness, etc.) are subordinate to the overarching Ego Development dimension, their psychometric differentiation illustrates clarification through demarcation.

In summary, exploratory test developers aim to represent each of several targeted traits with diverse candidate items that reflect alternative perspectives differing in inclusiveness. In this way, they seek to obtain informative convergent and discriminant correlational patterns that will lead, respectively, to construct elaboration and demarcation. They iteratively pursue these objectives, repeating as often as is productive the cycle of trait (re)formulation, item generation, and data collection and analysis.

APPROACH TO CONSTRUCTING THE MPQ

The Multidimensional Personality Questionnaire (MPQ) (Tellegen, 1982, 1995, 2003) was constructed in an exploratory manner over a 10-year period. It was not the purpose of this lengthy exploration to create another omnibus personality inventory for general use; only later did this become a consideration. It was to clarify and highlight the nature of several 'focal' dimensions repeatedly emphasized or adumbrated in the personality literature. Some of these traits seemed not to be well understood and were given conflicting interpretations, or were psychometrically neglected.

Data were collected with a series of seven sequentially expanded questionnaires. From each successive questionnaire, non-productive items were omitted and replaced by new items. Of the latter, some promised to clarify the meaning and bolster measurement of already included dimensions; others were intended to identify additional dimensions. The new items were generated by graduate students taking the first author's personality assessment seminar, and by the first author and his colleagues. Other items were adapted from existing sources. Item contributors first discussed among themselves the trait constructs in question, but were encouraged to submit items reflecting their own interpretations based on inspection of previously identified trait markers. A pluralism of alternative constructs for the same cluster of descriptors was thus encouraged to maximize the diversity and potential informativeness of new candidate descriptors for each hypothesized trait. All items were edited to improve clarity and simplicity. As was expected, only a minority of items included in the research questionnaires (276 items out of 1,082) survived as MPQ items.

Factor analysis (principal factors) with orthogonal simple structure rotation (varimax) was used to investigate the correlational structures of the successive multi-trait data sets. Rotations of varying numbers of dimensions were obtained to provide empirical indications of the number needed to represent salient and meaningful item concentrations. Factor-analytic solutions were thus used to provide corrective and suggestive feedback for improving and possibly adding constructs

in preparation for the next iteration of item writing, data collection, and data analysis.

In the pursuit of diverse trait indicators, it was important to distinguish true covariation between seemingly disparate response measures from chance patterns. It was required that each factor and each item identified as a factor marker be replicated in subsequent rounds of data analysis. Factor replicability was evaluated separately in both sexes with samples large enough ($n > 250$) to keep the probability of discarding good items tolerably low. Factor replication typically involved two stages: first, a subset of items consisting of established markers of each scale was factor-analyzed; this rarely resulted in item removals. Next, the remaining items, consisting largely of new candidates, were correlated with the replicated marker scales, and items showing a good convergent-discriminant pattern in both sexes were retained.

No special effort was made to produce scales of equal length. For each scale the number of items was determined by how many were needed to ensure adequate reliability and by how many distinctive content areas were identified in the course of construct elaboration.

Although both true-keyed and false-keyed candidate items were written for each scale, the scales were not required to contain an equal number of both (to have 'balanced' keys). The critical attributes determining inclusion of an item were its convergent and discriminant correlational properties. It was not assumed, and it appeared not to be the case, that any given construct is represented equally well and 'naturally' by true- and false-keyed items.

A familiar rationale for balanced keying is to control for 'acquiescent versus counter-acquiescent' response style (a fixed-response tendency to endorse items or not endorse items irrespective of item content). If (counter-)acquiescent responders complete a balanced scale, they are expected to lose as many points on one of the half-scales, keyed in one direction, as they are expected to gain on its counterpart, keyed in the opposite direction. But if the (counter-)acquiescent tendency is pronounced, a balanced scale should be expected to yield a score whose value approaches half the number of scale items (which may or may not be similar to the raw-score mean), rather than control response style. An alternative to controlling (counter-)acquiescence is to *measure* it, so that problematic individual records can be identified. The true-response inconsistency (TRIN) scale was constructed for that purpose. It is designed to detect the characteristic inconsistencies in response content that are the result of a (counter-) acquiescent style. TRIN is one of two MPQ inconsistency measures, the second being the variable-response inconsistency (VRIN) scale (for a discussion of TRIN and VRIN and of inconsistency assessment generally, see Tellegen, 1988).

The current MPQ (Tellegen, 1995, 2003) consists of 276 binary, mostly true–false, items. The 11 primary scales are composed of 262 items (the remaining 14 items make up the Unlikely Virtues scale, and are not discussed here). An earlier version (Tellegen, 1982) consisted of 300 items and was used in several of the studies considered here. It is nearly identical to the 276-item version, with the exception of containing an experimental validity scale, Associative Slips, which has subsequently been dropped.

In the next section we retrace the sequential development of the MPQ primary factor scales. Our account focuses on the process of construct (re)formulation, elaboration, and demarcation that resulted in the 11-factor structure.

DEVELOPING THE MPQ PRIMARY SCALES

Moving beyond N and E by testing ideas about hypnosis and personality

Construction of the MPQ began as an explo-ratory study focusing on personality characteristics related to individual differences in hypnotic susceptibility. The personological meaning of hypnotic responsiveness had long been of considerable interest to hypnosis researchers, but studies correlating measures of hypnotic responsiveness (to hypnotic suggestions) with scales from standard omnibus personality inventories had produced surprisingly negative findings (Barber, 1969; Hilgard, 1965). The personological significance of hypnotic responsiveness was either illusory or had eluded mainstream personality assessment. There were indications that the latter might be the case.

Several hypnosis researchers had published reports that certain 'hypnosis-like' experiences and related experiential tendencies correlate with hypnotic susceptibility. Tellegen and Atkinson (1974) assembled *Questionnaire I*, consisting in part of old items taken with minor changes from the studies just alluded to, and in part of specially written new items. The questionnaire items represented a variety of ideas about personal characteristics that could underlie hypnotic responsiveness such as trust, ability to relax, dissociative tendencies, tendency to become caught up in sensory and imaginative experiences, spontaneity, and so on. These items were grouped in 11 short and homogeneous scales based on item factor analysis. Subjects also completed measures of ego resiliency (ER) and Ego Control (EC) (Block, 1965). These two well-validated scales represent the two 'superfactors' that play a dominant role in almost every major personality inventory, and are best known by their Eysenckian labels N (Neuroticism) and E (Extraversion) (Eysenck and Eysenck, 1991). ER served as a reversed N marker, and EC as a reversed E marker.

Our factor analyses revealed three major dimensions, two easily identifiable as N and E, and a third we called 'Absorption'. Of the three factor scales, only Absorption correlated (moderately) with hypnotic susceptibility. Absorption had the appearance of a major personality trait like N and E: structurally coherent but diverse in content. We interpreted the trait as openness to absorbing and even 'self-altering' experiences. Our multidimensional approach also led to construct demarcation, since some of the 11 scales in our questionnaire proved, as expected, to be markers of N or E, not of Absorption.

McCrae and Costa (1985b) have referred to this early three-factor structure of N, E, and Absorption or Openness as a first formulation of the NEO model they developed independently a few years later. Interestingly, they found that Absorption and the McCrae and Costa Openness scale are substantially correlated ($r = 0.55$ and 0.56). Wild et al. (1995) subsequently reported a similar value ($r = 0.64$).

Re-examining and remapping N, E, and P domains

The Tellegen and Atkinson three-factor structure was a beginning. The N and E scales had not been analyzed at the item level and our E measure, in particular, looked complex and possibly multidimensional. The results also raised questions about the range and demarcation of absorption. Some absorption items suggested loose and unconventional thinking. Perhaps absorption also encompassed more radical departures from realistic thinking, even 'Psychoticism'. Eysenck had advocated Psychoticism, or P, as a third superfactor complementing N and E (Eysenck and Eysenck, 1985).

Questionnaire II was assembled from the viable items in Tellegen and Atkinson's questionnaire, augmented with new candidate N, E, and Absorption markers. Some of the new items came from the large N and E factors that Sells et al. (1968) had identified in their landmark study of a 600-item inventory composed equally of items provided by Cattell and Guilford. Also included in Questionnaire II were some 40 items selected from several sources to represent broadly the psychoticism domain, including several P items (Eysenck and Eysenck, 1968) and MMPI items, the latter mostly from the Schizophrenia scale (Butcher et al., 2001). These candidate Psychoticism items covered a broad area of self-description: aberrant experiences and thoughts, poor interpersonal relations, suspiciousness, and feelings of victimization.

The factor-analytic data collected with Questionnaire II produced a better delineated N factor; its corresponding scale was the precursor of the current MPQ stress reaction scale. The analyses also showed that the assembled pool of E items defined three distinctive dimensions, which through replication and elaboration studies evolved into the MPQ Social Potency, Social Closeness, and Control-versus-Impulsivity scales.

The division of E into three dimensions draws a clear distinction, more in accord with Guilford's than with Eysenck's views, between impulsivity and interpersonal behavior (Eysenck, 1977; Guilford, 1975, 1977). Within the interpersonal domain, Social Potency and Social Closeness represent a second basic distinction. We have suggested (Tellegen et al., 1988) that these two traits represent the two fundamental dimensions of Interpersonal Theory, namely, Power (dominance) and Love (affiliation), respectively (Kiesler, 1983; Leary, 1957; Wiggins, 1979).

The candidate Psychoticism items did not contribute clear Absorption markers, nor did they define a separate major Psychoticism-like dimension. A small factor reflecting distrust and a sense of victimization came closest to suggesting a distinctive trait in this domain. Using this small factor as a starting point, larger and more diverse item sets were generated for later questionnaires and subsequent data collections and analyses. Out of these analyses came eventually the current MPQ Alienation scale. People with high Alienation scores describe themselves as victims of malicious and exploitive treatment. They perceive in personal ('self-referential') terms the social world around them as malevolent. This perception may or may not have a basis in consensual reality but is salient in their own experience. Although Alienation and Stress Reaction are distinctive dimensions, they are moderately intercorrelated and were later found to be markers of the same higher-order dimension, Negative Emotionality.

The content of the Alienation scale has not moved as far from the original psychoticism concept as has Eysenck's P scale (Eysenck and Eysenck, 1991). The latter describes a careless, callous, cruel, and antisocial individual, and the P label no longer seems appropriate. Probably, the initial more plausible item pool for P, upon being found too close to N, was gradually shifted to its current content and location away from N (but claiming the impulsive region of E). The shift in the P-item pool appears to be a case of psychometric drift with conceptual lag. As we will see, the MPQ represents the current P-domain in a number of scales; for example, Aggression and (reversed) Control, as well as the (reversed) higher-order Constraint dimension. Although analyses did not yield a distinctive major Psychoti-cism dimension, let alone one subsuming Absorption or Alienation, the latter two may nevertheless be relevant to psychoticism-like phenomena. Specifically, a high level of Alienation, combined with a high Absorption level, may indicate a predisposition for episodes of psychosis-like aberrant thinking (see discussion below of Sellbom and Ben-Porath, 2005).

We now had the beginnings of six scales: Stress Reaction, Alienation, Social Potency, Social Closeness, Control, and Absorption. The subsequent item-generation and data-collection rounds, conducted with Questionnaires III and IV, resulted in improvements of these scales, reflecting further construct elaborations and demarcations. The two questionnaires also incorporated questions and conjectures that would lead to four additional scales, namely Traditionalism, Harmavoidance, Achievement, and Aggression.

Further exploring (un)conventionality

One demarcation issue again arose from the observation that some absorption items described unusual and unconventional thinking. As just reported, the initial issue concerned the distinction between absorption and psychoticism. But it was also noted that Sells et al. (1968), in their large-scale study, had identified a 'Conscientiousness' factor marked by statements expressing conforming, conventional, and moralistic attitudes (not to be confused with Big Five conscientiousness). Several of these conscientiousness items had an authoritarian ring (e.g. acceptance of parental authority, advocacy of strict discipline). Authoritarianism is itself an important focal construct in psychology. The place of conformity, conventionality, and authoritarian beliefs and attitudes warranted further exploration.

The pool of additional items assembled for *Questionnaire* III was adapted from several sources: Sells et al.'s (1968) conscientiousness dimension, Lee and Warr's (1969) revised F scale, Rokeach's (1960) dogmatism scale, and Ernhart and Loevinger's (1969) measure of Authoritarian Family Ideology. These added items clearly identified a distinctive factor that replicated in subsequent data sets. As usual, some candidate items had to be discarded, others were retained or modified, and still others were added later. The final result is the MPQ Traditionalism scale, first called Authoritarianism before David Lykken suggested its current more descriptive label.

At the same time that Alienation and Traditionalism were identified, Absorption became more delineated. Items with primarily interpersonal content (e.g. trust and autonomy) did not survive as markers. A high score on the current Absorption scale is not indicative of a particular interpersonal orientation and is compatible, for example, with either low or high Alienation or Social Closeness scores. The current Absorption scale measures more purely the tendency to become immersed in self-involving and self-altering experiences triggered by engaging external and imaginal stimuli (Tellegen, 1981, 1992).

Exploring anxiety/avoidance/ fearfulness/risk-taking

Another demarcation question concerned Stress Reaction. As the Stress Reaction scale took shape, tension, jumpiness, and worry-proneness emerged as salient themes, suggesting trait anxiety. Although 'anxiety' would seem an underinclusive characterization of the dimension as a whole (as noted earlier), other scales in the same family as Stress Reaction have been interpreted as measures of anxiety; for example, Taylor's (1953) Manifest Anxiety scale, Welsh's (1956) MMPI A scale, Cattell's Adjustment-versus-Anxiety second-order factor scale (Cattell et al., 1970). Anxiety also figures prominently in Block's concept of low Ego Resilience (Block, 1965, 2002). Indeed, in personality theory, few concepts have been as prominent as anxiety.

However, the psychological literature provides an important alternative perspective on anxiety and its assessment. Murray (1938: 199ff.) linked the concept of anxiety to a motivational concept, 'avoidance reactions', which he divided into three classes: Harmavoidance, Blamavoidance, and Infavoidance. His own deductive items were a mixture. Some, indeed, described avoidance tendencies ('I avoid passing through certain districts at night on account of a vague fear of assault,' 'I do many things just to avoid criticism,' 'I often avoid open competition because I fear I may appear in a bad light'). Other items were more suggestive of emotional reactivity ('I am conscious of a vague fear of death,' 'I feel mortified if I'm told that I have acted selfishly,' 'I feel nervous when I have to meet new people'), and did not refer directly to avoidance.

Subsequently, others have developed scales focusing more exclusively on avoidance of fear-arousing situations. Jackson's PRF Harmavoidance scale (Jackson, 1974) is based explicitly on Murray's motivational concept. Wessler and Loevinger (1969) remarked that among the PRF scales, Harmavoidance came closest to a measure of anxiety. Jackson's items include avoidance statements, but also negatively keyed statements describing stimulus-seeking enjoyment of various risky activities (walking a tight rope, going into a dangerous section of town). The structural integrity of Jackson's scales assured us that the risk avoidance and enjoyment components of his Harmavoidance scale formed an internally coherent correlational structure.

Like the PRF Harmavoidance scale, Lykken's Activity Preference Questionnaire (APQ) covers a wide range of dangerous and potentially frightening situations. The APQ presents pairs of situations, each pair made up of one fear-arousing situation or activity and one with closely matching features but of an onerous or tedious nature, and invites respondents to select from each pair the situation they prefer or dislike less. Lykken himself considered the APQ a trait anxiety measure (Lykken et al., 1973).

It became apparent that Harmavoidance versus Danger Seeking items were needed to clarify the dimensional structure of the broader 'anxiety' domain. We included in *Questionnaire IV* a group of candidate Harmavoidance items, some of which required preference responses, for which the more discriminating APQ physical anxiety items were used, while others were of the traditional 'single-stimulus' true–false variety. Factor analyses of the expanded questionnaire showed that Harmavoidance items of both types formed one dimension, clearly distinct from Stress Reaction. The Harmavoidance dimension proved replicable in subsequent analyses, and with further refinements, deletions, and additions the current Harmavoidance scale was formed.

The empirical distinctness of Stress Reaction and Harmavoidance required a corresponding conceptual distinction. As noted earlier, the label 'anxiety' has been applied to representatives of both dimensions. 'Anxiety' can be explicated as 'intense fear experienced when an individual believes s/he is in great danger and is eager to escape, but appraises the threat as virtually overwhelming, and in some cases as poorly known or understood, and feels unsure that s/he can escape or avert it'. These basic features include a *feeling* of fear, a *wish* to escape, and a *perception* of impending harm appraised as virtually inescapable. We call this 'state anxiety,' and define 'trait anxiety' as proneness to experience this state in daily life. We do not believe that 'trait anxiety' applies to either Stress Reaction or Harmavoidance.

Beginning with Harmavoidance, we interpret this trait dimension as a propensity to *avoid* versus a propensity to *seek* physically dangerous situations and activities (e.g. skydiving, firefighting, floods). We assume that high-scoring persons avoid these situations out of *fear*. But fearfulness does not entail trait anxiety as we define it. Since Harmavoidant persons prefer to restrict themselves to relatively safe situations, they will *because* of fearfulness experience little or no anxiety attributable to physical danger, provided their avoidance efforts are successful. The active seeking and enjoyment of danger associated with low Harmavoidance may at least in part be a compensatory effort to increase arousal, which is low because of lack of fear. Zuckerman (1979) has highlighted the importance of arousal regulation as a factor underlying individual differences in this trait domain. Harmavoidance, then, is a motivational trait that underlies specific avoidance-approach tendencies, linked to basic individual differences in fearfulness versus enjoyment of physically dangerous situations.

Stress Reaction is not primarily a motivational-behavioral trait. Its most salient manifestations are systematic individual differences in frequency and intensity of negative emotional states (anxiety, anger, distress, guilt feelings) experienced in everyday life. Highly Stress-Reactive persons may view their own emotional responses as unwarranted overreactions or even as inexplicable. They acknowledge responding 'catastrophically' to minor mishaps and setbacks referred to as 'daily hassles' (Kanner et al., 1981). A high Stress Reaction score does not intrinsically entail a pattern of avoidance. Many daily hassles are, in fact, difficult to avoid – one reason why a person's Stress Reaction level tends to be revealed by the frequency of her/his negative emotional responses. Whereas high Harmavoidance is the tendency to avoid disaster, high Stress Reaction is the tendency to expect, perceive, and (re-) experience disaster.

A way to cope with everyday adversities is through 'cognitive maneuvering' (Lazarus and Folkman, 1984) whereby one avoids negative emotions without having to avoid potentially upsetting events, by appraising these events less alarmingly. Cognitive behavioral therapists do not teach their highly stress-reactive clients how to avoid losing their car keys or missing their plane, but focus on this kind of cognitive restructuring.

In sum, we do not interpret either Harmavoidance or Stress Reaction as trait anxiety. Rather, we distinguish between fearfulness and trait anxiety, and propose fearfulness about physical danger as a component of Harmavoidance, and trait anxiety, defined as proneness to experience state anxiety in everyday life, as a component of Stress Reaction.

Further exploring effectance

As the Social Potency scale evolved, and its content conveyed broad interpersonal effectiveness and a desire to make an impact on others, its boundaries became another demarcation issue. Effectiveness and impact are not limited to the strictly interpersonal sphere and are also salient in the world of work. Does an extended effectiveness domain define, motivationally or otherwise, a single broad dimension or is it multidimensional?

White's (1959, 1960) concept of effectance motivation refers to a unitary structure. The same applies to mastery motivation (Yarrow et al., 1983). Murray (1938) pointed to connections between Dominance and Achievement needs, suggesting that *n* Dominance may be 'subsidiary' to *n* Achievement, and took note of the view that *n* Achievement, conceived as Adlerian 'will-to-power', is the dominant psychogenic need. Similarly, the Power dimension of the 'Interpersonal Circle' (Kiesler, 1983), as measured by Wiggins' Interpersonal Adjective Scales (IAS), was originally defined as Ambitious/Dominant versus Lazy/Submissive (Wiggins, 1979).

On the other hand, Murray also conceived of *n* Dominance and *n* Achievement as distinct motives. Jackson accordingly constructed separate Dominance and Achievement scales, and other trait psychologists have focused on the study of either Achievement (McClelland et al., 1953; Atkinson, 1964) or Power (McClelland, 1975; Winter, 1973). Achievement motivation has been studied intensively for years, and clearly has been a distinctive focal dimension in psychology.

To explore the effectance domain more broadly along Achievement lines, a set of diverse items dealing with effort, work, persistence, and perfectionism were also included in Questionnaire IV. Factor analyses identified these themes as features of a single dimension. The factor proved replicable, and from analyses of successive questionnaires better items were retained, others were revised, new ones were added, resulting in the current MPQ Achievement scale. Although the findings clearly indicate that Social Potency and Achievement are distinct dimensions in the effectance domain, the two scales are modestly correlated (0.2 to 0.3), and are markers of the same higher-order factor, Agentic Positive Emotionality, as we will see. The data, then, support distinctive dimensions as well as a generalized effectance theme.

Further exploring the interpersonal domain

Still another demarcation issue involved the nature of Social Closeness. Interpersonal Theory has placed friendliness or agreeability at one pole of its Love dimension, and hostility or quarrelsomeness at the other. However, the Social Closeness items that had been identified so far contrasted warmth and need for intimacy with distance and preference for solitude. Should 'hostility' be considered a separate dimension? Friendliness and hostility as relatively independent dimensions would accommodate a more complex and potentially ambivalent picture of interpersonal motivation and behavior than as opposite poles of one dimension.

Accordingly, we added to Questionnaire IV a set of items describing aggressive, vindictive, and victimizing propensities. Factor-analyzed along with the other inventory items, these candidate Aggression markers defined a separate dimension distinguishable from Social Closeness. The final Social Closeness and Aggression scales correlated about −0.1, hardly suggesting a primary or even higher-order bipolar affiliation versus hostility dimension. Wiggins et al.'s (1988) removal of the 'quarrelsome' category from the non-friendly pole of the Love dimension is consonant with these findings, and was based on a correlational analysis of the revised Interpersonal Adjective Scales (IAS-R).

At this point, four basic and distinctive interpersonal dimensions had been identified: Social Potency, Social Closeness, Aggression, and Alienation. In light of this outcome, the Interpersonal Circle model adopted by some proponents of Interpersonal Theory has to be considered overinclusive. It forces the above four interpersonal dimensions as well as the achievement dimension as vectors into its two-dimensional framework: Social Potency and Achievement as fused markers of the Power/Ambition versus Submissiveness/Laziness vector, Social Closeness and Aggression as opposite poles of the Friendliness versus Hostility vector, and Alienation as an intermediate Trust versus Mistrust vector, with Trust placed between Love and Submissiveness (Kiesler, 1983).

The reluctance to give up a two-dimensional model is understandable. Even one extra dimension creates room for infinitely many circles. But to hold down dimensionality, one must choose rather than confound dimensions. As noted earlier, we believe that of the four dimensions, Social Potency and Social Closeness represent the Power and Love vectors of Interpersonal Theory. In subsequent refinements of the IAS, Wiggins appears to have moved toward such a representation (Wiggins, 1995; Wiggins et al., 1988).

Examining ten identified MPQ personality traits from a multi-faceted emotional perspective, and adding the eleventh trait: Wellbeing

The previous rounds of scale development focused on improving the representation of particular personality traits in particular areas. The purpose of round five was to evaluate whether, in some stipulative but meaningful sense, adequate representation of the personality *domain* had been achieved. After four rounds, the MPQ comprised ten scales close to their current form. At that point it became apparent that many MPQ items refer to emotional states: enjoyment, excitement, interest, warmth, anxiety, guilt, anger, disgust, fatigue. Each MPQ scale, in fact, contains items describing or implying certain emotional and related feeling dispositions. The Stress Reaction scale, in particular, is replete with emotional references.

The references to affect suggested an evaluation of the MPQ as an emotional-temperament inventory. Such an appraisal could be made by administering the MPQ together with a comprehensive measure of current mood, and looking for relations between emotional state dimensions and corresponding MPQ trait dimensions. The idea of systematic state–trait congruencies was not farfetched. Spielberger had demonstrated substantial correlations between his state anxiety scale and various trait measures, including his trait anxiety scale (Spielberger et al., 1970).

A 60-item mood inventory (cf. Zevon and Tellegen, 1982), covering a wide range of recognized emotional categories, or 'discrete emotions' (Izard, 1972), was administered along with *Questionnaire V*, the ten-scale precursor of the MPQ. Several salient state-trait correlations were found. Stress Reaction, Alienation, and Aggression correlated with several negative moods such as fear and anger. Mood correlations with the Stress Reaction scale were particularly numerous and strong, which was not surprising given the pervasively emotional content of this scale. Social Potency, and to a lesser degree Achievement and Social Closeness, tended to correlate with positive mood states (such as joy and enthusiasm). However, trait correlates of negative mood were more pronounced. Absent on the positive side was a counterpart of Stress Reaction, a 'Wellbeing' scale assessing a positive-emotional disposition (as distinct from the absence of negative-emotional tendencies).

If a separate Wellbeing dimension were to be identified, then addition of a Wellbeing scale would of course make the MPQ a more complete temperament inventory. Potential Wellbeing markers were generated and were included in *Questionnaire VI*. A distinctive Wellbeing factor did emerge, although it took a final round of item writing, and data collection with *Questionnaire VII*, to complete the empirical item selection for the current Wellbeing scale. The outcome of an attempt to clarify the personality domain from an emotional-temperament perspective, the Wellbeing scale proved to be an important marker of the higher-order Positive Emotionality dimension, which emerged when the 11 MPQ scales were factor-analyzed.

ATTRIBUTES OF THE MPQ

Once the 11 MPQ primary scales were in place, several basic studies of the completed inventory could be carried out. A comprehensive item content analysis was undertaken, first- and second-order factor structures and psychometric scale properties were examined, and the first external-correlate studies were conducted. We report results in the next three sections, labeled 'Content', 'Structure', and 'External correlates', respectively.

Content

Although item content was monitored throughout the scale construction phase, upon completion of the MPQ, a formal consensual content analysis was performed on each individual scale. Ten to twelve graduate psychology students participating in the first author's personality assessment seminar independently carried out the following sorting task. They received for each scale a deck of cards, each card showing a different item along with its direction of keying, and were asked to form groups of items whose content, as keyed in the scale, they considered very similar. Sorters were allowed to form as many or as few categories as they thought necessary and were encouraged to try different groupings until they found one that was satisfactory. The individual sortings were combined into a co-occurrence matrix.

A co-occurrence matrix is analogous to a correlation matrix; it can be interpreted as a matrix of 'proximities' or similarities between the members of a set of 'objects' (e.g. items). For example, if a scale consists of 20 items, then for each of the 190 items pairs one can determine the number of judges who sorted both pair members in the same group. Many same-group sortings, or co-occurrences, of two items would indicate a strong consensus that the two are similar. With ten judges, the number of possible co-occurrences would range from 0 to 10. A co-occurrence matrix, like a correlation matrix, can be cluster- or factor-analyzed. In all, 59 clusters were identified. Table 13.1 is based on these analyses; the second column ('Self-descriptors of high scorers') provides summaries of each cluster, separated by semicolons.

Structure

Factor analysis of content subscales

Content clusters not only aid systematic description of content but can also be used to assess structure. The 59 clusters were scored and factor-analyzed in several samples of college and community adults. None of the samples had been used in the derivation of the scales. The analyses consistently replicated an 11-factor structure corresponding to the 11 primary MPQ factor scales.

Results of one of these analyses, obtained on a sample of 889 male college students and shown in Table 13.2, reveal a maximally 'simple' convergent-discriminant pattern that clearly replicates the MPQ primary factor structure. Clusters from the same MPQ scale converge on the same factor, and clusters from different scales mark different factors, so that each scale defines its own dimension. Of the maximum number of 590 discriminant factor loadings, 571 (97%) are smaller than 0.20, suggesting that the effort to develop relatively independent scales was successful. Additional factor analyses were undertaken in which clusters were replaced by two items from each cluster (for a total of 118 items). The results again replicated near-perfectly the expected 11-factor configuration. By virtue of concisely summarizing the content and structure of the 11 MPQ first-order dimensions, Tables 13.1 and 13.2 also provided the necessary background for describing and interpreting the MPQ higher-order dimensions.

Discovering the higher-order MPQ dimensions

Consistent with the illustrative findings, shown in Table 13.2, of a clean first-order orthogonal factor structure, the correlations between MPQ scales are generally low. Even so, the scale intercorrelations were found to define a meaningful higher-order structure (reflecting the pattern of secondary item loadings on the primary factors). Table 13.3 shows the representative results obtained by factor analyzing a large composite sample of 4,340 participants, aged 17–59, comprising both college and general population samples (the latter was recruited from the Minnesota Twin Registry, to be described shortly).

The first three numerical columns of Table 13.3 display a structure of three higher-order factors (similar structures were also recovered separately from samples of college men and women, see Tellegen, 1985: 695, table 37.1). Tellegen (1985) has interpreted these factors as Positive Emotionality (PEM),

Table 13.1   Content Summaries of the 11 MPQ Primary Trait Scales

Scale	Self-Descriptors of High Scorers	Self-Descriptors of Low Scorers
1. Wellbeing	Has a cheerful, happy disposition, feels good about self; sees a bright future ahead, is an optimist; lives an interesting, exciting life; enjoys the things he or she is doing.	Is not a naturally cheerful person, is seldom really happy; does not seem to experience a lot of excitement and fun in life.
2. Social Potency	Is forceful and decisive; is persuasive and likes to influence others; enjoys or would enjoy leadership roles; enjoys being noticed, being the center of attention.	Prefers others to take charge and make decisions; does not like to persuade others; does not aspire to leadership; does not enjoy being the center of attention.
3. Achievement	Works hard, drives self; enjoys working hard; welcomes difficult and demanding tasks; persists where others give up; is ambitious, puts work and accomplishment before many other things; sets high standards, is a perfectionist.	Does not like to work harder than is strictly necessary; avoids very demanding projects; sees no point in persisting when success seems unlikely; is not terribly ambitious or a perfectionist.
4. Social Closeness	Is sociable, likes to be with people; takes pleasure in and values close interpersonal ties; is warm and affectionate; turns to others for comfort and help.	Likes to be alone; can do without close ties; is aloof and distant; prefers to work problems out on her (his) own.
5. Stress Reaction	Is tense and nervous; is sensitive, feels vulnerable; is prone to worry and feel anxious; is irritable and easily upset; has changing moods; can feel miserable without reason; is troubled by feelings of guilt and unworthiness.	Does not feel vulnerable; can put fears and worries out of her (his) mind; quickly gets over upsetting experiences; is not troubled by emotional turmoil or guilt feelings.
6. Aggression	Is physically aggressive; enjoys upsetting and frightening others; enjoys scenes of violence (fights, violent movies); victimizes others for own advantage; will retaliate, is vindictive.	Is not violent; does not enjoy others' distress; does not like to witness physical aggression; will not take advantage of others; would rather turn the other cheek than seek revenge.
7. Alienation	Believes that others wish her (him) harm; is a victim of false and nasty rumors; has been betrayed and deceived; feels used by "friends"; feels pushed around; has had a lot of bad luck.	Does not see self as victim; does not feel taken advantage of; feels treated fairly.
8. Control vs. Impulsivity	Is reflective; is cautious, careful, plodding; is rational, sensible, level-headed; likes to plan her (his) activities in detail.	Is impulsive and spontaneous; can be reckless and careless; makes no detailed plans, preferring to "play things by ear".
9. Harmavoidance	Does not or would not enjoy: participating in dangerous adventures or activities (e.g., skydiving); being in some natural disaster (e.g., a forest fire); being caught in a sudden and dangerous emergency (e.g., a hold-up); deliberately risking serious bodily injury (e.g., riding a runaway horse). Instead, prefers safer activities and experiences, even if they are tedious or aggravating.	Does or would enjoy dangerous and exciting experiences and activities; prefers these over safer ones that are tedious or aggravating.
10. Traditionalism	Endorses high moral standards; endorses religious values and institutions; expresses positive regard for parents; endorses strict child-rearing practices; values conventional propriety and a good reputation; opposes rebelliousness and unrestricted freedom of expression; condemns selfish disregard of others.	Does not belabor the importance of high morals; considers traditional religion outdated; does not believe in punitive discipline; is not prudish or very concerned over what is "proper"; sees value in rebelliousness and free expression; does not reject selfishness.

Continued

Table 13.1   Content Summaries of the 11 MPQ Primary Trait Scales—cont'd

Scale	Self-Descriptors of High Scorers	Self-Descriptors of Low Scorers
11. Absorption	Is responsive to evocative sights and sounds (e.g., a sunset); is readily captured by entrancing stimuli (e.g., overpowering music); tends to think in images; has "crossmodal" experiences, including synesthesia (e.g., sounds evoke color experiences); is capable of vivid and compelling imaginings; can vividly re- experience the past; becomes deeply immersed in own thoughts and imaginings; experiences episodes of expanded (e.g., ESP-like) awareness; experiences states of altered awareness (e.g., of "stepping outside oneself").	Is not easily caught up in sensory and imaginative experiences; does not readily relinquish a realistic frame of reference.

Table 13.2   Factor Analysis of Sorted Content-Homogeneous MPQ Item Clusters

		WB	SP	AC	SC	SR	AG	AL	CO	HA	TR	AB
WB	1.Optimistic, hopeful	56				-35						
	2.Has cheerful disposition	59										
	3.Has interesting experiences	67										
	4.Engages in enjoyable activities	60										
SP	1.Forceful decisive		66									
	2.Persuasive		65									
	3.Seeks leadership roles		65									
	4.Enjoys visibility		63									
AC	1.Works hard			42								
	2.Enjoys effort			57								
	3.Welcomes challenges			53								
	4.Persistent			54								
	5.Ambitious			51								
	6.Perfectionistic			38								
SC	1.Sociable				66							
	2.Values close relationships				49							
	3.Warm, affectionate				52							
	4.Seeks support				59							
SR	1.Tense, nervous					61						
	2.Sensitive, vulnerable					49						
	3.Worry-prone, anxious					64						
	4.Easily upset					61						
	5.Unexplainable negative emotions					60						
	6.Prone to feel guilty					54						
AG	1.Physically aggressive						51					
	2.Enjoys distressing others						59					
	3.Enjoys witnessing violence						47					
	4.Victimizes for own gain						32					
	5.Vengeful, vindictive						55					
AL	1.Target of malevolence							62				
	2.Victim of false rumors							53				
	3.Betrayed, deceived							50				
	4.Exploited							64				
	5.Pushed around							58				
	6.Unlucky							44				

Table 13.2   Factor Analysis of Sorted Content-Homogeneous MPQ Item Clusters—cont'd

		WB	SP	AC	SC	SR	AG	AL	CO	HA	TR	AB
CO	1.Reflective								62			
	2.Cautious, careful								58			
	3.Level-headed, sensible								69			
	4.Makes detailed plans								65			
HA	1.Dislikes risky adventures									62		
	2.Avoids disaster areas									62		
	3.Dislikes emergencies									62		
	4.Avoids injury									57		
TR	1.Moralistic										65	
	2.Endorses religion										59	
	3.Positive regard for parents										51	
	4.Endorses strict rearing										52	
	5.Values "proper" conduct										47	
	6.Opposes rebelliousness										43	
	7.Condemns selfishness										38	
AB	1.Responds to evocative stimuli											53
	2.Responds to involving stimuli											65
	3.Thinks in images											40
	4.Has "crossmodal" experiences											65
	5.Can imagine vividly											65
	6.Can relive past											39
	7.Absorbed in own thoughts											47
	8.Expanded awareness											50
	9.Altered awareness											63

Note: WB = Wellbeing; SP = Social Potency; AC = Achievement; SC = Social Closeness; SR = Stress Reaction; AG = Aggression; AL = Alienation; CO = Control versus Impulsiveness; HA = Harmavoidance; TR = Traditionalism; AB = Absorption. Sample: 889 college men. Only loadings > |.30| are shown. Decimal points are omitted.

Negative Emotionality (NEM), and Constraint (CON). These labels refer to 'open' concepts (Meehl, 1978), which leave much unspecified, but do not lack specific content and can serve a heuristic function. We offer the following descriptive and interpretive summaries.

PEM and NEM. Table 13.3 shows that PEM is associated with Wellbeing, Social Potency, Achievement, and Social Closeness, and less specifically with Absorption. Of these markers, Wellbeing represents *the tendency to experience positive emotions*, Social Potency and Achievement represent *effectance motivation and mastery*, and Social Potency and Social Closeness *the tendency to be involved in interpersonal transactions*; the Absorption loading probably reflects the emotional responsiveness component of this trait. The self-descriptive terms in Table 13.1 indicate that persons with high scores on these PEM markers present themselves as efficacious, as actively involved in their social and work environments, and as ready to experience the positive emotions congruent with these involvements. A high

Table 13.3   Higher-Order Factor Analysis of MPQ Scales Labeled Factors

Scale	PEM	NEM	CON	PEM-A	PEM-C
Wellbeing	**60**	−16	−07	**48**	**38**
Social Potency	**50**	03	**−32**	**42**	28
Achievement	**34**	−05	06	**54**	−06
Social Closeness	**37**	−16	04	03	**49**
Stress Reaction	−17	**61**	08	−08	−17
Aggression	01	**49**	−26	03	−02
Alienation	−09	**57**	08	02	−14
Control	−05	−29	**42**	08	−15
Harmavoidance	−13	−04	**47**	−26	07
Traditionalism	02	08	**44**	01	02
Absorption	**35**	**32**	−16	**43**	06

Note: In three-factor solution: PEM = (general) Positive Emotionality; NEM = Negative Emotionality; CON = Constraint. In four-factor solution PEM divides into PEM-A = Agentic Positive Emotionality and PEM-C = Communal Positive Emotionality. Sample: 4,340 college and community men and women. Loadings > |.30| are shown in boldface. Decimal points are omitted.

PEM pattern may be the implied focus of contemporary Positive Psychology (Seligman and Csikszentmihalyi, 2000). Persons with low PEM scores convey less self-efficacy, less active social and work involvement, and a higher threshold for positive emotional experiences.

NEM (or Negative Affectivity, Tellegen, 1982; Watson and Clark, 1984) is associated with Stress Reaction and Alienation, somewhat less strongly with Aggression, and secondarily with Absorption and (reversed) Control. Of these NEM markers, Stress Reaction represents *the tendency to experience negative emotions*, and Aggression and Alienation *the tendency to be involved in adversarial interpersonal transactions* as victimizer and victim, respectively. The secondary Absorption loading may represent the emotional reactivity component of this trait (as in the case of PEM), while the secondary negative Control loading suggests an element of disorganization. Individuals with high scores on the primary NEM markers describe themselves as often stressed and harassed, prone to react with strong negative emotions (e.g. anxiety and anger) to everyday vicissitudes, and being enmeshed in negative relationships. Scores of low NEM persons suggest a higher threshold for negative emotional responses and a less adversarial interpersonal outlook.

The PEM and NEM labels are meant to suggest that both traits are basic parameters of emotional temperament. The underlying structure of each is thought to include a major and distinctive emotional response system influencing cognitive and behavioral manifestations of the trait. In support of these conjectures we offer the following observations:

1   Both PEM and NEM have a 'pure-emotional' component: Wellbeing represents the disposition to experience positive emotions and is a salient marker of PEM, while Stress Reaction represents the disposition to experience negative emotions and is a salient NEM marker. Consistent with this observation, the PEM and NEM trait dimensions correlate in a convergent-discriminant pattern with the two major self-report emotional state

dimensions, positive affect (PA) and negative affect (NA) (Tellegen, 1985; Watson and Tellegen, 1985)[2]. In samples of men and women college students ($n = 222$ and 168, respectively) PEM was substantially correlated with PA ($r = 0.50$ and 0.42) and weakly with NA ($r = -0.09$ and -0.24), while for NEM, the correlations with PA and NA showed the opposite pattern ($r = -0.20$ and -0.17, and 0.53 and 0.50, respectively) (Tellegen, 1982, table 5). This pattern of correlations between traits and states supports our interpretation of PEM and NEM as emotional temperament parameters.

2   There is also telling content similarity between the PEM and NEM traits and their state counterparts. Tellegen's factor analyses of mood questionnaires demonstrated that PA and NA are multi-faceted higher-order dimensions subsuming a variety of 'discrete emotions', some emerging as lower-order dimensions (Tellegen et al., 1999a, 1999b; Zevon and Tellegen, 1982). PA includes not only such pure-emotional descriptors as 'joyful' and 'enthusiastic,' but also 'warm-hearted' and 'proud.' NA not only includes 'upset' and 'fearful,' but also 'angry' and 'ashamed.' Clearly, PA and NA states, like PEM and NEM traits, include interpersonal components. If social *states* can be considered part of *temper*, we can similarly consider social *traits* as part of *temperament*. In other words, if presence of social components does not argue against viewing PA and NA as emotional states, then neither does it argue against viewing both PEM and NEM as emotional traits.

3   Since both PEM and NEM, like PA and NA, have pure-emotional and social components, we may conclude that PEM is no less emotional than NEM and that NEM is no less interpersonal than PEM. The important remaining distinction between the two dimensions is that one is 'positive' and the other 'negative'. But 'positive' and 'negative' (psychologically speaking) are hedonic and attitudinal qualities that are, broadly speaking, affective. The distinctiveness of PEM and NEM appears to have an affective basis, which the PEM and NEM constructs underscore.

4   PEM and NEM can each be thought of as a *synergistic* emotional/cognitive/behavioral system: the emotions expressing the emotion-dispositional component of the trait seem to play a crucial role in priming and organizing its cognitive and behavioral (e.g. interpersonal) manifestations. These cognitions and behaviors in turn facilitate

and intensify trait-expressive emotions. For example, positive emotions prime positive social expectancies and rewarding social behaviors, which are in turn conducive to positive emotional experiences.

PEM-A and PEM-C   The MPQ also supports a meaningful four-factor higher-order pattern wherein PEM bifurcates into 'Agentic Positive Emotionality' (PEM-A) and 'Communal Positive Emotionality' (PEM-C). We borrowed 'agentic' and 'communal' from Bakan (1966) and use these terms in a sense roughly corresponding to his concepts of Agency and Communion. To increase comparability of the three- and four-factor solutions, the three-factor solution was obtained by extracting and rotating the four-factor structure and defining PEM as the intermediate vector between PEM-A and PEM-C. Thus NEM and CON are identical in the three- and four-factor structures.

The PEM-A and PEM-C factor loadings are shown in the last two columns of Table 13.3. PEM-A and PEM-C resemble PEM and one another in that all three have (near-) salient loadings on Wellbeing and Social Potency. However, PEM-A is distinguished by a strong loading on Achievement and virtually no loading on Social Closeness, while PEM-C has a strong loading on Social Closeness and virtually no loadings on Achievement and Absorption. Given the descriptions in Table 13.1, PEM-A emphasizes positive emotional responsiveness and effectance (or Agency), while PEM-C combines positive emotions with interpersonal connectedness (or Communion). We can add to our earlier suggestion that Social Potency and Social Closeness are main vectors of the Interpersonal Circle the observation that PEM-A and PEM-C form a more general Positive-Emotional plane in which there is room for both interpersonal and effectance vectors, as in Wiggins' original IAS (Wiggins, 1979).

CON   This higher-order factor is primarily associated with Control, Harmavoidance, and Traditionalism, and secondarily (and negatively) with Social Potency and Aggression. The three primary loadings characterize this higher-order dimension as one of *self-restrictive caution, safety-consciousness, and conventionality*. The secondary negative CON loadings of Social Potency and Aggression are congruent with the primary ones in conveying a *reluctance to be expansive and intrusive*. Self-descriptions of persons with high scores on CON markers indicate caution, planfulness, avoidance of danger, conventionality, and adherence to traditional values, while low CON scores suggest impulsiveness, danger-seeking, and rejection of conventional and traditional behavioral strictures.

Of the three Eysenckian superfactors (N, E, and P), CON covaries most (and negatively) with P (as discussed below). Earlier we questioned, as others have, the fit of the psychoticism construct to the P scale itself. Given its salient primary factor loadings, 'high versus low behavioral constraint' is a more accurate designation for this P-related higher-order MPQ dimension. Zuckerman has similarly suggested that *psychopathy* is a more appropriate label than psychoticism (Zuckerman, 1989). Possibly underlying this dimension is a general response inhibition system, a behavioral temperament trait, varying in strength across individuals and influencing behavior over a wide range of situations (Tellegen, 1985).

Internal consistency and stability

Alpha coefficients were computed on several samples of men and women. The first two of the four sets of alphas, shown in Table 13.4, are based on college student samples; the other two were obtained from samples of young adults, aged 18–30, consisting of identical and fraternal twins and their siblings recruited from the Minnesota Twin Registry. Other than containing twins, the latter two samples were representative of the general Minnesota population. Their recruitment has been reported elsewhere (e.g. Krueger and Johnson, 2002; Lykken, 1982). None of the alpha coefficients in the four samples was

Table 13.4   MPQ Reliability, Stability, External Correlational, and Heritability Data

	Alpha Coefficients					Stability	External Correlations	Heritability
	1	2	3	4	$\overline{r}_{ii}$			
Wellbeing	89	89	89	88	24	90	49	48
Social Potency	87	89	89	88	22	82	58	54
Achievement	84	84	85	80	19	88	51	39
Social Closeness	85	85	78	82	18	92	50	40
Stress Reaction	89	89	87	90	23	89	39	53
Aggression	84	76	88	77	18	82	29	44
Alienation	87	81	87	86	22	87	19	45
Control	83	86	80	84	17	82	45	44
Harmavoidance	84	84	82	83	15	88	56	55
Traditionalism	83	85	79	80	14	90	49	45
Absorption	88	88	89	88	18	91	21	50
I. Positive Emotionality	--	--	--	--	--	89	52	40
II. Negative Emotionality	--	--	--	--	--	89	25	55
III. Constraint	--	--	--	--	--	89	53	58

Note: The four sets of alpha coefficients were obtained on, respectively, 300 college men, 500 college women, 223 community men, and 391 community women; $\overline{r}_{ii}$ is the estimated mean inter-item correlation. The stability coefficients are 30-day test retest data on 75 college men and women. The external correlations are MPQ correlations with trait ratings of 223 college men and women (Harkness, Tellegen, & Waller, 1995). The heritabilities are from Tellegen et al. (1988). Decimal points are omitted

below 0.75 (median r = 0.85). Also shown is the mean inter-item correlation, $\overline{r}_{ii}$, estimated for each scale across the four samples, using the step-down Spearman–Brown correction (median $\overline{r}_{ii}$ = 0.18). The one-month test–retest correlations, obtained on a college sample, yielded a median value of 0.89. Overall, these results indicate acceptable internal consistencies and reliabilities, and compare favorably with those reported for other personality inventories.

External correlates

So far, we have focused on how the MPQ was developed by using exploratory methodology to elaborate and demarcate psychologically meaningful self-report dimensions. Once the MPQ scales were in (near-)final form, it was possible to explore external correlates.

Congruences with other self-report personality inventories

Current personality inventories differ and overlap in important ways. Overlap is especially interesting if (1) it is not piecemeal but systematic, for example if different

inventories have similar higher-order dimensions; and (2) the inventories differ substantially in their development and specific content. Higher-order convergences in spite of such differences could be considered evidence that each inventory represents, broadly speaking, the personality domain. Similar higher-order structures would also make it possible to compare seemingly very different inventories in mutually clarifying ways.

Joint factor analyses of MPQ, CPI, and EPQ The MPQ, CPI (Gough and Bradley, 1996), and EPQ (Eysenck and Eysenck, 1991) are very different instruments. The 11 MPQ scales were constructed by exploring, elaborating, and demarcating focal personality-psychological themes factor-analytically; the MPQ scale intercorrelations tend to be low. The primary CPI scales were intended to capture folk concepts and were largely derived through external keying; many CPI scales are substantially intercorrelated. The EPQ was intended to represent basic normal and abnormal personality variations; yet with its three near-orthogonal primary factor scales it is the most economical of the three inventories.

Despite these differences, the three inventories share one basic feature: each is the vehicle of three very broad dimensions. The CPI and MPQ supertraits emerged as higher-order factors from analyses of the primary scales. The CPI higher-order factors used here are those Nichols and Schnell (1963) had derived from the primary scale intercorrelations. One, Person Orientation, is a broad extraversion-like dimension; the second, Value Orientation, taps emotional adjustment; the (unnamed) third dimension is primarily marked by three CPI scales: Flexibility versus Rigidity, Achievement-via-Independence, and (reversed) Communality. In the EPQ, the primary scales themselves are superfactor measures. It seemed worthwhile to examine possible convergences between the three inventories at this level.

The MPQ, CPI, and EPQ were administered to a group of 155 college students. The nine broad factor measures (three sets of three) were factor-analyzed separately for each gender group and for the combined sample. In all three groups the sizes of the principal components indicated three dominant dimensions: the first six eigenvalues for the combined sample were: 2.9, 1.9, 1.8, 0.7, 0.5, and 0.4. Table 13.5 shows that the three triads of factor scores were highly congruent, defining a single three-dimensional structure interpretable as a PEM-NEM-CON space; the relatively weak negative loading of the EPQ P scale is partially attributable to its low internal consistency. Although the three inventories are not interchangeable, at the highest-order level they define similar personality domains.

Joint factor analyses of MPQ, 16PF, and PRF Although each of these three inventories was developed through internal consistency methods, they differ markedly. The 16PF (Cattell et al., 1970) originated from a dimensional distillation of the corpus of everyday personality trait descriptors (assembled by Allport and Odbert, 1936), and its 16 dimensions were designed to encompass the personality domain (cf. Cattell and Cattell, 1995). Whereas in the construction of the MPQ orthogonal simple-structure rotations

Table 13.5 Factor Analysis of Higher-Order Factor Scores Derived from the MPQ, CPI and EPQ

	Labeled Factors		
	PEM	NEM	CON
MPQ Positive Emotionality	**74**	−04	21
CPI Person Orientation	**80**	−22	−17
EPQ Extraversion	**78**	−13	−06
MPQ Negative Emotionality	−12	**79**	11
CPI Value Orientation (reversed)	−05	**80**	−16
EPQ Neuroticism	**−31**	**69**	12
MPQ Constraint	−12	04	**78**
CPI Rigidity	14	32	**69**
EPQ Psychoticism (reversed)	00	−28	**50**

Note: PEM = Positive Emotionality; NEM = Negative Emotionality; CON = Constraint. Sample = 155 college men and women. Loadings > |.30| are shown in boldface. Decimal points are omitted.

were used to enhance scale distinctiveness, Cattell, in developing the 16PF, applied an oblique simple-structure methodology, resulting in relatively high correlations between the primary factor scales. Unlike the 16PF and MPQ, Jackson's (1974) PRF was constructed deductively, its scales being largely modeled after Murray's (1938) classification of needs. Jackson (1970) used a sequential methodology to prune empirically an initial set of purely deductive (rational) scales in a manner designed to enhance internal consistency and distinctiveness of the scales.

The three inventories were administered to 288 college students, permitting a factor analysis of the 46 primary scales (excluding the 16PF Intelligence measure). Extraction of principal components revealed four salient dimensions (the eight successive eigenvalues were: 6.5, 6.1, 4.3, 4.0, 2.3, 1.6, 1.5, and 1.2). The rotated four-factor solution is shown in Table 13.6. A five-factor solution, not shown here, was virtually identical to the four-factor solution, augmented with a fifth factor identifiable as an aggression dimension.

Table 13.6 reveals a clean factor structure, with most variables showing only one clearly salient loading. The MPQ loadings correspond closely to those shown in Table 13.3, obtained when the MPQ was analyzed alone. A separate analysis of the scale intercorrelations

Table 13.6   Joint Factor Analysis of the MPQ, 16PF and PRF

SCALE	Labeled Factors			
	PEM-A	PEM-C	NEM	CON
MPQ				
Wellbeing	**31**	**43**	−25	−05
Social Potency	**55**	**53**	15	−06
Achievement	**71**	−08	−14	22
Social Closeness	−18	**71**	−23	04
Stress Reaction	−12	−15	**65**	07
Aggression	−02	00	**70**	−19
Alienation	−01	−17	**52**	11
Control	07	−13	−10	**66**
Harmavoidance	**−32**	03	03	**55**
Traditionalism	−05	03	08	**56**
Absorption	29	09	23	−03
16PF				
A outgoing	03	**40**	−03	13
C emotionally stable	20	11	**−65**	−02
E assertive	**50**	**31**	15	−29
F happy-go-lucky	06	**65**	00	**−32**
G conscientious	28	11	−01	**69**
H venturesome	**48**	**62**	−16	−02
I tender-minded	−14	01	−04	05
L suspicious	12	03	**65**	−10
M imaginative	07	−11	−17	−23
N shrewd	−23	−05	−04	24
O apprehensive	−15	−18	**59**	00
Q1 experimenting	22	01	07	**−33**
Q2 self-sufficient	14	**−54**	06	−01
Q3 controlled	15	−02	−28	**55**
Q4 tense	−14	−06	**72**	01
PRF				
Abasement	01	−05	**−31**	10
Achievement	**71**	−08	−19	20
Affiliation	−04	**73**	−22	−06
Aggression	14	11	**79**	−08
Autonomy	**46**	**−31**	03	**−44**
Change	**31**	20	08	**−46**
Cognitive Structure	04	−05	06	**73**
Defendence	20	−03	**60**	−07
Dominance	**65**	**43**	12	−08
Endurance	**67**	−04	−25	20
Exhibition	21	**66**	22	−17
Harmavoidance	**−36**	−04	04	**67**
Impulsivity	−10	24	28	**−70**
Nurturance	21	**42**	−29	12
Order	16	18	−05	**62**
Play	−17	**46**	16	**−46**
Sentience	**37**	23	−04	−13
Social Recognition	−16	**44**	**32**	16
Succorance	**−49**	**37**	23	29
Understanding	**35**	−08	−07	02

Note: PEM-A = Agentic Positive Emotionality; PEM-C = Communal Positive Emotionality NEM = Negative Emotionality; CON = Constraint. Sample: 288 college men and women. Loadings > |.30| are shown in boldface. Decimal points are omitted

in the PRF manual (Jackson, 1974) likewise revealed four dominant dimensions (the eigenvalues of the first eight principal components obtained from the combined female/male correlation matrix were 3.6, 3.2, 2.8, 2.1, 0.9, 0.8, 0.8, and 0.6), and produced a rotated four-factor structure similar to that in Table 13.6. These results support the representativeness of the four MPQ higher-order factors.

MPQ and the lexical Big Five The Big Five factors of personality are said to represent the major dimensions of the English-language adjectival personality-descriptive lexicon (see Digman and Takemoto-Chock, 1981; Goldberg, 1990, 1993; McCrae and Costa, 1987). Unlike the 16PF, which evolved beyond its lexical origin, the lexical Big Five model has remained strictly lexicon-based. Repeatedly rediscovered through exploratory factor analyses of various adjectival descriptor sets, its quasi-orthogonal dimensional framework has become the most influential embodiment of the lexical approach. In the context of this chapter, the view that the adjectival lexicon is a sufficient source of important personality distinctions warrants a few comments.

Arguably, lexical factor dimensions, being rooted in everyday language, correspond to (1) basic distinctions people make in everyday personality descriptions (i.e. 'folk concepts'); and (2) actual salient and important behavioral variations. In personality assessment, folk distinctions may well be an indispensable starting point. But, inevitably, personality psychologists find it necessary to introduce other trait concepts considered essential to basic description and causal understanding of behavior. Such 'psychological concepts' are potentially distinct from folk concepts (Tellegen, 1993). As these explanatory psychological concepts mature, some folk concepts may increasingly be seen as social-cognitive structures to be explained, not as basic constructs that explain. Insofar as they represent common person-perceptual structures that influence people's lives, folk concepts warrant our interest. Some psychological concepts rely on measures that correspond rather closely to folk dimensions. But others represent discriminations or combinations that folk concepts do not provide, or call for observations that fall outside the folk domain. It would have been surprising had it been otherwise (no less surprising than if clinical medicine had not gone beyond folk health complaints). We would expect an inventory mapping folk concepts to overlap, but not to be consistently congruent with scales from an instrument such as the MPQ.

The MPQ and a Big Five questionnaire were administered to 1,015 community adults from the Minnesota Twin Registry. The Big Five inventory consisted of 46 pairs of adjectival descriptors that were part of a larger set of markers used in self- and peer-rating studies by McCrae and Costa (1985a, 1987). These pairs were chosen because they marked the same traits in both studies and used relatively simple language.

Our community sample produced a close replication of the Big Five structure, as well as the distinctive pattern of correlations presented in Table 13.7, linking the Big Five factor scores to the MPQ. Table 13.7 shows that four of the Big Five correlated at least |0.50| with one MPQ scale: Extraversion with Social Closeness, Agreeability (negatively) with Aggression, Neuroticism with Stress Reaction, and Conscientiousness with Control. Openness correlated most with Absorption, but the correlation was lower

and not at the same level as the earlier noted correlations with the NEO openness scale.

Table 13.7 also shows that the Big Five factors, as measured here, and as 'diffracted' through the MPQ scales, differ in complexity. At one extreme, neuroticism is strongly convergent with a single MPQ scale, stress reaction, and is roughly its equivalent (an indication that negative emotionality is broader than neuroticism). At the other extreme, extraversion and especially openness are, in MPQ terms, complex. Extraversion is a measure of Communal Positive Emotionality, given its salient correlations with Wellbeing, Social Potency, and Social Closeness. Openness shows three distinctive correlational features: it correlates (near-) saliently (1) with Absorption; (2) with the Agentic Positive Emotionality markers (Wellbeing, Social Potency, and Achievement); and (3) (negatively) with the Constraint markers (Control, Harmavoidance, Traditionalism).

Taking these results into account, a comparison of the two inventories suggests that the iterative rational-empirical method of developing and measuring the MPQ constructs has resulted in a number of valid differentiations and connections not recognized by folk concepts. For example, the Big Five do not differentiate between 'anxiety' (a component of Neuroticism and Stress Reaction) and 'fear' (a Harmavoidance component). Big Five Conscientiousness does not distinguish

Table 13.7   Correlations of MPQ Lower-Order Scales with Big Five Factor Scores

| | Labeled Big Five Factors | | | | |
	Extraversion	Agreeability	Neuroticism	Conscientiousness	Openness
PEM Well-Being	**31**	12	**−39**	10	**31**
Social Potency	**42**	−26	−16	04	**35**
Achievement	07	−07	−09	**42**	**32**
Social Closeness	**61**	27	03	03	−10
NEM Stress Reaction	−08	−12	**73**	−02	−02
Aggression	00	**−50**	11	−17	07
Alienation	−10	−21	27	−13	09
CON Control	−11	03	−08	**52**	−24
Harmavoidance	04	15	23	15	**−35**
Traditionalism	10	14	−06	23	−28
Absorption	04	−13	09	11	**40**

Note: Sample: 1015 community men and women. Correlations > |.30| are shown in boldface. Decimal points are omitted

between Achievement (PEM-related gency), and Control (CON-related self-regulation). The diffuseness of Big Five Openness (also called 'Intellect') suggests a lack of differentiation as well – and is perhaps responsible for disagreement among Big Five advocates over the specific nature of this factor (Goldberg, 1993: 27). On the other hand, Big Five Extraversion and Neuroticism are conceptually unconnected, whereas the MPQ counterparts, PEM and NEM, are complementary affective-social constructs.

Biographical correlates

Kamp (1986) examined correlations between the MPQ and a wide range of behaviors and experiences in college settings. He administered the MPQ and a biographical inventory to 224 college students, and derived a number of biographical item clusters. His MPQ findings include the following correlations: (1) 0.45 between Social Potency and Leadership (sample items: number of times held office – high school or later; number of extracurricular speeches given – lifetime); (2) 0.61 between Positive Emotionality and Social Activities (sample items: number of different people dated – lifetime; fraternity/ sorority member – current); (3) 0.51 between Stress Reaction and a 'Neurotic' cluster (sample items: missing school due to emotional problems; frequent headaches); (4) 0.50 between Aggression and an 'Antisocial Aggression' cluster (sample items: number of physical fights – past two years; vandalism – lifetime); (5) –0.51 between Constraint and Alcohol and Drug Use (sample items: age at which drinking started, keyed negatively; selling illegal drugs other than marijuana – at least once, past two years); and (6) 0.46 between Absorption and Esthetic Activity (sample items: number of times gone to dramatic productions – past two years; number of concerts attended – past two years). Kamp's findings show that MPQ constructs and measures cover a wide range of adaptations encountered in a college setting.

Links to psychopathology

The PEM and NEM constructs have been applied to the distinction between anxiety and depression, the high comorbidity of which was increasingly seen as problematic (Maser and Cloninger, 1990; Tuma and Maser, 1985). Tellegen attributed the high correlations between measures of anxiety and depression to the pervasiveness of a general dimension of emotional discomfort or demoralization. But he also argued and illustrated empirically (1985: 693, fig. 37.2) that within the two-dimensional framework of the PA and NA dimensions, core depression should be recognizable as distinctively a state of low PA (or 'anhedonia'), as such largely unrelated to NA, and core anxiety as distinctively a state of high NA, largely unrelated to PA. Extrapolating from emotional states to emotional temperament, he linked an anhedonic-depressive disposition to low PEM, and anxiousness to high NEM.

SUBSEQUENT FINDINGS

This chapter focuses on exploratory test development. A comprehensive review of the numerous studies in which the MPQ has been used and examined (following its construction and initial construct validation) falls outside its scope. Instead, we will report illustrative findings from a number of diverse and broadly informative contributions.

Structure

Corroboration of primary and higher-order factors

Ben-Porath et al. (1995) replicated the 11 primary factors and the PEM, NEM, and CON higher-order dimensions of the MPQ in a sample of Israeli respondents who completed a Hebrew version. Church and Burke (1994) recovered from their college sample a three- and four-dimensional hierarchical pattern similar to the one we have found, supporting the overall MPQ structure. PEM, NEM, and CON (reflected and labeled 'disinhibition') also emerged as one of the levels identified in the Markon et al. (2005) hierarchical factor analysis of the meta-analytically estimated correlations between the scales of five personality inventories, including the MPQ.

Stability

McGue et al. (1993) analyzed data from pairs of same-sex twins participating in the Minnesota Twin Registry who had completed the MPQ at mean ages 20 and 30. They observed for the 11 primary scales a median 10-year stability coefficient of 0.54, consistent with results of other longitudinal personality studies. Participants in the Minnesota Twin Study of Adult Development and Aging (Finkel et al., 1995) completed the MPQ at mean ages 59 and 64. Over this average interval, the median stability for this community sample was 0.79 (Johnson et al., 2005).

IRT analyses

The earlier reported alpha coefficients are global indices of consistency. Like other classically derived reliability indices (Gulliksen, 1950), alpha coefficients do not reveal how precisely (reliably) a scale measures at any particular point along the trait continuum. This is a limitation of classical test theory since measurement errors are typically not of the same magnitude across the entire trait range. For example, some scales measure very reliably over a narrow trait zone, while other scales are moderately precise across the entire range.

Item response theory (IRT) (Embretson and Reise, 2000; Hambleton and Swaminathan, 1985), or latent trait theory (Lord, 1980) has been developed partly in recognition of the variability of measurement error across different trait levels. The IRT model makes it possible to estimate the contribution of each individual item to the measurement precision of an examinee's trait score. This contribution (item information) may differ at different trait levels. Thus, an item may provide a substantial amount of information (i.e. will substantially reduce measurement error) at one trait level, while contributing only

meager information at another level. The function that describes the item information available at each trait level is called the item information curve.

To derive item information curves it is necessary to estimate certain parameters of the individual items, such as the sensitivity of each item as a trait indicator, or *discrimination* value, and its location on the trait continuum, or *difficulty*. Estimates of these parameters, based on the IRT model, allow a fine-grained evaluation of the measurement properties of a scale. Before deriving these estimates it is necessary to determine whether a scale satisfies assumptions of the model, including the requirement that a scale be unidimensional.

Reise and Waller (1990) applied the two-parameter logistic IRT model (Birnbaum, 1968), which requires estimates of item discrimination and difficulty values, to the 11 MPQ primary scales. Upon finding that the MPQ scales fit the model assumptions, they derived discrimination and difficulty parameter values for the items of each scale and used these to produce item and scale information curves. This was the first attempt to fit an IRT model to an entire multi-scale personality inventory.

Reise and Waller concluded from their results that item response models hold promise for aiding the development and evaluation of personality assessment instruments. But they also recommend (and illustrated in their own analyses) sensitivity to the statistical and theoretical challenges to be expected in the realm of personality traits. For example, the MPQ Alienation scale stands out because its distribution is markedly peaked and positively skewed, characteristics that have persisted in spite of efforts during scale development to achieve a more uniform distribution. Should one conclude that a peaked distribution is inherent to this trait? We believe that questions such as these warrant additional studies in which IRT can play a significant role.

Computerized adaptive testing (CAT) (Weiss, 1985) uses the IRT model to administer individually tailored tests. The basic principle of CAT is straightforward: items are administered one at a time via a computer terminal, such that at any point during the assessment the item that will reduce measurement error most is presented to the examinee. Because at each step the most informative item available is selected, not all items need be administered for CAT to secure precise trait estimates in a fraction of the time needed for more traditional testing methods. When Waller and Reise (1989) applied CAT methodology to the MPQ Absorption scale, they found it possible to administer individually tailored tests approximately half the length of the original Absorption scale, without sacrificing measurement precision. For other applications of item response models to the MPQ, see Reise and Waller (1993), Waller and Reise (1992), and Waller et al. (1996).

External correlates

Correlations with other self-report measures

The five-factor model (FFM), represented by the NEO and NEO-PI-R (Costa and McCrae, 1985, 1992) and the lexical Big Five are closely related but not equivalent. The FFM is a conceptual elaboration of the lexical Big Five, with a hierarchy of traits and trait facets. Church's (1994) correlational and joint factor analyses of the MPQ and NEO identified clarifying linkages between the two inventories. At the highest levels he found that PEM maps onto Extraversion and the surgent aspect of Conscientiousness, NEM onto Neuroticism and Agreeableness, and CON onto the controlled aspect of Conscientiousness and much of Openness to experiences.

Patrick et al. (2002) further extended the correlational network connecting the MPQ to well-known personality measures. For example, they found substantial correlations linking (1) the MPQ Social Potency scale to Raskin and Terry's (1988) narcissistic personality measure ($r = 0.60$), and (2) the MPQ Social Closeness, Stress Reaction, and Control scales to Buss and Plomin's (1984)

Sociability ($r = 0.63$), Distress ($r = 0.64$), and Impulsivity ($r = -0.52$) scales, respectively.

In the vocational interest area, Larson and Borgen (2002) and Staggs et al. (2003), using the Strong Interest Inventory (e.g. Hansen et al., 1994), identified in their college samples a distinctive pattern of correlations between MPQ traits and specific interest areas; for example, correlations linking (1) MPQ Social Potency to interest in Public Speaking ($r = 0.39$); (2) MPQ Absorption to Artistic interests ($r = 0.43$); and (3) MPQ Harmavoidance to Realistic interests ($r = -0.51$). Larson and Borgen (2006) reported that the correlations of personality traits with areas of vocational confidence (self-efficacy) followed the same pattern as was found for vocational interests, and that, in addition, PEM contributed to the average level of vocational confidence ($r = 0.41$ to 0.48).

Sellbom and Ben-Porath (2005), also using data from a college sample, examined correlations of the MPQ scales with the MMPI-2 Clinical Scales (Butcher et al., 2001) and the MMPI-2 Restructured Clinical (RC) Scales (Tellegen et al., 2003). Their intent was to test hypothesized linkages between a normal-range personality inventory, the MPQ, and the clinically oriented MMPI-2, particularly the new MMPI-2 RC scales. Among several links, two are of special interest here. One is the pattern of differential correlations linking the MPQ PEM scale more strongly to the RC depression measure ($r = -.67$) than to the RC anxiety measure ($r = -19$), and the MPQ NEM scale more strongly to the latter ($r = .71$) than to the former ($r = .27$), supporting Tellegen's (1985) PEM-depression/NEM-anxiety model, especially in the case of the RC Scales. Also noteworthy, given our conjectures linking Absorption to psychoticism, is the correlation of Absorption with the RC measure of thought disturbance ($r = .52$).

Correlations with observer ratings

Harkness et al. (1995) arranged for 228 college students to complete the MPQ and be rated by parents and a friend on MPQ trait rating scales. The correlations between the MPQ self-report scores, or S-data, and ratings by others, or O-data, are presented in Table 13.4. These S–O correlations (median $r = 0.48$) compare favorably with those reported for other inventories. The authors concluded that aggregating O-ratings is generally appropriate, but that the differing perspectives of fathers, mothers, and friends influence ratings, particularly within subdomains of negative emotionality.

Kremen and Block (2002) examined correlations between the MPQ Absorption scale and items of the California Adult Q-set (Block, 1978), using the sample of young adult participants in the Longitudinal Study of Personality (Block and Block, 1980). The authors concluded that their correlational findings were consistent with interpreting Absorption as a 'disposition to destructure conventional modes of cognitive and perceptual processing' (1980: 252). For a wide range of additional Absorption correlates, see Rader and Tellegen (1987) and Wild et al. (1995).

Links to psychopathology and to problem behaviors

Watson et al. (1988) corroborated in a clinical sample the PEM/depression portion of Tellegen's (1985) model. They found that an abbreviated MPQ PEM scale was consistently (negatively) correlated with depression indicators and negligibly with anxiety indicators. There was no corresponding confirmation of the NEM/anxiety portion of the model: an abbreviated MPQ NEM measure was substantially correlated with both anxiety and depression. In the same sample, DiLalla et al. (1993) found that high aggression and low harmavoidance scores distinguished the MPQ profiles of antisocial patients.

Krueger et al. (2000) offered an integrative review of studies relating personality to a broad spectrum of emotional and behavioral problems. They included several analyses of data from participants in the Dunedin project (Silva and Stanton, 1996) who were assessed

at age 21, but had completed the MPQ at age 18. The MPQ correlates observed at age 21 clearly linked high NEM to subsequent clinically significant emotional disturbance, and the combination of high NEM and low CON to subsequent problem behaviors, including violent crime and substance dependence. In the same cohort, Arseneault et al. (2000) found that among individuals with schizophrenia-spectrum disorders at age 21, violence was best explained by excessive perceptions of threat as indexed at age 18 by the MPQ Alienation scale.

Miller (2003, 2004) has used the PEM, NEM, and CON trait constructs as a framework for characterizing emotional and behavioral dispositions of individuals suffering from PTSD. He proposed, consistent with Miller et al.'s (2003) MPQ findings on combat-exposed veterans, that high NEM is the primary personality risk factor for developing PTSD, and that PEM and CON serve to sort out the observed heterogeneity of post-traumatic responses. The combination of high NEM and low CON is associated with behaviorally disordered *externalizing* manifestations, while high NEM and low PEM are associated with an anhedonic-depressive *internalizing* response.

Genetic/environmental influences

Given our view of the MPQ as an emotional-temperament inventory, it made sense to inquire about genetic factors. In the Tellegen et al. (1988) study, the MPQ was administered to adult monozygotic and dizygotic twin pairs either reared together (community sample recruited by Lykken and later incorporated in the Minnesota Twin Registry) or separated at an early age and reared apart (Bouchard, 1994). Biometric analyses showed that solely environmental models did not achieve a good fit; only a model incorporating genetic and environmental components provided a satisfactory account. The authors found that under such a model the contribution of a systematic 'family-environment' effect was negligible. Twins reared apart were hardly less similar (as indicated by intraclass correlations) than twins reared together. In each of the scales, the genetic component was far more salient, with heritabilities (Table 13.3) ranging between 0.39 and 0.58.

McGue et al.'s (1993) biometric analyses indicated that between ages 20 and 30, most of the stable individual differences in MPQ personality traits were associated with genetic factors, while personality changes were largely associated with non-shared environmental factors. Johnson et al. (2005) showed that from ages 59 to 64, individuals' distinctive personality characteristics were not only stable (as noted earlier), but that stable personality components assessed at age 64 reflected the combined influence of virtually the same genetic factors and very similar non-shared environmental factors as those operating five years earlier.

Genetic and non-shared environmental components of personality variation have also been examined from a dimensional-structural perspective. Krueger's (2000) analyses of twin data recovered the MPQ higher-order three-factor structure separately and independently from both the genetic and the non-shared environmental components of the lower-order structure – near perfectly from the former, approximately from the latter, thus adding a genetic/environmental dimension to this hierarchical structure.

CONCLUDING COMMENT: THE MULTIPLE MEANINGS OF SELF-REPORT

The exploratory development of the MPQ was intended to identify and clarify major distinctive self-report dimensions of personality. The extensive external correlates and the genetic underpinnings of the primary and higher-order MPQ scales are indications that these measures represent more than subjective self-appraisals. We have proposed

an interpretation of PEM and NEM as emotional temperament dimensions, and of CON as a basic response inhibition trait. In support of this perspective, Depue and Collins's neurobiological personality model interprets PEM-A as a positive incentive motivational system, Stress reaction (the main marker of NEM) as a stress response system, and CON as a generalized response threshold regulation system (Depue, 1996; Depue and Collins, 1999).

However, we do not view MPQ scales as mere surrogates for more important variables. As S-data, MPQ scores have meanings that their correlations with other types of data do not exhaust. For example, S–O correlations rarely exceed 0.50, often being lower. This leaves room for reliable S–O discrepancies that are potentially informative and should not be dismissed as simply demonstrating the fallibility of self-report.

It is not 'psychometric error' if someone describing herself as highly stress reactive is not so viewed by others; or when someone sees himself as a strong leader but is rated ineffectual by colleagues. The MPQ provides organized self-descriptions. Each scale stands for a broad family of thematically connected statements. These statement families are empirically based, having been derived from observed patterns of covariation. Individual scale scores indicate levels of broad or 'generic' self-descriptive attributes. Hogan and Nicholson's (1988) self-presentational analysis, though placing a stronger emphasis on manipulative (operant) aspects of S-data, is substantially congruent with our view.

The MPQ can be useful in clinical and counseling applications and in research. In any setting, MPQ scores can be used to provide constructive individual feedback, which goes beyond repeating to the respondent what s/he reported. With use of appropriate norms, feedback can contribute to self-clarification by translating a series of discrete statements into telling and coherent self-characterizations.

NOTES

1 If the common factors accounting for correlation matrices, $\mathbf{R}_i$ and $\mathbf{R}_j$, number m_i and m_j, respectively, then, given orthogonal factor solutions, pure factor markers, and the same number of markers for each factor in both matrices, it can be readily shown that

$$DC_i = \frac{m_i - 1}{m_j - 1} DC_j \qquad (13.1)$$

where DC_i is the ratio of the number of discriminant correlations to the number of convergent correlations in matrix $\mathbf{R}_i$, and DC_j is the corresponding ratio in $\mathbf{R}_j$. Substituting the values from our example, such that $m_i = 10$ and $m_j = 2$, we find: $DC_i = 9DC_j$. Equation (13.1) and the example show that if $\mathbf{R}_i$ is accounted for by a larger number of factors than is $\mathbf{R}_j$, then (under the stated conditions) the ratio of discriminant correlations to convergent correlations is larger in $\mathbf{R}_i$ than it is in $\mathbf{R}_j$.

2 For greater clarity, Watson and Tellegen have renamed the PA and NA dimensions 'positive activation' and 'negative activation', respectively, without changing the abbreviations (Tellegen et al., 1999a, 1999b; Watson et al., 1999). In this article, 'PA' and 'NA' refer to states only, and 'PEM' and 'NEM' to traits only.

REFERENCES

Allport, G.W. and Odbert, H.S. (1936) 'Trait-names: A psycho-lexical study', *Psychological Monographs*, 47: No. 211.

Arseneault, L., Moffitt, T.E., Caspi, A., Taylor, P.J. and Silva, P.A. (2000) 'Mental disorders and violence in a total birth cohort', *Archives of General Psychiatry*, 57(10): 979–86.

Atkinson, J.W. (1964) *An Introduction to Motivation*. Princeton, NJ: Van Nostrand.

Bakan, D. (1966) *The Duality of Human Existence*. Chicago: Rand McNally.

Barber, T.X. (1969) *Hypnosis: A Scientific Approach*. New York: Van Nostrand Reinhold.

Ben-Porath, Y.S., Almagor, M., Hoffman-Chemi, A. and Tellegen, A. (1995) 'A cross-cultural study of personality with the Multidimensional Personality Questionnaire', *Journal of Cross-Cultural Psychology*, 26(4): 360–73.

Birnbaum, A. (1968) 'Some latent trait models and their use in inferring an examinee's ability', in F.M. Lord and M.R. Novick (eds), *Statistical Theories of Mental Test Scores*. Reading, MA: Addison Wesley.

Block, J. (1965) *The Challenge of Response Sets*. New York: Appleton-Century-Crofts.

Block, J. (1978) 'The Q-sort method in personality assessment and psychiatric research', Palo Alto, CA: Consulting Psychologists Press. (Originally published in 1961).

Block, J. (2002) *Personality as an Affect-Processing System: Toward an Integrative Theory*. Mahwah, NJ: Lawrence Erlbaum Associates.

Block, J.H. and Block, J. (1980) 'The role of ego-control and ego-resiliency in the organization of behavior', in W.A. Collins (ed.), Minnesota *Symposia on Child Psychology* (Vol. 13). Hillsdale, NJ: Erlbaum, pp. 39–101.

Bouchard, T.J. Jr. (1994) 'Genes, environment, and personality', *Science*, 264(5166): 1700–1.

Burisch, M. (1984) 'Approaches to personality inventory construction', *American Psychologist*, 39(3): 214–27.

Buss, A.H. and Plomin, R. (1984) *Temperament: Early Developing Personality Traits*. Hillsdale, NJ: Erlbaum.

Butcher, J.N., Graham, J.R., Ben-Porath, Y.S., Tellegen, A. and Kaemmer, B. (2001) *Minnesota Multiphasic Personality Inventory: Manual for Administration, Scoring, and Interpretation, Revised Edition*. Minneapolis, MN: University of Minnesota Press.

Cattell, R.B. (1966) 'Psychological theory and scientific method', in R.B. Cattell (ed.), *Handbook of Multivariate Experimental Psychology*. Chicago: Rand McNally. pp. 1–18.

Cattell, R.B. (1978) *Use of Factor Analysis in Behavioral and Life Sciences*. New York: Plenum.

Cattell, R.B. and Cattell, H.E.P. (1995) 'Personality structure and the fifth edition of the 16PF', *Educational and Psychological Measurement*, 55(6): 926–57.

Cattell, R.B., Eber, H.W. and Tatsuoka, M.M. (1970) *Handbook for the Sixteen Personality Factor Questionnaire*. Champaign, IL: Institute for Personality and Ability Testing.

Church, A.T. (1994) 'Relating the Tellegen and Five-Factor models of personality structure', *Journal of Personality and Social Psychology*, 67(5): 898–909.

Church, A.T. and Burke, P.L. (1994) 'Exploratory and confirmatory tests of the Big Five and Tellegen's three- and four-dimensional models of personality structure', *Journal of Personality and Social Psychology*, 66(1): 93–114.

Costa, P.T. Jr. and McCrae, R.R. (1985) *The NEO Personality Inventory Manual Form S and Form R*. Odessa, FL: Psychological Assessment Resources.

Costa, P.T. Jr. and McCrae, R.R. (1992) *Revised NEO Personality Inventory (NEO PI-R) and NEO Five-Factor Inventory (NEO-FFI) Professional Manual*. Odessa, FL: Psychological Assessment Resources.

Depue, R.A. (1996) 'Neurobiology and the structure of personality: Implications for the personality disorders', in J. Clarkin and M. Lenzenweger (eds), *Major Theories of Personality Disorders*. New York: Guilford, pp. 391–453.

Depue, R.A. and Collins, P.F. (1999) 'Neurobiology of the structure of personality: Dopamine, facilitation of incentive motivation, and extraversion', *Behavioral and Brain Sciences*, 22(3): 491–569.

Digman, J.M. and Takemoto-Chock, N.K. (1981) 'Factors in the natural language of personality: Re-analysis, comparison, and interpretation of six major studies', *Multivariate Behavioral Research*, 16(2): 149–70.

DiLalla, D.L., Gottesman, I.G. and Carey, G. (1993) 'Normal personality traits in an abnormal sample: Dimensions and categories', in L. Chapman and D. Fowles (eds), *Progress in Experimental and Psychopathology Research* (Vol. 16). New York: Wiley, pp.137–62.

Embretson, S.E. and Reise, S.P. (2000) *Item Response Theory for Psychologists*. Mahwah, NJ: Erlbaum.

Ernhart, C.B. and Loevinger, J. (1969) 'Authoritarian family ideology: A measure, its correlates, and its robustness', *Multivariate Behavioral Research Monographs*, No. 69-1: 3–82.

Eysenck, H.J. (1977) 'Personality and factor analysis: A reply to Guilford', *Psychological Bulletin*, 84: 405–11.

Eysenck, H.J. and Eysenck, M.W. (1985) *Personality and Individual Differences: A Natural Science Approach*. New York: Plenum.

Eysenck, H.J. and Eysenck, S.B.G. (1968) 'A factorial study of psychoticism as a dimension of personality', *Multivariate Behavioral Research, Special Issue*: 15–31.

Eysenck, H.J. and Eysenck, S.B.G. (1991) *The Eysenck Personality Questionnaire-Revised*. Sevenoaks: Hodder & Stoughton.

Finkel D., Pedersen N.L., McGue M. and McClearn, G.E. (1995) 'Heritability of cognitive abilities in adult twins: Comparison of Minnesota and Swedish data', *Behavior Genetics*, 25(5): 421–31.

Goldberg, L.R. (1990) 'An alternative "Description of personality": The Big-Five factor structure', *Journal of Personality and Social Psychology*, 59(6): 1216–29.

Goldberg, L.R. (1993) 'The structure of phenotypic personality traits', *American Psychologist*, 48(1): 26–34.

Gough, H.G. and Bradley, P. (1996) *CPI Manual* (3rd edn). Palo Alto, CA: Consulting Psychologists Press.

Guilford, J.P. (1975) 'Factors and factors of personality', *Psychological Bulletin*, 82(5): 802–14.

Guilford, J.P. (1977) 'Will the real factor of extraversion-introversion please stand up! A reply to Eysenck', *Psychological Bulletin*, 84(3): 412–16.

Gulliksen, H. (1950) *Theory of Mental Tests*. New York, NY: Wiley.

Hambleton, R.K. and Swaminathan, H. (1985) *Item Response Theory: Principles and Applications*. Boston: Kluwer-Nijhoff.

Hansen, L.W., Hansen, J.C., Borgen, F.H. and Hammer, A.L. (1994) *Strong Interest Inventory Applications and Technical Guide*. Palo Alto, CA: Consulting Psychologists Press.

Harkness, A.R., Tellegen, A. and Waller, N.G. (1995) 'Differential convergence of self-report and informant data for Multidimensional Personality Questionnaire traits: Implications for the construct of Negative Emotionality', *Journal of Personality Assessment*, 64(1): 185–204.

Hilgard, E.R. (1965) *Hypnotic Susceptibility*. New York: Harcourt Brace & World.

Hogan, R. and Nicholson, R.A. (1988) 'The meaning of personality test scores', *American Psychologist*, 43(8): 621–6.

Izard, C.E. (1972) *Patterns of Emotions: A New Analysis of Anxiety and Depression*. New York: Academic.

Jackson, D.N. (1970) 'A sequential system for personality scale development', in C.D. Spielberger (ed.) *Current Topics in Clinical and Community Psychology*. (Vol. 2). New York: Academic.

Jackson, D.N. (1971) 'The dynamics of structured personality tests: 1971', *Psychological Review*, 78(8): 229–48.

Jackson, D.N. (1974) *Personality Research Form Manual*. Goshen, New York: Research Psychologists Press.

Johnson, W., McGue, M. and Krueger, R.F. (2005) 'Personality stability in late adulthood: A behavioral genetic analysis', *Journal of Personality*, 73(2): 523–51.

Kamp, J. (1986) 'A demonstration of principles for improving the prediction of behavior from personality inventories' Unpublished manuscript.

Kanner, A.D., Coyne, J.C., Schaefer, C. and Lazarus, R.S. (1981) 'Comparison of two modes of stress measurement: Daily hassles and uplifts versus major life events', *Journal of Behavioral Medicine*, 4(1): 1–39.

Kiesler, D.J. (1983) 'The 1982 interpersonal circle: A taxonomy for complementarity in human transactions', *Psychological Review*, 90(3): 185–214.

Kremen, A.M. and Block, J. (2002) 'Absorption: Construct explication by Q-sort assessments of personality', *Journal of Research in Personality*, 36(6): 252–9.

Krueger, R.F. (2000) 'Phenotypic, genetic, and nonshared environmental parallels in the structure of personality: A view from the Multidimensional Personality Questionnaire', *Journal of Personality and Social Psychology*, 79(6): 1057–67.

Krueger, R.F., Caspi. A. and Moffitt, T.E., (2000) 'Epidemiological personology: The unifying role of personality in population-based research on problem behaviors', *Journal of Personality*, 68(6): 967–98.

Krueger, R.F. and Johnson, W. (2002) 'The Minnesota Twin Registry: Current status and future directions', *Twin Research*, 5(5): 488–92.

Larson, L.M. and Borgen, F.H. (2002) 'Convergence of vocational interests and personality: Examples in an adolescent gifted sample', *Journal of Vocational Behavior*, 60(1): 91–112.

Larson, L.M. and Borgen, F.H. (2006) 'Do personality traits contribute to vocational self-efficacy?', *Journal of Career Assessment*, 14(3): 295–311.

Lazarus, R.S. and Folkman, S. (1984) *Stress, Appraisal, and Coping*. New York: Springer.

Leary, T. (1957) *The Interpersonal Diagnosis of Personality*. New York: Ronald.

Lee, R.E. and Warr, P.B. (1969) 'The development and standardization of a balanced F scale', *Journal of General Psychology*, 81(1): 109–29.

Loevinger, J. (1957) 'Objective tests as instruments of psychological theory', *Psychological Reports*, Monograph Supplement 9:635–94.

Loevinger, J. and Wessler, J. (1970) *Measuring Ego Development* (Vol. 1). San Francisco: Jossey-Bass.

Lord, F.M. (1980) *Applications of Item Response Theory to Practical Testing Problems*. Hillsdale, NJ: Erlbaum.

Lykken, D.T. (1982) 'Research with twins: The concept of emergenesis', *Psychophysiology*, 19(4): 361–73.

Lykken, D.T., Tellegen, A. and Katzenmeyer, C. (1973) *Manual for the Activity Preference Questionnaire (APQ)*. Department of Psychiatry, University of Minnesota.

Markon, K.E., Krueger, R.F. and Watson, D. (2005) 'Delineating the structure of normal and abnormal personality: An integrative hierarchical approach', *Journal of Personality and Social Psychology*, 88(1): 139–57.

Maser, J.D. and Cloninger, C.R. (1990) *Comorbidity of Mood and Anxiety Disorders*. Washington, DC: American Psychiatric Association.

McClelland, D.C. (1975) *Power: The Inner Experience*. New York: Irvington.

McClelland, D.C., Atkinson, J.W., Clark, R.A. and Lowell, E.L. (1953) *The Achievement Motive*. New York: Appleton.

McCrae, R.R. and Costa, P.T. Jr. (1985a) 'Updating Norman's "adequate taxonomy": Intelligence and personality dimensions in natural language and in questionnaires', *Journal of Personality and Social Psychology*, 49(3): 710–21.

McCrae, R.R. and Costa, P.T. Jr. (1985b) 'Openness to experience', in R. Hogan and W.H. Jones (eds), *Perspectives in Personality*, (Vol. 1). Greenwich, CT: JAI Press, pp. 145–72.

McCrae, R.R. and Costa, P.T. Jr. (1987) 'Validation of the five-factor model of personality across instruments and observers',

Journal of Personality and Social Psychology, 52: 81–90.

McGue, M., Bacon, S. and Lykken, D.T. (1993) 'Personality stability and change in early adulthood: A behavioral genetic analysis', *Developmental Psychology*, 29(1): 96–109.

Meehl, P.E. (1978) 'Theoretical risks and tabular asterisks: Sir Karl, Sir Ronald, and the slow progress of soft psychology', *Journal of Consulting and Clinical Psychology*, 46(4): 806–34.

Meehl, P.E. (1986) 'Trait language and behaviors', in T. Thompson and M.D. Zeiler (eds), *Analysis and Integration of Behavioral Units*. Hillsdale, NJ: Erlbaum, pp. 315–34.

Miller, M.W. (2003) 'Personality and the etiology and expression of PTSD: A three-factor model perspective', *Clinical Psychology: Science and Practice*, 10(4): 373–93.

Miller, M.W. (2004) 'Personality and the development and expression of PTSD', *PTSD Research Quarterly*, 15(3): 1–8.

Miller, M.W., Greif, J.L. and Smith, A.A. (2003) 'Multidimensional Personality Questionnaire profiles of veterans with traumatic combat exposure: Externalizing and internalizing subtypes', *Psychological Assessment*, 15(2): 205–15.

Murray, H.A. (1938) *Explorations in Personality*. New York: Oxford.

Nichols, R.C. and Schnell, R.R. (1963) 'Factor scales for the California Psychological Inventory', *Journal of Consulting Psychology*, 27(3): 228–35.

Patrick, C.J., Curtin, J.J. and Tellegen, A. (2002) 'Development and validation of a brief form of the Multidimensional Personality Questionnaire', *Psychological Assessment*, 14(2):150–63.

Rader, C.M. and Tellegen, A. (1987) 'An investigation of synesthesia', *Journal of Personality and Social Psychology*, 52(5): 981–7.

Raskin, R. and Terry, H. (1988) 'A principal components analysis of the Narcissistic Personality Inventory and further evidence of its construct validity', *Journal of Personality and Social Psychology*, 54(5): 890–902.

Reise, S.P. and Waller, N.G. (1990) 'Fitting the two parameter model to personality data: The parameterization of the Multidimensional Personality Questionnaire', *Applied Psychological Measurement*, 14(1): 45–58.

Reise, S.P. and Waller, N.G. (1993) 'Traitedness and the assessment of response pattern scalability', *Journal of Personality and Social Psychology*, 65(1): 143–51.

Rokeach, M. (1960) *The Open and Closed Mind*. New York: Basic Books.

Seligman, M.E.P. and Csikszentmihalyi, M. (2000) 'Positive psychology: An introduction', *American Psychologist*, 55(1): 5–14.

Sellbom, M. and Ben-Porath, Y.S. (2005) 'Mapping the MMPI-2 Restructured Clinical (RC) Scales onto normal personality traits: Evidence of construct validity', *Journal of Personality Assessment*, 85(1): 179–87.

Sells, S.B., Demaree, R.G. and Will, D.P. Jr. (1968) *A Taxonomic Investigation of Personality: Conjoint Factor Structure of Guilford and Cattell Trait Markers*. US Office of Education, Department of Health, Education, and Welfare: Technical Report.

Silva, P.A. and Stanton, W.R. (1996) *From Child to Adult: The Dunedin Multidisciplinary Health and Development Study*. New York: Oxford University Press.

Staggs, G.D., Larson, L.M. and Borgen, F.H. (2003) 'Convergence of specific factors in vocational interests and personality', *Journal of Career Assessment*, 11(3): 243–61.

Spielberger, C.D., Gorsuch, R.L. and Lushene, R.E. (1970) *State-Trait Anxiety Inventory Test Manual for Form X*. Palo Alto: Consulting Psychologists Press.

Taylor, J.A. (1953) 'A personality scale of manifest anxiety', *Journal of Abnormal and Social Psychology*, 48(2): 285–90.

Tellegen, A. (1981) 'Practicing the two disciplines for relaxation and enlightenment: Comment on Qualls and Sheehan', *Journal of Experimental Psychology: General*, 110(2): 217–26.

Tellegen, A. (1982) 'Brief manual of the Multidimensional Personality Questionnaire', Unpublished manuscript University of Minnesota.

Tellegen, A. (1985) 'Structure of mood and personality and their relevance to assessing anxiety, with an emphasis on self-report', in A.H. Tuma and J.D. Maser (eds), *Anxiety and the Anxiety Disorders*. Hillsdale, NJ: Erlbaum, pp. 681–706.

Tellegen, A. (1988) 'The analysis of consistency in personality assessment', *Journal of Personality*, 56(3): 621–63.

Tellegen, A. (1991) 'Personality traits: Issues of definition, evidence and assessment', in D. Cicchetti and W. Grove (eds), *Thinking Clearly about Psychology: Essays in Honor of Paul Everett Meehl*. Minneapolis: University of Minneapolis Press, pp. 10–35.

Tellegen, A. (1992) 'Note on the Structure and Meaning of the MPQ Absorption Scale', Unpublished manuscript, University of Minnesota.

Tellegen, A. (1993) 'Folk concepts and psychological concepts of personality and personality disorder', *Psychological Inquiry*, 4(2): 122–30.

Tellegen, A. (1995) 'Multidimensional Personality Questionnaire', Unpublished document, University of Minnesota.

Tellegen, A. (2003) 'MPQ Scales' Unpublished document, University of Minnesota.

Tellegen, A. and Atkinson, G. (1974) 'Openness to absorbing and self-altering experiences ("absorption"), a trait related to hypnotic susceptibility', *Journal of Abnormal Psychology*, 83(3): 268–77.

Tellegen, A., Ben-Porath, Y.S., McNulty, J.L., Arbisi, P.A., Graham, J.R and Kaemmer, B. (2003) *The MMPI-2 Restructured Clinical (RC) Scales: Development, Validation, and Interpretation*. Minneapolis: University of Minnesota Press.

Tellegen, A., Watson, D. and Clark, L.A. (1999a) 'On the dimensional and hierarchical structure of affect', *Psychological Science*, 10(4): 297–303.

Tellegen, A., Watson, D. and Clark, L.A. (1999b) 'Further support for a hierarchical model of affect: Reply to Green and Salovey', *Psychological Science*, 10(4): 307–9.

Tellegen, A., Lykken, D.T., Bouchard, T.J. Jr., Wilcox, K., Segal, N.L. and Rich, S. (1988) 'Personality similarity in twins reared apart and together', *Journal of Personality and Social Psychology*, 54(6): 1031–9.

Tuma, A.H. and Maser, J.D. (1985), *Anxiety and the Anxiety Disorders*. Hillsdale, NJ: Erlbaum.

Waller, N.G. and Reise, S.P. (1989) 'Computerized adaptive personality assessment: An illustration with the Absorption scale', *Journal of Personality and Social Psychology*, 57(6): 1051–8.

Waller, N.G. and Reise, S.P. (1992) 'Genetic and environmental influences on item response pattern scalability', *Behavior Genetics*, 22(2): 135–52.

Waller, N.G., Tellegen, A., McDonald, R.P. and Lykken, D.T. (1996) 'Exploring nonlinear models in personality assessment: Development and preliminary validation of a Negative Emotionality scale', *Journal of Personality*, 64(3): 545–76.

Watson, D. and Clark, L.A. (1984) 'Negative affectivity: The disposition to experience aversive emotional states', *Psychological Bulletin*, 26(3): 465–90.

Watson, D., Clark, L.A. and Carey, G. (1988) 'Positive and negative affectivity and their relation to anxiety and depressive disorders', *Journal of Abnormal Psychology*, 97(3): 346–53.

Watson, D. and Tellegen, A. (1985) 'Towards a consensual structure of mood', *Psychological Bulletin*, 98(2): 219–35.

Watson, D., Wiese, D., Vaidya, J. and Tellegen, A. (1999) 'The two general activation systems of affect: Structural findings, evolutionary considerations, and psychobiological evidence', *Journal of Personality and Social Psychology*, 76(5): 820–38.

Weiss, D.J. (1985) 'Adaptive testing by computer', *Journal of Consulting and Clinical Psychology*, 53(6): 774–89.

Welsh, G.S. (1956) 'Factor dimensions A and R', in G.S. Welsh and W.G. Dahlstrom (eds), *Basic Readings on the MMPI in Psychology and Medicine*. Minneapolis: University of Minnesota Press, pp. 264–81.

Wessler, R. and Loevinger, J. (1969) 'Jackson, D.N. Personality Research Form (review)', *American Educational Research Journal*, 6(3): 302–6.

White, R.W. (1959) 'Motivation reconsidered: The concept of competence', *Psychological Review*, 66(5): 297–333.

White, R.W. (1960) 'Competence and the psychosexual stages of development', in M.R. Jones (ed.), *Nebraska Symposium on Motivation* (Vol. 8). Lincoln, NE: University of Nebraska Press, pp. 97–141.

Wiggins, J.S. (1979) 'A psychological taxonomy of trait-descriptive terms: The interpersonal domain', *Journal of Personality and Social Psychology*, 37(3): 395–412.

Wiggins, J.S. (1995) *Interpersonal Adjective Scales: Professional Manual*. Odessa, FL: Psychological Assessment Resources.

Wiggins, J.S., Trapnell, P. and Phillips, N. (1988) 'Psychometric and geometric characteristics of the revised Interpersonal Adjective Scales (IAS-R)', *Multivariate Behavioral Research*, 23(4): 517–30.

Wild, T.C., Kuiken, D., Schopflocher, D. (1995) 'The role of Absorption in experiential involvement', *Journal of Personality and Social Psychology*, 69(3): 569–79.

Winter, D.G. (1973) *The Power Motive*. New York: Free Press.

Yarrow, L.J., McQuiston, S., MacTurk, R.H., McCarthy, M.E., Klein, R.P. and Vietze, P.M. (1983) 'Assessment of mastery motivation during the first year of life: Contemporaneous and cross-age relationships', *Developmental Psychology*, 19(3): 159–71.

Zevon, M.A. and Tellegen, A. (1982) 'The structure of mood change: An idiographic/nomothetic analysis', *Journal of Personality and Social Psychology*, 43(1): 111–22.

Zuckerman, M. (1979) *Sensation Seeking: Beyond the Optimal Level of Arousal*. Hillsdale, NJ: Erlbaum.

Zuckerman, M. (1989) 'Personality in the third dimension: A psychobiological approach', *Personality and Individual Differences*, 10(4): 391–418.

PART III

Assessment of Biologically Based Traits

14

Psychophysiological Window on Personality: Pragmatic and Philosophical Considerations

John J. Furedy

INTRODUCTION

The purpose of this chapter is to provide useful information to those personality researchers who want to employ objective psychophysiological measures to differentiate among various psychological functions. From the perspective of these researchers, the various psychophysiological measures and the many technical problems involved in their recording are of little intrinsic interest. What is critical is how much these measures can add to information gleaned from behavioral and introspective (subjective) personality measures including self-report inventories and questionnaires. In terms of the window metaphor to which my title alludes, the issue is to what extent the psychophysiological window provides a useful additional perspective on the psychological functions that underlie personality differences.

For personality researchers to make informed decisions about which, if any, additional psychophysiological measures to employ, I shall argue that they need to consider at least the following distinctions: peripheral versus central measures, baseline versus response-to-challenge measures, tonic versus phasic measures; uniphasic versus multiphasic measures; lo-tech versus hi-tech measures; physiological 'respectability' versus psychological validity; temporal versus localization measures; specific versus reactive sensitivity; psychophysiological versus behavioral measures; and reliability versus validity.

The first section of the chapter elaborates the rationale of the psychophysiological approach. The next section will provide a detailed, pragmatic discussion of the distinctions that, in my view, have to be considered by personality the researchers. The concluding, meta-theoretical section briefly summarizes the underlying realist philosophy-of-science position that should constitute the basic approach to all areas of the science of psychology. A central thesis of this realist approach is that, as argued by a number of psychologists (e.g. Furedy, 1988, 1991a, 1991b, 1991c; Maze, 1983; Mitchell. 1988), it is crucial for empirical researchers to reflect on such philosophical considerations as the choice between realism and instrumentalism in the way that scientific research is carried out in psychology.

RATIONALE OF THE CHAPTER AND ITS RELEVANCE FOR PERSONALITY RESEARCHERS

This section will present a view of psychophysiology that attempts to provide a coherent account of the relation of this sub-area to the discipline of psychology. It also allows a rational assessment of the way in which objective psychophysiological measures can contribute to increase our scientific understanding of the psychological functions that contribute to personality differences, as well as improving those applications that are based on those increases in our scientific understanding. The section will discuss the special potential of psychophysiological measures for studying certain non-cognitive psychological functions, including individual differences in personality. In addition, it will consider the current practical problem of an ever-increasing armamentarium of psychophyisological measures that confront the personality researcher, who has to make informed and cost-effective choices among those many measures. Finally, I shall list certain crucial distinctions among psychophysiological measures that are of relevance to the personality researcher, rather than to the more specialized interests of psychophysiologists themselves.

Psychophysiology as the use of physiological measures to study psychological functions

There probably is no area of psychology about which there is so much conceptual confusion than psychophysiology. One symptom of this confusion is that as late as the mid-eighties, even specialists in this area, at least outside the English-speaking world, did not distinguish between psychophysiology and physiological psychology in terms of labeling their own special interests. And even today, researchers who are not specialists in psychophysiology, and have not employed psychophysiological measures in their research, cannot state what the distinction is between these two related, but quite different areas of psychology.

Although the term 'psychophysiology' only came into common usage in the early 1960s with the formation of the Society for Psychophysiological Research (SPR) and initiation of its research journal *Psychophysiology* in the US, psychophysiological research itself (using autonomic measures on human subjects) has a much longer history. More than 50 years ago, Woodworth and Schlosberg's (1954) textbook on experimental psychology had an extensive discussion on the galvanic skin response (GSR) that highlighted the difference between phasic skin conductance response (SCR) and tonic skin conductance level (SCL). Even earlier, in the 1930s, Skinner had reported a lack of success in operantly conditioning the peripheral vasomotor response. Skinner's (psychophysiological) research formed the basis of a tenet long accepted by learning theorists, with the first influential challenge being Miller's (1969) paper on operant conditioning (later known as 'biofeedback') of animal autonomic responses. The challenge proved successful to some extent, so that by the late 1980s, even the research community seemed to be accepting the notion of operant autonomic conditioning (see Furedy, 1987b; Riley and Furedy, 1981) despite clear evidence that for target responses like heart rate deceleration, operant conditioning or biofeedback was not effective when the requisite non-contingent control conditions were run (e.g. Elder et al., 1986; Engel, 1972; Green and Green, 1978).

The issue of how psychophysiology should be defined was debated at a symposium on the definition of psychophysiology at the inaugural 1982 Montreal conference of the International Organization of Psycho-physiology (IOP) chaired by *Psychophysiology*'s founding editor (Albert Ax). Whereas in the West, the distinction between physiological psychology and psychophysiology was relatively clear in practice, researchers in the Soviet bloc whose work was primarily psychophysiological, labeled themselves as physiological psychologists. The definition of psychophysiology offered in Furedy (1983) was one that defined the area as involving the use of physiological measures to study and to differentiate among various psychological functions including personality variables. The most important taxonomic feature of this definition is that the criterion of demarcation for this area of psychology is what the central interest of the researcher is, rather than who the researcher is, or what sorts of manipulations and dependent variables that s/he employs (see Furedy, 1983: 15–16; and Furedy, 1984). A consequence of adopting this definition is that the focus of the area is seen to be the 'psyche' rather than physiology, even though, to the extent that physiological factors affect the validity of psychophyisological measures, they must be taken into account (for a discussion of physiological versus psychological approaches to psychophysiology, see Furedy, 1983: 17–18; for the opposing 'biological' approach to psychophysiology, see Obrist, 1981).

Like any dependent variable employed in psychology, the validity of a psychophysiological measure is the extent to which it reflects the specific psychological functions it is purported to measure (e.g. for the purpose of this discussion, personality traits). The unique potential contribution of psychophysiological measures as adjuncts to behavioral and introspective self-report and rating measures is that they are not available to consciousness, and hence, at least under normal circumstances, are not under voluntary control. This is always the case with central measures of brain activity such as the evoked potential response (ERP) or the more recently employed functional magnetic resonance imaging (fMRI). However, lack of voluntary control

also holds for those autonomically controlled, relatively small physiological changes in such functions as heart rate (HR), where we are dealing with HR changes of 10% or less, or respiratory rate or short periods of apnea, where again the changes being measured are small enough not to be under voluntary control. It bears emphasis that this unique contribution of these measures is only a potential one. Even though the measures are objective in the sense that they can be specified consistently and communicated with precision from one observer to another, they will have no value if they are not valid. In particular, there may be problems of confounding. For example, in comparing the relative aversiveness of signaled and unsignaled shocks, it may seem that the objective SCRs elicited by the two sorts of shocks provide a more valid index of aversiveness than the subjective psychophysical magnitude-estimation measure.

However, as we have argued (e.g. Furedy and Klajner, 1973), and contrary to Lykken and Tellegen (1974), the signaled-shock elicited SCR is confounded (reduced) because of the fact that, with this phasic electrodermal response, the SCR elicited by the preceding signal reduces the SCR elicited by the following shock. This response-interference factor (known in physiology as the relative refractory period) operates in the case of the SCR at least up to interstimulus intervals of 20 seconds (Furedy and Scull, 1971), and is therefore a significant source of confounding for the five-second-duration signals that have typically been employed in the signaled-shock preparation. Yet another more practical problem in research into human personality is that some psychophysiological measures are too obtrusive, inasmuch as their use demands too much of the experimental subjects. The carotid dp/dt measure of sympathetic influence is a case in point. As noted by Furedy (1983: 16), this measure requires the subject not to swallow for the entire period that the experiment is being conducted, and therefore may interfere with both behavioral and introspective dependent variables that the experimenter is interested in. A final practical problem arises if the measure is very expensive to implement. In particular, for the researcher whose central interest is not psychophysiology, but rather the use of psychophysiological measures to investigate specific psychological functions, the cost of implementing a measure like the fMRI can be prohibitive. A by-product of this problem for the scientific community is that replication of phenomena of interest across laboratories is too rare, so that in the extreme case, reliability cannot be checked across laboratories. So, in some instances at least, less expensive, low-tech measures (e.g. electrodermal activity) have a practical advantage over more expensive, hi-tech measures (e.g. cardiac output).

Special potential of psychophysiological measures for personality researchers: non-cognitive psychological functions

Following the 'cognitive paradigm shift' (Segal and Lachman, 1972), the qualifier 'cognitive' came to have such a broad connotation as to apply to all psychological functions (cf. Furedy and Riley, 1987: 2–3). However, in an area like personality, it is clear that behavior has a number of non-cognitive determinants such as differences in motivation and feelings (i.e. also involving connative and affective variables). Of late, even the information-processing approach to psychology (the 'cognitive' approach) has recognized the importance of motivational and affective variables by referring to concepts like 'hot cognition', but such attempts amount to little more than metaphorical accounts of these non-cognitive variables.

The neglect of non-cognitive influences on behavior precedes the cognitive revolution of the 1960s, and can be traced back to the cognitive theories of the behaviorist Edward Tolman, who was subject to Guthrie's jibe that Tolman's theory left his rats 'buried in thought'. But whereas Tolman and his students had to contend directly with their S-R rivals like Hull and Spence, who did recognize

affective ('drive') and motivational ('incentive motivation) variables, the heirs of psychology's cognitive revolution have had the theoretical field all to themselves, with all psychological functions being essentially described in cognitive terms. However, personality researchers, whether they have a primary scientific or applied interest, need to take into account these non-cognitive psychological functions both in constructing explanations for the behavior of living organisms (not computers), and in attempting to improve prediction of that behavior. These non-cognitive personality, motivational and affective factors, moreover, are more difficult than cognitive ones both to measure objectively and to manipulate in experiments (but see Cattell and Child, 1975, for objective measurement of motivation). In comparison, it is relatively simple to assess differences in the ability to remember words, or the ability to do arithmetical problems, or to manipulate the difficulty level of such tasks.

On the other hand, even performance on these cognitive tasks is affected by the degree to which the subject is trying to perform them, and certainly other behaviors (such as choosing between alternatives) are affected by these non-cognitive factors. While dependent variables such as reaction time (RT) or number of correct answers may be adequate for assessing cognitive abilities, these measures do not allow differences due to such non-cognitive influences as changes in mood or differences in motivation to be assessed. Nor is it of much use to rely on subjective self-reports, both because these may not be honest, but also because (more importantly) our language is not useful for making these distinctions, especially between individuals – if one individual says s/he was excited about the experiment, and the other says s/he was very excited about the experiment, can we conclude that the latter subject was more aroused during the experiment (and hence was trying harder, if there was a cognitive task to be completed) than the former?

Experimental psychology that employs humans as subjects, moreover, has special difficulties in manipulating these non-cognitive factors, because of ethical (treatment of subjects) considerations. So, while the cognitive factor of task difficulty can be readily manipulated in memory experiments, it is much harder to manipulate arousal levels or the motivation to perform at one's maximal capacity. What is frequently assumed in these memory experiments is that the subject is allocating most of his/her attention to the task, and that the only variable of major importance in determining outcomes is the subject's cognitive (or 'processing') capacity.

Psychophysiological measures do not, of course, get over the difficulties of manipulating these non-cognitive variables. One cannot, for example, vary food deprivation over the wide range possible with rat subjects, and so orthogonally and effectively manipulate the hunger drive in an experiment that employs the Morris water maze to assess spatial cognitive ability. What can be done, however, is to employ a measure like skin conductance level (SCL) to determine whether there is greater arousal during the performance of a difficult cognitive task as compared to that of an easy task. Moreover, the SCL measure could also be used to assess individual differences in these SCL differences: perhaps more anxious individuals show more marked SCL differences than less anxious ones, even though their actual performance on the tasks do not differ as a function of this personality difference.

Current complexities facing personality researchers in employing psychophysiological measures

Up to the 1960s personality researchers who were considering the use of objective psychophysiological measures essentially had to deal only with the question of whether they wished to measure the GSR or electrodermal activity that was controlled by the autonomic nervous system (ANS). Although even the use of the GSR often presented some conceptual difficulties, such as the failure to distinguish between tonic changes (i.e. skin conductance level – SCL) and phasic (stimulus-elicited) changes (i.e. skin conductance response – SCR), understanding of the GSR was relatively simple, and its measurement was cheap to implement.

Consider, in contrast, the problems and choices presented to personality researchers in the first decade of the twenty-first century, who need to make decisions about whether to use objective psychophysiological measures, which ones to use, and how to quantify the changes they observe. The choices open to the personality researcher are many, not only among autonomically controlled measures such as electrodermal activity, cardiac performance measures, and measures of blood pressure, but also among central measures such as the electroencephelograph (EEG), evoked response potential (ERP), and functional magnetic resonance imaging (fMRI). A prime consideration in choosing among these many measures is that the choice depends on what is known about how well a particular candidate measure reflects the psychological function in which the researcher is interested. This is often difficult to decide, because those who are the first to introduce new measures tend to be optimistic about the range of psychological functions for which the new measure is valid. The literature to be considered by the personality researcher must also include critical scrutiny of such measures.

Thus, an important condition for an informed choice is that the researcher is clear about, precisely, what psychological function, and what aspects of that function are, of interest. For example, if the researcher is interested in the psychological function of mental effort, and wishes to focus on that aspect of mental effort that differentiates if from effortless mental functions, then it is important to use a psychophysiological measure that differentiates between the two sorts of mental functions. A physiological distinction between tasks that are more effortful and conscious (conceptual) as opposed to less effortful (perceptual) tasks is that only the former involves excitation of the sympathetic nervous system (SNS), whereas both involve approximately the same degree of withdrawal of the parasympathetic nervous system (PNS). Until the work of Obrist (1981), it had been common practice of even specialist psychophysiologists who were sensitive to the distinction between SNS excitation and PNS withdrawal to employ heart-rate (HR) acceleration as an index of this SNS-mediated fight/flight response. But as Obrist pointed out, because the atrium of the heart has both PNS and SNS connections, HR acceleration is a 'mixed' index of SNS activation. In particular, the small HR changes (that Obrist labeled 'biologically insignificant') of the sort observed in psychological manipulations could be solely due to PNS withdrawal and not at all to any SNS activation. Accordingly, Obrist correctly insisted that for any cardiac performance measure to validly reflect SNS activation (and hence, in our example, mental effort), it must be based on ventricular rather than atrial myocardial function.

The issue of which ventricular index has the greatest utility remains contentious, and will be commented on in the section entitled 'Physiological "respectability" vs. psychological validity' below, but in the iterative-subtraction task example (e.g. Heslegrave and Furedy, 1979), it was the ventricular T-wave amplitude (TWA) measure that was employed along with HR. The results showed that in this and other studies (for a review, see Furedy, 1987a), although HR acceleration was manifested both when subjects were listening to the two numbers to be operated on as well as during the iterative subtraction task itself, TWA attenuation occurred only during the (more effortful) task itself.

The use of TWA to differentiate effortful and non-effortful cognitive psychological functions requires both some knowledge about physiological differences (e.g. between atrial and ventricular myocardial functions), as well as clarity about the psychological function of interest. If, for example, the psychological taxonomy merely refers to a 'cognitive' task, then both the listening to numbers and operating on the numbers are 'cognitive', and the difference between TWA and HR indices

loses its psychological meaning. We are left only with the physiological distinctions such as that between SNS activation versus PNS withdrawal, or that between atrial versus ventricular functions. The most common current meaning of 'cognitive' is essentially the same as psychological, with the acceptance of the computer-metaphorical, information-processing view of all psychological functions (Neisser, 1967). It will be noted that both the listening and the iterative subtraction tasks involve, on this account, information processing by a system which is either a computer itself (hardware, analogous to the brain – a physiological system) or some computer programs (software, analogous to the mind – a psychological system). However, in this information-processing, computerized framework or taxonomy, both physiological distinctions (e.g. that between ventricular and atrial cardiac functions) and psychological ones (e.g. effortful, conscious, and conceptual versus effortless, unconscious, and perceptual) can be made only in a metaphorical sense.

The inability of the information-processing approach to differentiate adequately among psychological functions is apparent even for the experimental psychologist interested in manipulations. For example, in humans, one can transform the iterative subtraction task into an effortless cognitive one (for all except those very few who are totally innumerate) by employing the numbers 2 and 100 instead of 17 and 3,827. Or one can manipulate the effort required by only somewhat decreasing it (e.g. 12 and 3,000) or somewhat increasing it (e.g. 97 and 4,873). None of these manipulations would work on a computer, unless one used astronomically large numbers, and even then one would hesitate to assert that more mental effort (i.e. arousal of an SNS-like system) was required (with all its emotional concomitants such as an increase in anxiety), rather than a mere increase in computing time or capacity.

Moreover, in humans there are conditions under which an increase of mental effort that is required produces a 'giving up' phenomenon, where the individual decides no longer to engage in the task. In real life, this sort of non-computer-like behavior probably occurs in children who are not good at mathematics, and decide to no longer pay any attention to solving math problems. An experimental psychophysiological form of this 'giving up' phenomenon was reported by Muter et al. (1992), who manipulated the user-friendly aspect of a computer program given to subjects presented with some automated teller machine (ATM) tasks, and employed the electrodermal skin conductance level (SCL) as an index of (sympathetic) arousal. They found that the user-hostile condition produced an increase of SCL in most subjects, except for a small subset whose performance on the ATM task showed that, under the user-hostile condition, they had ceased to try to do the task. The SCL values for these 'task-rejecting' subjects were lower than for the subjects still engaged with the task (i.e. were obeying the experimental instructions), suggesting that they were devoting no mental effort at all to the task. Needless to say, giving-up behavior is only partly influenced by cognitive ability. It is also a significant function of personality characteristics that are unrelated to sheer cognitive ability. In the Muter et al. study, HR was also measured, and again, as in the TWA studies (Furedy, 1987a), this mixed index did not reflect mental effort as accurately as did the sympathetic SCL measure.

Differentiating between parasympathetic and sympathetic psychophysiological indices is also relevant for other personality characteristics. For example, Scher et al. (1986) found TWA but not HR differentiated the Type 'A' versus Type 'B' personality difference (cf. Friedman, 1996), while Shulhan et al. (1986) reported that TWA, but not HR, identified an interaction between physical fitness (a physiological function) and reactivity to mental challenge (a psychological, personality function) which suggested that physical fitness may protect against an overblown flight-or-flight sympathetic reaction to a real-life psychological challenge such as an executive

being told by his superior that s/he is no longer required by the organization. And in neither study did behavioral (performance) measures yield any information about these non-cognitive psychological functions, even though in terms of sensitivity to (cognitive) task difficulty the performance measures were most sensitive, followed by HR, with TWA being the least sensitive (for a more extensive discussion of specific versus reactive sensitivity, see below).

In addition to these theoretical issues that are relevant for the adequate differentiation among (and measurement of) psychological functions, the personality researcher also faces more practical problems. For example, if the fMRI is the ideal psychophysiological measure for a specific psychological function, the financial cost of both setting up and using this sort of very hi-tech equipment must be considered. This is an issue of evaluating cost effectiveness, where that evaluation needs to be relatively independent of advice from specialists who offer their own favorite measures, and tend to overestimate the utility of such measures.

The difficulties for the personality researcher's interest in evaluating cost effectiveness have been exacerbated by the recent fractionation of psychophysiology not in terms of an interest in various psychological functions, but in terms of the various physiological dependent variables employed. Even among those whose main interest is in autonomic dependent variables, there is a split between those who employ electrodermal measures, and those who employ cardiac performance measures. But there is a veritable conceptual chasm between those employing autonomic, peripheral measures, and those using central measures like the ERP, if only because the experimental manipulations that can be used for the shorter-latency ERP cannot be employed with the longer-latency electrodermal SCR. Part of the reason for this fractionation by measures instead of by interests is that, especially in the case of central measures, there is a great amount of technical expertise required not only for setting up the measures, but also in terms of the quantification of results. Another more deleterious influence that produces conceptual fractionation is the increasing separation among specialists using different measures in terms of the literature they read, and the presentations they attend at psychophysiological conferences (e.g. electrodermal versus ERP). This fractionation, moreover, also occurs within autonomic measures, and can result in the researchers of individual differences to neglect the right sort of autonomic measures.

A recent example of this occurred following a study (Algan et al., 1997) that examined sexual dimorphism influences in an acute smoking manipulation, which compared a group of deprived smokers given one cigarette to smoke in a 15-minute rest period between two cognitive tasks, with a group of non-smokers who simply rested for 15 minutes. There were no performance differences (reaction time, accuracy, and subjective confidence) due to this acute-smoking manipulation, but it was hoped that psychophysiological differences would be obtained, as a vast array of cardiac performance measures as well as the phasic electrodermal SCR were measured in a fully computerized laboratory. Although sophisticated psychophysiological data was obtained, the much lower-tech (and hand-readable) tonic electrodermal skin conductance level (SCL) autonomic measure yielded clear and interesting sex-differential effects, with one cigarette apparently producing relaxation in males, and an increase in tension in females (Furedy et al., 1999). This result was the inverse of the well-established introspective self-reports that suggest that males smoke for stimulation, while females smoke to reduce tension (e.g. Best and Hakstian, 1978; Ikard and Tomkings, 1978; Spielberger, 1986). It is likely that a personality researcher being advised by a psychophysiologist who is a cardiac specialist rather than an electrodermal specialist would miss out altogether on these psychophysiological results. The SCR literature, by the way, has long contained such abstruse specialist issues as to whether the optimal

window of measurement should be 1–5 seconds (used most often) or the shorter 1–3 second window. There is nothing like controversies about such relatively esoteric issues of measurement to narrow one's conceptual focus on specific measures, rather than what those measures purport to measure. And of course, this narrowing of conceptual focus means that the potentiality of the psychophysiological 'window' for the personality researchers is also diminished.

The next section will be a pragmatic one that deals with certain distinctions that are relevant for personality researchers who have decided to invest in psychophysiological measures. None of the distinctions are ones that occupy specialists in psychophysiology (e.g. whether to use the 1–5 or 1–3 second intervals to define an SCR, or the proper statistical treatment of heart-rate variability differences). Rather, the distinctions are all relevant for researchers in other areas of psychology who are interested in using objective psychophysiological measures to differentiate among psychological functions. These distinctions, moreover, will be presented as applying to all psychophysiological measures, rather than focusing on a specific class of measures (e.g. autonomic versus central), or even on a single measure (e.g. ERP versus fMRI).

Because most of my experience has been with autonomic measures, my illustrative examples will generally be taken from the autonomic sub-area of psychophysiology. I shall use, as the basic criterion of evaluation for the personality researcher, the concept of utility, defined as sensitivity to differences in psychological functions. A crude index of this sort of utility is the ability of a given measure to yield significant differences on independent variables manipulated in experimental psychology, or observed by differential psychology (Buss and Greiling, 1999). A final, theoretical section will put forward the philosophical perspective of direct realism that underlies the claims made above. Central is the claim by Maze (1983) that it is crucial, even for researchers concerned only with empirical issues (cf. Furedy, 1988), to reflect on the choices that they implicitly make, such as the choice between realist and instrumentalist approaches to the philosophy of science.

RELEVANT DISTINCTIONS FOR PSYCHOPHYSIOLOGICAL MEASUREMENT

The aim of this section is to provide and briefly discuss a list of distinctions that, for practical measurement purposes, personality researchers (and practitioners) should consider before they embark on objective psychophysiological measurement.

Peripheral versus central measures

The peripheral/central distinction refers to the difference between measures such as the electrodermal skin conductance response (SCR), heart rate (HR), and pulse transit time (PTT) on the one hand, and those such as the evoked response potential (ERP), functional magnetic resonance imaging (fMRI), and the electroencephalograph (EEG) on the other hand. One false distinction that is often espoused is the idea that the central measures, being 'closer' to the brain than peripheral measures, therefore reflect mental or cognitive functions more sensitively than do peripheral measures. All psychophysiological measures reflect psychological functions of the organism as a whole (Furedy, 1983), so the issue of whether one measure reflects a particular psychological function better than another is a purely empirical question. For example, at least in the current literature, the lower-tech peripheral electrodermal measure is a more sensitive indicator of the orienting functions of sensitivity to change than higher-tech central measures like the ERP (e.g. Furedy et al., 2001, reported that the electrodermal measure was sensitive to the phenomena of habituation to change, dishabituation, reinstatement, and 'super' reinstatement). One reason for this peripheral

superiority is that the skin conductance response (SCR) can be assessed on individual trials, whereas the ERP requires averaging over many trials for its assessment.

However, there is a real epistemological divide not between the two sorts of measures, but between those specialists who employ those measures. This divide is partly caused by the fact that there are different technological requirements for sound measurement for the two sorts of measures. Aside from strictly electronic engineering differences, peripheral and central measures also require different sorts of expertize. For a measure like the SCR, the psychophysiologist must engage in such questions as the optimal window of latencies employed for determining whether a change in conductance following a stimulus is 'spontaneous' or 'stimulus elicited'. Most electrodermal psychophysiologists favor a 1–5 second window, but specialists like Barry (1990) have produced persuasive evidence that a 1–3 second window is superior. Again, specialists working with the SCR need to be aware of the influence of the 'law of initial values', even if this 'law' is far from universal for all elicited peripheral measures (e.g. Furedy and Scher, 1989; Jamieson, 1987, 1993; Yu-Kang and Gilthorpe, 2006).

Finally, at a more basic level, personality researchers working with the electrodermal measure need to be aware of the distinction between phasic and tonic electrodermal measure. On the other hand, expertize in the use of a central measure like the ERP requires knowledge of averaging techniques that are not required with a measure like the SCR, which can be assessed on individual trials. Among the statistical techniques needed is that of 'bootstrapping', first introduced by Rosenfeld et al. (1988) and by Farwell and Donchin (1991) to assess the sensitivity of the ERP in a central-measures version of the polygraph guilty knowledge test (GKT). Researchers using the SCR for the GKT widely used as a scientifically based (the GKT is scientifically based in contrast to the more commonly used 'control' question 'test' that Lykken opposed) way of detecting guilt with autonomic dependent variables both in the laboratory and in the field (e.g. Reiko et al., 2004) do not need bootstrapping, as they are employing a measure that is assessable on single trials.

These epistemological splits between the two sorts of measures on the dependent-variable side also exist on the independent-variable side. The way in which variables can be manipulated in experiments differs significantly. The most obvious difference is between two phasic elicited measures like the SCR and the ERP. Not only are the onset latencies of the two different (more than 1 second for the SCR, while ERP latencies as short as 50 ms are observed), but more importantly, for the peripheral SCR measure, which has a long relative-refractory period (Furedy and Scull, 1971), inter-trial or inter-stimulus intervals need to be at least 25 seconds to avoid a response on trial x being interfered with by a response on trial $x-1$. This is of crucial methodological importance if the nature of the trials during the series differs, but even with homogeneous trials, if an interstimulus interval of less than 10 seconds is employed then it is unlikely that any significant SCRs will be observed at all. On the other hand, for the ERP, trials can be separated by as little as 2 seconds without any of this sort of response interference. This difference in experimental designs means that it is impractical to assess both SCRs and ERPs in the same experimental protocol, and specialists in the two sorts of measures will tend to think in terms of different experimental designs with very different numbers of trials given to subjects. Assuming that both groups of specialists are interested in the same psychological function (e.g. the detection of guilt), this is one case where specialization prevents epistemological progress.

Personality researchers who want to use objective psychophysiological measures need to be aware of these epistemological and methodological differences between 'central' and 'peripheral' psychophysiological specialties, so that their own interests do not get subjugated to what are often territorial disagreements between the two sub-specialties.

Baseline differences versus reaction-to-challenge differences

Although the medical literature tends to stress individual baseline or 'resting' level differences in such measures as blood pressure and heart rate, these differences, perhaps because they indicate differences in physiological (e.g. integrity of cardiac functioning) rather than psychological (e.g. ability to cope with threatening stimuli in the environment) functions, are often not sensitive to psychological individual differences (Boyle and Saklofske, 2004). An additional reason why resting-level differences are not sensitive to psychological variables is that they are often overshadowed by the enormous 'random' individual differences that occur in the population, differences that are due to physiological rather than psychological factors. This is certainly the case with skin resistance levels, which range between 5,000 and 200,000 ohms in any population, while mean differences in the increases in resistance levels to psychological stress are of the order of merely hundreds of ohms.

One psychophysiological measure which provides a dramatic illustration of personality differences that are not indexed at all by baseline differences is T-wave amplitude (TWA). Scher et al. (1980) reported that TWA attenuated more in Type A than in Type B personalities when subjects were faced with a psychological challenge (iterative subtraction task), while no A/B differences emerged in baseline levels. There is also clear evidence in the literature (see Furedy 1987a, for review) that TWA differences emerge only to the iterative subtraction task challenge, and not at all in resting TWA baselines, whereas, of course, it is the latter that are more significant for cardiologists monitoring patients in intensive care wards, or even those in whom pathology in cardiac functioning is suspected.

Another less thoroughly documented differential sensitivity to individual differences is in the skin resistance level (SRL) measure. Furedy et al. (1999) reported that a challenge consisting of one cigarette smoked after 10 hours of deprivation yielded a decrease of arousal in males (who, according to introspective self-reports, smoke for stimulation) and an increase in arousal in females (who, according to self-reports, smoke for relaxation).

Tonic versus phasic

For personality researchers interested in objective measurement rather than subjective self-reports or ratings, the relevance of the tonic/phasic distinction is most pertinent in the peripheral electrodermal measure. As reported by Furedy et al. (2001), only the less frequently measured tonic skin conductance level (SCL) but not the more commonly used phasic skin conductance response (SCR) differentiated male schizophrenics from the other five cells of a three (schizophrenics, depressives, and normals) by two (male and female) factorial design of six independent groups. However, perhaps the tonic/phasic distinction applied to the EEG and ERP central measures will also prove relevant in an analogous way for personality researchers. My speculation is that the EEG, though not the ERP, will show different levels of consciousness as measured by the frequency of alpha waves as a function of personality and even normal/abnormal differences. Currently, EEG and ERP psychophysiologists operate in different literatures, and in this regard my phasic-oriented electrodermal bias caused a similar blindness to the relevance of the tonic SCL measure for some 30 years. Until now, I, like most other 'GSR' workers, regarded tonic SCL or the previously measured skin resistance level (SRL) as a 'nuisance' variable to be controlled (the method, when using the skin resistance response, was to use a transformation that would eliminate the substantial correlation between SRL and the skin resistance response (SRR) – transforming to SCL and SCR usually did the trick, as that the SCL/SCR correlation is close to zero), rather than another potentially useful psychophysiological measure that complemented the phasic response measure, and was

actually more informative than the phasic measure for such areas as personality research.

Uniphasic, biphasic, and multiphasic measures

All these phasic measures are responses to stimuli that occur within a specified short period of time following a stimulus. Examples of uniphasic measures are the electrodermal SCR (this response is unidirectional, being always an increase in conductance), the peripheral vasomotor response (always a vascular constriction usually recorded from the finger), and specific central ERP measures such as the P300 (always a positive waveform occurring, as the name suggests, around 300 ms following stimulus onset: P300 was made popular with psychophysiologists who considered themselves to be 'cognitive psychophysiologists' (see Donchin, 1981), and has been widely used since then for a wide variety of psychological functions (e.g. Deslandes et al., 2004; Reinsel et al., 2004).

Examples of biphasic measures are heart rate changes (acceleration or deceleration) and breathing rate changes (again, acceleration or deceleration). Examples of multiphasic changes are the triphasic measures (deceleration, acceleration, and then deceleration) that some argued characterized the conditional heart-rate response in human Pavlovian conditioning (for a review, see Furedy and Poulos, 1976) and stimulus-induced changes in respiration pattern. In another example, polygraphers who use the 'control' question 'test' employ two of their four channels to measure respiration changes to questions, and claim that they can differentiate between 'deceptive' and 'truthful' individuals by assessing complex (and usually unspecified) changes in respiratory patterns to certain questions.

As a general rule, uniphasic measures are most sensitive in terms of measurement sensitivity of a defined psychological function. So it is no accident that the most commonly employed and replicable measures of a function like human Pavlovian conditioning (see Schwartz and Reisberg, 1990), use uniphasic measures like the SCR, or a heart-rate change that is only in a single (deceleratory) direction (e.g. Arabian and Furedy, 1983; Furedy and Klajner, 1978; Furedy and Poulos, 1976). Multiphasic measures are best if one hopes to use a single measure to differentiate among psychological functions. At present, only the biphasic psychophysiological measures have a significant and scientifically specifiable literature. One well-known example of this biphasic differentiation is the use of heart-rate acceleration and deceleration, respectively, to differentiate between the Sokovian defensive and orienting reaction, a position put forward in their citation-classic paper by Graham and Clifton (1976), and one that was not without its critics (e.g. Barry and Matlzman, 1985).

Low versus high-tech measures

Contrary to a commonly held but unexamined assumption, the higher-tech (and often newer) measure does not necessarily have greater utility for differentiating individual differences in personality. An extreme illustration of a reversal of this assumption is the fact that the oldest and most low-tech measure of tonic electrodermal activity appears to be a better marker of male schizophrenia than not only the somewhat higher-tech phasic electrodermal response (Furedy et al., 2001), but also than the much higher-tech ERP. Moreover, for the user of these measures, there must be clear evidence that the higher-tech (and hence more costly) measure has significantly greater utility than the lower-tech measure for the former to be chosen over the latter.

Physiological 'respectability' versus psychological validity

This distinction is illustrated by arguments in the 1980s of the relative merits of two cardiac performance measures which were rival ventricular indices of sympathetic excitation

of the sort involved in psychological functions such as mental effort and emotional stress. The two candidate indices were carotid dp/dt and T-wave amplitude (TWA) which were favored, respectively, by Paul Obrist's Chapel Hill laboratory (e.g. Obrist, 1981) and my Toronto laboratory (e.g. Furedy, 1987a), who had earlier convinced psychophysiologists that an atrial index like HR acceleration was grossly inadequate as a sympathetic index, because the atrium is under both sympathetic and parasympathetic influences (Obrist, 1981).

Carotid dp/dt is based on cardiac contractile strength, so the physiological mechanism that links it to sympathetic, beta-adrenergic excitation is well-known. On the other hand, TWA is an electrophysiological index, and the connection between it and sympathetic excitation is not physiologically clear. Similarly, while the electrodermal SCR or GSR has been the subject of many psychological investigations, the physiological mechanisms involved remain obscure, despite many years of physiological investigations.

So carotid dp/dt had greater physiological 'respectability' than TWA, and most psychophysiological researchers agreed with Obrist that his index was superior to TWA as a psychophysiological measure of sympathetic excitation. However, as detailed by Heslegrave and Furedy (1980), carotid dp/dt was severely limited for use in human experimental preparations. Among its most obvious flaws were the necessity for the subject not to swallow for the duration of the experiment (i.e. the index was obtrusive, though not invasive), and a reported data loss of over 20%.

Psychophysiological practice was consistent with the lack of psychological validity of carotid dp/dt, and even Obrist's laboratory, in a reply to Heslegrave and Furedy (1980), stated that they had abandoned this index, which did, in fact, disappear from the psychophysiological literature. Instead, the 'competition' that TWA currently faces is the contractile peripheral pulse transit time (PTT), which does not have the disadvantages that carotid dp/dt had (for evidence and arguments favoring PTT over TWA, see Weiss and Schwartz, 1983). More recently, some studies have suggested that the story is not one of a clear victory of one side over the other, but that TWA is superior as a measure of mental sympathetic stress, whereas PTT is superior as a measure of physiological sympathetic stress induced by challenging physical exercise (Furedy et al., 1996; Szabo et al., 1994).

Temporal versus localization (central) measures

With the development of central psychophysiological measures that have made it possible to record and observe physiological brain functioning, these central, brain-function measures can be classified into temporal measures like the P300 component of the ERP that reflects the total activity of the brain as a whole, and localization measures like fMRI that record activity from different parts of the brain. In both sorts of measures, the dependent variable is expressed in terms of response magnitude. For personality researchers, temporal measures have the greatest potential use for differentiating individuals in terms of general psychological functions like decision making, while localization measures can be used to differentiate among different sorts of cognitive abilities, as well as the role that emotion and even motivation plays in influencing behavior.

Complementary use of psychophysiological, behavioral, and introspective measures

The psychological functions that are measured by these three sorts of dependent variables are equally real and important. There are many cases where the three sorts of measures are employed in a complementary way to shed light on what are a complex set of influences that produce certain outcomes. For example,

in an experimental study of the effects of chronic smoking and an acute-smoking manipulation, behavioral or performance dependent variables alone indicated a beneficial effect of smoking on male cognitive verbal function (Algan et al., 1997). On the other hand, skin resistance level was unique in showing that the acute smoking manipulation of smoking one cigarette after 10 hours of deprivation, increased female arousal while decreasing male arousal (Furedy et al., 1999). Finally, this psychophysiological sex difference was in contrast to well-known survey results (i.e. introspective measures) that females tend to smoke for relaxation, while males do so for stimulation (Neumann et al., 2007).

Reliability versus validity

Psychophysiology's arguably most salient purported application is the polygraph or lie detection, which involves the classification of individuals (truthful vs. deceptive regarding certain important, often criminal, issues) by means of psychophysiological measures. In North America, the polygraph has also been employed by security organizations like the CIA and FBI to classify individuals in terms of whether they are security risks, or suitable for employment in these organizations. Even after they have been hired, employees in these security organizations are frequently 'polygraphed' to check whether they are still loyal. Of late, computer programs have been used to score the autonomic responses from these 'truth tests', and in such cases, at least the recorded reading itself is completely reliable in the sense that two users of the program get exactly the same outcome. And, even without the use of computers, the verdict of polygraphers based on their visual scoring of records have been close to 100% reliable in the sense that a 'blind' reading of records obtained by a polygrapher who classifies the examinee as 'truthful', 'deceptive', and 'inconclusive' will produce agreement between the two polygraphers close to 100% of the time.

On the other hand, while most of the scientific community do not take my 'extreme' position that the polygraph is not more than a North American flight of technological fancy whose real methodological status as a 'test' is the same as that of entrails reading during the Roman empire (e.g. Furedy, 1996, 2003), the majority of that community do agree (e.g. Iacono, 2001) that the polygraph's *validity* is insufficient for use as a classification device for discriminating between truthful and deceptive individuals, or even innocent and guilty ones. More generally, it is important for the personality researcher to be alert to this basic distinction between reliability and validity, because in areas other than the polygraph, proponents of a measure will often provide information only about reliability and not validity. Without adequate systematic evidence of validity, the potential utility of any psychophysiological measure that is employed to assess a psychological function is zero.

UNDERLYING PRE-SOCRATIC REALIST PHILOSOPHY-OF-SCIENCE POSITION

The philosophical position that underlies this chapter follows that put forward by the philosopher, John Anderson (e.g. Anderson, 1961). The most systematic application of Anderson's realism to psychology was by Maze (1983), one of Anderson's students, whose special expertize was theoretical psychology (cf. Furedy, 1988, 1989, 2001; Furedy and Riley, 1987; Riley and Furedy, 1985). My own experimental work in such areas as whether signaling the time of occurrence of a noxious unmodifiable event is preferred by humans (e.g. Furedy, 1975, vs. D'Amato, 1974) and animals (e.g. Biederman and Furedy, 1979, vs. Badia and Harsh, 1977), or whether the 'truly random' or 'explicitly unpaired' conditional stimulus constitutes the proper control for human autonomic Pavlovian conditioning (e.g. Furedy et al., 1975, vs. Rescorla, 1988) has benefited from the realist approach. These benefits are not only the

new and more valid scientific information that has been generated, but also some potentially useful applied implications that stem from this research, such as the use of 'imaginational' Pavlovian conditioning to teach relatively large-magnitude, difficult-to-learn and medically relevant HR decelerations (e.g. Furedy and Klajner, 1978).

More recently, and consistent with the recommendation that research should 'meld' differential and experimental methods, particularly in interdisciplinary work that combines psychological and physiological methods, research on sex differences in cognitive functioning has yielded distinctions such as conscious versus unconscious, male versus female, early versus late acquisition, perceptual versus conceptual, and preference for contrasting cognitive styles in which cortical versus hippocampal functions are involved. This biobehavioral research, performed at Ege University in Professor Pöğün's laboratory, has examined sex and smoking as individual-differences-related variables (Furedy and Pöğün, 2001).

For the science and applications of psychology, 'saving the appearances' is a matter of employing explanations that take account of such differences observed in living organisms as that between cognitive versus non-cognitive, ability versus drive, conscious versus unconscious, the emotions of anger versus fear, and all other individual differences that living organisms manifest. The secret, then, for the scientific and successful applied use of psychophysiological measures by personality researchers is to assess these measures not in terms of how currently fashionable they are, but in terms of their potential for providing complementary information about human individual differences.

ACKNOWLEDGEMENTS

This chapter is based on some 40 years of experience as a researcher in experimental psychophysiology in North America funded by various Canadian and American governmental agencies. In addition, I am grateful not only to my collaborators, many of whom are listed as co-authors in the references, but also to those with whom I engaged in published controversies in psychophysiology. I have learned a lot from both groups of scholars, even if at times the lessons were not received with great comfort. The chapter, however, is dedicated to the memory of the late supervisor of my BA, MA, and PhD research, Dick Champion, who taught me the art of experimental psychological design, the main skill of which is the ability to recognize significant empirical confounds, and, through discussion with one's collaborators, design one's research in such a way that hypotheses can be tested with increasing precision. He believed that in this way progress in real understanding of the sort that is common in the harder sciences, can also be made in psychology.

REFERENCES

Anderson, J. (1961) *Studies in Empirical Philosophy*. Sydney: University of Sydney Press.

Arabian, J.M. and Furedy, J.J. (1983) 'Individual differences in imagery ability and Pavlovian HR decelerative conditioning', *Psychophysiology*, 20(3): 325–31.

Badia, P. and Harsh, J. (1977) 'Preference for signaled over unsignaled shock schedules: A reply to Furedy and Biederman', *Bulletin of the Psychonomic Society*, 10(1): 13–16.

Barry, R.J. (1990) 'Scoring criteria for response latency and habituation in electrodermal research: A study in the context of the orienting response', *Psychophysiology*, 27(1): 94–100.

Barry, R.J. and Maltzman, I. (1985) 'Heart rate deceleration is not an orienting reflex; heart acceleration is not a defensive reflex', *Pavlovian Journal of Biological Science*, 20(1): 15–28.

Best, J.A. and Haksman, A.R. (1978) (eds), 'A stimulus specific model of smoking behavior', *Addictive Behavior*, 3(1): 79–82.

Biederman, G.B. and Furedy, J.J. (1979) 'A history of rat preference for signaled shock: From paradox to paradigm', *Australian Journal of Psychology*, 31(2): 101–18.

Boyle, G.J. and Saklofske, D.H. (2004) (eds), *Sage Benchmarks in Psychology: The Psychology of Individual Differences*. London: Sage.

Cattell, R.B. and Child, D. (1975) *Motivation and Dynamic Structure*. London: Holt, Rinehart & Winston.

Deslandes, A., Ferreira, C., Veiga, H., Cagy, M., Piedade, R., Pompeu, F. and Ribero, P. (2004) 'Effects of caffeine on electrophysiological and neuropsychological indices after sleep deprivation', *Neuropsychobiology*, 54(2): 126–33.

Donchin, E. (1981) 'Presidential address: Surprise, surprise!', *Psychophysiology*, 8(5): 493–513.

D'Amato, M.R. (1974) 'Derived motives', *Annual Review of Psychology*, 25: 83–106.

Elder, S.T., Lashley, J.K., Kedouri, N. and Regenbogen (1986) 'Can subjects be trained to communicate through the use of EEG biofeedback?', *Clinical Biofeedback and Health: An International Journal*, 9(1): 42–7.

Engel, B.T. (1972) 'Operant conditioning of cardiac function: A status report', *Psychophysiology*, 9(2): 161–77.

Farwell, L.A. and Donchin, E. (1991) 'The truth will out: Interrogative polygraphy ("lie detection") with event-related potentials', *Psychophysiology*, 28(5): 531–47.

Friedman, M. (1996) *Type A Behaviour: Its Diagnosis and Treatment*. New York: Plenum/Kluwer.

Furedy, J.J. (1975) 'An integrative progress report on informational control in humans: Some laboratory findings and methodological claims', *Australian Journal of Psychology*, 27(1): 61–83.

Furedy, J.J. (1983) 'Operational, analogical, and genuine definitions of psychophysiology', *International Journal of Psychophysiology*, 1(1): 13–19.

Furedy, J.J. (1984) 'Generalities and specifics in defining psychophysiology: Reply to Stern (1964) and Stern (1984)', *International Journal of Psychophysiology*, 2(1): 2–4.

Furedy, J.J. (1987a) 'Beyond heart-rate in the cardiac psychophysiological assessment of mental effort: The T-wave amplitude component of the electrocardiogram', *Human Factors*, 29(2): 183–94.

Furedy, J.J. (1987b) 'On some research-community contributions to the myth and symbol of biofeedback', *International Journal of Psychophysiology*, 4(4): 293–97.

Furedy, J.J. (1988) 'On the relevance of philosophy for psychological research: A preliminary analysis of some influences of Andersonian realism', *Australian Journal of Psychology*, 40(1): 71–77.

Furedy, J.J. (1989) 'On the relevance of philosophy for psychological research: Fashions versus fundamentals', *Australian Journal of Psychology*, 41(2): 131–3.

Furedy, J.J. (1991a) 'Realism, instrumentalism, and the distinction between epistemological and ontological certainty: Comments elicited by the Meehl and Mos manuscripts', *History and Philosophy Psychology Bulletin*, 3(1): 23–5.

Furedy, J.J. (1991b) 'Realist versus instrumentalist approaches to clarifying the conditions for orienting response habituation', *Journal of Experimental Psychology: General*, 12(1): 106–9.

Furedy, J.J. (1991c) 'Cognitivism and the conflict between realist and instrumentalist approaches to scientific theorising', *Canadian Psychologist*, 32(3): 461–3.

Furedy, J.J. (1993) 'Electrodermal activity as a tool for differentiating psychological processes in human experimental preparations: Focus on the psyche of psychophysiology', in J-C Roy, W. Boucsein, D.C. Fowles and J.H. Gruzelier (eds), *Progress in Electrodermal Research*. New York: Plenum, pp. 61–71.

Furedy, J.J. (1996) 'The North American polygraph and psychophysiology: Disinterested, uninterested, and interested perspectives', *International Journal of Psychophysiology*, 21(2–3): 97–105.

Furedy, J.J. (1997) 'Interdisciplinary interactions across the behavioral divide: A Pre-Socratic perspective', in S. Pöğün (ed.), *Neurotransmitter Release and Uptake*. Berlin: Springer, pp. 317–26.

Furedy, J.J. (2001) 'An epistemologically arrogant community of contending scholars: A pre-Socratic perspective on the past, present, and future of the Pavlovian society', *Integrative Physiological and Behavioral Science*, 36(1): 5–14.

Furedy, J.J. (2003) 'The North American polygraph as entrails reading: Lay, legal, and scientific reactions', Presented at the University of California, Long Beach Psi Chi Chapter meeting, Los Angeles, October 12, 2003.

Furedy, J.J. (2004) 'Aping Newtonian physics but ignoring brute facts will not transform Skinnerian psychology into genuine science or useful technology', *Behavioral and Brain Sciences*, 27(5): 693–4.

Furedy, J.J., Algan, O., Vincent, A., Demirgoren, S. and Pöğün, S. (1999) 'Sexually dimorphic effect of an acute smoking manipulation on skin resistance but not on heart-rate during a cognitive verbal task', *Integrative Physiological and Behavioral Science*, 34(4): 207–14.

Furedy, J.J. and Klajner, F. (1973) 'On evaluating autonomic and verbal indices of negative perception', *Psychophysiology*, 11(1): 121–4.

Furedy, J.J. and Klajner, F. (1978) 'Imaginational Pavlovian conditioning of large-magnitude cardiac decelerations with tilt as US', *Psychophysiology*, 15(6): 538–43.

Furedy, J.J. Morrison, J.W. and Flor-Henry, P. (2001) 'Skin conductance levels reveal unique deficits in allocation of attention to repetition and change in male schizophrenics', *Psychophysiology*, 38(3): S69 (abstract).

Furedy, J.J. and Pöğün, S. (2001) 'An investigative biobehavioral approach to sex differences in cognitive functioning', *Sexuality and Culture*, 5(1): 13–21.

Furedy, J.J. and Poulos, C.X. (1976) 'Heart-rate decelerative Pavlovian conditioning with tilt as UCS: Towards behavioral control of cardiac dysfunction', *Biological Psychology*, 4(2): 93–106.

Furedy, J.J., Poulos, C.X. and Schiffmann, K. (1975) 'Contingency theory and inhibitory conditioning: Some problems of assessment and interpretation', *Psychophysiology*, 12(2): 98–105.

Furedy, J.J. and Riley, D.M. (1987) 'Human Pavlovian autonomic conditioning and the cognitive paradigm', in G. Davey (ed.), *Conditioning in Humans*. Sussex: Wiley, pp. 1–25.

Furedy, J.J. and Scher, H. (1989) 'The Law of Initial Values: Differential testing as an empirical generalization versus enshrinement as a methodological rule', *Psychophysiology*, 26(2): 120–2.

Furedy, J.J. and Scull, J. (1971) 'Orienting-reaction theory and an increase in the human GSR following stimulus change which is unpredictable but not contrary to prediction', *Journal of Experimental Psychology*, 88(2): 292–4.

Furedy, J.J., Szabo, A. and Peronnet, F. (1996) 'Effects of psychological and physiological challenges on heart-rate, T-wave amplitude, and pulse-transit time', *International Journal of Psychophysiology*, 22(2): 173–83.

Green, A.M. and Green, E.E. (1978) 'Some problems in biofeedback research', *Journal of Transpersonal Psychology*, 10(2): 135–42.

Heslegrave, R.J. and Furedy, J.J. (1979) 'Sensitivities of HR and T-wave amplitude for detecting cognitive and anticipatory stress', *Physiology and Behavior*, 22(1): 17–23.

Heslegrave, R.J. and Furedy, J.J. (1980) 'Carotid dp/dt as a psychophysiological index of sympathetic myocardial effects: Some considerations', *Psychophysiology*, 17(5): 482–94.

Iacono, W.G. (2001) 'Forensic "Lie Detection": Procedures without a scientific basis', *Journal of Forensic Psychology Practice*, 1(1): 75–86.

Ikard, F.F. and Tomkins, S. (1973) 'The experience of affect as a determinant of smoking behavior. A series of validity studies', *Journal of Abnormal Psychology*, 81(2): 79–82.

Jamieson, J.J. (1987) 'Bilateral finger temperature and the law of initial values', *Psychophysiology*, 24(6): 666–9.

Jamieson, J. J. (1993) 'The law of initial values: Five factors or two?', *International Journal of Psychophysiology*, 14(3): 233–9.

Lykken, D.T. and Tellegen, A. (1974) 'On the validity of the perception hypothesis', *Psychophysiology*, 11(2): 125–32.

Maze, J.R. (1983) *The Meaning of Behaviour*. London, UK: Allen & Unwin.

Michell, J. (1988) 'Maze's direct realism and the character of cognition', *Australian Journal of Psychology*, 40(3): 227–49.

Miller, N.E. (1969) 'Learning of visceral and glandular responses', *Science*, 163(3866): 434–45.

Mulholland, T.B. (1982) 'Comments on the Furedy and Riley and Tursky chapters', in L. White and B. Tursky (eds), *Clinical Biofeedback: Efficacy and Mechanisms*. New York: Guilford, pp. 133–5.

Mulholland, T.B., Boudrot, R. and Davidson, A. (1979) 'Feedback delay and amplitude threshold and control of the occipital EEG', *Biofeedback and Self Regulation*, 4(2): 93–102.

Muter, P.M., Furedy, J.J., Vincent, A. and Pelcowitz, T. (1992) 'User-hostile systems and patterns of psychophysiological activity', *Computers in Human Behavior*, 9(1): 105–11.

Neisser, U. (1967) *Cognitive Psychology*. New York: Appleton Century Crofts.

Neumann, D.L., Fitzgerald, Z.T., Furedy, J.J. and Boyle, G.J. (2007) 'Sexually dimorphic effects of acute nicotine administration on arousal and visual-spatial ability in non-smoking human volunteers', *Pharmacology, Biochemistry and Behavior*, 86(4): 758–65.

Obrist, P.A. (1976) 'The cardiovascular-behavioral interaction – As it appears today', *Psychophysiology*, 13(1): 95–107.

Obrist, P.A. (1981) *Cardiovascular Psychophysiology: A Perspective*. New York: Plenum.

Obrist, P.A., Gaebelein, C.J. and Langer, A.W. (1975) 'Cardiovascular psychophysiology: Some contemporary methods of measurement', *American Psychologist*, 30(3): 277–84.

Obrist, P.A., Gaebelein, C.J., Teller, E.S., Langer, A.W., Grignolo, A., Light, K.C. and McCubbin, J.A. (1978) 'The relationships among heart rate, carotid dp/dt, and blood pressure in humans as a function of type of stress', *Psychophysiology*, 15(1): 102–15.

Obrist, P.A., Howard, J.L., Lawler, J.E., Sutterer, J.R., Smithson, K.W. and Martin, P.L. (1972) 'Alterations in cardiac contractility during classical aversive conditioning in dogs: Methodological and theoretical considerations', *Psychophysiology*, 9(2): 246–61.

Obrist, P.A., Light, K.C., Howard, J.L., Smithson, K.W., Martin, P.L. and Manning, J. (1974) 'Sympathetic influences on cardiac rate and contractility during acute stress in humans', *Psychophysiology*, 11(4): 405–27.

Reiko, S., Nakayama, M. and Furedy, J.J. (2004) 'Specific and reactive sensitivities of skin resistance response and respiratory apnea in a Japanese concealed information test (CIT) of criminal guilt', *Canadian Journal of Behavioral Science*, 36(3): 202–19.

Reinsel, R.A., Veselis, R.A., Wronski, M. and Marino, P. (1995) 'The P300 event-related potential during propofol sedation: A possible marker for amnesia?', *British Journal of Anaesthesia*, 74(6): 674–80.

Rescorla, R.A. (1988) 'Pavlovian conditioning: It's not what you think it is', *American Psychologist*, 43(3): 151–60.

Riley, D.M. and Furedy, J.J. (1981) 'Effects of instructions and contingency of reinforcement on the operant conditioning of human phasic heart rate change', *Psychophysiology*, 18(1): 75–81.

Riley, D.M. and Furedy, J.J. (1985) 'Psychological and physiological systems: Modes of operation and interaction', in S. Burchfield (ed.), *Psychological and Physiological Interactions in the Response to Stress*. New York: Hemisphere, pp. 3–34.

Rosenfeld, J.P., Cantwell, B., Nashman, V.T., Wojfdec, V., Ivanov, S. and Mazzeri, L. (1988) 'A modified, event-related potential-based guilty knowledge test', *International Journal of Neuroscience*, 42: 157–61.

Scher, H., Hartman, L.M., Furedy, J.J. and Heslegrave, R.J. (1986) 'Electrocardiographic T-wave changes are more pronounced in Type A than in Type B men during mental work', *Psychosomatic Medicine*, 48(3): 159–66.

Schwartz, B. and Reisberg, D. (1991) *Learning and Memory*. New York: Norton.

Schwartz, P.J. and Weiss, T. (1983) 'T-wave amplitude as an index of cardiac sympathetic activity: A misleading concept', *Psychophysiology*, 20(6): 696–701.

Segal, E.M. and Lachman, R. (1972) 'Complex behavior or higher mental process: Is there a paradigm shift?', *American Psychologist*, 27(1): 46–55.

Shulhan, D., Scher, H. and Furedy, J.J. (1986) 'Phasic cardiac reactivity to psychological stress as a function of aerobic fitness level', *Psychophysiology*, 23(6): 562–66.

Slezak, P. and Albury, W.R (1988) (eds), *Computers, Brains and Minds: Essays in Cognitive Science*. Dordrecht: Reidel/Kluwer.

Spielberger, C.D. (1986) 'Psychological determinants of smoking behavior', in R.D. Tollison (ed.), *Smoking and Society: Towards a More Balanced Assessment*. Lexington, MA: Lexington Books, pp. 89–134.

Szabo, A., Peronnet, F., Gauvin, L. and Furedy, J.J. (1994) 'Mental challenge elicits "additional" increases in heart rate during low and moderate intensity cycling', *International Journal of Psychophysiology*, 17(3): 197–204.

Weiss, T., Del Bo, A., Reichek, N. and Engelman, K. (1980) 'Pulse transit time in the analysis of autonomic nervous system effects on the cardiosympathetic system', *Psychophysiology*, 17: 202–7.

Woodworth, R.S. and Schlosberg, H. (1954) *Experimental Psychology*. London, UK: Methuen.

Yu-Kang, T. and Gilthorpe, M.S. (2006) 'Revisiting the relationship between change and initial value: A review and evaluation', *Statistics in Medicine*, 26(2): 443–57.

15

Psychophysiological Measurement of Personality

Eco de Geus and David L. Neumann

INTRODUCTION

Whereas the environment is in constant flux and causes changes in an individual's behavior over time, personality is considered the constant factor that causes stability in behavior. This constancy is likely to be hard-wired in our biology, and the brain seems the obvious place for such hard-wiring. Can we measure this hard-wiring of behavior? In this chapter we review attempts to correlate personality traits to individual differences in central nervous system functioning using psychophysiological recording techniques. This relatively small literature has been motivated by two different goals. The first has emerged from concerns about the validity of paper-and-pencil personality assessment (Eisenberger et al., 2005). Virtually all major personality inventories are based on potentially flawed subjective linguistic self-report. To further advance personality testing, it may be necessary to move to objective tests that avoid most of the motivational and response distortion associated with item transparency of self-report instruments. Psychophysiological testing seems a promising method to do so, because voluntary control over the recorded biological signals is limited

if not absent. A second motive to use psychophysiological testing in personality research is to elucidate the biological processes underlying the major dimensions of personality. Several influential models of personality, such as those by (Eysenck 1967, 1990; Eysenck and Eysenck, 1985) and (Gray 1982; Gray and McNaughton, 2000) have been strongly informed by biological theory.

The two central constructs in Eysenck's theory are neuroticism and extraversion. Neuroticism is related to activation levels in the limbic system. The limbic system includes the hippocampus, amygdala, septum, and hypothalamus and regulates emotional states such as fear and aggression. Neurotic individuals are hypothesized to have higher activation levels in the limbic system leading to lower thresholds for emotional responses. Neurotic individuals are more likely to report feelings of anxiety, guilt, and tension. Emotionally stable individuals, on the other, hand, have lower activation and higher thresholds in the limbic system, leading to attenuated responses to emotional challenges. The extraversion–introversion dimension is thought to be regulated by the ascending reticular activating system that is involved in regulating cortical arousal. An individual's comfort level at any given time will depend on the interaction between their basal cortical arousal and the type of situation they are in; being under- or over-aroused are both less desirable than a moderate level of arousal. Introverts are prone to be overstimulated by sensory stimuli and consequently tend to withdraw from social situations, are less active, and less willing to take risks. In contrast, due to their lower base level of cortical arousal, extraverts tend to be more lively and sensation seeking and will be attracted to social situations.

In the view of Gray and colleagues, there are two basic systems that control behavior. The behavioral inhibition system (BIS) is activated by novelty and stimuli associated with punishment; that is, aversive stimuli or omission of reward. The behavioral approach system (BAS) is activated by stimuli associated with reinforcement; that is, reward or termination of punishment. Gray and colleagues located these systems in the septohippocampal system (to which the amygdala was later added) and the ventral striatum (including the nucleus accumbens). Engagement of both systems is associated with arousal as reflected in changes in autonomic nervous system activity and hormonal secretion. Gray and colleagues proposed that the most salient individual differences reflect the variation in sensitivity to stimuli associated with punishment or reinforcement and the coupled behavioral tendencies of avoidance and approach. Specifically, individual differences in the functioning of the reward system in response to appetitive stimuli are implicated in the personality traits of extraversion and novelty seeking/impulsivity. Individual differences in the punishment system in response to aversive stimuli are implicated in the personality traits of neuroticism and harm avoidance.

Psychophysiological testing

Psychophysiological testing can be used to corroborate the hypothesized biological correlates of personality, and ultimately chart the various intermediate steps in the biological pathways connecting variation in brain function to variation in behavior. In the current chapter, we will focus on the electromyographic (EMG) recording of the startle blink reflex, electroencephalographic (EEG) recording of cortical electrical activity either recorded continuously or evoked by stimulus events, and changes in brain blood flow assessed by functional magnetic resonance imaging (fMRI). These signals can, first of all, be recorded under pure resting conditions. In such a setting, subjects are typically instructed to relax, focus their attention on a fixation point and in general made to avoid engaging in any particular state of mind. In keeping with a dispositional model of personality, the idea is that this will allow their 'underlying' or 'true' level of nervous system activity to manifest. For example, if extraverted individuals are characterized by positive and neurotic individuals by negative affect as assessed by affect scales like the PANAS (Watson et al., 1988) these differences in dispositional affect should be detectable by the measurement of resting brain blood flow and electrical activity in brain regions known to be implicated in affective processing. A number of studies have indeed reported such correlations (Davidson, 1998; Ebmeier et al., 1994; Stenberg et al., 1990, 1993; Youn et al., 2002).

By contrast, Wallace (1966) conceptualized personality attributes as abilities, an approach he termed the capability model of personality. Others have proposed similar formulations of personality (Mischel and Shoda, 1995). The capability model encourages the measurement of individual differences in 'brain behavior' during controlled laboratory challenges, much as one might test intelligence or high-jumping ability. Subjects can, for instance, be made to anticipate and actually gain a reward (e.g. 5 cents per correct answer) or be punished (e.g. shock or monetary loss) during a mentally challenging task. Alternatively, they can be shown series of words with strong negative (e.g. 'sick', 'murder', 'hate', 'rape') or positive connotations (e.g. 'happy', 'wedding', 'love', 'party'). Two popular sets of affective stimuli are a series of faces compiled by Ekman and

Friesen (1978) showing primary emotions like sadness, happiness, fear or anger, and a series of images compiled by Lang et al. (1998, 2001) in the International Affective Picture System (IAPS). The IAPS stimuli are complex visual scenes that were extensively normalized for emotional valence and arousal. For instance, unpleasant images depicted snarling dogs, spiders, sharks, disgusting objects, violence, severe burns, or corpses, whereas pleasant images depicted happy babies, appetizing foods, puppies and kittens, joyful people and loving couples. Response to these emotional valenced images are usually contrasted to those seen during neutral images of, for instance, a basket, books, or fractal images.

Most of the recent work on EEG, ERP, and EMG startle blink correlates of personality and almost all of the fMRI studies, follow the capability model rather than the dispositional model. Instead of assessing differences in resting levels of the EMG startle reflex, EEG or hemodynamic brain activity, these studies have looked at the magnitude, timing, and topography of changes in these measures during experimentally induced changes in psychological state.

EMG startle reflex

The startle reflex is a defensive response elicited by intense and abrupt stimuli. In humans, the startle reflex is measured by recordings of the *orbicularis oculi* muscle around the eye (Blumenthal et al., 2005). Blinks can be reliably elicited by presenting a brief (about 50 ms) and moderately intense tone, or white noise. Typically, participants are presented with a lead stimulus that might be neutral or emotionally toned and the startle eliciting probe stimulus is presented at a certain time, termed a lead interval, following the lead stimulus onset. Startle modulation is observed when the size of the startle reflex is altered by the lead stimulus. Lead intervals less than 50 ms can produce very short lead interval facilitation (Neumann et al., 2004). Lead intervals of 50 to 500 ms produce short

lead interval inhibition, often termed pre-pulse inhibition (PPI), with maximal inhibition at lead intervals around 100 ms (Neumann et al., 2004).

EEG power and EEG asymmetry

The EEG reflects the electrical activity generated by clusters of neurons in the cortex that show synchronized changes in membrane potential due to neural activity in that brain location. EEG recordings are made from multiple electrodes affixed to the scalp (the exact number varies across studies from the standard 18 scalp electrodes up to 128 scalp electrodes). The most striking feature of the brain activity recorded by an EEG is its oscillatory character. Quantification of EEG data reflects this, in that the energy (or power) in various frequency bands is used as a main index. EEG recording has many important clinical applications because there are predictable EEG signatures associated with different behavioral states. A relaxed resting state, for instance, is characterized by high power in the alpha (8–12 Hz) frequency band, whereas under-condition of mental load power in the beta band (12–30 Hz) increases in relative strength. In addition to its sensitivity to within-subject changes in behavioral state, EEG power can also be compared across subjects, for instance as a function of personality. Because right and left hemispheres are suspected to play a differential role in emotional processing, most attention has gone to individual differences in the degree of asymmetry in left and right EEG power (Sutton and Davidson, 1997).

Event-related potentials

The event-related potential (ERP) is a stereotyped short-term change in EEG activity that is time-locked to stimulus or cognitive events. Different ERP components can be identified according to whether the voltage fluctuation is positive or negative and the time (latency) at which the peak voltage fluctuation is seen.

For instance, the P300 (or P3) reflects a positive voltage change that peaks around 300 ms following stimulus onset. These changes in amplitude and timing of the voltage can be further differentiated as a function of spatial location. Thus, it can be determined whether individuals with different personality traits show different latencies, amplitudes, or patterns in the spatial distribution of their ERPs. The ongoing nature of psychological processes means that the ERP will consist of several potentially overlapping components (Fabiani et al., 2000). The major ERP components are N1, P2, N2, and P3, followed by slow wave components that return the EEG signal to baseline. Various other components may also be identified according to specific experimental conditions, such as the error-related negativity (ERN) and the contingent-negative variation (CNV).

fMRI

In a typical fMRI experiment, a high-resolution structural scan is taken initially that allows separation of gray and white matter from each other and other tissues (cerebrospinal fluid, skull, skin, etc.). Next, the subject is exposed to repeated stimuli, for example, pictures from the IAPS. When nerve cells are activated by these stimuli they consume extra oxygen which is carried by hemoglobin in red blood cells from local capillaries. The local response to this oxygen utilization is decrease in oxygenated blood followed by an increase in blood flow, occurring after a delay of approximately 1–5 seconds. Corresponding changes in the relative concentration of oxyhemoglobin and deoxy-hemoglobin can be detected using an appropriate magnetic resonance pulse sequence that gives rise to a so-called blood oxygenation level dependent (BOLD) contrast. The average level of BOLD signal intensity can be compared in two sets of stimuli, for instance aversive pictures versus neutral pictures, to see which parts of the brain were

specifically activated or deactivated by the aversive stimulus compared to the neutral stimulus. Statistical maps that take into account the multiple testing across thousands of 1–1.5 mm^3 blocks of brain tissue – voxels – show the (de)activated areas as colored blobs. These can be rendered in 3D and plotted on top of the original high-resolution structural scan for anatomical interpretation. Individual differences in the BOLD signal intensity in certain regions-of-interest (ROI) can be correlated with major personality traits like neuroticism and extraversion.

NEUROTICISM

EMG startle reflex

Response size and habituation
As a defensive response, the absolute size of the startle reflex should be larger and habituate more slowly in individuals with high neuroticism because of the association of this personality trait to hypersensitivity to aversive sensory stimuli (Eysenck et al., 1985). However, results have generally failed to support this prediction. No association has been found between startle reflex magnitude and neuroticism in a sample of male patients with schizophrenia or matched healthy controls (Akdag et al., 2003). In addition, the same study found no association between neuroticism and the rate of habituation from an early to a late block of trials. A similar failure to find any relationship between neuroticism and startle reflex magnitude has also been reported in other investigations (Hawk and Kowmas, 2003; Kumari et al., 1996).

Prepulse inhibition (PPI)
In contrast to the absolute size of the startle reflex, PPI has shown a stronger association with neuroticism. Prepulse inhibition is an index of automatic sensorimotor gating that serves to protect the processing of the prepulse from interruption from the startle stimulus

(Graham, 1979). High levels of neuroticism are associated with low levels of PPI at lead intervals of 30, 60, and 120 ms and the association may be stronger in earlier than in late trials (Swerdlow et al., 1995; Corr et al., 2002). This reduced PPI may reflect the hypersensitivity to aversive sensory stimuli thought to be present in neurotic individuals (Eysenck et al., 1985). Alternatively, neurotic individuals may allocate less attention to the processing of the prepulse and startle-eliciting stimulus, thus reducing the amount of PPI observed (Corr et al., 2002). Based on this explanation, it would be instructive to directly manipulate the participant's attention such as by using the discrimination and counting task (Filion et al., 1994). If PPI is attenuated in neurotic individuals during attended, but not ignored lead stimuli, it would suggest that the association between neuroticism and PPI is mediated by attention. A final reason for the association between neuroticism and PPI could be that it reflects the activation of emotion circuits during the task, which in turn reduces PPI due to overlapping neural systems between the circuits that govern PPI and emotion (Corr et al., 2002).

Affective modulation

According to the motivational priming interpretation of affective startle modulation (Lang et al., 1997), there will be startle potentiation when the lead stimulus induces an affective state congruent with the startle stimulus (i.e. unpleasant or aversive lead stimuli) and startle attenuation when the lead stimulus induces an incongruent affective state (i.e. pleasant or appetitive lead stimuli). Hence, affective startle modulation will be influenced by personality characteristics if these characteristics mediate responses to aversive or appetitive stimuli. In particular, individuals high in neuroticism or on the BIS scale would be expected to show enhanced startle potentiation due to their heightened sensitivity to aversive stimuli (Eysenck et al., 1985; Gray and Me Naughton., 2000). However, prior research has not always been consistent with these predictions. Startle latency potentiation during unpleasant compared to neutral pictures has been found in participants low in neuroticism, but not in those high in neuroticism (Corr et al., 1995). High BIS participants have shown increased attenuation of startle magnitude during pleasant pictures compared to neutral pictures, which was not found in low BIS participants (Hawk et al., 2003). However, the expected startle potentiation during unpleasant compared to neutral pictures in high BIS participants was not found. Absence of a relationship between neuroticism and affective startle modulation has also been reported (Kumari et al., 1996). Various explanations have been put forward to explain why the results are inconsistent with predictions, including ceiling effects or reduced attention to unpleasant stimuli in neurotic individuals (Corr et al., 1995), or that it reflects the nature of stimuli used in terms of their arousal level (Kumari et al., 1996) or content (Kumari et al., 1996; Hawk and Kowmas., 2003).

The nature of the unpleasant stimuli may be a crucial factor in the association between neuroticism and affective startle modulation. Startle potentiation is greater when stimuli are fearful than when disgusting (Kaviani et al., 1999). Moreover, the amygdala is implicated in the fear response and it plays a central role in startle potentiation (Lang et al., 1997). The BIS is closely associated with anxiety and fear and the amygdala has been included in this formalization (Gray et al., 2000). Accordingly, a closer association between neuroticism and affective startle modulation may be found if images of fear, rather than disgust, are used. In a re-examination of the data reported by Kumari et al. (1996), it was found that low-neuroticism participants showed greater startle potentiation to low fear–high disgust film clips than high-neuroticism participants (Wilson et al., 2000). In a study that systematically manipulated the nature of unpleasant pictures, high-BIS participants, but not low-BIS participants, exhibited startle potentiation during fear pictures (Caseras et al., 2006). The high-BIS participants showed significant differences in startle modulation between pleasant and neutral, pleasant and blood-disgust, and pleasant and fear pictures. The low BIS participants showed significant differences in startle modulation between pleasant and neutral, pleasant and blood-disgust, and blood-disgust and fear stimuli. The findings support the conclusion that individual differences in BIS functioning (and by extension, neuroticism) is associated with startle modulation during fear eliciting scenes.

EEG asymmetry

One of the most widely studied correlates of personality traits is frontal EEG alpha asymmetry; that is, asymmetry in EEG activity in the alpha frequency range (8–12 Hz) on frontal electrodes (Coan and Allen, 2004; Davidson, 2004; Davidson et al., 1985; Fox, 1991; Hewig et al., 2006). From their pioneer studies onward, Davidson and colleagues have linked frontal cortical asymmetry to an approach and a withdrawal system which bear strong resemblance to Gray's BAS and BIS system (Sutton et al., 1997). The approach system is activated by the perception of goals, elicits approach related (pre-goal-attainment) positive affect, and initiates appetitive behavior towards these goals. The neuroanatomical basis of the system is located in the left dorsolateral and medial prefrontal cortex and the basal ganglia. The withdrawal system is activated by aversive stimulation, elicits negative emotions, and leads to withdrawal behavior. The neuroanatomical basis of this system is thought to be the right dorsolateral prefrontal cortex, the right temporal polar region, the amygdala, the basal ganglia, and the hypothalamus. The amygdala may be a central structure connecting the activity of both systems (Ochsner et al., 2002).

Although EEG asymmetry seems a perfect candidate to act as a psychophysiological indicator of neuroticism, the extant literature shows large inconsistencies in statistical associations between frontal EEG asymmetry and neuroticism (and other related trait measures of personality), and it is unlikely that the methodological differences across laboratories can completely account for those inconsistencies (Allen et al., 2004; Coan and Allen., 2004; Davidson, 2004; Hagemann, 2004; Smit et al., 2007). From a conceptual point of view, Coan and colleagues (Coan et al., 2006) question the wisdom of the widespread use of measuring frontal asymmetry in resting conditions. The use of resting conditions derives from a near axiomatically accepted dispositional model of frontal affective style in this field. In this model individuals are thought to possess a general tendency to predominantly respond with either approach-related affect (indexed by relatively greater left frontal activity) or withdrawal-related affect (indexed by relatively greater right frontal activity) across all or most situations. Instead, the capability model of frontal EEG asymmetry may be more appropriate (Coan et al., 2006). As outlined before, this model posits that meaningful individual differences in frontal EEG asymmetry exist, but that those individual differences are best thought of as interactions between the emotional demands of specific situations and the emotion-regulatory abilities individuals bring to those situations. During emotional challenges, individual differences in frontal EEG asymmetries were indeed shown to be more pronounced than during a resting condition. Moreover, they were much more reliable; that is, more resistant to measurement error induced by variation in EEG methodology, and had a more reliable relationship with criterion measures of ongoing emotional state. These findings suggest that future use of evoked changes in EEG frontal asymmetry by emotion induction rather than resting EEG may yield more robust links to personality.

ERP

Early ERP components
Early ERP components can be influenced by the sensory characteristics of stimuli, such as their intensity. Based on the hypothesized hypersensitivity to sensory stimuli, neuroticism is expected to influence these components. However, research has generally failed to find

an association between neuroticism and N1, P2, and N2 amplitude or latency (De Pascalis, 1993; De Pascalis et al., 1996; Fjell et al., 2005). The error-related negativity (ERN), however, may be influenced by neuroticism. The ERN occurs when participants make errors in a sensorimotor task (Luu et al., 2000) or when outcomes are 'worse than expected' (Holroyd and Coles, 2002) and is thought to be generated by the anterior cingulate cortex (Van Veen and Carter, 2002). The negativity peaks around 150 ms following response onset and shows a fronto-central scalp distribution (Dehaene et al., 1994). Adult participants who scored high on measures of negative affect and emotionality have shown larger ERN than participants with low scores during a visual flanker task (Luu et al., 2000). No relationship between neuroticism and ERNs at a fronto-central site during a visual flanker task has also been reported (Santesso et al., 2005), although the lack of an association may reflect the use of 10-year-old children in this study.

P3

The P3 can be elicited in an oddball task in which infrequently presented pure tones (oddballs) are randomly interspersed among frequently occurring tones of a different pitch (standards). Stelmack and Houlihan (1995) present a comprehensive review of the earlier research on P3 and personality. In one of their own studies, participants high in neuroticism had a shorter P3 latency than participants low in neuroticism (Stelmack et al., 1993). The difference may reflect that the former spend less time to evaluate a stimulus (Plooij-van Gorsel, 1981). Alternatively, the increased worrying and susceptibility to stress, which are regarded as important elements of neuroticism that adversely influence cognitive performance (Eysenck et al., 1985), may also influence P3 latency (Stelmack et al., 1993). In addition, neuroticism level produced contrasting results for P3 latency and RT in that high neuroticism was associated with faster P3 latency but slower RT. This finding was interpreted to reflect that individuals with high neuroticism have a hasty and worried

evaluation of a stimulus (short P3 latency) that requires additional processing or checking to initiate a response leading to long RT (Stelmack et al., 1993).

No relationship between P3 and neuroticism has been found in a word/non-word detection task (De Pascalis et al., 1996), an auditory oddball task (Polich and Martin, 1992; Pritchard, 1989), and auditory startle probes presented during emotionally toned slides (Bartussek et al., 1996). It is possible that some discrepant results reflect differences in the task requirements or methodological features of the experiment. For instance, using a variety of visually presented tasks, Stelmack et al. (1993) found an association between neuroticism and P3 latency with some tasks, but not others. At least in terms of amplitude, the scalp distribution may be an important variable in that high and low neuroticism participants show similarities in P3 amplitude at some electrode sites and not others. Low neuroticism participants have shown the usual scalp distribution with a clear parietal maximum, whereas high neuroticism participants show a flat scalp distribution with nearly the same level of P3 amplitude at all electrode sites with both a structural (deciding if a word was longer or shorter than six letters) and affective (rating emotional valence of pleasant, neutral, and unpleasant pictures) processing task (Bartussek et al., 1996, experiment 1). Finally, the sampling of participants may be important in that gender and age may modulate the effects of neuroticism on the P3 (Gurrera et al., 2005; Pritchard, 1989).

Several personality researchers have also examined a component of the P3 that follows a third infrequent non-target stimulus that can be embedded in an oddball task. This P3a, or novelty-P3, is an earlier, frontally distributed potential arising in part from the anterior superior temporal gyrus and anterior cingulate gyrus and may be regarded as an index of the orienting response (Soltani and Knight, 2000). The amplitude of the P3a reflects the amount of attention a participant invests in the irrelevant, unexpected, and distracter stimuli.

A negative association between neuroticism and P3a amplitude to novel environmental stimuli embedded in an auditory oddball task has been found at frontal left, frontal right, frontal centre, and parietal centre locations (Gurrera et al., 2001). A similar, though statistically non-significant, association for P3a amplitude to irrelevant auditory distracter items has also been reported (Fjell et al., 2005). In a comparison between target and novel stimuli, stronger correlations with neuroticism were generally found for the P3 amplitude during novel stimuli (Fjell et al., 2005). The authors suggested that the stronger association may reflect that individuals high in neuroticism are more susceptible to distraction and less able to inhibit responses to non-target stimuli, which accords with Eysenck's notion of hypervigilance in these individuals.

fMRI

Although emotion research has been one of the largest beneficiaries of the new brain imaging techniques (Critchley, 2003; Davidson et al., 2000; Drevets, 2001), there is a surprising paucity of studies investigating the correlation between neuroticism and fMRI responsivity. That is, there is a large literature on deviant fMRI responses in psychopathology, but most of these studies used patients with clinical anxiety disorders or depression. In these studies, it becomes hard to separate the effects of having a psychiatric disorder itself, including toxic brain effects of co-morbid hypercortisolism (Sapolsky et al., 1986), from the effects of neuroticism *per se*. Fortunately, there is an increasing number of studies that address fMRI correlates of neuroticism in samples of healthy subjects (Canli et al., 2001; Eisenberger et al., 2005; Etkin et al., 2004; Guyer et al., 2006; Most et al., 2006; Paulus et al., 2003; Schwartz et al., 2003).

Most of these fMRI studies have implied amygdala hyper-reactivity in subjects scoring high on neuroticism. Activity in the amygdala robustly increases in response to unpleasant stimuli, most prominently to fearful and angry faces, even when these stimuli are rapidly masked to prevent conscious awareness. Neuroticism was found to be associated with larger amygdala responses to unpleasant pictures from the IAPS (Canli et al., 2001). Related traits of anxiety and harm avoidance were similarly associated with a larger amygdala fMRI response to angry or fearful faces (Etkin et al., 2004; Most et al., 2006). Finally, enhanced amygdala activity was found in response to novel, neutral face stimuli in adults who had been classified as inhibited as toddlers compared with adults who were not classified as such (Schwartz et al., 2003).

Harm avoidance was also associated with larger anterior cingulate cortex (ACC) reactivity while viewing aversive pictures (Most et al., 2006). Neuroticism was similarly associated with a significant increase in the activation of the dorsal ACC in response to an oddball task (Eisenberger et al., 2005). Intriguingly, the accuracy of the detection of interoceptive signals measured as heart beat perception was much better accounted for by ACC reactivity to the odd ball stimuli ($r_2 = 0.74$) than by self-reported neuroticism ($r_2 = 0.16$) This led the authors to suggest 'that neural reactivities may provide a more direct measure of personality than self-reports do' (Eisenberger et al., 2005: 196).

Paulus et al. (2003) had subjects perform a risk-taking decision-making task in which subjects could opt to try to win a small gain at low risk or larger gains at higher risk. Harm avoidance ($r = 0.54$) and neuroticism ($r = 0.59$) significantly predicted the degree of (mostly right) anterior insula activation during a punished response. They speculate that the insular cortex may be critical for the generation of anticipatory aversive somatic markers that guide risk-taking behavior (Damasio, 1999) and for aversive outcome processing once a decision has been made. Neuroticism appears to be associated with hyper-reactivity of this structure.

There is also some evidence for an effect of neuroticism on reactivity of the frontostriatal circuitry engaged in reward processing.

Forty-four children screened for behavioral inhibition (shyness) at 4 months were retested with fMRI in adolescence (Guyer et al., 2006). This study used the cued reaction time task by Knutson and colleagues (described in more detail below) that had been found to consistently engage the caudate nucleus, putamen, and nucleus accumbens (Knutson and Bhanji, 2006; Knutson et al., 2001, 2003). In all adolescents, activation of these structures became larger as the amount of monetary reward to be gained or lost increased, but the effect was much stronger in the group that had been behaviorally inhibited at 4 months.

EXTRAVERSION

EMG startle reflex

Response size and habituation

The hypothesized lower cortical arousal in the ascending reticular activating system in extraverts suggests that extraversion will be associated with smaller startle responses and faster, more rapid rates of habituation (Blumenthal, 2001). The startle reflex is particularly relevant to test such a hypothesis as the nucleus reticularis pontis caudalis has been implicated in regulating cortical arousal (Gottesmann et al., 1995) and forms part of the acoustic startle pathway (Davis et al., 1999). In support of Eysenck's conceptualization, introverts show larger startle magnitude (Blumenthal et al. 1995; Blumenthal, 2001) than extraverts. Introversion also appears to be associated with a faster response latency to 85 dB(A) than to 60 dB(A) acoustic stimuli, whereas extraverts do not show this difference, suggesting that introverts respond more to higher intensity stimuli (Britt and Blumenthal, 1991). However, differences in response magnitude between introverts and extraverts have not always been found (Akdag et al., 2003). No relationship between BAS scores and startle magnitude was found during the intertrial intervals of an affective startle

modulation experiment (Hawk et al., 2003). There is at least one report of an overall greater response probability (indicating more reactivity) in extraverts than introverts, although this was in the context of an affective startle modulation experiment (Kumari et al., 1996).

Blumenthal (2001) showed that selective attention may influence startle magnitude differently in introverts and extraverts. Introverts showed reduced startle amplitude when they directed attention towards a visual display (and away from an acoustic startle-eliciting stimulus). In contrast, startle amplitude tended to increase when extraverts direct attention towards a visual display. The difference may reflect that introverts were better able to allocate attention to the visual task, and were less distracted by the acoustic startle stimulus as less startle reactivity would be expected when attention is directed away from the modality of the eliciting stimulus (Neumann, 2002). Blumenthal (2001) also showed that the rate of startle habituation was faster in extraverts to 90 dB startle pulses than in introverts. The faster habituation in extraverts has been replicated in a study that examined habituation across individual trials during a picture slide presentation and during the intervals between the slides (LaRowe et al., 2006).

Prepulse inhibition

No association between extraversion and PPI has been found across two independent samples (Corr et al., 2002). However, a component measure of Gray's BAS activity, termed BAS-drive, is negatively correlated with PPI at lead intervals of 30, 60, and 120 ms (Corr et al., 2002). The association between BAS and PPI is further supported by an experiment that assessed PPI to an auditory stimulus during and in between picture presentations (Hawk and Kowmas, 2003). PPI assessed during a picture presentation was marginally greater among high BAS participants compared to low BAS participants. Although not statistically reliable, the same difference was found when PPI was assessed during the intertrial intervals. However, as PPI was assessed during slides that were emotionally toned, it is not clear whether the observed effects were influenced by the affective or attentional effects of the slides. Similar to the association between neuroticism and PPI, the association between BAS and PPI may reflect that high BAS participants attend more strongly to the prepulse stimuli and that this effect may have increased PPI. Further research which systematically manipulates attention to the lead stimulus is required to test this interpretation.

Affective modulation

Predictions of the relationship between affective startle modulation and levels of extraversion are not clear. For instance, extraverts might show greater startle attenuation during pleasant lead stimuli if extraversion is associated with higher levels of positive affect. On the other hand, greater attenuation during pleasant and greater potentiation during unpleasant lead stimuli might be expected in introverts due to their higher level of arousal in the ascending reticular activating system (Kumari et al., 1996) and the observation that lead stimuli that are higher in arousal elicit more pronounced affect startle modulation effects (Lang et al., 1997). An interaction between the valence of pictures and responses latency has been reported (Corr et al., 1995). The interaction reflected that only extraverted participants showed the expected linear pattern of modulation, although the effect seemed to be strongest for fear potentiation as only the difference between unpleasant and neutral slides was statistically significant. No association between extraversion and startle modulation during emotionally toned film clips has also been reported (Kumari et al., 1996).

Gray's model would suggest enhanced affective startle modulation among high BAS and high BIS participants relative to low BAS and low BIS participants. The main difference for BIS and BAS is that the enhanced modulation for high BAS participants should reflect greater attenuation during pleasant stimuli because of the association that pleasant stimuli have

with positive reinforcement. In contrast, the enhanced modulation for high BIS participants should reflect greater potentiation during unpleasant stimuli due to the association that unpleasant stimuli have with punishment. Consistent with these predictions, robust affective startle modulation has been observed for high BAS participants, but not for low BAS participants (Hawk and Kowmans, 2003). Although no groups showed facilitation during unpleasant pictures compared to neutral pictures, only the high BAS participants showed greater startle attenuation during pleasant pictures relative to neutral pictures.

A particularly novel way to examine the relationship between extraversion and psychological processes during emotionally toned situations is to examine startle modulation during a social encounter. In such a situation, it might be hypothesized that introverts will direct their attention inwards more than extraverts (Blumenthal et al., 1995). To test this hypothesis, an experimental assistant entered the participant's room and sat behind the participant while pretending to take notes. High extraversion participants did not differ in startle amplitude between the social encounter condition and a control (no social encounter) condition (Blumenthal et al., 1995). However, in support of the predictions, low extraversion participants showed smaller startle amplitude in the social encounter condition than in the control condition (Blumenthal et al., 1995). The examination of startle modulation during a social encounter may provide a means to specifically target the modulation of startle along the extraversion/introversion dimension, in much the same way that affective startle modulation with fear-provoking stimuli, rather than disgust-provoking stimuli, may more specifically target neuroticism (Wilson et al., 2000).

ERP

Early ERP components

Early research indicated that introverts have a greater N1-P2 amplitude than extraverts when elicited by infrequent tones (Stelmack et al., 1977), possibly reflecting that introverts attended to the tones more than extraverts. De Pascalis (De Pascalis, 1993) did not observe any direct association between N1 amplitude and extraversion, but did find a positive association between extraversion and auditory and visual N1 frontal ratios. The association reflected that extraverts showed predominantly left hemisphere engagement. These results support earlier findings in which P2 amplitude differed between extraverts and introverts when measured from the left hemisphere, but not when measured from the right hemisphere (De Pascalis and Montirosso, 1988).

Differences in attentional engagement also appear to underlie differences between introverts and extraverts in the N2. Extraverts have a shorter N2 latency than introverts to task irrelevant tone pipes that are superimposed over meaningful and meaningless speech (De Pascalis and Montirosso, 1988). In addition, the N2 amplitude is larger during meaningful speech than during meaningless speech for the extraverts, whereas the opposite difference is found for introverts (De Pascalis and Montirosso, 1988). The difference may reflect that the extraverts are more engaged or attended to the stimuli when the speech is meaningful than when it is meaningless, resulting in the greater N2 amplitude for the former condition. A more positive N2 amplitude in extraverts during a gambling task in which tones indicated a win or a loss has also been reported (Bartussek et al., 1993), although this difference was not due to a distinct effect on N2, but a consequence of a generally more positive ERP amplitude of the extraverts at the time between 250 and 400 ms after stimulus onset. The N2 amplitude of the extraverts in this study was always more positive when the tone indicated a win than a loss (Bartussek et al., 1993). Introverts, however, showed more positive N2 amplitudes to the tones indicating a loss than a win (Bartussek et al., 1993). The data appear consistent with the prediction that extraverts show larger reactivity to stimuli associated with reward than to stimuli associated with

punishment due to the activation of the BAS, whereas the opposite pattern will be found for introverts due to the activation of the BIS (Gray, 1982; Gray et al., 2000).

P3

The P3 amplitude elicited during the oddball paradigm and other similar tasks is smaller in extraverts than in introverts (Daruna et al., 1985; Polich et al., 1992; Pritchard, 1989; Wilson and Languis, 1990) and is likely to reflect the reduced attentional engagement in extraverts. Extraversion may also be related to the habituation of P3 amplitude across trials in that extraverts have displayed a greater decrease in P3 amplitude to the infrequent target stimuli across trial blocks than introverts (Ditraglia and Polich, 1991). Longer P3 latency has also been associated with higher levels of extraversion in a category matching and a same–different judgment task (Stelmack et al., 1993), a simple RT task (Doucet and Stelmack, 2000), and a reaction time task that varied stimulus and response location (Brebner, 1990). In contrast to these findings, P3 amplitude has been found to be greater in extraverts than in introverts (Cahill and Polich, 1992; Gurrera et al., 2001, 2005). Others investigations have found no relationship between extraversion and P3 (Ditraglia et al., 1991; Plooij-van Gorsel, 1981; Pritchard, 1989). One interpretation for the inconsistent pattern of results is that it reflects features of the experimental procedure. For instance, if extraverts habituate more rapidly to repetitive stimuli than introverts do (Ditraglia et al., 1991; Polich et al., 1992), different results may emerge depending on the number of trials used in the experiment (Gurrera et al., 2005). The use of community samples may also be more likely to yield a relationship than undergraduate student samples due to a greater range of extraversion scores in such samples (Gurrera et al., 2001).

The P3 elicited following the presentation of emotionally toned words may also vary as a function of extraversion for the same reasons that extraversion should be related to affective startle modulation. Bartussek et al. (1996, experiment 1) found that a complex relationship emerged when emotionally toned and neutral words were presented during a structural processing task, requiring a decision about whether a word is longer or shorter than six letters, and an affective processing task, requiring a rating of the affective valence of emotionally toned words. In extraverts, P3 amplitudes during the structural processing task showed a maximum amplitude at parietal electrode sites and a larger amplitude for pleasant and unpleasant words than neutral words. The difference between the emotionally toned and neutral words became less pronounced at a central electrode and was not present at a frontal electrode. In contrast, introverts showed higher P3 amplitudes during the emotionally toned words than during the neutral words at a parietal site only during the affective processing task. The results seem to indicate that extraverts reacted differentially to the emotional arousal associated with the words even in a task that did not require attention to be directed towards the emotional content. For the introverts, P3 amplitude at a frontal electrode was also larger to unpleasant and neutral words than to pleasant words, a result consistent with Gray's theory of an increased sensitivity of the BIS, and thus greater reactivity to stimuli associated with punishment. In a similar vein, results from the gambling task described above found that extraverts showed larger P3 amplitudes after a loss in the preceding trial, compared to winnings (Bartussek et al., 1993). The opposite was true for the introverts as P3 amplitude was larger when having won in the preceding trial than after a loss (Bartussek et al., 1993). Signals presented after a win may have been perceived as more negative as participants were likely to expect that the next trial would be a loss because an equal number of trials resulted in a win and loss. Likewise, signals presented after a loss were interpreted as positive because participants expected that the next trial would result in a win (Bartussek et al., 1993). Based on this interpretation of the meaning of the signals, the greater P3 amplitudes to signals presented after a loss for extraverts and greater P3 amplitudes to signals presented after a win in introverts is consistent with Gray's theory.

fMRI

The link between extraversion and functional MRI reactivity has been most systematically studied by Canli and colleagues (Canli, 2004; Canli et al., 2001, 2002, 2004). In a first study (Canli et al., 2001) they showed that the neural representation of personality traits may be widely distributed throughout the brain. In 15 different brain regions extraversion from the NEO-PI showed a significant correlation to an increase in the fMRI BOLD signal that was selective to pleasant images from the IAPS contrasted to unpleasant images. Two regions clearly stood out: the amygdala and the anterior cingulate cortex (ACC). Differential activation of these regions in extraverts has since then been replicated in different task settings (Amin et al., 2004; Canli et al., 2002). The larger response of the amygdala to pleasant IAPS pictures (Canli et al., 2001) as well as happy facial expressions (Canli et al., 2002) in extraverts is of particular interest because this structure had been primarily associated with the processing of negative affect. Indeed, as we saw, neuroticism increases the amygdala response to negatively valenced stimuli. Canli et al. (2002) clearly showed that the extraversion also influences this structure, albeit only during the processing of positive affect. Interestingly, the activation of the amygdala was left-lateralized; that is, located within the hemisphere that has been associated with positive emotions and with approach-related behavior in the EEG asymmetry literature (Davidson et al., 2000).

Because the ACC has been associated with attention to emotional stimuli (Whalen et al., 1998) the finding of larger ACC reactivity in response to pleasant stimuli would be compatible with the hypothesized attentional bias for reward stimuli in extraverted subjects (Derryberry and Reed, 1994). However, some caution is in order with the interpretation of ACC reactivity as purely reflecting the activation of an attentional system. Critchley and colleagues have repeatedly shown that the ACC is activated by afferent and efferent activity of the autonomic nervous system (Critchley, 2003; Critchley et al., 2000, 2004, 2005). The autonomic nervous system is activated by any form of arousal, either related to fear, anger, or excitement. The larger ACC reactivity seen in extraverts may therefore also reflect a greater arousability. That this greater arousability is selective to pleasant stimuli would fit the hypothesized higher sensitivity to reward in extraverts.

In keeping, extraversion has been linked to activity in the mesolimbic dopaminergic reward processing system running from the ventral tegmental area to the lateral hypothalamus, the ventral striatum (most prominently the nucleus accumbens) and parts of the medial prefrontal cortex (Knutson and Bhanji, et al., 2006). To test reactivity of this system with fMRI recordings, Knutson et al. (2001, 2003, 2006) developed a monetary incentive-processing task in which participants see a cue indicating whether they can gain or avoid losing money and how much is at stake. After a short delay subjects must rapidly respond to a presented target. Feedback on their success (i.e. were they fast enough?) is immediate and they are presented with the amount lost or gained and their cumulative total. Functional MRI recording during this task showed that potential losses only activated the thalamus and caudate nucleus, but that the nucleus accumbens was additionally activated by the anticipation of potential gain. Large individual differences in the degree of nucleus accumbens activation were found that corresponded to the subjectively experienced cue-elicited happiness in this study and to excitement in another study (Bjork et al., 2004). Activation of the nucleus accumbens was selective to gain anticipation rather than gain outcome, since the increase in BOLD fMRI signal intensity ceased after feedback of success (Knutson et al., 2001). In contrast, gain outcome, but not gain anticipation, did engage the medial prefrontal cortex (Knutson et al., 2003). Pooling across their studies extraversion was found to correlate with activation in the nucleus accumbens, medial caudate, and MPFC for gain versus non-gain anticipation, but not to loss versus non-loss anticipation (Knutson et al., 2006). The larger reactivity of these areas in extraversion was corroborated by another study (Cohen et al., 2005), although in this study reward evaluation rather than reward anticipation seemed to be more important.

The effects of extraversion on brain functioning are not limited to affective processing but are also evident during cognitive processing (Kumari et al., 2004; Stenberg et al., 1990). One study examined the influence of extraversion in fMRI activity during an 'n-back' task involving memory loads (0-, 1-, 2-, and 3-back) and a rest condition in healthy men (Kumari et al., 2004). As predicted by Eysenck, maintaining adequate cognitive performance required a larger increase in cortical arousal in the extraverts as evidenced by greater changes in fMRI signal intensity from rest to the 3-back condition in the ACC and the dorsolateral prefrontal cortex. In further keeping with the neurobiological underpinnings of Eysenck's model, higher extraversion scores were negatively associated with resting fMRI signals in the bilateral thalamus, cuneus and left hemisphere language areas, suggesting lower baseline arousal in these areas, possibly due to extraverts engaging in less internal self-talk than introverts.

DISCUSSION

The above review identified a number of theoretically meaningful and reproducible correlations between psychophysiological measures and personality traits measured by some of the major questionnaires used in the field (Carver and White, 1994; Cloninger et al., 1991; Costa and McCrae, 1992; Eysenck and Eysenck, 1994). Neuroticism and related traits have been related to larger startle modulation during fear eliciting scenes (Caseras et al., 2006; Wilson et al., 2000). These findings are in accord with Eysenck's notion of hypervigilance to threat/danger in these individuals. Such hypervigilance is also compatible with the gist of studies comparing fMRI responses in low and high neurotic subjects. These studies tended to converge on areas involved in the processing of stimuli signaling conflict threat or disgust; that is, the amygdala, the insula, and the ACC (Canli et al., 2002; Eisenberger et al., 2005; Paulus et al., 2003). Research on extraversion has shown that introverts are generally more reactive with startle amplitude than extraverts, with or without instructions to attend (Blumenthal, 2001). Furthermore, trial-by-trial habituation of the startle reflex is more rapid in extraverts. The N2 amplitude of extraverts was found to be more positive when the signal indicates a win than when the signal indicates a loss whereas the opposite pattern is found for introverts. This is consistent with the prediction that extraverts compared to introverts will show larger reactivity to stimuli associated with reward than to stimuli associated with punishment. In keeping, functional MRI studies have found extraversion to correlate with the extent of activation in the nucleus accumbens, medial caudate, and MPFC in gain versus non-gain anticipation trials (Knutson et al., 2006) and with the extent of activation in the nucleus accumbens and MPFC in response to actual reward (Cohen et al., 2005). Pleasant stimuli (e.g. happy faces) only engage the amygdala and the anterior cingulate cortex (ACC) in extraverts (Amin et al., 2004; Canli et al., 2002).

In summary, despite small sample sizes and the absence of special subject selection in most studies, significant correlations exist between psychophysiological reactivity and paper-and-pencil-based assessment of personality. These correlations are generally modest but reach into the range of large effects sizes ($r > 0.70$) where up to half of the variance in evoked EMG, EEG, or fMRI activity and self-reported personality derives from a shared underlying factor. Note, however, that

we can also turn that argument around: a large part of the variance in paper-and-pencil-based personality is not shared with psychophysiological reactivity. This raises the question of which of these types of measures best captures the theoretical construct of personality. Before we can compare their relative merit, psychophysiological indices must first be subjected to the same rigorous psychometric demands as paper-and-pencil tests. Put otherwise, they must be shown to have good test–retest reliability, validly index the brain processes they claim to index (construct validity) and to predict behavior across a wide range of situation (predictive validity). This is a huge challenge, both in terms of person-power and finance, because the complexities in the data acquisition and data analysis in psychophysiological research often reduce the sample size to very small numbers, particularly when compared with questionnaire based research.

The test–retest reliability for some psychophysiological measures has been shown to be moderate to high. For instance, good to excellent reliability has been reported for the P3 (Smit et al. in press), fMRI activation during memory encoding (Aron et al., 2006; Wagner et al., 2005), and the habituation and prepulse inhibition of the startle eye-blink reflex (Abel et al., 1998; Flaten, 2002). However, it has been disappointingly low for other measures, including affective startle modulation (Anokhin et al., 2007), EEG asymmetry (Smit et al., 2007), and fMRI activation during a working memory task (Manoach et al., 2001). This may be due to the inherent complexity of signal generation, flaws in recording techniques and strategies, or a failure to standardize testing conditions (e.g. stimuli, instructions, participant-experimenter interaction), all of which can reduce reliability.

Based on a large body of experimental studies in animals and neurological patients, the construct validity of brain activity as the basis for behavioral tendencies is very large (Kandel et al., 2000). However, there is no perfect one-to-one mapping of psychophysiological indices on brain activity. Although the temporal resolution of EEG recordings is excellent, it is hard to estimate the exact sources in the brain generating the observed patterns of electrical activity. This so-called inverse problem arises because an infinite number of possible charge distributions in the head could lead to the same pattern on the scalp. Although clever modeling techniques have been successfully used to tackle this problem, signals that arise from more than a few dipoles remain hard to localize with precision. Localization of the source of brain activity is much better with fMRI than with EEG, but the relation between the recorded signal (blood oxygenation) and underlying neural activity remains a matter of debate. Although it is commonly assumed that it represents excitatory neural activity, there is disagreement about whether it cannot also represent inhibitory neural activity (Waldvogel et al., 2000). Second, an increase in activation during one condition is equivalent to a decrease during the other condition. What is interpreted as an increase in activation to pleasant pictures, for instance, could instead have represented a decrease in activation to unpleasant pictures. Finally, correlation does not equal causation. A brain region that is activated during a task may not play a critical role in the task's performance. The region may merely be 'listening in' to the activity in other brain areas that constitute the true sources of individual differences.

To date surprisingly little is known about the predictive validity of psychophysiological reactivity. There are a number of studies showing predictive validity of psychophysiological reactivity to the development of psychopathology; for example, in the areas of schizophrenia (Keshavan et al., 2005) and alcoholism (Hill and Shen, 2002). However, this literature is much less well developed than that for paper-and-pencil measures of personality that are known to significantly predict anxiety disorders, depression, drug abuse, and antisocial behavior (Cloninger et al., 2006; Masse and Tremblay, 1997). Also, no studies known to us have addressed the predictive validity of psychophysiology for lifestyle parameters (smoking, exercise, sexual practices) or behavioral outcomes like career choices or job success.

In short, reliability of psychophysiological measures is currently less convincing than those for paper-and-pencil measures and validity has been far more rigorously tested for the latter. It is of note, however, that many of the studies reviewed here have silently adopted the stance that a *single* psychophysiological measure should index personality. This makes for an unfair comparison to paper-and-pencil tests that use multiple weighed items to arrive at a summary score. We believe a large increase in reliability and validity of a psychophysiological test battery could be achieved by looking at patterns of psychophysiological responding on multiple measures and to multiple types of stimuli rather than a single measure on a single class of stimuli. Ideally, multiple psychophysiological responses (ECG, SCL ERP, and fMRI) would need to be recorded consecutively, or even more ideally simultaneously, in the same subject in response to various classes of stimuli (e.g. emotional pictures, reward, and punishment). The response of each measure to each particular class of stimuli can be considered a single psychophysiological 'item'. These items would be subjected to factor analyses just as the items of personality inventories to obtain a factor structure and ultimately sum scores. Indeed 'ordinary' items for a personality inventory may be merged with psychophysiological items to obtain a hybrid 'subjective/objective' personality measure. This has the potential to anchor the new personality measure to the large existing theoretical framework based on paper-and-pencil while adding biological foundation. Therefore, rather than pitch psychophysiological recordings as more scientific alternatives to paper-and-pencil assessment, we propose to use these measurements as a way to support theory-building on the neurobiological basis of personality.

Implications for neuroscience

Although much work remains, the psychophysiological studies on personality research reviewed in this chapter already convey a very important message to the field of neuroscience. Mainstream neuroscience is still very much focused on universal affective and cognitive brain processes at the expense of individual differences (Kosslyn et al., 2002; Plomin and Kosslyn, 2001). By not taking individual differences into account, or considering them a mere nuisance variable, many neuroscience studies may have failed to detect a link between a brain structure and the putative affective and cognitive processes in which it is involved. It had, for instance, been assumed from group fMRI recordings that the amygdala is not involved in the processing of stimuli with a positive emotional value. By bringing personality into the equation, Canli et al. (2002) have proven this wrong. The amygdala does strongly influence such processing, but its total activation is a function of the level of extraversion. In short, by not taking personality differences into account, neuroscience runs the risk of presenting us with 'universal processes' in affect and cognition that reflect the average pattern of brain activity across many individuals, but do not really occur in any single individual.

REFERENCES

Abel, K., Waikar, M., Pedro, B., Hemsley, D. and Geyer, M. (1998) 'Repeated testing of prepulse inhibition and habituation of the startle reflex: A study in healthy human controls', *Journal of Psychopharmacology*, 12: 330–37.

Akdag, S.J., Nestor, P.G., O'Donnell, B.F., Niznikiewicz, M.A., Shenton, M.E. and McCarley, R.W. (2003) 'The startle reflex in schizophrenia: Habituation and personality correlates', *Schizophrenia Research*, 64(2-3): 165–73.

Allen, J.J., Coan, J.A. and Nazarian, M. (2004) 'Issues and assumptions on the road from raw signals to metrics of frontal EEG asymmetry in emotion', *Biological Psychology*, 67(1-2): 183–218.

Amin, Z., Constable, R.T. and Canli, T. (2004) 'Attentional bias for valenced stimuli as a function of personality in the dot-probe task', *Journal of Research in Personality*, 38(1): 15–23.

Anokhin, A.P., Golosheykin, S. and Heath, A.C. (2007) 'Genetic and environmental influences on emotion-modulated startle reflex: A twin study', *Psychophysiology*, 44(1): 106–12.

Aron, A.R., Gluck, M.A. and Poldrack, R.A. (2006) 'Long-term test–retest reliability of functional MRI in a classification learning task', *Neuroimage*, 29(3): 1000–6.

Bartussek, D., Becker, G., Diedrich, O., Naumann, E. and Maier, S. (1996) 'Extraversion, neuroticism, and event-related brain potentials in response to emotional stimuli', *Personality and Individual Differences*, 20(3): 301–12.

Bartussek, D., Diedrich, O., Naumann, E. and Collet, W. (1993) 'Introversion extroversion and event-related potential (Erp) – A test of Gray, J.A. theory', *Personality and Individual Differences*, 14(4): 565–74.

Bjork, J.M., Knutson, B., Fong, G.W., Caggiano, D.M., Bennett, S.M. and Hommer, D.W. (2004) 'Incentive-elicited brain activation in adolescents: Similarities and differences from young adults', *Journal of Neuroscience*, 24(8): 1793–802.

Blumenthal, T.D. (2001) 'Extraversion, attention, and startle response reactivity', *Personality and Individual Differences*, 31(4): 495–503.

Blumenthal, T.D., Chapman, J.G. and Muse, K.B. (1995) 'Effects of social anxiety, attention, and extraversion on the acoustic startle eyeblink response', *Personality and Individual Differences*, 19(6): 797–807.

Blumenthal, T.D., Cuthbert, B.N., Filion, D.L., Hackley, S., Lipp, O.V. and van Boxtel, A. (2005) 'Committee report: Guidelines for human startle eyeblink electromyographic studies', *Psychophysiology*, 42(1): 1–15.

Brebner, J. (1990) 'Psychological and neurophysiological factors in stimulus-response compatibility', in R.W. Proctor and T.G. Reeves (eds), *Stimulus–response Compatibility*. Amsterdam: Elsevier, pp. 241–60.

Britt, T.W. and Blumenthal, T.D. (1991) 'Motoneuronal insensitivity in extraverts as revealed by the startle response paradigm', *Personality and Individual Differences*, 12(5): 387–93.

Cahill and Polich, J. (1992) 'P300, probability, and introverted/extraverted personality types', *Biological Psychology*, 33(1): 23–35.

Canli, T. (2004) 'Functional brain mapping of extraversion and neuroticism: Learning from individual differences in emotion processing', *Journal of Personality*, 72(6): 1105–32.

Canli, T., Amin, Z., Haas, B., Omura, K. and Constable, R.T. (2004) 'A double dissociation between mood states and personality traits in the anterior cingulate', *Behavioral Neuroscience*, 118(5): 897–904.

Canli, T., Sivers, H., Whitfield, S.L., Gotlib, I.H. and Gabrieli, J.D. (2002) 'Amygdala response to happy faces as a function of extraversion', *Science*, 296(5576): 2191.

Canli, T., Zhao, Z., Desmond, J.E., Kang, E., Gross, J. and Gabrieli, J.D. (2001) 'An fMRI study of personality influences on brain reactivity to emotional stimuli', *Behavioral Neuroscience*, 115(1): 33–42.

Carver, C.S. and White, T.L. (1994) 'Behavioral-inhibition, behavioral activation, and affective responses to impending reward and punishment – the Bis Bas Scales', *Journal of Personality and Social Psychology*, 67(2): 319–33.

Caseras, F.X., Fullana, M.A., Riba, J., Barbanoj, M.J., Aluja, A. and Torrubia, R. (2006) 'Influence of individual differences in the Behavioural Inhibition System and stimulus content (fear versus blood-disgust) on affective startle reflex modulation', *Biological Psychology*, 72(3): 251–6.

Cloninger, C.R., Przybeck, T.R. and Svrakic, D.M. (1991) 'The Tridimensional Personality Questionnaire: US normative data', *Psychological Reports*, 69(3pt1): 1047–57.

Cloninger, C.R., Svrakic, D.M. and Przybeck, T.R. (2006) 'Can personality assessment predict future depression? A twelve-month follow-up of 631 subjects', *Journal of Affective Disorders*, 92(1): 35–44.

Coan, J.A. and Allen, J.J. (2004) 'Frontal EEG asymmetry as a moderator and mediator of emotion', *Biological Psychology*, 67(1–2): 7–49.

Coan, J.A., Allen, J.J. and McKnight, P.E. (2006) 'A capability model of individual differences in frontal EEG asymmetry', *Biological Psychology*, 72(2): 198–207.

Cohen, M.X., Young, J., Baek, J.M., Kessler, C. and Ranganath, C. (2005) 'Individual differences in extraversion and dopamine genetics predict neural reward responses', *Cognitive Brain Research*, 25(3): 851–61.

Corr, P.J., Tynan, A. and Kumari, V. (2002) 'Personality correlates of prepulse inhibition of the startle reflex at three lead intervals', *Journal of Psychophysiology*, 16(2): 82–91.

Corr, P.J., Wilson, G.D., Fotiadou, M., Kumari, V., Gray, N.S., Checkley, S.A. et al. (1995) 'Personality and affective modulation of the startle reflex. *Personality and Individual Differences*, 19(4): 543–53.

Costa, P.T. and McCrae (1992) *Professional Manual of the revised NEO Personality Inventory (NEO-PI-R) and NEO Five Factor Inventory (NEO-FFI)*. Odessa, FL: Psychological Assessment Resources.

Critchley, H. (2003) 'Emotion and its disorders', *British Medical Bulletin*, 65: 35–47.

Critchley, H.D., Elliott, R., Mathias, C.J. and Dolan, R.J. (2000) 'Neural activity relating to generation and representation of galvanic skin conductance responses: A functional magnetic resonance imaging study', *Journal of Neuroscience*, 20(8): 3033–40.

Critchley, H.D., Tang, J., Glaser, D., Butterworth, B. and Dolan, R.J. (2005) 'Anterior cingulate activity during error and autonomic response', *Neuroimage*, 27(4): 885–95.

Critchley, H.D., Wiens, S., Rotshtein, P., Ohman, A. and Dolan, R.J. (2004) 'Neural systems supporting interoceptive awareness', *Nature Neuroscience*, 7(2): 189–95.

Damasio, A.R. (1999) *The Feeling of What Happens: Body and Emotion in the Making of Consciousness*. New York: Harcourt Brace.

Daruna, J.H., Karrer, R. and Rosen, A.J. (1985) 'Introversion, attention, and the late positive component of event-related potentials', *Biological Psychology*, 20(4): 249–59.

Davidson, R.J. (1998) 'Affective style and affective disorders: Perspectives from affective neuroscience', *Cognition and Emotion*, 12(3): 307–30.

Davidson, R.J. (2004) 'What does the prefrontal cortex "do" in affect: Perspectives on frontal EEG asymmetry research', *Biological Psychology*, 67(1–2): 219–33.

Davidson, R.J., Jackson, D.C. and Kalin, N.H. (2000) 'Emotion, plasticity, context, and regulation: Perspectives from affective neuroscience', *Psychological Bulletin*, 126(6): 890–909.

Davidson, R.J., Schaffer, C.E. and Saron, C. (1985) 'Effects of lateralized presentations of faces on self-reports of emotion and EEG asymmetry in depressed and non-depressed subjects', *Psychophysiology*, 22(3): 353–64.

Davis, M., Walker, D.L. and Lee, Y. (1999) 'Neurophysiology and neuropharmacology of startle and its affective modulation', in M.E. Dawson, A.M. Schell and A.H. Bohmelt (eds), *Startle Modification: Implications for Neuroscience, Cognitive Science, and Clinical Science*. Cambridge, Cambridge University Press, pp. 54–9.

De Pascalis V., and Montirosso R., (1988) 'Extraversion (neuroticism and individual differences) in event-related potentials', *Personality and Individual Differences*. 9: 353–60.

De Pascalis, V. (1993) 'Hemispheric asymmetry, personality and temperament', *Personality and Individual Differences*, 14(6): 825–34.

De Pascalis, V., Fiore, A.D. and Sparita, A. (1996) 'Personality, event-related potential (ERP) and heart rate (HR): An investigation of Gray's theory', *Personality and Individual Differences*, 20(6): 733–46.

Dehaene, S., Posner, M.I. and Tucker, D.M. (1994) 'Localization of a neural system for error detection and compensation', *Psychological Science*, 5(5): 303–5.

Derryberry, D. and Reed, M.A. (1994) 'Temperament and the self-organization of personality', *Development and Psychopathology*, 6(4): 653–76.

Ditraglia, G.M. and Polich, J. (1991) 'P300 and introverted/extraverted personality types', *Psychophysiology*, 28(2): 177–84.

Doucet and Stelmack, R.M. (2000) 'An event-related potential analysis of extraversion and individual differences in cognitive processing speed and response execution', *Journal of Personality and Social Psychology*, 78(5): 956–64.

Drevets, W.C. (2001) 'Neuroimaging and neuropathological studies of depression: Implications for the cognitive-emotional features of mood disorders', *Current Opinion in Neurobiology*, 11(2): 240–49.

Ebmeier, K.P., Deary, I.J., Ocarroll, R.E., Prentice, N., Moffoot, A.P.R. and Goodwin, G.M. (1994) 'Personality associations with the uptake of the cerebral blood-flow marker (99m)Tc-exametazime estimated with single-photon emission tomography', *Personality and Individual Differences*, 17(5): 587–95.

Eisenberger, N.I., Lieberman, M.D. and Satpute, A.B. (2005) 'Personality from a controlled processing perspective: An fMRI study of neuroticism, extraversion, and self-consciousness', *Cognitive and Affective Behavioral Neuroscience*, 5(2): 169–81.

Ekman, P. and Friesen, W. (1978) *The Facial Action Coding System*. Palo Alto, CA: Consulting Psychologists Press.

Etkin, A., Klemenhagen, K.C., Dudman, J.T., Rogan, M.T., Hen, R., Kandel, E.R. et al. (2004) 'Individual differences in trait anxiety predict the response of the basolateral amygdala to unconsciously processed fearful faces', *Neuron*, 44(6): 1043–55.

Eysenck, H.J. (1967) *The Biological Basis of Personality*. Springfield, IL: Thomas.

Eysenck, H.J. (1990) 'Biological dimensions of personality', in L.A.Pervin (ed.), *Handbook of Personality: Theory and Research*. New York: Guilford, pp. 100–2.

Eysenck, H.J. and Eysenck, M.W. (1985) *Personality and Individual Differences*. New York: Plenum Press.

Eysenck, H.J. and Eysenck, S.B.G. (1994) *Eysenck Personality Questionnaire – Revised*. San Diego: Educational and Industrial Testing Service.

Fabiani, M., Gratton, G. and Coles, M.G. (2000) 'Event-related brain potentials', in J.T. Cacioppo, L.G. Tassinary and G. Berntson (eds), *Handbook of Psychophysiology* (2nd edn). Cambridge: Cambridge University Press, pp. 53–84.

Filion D.L., Dawson M.E., Schell A.M. et al. (1994). 'Probing the Orienting Response with Startle Modification and Secondary Reaction-Time', *Psychophysiology*, 31(1): 68–78.

Fjell, A.M., Walhovd, K.B., Meling, S. and Johansen, M.B. (2005) 'Basic information processing of neurotics and stable: An experimental ERP approach to personality and distractibility', *Scandinavian Journal of Psychology*, 46(6): 493–502.

Flaten, M.A. (2002) 'Test–retest reliability of the somatosensory blink reflex and its inhibition', *International Journal of Psychophysiology*, 45(3): 261–5.

Fox, N.A. (1991) 'If it's not left, it's right. Electroencephalograph asymmetry and the development of emotion', *American Psychologist*, 46(8): 863–72.

Gottesmann, C., Gandolfo, G. and Zernicki, B. (1995) 'Sleep-waking cycle in chronic rat preparations with brain stem transected at the caudopontine level', *Brain Research Bulletin*, 36(6): 573–80.

Graham, F.K. (1979) 'Distinguishing among orienting, defence, and startle reflexes', in H.D. Kimmel, E.H. van Olst and J.F. Orlebeke (eds), *The Orienting Reflex in Humans*. Hillsdale, NJ: Erlbaum, pp. 137–67.

Gray, J.A. (1982) *The Neuropsychology of Anxiety: An Enquiry into the Functions of the Septo-hippocampal System*. Oxford: Oxford University Press.

Gray, J.A. and McNaughton, N. (2000) *The Neuropsychology of Anxiety: An Enquiry into the Functions of the Septo-hippocampal System* (2nd edn). Oxford: Oxford University Press.

Gurrera, R.J., O'Donnell, B.F., Nestor, P.G., Gainski, J. and McCarley, R.W. (2001) 'The P3 auditory event-related brain potential indexes major personality traits', *Biological Psychiatry*, 49(11): 922–9.

Gurrera, R.J., Salisbury, D.F., O'Donnell, B.F., Nestor, P.G. and McCarley, R.W. (2005) 'Auditory P3 indexes personality traits and cognitive function in healthy men and women', *Psychiatry Research*, 133(2–3): 215–28.

Guyer, A.E., Nelson, E.E., Perez-Edgar, K., Hardin, M.G., Roberson-Nay, R., Monk, C.S. et al. (2006) 'Striatal functional alteration in adolescents characterized by early childhood behavioral inhibition', *Journal of Neuroscience*, 26(24): 6399–405.

Hagemann, D. (2004) 'Individual differences in anterior EEG asymmetry: Methodological problems and solutions', *Biological Psychology*, 67(1–2): 157–82.

Hawk, L.W. Jr. and Kowmas, A.D. (2003) 'Affective modulation and prepulse inhibition of startle among undergraduates high and low in behavioral inhibition and approach', *Psychophysiology*, 40(1): 131–8.

Hewig, J., Hagemann, D., Seifert, J., Naumann, E. and Bartussek, D. (2006) 'The relation of cortical activity and BIS/BAS on the trait level', *Biological Psychology*, 71(1): 42–53.

Hill, S.Y. and Shen, S. (2002) 'Neurodevelopmental patterns of visual P3b in association with familial risk for alcohol dependence and childhood diagnosis', *Biological Psychiatry*, 51(8): 621–31.

Holroyd, C.B. and Coles, M.G. (2002) 'The neural basis of human error processing: Reinforcement learning, dopamine, and the error-related negativity', *Psychological Review*, 109(4): 679–709.

Kandel, E.R., Schwartz, H.S. and Jessel, T.M. (2000) *Principles of Neural Science* (4th edn). New York: McGraw-Hill.

Kaviani, H., Gray, J.A., Checkley, S.A., Kumari, V. and Wilson, G.D. (1999) 'Modulation of the acoustic startle reflex by emotionally-toned film clips', *International Journal of Psychophysiology*, 32(1): 47–54.

Keshavan, M.S., Diwadkar, V.A., Montrose, D.M., Rajarethinam, R. and Sweeney, J.A. (2005) 'Premorbid indicators and risk for schizophrenia: A selective review and update', *Schizophrenia Research*, 79(1): 45–57.

Knutson, B. and Bhanji, J. (2006) 'Neural substrates for emotional traits? The case of extraversion', in T.Canli (ed.), *Biology of Personality and Individual Differences*. New York: Guilford, pp. 116–32.

Knutson, B., Fong, G.W., Adams, C.M., Varner, J.L. and Hommer, D. (2001) 'Dissociation of reward anticipation and outcome with event-related fMRI', *Neuroreport*, 12(17): 3683–7.

Knutson, B., Fong, G.W., Bennett, S.M., Adams, C.M. and Hommer, D. (2003) 'A region of mesial prefrontal cortex tracks monetarily rewarding outcomes: Characterization with rapid event-related fMRI', *Neuroimage*, 18(2): 263–72.

Kosslyn, S.M., Cacioppo, J.T., Davidson, R.J., Hugdahl, K., Lovallo, W.R., Spiegel, D.et al. (2002) 'Bridging psychology and biology. The analysis of individuals in groups', *American Psychologist*, 57(5): 341–51.

Kumari, V., Corr, P.J., Wilson, G.D., Kaviani, H., Thornton, J.C., Checkley, S.A. et al. (1996) 'Personality and modulation of the startle reflex by emotionally-toned filmclips', *Personality and Individual Differences*, 21(6): 1029–41.

Kumari, V., Ffytche, D.H., Williams, S.C. and Gray, J.A. (2004) 'Personality predicts brain responses to cognitive demands', *Journal of Neuroscience*, 24(47): 10636–41.

Lang, P.J., Bradley, M.M. and Cuthbert, B.N. (1997) 'Motivated attention: Affect, activation, and action', in P.J. Lang, R.F. Simons and M.T. Balaban (eds), *Attention and Orienting*. Cliffside, NJ: Lawrence Erlbaum, pp. 97–136.

Lang, P.J., Bradley, M.M. and Cuthbert, B.N. (1998) 'Emotion, motivation, and anxiety: Brain mechanisms and psychophysiology', *Biological Psychiatry*, 44(12): 1248–63.

Lang, P.J., Bradley, M.M. and Cuthbert, B.N. (2001) *International Affective Picture System*. Gainesville: Center for Reserach in Psychophysiology, University of Florida.

LaRowe, S.D., Patrick, C.J., Curtin, J.J. and Kline, J.P. (2006) 'Personality correlates of startle habituation', *Biological Psychology*, 72(3): 257–64.

Luu, P., Collins, P. and Tucker, D.M. (2000) 'Mood, personality, and self-monitoring: Negative affect and emotionality in relation to frontal lobe mechanism of error monitoring', *Journal of Experimental Psychology: General*: 129(1): 43–60.

Manoach, D.S., Halpern, E.F., Kramer, T.S., Chang, Y., Goff, D.C., Rauch, S.L. et al. (2001) 'Test–retest reliability of a functional MRI working memory paradigm in normal and schizophrenic subjects', *American Journal of Psychiatry*, 158(6): 955–8.

Masse, L.C. and Tremblay, R.E. (1997) 'Behavior of boys in kindergarten and the onset of substance use during adolescence', *Archives of General Psychiatry*, 54(1): 62–8.

Mischel, W. and Shoda, Y. (1995) 'A cognitive-affective system-theory of personality – reconceptualizing situations, dispositions, dynamics, and invariance in personality structure', *Psychological Review*, 102(2): 246–68.

Most, S.B., Chun, M.M., Johnson, M.R. and Kiehl, K.A. (2006) 'Attentional modulation of the amygdala varies with personality', *Neuroimage*, 31(2): 934–44.

Neumann, D.L. (2002) 'Effect of varying levels of mental workload on startle eyeblink modulation', *Ergonomics*, 45(8): 583–602.

Neumann, D.L., Lipp, O.V. and Mchugh, M.J. (2004) 'The effect of stimulus modality and task difficulty on attentional modulation of blink startle', *Psychophysiology*, 41(3): 407–16.

Ochsner, K.N., Bunge, S.A., Gross, J.J. and Gabrieli, J.D. (2002) 'Rethinking feelings: An FMRI study of the cognitive regulation of emotion', *Journal of Cognitive Neuroscience*, 14(8): 1215–29.

Paulus, M.P., Rogalsky, C., Simmons, A., Feinstein, J.S. and Stein, M.B. (2003) 'Increased activation in the right insula during risk-taking decision making is related to harm avoidance and neuroticism', *Neuroimage*, 19(4): 1439–48.

Plomin, R. and Kosslyn, S.M. (2001) 'Genes, brain and cognition', *Nature Neuroscience*, 4(12): 1153–5.

Plooij-van Gorsel, E. (1981) 'EEG and cardiac correlates of neuroticism: A psychophysiological comparison of neurotics and normal controls in relation to personality', *Biological Psychology*, 13: 141–56.

Polich, J. and Martin, S. (1992) 'P300, cognitive capability and personality: A correlational study of university undergraduates', *Personality and Individual Differences*, 13(5): 533–43.

Pritchard, W.S. (1989) 'P300 and EPQ/STPI personality traits', *Personality and Individual Differences*, 10(1): 15–24.

Santesso, D.L., Segalowitz, S.J. and Schmidt, L.A. (2005) 'ERP correlates of error monitoring in 10-year olds are related to socialization', *Biological Psychology*, 70(2): 79–87.

Sapolsky, R.M., Krey, L.C. and McEwen, B.S. (1986) 'The neuroendocrinology of stress and aging: The glucocorticoid cascade hypothesis', *Endocrinology Reviews*, 7(3): 284–301.

Schwartz, C.E., Wright, C.I., Shin, L.M., Kagan, J., Whalen, P.J., McMullin, K.G. et al. (2003) 'Differential amygdalar response to novel versus newly familiar neutral faces: A functional MRI probe developed for studying inhibited temperament', *Biological Psychiatry*, 53(10): 854–62.

Smit, D.J., Posthuma, D., Boomsma, D.I. and De Geus, E.J. (2007) 'Genetic contribution to the P3 in young and middle-aged adults', *Twin Research and Human Genetics* 10(2): 335–47.

Smit, D.J., Posthuma, D., Boomsma, D.I. and De Geus, E.J. (2007) 'The relation between frontal EEG asymmetry and the risk for anxiety and depression', *Biological Psychology*, 74(1): 26–33.

Soltani, M. and Knight, R.T. (2000) 'Neural origins of the P300', *Critical Reviews in Neurobiology*, 14(3–4): 199–224.

Stelmack, R.M., Achorn, E. and Michaud, A. (1977) 'Extraversion and individual differences in auditory and evoked responses', *Psychophysiology*, 14(4): 368–74.

Stelmack, R.M. and Houlihan, M. (1995) 'Event-related potentials, personality and intelligence: Concepts, issues and evidence', in D.H. Saklofske and M. Zeidner (eds), *International Handbook of Personality and Intelligence.* New York: Plenum Press.

Stelmack, R.M., Houlihan, M. and McGarry-Roberts, P.A. (1993) 'Personality, reaction time, and event-related potentials', *Journal of Personality and Social Psychology*, 65(2): 399–409.

Stenberg, G., Risberg, J., Warkentin, S. and Rosen, I. (1990) 'Regional patterns of cortical blood-flow distinguish extroverts from introverts', *Personality and Individual Differences*, 11(7): 663–73.

Stenberg, G., Wendt, P.E. and Risberg, J. (1993) 'Regional cerebral blood-flow and extroversion', *Personality and Individual Differences*, 15(5): 547–54.

Sutton, S.K. and Davidson, R.J. (1997) 'Prefrontal brain asymmetry: A biological substrate of the behavioral approach and inhibition systems', *Psychological Science*, 8(3): 204–10.

Swerdlow, N.R., Filion, D., Geyer, M.A. and Braff, D.L. (1995) '"Normal" personality correlates of sensorimotor, cognitive, and visuospatial gating', *Biological Psychiatry*, 37(5): 286–99.

van Veen, V. and Carter, C.S. (2002) 'The timing of action-monitoring processes in the anterior cingulate cortex', *Journal of Cognitive Neuroscience*, 14(4): 593–602.

Wagner, K., Frings, L., Quiske, A., Unterrainer, J., Schwarzwald, R., Spreer, J. et al. (2005) 'The reliability of fMRI activations in the medial temporal lobes in a verbal episodic memory task', *Neuroimage*, 28(1): 122–31.

Waldvogel, D., van Gelderen, P., Muellbacher, W., Ziemann, U., Immisch, I. and Hallett, M. (2000) 'The relative metabolic demand of inhibition and excitation', *Nature*, 406(6799): 995–8.

Wallace, J. (1966) 'An abilities conception of personality – Some implications for personality measurement', *American Psychologist*, 21(2): 132–8.

Watson, D., Clark, L.A. and Tellegen, A. (1988) 'Development and validation of brief measures of positive and negative affect – The Panas scales', *Journal of Personality and Social Psychology*, 54(6): 1063–70.

Whalen, P.J., Bush, G., McNally, R.J., Wilhelm, S., McInerney, S.C., Jenike, M.A. et al. (1998) 'The emotional counting Stroop paradigm: A functional magnetic resonance imaging probe of the anterior cingulate affective division', *Biological Psychiatry*, 44(12): 1219–28.

Wilson, G.D., Kumari, V., Gray, J.A. and Corr, P.J. (2000) 'The role of neuroticism in startle reactions to fearful and disgusting stimuli', *Personality and Individual Differences*, 29(6): 1077–82.

Wilson, G.D. and Languis, M.L. (1990) 'A topographic study of differences in the P300 between introverts and extraverts', *Brain Topography*, 2(4): 269–74.

Youn, T., Lyoo, I.K., Kim, J.K., Park, H.J., Ha, K.S., Lee, D.S. et al. (2002) 'Relationship between personality trait and regional cerebral glucose metabolism assessed with positron emission tomography', *Biological Psychology*, 60(2–3): 109–20.

16

Genomic Imaging of Personality: Towards a Molecular Neurobiology of Impulsivity

Eliza Congdon and Turhan Canli

Research on the biological basis of personality has made large leaps forward with the application of noninvasive neuroimaging methods and, most recently, with molecular genetic studies of common variations in genetic nucleotide sequences that are associated with personality traits (Canli, 2004; Canli, 2006a). In this review, we will introduce the reader to these methodologies, as they are applied to investigations of the personality trait of impulsivity. We begin with a discussion of the current limitations of impulsivity as a construct in personality research and in clinical psychology. These limitations motivate research on the biological basis of impulsivity, using both noninvasive neuroimaging and molecular genetic approaches. We will therefore discuss each of these methodologies in turn and highlight their respective contributions to recent discoveries on the biological basis of impulsivity. We will close chapter with a view toward the future, which we suggest will see a theoretically constrained integration of both neural and genetic mechanisms.

IMPULSIVITY AS A CONSTRUCT IN PERSONALITY RESEARCH

Impulsivity in personality assessments and models

Although 'impulsivity' is a commonly used term in both research and clinical settings, it has a broad set of meanings and definitions. Impulsive actions tend to lack forethought or planning and often carry the connotation of being negative in that they are inaccurate or maladaptive. Behavioral manifestations are numerous, such as responding before instructions are given or completed, responding without considering all options, inability to refrain from responding to an inappropriate stimulus, or acting without considering the full set of consequences (Solanto et al., 2001).

Similarly, there is a wide range of impulsivity assessments, reflecting different conceptualizations of the trait. One of the most widely used measures of impulsivity, the Barratt Impulsiveness Scale – version 11 (BIS-11), conceptualizes impulsivity in terms of three components: a nonplanning component, in which the individual does not plan or think carefully; a motor component, characterized by a tendency to act without thinking or an inability to withhold responses; and a cognitive component, characterized by a difficulty in paying attention (Patton et al., 1995). Other instruments focus on a distinction between functional and dysfunctional impulsivity (Dickman Impulsiveness Scale) (Dickman, 1990), the degree of efficiency of information processing in the face of rewarding stimuli ('Lifetime History of Impulsive Behaviors Interview') (Schmidt et al., 2004), or the distinction between conscious and unconscious risk-taking (I-7) (Eysenck et al., 1985).

Given that impulsivity has been conceptualized in different ways, it may not be surprising that influential personality models do not regard impulsivity as a higher-order trait, but rather the combination of other lower-order traits (Evenden, 1999). For example, in Costa and McCrae's five-factor model, impulsivity mostly reflects low conscientiousness (Costa and McCrae, 1992), while in Cloninger's three-factor model, impulsivity reflects a combination of low harm avoidance and high novelty seeking (Cloninger et al., 1993).

The multidimensional nature of impulsivity is more formally revealed with quantitative tools. For example, Flory and colleagues conducted a principal components analysis of impulsivity using a range of personality assessments (Flory et al., 2006). They assessed impulsivity-related traits using the Tridimensional Personality Questionnaire (TPQ)/Temperament and Character Inventory (TCI), the Zuckerman Sensation Seeking scale (SS-V), the Barratt Impulsiveness scale (BIS-11), the NEO Personality Inventory (NEO-PI-R), and the Buss Perry Aggression Questionnaire (BPAQ). Principal component analysis supported a three-factor model, in which nonplanning, disinhibition, and thrill seeking were identified as independent dimensions of impulsivity (Flory et al., 2006).

The complex nature of the impulsivity construct poses a challenge for biological investigations, because different conceptualizations of the trait demand different self-report measures or task paradigms. If there is no higher-order trait of impulsivity, then investigators have to operationalize impulsivity in terms of lower-order behaviors that can more easily be mapped onto neural circuits that may mediate these behaviors. On the other hand, there is a great opportunity for biological investigations to contribute to the development of more sophisticated psychological models of human personality, because they can provide the data that can constrain future models and generate testable hypotheses of how particular aspects of impulsive behavior ought to activate specific neural circuits.

Impulsivity in psychopathology

Impulsive behavior figures prominently in clinical diagnoses of psychopathology. Indeed, impulsivity in its extreme form is associated with a wide range of mental disorders, such as antisocial and borderline personality disorder (Newman, 1997; Links et al., 1999; Conrod et al., 2000; Bagge et al., 2004; Fossati et al., 2004), disorders related to abuse and addiction (Sher et al., 2000), mood disorders (Swann et al., 2003), suicide (Esposito, 2003; Dougherty et al., 2004; Swann et al., 2004; Yen et al., 2004), impulse control disorders (ICDs), and attention-deficit/hyperactivity disorder (ADHD) (Schachar et al., 1993; Barkley, 1997; Beauchaine et al., 2001; Avila et al., 2004; Lijffijt et al., 2005). These disorders affect a large percentage of the general population; even when limiting the analysis to ICDs and ADHD alone, they add up to a 12-month prevalence rate of 8.9% and a lifetime prevalence of 24.8% in the general population (Kessler et al., 2005a, 2005b). Because a comprehensive review of impulsivity in clinical practice is beyond the scope of this chapter, we will only offer a brief overview of some of the major diagnostic categories, in which impulsive behavior constitutes one aspect of the disease symptomatology.

Cluster B personality disorders (PDs) are characterized by impulsivity (Casillas and

Clark, 2002), and most research related to impulsivity has been conducted on two patient populations in particular: those diagnosed with antisocial personality disorder (ASPD) and those diagnosed with borderline personality disorder (BPD). According to the DSM-IV-TR (American Psychiatric Association, 2000), ASPD in adults is characterized by an 'impulsivity or failure to plan ahead'. Indeed, studies looking at the relationship between impulsive personality traits in samples with increased antisocial traits or behaviors (Newman et al., 1997; Conrod et al., 2000; Taylor et al., 2006), and samples with increased aggression (Newman, 1997; Barratt et al., 1999; Stanford, 2003) support the centrality of impulsivity in ASPD or antisocial behaviors. BPD is characterized by 'marked impulsivity beginning by early adulthood and present in a variety of contexts' (American Psychiatric Association, 2000). This impulsivity may manifest 'in atleast two areas that are potentially self-damaging (e.g., spending, sex, substance abuse, reckless driving, binge eating)' or in 'recurrent suicidal behavior, gestures, or threats, or self-mutilating behavior' (American Psychiatric Association, 2000). Support for this comes from reports that impulsivity is predictive of borderline psychopathology and poorer treatment outcome over time, is the most stable of traits associated with BPD, and is the most important distinguishing factor between persistent and remitted BPD individuals (Links et al., 1999; Bagge et al., 2004; Fossati et al., 2004).

Disorders related to abuse and addiction are also characterized by high levels of impulsivity. Although impulsivity is not explicitly listed as a criterion necessary for diagnosis, disorders of abuse and dependence are clearly characterized by deficits in behavioral inhibition. Impulsivity is significantly associated with increased rates of cocaine and alcohol abuse, in addition to higher rates of ASPD (Conrod et al., 2000; Taylor et al., 2006) or cluster BPDs (Dom et al., 2006), and impulsivity has been shown to predict rates of substance– abuse disorders,

cross-sectionally and prospectively (Sher et al., 2000).

Mood disorders, characterized by manic and depressive episodes, are also characterized by impulsivity, particularly during a manic episode (American Psychiatric Association, 2000; Leyton et al., 2001; Swann et al., 2003). However, impulsivity is not limited to manic episodes, but can remain at elevated levels in inter-episode bipolar disorder (Swann et al., 2003). During a depressed episode, patients can become highly impulsive and this often manifests itself in recurrent suicidal ideation or suicide attempts (American Psychiatric Association, 2000). Indeed, suicide potential is highest in bipolar disorder during a depressive or mixed manic episode, and increases further with co-morbid alcohol or substance abuse (Dougherty et al., 2004). In fact, suicide is a serious complication to many of the disorders reviewed here. Although not a diagnostic category in the DSM framework, there is ample evidence relating suicide to elevated impulsivity (Dougherty et al., 2004). For example, the impulsivity criteria for BPD significantly predicts suicidal behaviors (Yen et al., 2004), leading some to suggest that impulsivity is the underlying behavior shared between suicide, substance abuse, bipolar disorder, BPD and ASPD (Dougherty et al., 2004; Swann et al., 2004; Dom et al., 2006).

The prominence of impulsivity in attention-deficit/hyperactivity disorder (ADHD) has meant that a large portion of the literature addressing impulsivity is based on data from ADHD patients. ADHD is a childhood-onset disorder that is primarily characterized by inattention and/or hyperactivity-impulsivity. Impulsivity in ADHD 'manifests itself as impatience, difficulty in delaying responses, blurting out answers before questions have been completed, difficulty awaiting one's turn, and frequently interrupting or intruding on others to the point of causing difficulties in social, academic, or occupational settings' (American Psychiatric Association, 2000). In other words, ADHD is characterized by deficits in inhibition and this is readily seen in behaviors that are most relevant to individuals of this age (Schachar et al., 1993; Barkley, 1997; Beauchaine et al., 2001; Avila et al., 2004; Lijffijt et al., 2005).

Finally, the DSM recognizes a class of disorders that are primarily characterized dysfunction in impulsivity, and therefore named impulse control disorders (ICDs). ICDs include trichotillomania, intermittent explosive disorder (IED), pathological gambling, kleptomania, pyromania, and not otherwise specified (which includes impulsive sexual behaviors, repetitive self-mutilation, and compulsive shopping), although ICDs have been used in the literature to refer to a wider range of disorders, including disorders relating to externalizing behavior (including oppositional-defiant disorder, conduct disorder and ADHD) (Kessler et al., 2005a; 2005b). These disorders are clearly characterized by a strong impulse towards an ultimately maladaptive behavior, but our understanding of the ICDs is, at present, limited by the high co-morbidity of ICDs with PDs, mood disorders, anxiety disorders, substance abuse, and eating disorders (Hollander and Rosen, 2000; Grant and Potenza, 2004; Grant et al., 2005; Dell'Osso et al., 2006).

The prevalence of impulsivity-related psychopathology motivates efforts to attain a deeper understanding of the biological basis of this trait. One practical application of such knowledge would be the development more effective pharmacological treatments for patients. Another application could be the opportunity to identify vulnerable individuals before impulsivity has reached dysfunctional levels, and develop effective interventions for these individuals. Yet the fact that patients are classified based on a taxonomy that is not biologically based, poses a serious challenge to efforts to investigate the biological basis of impulsivity. Indeed, because patients are categorized based on diagnoses that summarize a heterogeneous constellation of symptoms, impulsivity is rarely studied in isolation of these other symptoms. Therefore, any study of impulsivity-related behaviors in patients is usually confounded with a disease-specific symptomatology.

BIOLOGICAL APPROACHES TO IMPULSIVITY

The previous section has highlighted the multidimensional nature of impulsivity, both in the personality structure of healthy individuals and in a wide range of patient populations. As we pointed out above, studies of the biological basis of impulsivity are motivated for several reasons. One is that biological data can constrain the models of normal personality structure developed by psychologists. Another is that such studies could lead to novel and biologically based clinical treatment or intervention approaches for patients. Investigators have followed two different, and to date largely independent, research approaches. One utilizes noninvasive brain imaging technology to identify the neural circuitry that mediates impulsive behavior. The other utilizes molecular genetic techniques to associate individual differences in impulsivity with genetic variation. We will next turn to each of these approaches and highlight its contributions to our current understanding of the biological basis of impulsivity.

Neuroimaging

One way to operationalize impulsivity is in terms of inhibitory control. For example, Nigg (2000) offers a taxonomy of impulsivity that differentiates executive inhibition processes (interference control, cognitive inhibition, behavioral inhibition, and oculomotor inhibition) from motivational inhibition processes (response to punishment cues and response to novelty). Of these processes, behavioral inhibition has received considerable attention from cognitive neuroscientists.

To identify the neural circuit that is engaged in behavioral inhibition, cognitive neuroscientists have relied on task paradigms in which participants have to either execute or inhibit a motor response. The two most commonly used tasks, the Go/NoGo and Stop-signal tasks, both share the characteristic that successful performance requires the inhibition of a prepotent response. The Go/NoGo task requires a participant to respond to one set of frequent stimuli (for example, every letter but 'X'), but to inhibit responding to a separate set of infrequent stimuli (in this example, 'X'). Despite its popularity, the Go/NoGo task is an imperfect measure of impulsivity because it does not control for the so-called 'oddball' effect, which refers to the fact that infrequent stimuli draw more attention than frequent stimuli. In the case of the Go/NoGo paradigm, Go stimuli are presented more frequently than NoGo stimuli. Therefore, neural response to a NoGo stimulus confounds processes of behavioral inhibition with attentional processes that detect infrequent stimuli.

The Stop-signal task is similar to the Go/NoGo, but makes greater demands on participants' inhibitory control. In the Stop-signal task, a Stop signal appears *after* the onset of a Go signal on a subset of trials, requiring the participant to interrupt a response to the Go signal that has already been triggered. The longer the delay between the Go signal and the Stop signal, or the closer in time that the Stop signal is to the actual response, the more difficult it is to inhibit a response. This task is based on a 'horse-race' model, which assumes that a Go process and a Stop process are in a race, and are independent of each other (Logan, 1994). This assumption of independence allows for the estimation of Stop-signal reaction time (SSRT), the primary dependent measure of the Stop-signal task. The SSRT is a measure of an individual's stopping process, or inhibitory function, and has been shown to distinguish samples with impaired inhibitory control from controls (Rucklidge and Tannock, 2002; Lijffijt et al., 2005).

There are a considerable number of neuroimaging studies of behavioral inhibition, which have accumulated evidence for a neural circuit involving prefrontal and striatal brain regions (Figure 16.1). In one of the first event-related (ER) fMRI studies to examine response inhibition, participants performed a Go/NoGo task (Konishi et al., 1998). In response to NoGo trials, as compared to Go trials, each participant showed significant activation in

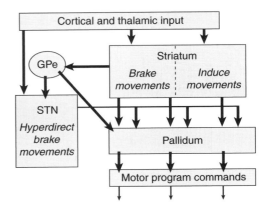

Figure 16.1   A frontostriatal neural circuit of behavioral inhibition. The hyperdirect pathway (cortiocothalamic input sent to subthalamic nucleus (STN) results in direct inhibition of pallidal output) enables rapid termination of already intiated motor response. (GPe = globus pallidus external segment). Red arrows = excitatory; black arrows = inhibitory

the right hemisphere of the prefrontal cortex, specifically the posterior part of the right inferior frontal sulcus (BA 45). Three subsequent ER-fMRI studies using a Go/NoGo task provided further support for a right-lateralized behavioral inhibition network involving activation in the right ventrolateral prefrontal cortex (BA 44), lateral prefrontal cortex (BA 10), dorsolateral prefrontal (9/46), parietal areas, SMA, and a subregion of the anterior cingulate cortex (BA 32) (Garavan et al., 1999; Braver et al., 2001; Liddle et al., 2001). One study compared activation in both the Go/NoGo and Stop-signal tasks and found a more strongly right-lateralized activation pattern in the Stop-signal task than the Go/NoGo task (Rubia et al., 2001). However, there was also considerable overlap in activation during both tasks, which was most consistently observed in the right inferior frontal cortex (IFC), which is argued to be specific to behavioral inhibition, while the other areas likely reflect other non-inhibitory functions, such as motor planning and response selection (Rubia et al., 2001). The central role of the IFC in behavioral inhibition has been more formally recognized in a recent meta-analysis of studies using the WCST, task-switching, and the Go/NoGo paradigms (Buchsbaum et al., 2005).

Subcortical contributions to the inhibition of a motor response that has already been initiated have been carefully delineated by Aron and Poldrack (2006). Using a tracking Stop-signal task in order to ensure comparable performance across participants, they were able to define the pattern of activation underlying response execution, successful inhibition and failed inhibition. These analyses showed that successful inhibition was characterized by activation in both cortical regions (the right IFC, pre-supplemental motor area or SMA, right parietal cortex), as well as several subcortical regions including the insula and regions within the basal ganglia, particularly the the globus pallidus (GP) and subthalamic nucleus (STN). The basal ganglia serve as a relay between corticothalamic and brainstem motor program commands, and represent the neural mechanisms responsible for selecting a motor program.

Among the regions of this right-lateralized neural circuit of behavioral inhibition, the IFC and STN appear to play a special role. As reviewed above, the IFC is believed to play a central role in controlling behavioral inhibition (as opposed to motor planning or response selection). The STN, on the other hand, plays a central role in the stopping of a motor response, and its position within this frontostriatal circuit is particularly well suited for braking ongoing motor commands that are in the later stages of being processed by the brain (Mink, 1996; Gerfen, 2000; Nambu et al., 2002; Aron and Poldrack, 2006). Further support for a central role of both IFC and STN in behavioral inhibition comes from the observation that activation in these two structures is positively correlated (Aron and Poldrack, 2006), suggesting that recruitment of both these areas together is required for successful inhibition.

Individual differences in the frontostriatal circuit further strengthen the link to impulsive behavior. The first report of an individual differences approach to impulsivity

consisted of a correlation between activation elicited by a Go/NoGo task with absentmindedness, a personality trait that is measured by the Cognitive Failures Questionnaire, that positively correlates with self-report measures of impulsivity (including the BIS-11) (Garavan et al., 2002). Activation of the right IFG (BA 44) was associated with successful response inhibition in the entire sample. Other brain regions, on the other hand, showed significant individual differences in activation that correlated with the personality trait of absentmindedness, leading the authors to conclude that individuals who scored high or low in absentmindedness, respectively, used distinct cortical systems when engaging in inhibitory control. Given that absentmindedness is not a direct measure of impulsivity and is confounded with cognitive failure, we are cautious in drawing firm conclusions on impulsivity based on this data.

Neural activation elicited by a Go/NoGo task was associated with specific measures of impulsivity, as assessed by Eysenck's impulsiveness scale and the BIS-11 (Horn et al., 2003). For the group as a whole, the authors reported significant right-hemisphere activation, including the right IFG, during inhibition. Impulsivity, as measured with Eysenck's impulsiveness scale, correlated positively with activation in the right IFG (BA 44/45) during inhibition. Impulsivity, as measured with BIS-11, correlated positively with activation in the left superior temporal gyrus during inhibition. Thus, two self-report instruments, that ostensibly measure the same construct and that were administered to the same subjects, were associated with two distinct sets of brain regions. However, both self-report instruments conceptualize impulsivity differently and are related to different executive inhibitory processes. The discrepancy between the Eysenck and BIS-11 instruments illustrates the difficulty in mapping individual differences based on different self-report measures onto neural circuits.

The same self-report measure can also yield different answers as a function of task paradigm. For example, whereas the BIS-11 correlated with individual activation differences in the left superior temporal gyrus during inhibition in the Go/NoGo task (Horn et al., 2003), it was associated with activation in the bilateral dorsolateral prefrontal cortex (DLPFC) during performance of the Immediate and Delayed Memory Task (IMT/DMT) (Valdes et al., 2006), which is proposed to assess both impulsivity and aspects of working memory. Thus, an interaction between choice of self-report measures and impulsivity-related task paradigms, further complicates the interpretation of available data.

The individual differences approach can be extended to structural brain features. Several studies have examined the structural features of the frontostriatal pathway, and investigated their association with individual differences in impulsivity. In particular, two sets of studies have quantified white matter microstructure and myelination and gray matter volume and density in relation to impulsivity.

Studies of white matter have used diffusion tensor imaging (DTI) and investigated fractional anisotropy (FA), a measure of axonal and/or myelin fiber integrity, and found it reduced in clinical samples characterized by elevated impulsivity as compared to controls, particularly in frontal cortical regions (Hoptman et al., 2004; Moeller et al., 2005; de Win et al., 2006). For example, white matter integrity in the corpus callosum was found to be reduced in cocaine-dependent individuals, compared to controls, which implicates degeneration of the prefrontal cortex (Moeller et al., 2005). In addition, impulsivity (as measured by either self-report or task performance) was negatively correlated with FA in these regions (Hoptman et al., 2004; Moeller et al., 2005; de Win et al., 2006). This relationship is not limited to clinical samples, however. For example, white matter myelination of the right frontostriatal network varies considerably between healthy adults, and is correlated with individual differences in behavioral inhibition, as measured by reaction time during performance of the Go/NoGo task (Liston et al., 2006). Elevated impulsivity is, therefore, associated with poor axonal and/or myelin fiber integrity,

and individual differences in white matter microstructure appear to predict behavioral inhibition in healthy adults.

Studies of gray matter have used high-resolution structural MRI and reported a reduction in gray matter volume in clinical samples characterized by elevated impulsivity (particularly ADHD), compared to controls (Carmona et al., 2005). For example, a significant correlation between age and right caudate volume was reported for healthy controls, but not for ADHD boys (Casey et al., 1997b). Self-reported impulsivity has also been correlated with gray matter volume in samples characterized by elevated impulsivity, although the direction of relationship varies across clinical samples (Hazlett et al., 2005; Antonucci et al., 2006). In healthy boys, volumetric measures of right prefrontal region and basal ganglia structures have been positively correlated with performance on several tasks of inhibitory control (Casey et al., 1997a); however, there continue to be drastic changes in gray matter throughout adolescence, making it difficult to draw any conclusions from this data about the relationship between impulsivity and gray matter volume in adults. Elevated impulsivity is therefore associated with reduced gray matter density, and individual differences in gray matter volume appear to correlate with behavioral inhibition (at least in healthy boys).

Neuroimaging studies implicating a right-lateralized frontostriatal network during behavioral inhibition or individual differences related to impulsivity are consistent with studies that interrupt brain activation with transcranial magnetic stimulation (TMS) or that study brain-damaged patients (Aron and Poldrack, 2005; Chambers et al., 2006). For example, temporary deactivation of the right IFC with TMS impairs the ability to stop an initiated action, but not the ability to execute an action (Chambers et al., 2006). A study of brain-damaged patients compared performance on a Stop-signal task between patients with unilateral right frontal lobe lesions and non-lesioned controls, and found that only the inferior frontal gyrus (IFG) (specifically the pars opercularis (BA 44)) was critical for response inhibition (Aron et al., 2003). Furthermore, the extent of right IFG damage (particularly in the pars opercularis), as measured with MRI, correlated with the SSRT, such that greater damage was associated with slower inhibition (Aron et al., 2003).

Molecular genetics

Although impulsivity is a multidimensional construct, there is a support for a significant genetic component of impulsivity. Familial transmission of impulsivity has been demonstrated both outside of DSM categories of mental disorders (defined as commission errors on a task designed to measure impulsive responding) (Dougherty et al., 2003) and within DSM categories (defined as impulsive personality disorder traits assessed with interviews) (Silverman et al., 1991). Data from twin studies support a genetic component of impulsive traits, as defined by a dissocial dimension characterized by impulsivity (Livesley et al., 1998; Seroczynski et al., 1999; Taylor et al., 2003), and also as defined by a impulsive/irresponsible dimension related to psychopathic personality (Larsson et al., 2006). Evidence from twin studies suggests that around 45% of the variance in self-reported impulsivity, as assessed by both the Karolinska Scales of Personality and the BIS-11, is accounted for by non-additive genetic factors (Pedersen et al., 1988; Seroczynski et al., 1999).

Impulsivity is not believed to be influenced by a single gene of large effect, rather, multiple genes of small effect size are thought to contribute to impulsive behavior (Faraone et al., 2002). Such genes contributing to genetic variance in continuous traits are called quantitative trait loci (QTL), and they refer to a model of transmission in which multiple genes of varying effect size influence the trait of interest (multigenic or polygenic mode of transmission) (Faraone et al., 2002). To investigate the possible effect of a QTL on a behavior of interest, association studies examine the correlation between a phenotype and genes that contain common variations in their nucleotide sequence (known as 'polymorphisms') that are common in the population (Plomin et al., 1994; Faraone et al., 2002).

Advances in molecular genetics have begun to identify gene polymorphisms that may be related to impulsivity. The genetic contributions to impulsivity may be mediated through many channels, including genetic mediation of neurotransmitter systems such as serotonin and dopamine (Evenden, 1999; Robbins, 2005). Indeed, the role of serotonin in impulsivity is well recognized, and interested readers are refered to these reviews (Evenden, 1999; Carver and Miller, 2006). In this chapter, we will focus on dopamine, because the neural substrate mediating behavioral inhibition, which we use as a proxy for impulsivity, is known to be under dopaminergic modulatory control.

Variations in dopamine-related genes are of particular interest for research on impulsivity, given dopamine's role in impulsivity (Congdon and Canli, 2005). Two candidate gene polymorphisms of interest are the dopamine D4 receptor (DRD4) and the dopamine transporter (DAT). The dopamine D4 receptor (DRD4) plays a role in dopaminergic signaling, particularly in the prefrontal cortex, which includes region such as the IFC involved in behavioral inhibition (Meador-Woodruff et al., 1996; Mulcrone and Kerwin, 1997). The gene that codes for the D4 receptor is polymorphic: it contains a particular nucleotide sequence that repeats a variable number of times, generating a range of so-called 'variable number of tandem repeats' (VNTR),[1] with the 2-, 4-, and 7-repeat variants being most common (Asghari et al., 1995). In patients diagnosed with ADHD, there is a small but significant association between presence of the DRD4 7-repeat variant and diagnosis of the disorder, according to two meta-analyses (Faraone et al., 2001; Li et al., 2006). It is therefore possible that presence of the DRD4 7-repeat variant contributes to impulsivity.

The dopamine transporter (DAT) is responsible for removing dopamine from the synapse, primarily throughout the midbrain (Sesack et al., 1998; Lewis et al., 2001), which includes subcortical regions associated with the behavioral inhibition circuit reviewed above. Similar to the *DRD4* polymorphism, the *DAT*[2] has a VNTR polymorphism, resulting in variants that range from 3 to 13 repeats, with 9 and 10 repeats occurring most commonly (Bannon et al., 2001). There have been a number of association studies with the *DAT*, with particular focus on ADHD or ADHD-related variables, which have suggested that presence of the *DAT* 10-repeat variant or more specifically the *DAT* 10/10 genotype (two copies of the 10-repeat variant) constitutes a risk factor for ADHD (Faraone et al., 2005). Other data suggest that the effect of *DAT* on ADHD may be moderated through interaction with other variables, such as subject demographics (Cornish et al., 2005) or other gene polymorphisms, including *DRD4*. For example, increased hyperactive-impulsive scores were reported in ADHD children with at least one 7-allele of the *DRD4* and both 10-alleles for the *DAT* (Roman et al., 2001). In another study, ADHD children were reported to have elevated frequencies of at least one *DRD4* 7-repeat variant and two copies of the *DAT* 10-repeat variant (Carrasco et al., 2006). It is, therefore, possible that presence of the *DAT* 10-repeat variant, particularly the *DAT* 10/10 genotype, contributes to impulsivity.

THE ENDOPHENOTYPE APPROACH

Separately, neuroimaging and molecular genetic studies provide support for neural and genetic and neural correlates of impulsivity, specifically of behavioral inhibition. This work, however, is largely limited by two major factors. First, most studies use samples constrained to diagnostic categories. This is particularly the case in association studies, in which psychiatric groups are compared to controls. This is problematic because it confounds impulsivity with disease-specific symptoms, which prevents the identification

of phenotypes closer to the influence of genetic variants (Gottesman and Gould, 2003). In addition, DSM criteria have been criticized for creating heterogeneous categories in that one diagnostic category may contain multiple subtypes, each of which may represent a different etiology (Gottesman and Gould, 2003). Each of these issues is problematic because they can create 'noise', thereby obscuring the relationship between a genotype and phenotype of interest.

Second, previous molecular genetic and neuroimaging studies relevant to impulsivity have been limited by over-reliance on self-report measures. Most studies have not measured impulsivity per se, but have relied on self-reported traits such as novelty seeking. Self-report inventories assessing higher-order traits, not necessarily rooted in a biological hypothesis, may be an insensitive measure that carries only a small effect size for genetic influences (Gottesman and Gould, 2003; Hariri and Weinberger, 2003). Furthermore, different conceptualizations of personality, and the use of divergent measures across studies, make it difficult to identify a useful phenotype. Again, these issues are problematic because they can create 'noise', serving to obscure any effect that a genotype may have on the phenotype of interest, especially when the size of the effect is small.

In answer to these limitations, an endophenotype approach is particularly useful for addressing impulsivity. It is widely acknowledged that complex behaviors have polygenic origins, where each gene may only contribute a small amount of variance to the phenotype (Gottesman and Gould, 2003; Abdolmaleky et al., 2005). Furthermore, any particular gene of interest may affect phenotypes that cut across behaviors or traits. The complexity of these relations can be reduced by considering an endophenotype approach (de Geus et al., 2001; Castellanos and Tannock, 2002; Gottesman and Gould, 2003; New and Siever, 2003; Hasler et al., 2004; Baud, 2005; MacQueen et al., 2005), which replaces complex phenotypes (e.g. diagnostic categories combining heterogeneous symptoms) with simpler endophenotypes (e.g. isolated cognitive processes or localized brain measures) that are presumed to be more closely linked to the biological processes regulated by genes of interest.

We set out to conduct an explicit test on the role of dopaminergic gene variation on impulsivity, using the endophenotype approach. Based on the clinical observations regarding the *DRD4* and *DAT* reviewed in the previous section, we set out to test whether these polymorphisms were associated with impulsivity in a sample of healthy individuals (Congdon et al., 2008). We expected that an endophenotype of impulsivity would be more sensitive to these gene effects than a more traditional phenotype measure, such as self-report. We therefore planned to compare the role of *DRD4* and *DAT* polymorphisms on self-reported impulsivity, using the BIS-11 questionnaire, against an endophenotype of impulsivity, which we operationalized as behavioral inhibition, and measured using the tracking Stop-signal task (Logan, 1994; Logan et al., 1997). In general, we expected that the endophenotype measure would be more sensitive to any gene effects than the self-report measure. More specifically, based

on the clinical data reviewed earlier we expected that the risk-variants of *DRD4* (presence of the 7-repeat variant) and *DAT* (10/10 genotype) would be associated with increased impulsive responding. We further expected that there would be an interaction between these risk variants on impulsive responding, such that participants with both risk variants/genotype would show the greatest impairment in behavioral inhibition.

To test these predictions, we genotyped 86 participants for the *DRD4* and *DAT* polymorphisms who completed the BIS-11 questionnaire and performed the Stop-signal task. Thus, the two principal dependent variables were self-reported impulsivity and Stop-signal reaction time (SSRT), or duration of the stopping process, where longer SSRT values reflect poorer inhibitory control. Analysis of the self-report responses failed to reveal any significant effect of genetic variation on the BIS-11 total score, or on any of its subscores.

On the other hand, analysis of the behavioral data revealed a significant interaction between *DRD4* and *DAT* genotypes on SSRT (Figure 16.2). Inspection of the data revealed

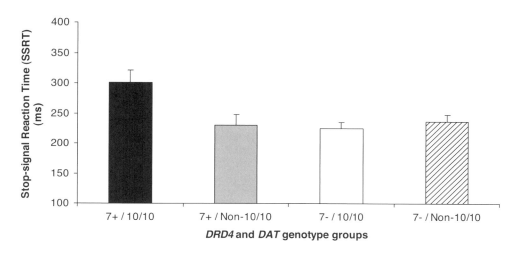

Figure 16.2   Stop-signal reaction time (SSRT) as a function of *DRD4* and *DAT* genotypes. *DRD4* 7-allele present (7+) vs. absent (7−) and *DAT* 10/10 genotype (10/10) vs. non-10/10 genotype (non-10/10) were combined to form four groups. There was a significant difference between groups on SSRT. Longer SSRT (ms) reflects greater difficulty inhibiting a behavioral response to a Stop-signal. Reprinted with permission from Congdon, Lesch, and Canli (2008)

that those individuals with both risk variants/genotype had the highest SSRT, while those with neither risk variants/genotype of both genes had the lowest SSRT. Thus, the individuals who carried both a *DRD4* 7-repeat variant *and* who also carried two copies of the *DAT* 10-repeat variant exhibited the poorest behavioral inhibition in this Stop-signal task. There was also a significant main effect of *DRD4* and a trend towards an effect of *DAT* on SSRT. For *DRD4*, those individuals who carried the *DRD4* 7-repeat variant had a higher mean SSRT than non-carriers, confirming our prediction that presence of the 7-repeat variant is associated with poorer behavioral inhibition. The effect was not as strong for the *DAT* 10/10 genotype, but was significant when the interaction of both genes was investigated.

These observations are consistent with the argument that the endophenotype approach is more sensitive to the effects of gene polymorphisms than more traditional measures of phenotypic expression. Given the dearth of data, however, it is prudent to be cautious not to over-interpret this single result. Although the Stop-signal task is more sensitive to the effects of dopaminergic genetic variation than a self-report measure of trait impulsivity, the SSRT and BIS-11 scores do not necessarily address the same components of impulsivity. Instead, we suggest that behavioral inhibition (as indexed by SSRT) is a more suitable endophenotype of impulsivity when testing for the effects of dopaminergic genetic variation than multifaceted, high-order traits (assessed with self-report measures) are. The implication of this conclusion is that the BIS-11 and its subscales may be less suitable for assessing behavioral inhibition, but may be more suited for assessing other components of impulsivity, which are potentially influenced by other neurotransmitter systems (such as serotonin).

INTEGRATION: GENOMIC IMAGING

As discussed above, neuroimaging studies of behavioral inhibition have reported activation within a frontostriatal network, particularly the right IFC, during inhibition. Furthermore, several studies have linked individual differences in impulsivity to variation within this network, which is consistent with the idea that dopaminergic gene variation may alter structural or functional aspects of this circuit to generate individual differences in behavioral inhibition. Indeed, this idea has already received considerable empirical support from studies that have integrated neuroimaging and molecular genetic approaches, which we refer to as 'genomic imaging' studies (Canli, 2006b) and others refer to as 'imaging genomics' studies (Hariri and Weinberger, 2003).

With regard to genomic influences on brain structure, differences in brain volume as measured with anatomical MRI scans have been reported between the *DAT* and the *DRD4*, such that ADHD boys with the *DAT* 10/10 genotype had smaller caudate volumes than those without the 10/10 genotype, and the unaffected siblings of ADHD boys with the *DRD4* 4/4 genotype had smaller prefrontal gray matter volumes than those without the 4/4 genotype (primarily a 7- or 2-repeat allele) (Durston et al., 2005).

With regard to genomic influences on brain functional activation, single photon emission computed tomography (SPECT) has reported higher perfusion (an indicator of metabolism) in the right middle temporal gyrus in ADHD children who had the 10/10 *DAT* genotype and at least one *DRD4* 7-allele, as compared to all other groups (Szobot et al., 2005). The functional significance is that DAT binding sites are located in the temporal cortex. Although the relationship between the higher perfusion in the medial temporal cortex and behaviors related to ADHD is less clear, the results highlight the increased sensitivity of an approach which addresses the possible effect of genetic variation on the actual response of brain regions. Overall, studies testing for differences in neural activity as a function of *DAT* have reported evidence for different patterns of neural responding between *DAT* genotype groups (Bertolino et al., 2006; Schott et al., 2006), with the exact pattern differing across tasks used.

Greater activation in the right IFC (BA 45 and 47) during a Go/NoGo task, as well as a NoGo-Flanker task, has been reported in individuals who carry the high-activity variant of *MAO-A* (an enzyme that is responsible for the catabolism of both serotonin and dopamine) as compared to individuals who carry the low-activity variant (Meyer-Lindenberg, 2006; Passamonti et al., 2006). In addition, the relationship between right IFC activation and self-reported impulsivity varied as a function of MAO-A genotype. Individuals who carried the high-activity variant exhibited a positive correlation between self-reported impulsivity and neural activation during inhibition, whereas individuals who carried the low-activity variant exhibited a negative correlation between self-reported impulsivity and neural activation during inhibition (Passamonti et al., 2006). The significant role that MAO-A plays in dopamine catabolism and the significant role the dopamine plays in prefrontal function suggests that these findings can be offered as preliminary support for the sensitivity of the imaging genomics approach in addressing the genetic and neural bases of behavioral inhibition.

CONCLUSIONS AND FUTURE DIRECTIONS

As we noted before, impulsivity is a multidimensional construct that inspired a wide range of definitions and self-report measures, and is implicated in a variety of DSM-based classifications of psychopathology. Such variety makes it difficult to generalize and compare research findings across studies. We suggested that a better approach is one that is based in neurobiology, particularly the endophenotype approach, which would arrive at a deeper understanding of impulsivity by combining neuroimaging and molecular genetic methods to account for individual differences in dopamine-related genes, impulsivity and inhibitory control, and the pattern of neural activation seen during inhibition of a motor response.

Paradigms such as the Go/NoGo and Stop-signal tasks yield quantitative, precise measures of specific forms of impulsive behaviors. The advantage of these paradigms is that impulsivity is operationalized in terms that do not rely on self-report or are susceptible to potential clinical observer bias. Although we acknowledge that other paradigms, such as delay discounting and reward processing, also capture important aspects of impulsivity, we have chosen to focus on tasks that measure behavioral inhibition in this chapter. We have done so because the neural circuit that mediates this behavior is well characterized and is regulated, in part, by dopaminergic genes.

Genetic approaches towards impulsivity acknowledge a significant role both for serotonin and dopamine. We chose to focus on dopamine, because reviews on the role of serotonin and impulsivity already exist (Evenden, 1999) and because the neural circuitry associated with behavioral inhibition is a candidate for studies assessing variations in dopaminergic tone. We noted that variation within several dopaminergic genes such as *DRD4* and *DAT* are associated with personality traits related to impulsivity and to DSM-based diagnostic categories that include impulsivity-related symptoms, but we pointed out the limitations of indirect, self-report measures and diagnostic classification schemes.

We see a number of exciting future directions for the endophenotype approach to the study of impulsivity. One direction is the development of predictive, theoretically and biologically constrained models of behavioral inhibition. In this chapter, we introduced the reader to a frontostriatal neural circuit that mediates inhibition. We also highlighted the role of some dopaminergic gene polymorphisms associated with impulsivity. Interestingly, these genes are not uniformly distributed across the brain. For example, DAT is predominantly found in the midbrain subcortical but not cortical brain regions (Melchitzky and Lewis, 2001; Mazei et al., 2002), whereas the DRD4 is primarily observed in cortical but not subcortical regions (Durston et al., 2005). From such spatial distribution, and from detailed biophysical models of dopaminergic function, it is possible to begin to develop computational models that predict the behavior of the frontostriatal circuit as a function of dopaminergic gene variation (Grace, 1991; Cohen et al., 2002; Bilder et al., 2004; Seamans and Yang, 2004; Robbins, 2005). The development of such models would signal a profound leap forward in our understanding of personality traits, with implications for psychologists interested in the structure of trait impulsivity in healthy individuals, and for clinicians concerned with understanding the etiology and treatment of multiple forms of psychopathology related to impulsive behavior.[3]

NOTES

1 In keeping with naming conventions of the field, DRD4 refers to the receptor itself, whereas *DRD4* refers to the gene polymorphism associated with the gene that codes for the receptor.

2 `We keep with the same convention as for the other polymorphism, referring to DAT as the transporter itself and to *DAT* when referring to the gene polymorphism.

3 Some of the work discussed in this chapter was supported by the National Science Foundation Grant (BCS-0224221) to T.C. and by a National Institutes of Health (NIH) Ruth L. Kirchstein National Research Service Award (F31 MH07 9643) to E.C.

REFERENCES

Abdolmaleky, H.M., Thiagalingam, S. and Wilcox, M. (2005) 'Genetics and epigenetics in major psychiatric disorders: Dilemmas, achievements, applications, and future scope', *American Journal of Pharmacogenomics*, 5(3): 149–60.

American Psychiatric Association (2000) *Diagnostic and Statistical Manual of Mental Disorders (Fourth Edition, Text Revision) (DSM-IV-TR)*. Washington, DC: APA.

Antonucci, A.S., Gansler, D.A., Tan, S., Bhadelia, R., Patz, S. and Fulwiler, C. (2006) 'Orbitofrontal correlates of aggression and impulsivity in psychiatric patients', *Psychiatry Research,* 147(2–3): 213–20.

Aron, A.R., Fletcher, P.C., Bullmore, E.T., Sahakian, B.J. and Robbins, T.W. (2003) 'Stop-signal inhibition disrupted by damage to right inferior frontal gyrus in humans', *Nature Neuroscience,* 6(2): 115–6.

Aron, A.R. and Poldrack, R.A. (2005) 'The cognitive neuroscience of response inhibition: Relevance for genetic research in attention-deficit/hyperactivity disorder', *Biological Psychiatry,* 57(11): 1285–92.

Aron, A.R. and Poldrack, R.A. (2006) 'Cortical and subcortical contributions to Stop signal response inhibition: Role of the subthalamic nucleus', *Journal of Neuroscience,* 26(9): 2424–33.

Asghari, V., Sanyal, S., Buchwaldt, S., Paterson, A., Jovanovic, V. and Van Tol, H.H. (1995) 'Modulation of intracellular cyclic AMP levels by different human dopamine D4 receptor variants', *Journal of Neurochemistry,* 65(3): 1157–65.

Avila, C., Cuenca, I., Felix, V., Parcet, M.A. and Miranda, A. (2004) 'Measuring impulsivity in school-aged boys and examining its relationship with ADHD and ODD ratings', *Journal of Abnormal Child Psychology*, 32(3): 295–304.

Bagge, C., Nickell, A., Stepp. S., Durrett, C., Jackson, K. and Trull, T.J. (2004) 'Borderline personality disorder features predict negative outcomes 2 years later', *Journal of Abnormal Psychology*, 113(2): 279–88.

Bannon, M.J., Michelhaugh, S.K., Wang, J. and Sacchetti, P. (2001) 'The human dopamine transporter gene: Gene organization, transcriptional regulation, and potential involvement in neuropsychiatric disorders', *European Neuropsychopharmacology*, 11(6): 449–55.

Barkley, R.A. (1997) 'Behavioral inhibition, sustained attention, and executive functions: Constructing a unifying theory of ADHD', *Psychological Bulletin*, 121(1): 65–94.

Barratt, E.S., Stanford, M.S., Dowdy, L., Liebman, M.J. and Kent, T.A. (1999) 'Impulsive and premeditated aggression: A factor analysis of self-reported acts', *Psychiatry Research*, 86(2): 163–73.

Baud, P. (2005) 'Personality traits as intermediary phenotypes in suicidal behavior: Genetic issues', *American Journal of Medical Genetics C: Seminars in Medical Genetics*, 133(1): 34–42.

Beauchaine, T.P., Katkin, E.S., Strassberg, Z. and Snarr, J. (2001) 'Disinhibitory psychopathology in male adolescents: Discriminating conduct disorder from attention-deficit/hyperactivity disorder through concurrent assessment of multiple autonomic states', *Journal of Abnormal Psychology*, 110(4): 610–24.

Bertolino, A., Rubino. V., Sambataro. F., Blasi, G., Latorre, V., Fazio, L., Caforio, Nardini, M., Weinberger, D.R. and Scarabino, T, (2006) 'Prefrontal-hippocampal coupling during memory processing is modulated by COMT Val158Met Genotype', *Biological Psychiatry*, 60(11): 1250–8.

Bilder, R.M., Volavka, J., Lachman, H.M. and Grace, A.A. (2004) 'The catechol-O-methyl-transferase polymorphism: Relations to the tonic-phasic dopamine hypothesis and neuropsychiatric phenotypes', *Neuropsychopharmacology* 29(11): 1943–61.

Braver, T.S., Barch, D.M., Gray, J.R., Molfese, D.L. and Snyder, A. (2001) 'Anterior cingulate cortex and response conflict: Effects of frequency, inhibition and errors', *Cerebral Cortex*, 11(9): 825–36.

Buchsbaum, B.R., Greer, S., Chang, W.L. and Berman, K.F. (2005) 'Meta-analysis of neuroimaging studies of the Wisconsin card-sorting task and component processes', *Human Brain Mapping*, 25(1): 35–45.

Canli, T. (2004) 'Functional brain mapping of extraversion and neuroticism: Learning from individual differences in emotion processing', *Journal of Personality*, 72(6): 1105–32.

Canli, T. (2006a) (ed.), *Biology of Personality and Individual Differences*. New York: Guilford.

Canli, T. (2006b) 'Genomic imaging of extraversion', in T. Canli (ed.), *Biology of Personality and Individual Differences*. New York: Guilford, pp. 93–115.

Carmona, S., Vilarroya, O., Bielsa, A., Tremols, V., Soliva, J.C., Ravira, M., Tomas, J., Raheb, C., Gispert, J.D., Battle, S. and Bulbena, A. (2005) 'Global and regional gray matter reductions in ADHD: A voxel-based morphometric study', *Neuroscience Letters*, 389(2): 88–93.

Carrasco, X., Rothhammer, P., Moraga, M., Henriquez, H., Chakraborty, R., Aboitiz, F., Rothhammer, F. (2006) 'Genotypic interaction between DRD4 and DAT1 loci is a high risk factor for attention-deficit/ hyperactivity disorder in Chilean families', *American Journal of Medical Genetics B: Neuropsychiatric Genetics*, 141(1): 51–4.

Carver, C.S. and Miller, C.J. (2006) 'Relations of serotonin function to personality: Current views and a key methodological issue', *Psychiatry Research*, 144(1): 1–15.

Casey, B.J., Castellanos, F.X., Giedd, J.N., Marsh, W.L., Hamburger, S.D., Schubert, A.B., Vauss, Y.C., Vaituzis, A.C., Dickstein, D.P., Sarfatti, S.E. and Rapoport, J.L. (1997a) 'Implication of right frontostriatal circuitry in response inhibition and attention-deficit/hyperactivity disorder', *Journal of the American Academy of Child and Adolescent Psychiatry*, 36(3): 374–83.

Casey, B.J., Trainor, R.J., Orendi, J.L., Schubert, A.B., Nystrom, L.E., Giedd, J.N., Castellanos, F.X., Haxby, J.V., Noll, D.C., Cohen, J.D., Forman, S.D., Dahl, R.E. and Rapoport, J.L. (1997b) 'A developmental functional MRI study of prefrontal activation during performance of a Go-No-Go task', *Journal of Cognitive Neuroscience*, 9(6): 835–47.

Casillas, A. and Clark, L.A. (2002) 'Dependency, impulsivity, and self-harm: Traits hypothesized to underlie the association between cluster B personality and substance use disorders', *Journal of Personality Disorders*, 16(5): 424–36.

Castellanos, F.X. and Tannock, R. (2002) 'Neuroscience of attention-deficit/hyperactivity disorder: The search for endophenotypes', *Nature Reviews in Neuroscience*, 3(8): 617–28.

Chambers, C.D., Bellgrove, M.A., Stokes, M.G., Henderson, T.R., Garavan, H., Robertson, I.H., Morris, A.P. and Mattingely, J.B. (2006) 'Executive "brake failure" following deactivation of human frontal lobe', *Journal of Cognitive Neuroscience*, 18(3): 444–55.

Cloninger, C.R., Svrakic, D. and Przybeck, T. (1993) 'A psychobiological model of temperament and character', *Archives of General Psychiatry*, 50(12): 975–90.

Cohen, J.D., Braver, T.S. and Brown, J.W. (2002) 'Computational perspectives on dopamine function in prefrontal cortex', *Current Opinion in Neurobiology*, 12(2): 223–9.

Congdon, E. and Canli, T. (2005) 'The endophenotype of impulsivity: Reaching consilience through behavioral, genetic, and neuroimaging approaches', *Behavioral and Cognitive Neuroscience Reviews*, 4(4): 262–81.

Congdon, E., Lesch, K.-P. and Canli, T. (2008) 'Analysis of DRD4 and DAT polymorphisms and behavioral inhibition in healthy adults: Implications for impulsivity', *American Journal of Medical Genetics Part B: Neuropsychiatric Genetics*, 147B(1): 27–32.

Conrod, P.J., Pihl, R.O., Stewart, S.H. and Dongier, M. (2000) 'Validation of a system of classifying female substance abusers on the basis of personality and motivational risk factors for substance abuse', *Psychology of Addictive Behaviors*, 14(3): 243–56.

Cornish, K.M., Manly, T., Savage, R., Swanson, J., Morisano, D., Butler, N., Grant, C., Cross, G., Bentley, L. and Hollis, C.P. (2005) 'Association of the dopamine transporter (DAT1) 10/10-repeat genotype with ADHD symptoms and response inhibition in a general population sample', *Molecular Psychiatry*, 10(7): 686–98.

Costa, P.T. Jr. and McCrae, R.R. (1992) *Revised NEO Personality Inventory: Professional Manual.* Odessa, FL, Psychological Assessment Resources.

de Geus, E.J., Wright, M.J., Martin, N.G. and Boomsma, D.I. (2001) 'Genetics of brain function and cognition', *Behavior Genetics*, 31(6): 489–95.

de Win, M.M., Reneman, L., Jager, G., Vlieger, E.J., Olabarriaga, S.D., Lavini, C., Bisschops, I., Majoie, C.B., Booij, J., den Heeten, G.J. and van den Brink, W. (2006) 'A prospective cohort study on sustained effects of low-dose ecstasy use on the brain in new ecstasy users', *Neuropsychopharmacology*, 32(2): 458–70.

Dell'Osso, B., Altamura, A.C., Allen, A., Marazziti, D. and Hollander, E. (2006) 'Epidemiologic and clinical updates on impulse control disorders: A critical review', *European Archives of Psychiatry and Clinical Neuroscience*, 256(8): 464–75.

Dickman, S.J. (1990) 'Functional and dysfunctional impulsivity: Personality and cognitive correlates', *Journal of Personality and Social Psychology*, 58(1): 95–102.

Dom, G., De Wilde, B., Hulstijn, W., van den Brink, W. and Sabbe, B. (2006) 'Behavioural aspects of impulsivity in alcoholics with and without a cluster-B personality disorder', *Alcohol*, 41(4): 412–20.

Dougherty, D.M., Mathias, C.W., Marsh, D.M. Moeller, F.G. and Swann, A.C. (2004) 'Suicidal behaviors and drug abuse: Impulsivity and its assessment', *Drug and Alcohol Dependence*, 76(suppl. 1): S93–S105.

Dougherty, D.M., Bjork, J.M., Moeller, F.G., Harper, R.A., Marsh, D.M., Mathias, C.W. and Swann, A.C. (2003) 'Familial transmission of Continuous Performance Test behavior: Attentional and impulsive response characteristics', *Journal of General Psychology*, 130(1): 5–21.

Durston, S., Fossella, J.A., Casey, B.J., Hulshoff Pol, H.E., Galvan, A., Schnach, H.G., Steenhuis, M.P., Minderaa, R.B., Buitelaar, J.K.,

Kahn, R.S. and van Engeland, H. (2005) 'Differential effects of DRD4 and DAT1 genotype on fronto-striatal gray matter volumes in a sample of subjects with attention deficit hyperactivity disorder, their unaffected siblings, and controls', *Molecular Psychiatry*, 10(7): 678–85.

Esposito, C. and Spirito, A. (2003) *Behavioral Factors: Impulsive and Aggressive Behavior. Evaluating and Treating Adolescent Suicide Attempters: From Research to Practice.* San Diego, CA, Academic Press.

Evenden, J.L. (1999) 'Varieties of impulsivity', *Psychopharmacology (Berl)*, 146(4): 348–61.

Eysenck, S.B., Pearson, P.R., Easting, G. and Allsopp, J.F. (1985) 'Age norms for impulsiveness, venturesomeness and empathy in adults', *Personality and Individual Differences*, 6(5): 613–19.

Faraone, S.V., Doyle, A.E., Mick, E. and Biederman, J. (2001) 'Meta-analysis of the association between the 7-repeat allele of the dopamine D(4) receptor gene and attention deficit hyperactivity disorder', *American Journal of Psychiatry*, 158(7): 1052–7.

Faraone, S.V., Perlis, R.H., Doyle, A.E., Smoller, J.W., Goralnick, J.J., Holmgren, M.A. and Sklar, P. (2005) 'Molecular genetics of attention–deficit/hyperactivity disorder', *Biological Psychiatry*, 57(11): 1313–23.

Faraone, S.V., Tsuang, D. and Tsuang, M.T. (2002) 'Methods in psychiatric genetics', in M.T. Tsuang and M. Tohen (eds), *Textbook in Psychiatric Epidemiology* (2nd edn). New York: John Wiley & Sons, pp. 65–130.

Flory, J.D., Harvey, P.D. Mitropoulou, V., New, A.S., Silverman, J.M., Siever, L.J. and Manuck, S.B. (2006) 'Dispositional impulsivity in normal and abnormal samples', *Journal Psychiatric Research*, 40(5): 438–47.

Fossati, A., Barratt, E.S., Carretta, I., Leonardi, B., Grazioli, F. and Maffei, C. (2004) 'Predicting borderline and antisocial personality disorder features in nonclinical subjects using measures of impulsivity and aggressiveness', *Psychiatry Research*, 125(2): 161–70.

Garavan, H., Ross, T.J., Murphy, K., Roche, R.A. and Stein, E.A. (2002) 'Dissociable executive functions in the dynamic control of behavior: Inhibition, error detection, and correction', *NeuroImage*, 17(4): 1820–9.

Garavan, H., Ross, T.J. and Stein, E.A. (1999) 'Right hemispheric dominance of inhibitory control: An event-related functional MRI study', *Proceedings of the National Academy of Sciences USA*, 96(14): 8301–6.

Gerfen, C.R. (2000) 'Molecular effects of dopamine on striatal-projection pathways', *Trends in Neurosciences*, 23(suppl.1): S64–S70.

Gottesman, I.I. and Gould, T.D. (2003) 'The endophenotype concept in psychiatry: Etymology and strategic intentions', *American Journal of Psychiatry*, 160(4): 636–45.

Grace, A.A. (1991) 'Phasic versus tonic dopamine release and the modulation of dopamine system responsivity: A hypothesis for the etiology of schizophrenia', *Neuroscience*, 41(1): 1–24.

Grant, J.E., Levine, L., Kim, D. and Potenza, M.N. (2005) 'Impulse control disorders in adult psychiatric inpatients', *American Journal of Psychiatry*, 162(11): 2184–8.

Grant, J.E. and Potenza, M.N. (2004) 'Impulse control disorders: Clinical characteristics and pharmacological management', *Annals of Clinical Psychiatry*, 16(1): 27–34.

Hariri, A.R. and Weinberger, D.R. (2003) 'Imaging genomics', *British Medical Bulletin*, 65: 259–70.

Hasler, G., Drevets, W.C., Manji, H.K. and Charney, D.S. (2004) 'Discovering endophenotypes for major depression', *Neuropsychopharmacology*, 29(10): 1765–81.

Hazlett, E.A., New, A.S., Newmark, R., Haznedar, M.M., Lo, J.N., Speiser, L.J., Chen, A.D., Mitropoulou, V., Minzenberg, M., Siever, L.J. and Buchsbaum, M.S. (2005) 'Reduced anterior and posterior cingulate gray matter in borderline personality disorder', *Biological Psychiatry*, 58(8): 614–23.

Hollander, E. and Rosen, J. (2000) 'Impulsivity', *Journal of Psychopharmacology*, 14(2 suppl. 1): S39–44.

Hoptman, M.J., Ardekani, B.A., Butler, P.D., Nierenberg, J., Javitt, D.C. and Lim, K.O. (2004) 'DTI and impulsivity in schizophrenia: A first voxelwise correlational analysis', *Neuroreport*, 15(16): 2467–70.

Horn, N.R., Dolan, M., Elliott, R., Deakin, J.F. and Woodruff, P.W. (2003) 'Response inhibition and impulsivity: An fMRI study', *Neuropsychologia*, 41(14): 1959–66.

Kessler, R.C., Berglund, P., Demler, O., Jin, R., Merikangas, K.R. and Walters, E.E. (2005) 'Lifetime prevalence and age-of-onset distributions of DSM-IV disorders in the National Comorbidity Survey Replication', *Archives of General Psychiatry*, 62(6): 593–602.

Kessler, R.C., Chiu, W.T., Demler, O., Merikangas, K.R. and Walters, E.E. (2005) 'Prevalence, severity, and comorbidity of 12-month DSM-IV disorders in the National Comorbidity Survey Replication', *Archives of General Psychiatry*, 62(6): 617–27.

Konishi, S., Nakajima, K., Uchida, I., Sekihara, K. and Miyashita, Y. (1998) 'No-go dominant brain activity in human inferior prefrontal cortex revealed by functional magnetic resonance imaging', *European Journal of Neuroscience*, 10(3): 1209–13.

Larsson, H., Andershed, H. and Lichtenstein, P. (2006) 'A genetic factor explains most of the variation in the psychopathic personality', *Journal of Abnormal Psychology*, 115(2): 221–30.

Lewis, D.A., Melchitzky, D.S., Sesack, S.R., Whitehead, R.E., Auh, S., Sampson, A. (2001) 'Dopamine transporter immunoreactivity in monkey cerebral cortex: Regional, laminar, and ultrastructural localization', *Journal of Comparative Neurology*, 432: 119–36.

Leyton, M., Okazawa, H., Diksic, M., Paris, J., Rosa, P., Mzengeza, S., Young, S.N., Blier, P. and Benkelfat, C. (2001) 'Brain regional alpha-[11C]methyl-L-tryptophan trapping in impulsive subjects with borderline personality disorder', *American Journal of Psychiatry*, 158(5): 775–82.

Li, D., Sham, P.C., Owen, M.J. and He, L. (2006) 'Meta-analysis shows significant association between dopamine system genes and attention deficit hyperactivity disorder (ADHD)', *Human Molecular Genetics*, 15(14): 2276–84.

Liddle, P.F., Kiehl, K.A. and Smith, A.M. (2001) 'Event-related fMRI study of response inhibition', *Human Brain Mapping*, 12(2): 100–9.

Lijffijit, M., Kenemans, J.L., Verbaten, M.N. and van Engeland, H. (2005) 'A meta-analytic review of stopping performance in attention-deficit/hyperactivity disorder: Deficient inhibitory motor control?', *Journal of Abnormal Psychology*, 114(2): 216–22.

Links, P.S., Heslegrave, R. and van Reekum, R. (1999) 'Impulsivity: Core aspect of borderline personality disorder', *Journal of Personality Disorders*, 13(1): 1–9.

Liston, C., Watts, R., Tottenham, N., Davidson, M.C., Niogi, S., Ulug, A.M. and Casey, B.J. (2006) 'Frontostriatal microstructure modulates efficient recruitment of cognitive control', *Cerebral Cortex*, 16(4): 553–60.

Livesely, W.J., Jang, K.L. and Vernon, P.A. (1998) 'Phenotypic and genetic structure of traits delineating personality disorder', *Archives of General Psychiatry*, 55(10): 941–8.

Logan, G.D. (1994) 'On the ability to inhibit thought and action: A user's guide to the stop signal paradigm', in D. Dagenbach and T.H. Carr (eds), *Inhibitory Processes in Attention, Memory, and Language*. San Diego: Academic Press, pp. 189–239.

Logan, G.D., Schachar, R.J. and Tannock, R. (1997) 'Impulsivity and inhibitory control', *Psychological Science*, 8(1): 60–64.

MacQueen, G.M., Hajek, T. and Alda, M. (2005) 'The phenotypes of bipolar disorder: Relevance for genetic investigations', *Molecular Psychiatry*, 10(9): 811–26.

Mazei, M.S., Pluto, C.P., Kirkbride, B. and Pehek, E.A. (2002) 'Effects of catecholamine uptake blockers in the caudate-putamen and subregions of the medial prefrontal cortex of the rat', *Brain Research*, 936(1–2): 58–67.

Meador-Woodruff, J.H., Damask, S.P., Wang, J., Haroutunian, V., Davis, K.L. and Watson, S.J. (1996) 'Dopamine receptor mRNA expression in human striatum and neocortex', *Neuropsychopharmacology*, 15(1): 17–29.

Melchitzky, D.S. and Lewis, D.A. (2001) 'Dopamine transporter-immunoreactive axons in the mediodorsal thalamic nucleus of the macaque monkey', *Neuroscience*, 103(4): 1033–42.

Meyer-Lindenberg, A., Buckholtz, J.W., Kolachana, B., Hariri, A.R., Pezawas, L., Blasi, G., Wabnitz, A., Honea, R., Verchinski, B., Callicott, J.H., Egan, M., Mattay, V. and Weinberger, D.R. (2006) 'Neural mechanisms of genetic risk for impulsivity and violence in humans', *Proceedings of the National Academy of Sciences*, 103(16): 6269–74.

Mink, J.W. (1996) 'The basal ganglia: Focused selection and inhibition of competing motor programs', *Progress in Neurobiology*, 50(4): 381–425.

Moeller, F.G., Hasan, K.M., Steinberg, J.L., Kramer, L.A., Dougherty, D.M., Santos, R.M., Valdes, I., Swann, A.C., Barratt, E.S. and Narayana, P.A. (2005) 'Reduced anterior corpus callosum white matter integrity is related to increased impulsivity and reduced discriminability in cocaine-dependent subjects: Diffusion tensor imaging', *Neuropsychopharmacology*, 30(3): 610–7.

Mulcrone, J. and Kerwin, R.W. (1997) 'The regional pattern of D4 gene expression in human brain', *Neuroscience Letters*, 234(2–3): 147–50.

Nambu, A.S., Tokuno, H. and Takada, M. (2002) 'Functional significance of the cortico-sub-thalamo-pallidal "hyperdirect" pathway', *Neuroscience Research*, 43(2): 111–17.

New, A.S. and Siever, L.J. (2003) 'Biochemical endophenotypes in personality disorders', *Methods in Molecular Medicine*, 77: 199–213.

Newman, J.P., Wallace, J.F., Schmitt, W.A. and Arnett, P.A. (1997) 'Behavioral inhibition system functioning in anxious, impulsive and psychopathic individuals', *Personality and Individual Differences*, 23(4): 583–92.

Nigg, J.T. (2000) 'On inhibition/disinhibition in developmental psychopathology: Views from cognitive and personality psychology and a working inhibition taxonomy', *Psychological Bulletin*, 126(2): 220–46.

Passamonti, L., Fera, F., Magariello, A., Cerasa, A., Gioia, M.C., Muglia, M., Nocoletti, G., Gallo, O., Provinciali, L. and Quattrone, A. (2006) 'Monoamine oxidase – a genetic variations influence brain activity associated with inhibitory control: New insight into the neural correlates of impulsivity', *Biological Psychiatry*, 59(4): 334–40.

Patton, J.H., Stanford, M.S. and Barratt, E.S. (1995) 'Factor structure of the Barratt impulsiveness scale', *Journal of Clinical Psychology*, 51(6): 768–74.

Pedersen, N.L., Plomin, R., McClearn, G.E. and Friberg, L. (1988) 'Neuroticism, extraversion, and related traits in adult twins reared apart and reared together', *Journal of Personality and Social Psychology*, 55(6): 950–7.

Plomin, R., Owen, M.J. and McGuffin, P. (1994) 'The genetic basis of complex human behaviors', *Science*, 264(5166): 1733–9.

Robbins, T.W. (2005) 'Chemistry of the mind: Neurochemical modulation of prefrontal cortical function', *Journal of Comparative Neurology*, 493(1): 140–6.

Roman, T., Schmitz, M., Polanczyk, G., Eizirik, M., Rohde, L.A. and Hutz, M.H. (2001) 'Attention-deficit hyperactivity disorder: A study of association with both the dopamine transporter gene and the dopamine D4 receptor gene', *American Journal of Medical Genetics*, 105(5): 471–8.

Rubia, K., Russell, T., Overmeyer, S., Brammer, M.J., Bullmore, E.T., Sharma, T., Simmons, A., Williams, S.C.R., Giampietro, V., Andrew, C.M.

and Taylor, E. (2001) 'Mapping motor inhibition: Conjunctive brain activation across difference versions of Go/No-Go and Stop Tasks', *NeuroImage*, 13(2): 250–61.

Rucklidge, J.J. and Tannock, R. (2002) 'Neuropsychological profiles of adolescents with ADHD: Effects of reading difficulties and gender', *Journal of Child Psychology and Psychiatry*, 43(8): 988–1003.

Schachar, R.J., Tannock, R. and Logan, G. (1993) 'Inhibitory control, impulsiveness, and attention deficit hyperactivity disorder', *Clinical Psychology Review*, 13(8): 721–39.

Schmidt, C.A., Fallon, A.E. and Coccaro, E.F. (2004) 'Assessment of behavioral and cognitive impulsivity: Development and validation of the Lifetime History Of Impulsive Behaviors Interview', *Psychiatry Research*, 126(2): 107–21.

Schott, B.H., Seidenbecher, C.I., Fenker, D.B., Lauer, C.J., Bunzeck, N., Bernstein, H.G., Tischmeyer, W., Gundelfinger, E.D., Heinze, H.J. and Duzel, E. (2006) 'The dopaminergic midbrain participates in human episodic memory formation: Evidence from genetic imaging', *Journal of Neuroscience*, 26(5): 1407–17.

Seamans, J.K. and Yang, C.R. (2004) 'The principal features and mechanisms of dopamine modulation in the prefrontal cortex', *Progress in Neurobiology*, 74(1): 1–58.

Seroczynski, A.D., Bergeman, C.S. and Coccaro, E.F. (1999) 'Etiology of the impulsivity/aggression relationship: Genes or environment?', *Psychiatry Research*, 86(1): 41–57.

Sesack, S.R., Hawrylak, V.A., Matus, C., Guido, M.A. and Levey, A.I. (1998) 'Dopamine axon varicosities in the prelimbic division of the rat prefrontal cortex exhibit sparse immunoreactivity for the dopamine transporter', *Journal of Neuroscience*, 18(7): 2697–708.

Sher, K.J., Bartholow, B.D. and Wood, M.D. (2000) 'Personality and substance use disorders: A prospective study', *Journal of Consulting and Clinical Psychology*, 68(5): 818–29.

Silverman, J.M., Pinkham, L., Horvath, T.B., Coccaro, E.F., Klar, H., Schear, S., Apter, S., Davidson, M., Mohs, R.C. and Siever, L.J. (1991) 'Affective and impulsive personality disorder traits in the relatives of patients with borderline personality disorder', *American Journal of Psychiatry*, 148(10): 1378–85.

Solanto, M.V., Abikoff, H., Sonuga-Barke, E., Schachar, R., Logan, G.D., Wigal, T.,

Hechtman, L., Hinshaw, S. and Turkel, E. (2001) 'The ecological validity of delay aversion and response inhibition as measures of impulsivity in AD/HD: A supplement to the NIMH multimodal treatment study of AD/HD', *Journal of Abnormal Child Psychology*, 29(3): 215–28.

Stanford, M.S., Houston, R.J., Villemarette-Pittman, N.R. and Greve, K.W. (2003) 'Premeditated aggression: Clinical assessment and cognitive psychophysiology', *Personality and Individual Differences*, 34: 773–81.

Swann, A.C., Dougherty, D.M., Pazzagila, P.J., Pham, M. and Moeller, F.G. (2004) 'Impulsivity: A link between bipolar disorder and substance abuse', *Bipolar Disorder*, 6(3): 204–12.

Swann, A.C., Pazzagila, P., Nicholls, A., Dougherty, D.M. and Moeller, F.G. (2003) 'Impulsivity and phase of illness in bipolar disorder', *Journal of Affective Disorders*, 73(1–2): 105–11.

Szobot, C., Roman, T., Cunha, R., Acton, P., Hutz, M. and Rohde, L.A. (2005) 'Brain perfusion and dopaminergic genes in boys with attention-deficit/hyperactivity disorder', *American Journal of Medical Genetics B: Neuropsychiatric Genetics*, 132(1): 53–8.

Taylor, J., Loney, B.R., Bobadilla, L., Iacono, W.G. and McGue, M. (2003) 'Genetic and environmental influences on psychopathy trait dimensions in a community sample of male twins', *Journal of Abnormal Child Psychology*, 31(6): 633–45.

Taylor, J., Reeves, M., James, L. and Bobadilla, L. (2006) 'Disinhibitory trait profile and its relation to cluster B personality disorder features and substance use problems', *European Journal of Personality*, 20(4): 271–84.

Valdes, I.H., Steinberg, J.L., Narayana, P.A., Kramer, L.A., Dougherty, D.M., Swann, A.C., Barratt, E.S. and Moeller, F.G. (2006) 'Impulsivity and BOLD fMRI activation in MDMA users and healthy control subjects', *Psychiatry Research*, 147(2–3): 239–42.

Yen, S., Shea, M.T., Sanislow, C.A., Grilo, C.M., Skodol, A.E., Gunderson, J.G., McGlashan, T.H., Zanarini, M.C. and Morey, L.C. (2004) 'Borderline personality disorder criteria associated with prospectively observed suicidal behavior', *American Journal of Psychiatry*, 161(7): 1296–8.

17

Temperament from a Psychometric Perspective: Theory and Measurement

Jan Strelau and Bogdan Zawadzki

Conceptualizations of temperament go back to the ancient Greek typology developed by Hippocrates (4th century BC) and Galen (2nd century BC). The latter author in his work *De Temperamentis* (Lat. *temperare* – to mix, to combine in a proper proportion) described nine temperaments among which the four considered by him as primary temperament types are well known among laymen: sanguine, choleric, melancholic, and phlegmatic. Their names refer to those humors that predominate in a given body. Many philosophers adverted to this idea; one may for instance recall Kant's theory of temperament (see Figure 17.1A). For constitution-oriented psychologists like Sheldon (Sheldon and Stevens, 1942) and Kretschmer (1944), the ancient Greek typology served as a model for their own conceptualizations. Also the founder of experimental psychology, W. Wundt (1887), should be mentioned here as the initiator of the dimension-oriented approach to temperament (personality). Referring to Hippocrates and Galen, he interpreted the four mentioned

types in terms of dimensions (traits; see Figure 17.1B) – an idea later developed by Eysenck (1970).

There is no common understanding of the concept of 'temperament'. Some authors, going back to the definition of temperament proposed by G. Allport (1937), refer to temperament understood as relatively stable differences in the domain of broadly understood emotions (e.g. Eysenck, 1970; Gray, 1991). Other researchers claim that temperamental traits are expressed in all kinds of behavior (e.g. Strelau, 1998; Thomas and Chess, 1977). Nevertheless, all temperament researchers agree that temperament is present since early infancy, that it occurs in animals, and has a genetic background (e.g. Buss and Plomin, 1984; Kagan, 1994; Strelau, 1998). For the purpose of the chapter we define temperament as a set of relatively stable personality traits present since early infancy in people and animals. Although primarily determined by inborn neurobiochemical mechanisms, temperament undergoes during

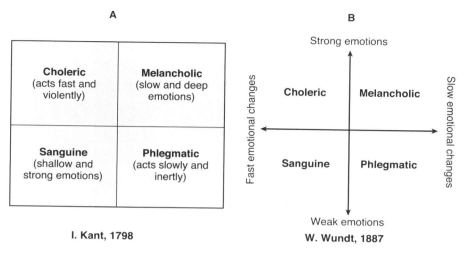

Figure 17.1   The Hippocrates–Galen typology expressed as a pigeonhole (A) and dimensional (B) model. From: *Psychologia różnic indywidualnych* **[***Psychology of Individual Differences***] by J. Strelau, 2002, p. 20. Copyright 2002 by Wydawnictwo Naukowe Scholar. Reprinted with permission**

ontogeny changes caused by maturation and individual-specific genotype–environment interplays.

THE FOUNDERS OF CONTEMPORARY CONCEPTUALIZATIONS OF TEMPERAMENT

Contemporary views on temperament have their roots in two theories which developed at the beginning of the second half of the twentieth century in Europe and the US. The European approach to temperament is based on Eysenck's theory of temperament and constitutes the starting point for theories which concentrate mainly on adult temperament. The modern American approach to temperament, on the other hand, has its roots in Thomas and Chess' theory and focuses on temperament in children. The reader may find the broadest review of temperament theories in Strelau's (1998) monograph, thus only a short presentation of both theories mentioned above will be portrayed here.

Eysenck's three superfactors theory of temperament (PEN)

Hans Eysenck's exhaustive factor analysis studies based on empirical data and on historical backgrounds going back to Hippocrates and Galen, C.G. Jung (1923) – the author of the term 'extraversion–introversion', and Pavlov's (1938) studies on basic nervous system properties, resulted in the development of a temperament (personality) theory which postulates a hierarchical structure composed of three dimensions – psychoticism (P), extraversion (E), and neuroticism (N). It must be added that Eysenck, despite using mostly the term 'personality' when describing his three dimensions, treated both terms – 'personality' and 'temperament' – as synonyms.

Most important in Eysenck's theory is the fact that he hypothesized a biological background for the PEN dimensions and adopted this assumption as a starting point for putting forward hypotheses regarding the role of these dimensions in human functioning under laboratory conditions as well as in everyday life situations. According to his preliminary view on the biological roots of extraversion–introversion (E–I), introverts occupy the excitation pole on the dimension of cortical excitation–inhibition balance, while extraverts are located on the inhibition pole. This view was influenced by Hull's (1943) concept of reactive inhibition and by Pavlov's (1938) typological theory of excitation and inhibition. Under the influence of studies demonstrating that the reticular formation of the brainstem produces unspecific activation, which is expressed in spontaneous EEG activity and known as cortical arousal, Eysenck changed his view regarding the biological background of the E–I dimension (Eysenck, 1967). He postulated that individual differences (ID) in the activity of the cortico-reticular loop are responsible for the individual's position on the E–I dimension. 'Introverts are characterized by higher levels of activity than extraverts and so are chronically more aroused than extraverts' (Eysenck and Eysenck, 1985: 197). Extraversion was the temperament trait whose biological background was in the center of his investigations.

The search for the biological background of neuroticism led Eysenck to the conclusion that the differential responsiveness of the sympathetic nervous system, constituting the basis for such emotional states as emotional excitability, tension, and anxiety, must be regarded as the physiological basis mediating differences in neuroticisms. In neurotic individuals, the reactivity of the sympathetic nervous system is higher as compared with emotionally stable individuals. This view – again owing to the discovery of the arousal phenomenon – became modified, and Eysenck located the physiological center of neuroticism in the visceral brain. It is the variability of the responsiveness of the hippocampus, amygdala, cingulum, septum, and hypothalamus that is responsible for ID in neuroticism (Eysenck, 1967; Eysenck and Eysenck, 1985). The physiological background of psychoticism is at least unclear, and in fact Eysenck did not develop a physiological theory of this personality dimension, which – as shown by psychometric studies in

the domain of the Big Five factors – seems to be composed of low conscientiousness and low agreeableness (McCrae and Costa, 1985). The idea to search for biological backgrounds of the PEN dimensions by referring to such constructs as 'arousal' and 'activation' constituted the basis for almost all biologically oriented temperament theories.

The PEN theory is extremely rich with regard to empirical data supporting the functional significance of the Eysenckian three superfactors expressed in behavior and in behavioral disorders. A detailed account of these studies may be found elsewhere (Eysenck and Eysenck, 1985; see also Strelau, 1998). Although many studies on the PEN dimensions were conducted under experimental conditions, Eysenck together with his co-workers developed several inventories for diagnosing the three superfactors. Among the most popular are: the Eysenck Personality Inventory (EPI) constructed by Eysenck and Sybil Eysenck (1964) and composed of three scales: extraversion (regarded as a composition of sociability and impulsivity), neuroticism, and the lie scale. Under the influence of empirical data the EPI was expanded by the psychoticism scale, what resulted in developing the Eysenck Personality Questionnaire (EPQ) (Eysenck and Eysenck, 1976) and, in the final stage of constructing inventories to measure the PEN factors, the Eysenck Personality Questionnaire – Revised (EPQ-R) (Eysenck et al., 1985). The EPQ-R, together with the EPI, has been adapted to many countries and languages and became the most popular inventory for measuring the PEN dimensions.

The interactional theory of temperament in children: Thomas and Chess' NYLS approach

In 1956, two psychiatrists, Alexander Thomas and Stella Chess, undertook a longitudinal study on temperament known as the New York Longitudinal Study (NYLS) (Thomas and Chess, 1977; Chess and Thomas, 1984).

In studying the interaction between temperament characteristics and the environment, the authors referred to the evolutional concept of goodness of fit which became a crucial construct in their so-called interactional theory of temperament. They claimed that temperament refers to the stylistic aspect of behavior. 'Temperament may be best viewed as a general term referring to the *how* of behavior. It differs from ability, which is concerned with the *what* and *how well* of behaving, and from motivation, which accounts for *why* a person does what he is doing' (Thomas and Chess, 1977: 9).

Their initial study on children's temperament at the age of 2–3 months was based on two cardinal assumptions: (1) children show individual differences in temperament; and (2) temperament plays an important role in normal and deviant development. Based on a study conducted on infants aged 2–3 months (part of which was followed up for over three decades), the authors postulated that the structure of children's temperament is composed of nine temperament categories (the term preferred by the authors):

- *Activity level*: the motor component in a child's behavior and the diurnal proportion of active to inactive periods.
- *Rhythmicity (Regularity)*: the regularity or irregularity of biological functions (e.g. sleep–wake cycle).
- *Approach or withdrawal*: the nature of the initial response to a new stimulus (e.g. food, toy, person); both are expressed in emotions and/or motor activity.
- *Adaptability*: the ease with which behavior can be changed in a desired direction.
- *Threshold of responsiveness*: the intensity of stimulation required to evoke a discernible response.
- *Intensity of reaction*: the energy level of the response, irrespective of its quality.
- *Quality of mood*: the extent of positive emotions as contrasted with negative ones.
- *Distractibility*: the effectiveness of extraneous stimuli in drawing attention away from the ongoing behavior.
- *Attention span and persistence*: the uninterrupted length of time a particular activity can be pursued (attention span) and the ability to continue the activity in the face of distractors (persistence).

On the basis of studies on normally developed children as well as on children with behavior disorders, the authors were able to distinguish three following constellations of temperament based on different compositions of temperament categories (traits): *difficult temperament* (irregularity, withdrawal, nonadaptability, intense reactions, and negative mood); *easy temperament* (high scores on regularity, approach, and adaptability, mild intense reactions and predominance of positive mood); and *slow-to-warm-up temperament* for which slow adaptability and negative reactions to new stimuli (situations) are the most typical. The authors' study concentrated mainly on the concept of difficult temperament present in about 10% of children. According to Chess and Thomas, difficult temperament 'placed a child at greater risk for behavior disorder development than did any other set of temperament characteristics' (1984: 186). But the lack of direct relationship between temperament constellations and behavior disorders led the authors to the concept of *goodness of fit* which occurs when the individual's capacities, temperament, and other individual characteristics are in accord with the demands and expectations of the surrounding world. A long-lasting dissonance between those variables may result in *poorness of fit* leading to maladaptive functioning and distorted development.

For assessing the categories of temperament as well for diagnosing the three temperamental constellations several inventories have been developed, taking into account the developmental specificity starting with 1-month-old infants. Most of them have been constructed by Carey and McDevitt (e.g. 1978, 1994). For children, but also for adolescents and adults, an inventory known as the Revised Dimensions of Temperament Survey (DOTS-R) developed by Windle and Lerner (1986) has gained much popularity. For a review of inventories corresponding or closely related to Thomas and Chess' theory of temperament see Strelau (1998).

The NYLS study on temperament is based on a fully descriptive theory, without any assumptions regarding the biological background of the temperamental traits postulated by Thomas and Chess. However, their theory stimulated many researchers to develop their own conceptualizations which, although of different origin, have several elements in common. These include the concentration on infants and children, searching for continuity and stability of temperament, underlining the contextual approach of this construct, and studying temperament as related to clinical, educational, and parental issues.

SELECTED THEORIES OF TEMPERAMENT IN CHILDREN

There is no way to present the majority of temperament conceptualizations which refer to infants and children in just one chapter (for a review, see Strelau, 1998). According to our insight, three of them gained the greatest popularity, namely Buss' and Plomin's behavior-genetic theory of temperament, the developmental model of temperament by Rothbart, and Kagan's theory of inhibited and uninhibited temperaments.

The behavior-genetic theory of temperament by Buss and Plomin

One of the first theories of children's temperament following Thomas and Chess' interactional model was the one developed by Buss and Plomin (1975). The authors defined temperament as 'inherited personality traits present in early childhood' (Buss and Plomin, 1984: 84). According to them temperament has an essential impact on personality development. In infancy, when internal cognitive structures are still lacking, the child's temperament constitutes his or her whole personality. Temperamental traits should be *broad*, by which they mean that they refer to a wide class of behaviors and situations. Buss and Plomin distinguished the three following temperamental traits: emotionality, activity, and

sociability (EAS, an acronym with which their temperament theory has often been labeled). They defined *emotionality* as a tendency to be aroused. 'Emotionality equals distress, the tendency to become upset easily and intensely' (Buss and Plomin, 1984: 54). The authors did not include positive emotions in their emotionality temperament arguing that the level of arousal of this kind of emotion is below that typical for negative emotions. According to Buss and Plomin, *activity* refers to the total energy output and is expressed in any kind of behavior. Activity consists of two components – vigor and tempo – positively correlated with each other. It is regarded as a stylistic trait because every response is accompanied by expended energy, and thus varies in vigor and tempo. The third trait, *sociability*, has a directional component – the seeking of other persons. Sociability, as expressed in social interactions which result in intrinsic rewards, is developmentally specific.

The authors postulate that the biology of EAS refers to three levels of arousal. As regards activity, it is behavioral arousal which may vary from deep sleep to high excitement. Emotionality is regulated by individual differences in autonomic arousal. Sympathetic dominance of the autonomic nervous system (ANS) is typical for individuals who receive high scores in emotionality. The authors postulate that sociability is highly related to Eysenckian extraversion (Buss and Plomin, 1984), thus the physiological basis of activity probably consists of brain arousal.

For measuring the EAS traits, the authors developed two inventories – one for children (parent-rating) and one for adults (self-report). They are known as the EAS – Temperament Survey (EAS-TS). Both versions have activity and sociability scales, but emotionality is represented by different, developmentally specific components of this trait. In the EAS-TS for children there are five emotionality scales: emotionality, shyness, distress, fearfulness, and anger; the EAS-TS for adults has three: distress, fearfulness, and anger. Curiously enough, the psychometric goodness of the EAS-TS inventories has never been fully elaborated.

The developmental model of temperament by Rothbart

The model of temperament developed by Mary Rothbart and her associates, which gained the highest popularity among developmental psychologists, may be described as a child-oriented (developmental), psychobiological, and multidimentional approach concentrated on children's whole behavior (Rothbart, 1989; Rothbart et al., 2000; Rothbart and Posner, 1985). Rothbart considers temperament in terms of constitutional differences in reactivity and self-regulation, whereby the term 'constitutional' refers to individual-specific biological make-up influenced by heredity, maturation, and experience. The construct *reactivity* refers to the arousability of the somatic, autonomic, neuroendocrine, and cognitive systems and is expressed in response parameters of threshold, latency, intensity, rise, and recovery time. *Self-regulation*, in turn, refers to processes that modulate reactivity by means of behaviors and reactions expressed in attention, approach, withdrawal, attack, behavioral inhibition, and self-soothing. As Rothbart wrote, the 'constructs of reactivity and self-regulation are very similar to Strelau's' (1989: 59). There is a continuous interaction between reactivity and self-regulation with an increasing influence of the latter on reactivity. By means of self-regulatory processes, which with age become subject to effortful (conscious) control, the individual is able to modulate reactivity. *Effort*, identified by means of the concept of will, is regarded as the ability to inhibit responses to stimuli when intentionally required.

Temperamental traits have their developmental specificity and the complexity of temperament structure growth with age. Whereas in newborn babies only distress, soothability, activity, attention, and approach-withdrawal may be observed, in early infancy, smiling and laughter, vocalization, stimulus seeking and avoidance, as well as frustration, are additionally present (Rothbart, 1989). For this very reason the scales of temperament inventories change with age.

The view on the biological bases of temperament has been subordinated by Rothbart to a developmental approach taking into account the fact that developmental changes in temperament go along with the maturation of the nervous system. These bases comprise the arousability of the ANS and the central nervous system (CNS), endocrine processes, and the activity of neurotransmitters, especially of norepinephrine, dopamine, and serotonin. All of these factors act as complex phenomena underlying ID in temperament.

Among the inventories developed by Rothbart and her associates, two of them are the best known: the Infant Behavior Questionnaire (IBQ), based on the Thomas and Chess theory of temperament; and the Children's Behavior Questionnaire (CBQ) (Rothbart et al., 2001). IBQ aimed at studying infants at the age of 3–12 months and contained six scales which have been extended in its revised form (IBQ-R; Garstein and Rothbart, 2003) to the following 14 scales: approach, vocal reactivity, high pleasure, smile and laughter, activity level, perceptual sensitivity, sadness, distress to limitations, fear, falling reactivity, low pleasure, cuddliness, duration of orienting, and soothability (Garstein and Rothbart, 2003). The CBQ, aimed at studying children aged 4–7 years, is composed of 15 scales, of which effortful control is the one which distinguishes it most from IBQ-R.

The theory of inhibited and uninhibited temperaments by Kagan

According to Kagan (1994), temperament refers to inherited profiles of behavior and biology, which are present in the infant and which mediate phenotypic displays depending on childhood experiences. Taking into account the observation that children differ in their initial reactions to unfamiliar events (people, objects, situations), he developed a theory around one dimension, the extremes of which result in two qualitatively different categories: inhibited and uninhibited temperament.

A child with an *inhibited temperament* is consistently shy, quiet, cautious, and emotionally reserved when confronted with unfamiliarity, whereas a child with an *uninhibited temperament* under the same conditions is sociable, talkative, and affectively spontaneous. Physiological, genetic, and behavioral patterns are specific for the two temperaments. As longitudinal studies conducted in Kagan's laboratory have shown (e.g. Kagan and Reznick, 1986; Kagan and Snidman, 1991), the two temperaments are relatively stable across age. Kagan (1994) suggests that the categories of inhibited and uninhibited temperament in children to a certain extent correspond to the approach–withdrawal tendency met in animals, as well as to introversion–extraversion as postulated by Eysenck. They also bear some similarity to the weak and strong types of the nervous system according to Pavlov (1938).

The physiological bases of the two temperaments refer to ID in reactivity thresholds of such CNS structures as the limbic system, especially the amygdala and hypothalamus, and systems connected with the latter (pituitary–adrenal axis, reticular activating system, and the sympathetic chain of the ANS). Inhibited children are characterized by lower reactivity thresholds of these structures. Instead of psychometric tools, Kagan and his co-workers used a whole set of physiological and biochemical markers of behavioral inhibition. Such measures as heart rate, heart rate variability, heart rate acceleration, pupillary dilation, level of urinary norepinephrine, adrenal axis cortisol levels, and so on, have been taken in conditions of psychological stress (unknown or unfamiliar situations) as indicators of ID in the two temperaments. Since correlations between the physiological and biochemical measures were rather low, an aggregate index of neurobiochemical activity was often used as the marker of inhibited temperament present in about 10% of children.

Since the chapter deals mainly with temperament constructs and dimensions assessed by means of inventories – this being the main diagnostic tool in the domain of temperament – we do not refer to Kagan's theory in the sections devoted to the assessment of temperament.

THE REGULATIVE THEORY OF TEMPERAMENT AS AN EXAMPLE OF A CONTEMPORARY APPROACH TO ADULT TEMPERAMENT

The list of temperament theories that refer to adults is rather scanty. One of the reasons is that several authors referring to traits (dimensions or factors) that fulfill the definitional criteria of temperament, such as biological roots, presence since infancy, and occurrence of their counterparts in animals, considered them – as Eysenck did – in terms of personality traits.

Selected temperament theories referring to adults

As examples of temperament theories, considered as personality ones with almost no place for the term 'temperament', such theories may serve as Gray's (1987, 1991) neuropsychological model of personality and Zuckerman's (1979, 1994) biological theory of sensation seeking. Both of them will be presented in separate chapters of the present handbook. A temperament theory which refers directly to adults and which gained high popularity during the last decade (especially among clinical-oriented researchers), is the psychobiological model of temperament developed by Cloninger and his co-workers (Cloninger, 1986; Cloninger et al., 1991, 1993; Svrakic et al., 1996). The authors made a clear distinction between temperament and character, the latter considered as one of the components of personality. In Russia the theory of adult temperament based on a functional systems approach developed by Rusalov (1989) gained some popularity. It is a conceptualization which refers to Pavlov's (1938) type of higher nervous activity interpreted in terms of Anokhin's (1978) theory of functional systems. (For a detailed description of this theory see

Strelau, 1998.) For the purpose of this chapter we will concentrate on the regulative theory of temperament postulated by Strelau (1983; 1998), which is considered to be one of the contemporary approaches to adult temperament that differs in several aspects from other theories of temperament.

Strelau's regulative theory of temperament (RTT)

The roots of the regulative theory of temperament (RTT) developed by Jan Strelau goes back to the Pavlovian typology of CNS properties according to which Pavlov (1938) himself distinguished three basic traits: strength of excitation, strength of inhibition, and the mobility of nervous processes. By applying a psychometric approach, the behavioral manifestations of these traits have been measured by means of the Strelau Temperament Inventory (STI) (Strelau, 1983) and a thoroughly modified version of STI developed by Strelau et al. (1999) known as the Pavlovian Temperament Survey (PTS). The final shape of the RTT was also influenced by Eysenck's PEN theory, the arousal theories initiated by Elisabeth Duffy (1957) and her followers, especially Gray's (1964) construct of arousability, and finally the theory of action as understood by Tomaszewski (1978).

According to the RTT, 'Temperament refers to basic, relatively stable personality traits expressed mainly in the formal (energetic and temporal) characteristics of behavior. These traits are present from early childhood and they have their counterpart in animals' (Strelau, 1998: 165). After a thorough psychometric study conducted on over 2,000 subjects (aged 15–80) Strelau and Zawadzki (1993: 327) described the structure of RTT temperament by the following six traits:

1   *Briskness* (BR): tendency to react quickly, to keep a high tempo in performing activities, and to shift easily in response to changes in the surroundings from one behavior (reaction) to another.
2   *Perseveration* (PE): tendency to continue and to repeat behavior or experience emotions after the cessation of stimuli (situations) which evoked this behavior or these emotions.
3   *Sensory sensitivity* (SS): ability to react to sensory stimuli of low stimulative value.
4   *Emotional reactivity* (ER): tendency to react intensively to emotion-generating stimuli, expressed in high emotional sensitivity and in low emotional endurance.
5   *Endurance* (EN): ability to react adequately in situations demanding long-lasting or high-stimulative activity and under intensive external stimulation.
6   *Activity* (AC): tendency to undertake behaviors of high stimulative value or to supply by means of behavior strong stimulation from the surroundings.

As postulated by the RTT, based on ten principles described elsewhere (Strelau, 2008), it is assumed that temperament traits take part in the regulation of the individual–environment relationship. This regulation consists of moderating all those behaviors and situations in which the energetic and temporal components play an important adaptive role. The adaptive role of the energetic components is especially evident when the individual is under intensive stimulation, experiences stress, and is confronted with demands requiring risk-taking activity. As far as temporal components are concerned, this role is manifested, among others, in behaviors and reactions requiring a speed of changes adequate to changes in the surrounding, and in the tempo of consecutive reactions (actions).

In contrast to some arousal-oriented temperament theories, the RTT does not postulate trait-specific neurophysiological and biochemical mechanisms. From the assumption that temperament refers to formal characteristics of behavior one may speculate that such features as sensitivity in synaptic transmission, the amount of neurotransmitters released, and the reactivity of neural structures to different kinds of stimuli take part in mediating ID in traits referring to the energetic characteristics of behavior. The temporal traits, such as perseveration and briskness, probably have their biological background in the neurophysiological and biochemical mechanisms responsible for the speed of elicitation, termination, and the course of nervous processes (Strelau, 1998). Since temperament is determined by individual-specific configurations of neurological (the physiology and biochemistry of the CNS and ANS) and endocrine systems regulating the energetic and temporal components of behavior, the term *neuroendocrine individuality* has been introduced (Strelau, 1983, 1998).

For measuring temperamental traits as postulated by the RTT, the questionnaire known as the Formal Characteristics of Behavior – Temperament Inventory (FCB-TI) has been developed by Strelau and Zawadzki (1993, 1995). The FCB-TI is composed of six scales, equivalent to the six traits composing the RTT temperament structure. The inventory has been developed in almost a dozen different cultures (languages) in two different forms referring to universal and culture-specific manifestations of temperament (the etic–emic version) as well as to universal manifestations only (the etic approach; see Zawadzki et al., 2001b).

THE PSYCHOMETRIC APPROACH TO TEMPERAMENT

Several methods are used to diagnose temperamental traits, but the most appropriate inventories are those based on self-report or on rating of behaviors and reactions (similarly to personality assessment). In some concepts the diagnosis is based on laboratory procedures (psychophysical and psychophysiological indices – see Kagan, 1994); however, low congruency among indices of the same temperamental characteristics suggested the necessity of using psychometric methods (see Strelau, 1983). The adoption of questionnaires in the assessment of temperamental traits linked temperament to the structure of personality, what resulted in the construction of temperamental instruments analogous to personality scales.[1] Thus, in modern concepts temperament is treated as a

part of personality and temperament instruments as similar to personality inventories. Based on the concept of temperament as biologically determined traits which constitute the core part of personality, several assumptions – underlying expected specificity of temperament traits and questionnaires – have been formulated as the basis for further consideration:

A   Temperamental traits regarded as personality dimensions should be measurable with high accuracy, which implies high homogeneity and reliability of temperamental scales (internal consistency; see Hubert et al., 1982; Slabach et al., 1991).

B   Temperamental traits might be diagnosed in humans from the very early ontogeny. Temperament instruments are designed to assess child as well as adult temperament – the former via self-report and rating by parents and teachers, the latter via self-report and peers (Buss and Plomin, 1984; Strelau, 1998).

C   Temperamental traits may be diagnosed in humans as well as in animals, although temperament inventories are designed to assess temperament in humans. Some attempts to diagnose animal temperament by laboratory procedures or behavior ratings are also made (Gosling and John, 1999; Strelau, 1998).

D   Temperamental traits are universal for all humans, in spite of cultural and demographic differences; traits may be identified in several cultures and demographic groups (Eysenck and Eysenck, 1985; Strelau, 1998). Temperament inventories are designed to assess temperament across cultures and demographic groups (see also point B).

E   Temperamental traits have a genetic background. Temperament inventories are designed to assess traits which should demonstrate high heritability (Buss and Plomin, 1984). Sometimes it is even suggested that their heritability should be higher than that of other personality dimensions (see Loehlin, 1992).

F   Temperamental traits are related to biological mechanisms. Temperamental traits assessed by inventories should demonstrate substantial relationships to psychophysical and neurobiochemical indices (Eysenck and Eysenck, 1985; Zuckerman, 1994).

G   Temperamental traits as a core and biologically determined part of personality should demonstrate high temporal stability. Temperamental instruments should show high test–retest reliability, or even higher than other personality traits (Buss and Plomin, 1984; Strelau, 1998).

H Temperamental traits manifest themselves in overt behavior, which implies their 'observability' (Angleitner and Riemann, 1991). Temperament inventories are designed to assess temperament via self-report and ratings (see also point B) with substantial congruence (Buss and Plomin, 1984).

I Temperamental traits determine behavior in every-day settings, yet they are the most strongly involved in the moderating of reactions to stress and in the pathogenesis of psychiatric and somatic illnesses. Temperament inventories should assess traits that have a substantial functional signifi-cance (Eysenck and Eysenck, 1985; Strelau, 1998).

J Finally, temperamental traits moderate (or mani-fest themselves in) normal and abnormal behav-ior; thus, temperament scales refer to such types of behavior as non-clinical, clinical, or to both, depending on the particular approach.

Taking into account all those assumptions, the chapter presents an overview of tempera-ment inventories and briefly describes the processes of their construction, their psycho-metric properties, and the type of data they provide.

Temperament inventories: Construction, psychometric properties, and data obtained by means of these instruments

Most temperament inventories are designed to assess either a child's or an adult's tem-perament only. In case of inventories for chil-dren, the assumption about the biological 'nature' of the assessed traits seems to be rea-sonable; however, a cross-demographic vali-dation should also be supplied. In case of adult temperament, it may be difficult to dis-tinguish temperament from other personality traits. The only method to prove that the assessed traits fulfill assumptions B and D is to develop a questionnaire aimed to assess both children and adults.

Another issue regarding the temperamental 'nature' of the measured traits is connected with the problem that all temperament inven-tories are designed to assess temperament in humans (what constitutes a limitation in obtaining data necessary to comply with assumption C). The diagnosis of temperament in animals obviously needs laboratory or experimental procedures (see Strelau, 1983); however, ratings are also sometimes applied (Gosling and John, 1999).

Typical instruments for children are based on ratings (parent or teacher), whereas inventories for adults rely on self-report. On the basis of the postulate of 'observatory' feature of tem-perament (Angleitner and Riemann, 1991), it may be also suggested that during the develop-ment of temperament inventories not only one but many sorts of data should be collected (assumptions B and H): in children, data based on both parent and teacher rating form (or forms), while in adults, data from self-report and rating. The procedure including both self-report and rating is paradoxically more fre-quent in personality studies than in the temperament approach (see Saucier and Goldberg, 2001) although it seems fully appropriate and necessary for temperamental instruments.

In summary, although temperament may be regarded as a cross-population phenomenon, temperament instruments are rarely designed to assess traits along the whole range of age in humans. The choice of inventories as basic tools for diagnosing temperament also consti-tutes a limitation of the applicability of these instruments in the case of animals. For animals either laboratory procedures or behavioral rat-ings may be applied (which evokes the ques-tion about the identity of the assessed traits). The different forms of temperament invento-ries are also rarely available – typically they are based on data from only one source (partic-ularly ratings or self-report). It may be there-fore concluded that far more sophisticated procedures are applied in the development of personality inventories than in the construction of strictly temperamental instruments.

Temperament and the structure of personality

Although recently over 30 temperament instruments and more than 80 temperament scales have been described in the literature, Strelau (1998) suggests their substantial similarity – many of the traits, differing in names, refer to similar psychological domains in the personality structure. It may also be expected that the common psychological domain is 'emotionality/neuroticism' and 'extraversion/activity', which refers to the broad concept of 'arousability'. The results of factor analysis, restricted to the five-factor solution, in respect to temperamental traits measured by means of PTS, FCB-TI, EAS-TS, DOTS-R, and EPQ-R questionnaires with the Big Five (OCEAN traits) assessed by the NEO-FFI inventory, were presented by Strelau (1998). The data indicate that most of the temperamental scales are located within the first two factors (recognized as 'emotionality/neuroticism' and 'extraversion/activity'), with the exception of rhythmicity (from DOTS-R loaded on 'openness' factor), task orientation (distractibility and persistence from DOTS-R loaded on the 'conscientiousness' factor) and psychoticim (from EPQ-R loaded on the 'agreeableness' factor). Moreover, highly specific temperamental dimensions, like activity-level sleep (DOTS-R) or sensory sensitivity (FCB-TI) may be found among scales sharing the same psychological content.

In summary, the results of factor analysis confirm the expectation of a broad five-factor domain of personality with temperamental scales located mainly in two 'arousability' factors: 'emotionality/neuroticism' and 'extraversion/activity'. Hubert et al. (1982) and Slabach et al. (1991) reviewed the psychometric properties of inventories designed to assess temperament in children, and concluded, among others, that their convergent and discriminant validity was unsatisfactory. The results of our factor analysis partially confirmed their conclusion: temperamental scales are mainly located on two factors, but at the same time they are not the 'best markers' of those factors and, in some cases they

demonstrate (sometimes due to broad theoretical concepts or to instrument failure) high secondary loadings on other factors, which suggests possible problems with discriminant validity.

The development of temperament inventories

Temperament inventories were developed similarly to other personality scales based on external (criterion-oriented), internal (inductive), or theoretical (deductive) strategies (Burisch, 1986). In the early attempts, temperament was seen as a clinical construct, and the external strategy was used (see Humm-Wadsworth Temperament Schedule; Humm and Wadsworth, 1935), which obviously resulted in low homogeneity of the scales. Very early on however, this strategy was replaced by the inductive one, and strictly empirical instruments were developed, like the Guilford-Zimmermann Temperament Survey (Guilford and Zimmermann, 1949) or the Thurstone Temperament Schedule (Thurstone, 1951). This classic strategy is applied in modern lexical studies (see e.g. Saucier and Goldberg, 2001). Recent psychometric instruments are most frequently based on either a theoretical strategy, applied for instance in PTS or FCB-TI studies, or on a mixed theoretical-inductive strategy, which was used in EPQ-R, EAS-TS, DOTS-R, as well as in several instruments for children. The advantage of such approaches is that they offer an opportunity to develop very homogenous scales, covering theoretically defined domains. Although factor analysis should lead to high homogeneity, the problem is the theoretical conceptualization – too broad definitions of the temperamental domains leading to the failure of validity of the instruments. Another – quite opposite – problem of the development of temperamental scales is related to the narrow definition of the temperamental domains, leading to a highly analytical approach and to the overextracting of the number of factors and scales, as exemplified by the CBQ or IBQ-R. As a result, a very similar content is assessed by several scales within the whole inventory, which means difficulty in demonstrating the discriminant validity of a particular scale (see for instance the DOTS-R rhythmicity scales), or even the convergent validity in the case of scales assessing highly specific temperamental features (see for instance activity-level sleep scale).

Another important issue in the development of temperament scales which may influence their validity is the lack of early validation. Temperament inventories are constructed similarly to other personality scales – the typical procedure focuses on the development of instruments via a psychometric approach and their subsequent validation in psychophysiological, genetic, cross-cultural, or clinical studies. The results indicate that temperament inventories, loosing their specificity in comparison to other personality instruments, sometimes demonstrate even weaker psychometric properties than personality scales. Only a few positive examples may be mentioned, and these seem to be rather exceptions in the development of temperamental instruments. For instance, in the EAS-TS studies on children (assumption B), an early genetic validation (see assumption E) and different sources of ratings (assumption H) were applied. The psychophysiological validation was conducted on the Vando R-A Scale (see Barnes, 1985; assumption F), the cross-cultural validation on PTS (assumption D), and the demographic validation on EQP-R and DOTS-R (assumption B and D).

In conclusion, it may be suggested that temperament inventories need a more precise theoretical definition of the temperamental domain and more sophisticated procedures of their development, including early validation. This is the only way to show the specificity of temperamental constructs and to improve the psychometric properties of temperament instruments.

Reliability (internal consistency) of temperamental scales

Angleitner and Riemann (1991) suggest that a reliability coefficient of about 0.70 is the borderline value for a personality instrument, but Slabach et al. (1991) regard internal consistency of about 0.80 as a good one. Hubert et al. (1982) demonstrated a weak internal consistency of several temperament inventories. In a later review of psychometric properties of temperament inventories for children, including new and revised instruments, Slabach et al. (1991) found a substantial improvement. Many of the analyzed inventories demonstrated a reliability of over 0.80, yet in the case of some of them it was lower than 0.70. Although the general overview seems to be very promising, some weak points may also be found – the authors concluded that there occurs a high variability of the internal consistency among the scales of a single inventory.

The German–Polish twin study, in which five temperament inventories were used (PTS, FCB-TI, EAS-TS, DOTS-R, and EPQ-R), may serve as an example of the reliability of temperament assessment in adults and adolescents (see Strelau, 1998). For all scales the internal consistency coefficients were calculated for self-report and peer ratings in both samples. Similar findings were obtained in both the Polish (the average reliability of 28 scales was 0.74 for self-report and 0.77 for peer rating) and the German sample (0.78 and 0.79, respectively). *Alpha* Cronbach exceeded the value of 0.70 in the case of 18 scales (64%) of self-report and 21 scales (75%) of peer rating in the Polish sample, and in the case of 24 (86%) and 25 (89%) scales, respectively, in the German sample. The value of 0.80 or higher was reached by 35% (German sample, self-report) and up to 50% of the scales (German sample, peer rating). The lowest estimation was obtained for EAS-TS and DOTS-R, probably due to the lowest number of items in the scales (4 items per scale in EAS-TS and from 3 to 7 in DOTS-R in comparison to longer scales in other inventories: 20 items in FCB-TI or from 21 to 32 in EPQ-R scales). As in the Slabach et al. (1991) review, a substantial variability of internal consistency within the instruments may be recorded – especially for EAS-TS and DOTS-R, but also for EPQ-R (P scale).

Although some temperamental scales demonstrate unsatisfactory reliability, in general, temperament inventories for children and adults offer, in comparison to other personality scales, sufficient reliability of the assessment of traits (assumption A).

Temporal stability of traits, assessed by temperament inventories

Meta-analyses of temporal stability mostly refer to personality inventories, but temperament instruments are included in these studies (see Roberts and DelVecchio, 2000). The results suggest that temporal stability depends on the length of the scale and its internal consistency, test–retest interval (lower estimation is obtained in the case of longer break), and the age of the respondents during the first inventory administration (higher estimation is reached for older subjects; see Schuerger et al., 1989). Probably for these reasons Roberts and DelVecchio (2000: 3) stated that 'temperament dimensions were less consistent than adult personality traits'. Taking into account that temperament inventories are broadly used to assess children's temperament via parent or teacher ratings (the shorter scales are typically used) and to demonstrate the long-term stability of traits (see Slabach et al., 1991), it seems obvious that temperament dimensions might be assessed as less temporarily stable. Slabach et al. (1991) suggest that in the case of children the short-term (test–retest) and long-term stability (over 6 months) should be distinguished. They found a high test–retest reliability of several temperament inventories (correlations higher than 0.70) and a substantially lower long-term stability (correlations of about 0.30), which may actually suggest a lower temporal consistency of temperamental traits. High temporal stability estimates of neuroticism (and affective dimensions) and extraversion (or activity) in children as well as in adults, however, indicate that temperamental traits may be not more, but also not less stable than other personality dimensions (Slabach et al., 1991). This means that the

assumption of high temporal stability, taken as a definitional criterion of temperament (see Buss and Plomin, 1984), is supported by empirical data only in a convergent but not in a discriminative sense – temperament is temporarily consistent, but probably not more stable than other personality characteristics (assumption G).

Inter-rater agreement and congruency between self-report and ratings of temperamental traits

Angleitner and Riemann (1991) stated that the specificity of temperament inventories is reflected in the items which refer to the observable (overt) forms of behavior. On the basis of this conclusion, they suggested that the 'observability' of temperamental traits may be regarded as a distinctive criterion of temperament dimensions (assumption B and H).

The reviews by Hubert at al. (1982) and Slabach et al. (1991) suggest, however, that this criterion is weakly fulfilled by temperamental inventories for children. Slabach et al. (1991: 225) concluded 'low and variable interparent or interrater agreement' of temperament assessment of children, which seems to be typical for temperament instruments in general (the mean of interparent agreement across five instruments was 0.43, ranging between 0.35 and 0.70). A more optimistic conclusion may be formulated in the case of temperamental instruments for adults. The German–Polish twin study may be mentioned as an example of the analysis of the 'observability' of temperamental traits (see Strelau, 1998). Self-report and two peer ratings (for each twin separately) were obtained for 27 temperamental traits (and the L scale for EPQ-R). The congruency indices between self-report and averaged peer rating, as well as between both ratings, were calculated independently for the Polish and the German sample. The results indicate that the average congruency between peers was 0.54 (range: 0.31–0.71) for the Polish and 0.55 (range: 0.20–0.72) for the German sample, while the mean congruency between self-report and peer rating was 0.47 (range: 0.23–0.66) and 0.48 (range: 0.29–0.69), respectively. The lowest congruency was recorded for DOTS-R (below the total mean – about 0.40) and the highest for EPQ-R (about 0.55). The highest indices were obtained for extraversion (EPQ-R) and activity (FCB-TI), which seem to be the most easily 'observable' traits.

In conclusion, it may be suggested that temperamental traits are observable and temperament inventories enable to obtain data confirming this expectation. However, it should also be noted that this criterion is fulfilled to a different extent by particular traits – some of them, like activity level-sleep or sensory sensitivity assessed in youth and adults, demonstrate lower observability, probably due to covert reactions applied in the items. It is also difficult to argue that temperamental traits are more observable than other personality dimensions because a similar congruency (about 0.50) between self-report and peer, spouse, or parent rating was obtained for various personality instruments (see McCrae and Costa, 2003).

Self-reported temperamental traits and laboratory (psychophysical and neurophysiological) indices

The assumption about the biological roots of temperament implies substantial relationships between temperamental measures and psychophysical and neurophysiological indices of arousability (assumption F). The psychophysical indices were mostly developed by Teplov and his co-workers and used to diagnose basic properties of the nervous system, and broadly applied also by Eysenck as indices of extraversion (see Strelau, 1998). The basic methods used for assessing, for instance, the strength of the excitation process were among others extinction with reinforcement, the absolute sensitivity threshold, the slope of the reaction time curve, described in details by Strelau (1983). The main limitations regarding the psychophysical or neurobiochemical indices as

indicators of individual arousability are related to the 'partiality' phenomenon – very low congruency among laboratory indices as well as low correlations with self-reported measures of temperament. Neurophysiologal correlates of temperamental traits referred to indices of autonomic activity: electrodermal activity or cardiovascular activity, and cortical activity: spontaneous EEG activity, evoked potentials, or cerebral asymmetry. More recently, hormones (like cortisol) and neurotransmmiters (norepinephrine, dopamine, and serotonin) and their enzymes (like MAO) were taken into account (see Strelau, 1998; Zuckerman, 1994). The results of several studies also showed that the correlations between neurophysiological indices and self-reported measures of temperament (neuroticism, extraversion, reactivity, sensation seeking, etc.) are very low, if they are significant at all (typically they do not exceed the value of 0.30, which is the 'personality coefficient' – a term coined by Mischel, 1968). As Strelau (1992) suggests, the reason for this discrepancy may be due to the fact that self-report temperament instruments refer to molar behaviors (characterized by transituational and temporal consistency), which occur in natural situations, while psychophysical and neurophysiological procedures record molecular reactions in laboratory (artificial) settings. It may be suggested that inventories assess traits as general dimensions, while laboratory measures assess states (specific reactions to particular stimuli).

In summary, the relationships between inventories and laboratory indices of temperament are very low, because of the substantial differences between the constructs measured by both methods and only weakly support the theory about the biological background of temperamental traits (assumption F).

TEMPERAMENT AS A CULTURALLY AND DEMOGRAPHICALLY UNIVERSAL PHENOMENON

The idea that temperament constitutes a core part of personality implies its universality across cultures and demographic groups (assumption B and D; Eysenck and Eysenck, 1985; Strelau, 1998). This statement is based on the assumption of common genetic mechanisms and similarity of eco-cultural influences for all humans. Several approaches have been proposed to show that basic temperamental traits may be identified in different cultures and demographic groups (see Zawadzki et al., 2001b). Triandis (1978) suggested that each instrument should be reconstructed within each culture, which may grasp the culture-specific manifestations of the trait (the 'emic' approach; Church and Katigbak, 1988). A completely different view claims that universal traits should be investigated by universal instruments, comprising the common aspects of traits and showing their identical properties in all cultures (the 'etic' approach; Van de Vijver and Leung, 1997). Berry (1989) links that both ideas and his approach is based on the assumption that each theoretical construct should cover culture-universal as well as culture-specific components (the combined 'etic–emic' approach). Each approach has its advantages and disadvantages (see Van Vijver and Leung, 1997; Zawadzki et al., 2001b) and all of them have been applied in cross-cultural as well as in demographic studies on temperament.

Cross-cultural studies on temperament

The 'emic' approach was applied in the classic form in lexical studies on the Big Five dimensions (Saucier and Goldberg, 2001). In cross-cultural studies on temperament, the 'etic' approach is the most popular. According to this strategy, temperament inventories are translated into the target language and their psychometric properties are examined and compared to the original ones. This approach was applied in studies on DOTS-R, EAS-TS, and CBQ (see Rothbart et al., 2000; Strelau, 1998). The most comprehensive project was carried out by Eysenck and co-workers for PEN

instruments (like EPI or EPQ), in which the similarity of factor structures across 34 cultures was demonstrated as a criterion of the universality of PEN (Barrett et al., 1998). The main advantage of this strategy is that it enables the analysis of the psychometric similarity on item and scale levels and to compare inventory scores across individuals (the within-culture level) and across cultures (the cross-culture level) (Van de Vijver and Leung, 1997). The main disadvantage is that psychometric characteristics are typically worse in target cultures than in the original one. The modern 'etic' strategy implies that inventories should be created simultaneously within all cultures under study (Van de Vijver and Leung, 1997). In the FCB-TI project the psychometric studies were performed in common analyses based on data obtained in eight cultures and a common version was developed (see Zawadzki et al., 2001b), and validated on individual and culture levels (against economical, demographic, and cultural indices).

The main problem of the 'etic' approach is that it neglects the culture-specific manifestations of traits, what may result in the loss of validity of the universal inventory in particular cultures. For this reason, the combined 'etic–emic' approach is suggested. This strategy, although relatively rare in temperament studies, was successfully applied in the study on PTS (Strelau et al., 1999). Three original language pools of the items (German, English, and Polish) served for translation to other languages and the instrument was reconstructed for each culture in psychometric analysis. As a result, each PTS version comprises a set of common items (about 50%) as well as a group of items specific only for a given country. The comparative analyses have shown psychometric similarity across 16 cultures, and each version was then widely used in within country studies.

In summary, although the choice of the 'etic' approach seems to be reasonable taking into account the universal nature of temperament, the idea of a simple translation of the final instrument developed in one culture only seems to be inappropriate. A more recent view suggests that temperamental inventories should be developed in common cross-cultural projects and ought to comprise truly culture-common aspects of the traits and/or their culture-specific manifestations.

Cross-demographic studies on temperament

The idea of temperament as a universal phenomenon refers also to demographic groups (Eysenck and Eysenck, 1985; Strelau, 1998), but it is rarely applied in the development of temperament instruments. For instance, EPQ-R was developed to cover the common aspects of PEN for both genders ('etic' approach), and a similarity of the factorial structure between females and males was demonstrated (Eysenck et al., 1985). DOTS-R was designed to assess temperament in all age groups – the items' content was adapted to the culture of all ages and similarity of the factor structures in different age groups was presented (Windle and Lerner, 1986). The 'emic' approach is also applied, especially when the original instrument was designed to assess temperament in adults and later adapted to diagnose temperament in children. In this approach, new items specific for children are generated and a completely new instrument is constructed, as exemplified by the Eysenck Personality Questionnaire – Junior (EPQ-J), a child version of the EPQ (see Eysenck and Eysenck, 1976).

Among demographic factors, typically only gender and age are taken into account, but specificity of the clinical groups should also be considered (assumption J). The most common view, apart from psychiatric models of temperament (see Akiskal, 2000) which refer to the clinical population (or the Eysenckian PEN model which refers to clinical and non-clinical groups), considers temperament as traits of the normal population (extended to disturbed individuals). It enables us to demonstrate the

importance of temperament in adaptation to everyday situations, but the limited validity of such an approach in clinical studies must also be taken into account.

GENETIC ANALYSES OF TEMPERAMENTAL TRAITS

Several behavior genetic studies have been conducted to verify hypothesis about genetic origin of temperamental traits (assumption E) and summarized by Eaves et al. (1989), Loehlin (1992), Plomin (1994), and Strelau (1998). The results of the German–Polish Twin Project may be mentioned as an example. The study was done on same-sex twins reared together (Polish sample: 546 pairs – 317 monozygotic and 229 dizygotic; German full sample: 1,009 pairs – 732 MZ and 277 DZ). All subjects filled out the PTS, FCB-TI, EAS-TS, and DOTS-R and were rated by two independent peers. This project enables the demonstration of the impact of genetic (additive and nonadditive) and environmental (common and specific) variance on the phenotypic variance of temperament traits. Traits were assessed by means of self-report and peer rating (the latter method enables to define a given trait as a latent variable by two peer ratings; see Oniszczenko et al., 2003).

The findings of the study showed that for almost all of the temperamental traits the impact of genetic factors may be demonstrated. The average estimation of the genetic factors for self-reported traits was about 40% (36% for all traits and 38% only for those 23 scales for which the genetic variance was extracted) and above 50% (52% and 59% for 21 scales, respectively) for ratings of traits. The lowest estimations were obtained for DOTS-R (probably due to the lowest reliability of the scales); the highest for FCB-TI (46% of the variance for self-report, 62% for both ratings). Other analyses for FCB-TI showed that the genetic factors explained 66% of the variance for self-report and averaged peer ratings (in a common analysis of both measures; see Zawadzki et al., 2001a). These results indicate that temperamental traits have a genetic background (what confirms assumption E); however, they address the question of differential heritability of temperament over other personality traits. The data of many studies do not support this hypothesis: a similar genetic estimation was obtained for temperament and personality variables (Loehlin, 1992). Another intriguing result is that only the specific environment factor may influence ID in temperament (or more broadly personality), with no or almost no impact of the common environmental factor. This relationship was studied in 'twins reared together' projects, but also in 'twins reared apart', as well as in family studies, including ordinary siblings, and in adoption studies (see Loehlin, 1992). The findings indicate resemblance only between biological family members, again demonstrating the heritability of traits, and no impact of the common environment (see Figure 17.2). It is also suggested that

additional genetic and environmental factors, and also their interactions or correlations, may influence temperament (Plomin, 1994).

The newest analyses are based on molecular genetic paradigms, focusing on the identification of particular genes influencing temperament. For instance, a significant relationship between emotional reactivity and polymorphism of the *DRD4* (dopamine receptor) gene was found (Oniszczenko and Dragan, 2005). It should be also mentioned that the most extended molecular genetic studies are conducted on the basis of Cloninger's model of temperament (see Benjamin et al., 2000).

THE FUNCTIONAL SIGNIFICANCE OF TEMPERAMENTAL TRAITS

The functional significance of temperament was evaluated within two broad areas: the role of traits in moderating the reaction to stress and health problems (psychiatric and somatic

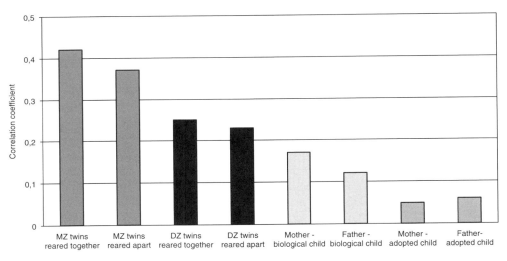

Figure 17.2   Average correlations (unweighted means) between neuroticism's scores among family members representing different genetic similarity. On the basis of data cited by Loehlin (1992: 53–54, table 3.5 – Britain and Minnesota study; table 3.7 – Finnland, Sweden and Minnesota study)

diseases) and the manifestation of traits in behavior in everyday life surroundings (assumption I and J). Taking into account the extraordinary high number of studies and the limited space of this chapter, the results of these studies will be presented in a much-abbreviated form.

Behavior in everyday life surroundings

One of the very frequently tested hypotheses refers to the expectation that temperamental traits are responsible for individual preferences of situations or actions of given energetic and temporal characteristics among children and adults. Several studies showed that styles of actions (individual styles of performing a given activity) are related to the strength of the nervous system or to reactivity (Strelau, 1983). It was also established that preferences of situations or kinds of activity depend on temperamental traits; for instance, the choice of job, the form of spending leisure time, and sport activity, are all related to strength of the nervous system, sensation seeking, reactivity, or the PEN dimensions (Eysenck et al., 1982; Strelau, 1998; Zuckerman, 1994). Several studies demonstrated that temperamental traits influence behavior in a given situation, such as child behavior in the classroom or at home or a child's interactions with the parents (Slabach et al., 1991). It was also shown that temperamental traits determine the level of performance – especially school and job achievements (Eysenck and Eysenck, 1985; Furnham, 1992; Martin, 1988; Strelau, 1998).

Reaction to stress and health problems

The main hypothesis concerned the direct or indirect relationship of temperament dimensions to health status and to adaptational problems. The main idea related temperament to individual reactions to stress and viewed behavioral problems as consequences of interactions between stressors and temperament. In several studies it was demonstrated (in laboratory as well as in natural settings) that temperament co-determines the level of performance as well as emotional reactions in stressful situations (Strelau, 1983; Strelau and Klonowicz, 2006). It was also demonstrated that temperament plays a crucial role in criminal incidents (Eysenck and Eysenck, 1985), behavioral problems (Caspi and Silva, 1995; Slabach et al., 1991), and psychiatric diseases in children and adults (Eysenck and Eysenck, 1985; Svrakic et al., 2002). The most controversial issue emphasizes the role of temperamental traits in the pathogenesis of somatic diseases, like coronary heart disease and cancer (Eysenck, 1991; Schapiro et al., 2001; Strelau and Zawadzki, 2005).

Studies demonstrating the functional significance of temperament suffer from many methodological problems, including a low validity of temperamental instruments. Hubert et al. (1981) in particular stressed their low convergent validity. Slabach et al. (1991) noted a substantial improvement but found a low discriminative validity of temperament inventories (probably due to the low homogeneity of temperament scales). Another problem is related to possible confounding of temperament inventories and behavioral criteria applied in particular studies, when both instruments assess the same or very similar behavioral phenomena (due to the item overlap) or are rated by the same persons (the same raters, even in the case of self-report) or used at the same time (to demonstrate concurrent validity). The limitations of these studies also refer to the most typical variable-centered approach in opposition to clusters or configurations of traits. Several studies, however, overcame these limitations, like the studies on 'difficult temperament' (understood as a pattern of traits), differential ratings of temperament and behavioral problems of children (parent rating of temperament and teacher rating of the child's adaptational problems), ratings of temperament *versus* observation or testing behavior in laboratory or natural settings, or prospective studies relating temperament to emotional disturbances in children and adults (Gil, 2005; Slabach et al., 1991; Strelau, 1998).

In summary, it should to be noted that temperamental scales demonstrate criterion-oriented validity with respect to clinical as well as in everyday behavior criteria, but it is difficult to determine whether they have higher validity than other personality instruments (McCrae and Costa, 2003).

TEMPERAMENT INVENTORIES – THE FINAL SENTENCE

Temperament concepts were continuously present in the studies on personality. From their early beginnings, temperament inventories were also applied to assess the basic biological dimensions of personality. For many years, temperament instruments suffered from psychometric invalidation. During the last few decades a substantial improvement may be observed; however, a lot of work is still to be done, especially with regard to the specificity of temperamental dimensions within the personality structure. Temperamental inventories need a more extended and precise theoretical basis and more sophisticated procedures of their development and validation to survive in modern personality studies. Otherwise, the concept of temperament as well as temperament instruments may completely sink in the OCEAN approach to personality.

ACKNOWLEDGEMENT

Preparation of the chapter was supported by Grant No 1H01F 071 28 from the Minister of Science and Higher Education.

NOTES

1 When using the expression "Personality Inventories" in the context of temperament inventories (scales) we mean personality scales which refer to other than temperament domains of personality.

REFERENCES

Akiskal, H. (2000) 'Temperament and mood disorders', *Harvard Mental Health Letter,* 16(8): 5–6.

Allport, G.W. (1937) *Personality: A Psychological Interpretation.* New York: Hold.

Angleitner, A. and Riemann, R. (1991) 'What can we learn from the discussion of personality questionnaires for the construction of temperament inventories?', in J. Strelau, and A. Angleitner (eds), *Explorations in Temperament: International Perspectives on Theory and Measurement.* New York: Plenum Press, pp. 191–201.

Anokhin, P.K. (1978) *Collected Works: Philosophical Aspects of the Functional System Theory.* Moscow: Nauka (in Russian).

Barnes, G.E. (1985) 'The Vando R-A Scale as a measure of stimulus reducing-augmenting', in J. Strelau, F.H. Farley and A. Gale (eds), *The Biological Bases of Personality and Behavior: Theories, Measurement Techniques, and Development* (Vol. 1). Washington: Hemisphere, pp. 171–80.

Barrett, P.T., Petrides, K.V., Eysenck, S.B.G. and Eysenck, H.J. (1998) 'The Eysenck Personality Questionnaire: An examination of the factor similarity of P, E, N, and L across 34 countries', *Personality and Individual Differences*, 25(5): 805–19.

Benjamin, J., Osher, Y., Kotler, M., Gritsenk, I., Nemanov, L., Belmaker, R.H. and Ebstein, R.P. (2000) 'Association between tridimensional personaliy questionnaire (TPQ) traits and three functional polymorphisms: Dopamine receptor D4 (DRD4), serotonin promoter region (5-HTTLPR) and catechol O-methyltransferase (COMT)', *Molecular Psychiatry*, 5(1): 96–100.

Berry, J.W. (1989) 'Imposed etics-emics-derived etics: The operationalization of a compelling idea', *International Journal of Psychology*, 24(6): 721–35.

Burisch, M. (1986) 'Methods of personality inventory development – A comparative analysis', in A. Angleitner and J.S. Wiggins (eds), *Personality Assessment via Questionnaires. Current Issues in Theory and Measurement.* Berlin-Tokyo: Springer-Verlag, pp. 109–19.

Buss, A.H. and Plomin, R. (1975) *A Temperament Theory of Personality Development*. New York: Wiley.

Buss, A.H. and Plomin, R. (1984) *Temperament: Early Developing Personality Traits*. Hillsdale, NJ: Erlbaum.

Carey, W.B. and McDevitt, S.C. (1978) 'Revision of the Infant Temperament Questionniare', *Pediatrics*, 61(5): 735–9.

Carey, W.B. and McDevitt, S.C. (1994) (eds), *Prevention and Early Intervention: Individual Differences as Risk Factors for the Mental Health of Children*. New York: Brunner/Mazel.

Caspi, A. and Silva, P.A. (1995) 'Temperamental qualities at age three predict personality traits in young adulthood: Longitudinal evidence from a birth cohort', *Child Development*, 66(2): 486–98.

Chess, S. and Thomas, A. (1984) *Origins and Evolution of Behavior Disorders: From Infancy to Early Adult Life*. New York: Brunner/Mazel.

Church, A.T. and Katigbak M.S.H. (1988) 'The emic strategy in the identification and assessment of personality dimensions in non-western culture. Rationale, steps, and a Philippine illustration', *Journal of Cross-Cultural Psychology*, 19(2): 131–52.

Cloninger, C.R. (1986) 'A unified biosocial theory of personality and its role in the development of anxiety states', *Psychiatric Developments*, 4(3): 167–226.

Cloninger, C.R., Svrakic, D.M. and Przybeck, T.R. (1991) 'The Tridimensional Personality Questionnaire: US normative data', *Psychological Reports*, 69(3): 1047–57.

Cloninger, C.R., Svrakic, D.M. and Przybeck T.R. (1993) 'A psychobiological model of temperament and character', *Archives of General Psychiatry*, 50(12): 975–90.

Duffy, E. (1957) 'The psychological significance of the concept of "arousal" or "activation"', *The Psychological Review*, 64(5): 265–75.

Eaves, L.J., Eysenck, H.J. and Martin, N.G. (1989) *Genes, Culture and Personality. An Empirical Approach*. London: Academic Press.

Eysenck, H.J. (1967) *The Biological Basis of Personality*. Springfield, IL: Thomas.

Eysenck, H.J. (1970) *The Structure of Human Personality* (3rd edn). London: Methuen.

Eysenck, H.J. (1991) *Smoking, Personality, and Stress. Psychosocial Factors in the Prevention of Cancer and Coronary Heart Disease*. New York: Springer-Verlag.

Eysenck, H.J. and Eysenck, M.W. (1985) *Personality and Individual Differences: A Natural Science Approach*. New York: Plenum Press.

Eysenck, H.J. and Eysenck, S.B.G. (1964) *The Eysenck Personality Inventory*. London: University of London Press.

Eysenck, H.J. and Eysenck, S.B.G. (1976) *Manual of the Eysenck Personality Questionnaire, (Junior and Adult)*. London: Hodder & Stoughton.

Eysenck, H.J., Nias, D.K.B. and Cox, D.N. (1982) 'Personality and sport', *Advances in Behaviour Research and Therapy*, 4(1): 1–56.

Eysenck, S.B.G., Eysenck, H.J. and Barrett, P. (1985) 'A revised version of the Psychoticism scale', *Personality and Individual Differences*, 6(1): 21–9.

Furnham, A. (1992) *Personality at Work*. London and New York: Routledge.

Garstein, M.A. and Rothbart, M.K. (2003) 'Studying infant temperament via the Revised Infant Behavior Questionnaire', *Infant Behavior and Development*, 26(1): 64–86.

Gil, S. (2005) 'Pre-traumatic personality as a predictor of post-traumatic stress disorder among undergraduate students exposed to terrorist attack: A prospective study in Israel', *Personality and Individual Differences*, 39(4): 819–27.

Gosling, S.D. and John, O.P. (1999) 'Personality dimensions in non-human animals: A cross-species review', *Current Directions in Psychological Science*, 8(3): 268–75.

Gray, J.A. (1964) 'Strength of the nervous system and levels of arousal: A reinterpretation', in J.A. Gray (ed.), *Pavlov's Typology*. Oxford: Pergamon Press, pp. 289–364.

Gray, J.A. (1987) 'Perspectives on anxiety and impulsivity: A commentary', *Journal of Research in Personality*, 21(4): 493–509.

Gray, J.A. (1991) 'The neuropsychology of temperament', in J. Strelau and A. Angleitner (eds), *Explorations in Temperament: International Perspectives on Theory and Measurement*. New York: Plenum Press, pp. 105–28.

Guilford, J.P. and Zimmerman, W.S. (1949) *The Guilford-Zimmerman Temperament Survey. Manual of Instructions and Interpretations*. Beverly Hills: Sheridan Supply.

Hubert, N.C., Wachs, T.D., Peters-Martin, P. and Gandour, M.J. (1982) 'The study of early temperament: Measurement of conceptual issues', *Child Development*, 53(3): 571–600.

Hull, C.L. (1943) *Principles of Behavior: An Introduction to Behavior Theory*. New York: Appleton-Century-Crofts.

Humm, D.G. and Wadsworth, G.W., Jr. (1935) 'The Humm-Wadsworth Temperament Scale', *American Journal of Psychiatry*, 92(1): 163–200.

Jung, C.G. (1923) *Psychological Types*. London: Routledge and Kegan Paul.

Kagan, J. (1994) *Galen's Prophecy: Temperament in Human Nature*. New York: Basic Books.

Kagan, J. and Reznick, J.S. (1986) 'Shyness and temperament', in W.H. Jones, J.M. Cheek and S.R. Briggs (eds), *Shyness*. New York: Plenum Press, pp. 81–90.

Kagan, J. and Snidman, N. (1991) 'Infant predictors of inhibited and uninhibited profiles', *Psychological Science*, 2(1): 40–4.

Kretschmer, E. (1944) *Körperbau and Charakter: Untersuchungen zum Konstitutionsproblem and zur Lehre von den Temperamenten* [Physique and character: Research concerning problems of constitution and knowledge on temperaments] (17–18th edn). Berlin: Springer.

Loehlin, J.C. (1992) *Genes and Environment in Personality Development*. Newbury Park: Sage.

Martin, R.P. (1988) 'Child temperament and educational outcomes', in A.D. Pellegrini (ed.), *Psychological Bases for Early Education*. Chichester: Wiley, pp.185–205.

McCrae, R.R. and Costa, P.T. Jr. (1985) 'Comparison of EPI and psychoticism scales with measures of the five-factor model of personality', *Personality and Individual Differences*, 6(5): 587–97.

McCrae, R.R. and Costa, P.T. Jr. (2003) *Personality in Adulthood: A Five-factor Theory Perspective*. New York: Guilford.

Mischel, W. (1968) *Personality and Assessment*. New York: Wiley.

Oniszczenko, W., Dragan, W. (2005) 'Association between dopamine D4 receptor exon III polymorphism and emotional reactivity as a temperamental trait', *Twin Research and Human Genetics*, 8(6): 633–7.

Oniszczenko, W., Zawadzki, B., Strelau, J., Riemann, R. and Angleitner, A. (2003) 'Genetic and environmental determinants of temperament: A comparative study based on Polish and German samples', *European Journal of Personality*, 17(3): 207–20.

Pavlov, I.P. (1938) *Twenty-five Years of Objective Study of the Higher Nervous Activity (Behaviour) of Animals*. Moskva-Leningrad, Russia: Narkomzdraw SSSR (in Russian).

Plomin, R. (1994) *Genetics and Experience: The Interplay Between Nature and Nurture*. Thousand Oaks: Sage.

Roberts, B.W. and DelVecchio, W.F. (2000) 'The rank order consistency of personality traits from childhood to old age: A quantitative review of longitudinal studies', *Psychological Bulletin*, 126(1): 3-25.

Rothbart, M.K. (1989) 'Temperament in childhood: A framework', in G.A. Kohnstamm, J.E. Bates and M.K. Rothbart (eds), *Temperament in Childhood*. Chichester: Wiley, pp. 59–73.

Rothbart, M., Ahadi, S.A. and Evans, D.E. (2000) 'Temperament and personality: Origins and outcomes', *Journal of Personality and Social Psychology*, 78(1): 122–35.

Rothbart, M.K., Ahadi, S.A., Hershey, K.L. and Fisher, P. (2001) 'Investigation of temperament at three to seven years: The Children's Behavior Questionnaire', *Child Development*, 72(5): 1394–408.

Rothbart, M.K. and Posner, M.I. (1985) 'Temperament and the development of self-regulation', in L.C. Hartlage and C.F. Telzrow (eds), *The Neuropsychology of Individual Differences: A Developmental Perspective*. New York: Plenum Press, pp. 93–123.

Rusalov, V.M. (1989) 'Object-related and communicative aspects of human temperament: A new questionnaire of the structure of temperament', *Personality and Individual Differences*, 10(8): 817–27.

Saucier, G. and Goldberg, L.R. (2001) 'Lexical studies of indigenous personality factors: Premises, products, and prospects', *Journal of Personality*, 69(6): 847–79.

Schapiro, I.R., Ross-Petersen, L., Sælan, H., Garde, K., Olsen, J.H. and Johansen, C. (2001) 'Extroversion and neuroticism and the associated risk of cancer: A Danish cohort study', *American Journal of Epidemiology*, 153(8): 757–63.

Schuerger, J.M., Zarella, K.L. and Hotz, A.S. (1989) 'Factors that influence the temporal stability of personality by questionnaire',

Journal of Personality and Social Psychology, 56(5): 777–83.

Sheldon, W.H. and Stevens, S.S. (1942) *The Varieties of Temperament: A Psychology of Constitutional Differences*. New York: Harper & Brothers.

Slabach, E., Morrow, J. and Wachs, T.D. (1991) 'Questionnaire measurement of infant and child', in J. Strelau and A. Angleitner (eds), *Explorations in Temperament: International Perspectives on Theory and Measurement*. New York: Plenum Press, pp. 205–34.

Strelau, J. (1983) *Temperament, Personality, Activity*. London: Academic Press.

Strelau, J. (1992) 'Are psychophysical scores good candidates for diagnosing temperament/personality traits and for a demonstration of the construct validity of psychometrically measured traits?,' *European Journal of Personality*, 5(5): 323–42.

Strelau, J. (1998) *Temperament: A Psychological Perspective*. New York: Plenum Press.

Strelau, J. (2008) *Temperament as a Regulator of Behavior: After Fifty Years of Research*. Clinton Corners, NY: Eliot Werner Publications.

Strelau, J., Angleitner, A. and Newberry, B.W. (1999) *Pavlovian Temperament Survey (PTS). An International Handbook*. Göttingen: Hogrefe & Huber.

Strelau, J. and Klonowicz, T. (2006) (eds), *People Under Extreme Stress*. New York: Nova Science Publishers.

Strelau, J. and Zawadzki, B. (1993) 'The Formal Characteristics of Behaviour–Temperament Inventory (FCB-TI): Theoretical assumptions and scale construction', *European Journal of Personality*, 7(5): 313–36.

Strelau, J. and Zawadzki, B. (1995) 'The Formal Characteristics of Behavior–Temperament Inventory (FCB-TI): Validity studies', *European Journal of Personality*, 9(3): 207–29.

Strelau, J. and Zawadzki, B. (2005) 'The functional significance of temperament empirically tested: Data based on hypotheses derived from the regulative theory of temperament', in A. Eliasz, S.E. Hampson and B. de Raad (eds), *Advances in Personality Psychology* (Vol. 2). Hove, East Sussex: Psychology Press, pp. 19–46.

Svrakic, D.M., Draganic, S., Hill, K., Bayon, C., Przybeck, T.R. and Cloninger, C.R. (2002) 'Temperament, character, and personality disorders: Etiologic, diagnostic, treatment issues', *Acta Psychiatrica Scandinavica*, 106(3): 189–95.

Svrakic, N.M., Svrakic, D.M. and Cloninger, C.R. (1996) 'A general quantitative theory of personality development: Fundamentals of a selforganizing psychobiological complex', *Development and Psychopathology*, 8(1): 247–72.

Thomas, A. and Chess, S. (1977) *Temperament and Development*. New York: Brunner/Mazel.

Thurstone, L.L. (1951) 'The dimensions of temperament', *Psychometrika*, 16(1): 11–120.

Tomaszewski, T. (1978) *Tätigkeit und Bewusstsein: Beiträge zur Einführung in die polnische Tätigkeitspsychologie* [Action and consciousness: Contribution to the introduction to Polish theory of action]. Weinheim and Basel: Beltz Verlag.

Triandis, H.C. (1978) 'Some universals of social behavior', *Personality and Social Psychology Bulletin*, 4(1): 1–16.

Van de Vijver, F. and Leung, K. (1997) 'Methods and data analysis of comparative research', in Berry, J.W. Poortinga, Y.H. and Pandey, J. (eds), *Handbook of Cross-cultural Psychology: Theory and Method* (Vol. 1). Boston: Allyn & Bacon, pp. 257–300.

Windle, M. and Lerner, R.M. (1986) 'Reassessing the dimensions of temperament individuality across life span: The Revised Dimensions of Temperament Survey (DOTS-R)', *Journal of Adolescent Research*, 1(2): 213–30.

Wundt, W. (1887) *Grundzüge der physiologischen Psychologie* [Outlines of physiological psychology] (Vol. 2, 3rd edn). Leipzig: Verlag von Wilhelm Engelmann.

Zawadzki, B., Strelau, J., Oniszczenko, W., Riemann, R. and Angleitner, A. (2001a) 'Genetic and environmental influences on temperament: The Polish–German twin study, based on self-report and peer-rating', *European Psychologist*, 6(4): 272–86.

Zawadzki, B., Van de Vijver, F.J.R., Angleitner, A., De Pascalis, V., Newberry, B., Clark, W., Van den Berg, P.T., Hyun, M.H., Kim, I.S., Mitina, O., Menchuk, T. and Kufel, M. (2001b) 'The comparison of two basic approaches of cross-cultural assessment of Strelau's temperament dimensions in eight countries', *Polish Psychological Bulletin*, 33(3): 133–41.

Zuckerman, M. (1979) *Sensation Seeking: Beyond the Optimal Level of Arousal*. Hillsdale, NJ: Erlbaum.

Zuckerman, M. (1994) *Behavioral Expressions and Biosocial Bases of Sensation Seeking*. New York: Cambridge University Press.

PART IV

Assessment of Self-Regulative Traits

18

From Situation Assessment to Personality: Building a Social-Cognitive Model of a Person

Vivian Zayas, Donna D. Whitsett, Jenna J.Y. Lee, Nicole Wilson and Yuichi Shoda

INTRODUCTION

Cross-situational variability has posed a puzzle for personality psychology: How does one reconcile the fact that any given person's behavior varies across situations and from moment-to-moment with a central assumption of personality theories that personality is stable and consistent across situations? In other words, how does one account for the invariance of personality while at the same time taking into account the dynamic changes in the cognitions, affects, and behaviors experienced by the individual?

Take, for example, David Letterman. He has been a stand-up comic since 1975 and has been the host of one of the most watched late night shows in America. Each evening, he tells witty jokes, engages in playful banter with his audience, interviews his guests, and entertains millions of TV viewers with his trademark gap-toothed smile. It is therefore surprising to learn that in his personal life he is extremely shy and introverted

(Walters, 1992). How does one account for such variability?

In the last decade, research has shown that it is possible to identify predictable patterns of variability across situations. These patterns of cross-situational variability can be seen in stable *if ... then ...* situation-behavior profiles, or 'behavioral signatures' that characterize each individual (Shoda et al., 1994). They capture how a person's behavior varies reliably as a function of the particulars of the situation a person encounters. For example, David Letterman's behavioral signature could be described as: *if* David Letterman is performing on stage in front of thousands of people, *then* he is talkative, extraverted, and outgoing. *If* instead he is at a small, intimate gathering, *then* he is reclusive, withdrawn, and shy. But *what* about these situations is responsible for this pattern? Is it because the TV audience is anonymous and impersonal, or is it because there are well-defined scripts and props on the set, for example?

In the present chapter, we propose that a key for understanding stable individual differences in people's behaviors, as well as the patterns of intraindividual variability for each person, is in knowing the features of situations that are *psychologically active* for a given person. Psychologically active features trigger particular cognitive and affective processes that ultimately lead to predictable responses in feelings, thoughts, and actions. This chapter will summarize and discuss recent conceptual and methodological advances in the identification of situational features. Three research examples illustrate six steps that can be used to identify (1) a set of psychological features that capture important aspects of a given situation, and (2) the features that are particularly salient for a given individual or groups of individuals. This approach, in turn, allows the assessment of each person's stable and distinctive 'behavioral signature', or *if ... then ...* situation-behavior profile, relating a person's thoughts, feelings, and behaviors to the situation, both external and internal, that the person encountered.

MAKING SENSE OF CROSS-SITUATIONAL VARIABILITY: *IF ... THEN ...* SITUATION-BEHAVIOR PROFILES

Some of the early evidence that cross-situational, intraindividual behavioral variability is meaningful (as opposed to error variance that needs to be removed or controlled) was obtained in a study of children at a residential summer camp (Shoda, 1990; Shoda et al., 1989, 1993a, 1993b, 1994; Wright and Mischel, 1987, 1988). Countless hours of observations revealed that each child's aggressive behaviors were systematically related to the features present in his or her situation. For example, for some children, being teased by peers elicited high levels of aggressive behavior, but being reprimanded by a counselor did not. Other children showed the opposite pattern; being scolded

by a counselor elicited high levels of aggressive behaviors, but being teased by peers did not. Thus, each child was characterized by a unique 'behavioral signature', or *if ... then ...* situation-behavior profile (e.g., *if* teased by peers, *then* the child is aggressive.). Most importantly, these situation-behavior profiles proved to be highly stable across time. The child who showed the '*if* teased by peers, *then* the child is aggressive' pattern during one half of the summer session showed a similar *if ... then ...* profile in the other half of the summer session.

THE MIND AS A COGNITIVE-AFFECTIVE PROCESSING SYSTEM

In response to the discovery of *if ... then ...* situation-behavior profiles, Mischel and Shoda (1995) proposed a reconceptualization of personality that could account for both the variability of a person's behavior across situations as well as consistency in a person's behavior over time. Inspired by cognitive and neural network models of the mind, the cognitive-affective processing system (CAPS) approach (Mischel and Shoda, 1995; Shoda and Mischel, 1998) conceptualizes each person's mind as a network of interconnected cognitions and affects. Figure 18.1 provides schematic representations of the CAPS networks of two hypothetical individuals.

A key premise of the CAPS approach is that each person's network remains unchanged from situation to situation. What changes from situation to situation are the particular cognitions and affects that become activated within the network, which in turn influence the corresponding behaviors that become expressed. Each person's unique and stable network is responsible for mediating the effect of the situation on behavior by guiding how a person encodes and construes a particular situation. The network also guides the goals, expectations, values, and strategies that become activated in the particular situation. The pattern and strength of

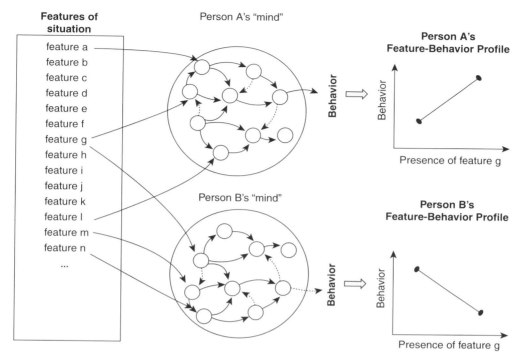

Figure 18.1 Schematic representation of the cognitive-affective processing system (CAPS) for two hypothetical individuals (i.e., person *A* and person *B*). Each person's mind is conceptualized by a stable network of interconnected cognitions and affects that mediates the effect of the situational features on behavior. Solid lines within and outside of the network represent excitatory associations (e.g., activation of one cognition automatically activates associated cognitions). Dotted lines within and outside of the network represent inhibitory associations (e.g., activation of one cognition makes it more difficult to activate associated cognitions). In the above illustration, each person encounters the same situation that consists of a common set of features (e.g., *a* through *n*). Because not all features are meaningful for all people, Person *A* and Person *B* differ in the specific situational features that activate (or inhibit) certain cognitions and affects within each person's network, which in turn lead to a behavioral response.

associations among the cognitions and affects guide the activation of thoughts and feelings within the network. For example, when two cognitions are strongly associated with one another, the activation of one will automatically *spread* and activate the other. In contrast, when two cognitions are weakly associated or unassociated with one another, the activation of one will not necessarily activate the other. Associations among cognitions may also be inhibitory such that activation of one concept will make it more difficult to activate another.

The networks of the two individuals illustrated in Figure 18.1 are assumed to differ in the cognitions and affects that are available within each person's network, the strengths of associations among those available that influence the accessibility of particular cognitions and affects, and the strengths of associations between external features and cognitions and affects within the network.

The interactions among cognitive-affective processes within a person's network and the sensitivity of the network to situational, external or internal, influences give rise to observable, stable, and predictable patterns of *if ... then ...* situation-behavior profiles. For example, a situation may elicit an initial fear response in most individuals. For one individual the fear response may lead to increased attention and hypervigilance. For another individual, however, the fear response may lead to avoidance of the fear-eliciting stimulus. The first individual is characterized by an '*if* afraid, *then* hypervigilance' pattern, whereas the second individual is characterized by an '*if* afraid, *then* avoidance' pattern (Miller, 1987).

To summarize, at the surface level a person's behaviors may vary considerably from moment to moment and across a number of different situations, and may even appear disparate and inconsistent. Nonetheless, within this variability there may be stable and meaningful intraindividual patterns of consistency represented by *if ... then ...* situation-behavior profiles that uniquely characterize each individual. The '*if*' is the situation, either external (e.g., a request for public speaking) or internal (e.g., fear responses), and the '*then*' is the affective, cognitive, and behavioral responses to the '*if*'.

PSYCHOLOGICALLY ACTIVE FEATURES OF SITUATIONS

Because the nature of a person's network is revealed in observable *if ... then ...* situation-behavior profiles, predicting each person's behavior requires conceptualizing and assessing situations. What are the most important *psychological features* of a given situation? The first step is then to identify, for a given individual, those features that are 'psychologically active' and that trigger particular cognitive-affective processes within a person's network and lead to behavioral responses.

How does one conceptualize and assess a situation, particularly the psychologically important features of a situation? Initial efforts at classifying situations were based on *nominal* features, such as whether a behavior occurred in a playground or cafeteria

(Hartshorne and May, 1928; Newcomb, 1929). A limitation of this approach is that it is unclear how to generalize the results to other situations. For example, if a child behaves aggressively at the playground, but is friendly and agreeable in the cafeteria, what would one predict her behavior to be in a classroom? When situations are defined nominally, knowledge of past behavior (e.g., aggressive at the playground) is useful in predicting behavior only in that exact situation, but shows little generalizability to other situations (e.g., aggressive when working on homework with peers; Hartshorne and May, 1928).

Going beyond this limitation requires understanding, for a given person, the most influential *psychological features* of the situation. What feature or features of the situation most strongly affect that individual's behavior? For example, imagine one knows that the reason why the child is aggressive at the playground is because she becomes insecure when she feels that she is being excluded by her classmates. Then one may predict that even in a cafeteria, which shows little physical resemblance to the playground, she will become aggressive if her peers start talking about their weekend plans to spend time together but do not invite her.

Social psychology has uncovered situational determinants of various behaviors (e.g., aggression, conformity, affiliation) and often focuses on the most important psychological features of situations, such as the effects of power, fear, authority, and group pressure. Despite the vast research on situational influences on social behavior, a systematic effort to develop a taxonomy of situations has only begun (Kelley et al., 2003). Furthermore, it is quite possible that a 'one-size-fits-all' taxonomy may not be adequate. That is, the features of psychological situations serving as the '*ifs*' in individuals' characteristic *if ... then* situation-behavior profiles may depend on the particular individual as well as the particular situation and behavior in question. For example, for the child who becomes aggressive when she feels excluded by her peers, the feature of the situation involves interpersonal rejection, perceived or actual, by her peers. This feature, however, may be of lesser or no importance to another child who instead becomes aggressive and belligerent when teachers give him poor marks on assignments. For the first child, the psychologically active feature is peer rejection. For the second child, it is negative evaluations from an authority figure.

METHODS FOR IDENTIFYING PSYCHOLOGICAL FEATURES OF SITUATIONS

Consider the myriad ways in which a situation can be conceptualized and operationalized. Is it even possible to find a small enough number of features that can provide a reasonably comprehensive description of the situations, which in turn can be used to characterize *if ... then ...* situation-behavior profiles? Ultimately, this is an empirical question. However, following the success in identifying the psychological features of situations influencing children's behaviors in the summer camp, methods for assessing *if ... then ...* profiles in a number of different domains have been developed.

Three examples of research programs aimed at identifying psychological features of situations are presented below. In a departure from techniques used in the original summer camp study (e.g., Shoda et al., 1994), the three illustrations introduce a new approach for assessing *feature-behavior* profiles. Instead of classifying '*ifs*' on discrete categories (e.g., peer teasing vs. teacher praise), the latest techniques attempt to assess on continuous scales the degree to which each psychological feature was present in a given situation. As will be described, the use of continuous indices of situational features allows the use of multi-level analysis to simultaneously estimate (i) the expected effect of a feature on the average individual's behavioral response (conceptually similar to the main effect of the feature), (ii) the effect of the feature on a given individual's behavioral response, and (iii) interindividual differences in behavioral responses to the feature.

One goal of such research is to determine a common set of features influencing a particular response. For example, as illustrated in Figure 18.1, a situation may consist of features *a*, *b*, *c*, *d*, *e*, and so on. In addition, this type of research aims to identify those features that are particularly salient for a given individual or groups of individuals. Such features are considered 'psychologically active features' or 'psychologically active ingredients' of situations. For example, as illustrated in Figure 18.1, person *A*'s behavior may be highly influenced by features *a*, *g*, and *l*. Person *B*'s behavior may be highly influenced by features *g*, *m*, and *n*. And yet another person's behavior may not be affected by any of the features. Thus, the process of feature identification – both to obtain a common set of features as well as to identify those features that are 'psychologically active' to a particular individual or group of individuals – is akin to identifying a set of environmental allergens to which some individuals have a strong reaction, while other individuals do not.

Often, the presence of psychologically active features triggers particular cognitive-affective processing dynamics within a person's network that leads to an *increase* in the expression of a particular behavior. For example, someone who enjoys novel experiences may express greater positive affect in response to novelty-related features. Such *feature-behavior* links are excitatory. However, psychologically active features can also activate cognitive-affective processing dynamics that may lead to a *decrease* in the behavior of interest. Such *feature-behavior* profiles may be considered inhibitory in nature. For example, in the classic bystander intervention studies (e.g., Darley and Latané, 1973), the number of other people present in a situation can be considered an important active feature of the situation for some individuals in that the feature suppresses the helping behavior that they may have otherwise engaged in. As will be discussed in the 'Further Considerations' section, the relation between the presence of a feature and resulting response may not necessarily reflect a one-to-one correspondence.

Rather, it may be influenced by the occurrence of other features also present in the situation. However, as a first step in feature identification and its effect on subsequent responses, this chapter will focus on the identification of features that have been shown to singularly influence behaviors.

To determine the psychological features of a situation – both the set of features that captures the most important psychologically meaningful aspects of situations as well as those features that are psychologically active for a given individual or group of individuals – one method is to use a top-down approach, basing identification of features on preexisting theory and research. This entails culling the literature for features of situations that are likely to influence the behavior of interest and developing stimuli that differ on the features selected. For example, if one were interested in the features of situations influencing partner preference, one might turn to past research that has identified the characteristics of potential dating partners (e.g., physical appearance, similarity to self) influencing perceived attractiveness. Another method for identifying features of situations involves using a bottom-up approach. In this approach, people's responses to a number of situations are recorded. One then asks: which situations elicit similar responses among different people and what do these situations have in common? Finally, a combination of the two approaches may at times be used.

The following sections provide step-by-step illustrations of three approaches for identifying psychological features of situations. Although the three approaches differ procedurally, they all employ the following six steps to identify psychological features of situations:

1 One needs to identify the domain of situations in which the behavior of interest occurs (Shoda et al., 1994).
2 The researcher then needs to develop (e.g., by conducting a separate study) or obtain, if possible, (e.g., from prior research) a relatively large number of stimuli that represent the situations of interest.
3 The next step is to identify a common set of psychological features that capture the most

important aspects of the situations and that are likely to influence the behavior of interest.
4 Objective indices reflecting the extent to which each of the features is present in the stimuli are derived.
5 In a sample of individuals whose behavioral signatures the researcher is seeking to understand, a *highly repeated* within-subjects research design (Shoda, 2003) is used to observe and record participants' behavioral responses across the different situations.
6 Through the use of multi-level analyses, it is then possible to determine the effect of individual features and interactions among features, on a given individual's responses as well as to identify 'psychologically active features' for a given individual or group of individuals.

Top-down approach to identifying psychological features of situations influencing partner preference

For some research questions, it may be useful to turn to past research and theory to identify candidate features of situations that are likely to influence a given behavior. For example, research and theory in social psychology has extensively examined the situational factors influencing person perception, attribution, impression formation, and spontaneous inference, to name just a few. This body of knowledge is a good starting point in identifying a common set of psychological features. Similarly, research on response to failure and experience of threat, as well as work on stereotypes, is also likely to inform the initial feature identification process. Ultimately, these possible features need to be empirically validated using methods such as those described in this chapter.

An illustration of a top-down approach is given in a study by Zayas and Shoda (2007), who set out to examine the question: Are women who have been the victim of psychological abuse in the past more likely to prefer an abusive dating partner in the future? This question was motivated by the widespread belief among lay persons, academics, and professionals alike that some people may be recreating negative relationship experiences through the dating partners they select, or attract. In a departure from traditional conceptualizations of situations, the researchers defined situations as another person (i.e., a potential dating partner). In this context, psychological features can be conceptualized as the personality characteristics of the potential dating partners (Zayas et al., 2002). In the present example, the features were identified *a priori* using existing research on the characteristics associated with victimized women and abusive men. Zayas and Shoda then tested the hypothesis that personality characteristics associated with abusive individuals (e.g., possessiveness and aggressive behaviors) in male potential partners may be the 'active psychological ingredients' that attract some women and repel others. The following section discusses the Zayas and Shoda (2007) study as a way of providing a step-by-step illustration of a theory-driven top-down approach for identifying psychological features.

Step 1: Identify the situations in which the behavior of interest is likely to take place

As a first step in identifying the psychological features of situations, the researcher must identify the situations in which the behavior of interest is likely to take place. In the present research illustration, the behavior of interest was college-aged women's preferences for male college-aged dating partners who may be potentially psychologically abusive. Thus, in this context, situations were operationalized as descriptions of potential dating partners in the form of personal ads. Features of the situations were the characteristics of the dating partners conveyed in the personal ads that were hypothesized to influence behaviors (i.e., preferences). Ideally, in this initial step, the researcher aims to identify the *universe* of situations in which the behavior of interest is likely to occur. Given the difficulty of this task, the researcher may choose to refine and narrow his or her definition of the behavior of interest. For example, in the present example the researchers focused on

preferences for college-aged dating partners, rather than dating partners of all ages or non-college students.

Step 2: Gather specific stimuli representing the situations of interest

To develop stimuli for the study, 112 male college students wrote short descriptions of themselves in the form of personal ads. Because the researchers were specifically interested in whether characteristics associated with an abusive personality were psychological features of situations influencing women's preferences in potential partners, it was necessary to assess whether the stimuli generated (i.e., 112 personal ads) possessed these characteristics. Three female undergraduate research assistants, who were unaware of the research hypotheses, provided initial evaluations of all 112 personal ads with regard to the degree to which the men described in the ads would be perceived by women, on average, as being (1) potentially abusive, and (2) desirable as a dating partner. Coders' evaluations, however, indicated that none of the ads were perceived as both potentially abusive *and* highly desirable, and that only 4 of the 112 ads were consensually evaluated as potentially abusive. Because it was not feasible to have participants in a study read all 112 ads, the following three types of dating partners were selected for the study: (1) four ads that described potential dating partners that were rated high on abusiveness and low on desirability (*abusive*); (2) eight ads that described potential dating partners that were rated low on abusiveness and low on desirability (*undesirable*); and (3) four ads that described potential dating partners that were rated low on abusiveness and high on desirability (*desirable*).

Step 3: Identify a common set of features that could be used to capture the most psychologically important aspects of the situation of interest

The next step is to identify features of the situation of interest. Past research and theory were used to identify the relevant features *a priori*. In particular, past research has linked characteristics such as jealousy, impulsivity, dependence, and violence with an abusive personality in men (e.g., Dutton et al., 1996; Dutton and Browning, 1988; Murphy et al., 1994; Walker, 1979). Thus, a top-down approach involves validating the extent to which the *a priori* features were present in the stimuli.

Step 4: Code the stimulus set according to a list of relevant features and derive indices reflecting presence of features

Construct validation and continuous indices of the features were obtained by having separate samples of female college students evaluate the descriptions. Specifically, some women (*n* = 24) rated the extent to which they perceived the man described in each of the 16 personal ads to be potentially abusive, psychologically and physically, with a romantic partner. A different sample of female college students (*n* = 22) rated the extent to which the man described in each ad was a desirable dating partner and someone they would be interested in dating. (These two ratings were averaged within each rater to index the desirability associated with each male dating partner.) In addition, both samples of female raters indicated the extent to which each male dating partner possessed personality characteristics that past research has linked to an abusive personality in men, including jealousy, impulsivity, dependence, and violence.

To create continuous indices that characterized each of the 16 male dating partners in terms of the psychological features (e.g., potential for abusiveness, aggressiveness, desirability, impulsivity, possessiveness), all the ratings were averaged across raters. Cronbach's alpha estimate (α) of the reliability of the index was computed to estimate the reliability of each index. Cronbach's alphas were 0.93 and 0.89 for the potential for abusiveness and desirability indices, respectively, and ranged from 0.72 to 0.87 for the specific personality characteristics (e.g., aggressiveness, jealousy, impulsiveness).

Not only did the women's ratings provide a continuous measure of the features present in each ad, they also provided support for the initial classification of the ads. Specifically, the abusive dating partners were rated as significantly more likely to inflict psychological as well as physical abuse than the undesirable and desirable dating partners. The desirable dating partners were rated as significantly more desirable than the undesirable and abusive men, which were rated as approximately equally undesirable. Adding further validity to the ads used as stimuli, abusive dating partners were rated as more impulsive, jealous, possessive, dependent, clingy, aggressive, hostile, violent, and angry than the undesirable and desirable dating partners. Undesirable and desirable ads did not differ from each other on any of these characteristics. As an additional step in the construct validation of the 16 personal ads, the relation between female raters' judgments of the ads and the male ad writers' own self-reported characteristics was examined. Correlations between men's self-reports and the female raters' judgments of the ads showed moderate to high convergence. Specifically, women's ratings of each ad writer's potential for psychological abuse were positively correlated in the expected direction with ad writer's self-reported hostility, impulsivity, jealousy, and past experiences behaving in psychologically abusive ways (e.g., controlling, jealous, verbally abusive).

Step 5: Use a highly repeated within-subjects design to observe and record responses to stimuli

In this study, the research employed a highly repeated, multi-level approach (Shoda, 2003) in which a person's preference was assessed across 16 potential dating partners, who varied systematically on key personal characteristics or 'psychological ingredients' (Zayas et al., 2002). Given that the behavior of interest was preferences for dating partners, the situations involved providing individuals with the opportunity to express their preferences. Therefore, the study procedures employed an Internet dating service paradigm in which participants read about the different potential dating partners and indicated through a four-round selection process who they wanted to get to know better.

Step 6: Analyze each participant's responses as a function of the situation

The focus on the analysis of psychological features of situations, and identifying individuals' behavioral signatures with regard to such features, calls for a shift in the general paradigms used for social and personality psychology research. Specifically, the traditional 'one-shot' data collection approach, which examines individual differences at one time in one situation, has intrinsic limitations for discovering patterns of psychological regularities within each person. An alternative approach, which might be called a 'highly repeated, within-subjects design' (Shoda, 2003) allows a systematic and quantitative characterization of *if … then …* situation-behavior profiles, for each person, by within-subject regression analyses. These individual-level characterizations can in turn be predicted from individual difference variables, using a multi-level modeling approach (e.g., HLM, hierarchical linear modeling). The set of level-1 coefficients from such analyses, describes the effect of each situation feature within a given individual. Thus, it is a behavioral signature, specifically, a feature-behavior profile, that can be computed with continuous, rather than categorical, characterization of situations with regard to

the *degree* to which each psychological feature is present.

To illustrate, Zayas and Shoda (2007) used multi-level modeling to predict, for each woman, the effects of psychological features on partner preference.[1] Specifically, as shown in equation (18.1), the level-1 model examined, for each woman, the relation between the presence of particular features (e.g., aggressiveness and desirability) that characterized each potential dating partner and the behavior of interest (i.e., preference for each dating partner).[2] The level-1 model is as follows:

$$[\text{Preference for partner } i]_i$$
$$= b_{\text{aggressiveness } j} [\text{partner } i\text{'s aggressiveness}]$$
$$+ b_{\text{desirability } j} [\text{partner } i\text{'s desirability}] + r_{ij}$$
$$(18.1)$$

Because each woman can now be characterized by a $b_{\text{aggressiveness } j}$ and $b_{\text{desirability } j}$, these coefficients can be used to represent her feature-behavior profile. For example, Table 18.1 reports the level-1 regression equations for five participants. As shown, for participant 308 there is an inverse relation between the aggressiveness of the potential dating partner and her preference for the dating partner ($b_{\text{aggressiveness } j} = -0.80$); she was less likely to prefer a potential dating partner who was perceived by other women to be aggressive. This woman also shows a slight positive relation between the desirability of the dating partner and her preference ($b_{\text{desirability } j} = 0.13$), such that the more desirable the

Table 18.1 Level-1 regression equations predicting for each participant the effect of partner aggressiveness and desirability on her partner preference

Participant	PMI	Level-1 regression equation
308	0.02	[Preference for partner i]$_j$ = −0.80[partner i's aggressiveness] + 0.13 [Partner i's desirability] + r_{ij}
241	0.05	[Preference for partner i]$_j$ = −0.04[partner i's aggressiveness] + 1.38[partner i's desirability] + r_{ij}
293	0.08	[Preference for partner i]$_j$ = −0.53[partner i's aggressiveness] + −0.02[partner i's desirability] + r_{ij}
287	2.13	[Preference for partner i]$_j$ = 0.41 [partner i's aggressiveness] + 0.61[partner i's desirability] + r_{ij}
289	2.24	[Preference for partner i]$_j$ = 0.89[partner i's aggressiveness] + 1.58[partner i's desirability] + r_{ij}

Notes: Each participant's regression equation predicts her preferences for each dating partner as a function of the dating partner's aggressiveness and desirability. Each woman's score on the self-report measure assessing frequency of experiencing psychological abuse in her most recent romantic relationship is reported in the second column (range of possible scores = 0–4). PMI = Psychological Maltreatment Inventory.

partner, the more likely she was to select him. Visually scanning the coefficients for the different women in the study, one sees that the pattern differs for each one. For participant 287, aggressiveness is *positively* related to her partner preference ($b_{\text{aggressiveness } j} = 0.41$) and so is desirability ($b_{\text{desirability } j} = 0.61$). It is important to keep in mind that features that do not appear to have an effect on responses, as indexed by regression coefficients that are not statistically different from zero, may still be psychologically meaningful, but may not lead to observable responses.

Are the differences in women's profiles, as represented by the level-1 regression coefficients meaningful? To the extent that the answer is yes, one would expect that these coefficients could be predicted by individual difference measures. For example, do women who have experienced more instances of psychological abuse show a preference for potentially abusive dating partners? To identify the features of situations that may be particularly salient (i.e., 'active') for women with a higher incidence of experiencing psychological abuse in a past romantic relationship, the set of level-1 coefficients can, in turn, be predicted by individual difference variables, such as a woman's past relationship experiences. Specifically, the level-2 model is a between-subjects analysis that predicts each woman's preference for potentially abusive dating partners, as reflected in $b_{\text{aggressiveness } j}$, from the degree to which she had experienced psychologically abusive behaviors in her past romantic relationship as assessed by the Psychological Maltreatment Inventory (PMI; Kasian and Painter, 1992). The level-2 model is as follows:

$$b_{\text{aggressiveness } j} = \gamma_{\text{aggressiveness } 0} + \gamma_{\text{aggressiveness } 1}$$
[participant j's past experiences of psychological abuse] $+ \mu_{\text{aggressiveness } j}$
$$(18.2)$$

$$b_{\text{desirability } j} = \gamma_{\text{desirability } 0} + \gamma_{\text{desirability } 1} \text{ [participant}$$
j's past experiences of psychological abuse] $+ \mu_{\text{desirability } j}$
$$(18.3)$$

In these equations, the level-2 intercepts, $\gamma_{\text{desirability } 0}$ and $\gamma_{\text{aggressiveness } 0}$, can be interpreted as the expected average effect of partners' desirability and potential for aggressiveness, respectively, on partner preference, from a participant who was average on the level-2 predictor (because all level-2 variables were centered, level-2 intercepts predict the level-1 coefficients for participants at the mean of the distribution).

The results of the Zayas and Shoda study showed that the frequency with which women reported experiencing psychologically abusive relationships in their past was positively related to preferences for aggressive dating partners, even though the effect of desirability was statistically controlled in the level-1 model ($\gamma_{\text{aggressiveness } 1} = 0.28$, $p < 0.001$). In addition, when the HLM analysis was repeated in order to examine the effect of different features on preference, the results showed that women who reported more psychological victimization in their most recent romantic relationship showed a stronger preference for dating partners who had been judged to be impulsive, jealous, possessive, hostile, and violent. All of these characteristics have been linked to personality characteristics of abusive men (e.g., Dutton et al., 1996). Thus, these characteristics are the features of situations or 'psychological ingredients' that differentially affected women's partner preferences.

In addition to identifying features of situations that have high functional significance for a given person, the analysis also allowed one to see how a person's partner preference varies as a function of a common set of 'psychological ingredients' present in the situation. For this analysis, situations were classified into '*abusive*', '*undesirable*', and '*desirable*', allowing each woman's 'behavioral signature' to be assessed using the more categorical approach to situation assessment used in earlier work (Shoda et al., 1994). For example, as shown in Figure 18.2, the 'behavioral signature' for women who had experienced psychological abuse differed meaningfully from the

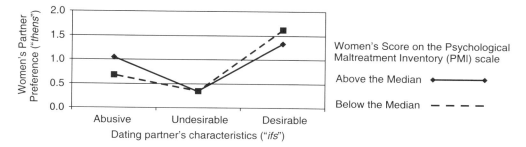

Figure 18.2   The characteristics of the potential dating partners (i.e., desirability and potential for abusiveness) are the 'psychological ingredients' of the situation, and partner preference ('*thens*') varied systematically as a function of the dating partner's characteristics ('ifs'). Women who had been the victim of psychological abuse (i.e., scoring above the median on the PMI) showed *if ... then ...* (situation-behavior) profiles that were distinct from the profiles that characterized women who had experienced less abuse (i.e., scoring below the median on the PMI). Figure is reproduced from Zayas and Shoda (2007).

if ... then ... 'behavioral signature' for women who had not.

BOTTOM-UP APPROACH TO IDENTIFYING PSYCHOLOGICAL FEATURES OF SOCIAL SUPPORT SITUATIONS

Given that the endeavor of identifying features of situations is relatively new, even in well-developed research areas, it is possible that not all the relevant psychological features affecting individual differences in behavior have been identified. Thus, for some research questions, it may be useful to utilize bottom-up approaches in which identifying the psychologically active features of situations is based on responses provided from individual participants rather than from existing theory and research.

The research below illustrates a bottom-up approach to answer the question: What are the features of situations that influence whether one person perceives that another needs help, specifically social support? Certainly, it is not simply a matter of hearing the person say 'I need help', because distressed individuals may have good reason to *not* express an explicit desire for help.

A direct request for help involves the possibility of rejection or stigmatization, can be associated with feelings of loss of independence, and comes with the knowledge that one could be burdening the listener (Goldsmith and Parks, 1990). If people in distress do not directly ask for support, what situational features do potential support providers (PSPs) rely on to determine whether someone needs help? Is a person who clearly and freely expresses nonverbal signals of distress (e.g., a large variety and high frequency of negative facial expressions) more likely to be perceived as needing help compared to someone who attempts to manage their distress (e.g., attempting to suppress the expression of negative emotions)? The research described below examined the support seeker's verbal and nonverbal communication as possible key ingredients of the situations that PSPs encounter.

Step 1: Identify the situations in which the behavior of interest is likely to take place

The present research example focuses on situations in which one person is distressed and another person has the opportunity to provide support. Distress signals may differ depending on the nature of the distress-eliciting event and context in which they occur.

For example, it may be perceived as more acceptable to freely express sadness and grief in response to a family member's death, but less so in response to a loss at an athletic event or competition. As a first effort in understanding the features of situations that are 'active' and addressing the question, 'What features of situations do PSPs rely on to determine whether someone needs help?', the researchers deliberately limited their focus to situations in which individuals believed that they would have to engage in an aversive behavior (i.e., eating dried worms). By equating the nature of the distressing situation encountered, the range of psychological features that could play a role in determining potential support providers' responses (e.g., perceptions that a discloser needs help) was restricted. Constraining the range of psychological features affects the generalizability to other kinds of distressing situations. Nonetheless, it is a first step in determining the effectiveness and feasibility of such an approach.

Step 2: Gather specific stimuli representing the situations of interest

The next step is to identify a set of stimuli that capture the most psychologically important aspects of the situation of interest. For this purpose, a sample of situations was developed by asking 65 different people to serve as disclosers. Upon arriving in the laboratory, the disclosers were led to believe they were in a taste-testing study in which they would be eating dried worms. Past research has shown that individuals react negatively in response to this procedure (Johnson, 2006). Prior to performing the presumed dried worm taste-test, a video recording was made of each of these 65 disclosers while they were interviewed, 'so that future participants would know what the study was like.' Disclosers were asked to describe their experience, say how they felt about it (positive, negative, or neutral) and to elaborate on their response. Each interview lasted approximately five minutes.

Videotaped interviews were edited in order to delete the interviewer's questions and focus solely on disclosers' responses. Any responses not having to do with the discloser's response to the worms (e.g., disclosers' descriptions of the study procedures) were also deleted. The final clips were between 20 and 25 seconds in length. Therefore, after completing this step in the process, there were 65 clips that could be presented to a new group of participants.

Step 3: Identify a common set of features that could be used to capture the most psychologically important aspects of the situation of interest

All the video clips developed from the first study were then presented to a different sample (from the same population of interest) to identify the psychological features of the situation; namely, the features of situations to which people respond when deciding whether or not another person needs help (Whitsett and Shoda, 2007). Participants ($N = 58$) viewed randomly assigned pairs of clips, with each video depicting a different person describing his or her response to the distressing event.[3] Participants selected one clip from each pair in terms of who they thought needed more help, which was defined to participants in the following way: 'By "needs help" we mean that the person would benefit from someone providing some comforting words of support. An example of this type of help is someone saying, "I know how you feel" to the person'. To identify the features that affected their judgment of who needed more help, they were asked to reply to an open-ended question asking why they chose one individual over the other. Participants were asked to type a few sentences explaining their choice for each pair. In a variation of this method, participants could be asked to rate the extent to which each person needed help instead of making a choice between two disclosers, and then explain why they gave each person the rating they did.

The result of this step was a large qualitative dataset, which consisted of reasons participants spontaneously provided for perceiving one discloser as needing more help compared to another discloser (32 video pairs × 58 participants = 1,856 responses). Several steps were taken to extract the important psychologically meaningful features from these data, which entailed creating a bottom-up coding system (Lampert and Ervin-Tripp, 1993). First, two coders read through all responses, noting any features that were consistently mentioned by a number of participants. Features were quite diverse, including demographics (e.g., gender), personality characteristics (e.g., shyness), and specific behaviors (e.g., fidgeting). A list of 99 themes was developed, providing a preliminary list of psychological features.

The open-ended responses were then read through a second time, with the goal of coding every response using the preliminary list of 99 features. In cases when coders encountered a response that could not be coded using the preliminary list of features, a new code was added. As a result, there were 120 features in the preliminary list. Next, each rater coded 60% of the responses and determined how frequently each of the 120 features was mentioned in each participant's response. Because there was a 20% overlap between coders, it was possible to compute inter-rater reliabilities, using Cronbach's alpha, for each feature. To reduce

the list of 120 features, only the 30 of the 120 features that were reported by at least 10% of participants and had a Cronbach's alpha of greater than 0.70 were retained. These features are listed in Table 18.2. Given that participants' responses were obtained in open-ended format questions, 10% of participants spontaneously reporting the same feature is considerable.[4] To summarize, the coding procedure reduced the preliminary list of 120 features to a more manageable list of 30 features.

Step 4: Code the stimulus set according to a list of relevant features and derive indices reflecting presence of features

After establishing a list of features relevant for the situations, the next step was to rate each video, on a 7-point Likert scale, according to the degree to which each feature was present in the clips. A new group of individuals, similar in characteristics to those participating in the final study of interest, rated the videos with regard to the list of features. In this way, the presence of psychological features of situations in the set of stimuli is rated from the perspective of the individuals who are similar to the eventual test participants. In addition, given that these judgments will be used to develop a consensually agreed-upon index to capture the extent to which each feature is present in a situation, the greater the number

Table 18.2 List of 30 features identified as describing the most psychologically important aspects of one type of distressing situation

1. Negative expectations about what is to come next	16. Tense body
2. Disgust	17. Nervous tics (playing with earlobe, hair, etc.)
3. Lack of confidence	18. Looks at worms
4. Distressed/upset	19. Looks down
5. Angry	20. Voice in general indicates a negative state
6. Scared	21. Quiet voice
7. Anxious	22. Words that are used indicate a negative state
8. Surprised	23. Relays a negative personal memory
9. Negative attitude	24. Focuses on negative aspects of the task
10. 'Playing it cool'/covering up true feelings	25. Is willing to try the worms/open-minded
11. Convincing self	26. Task seems difficult for the discloser
12. Conveys a forced/ fake smile	27. Willing to try the worms, but with reservations
13. Conveys nervous laughter	28. Not open to experience/opposed to trying worms
14. Body movements in general indicate a negative state	29. Has no previous experience with worms
15. Engages in fidgeting/squirming	30. Participant can relate to person/understand point-of-view

of raters, the more reliable the index becomes.

In order to make the task more manageable for raters, each rater was responsible for only one feature. Ten raters were assigned to each feature, and their responses were averaged for each video clip. By having multiple raters per feature, idiosyncratic responses cancel each other out when averaged with the responses of other raters. After averaging across raters, each video has a value assigned to it for each feature, indicating the level of each feature contained in each of the 65 video clips. The reliability of these indices can be computed using inter-rater correlations, Cronbach's alpha, or both.

Step 5: Use a highly repeated within-subjects design to observe and record responses to stimuli

Now that the important features and the level of presence in each of the videos are known, it is possible to examine how responses to the clips are based on features contained in the clips. A new group of participants served as the PSPs and were asked to view the videos and respond, for each one, with how much help (on a Likert scale) they think each person needs.

Step 6: Analyze each participant's responses as a function of the features of the situation

For each individual PSP, his or her perception of disclosers' need for help can be predicted as a function of the various features of the film clips. Specifically, multi-level

modeling can be used to predict, for each potential support provider, the effects of psychological features on perceived need for help. As shown in equation (18.4), the level-1 model predicts, for each PSP, the extent to which disclosers' negative expectations and expressions of disgust influence his or her perception that a discloser needs help. The level-1 model is as follows:

$$[\text{Perceived need for help } i]_j = b_0 + b_{\text{neg.expectations } j} [\text{discloser } i\text{'s} \text{ negative expectations}] + b_{\text{disgust } j} [\text{discloser } i\text{'s disgust}] + r_{ij}$$
(18.4)

Table 18.3 reports the regression equations for five participants. As shown, for PSP 1, the more negative expectations and disgust that a discloser displays, the more likely she is to perceive that the discloser needs help. The feature-behavior profile for PSP 2 is somewhat different. As for PSP 1, the more a discloser displays negative expectations, the more PSP 2 is likely to help. However, unlike PSP 1, disgust does *not* appear to be a relevant feature for PSP 2.

It can also be determined if there are systematic differences between PSPs in what features of the disclosers' expressions of distress prompt the perception that help is needed. Recall that individual level characterizations that result from the level-1 model can be predicted from individual difference measures. In this particular study, the focus was on examining individual differences in

Table 18.3   Level-1 regression equations predicting for each participant the effect of the discloser's negative expectations and disgust on each participant's perception of whether the discloser needs help

Participant	ECR	Level-1 regression equation
1	2.22	$[\text{Perceived need for help } i]_j = b_0 + 0.36(\text{negative expectations}) + 0.58 (\text{disgust}) + r_{ij}$
2	1.83	$[\text{Perceived need for help } i]_j = b_0 + 0.97(\text{negative expectations}) - 0.07(\text{disgust}) + r_{ij}$
3	1.50	$[\text{Perceived need for help } i]_j = b_0 - 0.12(\text{negative expectations}) + 0.92(\text{disgust}) + r_{ij}$
4	4.11	$[\text{Perceived need for help } i]_j = b_0 + 0.47(\text{negative expectations}) + 0.35(\text{disgust}) + r_{ij}$
5	5.33	$[\text{Perceived need for help } i]_j = b_0 + 0.79(\text{negative expectations}) + 0.06(\text{disgust}) + r_{ij}$

Notes: Each participant's regression equation predicts his or her perceptions of whether the discloser needs help as a function of the discloser's negative expectations and disgust. Each participant's score on the avoidance dimension of the experiences in close relationship (ECR) scale is reported in the second column (range of possible scores = 1 to 7).

attachment avoidance. The level-2 model for the slopes predicts the magnitude and direction of the association between features of disclosers' communication and perceived need for help as a function of the PSP's attachment avoidance score as measured by the Experiences in Close Relationships Questionnaire (ECR; Brennan et al., 1998). In other words, the level-2 model examines whether attachment avoidance moderates the relation between features of disclosers (i.e., whether disclosers were perceived as having negative expectations and expressing disgust) and perceived need for help. The level-2 model is as follows:

$$b_{neg.expectations\,j} = \gamma_{neg.expectations\,0} + \gamma_{neg.expectations\,1}$$
[PSP j's avoidance score] + $\mu_{neg.expectations\,j}$
(18.5)

$$b_{disgust\,j} = \gamma_{disgust\,0} + \gamma_{disgust\,1}\,[\text{PSP } j\text{'s}$$
avoidance score] + $\mu_{disgust\,j}$
(18.6)

The level-2 intercepts, $\gamma_{neg.expectations\,0}$ and $\gamma_{disgust\,0}$, can be used to examine perceived need for help in relation to negative expectations and disgust. In general, results showed that the more the discloser in a video clip displayed negative expectations, the greater the perceived need for help ($\gamma_{neg.expectations\,0} = 0.50$, $t(39) = 11.31$, $p < 0.0001$). In addition, the more the discloser in a video clip displayed disgust, the greater the perceived need for help ($\gamma_{disgust\,0} = 0.47$, $t(39) = 10.91$, $p < 0.0001$).

Rather than assessing the moderating effect of attachment avoidance via product term interactions, multi-level modeling determines the extent to which the slopes in the level-1 model for situation features (i.e., disclosers' negative expectations and disgust, represented by $b_{neg.expectations\,j}$ and $b_{disgust\,j}$, respectively) varied as a function of participants' attachment avoidance. Attachment avoidance did not appear to moderate the relationship between negative expectations and perceived need for help ($\gamma_{neg.expectations\,1} = 0.06$, $t(39) = 1.52$, $p = 0.14$), but it was found

to be an important moderator of the relation between disgust and perceived need for help ($\gamma_{disgust\,1} = -0.10$, $t(39) = -2.80$, $p = 0.008$). Participants with low attachment avoidance, compared to those with high attachment avoidance, showed a stronger relation between disclosers' expressions of disgust and their perception that help was needed.

COMBINED (TOP-DOWN AND BOTTOM-UP) APPROACH TO IDENTIFYING PSYCHOLOGICAL FEATURES INFLUENCING SELF-RELEVANT EVALUATIONS

In some cases, using a bottom-up approach – in which individuals describe the features of situations that are most psychologically meaningful – may result in more features than one may wish to, or is able to, address within a study. In such cases, it may be useful to identify potentially important psychological features by combining a bottom-up approach with a top-down approach. Pre-existing theory-driven concepts are used to pare down the number of features studied. This approach is illustrated by the following research example identifying those psychological features of situations that are likely to differentially influence how people feel about themselves, that is, people's affective self-evaluation. This study further demonstrates the stability of individuals' *feature-behavior* profiles by using the profiles from one time point to predict affective self-evaluative responses to situations at a second time point more than one week later.

Step 1: Identify the situations in which the behavior of interest is likely to take place

As mentioned in the first two research examples, the researcher must identify where the behavior of interest is likely to take place. The behavior of interest in this study was affective self-evaluation. Therefore, the researchers aimed to find situations in which individuals would feel positively or negatively about themselves.

Step 2: Gather specific stimuli representing the situations of interest

In contrast to the previous two illustrations, the present study used existing stimuli. Kitayama and colleagues (Kitayama et al., 1992, 1997) had participants describe situations in which their self-esteem increased or decreased. This resulted in 200 positive and 200 negative situations. Each situation described a single social episode and was usually one sentence in length (e.g., 'In an attempt to get a person's attention, I poked my nose into that person's affair and he/she became upset at me').

Step 3: Identify a common set of features that could be used to capture the most psychologically important aspects of the situation of interest

Next, a bottom-up strategy was used to identify features that might differentially predict how individuals will feel about themselves. Participants ($N = 194$) first completed a *situation-self-evaluation* task. This task consisted of two ten-minute blocks. In one block, negative situations from the stimulus set described in Step 2 were presented in random order one at a time on a computer screen. In the other block, positive situations were presented in random order. After reading each situation, participants rated how positively they would feel about themselves in that situation, how negatively they would feel about themselves in that situation, and how frequently they encountered each situation. A 5-point scale ($0 = $ never; $4 = $ frequently) was used to assess the frequency with which participants experienced each situation. Situations with mean frequency ratings less than 1.05, indicating that they were infrequently experienced by the majority of participants, were excluded from the stimulus set of future studies (i.e., those described in Steps 4 and 5). This reduced the list to 139 negative and 168 positive situations. On average, participants rated 38 different situations ($SD = 13.56$) per block.

Next, participants completed a *situation comparison* task in which they were prompted to identify the features of the situations that led them to feel positively or negatively about themselves. In one of the four blocks

of this task, participants saw two lists of situations, one on either side of their computer screen. For each participant, one list consisted of ten negative situations that he or she evaluated most negatively. The other list consisted of ten negative situations that he or she evaluated least negatively.[5] The two lists were randomly assigned to either side of the computer screen. Participants were instructed to write a list of characteristics that the situations within each list all shared and the characteristics on which the two lists differed from one another. The remaining three blocks of the situation comparison task followed the same procedure. The only difference was that pairs of lists varied such that participants compared *negative* situations that they evaluated most and least positively, *positive* situations that they evaluated most and least positively, and *positive* situations that they evaluated most and least negatively. The order of these blocks was counterbalanced between participants. After the situation comparison task, all participants were asked to list any additional situation characteristics that also may have led them to feel positively or negatively about themselves. The situation comparison task and the follow-up question resulted in a list of approximately 2,700 free-response items. Using the instructions for constructing a bottom-up coding system outlined by Lampert and Ervin-Tripp (1993), the free-response data were segmented into potential coding categories (i.e., situation features). This step yielded a large and diverse set of approximately 85 potential situation features.

As a first pass, a top-down approach was applied to reduce this list of situation features to those considered to have theoretical value in the field of social psychology. Two researchers independently analyzed social psychology textbooks (Brown, 2006; Sears et al., 1991) and identified topics from the textbooks that were also reflected in the bottom-up coding categories derived from the free-response data. Those categories identified by both researchers as being represented in the free-response data *and* in at least one of the textbooks were selected as features to be used for this study. For example, one of the categories identified with this approach was 'conformity due to presence of an authority figure'. Using this procedure, 46 features were selected.

Step 4: Code the stimulus set according to a list of relevant features and derive indices reflecting presence of features

A separate sample of participants ($N = 318$) rated the extent to which each of the situations in the stimulus set contained the situation features identified from Step 3. Situations were randomly selected without replacement from the stimulus set of 307 situations and presented one at a time on a computer screen. Participants were assigned one of the 46 situation features, and they rated the extent to which their assigned feature was present in each situation.[6]

Inter-rater reliabilities for each of these features were indexed by Cronbach's alpha (α). Eleven of the features had alphas greater than 0.80, and they were selected for the present study (see Table 18.4 for the 11 features). The degree to which a situation reflected the presence of a feature was indexed by the mean rating of these participants.

Step 5: Use a highly repeated within-subjects design to observe and record responses to stimuli

A third set of participants ($N = 37$) completed a two-session study. In each session, participants read situations one at a time on the computer screen and rated, on two separate scales, how negatively and how positively they would feel about themselves in each situation. The scale consisted of 26 vertically aligned points anchored at the first and twenty-sixth points (e.g., 'I would not feel *negative* about myself' and 'I would feel extremely *negative* about myself', respectively.) In both sessions, participants evaluated one block of 40 negative situations randomly selected without replacement from the negative stimulus set and one block of 40 positive situations randomly selected without replacement from the positive stimulus set. Both positive and negative self-evaluations were measured in order to evaluate individual differences in within-person relations between negative and positive self-evaluation (Wang et al., 2007). For the purpose of illustration, this example will focus only on negative self-evaluation ratings in negative situations.

Step 6: Analyze each participant's responses as a function of the features of the situation

As discussed in the previous two research examples, participants' *feature-behavior* profiles were indexed by intraindividual slope coefficients predicting negative self-evaluation to situations from the degree to which features were present in the situations. Within each session, a standardized slope

Table 18.4   The stability of individual *feature-behavior* profiles for situation features between time 1 and time 2

Situation feature	rank-order correlation	p
Shared success	0.67	9.03×10^{-6}
Receipt of social support	0.44	0.007
Academics	0.38	0.02
Receipt of negative feedback from others	0.38	0.02
Being alone	0.37	0.03
Poor performance due to the presence of others	0.35	0.03
Competition	0.35	0.04
Achieving success alone	0.29	0.08
Being misunderstood or misperceived	0.27	0.1
Physical activity (e.g., exercise)	0.26	0.1
Receipt of positive feedback	0.13	0.4

Notes: The stability of the profiles for each feature was indexed by Spearman's rank-order correlation coefficient predicting individuals' time 2 *feature-behavior* profile signatures from their time 1 signatures. Only cues with standardized Cronbach's alphas (α) greater than 0.80 were included in this table.

coefficient was computed for each individual for each feature. Specifically, the level-1 model was as follows:

[Negative self-evaluation in situation i]$_j$
= β_{0j} + $\beta_{\text{neg.feedback } j}$ [negative feedback in situation i] + r_{ij}

(18.7)

The top panel of Figure 18.3 illustrates the data for 37 participants' negative self-evaluative responses to negative situations as a function of receiving negative feedback (e.g., criticism) at time 1. Each scatterplot represents the data for one participant. The inset to the right of Figure 18.3 presents the data of participants 33, 34, and 35.

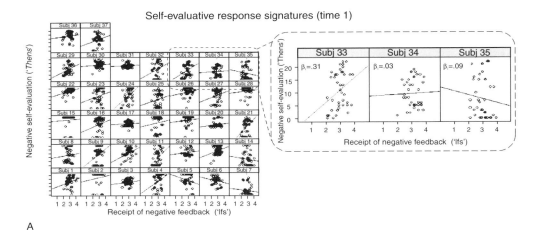

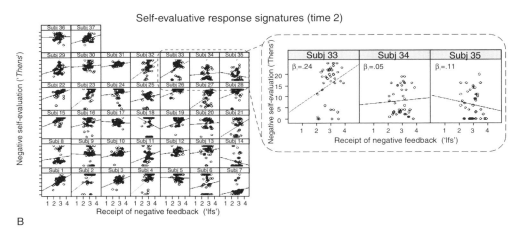

Figure 18.3   Top panel (panel A) depicts scatterplots representing the relation between the feature of the situation (i.e., receipt of negative feedback) and negative self-evaluation, for each participant at time 1. In each graph, the _x_-axis represents the degree to which the situations involved receiving negative feedback. The _y_-axis represents participants' negative self-evaluation ratings in response to each situation. The inset to the right illustrates that, for participant 33, the greater the negative feedback present in the situation, the more he reported negative self-evaluations. The same feature had almost no effect on participant 34 and slightly an inverse effect on participant 35. Lower panel (panel B) shows scatterplots representing the relation between the same feature of the situation (i.e., receipt of negative feedback) and negative self-evaluation, for each participant at time 2.

For participant 33, *if* the situation involves receiving negative feedback, *then* he is more likely to feel negatively about himself. This is reflected by a positive beta-coefficient of 0.31. In contrast, for participant 35, the same feature predicted less negative self-evaluations ($\beta_{neg.feedback} = -0.09$). For participant 34, this feature was not predictive of negative self-evaluations ($\beta_{neg.feedback} = 0.03$).

The present study also looked at the stability, or predictive utility, of participants' *feature-behavior* profiles. The bottom panel of Figure 18.3 illustrates data for the same 37 participants at time 2. The stability of the profiles for each feature was indexed by a Spearman's rank-order correlation coefficient predicting individuals' time 2 *feature-behavior* profile from their time 1 *feature - behavior* profile. Table 18.4 illustrates the stability of the *feature-behavior* profiles for all the features. For any given feature, the more positive a correlation coefficient, the greater the stability of participants' *feature-behavior* profiles between sessions 1 and 2.

This research provides an illustration of a method used to identify potentially important psychological features by combining a bottom-up approach – in which individuals' self-reports of what influences their feelings about themselves were solicited – with a top-down approach in which pre-existing concepts within the field of social psychology were used to pare down the features resulting from the bottom-up approach. Variability in individuals' *feature-behavior* profiles suggests that they may trigger cognitive-affective processes that lead to a behavioral response, in this case, negative feeling about the self. This research also provides an example of how to identify features that yield temporally stable *feature-behavior* profiles. The Spearman's rank-order correlation coefficients in Table 18.4 suggest that the stability of *feature-behavior* profiles are strong for some features and weak for others.

Strengths and limitations

Research strategies such as the ones described in this chapter that use top-down or bottom-up approaches, or a combination of the two, allow identification of features of situations. Each approach has its own strengths and limitations and it is up to the researcher to determine the most suitable strategy for addressing a specific research question. An obvious strength of top-down approaches is that identification of features is supported by existing evidence collected from various researchers. These previous research findings can be used to identify features of situations hypothesized to affect behavior and to test specific hypotheses about the role of specific features on behavior. A weakness of top-down approaches is that they are limited to those features that have been studied in the literature. In addition, those psychological features that have been identified may be specified at varying levels of abstraction (see section on 'Feature identification and level of analyses'). Moreover, it is highly likely that not all the relevant psychological features affecting individual differences in behavior have been identified. In contrast, bottom-up approaches are based on individuals' responses, and therefore are not limited by previous research and theory. However, a limitation of bottom-up approaches is that they require that at least some participants are aware and willing to reveal the factors that affected their behaviors. Given that many processes involved in judgment, decision-making, and producing a behavioral response may be automatic and unconscious, individuals may not be aware of all the factors influencing their decision-making and behaviors. Social desirability processes, whether to present one's self in a positive light to others or to oneself, may also likely to affect the responses that participants provide. Finally, in some cases, a feature may be important, but may not be one that spontaneously comes to mind.

FURTHER CONSIDERATIONS

The research projects described above illustrate approaches for identifying the psychological features of situations in different domains – situations involving preferences for and selection of potential dating partners, to those involving deciding whether an individual needs social support, to situations that may influence one's affective self-evaluations. As with any research paradigm, there are issues that each researcher needs to consider in light of his or her specific research goal. Below is a brief discussion of considerations involved in the process of feature identification.

Feature identification and level of analyses

As may be evident from the research illustrations presented so far, psychological features can be conceptualized at different levels. In the Zayas and Shoda (2007) study described earlier, for example, the level of analysis was general perceptions of personality characteristics, such as whether a potential dating partner was aggressive, impulsive, and so on. However, other researchers might have focused on more micro features such as potential partner's tone of voice or how they cope with temptation, to examine how such micro features give rise to more general perceptions of potential dating partners. A focus on more micro-level features, such as subtle nonverbal behaviors (e.g., eye gaze or vocal intonation) would address a different question: what are the features of situations that give rise to perceptions that another person is, for example, jealous or impulsive or needs help? Specifying the level of analyses for a particular project is analogous to the study of linguistics in which one goal is to understand how written words are encoded and assigned meaning. In linguistics, the first level involves orthographic analysis. Successful analysis is required for the identification of

morphemes, the smallest unit of meaning, such as prefixes (un-, ad-) and suffixes (-less, -ness). These in turn may combine with other morphemes to form words. Similarly, in personality and social psychology, the process of feature identification is likely to involve stages and the researcher must decide which stage and corresponding level of analyses to focus on. Given that conceptualization and operationalization of situational features is still in the early stages, it is up to future research to derive a vocabulary for describing different levels, how the different levels correspond with one another, and the most effective demarcation of levels.

Highly repeated within-subjects approach

The techniques described in the three illustrations are useful in identifying *feature-behavior* profiles that differ in notable ways from those used in the original summer camp study (e.g., Shoda et al., 1994). Most important, these techniques no longer classify '*ifs*' on discrete categories (e.g., peer teasing vs. teacher praise). Rather, continuous scales are used to assess the degree to which each psychological feature is present in a given situation. The use of continuous indices of situational features has also changed the statistical methods available for the analysis of the effects of situation features. Specifically, multi-level modeling allows one to simultaneously estimate the expected effect of a feature on the average individual (conceptually similar to the main effect) as well as the effect of the feature for a given individual. It does so without requiring that a situation be classified into mutually exclusive categories. Multi-level modeling also allows the analysis of the role of individual difference variables, such as attachment avoidance, without requiring that the sample be divided into discrete groups (e.g., high avoidance vs. low avoidance).

Predicting future behavior: generalizability of 'ifs'

Ultimately, most researchers wish to say more than how a person will respond to the features of the specific stimulus set that was presented in a particular research paradigm. For example, a researcher may wish to go beyond the psychologically active features of expressions of distress in response to the specific situation of having to eat dried worms to expressions of distress elicited by a broader class of aversive situations. If one is successful in identifying psychological features that are important, identifying a particular person's *feature-behavior* profile in a specific research paradigm should enable us to predict what the person will do in new situations that contain the same psychological feature, even if they are nominally different situations. For example, the level-1 coefficients from the Whitsett and Shoda (2007) study, such as those that index the effect of negative expectations and disgust on perceptions of whether another person needs help, may allow one to predict each person's perception of an individual's suffering under different sources of distress, such as being unprepared for an upcoming exam.

The meaning and impact of particular psychological features often depend on the other features present in the same situation. For example, although a situation may possess fear-eliciting features that may in themselves lead to withdrawal, the situation may also possess other features, such as a highly desired goal, that simultaneously activate processing dynamics that may lead to approach, thus overriding the fear–withdrawal response. It is the set of cognitions and affects activated, rather than a single cognition that influences a person's response. This possibility can be addressed empirically by testing for interactions among features. Of course with the presence of multiple features in a given situation, the number of interactions quickly becomes unwieldy. Thus, even for bottom-up approaches, past research and theory may inform which particular interactions to examine.

Building a Model of a Person

Identifying meaningful and stable *if ... then ...* situation-behavior profiles, or 'behavioral signatures', is one step in building a model of a person. Ultimately, however, one needs to understand how, within a given individual, a particular situational feature (e.g., Joe's facial features that remind Mary of her father) activates cognitive (e.g., a memory of his disdain for mediocrity) and emotional (e.g., anxiety) reactions that mediate the effect of situation features on behavior. But how would one go about directly assessing such internal *if ... then ...* relations?

Assessing internal *if ... then ...* relations is a significant challenge because individuals are often not aware of the associations among their thoughts. However, there are now some promising methodologies for the assessment of automatic (i.e., not consciously controlled) associations among cognitions and affects. Recent research has shown the importance and feasibility of assessing links between specific cognitive, affective, and behavioral reactions. For example, links between situation features and cognitive and emotional reactions have repeatedly been shown to underlie the phenomenon of 'transference' (Andersen and Chen, 2002).

One approach for assessing strengths of automatic associations within each individual's CAPS network utilizes implicit measures, such as the Implicit Association Test (Greenwald et al., 1998). For example, people with secure attachment styles, compared to those with insecure styles, were shown to have stronger automatic associations between the concept of their current romantic partner and positive reactions (Zayas and Shoda, 2005). For these securely attached individuals, thoughts about their partner more strongly (compared to insecurely attached individuals) automatically activated positive reactions. Furthermore, the strength of such associations was found to be meaningfully related to relationship outcomes, such as greater satisfaction and emotional commitment.

Another approach builds on basic findings in research on brain activities. Specifically, a particular component of Event Related Potentials (ERP) waves in response to an event, called N400, has been shown to be magnified when participants analyze the semantic meaning of words. A typical finding using the N400 as an index, for example, is that targets preceded by an unrelated prime are more difficult to process (than targets preceded by a related prime), presumably because they require greater semantic analysis. Applying this finding and methodology to the social and personality domain, greater N400 reactions are observed when women encounter a negative interpersonal outcome (e.g., partner's inattention) in response to a bid for a partner's support compared to encountering the same situation in more neutral contexts (Zayas et al., under review). Moreover, according to research in adult attachment, the negative interpersonal information encountered in response to a bid for partner's support may be a psychologically salient feature of the situation, particularly for insecurely attached women (compared to securely attached women). However, given that women with insecure styles may cope with interpersonal rejection in distinctive ways – women who are considered preoccupied turn their attention *towards* threatening information whereas women who are highly avoidant turn their attention away from threatening information – the greatest reaction should be observed among women with a preoccupied attachment style. In other words, these women show not only a sensitivity to threatening information, but once encountered have a difficult time disengaging from it. Consistent with these ideas, women who were anxiously attached and low in attachment avoidance (also referred to as preoccupied with attachment) showed the

greatest reaction to rejection words as assessed by the N400.

CONCLUSIONS

The finding that people can be characterized by stable *if ... then ...* situation-behavior profiles led to two related developments in the study of personality. First, there was a recognition that the field needed to reconcile the fact that people's behavior varies across situations with the core assumption of the field itself, that people possess a stable and coherent personality. This led to a reconceptualization of personality. Instead of focusing on traits, social cognitive approaches assumed that each person is characterized by a unique network of interconnected cognitions, which itself remains constant, even if the specific behaviors that arise from the network vary from one situation to another. This then suggested that that *if ... then ...* profiles provide clues for identifying individuality and personality coherence within individuals' cross-situational variability. This variability need not be considered a source of error to be eliminated.

But what are the '*ifs*'? As a first step in constructing a cognitive social model of personality, this chapter discussed three approaches for identifying psychological significant '*ifs*', or psychological features of situations. They illustrate different approaches used to identify the features of situations, and the different level of analysis involved in the conceptualization of the situation and the psychological features embedded within it.

Certainly, the task of identifying a set of psychological features that are particularly relevant for a given individual is not an easy one. But once a list of features that represent the most important features of the situation is developed, stimuli that differ in the presence of these features can the be used to examine questions such as: What features of situations activate a given individual's encodings of situations and generate behavior, reflecting a person's unique and stable cognitive-affective processing system?

NOTES

1 Due to the design of the Internet dating service (IDS) procedure used to assess partner preference (Zayas and Shoda, 2007), all participants (in study 1 and 2) obtained the same *average* preference score. Because the average preference for all participants was zero after centering, the intercept, b_{0j}, which reflects each participant's average preference score for the 16 dating partners, was not included in the level-1 model. Details regarding model specification for the HLM analysis are described in Zayas and Shoda (2007).

2 To examine the effect of the presence of specific personality traits, the HLM models were specified exactly as those described in equations (18.1), (18.2), and (18.3), except that the aggressiveness index was replaced by each personality index (e.g., impulsivity, jealousy), one at a time, as the level-1 predictor.

3 Each participant viewed 64 of the 65 video clips randomly selected. All 65 video clips were presented an approximately equal number of times.

4 It is not necessarily the case that codes with poor inter-rater reliabilities are not useful. The low reliabilities could be due to low frequency of the feature across stimuli or simply the fact that these cues might be perceived differently by different people. In other words, they could be highly relevant for most or some people, but the effect of the feature on behavior could vary greatly from individual to individual.

5 If participants evaluated fewer than 20 negative situations, the two lists were generated by splitting the evaluated situations into the most and least negatively rated.

6 Participants who evaluated fewer than 224 (90%) of the situations were not included in the calculation of the presence of features in situations. They did not evaluate enough situations to establish whether there was high inter-rater reliability regarding the presence of features in the situations. For the same reason of needing to establish consensus, features were also required to have been assigned to at least five participants. The reasons why only 25 of the 46 features fit the criteria described are two-fold. The main reason was because the initial computer program for this study randomly assigned participants to 1 of the 46 features. Random assignment led to an uneven distribution such that certain features were assigned to participants more frequently than others.

Once this problem was identified, block random assignment was used and participants were no longer assigned to oversampled situation features. Some features also failed to have a sufficient number of raters (i.e., five or more) because participants assigned to these features were unable to rate at least 224 (90%) of the 307 situations. These criteria resulted in 25 features.

REFERENCES

Andersen, S.M. and Chen, S. (2002) 'The relational self: An interpersonal social-cognitive theory', *Psychological Review*, 109(4): 619–45.

Brennan, K.A., Clark, C.L. and Shaver, P.R. (1998) 'Self-report measurement of adult attachment: An integrative overview', in J.A. Simpson and W.S. Rholes (eds), *Attachment Theory and Close Relationships*. New York: Guilford Press, pp. 46–76.

Brown, J.D. (2006) *Social Psychology*. New York: McGraw-Hill.

Darley, J. M. and Latané, B. (1968) 'Bystander intervention in emergencies: Diffusion of responsibility', *Journal of Personality and Social Psychology*, 8(4): 377–83.

Dutton, D.G. (1994) 'Patriarchy and wife assault: The ecological fallacy', *Violence and Victims*, 9: 167–82.

Dutton, D.G. and Browning, J.J. (1988) 'Power struggles and intimacy anxieties as causative factors of violence in intimate relationships', in G. Russell (ed.), *Violence in Intimate Relationships*. New York: PMA Publishing.

Dutton, D.G., Starzomski, A. and Ryan, L. (1996) 'Antecedents of abusive personality and abusive behavior in wife assaulters', *Journal of Family Violence*, 11(2): 113–32.

Goldsmith, D. and Parks, M.R. (1990) 'Communicative strategies for managing the risks of seeking social support', in S. Duck and R.C. Silver (eds), *Personal Relationships and Social Support*. Newbury Park, CA: Sage, pp. 104–21.

Greenwald, A.G., McGhee, D.E. and Schwartz, J.K.L. (1998) 'Measuring individual differences in implicit cognition: The Implicit Association Test', *Journal of Personality and Social Psychology*, 74(6): 1464–80.

Hartshorne, H. and May, M.A. (1928) *Studies in the Nature of Character: Vol. 1. Studies in Deceit*. New York: Macmillan.

Johnson, K.L. (2006) 'Dreading to a better end: How anticipation affects intertemporal evaluative judgments', Unpublished manuscript, New York University.

Kasian, M. and Painter, S.L. (1992) 'Frequency and severity of psychological abuse in a dating population', *Journal of Interpersonal Violence*, 7(3): 350–64.

Kelley, H.H., Holmes, J.G., Kerr, N., Reis, H., Rusbult, C.E. and Van Lange, P.A. (2003) *An Atlas of Interpersonal Situations*. Cambridge: Cambridge University Press.

Kitayama, S., Markus, H.R., Matsumoto, H. and Norasakkunkit, V. (1997) 'Individual and collective processes in the construction of the self: Self-enhancement in the United States and self-criticism in Japan', *Journal of Personality and Social Psychology*, 72(6): 1245–67.

Lampert, M.D. and Ervin-Tripp, S.M. (1993) 'Structured coding for the study of language and social interaction', in J.A. Edwards and M.D. Lampert (eds), *Talking Data: Transcription and Coding in Discourse Research*. Hillsdale, NJ: Erlbaum, pp. 169–206.

Miller, S.M. (1987) 'Monitoring and blunting: Validation of a questionnaire to assess styles of information seeking under threat', *Journal of Personality and Social Psychology*, 52(2): 345–53.

Mischel, W. and Shoda, Y. (1995) 'A cognitive-affective system theory of personality: Reconceptualizing situations, dispositions, dynamics, and invariance in personality structure', *Psychological Review*, 102(2): 246–68.

Murphy, C.M., Meyer, S.L. and O'Leary, K.D. (1994) 'Dependency characteristics of partner assaultive men', *Journal of Abnormal Psychology*, 103(4): 729–35.

Newcomb, T.M. (1929) 'The consistency of certain extrovert-introvert behavior patterns in 51 problem boys', *Contributions to Education*, No. 382, Columbia University, New York.

Sears, D.O., Peplau, L.A. and Taylor, S.E. (1991) *Social Psychology*. New Jersey: Prentice Hall.

Shoda, Y. (1990) 'Conditional analyses of personality coherence and dispositions', PhD dissertation, Columbia University.

Shoda, Y. (2003) 'Individual differences in social psychology: Understanding situations to understand people, understanding people to understand situations', in C. Sansone, C.C. Morf and Panter, A.T. (eds), *The Sage Handbook of Methods in Social Psychology*. Thousand Oaks, CA: Sage, pp. 117–41.

Shoda, Y. and Mischel, W. (1998) 'Personality as a stable cognitive-affective activation network: Characteristic patterns of behavior variation emerge from a stable personality structure', in S.J. Read and L.C. Miller (eds), *Connectionist and PDP Models of Social Reasoning and Social Behavior*. New Jersey: Lawrence Erlbaum, pp. 175–208.

Shoda, Y., Mischel, W. and Wright, J.C. (1989) 'Intuitive interactionism in person perception: Effects of situation-behavior relations on dispositional judgments', *Journal of Personality and Social Psychology*, 56(1): 41–53.

Shoda, Y., Mischel, W. and Wright, J.C. (1993a) 'The role of situational demands and cognitive competencies in behavior organization and personality coherence', *Journal of Personality and Social Psychology*, 65(5): 1023–35.

Shoda, Y., Mischel, W. and Wright, J.C. (1993b) 'Links between personality judgments and contextualized behavior patterns: Situation-behavior profiles of personality prototypes', *Social Cognition*, 4(11): 399–429.

Shoda, Y., Mischel, W. and Wright, J.C. (1994) 'Intra-individual stability in the organization and patterning of behavior: Incorporating psychological situations into the idiographic analysis of personality', *Journal of Personality and Social Psychology*, 67(4): 674–87. (Article also reprinted as a chapter in Cooper, C.L. and Pervin, L.A. (1998) *Personality: Critical Concepts in Psychology*. New York/London: Routledge.)

Walker, L.E. (1979) *The Battered Woman*. New York: Harper & Row.

Walters, B. (1992) [Interview of David Letterman, January 29, 1992].

Wang, J., Lee, J.J., Shoda, Y. and Leu, J. (2007) 'Culture and self evaluation: An idiographic approach', Poster presented at the Annual Meeting of the Society for Personality and Social Psychology, Memphis.

Whitsett, D.D. and Shoda, Y. (2007) 'Providing emotional support to individuals in distress: Women's utilization of nonverbal cues',

Poster presented at the Annual Meeting of the Society for Personality and Social Psychology, Memphis.

Wright, J.C. and Mischel, W. (1987) 'A conditional approach to dispositional constructs: The local predictability of social behavior', *Journal of Personality and Social Psychology*, 53(6): 1159–77.

Wright, J.C. and Mischel, W. (1988) 'Conditional hedges and the intuitive psychology of traits', *Journal of Personality and Social Psychology*, 55(3): 454–69.

Zayas, V. and Shoda, Y. (2005) 'Do automatic reactions elicited by thoughts of romantic partner, mother, and self relate to adult romantic attachment?', *Personality and Social Psychology Bulletin,* 31(8): 1011–25.

Zayas, V. and Shoda, Y. (2007) 'Predicting preferences for dating partners from past experiences of psychological abuse: Identifying the "psychological ingredients" of situations', *Personality and Social Psychology Bulletin*, 33(1): 123–38.

Zayas, V., Shoda, Y. and Ayduk, O.N. (2002) 'Personality in context: An interpersonal systems perspective', *Journal of Personality*, 70(6): 851–900.

Zayas, V., Shoda, Y., Osterhout, L., Takahashi, M.M. and Mischel, W. (under review) 'Neural responses to partner rejection cues'.

19

The Angry Personality: A Representation on Six Dimensions of Anger Expression

Ephrem Fernandez

As in my chapter with Kerns (Vol. 1 of this handbook) I draw from affect science and phenomenology in conceptualizing emotion. I situate emotion within a triad of feeling-related phenomena, with mood and temperament as the other two close relatives of emotion. This means that anger, like any feeling, not only has quality and quantity but also has form. Qualitatively, it is unpleasant yet categorically different from other discrete emotions such as sadness and fear. Quantitatively, it varies on a continuum of intensity or arousal from low levels called annoyance to high levels called rage. Additionally, anger can assume the form of an emotion, a mood, or a temperament, depending on whether it is phasic, tonic, or cyclic. It is the temperament form of anger that is the focus of this chapter. Specifically, boundaries between anger and related concepts are explored, past measures of dispositional anger are surveyed, and a new set of dimensions is presented for a more comprehensive assessment of the 'angry person'.

DEFINITIONS OF ANGER

As with other emotions, anger has been defined in a myriad of ways. Averill called it:

> A conflictive emotion that, on the biological level, is related to aggressive systems, and even more important, to the capacities for cooperative social living, symbolization, and reflective self-awareness; that on the psychological level, is aimed at the correction of some appraised wrong; and that, on the sociocultural level, functions to uphold accepted standards of conduct. (1982: 317)

Embedded in this definition is the assumption of perceived wrongdoing. The definition of anger is also couched within the context of interpersonal relations and social norms. Finally, the definition hints at the predominant avenues through which anger is expressed.

Lay notions of anger are also informative. According to Smedslund, beneath common sense views of anger lies a logical structure that points to 'a feeling involving a belief that a person one cares for has, intentionally or through neglect, been treated without respect, and a want to have that respect reestablished'

(1992: 30). By way of clarification, the person one cares for is usually the self but may extend to significant others, idealized personages, or strangers. To be treated without respect may entail being treated discourteously, unjustly, or in any way deemed to be offensive. Re-establishing respect means redressing or undoing the wrongdoing. This, according to Smedslund, is the classical definition of anger, one that pervades lay usage of the term.

Emphasizing the cognitive structure of emotions, Ortony et al. (1988) propose that anger is a compound emotion linking an attribution about the action of an agent to an assertion about one's wellbeing. Specifically, disapproval of someone else's blameworthy action (reproach) is combined with displeasure at the undesirable consequences of such action (distress).

Frijda (1986), on the other hand, underscores the action tendencies unique to each emotion. In the case of anger, these may entail the inclination to aggress or antagonize in any way so as to restore control, seek redress, or remove obstruction (Frijda, 1986; Frijda et al., 1989).

In short, anger, like any emotion, combines a cognitive appraisal with an action tendency. These features are mirrored in most scholarly definitions of anger, though with varying degrees of clarity. Even the so-called common sense characterizations, as analyzed by Smedslund (1992), share references to 'belief' and 'want' which are essentially the same as cognitive appraisal and action tendency, respectively. The appraisal is about some kind of wrongdoing, be it assault, exploitation, abandonment, or deceit. The ensuing tendency is to remedy or redress the wrongdoing and this opens up an array of anger expression styles which will be described later.

they are not identical in meaning. Aggression is behavior that is intended to injure (Worchel et al., 2000). This behavior may be verbal or nonverbal. Of course, such aggressive acts might emerge out of action tendencies fueled by anger. Alternatively, they may be motivated by thrill (as in pyromania), lust (as may be the case in rape), or sheer greed (as in armed robbery).

The injurious consequences of aggression may be bodily harm, psychological hurt, and/or material damage. Violence is that subtype of aggression in which physical harm is inflicted upon an individual. Not uncommonly, violent acts are attributed to anger, though (as with other acts of aggression) greed, lust, thrill, or mere obedience to authority may also be contributory factors. There is ample evidence of violence occurring everywhere from domestic settings to international battlefields. The World Health Organization (2002) reported 520,000 homicides and 310,000 war-related deaths across the world in the year 2000; the latter has probably risen steeply since then. If non-fatal violence is added, the statistics are much higher. Just focusing on adolescent males in secondary schools, the same WHO report revealed that physical fighting had a prevalence of 44% in the US, 76% in Jerusalem, Israel, and 22% in Sweden. Although aggression is not to be viewed as a proxy for anger, its rate of occurrence can tell us something about the prevalence of anger in the world.

In short, anger is a subjective feeling of unpleasantness bound up with the interpretation of an action as wrongful and tied to the inclination toward defiance or antagonism. One of the ensuing behaviors may involve aggression, and physical aggression may culminate in physical injury through acts of violence.

ANGER, AGGRESSION, AND VIOLENCE

The words anger, aggression, and violence are often used as if they are substitutable, yet

ANGER IN DISPOSITIONAL FORM

Unlike the episodic or phasic nature of anger as an emotion and unlike the prolonged or tonic nature of anger as a mood, the temperament of anger is one in which anger occurs with a frequency that suggests the individual is anger-prone. Such a person may also be deemed to have an angry disposition, meaning that the anger is not just peculiar to a particular situation. An alternate term may be angry personality. However, it must be borne in mind that in comparison to temperament, which is typically reserved for affect, a personality goes beyond feeling to encompass a complex of behaviors, cognitions, and other psychological processes that occur with a certain consistency in/across situations (Boyle, 1995; Larsen and Buss, 2002; Matthews, 1998; Saklofske and Zeidner, 1995).

A person who is habitually angry is often referred to as hostile. Hostility has been construed by some as an attitudinal bias predisposing the individual to regard others as untrustworthy, undeserving, and immoral (Barefoot, 1992) and as likely sources of provocation and mistreatment (Smith and Christensen, 1992). Not all scholars concur on the attributions of immorality, but there is consensus that hostility is a disposition to get angry. One who is hostile is not merely angry momentarily but inclined to get angry repeatedly. Hence, high frequency of anger is tantamount to habitual anger which has been labeled as hostility (Buss, 1961; Siegel, 1986), even though the instances of such anger need not be intense or prolonged. Hostility may thus be viewed as a temperament, not to be confused with the emotional state of anger or the mood of irritability/irascibility.

This brings us to the important distinction between state and trait anger. As defined by Spielberger et al. (1983), state anger is a transitory emotional episode, whereas trait anger pertains to a relatively stable pattern of personality attributes akin to hostility. Some caveats about this distinction are raised later in the evaluation of anger scales. Another common dichotomy found in clinical discourse on anger is anger-in versus anger-out. As defined by Spielberger et al. (1988), anger-in refers to the suppression of angry feelings whereas anger-out is aggressive

behavior motivated by angry feelings. However, the outward expression of anger need not be aggressive, and verbal communication of anger also counts as anger-out. On the other hand, anger-in would entail neither aggression nor communication. The terms 'internalization' versus 'externalization' have also been used as substitutes for anger-in and anger-out, respectively.

HOSTILITY/TRAIT ANGER

Due to a lack of psychophysiological specificity in the measurement of emotions, self-report measures continue to be the preferred approach to assessment in this domain. In the case of anger, for example, it is inadvisable to rely on measures such as blood pressure and heart rate which may correlate with anxiety, other affective qualities, or even stress in general. Self-report measures therefore remain the predominant approach to assessment of anger and hostility, and these are the focus of the present section.

In describing the self-report questionnaires, attention is paid mainly to the content and underlying constructs. This is in keeping with the overall theoretical and phenomenological orientation of this treatise, where the main goal is to characterize and systematize the various dispositional styles of anger expression. Detailed psychometric statistics are beyond the scope of this chapter. The reader may locate such statistical details in reviews by Biaggio (1980), Spielberger et al. (1983), Biaggio and Maiuro (1985), Barefoot (1992) and Eckhardt et al. (2004).

Buss–Durkee Hostility Inventory (BDHI)

Developed by Buss and Durkee (1957), this is the most widely used self-report measure of hostility. Its two underlying factors are neurotic aspects of hostility as measured on two subscales (suspicion and resentment) and behavioral-expressive aspects of hostility as measured on five subscales (assault, indirect hostility, verbal hostility, negativism, and irritability). There is an additional subscale designated 'guilt'; though this may accompany anger, it is clearly a separate or secondary emotion by comparison. The negativism scale is also rather broad and hence not anger-specific. The distinction between hostile outlook and hostile presentation seems valuable, but of additional value would have been some differentiation among various forms of hostile expression ranging from the passive to the active. It must be noted too that BDHI scores are influenced by social desirability as indexed by the Marlowe-Crowne Social Desirabilty Scale (Crowne and Marlowe, 1960). In other words, they probably lead to an underestimation of hostility levels.

Overcontrolled-Hostility Scale (O-H scale)

The O-H scale of Megargee et al. (1967) comprises select MMPI items designed to assess the tendency toward rigid overcontrol of aggressive impulses; such inhibition or denial may produce a cumulation of anger and frustration to the point of intense outbursts of aggression as seen in homicidal acts. Thus, the O-H scale has been used to identify those at risk of committing violent crime despite never having had a criminal history (Lane and Kling, 1979). It may also be suited to investigations of the unassertive individual who is reluctant to express anger because of its presumed social undesirability and/or its connotations of psychopathology. The O-H scale was developed exclusively in male subjects who remained the sample of choice in subsequent studies and it has been tested mainly in forensic populations. This limits the applicability of this test to females or to non-criminals who may yet have overcontrolled hostility. There has also been some concern about negative response bias arising from the way the test items have been framed.

Hostility and Direction of Hostility Questionnaire (HDHQ)

Unlike the O-H scale, which taps into impunitiveness, the HDHQ (Caine et al., 1967) assesses intropunitiveness as well as extrapunitiveness. The former factor comprises subscales of delusional guilt and self-criticism, while the latter includes delusional hostility, criticism of others, and hostile acting out. This is analogous to the anger-in, anger-out distinction to be described at greater length later. The distinction is an important one to make because, as explained earlier, intropunitiveness has been implicated in depression, while the externalization of hostile impulses often foments interpersonal conflict. Items on the HDHQ can be easily culled from the MMPI, which by virtue of widespread use, lends itself to the assessment of the direction of hostility. By the same token, using the HDHQ outside the context of the MMPI should be attempted with care because many of its items refer to pathognomic qualities (e.g. paranoia) and are also susceptible to social desirability effects. Within the framework of the MMPI however, HDHQ scores can be interpreted in conjunction with concurrent information from MMPI validity scales. Like the O-H scale, the HDHQ has declined in use within psychology.

Cook–Medley Hostility Scale (HO scale)

Another offshoot of the MMPI even more commonly used than the HDHQ is the Cook–Medley hostility scale (Cook and Medley, 1954). This so-called Ho scale supposedly taps into the cognitive components of hostility, namely attitudinal variables such as resentment and suspiciousness. Therefore, the underlying construct is referred to as cynical hostility. However, research has shown that the construct is even more diffuse, tapping into social maladjustment, coping difficulties, and neuroticism (Blumenthal et al., 1987). This is not surprising since the Ho scale was originally put together to identify teachers who described themselves as hostile and viewed students as untrustworthy and lazy; it was then serendipitously shown to predict coronary artery disease. The conclusion reached by various researchers is that items of the Ho scale are diverse in content and not well suited to broadly representing various levels of hostility (Barefoot et al., 1989; Steinberg and Jorgensen, 1996). It has consequently been overshadowed by newer alternatives for assessing anger/hostility.

Anger Self-Report (ASR)

The ASR (Zelin et al., 1972) draws 64 items from various anger/hostility assessment instruments in order to distinguish between the awareness of anger and the expression of anger. A total expression score is derived as a function of what the authors term physical expression, verbal expression, and general expression. In addition to such ways of externalizing anger, there are subscales for assessing intropunitive feelings such as guilt and condemnation of anger. There is also a subscale for assessing mistrust. Many of the subscale scores correlate with those on the BDHI and (like the latter) tend to be influenced by self-presentation bias. Basically, the ASR was built around psychodynamic formulations of anger and since its release in the 1970s, has not attracted much interest as an object of research or as a tool for application.

Reaction Inventory (RI)

A contemporary of the ASR is the RI (Evans and Strangeland, 1971), an instrument that has also been on the periphery of anger assessment methodology. This instrument employs hypothetical scenarios distributed across ten factors: minor chance annoyances, destructive people, unwarranted delays, inconsiderate people, self-opinionated people, frustration at work, criticism, major chance annoyances, people being personal, and

authority. Imagination of these scenarios has the potential to evoke anger, and thereby offer clues about the test-taker's propensity for anger arousal. However, hypothetical scenarios of the kind featured in the RI, often run the risk of being over-specific and thus of limited generalizability across test-takers.

Anger Inventory (AI)

Nearly identical in format to the RI is the AI (Novaco, 1974). It also attempts to assess anger-arousability in response to a variety of hypothetical provocations. Like the RI, the AI is correlated with scores on the BDHI. The test has undergone successive revisions, the most recent being a list of 25 anger-provoking scenarios incorporated into the Novaco anger scale and Provocation Inventory (Novaco, 2003). Some of these scenarios are:'You have hung up your clothes, but someone knocks them to the floor and fails to pick them up'; 'Stepping on a lump of chewing gum'; 'You need to get somewhere quickly, but the car in front of you is going 40 km/h in a 60 km/h zone, and you can't pass'. Psychometrically, the test has achieved retest reliability and discriminant validity, though it would be interesting to see how such specific scenarios fare in terms of cross-cultural validity. The second part of the NASPI comprises 60 items tapping into the experience of anger; in particular, the cognitive, behavioral, and arousal-related features, in addition to efforts at regulating anger.

Multidimensional Anger Inventory (MAI)

Siegl (1986) developed the MAI, which is quite brief but more comprehensive than many of its forerunners described above. It poses a variety of anger-eliciting situations, but also measures the frequency, intensity, and duration of anger as they load on a factor called anger arousal. Hostile outlook is also assessed, and a distinction is made between two modes of expression of anger: anger-in and anger-out. Originally designed to assess cardiovascular patients, its factor structure has been replicated in two populations that differ in age, geographic location, gender composition, and lifestyle.

The State–Trait Anger Expression Inventory (STAXI)

Driven by success in the state–trait assessment of anxiety, Spielberger and colleagues developed the STAXI (Spielberger, 1988). It is really an amalgamation of two precursors, the state–trait anger scale or STAS (Spielberger et al., 1983) and the anger expression (AX) scale (Spielberger et al., 1985). It has been revised into the STAXI-2 (Spielberger, 1999). What sets the STAXI apart from most of its forerunners is its attempt to distinguish transient anger from dispositional anger (i.e. hostility) in addition to assessing the modes of anger expression (anger-in vs. anger-out). There is also a sub-scale for assessing the ability to control anger. Clearly, the STAXI is the most thorough instrument of its kind. Results from this test can aid in case formulation about whether an individual's anger is primarily related to frustration and perceived maltreatment (state anger) or else a sign of (premorbid) anger-proneness (trait anger). Overt expression of anger (anger-out) may be minimal but anger may still be present if anger-in scores are high. The individual's handling of anger can lie between overcontrol and undercontrol and thereby serve as a guide for treatment planning.

Psychometrically, the factor structure of the STAXI does support the construct validity of this instrument (Fuqua et al., 1991). High coefficients of reliability and internal consistency have been reported for the STAS and AX segments of the STAXI (Spielberger and Sydeman, 1993). Concurrent validity has been supported by correlations between the STAXI trait anger and hostility measures such as the BDHI, while discriminant validity has been reflected in the negative correlations between anger-out and anger-in and between anger-out and anger control. Data are not available on the relationship between the STAXI and the Marlowe–Crowne, but there are some indications that test-taking attitudes influence results. For example, Spielberger and Sydeman (1993) found that small negative correlations emerged between trait anger and the lie scale of the Eysenck Personality Questionnaire (Eysenck and Eysenck, 1975).

The operationalization of state versus trait anger by asking subjects to report how they feel 'right now' and 'how they feel generally' is somewhat misleading. Saying that I am angry right now could mean that the anger began two minutes ago or that it has been around for two days. On the other hand, saying that I am generally angry is also ambiguous since it could suggest that my anger is unremitting or that my anger is frequent. As pointed out in the Fernandez and Kerns chapter in Vol. 1, the state–trait dichotomy obscures the phenomenon of mood. A lesser problem is that patients may be puzzled by the repetitive nature of many of the test items. Some test-takers fail to see the purpose of being asked to respond to such similar statements as 'I feel furious', 'I feel angry', 'I am mad', etc. There is also room for improvement in assessing the styles of anger expression. Anger-in and anger-out are not the only ways in which people differ in anger expression. As will be shown in the next section, there are several additional dimensions for characterizing the angry personality. These dimensions serve as building blocks upon the already available foundations of anger assessment that have been put in place over the last half century.

DIMENSIONS OF ANGER EXPRESSION

It is proposed that there are six main dimensions in the expression of anger, and each of these dimensions is anchored by a pair of distinct markers. As shown in Table 19.1, the first dimension is the 'direction of anger' which can vary between reflection and deflection. Dimension II is labeled 'locus of anger' which can range from internal to external; the corresponding expression styles are internalization and externalization. Dimension III refers to 'anger reaction' which is bounded by resistance at one end and retaliation at the other end. Dimension IV refers to the 'modality of anger' which can be verbal at one end and physical at the other. The fifth dimension relates to 'impulsivity' which varies between controlled and uncontrolled. Finally, the sixth dimension is the 'objective of anger' which can be restorative at one extreme and punitive at the other.

Each dimension is presented as a continuum on which some numerical rating can be provided. The anchors are guideposts for selecting or adjusting the rating. The continuum can be depicted as a visual analog scale which the subject crosses or hatches at a point denoting where s/he lies between the two guideposts. The distance between the hatch on the horizontal line and a particular endpoint is a measure of that person's 'psychological proximity' to the particular expression style specified by that anchor. A mark equidistant between the two anchors (e.g. controlled vs. uncontrolled), would indicate that the individual is at neither extreme but intermediate on that dimension (in this case, impulsivity). It should be noted that on the dimension of 'modality', it is possible for both anchors (physical and verbal) to be endorsed, and hence two ratings may be made. Additionally, it bears mentioning that the six dimensions are theoretically independent in

Table 19.1 Dimensions and anchors of anger expression

Dimensions	Anchors	
I	a. Reflection	b. Deflection
II	a. Internalization	b. Externalization
III	a. Resistance	b. Retaliation
IV	a. Verbal	b. Physical
V	a. Controlled	b. Uncontrolled
VI	a. Restorative	b. Punitive

that no point on any particular scale dictates what the rating should be on another scale. However, some ratings toward one end of a particular dimension may be more consistent with ratings toward a particular end of another dimension. For example, a retaliatory style of expressing anger may be consistent with a punitive style of expression anger. Yet, this is not necessarily the case, and the dimensions have therefore been separated to allow for as many possible patterns of endorsement as human idiosyncrasies may require.

In the next section, each dimension is described and so are its respective anchors. The conceptualization is primarily psychological and references are made to clinical lore where available. These are embellished with excerpts from celebrated literary sources. The idea behind citing literary material is not new; it is particularly helpful in providing qualitative characterizations of anger especially where empirical data have not yet emerged. Such literature is, after all, the product of efforts by authors to intuitively mirror the rich reality of human nature, in this case, with special reference to anger.

I: Anger Direction – Reflection versus Deflection

Dimension I, the direction of anger, refers to the target of one's anger at which one takes aim. This can prompt the angered person to reflection or to deflection. Reflection is basically an act of reciprocation. Popularly called 'hitting back', the anger is reflected toward the source of provocation, especially when turning on others would not do, the aggrieved individual turns on the offender. The offender is repaid, measure for measure, at other times twofold or more, and at yet other times only a fraction of what was received. This may become a vicious cycle in which each party takes turns dishing out anger toward each other or gets locked in conflict. The 'duel', however, is somewhat confined because of the specificity of the targets. The targets are restricted to those deemed responsible, though this can certainly change over time if other entities also get embroiled in the conflict process.

The tendency to reflect anger back to the offending person is illustrated in a conversation in Charlotte Bronte's book *Jane Eyre*:

> When we are struck at without a reason, we should strike back again very hard; I am sure we should – so hard as to teach the person who struck us never to do it again.

> You will change your mind, I hope, when you grow older: as yet you are but a little untaught girl.

> But I feel this, Helen; I must dislike those who, whatever I do to please them, persist in disliking me; I must resist those who punish me unjustly. It is as natural as that I should love those who show me affection, or submit to punishment when I feel it is deserved. (1850: 76)

A key element in this passage is the select reference to 'the person' who struck, 'those' who persist, and 'those' who are unjust. This is consistent with the practice of anger reflection which is restricted to the offending stimulus rather than visited upon bystanders, relatives, or the populace at large.

Deflection is much like the Freudian ego-defense mechanism called 'displacement'. Here, the angered person turns to victimization of the innocent which may include people, animals, and other life forms, or even inanimate objects. Sometimes, the target of anger is determined by group membership, mere proximity to the offender, or else a symbolic association. For example, family members have been tormented for what may have been the infraction of a particular family member, whole neighborhoods have suffered for the crimes of a few, and historic places of worship have been desecrated in fits of rage ignited by a handful of individuals. Yet other times, the anger may be taken out on a totally random target. This kind of deflection may be because the original target is somehow inaccessible or unassailable. In everyday life, employers often fall into this category of being 'beyond reach', for to reproach them may incur the loss of one's job and livelihood. Law enforcement officials, parents, anyone in a position of authority over another may be spared anger because of

the potential for reprisal. The result is an adaptational move by which the anger is transferred to a more convenient but less culpable victim.

An illustration of deflection can be found in Sidney Lanier's *Tiger Lillies: A Novel*. Here, the redirection of anger from the self to another:

> Perhaps anger is the most complex deceit of them all, shifting its wrath from one's self, richly deserving to some other self, undeserving ... And so, John Cranston, instead of cursing his own crime, or gnashing his teeth over the insane folly which had prompted him to betray himself, cursed Rubetsahl instead, and snarled at him. (1867.61)

II: Anger Locus – Internalization versus Externalization

Dimension II, the locus of anger, as the term implies, refers to the seat or primary location of one's anger. This can be internalized within oneself or else externalized upon others or the world at large. Anger internalized is essentially a subtype of what psychodynamic theorists had long called emotional suppression. It runs counter to spontaneous expression. The greater the anger, the more effortful the suppression. Internalized anger does not mean self-blame but rather that one's ire is stuffed within and hidden from the awareness of the others. When the suppressive effort is exceeded by the force of anger, the anger may be released to the outside world or break free to the offending person. Until then, the aggrieved person carries anger within and keeps others from knowing how angry s/he really is. This may serve the purpose of protecting oneself from embarrassment or disapproval, or maybe even protecting others from being hurt by the anger in the first place. Moreover, anger that is concealed can be actualized secretively or subversively executed without the risk of being traced back to oneself. In this way, a further goal of revenge may be realized without incurring counter-attacks. This is a kind of covert anger. But not all internalized anger is the veil for a sinister or insidious operation, for sometimes, concealment is an end in itself.

A literary description of the struggle to internalize anger can be found in a brief excerpt from Eleanor Porter's book *Miss Billy – Married*: 'Outwardly, through it all, Billy was gayety itself. Inwardly, she was burning up with anger and mortification' (1914: 129). It appears that Billy was putting up on a front that was quite the opposite of the anger she experienced.

About 100 years ago, Hans Gross in his manual on criminal psychology, claimed to be able to recognize suppressed anger:

> The hand lies in the lap apparently inert, but the otherwise well concealed anger slowly makes a fist of it, or the fingers bend characteristically forward as if they wished to scratch somebody's eyes out ... In anger, when they cannot, because it would be suggestive, stamp their feet, the women press their toes closely to the ground. (1911: 104)

Whether the gender differences he observed were correct or not, Gross was observant of the cues to concealment or suppression which can become transparent. He was also alert to the amount of effort involved in concealing anger.

Externalized anger is the expression of anger outside the self. Anger is part and parcel of the repertoire for responding to offensive stimuli (as explained in my chapter with Kerns), and its natural course when unimpeded or unregulated is to be externalized. The greater the anger, the more likely it will demand expression. The precise way in which it is expressed may vary from reflexive vocalizations and facial contortions through limb movements to engaging the whole body in complex goal-directed behavior. It can also be interwoven with self-blame or blaming others. Occasionally, this manifestation may occur when a person has reached the limit of suppression, and like the surge of water when a dam bursts, his/her anger emerges suddenly in an almost explosive manner. In other cases, anger may be a normal feature of a person who simply has no reservations about showing any anger any

time. The latter is illustrated in an excerpt from the volume III of the *Purcell Papers* by Joseph Sheridan Le Fanu:

> There was something in her face, though her features had evidently been handsome, and were not, at first sight, unpleasing, which, upon a nearer inspection, seemed to indicate the habitual prevalence and indulgence of evil passions, and a power of expressing mere animal anger, with an intenseness that I have seldom seen equalled, and to which an almost unearthly effect was given by the convulsive quivering of the sightless eyes. (1975: 91–92)

III: Anger Reaction – Resistance versus Retaliation

Dimension III, the anger reaction, is the term given to the particular interpersonal dynamic that results when one is provoked. This can range from passive resistance to outright retaliation. Resistance qualifies as a reaction but instead of paying back the offender in kind, the respondent adopts a rigidly defensive stance. The anger is behaviorally communicated in a manner typically suggesting non-cooperation rather than overt aggression; thus it may take the form of procrastination, disengagement, non-compliance, defiance, and the like. In clinical parlance, this is often called passive-aggressiveness. At the societal level, it has been called civil disobedience, as expounded by Mohandas Gandhi, Henry David Thoreau, and Martin Luther King, Jr. Passive-aggressiveness may be inconspicuous in comparison to active aggressiveness but its impact on the offending party may be no less potent, often taking its toll by confusing, frustrating, and eroding the morale of the opponent. This style of obstinate resistance toward others may itself be pathological when it becomes so enduring and pervasive as to be dysfunctional. Thus, it appeared in DSM-III as a personality disorder, was discontinued in DSM-III-R, but later returned to DSM-IV as a disorder warranting further study. Another DSM disorder with an element of passive-aggressiveness is 'oppositional defiant disorder'.

Anthony Trollope in volume 2 of *Rachel Ray* wrote:

> He had never determined that there should be a quarrel between them. But he was angered, and he would stand aloof from her. He would stand aloof from her, and would no longer acknowledge that he was in anyway bound by the words he had spoken. (1863: 218)

Standing aloof, in this instance, is a non-aggressive but uncooperative stance that qualifies as resistance or distancing.

In the case of retaliation, on the other hand, attack is repelled with counter-attack. The opponent is essentially paid back in kind. Thus, a punch is met with a punch, an insult is returned with an insult, and soon the impression emerges that the provocateur and the provoked are simply trading arsenal. Note that the retaliation is not defined by the target but by the behavioral response. In the arena of international relations, this is often referred to as open warfare and it can turn into a calamity where casualties mount. At the interpersonal level, it can also become a point-scoring exercise that seems endless even as damage is sustained by both parties. The pathological proportions of this kind of exchange are especially apparent when the individual deteriorates in functioning as his/her resources are depleted from the fight. Some DSM disorders which contain aggressive retaliatory behavior among the diagnostic criteria are conduct disorder, borderline personality disorder, and antisocial personality disorder.

In volume 2 of *The Wigwam and the Cabin*, William Gilmore Simms provides a graphic account of retaliation driven by intense anger:

> They found Barnacle Sam still upon his knees. The sight of their comrade suspended from the tree, enkindled all their anger. They laid violent hands upon his executioner ... To what lengths their fury would have carried them may only be conjectured, but they had found a rope, had fitted a noose, and in a few moments more they would, in all probability, have run up the offender to the same tree from which they had cut down his victim. (1845: 75)

IV: Anger Modality – Verbal versus Physical

Dimension IV, anger modality, refers to the medium of anger expression. This takes two main forms, the verbal and the nonverbal or physical. An individual's utterances can possess content as well as auditory properties for conveying anger. Spectral and formant analyses of voice have revealed certain acoustic correlates of emotion. Anger, for instance, has a pattern of high pitch level, some variability of pitch, loud volume, and fast tempo (Scherer, 1989; Goldbeck et al., 1988) in addition to a coarse tone. Acoustics aside, the content of angry utterances may encompass a litany of statements of blame possibly interspersed with expletives or profanities that do not necessarily add meaning yet evince the magnitude of the emotion. Various combinations of content and acoustics are possible. Some individuals may yell, scream, and vociferously heap curses upon the target of their anger, whereas others may resort to relatively soft-spoken sarcasm. This reminds us of the amount of rich detail that is possible in the mere verbal/vocal communication of anger.

Joseph Conrad in *Youth and Two Other Stories* provided an account of language so angry that it almost seemed violent:

> And then, before I could open my lips, the East spoke to me, but it was in a Western voice. A torrent of words was poured into the enigmatical, the fateful silence; outlandish, angry words, mixed with words and even whole sentences of good English, less strange but even more surprising. The voice swore and cursed violently; it riddled the solemn peace of the bay by a volley of abuse. It began by calling me Pig, and from that went crescendo into unmentionable adjectives – in English. The man up there raged aloud in two languages, and with a sincerity in his fury that almost convinced me I had, in some way, sinned against the harmony of the universe. (1903: 44)

Nonverbal communication of anger takes place largely through visual-motor channels. It may be displayed in the face. Extending a line of enquiry begun by Darwin (1872/1965), Ekman and Friesen (1978) have proposed a facial action coding system (FACS) for deciphering discrete emotions according to the different configurations of muscle movement in the face. Anger, for instance, is indicated by movement of the corrugator supercilii, medial frontalis, and obicularis oculi. This may be supplemented by other aspects of body language such as hand gestures, posture, and gait that may portend even more purposive motor behaviors such as striking, pushing, and kicking. The physical expression of anger is often dreaded because of its potential for violence. This has earned it a place at the opposite end of verbal anger which can also be hurtful but in a psychological sense; violence, on the other hand inflicts damage to the physical or material wellbeing of others.

Literature is replete with vivid descriptions of violence. One excerpt worthy of quoting comes from Edwin Arnold's book *Gulliver of Mars*:

> In an instant, though but half awake, with a yell of surprise and anger I grappled with the enemy, and exerting all my strength rolled him over. Over and over we went struggling towards the fire, and when I got him within a foot or so of it I came out on top, and digging my knuckles into his throttle, banged his head upon the stony floor in reckless rage, until all of a sudden it seemed to me he was done for. (1935: 129)

What is interesting is that the victim of violence in this case was already dead at the time of contact, yet perceived provocation was high enough to motivate violent behavior toward this corpse of an enemy.

The verbal and nonverbal must not be viewed as mutually exclusive, especially in the expression of anger. Even though clinical lore makes a distinction between verbal abuse and physical abuse, the social reality is that a person is likely to resort to both verbal and nonverbal behaviors for expressing anger in any single instance. Across instances, the alternation of verbal and physical expression of anger is even more likely, so that as a whole, one may witness both at work. Maria S. Cummins in her book *Mabel Vaughan* wrote:

> The subdued voice of Louise was changed to loud tones of reproach; words of sudden anger took the place of her usual languid accents, and the little hand, so perfect in contour, so graceful in gesture, now added force to her words, as she inflicted with it a sudden blow upon Murray's offending palm. (1857: 66)

Here, Louise combines reproachful words with a loud voice. This is further strengthened by a strike from her hand.

V: Anger Impulsivity – Controlled versus Uncontrolled

Dimension V, anger impulsivity, refers to the degree to which a person regulates his/her anger. At one extreme, this is marked by uncontrolled anger, and at the other extreme, it is marked by controlled anger. The control of anger is a topic that has occupied philosophers, theologians, and psychologists alike, in addition to the many challenges it poses to people in everyday life. Typically, it involves cogitation and behavior modification (Fernandez, 2003a, 2003b; Fernandez and Beck, 2001). In that sense, it entails being reflective as opposed to reflexive. Anger control does not imply anger suppression or anger internalization and certainly does not require the elimination of anger altogether. Rather, it is an attempt to keep anger within manageable limits. In other words, this is an exercise in regulating anger – perhaps by contemplating the antecedents and consequences of one's anger, taking other's perspectives, brainstorming for alternatives, self-calming, and so on. When the outcome is adaptive, the individual has, in effect, constructively handled the anger-provoking situation. The role of reflection and reappraisal in controlling mass anger is emphasized by William Roscoe Thayer in his account of the aftermath of the bombing of the USS *Maine* in 1898:

> The next morning the newspapers carried the report to all parts of the United States, and indeed, to the whole world. A tidal wave of anger surged over this country. 'That means war!' was the common utterance. Some of us, who abhorred the thought of war, urged that at least we wait until the guilt could be fixed. The reports of the

catastrophe conflicted. Was the ship destroyed by the explosion of shells in its own magazine, or was it blown up from outside? If the latter, who set off the mine? The Spaniards? It seemed unlikely, if they wished war, that they should resort to so clumsy a provocation! (1919: 117)

In this narrative, a few people paused to reappraise the incident (with additional evidence and alternative hypotheses) instead of rushing to rage. In doing so, they were exerting control over what was otherwise 'knee-jerk' anger on the part of the masses.

Antithetical to the control of anger is the unbridled anger that is also alluded to in the foregoing narrative. At the individual level, such uncontrolled anger may meet criteria for the DSM diagnosis called intermittent explosive disorder, if it is transformed into aggression that is grossly out of proportion to the precipitating psychosocial trigger. As a reminder, it should be emphasized that the aggression need not be physical and may in fact consist of invectives and other verbalizations that also result from loss of control.

If rethinking is part and parcel of anger control, 'acting without thinking' is what often constitutes failure to control anger. No doubt, this leaves room for some pondering after action, but by that time it will probably have to make room for remorse as well. Leo Tolstoy, in his short story 'Father Sergius' presents a character strong in many ways but weak in anger control:

He would have been an altogether exemplary cadet had it not been for his quick temper. ... The only faults that marred his conduct were fits of fury to which he was subject and during which he lost control of himself and became like a wild animal. He once nearly threw out of the window another cadet who had begun to tease him about his collection of minerals. (1967: 503)

VI: Anger Objective – Restorative versus Punitive

Dimension VI, anger objective, refers to the functional consequence of one's anger. Emotions have an implicit goal significance (Lazarus, 1991). In the case of anger, this can

be restorative or at the other extreme, can be punitive. When restoration is the objective, the angered individual tries to 'get over it' as the popular adage goes. An apology, return of what was lost, damage repair, or some reparation is usually sufficient to make this eventuate. In the absence of reparation, the individual still remains motivated to overcome the disquiet of anger. To this end, the aggrieved individual may even choose to forgive and forget the offending person. Of course, this is dependent on the gravity of the offense, but the fundamental urge to 'get over' the provocation and 'move on' is what serves as a catalyst for this individual's recovery from anger. This represents another constructive handling of anger. Some of the elements in this style of anger are illustrated in volume 3 of *Tales of a Traveller* by Irving Washington (under the pen name of Geoffrey Crayon):

I obeyed, of course, stifling the fury that raged within me, though I felt for the moment that he was my most deadly foe.

On my way, however, a ray of reflection came across my mind. I perceived that the captain was but following with strictness the terrible laws to which we had sworn fidelity. That the passion by which I had been blinded might with justice have been fatal to me but for his forbearance; that he had penetrated my soul, and had taken precautions, by sending me out of the way, to prevent my committing any excess in my anger. From that instant I felt that I was capable of pardoning him. (1824: 112–113)

If reparation is the hallmark of restorative anger, then retribution is the cornerstone of punitive anger. Instead of 'getting over it', the aggrieved individual in this case tries to 'get even' with the offender. Notwithstanding apologies, and gestures of compensation, the anger is likely to persist till the person responsible is punished or suffers. This is not uncommon in survivors of grievous crime who may obsess about their victims till the latter are tried and executed. However, the hunger to be avenged may persist in much more trivial wrongdoings as may occur in family life or professional interactions. Instead of moving on, the individual remains fixated on the provocation and hurt; there is minimal ability to forget, let alone forgive; redemption, if any, is only accorded when a rather personalized demand for justice has been served. A pithy depiction of this style is found in Edgar Rice Burroughs' *The Mad King*:

> Then too, righteous anger and a desire for revenge prompted his decision. He would run Maenck to earth and have an accounting with him. It was evident that his life would not be worth a farthing so long as the fellow was at liberty. (1914: 124)

Looking back at the literary material, it is quickly apparent that multiple aspects of anger expression are present within some narratives. For example, the excerpt from *Tales of a Traveler* reveals control of anger as well as restorative anger. Therefore, it behooves us to attempt a multidimensional characterization of anger in a single situation and in the same individual. The pattern linking different points on each dimension becomes a sort of profile of that individual's anger in that situation. Averaging across profiles would then lead us closer to the dispositional features in the expression of anger.

SAMPLE PROFILES OF ANGER BASED ON THE SIX DIMENSIONS

We now turn to sample profiles based on the six dimensions of anger expression and their respective anchors. This has the advantage of integrating the different dimensions and their anchors into whole configurations. Thus, one may simply 'eyeball' the profile to perform a quick configural analysis of an individual's anger expression styles. For the sake of brevity and mere exemplification, four configurations are presented.

As can be seen in Figures 19.1–19.4, the top panel of each graph is reserved for charting the more pathological and problematic aspects of anger expression whereas the bottom panel represents less pathological and less problematic ways of handling anger. For example, deflection, regarded as a more unreasonable response than reflection, is

placed in the top panel; uncontrolled anger is placed on top, controlled anger on the bottom; punitive anger is placed on top, and restorative anger is on the bottom. The resulting elevations in the top panel are isomorphic with pathology, just as dips in the bottom panel are isomorphic with more adaptive responding. Ideally, the higher the elevation at the top, the lower the dip at the bottom, unless an individual is 'bipolar' in the sense of conflating or alternating between extremes.

Figure 19.1 profiles an individual with what is clinically labeled as passive-aggressiveness. As can be seen, this individual is low in externalization and high in internalization, low in retaliation but high in resistance. As would be expected, the individual is highly controlled but when it comes to the objective of anger, the individual is far more punitive than restorative. It is this punitive feature of the passive-aggressive that can be particularly problematic in interpersonal relations.

Figure 19.2 is a profile of what in DSM would be called 'intermittent explosive disorder'. The configuration shows elevations in nearly all of the top panel: almost total loss of control that explains this person's externalization of anger, heavy retaliation, physical expression of anger possibly co-occurring with verbal abuse, and a punitive outlook. Note that this individual may reflect or deflect during this state of uncontrolled anger.

Figure 19.3 is a profile of anger repressed. There are hardly any elevations in the top panel of the graph, but two prominent dips in the lower panel, one showing internalization and the other representing controlled anger. The low point for restorative efforts indicates that the anger is not absent but merely dealt with privately. The absence of resistance suggests that there is no covert anger either. For whatever reason (be it social propriety or otherwise), such an individual spares others his/her anger by keeping it within.

Figure 19.4 represents one of many possible profiles of constructive anger. There are

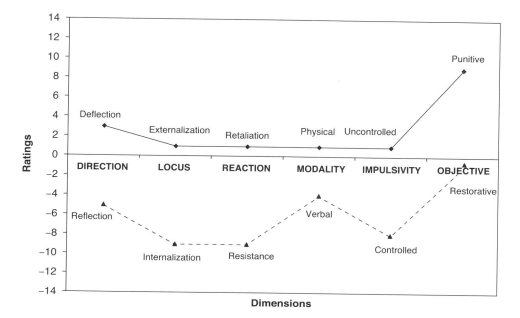

Figure 19.1   Profile of passive-aggressive anger

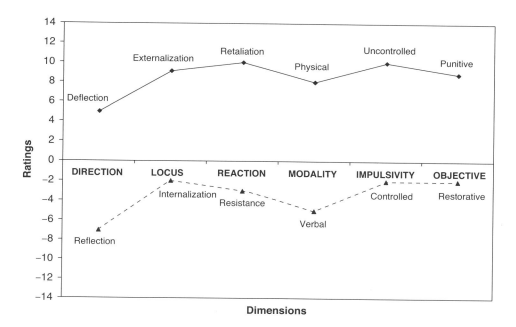

Figure 19.2   Profile of explosive anger

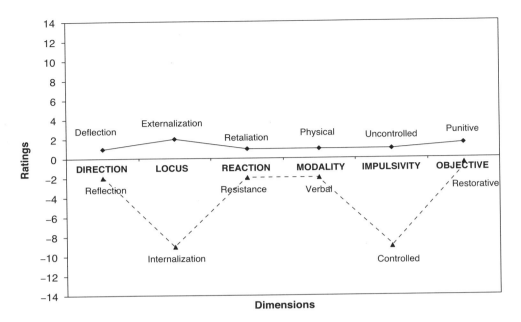

Figure 19.3   Profile of repressive anger

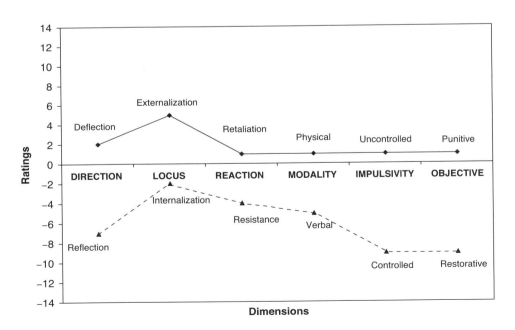

Figure 19.4   Profile of constructive anger

no elevations in the top panel with the exception of a moderate level of externalized anger. The bottom panel shows an interesting pattern of minimal anger suppression, some attempt to resist, and some tendency to reflect anger at the offending person but primarily through the mode of verbal communication. All this proceeds within a style of controlled or self-regulated anger which is ultimately in the service of recovery or restoration of balance.

CONCLUSION

In this chapter, six dimensions of anger expression have been presented, each with a pair of anchors representing ends of the continuum. Thus, the direction of anger is bounded by reflection versus deflection, locus of anger may range from internal to external, the anger reaction can be retaliatory at one extreme or resistant at the other, the modality of anger expression can be predominantly physical or verbal, anger impulsivity can vary between the controlled and the uncontrolled, and the objective of the anger can range from being restorative to being punitive. In this way, the expression of anger can be comprehensively represented with reference to a total of 12 criteria or six pairs of coordinates. While the focus of this chapter has been on anger expression as a disposition or an enduring and pervasive style, the very same expressions presented here can be used to characterize individual situations involving anger.

As an integrated framework, these dimensions and anchors of anger expression are novel. They were formulated primarily on the basis of theorizing and preliminary empirical exploration. Having also reviewed some of the existing psychological tests and theories of anger within this chapter, the relevant precursors and foundations laid by other forerunners in the field are recognizable. Finally, as evident from the literary material cited in this chapter, this new framework of anger expression styles has been illustrated in no small degree by the many written and spoken narratives about human anger.

ACKNOWLEDGEMENTS

Thanks to PF, HK, and MW for the valuable cross-disciplinary discussions. Thanks also to Garrett Nikolaus and Daniel Nguyen for assistance with the bibliography and with the preparation of graphs and tables in this chapter.

REFERENCES

Arnold, E.L.L. (1935) *Gulliver of Mars*. New York: Ace Books.

Averill, J.R. (1982) *Anger and Aggression: An Essay on Emotion*. New York: Springer-Verlag.

Barefoot, J.C. (1992) 'Developments in the measurement of hostility', in H.S. Friedman (ed.), *Hostility, Coping and Health*. Washington, DC: American Psychological Association, pp. 13–31.

Barefoot, J.C., Dodge, K.A., Peterson, B.L., Dahlstrom, W.G. and Williams Jr., R.B. (1989) 'Cook–Medley Hostility scale: Item content and ability to predict survival', *Psychosomatic Medicine*, 51(1): 46–57.

Biaggio, M.K. (1980) 'Assessment of anger arousal', *Journal of Personality Assessment*, 44(3): 289–98.

Biaggio, M.K. and Maiuro, R.D. (1985) 'Recent advances in anger assessment', in C.D. Spielberger and J.N. Butcher (eds), *Advances in Personality Assessment*. Hillsdale, NJ: Erlbaum, pp. 71–112.

Blumenthal, J.A., Barefoot, J., Burg, M.M. and Williams, R.B. Jr. (1987) 'Psychological correlates of hostility among patients undergoing coronary angiography', *British Journal of Medical Psychology*, 60(4): 349–55.

Boyle, G.J. (1995) 'Measurement of intelligence and personality within the Cattellian psychometric model', *Multivariate Experimental Clinical Research*, 11(1): 47–59.

Bronte, C. (1850) *Jane Eyre: An Autobiography* (Vol. I). Leipzig: B. Tauchnitz.

Burroughs, E.R. (1914) *The Mad King*. New York: Ace Books (Grosset & Dunlap).

Buss, A.H. (1961) *The Psychology of Aggression*. New York: Wiley.

Buss, A.H. and Durkee, A. (1957) 'An inventory for assessing different kinds of hostility', *Journal of Consulting Psychology*, 21(4): 343–9.

Caine, T.M., Foulds, G.A. and Hope, K. (1967) *Manual of the Hostility and Direction of Hostility Questionnaire*. London: University of London.

Conrad, J. (1903) *Youth and Two Other Stories*. New York: McClure, Phillips & Co.

Cook, W.W. and Medley, D.M. (1954) 'Proposed hostility and pharisaic-virtue scales for the MMPI', *Journal of Applied Psychology*, 38(6): 414–8.

Crowne, D.P. and Marlowe, D. (1960) 'A new scale of social desirability independent of psychopathology', *Journal of Consulting Psychology*, 24(4): 349–54.

Cummins, M.S. (1857) *Mabel Vaughan*. Boston: John P. Jewett & Company.

Darwin, C. (1872/1965) *The Expression of the Emotions in Man and Animals*. Chicago: University of Chicago Press.

Eckhardt, C.I., Norlander, B. and Deffenbacher, J.L. (2004) 'The assessment of anger and hostility: A critical review', *Aggression and Violent Behavior*, 9(1): 17–43.

Ekman, P. and Friesen, W.V. (1978) *Facial Action Coding System: A Technique for the Measurement of Facial Movement*. Palo Alto, CA: Consulting Psychologists Press.

Evans, D.R. and Strangeland, M. (1971) 'Development of the Reaction Inventory to measure anger', *Psychological Reports*, 29(2): 412–4.

Eysenck, H.J. and Eysenck, S.B.G. (1975) *Manual of the Eysenck Personality Questionnaire*. London: Hodder & Stoughton.

Fernandez, E. (2003a) 'Anger regulation in adolescence', in T.P. Gullotta and M. Bloom (eds), *Encyclopedia of Primary Prevention and Health Promotion*. New York: Kluwer Academic/Plenum, pp. 195–9.

Fernandez, E. (2003b) 'Anger regulation in childhood', in T.P. Gullotta and M. Bloom (eds), *Encyclopedia of Primary Prevention and Health Promotion*. New York: Kluwer Academic/Plenum, pp. 190–95.

Fernandez, E. and Beck, R. (2001) 'Cognitive-behavioral self-intervention versus self-monitoring of anger: Effects on anger frequency, duration, and intensity', *Behavioural and Cognitive Psychotherapy*, 29(3): 345–56.

Frijda, N.H. (1986) *The Emotions*. Cambridge: Cambridge University Press.

Frijda, N.H., Kuipers, P. and Terschure, E. (1989) 'Relations among emotion, appraisal, and emotional action readiness', *Journal of Personality and Social Psychology*, 57(2): 212–28.

Fuqua, D.R., Leonard, E., Masters, M.A., Smith, R.J., Campbell, J.L. and Fischer, P.C. (1991) 'A structural analysis of the State–Trait Anger Expression Inventory', *Educational and Psychological Measurement*, 51(2): 439–46.

Goldbeck, T., Tolkmitt, F. and Scherer, K.R. (1988) *Facets of Emotion: Recent Research*. Hillsdale, NJ: Erlbaum.

Gross, H. (1911) *Criminal Psychology: A Manual for Judges, Practitioners, and Students*. Montclair, New Jersey: Patterson Smith.

Lane, P.J. and Kling, J.S. (1979) 'Construct validation of the overcontrolled hostility scale of the MMPI', *Journal of Consulting and Clinical Psychology*, 47(4): 781–2.

Lanier, S. (1867) *Tiger-Lilies: A Novel*. New York: Hurd & Houghton.

Larson, R.J. and Buss, D.M. (2002) *Personality Psychology: Domains of Knowledge About Human Nature*. New York: McGraw-Hill.

Lazarus, R.S. (1991) *Emotion and Adaptation*. New York: Oxford University Press.

Le Fanu, J.S. (1975) *The Purcell Papers* (Vol. III). New York: AMS Press.

Matthews, G. (1998) *Personality Traits*. Cambridge: Cambridge University Press.

Megargee, E.I., Cook, P.E. and Mendelsohn, G.A. (1967) 'Development and validation of an MMPI scale of assaultiveness in overcontrolled individuals', *Journal of Abnormal Psychology*, 72(6): 519–28.

Novaco, R.W. (1974) 'The effect of disposition for anger and degree of provocation on self-report and physiological measures of anger in various modes of provaocation', Unpublished manuscript, Indiana University, Bloomington.

Novaco, R.W. (2003) *The Novaco Anger Scale and Provocation Inventory (NAS-PI)*. Los Angeles: Western Psychological Services.

Ortony, A., Clore, G. and Collins, A. (1988) *The Cognitive Structure of Emotions*. Cambridge: Cambridge University Press.

Porter, E.H. (1914) *Miss Billy – Married*. New York: Grosset & Dunlap.

Saklofske, D.H. and Zeidner, M. (1995) *International Handbook of Personality and Intelligence*. New York: Plenum.

Scherer, K.R. (1989) 'Vocal measurement of emotion', in R. Plutchik and H. Kellerman (eds), *Emotion Theory, Research, and Experience, Volume 4: The Measurement of Emotions*. San Diego, CA: Academic, pp. 233–59.

Siegel, J.M. (1986) 'The Multidimensional Anger Inventory', *Journal of Personality and Social Psychology*, 51(1): 191–200.

Simms, W.G. (1845) *The Wigwam and the Cabin* (Vol. 2). New York: Wiley and Putnam.

Smedslund, J. (1993) 'How shall the concept of anger be defined?', *Theory and Psychology*, 3(1): 5–33.

Smith, T.W. and Christensen, A.J. (1992) 'Hostility, health, and social contexts', in H.S. Friedman (ed.), *Hostility, Coping, and Health*. Washington, DC: American Psychological Association, pp. 33–48.

Spielberger, C.D. (1988) *Manual for the State–Trait Anger Expression Inventory (STAXI)*. Odessa, FL: Psychological Assessment Resources.

Spielberger, C.D. (1999) *STAXI-2: State–Trait Anger Expression Inventory Professional Manual*. Odessa, FL: Psychological Assessment Resources.

Spielberger, C.D. and Sydeman, S.J. (1993) 'State–Trait Anxiety Inventory and State–Trait Anger Expression Inventory', in M.E. Maruish (ed.), *The Use of Psychological Tests for Treatment Planning and Outcome Assessment*. Hillsdale, NJ: Erlbaum, pp. 292–321.

Spielberger, C.D., Jacobs, G., Russell, S. and Crane, R.S. (1983) 'Assessment of anger: The State–Trait Anger Scale', in J.N. Butcher and C.D. Spielberger (eds), *Advances in Personality Assessment* (Vol. 2). Hillsdale, NJ: Erlbaum, pp. 159–87.

Spielberger, C.D., Johnson, E.H., Russell, S.F., Crane, R.J., Jacobs, G.A. and Worden, T.J. (1985) 'The experience and expression of anger: Construction and Validation of an anger expression scale', in M.A. Chesney and R.H. Rosenman (eds), *Anger and Hostility in Cardiovascular and Behavioral Disorders*. New York: Hemisphere, pp. 5–30.

Spielberger, C.D., Krasner, S.S. and Solomon, E.P. (1988) 'The experience, expression and control of anger', in M.P. Janisse (ed.), *Health Psychology: Individual Differences and Stress*. New York: Springer-Verlag, pp. 89–108.

Steinberg, L. and Jorgensen, R.S. (1996) 'Assessing the MMPI-based Cook–Medley hostility scale: The implications of dimensionality', *Journal of Personality and Social Psychology*, 70(6): 1281–7.

Thayer, W.R. (1919) *Theodore Roosevelt: An Intimate Biography*. Boston: Houghton Mifflin.

Tolstoy, L.G. (1967) 'Father Sergius', in *The Great Short Works of Leo Tolstoy* (Translated by Aylmer and Louise Maude). New York: Harper & Row.

Trollope, A. (1863) *Rachel Ray* (Vol. 2). New York: Arno Press.

Washington, I. (1824) *Tales of a Traveler*. Philadelphia: H.C. Carey and I. Lea.

Worchel, S., Cooper, J., Goethals, G.R. and Olson, J.M. (2000) *Social Psychology*. Belmont, CA: Wadsworth.

World Health Organization (2002) *World Report on Violence and Health*. Geneva; World Health Organization.

Zelin, M.L., Adler, G. and Myerson, P.G. (1972) 'Anger self-report: An objective questionnaire for the measurement of aggression', *Journal of Consulting and Clinical Psychology*, 39(2): 340.

20

Interpersonal Theory and the Measurement of Interpersonal Constructs

Leonard M. Horowitz, Bulent Turan, Kelly R. Wilson and Pavel Zolotsev

This chapter describes personality measures that are derived from modern theories about dyadic interactions. Modern theories emphasize two prominent themes or dimensions that allow us to organize interpersonal behaviors systematically and draw inferences about them. The first dimension (*communion*) refers to the degree of connection between two people that is fostered by different kinds of interaction. An exchange of intimacy, for example, promotes communion. The second dimension (*agency*) refers to the degree of influence that one partner has upon the other when they interact. If one person dominates and the other yields, the dominating partner's behavior is said to be highly agentic.

As shown below, these two theoretical dimensions have led to the construction of various personality measures for assessing interpersonal behaviors, interpersonal traits, interpersonal motives, interpersonal problems, and the interpersonal impact of one person upon another. In this chapter, we describe the rationale, purpose, construction, and interpretation of each measure. In doing so, however, we first need to describe the theoretical framework from which the measures are derived. The interpersonal theory that we present will help explain why and how the measures were constructed. We therefore begin this chapter with a theoretical model of interpersonal interactions. Then we use the theory to describe the measures themselves, show how they may be applied, and explain important properties that they share.

DESCRIPTION OF INTERPERSONAL BEHAVIOR AND INTERPERSONAL MOTIVES

Interpersonal theory

Interpersonal theories (e.g. Leary, 1957; Sullivan, 1953) first began to emerge in the 1940s and 1950s as a way of explaining phenomena associated with the study of personality and social interaction. These theories were typically a reaction against prevailing theories of the time, particularly a reaction against psychoanalysis and behavioral theories of learning. Interpersonal theories were especially appealing because they incorporated new insights about human interaction, but still managed to sidestep the controversial assumptions of behaviorism and psychoanalysis.

Over the past 50 years a variety of interpersonal models have evolved from those early efforts (see review by Kiesler, 1996). Harry Stack Sullivan's (1953) writing introduced original ideas into American psychiatry that departed substantially from the psychoanalytic thinking of his day. Sullivan's theory emphasized 'what people do to one another' when they interact in a given situation. This view contrasted sharply with earlier views that implicitly viewed two interacting people as though they were each behaving autonomously. Sullivan's theory was particularly influenced by Lewin's (1938) field theory, with its emphasis on the contemporaneous, bidirectional influences that people have upon one another in a particular situation.

Timothy Leary (1957) tried to operationalize Sullivan's concepts with concrete measurement procedures. Using the language of clinicians to describe what patients do to each other (and to themselves) in group psychotherapy, he tried to capture empirically how various behaviors can be organized graphically within a two-dimensional interpersonal space. We shall examine his method later in this chapter and use it to describe people's salient interpersonal characteristics.

In Sullivan's (1953) early theory, the 'theorem of reciprocal emotion' emphasized the reciprocity (or complementarity) that is evident when two partners interact. In later models this theorem became the principle of complementarity. Kiesler expressed the principle of complementarity this way: 'A person's interpersonal actions tend to initiate, invite, or evoke from an interactant complementary responses' (1983: 200–201). According to his version of the interpersonal

theory, a behavior and its complement are (a) similar with respect to affiliation (or communion) – hostility pulls for hostility, friendliness pulls for friendliness; and (b) reciprocal with respect to control (or agency) – dominance pulls for submission, submission pulls for dominance (Carson, 1969; Kiesler, 1983, 1996). One of the measures that we examine in this chapter will concern the impact that each partner has upon the other.

Horowitz et al. (2006) reviewed the literature on interpersonal models and concluded that interpersonal interactions can be best understood if we focus on the interpersonal *motives* that give rise to each person's interpersonal behavior. That is, people sometimes desire a *connection* with other people, but sometimes they desire *distance* from other people. Similarly, people sometimes want to control or influence other people; but sometimes they want to have other people take charge and lead. If we do not understand the motive behind a person's behavior, we do not understand what the person is trying to do, and we cannot anticipate the impact of the partner's reaction. For this reason, we need to examine the concept of an interpersonal motive and describe a way to assess interpersonal motives.

Interpersonal motives

Generally speaking, an interpersonal behavior is purposeful and goal-directed: Each person wants something from the other person. When one person brags to another, for example, we assume that the person wants admiration or respect from the partner. The partner's reaction may be one that does or does not satisfy the person's motive. Positive affect occurs when an important motive is satisfied, and negative affect occurs when an important motive is frustrated (Lazarus, 1991). The person is not necessarily conscious of this motive, and the same motive may be trivial in some situations and vital in others. On average across time and situations, however, some motives are more important to one person than to another

(McAdams, 1985: 62). Being admired, for example, might be vitally important to one person, but relatively unimportant to another.

In contemporary psychology, motivational constructs are thought to differ in their breadth or level of abstraction. Therefore, motives vary hierarchically. A broad desire, such as a desire for intimacy, is more abstract (higher in the hierarchy) than a narrow desire, such as a desire to spend time with an attractive partner (which falls lower in the hierarchy). However, the lower desire is more abstract than a still narrower desire, such as a desire to schedule a date with the attractive person who lives next door. The level of abstraction thus reflects a construct's hierarchical position (Emmons, 1989). A desire for intimacy constitutes a relatively abstract category, which subsumes narrower categories, and they, in turn, subsume still narrower categories. The term motive usually refers to a high level of abstraction, whereas the term 'goal' usually refers to a lower, more concrete category that specifies a particular class of behavior. This way of conceptualizing motivation is common in contemporary psychology (Austin and Vancouver, 1996; Cantor and Kihlstrom, 1987; Cropanzano et al., 1992; Emmons, 1989; Horowitz, 2004; Horowitz et al., 2006; Klinger, 1987; Little, 1983; McAdams, 1985).

Interpersonal models assume that two very broad super-ordinate motivational categories – communion and agency – are at the top of the hierarchy (Bakan, 1966; see also McAdams, 1985; Saucier and Goldberg, 1996). A communal motive reflects a desire for a connection with one or more others – a desire to participate in a larger union with other people. It subsumes motives, such as a desire for intimacy and a desire to socialize with friends. An agentic motive, on the other hand, emphasizes the self as a distinct unit; it focuses on each person's desire for influence or control over the other person. It subsumes motives such as a desire for power, control, or autonomy.

A particular behavior may arise from more than one motive. A person who enjoys giving advice may do so for more than one reason – displaying competence and knowledge (agentic), influencing others (agentic), or connecting with others (communal). Similarly, a person may enjoy playing a sport for various reasons – belonging to the team (communal), displaying a skill (agentic), winning competitions (agentic), maintaining a family tradition (communal), and so on. The meaning of a behavior depends on all of the motives behind it. Sometimes, however, it is convenient theoretically to identify and examine the one or two most salient motives that energize and direct the behavior in question.

Coexisting motives may be behaviorally compatible, or they may conflict. A person who gives advice to another person may be trying to satisfy (a) a motive to influence the other person, as well as (b) a motive to connect with that person. In this example, the two motives are behaviorally compatible. Sometimes, however, coexisting motives conflict behaviorally. For example, an agentic motive may conflict with a communal motive: Suppose a woman competed with a good friend for an elective office and won the election. In the process of satisfying her own agentic motive, she may have disappointed and alienated her friend, thereby jeopardizing the friendship. Exline and Lobel (1999) have discussed this type of conflict, showing how strivings for personal mastery and superiority can clash with strivings for communion. For this reason, people sometimes conceal their success or downplay its significance (Brigham et al., 1997). Similarly, academically gifted students frequently conceal their superior abilities from peers through a variety of 'camouflaging' strategies (Arroyo and Zigler, 1995; Cross et al., 1991). The conflict seems especially salient among people with strong communal needs (Santor and Zuroff, 1997).

Conflicts between a communal motive and an agentic motive seem to be fairly common in everyday life. It should be noted, however, that two communal motives may also conflict; for example, a desire to be part of an admired group may conflict with a desire to remain friends with a non-group member. Likewise, two agentic motives may conflict; for example, a desire to hold a managerial position of power may conflict with a desire to express personal opinions freely. Conflicts such as these would follow the same principles as conflicts between communal and agentic motives.

Interpersonal behavior

Interpersonal behaviors may be represented graphically within two prominent dimensions that correspond to communion and agency. The reason these two themes are so prominent is that they reflect the two broad classes of motives that drive interpersonal behavior in the first place.

Interpersonal behaviors include all behaviors that fit the frame 'person A [does this to] person B' – 'A dominates B', 'A blames B', 'A ignores B', 'A yields to B', and so on. A variety of data-reduction methods (such as principal components analysis) have been used to expose the most salient dimensions of meaning that run through the domain of interpersonal behaviors. Numerous studies have consistently identified two particularly salient dimensions, as shown in Figure 20.1 (see reviews by Horowitz, 2004; Kiesler, 1996; Wiggins, 1991, 1996). Most investigators have concluded that these two salient

dimensions provide a good first approximation toward explaining co-variation among interpersonal behaviors. The exact amount of variance explained depends on the particular scaling method used, the items selected for study, and the context of the study. Dimensions beyond the first two would certainly add nuance to the meaning of the behaviors, but the first two dimensions seem to provide an adequate first approximation. These two dimensions are therefore used as a heuristic to help us conceptualize the meaning of different interpersonal behaviors.

The first dimension (represented by the x-axis) has been called connectedness, affiliation, love, warmth, or nurturance; we use the super-ordinate term *communion*. The second dimension (represented by the orthogonal y-axis) has been called influence, control, dominance, power, or status; we use the super-ordinate term *agency*. Communion, as the horizontal dimension, ranges in meaning from 'being disconnected, indifferent, or distant from the other person' to 'being connected, loving, or close'. Agency, as the vertical dimension, ranges in meaning from 'submitting, relinquishing control, or yielding to the other person' to 'influencing, controlling or dominating the other person'.

Scaling procedures such as principal components analysis that expose the two main dimensions also provide a pair of coordinates

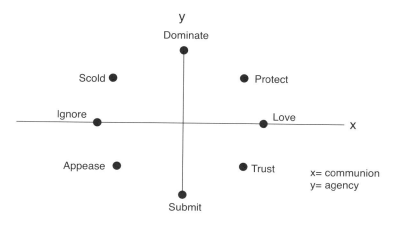

Figure 20.1   Interpersonal behaviors placed in a two-dimensional space

showing every behavior's location on each dimension. 'A protects B' is positive in communion and positive in agency; 'A scolds B' is negative in communion but positive in agency. Behaviors that are geometrically close to one another (similar co-ordinates on both dimensions) have similar meanings, so they are positively correlated: People who strongly exhibit one behavior also tend to exhibit other nearby behaviors. Behaviors that are diametrically opposite to one another have contrasting meanings, so they are negatively correlated. For example, behaviors that typically accompany dominating behavior rarely accompany submissive behavior. Thus, the closer two behaviors are on the graph, the higher their degree of correlation (Gurtman, 1994; Gurtman and Bakarishnan, 1998). Behaviors that are far apart are negatively correlated.

Over the past 50 years, many investigators have used variations of these methods to expose the most salient dimensions of meaning; the studies have yielded very similar results. LaForge and Suczek (1955) and Leary (1957) first characterized interpersonal traits in this way. Later investigators applied the procedures to a variety of other interpersonal domains, such as interpersonal *behaviors*, interpersonal *traits*, and interpersonal *goals*. Examples include work by Benjamin (1974, 1977, 1986, 1996), Berzins (1977), Bierman (1969), Carson (1969), DeVoge and Beck (1978), Kiesler (1983, 1996), Locke (2000), Lorr and Strack (1990), Moskowitz (1994), Moskowitz and Coté (1995), Strack (1987), Strack et al. (1990), Trobst (1999), Wiggins (1979, 1982), and Wiggins and Trobst (1997).

We assume that particular communal and agentic *motives* give rise to particular interpersonal behaviors, traits, and goals. That is, communion and agency apparently constitute fundamental dimensions of meaning because they reflect two broad classes of desires, wants, or needs that drive behavior from childhood on (cf. Angyal, 1941; Erikson, 1963). From an evolutionary perspective, Hogan and Roberts (2000) suggested that they reflect the two principal evolutionary

challenges of social adaptation, namely, 'getting along' (communion) and 'getting ahead' (agency). Other writers have described the two tasks as (a) connecting with other people to form a larger protective community and (b) achieving a reasonably stable and realistic sense of one's own competence and control, which helps facilitate instrumental action (e.g. Blatt, 1990; Horowitz, 2004). Let us now examine two very commonly used interpersonal measures that illustrate the application of interpersonal principles described so far.

Methods for assessing interpersonal traits and interpersonal motives

A measure of traits: interpersonal adjective scales (IAS)

Interpersonal traits such as *assertive* and *friendly* are often regarded as summary labels for a class of motivated behavioral acts that tend to co-occur (e.g. Alston, 1975; Buss and Craik, 1983). Because the acts are motivated, the traits (as aggregates of motivated acts) may also be organized in terms of the two broad classes of interpersonal motives, *communion* and *agency*.

To construct the IAS, Wiggins (1979) used principal components analysis to locate interpersonal personality traits in a two-dimensional space. Once the traits were organized in this way, Wiggins divided the two-dimensional space into eight equal regions (or octants), as shown schematically in Figure 20.2. One octant, for example, included traits that are high in agency but neutral in communion (e.g. assertive, self-confident, forceful). In Figure 20.2, we call this region *Octant 1*. Wiggins used the overarching label *assured-dominant* to refer to the traits in Octant 1; this higher-order label is more abstract than an isolated, one-word trait such as 'assertive' or 'forceful'.

Octant 7 contained traits that are high in communion but neutral in agency (e.g. kind, sympathetic, nurturant). That higher-order category was labeled *warm-agreeable*. Octant

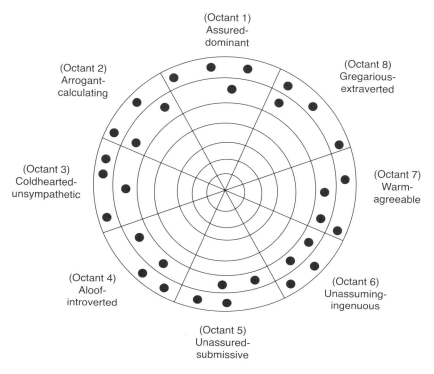

Figure 20.2   Two-dimensional graph divided into eight octants (to create eight scales)

8 contains traits that are relatively high on both dimensions simultaneously (e.g. jovial, enthusiastic, extraverted); that category was labeled *gregarious-extraverted*. In this way, Wiggins created eight separate scales to assess each of the eight higher-order (more abstract) octants. The eight scales, beginning with Octant 1, are: 'assured-dominant', 'arrogant-calculating', 'coldhearted-unsympathetic', 'aloof-introverted', 'unassured-submissive', 'unassuming-ingenuous', 'warm-agreeable', and 'gregarious-extraverted'.

When the IAS is administered, respondents are asked to describe themselves or another person. They consider each trait and make a rating to describe how well that trait describes the target person (self or other person). The rating scale ranges from 1 ('extremely inaccurate') to 8 ('extremely accurate'). The IAS contains of eight eight-item scales (altogether, 64 items). The score on a given scale is simply the sum of ratings for the eight traits in that scale.

In this way, we can use Wiggins's IAS to rate a person on (a) a narrow trait (such as assertive), or (b) a higher-order trait (such as assured-dominant). We can also assess the two highest-order trait categories, *communion* and *agency*. To assess *communion*, we would weight each scale's score by the proportion of the score that assesses communion and combine all relevant values. The formula is:

Net communion $(x) = 0.7$ (scale 6) + 1.0 (scale 7) + 0.7 (scale 8) − 0.7 (scale 2) − 1.0 (scale 3) − 0.7 (scale 4)

To assess agency, we would weight each scale's score by the proportion of the score that assesses agency and combine all relevant values. The formula is:

Net agency $(y) = 0.7$ (scale 8) + 1.0 (scale 1) + 0.7 (scale 2) − 0.7 (scale 4) − 1.0 (scale 5) − 0.7 (scale 6)

(See Horowitz, 2004, for the rationale and applications of this formula.) In brief, we can assess traits at different levels of abstraction – analogous to the levels of abstraction described earlier for motivational constructs.

The scales all have high internal consistency; the values of coefficient *alpha* for the different scales range from 0.80 to 0.90. From a sample of over 600 students, the authors found consistent (though sometimes very small) gender differences in the self-descriptions of men and women. On average, men presented themselves as more assured-dominant (5.9 vs. 5.7), arrogant-calculating (4.3 vs. 3.6), coldhearted-unsympathetic (3.0 vs. 2.5), and aloof-introverted (4.3 vs. 3.9). Women presented themselves as more unassured-submissive (4.1 vs. 3.9), unassuming-ingenuous (5.1 vs. 4.6), warm-agreeable (7.1 vs. 6.6), and gregarious-extraverted (6.5 vs. 6.2).

Wiggins and Trobst (1998) have published the IAS profile of a 44-year-old woman who was employed as a senior bank manager. Her T-scores on the eight scales of the IAS were: scale 1 (assured-dominant): 65; scale 2 (arrogant-calculating): 56; scale 3 (coldhearted-unsympathetic): 52; scale 4 (aloof-introverted): 40; scale 5 (unassured-submissive): 30; scale 6 (unassuming-ingenuous): 41; scale 7 (warm-agreeable): 49; scale 8 (gregarious-extraverted): 60. If we reduce each T-score by 50 and divide by 10, we obtain the woman's *z*-score (relative to the corresponding normative group), showing how many standard deviations her score is from the mean. Those *z*-scores, respectively, are: 1.5, 0.6, 0.2, −1.0, −2.0, −0.9, −0.1, and 1.0. Her highest score (1.5) is on scale 1 (assured-dominant), and her lowest score (−2.0) is diametrically opposite, scale 5 (unassured-submissive). She apparently exercises power over other people (taking charge, making decisions, trying to win arguments, and the like). According to her own self-report, her dominant-assured behaviors frequently occur both at work and in social contexts.

A measure of motives: circumplex scales of interpersonal values (CSIV)

Locke (2000) used a similar procedure to construct a test of interpersonal goals (or 'values'). He first compiled statements that describe interpersonal motives and goals mentioned in transcripts of psychotherapy sessions and in already existing personality inventories. The statements were put in the form: 'It is important to me that ...' Half of the statements focused on the self (e.g. 'It is important that I not make mistakes in front of other people'), and half focused on other people (e.g. 'It is important that I not make other people angry with me'). Participants were asked to rate the importance of each item on a scale from 0 ('not important to me') to 4 ('extremely important to me'). Then, using principal components analysis, Locke demonstrated that the first two dimensions corresponded to communion and agency. Finally, he selected eight items that best represented each octant of the two-dimensional interpersonal space.

In Locke's final measure, all items begin with the stem: 'When I am with another person, it is important to me that ...' The 64 items complete this stem, describing different interpersonal goals, motives, or values. Illustrative items are shown in Figure 20.3. The item 'It is important to me that I am obeyed when I am in authority' (Octant 1) is high in agency and neutral in communion. The item 'It is important to me that others approve of me' (Octant 6) is high in communion and low in agency. The items are organized into eight scales, and every scale contains eight items, making a total of 64 items. Responses to the eight items of a scale are summed to yield a score for that scale, and norms are available for each scale. The items of each scale are internally consistent, with the values of *alpha* ranging from 0.76 to 0.86, and the test–retest reliability is also adequate.

As usual, a scale measures a broader motivational category than a single item. Individual items of scale 1, for example, assess goals such as 'appearing self-confident',

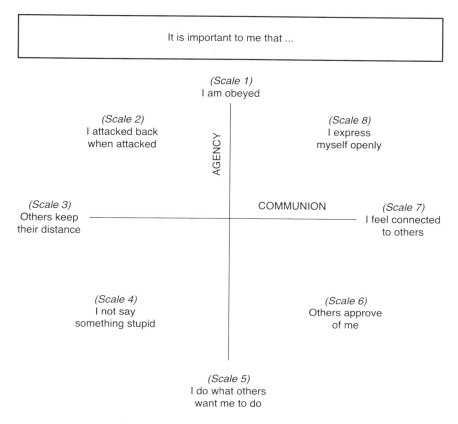

Figure 20.3   Illustrative items of the CSIV

'being obeyed', and 'not being told what to do'. The aggregate of items in scale 1 reflects a broader motive for autonomy, control, or self-assertion. Locke (2000) describes the content of scale 1 as 'appearing confident, correct, and in authority, not letting others boss me around'. Thus, people with high scores on scale 1 are strongly motivated to be in charge, to be seen as independent, correct, and confident. In brief, they have a strong agentic motive. Scale 2 (positive agency, negative communion) and scale 8 (positive agency, positive communion) are also high in agency. In contrast, scales 4, 5, and 6 are all low in agency. Scale 4, for example, describes a motive to 'avoid ridicule and rejection by avoiding blunders and concealing positive feelings' (Locke, 2000). Scale 6 describes a motive to 'get others to like and approve

of me by putting others' needs first'. Scale 5 (negative agency) reflects a motive to 'go along with what others want and expect'.

The scales also differ along the communion axis. Scales 6, 7, and 8 are high in communion. People with high scores on scale 7, for example, have strong goals 'to feel connected with others, to be genuinely cared about, and to be supported by others'. Scales 2, 3, and 4 reflect an absence of a communal motive. People with high scores on scale 3, for example, have a strong motive to appear cool, detached, and on guard, concealing private thoughts and feelings.

Thus, Locke's measure allows us to assess motives at different hierarchical levels. First, we can assess individual goals (single items). Second, we can assess broader motives using each of the eight (octant) scales. Third, as described above, we can also assess the overall strength of the two broadest (most abstract) motives, namely communion and agency.

Locke (2000) has shown that scores on the subscales correlate with other measures with which they ought to correlate (according to the interpersonal theory). For example, the Bem Sex Role Inventory (BSRI) (Bem, 1974) is a self-report inventory of traits containing stereotypically masculine traits and stereotypically feminine traits. Respondents indicate on a seven-point scale how well each trait describes themselves, and the instrument provides a measure of 'masculinity' and a measure of 'femininity'. The masculinity subscale is highly correlated with the Wiggins IAS scale that measures dominance, and the femininity subscale is highly correlated with the Wiggins IAS scale that measures nurturance (Wiggins and Holzmuller, 1981). Now, according to the interpersonal theory, self-descriptive traits (assertive, forceful, nurturant) partly reflect *motivated* behavior, so trait measures, such as the measures of masculinity and femininity, ought to correlate with the corresponding scales of Locke's CSIV. They do. The masculinity subscale was most positively correlated with scale 1 (agentic motivation) and negatively correlated with scale 4 (absence of agentic motivation). The femininity subscale was most positively correlated with scale 7 (communal motivation) and most negatively correlated with scale 3 (absence of communal motivation).

Another way in which Locke (2000) validated the CSIV scales was to correlate them with the different personality disorders. Most personality disorders may be interpreted in terms of the person's interpersonal motivation (Horowitz and Wilson, 2005). For example, people with a narcissistic personality disorder desire admiration and respect (agentic motivation). Therefore, Locke administered the Millon Clinical Multiaxial Inventory (MCMI) (Millon, 1983) together with his measure of motives. From the data he obtained, he was able to 'project' each personality disorder onto a two-dimensional space created by the two underlying motivational themes, communion and agency. He showed that people with a narcissistic personality disorder report positive agentic motivation (scale 1), whereas people with a dependent personality disorder report negative agentic motivation (scale 5). Similarly, people with an avoidant personality disorder report negative communion and negative agency (scale 4). People with a schizoid personality disorder report negative communion. People with a paranoid personality disorder report negative communion and positive agency. Thus, the CSIV appears to be a very promising self-report measure of motivation that helps clarify the goals (often self-protective goals) of people with different personality disorders.

DYNAMICS: INTERPERSONAL COMPLEMENTARITY

Interpersonal theory

As noted previously, an interpersonal behavior can be ambiguous. When a wife says to her husband, 'Let's straighten up before we go out', the goal driving her behavior may be primarily communal: She may primarily desire closeness and teamwork (the satisfaction of working together); or she may primarily desire to influence or control her husband's behavior. Therefore, the husband and wife may perceive the wife's remark quite differently. To say that a behavior is ambiguous is to say that the coordinates of the behavior on the interpersonal graph are not known: The underlying motive behind the behavior is unclear. When two people interpret the same behavior differently, that difference is a potential basis for a significant misunderstanding.

A difference in perspective frequently arises in troubled marriages (Fincham and Beach, 1999): A husband returns home late from work, and his wife reports that 'he thinks only about himself and his needs'.

Such conflict-promoting attributions impair problem solving, increase negative affect, and lower marital satisfaction (Bradbury and Fincham, 1992; Fincham and Bradbury, 1992; Karney and Bradbury, 1997). Soon we shall describe a third measure, the Impact Message Inventory, that can be used to document how the very same behavior may produce quite a different impact on two different observers.

When we *do* know the motive behind a behavior, then we *are able to* locate that behavior graphically. And if the motive is clear, we can also specify the person's desired reaction (see Figure 20.4). When person A unambiguously dominates person B, A wants B to yield. When A makes an unambiguous bid for intimacy, A wants B to reciprocate closeness. An unambiguous interpersonal behavior invites a desired class of reactions (which the partner may or may not provide), and those desired reactions constitute the *complement*: That is, the complement of a behavior is the reaction that would satisfy the motive behind it. In contrast, an ambiguous behavior has different possible complements, depending on the motive behind it.

What is the formal relationship between an unambiguous interpersonal behavior and its complement? An unambiguous behavior and its complement are similar with respect to the horizontal axis (connection invites connection, detachment invites detachment), and they are reciprocal with respect to the vertical axis (influence invites deference, and deference invites influence). Therefore, when person A gives friendly advice (warm influence) to person B, person A desires warm acceptance of the advice, as shown in Figure 20.4. When A tells B to 'leave me alone' (detached influence), A would like B to comply by withdrawing (detached deference). When A tells B that he feels 'stuck' over a problem (warm deference), A is inviting B to come to A's rescue (warm influence).

This relationship between an interpersonal behavior and its complement explains why we prefer to call the negative pole of the *x* dimension 'disconnected' or 'indifferent' behavior, rather than hostile behavior: When people exhibit hostile behavior toward a partner, they do not usually desire a hostile reaction. But when people exhibit a desire to be left alone, they do seem to desire that the other person leave them alone. According to the principle of complementarity, disconnectedness invites disconnectedness. When an important motive is frustrated, the

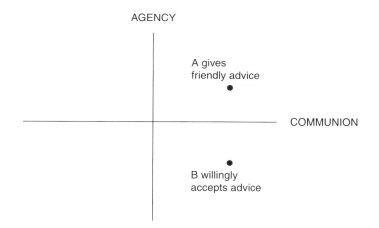

Figure 20.4   A pair of complementary behaviors

frustrated person experiences negative affect, so a person who wants to be left alone might become angry if a partner kept offering love (Moskowitz and Coté, 1995), and a person who wants intimacy might become angry if a partner were chronically unresponsive.

An interesting case arises when B reacts to A's dominance with dominance (or to A's deference with deference), thereby frustrating A's desire. If two people keep trying to influence each other (and neither yields), they may become stuck in a power struggle in which neither satisfies the goal of the other. Two people may also become frustrated (and irritated) if each keeps deferring to the other's invitation to take control – for example, 'After you, my dear Alphonse'. 'No, dear sir, after you!' 'No, no, I'll follow you'.

A measure of interpersonal impacts: Impact Message Inventory (IMI)

According to the interpersonal theory, person A's behavior invites a particular class of reactions from person B. B infers A's 'desired class of reactions' from A's behavior, and B may (or may not) provide the desired reaction. The invitation, as perceived, arouses a variety of reactions from B – including cognitions, action tendencies, and affect. The Impact Message Inventory (IMI) (Kiesler, Schmidt, and Wagner, 1997 Kiesler and Schmidt, 1993) assesses these immediate, internal reactions – the partner's feelings, perceived messages, and action tendencies. As usual, its items may be organized in a two-dimensional space. Whereas Wiggins's IAS (which measures traits) and Locke's CSIV (which measures values or goals) are concerned with characteristics of person A, Kiesler's IMI is concerned with the internal reactions of person B – before B has actually responded to A.

Following the same procedure described for the IAS and CSIV, Kiesler developed a list of possible reactions to a person's interpersonal behavior. A principal components analysis demonstrated an underlying pair of dimensions that correspond to communion and agency. The IMI contains eight scales. When the IMI was constructed, the two underlying dimensions were called *affiliation* (ranging from Hostile to Friendly) and *dominance* (ranging from dominant to submissive). The eight octants were therefore labeled: dominant (D), hostile-dominant (HD), hostile (H), hostile-submissive (HS), submissive (S), friendly-submissive (FS), friendly (F), and friendly-dominant (FD). Each scale contains seven items, making a total of 56 items. Respondents rate their reaction to a person along a scale from 1 ('not at all') to 4 ('very much so').

Items of the IMI that describe direct feelings begin with the frame: When I am with this person, he (or she) makes me feel .... Typical items are: 'bossed around' (scale D), 'important' (scale FS), and 'entertained' (scale F). Items that describe action tendencies begin with the stem: When I am with this person, he (or she) makes me feel that .... Typical items are 'I could relax and he'd take charge' (scale FD), 'I want to get away from him' (scale HD), and 'I should tell him not to be so nervous around me' (scale HS). Items that describe perceived evoking messages begin with the stem 'When I am with this person, it appears to me that ...' Typical items are 'he thinks he is inadequate' (scale HS), 'he's carrying a grudge' (scale HD), 'he'd rather be alone' (scale HD). Kiesler and Schmidt (1993) reported satisfactory levels of internal consistency. When female undergraduate students watched videotaped interviews of individuals and reported their reactions, the values of alpha across the different scales ranged from 0.78 to 0.91.

The IMI is unusual in that the respondent does not describe a partner's overt behavior, but rather his or her own inner reactions to that partner. The measure can be used in any two-person interaction: husband–wife, friend–friend, employer–employee, siblings, patient and therapist, two new acquaintances, and so on.

FRUSTRATED MOTIVES AND INTERPERSONAL PROBLEMS

Interpersonal theory

When an important goal or motive is chronically frustrated, the person experiences negative affect. We now ask why important interpersonal motives get frustrated and how those frustrated motives can be assessed.

A chronically frustrated goal or motive constitutes an interpersonal problem for one or both members of a dyad. Most people seem to be reasonably successful in finding ways to attain desired levels of intimacy, friendship, autonomy, influence, self-efficacy, and so on. Some people, however, are not successful and report interpersonal problems. A very shy person, for example, might yearn for intimacy but avoid social contact in order to avoid rejection. By withdrawing from others, the person unwittingly invites others to withdraw. In this way, the person's self-protective strategies frustrate the motive for intimacy.

Why do interpersonal motives get frustrated? Suppose a person has a strong desire to affirm the self through assertive behavior (an agentic motive), but the person finds it hard to be assertive (an interpersonal problem). How is this interpersonal problem to be understood? Among the possible answers, two are particularly evident from the interpersonal model.

Motives conflict

Psychodynamic writers (e.g. Strupp and Binder, 1984; Luborsky and Crits-Christoph, 1998) have emphasized the adverse effect of motivational conflict on a person's wellbeing. When two or more motives conflict within a person, the person has to sacrifice one in order to satisfy the others. For example, a person with a strong desire to behave assertively may forsake that motive in order to safeguard a communal motive (preserving harmony in relationships). Numerous laboratory studies have shown that people often camouflage or forfeit a desired agentic goal (such as successful competitive behavior with friends) in order to preserve a friendship

(e.g. Arroyo and Zigler, 1995; Brigham et al., 1997; Cross et al., 1991; Exline and Lobel, 1999; Santor and Zuroff, 1997). In addition, Emmons (1986; Emmons and King, 1988) assessed the amount of conflict people reported among their top-rated 'personal strivings' (goals). Participants listed up to 15 goals and rated, for each pair of goals, the extent to which the goals conflicted. The goal 'to appear more intelligent than I am', for example, was judged to conflict with the goal 'to present myself in an honest light'. The more conflict participants reported, the greater their level of negative affect, depression, psychosomatic complaints, physical illness, and number of visits to a health center. Riediger and Freund (2004) also showed that conflicting goals interfere with a person's subjective wellbeing.

Ambiguous behavior is misinterpreted

A second reason that motives get frustrated is that behavior is misinterpreted. A person who tries to be firm or assertive may come across as disagreeable. Other people, misinterpreting the behavior, may then react in ways that frustrate at least one of the person's motives. As noted previously, a trait may be regarded as a summary of frequent acts as well as the motives, goals, and values behind them. Following Allport (1937: 319–24), we would say that a sociable person wants company, an assertive person wants to have influence, a theatrical person wants attention, a dependent person wants to be cared for, a timid person wants safety, and a narcissistic person wants admiration. Observers, however, may misinterpret the observed behavior and frustrate the very motive that the person is trying to satisfy.

A measure of interpersonal problems: Inventory of Interpersonal Problems (IIP)

When an important interpersonal motive is chronically frustrated, the person reports interpersonal problems, such as 'It is hard for me to make friends', or 'I find myself alone too much'. Complaints of this kind may be assessed using the Inventory of Interpersonal Problems (Horowitz et al., 2000), a self-report measure that contains 64 items (problems) organized in two dimensions that correspond to communion and agency. Every item states a common interpersonal problem, and as usual the 64 items are organized into eight scales (eight items per octant).

The first step in developing this measure was to identify problems mentioned by patients during the interview before they began psychotherapy. Statements were identified that had one of two general forms: *inhibitions* ('It is hard for me to [do something]') and *excesses* ('I [do something] too much'). On average, the patients produced nearly seven problems of this type. A panel of 14 judges then judged whether each problem would be considered an interpersonal problem. On average, 5.2 problems per patient were considered interpersonal by at least 13 judges on the panel. Some specific examples were: 'I find it hard to make demands of my secretary', and 'I reveal personal things to my friends too much'.

The interpersonal problems were then transformed into a standardized form: For inhibitions, the frame was 'It is hard for me to *x* other people'. (*x* might refer to the problematic behavior 'say *no* to'). For excesses, the frame was 'I do *y* too much'. ('do *y*' might refer to the problematic behavior 'let other people take advantage of me'). An inventory was constructed from the resulting statements, and participants were asked to indicate 'how much you have been distressed by this problem in the last two weeks. They rated their distress on a scale from 0 (not at all) to 4 (extremely).

A principal components analysis was performed on people's ratings, and the analysis, as usual, yielded two components (factors). Items were then selected from each octant of the space to form eight eight-item scales. A summary score is obtained by summing the respondent's ratings of the eight problems within each scale. The sum of ratings across all 64 items provides a total score that reflects the person's overall distress from interpersonal problems (see Table 20.1).

Norms for the IIP-64 are based on a standardization sample of 800 people, representative of the US population of adults aged 18 to 89. The norms are presented by gender and by age – 100 individuals of each gender at each of four age levels. The internal consistency of the individual scales range from $alpha = 0.76$ to $alpha = 0.81$. The total score (across all 64 items) correlates significantly with scores on measures of anxiety and depression. Although the amount of distress reported from interpersonal problems correlates significantly with depression and anxiety, the correlations are not very strong (Horowitz et al., 2000); *interpersonal* distress is quite different from the symptomatic distress that we call depression and anxiety.

When people report an improvement through a brief dynamic psychotherapy, they also report a concomitant reduction in interpersonal distress (Horowitz et al., 1988). Moreover, the likelihood of improvement is related to the person's most salient type of problem before treatment begins. People who improve most through a brief dynamic psychotherapy tend to be people with initially high scores on scales 5, 6, and 7; those

Table 20.1 Sample items from the inventory of interpersonal problems

Scale	Label	Sample item
1	Domineering/controlling	I try to control other people too much.
2	Vindictive/self-centered	It is hard for me to put somebody else's needs before my own.
3	Cold/distant	It is hard for me to experience a feeling of love for another person.
4	Socially inhibited	It is hard for me to ask other people to get together socially with me.
5	Nonassertive	It is hard for me to be assertive with another person.
6	Overly accommodating	I let other people take advantage of me too much.
7	Self-sacrificing	I try to please other people too much.
8	Intrusive/needy	I tell personal things to other people too much.

with initially high scores on scales 1, 2, and 3 are more difficult to treat. In addition, a number of studies have shown that distinctive types of interpersonal problems are associated with the different personality disorders (for a summary, see Horowitz, 2004; Horowitz et al., 2006). Personality disorders that reflect a more difficult type of problem (scales 1, 2, and 3) are generally known to be among the more difficult personality disorders to treat. Thus, an assessment of interpersonal problems can be very useful in clarifying why the person is distressed and seeking treatment.

SUMMARY STATISTICS FOR THE FOUR MEASURES

The interpersonal measures described in this chapter are all based on the two dimensions that result from a principal component analysis. In all four cases, the two principal components (dimensions) may be interpreted in terms of communion and agency. In all four cases, it is possible to compute summary statistics in the same way. We illustrate these statistics by describing the interpersonal problems of two women on the IIP-64: Ms. D, a woman with a dependent personality disorder, and Ms. A, a woman with an avoidant personality disorder.

Ms. D's eight scores were reported as z-scores. Beginning with scale 1 (domineering/controlling), the z-scores were: 0.6, 0.4, 0.7, 1.0, 2.1, 2.7, 0.8, and 0.4. Figure 20.5 gives a graphical picture of these z-scores. The length of each vector reports the magnitude of the z-scores. The highest z-score – $z = 2.7$ on scale 6 (overly accommodating) – indicates that her distress on that scale was 2.7 standard deviations above the mean of the standardization group.

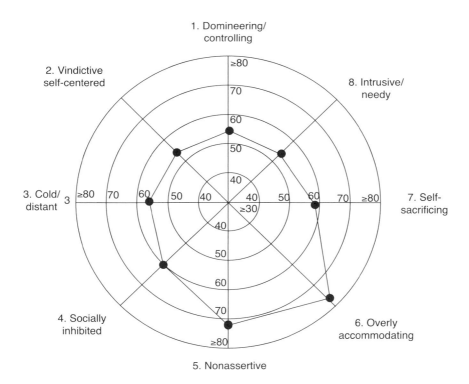

Figure 20.5   Pattern of z-scores on IIP-64 for Ms. D

The eight z-scores may be combined in a way that shows Ms. D's net distress on the communion (x) dimension and, separately, her net distress on the agency (y) dimension. That is, every vector may be analyzed into an x component (that reflects the projection of the vector onto the x-axis) and a y component (that reflects the projection of the vector onto the y-axis). (Once we have specified a vector's angle with respect to the x-axis, the x component may be computed using the sine of that angle; and the y component may be computed as the cosine of that angle.) Then we can average the eight x components to obtain the net distress on communion. Separately, we can also average the eight y components to obtain the net distress on agency.

To be specific, let us consider the x component of each vector. To obtain the x component of a vector, we multiply that vector by the cosine of its angle with the $x =$ axis. The vector of scale 8, for example, makes a 45° angle with the x-axis. To obtain its x component, we need to multiply the length of that vector (the z-score on that scale) by cos 45° (which equals 0.7). Since the length of the vector for scale 8 is 0.4, the length of the x component of the vector is: (cos 45°) (0.4) = (0.7) (0.4) = 0.28.

The cosine is positive for some scales; those scales – scales 6, 7, and 8 – reflect problems with too much communion. The cosine is negative for other scales; those scales – scales 2, 3, and 4 – reflect problems with too little communion. Once we have determined the x component of each vector, we sum the eight values algebraically to determine the net amount of communal distress:

Net communal (x) distress = 0.7 (scale 6) + 1.0 (scale 7) + 0.7 (scale 8) – 0.7 (scale 2) – 1.0 (scale 3) – 0.7 (scale 4)

Scale 1 and scale 5 do not reflect problems of communion at all since those problems are entirely agentic; in both cases, the cosine is 0. Therefore, scales 1 and 5 do not contribute

to the net communal distress and need not appear in the formula. When we apply the formula to Ms. D's z-scores:

Net communal (x) distress = 0.7 (2.7) + 1.0 (0.8) + 0.7 (0.4) – 0.7 (0.4) – 1.0 (0.7) – 0.7 (1) = 1.29

The net amount of communal distress is positive, so Ms. D seems to experience more distress from excessive communion than from a lack of communion.

Now we compute the net agentic distress by determining the y component of each vector. To compute the y component of a vector, we need to multiply each vector by the sine of its angle with the x-axis. Scale 8, for example, is at a 45° angle with the x-axis, so we multiply the z-score on that scale by sin 45° (which also equals 0.7); that is, 0.7 (0.4) = 0.28, which represents the component of the vector associated with Ms. D's agentic difficulties on scale 8. Following the same logic, we algebraically sum the y components to obtain the net agentic (y) distress.

Net agentic (y) distress = 0.7 (scale 8) + 1.0 (scale 1) + 0.7 (scale 2) – 0.7 (scale 4) – 1.0 (scale 5) – 0.7 (scale 6)

Scale 3 and scale 7 do not reflect problems of agency at all since those problems are entirely communal; in both cases, the cosine is 0. Therefore, scales 3 and 5 do not contribute to the net agentic distress and need not appear in the formula. When we apply the formula to Ms. D's z-scores:

Net agentic distress = 0.7 (0.4) + 1 (0.6) + 0.7 (0.4) – 0.7 (1) – 1.0 (2.1) – 0.7 (2.7) = –3.53

Thus, the net amount of agentic distress is negative; that is, the problems strongly reflect a *lack* of agency – yielding too much. To summarize, Ms. D's net distress on communion is positive, 1.29 (her problems largely reflect her report of being too connected with people), and her net distress on agency is negative, −3.53 (her problems largely reflect her report of yielding too readily to other people: −3.53). Her overall net distress therefore lies in the lower right-hand quadrant of the interpersonal space (as expected for someone with a dependent personality disorder).

Finally, we can imagine a point that summarizes the location of Ms. D's overall distress on both dimensions. It can be shown mathematically that we need to divide each net distress by 4 to retain the properties of a z-score. Leary (1957) used the term 'LOV' to denote the net communal distress (z-score form), and the term 'DOM' to denote the net agentic distress (in z-score form):

$$LOV = 1.29/4 = 0.32$$

$$DOM = -3.53/4 = -0.88.$$

If we wanted, we could plot the location of this point, [0.32, −0.88] on the graph in Figure 20.5 to show the point that locates Ms. D's net communal and agentic distress from interpersonal problems. Then, if we wanted to be even more precise, we might draw a vector from the origin to the point [0.32, −0.88] and compute the tangent of its angle with the x-axis: $\tan \theta = DOM/LOV = -0.88/0.32 = -2.75$. The angle whose tangent is '−2.75' is 290°. The summary vector is thus 290° from the x-axis, in the lower right-hand quadrant.

We can use the same procedure to describe the scores of Ms. A, a woman with an avoidant personality disorder. Expressed as z-scores, and beginning with scale 1, her z-scores are: 0.7, 0.9, 1.2, 3.2, 2.1, 1.0, 0.5, and 0.3. The above formulas may be used to compute the net communal (x) distress and the net agentic (y) distress: The net communal distress equals −2.66, and the net agentic distress equals −3.50. Dividing each sum by 4, we obtain the coordinates of the point [−0.66, −0.88]. The vector from the origin to this point would be analogous to an average of the eight vectors. This summary vector would be in the lower left-hand quadrant.

The tangent of the summary vector's angle with the x-axis is: (−0.88)/(−0.66) = 1.33. The angle with this tangent is 233°, which places Ms. A's overall distress due to interpersonal problems in the lower left-hand quadrant, as expected for someone with an avoidant personality disorder.

CONCLUSIONS

In this chapter we have reviewed four different interpersonal measures (of behaviors, traits, interpersonal goals, and interpersonal problems), all derived from the interpersonal model of personality. Each of the four measures contains eight subscales organized around the two interpersonal dimensions of communion (x-axis) and agency (y-axis). The summary thus provides a profile for each person showing the person's score on each of eight interpersonal variables which themselves may be located in a two-dimensional interpersonal space.

In each case, the eight subscales form a 'nomological net' of variables (Cronbach and Meehl, 1955; also see Gurtman, 1993, 1994, 1995; Gurtman and Bakarishnan, 1998). These eight variables may also be used to locate another interpersonal construct within the interpersonal space (e.g. Pincus and Gurtman, 1995). Doing so helps establish the 'construct validity' of a new interpersonal test.

In future research, it should also be possible to show how the four interpersonal measures (the IMI, IAS, IIP, and CSIV) may be used together to clarify other concepts in clinical psychology. For example, the personality disorders are vital to our description of psychopathology, but the personality disorders require conceptual clarification. We know that patients with different personality disorders differ systematically in the interpersonal problems that they report. Such data have been based on the IIP (see, for example, Horowitz, 2004; Pincus and Wiggins, 1990). Since an interpersonal problem may be conceptualized in terms of frustrated goals and motives (Horowitz et al., 2006), patients with different personality disorders should differ in the strength of particular motives. The behavioral strategies that people use to satisfy their most salient (but often frustrated) motives express characteristic behaviors, so patients with different personality disorders should also exhibit characteristic types of behaviors; these behavioral differences could be assessed using the IMI. Finally, traits are abstract summaries of frequent behaviors, so patients with different personality disorders should differ in their most salient traits, and characteristic traits associated with each personality disorder could be exposed using the IAS. In this way, the four scales may be used together in future research to provide a fuller understanding of the patient.

REFERENCES

Allport, G.W. (1937) *Personality: A Psychological Interpretation*. New York: Holt, Rinehart & Winston.

Alston, W.P. (1975) 'Traits, consistency, and conceptual alternatives for personality theory', *Journal for the Theory of Social Behaviour*, 5(1): 17–48.

Angyal, A. (1941) *Foundations for a Science of Personality.* New York: Commonwealth Fund and Harvard University Press.

Arroyo, C.G. and Zigler, E. (1995) 'Racial identity, academic achievement, and the psychological well-being of economically disadvantaged adolescents', *Journal of Personality and Social Psychology*, 69: 903–14.

Austin, J.T. and Vancouver, J.B. (1996) 'Goal constructs in psychology: Structure, process, and content', *Psychological Bulletin*, 120: 338–75.

Bakan, D. (1966) *The Duality of Human Existence: Isolation and Communion in Western Man*. Boston: Beacon.

Bem, S.L. (1974) 'The measurement of psychological androgeny', *Journal of Consulting and Clinical Psychology*, 42(2): 155–62.

Benjamin, L.S. (1974) 'Structural analysis of social behavior', *Psychological Review*, 81(5): 392–425.

Benjamin, L.S. (1977) 'Structural analysis of a family in therapy', *Journal of Consulting and Clinical Psychology*, 45(3): 391–406.

Benjamin, L.S. (1986) 'Adding social and intrapsychic descriptors of Axis I of DSM-III', in T. Millon and G. Klerman (eds), *Contemporary Issues in Psycholopathology*. New York: Guilford, pp. 599–638.

Benjamin, L.S. (1996) *Interpersonal Diagnosis and Treatment of Personality Disorders* (2nd edn). New York: Guilford.

Berzins, J.I. (1977) 'Therapist-patient matching', in A.S. Gurman and A.M. Razin (eds), *Effective Psychotherapy*. New York: Pergamon, pp. 221–51.

Bierman, R. (1969) 'Dimensions of interpersonal facilitation in psychotherapy and child development', *Psychological Bulletin*, 72(5): 338–52.

Blatt, S.J. (1990) 'Interpersonal relatedness and self-definition: Two personality configurations and their implications for psychopathology and psychotherapy', in J.L. Singer (ed.), *Repression and Dissociation*. Chicago, IL: University of Chicago Press, pp. 299–335.

Bradbury, T.N. and Fincham, F.D. (1992) 'Attributions and behavior in marital interaction', *Journal of Personality and Social Psychology*, 63(4): 613–28.

Brigham, N.L., Kelso, K.A., Jackson, M.A. and Smith, R.H. (1997) 'The roles of invidious comparisons and deservingness in sympathy and schadenfreude', *Basic and Applied Social Psychology*, 19(3): 363–79.

Buss, D.M. and Craik, K.H. (1983) 'The act frequency approach to personality', *Psychological Review*, 90(2): 105–26.

Cantor, N. and Kihlstrom, J.F. (1987) *Personality and Social Intelligence*. Englewood Cliffs, NJ: Prentice Hall.

Carson, R.C. (1969) *Interaction Concepts of Personality*. Chicago: Aldine.

Cronbach, L.J. and Meehl, P.E. (1955) 'Construct validity in psychological tests', *Psychological Bulletin*, 52(4): 281–302.

Cropanzano, R., James, K. and Citera, M. (1992) 'A goal hierarchy model of personality, motivation, and leadership', in L.L. Cummings and B.M. Staw (eds), *Research in Organizational Behavior* (Vol. 15). Greenwich, CT: JAI Press, pp. 267–322.

Cross, T.L., Coleman, L.J. and Terhaar-Yonkers, M. (1991) 'The social cognition of gifted adolescents in schools: Managing the stigma of giftedness', *Journal for the Education of the Gifted*, 15(3): 44–55.

DeVoge, J. and Beck, S. (1978) 'The therapist-client relationship in behavior therapy', in M. Hersen, R.M. Eisler and P.M. Miller (eds), *Progress in Behavior Modification* (Vol. 6). New York: Academic, pp. 203–48.

Emmons, R.A. (1986) 'Personal strivings: An approach to personality and subjective well-being', *Journal of Personality and Social Psychology*, 51(5): 1058–68.

Emmons, R.A. (1989) 'The personal striving approach to personality', in L.A. Pervin (ed.), *Goal Concepts in Personality and Social Psychology*. Hillsdale, NJ: Erlbaum, pp. 87–126.

Emmons, R.A. and King, L.A. (1988) 'Conflict among personal strivings: Immediate and long-term implications for psychological and physical well-being', *Journal of Personality and Social Psychology*, 54(6): 1040–8.

Erikson, E.H. (1963) *Childhood and Society* (2nd edn). New York: Norton.

Exline, J.J. and Lobel, M. (1999) 'The perils of outperformance: Sensitivity about being the target of a threatening upward comparison', *Psychological Bulletin*, 125: 307–37.

Fincham, F.D. and Beach, S.R.H. (1999) 'Conflict in marriage: Implications for working with couples', *Annual Review of Psychology*, 50: 47–77.

Fincham, F.D. and Bradbury, T.N. (1992) 'Assessing attributions in marriage: The Relationship Attribution Measure', *Journal of Personality and Social Psychology*, 62(3): 457–68.

Gurtman, M.B. (1993) 'Constructing personality tests to meet a structural criterion: Application of the interpersonal circumplex', *Journal of Personality*, 61(2): 237–63.

Gurtman, M.B. (1994) 'The circumplex as a tool for studying normal and abnormal personality: A methodological primer', in S. Strack and M. Lorr (eds), *Differentiating Normal and Abnormal Personality*. New York: Springer, pp. 243–63.

Gurtman, M.B. (1995) 'Personality structure and interpersonal problems: A theoretically-guided item analysis of the Inventory of Interpersonal Problems', *Assessment*, 2(4): 343–61.

Gurtman, M.B. and Bakarishnan, J.D. (1998) 'Circular measurement redux: The analysis and interpretation of interpersonal circle profiles', *Clinical Psychology: Science and Practice*, 5(3): 344–60.

Hogan, R. and Roberts, B.W. (2000) 'A socioanalytic perspective on person-environment interaction', in W.B. Walsh, K.H. Craik and R.H. Price (eds), *New Directions in Person–Environment Psychology*. Hillsdale, NJ: Erlbaum, pp. 1–24.

Horowitz, L.M. (2004) *Interpersonal Foundations of Psychopathology*. Washington, DC: American Psychological Association.

Horowitz, L.M., Alden, L.E., Wiggins, J.S. and Pincus, A.L. (2000) *Inventory of Interpersonal Problems*. San Antonio: The Psychological Corporation.

Horowitz, L.M., Rosenberg, S.E., Baer, B.A., Ureno, G. and Villasenor, V.S. (1988) 'Inventory of interpersonal problems: Psychometric properties and clinical applications', *Journal of Consulting and Clinical Psychology*, 56(6): 885–92.

Horowitz, L.M. and Wilson, K.R. (2005) 'Interpersonal motives and personality disorders', in S.N. Strack (ed.), *Handbook of Personology and Psychopathology*. New York: Wiley, pp. 495–510.

Horowitz, L.M., Wilson, K.R., Turan, B., Zolotsev, P., Constantino, M.J. and Henderson, L. (2006) 'How interpersonal motives clarify the meaning of interpersonal behavior: A revised circumplex model', *Personality and Social Psychology Review*, 10(1): 67–86.

Karney, B.R. and Bradbury, T.N. (1997) 'Neuroticism, marital interaction, and the trajectory of marital satisfaction', *Journal of Personality and Social Psychology*, 72(5): 1075–92.

Kiesler, D.J. (1983) 'The 1982 interpersonal circle: A taxonomy for complementarity in human transactions', *Psychological Review*, 90(3): 185–214.

Kiesler, D.J. (1996) *Contemporary Interpersonal Theory and Research: Personality, Psychopathology and Psychotherapy*. New York: Wiley.

Kiesler, D.J. and Schmidt, J.A. (1993) *The Impact Message Inventory: Form IIA Octant Scale Version*. Palo Alto, CA: Mind Garden.

Kiesler, D.J., Schmidt, J.A. and Wagner, C.C. (1997) 'A circumplex inventory of impact messages: An operational bridge between emotion and interpersonal behavior', in

R. Plutchik and H.R. Conte (eds), *Circumplex Models of Personality and Emotions*. p.424 Washington, DC: American Psychological Association, pp. 221–44.

Klinger, E. (1987) 'Current concerns and disengagement from incentives', in F. Halisch and J. Kuhl. (eds), *Motivation, Intention, and Volition*. Heidelberg: Springer-Verlag, pp. 337–47.

LaForge, R. and Suczek, R.F. (1955) 'The interpersonal dimension of personality: III. An interpersonal check list', *Journal of Personality*, 24(1): 94–112.

Lazarus, R.S. (1991) *Emotion and Adaptation*. New York: Oxford University Press.

Leary, T.F. (1957) *Interpersonal Diagnosis of Personality*. New York: Ronald Press.

Lewin, K. (1938) *The Conceptual Representation and Measurement of Psychological Forces*. Durham, NC: Duke University Press.

Little, B.R. (1983) 'Personal projects: A rationale and method for investigation', *Environment and Behavior*, 15(3): 273–309.

Locke, K.D. (2000) 'Circumplex Scales of Interpersonal Values: Reliability, validity, and applicability to interpersonal problems and personality disorders', *Journal of Personality Assessment*, 75(2): 249–67.

Lorr, M. and Strack, S. (1990) 'Wiggins' Interpersonal Adjective Scales: A dimensional view', *Personality and Individual Differences*, 11(4): 423–5.

Luborsky, L. and Crits-Christoph, P. (1998) *Understanding Transference: The Core Conflictual Relationship Theme method* (2nd edn). Washington, DC: American Psychological Association.

McAdams, D.P. (1985) *Power, Intimacy, and the Life Story: Personological Inquiries into Identity*. New York: Guilford.

Millon, T. (1983) *Millon Clinical Multiaxial Inventory manual* (3rd edn). Minneapolis: National Computer Systems.

Moskowitz, D.S. (1994) 'Cross-situational generality and the interpersonal circumplex', *Journal of Personality and Social Psychology*, 66(5): 921–33.

Moskowitz, D.S. and Coté, S. (1995) 'Do interpersonal traits predict affect? A comparison of three models', *Journal of Personality and Social Psychology*, 69: 915–24.

Pincus, A.L. and Gurtman, M.B. (1995) 'The three faces of interpersonal dependency: Structural analyses of self-report dependency measures', *Journal of Personality and Social Psychology*, 69(4): 744–58.

Pincus, A.L. and Wiggins, J.S. (1990) 'Interpersonal problems and conceptions of personality disorders', *Journal of Personality Disorders*, 4(4): 342–52.

Riediger, M. and Freund, A.M. (2004) 'Interference and facilitation among personal goals: Differential associations with subjective well-being and persistent goal pursuit', *Personality and Social Psychology Bulletin*, 30(12): 1511–23.

Santor, D.A. and Zuroff, D.C. (1997) 'Interpersonal responses to threats to status and interpersonal relatedness: Effects of dependency and self-criticism', *British Journal of Clinical Psychology*, 36(4): 521–41.

Saucier, G. and Goldberg, L.R. (1996) 'The language of personality: Lexical perspectives on the five-factor model', in J.S. Wiggins (ed.), *The Five-factor Model of Personality*. New York: Guilford, pp. 21–50.

Strack, S. (1987) 'Development and validation of an adjective checklist to assess the Millon personality types in a normal population', *Journal of Personality Assessment*, 51(4): 572–87.

Strack, S., Lorr, M. and Campbell, L. (1990) 'An evaluation of Millon's circular model of personality disorders', *Journal of Personality Disorders*, 4: 353–61.

Strupp, H.H. and Binder, J. (1984) *Psychotherapy in a New Key: Time-limited Dynamic Psychotherapy*. New York: Basic Books.

Sullivan, H.S. (1953) *The Interpersonal Theory of Psychiatry*. New York: Norton.

Trobst, K.K. (1999) 'Social support as an interpersonal construct', *European Journal of Psychological Assessment*, 15(3): 246–55.

Wiggins, J.S. (1979) 'A psychological taxonomy of trait-descriptive terms: The interpersonal domain', *Journal of Personality and Social Psychology*, 37(3): 395–412.

Wiggins, J.S. (1982) 'Circumplex models of interpersonal behavior in clinical psychology', in P.C. Kendall and J.N. Butcher (eds), *Handbook of Research Methods in Clinical Psychology*. New York: Wiley, pp. 183–221.

Wiggins, J.S. (1991) 'Agency and communion as conceptual coordinates for the understanding and measurement of interpersonal behavior', in W. Grove and D. Cicchetti (eds), *Thinking Clearly about Psychology: Essays in Honor of Paul E. Meehl* (Vol. 2). Minneapolis, MN: University of Minnesota Press, pp. 89–113.

Wiggins, J.S. (1996) 'An informal history of the interpersonal circumplex tradition', *Journal of Personality Assessment*, 66(2): 217–33.

Wiggins, J.S. and Holzmuller, A. (1981) 'Further evidence on androgyny and interpersonal flexibility', *Journal of Research in Personality*, 15(1): 67–80.

Wiggins, J.S. and Trobst, K.K. (1997) 'When is a circumplex an "interpersonal circumplex"? The case of supportive actions', in R. Plutchik and H.R. Conte (eds), *Circumplex Models of Personality and Emotions*. Washington, DC: American Psychological Association, pp. 57–80.

Wiggins, J.S. and Trobst, K.K. (1998) 'Principles of personality assessment', in A. Bellack, M. Hersen and C. Reynolds (eds), *Comprehensive Clinical Psychology*. Oxford, UK: Pergamon, pp. 349–70.

21

Measuring Emotional Intelligence as a Mental Ability in Adults and Children

Susan E. Rivers, Marc A. Brackett and Peter Salovey

Emotional intelligence (EI) refers to the capacity to both reason about emotion and use emotion to enhance thinking and problem solving. This capacity is developed through skills in four domains having to do with perceiving, using, understanding, and managing emotions (Mayer and Salovey, 1997; Salovey and Mayer, 1990). This conceptualization of EI, known as the ability model, is distinct from popularized conceptualizations of the construct that emerged in the mid-1990s. In this chapter, we describe EI assessments which are based on Mayer and Salovey's (1997) model of EI, the Mayer–Salovey–Caruso Emotional Intelligence Test (MSCEIT), for adults (Mayer et al., 2002a), and the youth version, the MSCEIT-YV (Mayer et al., 2005a).

EMOTIONAL INTELLIGENCE THEORY

Emotional intelligence refers to how thinking about emotion and integrating emotion into

cognitive processes both facilitate and enhance reasoning (Mayer and Salovey, 1997; Salovey and Mayer, 1990). Emotional intelligence theory emerged from research on intelligence and on emotion which, until the late 1980s, were two relatively divergent areas of inquiry. Similar to conceptualizations of intelligence, EI involves the capacity to engage in abstract reasoning, but about emotions in particular. Emotions convey regular signals and meanings about the status of individuals' relationships between themselves and their physical and social environment (e.g. Ekman, 1973; Lazarus, 1991). For example, anger signifies that someone or something is blocking one's goal, and fear signifies that someone or something in the environment poses a threat. Thus, recognizing and understanding emotions in the self and in others can influence behavior and decision making in adaptive ways. Further, emotions can facilitate or impede different types of thought processes. Studies of patients with prefrontal lobe brain damage demonstrate that the ability to integrate emotional information with rational decision making and other cognitive processes is essential for people to manage their daily lives (Damasio, 1994).

Mayer and Salovey (1997; Salovey and Mayer, 1990) identified four relatively distinct domains of emotion abilities: perceiving, using, understanding, and managing emotion, representing what they called the four-branch model of EI. The four abilities constituting EI are hypothesized to have developmental trajectories, such that abilities within each domain evolve from basic to more advanced and complex. The model further stipulates that the four abilities are hierarchical in structure with the abilities at the foundation (perceiving emotion) being necessary to develop and use skills across the other domains (outlined in Figure 21.1). Perceiving emotion is followed by using

emotion and understanding emotion, and managing emotion resides at the top of the hierarchy. The four-branch model of EI is measured by the Mayer–Salovey–Caruso Emotional Intelligence Test (MSCEIT) and adaptations of it (Mayer et al., 2002a).

Perceiving emotion, the first domain, is the ability to perceive and identify emotions in oneself and others through stimuli including people's facial expressions and voices, as well as stories, music, and artifacts (e.g. Ekman and Friesen, 1975; Nowicki and Mitchell, 1998; Scherer et al., 2001). This ability involves identifying and differentiating emotions in one's physical states (including bodily expressions), feelings, and thoughts, and in the behavioral expressions of others, as well as in the cues expressed in art, music, and other objects. More advanced perceiving emotion abilities encompass

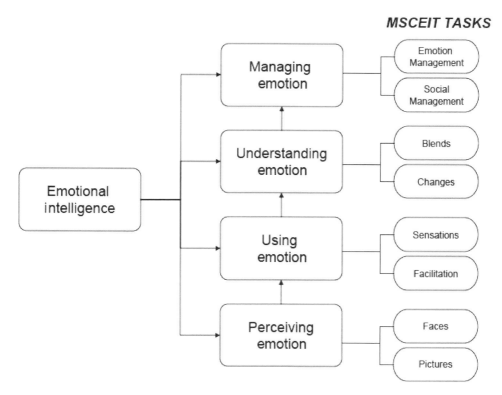

Figure 21.1   Mayer and Salovey's (1997) four-branch model of EI and the MSCEIT tasks for each domain of skills

adaptively expressing emotions and related needs, and discriminating between honest and false emotional expressions in others.

Using emotion to facilitate thought, the second domain, refers to the use of emotion both to focus attention and to think more rationally, logically, and creatively. The most basic aspects of this ability are prioritizing thinking by directing attention to important information about the environment or others. Different emotional states modify thinking processes, such that certain emotions are more and less adaptive for various kinds of reasoning tasks (Isen, 1987; Palfai and Salovey, 1993; Schwarz, 1990; Schwarz and Clore, 1996). For example, positive emotions are more useful in stimulating creative thought (Fredrickson, 1998; Isen and Daubman, 1984; Isen et al., 1987), and slightly negative moods are more tuned to solving deductive reasoning tasks (Palfai and Salovey, 1993). Generating vivid emotions to aid judgment and memory processes and generating moods to facilitate both consideration of multiple perspectives and different thinking styles (e.g. inductive versus deductive reasoning) reflects more advanced using emotion ability.

Understanding emotion, the third domain, includes, at its most basic level, labeling emotions accurately. Understanding the emotional lexicon and the manner in which emotions combine, progress, and transition from one to the other (e.g. the combination of fear and anger in a certain context to form jealousy and the progression from contentment to delight to elation) reflects more advanced understanding emotion ability. Understanding the language of emotion facilitates the process of analyzing emotions. Individuals who are skilled at understanding emotions have a particularly rich 'feelings' vocabulary and appreciate the relationships among terms describing different feeling states. They may be especially adept at identifying the core meaning or themes underlying various emotional experiences, such as anger indicating that one's goal has been blocked or happiness indicating that one's goal has been attained

(e.g. Lazarus, 1991). Understanding the causes and consequences of emotional states and the information they provide regarding the person–environment relationship guides attention, decision making, and behavioral responses.

Managing emotion, the fourth domain, refers to the ability to regulate moods and emotions in oneself and in other people. To manage emotions effectively, people must be able to monitor, discriminate, and label their own and others' feelings accurately, believe that they can improve or modify these feelings, assess the effectiveness of these strategies, and employ strategies that will alter these feelings. This ability involves attending and staying open to pleasant and unpleasant feelings as well as engaging in or detaching from an emotion depending on its perceived utility in a particular situation. Monitoring and reflecting on emotions in the self and others (e.g. processing whether the emotion is typical, acceptable, or influential) represents more complex emotion regulation ability. Managing emotions (e.g. reducing, enhancing, or maintaining) in the self and others without compromising the information value of the emotion reflects an especially advanced level of ability. Managing emotions effectively enables one to accomplish situational goals, express socially appropriate emotions, and behave in socially acceptable ways (Gross, 1998).

ASSESSING EMOTIONAL INTELLIGENCE

EI refers the capacity to use emotions in thinking, planning, and decision making (Salovey and Grewal, 2005). By this definition, measuring EI using performance tests or ability scales, as opposed to using self-report indices, is logical. Moreover, people's perceptions of their intelligence typically are not highly related to their actual or measured intelligence. Most people make inaccurate self-judgments about their intelligence, tending to either under or overestimate their performance on objective tests (Alicke, 1985; Dunning et al., 2003; Mabe and West, 1982). Indeed, Paulhus et al. (1998) report that correlations between self-reported and actual verbal intelligence tend to be below 0.30. Research from our laboratory showed that undergraduates' self-reports of their EI correlated less than 0.20 with their performance on an ability test of EI in three separate studies (Brackett et al., 2006). By dividing participants into quartiles based on their performance on a performance measure of EI, the MSCEIT, and plotting both performance on the MSCEIT as well as responses to a self-report measure of EI (which mapped onto the MSCEIT), the discrepancy between these two types of tasks is evident, as Figure 21.2 shows (Brackett et al., 2006, study 1). Participants scoring in the lower two quartiles overestimate their EI while those scoring in the higher two quartiles underestimate their EI.

Assessments that ask respondents how good they are at recognizing their emotions and those of others or how effectively they regulate anger, are prone to response biases such as social desirability. Performance tests like the MSCEIT are not associated with social desirability (Lopes et al., 2003). A recent meta-analyses of 13 studies (combined sample size of 2,442) revealed that the MSCEIT is relatively distinct from self-report indices of EI that are currently in use (overall $r = 0.14$) (Van Rooy and Viswesvaran, 2004), such as measures by Bar-On (1997, 2004) and Schutte et al. (1998). Moreover, unlike the MSCEIT, self-report indices of EI tend to overlap significantly with measures of personality traits and subjective wellbeing (Brackett and Mayer, 2003; O'Connor and Little, 2003). Thus, as with verbal or quantitative intelligence, ability scales should be the standard for measuring EI.

THE MAYER–SALOVEY–CARUSO EMOTIONAL INTELLIGENCE TEST (MSCEIT)

In adults, the four-branch model of EI is assessed using the Mayer–Salovey–Caruso Emotional Intelligence Test Version 2.0 (MSCEIT) (Mayer et al., 2002a). The MSCEIT is a 141-item test

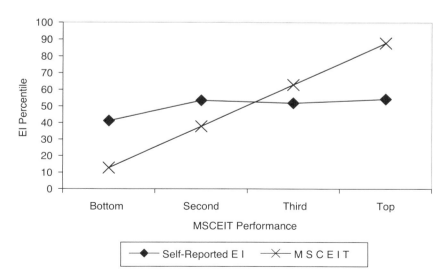

Figure 21.2 Discrepancy between self-reported EI and performance on the MSCEIT (Brackett et al., 2006)

comprised of a total of eight tasks. Two tasks measure each of the four ability domains, as Figure 21.1 shows.

The MSCEIT was based on the 402-item multi-factor emotional intelligence scale (MEIS) (Mayer et al., 1997a, 1999). Empirical studies with the MEIS provided evidence for an underlying unified structure for EI with three distinguishable subfactors (perception, understanding, and management), and that EI was distinguishable from general intelligence and self-reported empathy (see Mayer et al., 2002b). The MEIS was then modified into the 294-item MSCEIT Research Version 1.1 for two reasons. First, its extensive length made it impractical for use in both applied and research settings. Second, there was limited evidence for the using emotion factor (domain 2). The revised test included improved items and scales and has since been shortened to the MSCEIT Version 2.0.

The revised MSCEIT, available from Multi-Health Systems (MHS), can be administered individually or in groups using a paper-and-pencil or an online version; both versions are scored by the test publisher (MHS). Scores using the paper-and-pencil and online versions are indistinguishable (Mayer et al., 2003). Test administration takes approximately 30 to 45 minutes. Details on how the test is scored are described later in the chapter (see also <www.unh.edu/emotional_intelligence/>). The MSCEIT has a grade 8 reading level and has been normed on women and men aged 17 years or older (Mayer et al., 2002b). A separate EI test for individuals younger than 17 years, the MSCEIT-Youth Version (MSCEIT-YV) (Mayer et al., 2005a) has become available and is described in the second part of this chapter.

Description of tasks

The technical manual describes in detail the eight tasks that comprise the MSCEIT (Mayer et al., 2002b); here, we provide a brief summary of each.

Perceiving emotion

The ability to perceive emotion is assessed by asking respondents to identify and differentiate emotions expressed in photographs of people's faces (faces task) as well as emotions represented in artistic designs and landscapes (pictures task). Respondents first examine an image and then use a five-point scale to indicate the extent to which each of five emotions (e.g. happy, sad, fear) are expressed in the image (1 = none at all, 5 = extreme).

Using emotion

The ability to use emotion to facilitate thinking is assessed by asking respondents to compare emotional feelings to those of sensory modalities like taste, color, and temperature (sensations task). By way of this cross-modality matching task, respondents are asked to imagine feeling 'closed', 'dark', and 'numb' and then to use a five-point scale to evaluate how much this combination of sensations are similar to three different emotions (e.g. sad, content, calm; 1 = not alike, 5 = very much alike). In a second task, respondents identify the feelings that assist or interfere with performing various cognitive and behavioral activities (facilitation task). For example, respondents are asked, 'What mood(s) might be helpful to feel when composing an inspiring military march?' Respondents rate a list of possible moods (e.g. anger, excitement) using a five-point scale (1 = not useful, 5 = useful).

Understanding emotion

Understanding emotion and employing emotional knowledge is assessed by asking respondents to decompose emotion blends and to construct simple emotions to form complex feelings (blends task). For example, respondents are provided with the stem, 'Sadness, guilt, and regret combine to form ...', and are asked to identify from a list of five emotion words which best completes the sentence (i.e. grief, annoyance, depression, remorse, misery). In a second task, respondents are asked to identify transitions between emotions, such as identifying an event that would have happened to make a woman feel ashamed and then worthless (changes task). Respondents choose the most appropriate response from a list of five response alternatives (i.e. overwhelmed, depressed, ashamed, self-conscious, jittery).

Managing emotion

The ability to regulate emotion is assessed with the emotion management task which measures the ability to identify the effectiveness of various emotion management strategies to achieve a specified intrapersonal goal in a given situation (e.g. preserving a positive mood). For example, respondents read a short vignette about another person, and then evaluate the effectiveness of four different courses of action to cope with emotions in the story. A second task, social management, measures the ability to identify the effectiveness of three different strategies to manage others' emotions in various situations to achieve a specified interpersonal goal (e.g. maintaining a good relationship with a close friend). For both tasks, respondents use five-point Likert-type scales to rate the effectiveness of the strategies (1 = very ineffective, 5 = very effective).

Scoring the MSCEIT

Performance on the MSCEIT is calculated using two types of scoring approaches: consensus and expert. In consensus or normative scoring, each response option is weighted according to responses provided by the normative sample. If, for example, 82% of the sample selected option D and 16% of the sample selected option B, the score for a respondent who selected option D would be incremented 0.82 while the score for a respondent who selected option B would be incremented 0.16. Higher scores, using this method, reflect greater agreement with the general consensus. Consensus-based measurement (CBM) relies on two assumptions: (a) large samples of individuals converge on correct answers, and (b) knowledge

of a representative sample of individuals approximates how knowledge is used and applied (Legree, 1995; Legree et al., 2005). CBM is useful when a formal information source is not readily available (Legree et al., 2005), and is appropriate for the MSCEIT because knowledge related to the perception, use, understanding, and regulation of emotions is emerging and varies according to cultural norms. Expert scoring works in a similar way to consensus scoring except that responses are compared to those made by a panel of 21 international experts in research on emotion. Test administrators choose the scoring method employed by the publisher.

Expert and consensus scoring produce highly correlated test results ($r = 0.91$), with expert scoring yielding slightly higher scores than consensus scoring (Mayer et al., 2003; Palmer et al., 2005). The correspondence between the two scoring methods addresses criticisms raised about earlier versions of the MSCEIT (i.e. MEIS, MSCEIT Research Version 1.0) that the general consensus may identify qualitatively different responses than experts (e.g. Matthews et al., 2002). This topic is addressed in more detail by Mayer et al. (2003).

The MSCEIT yields seven scores: one for each of the four domains, two area scores, and a total EI score. Task scores are combined to form scores for each of the domains, as illustrated in Figure 21.1. *Experiential* EI, computed from the perceiving and using tasks, reflects the extent to which respondents recognize emotions, compare emotions to other sensations, and understand how emotions interact with thought processes. *Strategic* EI, computed from the understanding and management tasks, reflects the extent to which respondents understand emotional information and use that information for planning and management of the self and of others. The total score, computed from performance on each of the eight tasks, reflects overall EI. Task scores generally are not interpreted as these tend to be less reliable than domain, area, and total scores (Mayer et al., 2002b).

Individual respondents are compared to the normative sample of 5,000 respondents to derive scores, which are computed as empirical percentiles and then standardized to a normal scale, like intelligence, with a mean of 100 and a standard deviation of 15 (Mayer et al., 2002b). The MSCEIT technical manual provides guidelines for interpreting ranges of scores.

PSYCHOMETRIC PROPERTIES

Reliability

The technical manual reports split-half reliabilities, using the Spearman–Brown correction, for both types of scoring (general consensus and expert) for the overall test (r's $\geq$ 0.91), the two areas (r's $\geq$ 0.86), the four domains ($0.76 \leq r$'s ≤ 0.91), and the eight tasks ($0.56 \leq r$'s ≤ 0.88), based on the normative sample ($N = 5,000$) (Mayer et al., 2002b). Split-half reliability coefficients are used to test reliability, as they involve the orderly allocation of different item types to the two different halves of the test (Nunnally, 1978). We reviewed the literature and identified 26 published studies that used either the MSCEIT Research Version 1.1 or Version 2.0, (only English language versions). The average reliabilities reported in the literature generally replicate those in the technical manual. Where there are deviations from the reliabilities reported in the technical, the reliabilities of these published studies tend to be lower as the level of specificity increases (e.g. moving from the total score to the task level scores). The test–retest reliability of the MSCEIT among a sample of 60 undergraduates at a three-week interval is $r = 0.86$ (Brackett and Mayer, 2003).

Intercorrelations among scales

EI theory posits that the skills of perceiving, using, understanding, and regulating emotion reflect a unified set of abilities. Accordingly, the intercorrelations between tasks and scales on the MSCEIT should be moderate and positive. The intercorrelations of scores between tasks and scales, using the normative sample ($N = 5,000$), range from 0.14 to 0.57, with somewhat lower correlations reported between the tasks and somewhat higher correlations reported between the domains (Mayer et al., 2002b).

Structural validity

The design of the MSCEIT reflects the four-branch model of EI. In a confirmatory factor analysis of the eight MSCEIT tasks using a large portion of the standardized sample, Mayer et al. (2003) tested the fit of the one-, two-, and four-factor models. Each model fit fairly well. The four-factor solution was the best fit, as evidenced by the following goodness-of-fit indices using consensus and expert scoring methods, respectively: NFI = 0.98, 0.97; TLI = 0.96, 0.97; RMSEA = 0.05, 0.04. A reanalysis of Mayer et al.'s (2003) data yielded comparable results for the four-factor solution, but lower goodness-of-fit for both the one- and two-factor solutions (Gignac, 2005). The difference in fit can be traced to an unpublished change in the algorithm for Amos 4.0; Gignac used Amos 4.2 in the reanalysis (Mayer et al., 2005b). Using a different sample, Palmer et al. (2005) reported that a better one-factor model may be obtained by employing a hierarchical model. These data, however, did not support a four-factor model. Additional research is necessary to verify the optimal factor structure of the MSCEIT.

Concurrent, discriminant, and predictive validity

Emotional intelligence theory posits that emotion abilities represent an intelligence that is distinct from, but related to, general and verbal intelligence, and that these abilities contribute to effectiveness across a variety of domains. Accumulating research, described in this section, provides empirical evidence of these postulates, and attests to the validity of the MSCEIT (also see Brackett and Salovey, 2004; Mayer et al., 2004; Rivers et al., in press).

EI is related to but distinct from general and verbal intelligence

MSCEIT scores are distinguishable from intelligence, but (as predicted) there is some positive overlap as both are tapping into a type of intelligence. For example, in samples of college undergraduates, correlations between MSCEIT scores and verbal SAT scores (obtained from college registrars) range between 0.32 and 0.35 (Brackett and Mayer, 2003; Brackett et al., 2004). Gil-Olarte and colleagues (2006) replicated a positive, moderate correlation between MSCEIT scores and verbal intelligence ($r = 0.31$) in a sample of high-school students ($n = 77$) in Spain using the Spanish translation of the MSCEIT (Extremera et al., 2006) and a general intelligence test, the Factorial General Intelligence (IGF-5r, Yuste, 2002).

Promising studies examining MSCEIT scores and brain activity provide evidence that emotional intelligence is distinct from general intelligence. Jausovec and colleagues (2001) showed that MSCEIT scores predicted the amount of cognitive effort employed to solve emotion-related problems. While completing emotion-related tasks, individuals with high MSCEIT scores ($n = 120$) used less cognitive effort, assessed by patterns in theta and alpha frequency bands of electroencephalographic activity of the brain, compared to individuals with average MSCEIT scores ($n = 89$). In another study, Jausovec and Jausovec (2005) made EEG recordings of 30 participants during two types of problem-solving tasks: analytical (recognizing patterns of figures) and emotion-related (identifying emotions in faces). They compared recordings between participants who were high or average in intelligence (assessed with subscales of the WAIS), and between participants who were high or average in emotional intelligence (assessed with the MSCEIT). Significant differences in brain activity (i.e. event-related desynchronization/synchronization; ERD/ERS) during the *analytical tasks* emerged only between those high versus average in intelligence, while significant differences in brain activity during the *emotion-related tasks* emerged only between those high versus average in emotional intelligence. The authors interpret these findings as evidence that 'emotional intelligence and verbal/performance intelligence represent distinct components of cognitive architecture' (Jausovec and Jausovec, 2005: 223).

EI is related to but distinct from personality

Emotional intelligence theory posits that emotional intelligence does not vary as a function of personality characteristics (Mayer and Salovey, 1997). Individuals high (or low) in emotional intelligence are not expected to differ on major personality traits such as extroversion or neuroticism. Numerous empirical investigations show that personality accounts for a small amount of the variance in MSCEIT scores (Brackett and Mayer, 2003; Brackett et al., 2006; Gil-Olarte Marquez et al., 2006; Lopes et al., 2003; Mayer et al., 2004; Van Rooy and Viswesvaran, 2004; Warwick and Nettelbeck, 2004). Indeed, across five studies ($n = 1,584$) EI (measured by the MSCEIT or the MEIS) correlated moderately and positively with two of the Big Five personality traits: agreeableness (weighted $r = 0.21$) and openness (weighted $r = 0.17$); there were low but significant correlations with extraversion, neuroticism, and conscientiousness (weighted r's = 0.06, −0.09, and 0.11, respectively; Mayer et al., 2004). Each of these correlations is quite modest, and it is clear that the traits measured in the most prominent model of personality are generally unrelated to EI indicating that the MSCEIT is assessing a construct not currently measured by common personality inventories.

Associations of EI with other emotion-related abilities

Assessing the convergent validity of the MSCEIT is an area that has received limited attention in the literature. One study reported that the perception of emotion tasks on the MSCEIT did not correlate significantly with other measures of emotion perception (Roberts et al., 2006). However, there are few other empirical tests examining the relationship of the MSCEIT to other task-based assessments of emotion-related skills.

A recent set of studies examined the role of EI in the ability to accurately predict future feelings, or forecast affect (Dunn et al., 2007). Individual differences in EI, and in managing emotion domain in particular, predict accuracy in affective forecasting. For example, in study 1, on US election day, college undergraduates ($n = 84$) were asked to predict how they would feel if their choice for president won the election, and how they would feel if their candidate lost. Two days after the election, they were asked how they actually felt. Students scoring higher on the MSCEIT more accurately predicted their future feelings. This effect replicated across situations – anticipating feelings in response to receiving a grade on a term paper and in response to the outcome of a basketball game.

The finding that scores on the MSCEIT predict accuracy in affective forecasting is interesting and contributes important empirical evidence supporting both the validity of the MSCEIT and EI theory (Dunn et al., 2007). First, MSCEIT scores were used to predict an actual behavior (individuals making predictions about their future feelings) extending self-report evidence from previous research. Second, the findings provide support for emotional intelligence theory by showing that emotion abilities are relevant to an emotion-related task (predicting future feelings). Third, because domain scores in emotion management were the significant predictor of accuracy scores, these results shed some light on the plausible processes by which EI may contribute to

greater forecasting accuracy. As Dunn and colleagues suggest, individuals who score high in this domain likely are not just predicting how they will feel if a certain event occurs, but they probably also are calibrating the intensity and perhaps the direction of that feeling (positivity, negativity) according to the resources they have available, including emotion management strategies such as social support seeking, cognitive reappraisal, and meaning making (e.g. weighing the significance of the event against other events).

Relationship of EI to academic performance

Research from the US and Spain provides evidence that MSCEIT scores are related to academic performance. Among US college undergraduates ($n = 330$) there was a small but significant positive correlation ($r = 0.14$, $p < 0.01$) between MSCEIT scores and college GPA (obtained from the college registrar) (Brackett et al., 2004). Among high-school students in Spain ($n = 77$), MSCEIT scores collected at the start of the academic year predicted end-of-year grades ($r = 0.43$), after controlling for general intelligence (Gil-Olarte Marquez et al., 2006). The difference in the strength of the correlations between the samples from the US and Spain may be a result of restricted range in MSCEIT scores (and grades, for that matter) among American college student samples. These findings are corroborated by Mestre and colleagues (2006) who report a positive correlation between the Spanish version of the MSCEIT and teacher reports of academic performance in high school. After controlling for IQ and the Big Five personality traits, boys' ($n = 63$) scores on the strategic area of the MSCEIT (understanding and managing emotion) were positively related to teacher-ratings of the students' academic adaptation (e.g. student's average academic achievement, extent to which students completes homework and attends class, belief that student will fare well in life).

Relationship of EI to social functioning

Scores on a test of EI ought to be related to indicators of social functioning as emotion abilities are integral to effective social interactions (Mayer and Salovey, 1997). For example, recognizing the emotions of others facilitates perspective-taking, which promotes empathy and provision of social support; expressing emotions in a clear way leads to fewer misunderstandings, and regulating emotions can reduce the likelihood of expressing emotions at inappropriate times or to inappropriate persons (e.g. yelling at one's best friend after getting a parking ticket).

Across numerous studies, MSCEIT scores correlate with self-report measures of social functioning. In one study of 103 undergraduates, participants with higher scores on the managing emotions domains of the MSCEIT were more likely to report having better quality relationships including more positive relations with others and greater intimacy, companionship, and affection in their relationships (Lopes et al., 2003). In addition, participants with higher MSCEIT total scores were less likely to report having relationships that were rife with conflict and antagonism. These correlations remained significant after controlling for the Big Five and verbal intelligence.

In a daily diary study of 99 German undergraduates, scores on the managing emotion domain of the MSCEIT also correlated positively with perceived self-presentational success in opposite-sex interactions, even after controlling for personality characteristics (Lopes et al., 2004, Study 2). Participants scoring higher on the managing emotions domain of the MSCEIT were more likely to report that they had behaved competently and attractively when interacting with someone of the opposite sex, and that their opposite sex interaction partner perceived them positively (e.g. as intelligent and friendly).

A study of 86 heterosexual couples extended these findings (Brackett et al., 2005). Compared to couples where at least one member of the couple scored high on the MSCEIT, among couples where both individuals scored low on the MSCEIT, positive evaluations of the relationship were lower. Individuals in low EI couples reported being less satisfied with the relationship, and that the relationship was less supportive, secure, and important. One limitation of this study is that the majority of the participating couples had been dating for less than one year. In a follow-up study of couples in longer-term relationships, among couples where both individuals had low MSCEIT scores (low EI couples), evaluations of the relationship were more negative compared to couples where both individuals had high MSCEIT scores (high EI couples) (Brackett et al., 2005). Among couples where only one individual scored high on the MSCEIT (mixed couples), evaluations of the relationship fell in between those made by low and high EI couples.

The types of strategies couples use to resolve conflict in the relationship may mediate the relationships between emotional intelligence and relationship quality. Low EI couples reported using more destructive conflict resolution strategies (e.g. yelling) than high EI couples (Brackett et al., 2005). A study with college students lends additional support to this proposition (Brackett et al., 2006, Study 2). Among 139 men, MSCEIT total scores correlated with assessments of ineffective interpersonal strategies (range of r's = 0.22 to 0.33, p's < 0.05), controlling for personality, intelligence, wellbeing, and empathy. For example, in response to a conflict with a close friend or roommate, compared to men with higher EI, men with lower EI were more likely to respond by avoiding or screaming at the other person. Further, in response to a friend or roommate sharing good news (such as securing a great summer job or getting a good grade on a paper), men with lower EI were more likely to respond by pointing out a problem with the event or by not paying much attention, compared to men with higher EI. In this study, the relationship between MSCEIT total scores and interpersonal strategies was not significant for women ($n = 216$, r's < |0.14|).

Studies assessing the relationship between MSCEIT scores and peer-reports of social competence contribute additional evidence that emotional intelligence – managing emotions in particular – is related to social functioning. Individuals scoring higher on the managing emotions domain of the MSCEIT were more likely to be rated by two friends as having positive social interactions and less likely to be rated as having negative interactions, after controlling for gender and the Big Five personality characteristics (Lopes et al., 2004, Study 1). Similarly, among high-school girls in Spain, after controlling for IQ and personality, scores on the strategic areas (understanding and managing) of the MSCEIT were correlated positively with social adaptation, as derived from friendship nominations (Mestre et al., 2006). There was no relationship between MSCEIT scores and peer ratings of social adaptation among boys ($n = 63$). However, in this sample, teacher reports of social functioning were related to boys' MSCEIT scores. Controlling for IQ and the Big Five personality traits, scores on the strategic area of the MSCEIT for high-school boys were negatively related to engaging in conflict and being hostile toward classmates.

MSCEIT scores also predict real-time social behavior. In a laboratory-based study, participants ($n = 50$) interacted in a 'getting-to-know-you' waiting room task with an ostensible peer (actually a confederate of the experimenter). For men ($n = 22$), MSCEIT total scores positively correlated with several behavioral indicators of social competence, as evaluated by independent observers (r's = 0.47 to 0.60, p's < .05). Specifically, men with higher scores on the MSCEIT were more likely than men with lower scores on the MSCEIT to be rated as (a) showing greater interest in their interaction partner, (b) more socially engaged, (c) more socially competent, and (d) being a team player. These findings remained significant after statistically controlling for the Big Five in multiple regression analyses (Brackett et al., 2006).

Finally, two recent studies by cognitive neuroscientists provide further evidence that MSCEIT scores are related to social functioning (Reis et al., 2007). In Study 1 ($n = 48$), individuals with higher MSCEIT scores solved social problems more quickly and accurately than those with lower MSCEIT scores, after controlling for performance in solving comparable but problems of a non-social nature. In Study 2, functional magnetic resonance imaging (FMRI) was used to assess the neural activity of healthy adults ($n = 16$) as they engaged in social and non-social reasoning. MSCEIT scores selectively predicted neural activity in two brain regions linked to social reasoning: the frontal and anterior temporal lobes. Higher MSCEIT scores were related to less hemodynamic activation in these regions, which according to the authors suggests either that individuals with higher EI are more efficient in social reasoning, compared to those with lower EI, or that those with lower EI have more difficulty with social reasoning tasks, utilizing greater brain activity. Both interpretations are plausible.

Relationship of EI to workplace competence

EI should contribute to workplace competence, including success at work and leadership, as the skills of EI are instrumental in communicating effectively during social interactions, managing conflict and stress well, and operating under pressure (Lopes et al., 2006). Among 44 analysts and clerical employees at a Fortune 400 insurance company, scores on the MSCEIT correlated positively with objective erformance indicators including company rank and percent merit pay increases, r's > 0.35. Informant evaluations of social competence from peers and supervisors also correlated significantly with employees' MSCEIT scores. Employees with higher MSCEIT scores were rated to be more interpersonally sensitive, more social, and more likely to contribute to a positive work environment.

Similarly, EI was related to leadership behaviors in a sample of 41 senior level executives (Rosete and Ciarrochi, 2005). Executives with higher MSCEIT scores were more likely to be rated as demonstrating leadership behaviors (e.g. cultivating productive working relationships, as exemplifying personal drive and integrity). Follow-up analyses showed that scores on the perceiving emotions domain was the strongest predictor of leadership behaviors, after controlling for cognitive intelligence and personality. This study contributes to our knowledge of which domain of EI skills (perceiving emotion) may contribute most to effective leadership.

EI may matter more in the workplace when cognitive intelligence is lower. In a sample of 175 full-time workers at a public university, MSCEIT scores were positively related to job performance, but only among individuals with low cognitive intelligence (i.e. one standard deviation below the mean) (Cote and Miners, 2006). This same pattern occurred for organizational citizenship behavior directed at the organization; EI was positively related to citizenship behavior, but only among those individuals with low cognitive intelligence. All analyses controlled for personality and relevant demographic variables (e.g. level of education).

Relationship of EI to psychological well-being, at-risk behaviors and psychopathology

Identifying emotions and responding efficiently to the information they provide about one's relationship to the environment should direct action in ways the promote well-being. There is some evidence that EI is related to psychological well-being. Among college students, psychological well-being, as assessed by Ryff's (1989) measure correlated positively and significantly with total MSCEIT scores, range r's = 0.19 to 0.28, p's < 0.001 (Brackett and Mayer, 2003; Brackett et al., 2006, study 2). The generalizability of this relationship beyond college samples is unknown. One study did not find significant associations between subscale scores on the

MSCEIT (Research Version 1.1) and life or job satisfaction among Canadian military personnel (Livingstone and Day, 2005).

One pathway by which EI may promote well-being is that individuals high in EI may avoid risky behaviors. There is some evidence that individuals higher in EI are less likely to engage in behaviors that place their health and wellbeing at risk. For example, among male undergraduates (n = 89), MSCEIT total scores correlated negatively with drug and alcohol use (r's = −0.34 and −0.26, respectively) and with deviant behavior (r = −0.27) after controlling for personality and verbal intelligence (Brackett et al., 2004). Similarly, in a sample of 243 male and female college undergraduates, MSCEIT scores were negatively related to engagement in risky behaviors, including aggression, substance abuse, sexual, and criminal behaviors (range r's = −0.18 to −0.25, p's < 0.05) (Omori et al., 2006). Among 205 adolescents (106 boys, mean age = 12.6 years), Trinidad and Johnson (2002) found a significant negative correlation between total scores on the adolescent version of the MEIS (Mayer et al., 1997b) and use of tobacco and alcohol (r = −0.19, p < 0.05), which remained significant after controlling for age, gender, and self-reported grades. Thus, there is emerging evidence that EI may be a protective factor for risk taking.

We identified no studies examining MSCEIT scores in individuals diagnosed with psychopathology, such as unipolar depression, social anxiety disorder, and schizophrenia (Keltner and Kring, 1998). There is some preliminary evidence suggesting that there may be relevant associations. MSCEIT scores correlate negatively with depression (assessed by the Symptom Checklist-90-R) and anxiety (assessed by both the Symptom Checklist-90-R and the 16PF), r's = −0.25 and −0.24, respectively (David, 2005; O'Connor and Little, 2003).

Gender differences in MSCEIT scores

Gender differences exist on many emotion abilities. Women, for example, tend to outperform men on a variety of performance measures of emotional abilities (L.R. Brody and Hall, 1993, 2000), perhaps because parents tend to talk about emotions more with their daughters than their sons (Adams et al., 1995; Fivush, 1991, 1998; Fivush et al., 2000). On the MSCEIT, women tend to outperform men, at least among college student samples (Brackett and Mayer, 2003; Brackett et al., 2004, 2005, 2006). Effect sizes range from $\eta^2 = 0.034$ to 0.180, and differences are typically less than one standard deviation. Comparable gender differences emerged with the MEIS (Mayer et al., 1999).

There is evidence for the presence of gender differences in the relationship between EI and social functioning. For example, MSCEIT scores were related to social deviance (drug and alcohol use, aggressive acts) for men but not for women (Brackett et al., 2004). The evidence of gender differences in correlates of emotional abilities is not unique to the MSCEIT. Ability to regulate emotions effectively was related to social functioning for boys but not for girls (Eisenberg et al., 1995). In contrast, the ability to decode and encode emotions contributed to social competence for girls but not boys (Custrini and Feldman, 1989). Few theoretical explanations for these differences are offered in the literature. One plausible explanation may be that behaviors often are interpreted depending on the gender of the actor (Shields, 2002). Indeed, parents categorize children's social behaviors differently depending on the gender of the child (Bacon and Ashmore, 1985).

The reasons underlying gender differences in the correlations between MSCEIT scores and social functioning remain unclear. One reason may be due to a threshold (Brackett et al., 2006). There may be a minimum level of EI that is needed to function effectively in social situations, and the proportion of men who fall below this threshold may be higher than the proportion of women. Because women have higher MSCEIT scores than men, women (as a group) may have attained that threshold. Differences in scores for women, then, would not explain variance in

social competence. These hypotheses are in need to be tested in a sample with a large number of low-scoring women to see whether the effects are due to EI or gender.

Another possible explanation for gender differences in correlations between the MSCEIT and social functioning may be that the MSCEIT is not tapping into EI for women in the same way as it does for men (Brackett et al., 2006). Emotional abilities may manifest differently for men and women. For example, there is a stereotype that women in the US are more adept emotionally than men (e.g. L.R. Brody and Hall, 2000). These expectations may influence how emotional abilities operate in men and women. For both men and women, expressing emotions that violate social norms and display rules can lead to social consequences in daily interactions (Frijda and Mesquita, 1994; Saarni, 1999); thus, learning to regulate these emotions is adaptive (Goffman, 1959; Hochschild, 1983). However, the social norms governing 'appropriate' gendered behavior for men and women are different. Thus, it is possible that the MSCEIT is biased in that it better assesses the emotional abilities of men (and thus it better predicts relevant social outcomes for men), but it may not capture the abilities of women adequately (and thus is not related to social outcomes for women). More research is needed to explain the presence of gender differences in EI and its correlates.

Critiques of MSCEIT

That EI exists and is measured validly by the MSCEIT has been questioned. Such critiques are not surprising given the relatively recent introduction of EI in the scientific literature as well as the outrageous claims by the popular press that EI may be the best predictor of life success (Gibbs, 1995). In this section, we review some of the common critiques of the MSCEIT, in particular the content of the test and its scoring methods (see also N. Brody, 2004; Matthews et al., 2002).

The content of the MSCEIT is limited by its design. As a standardized, easy-to-administer, transportable test for researchers to use with individuals and groups, it is not possible to include direct assessments of all emotion abilities captured by the EI framework, especially higher order and more fluid skills, such as expressing emotions appropriately and accurately, using emotions to prioritize thinking about important information, and being open to and monitoring emotions for purposes of regulation. To assess these abilities, more complex procedures, such as behavioral indicators or reaction time tasks, may be required. Such procedures are not easily administered. The specific items that comprise the MSCEIT do not capture the full range of emotions or, for the perceiving emotion tasks in particular, or all channels of expression such as tone of voice, gesture, and physiological arousal (e.g. O'Sullivan and Ekman, 2004).

Assessing all relevant skills with one test may not be appropriate or realistic. To address some of the limitations of the content of the MSCEIT, research is needed examining the convergent validity of the MSCEIT with other performance-based tasks of emotion abilities, as well as comparing their predictive validity (e.g. Roberts et al., 2006). Few performance-based assessments are available for measuring each of the domains of skills delineated by the four-branch model, either individually or collectively (Rivers et al., 2007).

There also are critiques of the consensus and expert scoring methods. For example, it has been argued that the MSCEIT may not measure emotion skills, but rather convergence to popular opinion (Geher and Renstrom, 2004). As described in the section on scoring, high MSCEIT scores reflect greater agreement with a general consensus or with experts. Thus, as Day (2004) questions, 'Does the high EI individual know what everyone else knows or does the high EI individual know more and know better?' Reliance on response convergence may limit emotional creativity from contributing to emotion skills (Averill, 2004). Further, knowing how others identify an emotional expression is different from knowing what emotion is actually being conveyed by the expression (O'Sullivan and Ekman, 2004); the former is not contingent necessarily upon accuracy in identification. The strong correlation between the expert and consensus scoring methods suggests that experts rely, in part, on consensus judgment (Mayer et al., 2001); that is, being an expert means knowing the consensus better than the average person (see Rivers et al., in press). To our knowledge, there is no research documenting that expertise in emotion yields a distinct set of responses from responses derived by a consensus. However, it is possible that response sets do differ between experts and a consensus. Relying on veridical scoring to evaluate performance on the MSCEIT would provide an alternative to expert and consensus scoring methods (MacCann et al., 2004), however there is often more than one 'correct' response to emotion-laden problems. Alternative scoring methods such as those using flexible scoring whereby experts rank responses should be considered (Mayer et al., 2004).

Future directions

Evidence supporting the validity of the MSCEIT is accumulating rapidly. Importantly, this evidence also provides support for EI theory. To move beyond correlational evidence, prospective studies are warranted to examine causal links between emotion skills and relevant outcomes. One approach is to examine how EI operates in ongoing emotional situations. Powerful emotion situations, such as interpersonal conflict, preparing for an important exam, making a major life decision such as switching jobs or selecting a college, require greater use of emotion skills. Thus, EI should be especially influential in predicting outcomes in such circumstances. Identifying the mechanisms by which EI contributes to optimal performance during emotion-laden situations would provide a richer understanding of when and how individuals use emotion skills, and also which of the domains of skills (perceiving, using, understanding, and managing) contribute most (or least) to performance. These studies also would contribute to our knowledge of the extent to which the MSCEIT measures a person's ability to process and integrate emotional information when thinking critically about emotions *and* what a person will do in the context of daily emotional events (e.g. Van Rooy and Viswesvaran, 2004). Further, we know little about how the collective EI of groups or dyads contributes to performance of the group/dyad. As described earlier in the chapter, individuals' MSCEIT scores are related to various indicators of relationship quality, but when looking at characteristics of a group or dyad, the composite scores of the groups' members may contribute to interaction quality and performance (see Brackett et al., 2005). In summary, the aim of future research is to explore how EI contributes performance and functioning.

MEASURING EMOTIONAL INTELLIGENCE OF YOUTH WITH THE MSCEIT-YV

Until recently, testing the developmental postulates of EI theory (i.e. that emotional intelligence develops with age and experience) has been limited by available measurement instruments. A youth version of the MSCEIT – the MSCEIT-YV – is now available (Mayer et al., 2005). The MSCEIT-YV can be administered individually or in groups, and is appropriate for children aged 11 years to 17 years. In this section, we describe this test and report two studies examining its reliability and validity.

MSCEIT-YV: test description

The research version of the MSCEIT-YV contains 180 items divided among four sections, each representing one of the four domains of the four-branch model (Mayer and Salovey, 1997). Initial analyses by the test developers led to a revised scoring algorithm based on 97 items. Descriptions of the test and study results reported here use this revised scoring algorithm.

Perceiving emotions is assessed through identification of emotions in eight photographed faces. Respondents are asked to identify the extent to which each of four emotions (e.g. surprise, anger, fear, happiness) are present on each of the faces using a five-point Likert-type response scale (1 = none at all, 5 = a very strong feeling).

Using emotions is assessed by asking respondents to compare emotion labels to a variety of physical sensations. For example, in one task respondents are asked to imagine 'feeling surprised after getting an unexpected gift' and then are asked to rate the extent to which that feeling of surprise is like each of the following terms: yellow, cold, quick, and energetic. Responses are made using a five-point Likert-type scale (1 = does not feel this way; 5 = definitely feels this way).

Understanding emotions is assessed by asking respondents to identify the definition or causes of emotions. For example, on one task respondents match an emotion term with a description of a hypothetical situation, such as 'When you worry that something awful and dangerous is about to happen, you feel …'. Using a multiple-choice format, respondents select the best term from a list of five emotion terms (e.g. sadness, envy, fear, frustration, or jealousy).

Managing emotions is assessed by asking respondents to evaluate the effectiveness of several actions in making an individual feel a certain way. A situation is described wherein the target character is feeling one way but needs to feel a different way in order to complete a specified task (e.g. Li is excited about a party but needs to study). Several actions are described following this description (e.g. think about the importance of the grade and the test; watch TV; call a friend to talk). Respondents indicate the extent to which the action would help the target character achieve the specified goal using a five-point scale (1 = not at all helpful, 5 = very helpful).

Scoring the MSCEIT-YV

Performance on the MSCEIT-YV is calculated using veridical scoring (see Roberts et al., 2001). Three experts in emotion consulted the empirical literature and determined independently the best responses to each item on the test. The experts agreed upon the best responses. Where there was disagreement, the item was dropped. Responses that matched the experts were assigned two points. In cases where more than one response was deemed appropriate, each response option was assigned one point.

Similar to the MSCEIT, the MSCEIT-YV yields seven scores: one for each of the four domains (perceiving, using, understanding, and managing), two area scores (experiential [perceiving + using] and strategic [understanding + managing]), and a total EI score. To compute scores, individual respondents are compared to a normative sample of 2,000. Scores are computed as empirical percentiles and then standardized to a normal scale, like intelligence, with a mean of 100 and a standard deviation of 15.

Using two independent samples drawn from US public schools, we tested the reliability of the MSCEIT-YV and also conducted initial validity tests (Rivers et al., 2006). Sample 1 included 215 students (47% girls; mean age = 10.97 years, SD = 0.63 years) and sample 2 included 546 students (51% girls; mean age = 11.69 years, SD = 1.02 years).

Reliability

Two methods were used to compute the reliability of the MSCEIT-YV. For domain scores, Cronbach's alphas were computed and were acceptable, range of α's = 0.70 to 0.84. Split-half reliabilities with the Spearman–Brown correction were used to compute reliabilities for the total score and the two area scores, because response formats

across the test varied (i.e. Likert-type scale, multiple choice). The reliability for the total score was acceptable, r's = 0.89, as was the reliability for the experiential area, r's = 0.88. The reliability was low for the strategic area, r's = 0.62 to 0.64.

Gender and age differences in scores

There were no significant gender differences in sample 1, but in sample 2, girls scored significantly higher than boys overall, on the two strategic areas, and in three of the four domains (not perceiving), p's < 0.001. Age, generally, was unrelated to MSCEIT scores in both samples, r's < |0.15|. Thus, there was little evidence for developmental differences in EI within this age group.

Validity

Using school, social, and personal criteria, we conducted an initial validity test of the MSCEIT-YV (Rivers et al., 2006). In sample 1, we examined student and teacher reports of academic, social, and personal functioning using the Behavior Assessment System for Children (BASC) (Reynolds and Kamphaus, 1992). Students scoring higher on the MSCEIT were less likely to be rated by their teacher as having externalizing problems (e.g. hyperactivity, aggression, conduct problems), internalizing problems (e.g. anxiety, depression), or school problems (e.g. attention and learning problems), r's = |0.26| to |0.56|, p's < 0.001. Students scoring higher on the MSCEIT-YV also were more likely to be rated by their teachers as having adaptive skills including social skills, leadership, and study skills, $r = 0.37$, $p < 0.001$. Student self-reports correlated significantly with MSCEIT-YV total scores as well. Students scoring higher on the MSCEIT-YV were less likely to report negative attitudes toward school and toward their teachers ($r = -.30$, $p < .001$), and less likely to report emotional symptoms like anxiety, social stress, low self-esteem, and depression, r's = |0.19| to |0.30|, p's < 0.01.

In sample 2, we examined student self-reports of academic, social, and personal functioning using several subscales from the BASC-II (Reynolds and Kamphaus, 2004). Students scoring higher on the MSCEIT-YV were less likely to have negative attitudes toward school and toward their teachers, and were more likely to report having positive social relationships, high self-reliance, and positive relationships with their parents, r's = $|0.10|$ to $|0.37|$, p's < 0.05. These data provide initial evidence that emotional intelligence, as measured by the MSCEIT-YV is related to academic, social, and personal functioning among youth.

CONCLUSION

EI is a set of mental abilities that relies on both the emotion and cognitive systems to enhance reasoning and solve emotion-laden problems. The MSCEIT, for adults, and MSCEIT-YV, for youth and adolescents, are two assessment tools that operationalize EI as skills in four different domains: perceiving, using, understanding, and managing emotion. These tests require test-takers to apply their emotion-related abilities to solve emotion-based problems. Although research on the MSCEIT and the MSCEIT-YV is still in a relatively early stage, what we know about their reliability and validity is promising.

REFERENCES

Adams, S., Kuebli, J., Boyle, P.A. and Fivush, R. (1995) 'Gender differences in parent-child conversations about past emotions: A longitudinal investigation', *Sex Roles*, 33(5/6): 309–23.

Alicke, M.D. (1985) 'Global self-evaluation as determined by the desirability and controllability of trait adjectives', *Journal of Personality and Social Psychology*, 49(6): 1621–30.

Averill, J.R. (2004) 'A tale of two snarks: Emotional intelligence and emotional creativity compared', *Psychological Inquiry*, 15(3): 228–33.

Bacon, M.K. and Ashmore, R.D. (1985) 'How mothers and fathers categorize descriptions of social behavior attributed to daughters and sons', *Social Cognition*, 3(2): 193–217.

Bar-On, R. (1997) *Bar-On Emotional Quotient Inventory: Technical Manual*. Toronto, Canada: Multi-Health Systems.

Bar-On, R. (2004) 'The Bar-On Emotional Quotient Inventory (EQ-i): Rationale, description, and summary of psychometric properties', in G. Geher (ed.), *Measuring Emotional Intelligence: Common Ground and Controversy*. Hauppauge, NY: Nova Science Publishers, pp. 111–42.

Brackett, M.A., Cox, A., Gaines, S.O. and Salovey, P. (2005) 'Emotional intelligence and relationship quality among heterosexual couples', Unpublished manuscript.

Brackett, M.A. and Mayer, J.D. (2003) 'Convergent, discriminant, and incremental validity of competing measures of emotional intelligence', *Personality and Social Psychology Bulletin*, 29(9): 1147–58.

Brackett, M.A., Mayer, J.D. and Warner, R.M. (2004) 'Emotional intelligence and its relation to everyday behaviour', *Personality and Individual Differences*, 36(6): 1387–402.

Brackett, M.A., Rivers, S.E., Shiffman, S., Lerner, N. and Salovey, P. (2006) 'Relating emotional abilities to social functioning: A comparison of self-report and performance measures of emotional intelligence', *Journal of Personality and Social Psychology*, 91(4): 780–95.

Brackett, M.A. and Salovey, P. (2004) 'Measuring emotional intelligence with the Mayer-Salovey-Caruso Emotional Intelligence Test (MSCEIT)', in G. Geher (ed.), *Measuring Emotional Intelligence: Common Ground and Controversy*. Happauge, NY: Nova Science Publishers, pp. 179–94.

Brackett, M.A., Warner, R.M. and Bosco, J.S. (2005) 'Emotional intelligence and relationship quality among couples', *Personal Relationships*, 12(2): 197–212.

Brody, L.R. and Hall, J.A. (1993) 'Gender and emotion', in M. Lewis and J.M. Haviland (eds), *Handbook of Emotions*. New York: Guilford Press, pp. 447–60.

Brody, L.R. and Hall, J.A. (2000) 'Gender, emotion, and expression', in M. Lewis and J.M. Haviland (eds), *Handbook of Emotions* (2nd edn). New York: Guilford, pp. 338–49.

Brody, N. (2004) 'What cognitive intelligence is and what emotional intelligence is not', *Psychological Inquiry*, 15(3): 234–8.

Cote, S. and Miners, C.T.H. (2006) 'Emotional intelligence, cognitive intelligence, and job performance', *Administrative Science Quarterly*, 51(1): 1–28.

Custrini, R. and Feldman, R.S. (1989) 'Children's social competence and non-verbal encoding and decoding of emotion. *Journal of Child Clinical Psychology*, 18(4): 336–42.

Damasio, A.R. (1994) *DeCartes' Error: Emotion, Reason, and the Human Brain*. New York: Grosset/Putnam.

David, S.A. (2005) *Emotional Intelligence: Developmental Antecedents, Psychological and Social Outcomes*. Melbourne: University of Melbourne, Unpublished dissertation.

Day, A.L. (2004) 'The measurement of emotional intelligence: The good, the bad, and the ugly', in G. Geher (ed.), *Measuring Emotional Intelligence: Common Ground and Controversy*. Hauppauge: Nova Science Publishers, pp. 239–64.

Dunn, E.W., Brackett, M.A., Ashton-James, C., Schneiderman, E. and Salovey, P. (2007) 'On emotionally intelligent time travel: Individual differences in affective forecasting ability', *Personality and Social Psychology Bulletin,* 33(1): 85–93.

Dunning, D., Johnson, K., Ehrlinger, J. and Kruger, J. (2003) 'Why people fail to recognize their own incompetence', *Current Directions in Psychological Science*, 12(3): 83–7.

Eisenberg, N., Fabes, R.A., Murphy, B. et al. (1995) 'The role of emotionality and regulation in children's social functioning: A longitudinal study. *Child Development*, 66(5): 1360–84.

Ekman, P. (1973) *Darwin and Facial Expression: A Century of Research in Review*. Oxford: Academic Press.

Ekman, P. and Friesen, W.V. (1975) *Unmasking the Face: A Guide to Recognizing Emotions from Facial Clues*. Oxford: Prentice-Hall.

Extremera, N., Fernandez-Berrocal, P. and Salovey, P. (2006) 'Spanish version of the Mayer-Salovey-Caruso Emotional Intelligence Test (MSCEIT) Version 2.0: Reliabilities, age, and gender differences', *Psicothema*, 18(suppl): 42–8.

Fivush, R. (1991) 'Gender and emotion in mother-child conversations about the past', *Journal of Narrative and Life History*, 1(4): 325–41.

Fivush, R. (1998) 'Methodological challenges in the study of emotional socialization', *Psychological Inquiry*, 9(4): 281–3.

Fivush, R., Brotman, M.A., Buckner, J.P. and Goodman, S.H. (2000) 'Gender differences in parent-child emotion narratives', *Sex Roles*, 42(3–4): 233–53.

Fredrickson, B.L. (1998) 'What good are positive emotions?', *Review of General Psychology*, 2(3): 300–19.

Frijda, N.H. and Mesquita, B. (1994) 'The social roles and functions of emotions', in S. Kitayama and H.R. Markus (eds), *Emotion and Culture: Empirical Studies of Mutual Influence*. Washington, DC: American Psychological Association, pp. 51–87.

Geher, G. and Renstrom, K. (2004) 'Measurement issues in emotional intelligence research', in G. Geher (ed.), *Measuring Emotional Intelligence: Common Ground and Controversy*. Hauppauge, NY: Nova Science Publishers, pp. 1–17.

Gibbs, N. (1995) 'The EQ Factor', *Time Magazine*, 146 (October 2).

Gignac, G.E. (2005) 'Evaluating the MSCEIT V2.0 via CFA: Comment on Mayer et al. (2003)', *Emotion*, 5(2): 233–5.

Gil-Olarte Marquez, P., Palomera Martin, R. and Brackett, M.A. (2006) 'Relating emotional intelligence to social competences, and academic achievement among high school students', *Psicothema*, 18(suppl): 118–23.

Goffman, E. (1959) *The Presentation of Self in Everyday Life*. New York: Doubleday Anchor.

Gross, J.J. (1998) 'The emerging field of emotion regulation: An integrative review', *Review of General Psychology*, 2(3): 271–99.

Hochschild, A. (1983) *The Managed Heart: Commercialization of Human Feeling*. Berkeley: University of California Press.

Isen, A.M. (1987) 'Positive affect, cognitive processes, and social behavior', in L. Berkowitz (ed.), *Advances in Experimental Social Psychology* (Vol. 20). San Diego, CA: Academic Press, pp. 203–53.

Isen, A.M. and Daubman, K.A. (1984) 'The influence of affect on categorization', *Journal of Personality and Social Psychology*, 47(6): 1206–17.

Isen, A.M., Daubman, K.A. and Nowicki, G.P. (1987) 'Positive affect facilitates creative problem solving', *Journal of Personality and Social Psychology*, 52(6): 1122–31.

Jausovec, N. and Jausovec, K. (2005) 'Differences in induced gamma and upper alpha oscillations in the human brain related to verbal/performance and emotional intelligence', *International Journal of Psychophysiology*, 56(3): 223–35.

Jausovec, N., Jausovec, K. and Gerlic, I. (2001) 'Differences in event-related and induced electroencephalography patterns in the theta and alpha frequency bands related to human emotional intelligence', *Neuroscience Letters*, 311(2): 93–6.

Keltner, D. and Kring, A.M. (1998) 'Emotion, social function, and psychopathology', *Review of General Psychology*, 2(3): 320–42.

Lazarus, R.S. (1991) *Emotion and Adaptation*. New York: Oxford University Press.

Legree, P.J. (1995) 'Evidence for an oblique social intelligence factor established with a Likert-based testing procedure', *Intelligence*, 21(3): 247–66.

Legree, P.J., Psotka, J., Tremble, T. and Bourne, D.R. (2005) 'Using consensus based measurement to assess emotional intelligence', in R. Schulze and R.D. Roberts (eds), *Emotional Intelligence: An International Handbook*. Cambridge, MA: Hogrefe & Huber Publishers, pp. 155–79.

Livingstone, H.A. and Day, A.L. (2005) 'Comparing the construct and criterion-related validity of ability-based and mixed model measures of emotional intelligence', *Educational and Psychological Measurement*, 65(5): 757–79.

Lopes, P.N., Brackett, M.A., Nezlek, J.B., Schutz, A., Sellin, I. and Salovey, P. (2004) 'Emotional intelligence and social interaction', *Personality and Social Psychology Bulletin*, 30(8): 1018–34.

Lopes, P.N., Cote, S. and Salovey, P. (2006) 'An ability model of emotional intelligence: Implications for assessment and training', in V. Druskat, F. Sala and G. Mount (eds), *Linking Emotional Intelligence and Performance at Work*. Mahwah, NJ: Lawrence Erlbaum Associates, pp. 53–80.

Lopes, P.N., Salovey, P. and Straus, R. (2003) 'Emotional intelligence, personality, and the perceived quality of social relationships', *Personality and Individual Differences*, 35(3): 641–58.

Mabe, P.A. and West, S.G. (1982) 'Validity of self-evaluation of ability: A review and meta-analysis', *Journal of Applied Psychology*, 67(3): 280–96.

MacCann, C., Matthews, G., Zeidner, M. and Roberts, R.D. (2004) 'The assessment of emotional intelligence: On frameworks, fissures, and the future', in G. Geher (ed.), *Measuring Emotional Intelligence: Common Ground and Controversy*. Hauppauge, NY: Nova Science Publishing, pp. 19–50.

Matthews, G., Zeidner, M. and Roberts, R.D. (2002) *Emotional Intelligence: Science and Myth*. Cambridge, MA: MIT Press.

Mayer, J.D., Caruso, D.R. and Salovey, P. (1999) 'Emotional intelligence meets traditional standards for an intelligence', *Intelligence*, 27(4): 267–98.

Mayer, J.D., Caruso, D.R. and Salovey, P. (2005a) *The Mayer-Salovey-Caruso Emotional Intelligence Test-Youth Version (MSCEIT-YV), Research Version*. Toronto: Multi Health Systems.

Mayer, J.D., Panter, A., Salovey, P., Caruso, D.R. and Sitarenios, G. (2005b) 'A discrepancy in analyses of the MSCEIT – Resolving the mystery and understanding its implications: A reply to Gignac (2005)', *Emotion*, 5(2): 236–7.

Mayer, J.D. and Salovey, P. (1997) 'What is emotional intelligence?', in P. Salovey and D.J. Sluyter (eds), *Emotional Development and Emotional Intelligence: Educational Implications*. New York: Basic Books, pp. 3–34.

Mayer, J.D., Salovey, P. and Caruso, D.R. (1997a). *Emotional IQ Test* [CD-ROM]. Needham, MA: Virtual Knowledge.

Mayer, J.D., Salovey, P. and Caruso, D.R. (1997b) *Multifactor Emotional Intelligence Scale, Student Version*. Durham, NH.

Mayer, J.D., Salovey, P. and Caruso, D.R. (2002a) *The Mayer-Salovey-Caruso Emotional Intelligence Test (MSCEIT), Version 2.0*. Toronto: Multi Health Systems.

Mayer, J.D., Salovey, P. and Caruso, D.R. (2002b) *Mayer-Salovey-Caruso Emotional Intelligence Test (MSCEIT): User's Manual*. North Tonawanda, New York: Multi-Health Systems.

Mayer, J.D., Salovey, P. and Caruso, D.R. (2004) 'Emotional intelligence: Theory, findings, and implications', *Psychological Inquiry*, 15: 197–215.

Mayer, J.D., Salovey, P., Caruso, D.R. and Sitarenios, G. (2001) 'Emotional intelligence as a standard intelligence', *Emotion*, 3(1): 232–42.

Mayer, J.D., Salovey, P., Caruso, D.R. and Sitarenios, G. (2003) 'Measuring emotional intelligence with the MSCEIT V2.0', *Emotion*, 3(1): 97–105.

Mestre, J.M., Guil, R., Lopes, P.N., Salovey, P. and Gil-Olarte, P. (2006) 'Emotional intelligence and social and academic adaptation to school', *Psicothema*, 18(suppl): 112–17.

Nowicki, S. and Mitchell, J. (1998) 'Accuracy in identifying affect in child and adult faces and voices and social competence in preschool children', *Genetic, Social, and General Psychology Monographs*, 124(1): 39–59.

Nunnally, J.C. (1978) *Psychometric Theory*. New York: McGraw-Hill.

O'Connor, R.M., Jr. and Little, I.S. (2003) 'Revisiting the predictive validity of emotional intelligence: Self-report versus ability-based measures', *Personality and Individual Differences*, 35(8): 1893–902.

O'Sullivan, M. and Ekman, P. (2004) 'Facial expression recognition and emotional intelligence', in G. Geher (ed.), *Emotional Intelligence: Common Ground and Controversy*. Hauppauge, NY: Nova Science Publishers, pp. 89–109.

Omori, M., Rivers, S.E., Brackett, M.A. and Salovey, P. (2006) 'Emotion skills as a protective factor for risky behaviors among college students', Unpublished manuscript.

Palfai, T.P. and Salovey, P. (1993) 'The influence of depressed and elated mood on deductive and inductive reasoning', *Imagination, Cognition and Personality*, 13(1): 57–71.

Palmer, B.R., Gignac, G., Monocha, R. and Stough, C. (2005) 'A psychometric evaluation of the Mayer-Salovey-Caruso Emotional Intelligence Test version 2.0', *Intelligence*, 33(3): 285–305.

Paulhus, D.L., Lysy, D.C. and Yik, M.S.M. (1998) 'Self-report measures of intelligence: Are they useful as proxy IQ tests? *Journal of Personality*, 66(4): 525–54.

Reis, D.L., Brackett, M.A., Shamosh, N.A., Kiehl, K.A., Salovey, P. and Gray, J.R. (2007) 'Emotional intelligence predicts individual differences in social exchange reasoning', *Neuro Image*, 35(3): 1385–91.

Reynolds, C.R. and Kamphaus, R.W. (1992) *Behavior Assessment System for Children*. Circle Pines, MN: American Guidance Service.

Reynolds, C.R. and Kamphaus, R.W. (2004) *Behavior Assessment System for Children* (2nd edn). Circle Pines, MN: AGS Publishing.

Rivers, S.E., Brackett, M.A. and Salovey, P. (2006) 'Emotional intelligence and its relations to social, emotional, and academic outcomes among adolescents', Unpublished manuscript.

Rivers, S.E., Brackett, M.A., Salovey, P. and Mayer, J.D. (2007) 'Measuring emotional intelligence as a set of mental abilities', in G. Matthews, M. Zeidner and R.D. Roberts (eds), *The Science of Emotional Intelligence*. Oxford: Oxford University Press, pp. 230–57.

Roberts, R.D., Schulze, R., O'Brien, K., MacCann, C., Reid, J. and Maul, A. (2006) 'Exploring the validity of the Mayer-Salovey-Caruso Emotional Intelligence Test (MSCEIT) with established emotions measures', *Emotion*, 6(4): 663–9.

Roberts, R.D., Zeidner, M. and Matthews, G. (2001) 'Does emotional intelligence meet traditional standards for an intelligence? Some new data and conclusions', *Emotion*, 1(3): 196–231.

Rosete, D. and Ciarrochi, J. (2005) 'Emotional intelligence and its relationship to workplace performance outcomes of leadership effectiveness', *Leadership and Organization Development Journal*, 26(5): 388–99.

Ryff, C.D. (1989) 'Happiness is everything, or is it? Explorations on the meaning of psychological well-being', *Journal of Personality and Social Psychology*, 57(6): 1069–81.

Saarni, C. (1999) *The Development of Emotional Competence*. New York: Guilford.

Salovey, P. and Grewal, D. (2005) 'The science of emotional intelligence', *Current Directions in Psychological Science*, 14(6): 281–5.

Salovey, P. and Mayer, J.D. (1990) 'Emotional intelligence', *Imagination, Cognition and Personality*, 9(3): 185–211.

Scherer, K.R., Banse, R. and Wallbott, H.G. (2001) 'Emotion inferences from vocal expression correlate across languages and cultures', *Journal of Cross Cultural Psychology*, 32(1): 76–92.

Schutte, N.S., Malouff, J.M., Hall, L.E., Haggerty, D.J., Cooper, J.T., Golden, C.J, and Dornheim, L. (1998) 'Development and validation of a measure of emotional intelligence', *Personality and Individual Differences*, 25(2): 167–77.

Schwarz, N. (1990) 'Feelings as information: Informational and motivational functions of affective states', in E.T. Higgins and R.M. Sorrentino (eds), *Handbook of Motivation and Cognition: Foundations of Social Behavior* (Vol. 2). New York: Guilford, pp. 528–61.

Schwarz, N. and Clore, G.L. (1996) 'Feelings and phenomenal experiences', in E.T. Higgins and A.W. Kruglanski (eds), *Social Psychology: Handbook of Basic Principles*. New York: Guilford, pp. 433–65.

Shields, S.A. (2002) *Speaking From the Heart: Gender and the Social Meaning of Emotion*. New York: Cambridge University Press.

Trinidad, D.R. and Johnson, C.A. (2002) 'The association between emotional intelligence and early adolescent tobacco and alcohol use', *Personality and Individual Differences*, 32(1): 95–105.

Van Rooy, D.L. and Viswesvaran, C. (2004) 'Emotional intelligence: A meta-analytic investigation of predictive validity and nomological net', *Journal of Vocational Behavior*, 65(1): 71–95.

Warwick, J. and Nettelbeck, T. (2004) 'Emotional intelligence is...?', *Personality and Individual Differences*, 37(5): 1091–100.

Yuste, C. (2002) *Inteligencia General Factorial-Revisada* 5 *(IGF-r 5)*. Madrid: EOS.

22

The Measurement of Emotional Intelligence: A Decade of Progress?

Richard D. Roberts, Ralf Schulze and Carolyn MacCann

The past decade has seen interest in emotional intelligence (EI) increase from an obscure scientific trickle to a media- and research-saturated proverbial flood (Matthews et al., 2007). Empirical studies examining EI, and its application in education, business, and clinical fields, depend crucially on the accurate and meaningful measurement of EI. This measurement, in turn, depends crucially on an accurate and meaningful definition of the construct; that is, a logically and empirically justifiable theoretical model. Primary challenges to EI assessment emerge from two issues. First, there exists a diversity of theories; arguably sufficiently large and heterogeneous as to appear incoherent. Second, there exists an intrinsic difficulty with operationalizing emotion-related material.

The current chapter outlines the major theoretical models of EI, evaluating whether these different models actually describe the same entity, suggesting that ability-based models are the only appropriate ones to delineate, and hence investigate, emotional *intelligence*. The second challenge to EI measurement is the greater operational difficulty in interpreting, judging, or manipulating emotion-based stimuli as compared to the stimuli from conventional cognitive tests. This problem has resulted in scoring rubrics more often based on group judgment (i.e. expert-or consensus-based scoring) than on theory or bodies of knowledge (i.e. standards-based scoring). This difficulty has also resulted in very few ability-based instruments. After describing these challenges, some future directions and potential mechanisms for advancing the assessment of EI are suggested. Among these is the design of new instruments for the assessment of EI, to be used both in isolation and for collecting validity evidence on existing instruments.

BACKGROUND TO EMOTIONAL INTELLIGENCE: HISTORY, MODELS, AND CONCEPTS

The first noteworthy psychological publication on EI was in a scientific journal called

Imagination, Cognition, and Personality (Salovey and Mayer, 1989). Six years later, Goleman penned a bestseller on the topic, marking the beginning of intense interest in EI from both the general public and scientific researchers. The immense popularity of EI has in some ways hindered the field, particularly in terms of conceptual clarity – the sheer number of models and definitions of EI has meant that vastly different constructs exist under the same label. In turn, these various models have led to different and sometimes conflicting claims about what EI represents, its antecedents, and its consequences.

In an effort to bring order to the field, Mayer et al. (2000b) categorized models of EI into two types. In the first type of models, EI is conceptualized as a form of intelligence, involving cognitive processing of emotional information (referred to as ability models of EI). In the second type, EI is partly or wholly a personality-like trait, or behavioral disposition (referred to as mixed models of EI). An alternative and overlapping conceptualization of this bifurcation was proposed by Petrides and Furnham (2001), who categorized instruments according to their measurement approaches into ability-EI (also referred to as performance-based or information-processing EI; see Petrides and Furnham, 2000) and trait-EI. Generally, instruments designed to assess constructs in an EI model of abilities use a maximum performance method of measurement. Instruments following a mixed model conceptualization use self-report or other-report rating scales of typical performance. However, this characterization is somewhat imperfect – some self-report scales are constructed with the intention to assess constructs paralleling the ability model. In this chapter, instruments are classified as EI measures versus self-reports of EI. Since the chapter focuses on a conceptualization of EI that implies maximum performance measures, EI measures are contrasted to self-reports of EI by flagging (and indeed raising a number of limitations with) such self-reports.

The most commonly agreed-upon definition of EI is associated with the most prominent scientific model of EI, the four-branch model (see Mayer and Salovey, 1997; Mayer et al., 2001, 2008; Neubauer and Freudenthaler, 2005; Roberts et al., 2007). In this conceptualization EI consists of four branches of abilities that increase in complexity from the first to the fourth branch. The component abilities in the higher branches depend, or build, on abilities in the lower branches. At the simplest level, EI is the perception and expression of emotions (branch 1 – *perceiving and expressing emotion*). Branch 2 consists of the productive integration of emotions in thought processes (*assimilating emotions in thought*). Branch 3 includes the understanding of the use of emotion terms in language, relations between emotions, between emotions and circumstances and transitions among emotions (*understanding emotions*). Finally, the fourth and highest branch involves managing emotions in order to moderate negative, and enhance positive, emotions (*reflectively regulating emotions*).

Following Mayer et al. (2002), the first two branches are collectively referred to as *experiential EI* (expression, perception, and assimilation of emotions) and the last two as *strategic EI* (understanding and managing emotions). The model has variously been interpreted as a higher-order measurement model (Wilhelm, 2005). Empirical tests of corresponding factor-analytic models have not found support for the facilitation branch, but rather find that experiential EI is represented by perception alone. However, the division between strategic and experiential EI, and a further division between understanding and management are supported empirically (Ciarrochi et al., 2000; Mayer et al., 2003, 2005; Palmer et al., 2005; Roberts et al., 2001).

This theoretical model or its predecessor (see Neubauer and Freudenthaler, 2005) has also constituted a point of reference for some of the available self-reports of EI, either in part or as a whole. Among these self-report instruments are the Schutte et al. (1998) Assessing Emotions Scale (AES), the Multidimensional Emotional Intelligence Assessment (MEIA) (Tett et al., 2005), and the Self-Rated Emotional Intelligence Scale (SREIS) (Brackett et al., 2006). The AES was based on an earlier model of EI that essentially included only branches 1, 2, and 4. The same is true for the MEIA, which was subdivided into ten facets of EI. By contrast, the SREIS was, for all intents and purposes, based on the full four-branch model discussed previously. The Trait Emotional Intelligence Questionnaire (TEIque) (Petrides and Furnham, 2003) also includes components based on branches 1, 2, and 4, but adds additional components. However, the instruments most strictly following the basic tenets of this theory are the maximum performance measures: the Mayer–Salovey–Caruso Emotional Intelligence Test (MSCEIT) (Mayer et al., 2002) and its noncommercial precursor, the Multibranch Emotional Intelligence Scale (MEIS) (see Mayer et al., 1999; see also Mayer et al., 2008 for measures assessing specific branches).

SELF-REPORTS OF EMOTIONAL INTELLIGENCE

There exist a large and increasing number of self-report instruments allegedly measuring EI or the components of a model of EI. Scores on these instruments tend to relate strongly to personality traits, both conceptually and empirically (cf. De Raad, 2005; MacCann et al., 2003; Matthews et al., 2002). Many researchers have argued that EI ought to be an intelligence rather than a set of personality traits to justify the label emotional *intelligence* (see Austin and Saklofske, 2005; Matthews et al., 2002; Mayer et al., 2001; Neubauer and Freudenthaler, 2005; Roberts et al., 2001; Schulze et al., 2007; Wilhelm, 2005). Since EI is an aspect of intelligence, as the label suggests, it should be conceptually and empirically distinct

from personality, relating only as strongly as other cognitive abilities do (i.e. r between 0 and 0.30; see Ackerman and Heggestad, 1997; Ashton et al., 2000). In addition, EI scores should relate positively, and substantially, to scores obtained on standard tests of intelligence and related abilities. Mayer et al. (2000a) refer to these requirements as the correlational criteria. The paragraphs below evaluate whether self-reports of EI meet the two criteria of independence from personality and relationships to intelligence. In addition, these passages examine whether trait- and ability-based EI are in fact correlated, and should meaningfully share the same label.

Relationships with personality constructs

Pérez et al. (2005) listed 15 scientifically studied self-report instruments of EI, most of which are based on different theoretical models. After their list was compiled, three more instruments were published in scientific journals (Brackett et al., 2006; Freudenthaler and Neubauer, 2005; Tett et al., 2005), not to mention the plethora of instruments outside the arena of peer-review publication. We direct the reader to the Pérez et al. (2005) 15-instrument summary and the Tett et al. (2005) detailed evaluation of six instruments rather than reiterate this information here in its entirety.

Instead, we present information concerning the conceptual and empirical overlap between constructs assessed with self-reports of EI and the Big Five model of personality, as often assessed with the Neuroticism-Extraversion-Openness Personality Inventory Revised (NEO-PI-R) (Costa and McCrae, 1992). In what follows, the focus is put on the two emotion-related dimensions of the personality model (extraversion (E) and neuroticism (N)), as it is likely with these two constructs that the greatest overlap may be found. The relationships between these personality constructs and three of the most commonly used self-reports of EI are presented: (1) the AES (Schutte et al., 1998); (2) the EQ-*i* (Bar-On, 1997); and (3) the TEIque (Petrides and Furnham, 2003).

Table 22.1 shows the facets from the Big Five model of personality that the AES, EQ-*i*, and TEIque share relationships with, especially E and N. The constructs assessed with all three self-report instruments of EI show conceptual overlap with components of the Big Five model. The empirical overlap as assessed with correlations between facets of E and N on the one hand and subscales of the AES, EQ-*i*, and TEIque on the other, is also extremely high (note also that the correlations with the TEIque reach 0.84 for E and −0.87 for N after correcting for attenuation). At the very least, the estimates reported in Table 22.1 are consistent with the idea that the constructs assessed with self-report instruments of EI are located within the Big Five personality factor space. Indeed, correlations are high enough to indicate that the EQ-*i* and TEIque primarily assess N, and the AES primarily assesses E, rather than EI as a construct distinct from personality.

Lest the reader assume that the abovementioned overlap is limited to these particular three instruments, some brief examples are provided from other measures. Thus, the Freudenthaler and Neubauer (2005) self-report intrapersonal scale correlates $r = −0.67$ with N, while the Tett et al. (2005) self-regulation scale correlates $r = −0.61$ with anxiety. In summary, both conceptually and empirically, self-reports of EI assess constructs closely aligned with existing personality traits.

Relationships with intelligence

Self-reports of EI are generally not related to intelligence. For example, the EQ-*i* correlates 0.01 with the Wonderlic (Newsome et al., 2000). The AES correlates −0.06 with SAT scores, 0.04 with verbal SAT scores, 0.13 with Raven's Progressive Matrices scores, and variously at 0.06 and −0.21, with vocabulary (Bastian et al., 2005; Brackett et al., 2006; Schutte et al., 1998; Zeidner et al., 2005). Barchard and Hakstian's (2004) comprehensive structural analysis of different EI measures found that factors of self-report instruments were unrelated to verbal ability, verbal closure, visualization, and inductive reasoning (correlations ranged from −0.17 to 0.19 with the majority of lower magnitude than 0.10).

It is clear from the preceding that self-report instruments of EI do not meet the correlational

Table 22.1 Conceptual and empirical overlap of the constructs assessed with three self-report instruments of EI with extraversion (E) and neuroticism (N)

Instrument	Subscale of instrument ≈ corresponding facet of extraversion	Subscale of instrument ≈ corresponding facet of neuroticism	Correlations with E	Correlations with N
AES [a]	Optimism[b] ≈ Positive emotions		0.43 to 0.54	−0.21 to −0.64
EQ-*i* [c]	Assertiveness, positive emotions ≈ optimism and/or happiness	Impulsiveness, vulnerability (to stress) ≈ stress tolerance	0.46 to 0.53	−0.62 to −0.72
TEIque[d]	Assertiveness, positive emotions ≈ optimism and/or happiness	Impulsiveness, vulnerability (to stress) ≈ stress management	0.68	−0.70

[a]Correlations from Brackett et al. (2006), Engelberg and Sjöberg (2004), MacCann (2006), and Saklofske et al. (2003)
[b]The optimism factor appears combined with mood regulation in AES analyses reported by Austin et al. (2004), Austin et al. (2005), MacCann (2006), Petrides and Furnham (2000), and Saklofske et al. (2003)
[c]Correlations from Austin et al. (2005), Brackett et al. (2006), Dawda and Hart (2000), and O'Connor and Little (2003)
[d]Correlations from Petrides and Furnham (2003)

criteria demanded of a type of intelligence. In the domain of intelligence research, Guttman and Levy (1991) have posited the existence of what many scientists consensually agree is the first law of intelligence (see also Guttman, 1992). Briefly, this law acknowledges that reliable and valid intelligence measures, without exception, correlate positively with one another (of note too, generally these correlations are of a moderate to high magnitude). Self-report EI measures clearly violate this principle. The only conclusion that can be reached, based upon an established scientific standard, is that self-report EI measures do not assess a form of intelligence, and in the interests of psychological terminology should not be labeled as such.

Relationships with maximum performance measures of EI

The divergence between self-reports and maximum performance measures of EI is clearly more than a difference in measurement methodology, with ample empirical evidence to suggest the underlying constructs are weakly related to unrelated (e.g. Goldenberg et al., 2006; MacCann et al., 2003; Zeidner et al., 2005). For example, Brackett and Mayer (2003) reported correlations of $r = 0.18$ between the MSCEIT, the flagship of EI assessment, and AES total scores. The correlation with the EQ-i was estimated at $r = 0.21$. In addition, Brackett et al. (2006) found that the performance-based and self-report measures of EI based on the same four-branch structure and definition correlated $r = 0.19$ among men and $r = 0.27$ among women.

The use of the label EI for the constructs assessed by both self-reports and maximum performance measures appears to be another case of the jingle fallacy that Thorndike (1904) cautioned against over a century ago. A case in point is the meta-analysis of Van Rooy and Viswesvaran (2004), in which results from different instruments from both ability and self-report categories were aggregated to arrive at a pooled estimate. Since the constructs assessed by the different types of instruments are clearly different entities, researchers and practitioners must choose which one of these deserves the 'emotional intelligence' label, as keeping the label for both entities invites misinterpretation. It should be evident at this juncture which set of constructs we believe deserve further consideration.

Lest there be any doubt, it is worth noting that we are unaware of any large volume, high-stakes assessment that makes use of self-reported assessment to assess any form of cognitive ability. Indeed, all forms of intelligence, achievement, and aptitude have thus far been assessed by maximal performance measures. For example, we could find no measure of nearly 70 replicable factors of intelligence covered in Carroll's (1993) major review of the literature that used a self-report methodology to assess the underlying factor. Clearly, trait or mixed models should yield up the label of EI. It is also difficult to envisage how measures of such concepts would, or could, be used in many important practical, real-life applications, more so since research also suggests that they are especially prone to faking (Grubb and McDaniel, 2007). Instead, emotional *intelligence* should be conceptualized and assessed as a set of cognitive abilities. Based on this rationale, henceforth we reserve the phrase EI to refer to an ability-based concept that may only readily be assessed using maximum performance measures, of the type that are reviewed in the passages that follow.

MAXIMUM PERFORMANCE MEASURES OF EMOTIONAL INTELLIGENCE

The MSCEIT and its earlier manifestation (the MEIS) are virtually the only comprehensive maximum performance measures of EI. Thus, almost all that is known empirically about EI is based on studies using these instruments. The first wave of validity evidence for the MEIS/MSCEIT tests focused on two main hypotheses: (1) EI subtests should relate to previously established intelligence measures; and (2) EI subtests should relate to each other more strongly than to these previously established intelligence measures, showing unique EI-related variance that prior intelligence tests cannot account for (e.g. see Mayer et al., 2000a, 2001; Roberts et al., 2001).

An important issue within this debate is whether the unique variance may be just an effect of methodological aspects of EI assessment procedures, such as the unusual scoring of these tests. The MEIS and MSCEIT both use idiosyncratic scoring rubrics (proportion-based scoring) and an unusual response format (effectiveness ratings as commonly used in Situational Judgment Tests (SJTs)), certainly as compared to cognitive tests. These unusual methods of measurement may account for some of the unique variance. The important issue is just how much unique variance is due to the method of measurement rather than the EI construct. In the passages that follow, we take up these issues in greater detail.

Response format of the MSCEIT tasks

The eight tasks of the MSCEIT are described in Table 22.2, along with a description of the knowledge, skill, and ability components of the four-branch model (see Mayer and Salovey, 1997; Mayer et al., 2002).

All the tasks from branches 1, 2, and 4 have ratings as the response format: The presence of emotions, helpfulness of a mood, similarity of emotions to sensations, or effectiveness of responses to a given situation are each rated on a five-point scale. Tasks of the third branch are multiple-choice rather than ratings, mirroring traditional tests of cognitive ability. Two of the MEIS' four understanding tasks are also multiple-choice,

whereas ratings are used for the rest of the tasks. The rating format may cause common variance between EI branches and may lower relationships between EI and other forms of intelligence. Indeed, research thus far has found that understanding can be differentiated from other EI constructs by their higher correlations with traditional tests of intelligence (see Mayer et al., 2001). When the link between EI and such tests is examined at different branches, tests of understanding are either the ones that correlate significantly with other forms of intelligence, or that correlates much more strongly than tests from the other three branches. The available evidence is presented in Table 22.3.

This table shows correlations between scores of EI branches and fluid intelligence (Gf), crystallized intelligence (Gc), and a combination of Gf/Gc. It is notable that the correlations in this table were drawn from a number of independent research studies. The evidence of stronger relationships with established forms of intelligence found for the understanding branch than for other branches is consistent with the hypothesis of a response format effect. Since all MSCEIT understanding tasks are multiple-choice, and all tasks from other branches are based on ratings, it is impossible to assess the strength of a response format effect as compared to the strength of relationships of the constructs.

MacCann (2006) examined this response format issue further with an emotion management task, the Situational Test of Emotion Management (STEM). The STEM may be administered in either multiple-choice format or with ratings. The multiple-choice format correlated more highly with Vocabulary ($r = 0.40$, $n = 111$) than scores based on ratings ($r = 0.26$, $n = 86$). Such data also support the idea that the stronger understanding-intelligence link might be related to the common response format.

This specific methodological issue illustrates a more general point: For scientific research on EI to progress systematically, research needs to be conducted with many different task paradigms. When all research

Table 22.2   Structure of the four-branch higher-order model of EI, and descriptions of tasks from the Mayer–Salovey–Caruso Emotional Intelligence Test (MSCEIT), at each branch (adapted from Mayer and Salovey, 1997; Mayer et al., 2002)

Area and branch	Corresponding MSCEIT task
Area 1: Experiential EI	
Branch 1: Perceiving and expressing emotion	
Implied knowledge, skills, and abilities: Identification of emotion in physical states, feelings, and thoughts. Identification of emotions in other people, designs, and artwork, through language, sound, appearance or behavior. Expression of emotions and needs relating to emotions. Discrimination between accurate or inaccurate, and honest or dishonest emotional expression.	*Faces*: For each human face (presented as a photo), rate the presence of five emotions of from 1 (no emotion) to 5 (extreme emotion). *Pictures*: For each picture (photos or paintings not depicting humans), rate the presence of five emotions of from 1 (no emotion) to 5 (extreme emotion).
Branch 2: Assimilating emotions in thought	
Implied knowledge, skills, and abilities: Attention can be directed by prioritizing emotions over thinking. Generation of emotions to aid judgment and memory. Emotions change the individual's perspective, allowing multiple points of view. Emotional states can be self-induced to differentially encourage different problem solving approaches.	*Sensations*: For each scenario (verbal vignettes), rate the helpfulness of three different moods from 1 (not useful) to 5 (useful). *Facilitation*: For each statement, make three judgments on the similarity of an emotion to a physical sensation from 1 (not alike) to 5 (alike).
Area 2: Strategic EI	
Branch 3: Understanding emotions	
Implied knowledge, skills, and abilities: Labeling of emotions and recognition of relations among labeled emotions. Interpretation of meanings of emotions and circumstances. Understanding complex feelings and transitions among emotions.	*Blends*: Multiple-choice questions ask which emotions are related to particular situations (presented verbally). *Changes*: Multiple-choice questions ask which combinations of emotions form which complex emotions.
Branch 4: Reflectively regulating emotions	
Implied knowledge, skills, and abilities: Openness to feelings, both pleasant and unpleasant. Reflective engagement or attachment to emotion depending on its utility or information value. Reflective monitoring and judgment of emotions in self and others. Management of emotions in oneself and others: moderating negative and enhancing positive emotions.	*Management*: For each scenario (verbal vignettes), rate the effectiveness for mood-management of four actions from 1 (very ineffective) to 5 (very effective). *Relations*: For each scenario (verbal vignettes), rate the effectiveness of three responses from 1 (very ineffective) to 5 (very effective).

is conducted with the MSCEIT, there is effectively *one* task paradigm (ratings of stimuli scored with proportion-based weights) always used to measure *one* construct (EI). With such mono-operation and mono-method biases (Shadish et al., 2002), the disentanglement of method and construct effects through the use of multi-trait-multi-method (MTMM) designs cannot be undertaken. These methodological issues in EI measurement limit the claims that can be made about EI and its relationships with

other constructs and criteria. For example, we cannot know whether EI relates to tacit knowledge because (a) these constructs are measured with the same task paradigm, or (b) EI and tacit knowledge are similar or overlapping constructs.

Scoring of the MEIS and MSCEIT

In traditional aptitude or cognitive tests such as arithmetic, reasoning, spatial skills or

Table 22.3   Correlations Between MEIS/MSCEIT Scale Scores and Fluid and Crystallized Intelligence Constructs

	Fluid Intelligence (Gf)	Crystallized intelligence (Gc)	Combination Gf /Gc
Total score	$k = 3^a$	$k = 6^b$	$k = 3^c$
	$\bar{r} = 0.18$	$\bar{r} = 0.35$	$\bar{r} = 0.31$
	[0.09, 0.27]	[0.31, 0.38]	[0.23, 0.39]
Perception	$k = 4^d$	$k = 7^e$	$k = 3^f$
	$\bar{r} = 0.10$	$\bar{r} = 0.14$	$\bar{r} = 0.01$
	[0.02, 0.17]	[0.10, 0.17]	[–0.07, 0.09]
Assimilation	$k = 3^g$	$k = 6^h$	$k = 2^i$
	$\bar{r} = 0.03$	$\bar{r} = 0.18$	$r = -0.03$
	[–0.05, 0.12]	[0.14, 0.22]	$r = 0.20$
Understanding	$k = 3^g$	$k = 7^j$	$k = 3^k$
	$\bar{r} = 0.14$	$\bar{r} = 0.40$	$\bar{r} = 0.32$
	[0.06, 0.23]	[0.37, 0.43]	[0.25, 0.39]
Management	$k = 4^l$	$k = 8^m$	$k = 2^k$
	$\bar{r} = 0.13$	$\bar{r} = 0.18$	$r = 0.11$
	[0.05, 0.20]	[0.15, 0.22]	$r = 0.28$

Estimates for the mean effect size indicated by $\bar{r}$ and the 95%-confidence interval limit estimates given in brackets are calculated based on the approach by Olkin and Pratt (see Schulze, 2004), k denotes the number of studies. Due to the small number of studies per cell, estimates based on the random effects model of meta-analysis would be untrustworthy (Schulze, 2004), the fixed effects model of meta-analysis was used instead.

[a]Correlations from Bastian et al. (2005); Ciarrochi et al. (2000); Warwick and Nettelbeck (2004).
[b]Correlations from Bastian et al. (2005); Lopes et al. (2003); Mayer et al. (1999); Roberts et al. (2001); Zeidner et al. (2005).
[c]Correlations from Lam and Kirby (2002); O'Conner and Little (2003); Schulte, et al. (2004).
[d]Correlations from Bastian et al. (2005); Ciarrochi et al. (2000); Livingstone and Day (2005); Warwick and Nettelbeck (2004).
[e]Correlations from Bastian et al. (2005), Livingstone and Day (2005); Lopes et al. (2003); Mayer et al. (1999); Roberts et al. (2001); Zeidner et al. (2005).
[f]Correlations from Lam and Kirby (2002); Livingstone and Day (2005); O'Conner and Little (2003).
[g]Correlations from Bastian et al. (2005); Livingstone and Day (2005); Warwick and Nettelbeck (2004)
[h]Correlations form Bastian et al. (2005); Livingstone and Day (2005); Lopes et al. (2003); Roberts et al. (2001); Zeidner et al. (2005).
[i]Correlations from O'Conner and Little (2003), Livingstone and Day (2005).
[j]Correlations from Bastian et al. (2005); Livingstone and Day (2005); Lopes et al. (2003); Mayer et al. (1999); Roberts et al. (2001); Zeidner et al. (2005).
[k]Correlations from Lam and Kirby (2002); Livingstone and Day (2005); O'Conner and Little (2003).
[l]Correlations from Bastian et al. (2005); Livingstone and Day (2005); Lopes et al. (2005); Warwick and Nettelbeck (2004).
[m]Correlations from Bastian et al. (2005); Livingstone and Day (2005); Lopes et al. (2003; 2005); Mayer et al. (1999); Roberts et al. (2001); Zeidner et al. (2005).

vocabulary, organized systems such as mathematics, geometry, or semantics determine the correct answer logically. There are no equivalent systems for determining the correct answer to tests assessing EI (Roberts et al., 2001). This less than desirable state-of-affairs is the case because tasks from the strategic area (especially emotion management), for example, present situations that are designed to mirror the complexity of real-life situations. With such complexity,

unambiguously applying a set of specifications or rules about emotion management would appear difficult, even if such a set of rules were available. Systems grounded in psychological (or other) theories are not used as a basis for scoring the MEIS and MSCEIT. This is true even for emotion perception, where this is demonstrably possible through various procedures (e.g. see Ekman, 2004; Matsumoto et al., 2000; Scherer et al., 2001) that we take up later in this chapter.

Instead, solutions to the problem of determining the correct answer are undertaken in two main ways: (1) expert scoring and (2) consensus scoring. A discussion of these scoring rubrics follows.

1 *Expert scoring:* This form of scoring requires a panel of experts who determine the correct answer. Both the MEIS and MSCEIT use this as a scoring alternative. Expert scoring does not solve the problem of finding a unique correct solution to the problems presented in EI tests; it simply pushes the specification of the correct answer one step back, into the specification of criteria for expertise. Academic study of the psychology of emotions certainly leads to enhanced knowledge in this domain and can therefore be considered as a reasonable criterion for expertise. However, as Roberts et al. (2001) proposed, there might be multiple domains of expertise, of which academic knowledge is only one. Other domains might include experience and procedural knowledge acquired in professions like counseling, or experience in understanding and managing people's relationships and goals (e.g. human-resource-related careers).

2 *Consensus scoring:* In this form of scoring, a normative sample first completes the test and the proportion of participants choosing each option becomes the score that is awarded for that option. For example, if 61% of the normative sample selected a scale point of '1' for rating the presence of happiness in a face, a response of '1' would get a score of 0.61 (see also Legree et al., 2005; MacCann et al., 2004).

Using consensus to deduce the best answer might be conceptually problematic in some cases, particularly for ratings. As an example, people exceptionally good at facial expression recognition might perceive nuances of expression that the ordinary person would miss, and rate faces as showing some slight level of emotion where most people see no emotion. These exceptionally sensitive people would receive low scores with consensus scoring, despite a high level of skill.

Another concern with these scoring rubrics is that consensus and expert scores should be strongly related if they both represent valid scoring methods. MSCEIT consensus scores are indeed strongly related to MSCEIT expert scores ($r = 0.93$ to $r = 0.99$; Mayer et al., 2001). However, this convergence of scoring was not true of the earlier MEIS, particularly for emotion perception measures; where some correlations were near zero (Roberts et al., 2001). This discrepancy might have occurred because expert scores for the MSCEIT were scored based on the endorsement rates in a norm sample whereas MEIS expert scores were dichotomously scored (with one point awarded to ratings selected by only two experts).

Another potential issue with consensus scoring is that it introduces another methodological difference between EI measures and tests of other forms of intelligence. This difference in methodology may partly be responsible for the empirical distinctiveness of EI. However, MacCann (2006) found that consensus scoring made little difference to the distinction between EI and either Gf or Gc. Correlations at the factorial level were 0.49 for EI and Gf, and 0.73 for EI and Gc when tests were scored conventionally (i.e. consensus scores for EI tests and dichotomous standards-based scores for other intelligence tests). When both EI and other intelligence tests were scored by consensus, the correlation between EI and Gf was 0.40, and the one between EI and Gc was 0.79. Although this result certainly needs replication, it indicates that consensus scoring may not be a major factor accounting for empirical differences between EI and other forms of intelligence.

VALIDITY ISSUES FOR MAXIMUM PERFORMANCE MEASURES OF EI

Maximum performance tests of EI need to meet the same criteria as outlined earlier in this chapter. For example, constructs assessed with EI measures must not duplicate existing constructs. Scores on EI tests should converge to some degree with results from other cognitive tests if EI is to qualify as a new type of intelligence. In addition, for EI to be a useful concept, it ought to meaningfully relate to some real-world outcomes not already predictable by existing ability and personality tests. Since there are only two different maximum performance measures of EI, that sample the four-branches – the MEIS and its successor the MSCEIT – the following subsection concentrates on available evidence from these instruments.

Relationships with measures of other forms of intelligence

When examining available findings of the MEIS and MSCEIT through the 'lens' provided by Gf/Gc theory (Horn and Cattell, 1966), it is clear that EI relates more strongly to Gc than Gf. Data relevant for this assertion appear in the previously discussed Table 22.3, where correlations are reported separately for each branch, as well as the total score on the MEIS or MSCEIT. Of note, the understanding branch shares the most robust relation with Gc, $\bar{r}$ = 0.40. Although correlations with the other branches are almost uniformly positive, they

are quite low in magnitude. However, as suggested earlier, the evidence undermining the convergent validity of the other branches might be due, in part, to the different response formats of the EI tests as compared to tests of Gf and Gc. Note too that the correlation between total EI and intelligence constructs is quite high, because understanding is part of this composite.

Relationships with personality

Table 22.4 summarizes some of the research linking MSCEIT scores to the Big Five personality dimensions. Generally, MSCEIT scores are not strongly related to any personality dimension. Indeed, only management shows small correlations, relating to agreeableness, $\bar{r}$ = 0.27, and to a lesser extent with openness, $\bar{r}$ = 0.18. Given that intelligence tasks do tend to correlate with openness ($r \approx 0.30$; Ackerman and Heggestad, 1997) and assuming that EI is a form of intelligence, a relationship of medium strength with openness can be expected.

Table 22.4   Correlations Between the MSCEIT and the Big Five Model of Personality

	O	C	E	A	N
Total score[a]	k = 8	k = 8	k = 8	k = 8	k = 8
	$\bar{r}$ = 0.12	$\bar{r}$ = 0.07	$\bar{r}$ = 0.05	$\bar{r}$ = 0.22	$\bar{r}$ = −0.07
	[0.08, 0.17]	[0.03, 0.12]	[0.00, 0.10]	[0.18, 0.27]	[−0.11, −0.02]
Perception[b]	k = 7	k = 7	k = 7	k = 7	k = 7
	$\bar{r}$ = 0.04	$\bar{r}$ = 0.01	$\bar{r}$ = 0.00	$\bar{r}$ = 0.08	$\bar{r}$ = −0.08
	[−0.02, 0.10]	[−0.05, 0.07]	[−0.06, 0.06]	[0.02, 0.14]	[−0.14, −0.03]
Assimilation[b]	k = 7	k = 7	k = 7	k = 7	k =7
	$\bar{r}$ = 0.08	$\bar{r}$ = 0.07	$\bar{r}$ = 0.01	$\bar{r}$ = 0.13	$\bar{r}$ = −0.07
	[0.02, 0.14]	[0.01, 0.12]	[−0.04, 0.07]	[0.08, 0.19]	[−0.12, −0.01]
Understanding[b]	k = 7	k = 7	k = 7	k = 7	k = 7
	$\bar{r}$ = 0.14	$\bar{r}$ = 0.05	$\bar{r}$ = 0.02	$\bar{r}$ = 0.11	$\bar{r}$ = −0.06
	[0.08, 0.20]	[0.00, 0.11]	[−0.04, 0.08]	[0.05, 0.16]	[−0.12, −0.00]
Management[b]	k = 7	k = 7	k = 7	k = 7	k = 7
	$\bar{r}$ = 0.18	$\bar{r}$ = 0.12	$\bar{r}$ = 0.10	$\bar{r}$ = 0.27	$\bar{r}$ = −0.09
	[0.13, 0.24]	[0.07, 0.18]	[0.04, 0.15]	[0.22, 0.32]	[−0.14, −0.03]

O = Openness to Experience, C = Conscientiousness, E = Extraversion, A = Agreeableness, N = Neuroticism.
[a]Correlations with the total MSCEIT score from Austin et al. (2007); Bastian et al. (2005); Brackett and Mayer, 2003; Brackett et al. (2004, 2006); Lopes et al. (2003, 2004); Schulte et al. (2004); Warwick and Nettelbeck (2004).
[b]Correlations at the branch level from Austin et al. (2007), Bastian et al. (2005); Day and Carroll (2004); Lopes et al. (2003); Lopes et al. (2004); Warwick and Nettelbeck (2004).

Arguments have been presented as to why management, but not the other branches, might relate significantly to personality factors. Mayer et al. state that all branches assess cognitive abilities but that management must also 'balance many factors including the motivational, emotion, and cognitive' and has an 'interface with personality and personal goals' (2001: 235). Although all branches of EI require processing of information concerning emotions, management is the only one that involves judgments that clearly fall outside of the realm of the intelligence domain. For example, whether one cares if other people experience negative emotions is a type of judgment that influences responses to management tasks. A person very low on agreeableness may not consider a crying or angry workmate to be particularly disturbing or problematic, whereas someone high on agreeableness might view this as a serious disturbance. Responding to management items correctly requires a correct understanding of the situation (i.e. the processing required by other branches) and also the knowledge, ability, and proclivity to fix the situation. How the latter component can be conceptually subsumed under an intelligence construct is an interesting, and an as yet unresolved, issue.

In any case, the patterns of correlations amongst EI and personality factors are quite unlike the patterns found for self-reports of EI. For the latter, the strongest relationships were with E and N, whereas for maximum performance measures of EI, E and N show the weakest correlations. Note too that the significant correlations with A for management and total EI, albeit of theoretical interest, are not too high. Clearly, variables assessed with the MEIS and MSCEIT are distinctive enough from personality factors to suggest they are outside of this domain.

Relationships with further criteria

One of the possible advantages associated with EI is the prediction of valued criteria in formal academic and workplace environments, as well as areas of life where understanding emotions and their management may be more important than reasoning or knowledge (e.g. Bastian et al., 2005; Roberts et al., 2005; Saarni, 1999). Space precludes a detailed discussion of all such relations, though they have been the topic of a recent review (Mayer et al., 2008). Some representative relations between EI and criteria covered by these commentators include:

1 Total scores on the MEIS correlate negatively with self-reported use and intention to use tobacco and alcohol (Trinidad and Johnson, 2002; Trinidad et al., 2005). Scores from the MSCEIT, the strategic area in particular, have also been found to correlate negatively with self-reported illegal drug and alcohol use (Brackett et al., 2004).

2 Bastian et al. (2005) found small to moderate relationships between anxiety and perception and understanding branch scores assessed with the MSCEIT. They also found some evidence for the incremental predictive power of MSCEIT total scores. When other forms of intelligence and personality factors were controlled, MSCEIT scores predicted an additional 6% of the variance in anxiety.

3 Gohm et al. (2005) found significant relationships between MSCEIT subscale scores and coping styles. Understanding and management were related to behavioral disengagement ($r = -0.25$ and $r = -0.21$) and denial ($r = -0.30$ and $r = -0.21$), while management also related to seeking emotional support ($r = 0.25$), and seeking instrumental social support ($r = 0.23$).

4 Brackett et al. (2006) found that MSCEIT total scores significantly predicted constructive/destructive responses after controlling for the Big Five personality factors, psychological wellbeing, empathy, life satisfaction, and verbal SAT (partial correlations ranged from -0.22 to -0.33; negative correlations are expected because of the nature of the criteria). Notably, these relations were found only for the male participants.

5 Brackett et al. (2005) found that couples where both partners were low on EI reported (a) lower relationship depth, (b) lower support and positive relationship quality, and (c) higher conflict and negative relationship quality. Similarly, Brackett et al. (2006) found that MSCEIT scores predicted confederate and judge ratings of social behaviors after a social interaction, but only among men.

6   Lopes et al. (2004) found that the management subscale of the MSCEIT predicted self-reports of positive interactions with friends ($r = 0.31$). MSCEIT management also predicted reports by friends of positive and negative interactions and emotional support ($r = 0.33$; -0.30; and 0.26). After controlling for the Big Five personality factors and gender, almost all relationships remained significant.

In summarizing the available empirical evidence for the MEIS and the MSCEIT on predicting social and emotional outcomes, the management branch, and to a lesser extent understanding, appear to be the key predictors. On this basis, research approaches that examine relationships at the branch level are more promising than efforts targeted at the top level of the four-branch EI model. Instead of a discussion of what EI predicts, it might be more informative to couch research questions in terms of what the subconstructs management or understanding predict, as these two constructs appear to be the most promising on the basis of the available criterion-related evidence. Indeed, such findings augur well for the importance of considering each of various strata of EI, rather than a single, general EI factor.

ADDRESSING METHODOLOGICAL ISSUES

Scoring responses: objective standards versus group consensus

The quality of a test depends, among other aspects, on the quality of the scoring algorithms. In the ideal case, the scoring algorithm is not a contentious matter, but self-evident, unique, and undisputed. This precondition is true for most available intelligence tests, where logic and other rule systems can be used to uniquely determine the correct response. This type of scoring will be designated as standards-based scoring in the discussion that follows. As already noted, standards-based scoring cannot be used for most EI tests. Instead, most EI tests rely on expert or consensus scoring.

Assessment of emotion perception with standards-based scoring

Tasks to assess emotion perception can be argued to be the best candidates among EI task types for standards-based scoring. In fact, tests to assess emotion perception, which employ objective scoring procedures, already exist. However, they have been developed outside the realm of more recent EI research. For example, Paul Ekman has conducted considerable research on facial expressions of basic emotions, finding cultural invariance in the expression and recognition of these emotions (e.g. Ekman, 1992; Ekman and Keltner, 1997). Specific rules relating muscular changes to facial expressions were codified decades ago in the form of the Facial Action Coding System (FACS) (Ekman and Friesen, 1978; Ekman and Rosenberg, 1997). In addition to these efforts, individual differences measures and associated training tools have been created. Examples include the Japanese and Caucasian Brief Affect Recognition Test (JACBART) (Matsumoto et al., 2000), the Micro-Expression Training Tool (METT) as well as the Subtle Expression Training Tool (SETT) designed by Ekman (2004), the DANVA2 (Diagnostic Analysis of Nonverbal Accuracy Scales; Nowicki, 2004), and PONS (Profile of Nonverbal Sensitivity; Rosenthal et al., 1979). Similarly, a measure of emotion perception in vocal expression with unequivocally defined correct responses, called the Index of Vocal Emotion Recognition (Vocal-I), is also available (Banse and Scherer, 1996; Scherer et al., 2001).

Despite the fact that such measures have been available for several years, they have not often been used in EI research. Rare exceptions are the studies by Austin (2004) and Roberts et al. (2006). By using the above-mentioned measures, both studies provide important validity evidence for available EI measures.

Austin (2004) used three different tasks with standards-based scoring to assess emotion perception, where participants had to identify a facial expression as: (1) either happy or neutral; (2) either sad or neutral; or (3) one of happiness, sadness, anger, fear, disgust, or surprise. These tasks were mutually positively correlated, but were virtually unrelated to the AES self-report of EI. Only one of the four AES components (appraisal) was positively correlated at $r = 0.22$ with scores on tasks 1 and 2, and no component showed substantial correlations with the third task. The results are hardly surprising, given the lack of relationship between maximum performance measures of EI and self-reports; and again call into question the veracity of the self-report methodology.

In the Roberts et al. (2006) study, two tasks developed outside of EI research, the JACBART and Vocal-I, as well as the MSCEIT were used. The aim was to test whether the former emotion perception tasks and the ones in the MSCEIT actually assess the same latent variable. Given all these tasks have the same underlying measurement intention they all should load on a single common factor (in the parlance of factor-analysis). The results reported by Roberts et al. (2006) clearly showed that this was not the case, thereby raising some doubts about the validity of emotion perception measurement in the MSCEIT. Notwithstanding, correlations between various emotional perception measures have been found previously to be low (e.g. Buck, 1984); and this finding appears something that requires more detailed scientific investigation.

Standards-based assessment of understanding emotions

There are no tests of emotional understanding with standards-based scoring systems available that have a research background in peer-reviewed journals. However, there exists considerable empirical evidence on the antecedents of emotion generation that might be used as the starting point to develop such a scoring system. Appraisal theories include statements about the relationship between particular combinations of appraisals to the generation of specific emotions.

One such example of an appraisal theory is Roseman's (2001) model. It outlines which sets of appraisals (e.g. unexpected circumstance-caused, motive consistent) lead to which emotions (surprise). Roseman's structural theory of the emotions has extensive

empirical evidence supporting it. It also bears close correspondence with Scherer's sequential-check appraisal theory (Scherer, 2001), which makes similar predictions. These theories have in fact been modified and retested in line with accumulating empirical evidence (e.g. Roseman, 1991, 2001; Scherer, 1999; Scherer et al., 2006). Given the empirical support for the predictions made by these theories, it appears reasonable to use them in the design of tasks to assess EI, especially the understanding branch. Predictions about emotions being caused by particular appraisals could be used to create item stimuli where particular emotions are present or absent according to these rules. Correspondingly, scoring item responses would follow the theoretical rules for situational antecedents of emotion to make it a standards-based scoring of tasks in understanding.

MacCann (2006) developed a test of emotional understanding using Roseman's model. Items were generated by translating this model's appraisal dimensions into everyday language. For example, relief-generating appraisals of circumstance-cause, certainty, motive consistency, and aversive stimuli were translated into 'an unwanted situation becomes less likely or stops altogether'. Participants were then asked how the person involved is most likely to feel and given five possible emotions including the correct response (relief). Analogs representing workplace and personal-life contexts were also created for each emotion.

The internal consistency estimate for the measure created by this process was 0.71 (MacCann, 2006; $n = 200$). Scores correlated $r = 0.49$ with vocabulary, less than $r = 0.20$ with measures of the five superfactors of personality, and $r = 0.34$ with the MEIS Stories test (study 1, $n = 200$). In addition, factor scores correlated $r = -0.12$ with state depression; $r = -0.38$ to -0.54 with state anxiety; and $r = -0.16$ with state stress (study 2, $n = 149$). Results demonstrate that standards-based assessment of understanding is possible, with test scores showing similar reliability and validity evidence to consensus-based tests like the MEIS or MSCEIT. Such results are encouraging in that they indicate a new direction and methodology for test development in EI.

Approaches to test construction: the situational judgment test methodology

The Situational Judgment Test (SJT) methodology has been primarily used by industrial/organizational psychologists with the intention to assess noncognitive qualities relevant to performance in workplace situations. McDaniel and Nguyen (2001) summarized the SJT construction methodology into three basic steps: (1) item generation, where situations are collected from a sample with subject matter knowledge and used to create item stems; (2) response option generation, where item stems are presented to members of a second sample who generate responses to the situations which are used to create response options; and (3) expert scoring, where this final set of items is presented to a group of experts who determine which response options are the best. Hanson et al. (1998) argued that the methodology is particularly well suited to assess interpersonal skills and constructs involving judgment and decision making. Thus, it seems that the SJT methodology could be adapted for use in creating measures of emotion management.

There have been at least two attempts to create emotion management tests with the SJT technique: Freudenthaler and Neubauer's (2005) Intrapersonal and Interpersonal Emotional Abilities Test, and MacCann's (2006) Situational Test of Emotion Management (STEM). However, there are clear differences in the methodology employed by these two scales. Freudenthaler and Neubauer asked test-takers to choose the alternative that would best describe their actual behavior in the given situation, rather than asking for the most effective response, and used a four-option multiple-choice response format. MacCann asked test-takers to select the most effective response. At first glance, this might seem to be just a minor and innocuous difference, but it has been shown that this is in fact a critical difference in instruction. In the SJT literature this difference is discussed under the label of 'would-do' and 'should-do' instructions, where the former has been found to have more desirable characteristics and higher criterion-related correlations (Ployhart and Erhart, 2003). Freudenthaler and Neubauer (2007) examined the same set of items under 'would-do' and 'should-do' types of instructions. Significant relationships to intelligence but not personality were found for the 'should-do' condition, and significant relationships to personality but not intelligence were found for the 'would-do' condition. Given that EI should relate to maximal performance, these results indicate that the 'should-do' type of instruction appears more appropriate for the assessment of EI and its components, and the 'would-do' type of instruction for noncognitive characteristics.

Table 22.5 shows the correlations with Gf, Gc, and the Big Five factors for the Intrapersonal and Interpersonal Emotional Abilities Test and the STEM reported by Freudenthaler and Neubauer (2007) and MacCann (2006), respectively. The most obvious difference between the two measures is the different pattern of correlations with intelligence and personality factors.

The measure with the 'would-do' instruction (with one exception) evinces higher correlations with the Big Five personality factors than the 'should-do' type instrument. Correlations of the Intrapersonal test with personality factors are also comparable in size to those for self-report EI measures. In contrast, the correlations of the STEM with personality factors are similar to those reported for the emotion management subscale of the MSCEIT, and close to what is expected for a form of intelligence. The correlations with intelligence show the opposite pattern. In Table 22.5, relatively high correlations with Gc can be found for the STEM in comparison to the intrapersonal and

Table 22.5   Reliability estimates and correlations with intelligence and personality factors for SJT measures of emotion management

	Reliability	Gf	Gc	O	C	E	A	N
Intrapersonal	0.72	−0.02 to 0.07	0.01 to 0.06	0.21	0.23	**0.37**	0.11	**−0.51**
Interpersonal	0.70	−0.01 to 0.11	0.04 to 0.06	0.25	0.08	0.08	**0.35**	−0.08
STEM	0.74	*	**0.40**	−0.15	−0.01	0.08	0.23	−0.02

Correlations greater than 0.30 are in bold text. Data for Intra- and Interpersonal is taken from Neubauer and Freudenthaler (2005), the STEM data is taken from MacCann (2006).

interpersonal tests, which do not show substantial correlation with intelligence factors. Again, the pattern for the STEM is more consistent with what is generally found for intelligence measures.

Assessing emotional intelligence with different response formats

Consistent with the multimethod approach to the assessment of EI advocated at the beginning of this chapter, the use of different response formats to assess EI and its subconstructs appears to be desirable. Specifically, such a strategy would include: (1) using multiple-choice formats not only for the assessment of the understanding branch but for other branches as well, (2) using ratings also for the assessment of the understanding branch, (3) perhaps using other possible response formats for all EI sub-components (e.g. rank ordering of response options, for the assessment of all the branches) to enhance the diversity of methodological approaches, and more specifically (4) using constructed response formats.

Assessing EI with a constructed response format is not a new undertaking. Although not under the name of EI research, this has been done previously with the Levels of Emotional Awareness Scale (LEAS) (Lane et al., 1990). The LEAS consists of 20 scenes involving two protagonists, in which test-takers describe how each protagonist would feel simply by writing down their beliefs. Responses are scored in terms of complexity of the emotions expressed from Level 0 (where no emotion-related terms are given)

through to Level 5 (where detailed emotional content for both protagonists is provided, and this content is clearly differentiable for each protagonist). Essentially, the LEAS is used to assess the identification of emotions in vignettes, and needs to be hand-scored by experts.

The LEAS is significantly correlated with only one of the Big Five factors of personality, namely openness to experience ($r = 0.29$ to 0.33; Lane et al., 1990; Ciarrochi et al., 2003). That is, the LEAS performs like a conventional intelligence test with respect to personality correlates. Correlations with verbal ability were significant and medium in size ($r = 0.27$), as were correlations to a maximum performance measure of EI (Ciarrochi et al., 2003). The LEAS correlated $r = 0.20$ with a MEIS perception test (stories); $r = 0.21$ with a MEIS understanding test (relativity) but was uncorrelated with a MEIS assimilation test or the MEIS faces test of perception. Ciarrochi et al. (2003) found relationships between the LEAS and two aspects of alexithymia in one study ($r = 0.19$ with difficulty identifying feelings and $r = 0.29$ with difficulty describing feelings) but no significant relationships in a second study. Ciarrochi et al. (2003) also found no relationships between the LEAS and alexithymia.

The LEAS seems like a reasonably promising constructed-response test of EI, with validity evidence indicating a pattern of correlations with other forms of intelligence and personality factors that would be expected for a new form of intelligence. It also shows some promising links to emotion-related criteria. However, the LEAS is limited in that it appears factorially complex, assessing in near equal measure aspects of perception and understanding.

The test development exercise with the constructed response methodology can be extended to assess perceiving emotions, understanding, and managing branches of EI, a prototypical item exemplifying this methodology is shown in Figure 22.1.

In this methodology, the same vignettes are used to assess perception, understanding, and management. Although this limits some psychometric analysis due to response dependencies, it allows a direct test of the hierarchical relationship posited between perception, understanding, and management. That is, test-takers who cannot perceive the emotions also should neither have understood why such emotions occurred, nor how to handle these emotions. No comparable test of the hierarchical nature of the four-branch model has yet been undertaken. This research design therefore has the potential to provide a means to testing this aspect of EI theories. In addition, the use of alternative instructions of the 'would-do' and 'should-do' type of emotion management would allow a direct comparison between these two methods of measurement in the domain of EI.

SUMMARY AND CONCLUDING COMMENTS

EI assessment procedures may be divided into two categories: maximum performance and self-report measures. Our review of the correlates of self-report measures shows that such measures do *not* assess intelligence, and therefore should not be used to assess EI. Our conceptual arguments for a constrained definition of EI support this conclusion (more detailed descriptions of the underlying logic of such arguments are given in MacCann, 2006; Roberts et al., 2007; Schulze et al., 2007). Nevertheless, the study of emotionality within the personality field is an interesting and potentially fruitful undertaking. Roberts et al. (2007) describe how such research may be continued with self-reports, more correctly treating these measures as a detailed and focused expansion of research within the personality domain.

Situation:

John and his best friend Steve work together for the same firm. Both of them are in line for promotion and work hard to achieve this goal. One day an email is sent around the office indicating that Steve has received a major promotion and John has received only a very minor promotion.

| *Perception/Identification* | |
| What emotions would John feel? | What emotions would Steve feel? |

| *Understanding* | |
| Why would John feel like this? | Why would Steve feel like this? |

| *Management Form 1 (Would-Do instruction)* | |
| How would John handle these feelings? | How would Steve handle these feelings? |

| *Management Form 2 (Should-Do instruction)* | |
| What is the best way for John to handle these feelings? | What is the best way for Steve to handle these feelings? |

Figure 22.1   An example of a constructed response emotional intelligence item

In contrast, maximum performance assessments show better qualities as measures of EI, although there remains much work to be done. First, the very fact that only two measures (MEIS and MSCEIT) have a research background that goes beyond initial stages of test development is a suboptimal state of affairs. Additionally, considering that these measures are quite similar in the type of tasks used, mono-operation and mono-method biases may endanger the interpretation and generalizability of test results. We present some preliminary empirical evidence that these biases *do* change the interpretation of validity evidence. As such, we recommend that a balance of diverse response formats should be used across different sub-components of EI (e.g. ratings-based, multiple-choice, rank-order formats, and free-response formats). Such a diversity of measurement methods allows an examination of whether validity evidence generalizes across all the measurement-specific operationalizations of the construct.

Another similarity across all available EI measures is the scoring of responses according to human judgment (either expert or normative samples) rather than veridical standards. We showed that standards-based scoring is not only a theoretical possibility, but has in fact been done and should be done. Such scoring would not only constitute an important remedy for the mono-method bias within scoring, but would support the validity of the assessment procedures. Of course, such new scoring protocols for EI measures would need to be examined with respect to the strength of relationship to already established procedures as used in the MEIS and MSCEIT. However, since standards-based assessment procedures are grounded in theories, the validity evidence for other scoring methods like consensus scoring should be examined against the criterion of standards-based assessments and not vice versa.

More specifically, the measurement of emotion perception could be expanded using existing tests from related areas as adjuncts or alternatives to their MEIS/MSCEIT counterparts. Several emotion recognition measures have extensive theoretical and research backgrounds, and well-validated tests (e.g. DANVA2) that could be used for standards-based measurement of emotion perception. We also presented the possibility of developing standards-based assessments for the EI branches, in particular understanding emotions. Development procedures and instruments for these branches are less advanced, but appear a promising beginning. We recommend that standards-based assessment should be used wherever possible, with a standards-based approach to test construction expanded into the other branches of EI.

The last decade of EI research was characterized both by a cornucopia of instruments, publications, and findings, and at the same time by a very specific and narrow measurement methodology. Part of this apparent contradiction stems from the divide between self-report and maximal performance measures of EI. The overabundance of self-report instruments has to some extent obscured the fact that there has really only been *one* research tradition with *one* measurement model and methodology researching emotional *intelligence*. While self-report research has generated useful discussion on such issues as identifying a relevant criterion-space for EI; delineating the boundaries between emotion, personality, and cognition; and the importance of emotional phenomena in a variety of applied settings, we would argue that such research has been largely irrelevant to advancing the accurate measurement of EI. To achieve the goal of accurate and systematic measurement of EI, instrumentation needs to expand beyond a single paradigm to provide a more reliable estimate of the generalizability of the construct. This expansion is now just beginning, with researchers using new paradigms from emotions research, and new test construction techniques from I/O psychology. We are hopeful that the next decade will be one of exciting innovation within the field, and that the bridge between our knowledge of EI, and the popular demand for applications of EI will have narrowed.

ACKNOWLEDGEMENTS

This research was supported in part by Army Research Institute Contract W91WAW-07-C-0025 to the Educational Testing Service. We thank Helen Blank, Greg Boyle, Dan Eignor, Nathan Kogan, and Lydia Liu for helpful suggestions on earlier versions of this manuscript. The views expressed here are those of the authors and do not reflect on the Educational Testing Service. Correspondence concerning this article should be directed to Richard D. Roberts, Center for New Constructs, R&D, MS 16-R, Educational Testing Service, Rosedale Road, Princeton, NJ, 08541, US. E-mail: RRoberts@ets.org

REFERENCES

Ackerman, P.L. and Heggestad, E.D. (1997) 'Intelligence, personality and interests: Evidence for overlapping traits', *Psychology Bulletin*, 121(2): 219–45.

Ashton, M.C., Lee, K., Vernon, P.A. and Jang, K.L. et al. (2000) 'Fluid intelligence, crystallized intelligence, and the openness/intellect factor', *Journal of Research in Personality*, 34(2): 198–207.

Austin, E.J. (2004) 'An investigation of the relationship between trait emotional intelligence and emotional task performance', *Personality and Individual Differences*, 36(8): 1855–64.

Austin, E.J., Farrelly, D., Black, C. et al. (2007) 'Emotional intelligence, Machiavellianism and emotional manipulation: Does EI have a dark side?,' *Personality and Individual Differences*, 43(1): 179–89.

Austin, E.J. and Saklofske, D.H. (2005) 'Far too many intelligences? On the communalities and differences between social, practical, and emotional intelligences', in R. Schulze and R.D. Roberts (eds), *Emotional Intelligence: An International Handbook*. Cambridge, MA: Hogrefe & Huber, pp. 107–28.

Banse, R. and Scherer, K.R. (1996) 'Acoustic profiles in vocal emotion expression', *Journal of Personality and Social Psychology*, 70(3): 614–36.

Bar-On, R. (1997) *Bar-On Emotional Quotient Inventory (EQ-i): Technical Manual*. Toronto: Multi-Health Systems.

Barchard, K.A. and Hakstian, R.A. (2004) 'The nature and measurement of emotional intelligence abilities: Basic dimensions and their relationships with other cognitive ability and personality variables', *Educational and Psychological Measurement*, 64(3): 437–62.

Bastian, V.A., Burns, N.R. and Nettelbeck, T. (2005) 'Emotional intelligence predicts life skills, but not as well as personality and cognitive abilities', *Personality and Individual Differences*, 39(6): 1135–45.

Brackett, M.A. and Mayer, J.D. (2003) 'Convergent, discriminant, and incremental validity of competing measures of emotional intelligence', *Personality and Social Psychology Bulletin*, 29(9): 1147–58.

Brackett, M.A., Mayer, J.D. and Warner, R.M. (2004) 'Emotional intelligence and its relation to everyday behaviour', *Personality and Individual Differences*, 36(6): 1387–1402.

Brackett, M.A., Rivers, S.E., Shiffman, S., Lerner, N. and Salovey, P. (2006) 'Relating emotional abilities to social functioning: A comparison of self-report and performance measures of emotional intelligence', *Journal of Personality and Social Psychology*, 91(4): 780–95.

Brackett, M.A., Warner, R.M. and Bosco, J.S. (2005) 'Emotional intelligence and relationship quality among couples', *Personal Relationships*, 12(2): 197–212.

Buck, R. (1984) *The Communication of Emotion*. New York: Guilford.

Carroll, J.B. (1993) *Human Cognitive Abilities: A Survey of Factor-analytic Studies*. New York: Cambridge University Press.

Ciarrochi, J.V., Caputi, P. and Mayer, J.D. (2003) 'The distinctiveness and utility of a measure of trait emotional awareness', *Personality and Individual Differences*, 34(8): 1477–90.

Ciarrochi, J.V., Chan, A.Y.C. and Caputi, P. (2000) 'A critical evaluation of the emotional intelligence construct', *Personality and Individual Differences*, 28(3): 539–61.

Ciarrochi, J.V., Scott, G., Deane, F.P. and Heaven, P.C.L. (2003) 'Relations between social and emotional competence and mental health: A construct validation study', *Personality and Individual Differences*, 35(8): 1947–63.

Costa, P.T. Jr. and McCrae, R.R. (1992) *Revised NEO Personality Inventory (NEO-PI-R) and NEO Five-Factor Inventory (NEO-FFM) Professional Manual*. Odessa, FL: Psychological Assessment Resources.

Day, A.L. and Carroll, S.A. (2004) 'Using an ability-based measure of emotional intelligence to predict individual performance, group performance, and group citizenship behaviours', *Personality and Individual Differences*, 36: 1443–59.

De Raad, B. (2005) 'The trait-coverage of emotional intelligence', *Personality and Individual Differences*, 38(3): 673–87.

Ekman, P. (1992) 'Are there basic emotions?', *Psychological Review*, 99(3): 550–3.

Ekman, P. (2004) MicroExpression Training Tools (METT) and Subtle Expression Training Tools (SETT). Available from <http://www.paulekman.com/>.

Ekman, P. and Friesen, W.V. (1978) *Facial Action Coding System*. Palo Alto, CA: Consulting Psychologists Press.

Ekman, P. and Keltner, D. (1997) 'Universal facial expressions of emotion: An old controversy and new findings', in U.C. Segerstrale and P. Molnar (eds), *Non-verbal Communication: Where Nature Meets Culture*. Mahwah, NJ: Erlbaum, pp. 27–46.

Ekman, P. and Rosenberg, E.L. (1997) *What the Face Reveals: Basic and Applied Studies of Spontaneous Expression Using the Facial Action Coding System (FACS)*. New York: Oxford University Press.

Freudenthaler, H.H. and Neubauer, A.C. (2005) 'Emotional intelligence: The convergent and discriminant validities of intra- and interpersonal abilities', *Personality and Individual Differences*, 39(3): 569–79.

Freudenthaler, H.H. and Neubauer, A.C. (2007) 'Measuring emotional management abilities: Further evidence of the importance to distinguish between typical and maximum performance', *Personality and Individual Differences*, 42(8): 1561–72.

Gohm, C.L., Corser, G.C. and Dalsky, D.J. (2005) 'Emotional intelligence under stress: Useful, unnecessary, or irrelevant?', *Personality and Individual Differences*, 39(6): 1017–28.

Goldenberg, I., Matheson, K. and Mantler, J. (2006) 'The assessment of emotional intelligence: A comparison of performance-based and self-report methodologies', *Journal of Personality Assessment*, 86(1): 33–45.

Grubb, W.L. and McDaniel, M.A. (2007) 'The fakability of Bar-On's Emotional Quotient Inventory Short Form: Catch me if you can', *Human Performance*, 20(1): 43–59.

Guttman, L. (1992) 'The irrelevance of factor analysis for the study of group differences', *Multivariate Behavioral Research*, 27(2): 175–204.

Guttman, L. and Levy, S. (1991) 'Two structural laws for intelligence tests', *Intelligence*, 15(1): 79–103.

Hanson, M.A., Horgen, K.E. and Borman, W.C. (1998) 'Situational judgment: An alternative approach to selection test development', Paper presented at the 40th International Military Testing Association Conference, Pensacola, Florida.

Horn, J.L. and Cattell, R.B. (1966) 'Refinement and test of the theory of fluid and crystallized intelligence', *Journal of Educational Psychology*, 57(5): 253–70.

Lane, R.D., Quinlan, D.M., Schwartz, G.E., Walker, P.A. and Zeitlin, S.B. (1990) 'The Levels of Emotional Awareness Scale: A cognitive-developmental measure of emotion', *Journal of Personality Assessment*, 55(1–2): 124–34.

Legree, P.J., Psotka, J., Tremble, T. and Bourne, D.R. (2005) 'Using consensus based measurement to assess emotional intelligence', in R. Schulze and R.D. Roberts (eds), *Emotional Intelligence: An International Handbook*. Cambridge, MA: Hogrefe & Huber, pp. 155–79.

Livingstone, H.A. and Day, A.L. (2005) 'Comparing the construct and criterion-related validity of ability-based and mixed-model measures of emotional intelligence', *Educational and Psychological Measurement*, 65(5): 757–79.

Lopes, P.N., Brackett, M.A., Nezlek, J.B., Schütz, A., Sellin, I. and Salovey, P. (2004) 'Emotional intelligence and social interaction', *Personality and Social Psychology Bulletin*, 30(8): 1018–34.

Lopes, P. N., Salovey, P. and Straus, R. (2003) 'Emotional intelligence, personality, and the perceived quality of social relationships',

Personality and Individual Differences, 35(3): 641–58.

Lopes, P.N., Salovey, P., Cote, S. et al. (2005) 'Emotion Regulation Abilities and the Quality of Social Interaction', *Emotion,* 5(1): 113–18.

MacCann, C. (2006) 'New approaches to measuring emotional intelligence: Exploring methodological issues with two new assessment tools', Unpublished doctoral dissertation, University of Sydney, Australia.

MacCann, C., Matthews, G., Zeidner, M. and Roberts, R.D. (2003) 'Psychological assessment of emotional intelligence: A review of self-report and performance-based testing', *International Journal of Organizational Analysis*, 11(3): 247–74.

MacCann, C., Roberts, R.D., Matthews, G. and Zeidner, M. (2004) 'Consensus scoring and empirical option weighting of performance-based Emotional Intelligence (EI) tests', *Personality and Individual Differences*, 36(3): 645–62.

Matsumoto, D., LeRoux, J., Wilson-Cohn, C., Raroque, J., Kooken, K., Ekman, P. et al. (2000) 'A new test to measure emotion recognition ability: Matsumoto and Ekman's Japanese and Caucasian Brief Affect Recognition Test (JACBART)', *Journal of Nonverbal Behavior*, 24(3): 179–209.

Matthews, G., Zeidner, M. and Roberts, R.D. (2002) *Emotional Intelligence: Science and Myth*. Boston, MA: MIT Press.

Matthews, G., Zeidner, M. and Roberts, R.D. (2007) (eds), *The Science of Emotional Intelligence: Knowns and Unknowns*. Oxford: Oxford University Press.

Mayer, J.D., Caruso, D.R. and Salovey, P. (1999) 'Emotional intelligence meets traditional standards for an intelligence', *Intelligence*, 27(4): 267–98.

Mayer, J.D., Caruso, D.R. and Salovey, P. (2000a) 'Selecting a measure of emotional intelligence: The case for ability scales', in R. Bar-On and J.D.A. Parker (eds), *Handbook of Emotional Intelligence*. San Francisco: Jossey-Bass, pp. 320–42.

Mayer, J.D., Panter, A., Salovey, P., Caruso, D.R. and Sitarenios, G. (2005) 'A discrepancy in analyses of the MSCEIT – Resolving the mystery and understanding its implications: A reply to Gignac (2005)', *Emotion*, 5(2): 236–7.

Mayer, J.D., Roberts, R.D. and Barsade, S.G. (2008) 'Emerging research in emotional intelligence', *Annual Review of Psychology*, 59, 507–36.

Mayer, J.D. and Salovey, P. (1997) 'What is emotional intelligence?', in P. Salovey and D. Sluyter (eds), *Emotional Development and EI: Educational Implications*. New York: Basic Books, pp. 3–34.

Mayer, J.D., Salovey, P. and Caruso, D.R. (2000b) 'Models of emotional intelligence', in R.J. Sternberg (ed.), *Handbook of Intelligence*. Cambridge: Cambridge University Press, pp. 396–420.

Mayer, J.D., Salovey, P. and Caruso, D.R. (2002) *Mayer-Salovey-Caruso Emotional Intelligence Test (MSCEIT) User's Manual*. Toronto, Canada: Multi-Health Systems.

Mayer, J.D., Salovey, P., Caruso, D.R. and Sitarenios, G. (2001) 'Emotional intelligence as a standard intelligence', *Emotion*, 1(3): 232–42.

Mayer, J.D., Salovey, P., Caruso, D.R. and Sitarenios, G. (2003) 'Measuring emotional intelligence with the MSCEIT V2.0', *Emotion*, 3(1): 97–105.

McDaniel, M.A. and Nguyen, N.T. (2001) 'Situational judgment tests: A review of practice and constructs assessed', *International Journal of Selection and Assessment*, 9(1–2): 103–13.

Neubauer, A.C. and Freudenthaler, H.H. (2005) 'Models of emotional intelligence', in R. Schulze and R.D. Roberts (eds), *Emotional Intelligence: An International Handbook*. Cambridge, MA: Hogrefe & Huber, pp. 31–50.

Newsome, S., Day, A.L. and Catano, V.M. (2000) 'Assessing the predictive validity of emotional intelligence', *Personality and Individual Differences*, 29(6): 1005–16.

Nowicki, S. (2004) 'A manual for the Diagnostic Analysis of Nonverbal Accuracy tests (DANVA)', Unpublished manuscript, Department of Psychology, Emory University.

Palmer, B., Gignac, G., Manocha, R. and Stough, C. (2005) 'A psychometric evaluation of the Mayer-Salovey-Caruso Emotional Intelligence Test Version 2.0', *Intelligence*, 33(3): 285–305.

Perez, J.C., Petrides, K.V. and Furnham, A. (2005) 'Measuring trait emotional intelligence', in R. Schulze and R.D. Roberts (eds), *Emotional Intelligence: An International*

Handbook. Cambridge, MA: Hogrefe & Huber, pp. 181–202.

Petrides, K.V. and Furnham, A. (2000) 'On the dimensional structure of emotional intelligence', *Personality and Individual Differences*, 29(2): 313–20.

Petrides, K.V. and Furnham, A. (2001) 'Trait emotional intelligence: Psychometric investigation with reference to established trait taxonomies', *European Journal of Personality*, 15(6): 425–48.

Petrides, K.V. and Furnham, A. (2003) 'Trait emotional intelligence: Behavioural validation in two studies of emotion recognition and reactivity to mood induction', *European Journal of Personality*, 17(1): 39–57.

Ployhart, R. E. and Erhart, M. G. (2003) 'Be careful what you ask for: Effects of response instructions on the construct validity and reliability of situational judgment tests', *International Journal of Selection and Assessment*, 11(1):1–16.

Roberts, R.D., Schulze, R., O'Brien, K., MacCann, C., Reid, J. and Maul, A. (2006) 'Exploring the validity of the Mayer-Salovey-Caruso Emotional Intelligence Test (MSCEIT) with established emotions measures', *Emotion*, 6(4): 663–9.

Roberts, R.D., Schulze, R., Zeidner, M. and Matthews, G. (2005) 'Understanding, measuring, and applying emotional intelligence: What have learned? What have missed?', In R. Schulze and R.D. Roberts (eds), *Emotional Intelligence: An International Handbook*. Cambridge, MA: Hogrefe & Huber, pp. 311–41.

Roberts, R.D., Zeidner, M. and Matthews, G. (2001) 'Does emotional intelligence meet traditional standards for an intelligence? Some new data and conclusions', *Emotion*, 1(3): 196–231.

Roberts, R.D., Zeidner, M. and Matthews, G. (2007) 'Emotional intelligence: Knowns and unknowns', in G. Matthews, M. Zeidner and R.D. Roberts (eds), *The Science of Emotional Intelligence: Knowns and Unknowns*. New York: Oxford University Press, pp. 419–74.

Roseman, I.J. (1991) 'Appraisal determinants of discrete emotions', *Cognition and Emotion*, 5(3): 161–200.

Roseman, I.J. (2001) 'A model of appraisal in the emotion system: Integrating theory, research, and applications', in K.R. Scherer, A. Schorr and T. Johnstone (eds), *Appraisal Processes in Emotion: Theory, Methods, Research*. New York: Oxford University Press, pp. 68–91.

Rosenthal, R., Hall, J.A., DiMatteo, M.R., Rogers, P.L. and Archer, D. (1979) *Sensitivity to Nonverbal Communication: The PONS Test*. Baltimore, MD: Johns Hopkins University Press.

Saarni, C. (1999) *The Development of Emotional Competence*. New York: Guilford.

Salovey, P., Bedell, B.T., Detweiler, J.B. and Mayer, J.D. (2000) 'Coping intelligently: Emotional intelligence and the coping process', in C.R. Snyder (ed.), *Coping: The Psychology of What Works*. New York: Oxford University Press, pp. 141–64.

Salovey, P. and Mayer, J.D. (1989) 'Emotional intelligence', *Imagination, Cognition and Personality*, 9(3): 185–211.

Scherer, K.R. (1999) 'On the sequential nature of appraisal processes: Indirect evidence from a recognition task', *Cognition and Emotion*, 13(6): 763–93.

Scherer, K.R. (2001) 'Appraisal considered as a process of multilevel sequential checking', in K.R. Scherer, A. Schorr and T. Johnstone (eds), *Appraisal Processes in Emotion: Theory, Methods, Research*. New York: Oxford University Press, pp. 92–120.

Scherer, K.R., Banse, R. and Wallbott, H.G. (2001) 'Emotion inferences from vocal expression correlate across languages and cultures', *Journal of Cross-Cultural Psychology*, 32(1): 76–92.

Schulze, R. (2004) *Meta-analysis: A Comparison of Approaches*. Cambridge, MA: Hogrefe & Huber.

Schulze, R., Wilhelm, O. and Kyllonen, P.C. (2007) 'Approaches to the assessment of emotional intelligence', in G. Matthews, M. Zeidner and R.D. Roberts (eds), *The Science of Emotional Intelligence: Knowns and Unknowns*. New York: Oxford University Press, pp. 199–229.

Schutte, N.S., Malouff, J.M., Hall, L.E., Haggerty, D.J., Cooper, I.T., Golden, C.J. et al. (1998) 'Development and validation of a measure of emotional intelligence', *Personality and Individual Differences*, 25(2): 167–77.

Shadish, W.R. Jr., Cook, T.D. and Campbell, D.T. (2002) *Experimental and Quasi-experimental*

Designs for Generalized Causal Inference. Boston, MA: Houghton-Mifflin.

Tett, R.P., Fox, K.E. and Wang, A. (2005) 'Development and validation of a self-report measure of emotional intelligence as a multidimensional trait domain', *Personality and Social Psychology Bulletin*, 31(7): 859–88.

Thorndike, E.L. (1904) *An Introduction to the Theory of Mental and Social Measurements*. New York: Teachers College, Columbia University.

Trinidad, D.R. and Johnson, C.A. (2002) 'The association between emotional intelligence and early adolescent tobacco and alcohol use', *Personality and Individual Differences*, 32(1): 95–105.

Trinidad, D.R., Unger, J.B., Chou, C.-P. and Johnson, C. (2005) 'Emotional intelligence and acculturation to the United States: Interactions on the perceived social consequences of smoking in early adolescents',

Substance Use and Misuse, 40(11): 1697–706.

Van Rooy, D.L. and Viswesvaran, C. (2004) 'Emotional intelligence: A meta-analytic investigation of predictive validity and nomological net', *Journal of Vocational Behaviour*, 65(1): 71–95.

Warwick, J. and Nettelbeck, T. (2004) 'Emotional intelligence is?', *Personality and Individual Differences*, 37(5): 1091–100.

Wilhelm, O. (2005) 'Measures of emotional intelligence: Practice and standards', in R. Schulze and R.D. Roberts (eds), *Emotional Intelligence: An International Handbook*. Cambridge, MA: Hogrefe & Huber, pp. 131–54.

Zeidner, M., Shani-Zinovich, I., Matthews, G. and Roberts, R.D. (2005) 'Assessing emotional intelligence in gifted and non-gifted high school students: Outcomes depend on the measure', *Intelligence*, 33(4): 369–91.

PART V

Implicit, Projective and Objective Measures of Personality

23

The Nonverbal Personality Questionnaire and the Five-Factor Nonverbal Personality Questionnaire

Ryan Y. Hong and Sampo V. Paunonen

In this chapter, we describe the development and the psychometric properties of two new nonverbal personality questionnaires. The first measure is called the Nonverbal Personality Questionnaire (NPQ) and the second is the Five-Factor Nonverbal Personality Questionnaire (FF-NPQ). What makes these two measures novel is that they do not employ verbal item content. Nonverbal stimuli are used as items instead, in an otherwise standard paper-and-pencil personality questionnaire (Paunonen et al., 2004).

NONVERBAL PERSONALITY ASSESSMENT

Nonverbal measures of personality have, of course, existed for many years. Examples include the popular Rorschach inkblot test and the thematic apperception test (TAT).

Those measures, however, are different from the ones to be described in this chapter in at least three important ways: (a) the assessment of implicit/unconscious versus explicit/conscious personality characteristics, (b) the 'signs versus samples' based interpretation of test responses, and (c) the unstructured versus structured nature of item response alternatives.

The Rorschach and the TAT are examples of projective tests, in which test takers' responses to ambiguous pictorial stimuli are considered to represent their unconscious psychological motives. Interpretation of the Rorschach or TAT protocols may or may not corroborate results from more objectively scored measures of the same psychological constructs. For instance, non-correspondence has been found between the TAT and objective measures such as the Personality Research Form (PRF) (Jackson, 1984) on the same motives (e.g. affiliation, dominance).

The differences have been attributed to the different levels of awareness in processing self-information (McClelland et al., 1989). Specifically, the TAT is purported to tap unconscious implicit motives, whereas the PRF is supposed to capture conscious and explicitly articulated motives. The NPQ and FF-NPQ, despite their similarity to the TAT in using a nonverbal stimulus item format, are considered to be measures of personality characteristics and explicit psychological motives that are in conscious awareness, very much like the PRF.

The second difference between projective tests and the present nonverbal measures concerns the interpretation of test responses as either 'signs' of underlying psychological constructs or 'samples' of behaviors (Loevinger, 1957). Whereas projective tests are generally associated with the notion that test responses are behavioral signs that are symptomatic of inner psychological dispositions, the responses on the NPQ and FF-NPQ are to be considered as behavioral samples reflective of actual personality traits. Thus, a person's response to a dominance scale item is driven by his or her level of dominance, which in turn is reflective of that internal psychological trait. Therefore, to the extent that someone endorses the nonverbal items of an NPQ or FF-NPQ personality scale, he or she is manifesting behaviors consistent with the trait being assessed by those items, and the person would obtain a corresponding high trait score. This samples-based notion of test item responding underlies many paper-and-pencil personality questionnaires such as the PRF (Jackson, 1984) and the Jackson Personality Inventory (Jackson, 1994).

Another difference between most projective tests and the present nonverbal personality measures has to do with the possible response options to the items. Whereas the Rorschach and the TAT are both unstructured, in the sense that examinees are allowed to generate open-ended verbal responses to the items, the NPQ and FF-NPQ are structured measures. This means that a person completing the tests must choose his or her responses to each nonverbal item from a series of alternatives or response options. This allows for objective scoring of the scales and precludes problems with inter-scorer reliability.

THE NEED FOR NONVERBAL PERSONALITY MEASURES

A nonverbal measure of personality offers several advantages over verbal measures in the study of human behavior. These advantages, which are described in separate sections below, pertain to the assessment of special populations, the search for a universal structure to personality, the evaluation of the cultural effects on personality assessments, and the study of person perception.

Assessment of special populations

Standard verbal assessments of personality are limited to respondents who can read and understand the items contained in traditional paper-and-pencil forms. Sometimes, however, one might be interested in assessing individuals who are unable to comprehend such items. Such people could include: (a) young children who have not yet developed adequate reading skills; (b) specific groups of individuals having short attention spans who cannot concentrate long enough to respond to a long list of personality-relevant questions (e.g. some clinical patients); (c) illiterate adults who have never learned to read at a level necessary to understand the typical personality statement; and, of course, (d) people for whom the language of the test is not their primary language and who may not be able to read the test items (e.g. respondents in foreign cultures). The nonverbal items of the type found in the NPQ and the FF-NPQ can circumvent the problem of assessing personality in these special populations.

Testing a model of universal trait structure

Some researchers are interested in the extent to which there are cross-cultural differences and similarities in the structure of personality (see Rolland, 2002, and Triandis and Euh, 2002, for reviews). There is increasing evidence that the Big Five personality dimensions are universally replicable (e.g. McCrae et al., 2005; McCrae and Costa, 1997; Rolland, 2002; but see De Raad and Peabody, 2005). However, the vast majority of studies in this area of inquiry have relied predominantly on traditional verbal measures of personality where lingering concerns regarding equivalence of the different linguistic translations persist. The NPQ and FF-NPQ present researchers alternative tools to examine this issue, precluding the need for translations and the consequent problems of item equivalence. In particular, as noted by Rolland (2002: 12), nonverbal measures can minimize language effects in the structuring of personality trait data.

Another advantage of nonverbal assessments for structural studies of personality concerns the use of such measures among cross-cultural samples in which language proficiency is lacking (e.g. people with lower educational attainment). One criticism in this literature is that the vast majority of the cross-cultural replication studies of the five-factor model have involved well-educated college student samples who may be poorly representative of other members within those cultures. The NPQ and FF-NPQ can be easily administered to individuals with lower language skills to increase representativeness of cultural samples in this area of research. Unless more personality data are gathered from population-representative cross-cultural samples, the extent to which the Big Five personality factors are universal and replicable beyond well-educated individuals is still up for debate.

Cultural effects on personality assessments

In an increasingly globalized world, where individuals are often exposed to multiple cultural influences, psychologists are increasingly interested in the effects such varied cultural influences might have on people's cognitions, affective states, and behaviors. Indeed, there is some compelling evidence to suggest that bicultural individuals display attitudes, values, and self-construals consistent with either one culture or the other, depending on which cultural knowledge system is more cognitively accessible and salient at the moment. This phenomenon is called the cultural frame switching (CFS) effect (Y. Hong et al., 1997, 2000). For example, Hong Kong Chinese subjects familiar with American culture were, as predicted, more likely to provide external (vs. internal) causal attributions and show cooperative (vs. competitive) behaviors to in-group members when primed with Chinese (vs. American) cultural icons (Y. Hong et al., 2003, Wong and Hong, 2005). Similar CFS effects have been found with Dutch–Greek biculturals (Verkuyten and Pouliasi, 2002, 2006).

More recently, the CFS hypothesis has been applied to the domain of personality traits. Ramírez-Esparza et al. (2006) examined whether English–Spanish bilinguals exhibit cultural frame switching when describing their personalities, such that discernable personality differences can be elicited within a bilingual individual when different assessment languages are used. The authors, through a series of studies, demonstrated that English–Spanish bilinguals reported being more extraverted, agreeable, and conscientious when responding to the same personality inventory in English translation than in Spanish translation. Although the results were not entirely consistent with their hypothesis (e.g. bilinguals were also expected to report lower agreeableness in English than in Spanish), the authors interpreted their results as generally in support of the CFS hypothesis.

We see tremendous value in using a well-validated nonverbal personality instrument to address some of these issues revolving around the CFS effect in personality research. A nonverbal personality questionnaire can help ascertain whether the language effects found for personality assessments are substantive or spurious. Ramírez-Esparza et al. (2006), for example, have not entirely ruled out the possibility that the observed personality differences in their study were mere artifacts arising from wording differences, and their associated differences in meaning, characterizing their translated verbal questionnaires. With a nonverbal personality questionnaire, one can prime bilinguals into 'using' the different languages by presenting questionnaire instructions in the respective languages. In fact, one can even explicitly tell the bilinguals to think in a particular language when completing the nonverbal questionnaire. In such a scenario, any response differences cannot be due to the lack of equivalence between two language variants of the same item – all items are identical across conditions. Hence, if differences in personality are still found using such a strategy, then the charge of CFS effects merely reflecting spurious language effects due to problems in translation is weakened. In summary, given the increasing interest in the interplay between culture and personality, we see a unique opportunity for nonverbal personality questionnaires such as the NPQ and FF-NPQ to play an important role in exploring the CFS phenomenon.

Studies in person perception

The nonverbal items of the NPQ and the FF-NPQ were initially created for a study in person perception (Paunonen and Jackson, 1979). Those items were used in that study both as target descriptors and as measures of personality inferences. Observer judges were first presented with certain personality characteristics describing a hypothetical target person. The target description was either a verbal scenario consisting of statements describing some of the person's characteristic behaviors, or a nonverbal scenario depicting the same personality characteristics but consisting of behavior drawings taken from the NPQ item pool. Judges were then asked

to make inferences about that target's other personality characteristics. The judgments were recorded on the usual verbal personality scales or on equivalent nonverbal personality scales.

The purpose of the study by Paunonen and Jackson (1979) was to evaluate certain issues in person perception having to do with semantic determinants of personality attributions. But their procedure of describing target personality characteristics using nonverbal NPQ or FF-NPQ items can be used more generally. For example, someone might be interested in manipulating target personality in a classic person perception paradigm, but he or she might disapprove of standard verbal descriptions of target characteristics (not realistic enough) and be unwilling to use real targets (high cost, poor control of behaviors). Nonverbal illustrations depicting trait-relevant behaviors of the type found in the NPQ and the FF-NPQ might be a suitable compromise. Such behavior depictions have several advantages for studies in person perception: (a) they tend to have more realism than do verbal statements of behavior, potentially leading to studies with more external validity; (b) the nonverbal items have been constructed to be relatively pure exemplars of particular personality traits, allowing one to craft a carefully-prescribed target persona; and (c) target characteristics can be easily manipulated and standardized, resulting in excellent control across different experimental conditions.

THE NPQ

Construction of the NPQ

As mentioned above, the NPQ initially arose from research on person perception (Paunonen and Jackson, 1979) where drawings depicting a line-figure person engaging in specific behaviors under specific situational contexts were used. The illustrated behaviors were each intended to depict one of 17 traits in Murray's (1938) system of needs, with between 9 and 14 behavior scenarios each. Such needs, or traits, include affiliation, dominance, nurturance, and so on, and are measured by more traditional verbal personality inventories, such as the PRF.

In fact, the NPQ was designed as a nonverbal counterpart to the PRF. An example nonverbal item, depicting thrill-seeking behavior, can be seen in a reproduction of the NPQ instruction page shown in Figure 23.1. Other examples of NPQ items can be found in

NONVERBAL PERSONALITY QUESTIONNAIRE

Instructions

Attached is a **Picture Booklet** containing a series of illustrations depicting a *central figure* (the one with the *hair* drawn in) performing specific behaviors in certain situations.

Please look at each illustration and rate the *likelihood that you would engage in the type of behavior* shown.

Using the **Answer Sheet**, record your responses by selecting an appropriate number from the 7-point rating scale. Consider the example below:

Example

7 - **extremely likely** that I would perform this type of behavior
6 - **very likely** that I would perform this type of behavior
5 - **moderately likely** that I would perform this type of behavior
4 - **neither likely nor unlikely** that I would perform this type of behavior
3 - **moderately unlikely** that I would perform this type of behavior
2 - **very unlikely** that I would perform this type of behavior
1 - **extremely unlikely** that I would perform this type of behavior

Rating. *6*

In this example the person has responded that it would be *very likely* that he/she would engage in the kind of activity in which the central figure is engaging. Your own response might have been different.

In a similar manner, consider each illustration in the **Picture Booklet** and estimate the likelihood that you would engage in the type of behavior depicted by the central figure.

Please record your responses on the 7-point rating scales printed on the separate **Answer Sheet**. Do not mark the **Picture Booklet** or any other materials.

Figure 23.1   Reproduction of the NPQ instruction page

Paunonen and Jackson (1979) and Paunonen et al. (1990, 1996, 2001).

As seen in Figure 23.1, the instruction to a respondent completing the NPQ involves asking him or her to estimate 'the likelihood that you would engage in the type of behavior shown', using a seven-point rating scale. Respondents are not asked whether they have ever performed the depicted behavior, or even whether they are likely to perform the behavior exactly as illustrated. Instead, the rating instructions emphasize the idea that each behavior item in the questionnaire is an exemplar of a cluster or domain of related behaviors. Note that both male and female respondents should be able to identify with the depicted behaviors as the central character in each item is portrayed in a sex-neutral manner.

The scale development of the NPQ has been documented extensively elsewhere (Paunonen and Ashton, 2002; Paunonen et al., 1990, 2004), hence it is only briefly summarized here. As mentioned above, the NPQ was intended as a nonverbal counterpart to the verbal PRF. The PRF (form-E) consists of 20 trait scales and two validity scales; each scale has 16 behavior-in-situation type verbal items. In constructing the nonverbal item set, it became apparent that it was extremely difficult to create nonverbal items for three PRF scales (i.e. change, cognitive structure, and defendence) because these traits typically refer to cognitive and affective tendencies that are not directly observable. These three Murray needs were hence eliminated from further consideration in preparing the nonverbal items. Furthermore, the nonverbal abasement scale was also deleted later in the test construction process because of relatively poor item and scale properties.

Working with an initial item pool of 202 nonverbal items, efforts were then made to retain the best eight items for each nonverbal scale. The final product was the 136-item NPQ, consisting of 16 eight-item trait scales and one infrequency validity scale. The infrequency scale contains eight items that are likely to be endorsed only by someone who is completing the questionnaire thoughtlessly. In the latest NPQ version (Paunonen et al., 2004), the infrequency scale has been renamed the deviation scale, and it measures an individual's tendency to engage in socially deviant behaviors such as stealing and destroying property. High deviation scale scores can also mean random responding or purposeful distortion. Table 23.1 (top panel) presents the names and descriptions of the scales of the NPQ.

Psychometric properties

In this section, we review information concerning the psychometric properties of the NPQ in the context of several cross-cultural studies (Amelang et al., 2002; Lee et al., 2000; Paunonen et al., 1990, 1992, 1996, 2000). These data were collected from a wide variety of countries, including those from North America (Canada), Europe (Finland, Poland, Germany, Russia, England, the Netherlands, and Norway), Asia (Hong Kong and Korea), and the Middle East (Israel). Such a wide sampling of countries allowed us to examine the generalizability of the NPQ's psychometric properties across cultures.

Table 23.2 presents the average NPQ scale internal consistency reliabilities and convergent validities in 19 samples from 11 different countries. Convergent validities were estimated from the correlations between corresponding scales of the nonverbal NPQ and the verbal PRF. In each case, the verbal PRF items and NPQ instructions were translated into the culture's language by native speakers familiar with both the PRF scale definitions and the English language. Overall, the NPQ has demonstrated adequate internal consistencies, with a mean of 0.68 across all cultural samples. The lowest reliability came from the Chinese sample in Hong Kong (0.61) whereas the highest reliability came from one of the five Canadian samples (0.75). These values, in general, are considered quite acceptable in view of the fact that most reliabilities were based on short eight-item scales.

The mean NPQ-PRF convergent validities for the corresponding trait scales are shown

Table 23.1   NPQ and FF-NPQ trait scale names and descriptions

NPQ scale descriptions

Achievement	Works hard to attain excellence; willing to forgo leisure activities to achieve an academic, work-related, or physical goal.
Affiliation	Seeks warm and positive human relations; enjoys being in the company of other people; a high scorer has a gregariousness towards others.
Aggression	Willing to strike out at others both verbally and physically when angered; is easily aggravated or annoyed.
Autonomy	Prefers to engage in adventurous activities alone; unconcerned about the opinions of others; may not conform to social norms of dress.
Dominance	Readily assumes the role of a leader; gives directions clearly and forcefully; capable to rallying people to act.
Endurance	Work tirelessly at difficult projects until complete; does not give up quickly on tasks, either physical or mental.
Exhibition	Enjoys being the center of attention; likes to perform in front of audience; engages in humorous and/or risky behaviors to get noticed.
Thrill-seeking	Enjoys engaging in exciting, risky and/or dangerous activities; not overly concerned with personal safety.
Impulsivity	Will react quickly to situations without much forethought or planning; tends to have a low frustration tolerance.
Nurturance	Enjoys helping children, animals, and those in need; willing to come to the aid of the sick, infirm, or disabled.
Order	Prefers a working and living environment that is tidy and organized; dislike clutter or confusion.
Play	Seeks activities that are fun and pleasurable, such as sports and games; enjoys jokes and pranks.
Sentience	Engages in activities that arouse the senses, such as tasting food, smelling flowers, listening to music, and viewing art.
Social Recognition	Tries to gain the approval and esteem of others; draws attention to own accomplishments and possessions.
Succorance	Frequently seeks out other people for help, advice, and reassurance; craves emotional support.
Understanding	Interested in gaining knowledge through reading, observation, and experimentation in the arts and sciences.
Deviation	Admits to socially deviant behaviors, such as stealing and destroying property; high scores may result from careless or random responding or purposeful distortion.

FF-NPQ scale descriptions

Neuroticism	Has low threshold for physical fear (e.g. of small animals); needs emotional support and succor following disappointment; suspects and fears the hostility of others; is frequently sad or depressed.
Extraversion	Often entertains or leads others; enjoys social gatherings and parties; engages in conversations; likes to make new friends.
Openness to experience	Appreciates the arts (e.g. music, painting, sculpture); reads widely; is interested in scientific discovery; seeks contact with nature.
Agreeableness	Provides help and support for others; often assumes the role of care-giver; avoids confronting others; is reluctant to express aggression, either verbally or physically.
Conscientiousness	Maintains tidy and orderly surroundings; organizes personal effects; sets ambitious goals; is able to maintain attention and to work long hours.

Note: Adapted from S.V. Paunonen, D.N. Jackson and M.C. Ashton (2004) *Manual for Nonverbal Personality Questionnaire (NPQ) and Five-Factor Nonverbal Personality Questionnaire (FF-NPQ)* : pp. 7–8; p. 28. Reproduced by permission of SIGMA Assessment Systems, Inc. P.O. Box 610984, Port Huron, MI 48061-0984

in the last column of Table 23.2. In general, the NPQ-PRF convergent validities were satisfactory (mean $r = 0.43$) across the samples. It is noteworthy here that, perhaps, one should not be expecting the high levels of convergent validities sometimes found with other predictor-criterion test correlations. This is because nonverbal depictions of behaviors, unlike verbal ones, are constrained to behaviors that are directly observable. Hence, nonverbal items are often unable to represent unobservable cognitive and affective tendencies such as preferences, desires, and sentiments. Some of the items in PRF trait scales refer to behaviors that are not represented in the corresponding NPQ

Table 23.2   Summary of NPQ scale psychometric properties (averaged across scales) by country

Study	Country	N	Internal consistencies	Convergent validities [a]
Paunonen et al. (1990)	Canada	119	0.72	0.52
	Canada	90	0.71	0.54
Paunonen et al. (1992)	Canada	285	0.65	—
	Finland	88	0.70	0.50
	Poland	93	0.65	0.40
	Germany	102	0.67	0.47
Paunonen et al. (1996)	Canada	94	0.75	0.51
	Finland	92	0.67	0.39
	Poland	100	0.67	0.42
	Germany	90	0.66	0.39
	Russia	99	0.68	0.37
	Hong Kong	100	0.61	0.28
Paunonen et al. (2000)	Canada	103	0.71	0.44
	England	104	0.72	0.47
	Netherlands	316	0.70	0.42
	Norway	113	0.68	0.48
	Israel	142	0.65	0.27
Lee et al. (2000)	Korea	221	0.71	—
Amelang et al. (2002)[b]	Germany	190	0.67	0.45
Mean			0.68	0.43
Range			(0.61–0.75)	(0.27–0.54)

[a]Mean correlation with corresponding PRF scales, where applicable
[b]Only values from the self-report ratings collected during the straight-take testing session (session 1) are presented here

trait scales, a fact that will tend to attenuate their intercorrelations.

There are some discernable cultural differences in the convergent validities shown in Table 23.2. Canadian samples generally showed the highest convergent validities (mean $r = 0.50$) followed by the European samples (mean $r = 0.43$). Samples from Hong Kong and Israel exhibited the lowest convergent validities, r's $= 0.28$ and 0.27, respectively. These cultural differences could indicate that translations of the verbal criterion measures (i.e. PRF trait scales) into languages other than English may have not been optimal for some of the scales in some of the cultures. Or, the differences in validities might suggest that traits found in North American culture (or their behavior-in-situation exemplars) may not be relevant in other cultures, particularly in non-Western cultures. We will have more to say about these possibilities later in this chapter.

In addition to the adequate internal consistencies and convergent validities exhibited by the NPQ scales, other psychometric properties were also good. For instance, Paunonen et al. (1992) found that the absolute discriminant NPQ-PRF correlations were appropriately low; the mean correlations between NPQ scales and non-corresponding PRF scales were 0.16, 0.14, and 0.15 for Finland, Poland, and Germany, respectively. Amelang et al. (2002) reported that the mean test–retest reliability (one week apart) for the NPQ in Germany was 0.73, which was comparable to that of the PRF at 0.74. Those authors also found that the mean correlation between self- versus peer rated NPQ scales was 0.52 (across the scales; range = 0.43 to 0.59), which was similar to that of the PRF (mean $r = 0.56$; range = 0.43 to 0.71).

Factor structure across cultures

As discussed in the previous section, the NPQ scales possess good psychometric properties of internal consistency, test–retest stability, and convergent validity. Also pertinent to an NPQ evaluation is the determination of its structural properties. We now consider the structure of the NPQ and the generalizability of that structure across different cultures. One of the first studies of NPQ structure was reported by Paunonen et al. (1992), where NPQ and PRF data were available for four countries (i.e. Canada, Finland, Poland, and Germany). Factor analytic solutions of the four samples' verbal and nonverbal personality data were remarkably consistent. Using orthogonal Procrustes transformations (Schönemann, 1966) with reference to a target structure (i.e. the PRF factor structure reported by Skinner et al., 1976; cf. Ashton et al., 1998; Jackson et al., 1996), similar five-factor solutions were found across inventories and countries (with an average coefficient of congruence close to 0.90).

It was apparent to the investigators that the structural models recovered from those cross-cultural data referred to above, with both the verbal and the nonverbal personality inventories, closely resembled the Big Five personality dimensions. Costa and McCrae (1988) were among the first to extract a robust five-factor solution from PRF traits, which they interpreted as akin to the Big Five. Hence, with reference to the Costa and McCrae's PRF five-factor solution as a target structure, Paunonen et al. (1992) rotated their NPQ and PRF factors for each of the four cultures and computed coefficients of congruence. The mean congruence coefficient was 0.83 for NPQ data and 0.92 for PRF data, averaged across factors and countries. The slightly lower mean convergence for the nonverbal data was attributed to differences in behavioral representation in the nonverbal and verbal items. Perhaps the most intriguing finding was that the Big Five personality factors can be recovered within an assessment modality where no language is explicitly used.

Several subsequent studies have been conducted to further explore the factor structure of the NPQ across a wider range of cultures (Paunonen et al., 1996, 2000). In general, each of the data sets (by country) tended to yield five factors, all of which were then rotated with a Procrustes transformation (Schönemann, 1966)

to the theoretically based Big Five target structure presumably underlying the Murray needs (Costa and McCrae, 1988). The results of those orthogonal factor rotations showed very good convergences (approximately 0.90 on average) for the corresponding NPQ dimensions across cultures. In analyzing a sample of 221 Korean students, Lee et al. (2000) also demonstrated that the five factors extracted from the NPQ showed high congruence coefficients with the Costa and McCrae's PRF Big Five factors, ranging from 0.79 to 0.94 with a mean of 0.86.

In addition to the separate factor analyses conducted by country as described above, Paunonen et al. (2000) also employed a meta-analytic technique for factor analysis (Becker, 1996) to analyze a combined NPQ data set. In this technique, a weighted means procedure is used to combine the countries' individual product-moment correlation matrices for the questionnaire scales into a single pooled matrix. The variable intercorrelations are then disattenuated for unreliability before factoring, so that the resultant structure is not unduly affected by differential levels of measurement error. Five factors were extracted by Paunonen et al. (2000) from the NPQ trait scores in the aggregated data, accounting for 83.8% of the scales' variance. As before, the factors were then rotated to a target matrix representing Costa and McCrae's (1988) PRF Big Five factor structure. The results of that meta-factor analysis for the combined NPQ data set are shown in Table 23.3.

The NPQ meta-factor solution shown in Table 23.3 is clearly aligned with the Big Five, with most of the NPQ traits loading onto their targeted Big Five factors. However, two traits loaded more highly on a factor other than that targeted for the variable: (a) the NPQ dominance scale tended to load onto the extraversion factor instead of its targeted agreeableness factor, and (b) understanding appeared to define conscientiousness more than its intended openness to experience factor. Still, although dominance and understanding deviated somewhat from their targeted factors, their assignments to the non-targeted

Table 23.3   Procrustes rotated meta-factors of combined Nonverbal Personality Questionnaire (NPQ) data from five countries

Factor	*Factor*				
NPQ scale	*E*	*A*	*C*	*N*	*O*
Extraversion (E)					
Affiliation	**0.74**	0.44	0.12	0.32	0.23
Exhibition	**0.80**	−0.29	−0.16	0.13	0.25
Play	**0.68**	−0.50	0.03	0.04	0.15
Agreeableness (A)					
Nurturance	0.50	**0.61**	0.35	0.21	0.33
Aggression	0.20	**−0.80**	−0.27	0.27	0.03
Dominance	0.65	**−0.34**	0.24	0.21	0.39
Conscientiousness (C)					
Achievement	0.23	−0.19	**0.74**	0.26	0.46
Endurance	0.21	−0.06	**0.71**	−0.15	0.56
Order	0.03	0.22	**0.70**	0.45	0.02
Impulsivity	0.47	−0.42	**−0.54**	0.40	0.26
Neuroticism (N)					
Social recognition	0.40	−0.47	0.24	**0.64**	0.00
Succorance	0.10	0.20	−0.09	**0.83**	0.25
Openness to experience (O)					
Autonomy	0.12	0.00	0.08	−0.09	**0.93**
Thrill-seeking	0.39	−0.41	−0.08	−0.29	**0.66**
Sentience	0.18	0.41	0.17	0.43	**0.65**
Understanding	−0.06	−0.09	0.61	0.20	**0.56**

Note: Targeted loadings are in boldface. From S.V. Paunonen, M. Zeidner, H. Engvik, P. Oosterveld and R. Maliphant (2000) 'The nonverbal assessment of personality in five cultures', *Journal of Cross-Cultural Psychology*, 31: 232. © 2000 Sage Publishers

factors were not entirely unexpected. For example, dominant individuals are often perceived as leaders who assert their influence upon others (Paunonen et al., 2004). This conceptualization of the trait is not inconsistent with its loading on the broad personality dimension of extraversion, which is often viewed as encompassing dominance-like behaviors related to assertiveness (Costa and McCrae, 1992).

Note in Table 23.3 that the NPQ version of neuroticism is defined by social recognition and succorance only. This means that the factor is restricted to the assessment of excessive cravings for social approval and emotional assurances from others. This definition of neuroticism is arguably too narrow in relation to conventional conceptualizations of this construct, which often include the propensity to feel vulnerable and to experience frequent and intense negative moods. This is an issue we address again in the development of the FF-NPQ described later.

Relations with social desirability

Amelang et al. (2002) proposed that nonverbal personality questionnaires may have the advantage of low 'fakeability' compared to their verbal counterparts. They suggested that the ambiguity surrounding the meaning of nonverbal items should make them less susceptible to social desirable responding. The authors tested their hypothesis among 190 non-student German participants who completed the verbal PRF and the nonverbal NPQ, along with a measure of social desirability. In the first session, participants were given the standard (straight-take) instructions for completing the questionnaires. During a second session (one week later), half of the participants completed the same questionnaires under the straight-take instructions, whereas the other half received 'fake good' instructions. Ratings from two well-acquainted peers per study respondent were also collected.

On average, the PRF scales correlated 0.27 with social desirability scores whereas the NPQ scales correlated 0.21. When valid variance (as measured by peer ratings) was partialed out to obtain a more accurate measure of self-report bias (John and Robins, 1994), the partial correlations were 0.21 for PRF and 0.17 for NPQ. In terms of the experimentally manipulated 'faking good' effects, the PRF scale scores were elevated, on average, by 0.37 of a standard deviation whereas the NPQ scale scores increased, on average, by 0.30 of a standard deviation. The authors concluded that both PRF and NPQ showed equal (but small) associations with social desirability and similar levels of scale score inflation under the 'fake good' experimental manipulation.

Some conclusions

As reviewed in the sections above, the NPQ has shown some promising psychometric characteristics, including good reliability, convergent validity, and factorial validity. The scales are applicable across many cultures and thus can be used for cross-cultural personality assessment. The cross-cultural replicability of the NPQ factor structure (along with that of other personality questionnaires) further suggests that the structure of personality has some generality across cultures. Moreover, that structure tends to support the well-known five-factor model of personality, a fact that paved the way for the development of a nonverbal personality questionnaire based on that model – the FF-NPQ.

THE FF-NPQ

The FF-NPQ (Paunonen et al., 2004) contains 60 nonverbal items that measure the Big Five personality factors of neuroticism, extraversion, openness to experience, agreeableness, and conscientiousness (Digman, 1990; John and Srivastava, 1999). The FF-NPQ scale descriptions are presented in the bottom panel of Table 23.1. Those 60 items, with 12 items per scale, were mostly selected from the longer 136-item NPQ to represent each of the Big Five factor domains. In completing the FF-NPQ, the same rating instructions are given respondents as those shown in Figure 23.1 for the NPQ. Because of its short length of 60 items, most people finish the FF-NPQ in about 10 minutes.

Construction of the FF-NPQ

The construction of the FF-NPQ is briefly summarized here; interested readers are referred to Paunonen et al. (2001, 2004) and Paunonen and Ashton (2002) for more details. Instead of creating new nonverbal items for the FF-NPQ, Paunonen et al. (2001) decided to select representative nonverbal items from the existing NPQ item pool to develop the FF-NPQ. To verify the relevance of each NPQ trait scale to the traditional Big Five domains, the authors correlated those scales with known markers of the Big Five structure, specifically the factor scales of the NEO Five-Factor Inventory (NEO-FFI) (Costa and McCrae, 1992). Using a sample of 304 Canadian university students (112 men, 192 women), each NPQ scale was assigned to one of the Big Five factors if it correlated more than 0.30 with a NEO-FFI factor scale. Three NPQ scales (thrill-seeking, social recognition, and play) failed to correlate 0.30 or more with any NEO-FFI factor scale, and were thus excluded from the FF-NPQ item selection process.

The composition of each resultant FF-NPQ factor scale, in terms of the constituent NPQ trait scales in parentheses, was as follows: extraversion (affiliation, dominance, and exhibition); agreeableness (nurturance, and reverse-keyed aggression); conscientiousness (achievement, endurance, order, and reverse-keyed impulsivity); neuroticism (succorance); and openness to experience (autonomy, sentience, and understanding). Next, for each Big Five factor (except neuroticism which was represented by only one

NPQ trait scale), items from its constituent NPQ scales were pooled and subjected to a series of item selection processes. The best 12 items for each of the Big Five factors were retained based on the following criteria: (a) the item showed good within-factor item-total correlation, (b) the item showed low correlations with the total scores of other Big Five factors, and (c) the item depicted behaviors that have some cross-cultural generality. Note that none of the items from the impulsivity scale (assigned to the conscientiousness factor) survived this selection process.

An initial 56-item version of the FF-NPQ was constructed, the neuroticism factor being defined only by the NPQ succorance scale (Paunonen et al., 2001). Since then, the neuroticism scale has been revised and lengthened from 8 to 12 items. Moreover, items representing phobic behavior, paranoia, and depression, in addition to the need for succorance, have been incorporated into this new neuroticism scale to bring it more in line with its traditional definition (see Paunonen et al., 2004, and Paunonen and Ashton, 2002, for more details).

Psychometric properties

We now describe some psychometric properties of the FF-NPQ based on four Canadian college student samples (see Paunonen, 2003; Paunonen et al., 2001; R.Y. Hong et al., 2006). As seen in the first two columns of Table 23.4, the means and standard deviations of the FF-NPQ scales were relatively consistent across the four samples, with neuroticism showing the lowest mean scores and agreeableness exhibiting the highest mean scores. Gender differences were also consistent across the samples: women tended to report elevated levels of neuroticism (slightly over one standard deviation higher), agreeableness (about three-fourths of a standard deviation higher), and conscientiousness (about half a standard deviation higher) than men. Women and men showed approximately equal mean scores on extraversion and openness.

The five factor scales of the FF-NPQ demonstrate good psychometric properties related to reliability and validity, as shown in Table 23.4. Internal consistency reliabilities of the scales were uniformly high (mean alpha was approximately 0.80) across the four samples. Convergent validities with the corresponding scales from the NEO-FFI or the Revised NEO Personality Inventory (NEO-PI-R) (Costa and McCrae, 1992) were also good (fourth column, Table 23.4). Across samples and scales, these correlations ranged from 0.42 to 0.66, with an average convergence of approximately 0.53. This value is comparable to values normally obtained between different Big Five measures (e.g. Costa and McCrae, 1992: 54). Conversely, the discriminant validities between FF-NPQ and the NEO measures were appropriately low. The mean absolute discriminant correlations were 0.14 (Paunonen et al., 2001), 0.17 (Paunonen, 2003; sample 1), 0.12 (Paunonen, 2003; sample 2), and 0.15 (R.Y. Hong et al., 2006). As shown in the last column of Table 23.4, the self-peer correlations ranged between 0.38 and 0.45 (mean $r = 0.41$) in the Paunonen et al. (2001) study, and the correlations ranged between 0.33 and 0.44 (mean $r = .39$) in the R.Y. Hong et al. (2006) study. These values compare favorably against the 0.43 correlation between self- and peer ratings scores on NEO-PI-R domain scales (Costa and McCrae, 1992: 50). Furthermore, the self-peer discriminant correlations for the FF-NPQ scales were relatively weak, averaging 0.08 in the Paunonen et al. (2001) and 0.15 in the R.Y. Hong et al. (2006) study.

To investigate whether the Big Five dimensions as measured by the FF-NPQ scales occupy the same factor space as that of Big Five dimensions measured by other verbal questionnaires, common factor analysis was conducted on a sample of participants who completed three different self-report Big Five measures: the FF-NPQ, NEO-FFI, and a Big Five adjectives (B5-ADJ) (Goldberg, 1992) rating scale (R.Y. Hong et al., 2006). Principal axis factoring of the 15-factor measures with oblique (promax) rotation revealed the expected Big Five personality structure

Table 23.4 Means, standard deviations, internal consistencies, and convergent validities of the FF-NPQ scales among four Canadian samples

FF-NPQ scale	M	SD	Internal consistencies	Correlation with NEO	Self-peer correlation[a]
	Paunonen et al. (2001), $n = 304$				
Neuroticism[b]	33.3	7.7	0.75	0.45	0.39
Extraversion	48.9	11.9	0.81	0.53	0.45
Openness	57.3	11.1	0.82	0.55	0.38
Agreeableness	64.4	11.3	0.82	0.59	0.40
Conscientiousness	56.4	10.7	0.79	0.50	0.41
Mean			0.80	0.52	0.41
	Paunonen (2003) sample 1, $n = 135$				
Neuroticism	46.5	11.8	0.80	0.51	—
Extraversion	50.1	11.1	0.87	0.57	—
Openness	55.6	10.9	0.82	0.63	—
Agreeableness	61.8	10.9	0.80	0.58	—
Conscientiousness	57.1	9.2	0.74	0.46	—
Mean			0.81	0.55	—
	Paunonen (2003) sample 2, $n = 174$				
Neuroticism	43.3	12.3	0.81	0.57	—
Extraversion	52.3	13.1	0.87	0.49	—
Openness	55.8	12.4	0.85	0.66	—
Agreeableness	62.9	12.2	0.85	0.42	—
Conscientiousness	54.5	10.3	0.79	0.51	—
Mean			0.83	0.53	—
	R.Y. Hong et al. (2006), $n = 295$				
Neuroticism	45.7	12.0	0.80	0.46	0.33
Extraversion	50.4	11.5	0.82	0.50	0.44
Openness	54.7	10.8	0.80	0.48	0.43
Agreeableness	62.9	9.9	0.76	0.57	0.41
Conscientiousness	55.4	10.3	0.79	0.52	0.36
Mean			0.79	0.51	0.39

Note: All correlations are significant at $p < 0.01$. FF-NPQ = Five-Factor Nonverbal Personality Questionnaire; NEO = NEO Five-Factor Inventory or Revised NEO Personality Inventory. The NEO Five-Factor Inventory was used in all samples except in sample 1 of Paunonen (2003), where the Revised NEO Personality Inventory was used.
[a]Roommate ratings on the FF-NPQ were available on subsets of the Paunonen et al. (2001) sample ($n = 96$) and the R.Y. Hong et al. (2006) sample ($n = 124$).
[b]For this sample, the FF-NPQ neuroticism scale had only eight items.

(accounting for 61.21% of the variance), with measures of the same personality domain forming each of the factors (e.g. extraversion was defined by the extraversion scales of the FF-NPQ, NEO-FFI, and B5-ADJ). This provided empirical support for the assertion that the FF-NPQ assesses a factor structure similar to those of other established verbal measures of the Big Five.

Criterion-related validity

Having established that the FF-NPQ demonstrates good psychometric properties, it is also imperative to show that it has criterion-related validity in predicting non-test variables. More specifically, there is an interest in the extent to which the FF-NPQ is able to corroborate its verbal counterparts in the prediction of important criteria of some social significance. These criteria were assessed in several studies (Paunonen, 1998, 2003; Paunonen and Ashton, 2001) via the Behavior Report Form (BRF). The BRF is a self-report questionnaire designed to assess relatively objective and behaviorally quantifiable psychological outcomes, such as tobacco and alcohol consumption, the average number of parties attended per month, the number of

Table 23.5   Replicated partial correlations (with sex removed) between criteria and Big Five factor scales

Criterion	Factor scale	FF-NPQ (n = 178)	FF-NPQ (n = 142)	NEO-FFI (n = 273)	NEO-PI-R (n = 135)
Participant sex[a]	Neuroticism	0.53***	0.54***	0.31***	0.20*
	Agreeableness	0.33***	0.23**	0.25***	0.23**
	Conscientiousness	0.19**	0.30***	0.06	0.22*
Intelligence self-rating	Neuroticism	−0.23**	−0.12	−0.30***	−0.33***
	Openness	0.13*	0.24**	0.25***	0.32***
	Conscientiousness	0.07	0.17*	0.20***	0.36***
Alcohol consumption	Extraversion	0.30***	0.33***	0.14*	0.24**
	Conscientiousness	−0.21***	−0.15	−0.26***	−0.29***
Honesty self-rating	Agreeableness	0.23***	0.19*	0.17**	0.26**
	Conscientiousness	0.25***	0.12	0.27***	0.27***
Popularity self-rating	Extraversion	0.39***	0.36***	0.39***	0.51***
Parties attended	Extraversion	0.31***	0.33***	0.29***	0.33***
Grade point average	Conscientiousness	0.23***	0.13	0.27***	0.19*
Plays musical instruments	Openness	0.19**	0.24**	0.19**	0.20*
Attractiveness self-rating	Extraversion	0.25***	0.07	0.35***	0.18*
Tobacco consumption	Agreeableness	−0.23***	−0.16	−0.26***	−0.18*
Dating variety	Extraversion	0.17**	0.24**	0.07	0.28***
Routinely exercises	Extraversion	0.23***	0.18*	0.29***	0.14

Note: FF–NPQ = Five-Factor Nonverbal Personality Questionnaire; NEO-FFI = NEO Five-Factor Inventory; NEO–PI–R = Revised NEO Personality Inventory. From S.V. Paunonen (2003) 'Big Five factors of personality and replicated predictions of behavior' *Journal of Personality and Social Psychology*, 84: 417. © 2003 by the American Psychological Association
[a]Participant sex was not partialed
* $p < 0.05$; ** $p < 0.01$; *** $p < 0.001$

traffic violations one has had, and whether one regularly participates in sports, exercise, and volunteering activities, and so on. These criteria were selected on the basis that they represent important behavior outcomes that might have underlying personality determinants. The BRF has undergone minor revisions (with new items being added to it) over time; hence, the total number of criteria assessed differed slightly from study to study.

Paunonen et al. (2001, Table 6) reported that the multiple correlations of the FF-NPQ and NEO-FFI scales with each of 14 assessed behavioral criteria were comparable. The average multiple correlation across all 14 criteria (e.g. grade point average, alcohol consumption, blood donation frequency, etc.) was 0.25 both for the FF-NPQ and NEO-FFI, suggesting that the criterion-related validity of the nonverbal scales was equal to that of the more established verbal scales.

Using three different Big Five questionnaires (i.e. FF-NPQ, NEO-FFI, and NEO-PI-R) across two independent samples, Paunonen (2003) showed that there was substantial

agreement in the prediction of behavior criteria across the different personality assessments. Out of a total of 27 behavior criteria, 12 of them were reliably predicted by the same personality factors, as summarized in Table 23.5. The FF-NPQ showed remarkable consistency with both the NEO-FFI and NEO-PI-R in the prediction of those criteria. Besides these replicated predictions, Paunonen also evaluated the extent to which the null results were replicated; that is, that the different personality assessments agreed in terms of their lack of prediction of any particular criterion. He found that the majority of the factor-criterion combinations (not shown in Table 23.5) agreed in their (null) results across the different Big Five assessments (89%).

The criterion-related validity of FF-NPQ in relation to corresponding verbal personality questionnaires was evaluated again in a recent study (R.Y. Hong et al., 2006). In that study, participants completed three different Big Five measures (FF-NPQ, NEO-FFI, and B5-ADJ) and a newer version of the BRF measuring 36 criteria. For each criterion, three separate hierarchical regression analyses were conducted using, in each analysis, a different Big Five questionnaire. In all cases, sex of the participant was entered into the regression as a first step to partial out gender effects. The Big Five factors were then entered in the second step. An arbitrary decision rule concerning replicated predictions was applied. Specifically, the prediction of a particular criterion by a particular trait was considered replicated if (a) all three regression coefficients across the different Big Five measures were significant at $p < 0.05$ or better, or (b) any two of the three regression coefficients were significant beyond $p < 0.01$. The results for the replicated predictions on 21 criteria are presented in Table 23.6. The authors also examined the extent to which the Big Five measures agreed

Table 23.6 Replicated standardized regression coefficients (with sex controlled for) in predicting criteria from Big Five factor scales

Criterion	ΔR^2	Big Five factor	FF–NPQ	NEO–FFI	B5–ADJ
Participant sex[a]	0.19	Neuroticism	0.39***	0.30***	0.32***
		Extraversion	0.03	0.17**	0.24**
		Agreeableness	0.37***	0.21**	0.07
		Conscientiousness	0.08	0.21***	0.23**
Leadership self-rating	0.26	Extraversion	0.37***	0.45***	0.60***
		Agreeableness	0.05	−0.19**	−0.20**
		Conscientiousness	0.03	0.20***	0.19**
Popularity self-rating	0.25	Neuroticism	−0.18**	−0.17***	−0.13*
		Extraversion	0.44***	0.47***	0.50***
Alcohol consumption	0.15	Extraversion	0.37***	0.22***	0.31***
		Conscientiousness	−0.28***	−0.20**	−0.30***
Parties attended	0.15	Extraversion	0.41***	0.34***	0.30***
		Conscientiousness	−0.16*	−0.18**	−0.25***
Attractiveness self-rating	0.13	Neuroticism	−0.10	−0.29***	−0.23**
		Extraversion	0.25***	0.18***	0.30***
		Agreeableness	0.05	−0.17***	−0.25***
Honesty self-rating	0.13	Agreeableness	0.29***	0.25***	0.37***
Intelligence self-rating	0.12	Openness	0.14*	0.19***	0.27***
		Agreeableness	−0.08	−0.19***	−0.28***
		Conscientiousness	0.11	0.35***	0.22**
Tobacco consumption	0.12	Conscientiousness	−0.24***	−0.23***	−0.26***
Alcoholic drinks per week	0.10	Extraversion	0.21***	0.14*	0.26***
		Conscientiousness	−0.27***	−0.18**	−0.20**
Routinely exercises	0.10	Extraversion	0.17*	0.22***	0.38***
		Conscientiousness	0.11	0.23***	0.24***
Maximum speed traveled	0.08	Conscientiousness	−0.25***	−0.18***	−0.21***
Religiosity self-rating	0.07	Conscientiousness	0.24***	0.18**	0.16*
Plays organized sports	0.07	Extraversion	0.16**	0.19**	0.21**
Volunteering	0.07	Conscientiousness	0.14*	0.25***	0.24***
Dating variety	0.06	Extraversion	0.18**	0.22**	0.20**
		Conscientiousness	−0.14*	−0.13*	−0.14*
Liberal arts	0.06	Openness	−0.19**	−0.19**	−0.21**
High school graduating grade	0.05	Conscientiousness	0.14*	0.24***	0.15*
Long-term diet	0.05	Neuroticism	0.13*	0.21***	0.21**
Plays musical instruments	0.05	Openness	0.15*	0.20**	0.28***
Femininity self-rating	0.03	Agreeableness	0.11*	0.16**	0.12*

Note: FF-NPQ = Five-Factor Nonverbal Personality Questionnaire; NEO-FFI = NEO Five-Factor Inventory; B5-ADJ = Big Five Adjectives Rating Scale. ΔR^2 = Change in proportion of variance accounted for in the criterion by the Big Five factors after partialing out participant sex. For decision rule about replicated effects, see text

[a] Participant sex was not controlled for

* $p < 0.05$; ** $p < 0.01$; *** $p < 0.001$

in terms of their nonsignificant predictions. The decision rule concerning replicated nonsignificant predictions was that all three Big Five measures must yield nonsignificant predictions ($p > 0.05$).

Table 23.6 shows that, in general, the three Big Five measures in the R.Y. Hong et al. (2006) study were consistent in their prediction of various criteria. Upon close inspection, however, the nonverbal FF-NPQ tended to agree slightly less with the two verbal forms than the verbal forms did with each other. In terms of replicated predictions of the 36 BRF criteria according to the above-mentioned decision rules, the results were quite encouraging. Out of a total of 180 factor-criterion evaluations (5 factors × 36 criterion variables), 129 (72%) were replicated evaluations (significant and non-significant), and the remaining were non-replicated evaluations. This result thus suggested that the three Big Five measures were generally consistent in their predictions of a variety of important outcome variables.

In summary, the FF-NPQ appears to provide a level of criterion-related validity only slightly lower than that of the other more established verbal personality questionnaires. We acknowledge that the FF-NPQ may not attain similar levels of validity in part because the nonverbal items are inherently limited in their ability to represent certain internal cognitive, affective, or motivational proclivities in individuals. Nonetheless, the ability of the FF-NPQ to replicate most of the factor-criterion relations evaluated in the R.Y. Hong et al. (2006) study supported this new nonverbal measure as a viable alternative to traditional verbal measures of the Big Five personality factors.

Relations with response set

Using the R.Y. Hong et al. (2006) data, the extent to which the FF-NPQ is correlated with social desirable response sets was examined. Such response sets include self-deception enhancement, impression management (Paulhus, 1984, 2002), and general desirability responding. Self-deception enhancement

and impression management were assessed using the Balanced Inventory of Desirable Responding (Paulhus, 1991). Overall social desirability responding was assessed using the desirability subscale from the PRF. Response set contamination was also assessed in the personality responses gathered with the NEO-FFI and B5-ADJ questionnaires.

The correlations of self-deception enhancement, impression management, and social desirability with the three different Big Five measures are shown in Table 23.7. Both the B5-ADJ and NEO-FFI were moderately associated with self-deception enhancement scores, with mean absolute correlations of 0.25 and 0.21, respectively, whereas the FF-NPQ, with a value of 0.13, did not appear to be excessively contaminated with self-deception enhancement. The three personality questionnaires seemed to have equally weak correlations with impression management scores, with correlations ranging between 0.15 and 0.19. Finally, the FF-NPQ was the least correlated with the PRF desirability scale (mean $r = 0.16$) compared to NEO-FFI (mean $r = .39$) and B5-ADJ (mean $r = .23$). As far as the individual factor scales are concerned, the nonverbal measures of neuroticism and, especially, conscientiousness seemed to be less affected by response set than were the corresponding verbal measures.

To derive a more accurate estimate of self-serving bias in responding, some researchers have recommended partialing out the valid variance (in the form of peer ratings) from self-rated personality and social desirable responding (Amelang et al., 2002; John and Robins, 1994). Recall that a subset of the R.Y. Hong et al. (2006) study participants ($n = 124$) had roommates make peer ratings of their personality. Hence, we could obtain (partial) correlations between self-rated personality and response sets after controlling for peer rated personality scores. The absolute partial correlations between self-deception enhancement and personality, averaged across the five factors, were 0.15 (FF-NPQ), 0.21 (NEO-FFI), and 0.22 (B5-ADJ). The mean absolute partial correlations

Table 23.7 Correlations of three Big Five measures with self-deception enhancement, impression management, and desirability scales

	Self-deception enhancement (n = 291)			Impression management (n = 291)			Desirability (n = 124)		
	FF-NPQ	NEO-FFI	B5-ADJ	FF-NPQ	NEO-FFI	B5-ADJ	FF-NPQ	NEO-FFI	B5-ADJ
Neuroticism	−0.30***	−0.41***	−0.31***	−0.08	−0.16**	−0.07	−0.11	−0.59***	−0.36***
Extraversion	−0.01	0.11	0.21***	−0.19**	0.00	0.03	0.16	0.37***	0.24
Openness	0.01	−0.04	0.20**	−0.01	−0.14*	0.03	0.16	−0.10	−0.06
Agreeableness	0.29***	0.19**	0.26***	0.40***	0.34***	0.30***	0.28**	0.43***	0.20*
Conscientiousness	0.06	0.30***	0.26***	0.24***	0.32***	0.33***	0.10	0.44***	0.29**
Mean (absolute)	0.13	0.21	0.25	0.18	0.19	0.15	0.16	0.39	0.23

Note: FF-NPQ = Five-Factor Nonverbal Personality Questionnaire; NEO-FFI = NEO Five-Factor Inventory; B5-ADJ = Big Five Adjectives Rating Scale; self-deception enhancement and impression management are subscales of the Balanced Inventory of Desirable Responding (Paulhus, 1991); Desirability is a subscale of the Personality Research Form (Jackson, 1984)
* $p < .05$; ** $p < .01$; *** $p < .001$

between impression management and personality were 0.11 (FF-NPQ), 0.20 (NEO-FFI), and 0.11 (B5-ADJ). Finally, the mean absolute partial correlations between social desirability and personality were 0.15 (FF-NPQ), 0.34 (NEO-FFI), and 0.19 (B5-ADJ). In general, the magnitudes of the partial correlation were slightly smaller than their zero-order correlation counterparts, and slightly better for the nonverbal scales than for the verbal scales.

In sum, there is some preliminary evidence that FF-NPQ as a measure of the Big Five is not overly contaminated with social desirability. In fact, the associations found by R.Y. Hong et al. (2006) seem to mirror the correlations between NPQ scales and social desirability as reported in the Amelang et al. (2002) article. Together, these studies suggest that the nonverbal measures of personality described in this chapter are less susceptible to social desirability and self-deception enhancement effects compared to more established verbal counterparts.

Cross-cultural evaluations

To date, empirical evidence concerning the psychometric properties of the published FF-NPQ administered in cross-cultural contexts is sparse. However, we believe that the prospects for the cross-cultural applicability

of the FF-NPQ look promising given the success reported for the NPQ. Moreover, some relevant FF-NPQ information has been obtained from archival NPQ data. As reported by Paunonen et al. (2001), some samples of NPQ respondents, already described in this chapter, were used to provide an initial investigation of the FF-NPQ across cultures. They included 701 university students (447 women, 254 men) in Canada, England, Finland, Germany, Norway, Poland, and Russia. These participants completed the nonverbal NPQ scales, from which FF-NPQ scores could be calculated, in addition to the verbal PRF scales (some of the latter were in an abbreviated form).

Paunonen et al.'s (2001) results indicated that the means and standard deviations for men and women on the FF-NPQ scales for the international samples were similar to the values reported for the Canadian sample. Internal consistencies averaged across the seven countries were satisfactory: 0.64 for neuroticism, 0.75 for extraversion, 0.77 for openness, 0.72 for agreeableness, and 0.71 for conscientiousness. Internal consistencies averaged across the five scales varied slightly by country, ranging from 0.66 in Finland to 0.79 in England. The FF-NPQ scale intercorrelations were relatively small, with a mean absolute correlation of 0.22. In addition, those intercorrelations tended to be similar across the individual countries in that data set.

Paunonen et al. (2001) calculated correlations between the nonverbal measures of the Big Five (FF-NPQ scales) and the verbal measures of the Big Five (factor scales constructed from the PRF trait scales). To construct each PRF-based Big Five measure, the authors simply summed the PRF scales whose NPQ counterparts had provided items for the corresponding FF-NPQ factor measure (as described in an earlier section). Convergent correlations between the PRF and FF-NPQ measures of the Big Five ranged from 0.35 to 0.54, with a mean of 0.48. The mean convergent correlation differed slightly by country, ranging from 0.40 in Finland to 0.55 in Norway and in England. These values are considered to be quite satisfactory given (a) the relatively short length of the nonverbal factor scales, and (b) the fact that the verbal and nonverbal scales undoubtedly measure somewhat different aspects of the same personality constructs. The discriminant correlations between the PRF and FF-NPQ scales were generally small in this data set, having a mean absolute correlation of 0.10, and being similar in size across countries.

New empirical cross-cultural data on the FF-NPQ are beginning to emerge. For instance, Vorkapi et al. (2006) reported that the FF-NPQ demonstrated reasonably good psychometric properties in a sample of 320 Croatian students. Principal components analysis on the FF-NPQ items revealed the expected five-factor structure of personality, although the solution explained only 36.01% of the variance. The internal consistencies of the five FF-NPQ scales were good with an average of 0.78, slightly better than those reported in Paunonen et al.'s (2001) European samples. The mean absolute intercorrelations among the FF-NPQ scales in the Croatian data was relatively low (mean $r = 0.21$), with a range between 0.01 and 0.48.

Some conclusions

Like the NPQ, the FF-NPQ has performed remarkably well as a nonverbal personality questionnaire, with good internal scale consistency, convergent validity, criterion-related validity, and minimal contamination with social desirability response sets. Compared to its verbal counterparts, the FF-NPQ presents a viable alternative nonverbal measure of the Big Five personality dimensions. Although its criterion-related validity is perhaps slightly less than those of corresponding verbal measures, the FF-NPQ is possibly more independent of social desirable responding. The FF-NPQ's psychometric properties, as reported in this chapter, have been predominantly evaluated in Western cultures. But the extent to which they generalize to assessment in other cultures looks promising.

SOME CAUTIONARY NOTES

Having demonstrated the good psychometric properties of the NPQ and FF-NPQ questionnaires, we hasten to add that there are some important limitations in the use of those measures. As discussed in a previous article (Paunonen and Ashton, 2002), these limitations pertain to (a) the cultural-generality of the nonverbal items, (b) the predominantly etic (Berry, 1969) approach used in the development of those nonverbal measures, and (c) the comprehensiveness of the so-called five-factor model of personality structure.

Cultural-generality of the nonverbal items

The first limitation concerns the cultural-generality of the nonverbal items of the type described in this chapter. Although we have reported evidence supporting the cross-cultural applications of the NPQ and FF-NPQ, it should not be interpreted as a claim that the nonverbal items are entirely culture-free. Many of those items have culture-specific referents to behaviors that are typically performed by Western, educated, middle-class respondents (e.g. a person cooking a meal for friends using an outdoor barbecue grill).

Such item-level culture specificity effects may explain why some of the nonverbal scales showed lower levels of reliability and validity in some non-Western samples (Paunonen et al., 1996, 2000).

We do not intend to portray the NPQ or FF-NPQ as completely culture-free. We caution potential users of those questionnaires to consider carefully the extent to which their cross-cultural respondents would be able to relate to the individual nonverbal depictions of behavior. (The ages of the respondents should also be considered, as some items are relevant for adults only, such as a person driving a car.) Despite this limitation, it is our belief that the NPQ and FF-NPQ personality measures can be useful for research and assessment in many different cultures and contexts.

Etic approach to cross-cultural personality research

The second limitation with the present nonverbal personality measures concerns the etic approach that has been employed with those measures in evaluating the cross-cultural consistency in human personality. In this case, the NPQ and FF-NPQ have been exported for use in other (i.e. foreign) cultures, even though their development was largely based on North American culture. Some researchers are rightly concerned with the ability of such an imposed-etic approach to accurately assess personality structure similarity among diverse cultures. Instead, a balanced strategy can be advocated, combining both etic and emic (cultural-specific) approaches (Katigbak et al., 2002; Triandis and Euh, 2002). We concur with those who caution against the exclusive adoption of foreign assessment instruments in cross-cultural research. Nonetheless, based on the available evidence of the universality of most major personality dimensions (e.g. Katigbak et al., 2002; Rolland, 2002), we suspect that there are very few truly culture-specific dimensions of behavior (but see Cheung and Leung, 1998, for evidence of an emic 'Chinese tradition' factor).

Paunonen and Ashton (1998) have argued that the cross-cultural consistency of existing imposed-etic personality data supports the generality of personality traits across cultures. In other words, it would be hard to argue that the traits or behaviors assessed are not relevant to a culture if the imported measures show good levels of reliability, criterion validity, and factorial validity in that culture. But even if the psychometric properties of imported measures were substantially different across cultures, which could be due to a variety of reasons (i.e. response style contamination, test format issues, translation problems, and so on; see Paunonen and Ashton, 1998), this should not be taken to mean that a particular personality trait is nonexistent or irrelevant in a culture. In fact, if a trait were to exist in one culture but not in another, the implication must be that, in the latter culture, (a) no behavioral expressions of that postulated latent trait exist, or (b) the behaviors exist but they are manifestations of some other trait(s). We consider both of these alternatives as highly improbable. In all likelihood, the behavior exemplars depicted in some of the items (verbally or nonverbally) are irrelevant to the people in the one culture, and it is that irrelevance which is causing the cultural differences in test scores.

The idea that behavior exemplars of a trait can vary from one culture to another is hardly controversial; hence, different versions of a nonverbal questionnaire would ideally reflect that variation. To people who are intent on developing such a questionnaire, we encourage them to familiarize themselves with the indigenous cultures and to identify culture-specific behavior exemplars in developing their nonverbal item pool. Alternatively, one might attempt to create nonverbal items that are truly culture-free, assuming such items exist, and to cross-validate them in various cultures before incorporating them in their measures. Regardless of such endeavors, however, it is our belief that, although trait exemplars might very well be different in various cultures, most (if not all) of the postulated latent traits of personality exist in those cultures, and could be found with a systematic and rigorous program of construct validation (Paunonen, 2000).

Comprehensiveness of the five-factor model

Although many studies have been supportive of the generality of the five-factor model of personality across cultures, including studies using the present nonverbal measures, others have revealed inadequacies of that model in replicating across cultures (e.g. Cheung and Leung, 1998; De Raad and Peabody, 2005). It is not the purpose of this chapter to provide an extensive and critical review of the cross-cultural replicability of the five-factor model, but suffice it to say that researchers should be mindful of the possibility that some traits may lie outside the five-factor model factor space, and that the organization of those traits may differ from culture to culture.

Paunonen and colleagues, for example, have shown that there are several traits (e.g. integrity, seductiveness, femininity) that do not fall within the traditional factor space of the Big Five (Paunonen, 2002; Paunonen and Jackson, 2000). Furthermore, in one study (Paunonen et al., 2003), these personality traits appeared to have some value in behavioral prediction, with some of those predictions replicating across cultures. From the psycholexical approach to personality structure, there is also evidence to suggest an honesty-humility factor, in addition to the Big Five factors, that is cross-culturally replicable (Ashton et al., 2004; Ashton et al., 2000; Lee and Ashton, 2004). On the other hand, the so-called 'Chinese tradition' factor identified among some Asian samples (Cheung and Leung, 1998) is an example of a personality factor that (a) does not fall within the Big Five factor space, and (b) is not universal but is unique to a particular culture.

The putative existence of non-Big Five personality traits and factors demands that they be considered in cross-cultural studies of personality structure. The personality

questionnaires that are the focus of this chapter, the NPQ and FF-NPQ, unfortunately do not provide measures of proposed non-Big Five dimensions. But relevant verbal measures do exist (e.g. Paunonen, 2002), and they could form the basis for future developments in the nonverbal assessment of personality.

ACKNOWLEDGEMENTS

Ryan Y. Hong and Sampo V. Paunonen, Department of Psychology, University of Western Ontario. This research was supported by the Social Sciences and Humanities Research Council of Canada Research Grant 410-2006-1795 to Sampo V. Paunonen.

REFERENCES

Amelang, M., Schäfer, A. and Yoush, S. (2002) 'Comparing verbal and non-verbal personality scales: Investigating the reliability and validity, the influence of social desirability, and the effects of fake good instructions', *Psychologische Beiträge*, 44(1): 24–41.

Ashton, M.C., Jackson, D.N., Helmes, E. and Paunonen, S.V. (1998) 'Joint factor analysis of the Personality Research Form and the Jackson Personality Inventory: Comparisons with the Big Five', *Journal of Research in Personality*, 32(2): 243–50.

Ashton, M.C., Lee, K., Perugini, M., Szarota, P., de Vries, R.E., Di Blas, L., Boies, K. and De Raad, B. (2004) 'A six-factor structure of personality-descriptive adjectives: Solutions from psycholexical studies in seven languages', *Journal of Personality and Social Psychology*, 86(2): 356–66.

Ashton, M.C., Lee, K. and Son, C. (2000) 'Honesty as the sixth factor of personality: Correlations with Machiavellianism, primary psychopathy, and social adroitness', *European Journal of Personality*, 14(4): 359–68.

Becker, G. (1996) 'The meta-analysis of factor analyses: An illustration based on the cumulation of correlation matrices', *Psychological Methods*, 1(4): 341–53.

Berry, J.W. (1969) 'On cross-cultural comparability', *International Journal of Psychology*, 4(2): 119–28.

Cheung, F.M. and Leung, K. (1998) 'Indigenous personality measures: Chinese examples', *Journal of Cross-Cultural Psychology*, 29(1): 233–48.

Costa, P.T. Jr. and McCrae, R.R. (1988) 'From catalog to classification: Murray's needs and the five-factor model', *Journal of Personality and Social Psychology*, 55(2): 258–65.

Costa, P.T. Jr. and McCrae, R.R. (1992) *Revised NEO Personality Inventory (NEO-PI-R) and NEO Five-Factor Inventory (NEO-FFI) Professional Manual*. Odessa, FL: Psychological Assessment Resources.

De Raad, B. and Peabody, D. (2005) 'Cross-culturally recurrent personality factors: Analyses of three factors', *European Journal of Personality*, 19(6): 451–74.

Digman, J.M. (1990) 'Personality structure: Emergence of the five-factor model', *Annual Review of Psychology*, 41: 417–40.

Goldberg, L.R. (1992) 'The development of markers for the Big-Five factor structure', *Psychological Assessment*, 4(1): 26–42.

Hong, R.Y., Slade, H.P. and Paunonen, S.V. (2006) 'Consistency among three measures of the Big Five personality factors in the predictions of behavior', Poster session presented at the 7th Annual Meeting of the Society for Personality and Social Psychology, January, Palm Springs, California.

Hong, Y., Chiu, C. and Kung, T.M. (1997) 'Bringing culture out in front: Effects of cultural meaning system activation on social cognition', in K. Leung, Y. Kashima, U. Kim and S. Yamaguchi (eds), *Progress in Asian Social Psychology* (Vol. 1). Singapore: Wiley, pp. 135–46

Hong, Y., Morris, M.W., Chiu, C. and Benet-Martínez, V. (2000) 'Multicultural minds: A dynamic constructivist approach to culture and cognition', *American Psychologist*, 55(7): 709–20.

Hong, Y., Benet-Martínez, V., Chiu, C. and Morris, M.W. (2003) 'Boundaries of cultural influence: Construct activation as a mechanism for cultural differences in social perception', *Journal of Cross-Cultural Psychology*, 34(4): 453–64.

Jackson, D.N. (1984) *Personality Research Form Manual*. Port Huron, MI: Research Psychologists Press.

Jackson, D.N. (1994) *Jackson Personality Inventory – Revised Manual*. Port Huron, MI: Research Psychologists Press.

Jackson, D.N., Paunonen, S.V., Fraboni, M. and Goffin, R.G. (1996) 'A five-factor versus a six-factor model of personality structure', *Personality and Individual Differences*, 20(1): 33–45.

John, O.P. and Robins, R.W. (1994) 'Accuracy and bias in self-presentation: Individual differences in self-enhancement and the role of narcissism', *Journal of Personality and Social Psychology*, 66(1): 206–19.

John, O.P. and Srivastava, S. (1999) 'The Big Five trait taxonomy: History, measurement, and theoretical perspectives', in L.A. Pervin and O.P. John (eds), *Handbook of Personality: Theory and Research* (2nd edn). New York: Guilford, pp. 102–38.

Katigbak, M.S., Church, A.T., Guanzon-Lapena, M.A., Carlota, A.J. and del Pilar, G.H. (2002) 'Are indigenous personality dimensions culture specific? Philippine inventories and the Five-Factor model', *Journal of Personality and Social Psychology*, 82(1): 89–101.

Lee, K. and Ashton, M.C. (2004) 'Psychometric properties of the HEXACO personality inventory', *Multivariate Behavioral Research*, 39(2): 329–58.

Lee, K., Ashton, M.C., Hong, S. and Park, K.B. (2000) 'Psychometric properties of the Nonverbal Personality Questionnaire in Korea', *Educational and Psychological Measurement*, 60(1): 131–41.

Loevinger, J. (1957) 'Objective tests as instruments of psychological theory [Monograph]', *Psychological Reports*, 3: 635–94.

McClelland, D.C., Koestner, R. and Weinberger, J. (1989) 'How do self-attributed and implicit motives differ?', *Psychological Review*, 96(4): 690–702.

McCrae, R.R. and Costa, P.T. Jr. (1997) 'Personality trait structure as a human universal', *American Psychologist*, 52(5): 509–16.

McCrae, R.R., Terracciano, A. et al. (2005) 'Universal features of personality traits from the observer's perspective: Data from 50 cultures', *Journal of Personality and Social Psychology*, 88(3): 547–61.

Murray, H.A. (1938) *Explorations in Personality*. New York: Oxford Press.

Paulhus, D.L. (1984) 'Two-component models of socially desirable responding', *Journal of*

Personality and Social Psychology, 46(3): 598–609.

Paulhus, D.L. (1991) 'Measurement and control of response bias', in J.P. Robinson, P.R. Shaver and L.S. Wrightsman (eds), *Measures of Personality and Social Psychological Attitudes*. San Diego: Academic Press, pp. 17–59.

Paulhus, D.L. (2002) 'Social desirability responding: The evolution of a construct', in H.J. Braun, D.N. Jackson and D.E. Wiley (eds), *The Role of Constructs in Psychological and Educational Measurement*. Mahwah, NJ: Lawrence Erlbaum Associates, pp. 49–69.

Paunonen, S.V. (1998) 'Hierarchical organization of personality and prediction of behavior', *Journal of Personality and Social Psychology*, 74(2): 538–56.

Paunonen, S.V. (2000) 'Construct validity and the search for cross-situational consistencies in personality', in R.D. Goffin and E. Helmes (eds), *Problems and Solutions in Human Assessment: Honoring Douglas N. Jackson at Seventy*. Norwell, MA: Kluwer, pp. 123–40.

Paunonen, S.V. (2002) *Design and Construction of the Supernumerary Personality Inventory*. Research Bulletin 763. London, Ontario: University of Western Ontario.

Paunonen, S.V. (2003) 'Big Five factors of personality and replicated predictions of behavior', *Journal of Personality and Social Psychology*, 84(2): 411–24.

Paunonen, S.V. and Ashton, M.C. (1998) 'The structured assessment of personality across cultures', *Journal of Cross-Cultural Psychology*, 29(1): 150–70.

Paunonen, S.V. and Ashton, M.C. (2001) 'Big Five factors and facets and the prediction of behavior', *Journal of Personality and Social Psychology*, 81(3): 524–39.

Paunonen, S.V. and Ashton, M.C. (2002) 'The nonverbal assessment of personality: The NPQ and the FF-NPQ', in B. De Raad and M. Perugini (eds), *Big Five Assessment*. Göttingen, Germany: Hogrefe & Huber, pp. 171–94.

Paunonen, S.V., Ashton, M.C. and Jackson, D.N. (2001) 'Nonverbal assessment of the Big Five personality factors', *European Journal of Personality*, 15(1): 3–18.

Paunonen, S.V., Haddock, G., Forsterling, F. and Keinonen, M. (2003) 'Broad versus narrow personality measures and the prediction of behavior across cultures',

European Journal of Personality, 17(6): 413–33.

Paunonen, S.V. and Jackson, D.N. (1979) 'Nonverbal trait inference', *Journal of Personality and Social Psychology*, 37(10): 1645–59.

Paunonen, S.V. and Jackson, D.N. (2000) 'What is beyond the Big Five? Plenty!', *Journal of Personality*, 68(5): 821–35.

Paunonen, S.V., Jackson, D.N. and Ashton, M.C. (2004) *Manual for Nonverbal Personality Questionnaire (NPQ) and Five-Factor Nonverbal Personality Questionnaire (FF-NPQ)*. Port Huron, MI: Sigma Assessment Systems.

Paunonen, S.V., Jackson, D.N. and Keinonen, M. (1990) 'The structured nonverbal assessment of personality', *Journal of Personality*, 58(3): 481–502.

Paunonen, S.V., Jackson, D.N., Trzebinski, J. and Forsterling, F. (1992) 'Personality structure across cultures: A multimethod evaluation', *Journal of Personality and Social Psychology*, 62(3): 447–56.

Paunonen, S.V., Keinonen, M., Trzebinski, J., Forsterling, F., Grishenko-Rose, N., Kouznetsova, L. and Chan, D.W. (1996) 'The structure of personality in six cultures', *Journal of Cross-Cultural Psychology*, 27(3): 339–53.

Paunonen, S.V., Zeidner, M., Engvik, H., Oosterveld, P. and Maliphant, R. (2000) 'The nonverbal assessment of personality in five cultures', *Journal of Cross-Cultural Psychology*, 31(2): 220–39.

Ramírez-Esparza, N., Gosling, S.D., Benet-Martínez, V., Potter, J.P. and Pennebaker, J.W. (2006) 'Do bilinguals have two personalities? A special case of cultural frame switching', *Journal of Research in Personality*, 40(2): 99–120.

Rolland, J.-P. (2002) 'Cross-cultural generalizability of the Five-Factor model of personality', in R.R. McCrae and J. Allik (eds), *The Five-Factor Model of Personality Across Cultures*. New York: Kluwer Academic/Plenum, pp. 7–28.

Schönemann, P.H. (1966) 'A generalized solution of the orthogonal Procrustes problem', *Psychometrika*, 31(1): 1–10.

Skinner, H.A., Jackson, D.N. and Rampton, G.M. (1976) 'The Personality Research Form in a Canadian context: Does language make a difference?', *Canadian Journal of Behavioral Science*, 8(2): 156–68.

Triandis, H.C. and Euh, E.M. (2002) 'Cultural influences on personality', *Annual Review of Psychology*, 53(1): 133–60.

Verkuyten, M. and Pouliasi, K. (2002) 'Biculturalism among older children: Cultural frame switching, attributions, self-identification, and attitudes', *Journal of Cross-Cultural Psychology*, 33(6): 596–609.

Verkuyten, M. and Pouliasi, K. (2006) 'Biculturalism and group identification: The mediating role of identification in cultural frame switching', *Journal of Cross-Cultural Psychology*, 37(3): 312–26.

Vorkapić, S.T., Lučev, I. and Turčinović, S.M. (2006) 'Factor analysis of FF-NPQ used on a Croatian sample', Paper presented at the 15th Psychology Days Conference, May, Zadar, Croatia.

Wong, R.Y. and Hong, Y. (2005) 'Dynamic influences of culture on cooperation in the prisoner's dilemma', *Psychological Science*, 16(6): 429–34.

24

Using Implicit Association Tests for the Assessment of Implicit Personality Self-Concept

Konrad Schnabel, Jens B. Asendorpf and
Anthony G. Greenwald

Psychologists have long suspected that people do not have good access to their own thoughts and feelings and that self-exploration is subject to introspective limits. Empirical evidence supports this view (e.g. Nisbett and Wilson, 1977). What results is a compelling claim for measurement procedures suitable for the assessment of cognitive processes that remain obscured if people are simply asked to report them. Recently, social cognition research has made progress towards the development of such 'implicit' procedures. This chapter deals with a most prominent class of implicit procedures, the Implicit Association Tests (IATs) (Greenwald et al., 1998), and reviews theoretical and empirical contributions that explored IATs for the assessment of the personality self-concept.

Although the term 'implicit' was criticized because it left unclear whether it described the measure or the construct, we retain this term that is now firmly entrenched in the literature. Originally, 'implicit' was intended to be a label for the measure. In this chapter, we consider both aspects and refer to the implicit personality self-concept at the construct level and to features of the measurement procedure (e.g. unawareness or fakability) at the empirical level. Also, we refer to IAT measures in plural to indicate that they represent different applications of a general procedure rather than one specific test.

The chapter is organized into four main parts. The first section is devoted to the conceptualization of the explicit and the implicit personality self-concept. Following this, we describe essential characteristics of IAT procedures and discuss different theoretical accounts for IAT effects. The third section presents the psychometric properties of IATs including their reliability and their ability to predict criterion variance unpredicted by self-report measures (incremental validity). The section also discusses the extent to which IATs meet the demands of individual diagnosis. In the final section, we describe alternatives to IAT measures along with their advantages and disadvantages over the IATs and offer an outlook to future research.

IMPLICIT AND EXPLICIT PERSONALITY SELF-CONCEPT

Bearing in mind the mind's limited ability to introspect, current social cognition research developed *two-systems models* that differentiate between two ways of human information processing. In the following, we employ the reflective-impulsive model (Strack and Deutsch, 2004) to illustrate this approach although it remains debatable whether an implicit–explicit distinction strictly at the empirical level would be sufficient (Greenwald and Nosek, in press). Strack and Deutsch's model proposes that perception, thinking, and behavior are functions of two different systems of information processing, the reflective and the impulsive system. In the *reflective system*, behavior is the result of propositional reasoning. For instance, thinking about one's life may lead to the decision 'I am happy.' In this reasoning process, information is made available in the form of propositions. Propositions consist of concepts (e.g. 'I' and 'happy') that are linked by a relation (e.g. 'am'). Propositions are generated through introspection and may be considered as either true or false. In the *impulsive system*, information is processed by the spread of activation between concepts that are associatively linked (e.g. 'I'–'happy'). Associative links are activated spontaneously and are only indirectly accessible by introspection. They may vary in strength but they cannot be considered as true or false.

Dissociations between propositional and associative information processing are also relevant with respect to representations of one's own self. The entirety of one's self-representations is called the self-concept. The part of the self-concept that refers to personality describing attributes is named the personality self-concept (cf. Asendorpf et al., 2002). Considering the conceptualization of two-system models, the personality self-concept comprises both propositional and associative representations of one's personal characteristics. We call propositional representations of the personality self-concept the *explicit personality self-concept* and associative representations the *implicit personality self-concept*. The explicit personality self-concept consists of propositional categorizations that include the concepts of the self and personality describing attributes. The implicit personality self-concept consists of associative clusters between concepts of the self and personality describing attributes.

Although this dual-representation interpretation remains debatable (Greenwald and Nosek, in press) the differentiation between the explicit and the implicit personality self-concept may be useful to conceptualize implications for personality assessment. Given that the explicit personality self-concept contains conscious representations that are generated through a deliberate reasoning process, these representations correspond to answers in a questionnaire that asks respondents to inform about themselves. Consequently, these answers are subject to the limitations of explicit representations (Greenwald and Banaji, 1995). One limitation is that answers in a questionnaire rely on verbal report that is intentionally given to inform about the self. Therefore, questionnaire answers are susceptible to *self-presentational biases*. Second, questionnaire answers only refer to representations of the personality self-concept that are accessible through introspection. Therefore, they are bound to *introspective limits* and may not reflect the entirety of an individual's implicit knowledge about his or her personality. Due to these limitations, there is much interest in the field of personality assessment to have access to procedures that are freed of these limits of explicit questionnaire measures and that are suitable for the assessment of implicit self-representations. Progress has been made with the development of these implicit measures, especially with the development of chronometric procedures like the IAT (Greenwald et al., 1998) that will be described in the next section in more detail.

IAT PROCEDURES

IAT measures are designed to assess automatic associations between a contrasted pair of target (such as 'me' vs. 'others') and attribute (such as 'anxious' vs. 'confident') concepts through a series of discrimination tasks that require fast responding. Faster responses are expected when two highly associated categories (e.g. 'me' and 'confident') share the same response. IATs start by introducing participants to the target, and, subsequently, to the attribute concept. For instance, an IAT that assesses the personality self-concept of anxiousness[1] (see Table 24.1) *first* trains participants to press the left response key when a 'me' word is presented on the screen and the right response key when an 'others' word is presented (side assignments are arbitrary and may be counterbalanced, see below). In the *second* block, participants are trained to press left for 'anxious' words and right for 'confident' words. The *third* and *fourth* block combine the target and the attribute discrimination, and ask participants to respond left to 'me' or 'anxious' words, and right to 'others' or 'confident' words. The combined tasks are subdivided into one block of 20 trials and one block of 40 trials in standard IATs mostly due to historical reasons. Early IAT procedures labeled the first 20 trials as practice blocks and the following 40 trials as test blocks. Currently

used IAT procedures do not use practice and test instructions, and scoring algorithms also include data from the first 20 trials because this was shown to increase the IATs' psychometric properties (Greenwald et al., 2003). Nevertheless, the '20 + 40' subdivision is often retained and may help to reduce task demands in the otherwise overly lengthy combined blocks. The subsequent *fifth* block reverses the target discrimination, and assigns the left response to 'others' words and the right response to 'me' words. Finally, the *sixth* and *seventh* block combine again the attribute and the previously reversed target discrimination, and asks participants to respond left to 'others' or 'anxious' words, and right to 'me' names or 'confident' words.

The standard IAT procedure (cf. Nosek et al., 2007) (a) instructs participants to 'respond rapidly while occasional errors are acceptable', (b) displays category labels assigned to the right or left response key in the right or left upper screen corner throughout all tasks, (c) presents labels and stimuli of the target concept in a font (color or type) distinct from the attribute concept when both are represented by printed word stimuli, (d) alternates between target and attribute stimuli in the combined blocks, and (e) employs 60 trials

Table 24.1 Task sequence and stimuli of an Implicit Association Test to measure the implicit personality self-concept of anxiousness

			Response key assignment	
Block	No. of trials	Task	Left key	Right key
1	20	Target discrimination	Me	Others
2	20	Attribute discrimination	Anxious	Confident
3	20	First block of first combined task	Me, anxious	Others, confident
4	40	Second block of first combined task	Me, anxious	Others, confident
5	40	Reversed target discrimination	Others	Me
6	20	First block of second combined task	Others, anxious	Me, confident
7	40	Second block of second combined task	Others, anxious	Me, confident

	Target concept		Attribute concept	
Categories	Me	Others	Anxious	Confident
Sample stimuli	Me	Others	Anxious	Confident
	I	They	Timid	Daring
	Self	Them	Insecure	Secure
	My	You	Worried	Unconcerned
	Own	Your	Cautious	Carefree

Note: Sample stimuli correspond to Schnabel et al. (2006b)

(trial numbers can vary somewhat in typical use) in the combined blocks (each divided into an initial block of 20 trials and a main block of 40 trials), 20 trials in the first two simple discrimination blocks, and 40 trials in the third block (reversed target discrimination). For this block, 40 instead of only 20 trials are recommended because this was shown to reduce the well-known order effect for combined blocks (Nosek et al., 2005). Due to this order effect, mean IAT scores tend to show slightly stronger associations corresponding to the pairings of the combined block that is completed first. To control for this effect, it is often recommended to counterbalance the order of combined blocks between participants (e.g. Nosek et al., 2007).

However, the opinions are mixed concerning the experimental variation of procedural variables. When IATs are employed to assess the personality self-concept, and individual differences rather than cross-group differences are the matter of interest, it seems reasonable to keep procedural variables constant. Otherwise, procedural variance is confounded with interindividual variance (cf. Banse et al., 2001). Many procedural variables do not significantly affect IAT scores and their correlations (cf. Nosek et al., 2007, for a more detailed discussion), and may be set to current standards (usually five but at least two stimulus items per category, response-stimulus interval of 250 ms, fixed response key assignments). According to the same logic, the stimuli may be presented in a fixed random order – while alternating target and attribute trials – for all participants in correlational studies (cf. Schnabel et al., 2006a).

In contrast, there are two procedural variables, namely order of combined tasks and order of implicit–explicit measures, that many favor counterbalancing because they may have effects on IAT results. Experimental variation allows for the statistical compensation of these effects in regression designs and maximizes the generalizability of results. A recent meta-analysis revealed that correlations between IATs and explicit questionnaire measures are higher if the order of compatible and incompatible pairing is counterbalanced across participants (Hofmann et al., 2005a). There seems to be a better chance to have participants completing the IAT tasks in the order that is optimal for the valid assessment of their characteristic values if one counterbalances the sequence of the tasks. On the contrary, little or no effect on explicit–implicit correlations was found for the order of explicit self-report and IAT measures (Hofmann et al., 2005a; Nosek et al., 2005).

At present, order effects as well as their consequences for implicit–explicit correlations are not fully understood. It is quite plausible that answering explicit self-report measures has an effect on IAT responses, especially if the implicit representations are weak or generated on the basis of conscious reasoning (cf. Gregg et al., 2006). On the other side, it was shown that the incompatible block of a flower–insect attitude IAT (i.e. the block that combines 'flower' + 'negative' and 'insect' + 'positive') increases response latencies during explicit ratings of attitudes towards flowers and insects while it had no effect on the means of the ratings themselves (Klauer and Mierke, 2005). In conclusion, counterbalancing of the order of combined tasks and implicit–explicit measures may be an option in the absence of specific reasons for do otherwise especially in studies where the subsamples of different conditions are large enough to compare for correlational differences (at least $n = 50$, better $n = 100$, for each subsample).

The different opinions concerning variation of procedural variables reflect different research traditions in experimental and correlational psychology (see Cronbach, 1957). Experimental psychology often focuses on the internal validity of experimental procedures and considers individual differences as error variance. In contrast, correlational psychology is interested in the assessment of individual differences and rather considers procedural variance as unwanted error variance. While standards that are established in one tradition are often ignored in the other, both approaches can learn from each other. The most frequently ignored standard from correlational psychology is that correlational designs require adequate sample sizes. It should be noted that the 95% confidence interval for a correlation of 0.30 ranges from 0.11 to 0.47 for $n = 100$, and from 0.02 to 0.53 for $n = 50$. This questions the interpretability of correlations and correlational differences in studies with small samples (n considerably below 50, often even below 30) that are nevertheless frequently published even in first-tier journals.

Calculation of IAT scores

For the calculation of IAT scores (IAT effects), only the combined tasks are relevant. Scores are based upon the difference in mean response latencies in the second minus the first combined task (see Table 24.1). Thus, if participants are quicker in combining 'me' + 'anxious' and 'others' + 'confident' relatively to the reverse pairing, they attain low latencies in the first combined task and high latencies in the second combined task. This would result in a positive score in the anxiousness IAT. Consistent with the IAT's logic (Greenwald et al., 1998), positive scores in this case reflect *stronger associations* for 'me' + 'anxious' and 'others' + 'confident' *relatively* to 'me' + 'confident' and 'others' + 'anxious'.

As a refinement to this difference score, Greenwald et al. (2003) proposed an improved scoring algorithm that produces an interrelated set of *D measures*. These were shown to increase internal consistencies, correlations with self-report measures, and resistance to the influence of extraneous factors (e.g. general speed of responding). Their major feature is that they are individually calibrated by each respondent's standard deviation of response latencies. In detail, the algorithm for D measures includes the steps that are described in Table 24.2. If the IAT procedure does not prompt participants to correct errant responses (i.e. the standard procedure) and rather shows an error message (e.g. 800 ms) without the possibility to answer before continuing with the next trial, the D600 or D2SD measures are recommended. These require an extra step after step 2 and replace latencies of error trials by the block mean for correct trials plus an error penalty of either 600 ms or twice the standard deviation of the same block's correct responses (cf. footnote 2, Nosek et al., 2007). Prompting participants to correct errant responses saves them to simply wait during presentation of the error message and trains the correct use of response keys. Not requiring error correction allows participants to rush through the test by randomly pressing the right or left key. The latter may be controlled by excluding data of participants with high error rates. Given the lack of empirical evidence comparing these two procedural variations, we recommend to prompt participants to correct errant trials because this is the design that is used most

Table 24.2 Summary of IAT scoring procedures recommended by Greenwald et al. (2003)

Step	Procedure
1	Eliminate trials with latencies over 10,000 ms.
2	Exclude data from participants with more than 10% of trials showing latencies less than 300 ms.
3	Compute one 'inclusive' standard deviation for all trials in Blocks 3 and 6 and likewise for Blocks 4 and 7.
4	Compute separate means for trials in each of the Blocks 3, 4, 6, and 7.
5	Compute two mean difference scores ($\text{Mean}_{Block6} - \text{Mean}_{Block3}$ and $\text{Mean}_{Block7} - \text{Mean}_{Block4}$).
6	Divide each difference score by its associated standard deviation of step 3.
7	Resulting D measure represents the equal-weight average of the scores calculated in step 6.

Note: This table is adapted from Table 3 in Lane et al. (2007). An additional step is necessary if the IAT procedure does not prompt participants to correct errant responses (see text for details). Block numbers refer to blocks described in Table 24.1 SPSS and SAS syntax for this scoring algorithm are available at http://faculty.washington.edu/agg/iat_materials.htm and www.briannosek.com

often and that will increase comparability between different studies.

Calculation of internal consistencies

There exist various ways for calculating internal consistencies of IAT D measures. Some compute difference scores for every single trial of the combined blocks and treat them as separate items to calculate Cronbach's internal consistency alpha, some employ difference scores for blocks of 5, 10, 20, or more trials, some calculate split-half reliabilities over blocks with identical number of trials, and some over blocks with different numbers of trials. In order to control for response changes during completion of the IAT, odd-even like estimates may be more useful than block-wise estimates (cf. Schmukle and Egloff, 2006). Procedures that calculate internal consistency estimates over more than two subblocks may result in slightly higher scores, although this has not been systematically investigated. The standard procedure calculates split-half reliabilities over the difference scores of Block 6/3 and Block 7/4 (see Table 24.1).

Accounts for the IAT effect

IATs operate on the basic premise that responses are easier (i.e. quicker) if the concepts assigned to the same response key are strongly associated (Greenwald et al., 1998). Although there does not yet exist a comprehensive theoretical account, that explains underlying psychological mechanisms of this 'IAT effect' and elucidates method-specific influences, the process of developing such an account has been begun in several publications.

De Houwer's (2003a) approach referred to a *stimulus-response compatibility mechanism* and claimed that in the two combined blocks stimuli elicit either compatible or incompatible response tendencies. Whereas responses are unambiguously associated with a certain meaning in the block that is completed faster,

response representations are more ambiguous in the block that is completed more slowly. The combined block that is completed faster is often referred to as the 'compatible' IAT block. Of course, compatibility is a function of the participant, and blocks should rather be labeled as the, for example, 'me-anxious' or 'me-confident' pairing. For didactical purposes, De Houwer's stimulus-response compatibility account is explained using the flower–insect IAT because this IAT has a clear compatible ('flower' + 'positive' and 'insect' + 'negative') and incompatible ('flower' + 'negative' and 'insect' + 'positive') pairing. De Houwer proposes that responses to items of the target concept may be based on either their category membership (e.g. 'flower' vs. 'insect') or their evaluative meaning (e.g. 'positive' vs. 'negative'). Both the category-based and the valence-based response tendencies lead to correct responses in the compatible pairing (synergistic effect). In the incompatible pairing, these response tendencies interfere with each other and only the category-based response tendencies lead to correct responses in terms of key assignments (antagonistic effect).

Steffens and Plewe (2001) claimed that both a concept-based and a stimulus-based factor have an impact on the IAT effect. The concept-based factor refers to target-attribute associations at the concept level. It accounts for a simplified task representation during the compatible IAT task due to a dimensional overlap (e.g. 'good–bad') between the target (e.g. 'flower–insect') and the attribute (e.g. 'positive–negative') concept. The stimulus-based factor refers to individual features of target and attribute stimuli. It accounts for a modification of the concept effect depending on whether cross-category associations at the stimulus level are consistent (e.g. insect = cockroach, wasp) or inconsistent (e.g. insect = ladybird, firefly) with associations at the concept level. Steffens and Plewe (2001) manipulated cross-category associations in a gender IAT and showed that the IAT effect was larger for item sets with consistent rather than inconsistent cross-category associations.

However, inconsistent cross-category associations did not reverse the IAT effect. Steffens and Plewe (2001) concluded that the concept factor plays a major role in the IAT effect but may be substantially altered by stimulus features (for similar results, cf. Mitchell et al., 2003; Nosek et al., 2005; Rudman et al., 2001; for cross-category associations reversing the IAT effect, cf. Blümke and Friese, 2006; Govan and Williams, 2004). Concerning practical implications, these findings suggest to thoroughly select IAT stimuli in a way that they (a) well represent all relevant aspects of the concept category, and (b) may not be categorized according to features different from the category frame (Nosek et al., 2005).

Additional evidence for the key influence of the task factor on the IAT effect was presented by Olson and Fazio (2005). These authors developed personalized IAT variants in order to assess attitudes towards various targets (e.g. apple vs. candy bars, Bush vs. Gore). Simply by changing the category labels of the attribute concept from 'positive' and 'negative' to 'I like' and 'I dislike', they found higher implicit–explicit correlations for these personalized IATs than for standard IATs. The authors concluded that the personalized IATs reduced effects of extrapersonal associations and focused the IATs on more personal associations.

Extrapersonal or environmental associations (cf. Karpinski and Hilton, 2001) were assumed to reflect external estimations that one has encountered in society (e.g. 'Apples are healthier and should be judged more positively than candy bars.') and that do not necessarily correspond with one's personal attitudes (e.g. 'Sometimes, I really like to have a candy bar.'). It may be worthwhile to adapt self-concept IATs to this personalized form in order to reduce unwanted environmental effects. This adaptation may not be easy because many self-concept IATs do not employ an evaluative attribute concept and may not be adapted using Olson and Fazio's 'I like' and 'I dislike' category labels. Additionally, as a first step, empirical

evidence should be collected that shows that personal IATs are superior to standard IATs in the prediction of social behavior that is in turn a function of environmental and contextual influences. Recent studies suggest that the personalized IAT does not remove a confound of extrapersonal variation. Instead, the 'I like' and 'I dislike' labels for the target categories rather introduce a confound of task-recoding in which the target stimuli are more likely to be explicitly evaluated (Nosek and Hansen, 2007).

Mierke and Klauer (2001, 2003) reported a *task-switching* account of the IAT effect. Similarly to De Houwer (2003a), they stated that merely considering attribute-related information is sufficient for fast and accurate responding within the compatible IAT task. Consequently, participants may neglect to switch between target-based and attribute-based decisions in the compatible pairing. As participants neglect to switch they avoid task-switching costs that are inescapable in the incompatible task. Mierke and Klauer (2001) compared response latencies between trials that switched between target to attribute discrimination and trials that required a discrimination according to the concept of the preceding trial. Results showed that switching between target and attribute discrimination produced significantly more costs (i.e. longer response latencies) in the incompatible than in the compatible IAT task.

Another set of experiments showed that interindividual differences in task-switching performance produce reliable method-specific variance in IAT scores, although the improved scoring procedure (see above) seems to control for this effect. Mierke and Klauer (2003) demonstrated that IAT effects could be obtained with an IAT that was not based on pre-existing associations between target and attribute concept. For this purpose, they developed an IAT that experimentally imposed a contingency between the target features ('blue' vs. 'red') and the attribute features ('big' vs. 'small') of geometrical objects, in such a way that all blue objects were big and all red objects were small.

This geometrical objects IAT produced IAT effects that were internally consistent (Cronbach's $\alpha = 0.93$) and showed a significant correlation with the absolute scores of a self-concept IAT that measured extraversion ($r = 0.29$). The authors used absolute scores for the extraversion IAT because they expected interindividual differences in task-switching performance to primarily affect the incompatible IAT pairing. Whether a pairing is compatible or incompatible, however, is a function of the participant rather than a function of the IAT. Participants with poor task-switching performance decrease response latencies in the pairing that is their particular incompatible pairing (i.e. either the 'me-extraverted' or the 'me-introverted' pairing). Consequently, these participants add an extremity bias to their IAT results rendering them either more extraverted or more introverted. The extremity bias is better captured by absolute scores rather than by IAT raw scores. In contrast, absolute scores and raw scores were identical for the geometrical objects IAT because no participant showed negative scores in this IAT. Overall, there was no conceptual similarity concerning the content of the extraversion IAT and the geometrical objects IAT, and the significant correlation between both IATs could not be interpreted in terms of convergent validity. Thus, Mierke and Klauer's (2003) results indicated a reliable contamination of both IATs with method-specific variance. Interestingly, when Mierke and Klauer (2003) computed the IAT scores as D measures using the improved scoring algorithm presented by Greenwald et al. (2003), the correlation between the geometrical objects IAT and the extraversion IAT was substantially reduced and no longer significant ($r = 0.12$).

In a similar vein, Back et al. (2005) explored correlations between another IAT measuring task-switching abilities and a content-specific self-concept IAT measuring anxiousness. Their task-switching IAT differed from Mierke and Klauer's (2003) IAT in two aspects that aimed to improve structural closeness to features of content-specific IATs.

First, Back et al.'s IAT employed verbal material instead of geometrical objects, and the concept categories were 'letter' (e.g. M, B) versus 'number' (e.g. 4, 7) and 'word' (e.g. shirt, pen) versus 'calculation' (e.g. $7 - 4 = 3$, $4 + 5 = 9$). Second, it used the preexisting associations between these concept categories (i.e. between 'letter' and 'word', and between 'number' and 'calculation') instead of experimentally imposed contingencies between geometrical objects in order to avoid individual differences caused by learning the previously unknown associations.

Similar to the results by Mierke and Klauer (2003), Back et al.'s (2005) results showed that correlations between the task-switching and the anxiousness IAT can be significantly reduced if the improved D measures were used for the IATs (in a combined analysis of three studies, from $r = 0.29$ to $r = 0.17$). Differently from Mierke and Klauer, the remaining small correlation between the two conceptually unrelated IATs was still significant in Back et al.'s study. This may be attributed to the larger sample size in Back et al.'s study and the effect that their task-switching IAT may be more appropriate to capture task-switching costs in content-specific IATs. Together, these findings suggest that task-switching costs (greater costs when categories sharing a response key are not well associated) represent an important component of the IAT effect. Additionally, a residual small portion of the IAT measure seems to contain a component of task-switching ability that is independent of the association strengths being measured.

Rothermund and Wentura (2004) suggested a *figure-ground model* that posits that target and attribute categories are asymmetrical with respect to their salience. According to this model, the salient category of the target (e.g. 'Blacks') and the attribute (e.g. 'negative') concept serves as 'figure' on the 'ground' of the opposing non-salient categories (e.g. 'Whites' and 'positive'). When the salient categories are mapped to one response key and the non-salient categories are mapped to the other response key during the compatible pairing, participants can base their discrimination on the figure-ground asymmetries alone. In contrast, there is a mismatch of 'figure' and 'ground' categories in the incompatible pairing.

In a series of different experiments, Rothermund and Wentura (2004) dissociated effects of salience asymmetries from effects of associations between target and attribute concepts, and showed that salience asymmetries alone may produce IAT effects. However, this does not rule out that differences in association strength may also be a source of IAT effects, and that salience asymmetries themselves may be the result of such differences. For example, insects may be the salient category in the flower–insect IAT because insects are associated with negative valence. As a consequence, salience asymmetries may only distort IAT effects in artificial IATs that were designed to maximize salience asymmetries and to minimize associations between concept categories (Greenwald et al., 2005). Furthermore, results for the content-unspecific task-switching IATs (Back et al., 2005; Mierke and Klauer, 2003) imply that salience asymmetries are, like associations, not a necessary precondition for IAT effects. Thus, the salience asymmetry account has not yet established itself as an aid to understanding the mechanism of IAT effects.

A key role in many of the accounts listed before seems to be whether target and attribute categories share similar features (cf. De Houwer et al., 2005). The more similarity exists between target and attribute concepts, the more similar are the activation patterns that they produce. When similar activation patterns are matched to identical responses in the compatible IAT pairing, responses are facilitated. The origins of similarity may be manifold, and shared salience asymmetries may be just one source of similarity. In turn, features that are shared between different concepts may provide a basis for associations between concepts. If one is interested in the assessment of associations one has to consider whether the similarity between the concepts refers to the associations of interest rather than

to alternate features of shared similarity (e.g. word length, stimulus familiarity, salience asymmetries; cf. Dasgupta et al., 2000; Greenwald et al., 2005).

It is important to note that most of the accounts that aim to explain IAT effects refer to mechanisms that affect mean IAT effects. Only a few studies refer to effects on correlations between different IATs or between IATs and explicit measures. Notably, correlations between IATs and explicit measures may be unaffected even if IAT effects are reduced by procedural variations or stimulus features (e.g. Nosek et al., 2005; Steffens and Plewe, 2001). Only one account explicitly refers to an individual differences perspective and suggests that task-switching abilities constitute a (small) contaminant of IAT measures (Back et al., 2005; Mierke and Klauer, 2003). Generally, care should be taken if models concerning mean IAT effects are employed to draw conclusions about the correlations of IAT scores.

PSYCHOMETRIC PROPERTIES OF IATS

Evaluating whether IATs meet relevant psychometric criteria is especially important when IAT measures are employed for the assessment of individual differences. A proper assessment requires that IATs refer to relatively stable individual differences in implicit self-representations, and that these differences contribute significantly to the prediction of behavior. In this section, we review psychometric properties of IAT measures and refer particularly to IAT adaptations that deal with the assessment of the implicit personality self-concept.

Reliability

Various adaptations of IAT measures usually reach *internal consistency* estimates (split-half correlations or Cronbach's alphas) between 0.70 and 0.90 (e.g. Banse et al., 2001; Schmukle and Egloff, 2004). Such reliabilities are psychometrically satisfactory, and they are much higher than those found for other latency-based measures such as priming procedures (e.g. Bosson et al., 2000; Kawakami and Dovidio, 2001) the Go/No-Go Association Task (GNAT) (Nosek and Banaji, 2001) or the dot probe task (Schmukle, 2005). Although internal consistencies for IATs may depend on the method of calculation (see above), these influences have not yet been studied systematically and may be relatively minor.

Another measure of reliability, test–retest reliability, has been observed to show a median of 0.56 across different studies (Nosek et al., 2007) which is about 0.15 to 0.20 below the internal consistencies that are typically obtained for IAT measures (Greenwald and Farnham, 2000; Schmukle and Egloff, 2004; Schnabel et al., 2006b). The same is true if the retest is completed after a time span of up to one year (Egloff et al., 2005), or if the second test is a parallel test that employs parallel attribute stimuli (Asendorpf et al., 2002). Within the period of one year it seems rather irrelevant whether the retest is completed immediately or with relatively more time after the first test (cf. Nosek et al., 2007). The reasons for the discrepancy between a satisfactory internal consistency and a retest reliability that is somewhat too low for assessments of stable constructs are presently unclear. The lower test–retest reliability implies that there are systematic occasion-to-occasion variations in IAT scores that stem from changes in either (a) the association strengths being measured or (b) unidentified additional sources of variance in the measurement procedure. The first is plausible because of the numerous context effects that have been demonstrated for IAT measures (Blair, 2002).

Approaches that separated trait and state influences (Schmukle and Egloff, 2004, 2005) showed that IATs capture both reliable trait-specific and state-specific variation. However, state-specific variation in an anxiousness IAT could, in contrast to an increase in self-reported state-anxiety, not be explained

by an anxiety induction (Schmukle and Egloff, 2004). Importantly, Schmukle and Egloff (2004) found non-significant induction effects on the anxiousness IAT both when using a between-subjects design (IAT was presented after the anxiety induction and compared to a control group without anxiety induction) and a within-subjects design (IAT was presented before and after the anxiety induction). The usage of between-subjects designs for the exploration of state effects on IAT measures is indispensable due to the small but systematic attenuation of IAT effects from first to subsequent administrations (Greenwald et al., 2003). One option for repeated measures designs may be to include a non-relevant control IAT that is expected to be unaltered by the manipulation and to compare effects on the relevant IAT with effects on the control IAT (cf. Teachman and Woody, 2003). But even then, there remains some uncertainty about the comparability of repeated administration effects on the relevant and the control IAT.

Fakability

Investigations of the fakability of IATs revealed that they are, though slightly fakable, much less fakable than explicit self-reports (Asendorpf et al., 2002; Banse et al., 2001; Boysen et al., 2006; Egloff and Schmukle, 2002; Steffens, 2004). Fakability increased if participants were informed beforehand about how to fake (Kim, 2003). Importantly, faking effects on mean IAT scores are a threat to the validity of individual differences measured by IATs only if differential faking (different individuals fake to a different extent) occurs. Differential faking effects should change the rank order of participants' IAT scores and alter their correlations with external validation criteria that are expected to be immune to faking.

Schnabel and colleagues (2006b) explored differential faking effects on a shyness IAT and a parallel chronometric procedure, the shyness IAP, and revealed strong effects of differential faking for explicit self-report but not for implicit measures. The authors compared correlations between an experimental group that was instructed to appear non-shy and a control group without faking instructions. Results showed that (a) implicit–explicit correlations were moderate in the control group whereas they were significantly reduced in the experimental group, (b) faking instructions increased the correlation between explicit shyness and a social desirability scale whereas the correlation between implicit shyness and social desirability was low in both groups, and (c) faking instructions decreased the correlations with observer judgments of shyness for explicit but not for implicit measures of shyness. Thus, IATs seem to be more robust against faking attempts than explicit self-report measures with regard to both mean and differential faking effects.

The fact that IATs are slightly fakable suggests that they are not process pure in the sense of measuring solely the strength of automatic associations. A recent multinomial modeling approach differentiates between several automatic and controlled cognitive processes in implicit social cognition and provides evidence that IATs may also reflect controlled efforts to reduce automatic biases (Conrey et al., 2005). Future research should deal with the question of how making IAT measures less fakable. Another approach may be to develop algorithms that allow to empirically distinguish honest from faked IAT performance (Cvencek and Greenwald, 2006).

Validity

Convergent and discriminant validity with implicit measures

Correlations of IATs with other implicit measures are typically weak. Bosson et al. (2000) observed non-significant correlations between a self-esteem IAT and six other implicit self-esteem measures. Correlations between IATs and priming procedures tend to be small or non-significant (Olson and Fazio, 2003). For the assessment of individual differences in implicit self-representations, priming procedures are scarcely used mainly due to their unsatisfactory reliability (cf. Banse, 1999). If one accounts for the lack of reliability, the observed disattenuated correlations between priming procedures and IATs become more substantial (Cunningham et al., 2001). Insufficient reliability of other implicit measures may principally explain why their correlations with IAT measures are so small. This is true also for recently developed implicit procedures (for a description of these measures, see next section) like the GNAT (Nosek and Banaji, 2001) and the EAST (De Houwer and De Bruycker, 2007; Teige et al., 2004).

For a different new implicit procedure, the Implicit Association Procedure (IAP), correlations with an IAT were much higher (up to 0.50) and not much lower than the IAT's and the IAP's retest reliability (Schnabel et al., 2006b). The IAP procedure is similar to the IAT in that it measures relative association strengths by comparing response latencies of two combined discrimination tasks. Differently from the IAT, the IAP uses joystick movements towards or away from the participant instead of a right and left response key. Because the IAP is similar to the IAT in other methodological details, the correlation of approximately 0.50 between IAT and IAP found by Schnabel et al. (2006b) may indicate an upper bound to the construct validity, suggesting a substantial method variance in the IAT and similar procedures.

Convergent and discriminant validity with explicit self-report measures

In several fairly large samples ($n > 98$) Asendorpf and colleagues found small to moderate correlations between self-concept IATs and explicit self-ratings on IATs' attribute stimuli. For a shyness IAT, correlations ranged between 0.30 and 0.44 (Asendorpf et al., 2002; Schnabel et al., 2006b; Teige et al., 2004), for an angriness IAT between 0.11 and 0.39 (Schnabel et al., 2006a; Teige et al., 2004), and for an anxiousness IAT the implicit–explicit correlation was 0.25 (Schnabel et al., 2006a). The small correlation for the anxiousness IAT replicated results from studies by Egloff and colleagues who used 'anxious' versus 'calm' instead of 'anxious' versus 'confident' as attribute categories (Egloff and Schmukle, 2002, 2003). Steffens and Schulze-König (2006) explored implicit–explicit correlations for the Big Five in a total sample of $n = 89$ psychology students and found significant but small correlations (< 0.29) for neuroticism and conscientiousness, but non-significant correlations for the other Big Five traits (i.e. extraversion, openness, agreeableness). Together, these findings are in line with results from other areas of IAT research (e.g. attitudes, stereotypes) revealing that IATs and their corresponding explicit self-report measures show evidence for both convergent and discriminant validity and refer to related but distinct constructs (Nosek and Smyth, 2007).

Recent meta-analyses on correlations between IATs and explicit self-reports over numerous content domains (including attitude, self-concept, and stereotype IATs) revealed average implicit–explicit correlations of 0.24 (Hofmann et al., 2005a) and 0.37 (Nosek, 2005). The difference between these findings may be explained by the facts that: (a) the studies put a focus on different domains; and (b) Nosek (2005) used relative feeling thermometers as explicit measures exclusively that may correspond more closely with the IAT in the sense that they more readily tap into an affective component. Hofmann and colleagues (2005) included studies using various explicit measures and content domains that are likely to elicit only weak implicit–explicit consistency (e.g. racial attitudes) whereas most of Nosek's (2005) studies referred to attitude domains showing moderate to substantial implicit–explicit correlations.

Hofmann and colleagues (2005) organized variables that may moderate implicit–explicit consistency in a process model containing five primary factors. The *translation* factor refers to the interrelation between implicit and explicit representations. It includes aspects like representational strength (subjectively important or frequently processed representations), dimensionality (representations that

refer to either end of a bipolar continuum), social distinctiveness (representations thought to be distinct from other individuals), and awareness (introspectively accessible representations) that are all associated with greater implicit–explicit consistency (cf. Nosek, 2005). The factor *additional information integration* describes whether explicit representations assessed by verbal self-report are generated spontaneously or deliberately. Explicit representations that are generated spontaneously or with minimal use of cognitive resources show greater implicit–explicit consistency.

The factors *explicit assessment* and *implicit assessment* refer to reliability and method-specific variance (e.g. fakability) of explicit and implicit measures. With respect to the explicit assessment factor, differences in social desirability or self-presentational concerns may also moderate implicit–explicit consistency (Nosek, 2005), although this influence seems to be somewhat over-estimated (Hofmann et al., 2005b) and has not yet been found for correlations with self-concept IATs (Egloff and Schmukle, 2003). With respect to the implicit assessment factor, the situational malleability of implicit representations (e.g. Blair, 2002) may additionally play a role in decreasing implicit–explicit consistency. Finally, *design factors* such as variance restriction due to sampling biases and lack of conceptual correspondence between implicit and explicit measures were found to reduce implicit–explicit consistency.

Recently, Nosek (2007) provided a nice illustration that the correlational or convergent validity indicator of implicit–explicit consistency can vary independently from particular mean differences between implicit and explicit measures. The latter refer to whether implicit and explicit measures show different deviations of the sample means from theoretically expected zero points on the scales. Using attitude IATs as examples, Nosek showed that even if implicit and explicit preferences were at odds concerning the sample means (e.g. indicating explicit preferences for 'evolution' and implicit preferences for 'creationism') interindividual correlations of these preferences can be very high (in this case 0.60). Moreover, there was no systematic relationship across 58 different attitude objects between the consistency of implicit and explicit preferences concerning sample means and the consistency concerning the implicit–explicit correlations.

Predictive validity for behavioral measures

A recent meta-analysis (Greenwald, Poehlman, Uhlmann, and Banaji, in press) found compelling evidence for the predictive validity of IATs (but also explicit measures) across various behavioral domains. The predictive validity of explicit measures, differently from IAT measures, was reduced in domains that are hardly guided by conscious control or that are susceptible to social desirability concerns. IATs outperformed explicit measures in the domain of stereotyping and prejudice, whereas explicit measures outperformed IATs in studies that explored brand preferences or political candidate preferences. Perugini (2005) classified predictive models of implicit and explicit measures to into three different types: the additive, the multiplicative, and the double dissociation model. All three models postulate that implicit measures show incremental validity and increase the prediction of behavior. This aspect is crucial for judging the value of implicit procedures for the assessment of personality constructs. The *additive model* describes implicit and explicit measures explaining different portions of variance of a relevant criterion. Concerning self-concept IATs, additive validity of a shyness, an anxiousness, and an angriness IAT was found for the prediction of observer judgments of shy behavior (Schnabel et al., 2006b), anxious behavior (Schnabel et al., 2006a), but not angry behavior (Schnabel et al., 2006a), respectively.

In the *multiplicative model*, implicit and explicit measures interact in predicting relevant behavioral criteria. Interactive validity effects were found for self-esteem IATs indicating that persons with discrepant self-esteem (persons showing discrepancies between implicit and explicit self-esteem) exhibit more defensive behavior (rejection of negative feedback, exaggerated social consensus estimates) than individuals with congruent self-esteem (Jordan et al., 2003; McGregor et al., 2005; Schröder-Abé et al., 2007). Defensive behavior was explained by a lack of integration in self-representation for individuals with discrepant self-esteem. Interactive predictive validity for implicit and explicit self-esteem may explain why Greenwald and colleagues (in press) found no overall main effects for implicit self-esteem predicting relevant behavioral criteria.

The *double dissociation model* claims that implicit measures predict spontaneous behavior whereas explicit measures predict controlled behavior. Double dissociation models for IATs have rarely been realized probably due to the complexity of identifying relevant indicators of spontaneous and controlled behavior. McConnell and Liebold (2001) presented evidence that a race IAT measuring attitudes towards Blacks versus Whites significantly correlated with indicators of spontaneous behavior indicating negative Black prejudices (e.g. less smiling towards a Black than a White experimenter). In contrast, the explicit measure of prejudice did not correlate with any of these behavioral indicators. Concerning self-concept IATs, Egloff and Schmukle (2002) found that an anxiousness IAT predicted several behavioral indicators of anxiety during a stressful speech whereas the explicit anxiousness measure only accounted for self-reported state anxiety during the speech. In a similar vein, Steffens and Schulze-König (2006) showed that four of five self-concept IATs measuring the Big Five correlated significantly with relevant indicators of spontaneous behavior, but explicit self-reports of the Big Five did not.

In what seems to be the strongest finding of a double dissociation, Asendorpf and colleagues (2002) confirmed for shyness a full and strong double dissociation pattern. Their studies included valid indicators of both spontaneous and controlled shy behavior, and the IAT uniquely predicted spontaneous but not controlled behavior whereas self-reports uniquely predicted controlled but not spontaneous behavior. Double dissociation designs are highly recommendable to elucidate the construct validity of implicit measures and to demonstrate their specific contribution in the sense of incremental validity to explicit measures. They are the only way to show unique validity of implicit measures for the prediction of spontaneous behavior while simultaneously ensuring that this cannot be attributed to a general lack of validity of the corresponding explicit measure.

It should be noted that all self-concept IATs that were valid for the prediction of behavior employed attribute concepts that are confounded with positive and negative valence (e.g. anxious vs. confident, shy vs. non-shy, agreeable vs. disagreeable). To date, it is unclear to what extent IAT responses are based on the specific semantic meaning of the attribute categories or simply on their positive and negative valence (cf. Schnabel et al., 2006a). For future self-concept IATs, it will be useful to show construct validity for their specific semantic content as distinct from a general positive or negative evaluation. Rudman and colleagues (2001) employed gender IATs to show independent effects of stereotyping and evaluation in implicit gender associations. In a similar vein, Amodio and Devine (2006) separated stereotyping and evaluation effects in implicit race biases using evaluative (pleasant vs. unpleasant) and stereotyping (mental vs. physical) race IATs (Amodio and Devine, 2006).

ALTERNATIVE METHODS TO IAT PROCEDURES

Alternative methods intended to overcome the limitation that IATs are restricted to the assessment of relative association strengths and that the concepts need to have two categories. In fact, IAT scores reflect the association strength between one pairing of target and attribute categories relatively to the

reverse pairing. For instance, a positive score in the standard flower–insect IAT does not indicate that one evaluates flowers positively and insects negatively. The positive score rather reflects that one evaluates flowers more positively than insects. As the most radical alternative to dual-category concepts, Blanton et al. (2006) presented the Single Association Test (SAT).

The SAT assesses the association strengths between the concept categories separately in different tasks. In these tasks, one target and one attribute category is used to create one joint category (e.g. 'flower-positive', 'flower-negative', 'insect-positive', or 'insect-negative') that is contrasted to two control categories. Blanton and colleagues (2006) used 'furniture' (e.g. table, desk) and 'middle' (e.g. midpoint, halfway) as control categories (cf. Pinter and Greenwald, 2005). They expected the associations between these control categories to be constant for all participants. Consequently, individual differences in response latencies should only be influenced by the associations between the relevant concepts and not by associations between the control concepts. Blanton and colleagues explored the SAT using the categories 'Black' (African American names), 'White' (European American names), 'positive' (positively valenced words), and 'negative' (negatively valenced words) of the race IAT. Differently from current standards, they did not employ difference scores between the combined tasks nor scoring algorithms according to Greenwald et al.'s (2003) D measure in order control for interindividual differences in response latencies. Instead, they employed response latencies of a flower–insect IAT as a general response speed measure.

Using structural equation modeling and partialing general processing speed, Blanton and colleagues showed that the SAT data did not fit structural equation models that assumed that positive and negative evaluations of the racial groups were opposed to each other. Thus, response latencies in the 'Blacks' + 'positive' task did not correlate negatively with response latencies in the 'Blacks' + 'negative' task.

The same was true for the 'Whites' + 'positive' and 'Whites' and 'negative' tasks. Both would be required by standard IAT procedures that do no allow to assess these associations separately. In contrast, model fit of the SAT data was good, when response latencies in the four different SAT tasks were treated as separate attitude indicators. Additionally, only response latencies in the 'Blacks' + 'negative' task showed a significant relationship with the scores on a racism questionnaire, suggesting that the tendency to automatically associate Blacks with negative attributes is a key predictor of racism.

Unfortunately, Blanton and colleagues did not directly compare their method to control for general speed differences with algorithms that are usually employed for IAT measures (i.e. difference scores and D measures). Also, the study did not directly compare SAT results with results yielded from an IAT. Thus, it is somewhat difficult to estimate to what extent the SAT approach is superior to standard IAT methods. Most importantly, before the SAT will be broadly employed for the assessment of interindividual differences it needs to show satisfactory internal consistencies. Blanton and colleagues do not report any reliability indices. Additionally, Nosek and Sriram (2007) employed structural equation modeling to show that IAT scores represent *relative measures* that contrast performance between two interdependent conditions and that cannot be decomposed into additive combinations of two distinct indicators of the same construct. Structural equation models that respected the interdependence of the two IAT tasks by using difference scores resulted in very good model fits whereas models that considered the two IAT tasks as independent additive indicators fit poorly to the data.

A less radical approach to tackle the problem that four categories are confounded in standard IATs is presented by *single category IATs* (Karpinski and Steinman, 2006; Nosek and Banaji, 2001; Penke et al., 2006; Wigboldus et al., 2006). Single category IATs employ one unipolar concept (e.g. 'Blacks')

and one concept that includes two categories (e.g. 'positive' vs. 'negative'). There is a broad range of concepts that do not have a natural complement. As a consequence, it makes little sense to consider associations with these non-bipolar concepts in relation to another category (e.g. attitudes towards certain brands). Different variants of single category IATs were shown to show satisfactory internal consistencies and higher implicit–explicit correlations than corresponding standard IAT procedures (Karpinski and Steinman, 2006; Penke et al., 2006). For instance, Karpinski and Steinman showed that a self-esteem single category IAT (using 'positive' vs. 'negative' as attribute categories and 'me' as target category) was significantly correlated with an explicit self-esteem measures whereas a self-esteem IAT (using identical attribute categories and 'me' vs. 'others' as target categories) showed non-significant implicit–explicit correlations. Considering self-concept IATs, researchers may also wish to assess associations between the self and personality traits using single category IATs because these associations do not need to be inversely related to associations towards other persons.

However, IAT variants using single categories did not show satisfactory reliability indices in all instances (Nosek and Banaji, 2001; Wigboldus et al., 2006). This may be attributed to the fact, that categorizing stimuli in single category IATs may be facilitated by concentrating on the single category. Consider that in these tasks only one response key is assigned to a joint category (e.g. 'me' + 'positive') whereas the other response key is assigned to a single category (e.g. 'negative'). If participants base their responses on the single category and ignore the joint category, the task may no longer assess what one aims to measure, namely, associations within the joint categories. A similar logic may apply to Blanton et al.'s (2006) Single Association Test. Remember that in this task the control category, though it is a joint category (i.e. 'furniture' + 'middle'), remains constant throughout the whole task, while the joint categories containing the relevant concepts are changing. Similarly to single category IATs, participants may concentrate on the non-relevant control category in order to facilitate their responding. Also, it is not clear whether response windows as suggested by Karpinski and Steinman (2006) really decrease the likelihood that participants engage in such unwanted processing of the stimuli. Obviously, a lot of work needs to be done in order to know the conditions that make these IAT variants superior to the standard IAT procedure.

De Houwer (2003b) proposed the *Extrinsic Affective Simon Task* (EAST). Similarly to IATs, the EAST requires a double discrimination task including two concepts. Differently from IATs, there is only one double discrimination task in the EAST, and only one concept is categorized according to its relevant feature (e.g. 'positive' vs. 'negative') whereas the second concept (e.g. 'insect' vs. 'flower') is categorized according to a non-relevant feature (e.g. 'green' vs. 'red'). The task requires that half of the stimuli for both categories of the second concept are responded to with the same key as the 'positive' category, for example, and the other half are responded to with the same key as the 'negative' category. For instance, if the stimuli of the second concept have to be categorized according to their green or red color, half of the words representing the 'insect' category are displayed in red and the other half is displayed in green. The same is true for the 'flower' category. In contrast, the stimuli of the first category are displayed in black and have to be categorized according to their meaning (e.g. 'positive' vs. 'negative'). In contrast to the IAT, response key assignments are fixed for the whole task (e.g. 'positive' and 'green' are assigned to the left and 'negative' and 'red' are assigned to the right response key) but the stimuli for the categories of the second concept change their non-relevant feature (e.g. green or red color). Separate EAST scores can be calculated by comparing response latencies and error rates for 'flower' and 'insect' stimuli assigned to the 'positive' versus the 'negative' key.

In theory, the EAST allows for the assessment of multiple concepts that are each mutually assigned to the two categories of the non-relevant feature. Unfortunately, the internal consistencies of the EAST proved to be relatively weak (De Houwer, 2003b). Although some adaptations of the EAST reliably and validly assessed individual differences in fear of spiders (Huijding and de Jong, 2005; Ellwart et al., 2005), EAST adaptations for the assessment of associations between the self-concept and personality attributes showed insufficient reliability and validity and were clearly outperformed by the psychometric properties of corresponding IAT measures (Teige et al., 2004; De Houwer and De Bruycker, 2007). Consequently, the EAST does not seem to be promising for the assessment of the implicit personality self-concept.

Payne et al. (2005) developed a variant of affective priming, the *Affect Misattribution Procedure* (AMP). In this task, participants have to categorize neutral Chinese characters as pleasant or unpleasant. The Chinese characters are preceded by positive, negative, or neutral stimuli (i.e. the primes). Results showed that the judgment of the Chinese characters was influenced by the valence of the primes (misattribution effect). In contrast to other priming procedures, preference scores (calculated by comparing character judgments following positive vs. negative primes) were internally consistent and substantially correlated with self-reported preference measures. Theoretically, the AMP allows for the assessment of attitudes towards multiple unipolar targets and even for the assessment of single associations in the sense of the SAT (Blanton et al., 2006) if one uses neutral primes as a reference concept. However, none of these variants has been empirically tested so far. Also, it is not clear whether the AMP can be used for the assessment of the personality self-concept by using, for example, 'me' and 'others' as primes and asking to guess the semantic meaning of unknown characters as, for example, 'anxious' or 'confident'.

Recently, Greenwald (2005) proposed an IAT variant, the *Multifactor Trait IATs* (MFT-IATs), to allow for the assessment of multiple constructs and to deal with the problem that evaluative valence and specific semantic meaning are confounded in many self-concept IATs (cf. Schnabel et al., 2006a). The procedure employs attribute categories that are valence-matched (i.e. all attributes are either positive, negative, or neutral) to avoid category discriminations simply on the basis of their positive and negative valence. MFT-IATs require, similarly to standard IATs, one IAT per attribute concept. Different from standard IATs, attribute concepts in MFT-IATs have only one relevant category referring to the concept and one irrelevant category referring to the other attributes of the MFT-IAT.

For instance, a Big Five MFT-IAT assesses automatic associations between the concept of self and extraversion by using 'me' versus 'others' as target concept and 'extraversion' (e.g. energetic, bold, active, gregarious) versus 'other trait' (e.g. agreeableness, conscientiousness, emotional stability, openness) as attribute concept. The same logic applies for the remaining four Big Five traits. It is not yet clear, however, how many trials in the combined blocks are necessary for the reliable and valid assessment of traits using an MFT-IAT. Also, the procedure is relatively demanding because it requires one IAT for each trait of interest.

Positive aspects are that MFT-IATs allow for (a) using single category concepts and (b) balancing the valence of these concepts. Valence-matched concept categories are otherwise difficult to achieve because many dual-category concepts (e.g. anxious vs. calm, shy vs. non-shy, agreeable vs. disagreeable, conscientious vs. unconscientious) intrinsically comprise a positive–negative contrast. Another positive aspect of MFT-IATs may be that, differently from other single category IATs (see above), the attention is drawn on the relevant category because the non-relevant category includes various different attributes and can, therefore, not be used to simplify the task.

CONCLUSION

After the IAT procedure had been published (Greenwald et al., 1998), some psychologists feared that IATs were intended as a lie-detector, revealing associations from the deep and inaccessible parts of personality that are more telling than what people can tell about themselves. However, an important aspect of IATs is that they do not obscure the content of what is being assessed and that they allow participants to refuse cooperation. Although this raises a question about how 'implicit' IATs are (cf. De Houwer and Moors, 2007) this brings the important benefit that (in contrast to procedures such as subliminal priming) IATs cannot be employed against the will of examinees. In fact, we are not aware of any publication exploring the validity of IATs that endorses a lie-detector view on this procedure.

IATs are beginning to be used as clinical research tools and may help to evaluate therapy needs and outcomes with regard to spontaneous behavior and automatic cognitive biases. For these purposes, IATs are not employed as self-sufficient procedures but as a useful adjunct to diagnosis via explicit self-reports. Moreover, it is clearly premature to consider IATs as tools for individual diagnosis in selection settings or as a basis for decisions that have important personal consequences. The modest retest-reliability of IAT measures together with the unanswered questions concerning the explanation of IAT effects make evident that potential applications should be approached with care and scientific responsibility. Meanwhile, IATs are a fascinating research tool at the interface of social cognition and personality psychology that help to draw a more holistic picture of individual behavior and experience.

NOTES

1 We use the term 'anxiousness' rather than 'anxiety' to differentiate between the trait (anxiousness) and the state (anxiety) conceptualization of this construct.

REFERENCES

Amodio, D.M. and Devine, P.G. (2006) 'Stereotyping and evaluation in implicit race bias: Evidence for independent constructs and unique effects on behavior', *Journal of Personality and Social Psychology*, 91(4): 652–61.

Asendorpf, J.B., Banse, R. and Mücke, D. (2002) 'Double dissociation between implicit and explicit personality self-concept: The case of shy behavior', *Journal of Personality and Social Psychology*, 83(2): 380–93.

Back, M.D., Schmukle, S.C. and Egloff, B. (2005) 'Measuring task-switching ability in the Implicit Association Test', *Experimental Psychology*, 52(3): 167–79.

Banse, R. (1999) 'Automatic evaluation of self and significant others: Affective priming in close relationships', *Journal of Social and Personal Relationships*, 16(6): 803–21.

Banse, R., Seise, J. and Zerbes, N. (2001) 'Implicit attitudes towards homosexuality: Reliability, validity, and controllability of the IAT', *Zeitschrift für Experimentelle Psychologie*, 48(2): 145–60.

Blair, I.V. (2002) 'The malleability of automatic stereotypes and prejudice', *Personality and Social Psychology Review*, 6(3): 242–61.

Blanton, H., Jaccard, J., Gonzales, P.M. and Christie, C. (2006) 'Decoding the implicit association test: Implications for criterion prediction', *Journal of Experimental Social Psychology*, 42(2): 192–212.

Blümke, M. and Friese, M. (2006) 'Do features of stimuli influence IAT effects?', *Journal of Experimental Social Psychology*, 42(2): 163–76.

Bosson, J.K., Swann, W.B. and Pennebaker, J.W. (2000) 'Stalking the perfect measure of implicit self-esteem: The blind men and the elephant revisited?', *Journal of Personality and Social Psychology*, 79(4): 631–43.

Boysen, G.A., Vogel, D.L. and Madon, S. (2006) 'A public versus private administration of the Implicit Association Test', *European Journal of Social Psychology*, 36(6): 845–56.

Cvencek, D. and Greenwald, A.G. (2006) 'Faking of the Implicit Association Test is statistically detectable', Unpublished manuscript, University of Washington, Seattle.

Conrey, F.R., Sherman, J.W., Gawronski, B., Hugenberg, K. and Groom, C.J. (2005) 'Separating multiple processes in implicit social cognition: The Quad Model of implicit task performance', *Journal of Personality and Social Psychology*, 89(4): 469–87.

Cronbach, L.J. (1957) 'The two disciplines of scientific psychology', *American Psychologist*, 12(11): 671–84.

Cunningham, W.A., Preacher, K.J. and Banaji, M.R. (2001) 'Implicit attitude measures: Consistency, stability, and convergent validity', *Psychological Science*, 12(2): 163–70.

Dasgupta, N., McGhee, D.E., Greenwald, A.G. and Banaji, M.R. (2000) 'Automatic preference for white Americans: Eliminating the familiarity explanation', *Journal of Experimental Social Psychology*, 36(3): 316–28.

De Houwer, J. (2003a) 'A structural analysis of indirect measures of attitudes', in J. Musch and K.C. Klauer (eds), *The Psychology of Evaluation: Affective Processes in Cognition and Emotion*. Mahwah, NJ: Lawrence Erlbaum, pp. 219–44.

De Houwer, J. (2003b) 'The Extrinsic Affective Simon Task', *Experimental Psychology*, 50(2): 77–85.

De Houwer, J. and De Bruycker, E. (2007) 'The Implicit Association Test outperforms the Extrinsic Affective Simon Task as an implicit measure of interindividual differences in attitudes', *British Journal of Social Psychology*, 46(2): 401–21.

De Houwer, J., Geldof, T. and De Bruycker, E. (2005) 'The Implicit Association Test as a general measure of similarity', *Canadian Journal of Experimental Psychology*, 59(4): 228–39.

De Houwer, J. and Moors, A. (2007) 'How to define and examine the implicitness of implicit measures', in B. Wittenbrink and N. Schwarz (eds), *Implicit Measures of Attitudes*. New York: Guilford, pp. 179–94.

Egloff, B. and Schmukle, S.C. (2002) 'Predictive validity of an Implicit Association Test for assessing anxiety', *Journal of Personality and Social Psychology*, 83(6): 1441–55.

Egloff, B. and Schmukle, S.C. (2003) 'Does social desirability moderate the relationship between implicit and explicit anxiety measures?', *Personality and Individual Differences*, 35(7): 1697–706.

Egloff, B., Schwerdtfeger, A. and Schmukle, S.C. (2005) 'Temporal stability of the implicit association test-anxiety', *Journal of Personality Assessment*, 84(1): 82–8.

Ellwart, T., Becker, E.S. and Rinck, M. (2005) 'Activation and measurement of threat associations in fear of spiders: An application of the Extrinsic Affective Simon Task', *Journal of Behavior Therapy and Experimental Psychiatry*, 36(4): 281–99.

Govan, C.L. and Williams, K.D. (2004) 'Changing the affective valence of the stimulus items influences the IAT by redefining the category labels', *Journal of Experimental Social Psychology*, 40(3): 357–65.

Greenwald, A.G. (2005) 'The Multifactor Trait IAT', Unpublished manuscript, University of Washington, Seattle.

Greenwald, A.G. and Banaji, M.R. (1995) 'Implicit social cognition: Attitudes, self-esteem, and stereotypes', *Psychological Review*, 102(1): 4–27.

Greenwald, A.G. and Farnham, S.D. (2000) 'Using the Implicit Association Test to measure self-esteem and self-concept', *Journal of Personality and Social Psychology*, 79(6): 1022–38.

Greenwald, A.G., McGhee, D.E. and Schwartz, J.L.K. (1998) 'Measuring individual differences in implicit cognition: The implicit association test', *Journal of Personality and Social Psychology*, 74: 1464–80.

Greenwald, A.G. and Nosek, B.A. (in press) 'Attitudinal dissociation: What does it mean?', in R.E. Petty, R.H. Fazio and P. Briñol (eds), *Attitudes: Insights From the New Implicit Measures*. Hillsdale, NJ: Erlbaum.

Greenwald, A.G., Nosek, B.A. and Banaji, M.R. (2003) 'Understanding and using the Implicit Association Test: I. An improved scoring algorithm', *Journal of Personality and Social Psychology*, 85: 197–216.

Greenwald, A.G., Nosek, B.A., Banaji, M.R. and Klauer, K.C. (2005) 'Validity of the salience asymmetry interpretation of the IAT: Comment on Rothermund and Wentura (2004)', *Journal of Experimental Psychology: General*, 134: 420–25.

Greenwald, A.G., Poehlman, T.A., Uhlmann, E. and Banaji, M.R. (in press) 'Understanding and using the Implict Association Test: III. Meta-analysis of predictive validity', *Journal of Personality and Social Psychology.*

Gregg, A.P., Seibt, B. and Banaji, M.R. (2006) 'Easier done than undone: Asymmetry in the malleability of implicit preferences', *Journal of Personality and Social Psychology*, 90: 1–20.

Hofmann, W., Gawronski, B., Gschwendner, T., Le, H. and Schmitt, M. (2005a) 'A meta-analysis on the correlation between the Implicit Association Test and explicit self-report measures', *Personality and Social Psychology Bulletin*, 31: 1369–85.

Hofmann, W., Gschwendner, T., Nosek, B.A. and Schmitt, M. (2005b) 'What moderates implicit–explicit consistency?', *European Review of Social Psychology*, 16(10): 335–90.

Huijding, J. and de Jong, P.J. (2005) 'A pictorial version of the Extrinsic Affective Simon Task', *Experimental Psychology*, 52(4): 289–95.

Jordan, C.H., Spencer, S.J., Zanna, M.P., Hoshino-Browne, E. and Correll, J. (2003) 'Secure and defensive high self-esteem', *Journal of Personality and Social Psychology*, 85(5): 969–78.

Karpinski, A. and Hilton, J.L. (2001) 'Attitudes and the Implicit Association Test', *Journal of Personality and Social Psychology*, 81(5): 774–88.

Karpinski, A. and Steinman, R.B. (2006) 'The single category implicit association test as a measure of implicit social cognition', *Journal of Personality and Social Psychology*, 91(1): 16–32.

Kawakami, K. and Dovidio, J.F. (2001) 'The reliability of implicit stereotyping', *Personality and Social Psychology Bulletin*, 27(2): 212–25.

Kim, D.Y. (2003) 'Voluntary controllability of the Implicit Association Test (IAT)', *Social Psychology Quarterly*, 66(1): 83–96.

Klauer, K.C. and Mierke, J. (2005) 'Task-set inertia, attitude accessibility, and compatibility-order effects: New evidence for a task-set switching account of the Implicit Association Test effect', *Personality and Social Psychology Bulletin*, 37(2): 208–17.

Lane, K.A., Banaji, M.R., Nosek, B.A. and Greenwald, A.G. (2007) 'Understanding and using the Implicit Association Test: IV. What we know (so far)', in B. Wittenbrink and N. Schwarz (eds), *Implicit Measures of Attitudes* New York: Guilford, pp. 59–101.

McConnell, A.R. and Liebold, J.M. (2001) 'Relations among the Implicit Association Test, discriminatory behavior, and explicit measures of racial attitudes', *Journal of Experimental Social Psychology*, 37(5): 435–42.

McGregor, I., Nail, P.R., Marigold, D.C. and Kang, S.-J. (2005) 'Defensive pride and consensus: Strength in imaginary numbers', *Journal of Personality and Social Psychology*, 89(6): 978–96.

Mierke, J. and Klauer, K.C. (2001) 'Implicit association measurement with the IAT: Evidence for effects of executive control processes', *Zeitschrift für Experimentelle Psychologie*, 48(2): 107–22.

Mierke, J. and Klauer, K.C. (2003) 'Method-specific variance in the Implicit Association Test', *Journal of Personality and Social Psychology*, 85(6): 1180–92.

Mitchell, J.P., Nosek, B.A. and Banaji, M.R. (2003) 'Contextual variations in implicit evaluation', *Journal of Experimental Psychology: General*, 132(3): 455–69.

Nisbett, R.E. and Wilson, T.D. (1977) 'Telling more than we can know: Verbal reports on mental processes', *Psychological Review*, 84(3): 231–59.

Nosek, B.A. (2005) 'Moderators of the relationship between implicit and explicit evaluation', *Journal of Experimental Psychology: General*, 134(6): 565–84.

Nosek, B.A. (2007) 'Understanding the individual implicitly and explicitly', *International Journal of Psychology*, 42(3): 184–88.

Nosek, B.A. and Banaji, M.R. (2001) 'The go/no-go association task', *Social Cognition*, 19(2): 625–66.

Nosek, B.A., Greenwald, A.G. and Banaji, M.R. (2005) 'Understanding and using the Implicit Association Test: II. Method variables and construct validity', *Personality and Social Psychology Bulletin*, 31(2): 166–80.

Nosek, B.A., Greenwald, A.G. and Banaji, M.R. (2007) 'The Implicit Association Test at age 7: A methodological and conceptual review', in J.A. Bargh (ed.), *Automatic Processes in Social Thinking and Behavior*. New York: Psychology Press, pp. 265–92.

Nosek, B.A. and Hansen, J.J. (2007) 'The associations in our heads belong to us: Searching for attitudes and knowledge in implicit evaluation', Unpublished manuscript, University of Virginia, Charlottesville.

Nosek, B.A. and Smyth, F.L. (2007) 'A multi-trait-multimethod validation of the Implicit Association Test: Implicit and explicit attitudes are related but distinct constructs', *Experimental Psychology*, 54(1): 14–29.

Nosek, B.A. and Sriram, N. (2007) 'Faulty assumptions: A comment on Blanton, Jaccard, Gonzales, and Christie (2006)', *Journal of Experimental Social Psychology*. 43(3): 393–98.

Olson, M.A. and Fazio, R.H. (2003) 'Relations between implicit measures of prejudice: What are we measuring', *Psychological Science*, 14(6): 636–9.

Olson, M.A. and Fazio, R.H. (2005) 'Reducing the influence of extrapersonal associations on the Implicit Association Test: Personalizing the IAT', *Journal of Personality and Social Psychology*, 86(5): 653–67.

Payne, B.K., Cheng, C.M., Govorun, O. and Stewart, B.D. (2005) 'An inkblot for attitudes: Affect misattribution as implicit measurement', *Journal of Personality and Social Psychology*, 89(3): 277–93.

Penke, L., Eichstaedt, J. and Asendorpf, J.B. (2006) 'Single Attribute Implicit Association Tests (SA-IAT) for the assessment of unipolar constructs: The case of sociosexuality', *Experimental Psychology*, 53(4): 283–91.

Perugini, M. (2005) 'Predictive models of implicit and explicit attitudes', *British Journal of Social Psychology*, 44(1): 29–45.

Pinter, B. and Greenwald, A.G. (2005) 'Clarifying the role of the "other" category in the self-esteem IAT', *Experimental Psychology*, 52(1): 74–9.

Rothermund, K. and Wentura, D. (2004) 'Underlying processes in the Implicit Association Test (IAT): Dissociating salience from associations', *Journal of Experimental Psychology: General*, 133(2): 139–65.

Rudman, L.A., Greenwald, A.G. and McGhee, D.E. (2001) 'Implicit self-concept and evaluative implicit gender stereotypes: Self and ingroup share desirable traits', *Journal of Personality and Social Psychology*, 27(9): 1164–78.

Schmukle, S.C. (2005) 'Unreliability of the dot probe task', *European Journal of Personality*, 19(7): 595–605.

Schmukle, S.C. and Egloff, B. (2004) 'Does the Implicit Association test for assessing anxiety measure trait and state variance?', *European Journal of Personality*, 18(6): 438–94.

Schmukle, S.C. and Egloff, B. (2005) 'A latent state-trait analysis of implicit and explicit personality measures', *European Journal of Psychological Assessment*, 21(2): 100–7.

Schmukle, S.C. and Egloff, B. (2006) 'Assessing anxiety with Extrinsic Simon Tasks', *Experimental Psychology*, 53(2): 149–60.

Schnabel, K., Banse, R. and Asendorpf, J.B. (2006a) 'Assessment of implicit personality self-concept using the Implicit Association Test (IAT): Concurrent assessment of anxiousness and angriness', *British Journal of Social Psychology*, 45(2): 373–96.

Schnabel, K., Banse, R. and Asendorpf, J.B. (2006b) 'Employing automatic approach and avoidance tendencies for the assessment of implicit personality self-concept: The Implicit Association Procedure (IAP)', *Experimental Psychology*, 53(1): 69–76.

Schröder-Abé, M., Rudolph, A., Wiesner, A. and Schütz, A. (2007) 'Self-esteem discrepancies and defensive reactions to social feedback', *International Journal of Psychology*. 42(3): 174–83.

Steffens, M.C. (2004) 'Is the implicit association test immune to faking', *Experimental Psychology*, 51(3): 165–79.

Steffens, M.C. and Plewe, I. (2001) 'Items' cross-category associations as a confounding factor in the Implicit Association Test', *Zeitschrift für Experimentelle Psychologie*, 48(2): 123–34.

Steffens, M.C. and Schulze-König, S. (2006) 'Predicting spontaneous Big Five behavior with Implicit Association Tests', *European Journal of Psychological Assessment*, 22(1): 13–20.

Strack, F. and Deutsch, R. (2004) 'Reflective and impulsive determinants of social behavior', *Personality and Social Psychology Review*, 8(3): 220–47.

Teachman, B.A. and Woody, S.R. (2003) 'Automatic processing in spider phobia: Implicit fear associations over the course of treatment', *Journal of Abnormal Psychology*, 112(1): 100–9.

Teige, S., Schnabel, K., Banse, R. and Asendorpf, J.B. (2004) 'Assessment of multiple implicit self-concept dimensions using the Extrinsic Affective Simon Task (EAST)', *European Journal of Personality*, 18(6): 495–520.

Wigboldus, D.H.J., Holland, R.W. and van Knippenberg, A. (2006) 'Single target implicit associations', Unpublished manuscript.

25

The Objective-Analytic Test Battery

James M. Schuerger

INTRODUCTION

The idea of assessing personality as expressed in non-questionnaire behavior is not new. Projective tests such as the Rorschach inkblot test or Murray's thematic apperception test (TAT) predate systematic efforts by Thornton, Thurstone and others with broad samples of non-questionnaire variables. The abiding notion behind all attempts to measure personality, without asking the person directly for his/her subjective reports (whether in interview or on questionnaire), is that personality is revealed in all that we do. After initial work in this non-questionnaire area by a few pioneers, Raymond B. Cattell, one of the most highly cited personologists (Haggbloom et al., 2002), assembled a broad sample of non-questionnaire behaviors and searched the domain for non-questionnaire dimensions of personality using multivariate statistical procedures such as factor analysis (see Cattell, 1978, 1988).

The non-questionnaire objective-analytic (OA) test batteries that are the subject of this chapter are predominantly the work of Cattell and his colleagues (i.e. within the Cattellian School – see Boyle, 2006).

Historically, by the mid-1960s, Cattell had already listed well over 500 objective tests comprising more than 2,000 score responses (Cattell and Warburton, 1967) and had factor-analytically elucidated a number of personality dimensions from objective test data. These efforts culminated over subsequent years in the publication of three different collections (batteries) of objective test measures collectively known as the objective-analytic test batteries (see Cattell and Schuerger, 1978; Schmidt, 1988, 2006; Schmidt et al., 1975, 1985; Schuerger, 1986).

It is easy to misunderstand the kinds of behaviors subsumed under this heading. The key idea is that the individual taking the tests, as in any popular projective test, is asked to perform some task, rather than subjectively describe him/herself as in a questionnaire. How the task is scored is not known to the individual completing the task. The test is objective both as to scoring and the performance itself, since there is no opportunity for the assessee to slant the results either deliberately or by reason of unconscious motivation, except in the case of deliberate sabotage (cf. Cattell and Johnson, 1986; Miller, 1988).

Therefore, it is impossible for the examinee to portray a unified and purposeful impression of some kind of personality (see Boyle, 1985; Boyle and Saklofske, 2004; Boyle et al., 1995).

The multiple test behaviors are varied and scoring is often complex. Examples of variables include: faster speed of social judgment; wider peripheral visual span; slower speed on mirror tracking; higher fluency on animal names; larger number of things disliked; fewer alliterative and rhyming responses; longer estimates of time to do tasks; more skepticism about potential for success; quicker line-length judgment. The list is only minimally representative of the many objective tests listed by Cattell and his colleagues. In the measurement of personality by such objective tests (in Cattell's terminology, 'objective-analytic' tests), one can posit three domains or modalities of measurable human characteristics (not including the measurement of transitory mood states):

- Ability: what a person can do, his/her talents, skills, proficiencies. The archetypal statement in this realm is, 'I can do X.'
- Motivation: movement, drive, or tendency towards something or someone. The archetypal statement in this realm is, 'In this circumstance, I want X.'
- Personality: personal style. The archetypal statement in this realm is, 'in this circumstance, I am X.'

Again, one can posit three ways to know about a person, three data-sources or media of measurement (see Schuerger, 1986):

- Life data (L-data): personality is revealed in everyday behavior, usually reported by someone other than the person being evaluated. Examples are behavioral observations, ratings, school grades, medical history, and interview observations.

- Subjective questionnaire data (Q-data): the person's own conscious verbal self-presentation, in a given circumstance. The presentation may be oral, as in an interview, written in essay form, or in responses to multiple-choice questions, as on a personality questionnaire.
- Objective test data (T-data): personality is revealed by a person's response to a contrived situation, such as an objective ability test or a projective personality test. It is not conscious self-presentation, and the overt task is not subjective self-description. Personality characteristics are inferred from what the individual does rather than from what the individual says (i.e. subjective statements about what kind of person one is).

They can be arranged as in Table 25.1 with representative objective tests in the various cells. The cell of most interest here, of course, is that at which the column for personality intersects the row for test-data – the presentation of one's personal style by behavior on contrived tasks.

There are many possible entries in each cell of the table, and together they give a thorough picture of the realm of human assessment. The Q-data row is the only one in which the person being assessed makes subjective statements about him/herself. Data from this source are subject to various misrepresentations, inaccuracies and distortions, both conscious and unconscious. For example, this author has seen Sixteen Personality Factor Questionnaire (16PF – see Cattell et al., 2002) scores from a young man under two circumstances. When he was in a clinical setting, he portrayed himself as moderately introverted, more than a little anxious, sensitive and vulnerable, tending to dominance, and flexible, rather than highly rule-oriented. In contrast, when he was being evaluated as a candidate for a sales position, he looked

Table 25.1 Assessment procedures by domain and data-source

Domain Data source	Ability	Motive	Personality
Life	School grades	What one buys or has	Interview observations
Question	Self-reported skills	Career interest survey	16PF, MMPI-2
Test	Wechsler	Motivation Analysis Test, TAT	Rorschach, OA tests

extraverted, calm and sure of himself, and conscientious. As he commented on these differences, it became clear that it wasn't so much the fact that he was deliberately falsifying his portrayal of himself – he simply got into the role and became the person that a salesman needed to be. Objective tests (T-data) are not subject to such fluctuations in self-portrayal, except by the introduction of random error or sabotage (Schuerger, 1986).

L-data are subject to similar sources of inaccuracy, particularly when they are in the form of ratings of one kind or the other, since they frequently involve subjective human judgments about the performance or personality of another human being. Teacher reports, manager feedback on performance, and psychiatric notes are examples. L-data, it should be noted, is frequently used in correlational studies (e.g. where school grades or job performance ratings are frequent criteria – e.g. Schuerger et al., 1970). T-data differs from L-data and Q-data in that test scores are derived with no proximate imposition of human judgment (which is inherently subjective; Schuerger, 1986).

The remainder of this chapter is arranged into five sections. The section just below, 'Objective-analytic tests', with examples of objective tests, may serve to illustrate the kinds of variables included in OA measurement (cf. Cattell and Johnson, 1986; Miller, 1988). A second section discusses attempts to discover factors in OA (non-questionnaire) variables (e.g. Cattell and Schuerger, 1978; Schuerger, 1986). Two subsequent sections deal with the reliability and validity (both conceptual and criterion) of OA variables and factors, while a final section contains some evaluative comments with suggestions for further research.

OBJECTIVE-ANALYTIC TESTS

The key distinction between subjective self-report personality questionnaires or rating scales and Objective-Analytic (OA) tests is

the fact that the person being assessed does not know how a given test is being scored – 'what aspect of his/her behavior is actually being measured' – by the OA test. For example, a questionnaire might be used that requires an individual to subjectively choose levels of punishment for various foibles and crimes. Despite the appearance – that one's severity of judgment is being measured – the actual scoring might consider only the number of such judgments that one makes in a given length of time. On the other hand, an objective test might require the examinee to identify objects in pictures that are incompletely drawn or obscure in some other way. In this case the score might be the number of objects correctly identified, or simply the number of identifications attempted.

Tests like this have a history outside of Cattell's efforts to systematize their use and collect them in a discrete battery. One has only to recall the extensive literature on projective tests such as the Rorschach inkblot test or the TAT, both of which for many years have been scorable by systematic and validated methods (Exner, 1993; Spangler, 1992). Taking the simple difference between commercial tests of verbal and quantitative ability, Schuerger and his associates have shown significant correlations with a number of personality and interest variables. For example, individuals with an excess of quantitative ability over verbal ability tend towards intolerance of ambiguity (Schuerger et al., 1979).

Research with objective tests using factor analysis as an analytic procedure goes back to the work of Thornton, as reported by Hundleby et al. (1965), in their exhaustive review of known personality structure in OA tests at that time. Thornton was seeking the factor-analytic structure of various measures of persistence. Among the variables listed in the study were: longer total time in breath holding; longer time spent on perceptual ability test; higher verbal score on revised army alpha test; higher total score for hand grip; higher self-rating on persistence; and larger number of familiar words written in word-building test. The variety of modalities was impressive. Some tests tapped physical tasks, some tapped cognitive abilities, and some tapped subjective self-description by questionnaire. Thornton factored 22 variables with 189 subjects, and extracted six factors, among which were 'withstanding discomfort to achieve a goal', 'keeping on at a task', 'feeling of adequacy', and 'mental fluency'.

Thurstone (as reported in Hundleby et al., 1965) factored 43 variables from a sample of 194 persons, mostly undergraduate students at the University of Chicago. A sample of his variables included: faster speed of letter recognition; faster speed of gestalt closure (dotted outlines); wider peripheral vision span; longer time of decision (size–weight illusion); lower score (Koh's block designs); higher score primary mental abilities reasoning factor; and larger total number of Rorschach responses. Thurstone extracted 11 factors, among which were 'facility in perceptual closure', 'speed of perception', 'oscillation of perception of ambiguous stimuli', and others. Subsequent work has tentatively identified some of these factors by other names within the personality sphere.

These two studies may be enough to illustrate the variety and ingenuity of tests now classified as part of an objective-analytic test battery. In general, one finds tests that resemble ability tests of various kinds (verbal, quantitative, spatial, memory, perception, physical abilities), tests that tap physiological reactions (swaying, saliva produced under certain conditions, recovery of skin tone after pressure, etc.), and objective tests that superficially resemble questionnaires in appearance (such as the motivation analysis test and its downward extensions – e.g. see Boyle, 1988; Cattell and Johnson, 1986). Of the latter, the scoring for the most part is not what would be suggested by the content of the items themselves.

This author's favorite test in the OA realm is the 'fidgetometer', a device for measuring a subject's restlessness while the person is just waiting with nothing to do. It consisted of an old chair with loose joints, further loosened for the sake of measurement. The chair was fitted with an electrical contact that would make and break with motion of the chair. The contact was not visible to the subject, nor was the wiring. The same chair was later refitted in Cattell's lab for service in a motivation experiment, after considerable labor and ingenuity had been expended to make it look threatening – after the manner of an electric chair.

There are three systematic and commercially available versions of OA tests and batteries known to this author, all originating in Cattell's laboratory. Two of these are in English. One, the OA Battery (Cattell and Schuerger, 1976, 1978) is the prime focus here, formerly available as a single large booklet and three expendable booklets, along with a detailed manual (see Cattell and Schuerger, 1978). The other English version consists of a large series of individual tests which could be purchased in any combination depending on a researcher's or a practitioner's specific requirements. These have been researched and made available mostly to adult examinees. In addition, a German version (Schmidt, 1988, 2006; Schmidt et al., 1975, 1985) has been used in some recently published research. More detail will be presented below, although the remainder of the chapter will focus mainly on the OA Test Kit itself.

FACTORS IN OBJECTIVE-ANALYTIC TESTS

Uppermost in the Cattellian tradition is the extraction of factors within a given domain and their oblique rotation to maximum simple structure. Table 25.2 gives a sample of the factors designed to be measured in the OA Test Kit (Cattell and Schuerger, 1976, 1978). The table may also serve to expand the list of variables presented in the prior section, and the three modalities represented by OA variables: (1) ability-like variables, (2) physiological qualities and reactions, and (3) questionnaire-like variables. The OA Kit currently has no physiological measures, but

Table 25.2 Ten factors and associated variables

U.I	Title/comment	Parsimonious description (some variables in this battery)	Average of factor loadings this study	Congruence coefficient with prior studies
16	Ego standards/also called assertiveness, fast natural tempo	Speed – quicker social judgment, coding speed, letter-number comparison, calculation, etc.	0.53	0.88
19	Independence vs. subduedness/accuracy; related to Witkin's field independence	Focus, accuracy, and visual competence – accuracy in computation, more hidden figures seen in Gottschaldt figures, accuracy in picture memory, etc.	0.54	0.73
20	Evasiveness/high acquiescence and conformity to group norms	Insecurity, uncertainness – insecurity of opinion, pessimism, tendency to agree, logical inconsistency of attitudes, etc.	0.32	0.66
21	Exuberance/high level of verbal fluency and imperviousness to social suggestion	Fluency and speed – ideational fluency, more garbled words guessed, faster speed of closure, higher frequency of alternating perspective, etc.	0.32	0.81
23	Mobilization vs. regression/low rigidity, general competence, endurance of stress	Variety of tasks – greater accuracy in letter-number task, higher perceptual coordination, fewer threatening objects seen in complicated drawings, higher ability to state logical assumptions, faster backward writing, etc.	0.16	0.31
24	Anxiety/standard anxiety indicators like admitting frailties, being easily annoyed	Questionnaire-like tests – preference for outright rather than inhibited humor, more common frailties admitted, more emotionality of comment, more willingness to play practical jokes, etc.	0.41	0.82
25	Realism vs. tensidia/related to Eysenck's normality vs. psychoticism; groundedness	Memory, good sense – less pessimism, better immediate memory, digit-span accuracy, agreement with homely wisdom, memory for proper nouns, accuracy in counting letters and numbers, etc.	0.22	0.24
28	Asthenia vs. self-assurance/a complex pattern of indicators; prominence of pessimism, low trust in own prowess	Questionnaire-like tests – tendency to agree, endorsement of institutional values, cynicism, longer time estimates to do common tasks, external locus of control, importance of luck, longer time estimates for waiting periods, etc.	0.23	0.30
32	Exvia vs. invia/fluent with regard to others, but not generally; quick	Almost all are performance tests – quicker line-length judgment, greater willingness to decide on vague data, more correct attribute-naming responses, fluency on people's characteristics, faster backward signature writing, etc.	0.19	0.30
33	Discouragement vs. sanguineness/lack of confidence, pessimism	All are questionnaire-like – less confidence in unfamiliar situations, fewer friends, fewer likes, less happiness, goals seen as less attainable, severity and pessimism, etc.	0.34	0.79

does adequately represent the other categories. Among those factors that have a large number of ability-like variables, UI 16 (ego standards), for example, consists entirely of behavior samples which, with one exception, are all scored as the 'number completed'. That is, it is only the speed with which the answers are provided that is important. The exception in this case is accuracy of computation, which is scored for the number correct. UI 19 (independence) consists mostly of perceptual tests that are scored for the 'number correct/number completed', where perceptual accuracy is the key element.

Some factors, notably UI 24 (anxiety), consist mainly of questionnaire-like variables, but even in these, it would be difficult if not impossible for an examinee to determine how the test was scored. For example, the first test in the factor battery is called a 'humor test'. It requires the examinee to rate, by multiple choice, how funny each of a series of items is. Half of the items are mildly rude or suggestive. Scoring is in the direction of favoring such items, and was expected to load positively on UI 24 (anxiety). In fact, it did not (Cattell et al., 1976). A second test in the factor battery, called 'How do you like?' lists 16 leisure activities, some of them 'highbrow' and some of them not. An example of a highbrow activity would be attending a classical drama or symphony orchestra. A non-highbrow activity would be bowling, or going to the shopping mall. Being lower on highbrow activities loads positively on anxiety (Cattell and Schuerger, 1978).

An example of a factor that includes both ability-like tests and questionnaire-like tests is UI 25 (realism). The first test in the test kit, called 'Human nature II', consists of a number of statements that range from mild to fairly severe cynicism. A typical statement might be, 'People will talk about your failings behind your back.' To these statements the examinee responds on a five-point 'strongly agree' to 'strongly disagree' scale. The test is scored for higher pessimism, and is one of the few tests in the battery which is somewhat transparent in this respect.

A second questionnaire-like test in this factor is called 'Wise statements'. It consists of a number of statements that might have come straight from Aesop's fables, except that some make more sense than others. Examples might be, 'A fool and his money are soon parted,' or 'Sometimes you just need to get away.' Examinees choose which statements to endorse, and the score is the number endorsed divided by the total number of responses.

Of the ability-like tests contributing to this factor, three are memory tests – immediate memory, digit span, and memory for proper nouns. Another ability measure requires the examinee to count how many times a particular letter or number occurs in a column of number or letter clusters. The score is the number correct. One final test, not in either category, requires the examinee to choose, for each stimulus word, one of three possible responses. In each group of responses, one rhymes with the stimulus, one is alliterative with the stimulus, and a third is commonly associated with the stimulus in some other way. The test is scored for fewer rhyming or alliterative responses.

Variables in the first three factors presented above (UI 16, UI 19, and UI 24) all have high average loadings (with high defined as > 0.40) on their relevant factors, whereas UI 25 does not (see Table 25.2, column 4). These data are reported in detail in the main study supporting the OA Test Kit (Cattell et al., 1976). Overall, of the ten factors intended for measurement in the battery, only three (UI 16, 19, and 24) had loadings averaging above 0.41. Another three (UI 20, 21, and 33) had average loadings above 0.30. The other four factors did less well, with loadings on their relevant factors near or below 0.20. The same six UI factors (16, 19, 20, 21, 24, and 33) had high congruence coefficients between factors in this study and in an earlier study. Of the factors that did less well, their congruence coefficients ranged from 0.19 for UI 25 to 0.31 for UI 23. The average loadings for these weaker factors were correspondingly low, but all had at least some high loadings on one or more variables that had been hypothesized for the factor, based on earlier studies.

Two further factors will be presented in this section, to illustrate more of the complex coding procedures for this large body of psychological variables, and for one of these factors, to illustrate some of the deficiencies in measurement of the four weaker factors. Table 25.3 presents the first of these factors, UI 23.

The table illustrates much about the OA Kit and about measurement by these objective-analytic devices in general. Primary is the distinction between a test (T-number) and the variable that is derived from it in this instance (Master index or MI number). For example, the first variable is derived from a test titled 'Annoyances' (T38b) in the test booklet, and a variable (MI) called 'higher social annoyances to non-social'. The test consists of brief descriptions of a number of situations that might or might not be annoying to a person: stubbing one's toe, a bad smell where one has to work, people who are braggarts, people who are rude, and so on. From the same test at least three variables could be derived: overall annoyance, higher social annoyances (as here), or higher non-social annoyances. For reasons of this kind, the MI numbers are needed as well as the T-numbers.

A creative and detailed compendium of OA tests was presented in Cattell and Warburton's (1967) *Objective Personality and Motivational Tests*. A check for T38 in this large volume is revealing, both as to the richness of the compendium and the nature and theory of the test. After a brief description, this source lists no fewer than six variables that can be derived from one or the other versions of this objective test: overall annoyability, susceptibility to ego threats, social rather than non-social susceptibility, purposeful rather than non-purposeful annoyances, more extremity of response on a test of annoyances, and greater number of non-social relative to social annoyances. The section on T38 then continues with the theory and rationale that guided the original writing of the test, discusses the scoring, and gives sample items.

One aspect of Cattell's well-developed theories of motivation and dynamic structure (Cattell, 1985; Cattell, 1992) is the dictum that frustration is a necessary precondition for the rise of anxiety. From the point of view of test construction, one could expect that the anxious examinee, though perhaps unaware of the original frustration, would displace it to trivial annoyances. This objective test (T38), originally designed to measure anxiety, was found to do so in nine early research studies. This particular scoring (MI 242, ratio of social to non-social annoyances) was not expected to load primarily on anxiety, and is not as transparent to the examinee as a simple tally of annoyances endorsed by the examinee. As is seen in Table 25.3, it did not load well on this factor, nor did it load above 0.10 on any factor in the analysis.

In contrast to this variable's lack of loading, one that did work well in this factor was T112 (MI 609), titled in the table 'Higher perceptual coordination'. As is seen in the table, it had a loading of 0.48, one of two high loadings in the table. In its multiple-choice form,

Table 25.3 Codes, variables and loadings for UI 23 (mobilization vs. regression)

Test (T no.)	Variable – master index (MI) no.	Psychologist's title	Answered on	Factor loading
38b	242	Ratio social/non-social annoyances	Answer sheet	0.01
44c	120b	Ratio accuracy/speed letter number	Answer sheet	0.10
112	609	Higher perceptual coordination	Answer sheet	0.48
197	401	Less preference for competitive situation	Answer sheet	0.22
11b	36	Higher ability to state logical assumptions	Answer sheet	0.54
20b	105	Fewer threatening objects seen	Answer sheet	−0.04
224b	714	Fewer rhyming and alliterative words chosen	Answer sheet	0.00
1a	2a(1)	Lower perceptual-motor rigidity: backward writing	Special booklet	0.01

as in the American OA Kit and in the German version (Schmidt et al., 1975), this ingenious test consists of a page display about six by six inches, with characters of three kinds: letters in upper case, digits from 1 to 9, and the lower case letters from a to e. The lower case letters are mostly scattered through the center of the display. A question gives two pairs of coordinates of number or capital letter combinations. The examinee's task is to find the coordinate pairs, and then, imagining a line between each pair of coordinates, find the lower-case letter that is closest to the intersection of the two (imagined) lines. The multiple-choice responses allow for an answer from a to e, and the examinee marks the appropriate choice for each set of coordinates. An earlier form of the test also had a second task, for which the examinee did not have the help of the printed page but had to remember the position of the letters and numbers.

The simplest scoring of T112, the accuracy of response, is a ratio of those correct to those completed (MI 609). If desired, the numerator can be adjusted by subtracting one-fourth of the erroneous responses from those correct, in order to compensate for guessing. The test can also be scored for speed by simply counting responses, or for breaking the rules, by examining the test booklet for pencil lines drawn to connect the coordinates. As used here, scored for accuracy under the stress of having to imagine the lines, it loaded well on UI 23, as noted, and also on UI 19 (independence), but lower in the latter case. The test fits well with the understanding of UI 23 as ability to mobilize one's intellectual resources under stress. Persons of low mobilization have a strong need for environmental help in any problem-solving situation, and T112 provides an opportunity for problem-solving with all required operations being performed in the head.

The next test in the factor battery is T197 (MI 401), 'Less preference for competitive situation', and it was originally expected to load on UI 33, Discouragement versus sanguineness, based on both theory and prior research. As a matter of fact, it had a modest positive loading (0.11) on UI 33 as well as the 0.22 loading on UI 23. The loading here, contrary in fact to intuitive expectations, has not been satisfactorily explained.

The next test listed, T11b (MI 36), 'Higher ability to state logical assumptions', consists of a series of questions, all having the same general form. First a statement of some kind is made: 'Bossie is contented because she is a cow.' Then follows the statement, 'For this to be true, it must be true that . . .'. Finally, there are five statements having to do with animals, cows, contentment, and other relevant and irrelevant material, on the order of: 'All contented animals are cows.' The examinee must choose the one that is necessary to support the original statement. This variable is most commonly found with a negative loading on UI 20 (evasiveness), but does load saliently on UI 23 in one earlier study. The ability to identify logical assumptions does not seem incompatible with the concept of mobilization of resources, but it does lack the specificity to the concept that one would hope for.

Some of the objective tests in the existing version of the OA Kit require the examinee to write or perform some other action, and such tests cannot go in a booklet that uses a separate answer sheet. Among the factors represented in the OA Kit, UI 21 (exuberance) consists entirely of fluency measures that require a booklet that cannot be re-used. Also, about half of the tests in UI 32 (exvia) are of this nature. Such a test is the last one in the table for UI 23, T1a (MI 2a1). The separate booklet for this test (called in the OA Kit an 'expendable booklet'), after a page for name, date, age, and gender, consists of two pages that have numbered lines ready for a young person to write on. On the first page, the instruction is to write, on signal, as quickly as possible, the word 'ready'. On a second signal, the examinee writes, as many times as possible, the words 'ten big dogs'.

On the following page, similarly lined, the examinee is instructed to write the same word (or phrase, later) as many times as possible, but backwards. In addition to verbal instructions, the examinee is provided with a sample of backward writing complete with directional arrows. The score is the number of written words completed backwards divided by the number completed on the first page. In general, these young persons seemed to do about one-fifth as many words backwards as forwards.

This is believed to be a test of rigidity (flexibility, as it is scored in the OA Kit), in that the examinee is required to perform an action that runs against the grain of an already well-learned skill. This test is a particularly narrow expression of the concept, leaving aside all the possible socio-political and emotional contexts. It has a substantial history in Cattell's laboratory of loading UI 23, UI 16, and UI 33. In the large study with the OA Kit, it had a few trivial loadings (< 0.10) and a zero loading on UI 23. This finding is particularly bothersome, since the concept of mobilization of energy, central to the understanding of UI 23, had been expected to be represented by this test.

This discussion of UI 23 may provide some insight into the complexities of OA measurement, and in particular of the conceptual difficulties when factors do not come together as expected. Another factor, UI 21 (exuberance) is at the other pole from the UI 23 example, in that it has both high congruence with earlier studies and high average loadings. Table 25.4 is set up like Table 25.3, but for UI 21 instead of UI 23. UI 21, it will be recalled, consists entirely of expendable booklet tests, the only factor for which the examinees are required to do so much performance. Most of the others require selection of multiple-choice options in the OA Kit.

As can be seen from Table 25.4, the UI 21 variables all load saliently on the factor. What cannot be seen in the table is the fact that, with the exception of the first variable, MI 335b, 'faster marking speed', no variable has a higher loading on any other factor. Marking speed, measured here on a sheet with boxes such as a person would see on an ordinary machine-scorable answer sheet, has a slightly higher loading on UI 16 than it does on UI 21, consistent with the prior factor's emphasis on speed. The next test in the table, T43a (MI 271) is a classic measure of verbal fluency, requiring the examinee to list (1) words beginning with a given letter of the alphabet, and (2) objects that would appear at some spot in a room, or in an outdoor scene. Following that is T88a (MI 853), in which the examinee is faced with 48 one-inch-square cells, each with a very simple geometric drawing in it. The examinee is to modify the drawing such that it becomes 'either a pleasing design or so that it looks like something'. After completing the drawings, the examinee is asked to write in titles for the ones that are supposed to be something real. The score is a simple count of the ones named as something real.

There are two tests that require the examinee to write something that is only heard and not seen. The first of these, T164a (MI 699), presents examinees with tape-recorded 'garbled words' that are very difficult to make out. Score is simply the number of words written under these difficult conditions. Originally expected to be useful in separating those with psychotic potential from the more realistic, this test seems to tap willingness to

Table 25.4 Codes, variables, and loadings for UI 21 (exuberance)

Test (T no.)	Variable – master index (MI) no.	Psychologist's title	Answered on	Factor loading
411d	335b	Faster marking speed	Special booklet	0.21
43a	271	Higher ideational fluency	Special booklet	0.51
88a	853	More concrete drawing completion	Special booklet	0.29
164a	699	More garbled words guessed	Special booklet	0.46
2d	7	Faster speed of closure	Special booklet	0.30
3	8	Higher frequency of alternating perspective	Special booklet	0.14
51	28b	Greater dynamic momentum: dictation	Special booklet	0.34
136a	264	Faster speed of tapping	Special booklet	0.32

try something without close attention to accuracy or specificity. Similarly, T51 (MI 28b) requires examinees to write under increasingly difficult conditions – in this case, a story that is read at a raster and faster rate. The score, again, is simply the number of words written under increasingly impossible conditions. Two tests measure fluency in responding to pictorial material, T2d (MI 7) and T3 (MI 8). The first of these presents the examinee with pictures that are incompletely drawn. The examinee is to write the name of the object. In the second of these visual measures, the examinee is presented with one of the classic alternating perspective pictures, and is asked to record each time the perspective changes while he/she is watching. In both tests, the score is the number completed, regardless of accuracy, a key element in UI 21.

The presentation in this section was intended to give the reader, if unfamiliar with this kind of measurement, some appreciation of the richness of the potential variable set in the Cattellian OA tradition. Historically, interested readers will find many more tests and variables in the Cattell and Warburton (1967) compendium, in Hundleby et al.'s (1965) personality factors in objective test devices, as well as in the manual for the OA Kit itself (Cattell and Schuerger, 1978; Schuerger, 1986). The manual is available from the publisher (Institute for Personality and Ability Testing), while the others are readily available on the Internet.

RELIABILITY AND CONCEPTUAL VALIDITIES

Reliabilities of psychological measurement devices are usually reported as homogeneity coefficients (e.g. coefficient alpha) or some form of test–retest correlations (cf. Boyle, 1991). The former of these is considered inappropriate for theoretical reasons Therefore, reliabilities of the ten variables in the OA Kit are given in the manual as test–retest correlations over a few hours

(dependability coefficients) and over about a month (stability coefficients). The former of these run from a low of 0.62 for UI 25 (realism) to a high of 0.93 for UI 21 (exuberance), averaging 0.76 over all ten factors. For the longer term, about one month, the stabilities run from a low of 0.58 for UI 28 (asthenia) to a high of 0.85 for UI 24 (anxiety), and have an average of 0.70. These values compare well with typical short-term test–retest reliabilities for personality questionnaires (Schuerger et al., 1989).

On the topic of the validity of psychological measurements, a distinction among three kinds is frequently seen: Concept or construct validity, content validity, and applied validities, usually in the form of criterion correlations (Cattell and Johnson, 1986; Miller, 1988). Here, the concern is with conceptual or construct validity, evidence for the nature of the constructs measured by the factors. Applied validities are considered in the next large section.

Three important aspects of conceptual validity are: (1) internal relationships of parts to whole; (2) evidence that the variable being studied is not in fact simply some well-known variable in unfamiliar guise; and (3) evidence about the nature of the variable by reason of its relationships to variables outside of itself. For the OA Kit, the first of these in the Cattellian tradition, properly so-called 'concept validity', consists of the multiple correlation of the constituent parts of the variable with the pure factor that they represent (see Cattell, 1986). These values for the OA Kit were computed on a sample of 394 14–16-year-old boys and girls, approximately split as to gender. In this sample, the concept validities of the ten factors ranged from a low of 0.71 for UI 32 (exvia) to a high of 0.92 for UI 16 (ego standards) and UI 24 (anxiety), with an average of 0.78 across the ten factors.

The second aspect of conceptual validity, noted in just above, has to do with the possibility that OA variables are measuring variables known under other names. One candidate for this possibility is general mental ability. In the OA Kit several of the factors, as noted above, have a preponderance of ability-like variables, so the question naturally arises as to whether or not these factors are simply ability variables under new names. Early evidence from the adult experiments is inconclusive and not readily available. Fortunately, for the current OA Kit, this issue is addressed thoroughly in King's thesis (1976). The bottom of Table 25.5 summarizes the relationship between the relevant OA Kit factors and two measures of general mental ability, factor B from the High-School Personality Questionnaire (Cattell et al., 1984), and the Lorge-Thorndike IQ test (see King, 1976). Correlations between several OA factors and the ability measures are substantial, particularly for those factors that are wholly or partially made up of ability-like tests: UI 16 (ego standards), UI 19 (independence), UI 23 (mobilization), and UI 25 (realism). UI 21 (exuberance), marked in this battery entirely by expendable-booklet tests of fluency and speed, does not show any significant correlations with general ability, a finding that is consistent with Cattell's notion that there are several broad second-order factors in the ability realm, including fluid general ability, crystallized general ability, fluid general ability, and so on (Cattell, 1971; Cattell and Johnson, 1986). Negative correlations with general ability measures are seen for UI 24 (anxiety) and UI 28 (asthenia).

Correlations between general intelligence and some UI factors were expected in this research, as noted by Cattell and Warburton. The correlations reported here are either with the 'fitness' factors UI 16, 19, 23, and 25, or, negatively, with the factors that have expected negative effects on all forms of performance or competence, notably UI 24 (anxiety) and UI 28 (asthenia), and to a lesser extent UI 20 (evasiveness). It is also possible that the OA Kit data, from an adolescent population, represent a period during which the various traits are not so well delineated as during adulthood, the period from which most subjects came for research prior to the OA Kit. Nevertheless, these correlations, particularly those linking the Lorge-Thorndike and the OA Kit, are so high as to suggest a more parsimonious hypothesis, that the fitness factors represent mostly components of general mental ability. This topic will be re-entered a bit with the discussion of the top half of the table in the portion of the chapter that addresses criterion relationships.

The third aspect of conceptual validity is the relationships that the various OA factors may have with other known variables, to shed light on their nature. For the OA Kit, King's thesis (1976) is again helpful, providing correlations between the OA variables and primary questionnaire variables from the HSPQ (Cattell et al., 1984). Also helpful in this regard, particularly with regard to the second-order questionnaire factors, is the large-sample study reported by Schuerger et al. (1981). These data are presented in Table 25.6. In the top half of the table, with

Table 25.5 Correlations of OA factors with school achievement

Study	Factor Grade	n	UI 16	UI 19	UI 20	UI 21	UI 23	UI 24	UI 25	UI 28
					Correlations with school achievement					
Dielman et al., 1970	7, 8	211	NA	NA	NA	0.31	0.23		0.44	
Schuerger et al., 1970	7, 8, 9	232	0.23	0.26			NA	NA	NA	
King, 1976	9, 10	105		0.33	−0.18		0.28	−0.23	0.32	−0.23
Feo, 1980			0.26	0.30	−0.10	0.13	0.17	−0.23	0.23	−0.19
					Correlations with tested ability					
King, 1976; HSPQ factor B			0.21	0.46			0.48		0.24	−0.38
King, 1976; Lorge-Thorndike IQ			0.48	0.60			0.59	−0.24	0.34	−0.45

Table 25.6 Correlations between OA variables and HSPQ variables

	UI 16	UI 19	UI 21	UI 23	UI 24	UI 25	UI 28	UI 33
Schuerger et al., 1981; n = 840	*Correlations with HSPQ second-order factors*							
Extraversion (exvia)			0.17			0.12		−0.25
Anxiety					0.30			0.17
Tough poise	−0.11	0.19		0.11	0.10	0.26		−0.14
Independence								−0.17
King, 1976; n = 105	*Correlations with HSPQ primary factors*							
A: Warmth	0.30			0.26	−0.39			
C: Emotional stability					−0.28			−0.18
F: Cheerfulness				0.18	0.28			
G: Conformity		0.20			−0.50		−0.29	−0.29
H: Boldness	0.29		0.31					
I: Sensitivity					−0.19			
J: Withdrawal	−0.18	−0.22						
O: Apprehension	−0.21							
Q3: Self-discipline					−0.31			
Q4: Tension	−0.23				0.31			

its large sample size, correlations on the order of 0.07 are significant at the 0.05 level with a two-tail test. To avoid clutter, only correlations of 0.10 or higher have been reported there. In the bottom half of the table, correlations on the order of 0.20 are significant, but in a few instances correlations of 0.18 and 0.19 are reported in addition to those significant ones.

Very early work with OA variables posited, with some support from relevant data, correlations between UI 32 (exvia) and the second-order questionnaire factor extraversion (sometimes also called exvia). This alignment has not subsequently been found, and this OA factor, without any significant questionnaire correlations, has been left out of the table. UI 20 was left out for similar reasons, but in fact, among the correlations for primary factors of the HSPQ, it did correlate 0.21 with factor J (withdrawal). Questionnaire second-order factor extraversion, although it did not correlate significantly with UI 32, did show significant correlations with UI 21 (exuberance) and negatively with UI 33 (discouragement). There is a second-order factor in OA data called 'ardor of temperament', not previously mentioned in the chapter, that has high loadings on UI 21 and UI 33 in these directions.

It may be that the correlations indicated for extraversion reflect that variable's relationship between this OA second-order factor.

The significant correlation (0.30) between anxiety in both media has considerable historical support, both early and more recent. It must be considered very solid. Despite the fact that UI 19 did not correlate significantly with the questionnaire independence factor as expected, the significant and salient correlations between tough poise and both UI 19 (independence) and UI 25 (realism) are consistent with theoretical expectations. The person high on tough poise is objective and not greatly influenced by emotional issues when making decisions. Such persons often appear as tough-minded, and they can be insensitive to others. These characteristics are not incompatible with the high degree of control and competence (not speed) that are found in behaviors typical of UI 19 and UI 25.

The bottom of the table is based on a much smaller sample, and the correlations are with primary factors that are, by their nature, less durable personal descriptions. Nonetheless, they do give some 'flavor' to the understanding of the OA variables. The list of HSPQ primary factors is shortened from the full 14 primary factors in the instrument. Factor B (intelligence) is left out because is was included in Table 25.5. Factors D (excitability) and Q2 (self-sufficiency) showed no significant correlations with OA factors, and factor E (dominance) was left out because the data for that factor could not be recovered.

Prominent in the table are the large number of significant or salient (slightly below the level for significance at the 0.05 level) correlations involving UI 16 (ego standards) and UI 24 (anxiety). UI 16, for example, has positive correlations with questionnaire warmth (A) and boldness (H), and negative correlations with withdrawal (J), apprehension (O), and tension (Q4). The questionnaire picture of a person high on UI 16, with its emphasis on uncritical speed of processing, is that of an outgoing person at ease with self. In contrast, UI 24 (anxiety) correlates positively with tension (Q4) and – oddly – cheerfulness (F), and negatively with warmth (A), emotional stability (C), conformity (G), sensitivity (I), and self-discipline (Q3). It must be remembered that the subjects in this research were all adolescents, and the picture of an examinee high on UI 24 is that of an adolescent who is not well adjusted – undisciplined, tense and emotionally labile, unable to focus on others (A−, I−). Both of these patterns fit well with traditional concepts of the OA factors in question. The seemingly anomalous positive correlation between cheerfulness (F) and UI 24 is possibly understood by noting the party-going tendencies (from the items) of the F+ person. The author has noted this quality and also the F+ among adolescents who were known users of drugs or alcohol. It is a far reach, but one that may help to explain the anomalous positive loading.

Other correlations in the table are more scattered, but there are a few notable patterns. Questionnaire conformity (G), a measure of the positive orientation to rules and authority that is so important to adolescent achievement, has a positive correlation with UI 19 (independence), which has such notable correlations with IQ and school achievement (Table 25.5). Conformity also correlates negatively with UI 24 (anxiety) as noted above,

and with UI 28 (asthenia) and UI 33 (discouragement), also, possibly, because of the lack of self-assurance that comes from knowing that one is capable of sustained disciplined effort. UI 33 (discouragement) also shows a salient negative correlation with emotional stability (C), perhaps reflecting the lack of hope that accompanies emotional lability and its propensity to interrupt productive activity.

UI 23 (mobilization) correlates positively with warmth (A) and cheerfulness (F), and UI 21 correlates positively with boldness (H). These patterns strike me as being not inconsistent with the standard conceptual interpretations of these OA factors; neither are they particularly conclusive as to their nature.

The reader now has access to much of the data concerning the conceptual aspects of the factors in the OA Kit, if only in summary form. It seems clear that while the OA Kit represents decades of imaginative test construction and research, much further research urgently needs to be carried out. In fact, to the best of my knowledge, no-one other than Cattellian-influenced researchers has ever exactly verified the structures reported (see, for example, Howarth, 1972; Kline and Cooper, 1984; Häcker, 1982). Furthermore, Korth, as early as 1978, presented a reanalysis of data on Cattell's congruence coefficient that was highly critical of its use in the alignment of factors in OA data. He concluded that Cattell's data did not support the claim of matching factor structures across studies. In all studies, by his reckoning, the factors that were most consistent included UI 16, UI 17, UI 21, and UI 24. Korth's conclusions were based on analyses of adult studies prior to those of the OA Kit that is featured here. His list of the most consistent factors may be compared with the list above from the OA Kit itself (UI 16, 19, 20, 21, 24, and 33).

Even in the case of the OA Kit research, with a large sample collected in non-threatening circumstances by a team of experienced and dedicated researchers, only six of the expected factors had satisfactory loadings and congruences with earlier work. Evidently, much further work remains to be done. On the topic of the practical utility of the variables and factors, the picture is brighter, as the next section will show.

CRITERION RELATIONSHIPS OF OA TESTS AND FACTORS

Under the rubric of criterion relationships one ordinarily finds three headings: Educational, clinical, and industrial/organizational. The top of Table 25.5 gives a brief summary of the relationships between the OA Kit variables and school achievement. Only significant correlations are entered into the table. Feo's (1980) thesis was not available to this writer, except for a brief summary of the correlations used in the table, but it is known that his sample size numbered in the several hundreds, and his subjects, all male, were from about the eighth grade to about the eleventh. All studies used all ten factors from the OA Kit except those by Dielman et al. (1970) and Schuerger et al. (1981); for these two studies, the table has NA in the appropriate cell if a variable was missing from the study. Given these conditions, generalizations from the table are not difficult, since the findings are highly consistent across studies. Factors UI 19 and 25 are highly positively related to the school grade criteria, averaging about 0.30 for both factors. Less strongly related in the positive direction are UI 16, 21, and 23; negatively, UI 24, 28, and 20, in that order.

King (1976) extended his work beyond zero-order correlations and used multiple correlation analysis to compare various combinations of the factors, with and without the addition of IQ, in the prediction of school grades. Briefly, he found that from intelligence alone ($r = 0.36$) he could account for about 13% of the variance in grades. When an efficient combination of OA factors was added ($r = 0.48$), he could account for about 23% of the variance. This finding, that the addition of the personality variables to that of IQ gives about a 77% increase in predictability, mirrors similar findings in research on

questionnaire variables. Abstracting for now from issues of convenience and cost, both as to money and as to testing time, it seems clear that for young persons the OA medium does contribute significantly to the prediction of school achievement.

In the area of clinical psychology there are no data available from OA Kit research to the best of my knowledge. What can be summarized here is the successful and highly promising research in English that predates the OA Kit, and work in German that has followed it. The prominent article in English was the monograph by Cattell et al. (1972) in which an ambitious project was described that was designed to separate by discriminant function analysis, groups with various clinical diagnoses from one another, using OA factors as predictors. The samples were too small to allow for cross-validation, but using 17 factors in a discriminant analysis, the researchers achieved a separation among the groups that gave placements with 91% accuracy. On the basis of contributions to the first two roots, the most important factors were, in descending order, UI 19 (independence), UI 21 (exuberance), UI 23 (mobilization), UI 25 (realism), and UI 28 (asthenia). Noteworthy in this group of factors are those with many ability-like tests in their makeup: UI 19, 21, 23, and 25. Missing from these is UI 16; also missing from the list of the most important is UI 24 (anxiety), one of the most questionnaire-like OA factors.

This line of research has been pursued by a German research group. An early publication in this line (Schmidt et al., 1985) performed a similar study with a German version of the OA battery (48 variables), a number of personality questionnaires, and a few intelligence tests. Their results were equally impressive, but most impressive were two findings: (1) that OA data and questionnaire data were differentially valid, and that a combination of the two was most valid, with 90% accuracy overall, and cross-validation accuracy of 67%; (2) that very good results could be obtained (67% accuracy, with 56% accuracy on cross-validation) using only the ten most powerful OA variables instead of the factors. The ten variables were:

- T112 (MI 609) Spatial judgment: accuracy
- T37 (MI 206) Gottschaldt figures: accuracy
- T197 (MI 401) Preferences: competitive situations
- T21 (MI 106) Risk taking: unqualified statements
- T62 (MI 378) Risk taking: figures scanned
- T93 (MI 860) Name choosing: unusual names
- T36 (MI 105) Emotionality of comment
- T31 (MI 144) Aphorisms: acceptance
- T45 (MI 312) Line length judgment: accuracy
- T41 (MI 219) Common frailties admitted.

Lothar Schmidt seems to have been the leading person in this fruitful line of OA research, beginning with his return to Germany in the 1970s. Schmidt (1988) commented on the fact that among these tests, three of them feature accuracy of judgment. Furthermore, among these most powerful variables there is a wide variety of content: competition, risk-taking, unusual name preferences, emotionality, common frailties. He suggested that the content becomes, because of the discriminatory power of the tests, a mine of information about the nature of the various diagnoses. His point was in line with his other suggestion, that factor analysis of OA data from patients with a variety of psychiatric symptoms could lead to additional objective diagnostic criteria. More recently, in a thoughtful chapter on OA tests, Schmidt (2006), presented a strong case for the utility of this line of research, lamenting the ignorance of the Cattellian tradition displayed by current authors and researchers (cf. Haggbloom et al., 2002). He referred to the huge corpus of OA tests and variables created by Cattell and his co-workers (over 500 objective tests!) as a 'goldmine' from which modern researchers are not removing valuable ores.

In the realms of educational prediction and clinical diagnosis the research-based promise of OA tests is impressive. There is, unfortunately, no equivalent background from which to assess the potential of these tests for employee selection, placement, and development. However, the generally powerful predictions possible in the other two areas makes it likely that relevant research would show a utility for these tests in that arena as well. When the difficulty of faking on OA tests is taken into account, it seems highly likely that research in this area has high potential.

CONCLUDING COMMENTS

Cattell's active research in this complex and fascinating area of human personality spanned about 30 years, from 1950, say, to 1980. After this time he did conduct some research on motivational variables using objective data, but deprived of his individual differences' laboratory following his retirement from the University of Illinois, most of his subsequent publications were retrospective and theoretical. Examples may be seen in *Functional Psychological Testing* (Cattell, 1986), which he edited along with Ronald Johnson, and to which he contributed a number of relevant chapters.

Without recent programmatic research in the OA realm (probably because of its high cost in terms of number of subjects and subject time), we must base any critical conclusions on the earlier research and subsequent commentators. This hiatus allows us to take a measured view, unencumbered by recent argument or ambition. In any event, two solid conclusions may be drawn about OA testing: (1) that as to structure and other theoretical aspects, the personality structure elucidated by Cattell needs urgent refinement; and (2) regarding the utility of OA tests and factors, much is known that can be considered conclusive and promising. Regarding the first of these conclusions, one notes that even under the very good conditions under which the OA Kit research was conducted, the factor structure might be considered well demonstrated for only six of the hypothesized factors. In part, the value of the OA devices, beyond the enormous diversity of the objective test variables, lies in their proven utility and psychometric qualities. Even Korth's (1978) highly critical article left room for the possibility of cross-validated structure for several OA factors. Clearly though, the enormous potential of objective tests of personality variables has been almost universally overlooked during the past two decades. As Boyle (2006) in his DSc thesis concluded, questionnaire and rating scales of personality (based on subjective conscious reports) are based on flawed methodology, due to the problems of item transparency and resultant motivational and response distortion. The way forward is to construct objective (i.e. non-fakeable) T-data tests of personality, administered interactively, as advocated by Cattell several decades ago. Hopefully, the objective testing of personality constructs will be a major focus of research into more scientific methods of personality assessment in the years ahead, that is not plagued by the serious flaws of L-data and Q-data methodology.

With regard to the practical utility of the OA tests, it seems that the case has already been well made in educational and clinical areas. The work of the German researchers has been particularly encouraging in this respect, but only (to my knowledge) with regard to clinical diagnosis. In the educational arena, the pure prediction of achievement is well established, but the understanding of the process, by content analysis, of particularly salient factors or individual tests (as encouraged by Schmidt in the area of clinical diagnosis) is totally lacking. Much has been accomplished; much remains to be done.

An over-riding concern with the OA tests as they existed before the astounding rise of the microcomputer was the time and expense of testing. Testing with the OA Kit, we would often allot five or six hours with adolescents. In addition, the Kit required use of three expendable booklets that had to be scored by hand. It was an expensive and tedious process, and one that precluded commercial success for the Kit. Today, the OA Kit could be highly streamlined and presented on any microcomputer. With some special requirements, such as touch-screen capability and a pad on which the examinee could write, the most promising objective tests could be included with the

exercise of some ingenuity. Additionally, there is much more known today about brain–behavior connections than was known during the early developmental period of the OA tests. Addition of modern psychophysiological measures (including fMRI imaging), could further enhance this promising area of research into the objective measurement of human personality structure.

REFERENCES

Boyle, G.J. (1985) 'Self-report measures of depression: Some psychometric considerations', *British Journal of Clinical Psychology*, 24(1): 45–59.

Boyle, G.J. (1988) 'Elucidation of motivation structure by dynamic calculus', in J.R. Nesselroade and R.B. Cattell (eds), *Handbook of Multivariate Experimental Psychology* (2nd edn). New York: Plenum, pp. 737–87.

Boyle, G.J. (1991) 'Does item homogeneity indicate internal consistency or item redundancy in psychometric scales?', *Personality and Individual Differences*, 12(3): 291–4.

Boyle, G.J. (2006) 'Scientific analysis of personality and individual differences', DSc thesis, University of Queensland, St. Lucia.

Boyle, G.J. and Saklofske, D.H. (2004) 'Editors' introduction: Contemporary perspectives on the psychology of individual differences', in G.J. Boyle and D.H. Saklofske (eds), *Sage Benchmarks in Psychology: The Psychology of Individual Differences*. London: Sage, pp. xix–lvi.

Boyle, G.J., Stankov, L. and Cattell, R.B. (1995) 'Measurement and statistical models in the study of personality and intelligence', in D.H. Saklofske and M. Zeidner (eds), *International Handbook of Personality and Intelligence*. New York: Plenum, pp. 417–46.

Cattell, R.B. (1971) *Abilities: Their Structure, Growth, and Action*. New York: Houghton Mifflin.

Cattell, R.B. (1978) *The Scientific Use of Factor Analysis in Behavioral and Life Sciences*. New York: Plenum.

Cattell, R.B. (1985) *Human Motivation and the Dynamic Calculus*. New York: Praeger.

Cattell, R.B. (1986) The psychometric properties of tests: Consistency, validity, and efficiency', in R.B. Cattell and R.C. Johnson (eds), *Functional Psychological Testing: Principles and Instruments*. New York: Brunner/Mazel, pp. 54–78.

Cattell, R.B. (1988) 'The meaning and strategic use of factor analysis', in J.R. Nesselroade and R.B. Cattell (eds), *Handbook of Multivariate Experimental Psychology* (2nd edn). New York: Plenum.

Cattell, R.B. (1992) 'Human motivation objectively, experimentally analysed. *British Journal of Medical Psychology*, 65(3): 237–43.

Cattell, R.B., Boyle, G.J. and Chant, D. (2002) 'The enriched behavioral prediction equation and its impact on structured learning and the dynamic calculus', *Psychological Review*, 109(1): 202–5.

Cattell, R.B., Cattell, M.D.K. and Johns, E. (1984) *Manual and Norms for the High School Personality Questionnaire 'HSPQ'*. Urbana, IL: Institute for Personality and Ability Testing.

Cattell, R.B. and Johnson, R.C. (1986) (eds), *Functional Psychological Testing: Principles and Instruments*. New York: Brunner/Mazel.

Cattell, R.B., Schmidt, L.R. and Bjerstedt, A. (1972) 'Clinical diagnosis by the objective-analytic personality batteries', *Journal of Clinical Psychology*, 28(3): 239–312.

Cattell, R.B. and Schuerger, J.M. (1976) *The Objective-Analytic (O-A) Test Kit*. Champaign, IL: Institute for Personality and Ability Testing.

Cattell, R.B. and Schuerger, J.M. (1978) *Personality in Action: Handbook for the Objective-Analytic (O-A) Test Kit*. Champaign, IL: Institute for Personality and Ability Testing.

Cattell, R.B., Schuerger, J.M., Klein, G. and Finkbeiner, C. (1976) 'A definitive large-sample factoring of personality structure in objective measures, as a basis for the high school Objective-Analytic battery', *Journal of Research in Personality*, 10(1): 22–41.

Cattell, R.B. and Warburton, F.W. (1967) *Objective Personality and Motivation Tests: A Theoretical Introduction and Practical Compendium*. Chicago, IL: University of Illinois Press.

Dielman, R.E., Schuerger, J.M. and Cattell, R.B. (1970) 'Prediction of junior high school achievement from IQ and the objective-analytic personality factors U.I. 21, U.I. 23, U.I. 24 and U.I. 25', *Personality*, 1(2): 145–52.

Exner, J.E. (1993) *The Rorschach: A Comprehensive System* (Vol. 1, 3rd edn). New York: Wiley.

Feo, A.F. (1980) 'Relationship of the Objective-Analytic Test Battery with academic success', Unpublished MSc thesis, Cleveland State University, Cleveland.

Häcker, H. (1982) 'Objective tests zur messung der persönlichkeit', in K.J. Groffmann and L. Michel (eds), *Persönlichkeitsdiagnostik (Enzyklopädie der Psychologie* (Serie II, Vol. 4). Göttingen: Hogrefe, pp. 132–85.

Haggbloom, S., Warnick, R., Warnick, J.E., Jones, V.K., Yarbrough, G.L., Russell, T.M., Borecky, C.M., McGahhey, R., Powell III, J.L., Beavers, J. and Monte, E. (2002) 'The 100 most eminent psychologists of the 20th century', *Review of General Psychology*, 6(2): 139–52.

Howarth, E. (1972) 'A factor analysis of selected markers for objective personality factors', *Multivariate Behavioral Research*, 7(4): 451–76.

Hundleby, J.D., Pawlik, K. and Cattell, R.B. (1965) *Personality Factors in Objective Test Devices*. San Diego: Knapp.

King, L.D. (1976) 'Relationship of 10 HSOA factor scores to school related criteria and personality data from HSPQ', Unpublished MSc thesis, Cleveland State University, Cleveland.

Kline, P. and Cooper, C. (1984) 'A construct validation of the Objective-Analytic Test Battery (OATB)', *Personality and Individual Differences*, 5(3): 323–37.

Korth, B. (1978) 'A significance test for congruence coefficients for Cattell's factors matched by scanning', *Multivariate Behavioral Research*, 13(4): 419–30.

Miller, K.M. (1988) (ed.), *The Analysis of Personality in Research and Assessment: In Tribute to Raymond B. Cattell*. London: Independent Assessment and Research Centre.

Schmidt, L.R. (1988) 'Objective personality tests – some clinical applications', in K.M. Miller (ed.), *The Analysis of Personality in Research and Assessment: In Tribute to Raymond B. Cattell*. London: Independent Assessment and Research Centre.

Schmidt, L.R. (2006) 'Objective persön-lichkeitstests in der Tradition Cattells: Forshuchungslinien und Relativierungen', in T.M. Ortner, R.T. Proyer and K.D. Kubinger (eds), *Theorie und Praxis Objektiver Persönlichkeitstests*. Bern: Huber.

Schmidt, L.R., Häcker, H. and Cattell, R.B. (1975) *Objektive Testbatterie OA-TB 75 Testheft*. Weinheim: Beltz.

Schmidt, L.R., Häcker, H. and Schwenkmezger, P. (1985) 'Differentialdiagnostische Unter-suchungen mit Objectiven Persönlichkeitstests und Fragebogen im psychiatrischen Bereich', *Diagnostica*, 31(1): 22–37.

Schuerger, J.M. (1986) 'Personality assessment by objective tests', in R.B. Cattell and R.C. Johnson (eds), *Functional Psychological Testing*. New York: Bruner-Mazel.

Schuerger, J.M., Dielman, T.E. and Cattell, R.B. (1970) 'Objective-analytic personality factors (U.I. 16, 17, 19 and 20) as correlates of school achievement', *Personality*, 1(2): 95–101.

Schuerger, J.M., Feo, A.F. and Nowak, M.J. (1981) 'Personality matches across media in a large high school sample', *Multivariate Behavioral Research*, 16(3): 373–8.

Schuerger, J.M., Kepner, J. and Lawler, B. (1979) 'Verbal-quantitative differential as indicator of temperamental differences', *Multivariate Experimental Clinical Research*, 4(3): 57–66.

Schuerger, J.M., Zarrella, K. and Hotz, A. (1989) 'Factors which influence the stability of personality by questionnaire', *Journal of Personality and Social Psychology*, 56(5): 777–83.

Spangler, W.D. (1992) 'Validity of questionnaire and TAT measures of need for achievement: Two meta-analyses', *Psychological Bulletin*, 112(1): 140–54.

26

Behavioral Measures of Personality in Children

Ellen W. Rowe, Alyssa M. Perna and Randy W. Kamphaus

Although it may seem self-evident, the aim of behavioral assessment is to seek documentation on the occurrence of behaviors. More recently, behavioral assessment has expanded to include cognitions as a form of behavior (Kamphaus and Frick, 2005). It is worth noting, however, that with a behavioral approach, interpretation of these behaviors is usually not made in relation to deep-seated psychodynamic processes, nor is the goal to uncover long-standing dimensions of personality or character (Thorpe et al., 2003). Instead, responses or observations are viewed simply as reports on samples of behaviors that have or have not transpired. Personality measures, on the other hand, have traditionally sought to reveal pathological states, abnormal characteristics, or normal personality dimensions (Sattler and Hoge, 2006). In this way, behavioral assessments can be contrasted with many measures of personality or adult psychopathology. While they may appear distinct, though, these two approaches to assessment usually occur in some combination on the rating scales and self-report measures used to evaluate children and adolescents.

The depression construct and its indicators are but one example of the difficulty of labeling a particular scale as a measure of either behavior or personality, and not both. Measures of this construct are included on virtually all behavior rating scales and personality measures, including the Minnesota Multiphasic Personality Inventory (MMPI) (Hathaway and McKinley, 1942), the most well-known personality measure of all. Similarly, some personality theorists consider depression central to personality assessment by tracing its roots to Gall and his theory of the four humors, and specifically the melancholic temperament. As this example illustrates, current behavior rating scales are not always easily distinguished from traditional personality measures, if at all. Thus, the labeling of these measures is a convention with an associated amount of error. Future research may help to shed light on the issue.

Despite a certain lack of clarity in the distinction between behavior and personality, the use of rating scales for the psychological and psychoeducational assessment of children and adolescents has increased considerably over the past few decades (Kamphaus et al.,

2000; Reschly, 1998). In fact, most psychologists and mental health professionals now include some type of rating scale as a component of their comprehensive evaluations of children.

ADVANTAGES OF BEHAVIOR RATING SCALES

Given the advantages that rating scales provide, this increase is not surprising. To begin, rating scales provide a cost-efficient means of obtaining information about a child across multiple contexts in which the child functions (e.g. school and home). Additionally, clinicians can obtain a picture of the child from the perspective of the different adults with whom the child interacts (i.e. father, mother, or teacher) and, in many cases, from the child him/herself. Rating scales allow one to collect information about a child's behavior in a more objective manner than in an interview, and they allow one to collect information regarding low frequency or rare behaviors that might not be exhibited during a time-limited observation (Hart and Lahey, 1999). With the normative data that exists for commercially available rating scales, clinicians can compare ratings of a child's behavior to that of a national sample of same-age peers and obtain a quantitative measure of the degree of deviance. Furthermore, the dimensional nature of rating scales provides information on sub-threshold or subsyndromal symptomology (Cantwell, 1996). Subsyndromal symptoms are those that do not meet diagnostic criteria, but which nonetheless may cause some functional impairment. Finally, because ratings are summarized in a quantitative format, rating scales can be used to clearly document changes in behavior following an intervention or changes over time.

A brief history on the development of child rating scales provides some insight into the characteristics of rating scales that give rise to these advantages. This chapter begins with a short overview of the early development of

rating scales. Subsequently, we provide a review of some of the rating scales most commonly used in the assessment of children and adolescents. In the discussion of current rating scales, we first present an overview of several families of multidimensional, multi-source rating scales. By families of rating scales, we mean a set of behavior rating scales by the same author or authors. These families of rating scales are multi-source in that they have teacher, parent, and self-report forms. Rating scales that are considered multidimensional assess a variety of adjustment and/or problem areas such as social skills, depression, attention problems, and delinquent behavior in a single form.

Our presentation cannot be exhaustive due to space limitations. We are not able to provide an overview of many measures, such as those that do not include child, parent, and teacher report forms (e.g. Devereux Scales of Mental Disorders, DSMD) (Naglieri et al., 1994). Likewise, we were unable to include child/adolescent self-report instruments that measure a single construct such as the Children's Depression Inventory (CDI) (Kovacs, 1992), Reynolds Child Depression Scale (RCDS) (Reynolds, 1989) and Reynolds Adolescent Depression Scale, 2nd edition (RADS-2) (Reynolds, 2002), and Revised Children's Manifest Anxiety Scale (RCMAS) (Reynolds and Richmond, 1985). Rather than choosing to provide a compendium of available measures, we chose instead to place rating scale assessment in historical context and discuss some of the common problems and issues of which clinicians should be aware when using rating scales. We think that this approach provides a deeper understanding of the instruments and issues that will serve the reader well regardless of their choice of scale.

HISTORY OF RATING SCALE DEVELOPMENT

Although an initial step in the development of rating scales took place in the area of adult psychopathology, it had important ramifications for the study and classification of child psychopathology. In the early 1950s Wittenborn set out to develop a quantitative method for diagnosing adult psychiatric patients (Wittenborn, 1951). To this end, he created an instrument that consisted of 55 symptom items. Wittenborn called his items 'rating scales', and set forth the following eight criteria for his rating scales: the items must sample key symptoms found among patients; the rating scales should reflect current behavior, as opposed to a history of symptoms, so they could be used to identify improvements or changes in symptoms; the scales should produce ratings that are unrelated to the insights or theoretical orientation of the rater; the scales should reflect observable behaviors so as to minimize bias from the rater; the scales should allow for rating of each item with all patients; to the degree possible, the items should reflect mutually exclusive, independent behaviors; the scales should be simple, inexpensive, and convenient; and the scales should be reliable. A number of Wittenborn's (1951) innovations influenced the development of rating scales for children and adolescents. For instance, the criteria Wittenborn set forth for his items or rating scales became a standard for those interested in creating similar types of measures. Moreover, Wittenborn highlighted narrow-band factors, and others would attempt to elucidate similar narrow-band factors with samples of children.

A 1961 study by Peterson was a further step in the development of child rating scales. Peterson sought to develop a checklist of problematic behaviors or symptoms to be used with children. He began by reviewing 427 cases at a child guidance center and identifying the 58 most common referral problems. From these 'common' descriptions of problems, Peterson compiled a checklist. He then selected 28 teachers to rate 831 school children on a scale of 0 (no problem), 1 (mild problem), or 2 (severe problem) using the checklist. Peterson noted that he sought ratings of school children as opposed to referred

children in an attempt to better sample the entire dimension of behaviors. Peterson felt that using a sample of children undergoing treatment for mental health issues would result in his sampling children with more extreme behavior. Quay and Quay (1965) later replicated Peterson's findings with seventh- and eighth-grade students.

Three aspects of the Peterson (1961) and Quay and Quay (1965) studies are noteworthy. First, Peterson compiled a behaviorally oriented checklist to be used with children, and his items were identified from those common to children. These researchers also used teacher ratings of children, not the ratings of mental health workers or mental health professionals. In addition, they sought a non-referred sample of children in an attempt to obtain a picture of the distribution of these behaviors among normal school children. This study was the foundation for Quay and Peterson's (1967) 55-item Behavior Problem Checklist, one of the first rating scales designed for use with children.

Conners (1969) published a study that, like the Peterson (1961) and Quay and Quay (1965) studies, utilized teacher ratings of children's behavior. However, the goals of Conners' research and his reasons for using teacher ratings were quite different from those of Peterson and Quay and Quay. Conners sought to investigate the usefulness of teacher ratings in documenting treatment effects following a psychopharmacological intervention for children with behavior or learning problems. Conners hoped his rating scale would prove functional for use in outpatient settings such as clinics and practitioners' offices. Several rating scales were available at the time for use in inpatient settings, but these scales did not translate easily into an outpatient format (Conners, 1969). As a result, mental health workers were forced to rely upon their own observations of the child in their office or to rely upon anecdotal reports from parents. Conners recognized that teachers had the potential to be a rich source of information about children's adjustment or behavior and any changes therein. As Conners observed, teachers have the opportunity to observe a child for an extended period of time in a social context with his or her peers. In this context, the child is confronted on a daily basis with tasks that are appropriately challenging for his or her age and grade. Moreover, teachers have the added advantage of being able to compare a child with other children of the same age and at the same developmental level (Conners, 1969).

At pretreatment, comparisons of teacher ratings for the treatment and placebo groups revealed no significant differences (Conners, 1969). However, change scores from pre- to post-test revealed significantly more change for the treatment group as opposed to the placebo group. It should be noted that Conners' study was double blind, so neither the teachers completing the ratings nor the children or families knew which children were actually receiving medication (Conners, 1969). These findings support Conners' contention that teacher ratings of children are sensitive enough to document changes in behavior and symptomology following psychopharmacological intervention. The promise of behavior rating scales was confirmed, and these compelling early findings resulted in future development and improvement of the Conners and other rating scales. (The most recent edition of Conners' scales will be discussed later in this chapter.)

Thomas Achenbach published his first monograph on child behavior problems in 1966. According to Achenbach (1966), a primary goal of his study was to derive a more empirical and precise classification system for child psychopathology. To this end, Achenbach developed a 91-item symptom checklist, designed to rate child behavior problems. In his introduction, Achenbach referenced the study by Wittenborn and Holzberg (1951), and the criteria by which he selected items were similar to those used by Wittenborn (1951). Achenbach's 1966 checklist was a nascent form of his subsequent rating scales.

From the principal factor analysis with these data, Achenbach (1966) interpreted two factors. Although he conducted his analyses separately for boys and girls, the findings were consistent across the samples. Achenbach named the first principal factor 'internalizing versus externalizing'. He discussed the 'polar tendencies' of this factor but pointed out that the label was not meant to have dynamic implications. Instead, items that loaded at the 'externalizing' end of the factor appeared to relate to conflict with the environment, while those on the 'internalizing' end seemed to describe problems within the self. Examples of items that loaded highly on the 'externalizing' end were 'disobedient', 'stealing', and 'fighting'. Items that loaded highly on the internalizing side were 'phobias', 'fearful', and 'withdrawn'. The second principal factor, which appeared consistently in Achenbach's samples, was labeled 'severe and diffuse psychopathology'. Items that loaded on this factor included 'bizarre behavior' and 'fantastic thinking'.

Following the principal factor analysis, Achenbach (1966) rotated the factors to obtain a simple structure solution of more narrow-band factors. Achenbach interpreted seven factors in the male sample and eleven with females. Six factors that were common to both males and females were somatic complaints; delinquent behavior; obsessions, compulsions, and phobias; schizoid thinking and behavior; aggressive behavior; and hyperactive behavior. Among the factors that were unique to the female sample were depressive symptoms and anxiety symptoms. Thus, Achenbach's early research established the well-known dimensions of externalizing and internalizing psychopathology. These dimensions, as well as syndrome scales such as somatic complaints, aggressive behavior, and hyperactive behavior laid the foundation for measuring these constructs on many of the rating scales used today.

MULTIDIMENSIONAL BEHAVIOR RATING SCALES

Achenbach System of Empirically Based Assessment

Achenbach and Edelbrock continued Achenbach's (1966) work by creating a parent

Table 26.1　Child Behavior Checklist (CBCL). Developed by: Thomas M. Achenbach and Leslie Rescorla (2001)

Ages:	Items:	Normative data:
Preschool (P): 1½–5	100	$n = 700$
Child (C): 6–18	113	$n = 1{,}753$
Informant: Parent or Guardian	**Completion time:** 10–20 minutes	**Scaling:** 0–2

Competence scales: Activities, social, and school (all on C-form only)

Syndrome scales: Anxious/depressed, somatic complaints, attention problems, aggressive behavior, withdrawn/depressed (C only), social problems (C only), thought problems (C only), rule-breaking behavior (C only), emotionally reactive (P only), withdrawn (P only), and sleep problems (P only)

Total scores and syndrome groupings: Total competence (C only), externalizing problems, internalizing problems, and total problems

DSM-oriented scales: Affective problems, anxiety problems, attention deficit/hyperactivity problems, oppositional defiant problems, somatic problems (C only), Conduct Problems (C only), and pervasive developmental problems (P only)

rating scale, the CBCL (Achenbach, 1978; Achenbach and Edelbrock, 1983), a teacher rating scale, the TRF (Achenbach and Edelbrock, 1986) and a self-report scale, the YSR (Achenbach and Edelbrock, 1987). Tables 26.1 and 26.2 contain summary information on current versions of the CBCL and the TRF (respectively). Summary information on the YSR is presented in Table 26.3. Today, Achenbach's measures are among the most commonly used rating scales in child and adolescent assessment (Hart and Lahey, 1999; Reschly, 1998) and have been translated into at least 61 other languages (Achenbach and Rescorla, 2001). The CBCL and the TRF have both preschool and school-age forms for the assessment of children and adolescents, while the YSR has a school-age form (Achenbach and Rescorla, 2000, 2001).

ASEBA school-age forms

The school-age forms of the CBCL and TRS are normed for use with children and adolescents ages 6 to 18, and the YSR is normed for ages 11 to 18 (Achenbach and Rescorla, 2001). Both the CBCL/6–18 and the TRF consist of 113 problem items, and the YSR has 112. Each form takes approximately 15–20 minutes to complete. Response options for all three forms are 0 = *not true*, 1 = *somewhat or sometimes true*, and 2 = *very true or often true*. The three forms are considered parallel versions of one

Table 26.2　Teacher Report Form (TRF) and Caregiver-Teacher Report Form (C-TRF). Developed by: Thomas M. Achenbach and Leslie Rescorla (2001)

Ages:	Items:	Normative data:
Preschool (P): 1½–5	100	$n = 1{,}192$
Child (C): 6–18	113	$n = 2{,}319$
Informant: Teacher or caregiver	**Completion time:** 10–20 minutes	**Scaling:** 0–2

Adaptive functioning: Academic performance, working hard, behaving appropriately, learning, and happy (all on C-form only)

Syndrome scales: Anxious/depressed, somatic complaints, attention problems, aggressive behavior, withdrawn/depressed (C only), social problems (C only), thought problems (C only), rule-breaking behavior (C only), emotionally reactive (P only), and withdrawn (P only)

Total scores and syndrome groupings: Externalizing problems, internalizing problems, and total problems

DSM-oriented scales: Affective problems, anxiety problems, attention deficit/hyperactivity problems, oppositional defiant problems, somatic problems (C only), conduct problems (C only), and pervasive developmental problems (P only)

Table 26.3   Youth Self-Report (YSR). Developed by: Thomas M. Achenbach and Leslie Rescorla (2001)

Ages: 11–18	**Items:** 112	**Normative data:** $n = 1,057$
Informant: Child or adolescent	**Completion time:** 10–20 minutes	**Scaling:** 0–2

Competence scales: Activities and Social

Syndrome scales: Anxious/depressed, somatic complaints, attention problems, aggressive behavior, withdrawn/depressed, social problems, thought problems, and rule-breaking behavior

Total scores and syndrome groupings: Total competence, externalizing problems, internalizing problems, and total problems

DSM-oriented scales: Affective problems, anxiety problems, attention deficit/hyperactivity problems, oppositional defiant problems, somatic problems, conduct problems

another so that comparisons can be made among different raters or responders and contexts (Achenbach and Rescorla, 2001). At the same time, not all of the items are identical. For example, the TRF has 23 problem items not found on the CBCL/6–18 that involve group or school situations that teachers are more qualified to rate. Similarly, the YSR has a number of unique socially desirable items. Both the CBCL/6–18 and the YSR contain seven question areas that relate to skills and competence. Areas covered by these questions are activities (e.g. sports and hobbies), social activity and relations, and school. The TRF competence questions address only academic performance and adaptive areas such as degree of learning. The competence and adaptive functioning questions are not in the Likert-style format of the problem items. Instead, responders list activities such as sports, clubs, and academic subjects, and then rate the frequency and/or the degree of skill. All three forms also have a set of open-ended questions that ask about concerns and strengths. The descriptive information from the open-ended questions can help the clinician get a broader picture of the responder's view of the child/adolescent.

Hand-scored and computerized scoring results for the school-age forms are available for areas of competence and adaptive functioning, syndrome scales, composite scores such as internalizing, externalizing, and total problems, and DSM-oriented scales (Achenbach and Rescorla, 2001). Ratings on the problem

items yield scores for the empirically derived syndrome scales and the DSM-oriented scales. Unlike the syndrome scales, which were derived empirically, the DSM-oriented scales were created according to the diagnostic criteria of the *Diagnostic and Statistical Manual of Mental Disorders* (4th edn) (DSM-IV; American Psychiatric Association, 1994). The degree to which items matched diagnostic criteria was determined by a group of culturally diverse child psychiatrists and psychologists (Achenbach and Rescorla, 2001). Although the normative data is separate for boys and girls, the scales are the same for both sexes. It is worth noting, though, that the TRF Attention Problems Scale and the teacher-rated DSM-oriented Scale of Attention Deficit/Hyperactivity Problems have separate subscales for symptoms of inattention versus those of hyperactivity/impulsivity. These subscales are not found on the CBCL/6–18 or the YSR.

ASEBA preschool forms

The preschool CBCL and Caregiver–teacher Report Form (C-TRF) are for use with children ages one year and six months to five years old (Achenbach and Rescorla, 2000). Each form has 100 behavior problem items to which parents or teachers respond on a 0–1–2 scale. Like the school-age forms, the CBCL/1½–5 and the C-TRF are considered to be parallel to one another, although some of the items are different. These forms do not have questions regarding competencies or skills, but they do have open-ended questions about concerns or strengths.

As is the case with the school-age forms, the preschool ASEBA forms have hand-scored and computerized scoring options (Achenbach and Rescorla, 2000). Both scoring methods produce profiles and information for empirically derived scales, composites, and DSM-oriented scales. At the preschool level, the CBCL/1½–5 contains one scale, Sleep Problems, not found on the C-TRF. The normative data for the CBCL/1½–5 represents ratings of both boys and girls, while the normative data for the C-TRF are separate for boys and girls.

The ASEBA preschool and school-age computerized reports also provide cross-informant information (Achenbach and Rescorla, 2000, 2001). With this information, clinicians can compare ratings across raters on actual items, as well as scales. Moreover, Q correlations between raters are provided. Because the average correlations for rater comparisons are also printed, the clinician has an idea of the degree to which the agreement between particular raters is typical.

The ASEBA family of scales offers numerous advantages. To begin, the forms cover a wide range of ages for the assessment of toddlers through adolescents. Although the item content is not identical from form to form, the scales are relatively similar. This similarity provides clinicians and researchers the chance to evaluate the degree of similarity or dissimilarity across raters. The ASEBA scoring and forms are designed to facilitate this type of comparison. The addition of the DSM-oriented scales on the most recent revision is also a plus. Because the syndrome scales are empirically derived, they do not always align well with the DSM-IV (APA, 1994) diagnostic criteria. The DSM-oriented scales help to mitigate this. The inclusion of items measuring competencies and open-ended questions is also beneficial in that they provide a more comprehensive picture of the child that is not limited to problem behaviors. The availability of only separate subgroup

norms for boys and girls, and truncated score distributions are potential limitations that will be discussed later. Another possible limitation is the combination of data from different years for the TRF and C-TRF normative samples. Both sets of norms consist of data from current and previous normative samples (Achenbach and Rescorla, 2000, 2001). Although research suggests few changes in child behavior over the years during which the data were collected (Achenbach et al., 2002), new normative data collected at the same time is probably the ideal.

The Conners' Rating Scales – Revised

As was the case with the ASEBA scales, the Conners' Rating Scales (CRS) have a history that dates to the 1960s. Over the past 30 years, various versions of the CRS were introduced with the addition of several items; however, the most recent revision and restandardization took place in the 1990s and was the most significant to date. In contrast to the two types of scales (parent and teacher) developed for the original versions, three types of scales were created for the revision (parent, teacher, and self-report). Additionally, the CRS-R (Conners, 1997) provides short and long versions for each of the parent, teacher, and self-report forms. While the long forms are the most comprehensive because of the number of items and division into numerous subscales, as well as their inclusion of DSM-IV (APA, 1994) symptom subscales, the short forms are well-suited for situations when administration time is limited or when the clinician plans to readminister the scale on multiple occasions. In general, comparable results are obtained using either the long or short version.

Conners' Parent Rating Scale – Revised

The Conners' Parent Rating Scale – Revised (CPRS-R) (Conners et al., 1998a) was

Table 26.4   Conners' Parent Rating Scale – Revised (CPRS-R). Developed by: C. Keith Conners

Ages: 3–17	**Items:** 80 (L; long form) and 27 (S; short form)	**Normative data:** $n = 2,482$
Informant: Parent or guardian	**Completion time:** 10–15 minutes	**Scaling:** 0–3

Subscales: Oppositional, cognitive problems/inattention, hyperactivity, anxious-shy, perfectionism, social problems, and psychosomatic, Connors' global (vary depending on form)

Indexes: Conners' ADHD Index (L & S) and Conner's Global Index (subscales: total, restless-impulsive and emotional lability; all L only)

DSM-IV symptom scales: Inattentive, hyperactive-impulsive, and total (all L only)

developed because of the need for a normative sample more representative of the current population of children being assessed with the CPRS. Brief information on the CPRS-R is given in Table 26.4. The normative data for the CPRS-R include 2,200 students ranging from ages 3 to 17 from schools across the US and Canada. Other goals in the revision and restandardization were to address the lack of a definitive, established factor structure, update the item content to reflect modern day thinking about childhood disorders, and to address scale brevity and focus of item content.

Both the long and short versions of the CPRS-R are normed for use with children ages 3 to 17 years. Items are measured on a four-point Likert scale ranging from 0 if it *never*, *seldom*, or *very infrequently* occurs, to 3 if it occurs *very often* or *frequently*. The short form contains 27 items with 4 subscales, while the long form has 80 items and 14 subscales. *T* scores are calculated based on both age and gender norms, with five different age groups (i.e. ages 3–5, 6–8, 9–11, 12–14, and 15–17). It is worth noting that clinicians are advised to use the age categories with caution, particularly when the individual recently had or is on the verge of a birthday. Exploratory and confirmatory factor analysis revealed the following seven factors: cognitive problems, oppositional, hyperactivity-impulsivity, anxious/shy, perfectionism, psychosomatic, and social problems (Conners, 1997).

In general, the revision of the CPRS has produced a more psychometrically sound instrument, which contains fewer items, yet provides a more comprehensive assessment. Internal reliability coefficients were good

and ranged from 0.75 to 0.94 for males, and 0.75 to 0.94 for females. Additionally, the scales demonstrate good test–retest reliability and discriminative validity. The CPRS-R specifically addresses attention-deficit/hyperactivity disorder (ADHD) related behaviors and demonstrates effectiveness in discriminating ADHD children and adolescents from the non-ADHD population. The cognitive problems factor is a new addition to the parent scales and addresses symptoms consistent with inattention and academic problems (Conners et al., 1998a). The CPRS-R continues to be useful as a screening tool for part of a more comprehensive assessment, as well as to monitor treatment and to assess treatment outcome.

Conners' Teacher Rating Scale – Revised

Since its introduction in the 1960s, the Conners' Teacher Rating Scale (CTRS) has been utilized by clinicians and researchers at both the screening level and as part of a comprehensive assessment battery. The CTRS compliments parent ratings and provides clinicians with a measure of children's behavior within the school setting. Teacher reports have become increasingly critical to the assessment and diagnosis of attention deficit/hyperactivity disorder (ADHD) because of the need for cross-situational (home and school) evidence of behavior problems. Similar to the original parent scale, the revision of the CTRS (Conners, 1997) was prompted because of the need for updated norms based on a more representative sample of North American children; in order to determine a reliable and

Table 26.5   Conners' Teacher Rating Scale – Revised (CTRS-R). Developed by: C. Keith Conners

Ages: 3–17	**Items:** 59 (L; long form) and 28 (S; short form)	**Normative data:** $n = 1,973$
Informant: Teacher	**Completion time:** 10–15 minutes	**Scaling:** 0–3

Subscales: Oppositional, cognitive problems/inattention, hyperactivity, anxious-shy, perfectionism, and social problems (vary depending on form)

Indexes: Conners' ADHD Index (L & S) and Conner's Global Index (subscales: total, restless-impulsive and emotional lability; all L only)

DSM-IV scales: Inattentive, hyperactive-impulsive, and total (all L only)

empirically derived factor structure; and lastly, to update items so to better match current conceptualizations of childhood disorders.

The normative sample for the Conners' Teacher Rating Scale – Revised (CTRS-R) (Conners et al., 1998b) consisted of 1,702 participants ranging in age from 3 to 17 years from 49 of the US and all 10 Canadian provinces. The resulting CTRS-R contains 59 items on the long version and 28 items on the short version. The items are rated on a four-point Likert scale (0 = *not true at all* to 3 = *very much true*). The directions ask teachers to rate the child's behavior during the last month. As with the CTRS-R, norms are based on both age and gender. The long form contains the same subscales as the parent form, with the exception of the psychosomatic subscale, to allow for comparisons across informants. Confirmatory factor analyses supported interpretation of six factors: hyperactivity-impulsivity, inattention/cognitive problems, perfectionism, oppositionality, social problems, and anxious/shy. Similar to the original teacher scale, as well as the CPRS-R, the CTRS-R demonstrates good overall internal and test–retest reliability, with the exception of the inattentive/cognitive problems scale, which was shown to have lower test–retest reliability ($r = 0.47$). Table 26.5 contains summary information on the CTRS-R

Conners–Wells' Adolescent Self-report Scale

The Conners–Wells' Adolescent Self-report Scale (CASS) (Conners et al., 1997) were included in the revision of the CRS to provide a third source of information in addition to the parent and teacher reports. Information on the CASS is presented in Table 26.6. Self-reports are particularly important during adolescence as children spend less time with parents and switch classes and teachers throughout the course of the day. These developmental changes can affect the expression and symptomology of internalizing and externalizing disorders and environmental changes provide fewer opportunities for teacher observation (Conners, 1997).

The CASS (long form) contains 87 items, which follow the same four-point Likert scale format as the CPRS-R and CTRS

Table 26.6   Conners–Wells' Adolescent Self-Report Scale (CASS). Developed by: C. Keith Conners and Karen Wells

Ages: 12–17	**Items:** 87 (L; long form) and 27 items (S; short form)	**Normative data:** $n = 3,394$
Informant: Adolescent	**Completion time:** 10–15 minutes	**Scaling:** 0–3

Subscales: Family problem, emotional problems, conduct problems, cognitive problems/inattention, anger control problems, hyperactivity (vary depending on form)

Indexes: Conners' ADHD Index (L & S)

DSM-IV symptom scales: Inattentive, hyperactive-impulsive, and total (all L only)

described earlier. Norms are based on age (two groups: 12–14 years and 15–17 years), as well as gender. Scores are interpreted based on the six CASS subscales derived from confirmatory factor analysis. The six factors include family problems, emotional problems, conduct problems, cognitive problems, anger control problems, and hyperactivity (Conners, 1997). A potential weakness of the CASS is the lack of breadth in its measurement of specific problems. Analysis of the CASS suggests good test–retest reliability of the six factors (0.86) and internal reliability with coefficient alphas ranging from 0.83 to 0.92 (Conners et al., 1997).

The Personality Inventory for Children, 2nd edition; Personality Inventory for Youth; and Student Behavior Survey

Another rating scale with a history covering several decades is the Personality Inventory for Children (PIC). The original PIC was published in 1958 and consisted of over 600 items that assessed areas such as family relations, intellectual, and physical development, as well as aggression (Lachar and Gruber, 2003). This original version was based loosely on the MMPI (Kamphaus and Frick, 2005). The most recent version of the PIC, the Personality Inventory for Children, 2nd edition (PIC-2) was published in 2001 (Lachar and Gruber). Like its predecessors, the PIC-2 is a rating scale completed by parents. Also included in this family of measures is the Personality Inventory for Youth (PIY) (Lachar and Gruber, 1995), a self-report inventory, and the Student Behavior Survey (SBS) (Lachar et al., 2000), a teacher rating scale. Table 26.7 presents summary information on the PIC-2.

Tables 26.8 and 26.9 contain information on the PIY and the SBS, respectively.

Personality Inventory for Children, 2nd edition and Personality Inventory for Youth

The PIC-2 (Lachar and Gruber, 2001) consists of 275 statements to which parents or caregivers respond *true* or *false*. Completion of the entire form takes approximately 45 minutes (Lachar and Gruber, 2001). Responses can be computer or hand-scored, and yield scores for three validity scales and nine adjustment scales. An improvement over previous versions of the PIC is that the majority of items are scored on only one scale. A new feature of this version is the inclusion of scores for subscales that are subsumed under the nine adjustment scales. Each adjustment scale has two to three subscales. For example, the delinquency scale consists of the three subscales, antisocial behavior, dyscontrol, and noncompliance. Gender specific, representative norms are available for children ages 5–19. Scores for eight shortened adjustment scales can also be produced from completion of the first 96 PIC-2 items.

Like the PIC-2, most of the items on the PIY were adapted from previous versions of the PIC (Lachar and Gruber, 2003). The PIY consists of 270 true–false statements which take between 30 and 60 minutes to complete (Lachar and Gruber, 1995). The PIY has three validity scales and nine clinical scales that are analogous to those on the PIC-2. However, some of the 24 subscales comprising the nine adjustment scales are different. The PIY can be scored manually or by computer. National norms for males and females are available for students from age 4 to 18.

Table 26.7   Personality Inventory for Children, 2nd edition (PIC-2). Developed by: David Lachar and Christian P. Gruber (2001)

Ages: 5–19	**Items:** 275	**Normative data:** $n = 2,306$
Informant: Parent, Guardian	**Completion time:** 40 minutes	**Scaling:** True/false

Adjustment scales: Cognitive impairment, impulsivity and distractibility, delinquency, family dysfunction, reality distortion, somatic concern, psychological discomfort, social withdrawal, and social skills deficits
Validity scales: Inconsistency, dissimulation, and defensiveness

Table 26.8   Personality Inventory for Youth (PIY). Developed by: David Lachar and Christian P. Gruber (1995)

Ages: 9–18	**Items:** 270	**Normative data:** $n = 2,327$
Informant: Child or adolescent	**Completion time:** 30–60 minutes	**Scaling:** True/false

Clinical scales: Cognitive impairment, impulsivity and distractibility, delinquency, family dysfunction, reality distortion, somatic concern, psychological discomfort, social withdrawal, and social skills deficits

Validity scales: Inconsistency, dissimulation, and defensiveness

The three validity scales that appear on both the PIC-2 and the PIY are inconsistency, dissimulation, and defensiveness (Lachar and Gruber, 2003). The Inconsistency scales are elevated when a respondent does not respond in a consistent manner to 35 highly correlated item sets. Elevations in the dissimulation scales can be indicative of a tendency to 'fake bad', and high scores on the defensiveness scales signify a pattern of denying common problems. According to Lachar and Gruber (1995), the PIY validity scales can provide additional information that clarifies the meaning of the remaining scales.

The increased precision of construct measurement with most items loading on a single scale is a great improvement for the PIC-2. Also, the scales on the PIC-2 and PIY are very similar and allow clinicians to compare ratings from these instruments. The validity scales provide clinicians an extra degree of assurance in determining the validity of their assessment information. A disadvantage of the PIC-2 and the PIY is the increased time for completion as compared to other measures reviewed. Also, the reliabilities for some of the subscales are low, and thus greater emphasis on the interpretation of the adjustment/clinical scales is warranted.

Student Behavior Survey

The SBS (Lachar et al., 2000) is the teacher scale in the PIC family. As a teacher rating scale, a large proportion of SBS items are school specific. In fact, 58 out of 102 total items relate to school or class behaviors. As a result, the SBS scales are not necessarily parallel to those on the PIC-2 and PIY. For example, the SBS has two academic scales: academic performance and academic habits. The SBS parent participation scale is a unique scale that assesses parent support for academics and involvement with the school. Teachers respond to items in two formats. For items on the academic performance scale, the response options are deficient, below average, average, above average, and superior. The remaining items are rated on a four-point scale of never, seldom, sometimes, and usually. The SBS has normative data for boys and girls in two age groups: 5–11 and 12–18 years.

Table 26.9   Student Behavior Survey (SBS). Developed by: David Lachar, Sabine A. Wingenfeld, Rex B. Kline, and Christian P. Gruber (2000)

Ages: 5–18	**Items:** 102	**Normative data:** $n = 2612$
Informant: Teacher	**Completion time:** 15 minutes	**Scaling:** *Never, seldom, sometimes, usually* (all but first scale) or *deficient, below average, average, above average, superior* (first scale)

Adjustment scales: Academic performance, academic habits, social skills, parent participation, health concerns, emotional distress, unusual behavior, social problems, verbal aggression, physical aggression, behavior problems, attention-deficit/hyperactivity, oppositional defiant, and conduct problems

The fact that a majority of items on the SBS are school and class focused is an advantage for acquiring information from the school context. The inclusion of the parent participation scale can give clinicians some insight into parental involvement with the school or a teacher's perception of this involvement. At the same time, the lack of similarities with the PIC-2 and the PIY make comparisons with these reports less straightforward.

Behavior Assessment System for Children, 2nd edition

The last set of scales to be discussed is a relative newcomer. The original Behavior Assessment System for Children (BASC) (Reynolds and Kamphaus, 1992) was first published in the early 1990s. Although comparatively new, the BASC has become a popular set of measures for the assessment of children and adolescents. In a 1997 survey of school psychologists' test use, only five years after its publication, the BASC ranked fourteenth among the fifteen most widely used tests (Reschly, 1998). The Conners' and Achenbach scales were also among the fifteen most widely used tests in that survey (Reschly, 1998).

The BASC was recently revised, and the Behavior Assessment System for Children, 2nd edition was released in 2004 (BASC-2; Reynolds and Kamphaus). Like the BASC,

the BASC-2 assessment system includes parent rating scales (PRS), teacher rating scales (TRS), and the self-report of personality (SRP) measures. Table 26.10 contains information on the TRS, and Table 26.11 summarizes the essential information on the PRS. Table 26.12 provides a summary of the SRP. BASC-2 parent and teacher ratings scales exist across three age levels: preschool (TRS-P, PRS-P; ages 2–5), child (TRS-C, PRS-C; ages 6–11), and adolescent (TRS-A, PRS-A; ages 12–18). Self-report measures are available for children (SRP-I; ages 6–7 and SRP-C; ages 8–11), adolescents (SRP-A; ages 12–21), and college students (SRP-COL; ages 18–25). The BASC-2 parent and teacher forms are considered complementary and have similar scales that allow clinicians to compare ratings from these measures. The SRP forms have a number of dimensions that are common to the parent and teacher forms (e.g. anxiety, depression, and atypicality). At the same time, many of the scales on the SRP are unique to the self-report forms (e.g. attitude to school, locus of control, and self-esteem).

At the child level, the TRS-C consists of 139 items, while the PRS-C has 160 items (Reynolds and Kamphaus, 2004). The scales take approximately 10–20 minutes to complete. Raters respond to TRS and PRS items on a four-point scale of *never, sometimes, often*, and *almost always*. The number of

Table 26.10 Behavior Assessment System for Children, 2nd edition (BASC-2), Teacher Rating Scales (TRS). Developed by: Cecil R. Reynolds and Randy W. Kamphaus (2004)

Ages:	Items:	Normative data:
Preschool (P): 2–5	100	$n = 1,050$
Child (C): 6–11	139	$n = 1,800$
Adolescent (A): 12–21	139	$n = 1,800$
Informant: Teacher, caregiver	**Completion Time:** 10–20 minutes	**Scaling:** 0–3

Primary scales: Adaptability, aggression, anxiety, attention problems, atypicality, conduct problems (C & A only), depression, functional communication, hyperactivity, leadership (C & A only), learning problems (C & A only), social skills, somatization, study skills (C & A only), and withdrawal

Composites: Behavioral Symptoms Index, externalizing problems, internalizing problems, adaptive skills, and school problems (C and A only)

Content scales: Anger control, bullying, developmental social disorders, emotional self-control, executive functioning, negative emotionality, and resiliency

Validity indexes: F-index, Consistency Index, and Response Pattern Index

Table 26.11   Behavior Assessment System for Children, 2nd edition (BASC-2), Parent Rating Scales (PRS). Developed by: Cecil R. Reynolds and Randy W. Kamphaus (2004)

Versions: English and Spanish

Ages:	**Items:**	**Normative data:**
Preschool (P): 2–5	134	$n = 1,200$
Child (C): 6–11	160	$n = 1,800$
Adolescent (A): 12–21	150	$n = 1,800$

Informant: Parent, guardian	**Completion time:** 10–20 minutes	**Scaling:** 0–3

Primary scales: Adaptability, activities of daily living, aggression, anxiety, attention problems, atypicality, conduct problems (C & A only), depression, functional communication, hyperactivity, leadership (C & A only), social skills, somatization, and withdrawal

Composites: Behavioral Symptoms Index, externalizing problems, internalizing problems, and adaptive skills

Content scales: Anger control, bullying, developmental social disorders, emotional self-control, executive functioning, negative emotionality, and resiliency

Validity indexes: F-index, Consistency Index, and Response Pattern Index

TRS and PRS items at the preschool and adolescent levels range from 100 (TRS-P) to 150 (PRS-A). The SRP form has 139 items at the child level, 176 for adolescents, and 185 for those ages 18–25. The SRP items are written at approximately a third-grade reading level and take about 20–30 minutes to complete. Respondents reply with *true* or *false* to roughly the first third of items on the SRP. The responses for the remaining items range from *never* to *almost always*, in the format of the other rating measures.

The BASC-2 forms may be scored by hand or computer (Reynolds and Kamphaus, 2004). Ratings for all BASC-2 rating scales yield composite and primary scale scores. With the BASC-2 ASSIST Plus computerized scoring, clinicians also have the option of using and interpreting content scales. The TRS-C form has 5 composite scales, 15 primary scales, and 7 content scales. Ratings on the PRS-C produce scores for 4 composite scales, 14 primary scales, and 7 content scales. The TRS-C and TRS-A primary scales of learning problems

Table 26.12   Behavior Assessment System for Children, 2nd edition (BASC-2), Self-Report of Personality (SRP). Developed by: Cecil R. Reynolds and Randy W. Kamphaus (2004)

Versions: English and Spanish

Ages:	**Items:**	**Normative data:**
Child (C): 8–11	139	$n = 1,500$
Adolescent (A): 12–21	176	$n = 1,900$
College (COL): 18–25	185	$n = 706$

Informant: Child, adolescent, or young adult	**Completion time:** 20–30 minutes	**Scaling:** True/false and 0-3

Primary scales: Alcohol abuse (COL only), anxiety, attention problems, attitude to school (C & A only), attitude to teacher (C & A only), atypicality, depression, hyperactivity, interpersonal relations, locus of control, relations with parents, school adjustment (COL only), self-esteem, self-reliance, sensation seeking (A & COL only), sense of inadequacy, social stress, and somatization (A & COL only)

Composites: Emotional Symptoms Index, inattention/hyperactivity. internalizing personal adjustment, and school problems (C & A only)

Content scales: Anger control, ego strength, mania, and test anxiety

Validity indexes: F-index, L-index, V-index, Consistency Index, and Response Pattern Index

and study skills are found only with teacher ratings, as teachers have a unique picture of these school-oriented problems and skills. A scale of activities of daily living is found only with parent ratings. The BASC-2 scales were all based on theoretical, as well as empirical foundations. Clinicians have the option of scoring their results with general normative data or clinical norms. Same-sex or separate norms for males and females are available with both the general and clinical norms. Computerized scoring also provides a comparison of ratings from different raters, and the BASC-2 ASSIST Plus scoring highlights behaviors or symptoms that match criteria for DSM-IV (APA, 1994) diagnoses.

Of the 15 primary TRS-C scales, 5 scales assess adaptive constructs (Reynolds and Kamphaus, 2004). Together, these scales form the adaptive skills composite. The BASC-2 is relatively unique among child/adolescent rating scales due to the inclusion of a substantial number of items assessing adaptive behaviors on the rating scales. The adaptive items are interspersed among the behavior problem items and are measured and scored in the same manner. The additional ten scales measure problem behaviors. Among the ten problem behavior scales is the learning problems scale. On the TRS-C and TRS-A, the learning problems scale combines with the attention problems scale to form the school problems composite. The other higher-order composites representing problem behaviors are internalizing and externalizing.

As mentioned previously, the SRP instruments have some scales that overlap with the TRS and PRS forms, but many items and scales are unique to the SRP. Of the 14 primary scales on the SRP-C, 4 measure adaptive dimensions (Reynolds and Kamphaus, 2004). The attitude to school and attitude to teacher scales on the SRP-C combine to form the school problems composite, and the attention problems and hyperactivity scales combine to form the inattention/hyperactivity composite. The remaining composite is internalizing problems.

Content scales were not found on the original BASC, but content scales have long been used with the MMPI (Graham, 1990). The same seven content scales are available with the TRS and PRS (Reynolds and Kamphaus, 2004). The SRP forms have four content scales at the adolescent and college levels, but there are no content scales for the SRP at the child-level. Like the primary scales, the content scales represent both adaptive and problematic constructs. For example, ego strength and resiliency are adaptive, while anger control and bullying are problematic in nature. Reynolds and Kamphaus (2004) note that these scales can give a broader picture of the child/adolescent by providing further information that may be relevant to a case.

All of the BASC-2 rating forms also have scales designed to assess the validity of ratings. The TRS and PRS forms all have three indices that supply information about validity (Reynolds and Kamphaus, 2004). The first of these is the F-index, also known as 'fake bad'. An elevated F-index suggests that the rater may have rated the child in an excessively negative manner. Although a rater may feel that their excessively negative ratings reflect the child's actual behaviors, and they may in fact represent the child's behavior, only 1% or less of the ratings in the general normative sample were in the 'extreme caution' range on the F-index. The Response Pattern Index indicates the number of times a response differs from the proceeding response. Thus, a very low score might reveal a pattern of repeated *never* responses, but a very high score might suggest a rater that systematically responded *never, sometimes, often, almost always* in a repeating pattern. The Consistency Index identifies times where a rater responded differently to similar items.

The SRP also has an F-index, a Response Pattern Index, and a Consistency Index (Reynolds and Kamphaus, 2004). However, the SRP has two additional validity indices. One is the L-index or the 'look good' index. A high score on this index reveals a child/adolescent who is presenting themselves in a very positive manner. The V-index consists of nonsense or absurd items that the child/adolescent has endorsed. A high score on the V-index could result from the child not understanding the item or from a failure to cooperate with the assessment.

The inclusion of validity scales is an obvious strength for this family of instruments. Like previous measures reviewed, the BASC-2 forms also cover a wide age range. A further advantage of the BASC-2 scales is the presence of adaptive competencies which are measured in the same manner as the clinical scales. Research supports the importance of adaptive competencies in predicting children's behavioral and academic outcomes (Thorpe et al., 2000). Additionally, the separation of symptoms of hyperactivity and impulsivity from those of inattention can be helpful for practitioners interested in distinguishing among the subtypes of ADHD (Vaughn et al., 1997). The parallel nature of the TRS and the PRS forms allows for easy comparisons between these measures. The lack of scales assessing aggression or conduct problems on the SRP limits some of the comparisons that can be made with these forms. Moreover, the definitions for some of the constructs on the SRP are less familiar to clinicians and may initially take longer to interpret.

ISSUES IN THE USE OF BEHAVIOR RATING SCALES

In spite of the many advantages of behavior rating scales, there are issues involved in using this type of measure. To begin, different raters, particularly those rating a child in different contexts, rarely provide ratings that are highly correlated (Achenbach et al., 1987). In their oft-cited meta-analytic study, Achenbach and his colleagues (Achenbach et al., 1987) determined mean correlations for different sets of raters. Not surprisingly, correlations for raters who observe a child in similar contexts are higher than those observing in different environments. For example, the average correlation between parents (e.g. mother and father) was 0.59 (Achenbach et al.). The mean correlation between teachers was 0.64 and 0.54 for mental health workers. At the same time, the average correlation among parents

and teachers was 0.27, while that among parents and child self-reports was 0.25. Finally, the mean correlation among teachers and child self-reports was 0.20 (Achenbach et al.). Although some have interpreted these differences as a problem with reliability or a reason to cast doubt on the accuracy of ratings from one or more of the raters (Achenbach et al., 1987), Achenbach and his colleagues (Achenbach, 1995; Achenbach and McConaughy, 2003; Achenbach et al., 1987) have argued that these small associations most likely reflect disparity in the child's behavior across environments and across their interactions with raters. Given these differences, clinicians and researchers frequently stress the importance of obtaining behavioral ratings from different sources who interact with the child in different environments (Achenbach and McConaughy, 2003; Achenbach et al., 1987; Kraemer et al., 2003; Lachar and Gruber, 2003; Reynolds and Kamphaus, 2004). In support of this recommendation, Verhulst et al. (1994) found that inclusion of both parent and teacher ratings improved the prediction of children's future academic and behavior problems.

Another issue in the use of rating scales is discrepancies in construct definitions. Two of the most common classes of behavior discussed in the literature on child psychopathology are externalizing and internalizing behaviors. These constructs have appeared in the literature for decades, and general descriptions have been presented. However, there are no clear-cut, definitive definitions, and little research exists on their relationship to diagnosis, prognosis, or etiology of child psychopathology. Most child psychopathology research, for example, is aimed at understanding syndromes as defined by the DSM, rather than those defined by the internalizing and externalizing constructs. Achenbach's early goal to develop an alternative diagnostic system for child psychopathology is not impossible, but not yet realized.

As an example of lingering definitional issues, both the ASEBA and BASC offer scores for externalizing and internalizing problems, but there are differences in the scales that comprise the higher-order factors scores. On the ASEBA CBCL/6-18, the externalizing problem score is derived by summing scores on the rule-breaking behavior and aggressive behavior scales (Achenbach and Rescorla, 2001). On the BASC PRS-C, the scales of hyperactivity, aggression, and conduct problems are summed for the externalizing composite score (Reynolds and Kamphaus, 2004). The clear difference is the inclusion of hyperactivity on the BASC externalizing composite. Factor analytic information in the BASC-2 manual indicates that the hyperactivity scale loads on an externalizing factor at 0.77 (Reynolds and Kamphaus, 2004). Thus, its inclusion seems warranted. According to the *Manual for the ASEBA School-Age Forms and Profiles* (Achenbach and Rescorla, 2001), the attention problems scale, which includes items related to hyperactivity and impulsivity, loads on the externalizing factor at 0.55, but it loads on the internalizing factor at 0.25. Achenbach and Rescorla (2001) note that the difference in these loadings is much lower than the differences in loadings for aggressive behavior and rule-breaking behavior. As a result, the attention problems scale is not included on the ASEBA externalizing factor score. This position is defensible, but it is up to clinicians to be alert to the differences among constructs represented on various rating scales.

Clinicians should also be aware of the type of normative data against which the raw scores are compared. Most commercially available rating scales now include nationally representative normative data. As had been the tradition from the first, though, the Achenbach forms typically use separate norms for girls and boys (an exception is the CBCL/1½–5) due to discrepancies between boys and girls in the scores reported for some syndromes (Achenbach and Rescorla, 2000, 2001). The Conners' (Conners, 1997), the PIC-2 (Lachar and Gruber, 2001), and the DSMD (Naglieri et al., 1994) measures also use separate norms for boys and girls. At the same time, the BASC-2 provides both combined general norms, as well as separate norms for boys and girls (Reynolds and Kamphaus, 2004). Reynolds and Kamphaus (2004) note that if the difference in scores between girls and boys are real and not a measurement artifact, then only the use of combined norms will reflect these differences. Moreover, if a clinician is interested in the degree of deviance in ratings for a child in relation to the general population of same-age children, then combined norms are the better option. On the other hand, if the differences between boys and girls are thought to be the result of differences in reporting or some other form of measurement error, then separate-sex norms are a better choice. Thus, the use of combined or same-sex norms may depend on the clinician's questions, as well as their beliefs about symptom differences between boys and girls.

A final issue in the use of rating scales is the manner in which normative, standardized scores are derived. Most social emotional measures report scale scores with standardized T scores. The use of T scores provides a common metric that allows comparison of scores across scales. At the same time, it is easy to assume that standard scores are always derived in the same manner and that they follow the properties of a normal distribution. With many ratings of child behaviors, though, that is not necessarily the case.

On the ASEBA syndrome scales, for instance, T scores are truncated at a low of 50, and as a result, several raw score values can be assigned a T score value of 50 (Achenbach and Rescorla, 2001). The disadvantage to this approach is that clinicians cannot use T score values to distinguish among low scale scores. Nonetheless, as Achenbach and Rescorla (2001) point out, it is not usually clinically meaningful to differentiate between very low scores on clinical scales. Researchers, though, should keep this truncation in mind and use raw scores for statistical analyses. Also, because few children receive ratings above the 98th percentile, ASEBA T scores from 70 to 100 were assigned in only as many increments as there were raw scores left on the scale. Due to the truncation of scores at 50 and the positive skew among syndrome scale raw distributions, then, the ASEBA syndrome scores do not have the typical T score mean of 50 and standard deviation of 10.

The BASC-2 raw scores were transformed to T scores using linear transformations (Reynolds and Kamphaus, 2004). Linear transformation, which maintains the shape of the raw score distribution, can be contrasted to an area transformation that may change the shape of the raw distribution. Area transformations shift raw scores to a normal distribution. The advantage of a linear transformation with data such as that from behavior rating scales is that it maintains the distribution thought to exist in the actual population. Frequently with behavior problems such as aggression or thought problems, the normative data is skewed. At the same time, some adaptive areas such as social skills have a natural distribution that approximates a normal curve (Reynolds and Kamphaus, 2004). BASC-2 standardized scale scores do go below a T score of 50. However, the use of a linear transformation means that scores should not necessarily be interpreted in reference to a normal distribution (Reynolds and Kamphaus, 2004). In conclusion, clinicians should be aware of the manner in which standard scores are derived and make decisions about interpretation and statistical analyses accordingly.

CONCLUSION

In spite of the fact that behavior rating scales have limitations and associated issues, they offer many advantages and will undoubtedly continue to be a component of child and adolescent assessments in the foreseeable future. Moreover, informed clinicians can mitigate most, if not all, the potential problems associated with their use and interpretation. It is up to practitioners, therefore, to insure that they are well informed and knowledgeable about the instruments they use, psychometric standards (American Educational Research Association (AERA), American Psychological Association (APA), and National Council on Measurement in Education (NCME), 1999), and the ethical guidelines and principles for assessment. It should be also recognized that rating scales and self-report measures are not meant to function alone when making diagnoses or treatment decisions. Instead, they are to be used in conjunction with additional assessment information and under any ethical guidelines that apply.

Child behavior rating scales have become popular over the course of the last five decades due to time and cost efficiency, and the accumulation of large bodies of internal and external validity evidence. Further refinements of the technology will likely serve to increase this popularity but, most importantly, the validity of inferences about children that are drawn from such measures.

REFERENCES

Achenbach, T.M. (1966) 'The classification of children's psychiatric symptoms', *Psychological Monographs: General and Applied*, 80(7): 1–37.

Achenbach, T.M. (1978) 'The Child Behavior Profile: I. Boys aged 6–11', *Journal of Consulting and Clinical Psychology*, 46(3): 478–88.

Achenbach, T.M. (1995) 'Diagnosis, assessment, and comorbidity in psychosocial treatment and research', *Journal of Abnormal Child Psychology*, 23(1): 45–65.

Achenbach, T.M., Dumenci, L. and Rescorla, L.A. (2002) 'Is American student behavior getting worse? Teacher ratings over an 18-year period', *School Psychology Review*, 31(1): 428–42.

Achenbach, T.M. and Edelbrock, C. (1983) *Manual for the Child Behavior Checklist and Revised Child Behavior Profile*. Burlington, VT: University of Vermont.

Achenbach, T.M. and Edelbrock, C. (1986) *Manual for the Teacher Report Form and Teacher Version of Child Behavior Profile*. Burlington, VT: University of Vermont.

Achenbach, T.M. and Edelbrock, C. (1987) *Manual for the Youth Self-Report and Profile*. Burlington, VT: University of Vermont.

Achenbach, T.M. and McConaughy, S.H. (2003) 'The Achenbach System of Empirically Based Assessment', in C.R. Reynolds and R.W. Kamphaus (eds), *Handbook of Psychological and Educational Assessment of Children: Personality, Behavior, and Context*. New York: Guilford, pp. 406–30.

Achenbach, T.M. and McConaughy, S.H. and Howell, C.T. (1987) 'Child/adolescent behavioral and emotional problems: Implications of cross-informant correlations for situational specificity', *Psychological Bulletin*, 101(2): 213–32.

Achenbach, T.M. and Rescorla, L.A. (2000) *Manual for the ASEBA Preschool Forms and Profiles*. Burlington, VT: University of Vermont, Research Center for Children, Youth, Families.

Achenbach, T.M. and Rescorla, L.A. (2001) *Manual for the ASEBA School-Age Forms and Profiles*. Burlington, VT: University of Vermont, Research Center for Children, Youth, Families.

American Educational Research Association (AERA), American Psychological Association (APA) and National Council on Measurement in Education (NCME). (1999) *Standards for Educational and Psychological Testing* (3rd edn). Washington, DC: AERA.

American Psychiatric Association. (1994) *Diagnostic and Statistical Manual of Mental Disorders* (4th edn). Washington, DC: APA.

Cantwell, D.P. (1996) 'Classification of child and adolescent psychopathology', *Journal of Child Psychology and Psychiatry*, 37(1): 3–12.

Conners, C.K. (1969) 'A teacher rating scale for use in drug studies with children', *American Journal of Psychiatry*, 126(6): 884–8.

Conners, C.K. (1997) *Conners' Rating Scales – Revised Technical Manual*. North Tonawanda, NY: Multi-Health Systems.

Conners, C.K., Sitarenios, G., Parker, J.D.A. et al. (1998a) 'The Revised Conners' Parent Rating Scale (CPRS-R): Factor structure, reliability, and criterion validity', *Journal of Abnormal Child Psychology*, 26(4): 257–68.

Conners, C.K., Sitarenios, G., Parker, J.D.A. et al. (1998b) 'Revision and restandardization of the Conners Teacher Rating Scale (CTRS-R): Factor structure, reliability, and criterion validity', *Journal of Abnormal Child Psychology*, 26(4): 279–91.

Conners, C.K., Wells, K.C., Parker, J.D.A. et al. (1997) 'A new self-report scale for assessment of adolescent psychopathology: Factor structure, reliability, validity, and diagnostic sensitivity', *Journal of Abnormal Child Psychology*, 25(6): 487–97.

Graham, J. (1990) *MMPI-2: Assessing Personality and Psychopathology*. New York: Oxford University Press.

Hart, E.L. and Lahey, B.B (1999) 'General child behavior rating scales', in D. Schaffer, C.P. Lucas and J.E. Richters (eds), *Diagnostic Assessment in Child and Adolescent Psychopathology*. New York: Guilford, pp. 66–85.

Hathaway, S.R. and McKinley, J.C. (1942) 'A multiphasic personality schedule (Minnesota): III. The measurement of symptomatic depression', *Journal of Psychology*, 14: 73–84.

Kamphaus, R.W. and Frick, P.J. (2005) *Clinical Assessment of Child and Adolescent Personality and Behavior* (2nd edn). New York: Springer.

Kamphaus, R.W., Petoskey, M.D. and Rowe, E.W. (2000) 'Current trends in psychological testing of children', *Professional Psychology: Research and Practice*, 31(2): 155–64.

Kovacs, M.K. (1992) *Children's Depression Inventory (CDI) Manual*. North Tonawanda, NY: Multi-Health Systems.

Kraemer, H.C., Measelle, J.R., and Ablow, J.C. (2003) 'A new approach to integrating data from multiple informants in psychiatric assessment and research: Mixing and matching contexts and perspectives', *American Journal of Psychiatry*, 160(9): 1566–77.

Lachar, D. and Gruber, C.P. (1995) *Personality Inventory for Youth (PIY) Manual: Administration and Interpretation Guide*. Los Angeles: Western Psychological Services.

Lachar, D. and Gruber, C.P. (2001) *Personality Inventory for Children (PIC-2) Standard Format and Behavioral Summary Manual* (2nd edn). Los Angeles: Western Psychological Services.

Lachar, D. and Gruber, C.P. (2003) 'Multisource and multidimensional objective assessment of adjustment: The Personality Inventory for Children, Second Edition; Personality Inventory for Youth; and Student Behavior Survey', in C.R. Reynolds and R.W. Kamphaus (eds), *Handbook of Psychological and Educational Assessment of Children: Personality, Behavior, and Context*. New York: Guilford, pp. 337–67.

Lachar, D., Wingenfeld, S.A., Kline, R.B. and Gruber, C.P. (2000) *Student Behavior Survey (SBS) Manual*. Los Angeles: Western Psychological Services.

Naglieri, J.A., LeBuffe, P.A. and Pfeiffer, S.I. (1994) *Devereux Scales of Mental Disorders Manual*. San Antonio: The Psychological Corporation.

Peterson, D.R. (1961) 'Behavior problems of middle childhood', *Journal of Consulting Psychology*, 25(3): 205–9.

Quay, H.C. and Peterson, D.R. (1967) *Manual for the Behavior Problem Checklist*. Champaign, IL: Children's Research Center, University of Illinois.

Quay, H.C. and Quay, L.C. (1965) Behavior problems in early adolescence', *Child Development*, 36(1): 215–20.

Reschly, D.J. (1998) 'School psychology practice: Is there change?', Paper presented at the meeting of the American Psychological Association, August, San Francisco.

Reynolds, C.R. and Kamphaus, R.W. (1992) *Behavior Assessment System for Children*. Circle Pines, MN: American Guidance Service.

Reynolds, C.R. and Kamphaus, R.W. (2004) *Behavior Assessment System for Children Manual* (2nd edn). Circles Pines, MN: American Guidance Service.

Reynolds, C.R. and Richmond, B.O. (1985) *Revised Children's Manifest Anxiety Scale (RSMAS) Manual*. Los Angeles, CA: Western Psychological Services.

Reynolds, W.M. (1989) *Reynolds Child Depression Scale Professional Manual*. Odessa, FL: Psychological Assessment Resources.

Reynolds, W.M. (2002) *Reynolds Adolescent Depression Scale Professional Manual* (2nd edn). Lutz, FL: Psychological Assessment Resources.

Sattler, J.M. and Hoge, R.D. (2006) *Assessment of Children: Behavioral, Social, and Clinical Foundations* (5th edn). San Diego: Jerome M. Sattler.

Thorpe, J., Kamphaus, R.W. and Reynolds, C.R. (2003) 'The Behavior Assessment System for Children', in C.R. Reynolds and R.W. Kamphaus (eds), *Handbook of Psychological and Educational Assessment of Children: Personality, Behavior, and Context*. New York: Guilford, pp. 387–405.

Thorpe, J., Kamphaus, R.W., Rowe, E. et al. (2000) 'Longitudinal effects of child adaptive competencies, externalizing, internalizing behavior problems on behavioral and academic outcomes', Poster session presented at the Annual Meeting of the American Psychological Association, August, Washington, DC.

Vaughn, M.L., Riccio, C.A., Hynd, G.W. et al. (1997) 'Diagnosing ADHD subtypes: Discriminant validity of the Behavior Assessment System for Children (BASC) and the Achenbach parent and teacher rating scales', *Journal of Clinical Child Psychology*, 26(4): 349–57.

Verhulst, F.C., Koot, H.M. and Van der Ende, J. (1994) 'Differential predictive value of parents' and teachers' reports of children's problem behaviors: A longitudinal study', *Journal of Abnormal Child Psychology*, 22(5): 531–46.

Wittenborn, J.R. (1951) 'Symptom patterns in a group of mental hospital patients', *Journal of Consulting Psychology*, 15(4): 290–302.

Wittenborn, J.R. and Holzberg, J.D. (1951) 'The generality of psychiatric syndromes', *Journal of Consulting Psychology*, 15(5): 372–80.

27

The Projective Assessment of Personality Structure and Pathology

Mark A. Blais and Matthew R. Baity

The evaluation of personality structure and functioning has traditionally been an important component of psychological assessment. However, the rise of behaviorism in the 1970s greatly reduced the role of personality in psychology as a whole and assessment in particular. This trend was effectively countered by the inclusion of Axis II in the third edition of the *Diagnostic and Statistical Manual of Mental Disorders* (American Psychiatric Association, 1980). The establishment of the multi-axial diagnoses re-established the importance of personality and invigorated personality research. This development also reintroduced mental health professionals to the importance of including personality as part of a comprehensive diagnostic work up. In response to this reawakening, there has been an explosion of new instruments for assessing personality (Clark and Harrison, 2001) and intense efforts to refine traditional instruments to better measure this area (Huprick and Ganellen, 2006). Despite the proliferation of numerous assessment measures and techniques, assessing personality structure and its pathology continues to be a challenging clinical task. There remain conflicting views about the strengths and limitations of the various assessment methods in use today (self-report, informant, and projective) and poor cross-method agreement particularly for identifying the DSM-IV personality disorders (Zimmerman, 1994). In the face of these uncertainties, it has been argued that a multi-method assessment battery – one that combines self-report, informant, and projective (performance-based[1]) data – offers the best approach for obtaining a comprehensive evaluation of personality functioning (Blais et al., 2001; Hilsenroth et al., 1996). In this chapter we will review the benefits and limitations of the most common performance-based (projective) methods, the Rorschach inkblot method (RIM) (Weiner, 1996) and the Thematic Apperception Test (TAT) (Murray, 1943), available for the assessment of personality.[2] In the first part of the chapter we will review the general principles for assessing personality structure while the second part of the chapter will focus on the empirical research related to the performance-based assessment of specific personality disorders.

ASSESSING PERSONALITY STRUCTURE: WHAT TO EVALUATE

The American Psychiatric Association's (APA) *Diagnostic and Statistical Manual of Mental Disorders*, 4th edition, text revision (DSM-IV-TR) (APA, 2000), provides general diagnostic criteria for identifying the presence of a personality disorder (see Table 27.1). All patients must satisfy these general criteria before being assigned any of the ten specific personality disorder diagnoses.

These general criteria identify the necessary psychological features that must be covered in conducting a comprehensive assessment of personality. As Table 27.1 shows, the traits and behaviors associated with all personality disorders are 'enduring patterns of perceiving, relating to, and thinking about the environment and oneself that are exhibited in a wide range of social and personal contexts'(APA, 2000: 686). Although classified as personality disorders, these pervasive patterns of experiencing and behaving affect a wide range of psychological domains. Guided by the DSM criteria, a comprehensive psychological assessment of personality must therefore include the evaluation of: *cognition* (i.e. ways of perceiving and interpreting the self, other people and events), *affectivity* (i.e. range, intensity, lability and appropriateness of emotional response), *interpersonal functioning* and *impulse control*. Each of these domains in turn represents semi-independent psychological structures with their own dynamics and processes.

Psychological structures can be thought of as persistent and reliably activated psychological processes that, when engaged, produce specific patterns of thinking, feeling, and behaving (Westen et al., 2006). While patients can be asked directly about their attitudes and behaviors, the psychological structures that produce them generally operate outside of conscious awareness. Therefore performance-based assessment methods with their ability to tap into implicit psychological functioning (McClelland et al., 1989) are an essential component of personality assessment. Data obtained from performance-based measures have been shown to add incrementally to self-report data in the prediction of the DSM-IV personality disorder criteria (Blais et al., 2001). However, before we review the application of performance-based methods to the assessment of personality structure, it will be useful to integrate our empirically and clinically determined personality domains with a model of personality development and functioning.

Kernberg (1970 and 1975; Clarkin et al., 1999) has proposed a hierarchical model of personality development, structure and organization. This model places personality development on a continuum that runs from the lower *psychotic* pole, through *borderline* to the higher *neurotic* pole. The majority of the DSM-IV personality disorders (schizoid, paranoid, histrionic, narcissistic, antisocial and dependent) occupy a large intermediate level within the model while the more severe personality disorders (e.g. schizotypal and

Table 27.1 DSM-IV general diagnostic criteria for a personality disorder

A. An enduring pattern of inner experience and behavior that deviates markedly from the expectations of the individual's culture. This pattern is manifested into (or more) of the following areas:
   (1) cognition (i.e. ways of perceiving and interpreting self, other people, and events)
   (2) affectivity (i.e. range, intensity, lability, and appropriateness of emotional responses)
   (3) interpersonal functioning
   (4) impulse control
B. The enduring pattern is inflexible and pervasive across a broad range of personal and social situations
C. The enduring pattern leads to clinically significant distress or impairment in social, occupational, or other important areas of functioning
D. The pattern is stable and of long duration and its onset can be traced back at least to adolescence or early adulthood

Criteria adapted from the Diagnostic and Statistical Manual of Mental Disorders, 4th edition (APA, 2000).

borderline) lay closer to the psychotic end of the continuum. In contrast, the obsessive-compulsive personality disorder is found at the upper portion of the continuum closer to the neurotic pole (Clarkin et al., 1999). Given the developmental range represented by the DSM Axis II PDs, it is not surprising that they demonstrate such diversity in their symptom patterns and level of functional impairment. The extensive heterogeneities of the personality disorders make it difficult to conceptually organize them into meaningful groups. The DSM-IV three cluster grouping (cluster A, cluster B, and cluster C) has not been well supported (see Blais et al., 1997). Kernberg's model of personality structure provides a number of distinguishing psychological features that builds a clinically relevant foundation to help organize the personality disorders. These features are: *identity diffusion*, *poor object relations*, *lapses in reality contact*, and *reliance on primitive defenses* (splitting and projection) to maintain emotional regulation and *excessive aggression*. Interestingly, significant similarities can be seen between the DSM-IV general personality disorder criteria and Kernberg's markers of personality pathology. Both systems focus on disruptions in cognition, affect regulation, self-image, and interpersonal relationships. The DSM-IV criteria approach these domains from a descriptive and behavioral perspective, while Kernberg's model emphasizes the psychological structures that underlie these behavior patterns. Kernberg's model of personality structure continues to be influential among dynamically oriented assessment psychologists and has been seen as a powerful tool for organizing projective/performance assessment data (Lerner, 1991). The integration of these two personality systems (DSM and Kernberg) enhances our ability to assess and understand personality structure by using a multi-method assessment strategy. By evaluating overt behavior and attitudes (self-report inventories) and implicit psychological structures (performance-based methods), we obtain information at both the nomothetic and idiographic levels of personality functioning.

ASSESSING THOUGHT QUALITY

Both Kernberg's model of personality structure and the DSM-IV general criteria highlight the potential for personality-disordered patients to experience disturbances in the quality of their thinking. These disturbances can range from the odd and unusual beliefs to paranoid ideation and transient psychotic symptoms. Therefore, assessing the quality of a patient's thinking and the degree to which they maintain contact with reality is central in the identification of personality psychopathology. RIM (Weiner, 1996), with its ambiguous visual stimuli and minimal test instructions ('What might this be?'), has proven to be an ideal instrument for identifying thought disturbance and vulnerabilities in reality contact. In fact, the ability of the RIM to detect thought disturbance is one of the few things that both critics and proponents of the test agree upon (Wood et al., 2000). A number of excellent studies have documented the RIM's ability to detect clinically meaningful signs of impaired thinking. O'Connell et al. (1989) found that the quality of thinking as revealed by the RIM predicted the later appearance of psychotic symptoms in a group of inpatients better than a structured psychiatric interview. Kircher et al. (2001) successfully used functional magnetic resonance imaging (fMRI) and RIM scores to identify the neural–anatomical correlates of formal thought disorder.

In the comprehensive system (CS) (Exner, 1986a, 1993, 2002), thought quality is primarily measured along two dimensions; perceptual accuracy and associational quality. Perceptual accuracy refers to the ability of the subject to perceive stimuli as others do (accurately) and is reflected by the *form quality* (FQ) codes. FQ is the percentage of responses in the protocol that match the contours of the inkblot and includes scores for good (X+), moderate (Xu), or poor (X−) fits. Associational quality reflects the adequacy of the subject's logic or associational reasoning once the sensory stimuli have been perceived.

The CS contains six special scoring categories (called *special scores*) intended to measure the quality of a subject's thinking. In addition, the CS's Perceptual Thought Index (PTI), a recently revised version of the Schizophrenia Index (SCZI), quantifies the likelihood of thought disturbance across the complete RIM protocol.

Kleiger (1999) observed that when evaluating the thought quality of personality-disordered patients we should look for a vulnerability to primary process thinking (psychotic experiences), not the presence of 'hard core' signs of psychosis. Consistent with Kernberg's model, this means that we should look for indications of weak perceptual accuracy and slippages in logic that fall somewhere between the signs of frank psychosis and the more reality-based protocols of non-patients. Research and clinical experience has generally supported Kleiger's position. The overall RIM form quality scores (XA%; adequate form quality composed of X+ and Xu responses) achieved by personality-disordered patients generally approaches that of non-patients (0.88; Exner and Erdberg, 2005) and is superior to the form quality of psychotic patients. However, in achieving their adequate form quality, the personality-disordered patients give more unusual (Xu%) perceptions to the inkblots than do non-patients. Non-patients typically have X+ and Xu percentages of approximately 0.70 and 0.20 respectively while personality-disordered patients typically have X+ percentages between 0.50 and 0.60 and Xu percentages between 0.25 and 0.40. Patients with cluster C PDs (avoidant, dependent, obsessive-compulsive) are least likely to show perceptual disturbance on the RIM with their protocols more closely resembling those of non-patients on this dimension. A few specific personality disorders (schizotypal and borderline) may produce RIM records looking more similar to those of psychotic patients but can be distinguished by the fact that signs of psychosis are unlikely to be present on other tests (i.e. IQ tests, self-report, etc.) for the personality-disordered patient.

In the CS there are 13 responses that were given with sufficient frequency in the normative samples to be considered *popular* responses. The number of popular responses contained in a RIM protocol reflects the degree to which a person accepts or acknowledges conventional reality; in other words, how much a patient sees what most other people have seen. Non-patients produce six or seven popular responses on average while the majority of personality-disordered patients produce four or five. The reduced number of populars in PD samples is thought to reflect their idiosyncratic view of the world and helps to outline a possible source of the persistent interpersonal struggles experienced by this population. Some personality-disordered patients, particularly those with obsessive-compulsive personality features, may produce substantially more popular responses than non-patients indicating an overcommitment to conventional reality. In a similar way, personality-disordered patients tend to reveal more cognitive slippage (associational difficulties) than non-patients but far less slippage than would be seen in the record of psychotic or bipolar patients. The average number of *special scores* in the record of non-patients is two; personality-disordered patients generally have three or four special scores in their record while psychotic patients on average have five or more. The special scores are also assigned weights to reflect the seriousness of the form of thought slippage they denote. Non-patients in Exner's sample had an average weighted special score value (Wsum6) of seven, personality-disordered patients typically have weighted values between 10 and 17, and psychotic patients have an average Wsum6 score of 44 (Exner, 2002). Special scores are also classified as either level 1 (Lvl1) or level 2 (Lvl2) with the Lvl2 scores reflecting more extreme examples of slippage. It is very rare for non-patients to produce even one Lvl2 special score; however, personality-disordered patients will often give one such score in a protocol. In comparison, psychotic patients on average produce five Lvl2 special scores.

It seems reasonable to accept the commonly held notion that personality-disordered patients will frequently produce a couple of signs of mild to moderate thought disturbance on the RIM. However, the amount of thought disturbance evidenced by these patients is usually much less than that seen in the RIMs of psychotic patients. Unlike schizophrenic subjects, when personality-disordered patients misperceive the form of the RIM stimuli, it will usually be a milder violation of form quality (Xu). The nature of their cognitive slippage will also be mild to moderate and typically reflected in Lvl1 special scores. However, their weighted special score value will often approach or exceed the concerning level of >17 (Exner, 2002). Therefore we can think of personality-disordered patients as perceiving reality reasonably well (generally acceptable perceptual accuracy), but they may misinterpret their perceptions due to their idiosyncratic needs or overvalued ideas (showing excessive but not psychotic degrees of cognitive slippage). Table 27.2 provides a two-by-two matrix for classifying perceptional quality and associational accuracy. The majority of DSM-IV personality-disordered patients (those with avoidant, dependent, histrionic, narcissistic, anti-social, schizoid, paranoid) would typical fall within quadrant 3 showing acceptable perceptual accuracy and

Table 27.2 Relationship of Rorschach perceptual accuracy and associational quality to various diagnostic levels

Associational quality	Perceptual accuracy	
	Good	Poor
Good	1 Good/Good	2 Good/Poor
Poor	3 Poor/Good	4 Poor/Poor

Quadrants: 1 good perception (XA% > 0.70) and associations (Wsum6 < 13) normal suggests non-patient or neurotic; 2 = good associations and poor perception is the 'odd box' suggests possible neurological impairment; 3 = poor associations and good perception suggests personality disorders (most personality-disordered patients would be placed here); and 4 = poor associations and poor perceptions possible psychosis (some severe personality-disordered patients with borderline and schizotypal PD may be in this quadrant).

disturbed logic. Patients with the more severe DSM PDs, borderline and schizotypal, might show up in quadrant 4 given their closer association with frank psychosis. Lastly, patients with obsessive compulsive PD, the least functionally impairing PD (Blais, 1997), might fall within quadrant 1, looking more like a non-patient on these Rorschach variables.

THOUGHT QUALITY AND THE THEMATIC APPERCEPTION TEST

Christiana Morgan and Henry Murray developed the Thematic Apperception Test (TAT) (Murray, 1943) to be a measure of whole personality. The 30 cards that make up the TAT series were hand-drawn copies of paintings, photographs, and posters depicting people in various life and interpersonal situations. In the redrawing of the stimuli, important details or aspects were intentionally made vague to enhance the apperceptive process. In its original form, 20 TAT cards were administered to a subject over two assessment sessions. In modern practice, clinicians usually show subjects six to ten cards as part of a testing battery. Subjects are instructed to look at the pictures and tell a story with a beginning, middle, and end, and to tell what the people are feeling and thinking (Murray, 1943). According to Murray, 'when someone attempts to interpret a complex social situation he is apt to tell as much about himself as he is about the phenomena on which his attention is focused' (Murray, 1943: 309). With the increase of structure and reality orientation provided by the TAT pictures (the objects have some vague details but are clearly recognizable), it is unlikely that the majority of personality-disordered patients would produce frank signs of disturbed thinking on this test. However, when listening to TAT stories of personality-disordered subjects, one can often 'hear' evidence of their idiosyncratic perceptual style and their difficulties maintaining a logical flow to their narrative. In particular, the TAT stories of patients with personality disorders are often confused, convoluted and difficult to follow or understand. Another potential indicator of personality pathology is the introduction of overly personal material or self-references when telling TAT stories. Some patients with more severe personality disorders (borderline and schizotypal) may produce prominent signs of thought disturbance (severe misperceptions, ideas of reference or marked paranoia) on this test. While it remains one of the most widely used assessment tools, the status of the Thematic Apperception Test is uncertain. Its lack of a standardized administration method, a reliable scoring system, and an adequate normative sample means that some consider it more of a clinical technique than a test. Still the TAT has considerable value for assessing personality and some scoring systems have been developed in recent years that show great promise in helping to standardize this clinical measure.

Westen's Social Cognition and Object Relations Scale (SCORS) (Hilsenroth et al., 2004; Westen, 1995; Westen et al., 1985) is the most comprehensive scoring system available for the TAT (Stricker and Gooen-Piels, 2004) and has demonstrated adequate reliability and validity to support its use in clinical assessment. Table 27.3 provides a listing of the eight SCORS variables as well as scoring examples in the low (pathological), middle, and high range. One subscale, the Social Causality subscale, has been shown to be sensitive to the mild disruptions in thought quality seen in personality-disordered patients. As defined by Westen, the SCORS Social Causality scale measures the extent to which attributions about the causes of people's actions, thoughts, and feelings are logical and accurate. Low scores on this scale reflect poorly formed causal inferences regarding motives, actions, and feelings of others. As Westen has indicated, 'clinical experience with severe personality disorders suggests that these patients tend to make highly idiosyncratic, illogical and inaccurate attributions of people's intentions'

(1990: 679). Westen further suggests that limitations in this area may reflect a structural and cognitively based difficulty in generating accurate social attributions. Such a deficit may, in part, cause many personality-disordered patients to misperceive the actions and motivations of other people.

EVALUATION OF AFFECTIVITY

Both the general PD diagnostic criteria of the DSM-IV and Kernberg's model of personality development indicate that assessing the ability to modulate, control, and express affect is important in the evaluation of personality functioning. However, for the domain of affectivity there are few well-established guidelines for identifying personality difficulties. The majority of personality-disordered patients find emotions to be confusing, painful, and disruptive to their function. The CS (Exner, 2002) Affective Ratio (Afr) reveals the level of approach or avoidance a subject has toward experiencing their emotions. Non-patients have a mean Afr of 0.61 (the normal range is 0.50 to 0.80) while most personality-disordered patients typically have an Afr at the low end or below the expected range, suggesting these patients are less willing or interested in processing affective stimuli. Conversely, it is also common for patients with a personality disorder that includes a high affective arousability (e.g. histrionic and borderline disorders), to have Afr scores > 0.80 indicating an almost irresistible pull into emotionally arousing situations.

The ability to control and modulate feelings is reflected in the ratio of form color (FC) responses to color form (CF+C). The presence of form in a color response indicates the level of structure that an individual is placing on their perception of the blot with FC being the most form-dominated score (i.e. highly modulated) and a C being a response that completely lacks structure (unmodulated). In non-patients the FC:CF+C ratio is typically 2:1. For most personality-disordered patients the ratio will either be balanced or more heavily weighted to the CF side. However, some personality disorders, particularly those in cluster C, are noted for their excessive emotional control and may produce a ratio that is more heavily weighted toward the FC side (FC:CF+C = 3:1). The experience of emotional arousal often has a negative impact on the quality of functioning of patients with a personality disorder. It is possible to assess the degree of impact that emotional arousal has on functioning by computing the form quality (X+%) for the responses to the final three RIM cards (VIII, IX and X). These three cards have pastel colors (rather than mostly achromatic blots) and are thought to elicit emotional arousal when viewed by subjects. If the subject produces responses with weaker form quality (increase in XU and X−%) and more special scores on these cards relative to the preceding seven cards, then it can be inferred that affective arousal negatively impacts quality of thinking; a hallmark of some personality disorders.

A high level of negative affect (a mixture of depression, fear/worry, anger, and frustration) is common to most DSM personality disorders (Blais, 1997). On the RIM, negative affect is reflected in shading or achromatic color responses where an individual uses the light or dark (shading) or black and white (achromatic) features of the blot. Shading scores can include diffuse shading (e.g. 'The shading makes it look wispy'), texture (e.g. 'It looks furry because of the light and dark parts'), and vista (e.g. 'That part is lighter so its behind this front piece') responses. On average, non-patients have three shading responses while personality-disordered patients would be expected to give four to six shading responses. Reviewing the nature of the [(black–white (dysphoria), diffuse shading (anxiety) texture (loneliness/interpersonal longing), or vista (painful introspections)] can identify the specific negative emotion that dominates a patient's inner world.

The experience of excessive anger or aggression is common for many personality

disorders including all the cluster B disorders and most of the cluster A. On the RIM, anger is associated with responses that use or incorporate the white space of a blot (called space responses). On average, non-patients produce two white space responses while personality-disordered patients (particularly those with disorders in clusters A and B) typically produce three or more space responses. The CS has only one score to capture aggression on the RIM called Aggressive Movement (AG) and is scored when responses include some form of aggression occurring in the *present tense* (aggressive movement; e.g. 'This bug is attacking this fly'). While some research has demonstrated a relationship between this score and behavioral manifestations of aggression (reported in Exner, 2002), the requirement that the aggression must be in the present tense places a limitation on AG. Many patients, including those with personality disorders, tend to produce responses containing more primitive descriptions of anger, aggressive actions, or the aftermath of aggression (i.e. 'It looks like a bloody, smashed-up face', 'A nuclear explosion annihilated everything'). Reviewing the actual verbalized response (done best by reading it out loud) can identify instances of under-modulated primitive aggressions. Typically, aggressive responses that contain imagery or language that seems unsuitable to polite social interactions is considered to depict primitive aggression. Gacono and Meloy (1994) have developed a useful system for identifying aggression on the RIM. While considerable research has been done with these variables in child, adolescent, and adult samples, Gacono and Meloy's scores are not currently included in the CS. The extended variables include multiple aspects of aggression: Aggressive Content (AgC), Aggressive Past (AgPast), Aggressive Potential (AgPot), and Sado-Masochism (SM). Recent research has provided impressive support for the validity and utility of this system (see Baity and Hilsenroth, 1999; Baity, et al., 2000; Baity and Hilsenroth, 2002). A comprehensive review of the research, to date, with all the extended aggression scores was recently published in the yearbook of the International Rorschach Society (Gacono et al., 2005).

The extensive comorbidity of mood and personality disorders makes it important to evaluate a propensity to depression when assessing personality structure. In the CS, the Depression Index (DEPI) (Exner, 2002) indicates the likelihood that patients will experience affective disruptions (DEPI = 5) or episodes of a diagnosable mood disorder (DEPI > 5) at some point in their life. The research findings regarding the ability of DEPI to identify current depressive episodes is inconsistent so it is best to think of DEPI as reflecting an underlying vulnerability to depression or mood dysregulation rather than the indication of a current depressive episode (Exner and Erdberg, 2005). It is very common for subjects with a personality disorder to also elevate DEPI revealing their vulnerability to mood dysregulation.

In addition to the RIM, TAT stories can provide much helpful information for assessing affective functioning. The qualitative review of (or listening to) TAT stories for frequency, range (differentiation), and intensity of emotions can reveal a substantial amount regarding the patient's emotional functioning. The intensity of the affect aroused by the TAT cards differs with some cards being generally milder and others producing substantial emotional arousal. For example, Card 13 FM depicts a young man standing with a downcast head buried in his arm while behind him is the figure of a half-naked woman lying unconscious on a bed: viewing this card can produce an intense and uncomfortable emotional arousal even in non-patients. Identifying how this arousal impacts the quality of their function, typically by evaluating the quality of the narrative can help reveal how well affect and cognition are integrated. Westen's SCORS scoring system, especially the Experiencing and Managing Aggression (EMA) subscale, can help quantify the level of contained aggression. Ackerman et al. (1999) applied this subscale to the TAT stories of borderline,

narcissistic, antisocial and cluster C PD patients. They found that borderline subjects obtained significantly lower ratings (indicating more destructive aggression) on EMA than did NPD and cluster C PD subjects.

PERCEPTION OF OTHERS

Although not identical in their conceptualizations, disrupted or conflicted object relations/interpersonal relations are a central feature of both the DSM-IV personality disorders and Kernberg's diagnostic systems. The DSM, with its behavioral emphasis, tends to focus on the patient's external relationships, while Kernberg's developmental model focuses on deficits in the patient's internalized object representations. Many performance-based assessment techniques including the RIM, TAT and Early Memories Test (EMT) (Mayman, 1968) have proven valuable in evaluating the interpersonal functioning of patients with personality disorders.

A number of CS RIM variables are useful for assessing the nature and quality of interpersonal functioning. The Coping Deficit Index (CDI) (Exner, 2002) is an important place to start. The CDI is a composite index that identifies chronically poor interpersonal functioning. When CDI is positive, it indicates psychological immaturity and persistent difficulty relating to others. Personality-disordered patients will routinely have CDI scores between three and five. The Hypervigilance Index (HVI) (Exner, 1993) provides information about a specific type of interpersonal style. A positive score on the HVI indicates a hyper-alertness to potential danger or threats and deficits in the ability to trust the motives of others. Paranoid and some borderline and obsessive-compulsive PD patients will frequently elevate this index. In addition, the degree to which a patient generally expects others to be helpful or harmful is reflected in the ratio of cooperative (COP) to aggressive (AG) movement responses given. The expected ratio is about 2:1 favoring COP.

Patients with a personality disorder will often produce a ratio of 1:1 or 1:2 (COP: AG) revealing their propensity for viewing the world and others as hostile. RIM human movement (M) responses provide a wealth of information about psychological functioning including the degree of accuracy one has in perceiving and understanding other people. Two or more well-formed M (form quality of 'o' or 'u') responses indicate accurate empathy while M responses with poor form quality (M–) indicate marked difficulties understanding and relating to others (Exner, 2002). It is very rare for non-patients to produce a single M response whereas personality-disordered patients often have one such response in their records. Interestingly, the mean number of M responses for psychotic patients is two (Exner, 2002).

Extremes in interpersonal neediness and dependency are another hallmark of personality-disordered patients. Two RIM variables tap different aspects of dependency and neediness, the texture response of the CS (FT, Exner, 2002) and the Rorschach Oral Dependency scale (ROD) (Bornstein and Masling, 2005; Masling et al., 1967). The texture response (a response that uses shading in the inkblot as texture, i.e. 'it looks rough') reflects a type of immature dependency with a need to be (emotionally) held and a longing for an infantile dependency on others (Blais et al., 2001). Non-patients typically produce one texture response, while patients with an antisocial or paranoid personality disorder typically produce no T responses (revealing a distant interpersonal style). Similarly, patients with borderline, histrionic, dependent, and avoidant personality disorders often produce two or more T responses suggesting a greater need for closeness and a stronger than usual need to be dependent on others (Exner, 2002). ROD was developed to assess orality and interpersonal dependency (Masling et al., 1967). An impressive body of literature has developed linking ROD scores to dependent behavior in interpersonal interactions (Bornstein, 1998; Bornstein et al., 2000; Bornstein and

Masling, 2005). Extreme ROD scores have been associated with borderline, histrionic, and dependent personality disorders.

The Mutuality of Autonomy Scale (MOAS) (Urist, 1977) was developed to assess an individual's object relations and is, in part, based on Kernberg's conceptualization of borderline and narcissistic personalities. The main focus of the MOAS is to assess the level of separation-individuation in a RIM response and is only scored for those responses where there is portrayal of a relationship between two or more objects. The greater the recognition of objects in a response as separate, yet potentially cooperative, entities (e.g. 'This tiger is helping this other tiger climb onto this rock') the more that individual is believed to be able to see important people in their life as functionally independent from them. Conversely, the less separation indicated by a response, the greater the suggested pathology ('It's two animals joined together'). The lowest scores on the MOAS include those responses where there is little or no differentiation between objects and/or one object is exerting malevolent control over the other ('It looks like a Venus flytrap devouring this fly'). In addition to showing a high degree of convergent validity with behavioral ratings of interpersonal relationships (Ryan et al., 1985; Urist, 1977; Urist and Schill, 1982), scores on the MOAS have also been linked with TAT responses.

While a number of performance-based measures can provide information regarding a patient's interpersonal style and object relations, the usefulness of the TAT stands out in this area. In fact, Westen (1990, 1991) has argued that the TAT, with its moderately ambiguous drawings of human figures in various emotional and interpersonal situations, is uniquely suited among psychological tests for eliciting information regarding a patient's object relations. Westen's (1990) SCORS method for scoring TAT stories has subscales measuring the Affective Quality of Representations (AQR) and Emotional Investment in Representations (EIR). Research thus far has shown that more malevolent MOAS scores (lower scores) are related to TAT themes of aggression (Rosenberg et al., 1994). More recently, Ackerman et al. (2001) found that the expectations of relationships as assessed by the SCORS variable AQR was related to both healthy and malevolent MOAS scores. In other words, more pathological SCORS ratings were related to a greater number of high (more pathological) MOAS scores, while healthier ratings on the AQR were related to a greater number of lower (healthier) MOAS scores. Healthier ratings on the MOAS were also related to high scores on EMA (aggression) indicating socially appropriate expressions of aggression. Results from this study lead the authors to conclude that the affective variables from the SCORS were more related to the MOAS than the more cognitively based SCORS variables (Ackerman et al., 2001).

The Affective Quality of Representations (AQR) subscale of the SCORS measures the emotional tone of relationships depicted in narrative data along a seven-point scale. The lowest AQR rating (1) indicates a malevolent and abusive relationship, a middle-point rating (5) indicates a mixed positive and negative relationship, and the highest rating (7) depicts a positive and mutually beneficial relationship (see Table 27.3). Personality-disordered patients typically achieve ratings between two and four (Ackerman et al., 2001). The Emotional Investment in Relationships (EIR) subscale rates a balance between an exclusive focus on personal needs and motivation for mutual need satisfaction. Here again, lower scores reflect more self-centered efforts to meet one's needs while higher scores reflect an appreciation and an accommodation of the needs of others. Patients with personality disorders often score at the lower end of this scale reflecting an egocentric and self-absorbed nature.

The Early Memories Test (EMT) asks subjects to describe a number of different early memories, including their first and second earliest memories, earliest memory of mother, earliest memory of father, first day of school, feeding, being warm and snug, and interaction with a transitional object. In addition, inquiries are typically made regarding the feeling tone of each memory reported. The last three EM queries (feeding, warm and snug, and transitional object) were added by Fowler et al. (1995). A transitional object is based on the observations and clinical writings of Winnicott (1971, 1975) who astutely hypothesized that a child's ability to transition from the safety of the mother to an inanimate object can have significant

Table 27.3   Overview of Westen's Social Cognition and Object Relations Scale (SCORS)

Categories	1	5	7
Complexity of representations	Egocentric representations	Conventional representations	Differentiated and complex representations
Affective quality of representations	Malevolent and abusive	Mixed positive and negative	Mostly positive
Emotional investment in relationships	Self/need focused	Mixed focus on needs	Focus on meeting mutual needs
Investment in values and morals	Self-indulgent and remorseless	Invested in and tries to met moral values	Thoughtful and compassionate challenges convention
Understanding social causality (SC)	Confused and unusual view of SC	Straightforward view of SC	Complex and coherent view of mutual SC
Experiencing and managing aggression	Physically assaultive and destructive	Denies anger and avoids confrontations	Assertive and appropriate expression of anger
Self-esteem	Evil, loathsome self-image	Range of self-image with positive and negative	Realistic positive self-image
Identity and coherence of self	Fragmented sense of self	Adequately stable identity and sense of self	Integrated sense of self with long range goals and plans

Note: Lower scores reflect greater psychopathology

ramifications for that child's capacity for interpersonal relatedness. Comparing the EMs of a clinical sample to a university student sample, Fowler et al. found significantly greater negative affect and poorer object relations in the clinical sample.

SENSE OF SELF AND SELF-ESTEEM

A number of CS RIM variables provide important information regarding the nature of one's self-image and self-esteem. The Egocentricity Index (Ego) provides an indication of how or where the patient focuses their psychological attention on themselves, on others, or balanced between self and other. Egocentricity scores between 0.33 and 0.44 are considered average and suggest a balance between focusing on personal needs and those of others (Exner, 2002). Scores below 0.33 suggest too little focus on the self (excessive focus on others) and poor self-esteem while scores greater than 0.44 indicate excessive self-focus, little attention to others and a preoccupation with an inflated self-image. While personality-disordered patients can score at either extreme of the Egocentricity scale, most will typically score at the low end (< 0.33). However, patients with narcissistic, antisocial, histrionic, and even obsessive-compulsive personality disorders can score at the upper end (> 0.44) reflecting an overinvestment in themselves and overvaluation of their abilities.

One of the more interesting findings from recent RIM research is a strong association between reflection responses and the DSM narcissistic personality disorder (Blais et al., 2001; Hilsenroth et al., 1993). The presence of one reflection response (a response in which a mirror image is seen) suggests the presence of narcissistic defenses, while two or more reflections are strongly associated with narcissistic personality disorder. At the other end of the self-esteem spectrum, the presence of two or more morbid (MOR) responses suggests a self-image of being

damaged or injured and poor self-esteem. The RIM CS also provides information regarding the degree to which the patient engages in self-reflection (introspection) and whether this introspective process is positive or negative. The form dimension (FD) and vista (FV) responses both indicate introspection; however, the FV response denotes a painful form of self-evaluation. The presence of more than one FV responses indicates excessive self-evaluation with a focus on perceived negative features of the self-image. Personality-disordered patients typically produce one FD response per protocol (similar to non-patients) but are more likely than non-patients to produce a vista response.

Westen's SCORS provides a rating of self-esteem and identity integration and coherence. The SCORS Self-Esteem variable rates self-esteem from the most negative poll of evil and loathsome through a mixture of positive and negative self-qualities to a realistic but predominantly positive self-image. The Identity and Coherence of the Self-variable (ICS) measures the degree of fragmentation and stability present in one's self-image. As would be expected, patients with personality disorders typically score within the lower half of these scales indicating their generally poor self-esteem and difficulties maintaining an integrated stable self-image.

EMPIRICAL REVIEW

The following section provides a review of the published literature on assessing personality disorders as defined by the DSM series. The goal of this section is to both introduce the reader to the major findings for each personality disorder and to provide the motivation to seek out the original sources. We would also like to remind the reader that while assessment measures (e.g. MMPI-2, MCMI, PAI, RIM, etc.) can provide a wealth of relevant data and capture information that might not otherwise get covered in a clinical interview, no psychological assessment instrument (including the RIM and TAT) should be used on its own to determine the presence or absence of a personality disorder. These instruments are intended to take a wide-angled view of the patient and can be used to help infer the presence of certain clinical syndromes (i.e. depression, PTSD, self-harm), but typically do not map directly onto specific DSM criteria.

Cluster A (paranoid, schizoid, schizotypal)

Among all three PD clusters, it is arguable that the least amount of research has been done within cluster A. One explanation for this might be that individuals classified in this 'odd and eccentric' cluster are least likely to enter or remain engaged in treatment (Kaser-Boyd, 2006; Kleiger and Huprich, 2006) or research. Additionally, individuals with disorders from cluster A have a good chance of being misclassified as having a primary psychotic disorder (Foley, 1996) due to the idiosyncratic and rigid thinking style common to this character type. Much of the available published work are case studies that report the presence or absence of certain RIM variables as opposed to an empirical examination of scores and/or indexes common to cluster A PDs.

As would be expected, the limited data available seems to indicate that the primary differences in cluster A RIM protocols from non-clinical samples lie in the thought quality and interpersonal variables. Theoretical writings and clinical observations indicate that individuals with paranoid personality disorder (PPD) have a tendency to chronically misperceive reality and have a great deal of anxiety when dealing with others. In the RIM, this is translated into poorer form quality and a greater number of humanoid (rather than pure human) content than community norms but not below what is commonly seen in floridly psychotic samples (X–%; Kaser-Boyd, 2006). Of particular

interest with PPD samples is the Hypervigilance Index (HVI) from the CS (Exner, 1993), which was developed with a sample of patients diagnosed with paranoid schizophrenia, a sample of schizophrenic patients without paranoid features, and later, a small group of patients diagnosed with PPD (Exner, 2002). The majority of patients with paranoid features met a preponderance of the criteria for HVI. The index was later changed to have eight criteria, but with one variable, $T = 0$, accounting for more than half the variance. Therefore before other criteria for HVI are considered in any given protocol there must be no texture responses ($T = 0$). Texture responses are thought to indicate one's level of interpersonal neediness; more than two texture responses is common in dependent and avoidant personality styles while no texture responses indicate a low need for interpersonal reliance.

One of the difficulties in assessing cluster A PDs on the RIM is how similar individuals with these disorders can look to patients with schizophrenia, and this is especially true for schizotypal personality disorder (SPD). In fact, research has suggested that SPD is actually on a schizophrenia continuum and rests somewhere between frank psychosis and the absence of symptoms (Foley, 2006; Perry et al., 2003; Torgersen et al., 1993). Due to the odd thinking style nature of SPD, it would be expected that these individuals have many perceptual inaccuracies that would come across as misinterpretations of their environment, distorted flow of ideas, and even cognitive slippage. Recent data supports this and demonstrates that individuals with SPD give more responses with poor FQ (X–%) and have a greater number of special scores than non-patients, but that the severity of the SPD protocols does not match the level of pathology suggested in the RIM of schizophrenic patients (Erdberg, 2003; Exner, 1986b). Further evidence for the level of SPD impairment is found on the Ego Impairment Index (EII) (Perry and Viglione, 1991), which uses existing CS scores to create an index of thought and perceptual impairment. Perry et al.

(2003) compared the EII scores of inpatients diagnosed with schizophrenia to a range of groups with decreasing levels of pathology (i.e. outpatient schizophrenics, patients with SPD, first-degree relatives of a patient with schizophrenia, etc.) and non-patients. Results from this study showed that patients with SPD ($M = 0.61$, SD = 1.00) had significantly higher EII scores that the non-patients ($M = -0.35$, SD = 0.81) and significantly lower EII scores than those hospitalized individuals with chronic schizophrenia ($M = 1.21$, SD = 2.03). Individuals with SPD tend to have very distorted views of themselves and those around them and as a result, tend to engage more in fantasy-driven isolative activities (Foley, 2006). On the RIM, the SPD's reliance on their problem-solving capacity as opposed to making decisions based on their feelings means they will tend to create more introversive protocols (Exner, 2002) than non-patients. In addition, people will not be seen as integrated whole beings with a complex set of thoughts and emotions and the SPD individual will represent this by having a fewer number of whole human (H) responses on the RIM and an increased number of fictional humanoids (i.e. 'Bigfoot') or parts of the body.

Cluster B

The disorders that make up the cluster B PDs (narcissistic, histrionic, borderline, antisocial) are easily the most researched character styles in personality assessment and have a rich tradition in the theoretical writing arena. As such, the review of the performance-based testing research with these populations will be limited to more recently published works.

Histrionic Personality Disorder (HPD) is the least researched of the cluster B disorders on the RIM. Although some studies have suggested that patients who meet criteria for HPD might be more prevalent than would be expected (Blais and Norman 1997; Torgersen et al., 2001), the behavioral manifestations of this character style can be easily overlooked or misdiagnosed as signs of another cluster B PD. Blais et al. (1998) evaluated the relationship between pre-selected Rorschach variables and the DSM-IV HPD criteria, as well as how well the RIM can distinguish HPD from BPD and NPD. Results indicated that both (FC + CF + C) and T were strongly and specifically correlated with HPD. In addition, these two Rorschach variables were significantly correlated with seven of the eight HPD criteria. In a follow-up study, Blais et al. (2001) explored the incremental validity of Rorschach variables relative to MMPI-2 personality disorder scales (Colligan et al., 1994; Morey et al., 1985) for predicting DSM-IV cluster B criteria. In this study, two Rorschach variables (FC + CF + C and T) added incrementally above and beyond the MMPI-2 HPD scales in identifying DSM-IV HPD criteria. In a third study, Bornstein (1998) used the ROD to explore the relationship of covert versus overt dependency needs in HPD and DPD. Results from this study found that while HPD and DPD were significantly related to ROD scores (covert dependency), only DPD was related to patients' self-report (overt dependency) of their dependency needs. Bornstein interpreted these findings as supporting the idea that patients with HPD use psychological defenses to keep their underlying dependency needs out of awareness while DPD patients are more fully aware of their needs. Although the empirical studies are limited in number, the findings are impressively consistent and point to the link between the DSM-IV HPD and reinforcing the importance of considering both emotional expression and more covert dependency needs on the RIM when assessing HPD (Blais and Baity, 2006).

Narcissistic personality disorder (NPD) has been proposed as having both empirical and theoretical overlap with BPD and antisocial (ANPD) personality disorders. Gacono et al. (1992) looked at the similarities and differences among these three character styles on the Rorschach and found all three had a borderline level of organization based on Kernberg's (1970) model of personality development.

In addition, they suggested that NPD is different from ANPD in that protocols of the former have a greater frequency of T (interpersonal) and Y (painful affect) suggesting individuals with NPD have a greater capacity for interpersonal relatedness and emotional experience than individuals with ANPD (Gacono et al., 1992). Hilsenroth et al. (1993) found some similarities to Gacono at el. (1992) in that the NPD protocols had less aggression and less frequent use of primitive defenses (i.e. splitting, devaluation, etc.) than BPD protocols. NPDs, on the other hand, had higher levels of egocentricity as measured by a modified version of the Egocentricity Index found in the CS. The variable most frequently associated with narcissism on the Rorschach is the reflection response where a respondent indicates that an image is reflected based on the features of the blot. Two studies looking more directly at the relationship between the reflection response and NPD had very favorable results. Refection responses have been shown to discriminated NPD from all the DSM PDs (Hilsenroth et al., 1997), as well as add incrementally to MMPI-2 personality disorder scales in the prediction of NPD criteria (Blais et al., 2001). While the presence of one or more reflection response should never be used as a diagnostic equivalent for NPD, enough data exists to suggest these patients may have narcissistic tendencies that deserve a more thorough assessment.

Due to the richness of its theoretical and clinical history, BPD has received the most attention in terms of performance-based assessment. A comprehensive review of this research is beyond the scope of this chapter. However, two such reviews have recently been published (see Blais and Bistis, 2004; Mihura, 2006). The primary Rorschach variables that have been empirically related to BPD are: (1) poor thought quality, (2) disturbed self and other object relations, (3) use of more primitive defenses, and (4) modulated and unmodulated aggression. Research has consistently reported borderline patients achieving Rorschach form quality scores (X+ and F+ percentages) ranging from 0.65 to 0.70 (Gartner et al., 1989; Kleiger, 1999). This would place the form quality achieved by borderline patients nicely between that of schizophrenic subjects (who score about 10 points lower) and non-patients (who score 5 to 10 points higher) (Blais and Bistis, 2004). A recent study exploring the psychometric quality of the Rorschach Schizophrenia Index (SCZI) (Hilsenroth et al., 1998) found that BPD patients had a mean SCZI of 3.0, which was significantly less than a group of psychotic patients (mean SCZI 4.5), but significantly greater than a group of cluster C personality-disordered patients (SCZI = 1.8) and a non-clinical group (SCZI = 1.1). When compared to other PDs and Axis I disorders, BPD patients tend to produce protocols with higher (more pathological) MOAS scores (Blais et al., 1999) and dependency needs that seem to scale with level of care (Bornstein et al., 2000). The CS variable Morbid Content (MOR) is scored when a percept on the Rorschach is identified as either having a dysphoric quality ('a sad tree') or has been damaged in some way ('a headless woman') and is thought to indicate a poor self-image. Baity and Hilsenroth (1999) found that among several different aggression variables, MOR was the only one to predict the total number of BPD criteria. Although the assessment of defensive functioning is not a formal part of the CS, research has shown that BPD patients tend to have more examples of splitting and devaluation in their protocols than other cluster B PDs (Blais and Bistis, 2004). Affective instability and anger are possibly some of the easiest criteria to recognize with BPD, and their Rorschach tests tend to reflect this by having more instances of primitive and socially acceptable examples of aggression (Hilsenroth et al., 1993). BPD patients with a recent history of self-mutilation or suicidal ideation also tend to produce Rorschach tests with more primitive forms of aggression (Fowler et al., 2000; Baity et al., 2001).

Research with the TAT has also provided supportive evidence in distinguishing BPD from other PDs. The Social Causality scale of the SCORS focuses on the degree of logic and accuracy present in a patient's interpretation of social interactions. In a series of studies, several authors have found that patients with BPD produced TAT stories that had poor interpretations of the actions of others and highly illogical attributions (Westen et al., 1990a; Westen et al., 1990b) to a greater extent than patients with NPD (Ackerman et al., 1999). In a stepwise regression analysis, Ackerman et al. (1999) found that the SCORS variables AQR and EIR were predictive of the total number of DSM-IV BPD criteria. Affect was negatively related to BPD criteria while EIR was positively related. This was interpreted as indicating that patients with TAT stories that had more negative affect but expressed a greater desire to invest in relationships was predictive of the total number of BPD criteria. More recently, Stein et al. (2007) examined the relationship between early memory (EMT) narratives and the Borderline scale of the Personality Assessment Inventory (Morey, 1991) where the SCORS was used to code the EM. Results from their work found that the PAI Borderline scale was significantly related to the SCORS variable Complexity of Representations only within the sample of patients with borderline pathology.

The EMT asks patients to recount a series of memories based on certain events in their childhood where the stories have to be unique occurrences as opposed to routine behaviors (e.g. going to church every Sunday). Arnow and Harrison (1991) found that the DSM-III borderline patients produced significantly fewer positive affective early memories than those of paranoid schizophrenics and a group of neurotics (defined as clinical subjects without severe psychopathology), while also producing the most negatively (opposed to neutral) toned memories. Nigg et al. (1992) also used the EMT to explore the object world of borderline patients. When compared to the EMs of patients with MDD, the EMs of the borderline patients contained more malevolent and hurtful objects. The findings from both TAT and EM studies consistently reveal that borderline patients attribute more negative emotional qualities and more malevolent motives to others (and their internal representations of others) than do patients with other personality disorders.

As recently discussed by Loving and Lee (2006), the DSM-IV antisocial personality disorder (ANPD) only describes part of the greater construct known as psychopathy. Although these terms are erroneously used interchangeably, psychopathy includes interpersonal descriptors such as the lack of anxiety symptoms or superficial charm that are not part of the ANPD criteria. Therefore, investigators have begun to discriminate between psychopathic (P-ANPD) and non-psychopathic (NP-ANPD) antisocial personality disorder. Gacono et al. (1992) found that while NPDs, P-ANPD, and NP-ANPD did not significantly differ in the number of reflection responses, the NPD and P-ANPD groups had a significantly higher egocentricity ratio than the NP-ANPD. P-ANPDs had a significantly fewer T (interpersonal dependency) and Y (painful affect) responses than NPD, BPD, and NP-ANPD groups thus pointing out the lower need for interpersonal communication and a lack of negative affect in individuals with a psychopathic personality. The authors note that while P-ANPD and BPD groups had a similar primitive level of object relations, the P-ANPD group's higher egocentricity index, lower number of T, lower number of Y, and a greater number of personalized responses 'support the argument that psychopaths are a severely and pathologically detached variant of NPD' (1992: 45). A boon to the assessment of antisocial and psychopathic personality is based on the work of Meloy (1988), Meloy and Gacono (1992), and Gacono and Meloy (1994) and the extended aggression scores (AgC, AgPast, AgPot), who discuss how the CS score AG (aggressive movement) was actually lower in their psychopathic samples. The AgC score has emerged as being significantly related to DSM-IV ANPD (Baity and Hilsenroth, 1999), as well as real-world examples of aggression (Baity and Hilsenroth, 2002).

There has been limited research using the TAT to explore ANPD. However, Ackerman et al. (1999) found that when compared to NPDs, ANPDs had significantly (more pathological) lower scores on the Complexity of Representations, EIR and Understanding of Social Causality SCORS variables lending further evidence to the idea that ANPD is a more interpersonally pathological version of NPD. Among the SCORS variables that predict the total number of ANPD criteria, EIR loaded in a negative direction while AQR had a positive relationship. The authors interpret this combination to indicate the parasitic nature of ANPD while having little desire to fulfill the needs of others and quickly moving to other relationships when their own goals have been met.

Cluster C

Known as the 'anxious-avoidant' cluster, the cluster C PDs are all marked by recurring fearful thoughts that impair the ability to relate to others. The manner in which these fearful thoughts drive the interpersonal dysfunction and the effect of this dysfunction on the patient are where the Rorschach may have utility. A literature search by the authors of each cluster C personality disorder (avoidant, obsessive compulsive, dependent) and the Rorschach resulted in no studies that have formally looked at scores on the CS and any one of the cluster C disorders. This lack of data means that much of the work with performance-based testing and cluster C disorders remains theoretical in nature. One possibility for the lack of data with this set of disorders is the relatively mild clinical presentation compared the other PDs. In their examination of narcissism, defensive structure, and aggression, Hilsenroth et al. (1993) used a mixed group of patients with cluster C PDs (CPD) as a comparison group to BPDs and NPDs. Results from this study showed that the BPD group used significantly more primitive defences, had more instances of grandiosity, and more examples of primary and secondary process aggression when compared to CPD. The NPD group, on the other hand, only differed from the CPD group

by having a greater frequency of idealization in their Rorschach responses. Hilsenroth et al. (1998) found that outpatients with Cluster C PD had a significantly lower score on the Rorschach's main thought disorder index at the time (SCZI) than either a group of hospitalized patients with a psychotic disorder or a small group of outpatients diagnosed with a cluster A PD.

For avoidant PDs (AVPD), Ganellen (2006) indicates this can come across on a protocol with signs of introversion, a negative self-concept, and emotional constriction and distress. The AVPD protocol might be expected to show an increased interest in others (more pure H) than average but will not have the skills to feel comfortable opening up and forming relationships (T < 1). An increase in vista (FV, VF) responses where the patient uses the shading features of the blot to denote three-dimensional space is an indication of painful introspection. Due to the amount of conscious internal strife suffered by AVPD, other markers of psychological distress are likely such as an elevated DEPI, and responses with a high number of achromatic color (FC') or diffuse shading (Y). When coupled with a low desire to process emotions (Afr < 0.46), the AVPD individual is likely to harbor a great deal of uncomfortable affect and a poor self-image.

Obsessive-compulsive personality disorder (OCPD) is marked by an unrelenting tendency to exert control and orderliness over the environment. Though not receiving a great deal of attention since its inception, the Obsessive Style Index (OBS) from the CS has been shown to have utility in separating individuals with strong obsessive-compulsive tendencies as it was normed on patients with OCPD and the Axis I version, obsessive-compulsive disorder (OCD) (Exner, 2002). While the OBS would be expected to be elevated on the protocols of individuals with OCPD tendencies, a cross-validation study has not been done with this scale. The OCPD patient would be expected to have a great deal of difficulty with the ambiguity of the RIM, and as such may attempt to inject a great deal of form into their responses.

This can come across by having more form-dominated responses (FC, FY, FT, etc.), by giving an unusual number of responses using obscure and unimportant parts of the blot (Dd), and/or by trying (unsuccessfully) to incorporate all the pieces of the blot (Zd > 3.0; Schneider, 2006). Due to the immense amount of time these individuals spend ruminating and plotting their attempts at control, one might also expect the Intellectualization Index to be elevated in these protocols.

The Rorschach investigation of dependent personality disorder (DPD) has almost exclusively focused on the ROD (Masling et al., 1967). ROD scores tend to range from 0.40 (high dependency) to 0.00 (low dependency) with college students averaging a score of about 0.13 (Bornstein, 2006; Bornstein and Masling, 2005). While the ROD has been used to assess dependency in a wide variety of psychopathology (e.g. eating disorders, substance abuse, etc.) two studies comparing ROD with DPD have been published in recent years. When comparing the ROD scores to self-reported symptoms of all Axis II PDs in college students, those participants whose responses qualified them for a DPD from the self-report test had significantly higher ROD scores than students who qualified for other PDs. The exception was HPD, which had a similar ROD score as those students that qualified for DPD (Bornstein, 1998). Bornstein et al. (2000) compared the ROD of several PD groups and found that inpatient BPDs had the highest ROD score and was significantly higher than BPD outpatients, ANPD, and a college student control group. Although a dependent character style group was included, it did not have a significantly different ROD score from the other groups.

CONCLUSIONS

Personality has re-emerged as one of the principal areas of study within psychology. We believe that the comprehensive assessment of personality requires the combination of a multi-method and multi-perceptive (conceptual) approach. Psychometrically sound data regarding both implicit and explicit psychological functioning is necessary in order to establish the level of a patient's personality structure (development) and describe their typical pattern of intra and interpersonal functioning. Such information can only be obtained from a multi-method battery that combines self-report and performance-based instruments (Blais et al., 2001). Beyond instrumentation, our ability to understand personality functioning and to predict important real-life behaviors (i.e. how a patient will approach psychotherapy) is enhanced through the blending of descriptive/empirical psychiatry (as presented in the DSM-IV) and psychology with a model of personality development like Kernberg's (multi-perceptive). This chapter has reviewed the valuable contributions that performance-based instruments can provide to the comprehensive evaluation of personality. It is our hope that the material presented in this chapter will encourage researchers and clinicians alike to work toward integrating assessment instruments with theory in both their clinical and research endeavors.

NOTES

1 Traditionally, psychological tests have been classified as objective (self-report instruments) and projective (Rorschach, TAT, and other tests). This classification system has held for many years. However, with increased understanding of the phenomena that give rise to responses on tests like the Rorschach, these terms are increasingly inaccurate. The field is exploring new terms to classify these instruments with many of us favoring the term 'performance-based' tests. It is felt that this term better captures the psychological processes of the Rorschach response and the research showing that the Rorschach is more related to neuropsychological tests than self-report instruments (Meyer and Kurtz, 2006).

2 The psychometric quality and clinical utility of performance-based instruments, especially the RIM, have been widely debated. While respecting the diversity of opinions on this topic, the authors believe there is sufficient evidence for both the reliability and

validity of these methods. Readers interested in exploring this productive scholarly debate are referred to Meyer (1999) and the Society for Personality Assessment (2005).

REFERENCES

Ackerman, S.J., Clemence, A.J., Weatherill, R. and Hilsenroth, M.J. (1999) 'Use of the TAT in the assessment of DSM-IV cluster B personality disorders', *Journal of Personality Assessment*, 73(3): 422–48.

Ackerman, S.J., Hilsenroth, M.J., Clemence, A.J., Weatherill, R. and Fowler, J.C. (2001) 'Convergent validity of the RIM and TAT scales of object relations', *Journal of Personality Assessment*, 77(2): 295–306.

American Psychiatric Association (1980) *Diagnostic and Statistical Manual of Mental Disorders* (3rd edn). Washington, DC: APA.

American Psychiatric Association (2000) *Diagnostic and Statistical Manual of Mental Disorders – Text Revision* (4th edn). Washington, DC: APA.

Arnow, D. and Harrison, R.H. (1991) 'Affect in early memories of borderline patients', *Journal of Personality Assessment*, 56(1): 75–83.

Baity, M.R. and Hilsenroth, M.J. (1999) 'Rorschach aggression variables: A study of reliability and validity', *Journal of Personality Assessment*, 72(1): 93–110.

Baity, M.R. and Hilsenroth, M.J. (2002) 'Rorschach Aggressive Content (AgC) variable: A study of criterion validity', *Journal of Personality Assessment*, 78(2): 275–87.

Baity, M.R., Hilsenroth, M.J., Fowler, J.C., Padawer, J.R. and Blais, M.A. (2001) 'Primary process aggression and primitive defenses: Self-multination and the borderline patient', Paper presented at the Midwinter Meeting of Society for Personality Assessment, Philadelphia.

Baity, M.R., McDaniel P.S. and Hilsenroth, M.J. (2000) 'Further exploration of the Rorschach aggressive content (AgC) variable', *Journal of Personality Assessment*, 74(2): 231–41.

Blais, M.A. (1997) 'The five-factor model of personality and the DSM personality disorders', *Journal of Nervous and Mental Disease*, 185(6): 388–93.

Blais, M.A. and Baity, M.R. (2006) 'Rorschach assessment of histrionic personality disorder', in S.K. Huprich (ed.), *Rorschach Assessment of the Personality Disorders*. Mahwah, NJ: Lawrence Erlbaum Associates.

Blais, M.A. and Bistis, K. (2004) 'Projective assessment of borderline psychopathology', in M.J. Hilsenroth and D.L. Segal (eds), *Comprehensive Handbook of Psychological Assessment* (Vol. 2). Hoboken, NJ: Wiley, pp. 485–99.

Blais, M.A. and Norman, D.K. (1997) 'A psychometric evaluation of the DSM-IV personality disorders criteria sets', *Journal of Personality Disorders*, 11(2): 168–76.

Blais, M.A., Hilsenroth, M.J., Castlebury, F., Fowler, J.C. and Baity, M.R. (2001) 'Predicting DSM-IV Cluster B personality disorder criteria from MMPI-2 and Rorschach data: A test of incremental validity', *Journal of Personality Assessment*, 76(1): 150–68.

Blais, M.A. Hilsenroth, M.J. and Fowler J.C. (1998) 'Rorschach correlates of the DSM-IV histrionic personality disorder', *Journal of Personality Assessment*, 70(2): 355–64.

Blais, M.A., Hilsenroth, M.J., Fowler, J.C. and Conboy, C.A. (1999) 'A Rorschach exploration of the DSM-IV borderline personality disorder', *Journal of Clinical Psychology*, 55(5): 1–10.

Blais, M.A., McCann, J., Benedict, K. and Norman, D. (1997) 'Towards an Empirical/ Theoretical Grouping of the DSM–III-R Personality Disorders', *Journal of Personality Disorders*, 11(2): 191–8.

Bornstein, R.F. (1998) 'Implicit and self-attributed dependency needs in dependent and histrionic personality disorders', *Journal of Personality Assessment*, 71(1): 1–14.

Bornstein, R.F. (2006) 'Rorschach assessment of dependent personality disorder', in S.K. Huprich (ed.), *Rorschach Assessment of the Personality Disorders*. Mahwah, NJ: Lawrence Erlbaum Associates, pp. 289–310.

Bornstein, R.F., Hilsenroth, M.J., Padawer, J.R. and Fowler, J.C. (2000) 'Interpersonal dependency and personality pathology: Variations in Rorschach Oral Dependency Scores across axis II diagnoses', *Journal of Personality Assessment*, 75(3): 478–91.

Bornstein, R. and Masling, J. (2005) 'The Rorschach Oral Dependency Scale', in R. Bornstein and J. Masling (eds), *Scoring the Rorschach: Seven Validated Systems*. Mahwah, NJ: Lawrence Erlbaum ssociates.

Clarkin, J., Yeomans, F. and Kernberg, O. (1999) *Psychotherapy for the Borderline Personality*. New York: Wiley.

Clark, L. and Harrison, J. (2001) 'Assessment Instruments', in W.J. Livesley (ed.), *Handbook of Personality Disorders: Theory, Research and Treatment*. New York: Guilford, pp. 277–306.

Colligan, R., Morey, L. and Offord, K. (1994) 'The MMPI/MMPI-2 personality disorder scales: Contemporary norms for adults and adolescents', *Journal of Clinical Psychology*, 50(2): 168–200.

Erdberg, P. (2003) 'Rorschach Assessment of Personality Disorders', Symposia at the Meeting of the Society for Personality Assessment, San Francisco.

Exner, J.E. (1986a) *The Rorschach: A Comprehensive System Vol. 1: Basic Foundations* (2nd edn). New York: Wiley.

Exner, J.E. (1986b) 'Some Rorschach data comparing schizophrenics with borderline and schizotypal personality disorders', *Journal of Personality Assessment*, 50(3): 455–71.

Exner, J.E. (1993) *The Rorschach: A Comprehensive System, Vol. 1: Basic Foundations* (3rd edn). New York: Wiley.

Exner, J.E. (2002) *The Rorschach: A Comprehensive System. Basic Foundations and Principles of Interpretation* (4th edn). New York: Wiley.

Exner, J.E. and Erdberg, P., (2005) *The Rorschach: A Comprehensive System, Vol. 2, Advanced Interpretations* (3rd edn). New York: Wiley.

Foley, D.D. (2006) 'Rorschach assessment of Schizotypal Personality Disorder', in S.K. Huprich (ed.), *Rorschach Assessment of the Personality Disorders*. Mahwah, NJ: Lawrence Erlbaum Associates, pp.113–138.

Fowler, J.C., Hilsenroth, M.J. and Handler, L. (1995) 'Early memories: An exploration of theoretically derived queries and their clinical utility', *Bulletin of the Menninger Clinic*, 59(1): 79–98.

Fowler, J.C., Hilsenroth, M.J. and Nolan, E. (2000) 'Exploring the inner world of self-mutilating borderline patients: A Rorschach investigation', *Bulletin of the Menninger Clinic*, 64(3): 365–85.

Gacono, C.B., Bannatyne-Gacono, L., Meloy, J.R. and Baity, M.R. (2005) 'The Rorschach extended aggression scores', *Rorschachiana*, 27: 164–90.

Gacono, C.B. and Meloy, J.R. (1994) *The Rorschach Assessment of Aggressive and Psychopathic Personalities*. Hillsdale, NJ: Lawrence Erlbaum Associates.

Ganoco, C.B., Meloy, J.R. and Berg, J.L. (1992) 'Object relations, defensive operations, and affect states in narcissistic, borderline, and antisocial personality disorder', *Journal of Personality Assessment*, 59(1): 32–49.

Ganellen, R.J. (2006) 'Rorschach assessment of avoidant personality disorder', in S.K. Huprich (ed.), *Rorschach Assessment of the Personality Disorders*. Mahwah NJ: Lawrence Erlbaum Associates, pp. 265–88.

Gartner, J., Hurt, S.W. and Gartner, A. (1989) 'Psychological test signs of borderline personality disorder: A review of the empirical literature', *Journal of Personality Assessment*, 53(3): 423–41.

Hilsenroth, M.J., Fowler, J.C. and Padawer, J.R. (1997) 'Narcissism in the Rorschach revisited: some reflections on empirical data', *Psychological Assessment*, 9(2): 113–21.

Hilsenroth, M.J., Fowler, J.C. and Padawer, J.R. (1998) 'The Rorschach Schizophrenia Index (SCZI): An examination of reliability, validity, and diagnostic efficiency', *Journal of Personality Assessment*, 70(3): 514–34.

Hilsenroth, M.J., Handler, L. and Blais, M.A. (1996) 'Assessment of Narcissistic Personality Disorder: A multimethod review', *Clinical Psychology Review*, 16(7): 655–83.

Hilsenroth, M.J., Hibbard, S.R., Nash, M.R. and Handler, L. (1993) 'A Rorschach study of narcissism, defense, and aggression in borderline, narcissistic, and cluster c personality disorders', *Journal of Personality Assessment*, 60(2): 346–61.

Hilsenroth, M.J., Stein, M. and Pinkster, J. (2004) 'Social Cognition and Object Relations Scale–Global rating method (SCORS-G)', Unpublished manuscript, Derner Institute of Advanced Psychological Studies, Adelphi University, Garden City, New York.

Huprick, S. and Ganellen, R. (2006) 'The advantages of assessing personality disorders with the Rorschach', in S.K. Huprich (ed.), *Rorschach Assessment of the Personality Disorders*. Mahwah, NJ: Lawrence Erlbaum Associates, pp. 27–56.

Kaser-Boyd, N. (2006) 'Rorschach assessment of Paranoid Personality Disorder', in S.K. Huprich (ed.), *Rorschach Assessment of the Personality Disorders*. Mahwah, NJ: Lawrence Erlbaum Associates, pp. 57–86.

Kernberg, O. (1970) 'A psychoanalytic classification of character pathology', *Journal of the American Psychoanalytic Association*, 18(4): 800–22.

Kernberg, O. (1975) *Borderline Conditions and Pathological Narcissism*. New York: Aronson.

Kircher, T.T.J., Liddle, F.P., Brammer, M.J., Williams, S.C.R., Murray, R.M. and McGuire, P.K. (2001) 'Neural correlates of formal thought disorder in schizophrenia', *Archives of General Psychiatry*, 58(8): 769–74.

Kleiger, J.H. (1999) *Disordered Thinking and the Rorschach*. Hillsdale, NJ: The Analytic Press.

Kleiger, J.H. and Huprich, S.K. (2006) 'Rorschach assessment of Schizoid Personality Disorder', in S.K. Huprich (ed.), *Rorschach Assessment of the Personality Disorders*. Mahwah: NJ: Lawrence Erlbaum Associates, pp. 85–112.

Lerner, P. (1991) *Psychoanalytic Theory and the Rorschach*. Hillsdale, NJ: The Analytic Press.

Loving, J.L. and Lee, A.J. (2006) 'Rorschach assessment of antisocial personality disorder and psychopathy', in S.K. Huprich (ed.), *Rorschach Assessment of the Personality Disorders*. Mahwah: NJ: Lawrence Erlbaum Associates, pp. 139–70.

Masling, J., Rabie, L. and Blondheim, S. (1967) 'Obesity, level of aspiration, and Rorschach and TAT measures of oral dependence', *Journal of Consulting Psychology*, 31(3): 233–9.

Mayman, M. (1968) 'Early memories and character structure', *Journal of Projective Techniques and Personality Assessment*, 32(4): 303–16.

McCllelland, D., Koestner, R. and Weinberger, J (1989) 'How do self-attributed and implicit motives differ?', *Psychological Review*, 96(4): 690–702.

Meloy, J.R. (1988) *The Psychopathic Mind: Origins, Dynamics, and Treatment*. Northvale, NJ: Aronson.

Meloy, J.R. and Gacono, C.B. (1992) 'The aggression response and the Rorschach', *Journal of Clinical Psychology*, 48: 104–14.

Meyer, G.J. (1999) (ed.), 'The utility of the Rorschach for clinical assessment [Special section]. *Psychological Assessment*, 11(3): 235–302.

Meyer, G.J. and Kurtz J.E. (2006) Advancing personality assessment terminology: Time to retire "objective" and "projective" as personality test descriptors', *Journal of Personality Assessment*, 87(3): 223–5.

Mihura, J.L. (2006) 'Rorschach assessment of borderline personality disorder', in S.K. Huprich (ed.), *Rorschach Assessment of the Personality Disorders*. Mahwah, NJ: Lawrence Erlbaum Associates, pp. 171–204.

Morey, L.C. (1991) *The Personality Assessment Inventory Professional Manual*. Odessa, FL: Psychological Assessment Resources.

Morey, L.C., Waugh, M. and Blashfield, R. (1985) 'MMPI scales for the DSM-III personality disorders: Their derivation and correlates', *Journal of Personality Assessment*, 49(3): 245–51.

Murray, H.A. (1943) *Manual for the Thematic Apperception Test*. Cambridge, MA: Harvard University Press.

Nigg, J.T., Lohr, N.E., Westen, D., Gold, L.J. and Silk, K.R. (1992) 'Malevolent object representations in borderline personality disorder and major depression', *Journal of Abnormal Psychology*, 101(1): 61–7.

O'Connell, M., Cooper, S., Perry, J.C. and Hoke, L. (1989) 'The relationship between thought disorder and psychotic symptoms in borderline personality disorder', *Journal of Nervous and Mental Disease*, 177(5): 273–8.

Perry, W. and Viglione, D.J. (1991) 'The Ego Impairment Index as a predictor in melancholic depressed patients treated with tricyclic antidepressants', *Journal of Personality Assessment*, 56(3): 487–501.

Perry, W., Minassian, A., Cadenhead, K., Sprock, J. and Braff, D. (2003) 'The use of the Ego Impairment Index across the schizophrenia spectrum', *Journal of Personality Assessment*, 80(1): 50–7.

Rosenberg, S.D., Blatt, S.J. and Oxman, T.E. (1994) 'Assessment of object relatedness through a lexical content analysis of the TAT', *Journal of Personality Assessment*, 63(2): 345–62.

Ryan, R., Avery, R. and Grolnick, W. (1985) 'A Rorschach assessment of children's Mutuality of Autonomy', *Journal of Personality Assessment*, 49(1): 6–12.

Schneider, R.B. (2006) 'Obsessive-Compulsive Personality Disorder', in S.K. Huprich (ed.) *Rorschach Assessment of the Personality Disorders*. Mahwah: NJ: Lawrence Erlbaum Associates, pp. 311–44.

Society for Personality Assessment (2005) 'The status of the Rorschach in clinical and forensic practice: An official statement by the Board of Trustees of the Society for Personality Assessment', *Journal of Personality Assessment*, 85(2): 219–37.

Stein, M.B., Pinkster-Aspen, J.H. and Hilsenroth, M.J. (2007) 'Borderline personality and the Personality Assessment Inventory (PAI): An evaluation of criterion and concurrent validity', *Journal of Personality Assessment*, 88(1): 81–9.

Stricker, G. and Gooen-Piels, J. (2004) 'Projective assessment of object relations', in M. Hilsenroth and D. Segal (eds), *Comprehensive Handbook of Psychological Assessment*. Hoboken, NJ: Wiley, pp. 449–65.

Torgersen, S., Kringlen, E. and Cramer, V. (2001) 'The prevalence of personality disorders in a community sample', *Archives of General Psychiatry*, 58(6): 590–6.

Torgersen, S., Onstad, S., Skre, I., Edvardsen, J. and Kringlen, E. (1993) '"True" schizotypal personality disorder. A study of co-twins and relatives of schizophrenia probands', *American Journal of Psychiatry*, 150(11): 1661–7.

Urist, J. (1977) 'The Rorschach test and the assessment of object relations', *Journal of Personality Assessment*, 41(1): 3–9.

Urist, J. and Schill, M. (1982) 'Validity of the Rorschach Mutuality of Autonomy Scale: A replication using expected responses', *Journal of Personality Assessment*, 46(5): 450–4.

Weiner, I.B. (1996) 'Some observations on the validity of the Rorschach Inkblot Method', *Psychological Assessment*, 8: 206–13.

Westen, D. (1990) 'Towards a revised theory of borderline object relations: Contributions of empirical research', *International Journal of Psycho-Analysis*, 71(4): 661–93.

Westen, D. (1991) 'Clinical assessment of object relations using the TAT', *Journal of Personality Assessment*, 56(1): 56–74.

Westen, D. (1995) 'Social Cognition and Object Relations Scale: Q-Sort for Projective Stories (SCORS-Q)', Unpublished manuscript, Department of Psychiatry, Cambridge Hospital and Harvard Medical School, Cambridge, MA.

Westen, D., Gabbard, G.O. and Blagov, P. (2006) 'Back to the future: Personality structure as a context for psychotherapy', in R.F. Krueger and J.L. Tackett (eds), *Personality and Psychopathology*. New York: Guilford Press, pp. 35–384.

Westen, D., Lohr, N., Silk, K.R., Gold, L. and Kerber, K. (1990a) 'Object relations and social cognition in borderlines, major depressives, and normals: A Thematic Apperception Test analysis', *Psychological Assessment*, 2(4): 355–64.

Westen, D., Lohr, N., Silk, K., Kerber, K. and Goodrich, S. (1985) 'Measuring object relations and social cognition using the TAT: Scoring manual', Unpublished manuscript, University of Michigan, Ann Arbor.

Westen, D., Ludolph, P. and Lerner, H. (1990b) 'Object relations in borderline adolescents', *Journal of the American Academy of Child and Adolescent Psychiatry*, 29(3): 338–438.

Winnicott, D.W. (1971) *Playing and Reality*. New York: Routledge.

Winnicott, D.W. (1975) 'Transitional objects and transitional phenomena', in D.W. Winnicott (ed.), *Through Paediatrics to Psycho-analysis*. New York: Basic Books, pp. 229–42.

Wood, J.M., Lilienfeld, S.O., Garb, H.N. and Nezworski, M.T. (2000) 'The Rorschach test in clinical diagnosis: A critical review, with a backward look at Garfield (1947)', *Journal of Clinical Psychology*, 56(3): 395–430.

Zimmerman, M. (1994) 'Diagnosing personality disorders: A review of issues and methods', *Archives of General Psychiatry*, 51(3): 225–45.

PART VI

Abnormal Personality Trait Instruments

28

Modern Applications of the MMPI/MMPI-2 in Assessment

Edward Helmes

The year 2005 provided the 65th anniversary of the first official publication on the Minnesota Multiphasic Personality Inventory (MMPI) (Hathaway and McKinley, 1940). There are comparatively few psychological tests which continue to be in current clinical use from their original development. This length of use of a psychological test has few rivals. It is predated by some decades by the introduction of the Rorschach and the Stanford Binet and is roughly equal in age to the series of intelligence and memory tests that were begun by David Wechsler during the same period of time in the late 1930s. As with the Wechsler and Binet scales, and unlike the Rorschach, the venerable MMPI has undergone recent development and change, albeit not on as regular schedule or as extensive change as has been the case with the Wechsler scales. Since its introduction, there has also been criticism of the MMPI that has continued from early into modern times, with some of these criticisms directed at the very core functions of the MMPI. While the criticisms date to shortly after the introduction of the MMPI (see Helmes and Reddon, 1993, for a review), the MMPI-2

continues in wide use despite its manifest weaknesses. Some of these weaknesses derive from the origins of the MMPI, while others arise from the wide range of uses (and frequent misuses) to which the test has been put. Such uses have been driven by the implicit and at time explicit claims for the many diverse applications of the test into settings that its developers never foresaw. Still other weaknesses are inherent in more complex issues involving the entire field of personality assessment (Hathaway, 1972).

The scope of intended use of the original MMPI was initially rather restricted, but even in those areas of intended use, critics of the test have long noted the weakness of the test. Norman noted that at least five major goals had been promoted for the test: screening for psychopathology, psychiatric differential diagnosis, detecting malingering and dissimulation, measurement of personality traits, and operationalizing certain theoretical constructs, although others were also considered (1972: 61). Norman also noted significant weaknesses of the MMPI at the conceptual, methodological, and psychometric levels. Some of the weaknesses of the

MMPI no doubt were founded in the limited resources available at the time (the late 1930s) for serious work on developing the constituent scales (Archer, 2006). Nevertheless, the current standards for evaluating tests leave the MMPI/MMPI-2 wanting in many respects, as indicated by recent comments on the test, which have continued to be quite critical. Kline was blunt in his appraisal of the MMPI/MMPI-2: 'In its day, it was no doubt splendid but almost half a century later, with little evidence for validity other than a screening ability, it is surely time to turn to personality tests devised on a better psychometric rationale' (2000: 512). In his comments on the MMPI, Wiggins noted: 'The reasons why such an instrument that was constructed on such shaky foundations became the most widely used inventory in the world is one of the more intriguing stories in the history of personality assessment' (2003: 165). That story is best told by another, but the 'shaky foundations' refer to the use of the contrasted groups method of scale development that saw a period of popularity, one that Norman has referred to as 'empiricism gone mad as well as blind' (1972: 72). A large part of the test's continuing popularity despite such criticisms clearly derives from its introduction without serious competition into a growing community of psychologists when there was increasing demand for psychological assessment instruments. Another part of the likely reasons for its continued wide use is the formation of a body of enthusiastic promoters of the MMPI/MMPI-2 that has extolled its values and explained its properties through the use of workshops, specialized conferences, newsletters, and books. Once established within the curriculum of psychological training programs, the continuation of its use across generations of psychologists was assured.

There is a range of reference publications on the MMPI/MMPI-2, including both basic and advanced textbooks on the test in addition to the journal literature. Perhaps as a reflection of the complexity of the interpretation of the test, opinions in the psychological assessment literature on the MMPI and MMPI-2 are diverse, as noted above. The various reference and textbooks that are available on the MMPI consequently range from unabashed promotion of its utility in a wide range of applications from the less critical devotees of the test, to more sober and reflective evaluations. (Some but not all references for texts that cover the MMPI/MMPI-2 include: Butcher, 2005; Butcher and Williams, 2000; Friedman et al., 2001; Graham, 2006; Greene, 1991, 2000; and Nichols, 2001).

This literature is one index of the widespread use of the MMPI/MMPI-2 and of its many applications. There is of course no reason to believe that any psychological test is appropriate for all applications, although for much of the time in which it has been in use, the MMPI has lacked serious competition for the assessment of psychopathology. There have long been cautions that the test should not be used in applications in which there are more appropriate instruments (e.g. Butcher and Tellegen, 1978). This admonition does not, however, appear to have been very widely heeded. At the same time, the wide range of applications of the MMPI/MMPI-2 that are covered in books such as Butcher (2006) certainly provide the impression that there is empirical support in the research literature for such wide-ranging uses. As a result of such influences, unsophisticated or inexperienced users may have been led into inappropriate uses of the test, in populations and applications for which alternative modern measures would be less controversial and probably more effective. The actual support for many such promoted uses of the MMPI/MMPI-2 is actually quite mixed when the research literature on particular applications is examined in any depth.

The recent research literature on the many various applications of the MMPI/MMPI-2 cannot be covered in a chapter such as this. Its widespread use despite a lack of strong support for some applications is due in part to the strong support from the group of devoted MMPI/MMPI-2 users who argue, for example, that the changes to the MMPI-2 have resulted in a greatly improved test (e.g. Ben-Porath and Graham, 1991; Butcher, 2000). In their critical review that appeared shortly after the publication of the revision, Helmes and Reddon (1993) suggested that the revisions could have gone further and that had they done so, the result may have been a significantly improved test over what was actually published.

Approximately 1,000 articles (excluding dissertations) on the MMPI-2 were reviewed in some way for this chapter, and selection of those most relevant to the topics here reduced the number covered in any depth. This number does not cover the full range of publications on the MMPI-2 over this period of time. Butcher et al. (2004) estimate that approximately 225 new publications appear annually on the MMPI-2, which suggests there were almost twice as many publications that were not reviewed. (Those figures include publications on the MMPI-A, which is not covered in this review.) It should be noted that despite its popularity in clinical use, there are surprisingly few quantitative reviews of uses of the MMPI/MMPI-2 in the form of meta-analyses. The review for this chapter found fewer than a dozen meta-analyses that involved the MMPI-2; some of these are cited during this chapter, which itself cannot be regarded as quantitative in any sense.

The chapter begins with a review of the content of the MMPI/MMPI-2. The next section includes comments on the various sets of scales now available: Wiggins content, MMPI-2 content, content component subscales, and the latest development, the Restructured Clinical (RC) sets of scales. Prior to exploring the content scales is a discussion of the important issue of the interpretability of the accumulated literature on MMPI code types for the interpretation of MMPI-2 profile code types. The various factor analytic studies of the MMPI item pool are briefly mentioned here. The utility of the MMPI/MMPI-2 for diagnosis is covered, which includes a discussion of the use and interpretation of code types before a final section of concluding comments.

The utility of a broadband, multi-scale inventory such as the MMPI/MMPI-2 depends upon its range of content. The 567 MMPI-2 items cover a wide range of symptoms and attitudes, some of which continues to be relevant to modern diagnostic practices and systems, while the coverage of content related to other psychological disorders is limited. This topic is one that has major implications for many of the applications of the MMPI/MMPI-2 because of developments in psychiatric nosology over time. The body of research on psychological disorders has expanded tremendously in recent years, leaving aspects of the content covered in the MMPI/MMPI-2 inadequate, particularly for disorders that were defined after the original development of the scale.

MMPI CONTENT

Fundamental to modern applications of the MMPI-2 is the source of the content material that formed the MMPI. One of the stated goals of the Restandardization Committee that oversaw the development of the MMPI-2 from the MMPI was to preserve continuity with the existing research base on the MMPI (Butcher et al., 1989), which meant that the bulk of the MMPI item content remained on the MMPI-2. One element that has changed from the period in which the MMPI was developed is that accumulated research now makes obvious that a test cannot measure the presence and severity of a particular characteristic if the content of the items does not relate to that characteristic in some reasonably direct manner. However, this logic was not active in the development of the original MMPI clinical and validity scales. They were derived in the tradition of US mid-West 'dustbowl empiricism', in which overt item content was not relevant to the assignment of an item to a scale, as long as that item differentiated the clinical groups in question from a sample of 'normal' individuals. At the same time, the source of the items in the pool to be used was important for defining the areas of concern; not just any self-descriptive statement was included in the original item pool (although some original MMPI items may have had just such an appearance). Therefore the source of the original MMPI item content remains relevant today because many of the items selected at that time continue to be used on the MMPI-2. Hathaway and McKinley reported that 'items were formulated on the basis of previous clinical experience' and upon 'earlier published scales of personal and social attitudes' (1940: 249). They classified the items into a total of 25 different content areas, a set of statements that involve 'behavior of significance to the psychiatrist' (1940: 249). It should be remembered that the group of psychiatrists in question included not only McKinley but also those in the Minnesota state hospital system in the late 1930s, the period of time prior to the publication of the first edition of the *American Psychiatric Association's Diagnostic and Statistical Manual* in 1952 (Blashfield, 1998), a period of time in which psychoanalytic theories were widely popular. This is the era from which much of the MMPI content domain hails. To the extent that one is skeptical of the degree of progress in psychiatric diagnostic practices, one may not see this as a significant issue. Others may regard this as a more serious matter, particularly those who believe in a degree of progress in psychiatric nosology over time and that diagnoses based on the original system of Kraepelin may not be as applicable today as it was at the time of the development of the MMPI. Clark et al. (1995) and Widiger and Sankis (2000) outline current issues in the modern conceptualization and diagnosis of psychopathology. In many ways, it is evident that concerns in modern diagnostic practices are more complex than can be easily accommodated within the simple diagnostic model embodied in the MMPI/MMPI-2.

The basic issue underlying the question of the MMPI content is the extent to which that content remains relevant today. Clearly the number of disorders cataloged in the revised

fourth edition of the DSM (American Psychiatric Association, 2000) has greatly increased (Houts, 2002), but many of the disorders, especially the more common ones, remain similar symptomatically over the various modern editions, from DSM-III onwards (American Psychiatric Association, 1980). At the same time, the expansion in the number of personality disorders (Axis II), repeated revisions to the criteria for some disorders, and the introduction of new conditions, such as post-traumatic stress disorder, suggest that the changes over time in diagnostic practices are indeed significant and important from the perspective of instruments intended to assess those disorders. Despite the previous comments, it is also important to keep in mind that the MMPI-2 does comprise both original and new content: 82 items were rewritten and 154 new items were added to be evaluated on the 704-item MMPI-AX during the process of revision (Butcher et al., 1989), 89 of which survived into the final 567 items of the MMPI-2. The bulk of these new items are in the last section of the MMPI-2, with the first 400 items containing the items for the traditional clinical scales.

The empirical method of test construction used by Hathaway and McKinley has since been found to be less efficient than rational, theory-based methods (Burisch, 1984, 1986). The lack of cross-validation of the original item assignment to scales likely led to items being assigned by chance and being labeled as 'subtle items' with no clear relationship to the designated scale on which such items are keyed (Jackson, 1971). Opinions have been expressed both in favor of and against the subtle items, and the absence of definitive research has not yet resolved the issue in some eyes. Hollrah et al. (1995) reviewed the existing research on subtle items and the issues that are involved. They concluded that 'some uncertainty still remains regarding the validity of the MMPI subtle items' (1995: 295). One apparent use that Hollrah et al. note is in the detection of faking good in psychiatric settings. Others are more definite as to the limited value of such items.

As Weed (2006) notes, it is difficult to distinguish subtle items that reduce the correlation of scales with external criteria from useless items that perform in the same way. The concerns expressed about the subtle items apply to the clinical scales of the MMPI/MMPI-2, but are less relevant for the various sets of content scales that have been developed. Table 28.1 provides the titles and numbers of items for the content scales for the MMPI that were developed by Wiggins (1966) and by Butcher et al. (1990) for the MMPI-2. The table is organized to highlight parallel scales, where this is possible, and also indicates the number of content component scales that have been derived for the content scales (Ben-Porath and Sherwood, 1993).

There is substantial empirical support for the use of content scales as adjuncts to the clinical scales (Butcher et al., 1990). The MMPI-2 content scales are also intended to provide a means of incorporating some of the new content in the MMPI-2 that remains outside the domains covered by the clinical scales. The content component scales (Ben-Porath and Sherwood, 1993) provide additional

material that can clarify the nature and reasons for elevations on content scales. Green et al. (2006) examined the correlations of the content component scales with the Symptom Checklist-90, the Brief Psychiatric Rating Scale, and information extracted from patients' files in over 500 psychiatric inpatients. This report provides evidence for the validity of the content component scales using self-report, clinician rating, and biographical information. Interestingly, Green et al. do not make mention of the utility of the standard clinical or the RC scales in their study. This study also illustrates a common weakness in studies of the MMPI/MMPI-2 content scales. While the scoring of multiple MMPI/MMPI-2 scales from the same data set is commonplace, it does create the problem of dependency among the analyses, and the approach used by Green et al. that emphasizes that the use of external correlates is preferable in future studies.

The development of the original Wiggins (1966) content scales for the MMPI was one element in the recognition of the importance of the manifest content of personality items. Wiggins' work clearly influenced the development of the MMPI-2 content scales (Nichols, 2004). The later development of the Restructured Clinical scales (Tellegen et al., 2003) can also be seen as part of a growing emphasis in personality assessment on demonstrable relationships between item content, the constituent scale, and the underlying construct. This is now evident in recommendations for new MMPI scales (Butcher et al., 1995; Butcher, 2006: 27), perhaps an indication of a general, if overdue, shift in thinking away from the original Minnesota emphasis on empirical, contrasted groups methods of test construction.

Table 28.1 Domains of MMPI/MMPI-2 content defined by content scales

Wiggins MMPI content scales component	MMPI-2 content scales (number of subscales)
Poor health	Health concerns [3]
Depression	Depression [4]
Organic symptoms	—
Family problems	Family problems [2]
Authority conflict	—
Feminine interests	—
Religious fundamentalism	—
Manifest hostility	Anger [2]; cynicism [2]
Poor morale	—
Phobias	Fears [2]
Psychoticism	Bizarre mentation [2]
Hypomania	—
Social maladjustment	Social discomfort [2]
—	Anxiety [0]
—	Low self-esteem [2]
—	Obsessiveness [0]
—	Type A [2]
—	Work interference [0]
—	Negative treatment indicators [2]

RESTRUCTURED CLINICAL (RC) SCALES

The most recent development in terms of content scales for the MMPI-2 has been the derivation of the Restructured Clinical (RC) scales by Tellegen et al. (2003). These scales have attracted substantial interest and discussion in the current literature, and so warrant further discussion in this section. The major goal in the development of the RC scales was to reduce the covariation among the clinical scales caused by the overlapping content among scales (i.e. items keyed on more than one scale). The first step was to form a scale of 23 items to embody the theoretical construct of demoralization (*Dem*), which was seen as defining the core of the first factor of the MMPI, commonly referred to as Welsh's *A* (Welsh, 1956). This was followed by a complex sequential and iterative process that led to the final scales. Nichols (2006) documents anomalies in the report on the construction of *Dem*, and expresses a range of criticisms on both conceptual and empirical grounds. Tellegen et al. (2006) rebut Nichols' arguments and also provide additional information on the process of developing the RC scales. Nichols' comprehensive review and critique covers a wide range of issues involving the conceptualization and implementation of the RC scales that cannot be summarized here at any length. The interested reader is urged to consult the original and the accompanying commentary, some of which is reviewed below.

There have been several recent studies that support the method of deriving the RC scales, or at least support their utility in practice. Wallace and Liljequist (2005) replicated the essential findings of Tellegen et al. (2003) in an independent outpatient sample: lower correlations among RC scales than among the clinical scales and strong correlations between the RC scales and the parent clinical scale. This point was also made by Rogers et al. (2006) in their replication of the RC scales. They report similar figures for reliability and correlations among the RC scales to the original report and comment favorably upon the RC scales as representing a promising approach, but suggest that insufficient data exist as yet to support their use in clinical practice. They also report that code types

based on the RC scales have little congruence with those based on the traditional clinical scales and suggest that the literature on the clinical scale code types cannot be safely applied to the RC scales. The analyses reported by Sellbom et al. (2006b) note that agreement on clinically significant elevations between clinical and RC scales occurred in from 64 to 87% of cases in two large samples of respondents, with differences in scale elevations in 10 to 35% of cases. Depending upon the exact pair of scales, the contribution of the *Dem* content, the presence of subtle items, and the operation of the *K*-correction were the major influential factors in determining the differences between the corresponding pairs of the sets of scales.

The negative perspective on the RC scales was not shared by all other commentators on the Nichols (2006) paper. Both Caldwell (2006) and Finn and Kamphuis (2006) support the use of the RC scales. Finn and Kamphuis provide case studies that illustrate the ability of the RC scales to provide clearer interpretations in the case of profiles that have high elevations on many clinical scales. Caldwell points out that the construction of the RC scales reduced the impact of the general distress factor, but did not remove it completely. His paper also is notable for a clear demonstration of the importance of extensive experience in the interpretation of the MMPI/MMPI-2.

Sellbom and Ben-Porath (2005) correlated the clinical and RC MMPI-2 scales with those of Tellegen's unpublished Multidimensional Personality Questionnaire, and reported higher correlations on average for the RC scales than for the clinical scales. Using five existing samples, Sellbom et al. (2005a) compared three sets of MMPI-2 scales in terms of their ability to detect simulated under-reporting and over-reporting of symptoms. Their analyses found that the clinical, content, and RC scales were all sensitive to instructions to under-report symptoms (fake good), with the clinical scales being somewhat less susceptible due to the artifactual influence of the subtle subscales. All three sets of scales were equally susceptible to instructions to over-report symptoms (fake bad). Simms et al. (2005) evaluated the RC scales in two samples, one of psychology clinic clients and the other of military veterans, using structured diagnostic interviews and the Schedule for Nonadaptive and Adaptive Personality (SNAP) (Clark, 1993). They found the RC scales to be somewhat more internally consistent than the clinical scale equivalents and also to be more distinct in their pattern of correlations. Their analysis of the incremental validity of the RC scales suggested that they make a modest contribution to prediction over and above that provided by the standard clinical scales. Sellbom et al. (2006a) and Sellbom et al. (2006b) drew similar conclusions using clients from a university psychology clinic and private practices, respectively. In his commentary on Nichols' (2006) critique of the RC scales, Simms (2006) notes the importance of using non-MMPI data to evaluate the significance of the RC scales. This point needs to be emphasized, given the common practices in the literature of using one set of measures from the MMPI/MMPI-2 to correlate with another set of measures from the MMPI/MMPI-2 and to reanalyze existing sets of data.

The commentary on the RC scales in the *Journal of Personality Assessment* provides the reader with very mixed opinions on the value of the RC scales for the practitioner. The limited evidence to date on the RC scales suggests that they have met the broad goals that inspired their development, despite the concerns raised by Nichols (2006). Whether the RC scales provide any benefit over the existing content scales remains to be seen and Nichols' concerns about the ability of the RC scales to retain the interpretive features of the traditional clinical scales also remains to be investigated. The limited evidence provided by Rogers et al. (2006) suggests that the lore related to the clinical scale code types cannot be applied readily to the RC scales. The one study to date (Simms et al., 2005) suggests that the pattern of correlations

remains much the same for the RC scales as for the traditional clinical scales. The matter of the utility of the lore surrounding the traditional clinical scales will be a matter for further discussion later in this chapter.

FACTOR ANALYSIS OF THE MMPI

Factor analysis has been regarded as another form of empirical item selection, but the method has not been widely used in forming MMPI scales. Most sets of content-related scales have been derived by rational or mixed approaches to test construction. For example, the Wiggins content, content, and content component scales were all derived without empirical factor analysis of the full MMPI item set. At the time of Wiggins' (1966) analyses, computation of the calculations required to analyze a 550×550 MMPI item correlation matrix was not practical. With increases in computing power, such analyses have become possible, providing answers to the question as to what dimensions of content in the MMPI item pool can in fact be supported by empirical factor analytic methods.

Several efforts have been made to use factor analysis to uncover the basic dimensions of psychopathology in the MMPI/MMPI-2 item pool. Results have not been definitive, largely because of differences in purposes and methodologies among the authors. Only a few studies of fairly recent publication are technically sufficiently sophisticated as to be preferred over the ones in the older literature. A common concern is the use of phi or Pearson correlations with the binary response format used by the MMPI. Such correlations do not have a maximum correlation of 1.0 unless both items in the correlation have item means of 0.50. Tetrachoric correlations are preferred because they do not have this property, but are significantly more complex to calculate. Waller (1999) summarizes outcomes of the four item-level factor analyses conducted up to that time, which reported from 6 to 21 factors.

Waller's analysis used tetrachoric correlations rather than the more common, but technically more problematic phi coefficients and a sample of over 23,000. His final solution retained 16 factors, whose names are summarized in Table 28.2. The doctoral dissertation by Goh (2006) used tetrachoric correlations with a sample of 2,989 personal injury claimants with a wide range of diagnoses augmented with 241 normal individuals. She retained 35 components after applying Horn's (1965) parallel analysis criterion. Leonelli et al. (2000) used the MMPI-2 normative data of 1,138 males and 1,462 females, excluding the validity scale items and some redundant ones in an analysis of 518 items. They used a method based on item response theory, which avoids the calculation of any correlations, phi or tetrachoric. The method has the additional advantage of providing a statistical test of when to stop adding additional factors. Leonelli et al. stopped the process at ten factors, whose names are provided for comparison with those of Waller and Goh in Table 28.2.

One notable element in Table 28.2 is the relatively limited correspondence between the two solutions with a larger number of factors and Waller's solution with only ten retained factors. Part of this limited concordance is likely due to the likelihood of chance factors appearing with solutions that rotate larger numbers of retained factors. Such chance factors are much less likely to replicate across different samples. Closer agreement in constructs is apparent in Waller's Table 9.1 of older MMPI item factor analyses, in which at least five factors of the maximum of six that might be found in all four solutions can indeed be located (the exception being impulse expression, which likely is separated into smaller elements in the other solutions that extracted more factors). The differences among the three solutions summarized in Table 28.2 may be due to the differences in analytic methods, with perhaps some impact of removing the validity scales and other items by Leonelli et al. (2000). Until additional large samples are analyzed using modern methods of analysis, the question of the internal structure of the MMPI/MMPI-2 will remain without a definitive answer. The current limited factor analytic evidence to date does not provide a

Table 28.2   Descriptive labels for resulting structures from two analyses of the MMPI/MMPI-2 item pool

Waller (1999) MMPI	Leonelli et al. (2000) MMPI-2	Goh (2006)
General maladjustment (148)	Distrust (109)	Psychological distress (107)
Denial of somatic symptoms (51)	Self-doubt (93) Somatic complaints (26)	
Cynicism (36)	Fitness (62)	Negative interpersonal
	Rebelliousness (49) Delinquency (8)	Attitudes (29)
Antisocial tendencies (29)		
Psychotic ideation (40)	—	Psychotic symptoms (22)
Social inhibition (16)	—	Social withdrawal (29)
Stereotypic feminine interests (23)	Artistry (35)	Femininity (16)
Stereotypic masculine interests (16)	Instrumentality (42) Masculinity (9)	
Christian fundamentalism (13)	—	
Extroversion (15)	Sociability (29)	
Phobias (15)	—	Fears (12)
Family attachment (15)	—	Family difficulties (11)
Assertiveness (12)	Self-reliance (7)	Positive impression (9)
Dream (5)	—	Dreams (3)
Hypomania (7)	—	Elation (8)
Hostility (5)	—	Anger (15)
—	Serenity (53)	
—	Irritability (39)	Irritability (12)

Note: Number of items on that scale in parentheses

resolution to the questions of the number and nature of the MMPI/MMPI-2 domains of content. If anything, two of the three suggest that there are substantially fewer domains than are assessed by the standard 10 clinical and 15 content scales and that some number between these two seems more appropriate. The analysis by Goh (2006) does suggest that 25 components can be retained from the MMPI-2 item pool, but the resulting scales do not correspond well to the original clinical scales, and many are quite short and specific. The other consideration is that the item factor analyses generally include all the items, including those that are not scored on any clinical or content scale. Such items are likely to distort the final solution in some way and probably contribute to the large number of items that load Waller's large 'general maladjustment' and Leonelli et al.'s large 'distrust' and 'self-doubt' factors. The repeated identification of this large first factor in both these item-level analyses and also by analyses of the MMPI/MMPI-2 scales has been a matter of concern in the literature for some time. The pervasive influence of the general factor across all the clinical scales has been subject to many interpretations. One may interpret the general factor variously as social desirability (Edwards and Heathers, 1962), anxiety (Welsh, 1956), (absence of) ego resiliency (Block, 1965), or demoralization (Tellegen et al., 2003). However interpreted, its pervasiveness led to the development of the RC scales discussed above. It is also clear that the factors that have been identified to date do not correspond well to the scales that are commonly used and interpreted. This outcome is to be expected from the contrasted groups method used to derive the original MMPI clinical scales, which causes substantial confusion. Contrary to the interpretation of Nichols (2006), the clinical scales do not reflect clinical syndromes as that phrase is commonly interpreted (Weed, 2006), but an empirical association between the responses of a criterion group and a presumed normal group over 60 years ago.

Modern normal practices in the interpretation of MMPI/MMPI-2 clinical scales involve the use of code types, and the literature has seen an extensive debate over whether or not the literature on MMPI code types will generalize to the MMPI-2. While there is not sufficient space here to review all the arguments, the conclusions are that code types based upon highly salient scale elevations generalize better than code types based upon 'flat' profiles and that the percentage of code types that replicate across different forms is somewhat lower than the number that replicate across test–retest comparisons of the same form. As the literature on the correlates of the MMPI-2 increases (e.g. Arbisi et al., 2003; Sellbom et al., 2005b), it will be more possible to put aside any older questionable literature based on the original MMPI and the attendant interpretive complications of trying to apply its literature to the MMPI-2. At the same time, the utility of code types in diagnosis has its own share of controversy.

CODE TYPES AND DIAGNOSIS

Two common applications of the MMPI/MMPI-2 are in the diagnosis of psychological disturbance and in differential diagnosis. A test of psychopathology should be able to determine if relevant pathology is present, and what variety of pathology is being reported. The evolution of code types is part of the complex history of the MMPI/MMPI-2. While MMPI code types have been the standard approach to these issues for many years, they also provide one of the major sources of interpretive difficulties.

It is well known that the interpretation of the clinical scales of a typical MMPI/MMPI-2 profile is complex to the point of being arcane. This complexity has evolved over time, and is illustrated in the length of sections on interpretation found in most MMPI/MMPI-2 reference books. Such complexity increases the amount of time that a new user must invest in learning the correct interpretation methods, while also increasing the risk of misuse and misinterpretation by less knowledgeable, less well-trained individuals, and of oversight errors by trained and experienced users. While there is no doubt that any test can be misinterpreted (Rogers, 2003), the complexity of MMPI/MMPI-2 interpretive processes does increase that risk. No other modern self-report instrument intended for the assessment of psychopathology rivals the MMPI-2 in this regard, and such complexity cannot be regarded as a positive feature of the test. That complexity has evolved out of efforts to overcome a basic weakness in the MMPI/MMPI-2, namely its poor performance as a diagnostic instrument when simple relationships are sought between scale scores and diagnostic categories (Tellegen et al., 2006). Indeed, the limitations in the use of the MMPI as a diagnostic instrument are inherent in its structure, and have long been known, if ignored in some circles. In Warren Norman's words:

> From a strictly diagnostic viewpoint, the Multiphasic is a mess! Its original clinical criteria are anachronistic; its basic clinical scales are inefficient, redundant, and largely irrelevant for their present purposes; its administrative format and the repertoire of responses elicited are, respectively, inflexible and impoverished; and its methods for combining scale scores and for profile interpretation are unconscionably cumbersome and obtuse. (1972: 64)

Someone unfamiliar with the MMPI and reading this could well wonder why such an instrument is even still in use. Indeed, that question has been raised, as the quotations from Wiggins and Kline earlier in this chapter show, but sales of the MMPI-2 continue and it remains in wide use, along with its 'cumbersome and obtuse' interpretive practices. Whether some of these interpretive practices are justified is largely an empirical question.

Current interpretive practices for the MMPI/MMPI-2 involve the literature on the correlations of code types, including single scale 'high point' codes, with empirical criteria. The MMPI-2 manual (Butcher et al., 1989) uses the phrase 'correlates of the clinical scales', while Greene (2000) refers to 'empirically based interpretation' for the 'cumbersome and obtuse' process of scoring and interpreting MMPI/MMPI-2 code types. This approach has been standard since the early realization that there was no simple relationship between a high score on a scale and the disorder implied by the scale's title (see reviews of the MMPI in the *Third Mental Measurements Yearbook* (e.g. Benton, 1949)) and later studies that review its modest diagnostic accuracy (e.g. Pancoast et al., 1988). Thus for example, a diagnosis of schizophrenia is but one of several possible interpretations for having a highly elevated score on scale 8 (Schizophrenia). A correct interpretation also depends upon how many items the person endorsed as 'true', and what other scales may also be elevated.

Determining the similarity of a given profile to a prototypical 'type' can be done in several ways, and there has been some recent research on the topic, although probably not as much as would be desirable. In general, the relevant properties of a profile are its overall mean score (the profile's elevation), the degree of variation between the different components of the profile (the profile's standard deviation, or scatter), and the profile's configuration or pattern (shape) (Burger, 1991; Cronbach and Gleser, 1953). The common interpretive processes usually take into account overall elevation in some way, but relies mostly upon the profile shape. Some systems, such as that of Greene et al. (1998), calculate correlations between the individual profile and a set of master code types. Such methods based on correlations need not classify profiles in the same way as a method that looks only at the highest one, two, or three scales. Munley and Germain (2000) reported that 30% of one sample had identical profiles by both code type matching, while by correlation 39% were similar, and 31% had different profiles. From such figures, it is clear that the method of determining the correspondence of a given profile to a set of prototypic profiles does indeed significantly matter for at least approximately a third of cases assessed with the MMPI-2.

In addition, the question of the code type to be used in interpretation depends upon a decision as to whether scores in a profile differ from one another. The traditional psychometric approach to this issue has been the calculation of standard errors of measurement (SEMs), based upon the reliability of the scales and the variance of the scales involved. Recent debates in the MMPI-2 literature have focused upon 'well-defined' profiles, ones in which there is at least a five-point difference between scores (Butcher et al., 2004: 30). Interestingly, Butcher et al. (1995) recommend the use of SEMs, but the actual practice within the MMPI community is different. As Rogers and Sewell (2006) note, the use of SEMs has substantial implications for the interpretation of MMPI-2 profiles in that very often what are regarded as interpretable differences between scales may well not be 'true' differences when SEMs are calculated.

The MMPI/MMPI-2 clinical scales have comparatively modest internal consistency reliabilities and test–retest stability in comparison to some measures. Modest reliabilities for the scales have another consequence; they require larger differences among scales to show that code types or profiles of different diagnostic groups do indeed differ from one another. This in turn means that the MMPI/MMPI-2 is weak at differentiating groups and can reliably differentiate only fairly gross differences in profiles. Indeed, the literature on differences among MMPI code types goes back decades. Meehl (1946) reported figures on the agreement of judgments of three MMPI profile types (neurotic, psychotic, and conduct disorder) with consensus psychiatric diagnoses that were blind to the MMPI results. Goldberg's (1965) actuarial equations were established to classify MMPI profiles as similar psychotic, neurotic, and sociopathic types. Later research that used the compiled manuals of code types showed three common modal MMPI/MMPI-2 types

that correspond to the broad types initially identified by Meehl in the MMPI (Skinner and Jackson, 1978; Skinner, 1979). These broad types have shown some stability and clinical utility, e.g. (Morrison et al., 1994). However, the code type literature includes many distinctions between much smaller differences, including distinctions such as a 7-3 differing from a 3-7, involving at times differences of only one or two *T*-score points. Such distinctions are both psychometrically and clinically meaningless, and a practitioner who makes such distinctions is likely over-interpreting the test.

The MMPI-2 content scales (Butcher et al., 1990) were developed in part to improve the performance of the MMPI-2 in differential diagnosis. Ben-Porath et al. (1991) and Munley et al. (1997) found that the *DEP* and *BIZ* content scales were able to account for more variance over and above the clinical scales in differentiating individuals with schizophrenia from those with depression. This of course is also a differentiation of the broad neurotic ('left side elevated') MMPI modal profile from the broad psychotic ('right side elevated') type, which had been clearly identified in previous research. This is a distinction that the MMPI/MMPI-2 has long been known to be able to make with reasonable accuracy, and thus these two papers do not provide a critical test of the ability of the MMPI-2 to make those discriminations among disorders that are critical for most diagnostic work.

Practitioners need to consider seriously the applicability of the MMPI-2 for their assessment goals and not simply administer it automatically. The issues of discriminant validity and differential diagnosis should also be seriously considered. It may be that the clinical scales of the MMPI/MMPI-2 function better at a secondary level of evaluating general distress than at a lower level of separable constructs of anxiety, depression, and low self-esteem (Bagby et al., 2005). The context of the assessment is also an important consideration, given that the MMPI/MMPI-2 now has applications that were not considered at the time of its development. One example is how well the MMPI/MMPI-2 functions in medical, as opposed to psychiatric settings.

APPLICATIONS IN MEDICAL SETTINGS

The studies mentioned above indicate a degree of utility for the MMPI/MMPI-2 in assessing and differentiating broad categories of psychiatric disorders. The use of the MMPI/MMPI-2 for people with a range of medical conditions was perhaps not a priority among the original goals for the test by Hathaway and McKinley (1940), but data with the first card version of the MMPI were collected from the medical units of the Minneapolis hospitals and content involving medical symptoms was certainly included in the original set of items. The 1956 compendium of readings (Welsh and Dahlstrom, 1956) has no fewer than seven chapters included that involve medical, as opposed to psychiatric samples (albeit two on experimental semi-starvation). Of the 13 group profiles reported in that section, 10 were 1-2/2-1 or 1-3/3-1, despite the variety of medical conditions, which ranged from gunshot wounds to asthma to cancer. These 'neurotic' profiles were also very common among individual cases reported in that section. The reason for reviewing data from over 50 years ago is to point out the similarity in MMPI profiles obtained in widely different medical conditions. A review of modern data with the MMPI-2 would not differ greatly. Indeed, this point is made in the recent review of applications of the MMPI-2 in medical settings by Arbisi and Seime (2006).

Reviews such as that just mentioned as well as the attributions of others made on the basis of individual profiles and resulting code types have led to the impression that the use of the MMPI/MMPI-2 in medical settings has been widely accepted; such acceptance has usually been uncritical and controversy is evident. Such controversy may be particularly the case with regard to its use with people with chronic pain. The literature on medical applications of the MMPI/MMPI-2 cannot be dealt with in depth here, but illustrative examples will be introduced to emphasize specific points. Arbisi and Seime (2006) review applications of the MMPI-2 to populations with chronic pain, chronic fatigue and related conditions, coronary artery disease, as well as candidates for organ transplantation and gastric surgery, as well as in the context of smoking cessation programs. They argue for the utility of the MMPI-2 with medical populations, but their review is largely uncritical. They do downplay the use of the obsolete 'functional versus organic' dichotomy in the interpretation of MMPI-2 scores in medical populations and stress the importance of a considered interpretation of scales 1 to 3. They also note the likelihood of defensive under-responding among candidates for treatments that are scarce, such as organ transplants.

Despite the long history of use with medical populations, the question must be raised as to the actual value and efficiency of the MMPI/MMPI-2 in those contexts. Interpretations based upon psychiatric populations are complicated by the high rates of anxiety about physical health and mood disturbance among people who have serious medical illness, and the likelihood of serious demoralization being present in those with life-threatening conditions. This makes the differentiation of normal emotional reactions from abnormal ones more difficult, particularly if the interpretive process used traditional code types and their correlates based upon psychiatric populations and did not involve a hypothesis-testing approach such as that described by Senior and Douglas (2001). Their analysis was presented in the context of personal injury claimants, a rather atypical medical group because of the important role of litigation. As with virtually all medical conditions, this group also shows a common profile of group means with elevations on scales 1, 2, and 3. However, as

Arbisi (2006) notes, there are important differences between such medico-legal disability assessments and those in more traditional medical and psychiatric settings in that many disability assessments are more likely to occur in an adversarial context in which there are incentives for the client to distort their responses. In such contexts, the strength of the MMPI/ MMPI-2 in assessing a variety of forms of response distortion can make it a useful tool in determining the presence of clients' attempts to misrepresent their condition.

Psychologists experienced with the MMPI/ MMPI-2 can nevertheless be caught by the interpretive pitfalls inherent in the measure when dealing with medical patients, especially if litigation is involved and substantial incentives exist for exaggeration or misrepresentation. While the validity scales of the MMPI/MMPI-2 may detect such attempts at manipulation, the exclusive reliance on a single inventory cannot be recommended. Given this type of context, novice users would best be advised not to use it without extensive consultation with experts in its use, which could also be a policy adopted by those who are more accustomed to the use of other, perhaps more appropriate and less complex instruments, but use the MMPI/ MMPI-2 only occasionally.

Medical applications of the MMPI illustrate its history of the extension of its use into applications beyond those for which it was originally designed. Efforts are then made by some users to defend and promote the case for its application, even though the validity of the interpretations drawn in those applications might be questionable and the relevant literature inconclusive. Those efforts often seem to make rather tenuous arguments for the continuation of the use of the MMPI/ MMPI-2 in these new areas that lack a strong evidence base, as illustrated in several chapters in Butcher (2006) and other applications that were introduced in recent times in the literature in which an evidence base for applications of a test is increasingly emphasized.

EVIDENCE-BASED ASSESSMENT

A measure of how well an established test can be adapted to changes in practice and society is not only the extent to which practitioners will continue to use it over time, but how the test meets the changing pressures on professional practices. With the rise of managed care in the US, several aspects of professional psychological practice have been changing as well (Barlow, 2004; Fox, 1995; Karon, 1995, Phelps et al., 1998). One consequence of this has been increased interest in both the efficacy and effectiveness of psychological interventions, which has in turn been accompanied by increased interest in evidence-based assessment (Hunsley and Mash, 2005). The articles in the section edited by Hunsley and Mash highlight current developments in evidence-based assessment, and one index of the adaptability of the MMPI-2 is how the contributors to the special section of the journal regard the MMPI-2. Studies that use the MMPI-2 to evaluate the taxonicity hypothesis of depression are mentioned by Joiner et al. (2005), who cite the weaknesses of studies that only use measures from within the MMPI-2. Otherwise the MMPI-2 is not mentioned as a measure of depression, nor is it mentioned in the article on assessment of anxiety (Antony and Rowa, 2005). The Colligan et al. (1994) norms for the Morey personality disorder scales are cited by Widiger and Samuel (2005) in their section on the evidence-based assessment of personality disorders. Snyder et al. (2005) only mentioned the MMPI-2 and PAI in passing as tests likely to arouse negative reactions in couples seeking help for marital problems. Barlow (2005) comments on both the clinical scales of the MMPI-2 and the content scales as representing a 'traditional model' of psychological assessment. He points out that evidence-based assessment strategies are designed to be integrated with treatment, reflecting our best knowledge of disorders and their etiology. With large amounts of its content reflecting models of psychopathology that are decades old, it is difficult to see how the MMPI-2 can be adapted to more focused and targeted assessment strategies. Certainly it does not appear to be used to any extent in any of the reviewed domains of assessment covered in this issue of *Psychological Assessment* on evidence-based assessment.

CONCLUSION

Modern applications of the MMPI-2 continue to show the pattern that was shown with the original MMPI. That is to say, applications for its original purposes in the assessment of forms of psychopathology in mental health settings continue to be where it can be applied most successfully. Whether a 65-year-old instrument that has 567 items can be accurately described as a modern screening instrument may be arguable, but it is in this role that the MMPI/MMPI-2 functions best. Even then, its utility in practice may be quite limited. One example of this is the study of Ross et al. (2006). They evaluated the role of psychological disturbance (as reflected in selected clinical and content scales from the MMPI-2), severity of head injury, incomplete effort on a neuropsychological memory test, compensation-seeking status, and demographic factors as predictors of neuropsychological test performance. They found that injury severity and compensation seeking were predictive of three out of thirteen outcomes, but demographic factors and incomplete effort predicted all the neuropsychological indices, while the MMPI-2 measures of psychological disturbance predicted eight of thirteen indices. This result shows a degree of utility for the MMPI-2 in assessing psychological problems in a neuropsychological setting, but not evidence for widespread and comprehensive utility.

At the same time, it is clear that the MMPI was developed at a time when pressures for shorter and more focused measures that require less time to administer and score were less prominent than they are currently. Nevertheless, the use of the MMPI-2 to evaluate the presence of psychological distress continues to be of value. Whether shorter screening instruments can perform this role as well is largely an empirical question that has not been addressed to any appreciable extent in the current literature. The MMPI-2 can also reliably distinguish broad types of psychopathology from one another when appropriate methods of evaluating the profiles are used. The evidence as to whether it can make finer distinctions, as between anxiety and depression, or between schizophrenia and bipolar disorder, is much more equivocal. There is promise that the new RC scales will be better able to make such distinctions than the traditional clinical scales, but the relevant studies have yet to appear in print. The issue of the ability of the clinical scales to differentiate disorders has been highlighted by the recent publication of studies that have used the standard error of measurement to determine the confidence intervals for differences between scales. The size of the SEMS suggests that much of the clinical lore on code type differences among the clinical scales is not justified. Whether many years of experience in interpreting profiles can compensate for such factors has never really been addressed, but the literature on clinical judgment (Dawes, 1994), some of which is directly based on the MMPI, suggests that experience alone is not enough.

The fact that recent publications on evidence-based assessment hardly mention the MMPI-2 suggests that applications of the MMPI-2 beyond a simple screening for the presence of psychopathology may be shrinking in number. Certainly the evidence for the utility of the test in many applications outside of its original territory are frequently contradictory and fail to provide strong support for its continued use in those applications. Its length and the comparatively high reading level of the MMPI-2 (Butcher et al., 1989) place it at a disadvantage in comparison to newer and shorter broadband instruments, such as the Personality Assessment Inventory (PAI) (Morey, 1991). The fact that it has been used in many environments, in many languages, and in many cultures does not mean that it should continue to be used in those applications.

To return to Norman's set of issues, there is in general little evidence to suggest that the MMPI-2 has contributed much to our understanding of psychological disturbances. It has generally followed a simple psychiatric diagnostic model, but has not updated that model as psychiatric diagnostic practices have evolved except to add new scales derived from the old set of items. Rather than advancing our theoretical understanding of disorders, continued use of the MMPI-2 has tended to lock practitioners into a dated and now obsolete diagnostic model.

The matters mentioned above suggest that the primacy of the MMPI/MMPI-2 as a psychological test is under threat. Certainly there is now competition with other measures of psychopathology. This may be one factor that contributed to the pressures for the long-overdue revision of the MMPI that resulted in the 1989 publication of the MMPI-2. With the early identification of significant problems with the test, the fact that it continued without change for almost 50 years is remarkable, to say the least. Even though the revision brought aspects of the test into modern days, notably through the provision of a set of contemporary norms, other serious problems with the test were not addressed in order to maintain continuity with the existing body of research.

Consequently, high standards of professional practice are required for modern use of the MMPI-2. Unsupervised test administration, failure to assure the client comprehends the task and has sufficient reading skills to understand the test, and applications of the test into contexts for which it was never intended and which lack empirical evidence of its validity, are all practices that cannot be recommended. At the same time, it is disingenuous on the part of some of the test's promoters to suggest that the MMPI-2 can be readily applied to the entire range of applications in which its use has been suggested. The modern question is not so much whether the MMPI-2 can be applied in such a wide

range of contexts, but what other instrument might be more appropriate for such uses. Another modern question is: How much time is available to administer, score, and interpret this test for this use? These are questions that are likely to weigh more upon the minds of modern practitioners than the simple one of whether or not the MMPI-2 *can* be used in settings outside of those for which it was originally intended.

The MMPI-2 does not represent a highly sophisticated approach to assessment that is based on the state-of-the-art in diagnosis and conceptualizations of psychopathology. Successive introductions of new scales have modernized aspects of the interpretation of the test, at the cost of providing increased opportunities for conflicting scores that need to be reconciled during the overly complex interpretive process. The escalating collection of scales for the MMPI-2, with each successive set providing at best modest increases in incremental validity for some applications, simply multiply the number of potential sources of interpretive conflict.

The future of the MMPI/MMPI-2 thus remains difficult to predict. In its applications by multiple users in many settings, the MMPI/MMPI-2 is no doubt the most popular psychological test of the twentieth century. It is much less certain that it will retain this primacy into the current century, but as Archer (2006) notes, the MMPI/MMPI-2 continues to be a work in progress. The work of Goh (2006) in developing a new set of scales and structural summary from the MMPI-2 item pool suggests that new developments are still possible. Should such developments as this and the RC scales become widely accepted, and should the problematic and complex clinical scales fall from favor, a revised MMPI-3 might continue in widespread use in the coming decades.

REFERENCES

American Psychiatric Association (1952) *Diagnostic and Statistical Manual of Mental*

Disorders. Washington, DC: American Psychiatric Association.

American Psychiatric Association (1980) *Diagnostic and Statistical Manual of Mental Disorders* (3rd edn). Washington, DC: American Psychiatric Association.

American Psychiatric Association (2000) *Diagnostic and Statistical Manual of Mental Disorders* (Text revision, 4th edn). Washington, DC: American Psychiatric Association.

Antony, M.M. and Rowa, K. (2005) 'Evidence-based assessment of anxiety disorders in adults', *Psychological Assessment*, 17(3): 256–66.

Arbisi, P.A. (2006) 'Use of the MMPI-2 in personal injury and disability evaluations', in J.N. Butcher (ed.), *MMPI-2: A Practitioner's Guide*. Washington, DC: American Psychological Association, pp. 407–41.

Arbisi, P.A., Ben-Porath, Y.S. and McNulty, J.L. (2003) 'Empirical correlates of common MMPI-2 two-point codes in male psychiatric inpatients', *Assessment*, 10(3): 237–47.

Arbisi, P.A. and Seime, R.J. (2006) 'Use of the MMPI-2 in medical settings', in J.N. Butcher (ed.), *MMPI-2: A Practitioner's Guide*. Washington, DC: American Psychological Association, pp. 273–99.

Archer, R.P. (2006) 'A perspective on the Restructured Clinical (RC) Scale project', *Journal of Personality Assessment*, 87(2): 179–85.

Bagby, R.M., Marshall, M.B., Basso, R.M. et al. (2005) 'Distinguishing bipolar depression, major depression, and schizophrenia with the MMPI-2 clinical and content scales', *Journal of Personality Assessment*, 84(1): 89–95.

Barlow, D.H. (2004) 'Psychological treatments', *American Psychologist*, 59(9): 869–78.

Barlow, D.H. (2005) 'What's new about evidence-based assessment?', *Psychological Assessment*, 17(3): 308–11.

Benton, R.L. (1949) 'Review of Minnesota Multiphasic Personality Inventory', in O.K. Buros (ed.), *The Third Mental Measurements Yearbook*. Highland Park, NJ: Gryphon Press, pp. 104–7.

Ben-Porath, Y.S., Butcher, J.N. and Graham, J.R. (1991) 'Contribution of the MMPI-2 content scales to the differential diagnosis of schizophrenia and major depression', *Psychological*

Assessment: A Journal of Consulting and Clinical Psychology, 3(4): 634–40.

Ben-Porath, Y.S. and Graham, J.R. (1991) 'Resolutions to interpretive dilemmas created by the Minnesota Multiphasic Personality Inventory 2 (MMPI-2): A reply to Strassberg', *Journal of Psychopathology and Behavioral Assessment*, 13(2): 173–9.

Ben-Porath, Y.S. and Sherwood, N.E. (1993) *The MMPI-2 Content Component Scales: Development, Psychometric Characteristics, and Clinical Application*. Minneapolis, MN: University of Minnesota Press.

Blashfield, R.K. (1998) 'Diagnostic models and systems', in A.S. Bellack and M. Hersen (eds), *Comprehensive Clinical Psychology*. New York: Pergamon, pp. 57–80.

Block, J. (1965) *The Challenge of Response Sets*. New York: Appleton-Century-Crofts.

Burger, G.K. (1991) 'The role of elevation, scatter, and shape in MMPI profiles', *Journal of Personality Assessment*, 56(1): 158–67.

Burisch, M. (1984) 'Approaches to personality inventory construction: A comparison of merits', *American Psychologist*, 39(3): 214–27.

Burisch, M. (1986) 'Methods of personality inventory development: A comparative analysis', in A. Angleitner and J.S. Wiggins (eds), *Personality Assessment via Questionnaires: Current Issues in Theory and Measurement*. Berlin: Springer-Verlag, pp. 109–20.

Butcher, J.N. (2000) 'Revising psychological tests: Lessons learned from the revision of the MMPI', *Psychological Assessment*, 12(3): 263–71.

Butcher, J.N. (2005) *A Beginner's Guide to the MMPI-2* (2nd edn). Washington, DC: American Psychological Association.

Butcher, J.N. (2006) (ed.), *MMPI-2: A Practitioner's Guide*. Washington, DC: American Psychological Association.

Butcher, J.N., Atlis, M.M. and Hahn, J. (2004) 'The Minnesota Multiphasic Personality Inventory-2 (MMPI-2)', in M.J. Hilsenroth and D.L. Segal (eds), *Comprehensive Handbook of Psychological Assessment. Vol. 2. Personality Assessment*. Hoboken, NJ: Wiley, pp. 30–8.

Butcher, J.N., Dahlstrom, W.G., Graham, J.R., Tellegen, A. and Kaemmer, B. (1989) *Manual for Administration and Scoring MMPI-2:*

Minnesota Multiphasic Personality Inventory-2. Minneapolis, MN: University of Minnesota Press.

Butcher, J.N., Graham, J. R. and Ben-Porath, Y.S. (1995) 'Methodological problems and issues in MMPI, MMPI-2, and MMPI-A research', *Psychological Assessment: A Journal of Consulting and Clinical Psychology*, 7(3): 320–9.

Butcher, J.N., Graham, J.R., Kamphuis, J.H. et al. (2006) 'Evaluating MMPI-2 research: Considerations for practitioners', in J.N. Butcher (ed.), *MMPI-2: A Practitioner's Guide*. Washington, DC: American Psychological Association, pp. 15–38.

Butcher, J.N., Graham, J.R., Williams, C.L. and Ben-Porath, Y.S. (1990) *Development and Use of the MMPI-2 Content Scales*. Minneapolis, MN: University of Minnesota Press.

Butcher, J.N. and Tellegen, A. (1978) 'Common methodological problems in MMPI research', *Journal of Consulting and Clinical Psychology*, 46(4): 620–8.

Butcher, J.N. and Williams, C.L. (2000) *Essentials of MMPI-2 and MMPI-A Interpretation* (2nd edn). Minneapolis: University of Minnesota Press.

Caldwell, A.B. (2006) 'Maximal measurement or meaningful measurement: The interpretive challenges of the MMPI-2 Restructured Clinical (RC) scales', *Journal of Personality Assessment*, 87(2): 193–201.

Clark, L.A. (1993) *Schedule for Nonadaptive and Adaptive Personality: Manual for Administration, Scoring, and Interpretation*. Minneapolis, MN: University of Minnesota Press.

Clark, L.A., Watson, D. and Reynolds, S. (1995) 'Diagnosis and classification of psychopathology: Challenges to the current system and future directions', *Annual Review of Psychology*, 46: 121–53.

Colligan, R.C., Morey, L.C. and Offord, K.P. (1994) 'The MMPI/MMPI-2 Personality Disorder Scales: Contemporary norms for adults and adolescents', *Journal of Clinical Psychology*, 50(2): 168–200.

Cronbach, L.J. and Gleser, G. (1953) 'Assessing similarity between profiles', *Psychological Bulletin*, 6(6): 456–73.

Dawes, R.M. (1994) *House of Cards: Psychology and Psychotherapy Built on Myth*. New York: Free Press.

Edwards, A.L. and Heathers, L.B. (1962) 'The first factor of the MMPI: Social desirability or ego strength?', *Journal of Consulting Psychology*, 26(2): 99–100.

Finn, S.E. and Kamphuis, J.H. (2006) 'The MMPI-2 RC scales and restraints to innovation, or "What have they done to my song?"', *Journal of Personality Assessment*, 87(2): 202–10.

Fox, R. (1995) 'The rape of psychotherapy', *Professional Psychology: Research and Practice*, 26(2): 147–55.

Friedman, A.F., Lewak, R., Nichols, D.S. and Webb, J.F. (2001) *Psychological Assessment with the MMPI-2*. Mahwah, NJ: Lawrence Erlbaum Associates.

Goh, H.E. (2006) 'A new structural summary for the MMPI-2 in evaluating personal injury claimants', Unpublished doctoral dissertation, University of Southern Queensland, Toowoomba, Queensland, Australia.

Goldberg, L.R. (1965) 'Diagnosticians versus diagnostic signs: The diagnosis of psychosis versus neurosis from the MMPI', *Psychological Monographs*, 79 (9, Whole No. 602).

Graham, J.R. (2006) *MMPI-2: Assessing Personality and Psychopathology* (4th edn). New York: Oxford University Press.

Green, B.A., Handel, R.W. and Archer, R.P. (2006) 'External correlates of the MMPI-2 Content Component Scales in mental health inpatients', *Assessment*, 13(1): 80–97.

Greene, R.L. (1991) *The MMPI-2/MMPI: An Interpretive Manual*. Boston: Allyn & Bacon.

Greene, R.L. (2000) *The MMPI-2: An Interpretive Manual* (2nd edn). Needham Heights, MA: Allyn & Bacon.

Greene, R.L., Brown, R.C. and Kovan, R.E. (1998) *MMPI-2 Adult Interpretive System Professional Manual*. Odessa, FL: Psychological Assessment Resources.

Hathaway, S.R. (1972) 'Where have we gone wrong? The mystery of the missing progress', in J.N. Butcher (ed.), *Objective Personality Assessment: Changing Perspectives*. New York: Academic Press. pp. 24–43.

Hathaway, S.R. and McKinley, J.C. (1940) 'A multiphasic personality schedule (Minnesota): I. Construction of the schedule', *Journal of Psychology*, 10: 249–54.

Helmes, E. and Reddon, J.R. (1993) 'A perspective on developments in assessing psychopathology: A critical review of the MMPI and MMPI-2', *Psychological Bulletin*, 113(3): 453–71.

Horn, J.L. (1965) 'A rationale and test for the number of factors in factor analysis', *Psychometrika,* 30(2): 179–85.

Hollrah, J.L., Schlottmann, R.S., Scott, A.B. and Brunetti, D.G. (1995) 'Validity of the MMPI subtle items', *Journal of Personality Assessment*, 65(2): 278–99.

Houts, A.C. (2002) 'Discovery, invention, and the expansion of the modern Diagnostic and Statistical Manuals of Mental Disorders', in L.E. Beutler and M.L. Malik (eds), *Rethinking the DSM: A Psychological Perspective*. Washington, DC: American Psychological Association, pp. 17–65.

Hunsley, J. and Mash, E.J. (2005) 'Introduction to the special section on developing guidelines for the Evidence-Based Assessment (EBA) of adult disorders', *Psychological Assessment*, 17(3): 251–5.

Jackson, D.N. (1971) 'The dynamics of structured personality tests: 1971', *Psychological Review*, 78(3): 229–48.

Joiner, T.E. Jr., Walker, R.L., Pettit, J.W., Perez, M. and Cukrowicz, K.C. (2005) 'Evidence-based assessment of depression in adults', *Psychological Assessment*, 17(3): 267–77.

Karon, B. (1995) 'Provision of psychotherapy under managed health care: A growing crisis and national nightmare', *Professional Psychology: Research and Practice*, 26(1): 5–9.

Kline, P. (2000) *Handbook of Psychological Testing* (2nd edn). London: Routledge.

Leonelli, B.T., Chang, C.H., Bock, R.D. and Schilling, S.G. (2000) 'Interpretation of a full-information item-level factor analysis of the MMPI-2: Normative sampling and non-pathognomonic descriptors', *Journal of Personality Assessment*, 74(3): 400–22.

Meehl, P.E. (1946) 'Profile analysis of the Minnesota Multiphasic Personality Inventory in differential diagnosis', *Journal of Applied Psychology*, 30(5): 517–24.

Morey, L.C. (1991) *Personality Assessment Inventory Professional Manual*. Odessa, FL: Psychological Assessment Resources.

Morrison, T.L., Edwards, D.W. and Weissman, H.N. (1994) 'The MMPI and MMPI – 2 as predictors of psychiatric diagnosis in an outpatient sample', *Journal of Personality Assessment*, 62(1): 17–30.

Munley, P.H., Busby, R.M. and Jaynes, G. (1997) 'MMPI-2 findings in schizophrenia and depression', *Psychological Assessment*, 9(4): 508–11.

Munley, P.H. and Germain, J.M. (2000) 'Comparison of two methods of MMPI-2 profile classification', *Psychological Reports*, 87(2): 515–22.

Nichols, D.S. (2001) *Essentials of MMPI-2 Assessment*. New York: Wiley.

Nichols, D.S. (2004) 'Giving the self a voice in MMPI self-report: Jerry Wiggins and the content scales', *Multivariate Behavioral Research*, 39(2): 155–65.

Nichols, D.S. (2006) 'The trials of separating bath water from baby: A review and critique of the MMPI-2 Restructured Clinical scales', *Journal of Personality Assessment*, 87(2): 121–38.

Norman, W.T. (1972) 'Psychometric considerations for a revision of the MMPI', in J.N. Butcher (ed.), *Objective Personality Assessment: Changing Perspectives*. New York: Academic Press, pp. 59–83.

Pancoast, D.L., Archer, R.P. and Gordon, R.A. (1988) 'The MMPI and clinical diagnosis: A comparison of classification system outcomes with discharge diagnoses', *Journal of Personality Assessment*, 52(1): 81–90.

Phelps, R., Eisman, E. and Kohout, J. (1998) 'Psychological practice and managed care: Results of the CAPP survey', *Professional Psychology: Research and Practice*, 29(1): 31–6.

Rogers, R. (2003) 'Forensic use and abuse of psychological tests: Multiscale inventories', *Journal of Psychiatric Practice*, 9: 316–20.

Rogers, R., Sewell, K.W., Harrison, K.S. and Jordan, M.J. (2006) 'The MMPI-2 Restructured Clinical Scales: A paradigmatic shift in scale development', *Journal of Personality Assessment*, 87(2): 139–47.

Rogers, R. and Sewell, K.W. (2006) 'MMPI-2 at the crossroads: Aging technology or radical retrofitting?', *Journal of Personality Assessment*, 87(2): 175–8.

Ross, S.R., Putnam, S.H. and Adams, K.M. (2006) 'Psychological disturbance, incomplete effort, and compensation-seeking status as predictors of neuropsychological test performance in head injury', *Journal of Clinical and Experimental Neuropsychology*, 28(1): 111–25.

Sellbom, M. and Ben-Porath, Y.S. (2005) 'Mapping the MMPI-2 restructured clinical scales onto normal personality traits: evidence of construct validity', *Journal of Personality Assessment*, 85(2): 179–87.

Sellbom, M., Ben-Porath, Y.S. and Graham, J.R. (2006a) 'Correlates of the MMPI-2 Restructured Clinical (RC) scales in a college counseling setting', *Journal of Personality Assessment*, 86(1): 88–99.

Sellbom, M., Ben-Porath, Y.S., Graham, J.R., Arbisi, P.A. and Bagby, R.M. (2005a) 'Susceptibility of the MMPI-2 Clinical, Restructured Clinical (RC), and Content Scales to overreporting and underreporting', *Assessment*, 12(1): 79–85.

Sellbom, M., Ben-Porath, Y.S., McNulty, J.L., Arbisi, P.A. and Graham, J.R. (2006b) 'Elevation differences between MMPI-2 clinical and Restructured Clinical (RC) scales: Frequency, origins, and interpretive implications', *Assessment*, 13(4): 430–41.

Sellbom, M., Graham, J.R. and Schenk, P.W. (2005b) 'Symptom correlates of MMPI-2 scales and code types in a private-practice setting', *Journal of Personality Assessment*, 84(2): 163–71.

Senior, G. and Douglas, L. (2001) 'Misconceptions and misuse of the MMPI-2 in assessing personal injury claimants', *Neurorehabilitation, Special Issue: Controversies in neuropsychology*, 16(4): 203–13.

Simms, L.J. (2006) 'Bridging the divide: Comments on the Restructured Clinical Scales of the MMPI-2', *Journal of Personality Assessment*, 87(2): 211–16.

Simms, L.J., Casillas, A., Clark, L.A., Watson, D. and Doebbeling, B.N. (2005) 'Psychometric evaluation of the restructured clinical scales of the MMPI-2', *Psychological Assessment*, 17(3): 345–58.

Skinner, H.A. (1979) 'A model of psychopathology based on the MMPI', in C.S. Newmark (ed.), *MMPI Clinical and Research Trends*. New York: Praeger.

Skinner, H.A. and Jackson, D.N. (1978) 'A model of psychopathology based on an integration of MMPI actuarial systems', *Journal of Consulting and Clinical Psychology*, 46(2): 231–8.

Snyder, D.K., Heyman, R.E. and Haynes, S.N. (2005) 'Evidence-based approaches to assessing couple distress', *Psychological Assessment*, 17(3): 288–307.

Tellegen, A., Ben-Porath, Y.S., Sellbom, M., Arbisi, P.A, McNulty, J.L. and Graham, J.R. (2006) 'Further evidence on the validity of the MMPI-2 Restructured Clinical (RC) Scales: Addressing questions raised by Rogers et al. and Nichols', *Journal of Personality Assessment*, 87(2): 148–71.

Tellegen, A., Ben-Porath, Y.S., McNulty, J.L., Arbisi, P.A, Graham, J.R. and Kaemmer, B. (2003) *The MMPI-2 Restructured Clinical (RC) scales: Development, Validation, and Interpretation*. Minneapolis, MN: University of Minnesota Press.

Wallace, A. and Liljequist, L. (2005) 'A comparison of the correlational structures and elevation patterns of the MMPI-2 Restructured Clinical (RC) and Clinical Scales', *Assessment*, 12(3): 290–4.

Waller, N.G. (1999) 'Searching for structure in the MMPI', in S.E. Embretson and S. L. Herschberger (eds), *The New Rules of Measurement: What Every Psychologist and Educator Should Know*. Mahwah, NJ: Lawrence Erlbaum Associates, pp. 185–217.

Weed, N.C. (2006) 'Intrascale insouciance, paradigm shifts, and the future of validation research', *Journal of Personality Assessment*, 87(2): 217–22.

Welsh, G.S. (1956) 'Factor dimensions A and R', in G.S. Welsh and W.G. Dahlstrom (eds), *Basic Readings on the MMPI in Psychology and Medicine*. Minneapolis: University of Minnesota Press, pp. 264–81.

Welsh, G.S. and Dahlstrom, W.G. (1956) (eds), *Basic Readings on the MMPI in Psychology and Medicine*. Minneapolis, MN: University of Minnesota Press.

Widiger, T.A. and Samuel, D.B. (2005) 'Evidence-based assessment of personality disorders', *Psychological Assessment*, 17(3): 278–87.

Widiger, T.A. and Sankis, L.M. (2000) 'Adult psychopathology: Issues and controversies', *Annual Review of Psychology*, 51: 377–404.

Wiggins, J.S. (1966) 'Substantive dimensions of self-report in the MMPI item pool', *Psychological Monographs*, 80 (22, Whole No. 630).

Wiggins, J.S. (2003) *Paradigms of Personality Assessment*. New York: Guilford.

29

The Dimensional Assessment of Personality Pathology (DAPP)

W. John Livesley and Roseann M. Larstone

The Dimensional Assessment of Personality Pathology (DAPP) scales were originally developed to delineate and validate the basic structure of personality disorder. Emphasis was placed on developing scales to assess constructs that clinicians have traditionally found useful in understanding personality disorder. Work began shortly after the publication of DSM-III in 1980. Because the DSM-III drew attention to the importance of personality disorder and offered a new approach to description and classification by specifying diagnostic criteria for each condition, the initial plan was to evaluate the DSM-III proposal that personality disorders could be represented by 11 discrete diagnoses. Systematic definitions of each disorder were developed through an extensive review of the clinical literature. This resulted in lengthy lists of clinical features. These were organized into trait descriptions of each disorder using clinical judgments and rational methods. This process eventuated in a list of 100 traits. Self-report scales were developed to assess these traits. When the expectation that multivariate studies would reveal factors that resembled DSM diagnostic constructs

was not fulfilled, attention focused on explicating and measuring the basic or primary trait structure of personality disorder and establishing the higher-order or secondary structure underlying these traits. Unlike most measures of normal personality, the DAPP emphasizes primary traits as the major focus of assessment because this level is most appropriate for clinical and research purposes. For example, most clinical interventions, including medication, seek to change or modulate behaviors associated with primary traits rather changing global personality disorder or secondary traits.

OVERVIEW OF DAPP MEASURES

The DAPP-Basic Questionnaire (DAPP-BQ) consists of 18 factor-based scales: affective lability, anxiousness, callousness, cognitive dysregulation, compulsivity, conduct problems, identity problems, insecure attachment, intimacy problems, narcissism, oppositionality, rejection, restricted expression, self-harm, social avoidance, stimulus seeking, submissiveness, and suspiciousness (see Table 29.1). A social desirability scale is included. The 18 scales are organized into four higher-order factors labeled emotional dysregulation, inhibitedness, dissocial behavior, and compulsivity, although not all primary traits are related to a secondary domain. These factors resemble clinical diagnoses of borderline, schizoid/avoidant, antisocial, and obsessive-compulsive personality disorders, and the five-factor domains of neuroticism, introversion, agreeableness, and conscientiousness, respectively.

Since 18 scales were derived from factor analyses of an initial set of 100 traits, each primary trait consists of several sub-traits. The number of sub-traits forming each scale ranges from two to seven, so that a total of 69 sub-traits define the 18 basic dimensions. Sub-traits are assessed by a second self-report measure – the DAPP-Differential Questionnaire (DAPP-DQ). The items forming the DAPP-BQ are a subset of the DAPP-DQ items. Thus the DAPP system has three levels of construct – higher-order factors or secondary traits, basic or primary traits, and sub-traits – whereas most personality measures typically incorporate two levels, higher-order domains and their facets. This permits a detailed analysis of trait structure that has been particularly useful in exploring the genetic architecture of personality disorder.

The development of the DAPP was influenced by two related ideas. First, it was assumed that the development and evaluation of a classification of mental disorders, especially personality disorders, is best approached by applying the methods used to construct a multi-scale psychological test (Blashfield and Livesley, 1991). With this approach, disorders are assumed to be equivalent to scales and diagnostic criteria equivalent to test items. Second, this assumption implies that a classification of personality disorder is best developed through the systematic application of the construct validation approach to test construction described by Loevinger (1957) and applied to psychiatric classification by Skinner (1981, 1986; Livesley and Jackson, 1992).

Table 29.1   DAPP primary traits and sub-traits

Affective lability:	Labile anger, affective over-reactivity, affective lability, irritability, generalized hypersensitivity
Anxiousness:	Indecisiveness, trait anxiety, rumination, guilt proneness
Callousness:	Lack of empathy, exploitation, egocentrism, sadism, contemptuousness, interpersonal irresponsibility, remorselessness
Cognitive dysregulation:	Depersonalization or derealization, schizotypal cognition, brief stress psychosis
Compulsivity:	Orderliness, conscientiousness, precision
Conduct problems:	Interpersonal violence, addictive behavior, juvenile antisocial behavior, failure to adopt social norms
Identity problems:	Chronic feelings of emptiness and boredom, labile self-concept, pessimism, anhedonia
Insecure attachment:	Feared loss, secure base, proximity seeking, separation protest, intolerance of aloneness
Intimacy problems:	Avoidant attachment, desire for improved attachment relationships, inhibited sexuality
Narcissism:	Need for approval, attention-seeking, need for adulation, grandiosity
Oppositionality:	Passivity, oppositional, lack of organization
Rejection:	Dominance, rigid cognitive style, interpersonal hostility, judgmental
Restricted expression:	Restricted affective expression, restricted expression of angry affects, restricted expression of positive affects, reluctant self-disclosure, self-reliance
Self-harm:	Ideas of self-harm, self-damaging acts
Social avoidance:	Low affiliation, fearful of interpersonal hurt, defective social skills, desire for improved affiliative relationships, social apprehensiveness
Stimulus seeking:	Recklessness, impulsivity, sensation seeking
Submissiveness:	Need for advice and reassurance, suggestibility, submissiveness
Suspiciousness:	Suspiciousness, hypervigilance

As conceptualized by Loevinger, construct validity has three components (Livesley and Schroeder, 1990). First, the substantive component of construct validity requires the construction of a theoretical taxonomy that carefully defines diagnostic constructs and items. Second, the structural component is established by demonstrating that relationships among diagnostic constructs and items are congruent with the structure postulated by the theoretical taxonomy. Third, the external component requires evidence that diagnostic constructs are systematically related to external criteria such as other measures and significant outcome and etiological variables. These components form an iterative process in which the postulated theoretical structure is systematically tested and revised based on empirical findings leading to incremental increases in validity.

CONSTRUCTING A THEORETICAL TAXONOMY

The theoretical taxonomy was initially organized around the eleven disorders proposed by the DSM-III. However, DSM-III diagnostic criteria were not used as diagnostic items because there are several problems with the DSM-III from a measurement perspective that remain unresolved in subsequent editions. First, the classification was arbitrary in terms of diagnoses included and the diagnostic criteria proposed for each disorder. Criteria were developed on the basis of an informal sampling of clinical opinion rather than systematic definitions of diagnoses and a domain sampling approach. Second, many criteria were poorly defined. In some cases, the criteria for different disorders were worded differently but actually referred to the same behavior, leading to content overlap across disorders. For example, it was not clear how 'incessant drawing attention to oneself' (DSM-III histrionic personality disorder) differed from 'exhibitionism' (DSM-III narcissistic personality disorder).

Third, most criteria sets contained only a handful of the terms used in the clinical literature to describe a given disorder and there was no reason to believe that the items selected represented all features of the disorder. This creates an immediate threat to construct validity due to the potential for over-representing some features, under-sampling other aspects, or including irrelevant items (see Cook and Campbell, 1979; Messick, 1980, 1988; Livesley and Jackson, 1992). For these reasons, more systematic definitions of each disorder were developed using a modification of the lexical hypothesis used to explicate the structure of normal personality (Saucier and Goldberg, 1996).

The lexical hypothesis assumes that the natural language of personality is a repository of wisdom about personality that embodies distinctions that have important implications for adaptation. Similarly, it was assumed that accumulated clinical wisdom in the form of ideas or concepts that clinicians have traditionally found useful in describing and explaining personality pathology forms the most appropriate starting point for a theoretical taxonomy. Although this knowledge is largely informally organized, explicit accounts are found in the general clinical literature. This was content analyzed to identify the terms and phrases used to describe each disorder. The process began by examining Millon (1981), Lion (1981), Valliant and Perry (1980), and the DSM-III, and subsequently expanded to the sources cited in these texts and additional references identified through computerized literature searches. This eventuated in lists of between 57 and 83 items for each disorder.

Next, these lists were organized by identifying the key features of each disorder based on Rosch's (1978) concept of prototypical categorization. Prototypical categories are organized around prototypical examples, the best examples of the concept, with less prototypical examples forming a continuum away from these central cases. With personality disorder, both cases and descriptive items may be considered to fall along a gradient of prototypicality (Livesley, 1985a, 1985b). For example, the term 'socially withdrawn' is more prototypical of schizoid personality disorder than the term 'eccentric'. Prototypes were developed for each DSM-III disorder by asking samples of psychiatrists selected randomly from the membership lists of the Canadian and American Psychiatric Associations to rate the prototypicality of items for each diagnosis. The results indicated substantial agreement on the most prototypical features of each disorder (Livesley, 1986). These ratings were then used to rank items according to their prototypicality.

A review of the resulting prototypes indicated that they contained substantial redundancy because many features seemed to refer to the same characteristic. For example, items that are highly prototypical of paranoid personality disorder such as 'mistrustful', 'searches for hidden meanings', and 'sees the world as hostile and opposed to him/her' could all be considered aspects of 'suspiciousness'. Consequently, the prototype of each disorder was reduced to fewer items by grouping together items referring to the same trait. Traits were then defined based on these items with the greatest weight given to items with the highest prototypicality ratings. This procedure was followed for all 11 DSM-III personality disorders. Definitions of each trait were subsequently reviewed across all disorders to ensure that definitions were distinctive. This procedure as applied to borderline personality disorder is illustrated in Table 29.2.

This method established a theoretical taxonomy in which each DSM-III personality disorder was defined by a set of traits. Essentially, disorders were conceptualized as categories of trait dimensions (Livesley et al., 1985). Initially, the 11 disorders of DSM-III were defined by 79 traits. This increased to 100 traits as a result of attempts to construct internally consistent scales. These traits could be considered to constitute a lexicon of personality pathology derived from clinical concepts. The important question was whether the DSM-III assumption that the features of personality disorder are organized into 11 diagnoses was supported empirically. It was assumed that preliminary support for the taxonomy would be provided by evidence that internally consistent and distinct scales can be constructed to assess each dimension and that dimensions are organized into the 11 diagnoses proposed by DSM-III.

SCALE CONSTRUCTION

Consistent with the construct validation framework, scale construction followed the structured approach proposed by Jackson (1971). This approach emphasizes the importance of selecting items for conformity to theoretical definitions of constructs and the suppression of response biases.

Item development

Following the systematic definition of traits based on the prototypicality ratings, each trait was divided into facets or sub-traits based on the descriptive features used in the definition. Items were selected to assess each sub-trait and a rigorous process of item development was used to foster convergent and discriminant validity. Items were culled from multiple sources including literature review, expert judgment, and interviews with personality-disordered patients. An initial set of approximately 50 items per trait was reduced to 30 items by eliminating those that: (a) failed to conform to the definition of the dimension; (b) referred to several behaviors; or (c) were judged to be at the extremes of social desirability. Typical items include: social apprehensiveness ('People make me feel nervous'); submissiveness ('I am not very good at being assertive with others'); restricted affective expression ('I do not often show my feelings'); and impulsivity ('I usually act first and think about the consequences later'). The response format adopted was to rate items on

Table 29.2   Dimensions used to classify highly prototypical traits for borderline personality disorder

Affective lability	Affect changes are sudden, frequent, and sustained. Feels overwhelmed by intense affects
Traits	Frequently overwhelmed by intense affect, either hostility or depression
Separation protest	Reacts strongly to all anticipated, threatened, or actual separation from attachment figures
Traits	Reacts intensely to separation from others; fears and reacts strongly to actual or threatened abandonment
Brief stress psychosis	Transient psychotic symptoms which are stress-related; impaired reality testing under stress
Traits	Brief psychotic episodes during periods of extreme stress; shows impaired reality testing under stress
Egocentrism	Emphasizes own needs in regard of the needs of others; perceptions dominated by own point of view, interests, and concerns
Traits	Egocentric; selfish; puts self first; demanding
Exploitation	Contrives to control or use others for own ends; sees others as easily manipulated
Traits	Manipulative; exploitative
Impulsivity	Does things suddenly on the basis of an impulse or whim with little regard for the consequences
Traits	Impulsive; disregard for the consequences of his/her own actions; failure to learn from experiences; self-defeating cycle of behavior; lacks judgment and foresight
Interpersonal lability	Forms unstable relationships; feelings and attitudes toward others change rapidly; conflicting emotions of love, anger, and guilt felt toward close others; relationships alternate between extremes of idealization and devaluation
Traits	Unstable personal relationships
Labile anger	Rapid and frequent expression of intense anger
Traits	Unable to control anger; intense, irrational, inappropriate anger
Labile self-concept	Unclear self-concept; experiences self as different in different circumstances; lacks clarity regarding goals and beliefs; fears loss of self
Traits	Shows marked disturbance of self-identity; confusion about self-concept
Addictive behaviors	Habitual use of drugs; including alcohol
Traits	Substance abuse
Self-damaging acts	Attempts to hurt or mutilate self; attempts suicide
Traits	Mutilates self
Chronic feelings of emptiness	Troubled by feelings of emptiness; feels bored and uninterested regardless of what is happening
Traits	Feels empty
Intolerance of aloneness	Uncomfortable when alone even for brief periods; seeks to be continuously in the company of other people
Traits	Frequently feels lonely
Ideas of self-harm	Recurrent thoughts of physically hurting self; frequently thinks about suicide
Traits	Frequently threatens self-harm; frequently talks of suicide

From: Livesley and Schroeder (1991)

a five-point scale ranging from 'very unlike me' to 'very like me'. Ratings were used rather than a true/false format because they tend to yield higher item variance and greater scale reliability.

Preliminary psychometric analyses

Preliminary analyses of the psychometric properties of scales were based on data obtained by mailing questionnaires to a general population sample selected randomly from a street directory. The study was designed to provide approximately 100 responses per scale which was considered adequate for psychometric purposes. Responses were received from 3,256 subjects. Each subject received items for only three personality scales, two measures of social desirability – a scale used to develop the Personality Research Form and the Differential Personality Inventory (Jackson, 1984) – and the Marlowe-Crowne Scale (Crowne and Marlowe, 1960). An attempt was also made to identify items that were strongly associated with general psychiatric symptoms by including the short version of the General Health Questionnaire (Goldberg, 1972).

Coefficient alpha ranged from 0.98 (secure base) to 0.64 (need for adulation). Item analysis involved correlating each item with its own scale score (minus that item), each social desirability scale, and the symptom measure. Items were eliminated if they: (1) correlated less than 0.3 with their own scale; (2) had a highly skewed response pattern defined as less than 5% of endorsements on two adjacent rating points; (3) correlated higher with a desirability scale than with their own scale; (4) had a correlation greater than 0.5 with a social desirability scale; (5) a higher correlation with the symptom measure than with their own scale; and (6) correlated more than 0.5 with the symptom scale. Based on these analyses, scales were reduced to 18–20 items.

The construction of internally consistent scales necessitated revisions to the trait component of the theoretical taxonomy. Some constructs were combined because it was not possible to identify behaviors that discriminated between them. Scales for other constructs were subdivided or redefined because of difficulty establishing internally consistent item sets. The procedure followed was to examine scales with an alpha coefficient of less than 0.80 with principal components analysis. For some scales, these analyses indicated that scales contained several distinct sets of items. In these cases, scales were divided and new items developed if needed. For example, the theoretical taxonomy originally had provision for a scale labeled 'control' designed to assess the need to control situations and feelings. Factor analysis suggested two distinct sets of items: need to exercise control over interpersonal situations and fear of losing emotional control. This led to the construction of two new scales to represent these behaviors. New scales were also developed to accommodate new diagnostic criteria included in DSM-III-R which was

published when this work was in progress. Together these factors increased the number of dimensions from 79 to 100.

The next step was to cross-validate the internal consistency of the revised scales and construct distinctive scales by eliminating items that correlated higher with irrelevant scales than the scale for which they were developed. This required subjects to endorse items for all scales (1,943 items). A second, heterogeneous general population sample ($n = 110$; 62 women) was obtained. The results indicated that scales cross-validated satisfactorily; coefficient alpha was above 0.90 for 22 scales, 0.80 to 0.89 for 67 scales, 0.70 to 0.79 for 6 scales, and 0.68 for 1 scale. These data were used to construct scales with 16 items.

STRUCTURE OF PERSONALITY DISORDER

A personality measure with a large number of scales inevitably contains considerable redundancy. Hence the next step in test construction was to examine the structure underlying the 100 scales to identify a comprehensive set of primary traits.

Primary structure

The 16-item-per-scale questionnaire was administered to a heterogeneous sample of 274 subjects (125 men, 149 women: mean age 29.7 years, range 17–70 years; Livesley et al., 1989). Internal consistency of the final scales was satisfactory: coefficient alpha was above 0.90 for 31 scales, between 0.80 and 0.89 for 64 scales, and between 0.72 and 0.79 for 5 scales. The structure underlying the 100 scales was examined using principal components analysis. Decomposition of the correlation matrix yielded 15 eigenvalues greater than unity. Because a scree plot of eigenvalues did not reveal the number of components to retain, several solutions were evaluated for simple structure and theoretical meaningfulness. An oblique rotation was used because it would predictably be more interpretable than an orthogonal solution and other studies demonstrated high correlations between personality diagnoses and features (Kass et al., 1985; Livesley and Jackson, 1986).

A 15-component, obliquely rotated solution accounting for 75.1% of the total variance appeared to have the greatest theoretical meaning. Solutions with fewer than 15 components contained a greater degree of factorial complexity and solutions with more components yielded components with only one salient loading. The 15 components were labeled: affective reactivity, rejection, social apprehensiveness, compulsive behaviors, stimulus seeking, insecure attachment, diffidence (later relabeled 'submissiveness'), intimacy problems, interpersonal disesteem (later relabeled 'callousness'), narcissism, conduct problems, restricted expression, cognitive distortion, identity disturbance, and obsessionality.

The next step was to repeat this study on a clinical sample to determine similarity of factor structure across clinical and non-clinical samples. As Eysenck (1987) pointed out, this is a critical test of the categorical model for classifying personality disorder: evidence of similar structure across the two samples constitutes strong support for a dimensional representation of personality disorder. Responses from a sample of 158 patients with a primary diagnosis of personality disorder yielded 19 eigenvalues greater than unity (Livesley et al., 1992). However, after examining different solutions, a 15-component solution accounting for 74.4% of the variance was adopted because solutions with more components were less readily interpretable and yielded components with a single salient loading. Examination of the distribution of scores on all scales for the two samples yielded no evidence of the discontinuity predicted by the categorical model (Livesley et al., 1992). Comparison of the two solutions indicated considerable similarity (see Table 29.3).

These studies offered little support for the diagnostic constructs included in DSM-III and DSM-III-R. Moreover, the similarity in factor structure across the new samples did not support the implicit assumption underlying the DSM that there is a clear distinction between normal personality and personality disorder. Together these findings suggested that considerable revisions were needed to both the structure and content of the theoretical taxonomy.

Defining primary traits

Given the strong evidence in support of a dimensional model of personality disorder, the categorical model was replaced and the revised system was organized around a set of dimensional diagnostic constructs based on factors identified in the empirical analyses. In the process, a self-report measure – the DAPP-BQ – was constructed. Although 15 components were extracted from the correlational matrices for the general population, clinical, and combined samples, 18 scales

Table 29.3   Congruence coefficients for the 15-component solution of principal components analysis for clinical and general population samples

Factor	Congruence coefficients	Off-diagonal element	
		Highest	Mean
1	0.98	−0.57	0.24
2	0.97	0.61	0.24
3	0.93	−0.54	0.17
4	0.88	−0.31	0.09
5	0.93	0.61	0.22
6	0.68	0.26	0.12
7	0.94	−0.57	0.20
8	0.77	0.25	0.09
9	0.62	0.20	0.09
10	0.80	−0.31	0.14
11	0.83	−0.22	0.14
12	0.65	−0.16	0.07
13	0.82	−0.44	0.15
14	0.86	0.39	0.12
15	0.67	0.20	0.01

From: Livesley et al. (1992)

were developed for several reasons. First, many scales were salient on the first component which appeared to represent general distress and resemble neuroticism (Eysenck and Eysenck, 1985) or negative affectivity (Watson and Clark, 1984). The factor combined traits representing fearfulness and emotional distress with those representing self or identity problems. This was considered a problem because these behaviors have different clinical and theoretical implications. To reduce possible confusion, the first factor was divided into two separate scales, labeled 'anxiousness' and 'identity problems'. Second, suspiciousness was retained as a separate scale although it was not salient on any component because of the clinical significance of this trait. Finally, a scale of self-harm was developed for use in clinical assessment because of the practical importance of these behaviors although the scale does not actually represent a personality trait and scales to assess these behaviors did not load in a consistent way in the factor analyses. These changes resulted in a new theoretical structure consisting of 18 basic or primary traits and the 69 specific traits that define them (see Table 29.1).

The extent to which this structure could be confirmed empirically in the two samples was evaluated using a procrustes rotation (Helmes and Jackson, 1994). Only two dimensions, suspiciousness and intimacy problems, failed to show strong convergence across samples (see Table 29.4). This confirmed the hypothesis that the basic scales are defined and organized in the same way in samples of patients with personality disorder and the general population.

Secondary structure

The next step in explicating the structure of personality disorder traits was to investigate the higher-order structure underlying the 18 basic traits. The DAPP-BQ was administered to 939 general population subjects, 656 patients with a primary diagnosis of

Table 29.4 Convergent Factor Structure of the DAPP-BQ in Normal and Clinical Samples

Factor	DAPP scale	Congruence coefficient
I	Affective lability	0.971
II	Anxiousness	0.923
III	Cognitive distortion	0.963
IV	Compulsivity	0.979
V	Conduct problems	0.954
VI	Submissiveness	0.905
VII	Identity problems	0.963
VIII	Insecure attachment	0.901
IX	Callousness	0.986
X	Intimacy problems	0.747
XI	Narcissism	0.970
XII	Passive opposition	0.966
XIII	Rejection	0.956
XIV	Restricted expression	0.980
XV	Self-harm	0.911
XVI	Social avoidance	0.979
XVII	Stimulus seeking	0.972
XVIII	Suspiciousness	0.832

Based on Helmes and Jackson (1994)

personality disorder, and 686 twin pairs (Livesley et al., 1998). Principal components analysis yielded four components labeled emotional dysregulation, dissocial behavior, inhibitedness, and compulsivity that were remarkably similar across the three samples: congruence coefficients ranged from 0.94 to 0.99. The four-component structure of the DAPP-BQ has cross-cultural stability being reported in studies from North America (Livesley et al., 1998), Germany (Pukrop et al., 2001), China (Zheng et al., 2002) Holland (van Kampen, 2002), and Spain (Gutiérrez-Zotes et al., in press) (see Table 29.5).

The robustness of the four-factor structure across cultures suggests a universal structure to personality disorder traits. This in turn raises the possibility that this structure reflects the way personality is organized at a biological level. This conjecture is supported by evidence that the four-factor secondary structure reflects the genetic architecture of personality disorder. Multivariate genetic analyses (Carey and DiLalla, 1994) were used to explicate genetic contributions to the covariance structure underlying the 18 traits. The degree to which genetic and environmental effects

Table 29.5   Higher-order structure of the DAPP-BQ in different cultures

DAPP-BQ Scales	Gutiérrez-Zotes et al. (in press) Factors				Zheng et al. (2002) Factors			
	I	II	III	IV	I	II	III	IV
1. Submissiveness	0.92				0.86			
2. Cognitive distortion	0.79				0.71			
3. Identity problems	0.80				0.67			
4. Affective lability	0.71				0.52			
5. Stimulus seeking			0.74			0.52		−0.40
6. Compulsivity				0.93			0.91	
7. Restricted expression		0.77					0.70	
8. Callousness			0.78			0.87		
9. Oppositionality	0.68				0.79			
10. Intimacy problems		0.84						
11. Rejection			0.74			0.53	0.44	
12. Anxiousness					0.83			
13. Conduct problems			0.84			0.80		
14. Suspiciousness	0.41			0.40		0.58		
15. Social avoidance	0.75				0.75			
16. Narcissism	0.50		0.43					−0.43
17. Insecure attachment	0.68				0.65			−0.44

DAPP-BQ Scales	Livesley et al. (1998) Factors				Pukrop et al. (2001) Factors				van Kampen (2002) Factors			
	I	II	III	IV	I	II	III	IV	I	II	III	IV
1. Submissiveness	0.84				0.83				0.80			
2. Cognitive distortion	0.75				0.66				0.83			
3. Identity problems	0.74				0.75				0.84			
4. Affective lability	0.78				0.53	0.62			0.82			
5. Stimulus seeking		0.67				0.71			0.49	0.57		−0.43
6. Compulsivity			0.88				0.88					0.78
7. Restricted expression			0.74		0.52		0.53		0.67			
8. Callousness		0.74				0.72				0.83		
9. Oppositionality	0.69			−0.40	0.73				0.78	0.45		
10. Intimacy problems			0.86				0.84				0.86	
11. Rejection		0.82				0.71				0.80		
12. Anxiousness	0.89				0.86				0.90			
13. Conduct problems		0.76				0.76				0.75		
14. Suspiciousness		0.46			0.62				0.72	0.57		
15. Social avoidance	0.69				0.82				0.82			
16. Narcissism	0.60				0.43	0.55			0.62	0.57		
17. Insecure attachment	0.81				0.53		−0.46		0.69			

on two variables are correlated is indexed by genetic and environmental correlation coefficients estimated from twin data. Genetic and environmental correlation or covariance matrices may then be factored to provide information about the structures underlying these influences (Crawford and DeFries, 1978; Loehlin and Vandenberg, 1968). The factors extracted from matrices of phenotypic, genetic, and environmental correlations computed among the 18 traits were highly congruent, indicating that the four-factor phenotypic structure closely corresponds to genetic structure as does the structure of non-shared environmental effects (Livesley et al., 1998). Congruence coefficients computed between genetic and phenotypic factors derived from data from a sample of twin pairs yielded values of 0.97, 0.97, 0.98, and 0.95 for emotional dysregulation, dissocial, inhibition, and compulsivity, respectively. Those between phenotypic and non-shared environmental factors were 0.99, 0.96, 0.99, and 0.96, respectively. These observations are consistent with other studies showing that the structure of genetic and environmental influences corresponds to phenotypic structure (Plomin et al., 1990; Loehlin, 1989; Jang et al., 2002).

Most trait models of personality assume that traits are hierarchically organized with a few higher-order or secondary domains subdividing into multiple facet or primary traits. Typically each secondary domain is assumed to subdivide in the same number of facets, nine in the case of the Eysenck model (Eysenck and Eysenck, 1985) and six with the five-factor model (Costa and McCrae, 1992) and each facet trait is assumed to be part of a higher-order domain. With the DAPP model, the hierarchy is assumed to be incomplete so that some traits are not assigned to a secondary domain. Moreover, secondary domains differ in breadth. The emotional dysregulation domain, for example, includes substantially more primary traits than the dissocial or inhibitedness domains.

RELATIONSHIP WITH OTHER MODELS OF NORMAL AND DISORDERED PERSONALITY

The results of studies discussed thus far offer little support for the DSM-IV model of personality disorder. Confidence in the alternative dimensional representation of personality disorder emerging from this work would be strengthened by evidence of convergence between the DAPP and other measures of personality disorder traits. Similarly, the conclusion that individual differences in personality disorder are continuous with normal personality variation and that the same constructs may be used to represent normal and disordered personality would be supported by evidence

of convergence with commonly used measures of normal personality.

Personality disorder

The four-factor structure of personality disorder as assessed with the DAPP-BQ is consistent with other studies using different measures and methods of measurement (Mulder and Joyce, 1997; Trull and Durrett, 2005). Mulder and Joyce referred to these factors as the four As: asthenic, asocial, antisocial, and anankastic. This structure first emerged in clinical studies in the 1970s that examined the factor structure underlying traits selected to represent personality disorder (Presly and Walton, 1973; Tyrer and Alexander, 1979). Since then, the structure has been confirmed by studies based on DSM personality disorder criteria (Austin and Deary, 2000; Kass et al., 1985; Mulder and Joyce, 1997) and shown to be robust across different methods of measurement including structured interviews (Tyrer and Alexander, 1979; Austin and Deary, 2000) and self-report (Livesley et al., 1998).

Besides agreement on secondary structure, good agreement also exists across studies on the primary traits of personality disorder (Harkness, 1992). For example, conceptual comparisons between the DAPP-BQ and the only other measure specifically designed to assess personality disorder traits (as opposed to disorders), the Schedule for Nonadaptive and Adaptive Personality (SNAP) (Clark, 1993a), showed high convergence (Clark and Livesley, 1994, 2002; Clark et al., 1996). Although the SNAP has only 15 scales, neither measure incorporates content not included in the other. Differences in number of scales were due to some traits being divided into several scales by the other approach. For example, the SNAP dependency scale is represented in the DAPP by two scales, submissiveness and insecure attachment. Empirical comparison of the two measures confirmed similarities: 22 of the 24 predicted convergent correlations were above 0.40, the average correlation was 0.53, and the average discriminant correlation was 0.22. This degree of convergence is encouraging given the different origins of these measures. The SNAP emerged from a cluster analysis of clinicians' ratings of DSM-III diagnostic criteria (Clark, 1990). This resulted in 22 clusters which were reduced to 15 scales following an iterative series of analyses.

Normal personality

The similarity of factor structure across clinical and non-clinical samples suggests that DAPP dimensions are clinical variants of normal personality traits and that individual differences in personality disorder may be represented by the same constructs used to describe normal personality. This is borne out by the systematic relationships observed between the DAPP-BQ and normal personality. The four secondary dimensions show some correspondence with the five-factor domains of neuroticism, introversion, (dis)agreeableness, and conscientiousness (Widiger, 1998; Trull and Durrett, 2005). The most notable divergence is the failure to find a factor resembling openness in analyses based on clinical concepts of personality disorder (Clark, 1993b). Convergence between the DAPP model and the five-factor approach was explored by administering the DAPP-BQ and NEO-PI to a sample of 300 subjects (Schroeder et al., 1992). Principal components analysis of the 18 scales and five NEO-PI domains yielded five factors (see Table 29.6). The first factor was defined by neuroticism and eight DAPP scales that largely formed the emotional dysregulation factor. The second factor consisted of extraversion and DAPP-BQ stimulus seeking. The third factor seemed to represent the introversion–extraversion domain being defined by NEO-PI extraversion and agreeableness and DAPP restricted expression of affects (negative loading). The fourth factor consisted of agreeableness and negative loadings of DAPP scales related to dissocial or psychopathic

features along with suspiciousness. The final factor was defined by conscientiousness and compulsivity. The phenotypic relationship between the five factors appears to reflect genetic continuity between normal and disordered personality traits. A behavioral genetic analysis indicated that the genetic and non-shared environmental factors shared by the DAPP-BQ and NEO-FFI accounted for the significant phenotypic correlations between them and that the magnitude of the genetic correlations between scales from the two instruments were often higher than the corresponding environmental or phenotypic correlations (Jang and Livesley, 1999).

Although the five-factor model explains the domain of personality disorder traits reasonably well, the DAPP-BQ and NEO-PI-R are not equivalent measures. DAPP-BQ scales are more directly related to clinical concepts and assess clinically important traits such as insecure attachment, cognitive dysregulation, suspiciousness, and self-harm that are poorly represented in the NEO-PI-R (Schroeder et al., 1992). This suggests caution in accepting the suggestion that the five-factor model provides an integrating framework for classifying and studying personality disorder. As Davis and Millon (1995) noted, there is only partial overlap between the domains of normal and disordered personality. The primary or facet structure of the five-factor model in particular needs further development before it captures clinical concepts adequately (Livesley, 2001).

The secondary structure of personality disorder is also consistent with other models of normal personality, especially the three-factor structure proposed by Eysenck (1987). Principal components analysis of the EPQ-R, NEO-PI-R, and DAPP-BQ higher-order factors identified four factors related to neuroticism, psychopathic traits, introversion, and compulsivity (Larstone et al., 2002; see Table 29.7).

Similarly, a combined analysis of the DAPP-BQ and the Zuckerman–Kuhlman Personality Questionnaire yielded a five-factor structure in which four factors resembled the four secondary components of the DAPP with

Table 29.6   A combined analysis of the NEO-PI five-factor model of normal personality traits and the DAPP-BQ sixteen-factor model of personality disorders

	Factors				
	1	2	3	4	5
NEO-PI scales					
Neuroticism	0.84	−0.21	0.02	−0.16	−0.13
Extraversion	−0.18	0.72	−0.42	−0.05	0.08
Openness	−0.05	0.06	−0.41	0.09	−0.16
Agreeableness	−0.06	0.11	−0.09	0.86	0.01
Conscientiousness	−0.14	0.04	−0.05	0.08	0.94
DAPP-BQ scales					
Anxiousness	0.83	−0.19	0.09	−0.11	0.06
Affective lability	0.68	−0.01	−0.17	−0.35	0.00
Diffidence	0.64	0.08	0.32	0.25	−0.07
Insecure attachment	0.61	0.22	−0.02	−0.10	0.04
Social avoidance	0.59	−0.15	0.42	−0.07	−0.09
Identity problems	0.58	−0.04	0.53	−0.14	−0.11
Narcissism	0.58	0.32	0.00	−0.29	−0.06
Stimulus seeking	−0.01	0.64	−0.03	−0.27	0.00
Restricted expression	0.15	0.01	0.81	0.03	−0.03
Intimacy problems	−0.11	−0.16	0.58	−0.12	−0.08
Callousness	0.11	0.09	0.19	−0.76	0.01
Rejection	0.11	0.32	−0.03	−0.62	0.05
Suspiciousness	0.30	0.10	0.32	−0.58	0.13
Conduct problems	0.12	0.16	−0.08	−0.48	−0.18
Compulsivity	0.12	0.06	0.13	−0.05	0.72
Oppositionality	0.51	0.09	0.22	−0.06	−0.55

From: Schroeder et al. (1992)

Table 29.7   Varimax rotated principal components analysis of the EPQ-R scales, NEO-PI-R domain scales, and the DAPP-BQ higher-order dimensions

	Factors			
Measures and scales	1	2	3	4
EPQ-R				
Psychoticism	−0.06	−0.04	0.70	−0.24
Extraversion	−0.15	0.86	0.07	0.05
Neuroticism	0.71	−0.17	0.23	0.07
Lie	−0.21	−0.07	−0.56	0.14
NEO-PI-R				
Neuroticism	0.81	−0.30	0.12	−0.17
Extraversion	−0.35	0.82	0.09	−0.05
Openness	−0.50	−0.22	0.37	−0.20
Agreeableness	−0.65	0.20	−0.49	−0.19
Conscientiousness	−0.32	0.11	0.24	0.82
DAPP-BQ				
Emotional dysregulation	0.84	−0.19	0.04	−0.28
Dissocial behaviour	0.22	0.37	0.72	0.14
Inhibition	0.07	−0.78	−0.01	−0.07
Compulsivity	0.12	−0.01	−0.01	0.93

From: Larstone et al. (2002)

the fifth factor being defined by ZKPQ activity and DAPP conduct problems, self-harm, and compulsivity (Wang et al., 2004; see Table 29.8).

The DAPP-BQ is potentially a useful way to assess disordered personality for clinical and research purposes. The focus on primary traits as the basic descriptive unit provides a differentiated evaluation of the domain of personality disorder. This is consistent with current trends in clinical intervention that increasingly focus on specific features of personality pathology rather than global diagnoses. Because the DAPP was derived from clinical concepts, scales are described by concepts used by clinicians in everyday practice. This means that the instrument provides clinicians with an evaluation that can readily be translated into clinical interventions. Pharmacological interventions typically address clusters of symptoms and behaviors (Soloff, 2000) that are closely related to DAPP-BQ scales of anxiousness, affective lability, and cognitive dysregulation. Similarly, scales reference behaviors such as anxiousness, affective lability, submissiveness, insecure attachment, and self-harm, which are common targets for psychotherapeutic strategies. In many cases, specific interventions are available to treat behaviors represented by these traits, such as assertiveness training for problems with the low assertiveness component of submissiveness or anxiety management to deal with high levels of anxiousness.

The merits of a detailed assessment of personality pathology are readily illustrated by considering a typical case diagnosed as borderline personality disorder. With the DSM-IV-TR system, this diagnosis is made

Table 29.8   Principal Components Analysis of the DAPP-BQ and ZKPQ scales

Trait Scale	Factors				
	I	II	III	IV	V
ZKPQ					
Impulsive Sensation-Seeking	0.06	0.32	**0.54**	0.20	0.17
Neuroticism-anxiety	**0.78**	0.10	0.05	0.03	0.09
Aggression-hostility	0.05	**0.44**	0.26	0.35	0.39
Activity	0.13	0.04	0.04	0.03	**0.86**
Sociability	0.17	0.10	0.06	**0.64**	0.00
DAPP-BQ					
Affective Lability	**0.68**	0.34	0.21	0.35	0.03
Anxiousness	**0.85**	0.23	0.11	0.10	0.00
Callousness	0.26	**0.65**	0.35	0.14	0.08
Cognitive Distortion	**0.77**	0.13	0.24	0.06	0.06
Compulsivity	0.17	0.15	**0.68**	0.04	**0.43**
Conduct Problems	0.15	**0.40**	**0.65**	0.03	0.08
Identity Problems	**0.69**	0.19	0.18	0.24	0.09
Insecure Attachment	**0.65**	0.15	0.02	**0.47**	0.06
Intimacy Problems	0.03	0.11	0.31	**0.70**	0.05
Narcissism	0.27	**0.81**	0.12	0.05	0.17
Oppositionality	**0.58**	**0.42**	0.15	0.02	0.27
Rejection	0.03	**0.80**	0.05	0.18	0.06
Restricted Expression	**0.46**	0.06	0.32	**0.61**	0.15
Self Harm	**0.44**	0.06	**0.59**	0.19	0.18
Social Avoidance	**0.72**	0.29	0.13	**0.36**	0.02
Stimulus Seeking	0.28	**0.57**	0.31	0.27	0.07
Submissiveness	**0.77**	0.07	0.00	0.21	0.02
Suspiciousness	**0.50**	**0.46**	0.20	0.19	0.11
Eigenvalue	7.22	3.51	1.97	1.39	1.11
% Total variance	31.40	13.70	8.56	6.05	4.83

From: Wang et al. (2004).

when the patient shows behaviors that meet five or more of the nine criteria for this disorder. Because there are a couple of hundred ways the criteria can be met, there is considerable heterogeneity among patients with the diagnosis. Knowledge that a patient meets the criteria for this diagnosis provides little information on the behaviors that are problematic for that person. In contrast, a dimensional assessment based on the DAPP-BQ would provide considerable information on relevant behaviors including identity problems, affective lability, anxiousness, cognitive dysregulation, submissiveness, insecure attachment, and self-harm, which would provide the basis for detailed treatment planning. Dimensional assessment would not only help to identify potentially maladaptive expressions of key traits but also features that may have a positive relationship to outcome such as moderate levels of compulsivity.

The level of analysis adopted by the DAPP is also well suited to study the neurobiological and behavioral mechanisms underlying personality disorders. These require relatively more homogeneous phenotypes than DSM-IV-TR diagnoses. The measure should also be useful in studying links between personality and mental disorders classified on DSM-IV-TR Axis I. The emotional dysregulation cluster of traits appears to be genetically and phenotypically related to mood and anxiety disorders and the dissocial cluster appears to be related to alcohol misuse. The detailed structure of the DAPP system should help to clarify the nature of these relationships and contribute to the construction of etiological models.

CLASSIFICATION OF PERSONALITY DISORDER

Currently, there is considerable interest in dimensional classification of personality disorder either as an alternative to the current categorical system or a supplement to it. As Trull and Durrett noted, 'There is little compelling evidence that the categorical model should be retained to the exclusion of a dimensional model of personality pathology' (2005, p. 372). There is extensive evidence supporting a dimensional representation of personality disorder (Livesley et al., 1994; Livesley, 2003; Trull and Durrett, 2005; Widiger, 1993), and empirical evaluations of the two models invariably support a dimensional perspective. The traits assessed by the DAPP-BQ or similar dimensional measures offer a systematic way to develop an empirically based dimensional classification that reflects the etiological structure of personality disorder (Livesley, 2005).

It seems unlikely that such a radical change would be acceptable to many clinicians and investigators who are comfortable with the traditional categorical system despite its limitations. An alternative would be to incorporate a dimensional perspective into the current categorical system by representing each diagnosis by a set of traits based on the primary traits assessed by the DAPP-BQ and similar measures (Livesley, 2006; 2007). With this approach, the DSM-IV-TR definition of personality disorders as traits associated with significant impairment would be extended to define personality disorder as *categories of trait dimensions*. An integrated categorical/dimensional classification could then be constructed organized around an empirically derived set of primary traits. These traits could be evaluated using a variety of methods including diagnostic criteria such as those used currently by the DSM-IV-TR and self-report scales. Alternatively each primary trait could simply be rated on the basis of information elicited during an assessment interview. Primary trait evaluations could then be combined to yield either categorical or dimensional diagnoses. The merit of this approach is that continuity with traditional diagnostic systems would be retained and integrated with an evidence-based system that also reflects the etiological structure of personality disorder.

CONCLUSIONS

The development of the DAPP measures of personality disorder illustrates how a construct validation approach may be used to construct a classification of personality disorder. The value of this approach is that it follows an iterative sequence in which an initial theoretical taxonomy is systematically evaluated and revised with attendant increases in validity. It also incorporates a bottom-up approach in which diagnostic constructs evolve based on empirical evidence of the way the features of personality disorder are organized. The process contrasts with the more 'top-down' approach of the DSM in which disorders and diagnostic criteria are compiled on the basis of a non-representative sampling of clinical opinion. The result is that official classifications have adopted an accumulative approach in which diagnostic categories change little across successive editions and diagnostic criteria are modified largely on the basis of clinical opinion supplemented with limited empirical data. Evidence of the limitations of categorical diagnoses suggests the need for an iterative approach and a major revision of current diagnostic constructs.

A remarkable feature of application of the construct validation process is that empirical evaluation and revision of a theoretical taxonomy based on traditional clinical concepts yielded a structure that is remarkably similar to the structure of normal personality described by trait theories. This finding now seems unremarkable and rather obvious but it was not so obvious when the DSM-III was published a quarter of a century ago. At that time, the study of normal and disordered personality were separate disciplines with little cross-fertilization of constructs and methods. The convergence between the structure of normal and disordered personality is important. It promises to provide a more solid foundation for conceptualizing the psychopathology of personality and begins to integrate psychiatric concepts of personality and psychological conceptions of personality – a process that can only be of mutual benefit.

Although a consensus seems to have emerged on the secondary domains of personality disorder, much work is needed to clarify the nature of these domains and the factors responsible for trait covariation. Even more work is needed to establish a comprehensive understanding of the primary trait structure of normal and disordered personality. Future developments of the DAPP will concentrate on revising primary traits so that they reflect more closely the genetic architecture of personality.

ACKNOWLEDGEMENTS

The DAPP measures were developed in collaboration with the late Dr. Douglas N. Jackson. His advice, encouragement, and inspiration guided each step in the lengthy process of test development. Unfortunately, Doug passed way before our project was fully completed. The preparation of this chapter was supported by Grant MOP-74635 from the Canadian Institutes of Health Research.

REFERENCES

Austin, E.J. and Deary, I.J. (2000) 'The "four As": A common framework for normal and abnormal personality?', *Personality and Individual Differences*, 28(5): 977–95.

Blashfield, R.K. and Livesley, W.J. (1991) 'A metaphorical analysis of psychiatric classification as a psychological test', *Journal of Abnormal Psychology*, 100(3): 262–70.

Carey, G. and DiLalla, D.L. (1994) 'Personality and psychopathology: Genetic perspectives', *Journal of Abnormal Psychology*, 103(1): 32–43.

Clark, L.A. (1990) 'Toward a consensual set of symptom clusters for assessment of personality disorder', in J. Butcher and C. Spielberger (eds), *Advances in Personality Assessment* (Vol. 8). Hillsdale, NJ: Erlbaum, pp. 243–66.

Clark, L.A. (1993a) *Manual for the Schedule for Non-adaptive and Adaptive Personality (SNAP)*. Minneapolis: University of Minnesota Press.

Clark, L.A. (1993b) 'Personality disorder diagnosis: Limitations of the five factor model', *Psychological Inquiry*, 4(2): 100–4.

Clark, L.A. and Livesley, W.J. (1994) 'Two approaches to identifying the dimensions of personality disorder', in P.T. Costa, P.T. and T.A. Widiger (eds), *Personality Disorders and the Five Factor Model of Personality*. Washington DC: American Psychological Association, pp. 261–77.

Clark, L.A. and Livesley, W.J. (2002) 'Two approaches to identifying the dimensions of personality disorder: Convergence on the five-factor model', in P.T. Costa Jr. and Widiger, T.A. (eds), *Personality Disorders and the Five-Factor Model of Personality* (2nd edn). Washington, DC: American Psychological Association, pp. 161–76.

Clark, L.A., Livesley, W.J., Schroeder, M.L. and Irish, S.L. (1996) 'Convergence of two systems for assessing specific traits of personality disorder', *Psychological Assessment*, 8(3): 294–303.

Cook, D.T. and Campbell, D.T. (1979) *Quasi-experimentation: Design and Analysis Issues for Field Settings*. Chicago: Rand McNally.

Costa, P.T. and McCrae, R.R. (1992) *Revised NEO Personality Inventory (NEO-PI-R) and the NEO Five-Factor Inventory (NEO-FFI) Professional Manual*. Odessa, FL: Psychological Assessment Resources.

Crawford, C.B. and Defries, J.C. (1978) 'Factor analysis of genetic and environmental correlation matrices', *Multivariate Behavioral Research*, 13(3): 297–318.

Crowne, D.P. and Marlowe, D. (1960) 'A new scale of social desirability independent of psychopathology', *Journal of Consulting Psychology*, 24(4): 349–54.

Davis, R. and Millon, T. (1995) 'The importance of theory to a taxonomy', in W.J. Livesley (ed.), *The DSM-IV Personality Disorders*. New York: Guilford.

Eysenck, H.J. (1987) 'The definition of personality disorders and the criteria appropriate for their description', *Journal of Personality Disorders*, 1(3): 211–19.

Eysenck, H.J. and Eysenck, M.W. (1985) *Personality and Individual Differences: A Natural Science Approach*. New York: Plenum Press.

Goldberg, L.R. (1972) 'Some recent trends in personality assessment', *Journal of Personality Assessment*, 36(6): 547–60.

Gutiérrez-Zotes, J.A., Gutiérrez, F., Valero, J., Gallego, E., Baillés, E., Torres, X., Labad, A. and Livesley, W.J. (in press) 'Structure of personality pathology in normal and clinical samples: Spanish validation of the DAPP-BQ. *Journal of Personality Disorders*.

Harkness, A.R. (1992) 'Fundamental topics in the personality disorders: Candidate trait dimensions from the lower regions of the hierarchy', *Psychological Assessment*, 4(2): 251–59.

Helmes, E. and Jackson, D.N. (1994) 'Evaluating normal and abnormal personality using the same set of constructs', in S. Strack and M. Lorr (eds), *Differentiating Normal and Abnormal Personality*. New York: Springer, pp. 341–60.

Jackson, D.N. (1971) 'The dynamics of structured personality tests', *Psychological Review*, 78(3): 229–48.

Jackson, D.N. (1984) *The Personality Research Form*. Port Huron, MI: Sigma Assessment Systems.

Jang, K.L. and Livesley, W.J. (1999) 'Why do measures of normal and disordered personality correlate? A study of genetic comorbidity', *Journal of Personality Disorders*, 13(1): 10–17.

Jang K.L., Livesley, W.J., Angleitner, A., Riemann, R. and Vernon, P.A. (2002) 'Genetic and environmental influences on the covariance of facets defining the domains of the five-factor model of personality', *Personality and Individual Differences*, 33(1): 83–101.

Kass, F., Skodol, A.E., Charles, E. and Williams, J.B. (1985) 'Scaled ratings of DSM-III personality disorders', *American Journal of Psychiatry*, 142(5): 627–30.

Larstone, R.M., Jang, K.L., Livesley, W.J., Vernon, P.A. and Wolf, H. (2002) 'The relationship between Eysenck's P-E-N model of personality, the five-factor model of personality, and traits delineating personality disorder', *Personality and Individual Differences*, 33(1): 25–37.

Lion, J.R. (1981) (ed.), *Personality Disorders: Diagnosis and Management*. Baltimore: Williams & Wilkins.

Livesley, W.J. (1985a) 'The classification of personality disorder: I. The choice of category concept', *Canadian Journal of Psychiatry*, 30(5): 353–8.

Livesley, W.J. (1985b) 'The classification of personality disorder: II. The problem of criteria', *Canadian Journal of Psychiatry*, 30(5): 359–62.

Livesley, W.J. (1986) 'Trait and behavioral prototypes of personality disorder', *American Journal of Psychiatry*, 143(6): 728–32.

Livesley, W.J. (2001) 'An integrated approach to treatment', in Livesley W.J. (ed.), *Handbook of Personality Disorder*. New York: Guilford, pp. 570–600.

Livesley, W.J. (2007) 'A framework for integrating dimensional and categorical classifications of personality disorder', *Journal of Personality Disorders,* 21(2): 199–224.

Livesley, W.J. and Jackson, D.N. (1986). The internal consistency and factorial structure of behaviors judged to be associated with DSM-III categories of personality disorders', *American Journal of Psychiatry*, 143(11): 1473–4.

Livesley, W.J. and Jackson, D.N. (1992) 'Guidelines for developing, evaluating, and revising the classification of personality disorders', *Journal of Nervous and Mental Disease*, 180(10): 609–18.

Livesley, W.J., Jackson, D.N. and Schroeder, M.L. (1989) 'A study of the factorial structure of personality pathology', *Journal of Personality Disorders*, 3(4): 292–306.

Livesley, W.J., Jackson, D.N. and Schroeder, M.I. (1992) 'Factorial structure of traits delineating personality disorders in clinical and general population samples', *Journal of Abnormal Psychology*, 101(3): 432–40.

Livesley, W.J. (2005) 'Behavioral and molecular genetic contributions to a dimensional classification of personality disorder', *Journal of Personality Disorders*, 19(2):131–55.

Livesley, W.J., Jang, K.L. and Vernon, P.A. (1998) 'Phenotypic and genetic structure of traits delineating personality disorder', *Archives of General Psychiatry*, 55(10): 941–8.

Livesley, W.J. (2003) 'Diagnostic dilemmas in the classification of personality disorder', in K. Phillips, M. First and H.A. Pincus (eds), *Advancing DSM: Dilemmas in Psychiatric Diagnosis*. Washington DC: American Psychiatric Association Press, pp. 153–189.

Livesley, W.J., Schroeder, M.L., Jackson, D.N., and Jang, K.L. (1994) 'Categorical distinctions in the study of personality disorder: Implications for classification', *Journal of Abnormal Psychology*, 103(1): 6–17.

Livesley, W.J. (2006) 'The dimensional assessment of personality pathology (DAPP) approach to personality disorder', in S. Strack (ed), *Differentiating Normal and Abnormal Personality* (2nd edn). New York: Springer.

Livesley, W.J. and Schroeder, M.L. (1990) 'Dimensions of personality disorder: The DSM-III-R Cluster A diagnoses', *Journal of Nervous and Mental Disease*, 178(10): 627–35.

Livesley, W.J. and Schroeder, M.L. (1991) 'Dimensions of personality disorder: the DSM-III-R Cluster B diagnoses', *Journal of Nervous and Mental Disease*, 179(6): 320–8.

Livesley, W.J., West, M. and Tanney, A. (1985) 'Historical comment on DSM-III schizoid and avoidant personality disorders', *American Journal of Psychiatry*, 142(11): 1344–7.

Loehlin, J.C. (1989) 'Partitioning environmental and genetic contributions to behavioral development', *American Psychologist*, 44(10): 1285–92.

Loehlin, J.C. and Vandenberg, S.G. (1968) 'Genetic and environmental components in the covariation of cognitive abilities: An additive model', in S.G. Vandenberg (ed.), *Progress in Human Behavior Genetics*. Baltimore: Johns Hopkins Press.

Loevinger, J. (1957) 'Objective tests as instruments of psychological theory', *Psychological Reports*, 3: 635–94.

Messick, S. (1980) 'Test validity and the ethics of assessment', *American Psychologist*, 35(11): 1012–27.

Messick, S. (1988) 'Validity', in R.L. Linn (ed.), *Educational Measurement* (3rd edn). New York: MacMillan.

Millon, T. (1981) *Disorders of Personality: DSM-III, Axis II*. New York: Wiley.

Mulder, R.T. and Joyce, P.R. (1997) 'Temperament and the structure of personality disorder symptoms', *Psychological Medicine*, 27(1): 99–106.

Plomin, R., Defries, J.C. and McLearn, G.E. (1990) *Behavioral Genetics: A Primer*. New York: Freeman.

Presly, A.J. and Walton, H.J. (1973) 'Dimensions of abnormal personality', *British Journal of Psychiatry*, 122(568): 269–76.

Pukrop, R., Gentil, I., Steinbring, I. and Steinmeyer, E. (2001) 'Factorial structure of the German version of the Dimensional Assessment of Personality Pathology-Basic Questionnaire in clinical and nonclinical samples', *Journal of Personality Disorders*, 15(5): 450–6.

Rosch, E. (1978) 'Principles of categorization', in E. Rosch and B.B. Lloyd (eds), *Cognition and Categorization*. Hillsdale, NJ: Lawrence Erlbaum Associates.

Saucier, G. and Goldberg, L.R. (1996) 'The language of personality: Lexical perspectives on the five-factor model', in J.S. Wiggins (ed.), *The Five Factor Model of Personality*. New York: Guilford, pp. 21–50.

Schroeder, M.L., Wormsworth, J.A. and Livesley, W.J. (1992) 'Dimensions of personality disorder and their relationship to the big five dimensions of personality', *Psychological Assessment*, 4(1): 47–53.

Skinner, H.A. (1981) 'Toward the integration of classification theory and methods', *Journal of Abnormal Psychology*, 90(1): 68–87.

Skinner, H.A. (1986) 'Construct validity approach to psychiatric classification', in T. Millon and G.L. Klerman (eds), *Contemporary Directions in Psychopathology: Towards DSM-IV*. New York: Guilford.

Soloff, P.H. (2000) 'Psychopharmacology of borderline personality disorder', *Psychiatric Clinics of North America*, 23(1): 169–92.

Trull, T.J. and Durrett, C.A. (2005) 'Categorical and dimensional models of personality disorder', *Annual Review of Clinical Psychology*, 1(1): 355–85.

Tyrer, P. and Alexander, J. (1979) 'Classification of personality disorder', *British Journal of Psychiatry*, 135: 163–7.

Vaillant, G.E. and Perry, J.C. (1980) 'Personality disorders', in H. Kaplan, A.M. Freedman and B. Sadock (eds), *Comprehensive Textbook of Psychiatry III*. Baltimore: Williams & Wilkins, pp. 1562–90.

van Kampen, D. (2002) 'The DAPP-BQ in the Netherlands: Factor structure and relationship with basic personality dimensions', *Journal of Personality Disorders*, 16(3): 235–54.

Wang, W., Du, W., Wang, Y., Livesley, W.J. and Jang, K.L. (2004) 'The relationship between the Zuckerman-Kuhlman Personality Questionnaire and traits delineating personality pathology', *Personality and Individual Differences*, 36(1): 155–62.

Watson, D. and Clark, L.A. (1984) 'Negative affectivity: The disposition to experience aversive emotional states', *Psychological Bulletin*, 96(3): 465–90.

Widiger, T.A. (1998) 'Four out of five ain't bad', *Archives of General Psychiatry*, 55(10): 865–6.

Widiger, T. A. (1993) 'The DSM-III-R categorical personality disorder diagnoses: A critique and an alternative', *Psychological Inquiry*, 4(2): 75–90.

Zheng, W., Wang, W., Huang, Z., Sun, C., Zhu, S. and Livesley, W.J. (2002) 'The structure of traits delineating personality disorder in China', *Journal of Personality Disorders*, 16(5): 477–86.

30

The Personality Assessment Inventory

Leslie C. Morey and Suman Ambwani

TEST DESCRIPTION

The Personality Assessment Inventory (PAI) (Morey, 1991), a 344-item self-report inventory, assesses various domains of personality and psychopathology among adults and is designed for use in professional settings. The PAI comprises of 22 non-overlapping full scales, including 4 validity scales, 11 clinical scales, 5 treatment consideration scales, and 2 interpersonal scales (listed in Table 30.1). Individuals completing the PAI respond to items on a four-point Likert-type scale, ranging from *false* to *very true*, and are scored based on the intensity of their responses; the inventory typically takes about 50–60 minutes for administration. The present chapter reviews information such as development of the test, its use with different populations, as well as some recent research literature attesting to the validity of this instrument. Individuals seeking more detailed information regarding the PAI may wish to review various interpretive volumes (Morey and Hopwood, 2007; Morey, 2003; Morey, 1996) or the test manual (Morey, 2007a; Morey, 1991).

TEST DEVELOPMENT

The PAI was developed with emphasis on theoretical and empirical knowledge through a construct validation framework. This framework focuses on a theoretically informed approach to the generation and selection of test items, as well as emphasis on their stability and correlates. Two criteria were used in the selection of constructs measured by the PAI, including the stability of the syndromes' importance within the conceptualization of psychological disorders, and the significance of the syndromes in contemporary professional practice. Using these criteria, an examination of the literature led to the selection of 18 construct scales and 4 validity scales. The literature was then reviewed to identify the components that were most fundamental to an understanding of the constructs, and test items were constructed to assess these individual components. *Content validity*, or the adequacy of sampling of content across the construct of interest; and *discriminant validity*, or specificity to the construct of interest, were two facets of construct validity that

Table 30.1 PAI scale and subscale names and acronyms

Validity scales

ICN		Inconsistency
INF		Infrequency
NIM		Negative impression management
PIM		Positive impression management

Clinical scales and subscales

SOM		Somatic complaints
	SOM-C	Conversion
	SOM-S	Somatization
	SOM-H	Health concerns
ANX		Anxiety
	ANX-C	Cognitive
	ANX-A	Affective
	ANX-P	Physiological
ARD		Anxiety-related disorders
	ARD-O	Obsessive-compulsive
	ARD-P	Phobias
	ARD-T	Traumatic stress
DEP		Depression
	DEP-C	Cognitive
	DEP-A	Affective
	DEP-P	Physiological
MAN		Mania
	MAN-A	Activity level
	MAN-G	Grandiosity
	MAN-I	Irritability
PAR		Paranoia
	PAR-H	Hypervigilance
	PAR-P	Persecution
	PAR-R	Resentment
SCZ		Schizophrenia
	SCZ-P	Psychotic experiences
	SXZ-S	Social detachment
	SCZ-T	Thought disorder
BOR		Borderline features
	BOR-A	Affective instability
	BOR-I	Identity problems
	BOR-N	Negative relationships
	BOR-S	Self-harm
ANT		Antisocial features
	ANT-A	Antisocial behaviors
	ANT-E	Egocentricity
	ANT-S	Stimulus-seeking
ALC		Alcohol problems
DRG		Drug problems

Treatment consideration scales and subscales

AGG		Aggression
	AGG-A	Aggressive attitude
	AGG-V	Verbal aggression
	AGG-P	Physical aggression
SUI		Suicidal ideation
STR		Stress
NON		Nonsupport
RXR		Treatment rejection

Interpersonal scales

DOM		Dominance
WRM		Warmth

were particularly important in the development of the PAI. With regards to content validity, the development of the PAI sought to include scales that offered a balanced sampling of the most central elements of the constructs of interest, both in terms of their breadth and depth. For instance, to measure the breadth of content coverage in assessing depression, the PAI included items to assess physiological, cognitive, and affective symptoms of depression. To ensure adequate depth of content coverage, the scales were developed to include items addressing the range of severity of the construct, including its milder as well as most severe forms. Each item is designed to capture differences in severity of that particular feature of the construct by attributing different points based on the intensity of the feature. The four-alternative scoring allows scales to capture more variance per item, thus facilitating scale reliability, while also drawing attention to those instances in which a *slightly true* response, such as to a suicidal ideation item, may be clinically significant. An examination of item characteristic curves facilitated the selection of final items that provide information across the full range of syndrome severity, which vary across different constructs. For example, cognitive aspects of anxiety can vary from mild rumination to severe despair and panic, while suicidal ideation can range from vague and poorly articulated thoughts to immediate plans for self-harm. Thus, PAI items were selected to provide an assessment across severity range of the selected constructs.

With regards to discriminant validity, a significant challenge in test development lies in the ability of a scale to measure a construct that is specific and free from the influence of other constructs. An important threat to discriminability lies in test bias, as tests designed to assess psychological constructs should not measure demographic variables such as gender, racial/ethnic background, or age. Although items on psychological measures may indeed correlate with these demographic characteristics, the size of such correlations should not exceed that which might be expected theoretically. For instance, most indicators of antisocial behavior suggest that this construct is more prevalent among men than women, thus it would be expected that a measure for antisocial behavior would yield higher average scores for men than for women. However, the inventory should exhibit substantially greater correlations with other indicators of antisocial behavior than with gender, and such convergent validity correlations should be comparable across gender.

Several steps were taken to avoid test bias in the construction of the PAI. First, all test items were reviewed by a bias panel of lay and professional individuals from various backgrounds, who were asked to identify any items that may inadvertently measure external factors, such as sociocultural background, rather than the intended emotional and behavioral problems. Next, convergent validity correlations across demographic groups were examined to eliminate items that seemed to have differential functioning for different demographic groups. Thus, both conceptual and empirical strategies were employed to minimize the likelihood of test bias. Consistent with this notion, the PAI does not use separate norms for men and women, as items were selected to have the same meaning regardless of the gender of the respondent. Scale scores may indeed exhibit mean demographic differences, such as higher proportions of men attesting to stealing behavior than women, but these differences were designed to reflect genuine gender differences in prevalence, rather than being a function of test bias.

A particularly common problem in the field of psychological assessment is that measures designed to assess a particular construct may in fact be highly related to several other constructs, thus making the test results difficult to interpret. For instance, how would a clinician interpret an elevation on a scale assessing schizophrenia, if that scale also assesses alienation,

family problems, depression, and indecisiveness? To address this potential problem, the PAI items were selected that demonstrated large differences in their association with indicators of the construct of interest as opposed to indicators of other constructs. Thus, although many of the scales demonstrate positive intercorrelations (an assessment of the factor structure of the item pool using principal axis extraction suggested that the first unrotated factor accounts for 18.5% of the variance), these correlations should reflect natural comorbidity rather than artifacts, such as those caused by overlapping scales. The resulting relative specificity of the scales as measures of the constructs of interest facilitates a straightforward interpretation of the PAI results.

RANGE OF APPLICABILITY AND LIMITATIONS

The PAI was developed and standardized for use with adults aged 18 or older; a parallel version of the instrument designed for adolescents aged 12 to 18 is available (Morey, 2007b). The PAI is designed to provide information relevant to clinical diagnosis, treatment planning and screening for psychopathology; it is not designed to offer a comprehensive assessment of normal personality. Moreover, interpretive hypotheses from PAI test results should always be limited to the purposes for which the PAI is administered, and diagnostic and treatment decisions should never be based solely on the results of the PAI. Such decisions necessarily require multiple sources of information, such as case histories and other historical data, results of mental status exams and clinical interviews, as well as additional self-report and performance-based information.

Items were written to be easily understood and applicable across cultures; initial reading level analyses of the PAI test items indicated that reading ability at the fourth-grade level was necessary to complete the inventory. A comparative study of similar instruments by Schinka and Borum (1993) supported the conclusion that the PAI items are written at a grade equivalent lower than estimates for comparable instruments. However, it is to be noted that years of completed education is not a reliable indicator of reading ability; typically, grade-level ability of many individuals to read and comprehend is substantially below their completed grade level of education. In instances where the examiner suspects that the respondent may be unable to read at the fourth-grade level, it may be necessary to first administer a brief test of reading comprehension to determine whether testing with the PAI can proceed. For instance, the evaluator may ask the client to read aloud the instructions for the test and the first few test items to gauge his or her reading proficiency.

In instances where the respondent cannot read or has limited visual acuity, it is recommended that the clinician employ an audiotape version of the PAI, available through the publisher. An alternative is to read each item orally to the respondent; however, in any such instances it is strongly recommended that the respondent record his or her responses directly on the answer sheet, rather than communicate them verbally to an examiner. When such verbal communication takes place, the test resembles a structured interview, and the resulting information is of dubious comparability to norms established using self-reported symptomatology.

An assumption of valid administration of PAI is that the respondent is physically and emotionally capable of meeting the normal demands of testing with self-administered instruments. For instance, care should be taken with individuals whose cognitive abilities may be compromised by the effects of recent drug use, withdrawal from drugs or alcohol, or disorientation due to neurological deficits. Another significant consideration in administering the PAI lies in the working alliance between the evaluator and the client. If an alliance can be established before the completion of the PAI, the respondent may

be more likely to accurately represent his or her concerns and behaviors on the test. One approach to establishing this alliance that may be particularly useful is that of therapeutic assessment, in which the assessment is viewed as an intervention, rather than as merely an information gathering session (Finn and Tonsager, 1997).

Caution should also be employed in testing individuals who, by the nature of their psychological disorder, display confusion, psychomotor retardation, distractibility, or extreme emotional distress. Test administrators should be watchful of physical or sensorimotor deficits, such as motor weakness or lack of visual acuity, which could affect the respondent's ability to complete the PAI in a valid manner. Clinicians should not rely solely on the PAI validity scale patterns to determine whether PAI protocols are valid; the determination that an individual is able to respond to a self-report measure is a professional decision.

TEST STANDARDIZATION AND SCORING PROCEDURES

The PAI was developed and standardized for use in the clinical assessment of individuals in aged 18 years through adulthood. PAI scale and subscale raw scores are transformed to *T*-scores (with a mean of 50, and a standard deviation of 10) to provide interpretation relative to a standardization sample of 1,000 community-dwelling adults. The standardization sample was carefully selected to match 1995 US census projections on the basis of gender, race, and age; the educational level of the standardization sample was representative of a community group with the required fourth-grade reading level. For each PAI scale and subscale, the *T*-scores were linearly transformed from the means and standard deviations derived from the census-matched standardization sample.

Unlike several other clinical measures, the PAI does not calculate *T*-scores differently for men and women; instead, combined norms are used for both genders. Separate norms are only necessary when the scale contains some bias that affects the interpretation of a score based on the respondent's gender. To use separate norms in the absence of such bias would only misrepresent the natural epidemiological differences between genders. For instance, men are more likely than women to receive the diagnosis of antisocial personality disorder, and this is reflected in the higher mean scores for men on the antisocial features (ANT) scale. A separate normative procedure for men and women would result in similar numbers of each gender scoring in the clinically significant range, a result that does not reflect the established gender ratio for this disorder. As mentioned earlier, the development of the PAI included several procedures to eliminate items that might be biased due to demographic features. Items that exhibited any signs of being interpreted differently as a function of demographic characteristics were eliminated in the course of selecting final items for the test. With relatively few exceptions, differences as a function of demography were negligible in the community sample. The most noteworthy effects involve the tendency for men to score higher on the ANT and alcohol problems (ALC) scales relative to women, and for younger adults to score higher on the borderline features (BOR) and ANT scales than older adults.

As T-scores are derived from a community sample, they offer a useful way to determine if certain problems are clinically significant, because relatively few normal adults will obtain markedly elevated scale scores. However, other comparisons are often equally salient in clinical decision-making. For example, nearly all patients report experiencing symptoms of depression at their initial evaluation; thus, the pertinent question for the clinician considering a diagnosis of major depressive disorder is one of relative severity of symptomatology. Although it is important to know whether or not an individual's score on the PAI depression scale is elevated in comparison to the standardization

sample, a comparison of the elevation relative to a clinical sample may be more critical in forming diagnostic hypotheses.

To facilitate comparisons with a clinical sample, the PAI profile form also indicates the T-scores that correspond to marked elevations when referenced against a representative clinical sample of 1,246 patients selected from a wide variety of professional settings. This profile 'skyline' indicates the score for each scale and subscale that represents the raw score that is two standard deviations above the mean for a clinical sample. Thus, approximately 98% of clinical patients will obtain scores below the skyline on the profile form. Scores above this skyline represent a substantial elevation of scores relative to a clinical sample. Thus, PAI profiles may be interpreted by comparing test data to both non-clinical and clinical samples.

The PAI manual offers normative transformations for various comparisons, such as T-score transformations referenced against the clinical sample, a large sample of college students, as well as for various demographic subgroups of the community standardization sample. As noted earlier, the differences between demographic groups were generally quite small; however, in certain instances it may be useful to make comparisons with reference to particular groups. Thus, the raw score means and SDs required to convert raw scores to T-scores with reference to normative data provided by particular groups (men, women, African-Americans, and individuals over the age of 60 years) are provided in the manual. However, it is strongly recommended that for most clinical and research applications, the T-scores derived from the full normative data are employed because of their greater representativeness and larger sample size.

PSYCHOMETRIC PROPERTIES: RELIABILITY DATA

Several studies have examined the internal consistency (Alterman et al., 1995; Boyle and Lennon, 1994; Karlin et al., 2005;

Morey, 1991; Rogers et al., 1995; Schinka, 1995), test–retest reliability (Boyle and Lennon, 1994; Morey, 1991; Rogers et al., 1995) and configural stability (Morey, 1991) of the PAI scales and subscales. Internal consistency estimates for the PAI typically suggest adequate internal consistency, with full scales and subscales typically yielding alphas in the 0.80s and 0.70s, respectively. However, although internal consistency estimates are commonly employed in clinical research and practice, they should not be considered an ideal basis for deriving the standard error of measurement in clinical measures, as temporal instability is often of greater concern than inter-item correlations. For instance, a ten-item measure with 'I am depressed' as the sole repeated item would likely yield a perfect internal consistency estimate, but may offer little in terms of validity or even test–retest reliability.

In the standardization studies, the temporal stability (median test–retest reliability) of the 11 PAI clinical scales over a four-week interval was 0.86 (Morey, 1991), leading to SEM for these scales of about three to four T-score points, with 95% confidence intervals of +/− six to eight T-score points. Assessment of the mean absolute T-score change values for scales also revealed that the absolute changes over time were quite small, about two to three T-score points for most of the full scales (Morey, 1991). In their non-clinical sample, Boyle and Lennon (1994) reported a median test–retest reliability of 0.73 over 28 days.

As multiple-scale inventories are often interpreted configurally, the stability of configurations on the 11 PAI clinical scales should also be evaluated. One such analysis involved examining the inverse (or Q-type) correlation between each respondent's profile at time 1 and at time 2. Correlations were obtained for each of the 155 respondents in the full retest sample, and a distribution of the within-subject profile correlations was obtained. Following these procedures, the median correlation over time of the clinical scale configuration was 0.83, thus indicating

a substantial degree of stability in profile configurations over time (Morey, 1991).

PSYCHOMETRIC PROPERTIES: VALIDITY DATA

As indicated in the PAI test manual (Morey, 1991), to assess the validity of the measure a number of the best available clinical indicators were administered concurrently to various samples to determine their convergence with corresponding PAI scales. In addition, hypothesized relations between clinical judgments, such as diagnoses, and their PAI correlates were also evaluated. Moreover, numerous simulation studies were performed to determine the efficacy of the PAI validity scales in identifying response sets. A comprehensive review of available validity evidence for the various scales is beyond the scope of this chapter; the PAI manual alone contains information about correlations of individual scales with over 50 concurrent indices of psychopathology (Morey, 1991). The following paragraphs review some of the more noteworthy findings from such studies, organized into the four broad types of PAI scales: validity scales, clinical scales, treatment consideration scales, and interpersonal scales.

Validity scales

The PAI validity scales were designed to assess the potential influence of certain response tendencies on PAI test performance, including both random and systematic influences upon test responding. To model the performance of individuals responding to the PAI in a random manner, computer-generated profiles were created by generating random responses to individual PAI items and then scoring all scales according to their normal scoring algorithms. In total, 1,000 simulated protocols were generated for this analysis. A comparison of profiles from non-clinical respondents, clinical respondents, and the random response simulations demonstrated a clear separation of scores of actual respondents from the random simulations, and 99.4% of these random profiles were identified as such by either the inconsistency (ICN) or infrequency (INF) scales (Morey, 1991). An additional indicator of random responding was developed by Morey and Hopwood (2004), whose measure of back random responding (BRR) involved comparing front to back scaled scores on the alcohol (ALC) and suicide (SUI) scales. Their report that front to back scaled score discrepancies $\geq 5T$ on ALC and SUI offer satisfactory positive and negative predictive power across levels and base rates of BRR has been validated in an independent clinical sample (Siefert et al., 2006).

Although the need to gather data from the client's perspective is crucial in diagnosis and treatment planning, there are several reasons why this information may be inaccurate. Individuals may systematically distort their responses to standardized tests in positive or negative manner, thus, several PAI indicators have been developed to identify intentional distortion or exaggeration in client responses. The validation of such PAI indicators has been of considerable research interest, and the data suggest that these markers may even be useful in understanding similar distortions in information derived from other methods of assessment, including interviews and/or clinical observation (e.g. Alterman et al., 1996).

To assess the validity of these measures, participants in numerous studies were instructed to simulate certain response styles and their responses were compared to honest responders. The negative impression management (NIM) scale was developed to alert the interpreter to the possibility that the PAI test results may depict a more negative picture of the respondent than what might be warranted. The content of the NIM scale involves two types of items, those presenting an exaggerated impression of oneself and current circumstances, and those reflecting unusually bizarre and unlikely symptomatology. Given the tendency of individuals with certain forms of psychopathology to perceive themselves and their circumstances as more negative than what might be merited by an objective observer, individuals with severe emotional problems typically do present with elevated scores on NIM, and more disturbed populations obtain higher scores than those who are less impaired. Although these perceptual distortions are reflective of psychopathology, clinicians must remain cognizant of the influence of these perceptual styles in interpreting PAI profiles.

A number of studies examining the utility of the NIM scale support its use in distinguishing honest responders from those presenting with a negative response sets. For instance, Rogers et al. (1993) administered the PAI to naive and sophisticated simulators (advanced clinical and counseling graduate students) with a financial incentive to avoid detection as malingerers, and reported that the recommended NIM scale cutoff successfully identified 90.9% of participants attempting to feign schizophrenia, 55.9% of participants simulating depression, and 38.7% of participants feigning an anxiety disorder, whereas only 2.5% of control participants were identified as simulators. As described in the PAI manual, individuals scoring above the critical level of the negative impression management (NIM) scale were 14.7 times more likely to be in the malingering group than the clinical sample. In subsequent studies hit rates for NIM typically range from 0.50 to 0.80, and the data suggest that NIM sensitivity is negatively affected by coaching and is positively related to the severity of feigned disorders (Rogers et al., 1995).

The NIM scale is supplemented by the Malingering Index (MAL) (Morey, 1996) and the Rogers discriminant function (Rogers et al., 1996) to assess negative response sets. The MAL, a composite of eight configural features seen more commonly among profiles of individuals feigning psychological disorders than true clinical patients, is designed to measure malingering more directly than NIM, which is often affected by response styles consequent to psychopathology (e.g. exaggeration associated with depression) as well as overt attempts at negative dissimulation. Morey (1996) reported that each feature of MAL was observed with greater frequency in a simulated mental disorder group than in actual clinical or community samples, and Morey and Lanier (1998) observed that a cutting score of three demonstrated a specificity of 93.3% and sensitivity of 81.8% in naïve simulators feigning severe psychopathology. Feigning status in male inmates, identified by the Structured Interview of Reported Symptoms (SIRS) (Rogers et al., 1992), has also been found to be associated with Malingering Index scores in the anticipated direction (Wang et al., 1997). Further support for MAL was demonstrated by Gaies (1993), who reported that using a cutoff of three or greater as an indicator of malingering yielded a sensitivity of 56.6% for identifying the informed malingerers and 34.2% for identifying the naive malingerers; specificity of the index in a sample of clinically depressed patients was 89.3%, whereas non-clinical controls demonstrated a specificity of 100%. Another study reported a sensitivity of 45% and specificity of 94% in distinguishing malingered from true post-traumatic stress disorder (Scragg et al., 2000). In general, the research data attest to the validity of the MAL, but also suggest that its sensitivity declines when milder forms of psychopathology (such as depression or anxiety) are being simulated.

The Rogers Index, or the RDF, was designed to distinguish the PAI profiles of bona fide patients from those instructed (both naive and 'coached') to simulate such psychopathology. In contrast to NIM, which is relatively highly saturated with influences of psychopathology, the RDF is virtually free of such influences psychopathology, and thus offers a potentially significant way to differentiate negative exaggeration due to psychopathology versus due to deliberate feigning (Morey, 1996). Rogers et al. (1996) reported estimates of sensitivity and specificity in excess of 80% in both derivation and cross validation; these results were superior to the use of the NIM scale in isolation. Several studies support the utility of the RDF; for instance, a comparison of NIM, MAL, and RDF found RDF to be the most accurate in identifying individuals simulating psychopathology (1.96 standard deviation effect size), and using a cutting score of +0.53 resulted in 95.5% sensitivity and 95.6% specificity (Morey and Lanier, 1998).

The content of the positive impression management (PIM) scale involves the presentation of a highly favorable impression or denial of relatively minor faults, thus, elevated scores suggest that the respondent does not take many opportunities to say negative things about him- or herself. As indicated in the PAI manual, respondents scoring above 57T on PIM were 13.9 times more likely to have been in the positive dissimulation sample than a community sample (Morey, 1991). A series of different studies (reviewed in Morey, 2007) have suggested that 57T is the optimal cutting score for distinguishing between honest responders and those instructed to stimulate positive response sets (e.g. Cashel et al., 1995; Morey and Lanier, 1998). For instance, Peebles and Moore (1998) reported that a cutting score of 57T resulted in a hit rate of 85.1% in distinguishing forthright from defensive respondents, while Fals-Stewart (1996) reported that the same cut score had a sensitivity of 88% in identifying 'questionable responding' among substance abusers (e.g. forensic patients who denied substance use but had positive urine screens), and a specificity of 80% among honest responders.

The Defensiveness Index (DEF) (Morey, 1996) and the Cashel discriminant function (CDF) (Cashel et al., 1995) may be employed to augment PIM in assessing positive distortion among PAI respondents. For the DEF, a composite of eight configural features observed more frequently among individuals instructed to present a positive impression than those without instruction, hit rates for detecting 'fake good' profiles in simulation studies tend to range from the high 0.70s to mid 0.80s (Baer and Wetter, 1997; Peebles and Moore, 1998), although there is some evidence suggesting that these hit rates decrease when respondents are instructed on how to avoid detection (Baer and Wetter, 1997). The average score for a naive 'fake good' sample on the DEF was reported to be 6.23, as compared to 2.81 of these features in the normative community sample (Morey, 1996). Peebles and Moore (1998) reported a hit rate of 83.3% for the Defensiveness Index in distinguishing forthright from 'fake good' responding. However, a study performed by Cashel et al. (1995) reported a lower mean score on the Defensiveness Index among a group of positive dissimulators 'coached' about validity scales, although their scores were still approximately one standard deviation above the norm for community samples. This result suggests that the sensitivity of the Defensive Index may be lowered in samples coached for 'believability' in being defensive.

The CDF is an empirically derived function developed to maximize differences between honest responders and individuals instructed to 'fake good' in college student and forensic populations. Cashel et al. (1995) reported that the CDF demonstrated sensitivities ranging from 79% to 87% in identifying falsified profiles, with specificity of 88%. They suggested that the CDF was more accurate in identifying dissimulated responses than either PIM or DEF used in isolation. Morey and Lanier's (1998) results also lend support to the utility of the CDF, as they reported that a score of 148.44 on the CDF demonstrated 97.8% sensitivity and 71.1% specificity in distinguishing normal and 'fake good' college students.

Clinical scales

The PAI clinical scales assess the critical diagnostic features of 11 important clinical constructs. Numerous validity indicators have been employed to examine the convergent and discriminant validity of the PAI clinical scales. As reported in the PAI manual (Morey, 1991; Morey, 2007a), correlations tend to follow hypothesized patterns; for example, strong associations have been reported among neurotic spectrum scales such as anxiety (ANX), anxiety-related disorder (ARD), somatic complaints (SOM), and depression (DEP) and other psychometric measures of neuroticism (Baer and Wetter, 1997; Morey, 1991). Similarly, the ARD scale (particularly the traumatic experiences subscale, ARD-T) has been found to differentiate female psychiatric patients who did and did not experience childhood abuse (Cherepon and Prinzhorn, 1994). Moreover, patterns of correlations with external indicators vary for the ARD and ANX scales, suggesting that the ARD scale assesses more specific diagnostic content, whereas the ANX scale measures more diffuse anxiety. For instance, ARD exhibited its most significant correlations with the Mississippi PTSD scale ($r = 0.81$; Keane et al., 1988) and the Fear Survey Schedule ($r = 0.66$; Wolpe and Lang, 1964), and somewhat more modestly correlated with the NEO-PI-R anxiety facet ($r = 0.57$). The DEP scale exhibits its largest correlations with various widely used indicators of depression, such as the Beck Depression Inventory (range: $r = 0.70$–0.81; Beck and Steer, 1987) and the NEO-PI-R depression facet ($r = 0.70$). The ANX scale correlates strongly with the anxiety facet of the NEO-PI-R ($r = 0.76$; Costa and McCrae, 1992) and trait anxiety on the State-Trait Anxiety Inventory ($r = 0.73$; Spielberger, 1983).

With regards to more recent research on the somatic complaints (SOM), anxiety (ANX), anxiety-related disorders (ARD), and depression (DEP) scales, much attention has been devoted to assessing the predictive validity of these scales. For instance, some data suggest that as might be predicted, SOM is typically the highest average PAI elevation in medical samples (Osborne, 1994; Karlin et al., 2005; Keeley et al., 2000), and may be particularly high among those with a clear external motivation, such as those seeking worker's compensation (Ambroz, 2005). One study highlighted the potential usefulness of SOM in decision-making for psychopharmacological interventions, reporting that SOM was significantly higher among individuals who did not adhere to anti-depressant treatment due to side-effects ($80.8T$, SD = 7.1) than those who did ($65.2T$, SD = 12.4) (Keeley et al., 2000). Research data on the ANX scale indicate that it relates significantly to acculturative stress (Hovey and Magana, 2000), indices of anxiety sensitivity (Plehn et al., 1998), sexual dysfunction (Bartoi et al., 2000), and dissociation (Briere et al., 2005). One study employed the ANX scale as an outcome measure for the treatment of trichotillomania, reporting that therapy clients experienced a decrease in ANX scores (from $63.8T$ to $58.3T$), maintained at three-month follow-up ($57.2T$), in contrast to the observed average increase in ANX scores among the wait-list control group (Woods et al., 2006). Similarly, subsequent research on the anxiety-related disorders (ARD) scale also attests to its validity; for instance, the traumatic experiences subscale (ARD-T) is typically elevated among individuals who are diagnosed with PTSD, as well as those instructed to feign PTSD (e.g. Liljequist et al., 1998; McDevitt-Murphy et al., 2005). Moreover, research reports suggest that ARD-T can differentiate among women psychiatric patients who were and were not victims of childhood abuse (Cherepon and Prinzhorn, 1994). Finally, the depression (DEP) scale has demonstrated strong associations with other indicators of depression (e.g. Mascaro et al., 2004; Romain, 2001), and has also been shown to be useful as an outcome measure for anti-depressant treatment (Keeley et al., 2000).

Within the psychotic spectrum, PAI scales such as paranoia (PAR), mania (MAN), and schizophrenia (SCZ) have previously been shown to correlate with various indicators of severe psychopathology (Morey, 1991). As predicted, MAN correlated strongly with MMPI-2 scale 9 ($r = 0.53$). Of these scales, the PAR scale has been found to correlate particularly well with diagnostic assessments

of paranoia made via structured clinical interview (Rogers et al., 1998b). One study demonstrated that individuals with persecutory delusions obtained higher scores on the persecution subscale (PAR-P) than did individuals without such delusions (Gay and Combs, 2005). Another study indicated that individuals with relatively high PAR scores performed poorly on an emotion-perception task, sat further away from the examiner, and took longer to read the research consent forms than individuals with low PAR scores (Combs and Penn, 2004). Research on the schizophrenia (SCZ) scale has also supported its validity, as it has been found to be associated with the Rorschach Schizophrenia Index and to distinguish individuals with schizophrenia from non-psychotic clinical controls in an inpatient sample (Klonsky, 2004). Despite the robust literature supporting the use of these psychotic-spectrum clinical scales, further research along these lines is needed, and evaluating PAI profiles in conjunction with data from other assessment sources may be particularly important for the differential diagnosis of psychotic disorders.

The borderline features (BOR) scale and the antisocial features (ANT) scale are the two scales on the PAI assessing character pathology. The selection of these two constructs was based on the fact that they are historically stable with greater empirical and theoretical development than other personality disorders. Both the BOR and ANT scales have been found to relate to other measures of these constructs as well as to predict relevant behavioral outcomes (e.g. Trull et al., 1997; Salekin et al., 1998). As indicated in the PAI test manual, the BOR scale has been found to correlate strongly with the MMPI borderline scale ($r = 0.77$) and the NEO-PI neuroticism ($r = 0.67$) scale. Other studies have supported the validity and utility of this scale in diverse clinical contexts. The BOR scale has previously demonstrated an ability to distinguish individuals with borderline personality disorder from unscreened controls with an 80% hit rate, and to successfully identify 91% of these subjects as part of a discriminant function (Bell-Pringle et al.,

1997). Classifications made from the BOR scale have been validated in multiple domains relating to borderline functioning, including depression, personality traits, coping, Axis I disorders, and interpersonal problems (Trull, 1995). These BOR scale classifications also predicted two-year outcomes on academic indices among college students, even after controlling for the effects of academic potential and substance abuse (Trull et al., 1997). Moreover, recent research suggests that as might be predicted by the clinical conceptualization of borderline personality disorder, individuals with high scores on BOR exhibit low, fluctuating self-esteem (Zeigler-Hill and Abraham, 2006).

The ANT scale demonstrated its largest correlations in initial validation studies (Morey, 1991) with the MMPI antisocial personality disorder (Morey et al., 1985) and the Hare's self-report psychopathy test (range: $r = 0.54$–0.80; Hare, 1985). Subsequent research has supported the validity of ANT. For instance, Edens et al., (2000) examined the relationship of the ANT scale to the screening version of the Psychopathy Checklist (PCL:SV; Hart et al., 1995) and the Psychopathy Checklist-Revised (PCL-R; Hare, 1991), and reported moderately strong correlations between ANT and the PCL:SV ($r = 0.54$) and the PCL-R total score ($r = 0.40$). Similarly, Salekin et al. (1998) reported that the ANT and aggression (AGG) scales of the PAI significantly predicted recidivism among female inmates over a 14-month follow-up interval. In addition, ANT has demonstrated validity in predicting violence in an incarcerated clinical sample (Wang and Diamond, 1999), as well as predicting treatment course for women with borderline personality (Clarkin et al., 1994).

Two scales on the PAI, alcohol problems (ALC) and drug problems (DRG) directly inquire about behaviors and consequences related to alcohol and drug use, abuse, and dependence. The ALC scale has previously been demonstrated to differentiate individuals in an alcohol rehabilitation clinic from

individuals with schizophrenia (Boyle and Lennon, 1994) and non-clinical controls (Ruiz et al., 2002). The DRG scale has been shown to successfully discriminate drug abusers and methadone maintenance patients from general clinical and community samples (Alterman et al., 1995). Moreover, Morey (1991) reported correlations from the validation studies attesting to the convergent and discriminant validity of these scales. For instance, whereas ALC correlated strongly with the Michigan Alcohol Screening Test ($r = 0.89$; Selzer, 1971), it demonstrated a modest inverse correlation with the Drug Abuse Screening Test ($r = -0.31$; Skinner, 1982). Conversely, DRG correlated strongly with the Drug Abuse Screening Test ($r = 0.69$), and exhibited a modest negative correlation with the Michigan Alcohol Screening Test ($r = -0.25$). However, despite the demonstrated utility of these scales, some caution should be employed in their interpretation; specifically, as ALC and DRG test items inquire directly about substance use, the scales are susceptible to denial.

Treatment consideration scales

The five treatment consideration scales of the PAI are designed to assess variables that potentially complicate treatment and may not be immediately apparent from diagnostic information. Specifically, these include an assessment of aggression (AGG), suicidal ideation (SUI), stress (STR), nonsupport (NON), and treatment rejection (RXR). Correlations between the PAI treatment consideration scales and multiple validation measures support the construct validity of these scales. For example, substantial correlations have been identified between the aggression (AGG) scale and the trait anger scale ($r = 0.75$) of the State-Trait Anger Expression Inventory (STAXI) (Spielberger, 1988). As predicted, AGG also relates to a variety of Rorschach indicators of aggression in a non-clinical sample (Mihura et al., 2003).

In a study of recidivism among female inmates over 14-month follow-up, AGG was found to be significantly associated ($r = 0.29$) with recidivism (Salekin et al., 1998). The suicidal ideation (SUI) scale has been validated against similar measures (Morey, 1991) such as the suicide probability scale (SPS) (Cull and Gill, 1982) and the Beck hopelessness scale (Beck and Steer, 1988). Morey (1991) reported that nonsupport (NON) demonstrated strong inverse correlations with the perceived social support (PSS) scales (Procidano and Heller, 1983), while stress (STR) exhibited its strongest correlations with the Schedule of Recent Events ($r = 0.50$). Consistent with the notion that distress can be a motivator for treatment, the treatment rejection (RXR) scale demonstrated an inverse correlation with the NEO-PI vulnerability scale ($r = -0.54$). Caperton et al. (2004) also reported that the treatment rejection (RXR) scale was modestly effective at predicting treatment non-compliance in a correctional setting. More recent research (Hopwood et al., 2007) suggests that the Treatment Process Index (TPI) (Morey, 1996), a supplemental index, is a stronger predictor of non-compliance than RXR in an outpatient setting, but that among profiles with low RXR, severity of psychopathology was a greater predictor of premature therapy termination than it was for patients with high RXR scores.

Interpersonal scales

The interpersonal scales of the PAI were designed to assess the interpersonal style of respondents along two dimensions: (a) a warm/affiliative versus a cold/rejecting axis (WRM) and (b) a dominating/controlling versus a meek/submissive style (DOM). These axes offer a useful way to organize variation in normal personality and to guide the process of treatment (Tracey, 1993). The PAI manual reports a number of studies indicating that diagnostic groups differ on

these dimensions; for example, spouse-abusers obtain relatively high scores on the dominance (DOM) scale, whereas schizophrenics obtain low scores on the warmth (WRM) scale (Morey, 1991). Initial validation data indicated that the WRM scale was significantly associated with the NEO-PI gregariousness facet ($r = 0.46$) whereas DOM was correlated with the NEO-PI assertiveness facet ($r = 0.71$). Correlations with other related measures, such as the interpersonal adjective scales (Wiggins, 1979), provide support for the construct validity of these scales. For example, consistent with expectations, PAI DOM is associated with the IAS-R dominance vector, whereas PAI WRM is associated with the IAS-R love vector. The NEO-PI extroversion scale approximately bisects the high DOM/high WRM quadrant, as it is moderately positively correlated with both scales, a finding that is consistent with previous research (Trapnell and Wiggins, 1990).

Risk assessment

Decisions about risk, whether targeted towards harming oneself or others, are critical factors in treatment planning in most clinical contexts. There are several indicators of risk on the PAI, including measures to evaluate suicide potential, such as the suicidal ideation (SUI) scale and the Suicide Potential Index (SPI), as well as measures of violent behavior, such as the aggression (AGG), antisocial behaviors (ANT), and Violence Potential Index (VPI).

The SUI items relate to thoughts of suicide and similar behaviors, and can alert the clinician to the need for further evaluation and intervention for suicidality. As SUI is a suicidal ideation scale, rather than a suicide prediction scale, it is important to use supplemental information when making decisions regarding suicide risk. The Suicide Potential Index (SPI) comprises of 20 features of the PAI profile that are considered key risk factors for completed suicide (such as severe psychic anxiety, poor impulse control, hopelessness, and worthlessness) and the SPI is scored by counting the number of positive endorsements on these factors. In the original standardization sample, the SPI was shown to highly correlate with various indicators of suicidal ideation (Morey, 1991). More recent research has supported this assertion. For instance, one study reported that the largest correlations of PAI scales with the number of suicide risk assessments completed on inmates in a correctional setting were between the number of suicide risk assessments and SUI ($r = 0.45$), borderline features ($r = 0.32$), depression ($r = 0.29$), and the SPI ($r = 0.28$) (Wang et al., 1997). Another study with a sample of emergency referrals in correctional settings reported correlations between SUI and suicidal symptoms reported during structured clinical interviews (Rogers et al., 1998a).

In addition to the AGG and ANT scales, the Violence Potential Index (VPI) (Morey, 1996) combines a variety of risk factors for violence that have been found to be useful in the prediction of dangerousness, such as the explosive expression of anger, sensation seeking, and impulsivity. The VPI has been shown to correlate with indicators of hostility and poor judgment on the MMPI, with Hare's (1985) self-report measure of psychopathic features, and with a diagnosis of antisocial personality disorder made through structured clinical interview (Morey, 1996; Edens et al, 2000). Research has supported the validity of these various markers to predict violent behavior. For instance, one study of individuals in a corrections-based inpatient psychiatric facility examined the relationship between the overt aggression scale (OAS) (Yudofsky et al., 1986) and the PAI scales, subscales, and the VPI; and reported significant correlations between the OAS total score and subscales from BOR, ANT, and AGG (Wang et al., 1997). In addition, findings revealed that individuals with low-VPI scores had significantly lower OAS total scores compared to individuals in with moderate/marked VPI scores. A follow-up

investigation revealed that the three ANT subscales were helpful in predicting institutional aggression among offenders diagnosed with psychopathology within their first two months of hospitalization (Wang and Diamond, 1999).

CROSS-CULTURAL FACTORS

Items for the PAI were specifically constructed to be free from idiomatic phrases or specific cultural references that might limit its cross-cultural applicability. As noted earlier, several procedures were followed to maximize the cross-cultural applicability of the PAI during the item selection phase. As a first strategy, all of the PAI test items were reviewed by a bias panel (consisting of ethnically and racially diverse men and women of lay and professional backgrounds) to identify items that, although written to identify emotional and/or behavioral problems, might instead reflect other factors, such as sociocultural background. A second step involved examining the item psychometric properties as a function of demographic variables, such as ethnic background. As noted by Cleary et al., 'A test is considered fair for a particular use if the inference drawn from the test score is made with the smallest feasible random error and if there is no constant error in the inference as a function of membership in a particular group' (1975: 75). Thus, the intent of this strategy was to eliminate items with different meanings for different demographic groups. For instance, if an item about crying seemed to relate to other indicators of depression in women but not in men, then that item was eliminated because interpretation of the item would vary as a function of gender.

Consequent to these efforts to avoid test bias, validation studies suggested that differences in PAI scores attributable to race are generally less than or equal to the standard error of measurement for a given scale. For instance, in examining the PAI profiles of ethnically diverse (Hispanic and

African-American) methadone maintenance patients, Alterman et al. (1995) noted that their sample presented with similar psychometric properties to the PAI standardization sample. They noted good internal consistency for the clinical scales, except for drug-related problems (DRG; alpha = 0.61), which may have been due to a restriction of range, and reported that the scale intercorrelations were similar to those reported in the PAI manual. There are some data to suggest, however, that there may be some cross-cultural differences in the paranoia (PAR) scale, as African-American respondents typically score approximately $7T$ points higher than Caucasians. This discrepancy does not necessarily imply test bias, as it may in fact reflect a true cultural difference. Given that African-Americans continue to experience multiple levels of oppression, it is not surprising if, as a group, they tend to maintain a cautious stance and to report feelings of being treated unjustly, as implied by a modest PAR elevation. As noted earlier, evidence of test bias would be indicated by varying relations of PAI scales to criteria as a function of race, a finding that has not been supported by the research data.

In addition to its use within English-speaking populations in the US, the PAI has also been used successfully in other English-speaking countries, such as Australia (White, 1996), and has been translated into several languages, including Spanish, Hebrew, Norwegian, Swedish, French, Korean, Slovenian, Danish, and Arabic. However, there has been somewhat limited research on translated versions of the PAI. A Spanish translation of the test is commercially available from the publisher, including translations of both the test booklet and the answer sheet. One study noted that internal consistency estimates for PAI scales administered in Spanish were satisfactory (average alpha = 0.63; average alpha for clinical scales = 0.68), albeit somewhat lower than comparable values among English-speaking samples (Rogers et al., 1995). In a study with mono-lingual Spanish-speakers and bilingual (English and Spanish) outpatients, Rogers et al. (1995) reported a strong correlation between the clinical scales of the English and Spanish versions of the PAI ($r = 0.72$), and a good test–retest reliability for the Spanish clinical scales ($r = 0.79$). However, they noted that, as with any translation, the utility of the PAI among non-English speakers is most directly assessed by examining correlates, thereby necessitating future research in this area. In a study with Mexican-American, Puerto Rican, and other Hispanic men and women, Fantoni-Salvador and Rogers (1997) reported that Spanish PAI demonstrated moderate convergent validity that was at least equal, and superior in some respects, to a Spanish translation of the MMPI-2 (Fantini-Salvador and Rogers, 1997). Their study also found no effect of ethnicity on PAI scale scores after controlling for symptom status as determined via structured interview.

THE PAI SOFTWARE PORTFOLIO (PAI-SP)

The PAI offers a software portfolio (PAI-SP) (Morey et al., 2000) for computerized administration, scoring, and narrative feedback based on diagnostic algorithms, but it is not designed to be a replacement for professional knowledge and expertise. The automated interpretive report generated by this program is intended to serve to provide useful information to professionals, to be considered in the context of all available information about the client.

The software package may be used to score computer-administered or paper/pen administrations of the PAI. Moreover, several additional indices are computed by the PAI-SP that would be difficult or tedious to compute by hand, such as coefficients of configural profile fit with diagnostic groups from the standardization samples, as well as various supplemental indices, such as the Rogers and Cashel discriminant functions and the malingering and defensiveness indices. The interpretive report, typically

10–15 pages in length, is comprised of several components, including DSM-IV diagnostic considerations, rule-outs, and the aforementioned supplemental clinical indices. The report provides verbal descriptive interpretations and coefficients of fit between the respondent's obtained profile and a database of various clinical modal profiles. In addition, the report addresses aspects of the client's response style, such as indicators of positive impression management, defensiveness about circumscribed areas (e.g. substance abuse), negative impression management, and malingering. Sections of the report describe clinical features, interpersonal behavior, treatment considerations, diagnostic possibilities, test validity, and critical items endorsed by the respondent. Graphic profiles are created for each respondent, and the PAI-SP allows the user to overlay graphs with a wide variety of comparison profiles, such as response sets, diagnostic groups, and regression-based predictions of the profile based on information from the validity scales, as well as any prior administrations for that client.

The PAI has garnered particular acceptance in situations where there is a need for empirical risk appraisal, such as forensic settings (Edens et al., 2001); thus, interpretive software has been developed for forensic (Edens and Ruiz, 2005) and law enforcement personnel selection (Roberts et al., 2000) applications of the PAI.

There has been some research support demonstrating the utility of the PAI in predicting the job performance of law enforcement officials. For instance, Weiss et al. (2004) reported that physical aggression (AGG-P) scores were significantly correlated with the number of times the officer discharged his or her weapon in the line of duty, any acts of insubordination, an excess of civilian complaints, as well as whether or not the officer was still employed with the department. Similarly, verbal aggression (AGG-V) was associated with whether or not the individual was still employed by the agency, and aggressive attitude (AGG-A)

scores were associated with the number of suspensions or reprimands received by the individual. Scores on other clinical scales, such as ANT-E and ANT-S, have demonstrated significant correlations with excessive civilian complaints (Weiss et al., 2005), conduct mistakes, insubordination, and neglect of duty (Weiss et al., 2004). ANT-S has also been shown to correlate with whether or not the individual was still employed by the department at follow-up (Weiss et al., 2004). Another study demonstrated that scores on MAN-G predicted whether or not the police officer was employed 12 months after completing the initial assessment (Blazsanyik, 2003), with lower MAN-G scores associated with a greater likelihood of subsequent employment. Finally, scores on certain PAI validity scales (e.g. PIM and NIM) have also demonstrated significant associations with various job-related criterion variables, such as conduct mistakes and whether or not the officer demonstrated an inappropriate use of a weapon (NIM; Weiss et al., 2004).

The PAI Correctional Software (Edens and Ruiz, 2005) scores the PAI and transforms raw scores based on normative data gathered from multiple correctional settings, including, inmates in a pre-release treatment facility in New Jersey ($n = 542$), a treatment program for convicted sex offenders in Texas ($n = 98$), state prison inmates in Washington ($n = 515$), and forensic inpatients in New Hampshire ($n = 57$). The PAI Correctional Software offers several indices relevant to correctional populations are provided, such as an inconsistency scale focusing on criminal behavior and an addictive characteristics scale that facilitates the assessment of denial of substance use. The PAI Law Enforcement, Corrections, and Public Safety Selection Report Module (Roberts et al., 2000) scores PAI scales and provides T-transformations based on data from a large normative sample public safety applicants ($n = 17,757$), including a sample of individuals who have successfully completed a post-hiring probation period. The program employs actuarial prediction formulas based upon two samples of job applicants designed to predict suitabil-ity-for-hire ratings based upon various data, excluding the PAI.

A BRIEF SCREENER: THE PAS

The Personality Assessment Screener (PAS) (Morey, 1997) was designed as a rapid mental health screening instrument, as it sought to identify a combination of items from the PAI that were collectively maxi-mally sensitive to the broad range of clinical issues measured by the parent instrument. This approach places a strong emphasis on item sensitivity and upon breadth of content coverage. The resulting 22-item screening instrument organizes hierarchically into a total score and ten different element scores representing ten distinct domains of clinical problems. These elements include the fol-lowing: negative affect (NA), acting-out (AO), health problems (HP), psychotic fea-tures (PF), social withdrawal (SW), hostile control (HC), suicidal thinking (SC), alien-ation (AN), alcohol problems (AP), and anger control (AC). Thus, the PAS may be used as a screening instrument as part of a sequential assessment strategy that can greatly increase efficiency of testing resources, particularly in non-mental health settings, where the base rate of mental health problems is relatively lower than in clinical settings. In such a sequential assessment, PAS results that suggest potential mental health problems may be followed up with an evalu-ation conducted using the PAI or any other of a variety of clinical assessment methods.

using the PAI, to exploring various elements of PAI profiles to address broader assessment queries. Indeed, survey data suggest that the PAI is ranked as one of the most frequently used objective personality measures in clini-cal training and practice (Piotrowski, 2000). For instance, in a survey of objective person-ality measures used in internship programs, the PAI was ranked fourth by internship directors (Piotrowski and Belter, 1999). Similarly, a study of assessment instruments used by forensic psychologists in emotional injury cases demonstrated that the PAI was used in 11% of the emotional injury cases sampled (Boccaccini and Brodsky, 1999). Given these clinical and research applica-tions of the PAI, the purpose of the section is to explore areas requiring further study.

Given the increasing popularity of the PAI across multiple contexts and cultures, further research investigating the cross-cultural measurement equivalence of the PAI and its translations is required. Validation studies of the individual scales and subscales, as well as studies of the utility of the instrument for par-ticular applications, for instance, in predicting treatment compliance or job performance, may also be important directions for future research. Further, although the PAI was not designed to assess certain forms of psy-chopathology, such as eating disorders, recent research suggests that PAI test data may nonetheless be informative in understanding and treating individuals with eating disorders (e.g. Tasca et al., 2002, 2003). Consequently, future research attention may be directed towards broadening the applicability of the PAI to understanding the phenomenology of other psychological disorders.

FUTURE DIRECTIONS

Since the introduction of the PAI in 1991, the test has generated significant interest from the research community. These research efforts have ranged from validating individ-ual scales, examining cross-cultural issues in

REFERENCES

Alterman, A.I., Snider, E.C., Cacciola, J.S., Brown, L.S., Zaballero, A. and Siddiqui, N. (1996) 'Evidence for response set effects in structured research interviews', *Journal of Nervous and Mental Disease*, 184(7): 403–10.

Alterman, A.I., Zaballero, A.R., Lin, M.M., Siddiqui, N., Brown, L.S., Rutherford, M.J. et al. (1995) 'Personality Assessment Inventory (PAI) scores of lower-socioeconomic African American and Latino methadone maintenance patients', *Assessment*, 2(1): 91–100.

Ambroz, A. (2005) 'Psychiatric disorders in disabled chronic low back pain Workers' Compensation claimants. Utility of the Personality Assessment Inventory (abstract)', *Pain Medicine*, 6: 190.

Baer, R.A. and Wetter, M.W. (1997) 'Effects of information about validity scales on underreporting of symptoms on the Personality Assessment Inventory', *Journal of Personality Assessment*, 68(2): 402–13.

Bartoi, M.G., Kinder, B.N. and Tomianovic, D. (2000) 'Interaction effects of emotional status and sexual abuse on adult sexuality', *Journal of Sex and Marital Therapy*, 26(1): 1–23.

Beck, A.T. and Steer, R.A. (1987) *Beck Depression Inventory Manual*. San Antonio, TX: Psychological Corporation.

Beck, A.T. and Steer, R.A. (1988) *Beck Hopelessness Scale Manual*. San Antonio, TX: Psychological Corporation.

Bell-Pringle, V.J., Pate, J.L. and Brown, R.C. (1997) 'Assessment of borderline personality disorder using the MMPI-2 and the Personality Assessment Inventory', *Assessment* 4(2): 131–9.

Blazsanyik, A.J. (2003) 'Psychological profiles of successful law enforcement personnel', doctoral dissertation, Adler School of Professional Psychology, *Dissertation Abstracts International*, 64: 2907.

Boccaccini, M.T. and Brodsky, S.L. (1999) 'Diagnostic test usage by forensic psychologists in emotional injury cases', *Professional Psychology: Research and Practice*, 30(3): 253–9.

Boyle, G.J. and Lennon, T.J. (1994) 'Examination of the reliability and validity of the Personality Assessment Inventory', *Journal of Psychopathology and Behavioral Assessment*, 16(3): 173–87.

Briere, J., Weathers, F.W. and Runtz, M. (2005) 'Is dissociation a multidimensional construct? Data from the Multiscale Dissociation Inventory', *Journal of Traumatic Stress*, 18(3): 221–31.

Caperton, J.D., Edens, J.F. and Johnson, J.K. (2004) 'Predicting sex offender institutional adjustment and treatment compliance using the Personality Assessment Inventory', *Psychological Assessment*, 16(2): 187–91.

Cashel, M.L., Rogers, R., Sewell, K. and Martin-Cannici, C. (1995) 'The Personality Assessment Inventory and the detection of defensiveness', *Assessment*, 2(4): 333–42.

Cherepon, J.A. and Prinzhorn, B. (1994) 'The Personality Assessment Inventory (PAI) profiles of adult female abuse survivors', *Assessment*, 1(4): 393–400.

Clarkin, J.F., Hull, J., Yeomans, F., Kakuma, T. and Cantor, J. (1994) 'Antisocial traits as modifiers of treatment response in borderline patients', *Journal of Psychotherapy Practice and Research*, 3(4): 307–12.

Cleary, T., Humphreys, L., Kendrick, S. and Wesman, A. (1975) 'Educational uses of tests with disadvantaged students', *American Psychologist*, 30(1): 15–41.

Combs, D.R. and Penn, D.L. (2004) 'The role of subclinical paranoia on social perception and behavior', *Schizophrenia Research*, 69(1): 93–104.

Costa, P.T. Jr. and McCrae, R.R. (1992) *Professional Manual: Revised NEO Personality Inventory (NEO-PI-R) and NEO Five-Factor Inventory (NEO-FFI)*. Odessa, FL: Psychological Assessment Resources.

Cull, J.G. and Gill, W.S. (1982) *Suicide Probability Scale Manual*. Los Angeles: Western Psychological Services.

Edens, J.F., Hart, S.D., Johnson, D.W., Johnson, J. and Olver, M.E. (2000) 'Use of the PAI to assess psychopathy in offender populations', *Psychological Assessment*, 12(2): 132–9.

Edens, J.F., Poythress, N.G. and Watkins, M.M. (2001) 'Further validation of the Psychopathic Personality Inventory among offenders: Personality and behavioral correlates', *Journal of Personality Disorders*, 15(5): 403–15.

Edens, J.F. and Ruiz, M.A. (2005) *PAI Interpretive Report for Correctional Settings (PAI-CS) Professional Manual*. Lutz, FL: Psychological Assessment Resources.

Fals-Stewart, W. (1996) 'The ability of individuals with psychoactive substance use disorders to escape detection by the Personality Assessment Inventory', *Psychological Assessment*, 8(1): 60–8.

Fantoni-Salvador, P. and Rogers, R. (1997) 'Spanish versions of the MMPI-2 and PAI: An investigation of concurrent validity with Hispanic patients', *Assessment*, 4(1): 29–39.

Finn, S. and Tonsager, S. (1997) 'Information-gathering and therapeutic models of assessment: Complementary paradigms', *Psychological Assessment*, 9(4): 374–85.

Gaies, L.A. (1993) 'Malingering of depression on the Personality Assessment Inventory', Doctoral dissertation, University of South Florida, *Dissertation Abstracts International*, 55: 6711.

Gay, N.W. and Combs, D.R. (2005) 'Social behaviors in persons with and without persecutory delusions', *Schizophrenia Research*, 80(2–3): 361–2.

Hare, R.D. (1985) 'Comparison of procedures for the assessment of psychopathy', *Journal of Consulting and Clinical Psychology*, 53(1): 7–16.

Hare, R.D. (1991) *The Psychopathy Checklist-Revised*. Toronto: Multi-Health Systems.

Hart, S.D., Cox, D.N. and Hare, R.D. (1995) 'Psychopathy Checklist: Screening version. Toronto, Ontario', Canada: Multi-Health Systems.

Hopwood, C.J., Ambwani, S. and Morey, L.C. (2007) 'Predicting non-mutual therapy termination with the Personality Assessment Inventory', *Psychotherapy Research,* 17(6): 706–12.

Hovey, J.D. and Magana, C.G. (2002) 'Cognitive, affective, and physiological expressions of anxiety symptomatology among Mexican migrant farmworkers: Predictors and generational differences', *Community Mental Health Journal*, 38(3): 223–37.

Karlin, B.E., Creech, S.K., Grimes, J.S., Clark, T.S., Meagher, M.W. and Morey, L.C. (2005) 'The Personality Assessment Inventory with chronic pain patients: Psychometric properties and clinical utility', *Journal of Clinical Psychology*, 61(12): 1571–85.

Keane, T.M., Caddell, J.M. and Taylor, K.L. (1988) 'Mississippi Scale for Combat-Related Posttraumatic Stress Disorder: Three studies in reliability and validity', *Journal of Consulting and Clinical Psychology*, 56(1): 85–90.

Keeley, R., Smith, M. and Miller, J. (2000) 'Somatoform symptoms and treatment nonadherence in depressed family medicine outpatients', *Archives of Family Medicine*, 9(1): 46–54.

Klonsky, E.D. (2004) 'Performance of Personality Assessment Inventory and

Rorschach indices of schizophrenia in a public psychiatric hospital', *Psychological Services*, 1(2): 107–10.

Liljequist, L., Kinder, B.N. and Schinka, J.A. (1998) 'An investigation of malingering posttraumatic stress disorder on the Personality Assessment Inventory', *Journal of Personality Assessment*, 71(3): 322–36.

Mascaro, N., Rosen, D.H. and Morey, L.C. (2004) 'The development, construct validity, and clinical utility of the Spiritual Meaning Scale', *Personality and Individual Differences*, 37(4): 845–60.

McDevitt-Murphy, M.E., Weathers, F.W., Adkins, J.W. and Daniels, J.B. (2005) 'Use of the Personality Assessment Inventory in assessment of posttraumatic stress disorder in women', *Journal of Psychopathology and Behavior Assessment*, 27(2): 57–65.

Mihura, J.L., Nathan-Montano, E. and Alperin, R.J. (2003) 'Rorschach measures of aggressive drive derivatives: A college student sample', *Journal of Personality Assessment*, 80(1): 41–9.

Morey, L.C. (1991) *The Personality Assessment Inventory Professional Manual*. Odessa, FL: Psychological Assessment Resources.

Morey, L.C. (1996) *An Interpretive Guide to the Personality Assessment Inventory*. Odessa, FL: Psychological Assessment Resources.

Morey, L.C. (1997) *The Personality Assessment Screener: Professional Manual*. Odessa, FL: Psychological Assessment Resources.

Morey, L.C. (2003) *Essentials of PAI Assessment*. New York: Wiley.

Morey, L.C. (2007a) *The Personality Assessment Inventory Professional Manual* (2nd edn). Odessa, FL: Psychological Assessment Resources.

Morey, L.C. (2007b) *The Personality Assessment Inventory – Adolescent Professional Manual*. Odessa, FL. Psychological Assessment Resources:

Morey, L.C. and Hopwood, C.J. (2004) 'Efficiency of a strategy for detecting back random responding on the Personality Assessment Inventory', *Psychological Assessment*, 16(2): 197–200.

Morey, L.C. and Hopwood, C.J. (2007) *Casebook for the Personality Assessment Inventory*. Odessa, FL: Psychological Assessment Resources.

Morey, L.C. and Lanier, V.W. (1998) 'Operating characteristics for six response distortion indicators for the Personality Assessment Inventory', *Assessment*, 5(3): 203–14.

Morey, L.C. and PAR Staff (2000) *PAI Software System*. Odessa, FL: Psychological Assessment Resources.

Morey, L.C., Waugh, M.H. and Blashfield, R.K. (1985) 'MMPI scales for DSM-III personality disorders: Their derivation and correlates', *Journal of Personality Assessment*, 49(3): 245–51.

Osborne, D. (1994) 'Use of the Personality Assessment Inventory with a medical population', paper presented at the Meeting of the Rocky Mountain Psychological Association, April, Denver, CO.

Peebles, J. and Moore, R.J. (1998) 'Detecting socially desirable responding with the Personality Assessment Inventory: The Positive Impression Management Scale and the Defensiveness Index', *Journal of Clinical Psychology*, 54(5): 621–8.

Piotrowski, C. and Belter, R.W. (1999) 'Internship training in psychological assessment: Has managed care had an impact?', *Assessment*, 6(4): 381–9.

Piotrowski, C. (2000) 'How popular is the Personality Assessment Inventory in practice and training?', *Psychological Reports*, 86(1): 65–6.

Plehn, K., Peterson, R.A. and Williams, D.A. (1998) 'Anxiety sensitivity: Its relationship to functional status in patients with chronic pain', *Journal of Occupational Rehabilitation*, 8(3): 213–22.

Procidano, M.E. and Heller, K. (1983) 'Measures of perceived social support from friends and from family: Three validation studies', *American Journal of Community Psychology*, 11(1): 1–24.

Roberts, M.D., Thompson, J.A. and Johnson, M. (2000) *PAI Law Enforcement, Corrections, and Public Safety Selection Report Module*. Odessa, FL: Psychological Assessment Resources.

Rogers, R., Bagby, R.M. and Dickens, S.E. (1992) *Structured Interview of Reported Symptoms Professional Manual*. Odessa, FL: Psychological Assessment Resources.

Rogers, R., Flores, J., Ustad, K. and Sewell, K.W. (1995) 'Initial validation of the Personality Assessment Inventory-Spanish version with clients from Mexican American communities', *Journal of Personality Assessment*, 64(2): 340–8.

Rogers, R., Ornduff, S.R. and Sewell, K. (1993) 'Feigning specific disorders: A study of the Personality Assessment Inventory (PAI)', *Journal of Personality Assessment*, 60(3): 554–60.

Rogers, R., Sewell, K.W., Cruise, K.R., Wang, E.W. and Ustad, K.L. (1998a) 'The PAI and feigning: A cautionary note on its use in forensic-correctional settings', *Assessment*, 5(4): 399–405.

Rogers, R., Sewell, K.W., Morey, L.C. and Ustad, K.L. (1996) 'Detection of feigned mental disorders on the Personality Assessment Inventory: A discriminant analysis', *Journal of Personality Assessment*, 67(3): 629–40.

Rogers, R., Ustad, K.L. and Salekin, R.T. (1998b) 'Convergent validity of the Personality Assessment Inventory: A study of emergency referrals in a correctional setting', *Assessment*, 5(1): 3–12.

Romain, P.M. (2000) 'Use of the Personality Assessment Inventory with an ethnically diverse sample of psychiatric outpatients' doctoral dissertation, Pepperdine University, *Dissertation Abstracts International*, 61: 6147.

Ruiz, M.A., Dickinson, K.A. and Pincus, A.L. (2002) 'Concurrent validity of the Personality Assessment Inventory Alcohol Problems (ALC) Scale in a college student sample', *Assessment*, 9(3): 261–70.

Salekin, R.T., Rogers, R., Ustad, K.L. and Sewell, K.W. (1998) 'Psychopathy and recidivism among female inmates', *Law and Human Behavior*, 22(1): 109–28.

Schinka, J.A. (1995) 'Personality Assessment Inventory scale characteristics and factor structure in the assessment of alcohol dependency', *Journal of Personality Assessment*, 64(1): 101–11.

Schinka, J.A. and Borum, R. (1993) 'Readability of adult psychopathology inventories', *Psychological Assessment*, 5(3): 384–6.

Scragg, P., Bor, R. and Mendham, M.C. (2000) 'Feigning post-traumatic stress disorder on the PAI', *Clinical Psychology and Psychotherapy*, 7(2): 155–60.

Siefert, C.J., Blais, M.A., Baity, M.R. and Chriki, L. (2006) 'The effects of back random responding on the PAI in a sample of psychiatric patients', Paper presented at the Meeting of the Society for Personality Assessment, March, San Diego.

Selzer, M.L. (1971) 'The Michigan Alcoholism Screening Test: The quest for a new diagnostic instrument', *American Journal of Psychiatry*, 127(12): 1653–8.

Skinner, H.A. (1982) 'The Drug Abuse Screening Test', *Addictive Behaviors*, 7(4): 363–71.

Spielberger, C.D. (1983) *Manual for the State-Trait Anxiety Inventory*. Palo Alto, CA: Consulting Psychologists Press.

Spielberger, C.D. (1988) *State-Trait Anger Expression Inventory*. Odessa, FL: Psychological Assessment Resources.

Tasca, G.A., Illing, V., Lybanon-Daigle, V., Bissada, H. and Balfour, L. (2003) 'Psychometric properties of the Eating Disorders Inventory-2 among women seeking treatment for binge eating disorder', *Assessment*, 10(3): 228–36.

Tasca, G.A., Wood, J., Demidenko, N. and Bissada, H. (2002) 'Using the PAI with an eating disordered population: Scale characteristics, factor structure and differences among diagnostic groups', *Journal of Personality Assessment*, 79(2): 337–56.

Tracey, T.J. (1993) 'An interpersonal stage model of the therapeutic process', *Journal of Counseling Psychology*, 40(4): 396–409.

Trapnell, P.D. and Wiggins, J.S. (1990) 'Extension of the Interpersonal Adjective Scale to include the big five dimensions of personality', *Journal of Personality and Social Psychology*, 59(4): 781–90.

Trull, T.J. (1995) 'Borderline personality disorder features in nonclinical young adults: 1. Identification and validation', *Psychological Assessment*, 7(1): 33–41.

Trull, T.J., Useda, J.D., Conforti, K. and Doan, B.T. (1997) 'Borderline personality disorder features in nonclinical young adults: 2. Two-year outcome', *Journal of Abnormal Psychology*, 106(2): 307–14.

Wang, E.W. and Diamond, P.M. (1999) 'Empirically identifying factors related to violence risk in corrections', *Behavioral Sciences and the Law*, 17(3): 377–89.

Wang, E.W., Rogers, R., Giles, C.L., Diamond, P.M., Herrington-Wang, L.E. and Taylor, E.R. (1997) 'A pilot study of the Personality Assessment Inventory (PAI) in corrections: Assessment of malingering, suicide risk, and aggression in male inmates', *Behavioral Sciences and the Law*, 15(4): 469–82.

Weiss, W.U., Zehner, S.N., Davis, R.D., Rostow, C. and DeCoster-Martin, E. (2005) 'Problematic police performance and the Personality Assessment Inventory', *Journal of Police and Criminal Psychology*, 20(1): 16–21.

Weiss, W.U., Rostow, C., Davis, R. and DeCoster-Martin, E. (2004) 'The Personality Assessment Inventory as a selection device for law enforcement personnel', *Journal of Police and Criminal Psychology*, 19(2): 23–9.

White, L.J. (1996) 'Review of the Personality Assessment Inventory (PAI): A new psychological test for clinical and forensic assessment', *Australian Psychologist*, 31(1): 38–9.

Wiggins, J.S. (1979) 'A psychological taxonomy of trait-descriptive terms: The interpersonal domain', *Journal of Personality and Social Psychology*, 37(3): 395–412.

Wolpe, J. and Lang, P. (1964) 'A fear survey schedule for use in behavior therapy', *Behavior Research and Therapy*, 2(1): 27–30.

Woods, D.W., Wetterneck, C.T. and Flessner, C.A. (2006) 'A controlled evaluation of acceptance and commitment therapy plus habit reversal for trichotillomania', *Behaviour Research and Therapy*, 44(5): 639–56.

Yudofsky, S.C., Silver, J.M., Jackson, W., Endicott, J. and Williams, D. (1986) 'The Overt Aggression Scale for the objective rating of verbal and physical Aggression', *American Journal of Psychiatry*, 143(1): 35–9.

Zeigler-Hill, V. and Abraham, J. (2006) 'Borderline personality features: Instability of self-esteem and affect', *Journal of Social and Clinical Psychology*, 25(6): 668–87.

31

The Assessment of Clinical Disorders within Raymond Cattell's Personality Model

Samuel E. Krug

In the 1960s Raymond B. Cattell and his coworkers began a programmatic series of researches to place the measurement of clinically important behavior patterns within the broader context of total personality measurement. Although well-established instruments had existed for many years that measured clinical *or* normal aspects of personality functioning, none had been specifically designed to assess both simultaneously.

The measurement of clinical symptomatology has a history nearly as long as scientific psychology itself. The associative techniques of Jung, which were influenced by psychoanalytic theory and concepts, continued a tradition that Wundt had pursued several decades earlier. During World War I, American psychologist Robert Woodworth developed an objective questionnaire to measure the emotional stability of army recruits at the request of the American Psychological Association (Woodworth, 1930). He identified hundreds of symptoms in case histories of neurotic patients, which he put in the form of individual questions to be answered 'yes' or 'no'. Trials on normal subjects eliminated questions that were reported so frequently as to be diagnostically irrelevant. Additional validation studies on recruits and diagnosed adults led to the conclusion that the instrument was promising, but the end of the war and the experiments left the utility of Woodworth's Psychoneurotic Inventory (also known as the Personal Data Sheet) undocumented. Nonetheless the items proved robust, and many appeared in later instruments in one form or another. The MMPI, which is probably the most frequently used clinical instrument in the US today, eventually came to represent the pinnacle of this objective, empirically based tradition in instrument development. Other inventories such as the Millon (2000) scales, the Personality Assessment Inventory (Morey, 1991), and the Beck Depression Inventory (Beck et al., 1988) are also quite widely used and well regarded, although not uncritically (Boyle and Le Dean, 2000; Boyle and Lennon, 1994).

Cattell and his colleagues spent a significant amount of time mapping the domain of normal personality. At the adult level his work coalesced in the Sixteen Personality Factor Questionnaire (16PF) (R.B. Cattell et al., 1993; Krug and Johns, 1990), which became one of the world's most widely used instruments since its initial publication in 1949. Although focused primarily on normal-range characteristics, the instrument has been found to make important contributions to the understanding of some clinical problems (see, for example, H.B. Cattell, 1989; Meyer and Deitsch, 1995). Nevertheless certain areas remain where the 16PF traits do not provide much differentiation among various diagnostic groups or provide insight in potential pathology. This is particularly true with respect to the identification of disorders where depression and psychosis are central.

The wisdom of clinical practice argues strongly that neither instruments oriented solely to clinical characteristics nor those oriented principally to normal-range characteristics are entirely satisfactory in practice. Clients present not only with symptoms but also with personalities. How individuals approach problems and how they cope with stress, for example, is influenced by their personality. Understanding clients' total personality is as important as understanding their symptoms if we are to develop effective treatment plans (Krug, 2004).

With substance abuse clients, for example, a simple case history that records information such as onset and length of addiction or types of substance(s) used is not sufficient to suggest effective treatment procedures nor does it provide great insight into probable outcomes. Information about normal-range characteristics such as maturity and sensitivity prove to be very helpful in predicting the course of therapy and structuring a reasonable treatment plan. Cloninger (1987), for example, described two alcoholism syndromes in which personality dynamics are very different. One type is characterized by anxiety accompanied by feelings of guilt and shame, whereas the other type is characterized by antisocial personality characteristics, with impulsive consumption of alcohol that is often accompanied by fighting and subsequent arrest.

Other normal-range characteristics are helpful in anticipating who will have greater difficulty following through on a treatment plan. Normal-range personality characteristics are useful in sorting out primary and secondary problems and understanding differences between chronic and acute symptoms. Knowledge of such characteristics can often predict resistance to therapy. Research has also demonstrated that normal-range personality characteristics can be useful in determining choice of medication as an adjunct to treatment for depression (Neal, 1977).

The instrument, which was initially published as the Clinical Analysis Questionnaire (CAQ) and a later modification called the PsychEval Personality Questionnaire (PEPQ), added 12 clinical scales to the 16 normal-range personality scales of the 16PF to produce a truly multi-purpose instrument. The development of the 16PF scales is well documented in other sources to which the reader is referred (see H.E. Cattell, this volume, for example). The 12 clinical scales had their origin in two avenues of research that R.B. Cattell and his colleagues actively pursued in the 1960s.

For many years depression was treated mainly as a unidimensional, clinical phenomenon, and few made any effort to study it scientifically. One of the earliest attempts to analyze depression into its subcomponents was that undertaken by Grinker et al. (1961), who identified five factors among items that described the attitude and out-look of patients diagnosed as clinically depressed. R.B. Cattell and Bjerstedt (1967) used these findings as a point of departure for identifying and replicating seven distinct, though correlated primary depression factors. Each reflected different aspects of clinical depression, such as somatic complaints, sleep disturbances, guilt, worthlessness, and low self-esteem. All were found to be distinct from those previously established personality factors included in the 16PF[1] and represent the first seven of the clinical scales.

The remaining five clinical scales resulted from studies of the joint dimensionality of the 16PF and the MMPI (R.B. Cattell and

Bolton, 1969). The MMPI was developed in the late 1930s and originally intended to distinguish among diagnostic groups. Although the instrument has 10 clinical scales, the symptoms that the items represent are not unique to the 10 clinical syndromes after which the scales were originally named. Factor analytic studies led Cattell to the conclusion that five factors beyond those in the 16PF were required to explain the covariation among the scales of the MMPI.[2] Subsequent research (R.B. Cattell, 1973) confirmed that these five were factorially independent of the seven depression factors.

The 28-scale inventory consisting of the 16 normal-range scales plus the 12 clinical scales was first published in 1980 as the Clinical Analysis Questionnaire (CAQ). It consisted of 128 items designed to measure the 16 normal-range traits and 144 items designed to measure the 12 clinical traits. These items were selected from a total pool of more than 4,000 items that had been tested and refined in programmatic studies on personality measurement that began in 1946. Except for about 20% new items, those selected to measure the normal traits appeared in previous, published versions of the 16PF, although some were modified slightly or simplified in language. The clinical items were new items that had been validated and refined in the course of six factor-analytic validity studies. Although validity was the prime consideration in the selection of items for the final test form, sensitivity reviews eliminated items with potentially offensive content and those that lacked clarity. Later, the 128 normal-range items were replaced with form A of the 16PF, which was the most widely used version and which incorporated several validity scales that the CAQ lacked.

In the course of a revision in 1999, a new version of the instrument appeared as the PsychEval Personality Questionnaire (PEPQ) (H.E.P. Cattell et al., 2006b). The most important change was the replacement of normal-range items with the 5th edition of the 16PF, which had been published in 1993. However, the clinical items in the instrument were reviewed and updated at the same time.

About half were replaced. Because of some shifts in the meaning of the scales, both versions of the instrument – CAQ and PEPQ – remain in print and are available from the publisher (IPAT).

DESCRIPTION OF THE COMPONENT SCALES

The PEPQ contains 325 three-choice items of which 185 are used to measure the normal-range scales and 140 to measure clinical symptoms. The instrument is not timed but generally takes no more than an hour and a half to complete. Scores are reported on the *sten* scale, which has a mean of 5.5 and a standard deviation of 2.0 in the reference population. In the discussion of scale scores that follow, the term 'high scores' usually refer to sten scores of 8–10, which represent approximately the upper 15% of scores, and 'low scores' usually refer to sten scores of 1–3, which represent the lowest 15% of scores. This is not to suggest, however, that sten scores from 4 through 7, which represent about 70% of all scores, are meaningless.[3] They often represent a positive balance of the polar characteristics.

In addition to the 28 primary scales scores are also presented for a series of global characteristics, which combine the primary scales in different ways. These global characteristics offer a convenient way of beginning test interpretation (Krug, 1981a) by giving as they do a 'broad brush' perspective on personality.

NORMAN RANGE PERSONALITY SCALES

A: Warmth[4]

Individuals who score high on this scale are usually found to be warmhearted, personable, and easy to get along with. They are more likely to share their feelings with others. They are frequently more successful and more satisfied in occupations where interpersonal contact is critical, such as sales and customer service positions. McClain (1968) found this characteristic to be an important element in counselor effectiveness. There are also indications that it contributes to teaching success.

Occupationally social workers score above average on this scale. Artists and research scientists, who are typically more oriented to concepts and ideas than to people, tend to score significantly below average on this scale.

Karson et al. (1997) have pointed out that low-scoring individuals often fit the 'burnt child' syndrome, indicating a long history of unsatisfying interpersonal relationships. Extremely low scores on this scale may point to a pathological dislike and avoidance of close personal relationships. Extremely high scores can on occasion point to an unhealthy dependence on others and low self-esteem.

B: Reasoning

This is not strictly a personality characteristic, but Cattell incorporated it into the first edition of the 16PF, and it has remained an integral part of the 16PF profile for more than half a century. It provides a measure of overall cognitive ability within which to understand total personality functioning. Despite the fact that the scale is short (15 items) and is given under power conditions, there is reasonable evidence of its validity (Conn and Rieke, 1994). Nonetheless it should be considered only a gross measure of general ability.

There may be some clinical significance to low scores when other evidence (e.g. a college degree)[5] would suggest the individual should score higher. Severe depression, for example, may interfere with the person's ability to concentrate.

C: Emotional stability

Scores on this scale may be taken as an index of the individual's stress resilience and tolerance for ambiguity. In other self-reports high-scoring individuals say they are generally able to reach personal goals without particular difficulty. They focus more easily on tasks before them and report overall satisfaction with the way they have lived their lives. It is an important contributor to the global anxiety factor.

Occupationally, airline pilots score significantly above average on this scale as do many successful executives. Scores have been found to be significantly below average in the chronically unemployed. Low scores are associated with accident proneness and have been shown to have consistent relationships with physical illness, including coronary problems (Krug and Sherman, 1977).

Low scores on this scale are especially important clinically and reflect someone who is overwhelmed by the challenges of day, someone with little resilience to stress or psychological 'wear and tear'. Karson et al. (1997) noted that the prognosis for therapeutic outcome is generally poorer when scores on this scale are low.

E: Dominance

High-scoring individuals are generally more self-assertive and competitive, forceful, and generally very direct in interactions with others. They enjoy having things their own way. Occupationally, E has been shown to be important in many sales occupations where it seems to be especially related to closing ability. Athletes and judges also score significantly above average as groups.

Karson et al. (1997) pointed out that this scale is related to the individual's ability to externalize hostile feelings. The high-scoring individual can more readily vent angry feelings. The individual who is extremely low is not so fortunate, and when bottled up feelings pour out unexpectedly may display a passive-aggressive behavior pattern.

F: Liveliness

High scores on this scale are associated with happy-go-lucky, enthusiastic, uninhibited behavior patterns. H.B. Cattell (1989: 90–91) compared factor F's exuberance with the natural self-expression and spontaneity that children show before they are socialized and learn self-control. Low scores on this scale are not synonymous with depression (Krug and Laughlin, 1977). While it is true that depressed patients frequently score low on this scale, many non-depressed test takers do so also. People working in sales often score much above average on this scale where it may reflect a tendency to reach out to others in new situations.

Karson et al. (1997) spoke of factor F as one of four behavior-control factors among the 16PF primary scales. Thus, there is the suggestion that this characteristic in combination with three others (G, O, Q$_3$) points to whether the individual will externalize and 'act out' inner conflicts (F+) or internalize them (F−). F is also an important contributor to the broad extraversion factor.

G: Rule consciousness

People who score high on this scale tend to be more persistent, more respectful of authority, and more rigid about following rules than people who score low. There is a certain degree of inflexibility associated with extremely high scores on this scale. Low-scoring people may sometimes appear too flexible, but such scores are not a reliable signal of sociopathic tendencies.

Occupationally, military professionals and airport tower controllers have been found to score significantly above average on this scale, with university professors scoring below average. Flexibility is not a signal aspect of the highscorer's behavioral repertoires, and this may lower his or her ability to cope with extreme stress generated associated with novel situations.

H: Social boldness

High-scoring people are typically adventurous and risk-taking. They typically enjoy being the center of attention. For this reason, people who are successful in sales jobs are often above average on this scale. Based on a review of the literature, particularly medical research, Krug (1980) suggested that high-scoring people appear to have higher stress resistance and more psychological 'insulation'. Consequently, lower scores are usually more indicative of clinical problems than higher scores.

I: Sensitivity

High-scoring people are typically described as sensitive, artistic, and sometimes as dependent and insecure. They generally prefer to use reason rather than force to get things done (Krug, 1981a). Engineering groups have been found to score below average on this dimension, and some counselors have been found to score above the mean. High scores have also been associated with greater frequency of accidents.

Medical research has found high scores on factor I to be consistently related to the incidence of coronary artery disease, hypertension, and frequency of chronic illness. From a patient management perspective there is some suggestion that high-scoring people tend to exaggerate symptoms while low-scoring people tend to understate the severity of their symptoms. Skidmore (1977) has suggested some practical methods of implementing change on this dimension both of increasing and decreasing the individual's score.

L: Vigilance

People who score high on this scale may be described as suspicious, critical, and constantly on guard. It is important to keep in mind, however, that this is a normal-range characteristic, which is not to be confused with the paranoid ideation (PI) scale in part 2 of the instrument. People who score high also say that their upbringing was strict and demanding. They are concerned about what others think about them and tend to be critical of other people's work. Occupationally accountants score above average on this scale, and those in occupations where relating to other people is a key task usually score significantly below average.

Of the scales considered so far, this is the third of four important medical risk factors identified by Sherman and Krug (1977). In particular, high scores have been found to be a risk factor for heart disease. High scores on this scale are significant clinically. Karson et al. (1997) noted that low scores must be regarded as a healthy sign, regardless of how low they may be.

M: Abstractness

Among the 16 normal-range scales this is the 'absent-minded professor' scale. High-scoring people are typically unconcerned about everyday matters. They tend to forget things and are not interested in mechanical things. They also report that their parents are above average in intellectual interests.

Artists and research scientists have been found to score significantly above average. There are associations also with number of automobile accidents and higher creativity levels. There are no strong relationships to any physical illness syndrome, and M does not seem to be particularly significant clinically. In terms of patient management, however, there is the suggestion that high-scoring patients may require more careful management. On one occasion a rather puzzling profile of a successful suicide was presented at a 16PF clinical interpretation seminar. The victim had exhibited no advance warning signs, no note was left, and the profile showed none of the deviations on the anxiety scales that might be expected. The M score was highly elevated, however, and the clinician involved advanced the hypothesis that the suicide was not planned, rather an accidental overdose by a distracted individual.

N: Privateness

Marriage research points to N as playing an important role in relationships. People who are extremely high may be too detached and unable to respond appropriately to the emotional needs of their partner. Low-scoring people tend to be more open, more forthright, and more forthcoming. High scorers prefer to keep problems to themselves.

The work of Krug and Laughlin (1977) suggests that this dimension is also one of socialization and behavior control. That is to say, low-scoring people are not simply more straightforward, but they are generally less constrained by rules and standards. Other clinical associations have not been validated.

O: Apprehension

High-scoring people tend to be worried, guilty, and moody. Elevations on this scale are common in clinical syndromes of all types. High scorers describe themselves as anxious, brooding, downhearted, fearful, lonely, and easily upset. Low scorers appear more confident, more self-assured, and less troubled.

Although it might appear that only high scores on this scale are clinically significant, Karson et al. (1997) pointed out that when the O score is very low questions arise as to the adequacy of behavior controls. For this reason they described O as one of four superego factors among the 16 normal-range personality characteristics.

Q₁: Openness to change

People who score high on this scale tend to be analytic, liberal, and innovative. They trust logic rather than feelings and are quicker to break with established ways of doing things when they find them unsatisfactory or unworkable. Studies of small-group process have shown that high scorers were often rated as the most effective, but not necessarily the best liked, leaders. Karson et al. (1997) pointed to the critical nature of people who score extremely high, which may create significant problems in their relationships with others. Low scorers tend to be more accepting and uncritical.

Q_2: Self-reliance

People who score high on Q_2 are comfortable alone and enjoy making decisions by themselves. They don't typically need a great deal of group support. People who score low work more easily with others and prefer the support of groups. Occupationally low scorers tend to do better in occupations where close interactions with others and teamwork are important. High scorers tend to do better in occupations and roles in which they can act on their own decisions, occupations in which group consensus is relatively less important. Sherman and Krug's (1977) review did not identify Q_2 as a major medical risk factor but there are some associations of higher scores with the incidence of coronary artery disease, hypertension, and ulcers. By themselves, extremely high scores on Q_2 are probably not directly indicative of underlying pathology, but when combined with low scores on A and F and high scores on and Q_4, there may be some evidence of pathological withdrawal from others.

Q_3: Perfectionism

High-scoring people generally exert strong control over their emotional life and behavior. They prefer to get their thoughts organized before speaking out. Organization is a defining characteristic of their actions in general. Low scores are important clinically, although at the extreme upper end of the scale people may be excessively compulsive and difficult to be around. In this vein, Karson et al. (1997) pointed out that when high scores on Q_3 combine with high scores on O and Q_4 there is a tendency to excess compulsivity and obsessive behavior.

CLINICAL PERSONALITY SCALES

Q_4: Tension

This is a principal contributor to the global anxiety factor and a major medical risk factor. Cattell and others have pointed out there is evidence to suggest that higher scores are associated with frustration and inability to attain personal goals. High-scoring people report that they take a long time to calm down when they are upset, are easily irritated, have difficulty sleeping, and get angry too quickly.

Despite the fact that this is one of the largest contributors to the overall anxiety score, it may be less clinically significant than other contributing factors that have been previously discussed. Nevertheless, Karson et al. (1997) pointed out that high scores on Q_4 are always important because they signal an unmistakable cry for help when the items are so transparent as to be easily denied.

The twelve clinical scales can be thought of as falling into a group of six scales that assess depression symptoms, three scales that assess distorted thought patterns, two scales that assess risk taking, and one scale that measures overall feelings of inadequacy. With the exception of the two risk-taking scales, only elevations on the scales are generally clinically significant. Some redefinition of scales took place in the development of the PEPQ from the CAQ. The descriptions and scale designations provided here are consistent with those for the PEPQ.

HC: Health Concerns

The first of the six depression scales deals with concerns about health and non-specific physical complaints. High-scoring people feel that their health is worse than others' and report being generally run down. If the physical symptoms cannot be explained by an underlying physical condition, there is a basis for exploring diagnoses of a somatoform disorder. With respect to the MMPI scales HC has high, significant correlations with scales 1 (*Hs*), 2 (*D*), 7 (*Pt*), and 0 (*Si*).

ST: Suicidal Thinking

The item content of this scale centers on thoughts of self-destruction. High-scoring people report that they are disgusted with life and that life has become empty and meaningless. They entertain thoughts of death. Scores on ST are high in depressed patients. Even if these scores appear to take the form of suicide gestures only, they should still not be ignored because they signal a cry for help.

Correlations have been found with MMPI scales 7 (*Pt*), 1 (*Hs*), 8 (*Sc*), 0 (*Si*), and *F*, which, although originally conceptualized as a validity scale, Butcher et al. (2000) and others have shown to have clinical significance also.

AD: Anxious Depression

This is part of a global pattern of depression distinct from the global anxiety scale as measured by the normal-range personality scales. High-scoring people describe themselves as clumsy and shaky. They frequently obsess about frightening events, lack self-confidence, and are reluctant to speak out and say what they think. They are confused and unable to cope with sudden demands. It represents an aspect of depression that can be incapacitating and profoundly disturbing. AD tends to correlate with MMPI scales 0 (*Si*) and 7 (*Pt*).

LE: Low Energy State

Some of the other depression scales have fatigue as a secondary symptom, but here it is central. High-scoring people rarely wake up full of energy. They are worn out by the activities of the day and frequently feel sad and unhappy. LE tends to correlate positively with MMPI scales 0 (*Si*), 7 (*Pt*) and negatively with *K*. When LE and HC are both highly elevated, particularly in the absence of other clinical deviations in the profile, experience suggests that the client should be referred for a complete medical evaluation because treatable conditions frequently exist.

SR: Self-Reproach

This is the aspect of depression associated with a feeling of having committed unpardonable acts and experienced the sense of utter worthlessness that follows. People who score high report that they lie awake at night thinking of all the things they have done wrong during the day. They are self-critical and inclined to blame themselves when anything goes wrong. Nightmares in which desertion by others is the central theme are frequent. With respect to the MMPI, its highest correlation is a negative one with the *K* scale. Perhaps this should not be interpreted as a lack of defensiveness or openness on the part of the person but instead as indicating a total breakdown in the individual's system of ego defenses.

AW: Apathetic Withdrawal

Two main features characterize this scale: a feeling that life is too pointless to care and a tendency to avoid people. People who score high feel that they are too useless to interact effectively with others and, as a consequence, they are happier alone. With respect to the MMPI the highest correlation is with scale 0 (*Si*) but the correlation with scale 2 (D) is also significant.

PI: Paranoid Ideation

This is the first of two scales that assess thought disorder patterns, which are a central feature of schizophrenia and related disorders. High scores on this scale are associated with reports of suspicion, a sense of injustice, persecution, jealousy, cynicism, and a fear of being poisoned.

MMPI data show very significant correlations with the *F* scale followed by a somewhat lower but significant correlation with scale 0 (*Si*) and 6 (*Pa*).

OT: Obsessional Thinking

People who score high on this scale report obsessive types of behavior over which they have little control. Such behaviors include counting objects repetitively and unnecessarily and ideas and phrases that run though their minds endlessly. They worry about admittedly unimportant things, which often involve an underlying theme of harm, danger, or risk. There is also an element of phobic patterns as well. There are significant correlation between OT and MMPI scale 7 (*Pt*).

AP: Alienation and Perceptual Distortion

High-scoring people have difficulty getting their ideas into words, have strange impulses, and feel that other people push them around. They see themselves as being of little important to others, have memory lapses, have difficulty distinguishing real from unreal, and experience hallucinations. Scores on this scale are highly correlated with MMPI scale 8 (*Sc*) but also with scale 0 (*Si*) and *F* as well. Both AW and AP deal with withdrawal but the difference between them lies in the fact that AW mainly involves withdrawal from people and social settings while AP involves withdrawal from reality.

TS: Thrill-Seeking

TS is the first of two risk-taking scales. Correlations with the MMPI suggest a connection between scores on TS and what was originally conceived of as the hypomanic syndrome (scale 9–*Ma*). High-scoring people say they would like adventurous jobs and those in which they have to speak up and take charge. They crave excitement. Beneath the surface there may be something of a 'death wish', which might explain this restless love of adventure and risk.

In studies by R.B. Cattell and Bjerstedt (1967), this dimension first appeared among items designed to measure depression symptoms. However, Krug and Laughlin's (1977) large-scale study of the higher-order structure of the clinical scales did not find it to contribute to a broad, second-order depression dimension. With respect to TS low and high scores both represent significant clinical signs. Scores are low in those with anxiety disorders and schizophrenics but high in classes of drug abusers and those exhibiting symptoms of antisocial personality disorder.

TI: Threat Immunity

High-scoring people are generally less inhibited than the average person, by physical danger, pain, or society's criticism. Although scores are correlated with those on TS, elevations on TI appear to have more pathological implications. High scores on TS may reflect impulsivity, but high scores on TI appear to be more related to a sense of invulnerability. Among depressed patients, TI is often below average.

A number of correlations with the MMPI clinical scales are negative including scales 0 (*Si*), 2 (*D*), and 7 (*Pt*). It correlates positively with scale 9 (*Ma*).

Krug and Laughlin's (1977) study of the structure of the instrument's scales identified a second-order socialization dimension to which TI contributed negatively. With its insensitivity to inhibition, which appears to be a central feature of this scale, it may be that this scale would serve to reliably differentiate acting out disorders from those marked by withdrawal.

PI: Psychological Inadequacy

High-scoring people describe themselves as no good for anything. Reality distortion occurs in the area of factual self-worth. People who elevate on this scale think of themselves as doomed or condemned. This suggests the 'learned helplessness' pattern that Beck (1967) described in his analysis of depression. For this reason it is not surprising the PI is an important facet of the second-order depression factor. MMPI correlations are high with *F* and scales 8 (*Sc*), 0 (*Si*), and 7 (*Pt*).

VALIDITY SCALES

In addition to the 28 content scales, the PEPQ contains three validity scales: impression management (IM), infrequency (INF), and acquiescence (ACQ). They are designed to detect unusual response patterns that may invalidate or moderate an interpretation of the content scales.

Impression management assesses the degree to which the client endorses socially desirable responses consistently. High scores may indicate a deliberate attempt to present oneself in an untruthfully positive light. However, the scale may elevate when the client is being honest as well. Low scores may indicate a tendency toward extreme self-criticalness.

The Infrequency scale was developed empirically by identifying item responses with very low endorsement frequencies. For the 32 items in this scale, respondents in the normative population selected the 'a' or 'c' options nearly 95% of the time, leaving a very small group who answered 'b'. People who score high on the scale may have had difficulty reading the items or understanding the concepts. Or they may have trouble making decisions.

The acquiescence scale counts the number of times the test taker responds 'true' to 103 of the questions designed to measure the normal-range personality characteristics. Since the content of the questions is relatively balanced for positive and negative endorsement, people who score unusually high on this scale may appear inconsistent in their choices, saying, on the one hand, that they are bold and socially outgoing and, on the other hand, that they can go for long periods of time without wanting to speak to anyone.

Elevation on one or more of these validity scales does not automatically invalidate the profile. But it may give the examiner cause to delve more deeply in the interpretive process and look for external evidence to confirm the score profile.

GLOBAL OR SECOND-ORDER SCALES

The structure of correlations among the primary scales leads to identification of a set of second-order or global personality scales. These are often helpful in organizing the information contained in the profile and serve as a point of departure for test interpretation.

There are five global factors associated with the normal-range primaries: extraversion, anxiety, tough-mindedness, independence, and self-control. These are very similar to those described as the 'Big Five' in personality research. Krug and Laughlin (1977) identified several others that mainly involved the clinical scales or combinations of the clinical and normal-range scales. A scale they called 'socialization', for example, combined thrill seeking (TS) and threat immunity (TI) with normal-range characteristics that deal with aspects of behavior control, including G, Q1, and E. The socialization and self-control scales are correlated but factor-analytically separable. Another dimension Krug and Laughlin called 'psychoticism' combines scores on paranoid ideation (PI), alienation and perceptual distortion (AP), and obsessional thinking (OT). Krug and Laughlin's (1977) analysis was based on correlations among the test scores themselves. Boyle's (1987) second-order solution, which was based on the intercorrelations of the primary factors derived by Kameoka (1986: 11), produced a somewhat different set of factors.

Although the global scales do not convey any information about the person that is not contained in the primary scales, they can be very helpful in organizing that information and serve as a point of departure for test interpretation.

NORMS, RELIABILITY, AND VALIDITY

Norms for the normal-range scales are based on a sample of 10,261 adults. This sample tends to be younger and more highly educated than the general adult population. Norms for the 12 clinical scales are based on a sample of 1,763 non-diagnosed adults.

With the exception of the validity scales, which are converted to percentile ranks, the PEPQ raw scores are transformed to Cattell's *sten* scale, a standard score scale that has a mean of 5.5 and a standard deviation of 2.0 in the reference population. Sten scores of 8–10 are generally considered 'high', and sten scores of 1–3 are generally considered 'low'. Scores in the 4–7 range are thought to be average and of somewhat less importance in interpretation. On most scales, gender differences are not important enough to warrant separate norms, but on four (A, I, O, and TI) separate norms are available. Internal consistency reliabilities of the scales average about 0.78 for the content scales (cf. Boyle, 1991). Short-term test–retest reliabilities are somewhat lower. Reliabilities for the validity scales are not presented in the test manual (H.E.P. Cattell et al., 2006b).

Test validity is not so easily captured in a single coefficient or a table of values as the reliability because validity is an ongoing process of providing evidence for the accuracy of score interpretations. Some of this evidence may rest on correlations between test scores and external measures of similar constructs. Another source of evidence, particularly for clinical scales, is the demonstration that independently diagnosed patients exhibit characteristics consistent with the meaning of the separate scales.

Some relationships between the test and the MMPI have been already discussed in the description of those scales. The handbook (H.E.P. Cattell et al., 2006b) presents additional correlations between the clinical scales and those of the MMPI-2 (2006b: 49). Jones and Bedwell (2005) reported results of a series of regression analyses in which the MMPI clinical scales were predicted from the total set of 28 normal- and clinical-range scales. The analyses, which were based on a sample of 136, produced multiple correlations ranging from highs of 0.88 for scale 0 (*Si*) and 0.77 for scale 2 (*D*) to 0.54 for scale 1 (*Hs*) and scale 5 (*Mf*). Across the 10 basic MMPI scales the multiple correlations averaged 0.66.

The handbook also compares a sample of 529 clinically diagnosed, mainly depressed patients with the normal, standardization population. Group means were half a standard deviation or more apart on the six depression scales and on the psychological inadequacy (PI) scale. The groups differed by a similar amount on the threat immunity (TI) scale, but the direction was reversed with the clinical population scoring below normal adults. This may have been a reflection of the fact that depression was by far the most common diagnosis in the clinical group.

A large amount of validation evidence has accrued in areas involving screening for sensitive, high-stress positions and those involving protective services. Krug (1981b) constructed a formal screening model for use in screening nuclear power plant operators and Krug and Behrens (1981) described a similar application of the instrument in screening for weapons use suitability. Both reports marshaled an array of evidence for the reliability, validity, and utility of the approach.

Jones et al. (2006) examined PEPQ scores for a sample of 236 civilian police officers who applied for international peacekeeping assignments in countries such as Afghanistan, Iraq, and Kosovo. The applicant sample averaged about half a standard deviation below the PEPQ norm sample mean and a full standard deviation or more below the PEPQ clinical sample mean.

The test publisher, IPAT, has developed several computer-based reports specifically for use in protective service screening. The *Protective Services Report Plus*, which is based on the PEPQ scales, relates the individual's personal style to use of force, stress tolerance, and safety. The *Law Enforcement and Development Report*, which is based on the CAQ scales, focuses on issues in selecting applicants for enforcement and investigative services. Manuals for each of these reports summarize relevant validity information (H.E.P. Cattell et al., 2006a; IPAT staff, 1987).

CASE STUDIES

This section presents three sets of profiles. They were selected to illustrate typical applications of the instrument such as clinical evaluation and follow-up, marriage counseling, and forensic examination.

Case 1: Clinical evaluation and follow-up

This is the profile of a woman tested at the beginning of therapy and six months later. She was married and had two adult children who were no longer living at home. During the initial interview the client reported a very rigid upbringing, and there were unconfirmed suggestions of early sexual abuse by her father. She reported serious problems with depression, which is the reason she sought therapy. She was spending all of her time at home crying most of the day and had essentially withdrawn from all social activity.

As Figure 31.1 shows, all the pre-test depression primaries are in the extreme range, and the second-order depression factor score (9.4) is virtually the maximum obtainable. The other clinical scales are all within normal range, although the obsessional thinking (OT) scale is slightly elevated.

With regard to the normal-range primary scales, nine fall outside the average score range. The client describes herself as extremely conservative (Q1−) despite a very high score on M (abstractness). Three important anxiety scales (L+, O+, Q4+) and H(−) fall in the extreme score range. She is quite sensitive to threat (H−), suspicious (L+),

insecure (O+), and tense (Q4+). Rigidity is also an important element of the profile, with G, Q3, and L all highly elevated.

This case illustrates the utility of repeated testing during the course of therapy to monitor the effectiveness of intervention (Krug, 2004). Six months of treatment shows striking changes in this woman. This is evident primarily in the clinical scales: ten have gone down. Among the normal-range primaries, which represent more enduring aspects of personality, the shifts are much less, as might be expected. Factor O, which drops from 9 to 5, is the largest. Rigidity is still evident in the profile, but this may have some positive value as a defense in the presence of so much initial pathology. Her score on factor B also rose two sten score points in the six months. This is probably a reflection of depression interfering with her cognitive functioning at the time of initial testing.

Case 2: Forensic evaluation

This is the profile of a 34-year-old male who was convicted of two counts of murder. The profile is unique in the fact that the scores on the normal-range personality characteristics were obtained two months before the murder. Section 2 of the instrument was administered shortly before the trial.

The facts of the case are as follows. This man joined two others one evening who planned to rob a vacant farmhouse. As the evening progressed, plans changed, and they stopped two high-school seniors on a deserted highway whom they had spotted at a store picking up a six-pack of beer. One of the three, a 'leader' of sorts, shot the boys but did not kill them. The leader ordered his accomplice, whose profile is shown in Figure 31.2, to 'finish the job'. In his statement given at the time of his arrest, the 34-year-old maintained that the leader threatened to kill him if he didn't comply. The arrests followed a routine traffic stop.

Three of the clinical scales fall in the high range: anxious depression (AD), apathetic

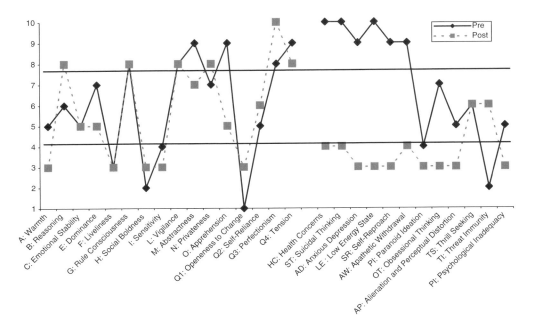

Figure 31.1

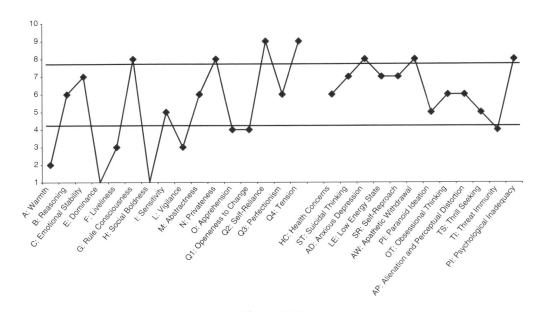

Figure 31.2

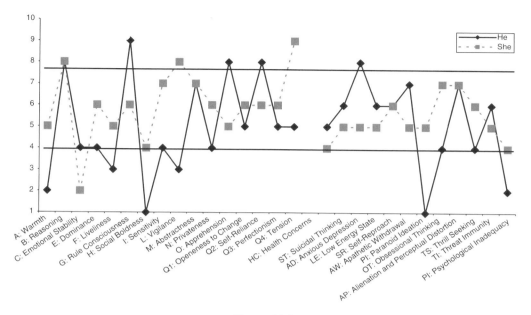

Figure 31.3

withdrawal (AW), and psychological inadequacy (PI). Withdrawal is also evident in very low scores on warmth (A–), liveliness (F–), and social boldness (H–). The extremely low score on H seems particularly revealing in light of his statement that he killed in response to a threat. H can be thought of as representing the individual's level of 'psychological insulation', with higher scores representing more insulation. People who score low are more vulnerable and sensitive to threat. When combined with the low score on dominance (E) the picture emerges of the type of person who must adapt to circumstances despite the personal costs involved in doing so. He is also significantly above average on G, and this, too, makes it very difficult for him to disobey orders.

The trial jury returned a guilty verdict and imposed the death penalty, which had just been restored in Illinois that year. The state Supreme Court, which automatically reviews all death penalty cases, drew heavily on testimony related to the psychological profile in vacating the death penalty. He was subsequently re-sentenced to 500 years in prison.

Case 3: Marriage counseling

Figure 31.3 presents the profiles of a couple seeking marital counseling. She is 26 years old, and he is 28. Both are college graduates, had been married two years at the time, and knew each other for a year and a half before marriage. There were no children. He was employed in a middle-level management role for five years.

During the initial interview she had trouble pinpointing what had led her to move out of the house a week earlier. Both reported a decline in the enjoyment and frequency of sex during the past year. She attributed much of this to the fact that her husband was unhappy with his job. He was afraid of being fired but refused to consider other job options. She felt that he brought his problems home from work and focused his anger on her.

The most extreme elements of her profile are found among the anxiety scales. Of those Q4 is nearly at the maximum level and C is equally deviant. She is bright (B+) and tends to be somewhat more sensitive than the average woman (gender-specific norms were used in converting raw to scale scores). She is inclined to be creative (I+, M+) but given her high-anxiety level it is doubtful whether she was able to channel her efforts as productively as she might like. None of her clinical scales fall outside the normal range.

His profile combines a maximum degree of threat sensitivity (H−) with conformity (G+). His extreme withdrawal is reflected in a global extraversion score of 1.2, which undoubtedly leads to difficulties in how he relates to others. He prefers to work and do things alone (Q2 = 8). Creative potential is high, but in the face of so many underlying conflicts it is unlikely that he will be able to harness these resources effectively. An anxiety disorder (see elevation on AD) would appear to underlie his current career crisis: he is afraid of being fired but refuses to look for other employment. Another depression scale, apathetic withdrawal (AW), is also elevated.

In both profiles there is evidence of elevated anxiety, underlying conflict, and some tendency toward obsessive behavior patterns. One important point to be noted in this case is that personality problems that have led to their problems are essentially contained within normal dimensions.

His extreme tendencies toward introversion undoubtedly place many demands on the relationship particularly with respect to communication. The score of 2 on A (warmth) is suggestive of a long history of unsatisfactory relationships. Counseling did not work in this situation, and they subsequently divorced.

SUMMARY

In the CAQ and PEPQ, Cattell and his colleagues created useful instruments for simultaneously assessing pathology and personality. The instruments provide a means of understanding symptoms within the context of total personality functioning. The scales are reliable and combine to form even more reliable composite or global scales.

Perhaps the single biggest disadvantage to the use of the CAQ (and PEPQ) is that the clinical scales, in particular, have not been as widely researched as many other multidimensional clinical inventories. The CAQ was published only a short time before Cattell's retirement, and no co-author has emerged to guide the subsequent research agenda for the instrument. The normal-range (16PF) scales in part 1 of the CAQ, of course, continue to be widely studied, but relatively little research has emerged in recent years relative to the clinical psychopathology scales in part 2 of the instrument.

Although the clinical scales have not enjoyed as wide use in general clinical evaluation, there are niches within which a significant body of research evidence points to the utility of the CAQ/PEPQ, particularly in the area of screening for protective services. Thus, the instrument has been used extensively in personnel selection, for example, by the Australian Army Psychology Corps (Boyle, 1989). Nevertheless, further research is clearly warranted in relation to the construct validity and utility of the clinical scales.

NOTES

1 Scales in the 16PF such as O (apprehension) involve some feelings of guilt and depressed mood. However, empirical studies demonstrated that O and the seven depression scales were factorially distinct.

2 Five 16PF primaries (C, H, L, O, Q4) captured much of the anxiety symptoms present in the MMPI item pool.

3 The score ranges described here refers to the theoretical distribution of sten scores. In practice, it is not possible to obtain 'high' or 'low' PEPQ sten scores in 19 of 96 instances for the normal scales and 24 of 72 instances for the clinical scales (Cattell et al., 2006b).

4 The 16PF handbook (Cattell et al., 1970) is the main source of information about the occupational,

educational, and social correlates of the scales and contains the primary references to the research studies, not otherwise noted here, from which much of the material is adapted.

5 The process of test interpretation requires the user to correlate test scores with background information, self-report, and other test scores in order to arrive at reasonable conclusions about the client's level of functioning. As often as not, discrepancies among these various sources of information will suggest useful questions for follow up inquiry.

REFERENCES

Beck, A.T. (1967) *Depression: Causes and Treatment*. Philadelphia: University of Pennsylvania Press.

Beck, A.T., Steer, R.A. and Garbin, M.G. (1988) 'Psychometric properties of the Beck Depression Inventory: Twenty-five years of evaluation', *Clinical Psychology Review*, 8(1): 77–100.

Boyle, G.J. (1987) 'Psychopathological depression superfactors in the Clinical Analysis Questionnaire', *Personality and Individual Differences*, 8(5): 609–14.

Boyle, G.J. (1989) *A Guide to the Use of the Sixteen Personality Factor Questionnaire and Clinical Analysis Questionnaire in Military Selection*. Canberra: Australian Army Directorate of Psychology, 1st Psychological Research Unit.

Boyle, G.J. (1991) 'Does item homogeneity indicate internal consistency or item redundancy in psychometric scales?', *Personality and Individual Differences*, 12(3): 291–4.

Boyle, G.J. and Le Dean, L. (2000) 'Discriminant validity of the Illness Behavior Questionnaire and Millon Clinical Multiaxial Inventory-III in a heterogeneous sample of psychiatric outpatients', *Journal of Clinical Psychology*, 56(6): 779–91.

Boyle, G.J. and Lennon, T.J. (1994) 'Examination of the reliability and validity of the Personality Assessment Inventory', *Journal of Psychopathology and Behavioral Assessment*, 16(3): 173–87.

Butcher, J.N., Williams, C.L. and Fowler, R.D. (2000) *Essentials of MMPI-2 and MMPI – An Interpretation* (2nd edn). Minneapolis: University of Minnesota Press.

Catell, R.B., Eber, H.W. and Tatsuoka, M.M. (1970) *Handbook for the 16 Personality Factor Questionnaire*. Champaign, IL: Institute for Personality and Ability Testing.

Cattell, H.B. (1989) *The 16PF: Personality in Depth*. Champaign, IL: Institute for Personality and Ability Testing.

Cattell, H.E.P., Bedwell, S. and Maraist, C.C. (2006a) *Protective Services Reports: Interim Manual*. Champaign, IL: Institute for Personality and Ability Testing.

Cattell, H.E.P., Russell, M.T. and Bedwell, S. (2006b) *PsychEval Personality Questionnaire Manual*. Champaign, IL: Institute for Personality and Ability Testing.

Cattell, R.B. (1973) 'A check on the 28-factor Clinical Analysis Questionnaire structure on normal and pathological subjects', *Journal of Multivariate Experimental Personality and Clinical Psychology*, 1(1): 3–12.

Cattell, R.B. and Bolton, L.S. (1969) 'What pathological dimensions lie beyond the normal dimensions of the 16PF? A comparison of MMPI and 16PF factor domains', *Journal of Consulting and Clinical Psychology*, 33(1): 18–29.

Cattell, R.B. and Bjerstedt, A. (1967) 'The structure of depression, by factoring Q-data, in relation to general personality source traits', *Scandinavian Journal of Psychology*, 8(1): 17–24.

Cattell, R.B., Cattell, A.K. and Cattell, H.E.P. (1993) *Sixteen Personality Factor Questionnaire Fifth Edition*. Champaign, IL: Institute for Personality and Ability Testing.

Cloninger, C.R. (1987) 'Neurogenetic adaptive mechanisms in alcoholism', *Science*, 236(4800): 410–16.

Conn, S.R. and Rieke, M.L. (1994) (eds), *The 16PF Fifth Edition Technical Manual*. Champaign, IL: Institute for Personality and Ability Testing.

Grinker, R.R., Miller, J., Sabshin, M., Nunn, R. and Nunnally, J.C. (1961) *The Phenomena of Depressions*. New York: Hoeber.

IPAT staff (1987) *Law Enforcement Assessment and Development Report Manual*. Champaign, IL: Institute for Personality and Ability Testing.

Jones, J.W. and Bedwell, S.E. (2005) *The PsychEval Personality Questionnaire: Introduction to Twenty Experimental Derivative Scores*. Champaign, IL: Institute for Personality and Ability Testing.

Jones, J.W., Newhouse, N.K. and Stowers, M.R. (2006) *Civilian Police Officer Profiles: An IPAT Technical Report*. Champaign, IL: Institute for Personality and Ability Testing.

Kameoka, V.A. (1986) 'The structure of the Clinical Analysis Questionnaire and depression symptomatology', *Multivariate Behavioral Research*, 21(1): 105–22.

Karson, M., Karson, S. and O'Dell, J. (1997) *16PF Interpretation in Clinical Practice: A Guide to the Fifth Edition*. Champaign, IL: Institute for Personality and Ability Testing.

Krug, S.E. (1980) *Clinical Analysis Questionnaire Manual*. Champaign, IL: Institute for Personality and Ability Testing.

Krug, S.E. (1981a) *Interpreting 16PF Profile Patterns*. Champaign: Institute for Personality and Ability Testing.

Krug, S.E. (1981b) 'Development of a formal measurement model for security screening in the nuclear power plant environment', *Multivariate Experimental Clinical Research*, 5(3): 109–23.

Krug, S.E. (2004) 'The Adult Personality Inventory', in M.E. Maruish (ed.), *The Use of Psychological Testing for Treatment Planning and Outcomes Assessment* (3rd edn, Vol. 3). Mahwah, NJ: Erlbaum, pp. 679–94.

Krug, S.E. and Behrens, G.M. (1981) 'Psychological screening for weapons use suitability: A formal decision model', *Proceedings of the 23rd Annual Conference of the Military Testing Association. Arlington, VA*, October 28.

Krug, S.E. and Johns, E.F. (1990) 'The 16PF', in C.E. Watkins Jr. and V.L. Campbell (eds), *Testing in Counseling Practice*. Hillsdale, NJ: Erlbaum.

Krug, S.E. and Sherman, J.L. (1977) 'Psychological trait analysis in preventive medicine', *Journal of the International Academy of Preventive Medicine*, 4(1): 48–56.

Krug, S.E. and Laughlin, J.E. (1977) 'Second-order factors among the normal and pathological primary personality traits', *Journal of Consulting Psychology*, 45(4): 575–82.

McClain, W.E. (1968) 'Sixteen Personality Factor Questionnaire scores and success in counseling', *Journal of Counseling Psychology*, 15(6): 492–6.

Meyer, R.G. and Deitsch, S.E. (1995) *The Clinician's Handbook: Integrated Diagnostics, Assessment, and Intervention in Adult and Adolescent Psychopathology* (4th edn). Boston: Allyn & Bacon.

Millon, T. (2000) *Personality Disorders in Modern Life*. New York: Wiley

Morey, L.C. (1991) *Personality Assessment Inventory – Professional Manual*. Odessa, FL: Psychological Assessment Resources.

Neal, W. (1997) 'The DI/AN formula for predicting patient response to antidepressant medication', in S.E. Krug (ed.), *Psychological Assessment in Medicine*. Champaign, IL: Institute for Personality and Ability Testing.

Sherman, J.L. and Krug, S.E. (1977) 'Personality-somatic interactions: The research evidence', in S.E. Krug (ed.), *Psychological Assessment in Medicine*. Champaign, IL: Institute for Personality and Ability Testing.

Skidmore, S. (1977) 'Translating psychological profiles into treatment procedures', in S.E. Krug (ed.), *Psychological Assessment in Medicine*. Champaign, IL: Institute for Personality and Ability Testing.

Woodworth, R.S. (1930) 'Autobiography of Robert S. Woodworth', in C.A. Murchison (ed.), *History of Psychology in Autobiography* (Vol. 2). Worcester, MA: Clark University Press, pp. 359–80.

32

The Logic and Methodology of the Millon Inventories

Theodore Millon

In seeking to identify and measure distinct trait dimensions that characterize individual differences, psychological tests tease out from each person only those features considered common to all persons. Yet by using such assessment instruments, we must ultimately put together in a reconstructive process the very individuality of each person we had just disassembled. In this disassembly and reconstructive sequence an assessment circle completes itself as an interpretive synthesis: from rich idiographic individuality, to nomothetic commonalities, and finally, to nomothetic individuality. We break down with our assessment tools the very person we ultimately must rebuild and thereby understand. The fractionated person, the person who has been dispersed across instruments and scales, must be put back together again as the integrated whole he or she once was.

How is such a venture to be achieved? First and foremost, I believe that assessment must be based on a sound theoretical foundation. The end goal, of course, is the integrated person, wherein every loose end has been tied up in a reconstruction of the person's unique psyche. Only theory can guide the synthesis of the person so that his or her traits can be addressed with confidence and useful understandings.

Although undoubtedly biased in my appraisal, I believe that no other group of assessment inventories offers as complete a synthesis of personality styles and classical psychiatric disorders as the Millon Inventories. Moreover, perhaps no other group of instruments is as coordinated with the official DSM and ICD taxonomies of personality disorders as the Millon Inventories, or as conceptually consonant with the multiaxial logic that underlies the DSM. In fact, the Millon Inventories are but one (essential) link in what has emerged as a theoretical schema by which to conceptualize both personality and abnormal behavior (Millon, 1969, 1981, 1990, 2004a). Since the test is embedded in a theoretical matrix, one must understand the theory to understand the tests. This requires a justification, not merely a dispensation. Most of the more theoretical material presented may be found in *Toward a New Personology: An Evolutionary Model* (Millon, 1990). Other concerns have been treated at a level of abstraction more gross than their gravity requires. Here must be included the descriptions, developmental pathways (all but omitted), and specific intervention opportunities for each of the personality disorders and their more common two-point variants. Much of this information is available in *Disorders of Personality* (Millon, 1981, 1996). In an ideal world, we should adopt ideal goals, but in a less than ideal world, we must often adopt pragmatic ones.

INTEGRATIVE LOGIC AND THE PROCESS OF ASSESSMENT

The word 'integrative' is now used so widely as to be platitudinous: Obviously, given an equivalence of purpose, that which is more integrated is better than that which is less integrated. However, integration neither springs into being fully formed, nor is it unveiled or discovered in a single conceptual leap. Instead, integration is perhaps better understood as a dynamic process. Such a conception sees knowledge building as an ongoing activity in which internal inconsistencies are generated and resolved or transcended at successively superordinate levels of conceptualization: While reality is undoubtedly integrated, our ideas about reality must be more or less so.

Pepper (1942) formalized the integrative means of knowledge building as a world view which he called 'organicism', one of his four relatively adequate 'world hypotheses' or metaphysical world views. Pepper describes seven categories of organicism. Translated into terms easily recognized, these are: (1) observations (fragments) lead one to (2) form inchoate theoretical propositions (nexuses), which, unfortunately, do not all mesh harmoniously, automatically producing (3) aggravating and ostensibly irreconcilable inconsistencies (contradictions) that are resolved through (4) a unified theory (organic whole), which, upon reflection, is (5) found to have been implicit in the observations (fragments) all along. Thus, (6) transcends

the initial naive inconsistencies among observations by reconceptualizing these observations in terms of a new, coherent theoretical model, one which (7) integrates or accounts for all the evidence (economizes) according to its new terms and relationships.

Undoubtedly, even this is a lot to digest in a paragraph or two. Extrapolating from the logic presented above, we might say that as a body of implicit theories is formalized, hiatuses are discovered, and the theories inevitably become enmeshed in inconsistencies and contradictions. Eventually, a new theory is formulated which unifies disparate observations and inconsistencies. What was believed to have been contradictory is discovered not to have been so at all, but only to have appeared contradictory, much as special cases are transcended by more general formulations.

By this account, science cannot exist merely as a descriptive venture which consists of observing, categorizing, and cross-correlating various phenomena at face value, but instead proceeds by establishing superordinate theoretical principles that unify the manifestations of a subject domain by explaining why these particular observations or formulations obtain rather than others.

Even if reliable observations of great or even perfect positive predictive power could be made through some infallible methodology, these indicators would stand simply as isolated facts unassimilated as scientific knowledge until unified through some theoretical basis. Predictive power alone does not make a science. Scientific explanations appeal to theoretical principles which operate above the level of superficialities, principles which are sufficient because they predict, and necessary because they explain.

The process of clinical assessment follows essentially the same logic. Modeling the following after Pepper but substituting the appropriate terminology: The individual scales, instruments, and other data are the (1) fragments. These possess (2) nexuses, implications, or (statistically) intercorrelations both with each other and with other clinical phenomena, leading to inchoate theories about the individual and his or her psychopathology. Inevitably these theories do not mesh, and cannot be assimilated to each other exactly, leading to (3) contradictions, gaps, or inconsistencies in the assessment thus far. One then steps back, seeking (4) a more integrative theory or organic whole which makes sense of the gaps or inconsistencies. This integrative theory is then found to have been (5) implicit in the scales, observations, and other data (otherwise an integrative assessment would not be possible at all), and to (6) transcend the foregoing inconsistencies, gaps, or contradictions by means of a coherent totality, which (7) makes sense of all the observations by tying up all loose ends.

In an integrative assessment, one is required to step outside the theoretical fecundity and inevitable contradictions of a morass of scales and data domains in order to develop a theory of the client in which all the data somehow makes sense. This superordinate theory lies literally at a higher level of formulation than the individual measures which constitute the 'raw data' of the assessment do. Thus, the 'loop' from idiographic individuality to nomothetic commonality to nomothetic individuality is brought to closure: Nomothetic individuality explicitly requires the re-integration of the individual who currently lies fractionated among various scales and dimensions. An integrative assessment, then, does not come into being of its own accord, but is constructed, and its validity is linked to the mode of its construction.

ON THE IMPORTANCE OF THEORY TO A TAXONOMY OF PERSONALITY DISORDERS

Philosophers of science are agreed that it is theory which provides the conceptual glue that binds a nosology together. Moreover, a good theory not only summarizes and incorporates extant knowledge, it possesses systematic import, in that it originates and develops new observations and new methods. In setting out a theory of personality prototypes, what is desired is not merely a *descriptive* list of disorders and their correlated attributes, but an *explanatory* derivation based on theoretical principles. Again, the question of interest is: Why these particular personality disorders rather than others?

To address this question, a taxonomy must seek a theoretical schema which 'carves nature at its joints', so to speak. The philosopher of science Carl Hempel (1965) clearly distinguished between natural and artificial classification systems. The difference, according to Hempel, is that natural classifications possess 'systematic import'. Hempel writes:

> Distinctions between 'natural' and 'artificial' classifications may well be explicated as referring to the difference between classifications that are scientifically fruitful and those that are not: in a classification of the former kind, those characteristics of the elements which serve as criteria of membership in a given class are associated, universally or with high-probability, with more or less extensive clusters of other characteristics. ... a classification of this sort should be viewed as somehow having objective existence in nature, as 'carving nature at the joints'. (1965: 146–147)

The biological sexes, male and female, and the periodic table of elements are both examples of classifications schemes which can be viewed as possessing 'objective' existence in nature. The items we seek to classify are not genders or chemical elements, however, but persons. In so doing, we seek the ideal of a classification scheme or taxonomy which is 'natural', one which 'inheres' in the subject domain, not 'imposed' on it. Such a scheme asserts its 'the-ness' rather than its 'a-ness': Not only is sufficient with respect to the phenomena of a subject domain, it is necessary.

The purpose of assessment is to develop a theory of the person. That anyone would want to develop an integrative theory of the person without a proportionally integrative theory of the constructs used to explain the person is somewhat puzzling, if not amazing. But when theory is ignored in favor of exclusively empirical inductions or factor-analytically derived orthogonal dimensions, that is essentially what is being done.

Does this mean that one has to buy into the theory which underlies the Millon Inventories to buy into the test? Not at all. While no other instrument is as coordinated with the official DSM taxonomy of personality disorders as the MCMI, the official position of the DSM with regard to all taxonomic categories, including personality prototypes, is atheoretical. Moreover, the MCMI, for example, was designed from the beginning to function as an explicitly clinical inventory. It is not set in stone. As substantive advances in knowledge take place, whether as the result of compelling empirical research or well-justified theoretical deduction, the MCMI has been upgraded and refined as well. Minor elaborations and modifications have been introduced since the original MCMI-I formal publication 30 years ago; these fine-tunings will continue regularly as our understanding of the MCMI's strengths, limits, and potentials develops further.

We must add, however, that to jettison the theory would be to sell the Millon Inventories short. In the absence of a theoretical foundation, the outline of this chapter could be effectively abbreviated. A theoretical perspective embodies well-ordered and codified links between constructs, providing a *generative* basis for making clinical inferences founded on a small number of fundamental principles. We now turn briefly to these principles.

THE POLARITY MODEL OF PERSONALITY DISORDERS

The theoretical model which follows is grounded in evolutionary theory. In essence, it seeks to explicate the structure and styles of personality with reference to deficient, imbalanced, or conflicted modes of ecological adaptation and reproductive strategy. The proposition that the development and functions of personologic traits may be usefully explored through the lens of evolutionary principles has a long, if yet unfulfilled tradition. Spencer (1870) and Huxley (1870) offered suggestions of this nature shortly after Darwin's seminal *Origins* was published. In more recent times, we have seen the emergence of sociobiology, an interdisciplinary science that explores the interface between human social functioning and evolutionary biology (Wilson, 1975, 1978).

Four domains or spheres in which evolutionary principles are demonstrated are labeled as *existence, adaptation, replication*, and *abstraction*. The first relates the serendipitous transformation of random or less organized states into those possessing distinct structures of greater organization; the second refers to homeostatic processes employed to sustain survival in open ecosystems; the third pertains to reproductive styles that maximize the diversification and selection of ecologically effective attributes; and the fourth concerns the emergence of competencies that foster anticipatory planning and reasoned decision making. Polarities derived from the first three phases (pleasure–pain, passive–active, self–other) are used to construct a theoretically embedded classification system of personality disorders.

These polarities have forerunners in psychological theory that may be traced as far back as the early 1900s. A formal summary of the concordance between evolutionary model polarities and modern psychological constructs across (1) principles of learning, (2) psychoanalytic concepts, (3) components of emotion/motivation, and (4) neurobiological substrates is presented in Millon (1990).

The first component of the theory, existence, concerns the maintenance of integrative phenomena, whether nuclear particle, virus, or human being, against the background of entropic decompensation. Evolutionary mechanisms derived from this stage regard life enhancement and life preservation. The former are concerned with orienting individuals toward improvement in the quality of life; the latter with orienting individuals away from actions or environments that decrease the quality of life, or even jeopardize existence itself. These may be called *existential aims*. At the highest level of abstraction such mechanisms form, phenomenologically or metaphorically expressed, a pleasure–pain polarity. Some individuals are conflicted in regard to these existential aims (e.g. the sadistic), while other possess deficits in these crucial substrates (e.g. the schizoid). In terms of neuropsychological growth stages (Millon, 1969, 1981, Millon and Davis 1996), the pleasure–pain polarity is recapitulated in a *sensory-attachment* phase, the purpose of which is the largely innate and rather mechanical discrimination of pain and pleasure signals.

Existence, however, is but an initial phase. Once an integrative structure exists, it must maintain its existence through exchanges of energy and information with its environment. The second evolutionary stage relates to what is termed the 'modes of adaptation'; it is also framed as a two-part polarity, a passive orientation, a tendency to accommodate to one's ecological niche, versus an active orientation, a tendency to modify or intervene in one's surrounds. These *modes of adaptation* differ from the first phase of evolution, being, in that they regard how that which is, endures. Unlike pleasure–pain and self–other, the active–passive polarity is truly unidimensional – one cannot be both active and passive at the same time. In terms of neurophysiological growth stages, these modes are recapitulated in a *sensorimotor-autonomy* phase, during which the child either progresses to active disposition toward his or her physical and social context, or perpetuates the dependent mode of prenatal and infantile existence.

Although organisms may exist well adapted to their environments, the existence of any life form is time-limited. To circumvent this limitation, organisms progress through a *replicatory phase* in by which they are prepared to leave progeny. This phase relates to what biologists have referred to as an *r-* or self-propagating strategy at one polar extreme, and a *K-* or other-nurturing strategy at the second extreme. Psychologically, the former strategy is disposed toward actions which are egotistic, insensitive, inconsiderate, and uncaring; while the latter is disposed toward actions which are affiliative, intimate, protective, and solicitous (Gilligan, 1982; Rushton, 1985; Wilson, 1978). Like pleasure–pain, this self–other polarity is not truly unidimensional. Some personality disorders are conflicted on this polarity, such as the compulsive and passive–aggressive. In terms of a neuropsychological growth stages, an individual's orientation toward self and others is recapitulated in the intracortical-initiative stage. A description of each of the derived personality patterns follows.

APPLYING THE POLARITY MODEL TO THE PERSONALITY DISORDERS

In this section, our goal is to apply the polarity model to the DSM personality disorders. Some personalities exhibit a reasonable balance on one or other of the polarity pairs. Not all individuals fall at the center, of course. Individual differences in both personality features and overall style will reflect the relative positions and strengths of each polarity component. Personalities we have termed *deficient* lack the capacity to experience or to enact certain aspects of the three polarities (e.g. the schizoid has a faulty substrate for both 'pleasure' and 'pain'); those spoken of as *imbalanced* lean strongly toward one or another extreme of a polarity (e.g. the dependent is oriented almost exclusively to receiving the support and nurturance of 'others'); and those we judge *conflicted* struggle with ambivalences toward opposing ends of a bipolarity (e.g. the passive–aggressive vacillates between adhering to the expectancies of 'others' versus enacting what is wished for one's 'self'). In the explications that follow, it is suggested that the reader not only attend to the trait content of the various patterns, but particularly to their embeddedness in the polarity model. Consistent with integrative logic, this theoretical foundation is central to Millon Inventory interpretation.

1 *Schizoid personality.* Schizoid persons are those in which both pleasure and pain polarity systems are deficient, that is, they lack the capacity, relatively speaking, to experience life's events either as painful or pleasurable.

2A *Avoidant personality.* The second clinically meaningful combination based on problems in the pleasure–pain polarity comprises clients with a diminished ability to experience pleasure, but with an unusual sensitivity and responsiveness to pain.

2B *Depressive personality.* Both avoidant and depressive personalities have in common a diminished ability to experience pleasure and a comparable tendency to be overly sensitive to pain, that is, events of a foreboding, disquieting, and anguishing character. However, avoidants have learned to anticipate and eschew these troublesome events. Depressives are notably more passive than the anxiously proactive avoidant.

3 *Dependent personality.* Following the polarity model, one must ask whether particular clinical consequences occur among individuals who are markedly imbalanced interpersonally by virtue of turning almost exclusively toward others or toward themselves. Dependents have learned not only to turn to others as their source of nurturance and security, but also to wait passively for their leadership in providing them.

4 *Histrionic personality.* Also turning to others as their primary strategy are a group of personalities that take an active dependency stance. They achieve their goal of maximizing protection, nurturance, and reproductive success by engaging busily in a series of seductive, gregarious, and attention-getting maneuvers.

5 *Narcissistic personality.* Persons falling into the 'independent' personality pattern also exhibit an imbalance in their replication strategy; in this case, however, there is a primary reliance on self rather than others. These individuals are noted by their egotistic self-involvement, experiencing primary pleasure simply by passively being or focusing on themselves.

6A *Antisocial personality.* Those whom we characterize as exhibiting the active-independent orientation resemble the outlook, temperament, and socially unacceptable behaviors of the DSM antisocial personality. These individuals act to counter the expectation of pain and depredation by engaging in duplicitous and often illegal behaviors.

6B *Sadistic personality.* In some patients the usual properties associated with pain and pleasure are conflicted or reversed. These clients not only seek or create objectively 'painful' events, but experience them as 'pleasurable'. Both the sadistic and self-defeating patterns are labeled as discordant patterns.

7 *Compulsive personality.* The DSM compulsive personality represents a pattern conflicted on the self-other polarity, but with a passive bent. They display a picture of distinct other directedness, consistency in social compliance, and interpersonal respect.

8A *Negativistic (passive–aggressive) personality.* This pattern is also conflicted on the self–other polarity, but instead assumes a more active orientation toward this reversal than does the compulsive. While this struggle represents an inability to resolve conflicts similar to those of the passive-ambivalent (compulsives); they behave obediently one time, and defiantly the next.

8B *Self-defeating (masochistic) personality.* Like the sadistic, these clients are conflicted on the pleasure–pain polarity. These individuals interpret events and engage in relationships in a manner that is not only at variance with this deeply rooted polarity, they relate to others in an obsequious and self-sacrificing manner.

S *Schizotypal personalities.* This personality disorder represents a cognitively dysfunctional and maladaptively detached orientation in the polarity theory. Schizotypal personalities experience minimal pleasure, have difficulty consistently differentiating between self and other strategies, as well as active and passive modes of adaptation.

C *Borderline personalities.* This personality disorder corresponds to the theory's emotionally dysfunctional and maladaptively ambivalent polarity orientation. Conflicts exist across the board, between pleasure and pain, active and passive, and self and other.

P *Paranoid personalities.* Here are seen a vigilant mistrust of others and an edgy defensiveness against anticipated criticism and deception. Driven by a high sensitivity to pain (rejection-humiliation) and oriented strongly to the self-polarity, these clients exhibit a touchy irritability, a need to assert themselves, but not necessarily in action.

DEVELOPMENT OF THE MILLON INVENTORIES

It may be of interest to record a few words regarding the origin and sequential development of the various forms of the Millon Inventories (Millon, 2008). A year or two after the publication in 1969 of *Modern Psychopathology* (Millon, 1969), I began, with some regularity, to receive letters and phone calls from graduate students who had read the book and thought it provided ideas that could aid them in formulating their dissertations.

As the number of these potential 'Millon' progenies grew into their teens, however, concern grew proportionately regarding both the diversity and adequacy of these representations of the theory. To establish a measure of instrumental uniformity for future investigators, as well as to assure at least a modicum of psychometric quality among tools that ostensibly reflected the theory's constructs, I was prompted (perhaps 'driven' is a more accurate word) to consider undertaking the test-construction task myself.

I became involved soon thereafter in the development of the DSM-III, playing a major role in formulating both the constructs and criteria that were to characterize its Axis II personality disorders. Although my assessment project was regularly refined and strengthened on the basis of theoretical logic and research data, an effort was made during this period to coordinate both its items and scales with the forthcoming syndromes of DSM-III. In the ensuing ten-year period numerous refinements of the inventory (retrospectively labeled MCMI-I) were introduced (e.g. corrections for response distorting tendencies such as current emotional state), as were expansions made to incorporate theoretical extensions and the subsequently published DSM-III-R (e.g. the addition of the self-defeating and sadistic personality disorder scales) and DSM-IV. The MCMI-II, reflecting the preceding changes and additions, was published in 1987. Ongoing investigations, further refinements in its undergirding theory, and

modifications in the DSM-IV personality disorders criteria served as the primary impetus to refashion the inventory into its latest form, the MCMI-III, published in 1994, designed to reflect its theory optimally, and to maximize its consonance with the most recent and empirically grounded official DSM classification system.

THE MCMI

A principal goal in constructing the MCMI, the first of the Millon Inventories, was to keep the total number of items small enough to encourage use in diverse diagnostic and treatment settings, yet large enough to permit the assessment of a wide range of clinically relevant behaviors. At 175 items, the final form is much shorter than comparable instruments.

The current form of the inventory (Millon, Millon and Davis, 1994), the MCMI-III, consists of 22 clinical scales, as well as 3 'modifier' scales available for interpretive analysis. The first three scales, disclosure, desirability, and debasement, represent modifier indices (X, Y, and Z); their purpose is to identify distorting tendencies that characterize clients and their responses. The next two sections constitute the basic personality disorder scales, essentially reflecting Axis II of the DSM. The first section (1 to 8B) appraises what are to be viewed as the moderately severe personality pathologies, ranging from the schizoid to the self-defeating scales; the second section (scales S, C, and P) represents more severe personality pathologies, encompassing schizotypal, borderline, and paranoid disorders. The following two sections cover several of the more prevalent Axis I disorders, ranging from the more moderate clinical syndromes (scales A to T) to those of greater severity (scales SS, CC, and PP). The division between personality and clinical disorders scales is congruent with multiaxial logic, and has important interpretive implications. MCMI-III scales are presented in Table 32.1.

Table 32.1   MCMI-III scales

Modifying indices	
X	Disclosure
Y	Desirability
Z	Debasement

Clinical personality patterns	
1	Schizoid
2A	Avoidant
2B	Depressive
3	Dependent
4	Histrionic
5	Narcissistic
6A	Antisocial
6B	Aggressive/sadistic
7	Compulsive
8A	Negativistic (passive-aggressive)
8B	Self-defeating

Severe personality pathology	
S	Schizotypal
C	Borderline
P	Paranoid

Clinical syndrome	
A	Anxiety disorder
H	Somatoform disorder
N	Bipolar: manic disorder
D	Dysthymic disorder
B	Alcohol dependence
T	Drug dependence
PT	Post-traumatic stress disorder

Severe syndrome	
SS	Thought disorder
CC	Major depression
PP	Delusional disorder

ADMINISTRATION AND SCORING

The MCMI is administered much like other self-report inventories. No special instructions are necessary to administer the test beyond those printed on the front page of the answer sheet itself, and these are self-explanatory. The entire answer booklet forms a single-fold, four-page sheet, complete with test directions, client information chart, and a special coding section for clinicians on the front page. Computer scoring is the fastest and most convenient method for obtaining MCMI profiles. The MCMI interpretive report, available from Pearson

Assessments consists of a computer plotted 'profile report' and a theoretically and empirically based narrative which integrates clients' primary Axis II personality styles and Axis I symptom features. These reports can be obtained from Pearson in several ways. By far the most popular, however, is computer administration through the Pearson Q-Local assessment software. Here the traditional paper and pencil format is bypassed completely in favor of computer administration and scoring. Results can be printed on most popular printers. Although item-weighting, modifying indices, and look-up tables greatly complicate hand-scoring (research indicates that most scorers make one or more errors, sometimes severe enough to change the resulting profile), scoring templates have been made available primarily for students, researchers, and public agencies.

INTERPRETATION

The MCMI offers several layers or levels of interpretation. Consistent with integrative logic, each level subsumes the previous one in an explanatory hierarchy, demanding a higher order of complexity and integration. At the first level, one merely examines the personality and clinical syndrome scales for single scale elevations. If these scales are sufficiently elevated, certain diagnoses may be warranted. At the second level, the interpretive process branches to follow one of two pathways, depending upon whether any of the severe personality pathology scales are elevated, or whether elevations are confined to the less severe personality pattern scales. Regardless of which branch the interpretive process follows, the goal at the second layer is to obtain an integrated picture of the patient's personality functioning and dynamics. The third layer seeks to integrate the client's Axis II personality disorders and Axis I clinical syndromes according to multiaxial logic.

Base rates

For MCMI neophytes, perhaps the first thing to notice is that, unlike other instruments, the elevation of each scale of the profile is given in terms of a base rate (BR) score rather than more familiar T-score or percentile rank. Each is a transformation of the raw scores, and each has the purpose of putting the raw scores on a common metric. Unlike T-scores or percentile ranks, however, the BR scores are created such that the percentage of the clinical population deemed diagnosable with a particular disorder falls (1) either at or above a common threshold (clinical scales), or (2) at a particular rank order in the profile (personality scales). Thus, if 5% of the clinical population is deemed to possess a schizoid pattern as its primary personality style, and another 2% the schizoid pattern as a secondary feature, then the raw scores have been transformed so that the normative sample reflects these *prevalence* or *base* rates.

Obviously, the BR score implies that we are not so much interested in the 'absolute quantity' of a particular trait as in the implications of that quantity for psychological functioning. While a certain level of narcissism is considered healthy in our society, the same level of antisocial behavior may not be; we might treat the second, but not the first. Thus, the BR concept recognizes that equal quantities of a trait or characteristic have differential pathological implications. Such scales have been equated in terms of the implications of a particular quantity for psychological functioning. The base rate score simply represents the most direct way of getting at such considerations. Base rate scores are superior to T-scores, which implicitly assume the converse: that pathology varies directly with the absolute quantity of a trait or pattern.

Conceptualization and diagnosis

The BR score is intended to suggest positive characteristics of psychopathology.

In Pepper's terms, it represents something of a fragment, in that it makes a prediction in and of itself without appealing to anything immediately outside itself; that is, auxiliary evidence, for corroboration. Consequently, there is a possibility of interpretive error in always diagnosing a personality disorder, or worse, multiple personality disorders, whenever base rate scores equal or exceed BR 75 or 85. While it has become traditional to view BR 75 as indicating the presence of either a significant personality trait or a personality disorder, there are, as with every test, always false positives and false negatives.

This prefigures another common way of falling into error, that of viewing personality disorders as medical illnesses for which some discrete pathogen can be found, or for which there exists some underlying unitary cause, either past or present. The use of such language as 'disorder' is indeed unfortunate, for personality disorders are not disorders at all in the medical sense. Instead, personality disorders are best conceptualized as disorders of the entire matrix of the person. Hence, we prefer the terms 'pattern' or 'style' rather than the intrinsically reifying 'disorder'. This misconception is more paradigmatic than diagnostic, but it leads to subsequent distortions in multiaxial logic, encouraging the view that classical clinical syndromes and personality disorders exist alongside each other in a horizontal relationship, rather than as clinical symptoms embedded in personality patterns. What threatens to undermine the interpretive process will surely undermine the intervention as well.

Configural interpretation of MCMI personality scales

The quality of information that can be deduced from the profile analysis of a test is a function of several factors, including the adequacy and generativity of the theory which provides the logic underlying its various scales, the overall empirical validity of the inventory, and its internal consistency and scale generalizability. An interpretation which in fact mirrors the patient's characteristic style of functioning as well as his or her current problems depends ultimately on the clinician's skill in weighing the degree to which a variety of client variables interact in order to corroborate, moderate, or even disqualify straightforward hypotheses, as well as suggest ones which are more subtle. As noted by Wetzler and Marlowe (1992), even the best inventory is only as good as the clinician interpreting it. Perfect construct validity and generalizability will not make up for inadequate knowledge of the theory undergirding an inventory or ignorance of fundamental principles of psychopathology.

Although examining the elevation of single scale may be useful for making diagnostic assignments, their interpretive value is greatly amplified when viewed in the context of the remaining profile of scales. Why? The explanation of this obvious and widely accepted tenet of test interpretation can be traced back to meta-theoretical assumptions addressed in the section of this chapter which dealt with what we called integrative logic. The short answer is that the process of profile interpretation is similar to that of knowledge building in the integrative world view. We are working our way toward a full conception of the patient, what we have called nomothetic individuality. In doing so, we take distance from the individual scales and diagnoses in order to reconstruct the personality as an organic whole: In the context of the entire profile, the meaning of each scale becomes something other than it would have been had that scale alone been available for interpretation. Thus, we want to know more than just 'avoidant' or 'schizoid'. In Pepper's (1942) more metaphysical terminology, each scale and even each diagnosis becomes a mere fragment to be transcended by successively more integrative formulations, the limit of the series being reality itself, that is, the patient. From the superordinate vista of this final product, it is little wonder that diagnoses, as such, often seem pathetic, inadequate, and next to useless, just as Ptolemy's crystal spheres must seem to modern astronomers.

Integrative configural logic is inherently nonlinear or nonmechanistic. Although it asks for a level of sophistication, in return it breaks the pattern of labeling patients and fitting them to discrete diagnostic categories: It conceptualizes diagnostic constructs as a beginning of an assessment rather than its endpoint. A narcissistic-antisocial pattern, for example, is somewhat different from either the purely prototypal narcissistic pattern or the purely prototypal antisocial pattern. Although the 'two-point' pattern in part resembles these focal constructs (nomothetic commonality), it is also more than either of these two patterns added together (nomothetic individuality), by virtue of the synergism of these elements. A narcissistic-antisocial pattern is something more than narcissism + antisocial behavior.

In making configural personality interpretations, a separation should be made between those scales pertaining to the *basic* clinical personality pattern (1–8B) and those pointing to the presence of more *severe* Axis II pathology, the borderline (C), schizotypal (S), and paranoid (P). These structural pathologies differ from the other clinical personality patterns by several criteria, notably deficits in social competence and frequent (but readily reversible) psychotic episodes. Less integrated in terms of their personality organization and less effective in coping than their milder counterparts, they are especially vulnerable to decompensation when confronted with the strains of everyday life. In terms of the theoretical model, these patterns are significantly less adaptable in the face of ecological vicissitudes. They are dysfunctional variants of the more moderately pathological patterns, a feature which leads to several predictions concerning these patterns and MCMI profiles.

GENERATING CLINICAL DOMAIN HYPOTHESES

Not all clients with the same personality diagnosis possess the same problem. A single diagnostic label rarely if ever provides information specific and comprehensive enough to serve as a sound basis for intervention efforts. Not only do patients differ with respect to the magnitude of their pathology within a diagnostic kind, they differ in the features with which they approximate the kind. Whether diagnostic taxons are derived through clinical observation, mathematical analyses, or theoretical deduction, clients differ in *how* they meet taxonic requirements, a fact institutionalized in DSM-III with the adoption of the polythetic model. In and of itself, then, a diagnosis alone *underspecifies* pathology, especially with regard to treatment considerations. Moreover, the vast majority of patients represent so-called mixed types. In moving toward nomothetic individuality, then we must ask 'what part of the mix' is relevant to interpreting the individual case.

One option is to systematically investigate characteristics associated with each MCMI suggested personality prototype in a *domain-oriented* fashion. Recall Hempel's (1965) remark that 'those characteristics which serve as criteria of membership in a given class [should be] associated, universally or with high probability, with more or less extensive clusters of other characteristics'. These characteristics or clinical domains have been usefully organized in a manner similar to distinctions drawn in the biological realm, that is, by dividing them into *structural* and *functional* attributes. Functional characteristics represent dynamic processes that transpire within the intrapsychic world and between the individual's self and psychosocial environment. They represent 'expressive modes of regulatory action'. Structural attributes represent a deeply embedded and relatively enduring template of imprinted memories, attitudes, needs, fears, conflicts, and so on, which guide experience and transform the nature of ongoing events in accord with these imprintings.

These domains are further differentiated according to their respective data level, reflecting the several major historic approaches that characterize the study of psychopathology (Millon, 2004a).

Several criteria were used to select and develop the clinical domains that comprise this assessment schema: (1) that they be varied in the features they embody; that is, not be limited just to behaviors or cognitions, but to encompass a full range of clinically relevant characteristics; (2) that they parallel, if not correspond, to many of our profession's current therapeutic modalities; (3) that they not only be coordinated to the official DSM schema of personality disorder prototypes, as well as its guiding model of evolutionary polarities, but also that each disorder be characterized by a distinctive feature within each clinical domain. Brief descriptions of these functional and structural domains have been given in several publications (Millon, 1986, 1987, 1990), and are printed in the MCMI manual as well (Millon, 2006).

THE GROSSMAN FACET SCALES

Since diagnoses exist as 'fragments' to be transcended in successively more integrative formulations, they are, in the final analysis, somewhat trivial. We have already noted that diagnosis represents an underspecification of pathology with regard to treatment planning. In fact, as more integrative formulations are achieved; that is, as the limit of the series is reached in the necessary theory of the patient, this theory becomes eminently more suitable for treatment planning than simple Axis I and Axis II diagnoses.

The MCMI-III Grossman facet scales represent an effort to elucidate finer distinctions than are expressed through the primary personality scales. For each of the clinical personality patterns scales (1–8B) and severe personality pathology scales (S, C, and P), three sub scales represent 'facets' of the primary personality pattern, drawn from the structural–functional domains described in earlier paragraphs. Thus, there are 42 total facet scales tied to the 14 primary personality scales. The facet scales were developed with the aim of maximizing the assessment specificity and therapeutic utility of the MCMI-III test and its overarching evolutionary theory (Millon, 1969/1983, 1990; Millon and Davis, 1996, Millon 1999; 2004a).

Both normal and abnormal personalities are multifaceted in their composition. As singular or reified entities, they can be captured using a categorical diagnostic label, but to be maximally useful clinically they require an in-depth understanding of their several compositional domains and the interactions among those domains. The Grossman facet scales uncover these clinically salient domains as a means of identifying and measuring specific problematic personality qualities.

A utilitarian purpose that the facet scales were designed to serve was the ability to examine discrepancies between elevations on the primary personality scales and their associated facet scales for purposes of treatment planning. Thus, the clinician would be in a position to determine not only what problematic personologic elements were most evident but also what subtype or admixture of personality expressions the individual may present. To maintain congruence with the theory and to satisfy the goal of maximal clinical value, a logical within-scale delineation was to base the facet scales on the eight functional and structural personologic domains identified by the theory: expressive acts, interpersonal conduct, cognitive style, regulatory mechanisms, self-image, object representations, morphologic organization, and mood/temperament.

Each of the 14 MCMI-III personality pattern facet development followed a three-stage process. The first stage involved deciding, for each of the 14 primary personality scales, which of the eight structural–functional domains would be represented with facet scales. For each prototypic personality

disorder, Millon (1990; Millon and Davis, 1996) posited that only two or three of its personologic domains would be most salient; one to three others will probably be of moderate (supportive) importance, and the remaining domains will probably be of only occasional importance. Which domain presents as the most salient according to prototypal structure differs among the prototypic personality disorders. For example, the prototypal *histrionic* is primarily identified by his or her interpersonal conduct and mood/temperament, with expressive behavior and cognitive style features playing a secondary role. In contrast, the *depressive* prototype, whose cognitive style and mood/temperament are likely to be most salient, displays three other domains in more moderate form.

The MCMI-III item pool accords with the theory and reflects judgments regarding the salience of each structural and functional domain for each personality pattern. Facet scale construction began with predictions about which item domains in each primary personality scale were likely to match the domains of the theory. For some scales, secondary domains were better represented than expected in the scale's item composition. Nevertheless, preliminary choices at this first stage were made based on which three domains for each personality pattern fit the theory best and on a rational examination of each scale's item composition.

The second stage involved testing the predictions generated in the first stage through statistical methodology. This work is described in detail in Grossman Del Rio (2005). As with the content or facet scales that have been developed for other inventories, factor analytic procedures were used to empirically substantiate these facet scales. Because of item overlap across the primary MCMI-III scales, the relatively small number of items on each primary scale, and the high covariance expected owing to the polythetic nature of the theory, most statistical methods were not expected to yield highly parsimonious results (Choca, 2004). To optimize the analysis, an alpha factoring method was chosen.

This procedure maximized the internal consistency of the extracted factors.

The third scale development stage involved subjecting the tentative scales that emerged from the factor analyses to final rational and statistical refinements. The factor analytic results were scrutinized for their concordance with the predicted personologic domains, and scale adjustments were made based on item domain content and levels of factor loadings. A major decision made at this point was to augment the facet scales for each personality pattern with items from related scales within the instrument (e.g. items from scale D: dysthymia were added to the cognitive style facet for scale 2B: depressive). This decision allowed the range of scores for some very short facet scales to increase, thereby stabilizing those scales, and increased the breadth of coverage of some of the theoretical constructs.

By examining the facet scale scores for the primary personality scales that are elevated, it is possible to identify the patient's most troublesome or clinically significant domains. For example, an individual with a high score on the avoidant scale may be most troubled by social interaction (interpersonally aversive), self-esteem issues (alienated self-image), or his or her perception of others (vexatious object representations). According to the theory, these are three of the most salient domains of this prototypal personality pattern. The facet scales directly reflect these constructs and help identify the relative salience of alternate domains.

Another use of the facet scales goes beyond within-scale or within-syndrome differentiation, often providing information that may not be obvious upon initial examination. Millon's evolutionary theory predicts that most personality presentations are not prototypal in nature. Rather, they are admixtures of two or more personality patterns that form what Millon terms subtypes (e.g. narcissistic with antisocial features, dependent with avoidant features, etc.). More than 60 subtype patterns have been identified in Millon's writings over the past decade (Millon and Davis, 1996; Millon et al., 2004), and descriptions of additional subtypes are forthcoming. Given that the theory specifies eight functional and structural domains, it is possible that a subtype pattern may be detected by examining the configuration of facet scale scores. For example, it would be possible to characterize a patient as 'antisocial with histrionic features' (identified by the theory as a *risk-taking antisocial*) by viewing elevations on the primary scales and examining facet scales such as expressively impulsive (one of the antisocial facets) and interpersonally attention-seeking (one of the histrionic facets). As a result of integrating facet scale findings across several primary scales, a more detailed clinical picture with great interpretive specificity and therapeutic utility emerges.

Implications for treatment planning and intervention

Possibly the greatest benefit that the facet scales provide clinicians is the ability to deduce theoretically substantiated, clinically sound case conceptualizations, treatment plans, and therapeutic directions. Because the facet scales are consonant with Millon's eight personologic domains, which in turn are congruent with contemporary therapeutic philosophies and treatment techniques, the clinician may use the facet scale scores to assist in generating effective, fully contextual, and integrative personologic therapeutic interventions.

Perhaps the clearest example of the therapeutic utility of the facet scales can be found in the *personalized psychotherapy* method (e.g. Millon 1999; Millon and Grossman, 2007a, 2007b, 2007c) that represents a direct outgrowth of the same guiding theory from which the facet scales were generated. This paradigm is integrative in nature, recognizing the eight personologic domains measured by the facet scales as key guides to appropriate therapeutic strategies. Each domain is aligned with one of the principal schools of thought in modern psychotherapy (e.g. cognitive, psychodynamic, pharmacologic, etc.). Taken together, however, these eight domains comprise the complex, interwoven spectrum of the individual's personality. The facet scales can help identify a patient's problematic personologic domains, thereby serving as a catalyst to efficient, personalized psychotherapeutic treatment planning and intervention.

THE M-PACI AND MACI: TWO CHILD-ORIENTED INVENTORIES

Since the 1970s there have been three versions of the adult MCMI test (Millon, 1977, 1987, 1994); since the 1980s there have been two versions of the adolescent test (MAPI (Millon, Green and Meagher, 1982); MACI (Millon and Davis 1993)); and recently an instrument for the pre-adolescent age group, the M-PACI test (Millon 2005). The present brief section of the chapter will provide a context for considering personality patterns and clinical syndromes with children and adolescents.

For the MACI inventory, its 12 personality patterns scales do not represent personality 'disorders' per se because personality disturbances in the adolescent population, on top of their inherent dispositions and life shaping experiences, may be partially related to their

attempts to adjust to and negotiate the many internal and external changes and challenges they face. Adolescent personalities are still evolving and remain malleable to a degree, although evidence is gaining that late adolescents, in particular, demonstrate a high degree of stability in their personalities and this enduring feature may contribute to significant problems as an adult. Pre-adolescent personalities appear to be even less differentiated and may be more reactive or responsive to influences from their environment. The M-PACI test reflects these notions since it measures only seven basic personality patterns. Table 32.2 illustrates the correspondences between the respective personality patterns scales measured by these instruments.

The Millon Pre-Adolescent Clinical Inventory (M-PACI) (Millon Tringone, Millon and Grossman 2005) is a multidimensional self-report inventory for use with 9- to 12-year-olds seen in clinical settings. It consists of 97 true/false items written at a third-grade reading level. The inventory has 14 *profile scales* grouped into two sets: *emerging personality patterns* and *current clinical signs*. Scores on these scales are reported as base rate scores, scaled to reflect the relative prevalence of the characteristics they measure. In addition to the profile scales, there are two M-PACI *response validity indicators*.

Careful attention was paid throughout the development of the M-PACI inventory to

Table 32.2   MACI and M-PACI test personality patterns scales

Theoretical position	MACI	M-PACI
Passive detached	Introversive	
Active detached	Inhibited	Inhibited
Passive pain	Doleful	
Passive dependent	Submissive	Submissive
Active dependent	Dramatizing	Outgoing
Passive independent	Egotistic	Confident
Active independent	Unruly	Unruly
Passive ambivalent	Conforming	Conforming
Active ambivalent	Oppositional	
Passive discordant	Self-Demeaning	
Active discordant	Forceful	
Severe ambivalent	Borderline tendency	Unstable

ensure that, despite its comprehensiveness, it is also easy for most 9- to 12-year-olds to complete. Recognizing that deficits in reading and attention are especially common among 9- to 12-year-olds seen in clinical settings, every effort was made to craft items that are short and simple and at the same time interesting to pre-adolescents and phrased in the language they use. Keeping the inventory to fewer than 100 items was another way in which the goal of ease of completion was addressed. Most 9- to 12-year-olds can complete the M-PACI inventory in 20 minutes or less.

The M-PACI inventory can help mental health professionals identify, predict, and understand a broad range of psychological issues that are common among 9- to 12-year-olds seen in clinical settings. These settings include private practices, residential treatment facilities, public mental health centers, and family guidance clinics, and others. The inventory is also appropriate for use in school settings when a child has been referred for evaluation and/or counseling due to apparent behavioral and/or emotional problems. Administration of the M-PACI inventory can be beneficial at many points during the assessment and treatment process: as part of the initial clinical assessment, to gauge progress and reevaluate issues during the course of treatment, and as a treatment outcome measure.

The Millon Adolescent Clinical Inventory (MACI) (Millon, 1993) is a 160-item, self-report inventory that was developed as a significant revision of the Millon Adolescent Personality Inventory (MAPI) (Millon and Davis, 1993). It has 31 scales that are divided into four sections: (1) 12 personality patterns scales, (2) eight expressed concerns scales, (3) seven clinical syndrome scales, and (4) one reliability scale and three modifying indices. The MACI test has advantages over other adolescent objective inventories since its personality patterns constructs are theoretically derived, it has a unique configuration where separate scales assess more acute and transient clinical syndromes associated with

Axis I disorders and more stable personality patterns associated with Axis II disorders, and it was fully normed with a clinical population from diverse clinical settings (McCann, 1997; Tringone, 1999).

The MACI test has a central set of expressed concerns scales that assess an adolescent's perceptions of important areas in their development. While the M-PACI expressed concerns scales demonstrated poor support statistically for their inclusion and were dropped, the MACI concerns scales provide keen insights into adolescent development and, in some instances, low scores may represent areas of support or, potentially, relative strengths. Two scales, identity diffusion and self-devaluation, focus on self-image issues, in particular, regarding one's identity and self-esteem. These scales tap one's impressions in terms of the present and the future. Another pair of self-oriented scales, body disapproval and sexual discomfort, addresses an adolescent's reactions toward their physical maturation and the onset of sexual thoughts and urges. Two key areas involve peer relations, measured by the peer insecurity scale, and family relations, measured by the family discord scale. While pre-adolescent subjects were not able to identify conflicts in these areas, adolescents, perhaps related to the significance of the separation–individuation struggle, communicate frequent elevations, in particular, on the latter scale. The childhood abuse scale assesses an adolescent's *reactions* (e.g. shame, disgust) to prior abuse and should *not* be interpreted as a measure of whether abuse occurred or not. These scales will elevate when an adolescent identifies their respective targets as a subjective concern. The exception to this rule involves the social insensitivity scale that will typically elevate in tandem with the unruly, forceful, delinquent predisposition, and impulsive propensity scales. Serious conduct disorder problems are then indicated.

The MACI clinical syndromes scales assess common behavior patterns and mood problems in the adolescent population.

While these syndromes may be distinct in their presentation, it is important to recognize their meaning and significance within the context of the adolescent's personality. The anxious feelings and depressive affect scales identify key features in the mood realm and the suicidal tendency scale functions as a measure of acute severity and safety risk as it assesses issues related to self-harm and suicidal ideation. As noted above, the delinquent predisposition and impulsive propensity scales address conduct disorder patterns. The eating dysfunctions and substance abuse proneness scales are important also, especially since an elevation on either scale might indicate the need for specialized treatment interventions.

The unique structure of the MACI test, with separate theoretically derived personality patterns scales, helps communicate valuable clinical insights that can then serve as a guide to enhanced psychotherapeutic interventions. As with the MCMI-III, the MACI also contains *Grossman facet scales* that are extremely useful in planning therapeutic interventions. While Axis I disorders may be initial therapy targets, it is imperative that clinicians also address Axis II traits or features given their reciprocally reinforcing nature, their associations with clinical syndromes, and the growing evidence that adolescent patterns, from early on, may be more stable and enduring than once thought.

THE MBMD: A PSYCHOSOCIAL MEDICAL INVENTORY

Sir William Osler, the eminent nineteenth century clinician, said 'the good physician will treat the disease, but the great physician will treat the whole patient'. The MBMD (Millon Behavioral Medicine Diagnostic) inventory is designed to provide the critical psychological information doctors need to treat the whole patient. The MBMD inventory represents a substantial upgrading of the MBHI inventory (Millon Behavioral Health Inventory; It is a 165-item, self-report inventory with 29 clinical scales, three response patterns scales, one validity indicator, and six negative health habits indicators. It is designed to assess psychological factors that can influence the course of treatment of medically ill patients. (Table 32.3 lists the MBMD scales and the number of items on each scale.)

The MBMD inventory and its forerunners were developed in consultation with physicians, psychologists, nurses, and other health professionals who work with the physically ill. As a result, these instruments reflect issues that are relevant to a thorough understanding of the attitudes, behavior, and concerns of medical patients. The inventory was developed for use in clinical practice, hospitals, outpatient settings, and research. It is useful for evaluating patients with discernable medical impairments, especially those in which psychosocial factors may play a role in the course of the disease and treatment outcome. There have been numerous clinical studies at diverse hospital settings that have shown that patients who receive behavioral interventions require fewer medical services than those who receive standard care and that integrating behavioral assessment and counseling into a patient's care significantly reduces healthcare costs and ultimately enhances patient work productivity.

Important advances relating to 'psychological factor[s] affecting medical condition[s]' (code #316) were introduced in the DSM-IV-TR (American Psychiatric Association, 2000). This designation highlights the need for attention on the part of clinical/health psychologists, psychiatrists, physicians, surgeons, nurses, and other healthcare professionals concerning the role of several of the MBMD domains.

To expand empirical support for the validity of the developing MBMD scales, a wide range of external correlates were gathered. Similarly, evidence in the form of staff ratings was obtained from clinical judges who were

Table 32.3   MBMD domains and scales

Response patterns	No. of items	
X	Disclosure	6
Y	Desirability	11
Z	Debasement	10
Negative health habits		
N	Alcohol	2
O	Drug	2
P	Eating	3
Q	Caffeine	2
R	Inactivity	3
S	Smoking	3
Psychiatric indications		
AA	Anxiety-tension	15
BB	Depression	23
CC	Cognitive dysfunction	14
DD	Emotional lability	18
EE	Guardedness	20
Coping styles		
1	Introversive	15
2A	Inhibited	17
2B	Dejected	13
3	Cooperative	15
4	Sociable	9
5	Confident	12
6A	Nonconforming	14
6B	Forceful	12
7	Respectful	17
8A	Oppositional	22
8B	Denigrated	17
Stress moderators		
A	Illness apprehension vs. Illness acceptance	21
B	Functional deficits vs. Functional competence	16
C	Pain sensitivity vs. pain tolerance	22
D	Social isolation vs. social support	20
E	Future pessimism vs. future optimism	16
F	Spiritual absence vs. spiritual faith	7
Treatment prognostics		
G	Interventional fragility vs. interventional resilience	17
H	Medication abuse vs. medication conscientiousness	10
I	Information discomfort vs. information receptivity	6
J	Utilization excess vs. appropriate utilization	17
K	Problematic compliance vs. optimal compliance	16
Management guides		
L	Adjustment difficulties	15
M	Psych referral	14

well acquainted with their patients. These data served as a means of validating the accuracy of a number of the MBMD scales. Indices were added to the MBMD inventory to identify and correct patients' distorting response patterns (i.e. tendencies to complain excessively regarding their medical state or to deny and cover up their symptoms, fears, and concerns). These controls on patient inclinations to distort their problems have proven useful in strengthening the instrument's accuracy. Of no minor import was the decision to make available in the MBMD Interpretive Report a one-page 'healthcare provider summary' containing the essential assessment findings and treatment recommendations for healthcare providers other than PhD psychologists, who will want to read the entire interpretive report.

THE MCCI: ASSESSING COLLEGE-LEVEL DIFFICULTIES

The Millon College Counseling Inventory (MCCI) is a multidimensional self-report counseling inventory designed for use with college students. It extends the series of Millon clinical inventories. College counseling centers are seeing more clients than ever because of the increased pressures and demands of college life, because there are more students with learning disabilities and psychological problems, and because there are more students overall attending college. College counselors are overwhelmed with this increased demand for their services and, as a result, need an instrument to help them assess students' problems more quickly and accurately.

The MCCI consists of 150 items and has 32 profile scales grouped into three sets: personality scales (the personality styles scales and the severe personality tendencies scale), expressed concerns, and clinical signs. Scores on these scales are reported as prevalence scores, scaled to reflect the relative prevalence of the characteristics they measure.

Research has demonstrated that these scales have strong reliability and adequate validity. In addition to the profile scales, there are four response tendencies scales. The MCCI scales are listed in Table 32.4.

The MCCI inventory provides comprehensive coverage of college students' psychological issues, distinguishing it from the single-construct assessment instruments that

Table 32.4   MCCI scales – scale set scale name

Personality styles	
1	Introverted
2A	Inhibited
2B	Dejected
3	Needy
4	Sociable
5	Confident
6A	Unruly
7	Conscientious
8A	Oppositional
8B	Denigrated
Severe personality tendencies	
9	Borderline
Expressed concerns	
A	Mental health upset
B	Identity quandaries
C	Family disquiet
D	Peer alienation
E	Romantic distress
F	Academic concerns
G	Career confusion
H	Abusive experiences
I	Living arrangement problems
J	Financial burdens
K	Spiritual doubts
Clinical signs	
AA	Suicidal tendencies
BB	Depressive outlook
CC	Anxiety/tension
DD	Post-traumatic stress
EE	Eating disorders
FF	Anger dyscontrol
GG	Attention (cognitive) deficits
HH	Obsessions/compulsions
II	Alcohol abuse
JJ	Drug abuse
Response tendencies	
V	Validity
X	Disclosure
Y	Desirability
Z	Debasement

are commonly used with college students. As would be expected for a multidimensional counseling assessment, the MCCI inventory includes measures of the psychological symptoms that are most prevalent among college students. In addition, because the MCCI measures personality styles, its reach and usefulness are extended beyond the realm of symptoms alone. The inclusion of scales measuring personality dimensions reflects the view that, among college students, clinically significant psychological problems are often grounded in expressions of stable personality traits.

It is recommended that clinicians working with college-age youngsters in other than college settings administer either the MACI or the MCMI-III. Although the MCCI may be helpful for clinicians who are working with college-age clients in other settings, caution should be used when interpreting the results because the MCCI was normed on students who sought therapy at college counseling centers (not in hospitals or with clinicians in private practice). Students who seek help at college counseling centers typically exhibit less severe psychopathology than those who are in treatment elsewhere. College students who enter college counseling centers with severe levels of stress or disturbance are often referred elsewhere for treatment.

It is important that counselors to keep in mind that even the most well-adjusted college students sometimes question their identity and experience stress because they are living away from home for the first time and experiencing significant changes in their lives. For that reason, the MCCI inventory is better viewed as a tool to help understand a student's current condition than as an aid to diagnosing him or her. The danger in diagnosing a student is that the diagnosis may be inaccurate as he or she learns to adjust to college life. Even when the assignment of a diagnosis is necessary, the counselor should remember that the patterns of thought, feeling, and behavior of students this age are rather malleable.

THE MIPS-R: ASSESSING NORMAL PERSONALITY STYLES

The Millon Index of Personality Styles Revised (MIPS-R) inventory is a 180-item true/false questionnaire designed to measure personality styles of normally functioning adults between the ages of 18 and 65. Most MIPS-R items require an eighth-grade education to complete. Most individuals finish it in 30 minutes or less.

The MIPS-R test consists of 24 scales grouped into 12 pairs. Each pair contains two juxtaposed scales. For example, the externally focused and internally focused scales are considered a pair. As shown in Table 32.5, the 12 pairs of MIPS-R scales are organized into three major areas: motivating styles, thinking styles, and behaving styles. In addition to the 12 pairs of content scales, the MIPS test contains three validity indicators: positive impression, negative impression, and consistency.

Three pairs of motivating styles scales assess the person's orientation in his or her environment. The first pair of scales examines how the respondent's behavior is basically reinforced: toward pleasures or away from pains. The second pair assesses the extent to which the individual's activities reflect an actively modifying or a passively accommodating way of dealing with the world. The third pair of scales focuses on where life's reinforcements are obtained, assessing the extent to which the person is primarily motivated by indulging-self or by nurturing-other.

Four pairs of thinking styles scales examine the way in which information is processed. The first two pairs in this area, externally focused or internally focused, and realistic/sensing or imaginative/intuiting, assess *information-gathering* strategies. The second two pairs, thought-guided or feeling-guided, and conservation-seeking or innovation-seeking, assess different styles of *processing information* once it has been gathered.

Five pairs of behaving styles scales assess the extent to which the person's style of relating to others is generally asocial/withdrawing or gregarious/outgoing, anxious/hesitating or confident/asserting, unconventional/dissenting or dutiful/conforming, submissive/yielding or dominant/controlling, and dissatisfied/complaining or cooperative/agreeing.

As a group, the MIPS-R scales have a rich theoretical foundation in a model of personality that is deeply rooted in biosocial and evolutionary theory. To capture personality more or less fully, we must find ways to characterize all three components of the sequence: the deeper feelings that orient individuals, the characteristic modes they utilize to construct and transform their cognitions, and the particular behaviors they have learned in order to relate to others. By characterizing and quantifying these three dimensions, we should be able to represent individual differences in accordance with the major features that define personality.

Table 32.5 The MIPS *revised* scales

Motivating styles	Thinking styles	Behaving styles
Pleasure-enhancing	Externally focused	Asocial/withdrawing
Pain-avoiding	Internally focused	Gregarious/outgoing
Actively modifying	Realistic/sensing	Anxious/hesitating
Passively accommodating	Imaginative/intuiting	Confident/asserting
Self-indulging	Thought-guided	Unconventional/dissenting
Other-nurturing	Feeling-guided	Dutiful/conforming
	Conservation-seeking	Submissive/yielding
	Innovation-seeking	Dominant/controlling
		Dissatisfied/complaining
		Cooperative/agreeing

The MIPS-R test can be administered, scored, and interpreted on a personal computer, administered in paper-and-pencil format and hand scored or scanned on a desktop scanner. A mail-in scoring service is also available. Computer-generated reports provide either a single-page profile (i.e. a graph) of the scores or a complete narrative interpretation of the profile pattern.

The MIPS-R test offers separate norms for adults and college students, and for genders, both separate and combined. The MIPS-R test provides prevalence scores (PS) for each scale (usually between 0 and 100). An individual who scores above PS 50 on any scale is likely to display some of the characteristics measured by that scale. The higher the score, the more pronounced the characteristics. The median split-half reliability for the MIPS-R scales is $r = 0.82$ in the adult sample ($n = 1,000$), and $r = 0.80$ in the college sample ($n = 1,600$).

CONCLUSIONS

As noted, the polarity schemas and clinical domains delineated in the various Millon Inventories serve as useful points of focus for corresponding modalities of therapy. Which domains and which polarities should be selected for counseling or therapeutic intervention is not, we contend, merely a matter of making 'the diagnosis', but requires a comprehensive assessment that appraises not only the overall configuration of polarities and domains, but differentiates their balance and degrees of salience. By careful homework, the clinician or counselor will arrive at what we have called a 'nomologically individuated' formulation, one necessary in a theoretical sense, and therefore sufficient to serve as an intervention guide. In aiming for theoretical necessity in the individual case, a compelling theory of the person, we achieve a certain superordinate level of complexity and sophistication in the conceptualization of that case. Any discussion of *personalized*

psychotherapy, as we have recently called it (Millon and Grossman, 2007a,b,c), must take place at a level of abstraction or integration commensurate with that of personality itself. Personality disorders and clinical syndromes cannot be remedied if the person is thoroughly integrated while the therapy is not. Therapy must be as individualized as the person.

REFERENCES

American Psychiatric Association (2000) *Diagnostic and Statistical Manual of Mental Disorders – TR* (4th edn). Washington, DC: American Psychiatric Publishing.

Choca, J.P. (2004) *Interpretive Guide to the Millon Clinical Multiaxial Inventory* (3rd edn). Washington, DC: American Psychological Association.

Gilligan, C. (1982) *In a Different Voice.* Cambridge, MA: Harvard University Press.

Grossman, S.D. and Del Rio, C. (2005) 'The MCMI-III Facet Subscales', in R.J. Craig (ed.), *New Directions in Interpreting the Millon Clinical Multiaxial Inventory-III (MCMI-III).* Hoboken, NJ: Wiley, pp. 3–31.

Hempel, C.G. (1965) *Aspects of Scientific Explanation.* New York: Free Press.

Huxley, T.H. (1870) 'Mr. Darwin's critics', *Contemporary Review*, 18: 443–76.

McCann, J.T. (1997) 'The MACI: Composition and clinical applications', in T. Millon (ed.), *The Millon Inventories: Clinical and Personality Assessment.* New York: Guilford, pp. 363–88.

Millon, T. (1969) *Modern Psychopathology.* Philadelphia: Saunders (reprinted 1983, Prospect Heights, IL: Waveland Press).

Millon, T. (1977) *Manual for the Millon Clinical Multiaxial Inventory (MCMI).* Minneapolis, MN: National Computer Systems.

Millon, T. (1981) *Disorders of Personality: DSM-III, Axis II.* New York: Wiley-Interscience.

Millon, T. (1986) 'Personality prototypes and their diagnostic criteria', in T. Millon and G.L. Klerman (eds), *Contemporary Directions in Psychopathology.* New York: Guilford.

Millon, T. (1987) *Manual for the Millon Clinical Multiaxial Inventory-II (MCMI-II).*

Minneapolis, MN: National Computer Systems.

Millon, T. (1990) *Toward a New Personology: An Evolutionary Model*. New York: Wiley

Millon, T. (1993) *Millon Adolescent Clinical Inventory (MACI) Manual*. Minneapolis, MN: National Computer Systems.

Millon, T. (2008) (ed.), *The Millon Inventories: Clinical and Personality Assessment*. New York, NY: Guilford.

Millon, T. (2005) 'Millon Pre-Adolescent Clinical Inventory Manual. Minneapolis', MN: NCS Pearson.

Millon, T. (1999) *Personality-guided Therapy*. Hoboken, NJ: Wiley.

Millon, T. (2004a) *Masters of the Mind: Exploring the Story of Mental Illness from Ancient Times to the New Millennium*. New York: Wiley.

Millon, T. (2004b) *Millon Index of Personality Styles Revised Manual*. Minneapolis, MN: Pearson Assessments.

Millon, T. (2006) *Millon Clinical Multiaxial Inventory-III Manual* (3rd edn). Minneapolis, MN: NCS Pearson.

Millon, T. and Davis, R.D. (1993) 'The Millon Adolescent Personality Inventory and the Millon Adolescent Clinical Inventory', *Journal of Counseling and Development*, 71(5): 570–74.

Millon, T. and Davis, R.D. (1996) *Disorders of Personality: DSM-IV and Beyond* (2nd edn). New York: Wiley.

Millon, T., Green, C.J. and Meagher, R.B. (1982) *Millon Adolescent Personality Inventory Manual*. Minneapolis, MN: National Computer Systems.

Millon, T. and Grossman, S. (2007 a). *Resolving Difficult Clinical Syndromes: A Personalized Psychotherapy Approach*. Hoboken, NJ: Wiley.

Millon, T. and Grossman, S. (2007b) *Overcoming Resistant Personality Disorders: A Personalized Psychotherapy Approach*. Hoboken, NJ: Wiley.

Millon, T. and Grossman, S. (2007c) *Moderating Severe Personality Disorders: A Personalized Psychotherapy Approach*. Hoboken, NJ: Wiley.

Millon, T., Grossman, S., Millon, C., Meagher, S. and Ramnath, R. (2004) *Personality Disorders in Modern Life* (2nd edn). Hoboken, NJ: Wiley.

Millon, T., Millon, C. and Davis, R. (1994) *Millon Clinical Multiaxial Inventory-III Manual*. Minneapolis, MN: National Computer Systems.

Millon, T., Tringone, R., Millon, C. and Grassman, S. (2005) *Millon Pre-Adolescent Clinical Inventory Manual*. Minneapolis, MN: Pearson.

Pepper, S.C. (1942) *World Hypotheses: A Study in Evidence*. Berkeley: University of California Press.

Rushton, J.P. (1985) 'Differential K theory: The sociobiology of individual and group differences', *Personality and Individual Differences*, 6(6): 441–52.

Spencer, H. (1870) *The Principles of Psychology*. London: Williams & Norgate.

Tringone, R. (1999) 'Essentials of MACI assessment', in S. Strack (ed.), *Essentials of Millon Inventories Assessment*. New York: Wiley, pp. 92–160

Wetzler, S. and Marlowe, D. (1992) 'What they don't tell you in test manuals: A response to Millon', *Journal of Counseling and Development*, 70(3): 427–8.

Wilson, E.O. (1975) *Sociobiology: The New Synthesis*. Cambridge: Harvard University Press.

Wilson, E.O. (1978) *On Human Nature*. Cambridge: Harvard University Press.

Subject Index

Name Index